SOCIETY OF BIBLICAL LITERATURE

1993 Seminar Papers

Society of Biblical Literature
Seminar Paper Series

Editor, Eugene H. Lovering, Jr.

Number 32
Society of Biblical Literature
1993 Seminar Papers
Editor, Eugene H. Lovering, Jr.

Society of Biblical Literature
1993 Seminar Papers

Editor, Eugene H. Lovering, Jr.

One Hundred Twenty-Ninth Annual Meeting
November 20–23, 1993
The Sheraton Washington and the Omni Shoreham Hotels
Washington, D.C.

Scholars Press
Atlanta, Georgia

Society of Biblical Literature
1993 Seminar Papers

Indexed in *Religion Index Two: Multi-Author Works*
published by the American Theological Library Association, Evanston, Illinois.
Indexing also available in the ATLA Religion Database
accessible through Dialog Information Services, Palo Alto, California.
Also available for compact-disk searching through ATLA.

ISBN: 1-55540-903-2
ISSN: 0145-2711

Printed in the United States of America

Contents

S7   Q Bibliography Supplement IV: 1993
David M. Scholer 1

S28   Philo's *Exposition of the Law* and Social History:
Methodological Considerations
Adele Reinhartz 6

S28   Philo's *Quaestiones et solutiones in Genesim*: A Synoptic Approach
Sze-kar Wan 22

S28   The Place of Judaism in Philo's Thought: Israel, Jews, and Proselytes
Ellen Birnbaum 54

S30   Divine Power in the Apocalypse to John: Revelation 4–5
in Process Hermeneutic
Ron Farmer 70

S30   The Apocalypse as Utopia: Ancient and Modern Subjectivity
Randall C. Webber 104

S42   Help for Interpreting Jesus' Exorcisms
Paul W. Hollenbach 119

S42   Jesus, an Exorcist of a Kind
John J. Rousseau 129

S42   Insights and Models for Understanding the Healing Activity
of the Historical Jesus
John J. Pilch 154

S42   Jesus' Healings of Women: Conformity and Non-Conformity
to Dominant Cultural Values as Clues for Historical Reconstruction
Joanna Dewey 178

S45   From Wrath to Justification: Tradition, Gospel and Audience
in the Theology of Romans 1:18–4:25
Andrew T. Lincoln 194

S45   The Story of Israel and the Theology of Romans 5–8
Frank Thielman 227

S60   The Function of the Oracles against Babylon in Isaiah 14 and 47
Chris A. Franke 250

S60   On the Question of Divisions Internal to the Book of Isaiah
       Christopher R. Seitz 260

S60   On Multiple Settings in the Book of Isaiah
       Marvin A. Sweeney 267

S60   The Book of Isaiah as a Human Witness to Revelation
       within the Religions of Judaism and Christianity
       Gerald T. Sheppard 274

S66   "With the Power of the Spirit": Plotting the Program
       and Parallels of Luke 4:14–37 in Luke-Acts
       Jeffrey L. Staley 281

S71   Narrative Outline of the Composition of Luke
       According to the Two Gospel Hypothesis
       Lamar Cope, David L. Dungan, William R. Farmer,
       Allan J. McNicol, David B. Peabody, Philip L. Shuler 303

S74   Betwixt and Between: The Samaritans in the Hasmonean Period
       Lester L. Grabbe 334

S79   What Do We Mean by "First-Century Jewish Monotheism"?
       Larry W. Hurtado 348

S87   ". . . you teach all the Jews . . . to forsake Moses, telling them
       not to . . . observe the customs" (Acts 21:21; cf. 6:14)
       David L. Balch 369

S87   The Seed of Abraham and the People of God: A Study of Two Pauls
       J. Bradley Chance 384

S129   Historical Jesus the Healer: Cultural Interpretations of the Healing
       Cults of the Graeco-Roman World as the Basis for Jesus Movements
       Ralph J. Coffman 412

S129   Jesus' Table Practice: Dining with "Tax Collectors and Sinners,"
       including Women
       Kathleen E. Corley 444

S129   From Public Ministry to the Passion: Can a Link Be Found
       between the (Galilean) Life and the (Judean) Death of Jesus?
       Craig A. Evans 460

S129   "Where No One Had Yet Been Laid": The Shame of Jesus' Burial
       Byron R. McCane 473

S132   Principal Orientations on the Relations between the Apocryphal Acts
       (*Acts of Paul* and *Acts of John*; *Acts of Peter* and *Acts of John*)
       F. Stanley Jones 485

S132   *The Acts of Paul* and *The Acts of John*: Which Came First?
       Dennis R. MacDonald 506

S133   Luke's Paul as the Legacy of Paul
        J. Christiaan Beker 511

S133   The Social Dimensions of *Sōtēria* in Luke-Acts and Paul
        Luke Timothy Johnson 520

S133   Who's Characterizing Whom and the Difference This Makes:
        Locating and Centering Paul
        Stephen E. Fowl 537

S145   Sexual Practice and the Structure of Prestige:
        The Case of the Disputed Concubines
        Ken Stone 554

S153   Matthew 28:16–20, Resurrection, Ecclesiology and Mission
        Pheme Perkins 574

S153   Matthew 28:16–20, Anticlimax or Key to the Gospel?
        Robert Harry Smith 589

S158   Narrative Outline of the Composition of Luke
        According to the Two Gospel Hypothesis
        Lamar Cope, David L. Dungan, William R. Farmer,
        Allan J. McNicol, David B. Peabody, Philip L. Shuler 303

S158   The Silence of the Messiah: The Function
        of "Messianic Secret" Motifs across the Synoptics
        Neil Elliott 604

S165   *The Acts of Peter* and *The Acts of John*: Which Came First?
        Dennis R. MacDonald 623

S165   The *Acts of Peter* as Intertext: Response to Dennis MacDonald
        Judith B. Perkins 627

S165   Apostolic Apocrypha: Where Do We Stand
        with Schneemelcher's Fifth Edition?
        Robert F. Stoops, Jr. 634

S193   Matthew and Marginality
        Dennis C. Duling 642

S193   A Sound Map of the Sermon on the Mount
        Bernard Brandon Scott and *Margaret E. Dean* 672

S196   The Death of Christ as Divine Patronage in Romans 5:1–11
        Raymond W. Pickett 726

S196   Seized by the Cross: The Death of Jesus
        in Paul's Transformative Discourse
        Alexandra R. Brown 740

S197   Prayers from Qumran: Issues and Methods
       E. Glickler Chazon 758

S197   Prayer in the New Testament in Light of Contemporary Jewish Prayers
       James H. Charlesworth 773

S197   The Phenomenology of Greco-Roman Prayer
       David E. Aune 787

S197   Prayer of Early Rabbinic Tradition: Representative Texts
       Asher Finkel 796

S197   The Praying Logos and the Christian at Prayer in Clement
   of Alexandria: Critical Issues in the Patristic Prayer Corpus
       Pamela Bright 808

Introductory Note

The papers in this volume were prepared for discussion at the One Hundred Twenty-ninth Annual Meeting of the Society of Biblical Literature, convened at the Sheraton Washington and Omni Shoreham Hotels, Washington, D.C., 20-23 November 1993. They represent, in most cases, experimental and initial research on a subject. Therefore, they should not be considered finished works but works in progress. The Society encourages this type of publication to stimulate discussion which may lead to the refinement and precision necessary in a journal article or monograph.

The Seminar Papers Series serves the program efforts of the SBL. Younger scholars and veterans are able to prepare their research for distribution in advance of the annual meeting. This frees time otherwise allotted for the reading of papers and permits significant discussion to occur at the annual meeting.

In keeping with their purpose, the papers in this volume appear substantially as they were received. Authors were encouraged to submit electronic manuscripts, and the latter have been converted from their native word-processing format and printed with limited editorial corrections. No effort has been made to conform the papers to a consistent style or format.

The editor expresses appreciation to the authors, who worked diligently to produce quality papers in advance of an early deadline; to the Program Unit Chairs, who were responsible for soliciting, collecting and proofreading the papers; to Anita C. Estner, who provided invaluable assistance at the editorial and composition stage—authors and readers alike owe more to her care and linguistic abilities than can be told—and to the staff of Scholars Press, who oversaw final production, distribution, and accounting details. On behalf of the whole society, the editor thanks the chairs of all annual meeting program units for their efforts in developing a stimulating program.

Eugene H. Lovering, Jr., Editor
Associate Executive Director
Society of Biblical Literature

Q Bibliography Supplement IV: 1993

David M. Scholer
North Park College and
Theological Seminary

Introduction

This brief listing supplements "Q Bibliography Supplement II: 1991," *Society of Biblical Literature 1991 Seminar Papers* (ed. D. J. Lull; SBLSPS 30; Atlanta: Scholars Press, 1991), 1-7, and "Q Bibliography Supplement III: 1992," *Society of Biblical Literature 1992 Seminary Papers* (ed. E. H. Lovering, Jr.; SBLSPS 31; Atlanta: Scholars Press, 1992), 1-4. Sixty-two items are listed in this Supplement. It is still my plan to complete a comprehensive Q bibliography through 1993.

Books and Reviews

Carr, D. M. *From D to Q* . . . .

    Lust, J. *Ephemerides Theologicae Lovanienses* 68 (1992), 413-14.

Hartin, P. J. *James and the Q Sayings* . . . .

    Bauckham, R. *Journal of Theological Studies* 44 (1993), 298-301.

    Catchpole, D. R. *Expository Times* 103 (1991/92), 26-27.

    Head, P. M. *Themelios* 18:1 (October 1992), 29-30.

    Kloppenborg, J. *Catholic Biblical Quarterly* 54 (1992), 567-68.

    Piper, R. A. *Evangelical Quarterly* 65 (1993), 84-86.

    Trevijano Etcheverria, R. *Salmanticensis* 39 (1992), 308-10.

Jacobson, A. D. *The First Gospel: An Introduction to Q.* (Foundations & Facets.) Sonoma: Polebridge Press, 1992.

Kloppenborg, J. *The Formation of Q* . . . .

    Anonymous. *ADRIS Newsletter* 16 (1986/87), 81-82.

    Fairchild, M. R. *Journal of the Evangelical Theological Society* 34 (1991), 123-24.

Kloppenborg, J. *Q Parallels* . . . .

Fuchs, A. *Studien zum Neuen Testament und seiner Umwelt* 16 (1991), 205-08.

Kloppenborg, J. S., Meyer, M. W., Patterson, S. J. and Steinhauser, M. G. *Q Thomas Reader* . . . .

Guenther, H. *Toronto Journal of Theology* 8 (1992), 336-39.

Matera, F. *Catholic Biblical Quarterly* 54 (1992), 394-95.

Schenke, H.-M. *Theologische Literaturzeitung* 117 (1992), 359-60.

Kosch, D. *Die eschatologische Tora des Menschensohnes in Q* . . . .

Dautzenberg, G. *Biblische Zeitschrift* 36 (1992), 93-103 (NTA 36.1240r).

Witherup, R. D. *Catholic Biblical Quarterly* 54 (1992), 357-58.

Zeller, D. *Theologische Revue* 88 (1992), 28-29.

Mack, B. L. *The Lost Gospel: The Book of Q and Christian Origins*. San Francisco: HarperSanFrancisco, 1993.

Moreland, M. *Bulletin of the Institute for Antiquity and Christianity* 20:1 (March 1993), 13.

Piper, R. A. *Wisdom in the Q Tradition* . . . .

France, R. T. *Evangelical Quarterly* 64 (1992), 174-75.

Hoffmann, P. *Cristianesimo nella Storia* 13 (1992), 421-27.

von Lips, H. *Theologische Revue* 87 (1991), 475-77.

Schüling, J. *Studien zum Verhältnis von Logienquelle* . . . .

Downing, F. G. *Biblica* 73 (1992), 276-79.

Schenk, W. *Theologische Literaturzeitung* 117 (1992), 842-43.

Söding, T. *Theologische Revue* 88 (1992), 376-77.

Articles

Aitken, E. B. "The Covenant Formulary in Q 6:20b-49," *Abstracts: American Academy of Religion/Society of Biblical Literature 1992* (ed. W. C. Frisina and E. H. Lovering, Jr.; Scholars Press, 1992), 223.

Anderson, S. "IQP in Bamberg and Claremont," *Bulletin of the Institute for Antiquity and Christianity* 20:1 (March 1993), 10-11.

Asgeirsson, J. Ma. and Robinson, J. M. "The International Q Project: Work Sessions 12-14 July, 22 November 1991," *Journal of Biblical Literature* 111 (1992), 500-08 (*NTA* 37.688).

Brodie, T. "Not Q but Elijah: The Saving of the Centurion's Servant (Luke 7:1-10) as an Internationalization of the Saving of the Widow and her Child (1 Kgs 17:1-16)," *Irish Biblical Studies* 14 (1992), 54-71 (*NTA* 37.198).

Catchpole, D. R. "Ein Schaf, eine Drachme und ein Israelit: Die Botschaft Jesu in Q," *Die Freude an Gott – unsere Kraft: Festschrift für Otto Bernhard Knoch zum 65. Geburtstag* (hrsg. J. J. Degenhardt; Stuttgart: Katholishes Bibelwerk, 1991), 89-101.

Catchpole, D. R. "The Mission Charge in Q," *Semeia* 55 (1991), 147-74 (*NTA* 36.1229).

Corley, K. E. "Jesus, Egalitarian Meals, and Q," *Abstracts: American Academy of Religion/Society of Biblical Literature 1992* (ed. W. C. Frisina and E. H. Lovering, Jr.; Scholars Press, 1992), 204-05.

Cotter, W. J. "The Parables of the Mustard Seed and the Leaven: Their Function in the Earliest Stratum of Q," *Toronto Journal of Theology* 8 (1992), 38-51 (*NTA* 37.204).

D'Angelo, M. R. "Theology in Mark and Q: *Abba* and 'Father' in Context," *Harvard Theological Review* 85 (1992), 149-74.

Downing, F. G. "Christians and Cynics in the 50's: The Q Document," Chapter 5 in *Cynics and Christian Origins* (Edinburgh: T & T Clark, 1992), 115-42.

Ernst, J. "Johannes der Täufer in der Logienquelle," 1. Kapitel, §II in *Johannes der Täufer: Interpretation–Geschichte–Wirkungsgeschichte* (BZNW 53; Berlin: de Gruyter, 1989), 39-80.

Guenther, H. O. "The Sayings Gospel Q and the Quest for Aramaic Sources: Rethinking Christian Origins," *Semeia* 55 (1991), 41-76 (*NTA* 36.1234).

Hartin, P. J. "'Yet Wisdom is Justified by Her Children': A Rhetorical and Compositional Analysis of Divine Sophia in Q," *Abstracts: American Academy of Religion/Society of Biblical Literature 1992* (ed. W. C. Frisina and E. H. Lovering, Jr.; Scholars Press, 1992), 225.

Horsley, R. A. "Q and Jesus: Assumptions, Approaches, and Analyses," *Semeia* 55 (1991), 175-209 (*NTA* 36.1235).

Horsley, R. A. "Social Conflict Reflected in the Synoptic Sayings Source Q," *Abstracts: American Academy of Religion/Society of Biblical Literature 1992* (ed. W. C. Frisina and E. H. Lovering, Jr.; Scholars Press, 1992), 224.

Jacobson, A. D. "The Sayings Gospel Q," *The Complete Gospels: Annotated Scholars Version* (ed. R. J. Miller; Sonoma: Polebridge Press, 1992), 248-300.

Kloppenborg, J. S. "Literary Convention, Self-Evidence and the Social History of the Q People," *Semeia* 55 (1991), 77-102 (*NTA* 36.1237).

Kloppenborg, J. S. and Vaage, L. E. "Early Christianity, Q and Jesus: The Sayings Gospel and Method in the Study of Christian Origins," *Semeia* 55 (1991), 1-14 (*NTA* 36.1238).

Lambrecht, J. "John the Baptist and Jesus in Mark 1.1-15: Markan Redaction of Q?" *New Testament Studies* 38 (1992), 357-84 (*NTA* 37.166).

Levine, A.-J. "Feminist Food for Thought: The Leavening of the Q Community," *Abstracts: American Academy of Religion/Society of Biblical Literature 1992* (ed. W. C. Frisina and E. H. Lovering, Jr.; Scholars Press, 1992), 204.

Mack, B. L. "Q and the Gospel of Mark: Revising Christian Origins," *Semeia* 55 (1991), 15-39 (*NTA* 36.1241).

Meadors, E. P. "The Orthodoxy of the 'Q' Sayings of Jesus," *Tyndale Bulletin* 43 (1992), 233-57 (*NTA* 37.692).

Myllykoski, M. "Dating Q," *Abstracts: American Academy of Religion/Society of Biblical Literature 1992* (ed. W. C. Frisina and E. H. Lovering, Jr.; Scholars Press, 1992), 223.

Piper, R. A. "The Language of Violence and the Aphoristic Sayings in Q," *Abstracts: American Academy of Religion/Society of Biblical Literature 1992* (ed. W. C. Frisina and E. H. Lovering, Jr.; Scholars Press, 1992), 224.

Reed, J. L. "The Social Map of Q: An Analysis of the Q Community's Locale," *Abstracts: American Academy of Religion/Society of Biblical Literature 1992* (ed. W. C. Frisina and E. H. Lovering, Jr.; Scholars Press, 1992), 222-23.

Schelkle, K. H. "Spruchquelle Q," §II.1 in *Israel im Neuen Testament* (Darmstadt: Wissenschaftliche Buchgesellschaft, 1985), 12-20.

Scholer, D. M. "Q Bibliography Supplement III: 1992," *Society of Biblical Literature 1992 Seminar Papers* (ed. E. H. Lovering, Jr.; SBLSPS 31; Atlanta: Scholars Press, 1992), 1-4.

Schottroff, L. "Feminist Observations on the Eschatology of Q," *Abstracts: American Academy of Religion/Society of Biblical Literature 1992* (ed. W. C. Frisina and E. H. Lovering, Jr.; Scholars Press, 1992), 203-04.

Seeley, D. "Blessings and Boundaries: Interpretations of Jesus' Death in Q," *Semeia* 55 (1991), 131-46 (*NTA* 36.1245).

Steinhauser, M. G. "The Violence of Occupation: Matthew 5:40-41 and Q," *Toronto Journal of Theology* 8 (1992), 28-37 (*NTA* 37.141).

Strecker, G. "Die Spruchquelle Q in den Evangelien," §4.2.3 in *Literaturgeschichte des Neuen Testaments* (Uni-Taschenbücher 1682; Göttingen: Vandenhoeck & Ruprecht, 1992), 161-70.

Theissen, G. "Die Logienquelle – palästinazentrierte Perspektiven in der Mitte des 1. Jahrhunderts," 5. Kapitel in *Lokalkolorit und Zeitgeschichte in den Evangelien: Ein Beitrag zur Geschichte der synoptischen Tradition* (Novum Testamentum et Orbis Antiquus 8; Freiburg: Universitätsverlag/ Göttingen: Vandenhoeck & Ruprecht, 1989), 212-45.

Theissen, G. "The Sayings Source: Palestine-Centered Perspectives at the Middle of the First Century," Chapter 5 in *The Gospels in Context: Social and Political History in the Synoptic Tradition* (trans. L. M. Maloney; Minneapolis: Fortress, 1991), 203-34.

Tuckett, C. M. "Q (Gospel Source)," *The Anchor Bible Dictionary* (ed. D. N. Freedman; New York: Doubleday, 1992), 5.567-72.

Vaage, L. E. "Monarchy, Community, Anarchy: The Kingdom of God in Paul and Q," *Toronto Journal of Theology* 8 (1992) 52-69 (*NTA* 37.282).

Vaage, L. E. "Q, Cynicism, and the Historical Jesus," *Abstracts: American Academy of Religion/Society of Biblical Literature 1992* (ed. W. C. Frisina and E. H. Lovering, Jr.; Scholars Press, 1992), 290.

Vaage, L. E. "The Son of Man Sayings in Q: Stratigraphical Location and Significance," *Semeia* 55 (1991), 103-29 (*NTA* 36.1248).

New Testament Abstract Listings To Be Added

Catchpole, D. R. "The Beginning . . . .": *NTA* 36.1228

Kosch, D. "Q und Jesus:" *NTA* 36.1239

Robinson, J. M. "A Critical Test . . . .": *NTA* 36.1243

Seeley, D. "Jesus' Death . . . .": *NTA* 36.1246

Tuckett, C. M. "Q and Thomas . . . .": *NTA* 36.1247

Philo's *Exposition of the Law* and Social History: Methodological Considerations

Adele Reinhartz
McMaster University

The various Philonic treatises grouped under the heading *Exposition of the Law* constitute a relatively orderly and literal (as opposed to allegorical) commentary on the "holy scriptures." These treatises have been mined for information about Philo's philosophical and intellectual background, such as his knowledge of Greek cosmology, Roman law, and rabbinic oral tradition, as well as for insight into the political organization and aspirations of the Alexandrian Jewish community.[1] The homiletical tone of the commentary and the frequent rhetorical use of the second person form of address, however, suggest that these treatises may also provide insight into other, more private issues and concerns of Philo's community, at least as he perceived them. Explicit discussions of parent-child relationships, divorce, inheritance, and other aspects of family life, raise the rather tantalizing possibility of using Philo's *Exposition* as a source for social history in general, and the history of the Jewish family in particular.[2]

This paper is a preliminary attempt to address the question of whether and how it may be possible to draw social-historical data from Philo's exegetical discussions in the *Exposition*. We will consider, first, the rather formidable methodological obstacles which block the way to such an approach and, second, the differing assumptions that would either prevent or facilitate this

---

[1] Cf. David T. Runia, *Philo of Alexandria and the Timaeus of Plato* (Leiden: Brill, 1986); E. R. Goodenough, *The Jurisprudence of the Jewish Courts in Egypt* (New Haven: Yale University Press, 1929); Samuel Belkin, *Philo and the Oral Law* (Cambridge, Mass.: Harvard University Press, 1940); Aryeh Kasher, *The Jews in Hellenistic and Roman Egypt: The Struggle for Equal Rights* (Tübingen: Mohr, 1985).

[2] Social history may be defined as the study of "people's relationships with each other in families, kinship groupings, status groupings, villages, urban neighbourhoods, regions and polities." Sheldon Watts, *A Social History of Western Europe 1450-1720* (London: Hutchinson University Library, 1984) 1. "Families in Former Times," as one such work is entitled, have become a subject of great interest on the part of historians in recent years, as indicated by the growing number of articles and monographs in this area. See Jean Louis Flandrin, *Families in Former Times* (Cambridge: Cambridge University Press, 1972); Thomas E. J. Wiedemann, *Adults and Children in the Roman Empire* (London: Routledge, 1989); Mark Golden, *Children and Childhood in Classical Athens* (Baltimore: Johns Hopkins University Press, 1990); Shaye J. D. Cohen, ed., *The Jewish Family in Antiquity* (BJS; Atlanta: Scholars Press, forthcoming).

enterprise. Finally, we will look at some examples of scriptural exposition related to family issues. These will be drawn from *Special Laws* (*Spec.*), with occasional forays into *On The Decalogue* (*Dec.*) and *On the Virtues* (*Virt.*).

Methodological Problems

The *Exposition* is an exegetical work, the structure and content of which for the most part are based directly on the Pentateuch as Philo read it. This is evident not only from its contents but also from explicit Philonic statements to that effect. In *On Abraham* (*Abr.*) 3 Philo describes his task in the *Exposition* as the "examination of the law in regular sequence."[3] In *Dec.* 1 he proposes "to give full descriptions of the written laws," while in *Spec.* he focuses on "the particular ordinances" which he considers to be grouped under the ten headings provided by the Decalogue (*Spec.* 1.1).[4]

It is its exegetical genre that is at the root of the methodological difficulties in tapping the *Exposition* for data pertaining to Jewish family life in Philo's Alexandria.[5] Three problems may be singled out. First, Philo makes no attempt to provide a comprehensive discussion of "the Jewish family;" any insights into his views on family-related issues must be gleaned from the various places where these topics arise in his ten-fold classification of Jewish law. So, for example, the laws pertaining to forbidden marriages, incest, and intermarriage, are discussed under the category of the sixth commandment, which forbids adultery (*Spec.* 3.8, 22-29). Many other issues, such as child mortality, average ages of betrothal and marriage, and belief and practices related to fertility and infertility are mentioned only briefly if at all.

Second, it is clear that his discussions of family issues often, though not always, arise when and where they do simply because they appear in the biblical text upon which he happens to be commenting. Hence we cannot determine with any certainly whether his discussion of a specific topic simply represents his thoughts on a particular biblical discussion, or whether it also reflects a concern with some aspect of contemporary life. For example, Philo's vivid condemnation of women who grab the genitals of men during a public brawl (*Spec.* 3.175) might give rise to speculation concerning the pugnacious behavior of women in the marketplace. But because this specific case is described in the text he is explicating (Deut 25:11-12), we cannot conclude that he is reflecting on the situation in his own community.

Third, while Philo's attitudes on particular issues are often crystal clear, it

---

3 All citations and quotations from Philo are from *Philo in Ten Volumes (and two supplementary volumes)* (trans. and ed. F. H. Colson et al.; Loeb Classical Library; London: Heinemann, 1929-62).

4 Cf. Richard D. Hecht, "Preliminary Issues in the Analysis of Philo's *De Specialibus Legibus*," *Studia Philonica* 5 (1978) 1-56.

5 On the importance of recognizing exegesis as Philo's primary activity in the *Exposition*, see David T. Runia, "How to Read Philo," *Exegesis and Philosophy: Studies on Philo of Alexandria* (Great Britain: Variorum, 1990) 191; Thomas H. Tobin, SJ, *The Creation of Man: Philo and the History of Interpretation*, CBQMS 14 Washington, D.C.: Catholic Biblical Association of America, 1983) 2-5; Burton L. Mack, "Philo Judaeus and Exegetical Traditions in Alexandria," *ANRW* II.21.2 (ed. Hildegard Temporini and Wolfang Haase; Berlin: Walter de Gruyter, 1984) 228.

is very difficult to discern the presence or nature of any *realia* pertaining to such issues. For example, Philo is very explicit about his abhorrence of homosexual practices (*Spec.* 2.50; 3.37-42). Yet it is virtually impossible to determine from his vitriolic outbursts whether or to what degree homosexuality was practised in his community. Nor can we say whether his negative views were a reflection or a critique of Jewish popular opinion and/or practice.

A further problem is posed by the paucity and unreliability of external data concerning the Jewish family in first-century Alexandria. Our social-historical endeavor would be on more solid ground if we could correlate Philo's comments with extra-Philonic evidence. While there are a number of papyri from Alexandria, only a few have any relevance for the history of the Jewish family. Notable among these are a deed of divorce,[6] a contract with a wet-nurse, and the annulment of such a contract.[7] While these provide interesting social-historical data, they do not correlate with any Philonic discussions and hence are of limited value for the present task.

Somewhat more relevant are Jewish inscriptions from Greco-Roman Egypt, some of which make reference to family relationships. Of special interest are tombstone inscriptions that speak of the love of parents for their children, or the sadness of young women who died childless or during pregnancy or childbirth.[8] These reflect family values which are also expressed throughout Philo's *Exposition*. Philo too waxes eloquent on the ties of affection in the family, particularly on the part of parents towards their children,[9] and attributes to women in general a strong desire for children.[10] Hence these inscriptions provide general corroboration for claims that Philo, at least in these two respects, is consistent with popular attitudes. They offer little, however, in the way of specific confirmation of other issues discussed in the *Exposition*.

More numerous and detailed are references to the Jewish family in the works of non-Jewish Greek and Roman authors. Such references are often ambiguous or incorrect and hence must be used with caution. Nor do they always reflect the situation in Alexandria. According to Strabo (first century, Pontus), Jews, like Egyptians, 'excise' female children.[11] Tacitus (first century, Rome) claims that while Jews abstain from intercourse with foreign

---

6 *CPJ* 144, in Victor A. Tcherikover and Alexander Fuks, eds., *Corpus Papyrorum Judaicarum*, vol. 2 (Cambridge, Mass.: Harvard University Press, 1960) 10-12.

7 *CPJ* 146-47 (Tcherikover, *CPJ*, 2.15-20).

8 See William Horbury and David Noy, ed., *Jewish Inscriptions of Graeco-Roman Egypt* (Cambridge: Cambridge University Press, 1992) 38, 61, 70, 90, 103, 114.

9 See *Abr.* 195; *Jos.* 4; *Spec.* 2.129, 239-40. It may be claimed that what Philo and his contemporaries actually meant by "love and affection" differed significantly from our own understanding of this affective bond. But see Golden (*Childhood*, 82ff.), who affirms that, contrary to what many scholars have argued, Athenian parents did love their children in the ways that modern parents do, despite the high mortality rate and the practice of infanticide in classical Greece.

10 See *Mos.* 1.13-14, where Philo attributes the eagerness of Pharaoh's daughter to adopt the infant Moses to her depression over the failure to conceive a child, "though she naturally desired one, particularly of the male sex . . . ."

11 *Geography* 17:2, 5.

women, among themselves nothing is unlawful,[12] a statement which ignores Jewish laws against incest (Lev 18:6-18) as well as the laws governing sexual intercourse between husband and wife (Lev 15:19-32; 18:19).

While these statements are clearly incorrect, others have been given more credence. A notable example is the assertion, made by the above-mentioned writers, that Jews rear all their children. Because infanticide and the exposure of infants are also discussed by Philo (*Spec.* 3.110-19; *Virt.* 131-33), scholars have taken these comments along with Philo's condemnation of these practices as evidence that Jews did not engage in these practices.[13] As we shall see below, however, the audience and intent of Philo's comments on this issue are open to question; furthermore, the assertions of Strabo and Tacitus appear in the same passages as the errors noted above. Although the presence of some errors does not mean that all comments are mistaken, it does highlight the need for caution in using Greco-Roman literature to illuminate Jewish life in Alexandria.

These considerations return us once again to the task of finding a way to extract social-historical data from the *Exposition* itself. Yet, as we have seen, the exegetical focus of these treatises renders this endeavor difficult indeed.

Scholarly Assumptions

The connection between Philo's scriptural expositions and the actual attitudes, activities, and practices of the Jewish community in first-century Alexandria has received little detailed treatment in Philonic scholarship. Studies of Philo's legal commentary have tended to focus on the question of its sources in Greek and Roman law and philosophy on the one hand, and/or Tannaitic or pre-Tannaitic oral tradition and halakhah on the other. E. R. Goodenough, for example, argued that many passages in *Spec.* reflect the legal practices of Philo's community.[14] What Philo has done in *Spec.*, suggests Goodenough, is to "rebuild the whole structure of Jewish law upon a foundation of Greek, Roman, and Alexandrine jurisprudence."[15] Samuel Belkin, while accepting that Philo's legal discussions are based on the decisions of local Jewish courts, argues that most of the laws described in the *Exposition* agree with the principles of Tannaitic law.[16] More recently, scholars have focused on the issue of Philo's dependence on or independence from Palestinian and/or Hellenistic Jewish exegetical traditions,[17] setting aside the question of Philo's own intellectual contribution[18] or the possibility that he may be reacting to or reflecting on real social issues.

---

12 *Histories* 5:5.

13 Cf. page XXX below.

14 Goodenough, *Jurisprudence*, 10 and passim.

15 Ibid., 14.

16 Belkin, *Oral Law*, 5-6, 19.

17 See Burton L. Mack, "Exegetical Traditions in Alexandrian Judaism: A Program for the Analysis of the Philonic Corpus," *Studia Philonica* 3 (1974-5) 106; Jacques Cazeaux, "Système implicite dans l'exégèse de Philon," *Studia Philonica* 6 (1979-80) 5; Yehoshua Amir, "Philo and the Bible," *Studia Philonica* 2 (1973) 1.

18 Mack, "Program," 108.

These trends in Philonic scholarship on the *Exposition* point to assumptions regarding Philo's involvement in the Jewish community. Many scholars consider Philo to be more concerned with scripture, philosophy, and law than with contemporary social and communal issues per se. Sandmel, for example, describes Philo as "an ivory tower figure, rather than a man engaged in committee work in the community," a description he infers from Philo's prodigious literary output.[19] Others, however, find this description inadequate, arguing that while Philo's concern with exegesis and philosophy is clearly paramount, his involvement in and concern for Jewish community life is not to be dismissed. Peder Borgen's Philo lives squarely "in the double context of the Jewish community and the Alexandrian Greek community,"[20] and is concerned to make the Pentateuch interpret Jewish community life.[21] Borgen concludes that "Philo was an exegete who interpreted the Pentateuch and Jewish exegetical traditions into his contemporary situation, without cutting off their historical basis in the Biblical events."[22]

Runia, Kasher, and McKnight assume that certain sections of Philo's work describe the history,[23] institutions,[24] or attitudes[25] of his own city and community. Such assumptions are also basic to Goodenough's discussion of Philo's politics[26] and legal rulings[27] and are expressed explicitly by Belkin, who asserts that "The general view prevalent among scholars that Philo had no interest in communal affairs and was, as is sometimes said, an 'individualist' by nature is open to doubt."[28]

A second set of assumptions concerns the nature of the Jewish family in antiquity, an issue closely related to that of the relationship of the Diaspora Jewish community to its non-Jewish social environment. Are we to picture the Jewish family as isolated, insular, and therefore in some sense inoculated against the problems of the gentile family in Alexandria? Or should we assume that Jewish family relationships may have been similar to and even influenced by those of non-Jews even when in contravention of what we perceive to be Jewish ideals? Scholars' answers to these questions may reflect not only their academic evaluations of Jewish political and social status in the Diaspora but also more personal issues, such as the tendency to idealize the Jewish family in antiquity. Such idealization is clearly expressed in modern

---

[19] Samuel Sandmel, "Philo Judaeus: An Introduction to the Man, his Writings, and his Significance," *ANRW* II.21.1, 5.

[20] Peder Borgen, "Philo of Alexandria: A Critical and Synthetical Survey of Research," *ANRW* II.21.1, 119.

[21] Ibid., 138.

[22] Ibid., 150.

[23] Runia, "Polis and Megalopolis: Philo and the Founding of Alexandria," *Exegesis and Philosophy*, 398.

[24] Kasher, *Jews*, 206, 256.

[25] Scot McKnight, "*De Vita Mosis* 1.147: Lion Proselytes in Philo?" *The Studia Philonica Annual*, vol. 1 (ed. David T. Runia; Atlanta: Scholars Press, 1989) 58-62.

[26] E. R. Goodenough, *The Politics of Philo Judaeus: Practice and Theory* (New Haven: Yale University Press, 1938).

[27] Goodenough, *Jurisprudence.*

[28] Belkin, *Oral Law,* 6.

Jewish popular writings intended to reinforce "traditional" Jewish family values. A recent book entitled *Love, Marriage, and Family in Jewish Law and Tradition* declares that

> In the past, virtually impervious to degenerative influences from the outside world, the Jewish home was universally respected as a model of stability, wholesomeness, and integrity. This is no longer the case [in assimilated, twentieth century Jewish life].[29]

The assumption of a pure, strong, stable family life, while not stated explicitly in scholarship on Jews in antiquity, may be lurking behind the conclusion that certain gentile practices were unknown among Diaspora Jews. This may explain the readiness of scholars to take the testimony of Strabo et al., that Jews rear all their children, at face value. Menahem Stern, for example, states emphatically that "the Jews' religious duty to rear all their children and their view that the exposure of new-born children is tantamount to murder offer a striking contrast to the Greek habit of killing . . . infants, a constant feature of Greek life . . . ."[30]

Historians and social scientists who study the history of the Jewish family suggest that the perfect, uncorrupted Jewish family in antiquity is a myth.[31] David Kraemer introduces a volume of essays on the Jewish family by stating that

> If we understand the dynamism of earlier social conditions, we will appreciate the fact that contemporary experience represents less of a break with the past than we might have believed.

What emerges from this volume, he continues,

> is a picture of immense variety and the realization that down through the ages the Jewish family has adapted almost "organically" to the many and varied environments within which it has had to survive.[32]

This picture is apparently shared by scholars such as John Boswell, who suggests that the Jewish family might not have differed substantially from its gentile counterpart, even with respect to something as difficult as abandonment of children.[33]

Assumptions regarding the nature of the Jewish family—pure or assimilated—may generate further, more specific assumptions concerning the relevance of Philo's *Exposition* for the history of the Jewish family in antiquity. Perhaps the most important issue of this sort concerns the relationship between legal prohibition and community practice. Does Philo's

---

29 Michael Kaufman, *Love, Marriage, and Family in Jewish Law and Tradition* (New Jersey: Aronson, 1992) xxii.

30 M. Stern, *Greek and Latin Authors on Jews and Judaism*, vol. 1 (Jerusalem: Israel Academy of Sciences and Humanities, 1974) 33.

31 Gerald B. Bubis, *Saving the Jewish Family: Myths and Realities in the Diaspora* (New York: University Press of America, 1987) x.

32 David Kraemer, ed., *The Jewish Family: Metaphor and Memory* (New York: Oxford University Press, 1989) 5.

33 John Boswell, *The Kindness of Strangers* (New York: Vintage, 1988) 139-152.

assertion that a particular act was forbidden by Mosaic law mean that it was in fact foreign to the experience of the Jewish community? Philo himself does not assume this to be the case. For example, he suggests that the laws penalizing men who falsely accuse their wives of infidelity are aimed at those persons "who show fickleness in their relations to women" (*Spec.* 3.79). His discussion of the laws about murder assumes the existence of murderers in the community (e.g. *Spec.* 3.83ff.). Similarly, he is of the conviction that such penalties serve as a deterrent, "as a considerable check on those who are eager to practice the like" (*Spec.* 3.42).

These passages would suggest that Philo's strong condemnation of certain behaviors, and his assertions that they are prohibited by Mosaic law, point to activities which he perceived to be practiced in his community. This would undermine Léonie Archer's conclusion that the fact that Philo, Josephus, and the Sibylline Oracles declare infanticide and exposure to be contrary to Jewish law means that "the practice of exposing unwanted infants . . . was not found among the Jews of the Greco-Roman period."[34]

Implicit in the above discussion is yet another assumption, namely, the issue of intended audience. Three possibilities may be suggested. If the intended audience of the *Exposition* is gentile, as Goodenough argued, then passages condemning practices such as infanticide and homosexuality may not reflect Jewish practice at all, but may rather be directed at activities of the gentile readership which are amply documented elsewhere.[35] Or, if the audience is also composed of Jews "on the threshold of apostasy," as Sandmel suggested, Philo may be exhorting his Jewish readers not to adopt the immoral practices of their gentile neighbors.[36] Many scholars, however, consider the *Exposition* to be addressed to the Jewish community as a whole.[37] This view is supported by Philo's assertion that the law, while universally applicable, is addressed in the first place to Jews and proselytes (*Spec.* 4.100, 219; *Virt.* 102).

A *priori* views of Philo as removed from community life, of the Jewish community in Alexandria as insulated and isolated, of Philo's declarations about Mosaic law as descriptive of Alexandrian reality, and of Philo's *Exposition* as addressed to a gentile audience work against the use of this exegetical work as a source for the history of the Jewish family. The contrary assumptions—of Philo as involved in community life, of the potential influence of gentile practices on Jewish family life, of legal prohibitions as

---

34 Léonie Archer, *Her Price is Beyond Rubies: The Jewish Woman in Graeco-Roman Palestine*, JSOTSup 60 (Sheffield: Almond Press, 1990) 28. Cf. also L. E. Stager, "Eroticism and Infanticide at Ashkelon," *BARev* 17/4 (July/August 1991) 46.

35 See, for example, Boswell, *Kindness*, 53-137; D. Engels, "The Problem of Female Infanticide in the Greco-Roman World," *CPh* 75 (1980) 112-30; W. V. Harris, "The Theoretical Possibility of Extensive Infanticide in the Graeco-Roman World," *CQ* 32 (1982) 114-16; M. Golden, "Demography and the Exposure of Girls at Athens," *Phoenix* 35 (1981): 316-31; Sarah B. Pomeroy, "Infanticide in Hellenistic Greece," *Images of Women in Antiquity* (ed. A. Cameron and A. Kuhrt; Detroit: Wayne State University Press, 1983) 207-22.

36 Samuel Sandmel, *Philo of Alexandria: An Introduction* (New York: Oxford University Press, 1979) 47.

37 Victor Tcherikover, "Jewish Apologetic Literature Reconsidered," *Eos* 48 (1965) 178-79.

directed against actual practice, and of a Jewish audience for the *Exposition*—would provide a basis for considering these treatises as a source for social history, and, as we have suggested, may be equally plausible.[38]

Scriptural Exposition and Social History

Support for the second set of assumptions is provided by a brief examination of Philo's exegetical strategies in the *Exposition*, and the hermeneutical presuppositions which these strategies imply. Philo's exegetical method in the *Exposition* has been considered primarily from three perspectives: his use of sources, whether Greco-Roman, Palestinian, or Alexandrian; his allegorical interpretation, and his grouping of the particular laws according to the ten "headings" of the Decalogue.[39] For the purposes of detecting social-historical information between the lines of exegesis, our focus shall be on the specific moves Philo makes with respect to the biblical text he is expounding.

Several different types of moves may be noticed.

1. In almost every passage, Philo provides a rationale for the biblical law where none is provided by the biblical text itself. In the course of doing so, he often also explains scripture's silence on issues that in his view might well have been included in biblical legislation.

2. Philo will often extend the laws explicitly discussed in scripture to cover other situations that seem to him to be analogous to or implicit in biblical law.

3. He reinterprets laws that reflect social conditions that are no longer operative in his place and time.

4. He provides specific instructions and more precise definitions in cases where biblical law provides only a general formulation.

These exegetical moves imply Philo's hermeneutical presuppositions vis-à-vis Mosaic law as set out literally in scripture. First, the law is divinely given and applicable to every era and to all Jews. Second, the law covers, either explicitly or implicitly, all aspects of private, family, communal, and ritual life. In doing so, it implies an absolute set of values that can be abstracted from the text and applied to many situations. Third, the law as set out in scripture requires explanation and interpretation in order that Jews may understand and therefore be able to follow it. Fourth, the law must therefore be explained in ways that will be meaningful to its contemporary audience. Finally, the law should be practised in its literal sense by all Jews, including those in Philo's community, a view expressed explicitly by Philo in *Mig.* 89-93.

These hermeneutical presuppositions tend to support the idea that Philo's commentary does reflect his concerns for his own community and addresses those issues in some way. The way that he does so may reflect only his own views and perceptions, but it is also possible that at certain points his work

---

38 This is not to say, of course, that these assumptions are incorrect, or that those scholars who refrain from discussing family issues hold to all or even any of these assumptions. For most scholars, their work on Philo simply reflects other legitimate research interests as well as the incontrovertible fact that Philo's *Exposition* is above all an exegetical work and not an analysis of public and private policy and practice.

39 Cf. Hecht, "Preliminary Issues," 1-56.

reflects practices and attitudes present in his own community, not only in what he says in a positive way but also in what his legal argumentation critiques. This in turn implies that we can look at his exegesis for hints regarding the texture of family life in his community. We will illustrate this possibility by looking briefly at examples of each of the strategies we outlined above.

1. Rationalization

The topics of many of Philo's discussions pertinent to family issues are generated by the text itself. His discussions of the widowed or divorced, childless daughter of a priest, who returns to live with her father (*Spec.* 1.129-30; cf. Lev 22:13), of the requirement to redeem one's first-born, if a son (*Spec.* 1.134-40; cf. Ex. 13:2; 22:29; Num. 18:15-16), and of the laws of inheritance, according to which "the heirs of parents are to be sons, or failing sons daughters" (*Spec.* 2.124-30; cf. Num 27:8-11), are only a few examples among many of discussions the topics of which are derived directly from biblical law.

a. Rationalization of biblical law

The rationales that he provides for these laws, however, do not necessarily find their explicit source in the biblical text. For example, the biblical commandment to redeem the first-born son appears in the context of the law concerning the sacrificial offering of first-born animals. No reason is given in Ex or Num for the requirement to redeem the first-born son with a financial redemption fee. Philo fills this gap by describing this redemption as "a thank-offering for the blessings of parenthood realized in the present and the hopes of fruitful increase in the future" (*Spec.* 1.138). The "consecration of a fixed sum of money" is intended to prevent the separation of parents from their children and vice versa, and to assign equal value to the birth of a child to poor parents as to rich (*Spec.* 1.139-40). This argument places a positive value on procreation and on preserving the integrity of the nuclear family, values expressed in other Philonic discussions.[40]

A second example of Philo's rationalization of biblical law concerns the laws of inheritance. The fact that sons take precedence over daughters in matters of inheritance is considered by Philo to be analogous to the law of nature: ". . . just as in nature men take precedence of women, so too in the scale of relationships they should take the first place in succeeding to the property and filling the position of the departed . . ." (*Spec.* 2.124). The biblical text makes no such deduction, though one may infer that according to the biblical view "men take precedence of women" in many legal matters.[41] Philo uses his own thoroughgoing patriarchal worldview to provide the rationale for this biblical law.[42]

---

[40] See, for example, *Virt.* 131-33.

[41] See Judith Romney Wegner, "Leviticus," *The Women's Bible Commentary* (ed. Carol A. Newsom and Sharon H. Ringe; Louisville, KY: Westminster/John Knox, 1992) 36-44.

[42] Philo was of course not unique among Greco-Roman writers in his patriarchal worldview. See Mary Lefkowitz and Maureen Fant, eds., *Women in Greece and Rome* (Toronto: Samuel Stevens, 1977); Sarah Pomeroy, *Goddesses, Whores, Wives, and Slaves* (New York: Schocken, 1975); Eva Cantarella, *Pandora's Daughters* (Baltimore: The Johns Hopkins

b. Rationalization of omissions from biblical law

In other passages, Philo provides a rationale for the silence of the biblical text. In *Spec.* 2.129-32, for example, he considers a question raised "by some inquirers," namely, "Why . . . does the Law when dealing with the regulations of inheritance mention kinsmen of every degree . . . but leaves parents alone unmentioned who would naturally inherit from the children as the children do from them?" (*Spec.* 2. 129). Philo reads into this biblical silence the law's desire to refrain from "sinister thoughts": the distressing possibility that parents might be predeceased by their children, a circumstance "out of tune with and discordant to the harmony and concord which prevails throughout the cosmic order" (*Spec.* 2.130). This rationale, like that of the laws of redemption of the first-born, assumes the affection of parents towards their children, a theme which appears frequently in Philo's discussion of parent-child relations.[43]

c. Use of contemporary examples

In the course of these rationalizations, Philo often makes use of contemporary examples, drawing on customs, experiences or events with which his readers may be familiar. For example, in *Spec.* 3.159-62, Philo illustrates the unjustified cruelty of some people with the example of a tax-collector "a little time ago in our own district." In *Spec.* 1.123-28, Philo seems to be speaking directly of the experience of himself and others of his class when he describes the relationships between masters and slaves:

> Our domestics are always with us and share our lives. They prepare the ordinary food and drink and additional dishes for their masters, stand by the table and carry out the remains. Whether we wish it or not, they will even if they do not take them openly, pilfer them on the sly . . .

Similarly, Philo attributes the misdeeds such as the taking of bribes to the way in which the offender was raised by the women of the household:

> Now the principal cause of such misdeeds is familiarity with falsehood which grows up with the children right from their birth and from the cradle, the work of nurses and mothers and the rest of the company, slaves and free, who belong to the household (*Spec.* 4.68).

d. Implications for the study of the Jewish family in Alexandria

One may speculate that the various ways in which Philo provides a rationale for what is present in or omitted from biblical law reflects his own views, regardless of whether these are paralleled in other Jewish or non-Jewish sources. The brief examples of family law that we have considered demonstrate his patriarchal worldview and his conviction concerning the similarity between Mosaic law and natural law, which justifies the general principle that "men take precedence over women" and that parents should predecease their children. Also evident are the positive evaluation of

---

University Press, 1987).

43 For a survey of Philo's views on this issue, see my "Parents and Children: A Philonic Perspective," *Jewish Family in Antiquity*, forthcoming.

procreation and familial togetherness, in recognition of which the law, as Philo sees it, makes every effort not to separate parents and children. Finally, Philo's disparaging description of childrearing in *Spec.* 4.68 implies the image of a household as being composed of many people of difficult classes and roles (slaves, nurses, mothers). This passage may also be indirect testimony to the important role of women in addition to the mother in the raising of children, at least among the higher classes with whom Philo, as suggested by his description of the master-servant relationship, may have been acquainted.

2. Extension of Biblical Topics

In addition to providing a rationale for biblical laws or the omissions therefore, Philo extends them to cover analogous situations not explicitly described in the biblical text. In doing so, he does not perceive himself as creating new laws, but rather as drawing out and making explicit various laws that are already implicit in the biblical formulation. This strategy is expressed in his comment that "in the fifth commandment on honouring parents we have a suggestion of many necessary laws drawn up to deal with the relations of old to young, rulers to subjects, benefactors to benefited, slaves to masters."

a. Extensions of the law to cover cases similar to but not explicitly mentioned in the biblical text

An example of this strategy is to be found in his extension of the biblical laws concerning rape to include sexual assault of widowed and divorced women, cases which are not discussed in the biblical text itself (*Spec.* 3.64).[44] A second example is to be found in Philo's discussion of inheritance, in which he extends the biblical law by claiming that girls who do not have dowries inherit from the father even when there are sons (*Spec.* 2.125).

This strategy, like 1(b) above, demonstrates Philo's perception of a gap in the literary text of the Pentateuch. In these cases, however, rather than rationalizing the gap, he eliminates it by inserting explanations of the laws that are unarticulated in the biblical text. Do these insertions point to issues of concern regarding his own community, or is Philo simply engaged in a theoretical exercise? While this question is difficult to answer in any definitive way, some clues might be provided by the length and tone of each individual discussion. Because it is short and theoretical in its tone, it may be argued that the extension of rape law to include the case of the formerly-married woman is based on Philo's perception that the biblical law has omitted one possible situation from its presentation. The case of unmarried daughters left fatherless, however, is explained in much more detail, with provision made for how, where, and by whom a husband is to be found for such girls. This may point to a situation which actually occurred frequently enough in Philo's community to warrant the development of precise procedures.

---

44 Cf. Deut 22:22-29. Colson, *Philo,* 7.514-15 notes the difficulty of determining whether "what he says reflects the practice of his time . . . or merely what he feels would be right." Goodenough (*Jurisprudence,* 90-91) suggests that this was an independent tradition of the Alexandrian courts.

b.   Extensions which cover cases only tangentially related to the biblical law under discussion

In *Spec.* 3.34-36 Philo sharply criticizes those "who plough the hard and stony land," namely, men who marry women known to be infertile. Although this discussion would seem to have no connection to any biblical verse,[45] it in fact is an elaboration of the preceding discussion of the laws pertaining to menstruation and intercourse (*Spec.* 3.32-33; cf. Lev 18:19). Philo's main point in the latter discussion is "that generative seed should not be wasted fruitlessly for the sake of a gross and untimely pleasure" (*Spec.* 3.32). The theme that seed should not be wasted is also prominent in his discussion of the former point: in mating with barren women, men are "in quest of mere licentious pleasure like the most lecherous of men," a quest which entails the purposeful destruction of "the procreative germs" (*Spec.* 3.34). The tone and length of the discussion conveys Philo's strong disapproval of a situation that no doubt was known to him from the community, and expresses his firm belief that the only legitimate purpose of marriage and marital intercourse is procreation.

Spec. 4.203 provides another example of this strategy. In this passage Philo links the biblical prohibition of the mixing of different species of animals with the prohibition of adultery which is not mentioned in the biblical passage under discussion (Lev 19:19; Deut. 22:9-11): "For by prohibiting the crossing of irrational animals with different species he [Moses] appears to be indirectly working towards the prevention of adultery." Like the previous example, this extension expresses the disapproval of a practice, namely, adultery, that was the subject of his extreme disapproval in many other passages in the *Special Laws*, and, we may reasonably assume, was not totally foreign to Philo's community.[46]

Philo's impassioned arguments against infanticide also fall into this category.[47] *Spec.* 3.110-19 is a comment on Exodus (Ex) 21:22, which discusses the penalties for foeticide. *Virt.* 131-33 is part of his discussion of Leviticus (Lev) 22:27, which stipulates that a newborn ox, sheep or goat must stay seven days with its mother before being offered by fire to the Lord. Neither of these biblical passages refers to infanticide or exposure of infants, yet they provide Philo with the framework and vocabulary for his condemnation of these practices. Hence he declares that if the law is concerned about the life of an unborn child, how much more must this be true about the life of a newly-born child (*Spec.* 3.111). And if "even in the case of irrational animals, the offspring should not be separated from their mother . . . " how much more so is this true of human beings (*Virt.* 133).

As we have already noted, most scholars consider Philo's arguments, together with the statements of non-Jewish Greco-Roman writers, to be evidence that Jews did not kill or expose their new born children. It may be

---

45 So Colson, *Philo* 7.497, 633-34. For an analysis of the rabbinic views on this issue, see Jeremy Cohen, *"Be Fertile and Increase, Fill the Earth and Master It": The Ancient and Medieval Career of a Biblical Text* (Ithaca: Cornell University Press, 1989) 135-40.

46 See *Spec.* 3:52-63; *Virt.* 37.

47 For detailed discussion of this issue, see my "Philo on Infanticide," *Studia Philonica Annual*, vol. 4 (ed. David T. Runia; Leiden: Brill, 1992) 42-58.

suggested, however, that the fact that Philo introduces this topic, not once but twice, into exegetical discussions of verses to which it is only tangentially related should make us suspect that he was indeed concerned with the actual or potential recourse to these methods of population control in his own community.[48] The length of his arguments, the rhetorical use of the second person form of address, and the general tone of his discussion point in the same direction. It may be argued that what he is objecting to so strongly is the gentile practice of exposure or infanticide. It must be noted, however, that his critique of "other nations" refers to their failure to condemn this "sacrilegious practice" (*Spec.* 3.110). Hence the contrast he is making is not between gentiles who engage in this practice and Jews who do not, but between gentile law which regards this practice complacently and mosaic law, which condemns it most strongly.

c. Implications for the study of the Jewish family in Alexandria

The above comments suggest that the directions in which Philo extends biblical laws, together with the length to which and the rhetorical tone in which he does so, may point to topics of particular concern to him. These topics express his point of view on these issues, as well as the principles which undergird his perspective. They may also, however, hint at actual practices and concerns of the Jewish community, including the ways in which that community dealt with orphaned unmarried girls, and the possibility that some members of the community resorted to infanticide or the exposure of infants.

3. Contemporization of an Obsolete Law

a. Example of contemporization

In some passages, Philo reinterprets a law that is no longer applicable to his time in such a way as to make it applicable. For example, *Spec.* 2.135-39 is a discussion of Deut 22:15-17, pertaining to matters of inheritance in a situation in which a man has two wives, one loved and the other unloved. Biblical law stipulates that the son of the disliked woman inherits twice what the son of the beloved wife inherits. At a time when bigamy and formal concubinage were apparently no longer practised in the Jewish community, Philo applies this law to a situation in which a man, legally married to a wife who has borne a son, is engaged in an adulterous relationship which has also resulted in a son. He likens the legal wife to the hated wife of the biblical passage, and argues that her son receives twice the portion of the other son, on the grounds that the son of the legal wife has suffered by being abandoned by his father. This law, according to Philo, "shews mercy and pity for the victims of injustice" and equalizes the situation of the two families (*Spec.* 2.138-39). This discussion expresses Philo's abhorrence of adultery, which he criticizes severely elsewhere (cf. also *Spec.* 3.79-83). It also indicates that his condemnation of adultery is based not only on the licentiousness of the act, but also on the fact that it has severe social consequences affecting the legal family.

---

[48] A third reference to exposure is to be found in *Mos.* 1.10-11, in Philo's description of the birth and rescue of the infant Moses.

b. Implications for the study of the Jewish family in Alexandria

Philo's condemnation of adultery expresses his disapproval of licentiousness and passion, which run counter to his views of ideal human behavior. His discussion may also be taken as evidence for the social norm of monogamy in his community, and also, plausibly, as a reflection of a contemporary social issue which the Alexandrian community had to address.

4. Specification of a general Biblical Law

a. Example of Specification

A good example of this procedure is to be found in Philo's treatment of the fifth commandment. The biblical law simply enjoins people to honor their mothers and fathers, without specifying precisely what it means to do so. Philo provides two precise definitions of this commandment. In *Dec.* 111-19 he defines honoring as taking care of one's parents in their old age, a *topos* common to Greek philosophy.[49] The length and eloquence of his discussions suggests that this was an area of immediate concern to Philo and/or his community.

A similar strategy is evident in *Spec.* 2.228-41. In this section, Philo defines honoring one's parents as "trying both to be good and to seem good, to be good by seeking virtue simple and unfeigned, to seem good by seeking it accompanied by a reputation for worth and the praise of those around you" (*Spec.* 2.235). Evident in this section is Philo's concern to define the role and authority of parents, though this is not at all the subject of the biblical text of the fifth commandment.

To this latter definition is attached a discussion of the biblical law specifying the death penalty for a rebellious son (Deut 21:18-21). Philo's discussion is considered by some scholars to have been influenced by Roman laws regarding *patria potestas*, according to which the father had the power of life and death over the members of his household. This raises the interesting possibility that these laws, or a variation of them, were also operative in family relationships in the Jewish community. Whether or not that is the case, Philo's discussion does not necessarily mean that rebellious sons were actually executed, since this topic is generated by the biblical text itself. It does emphasize, however, the importance to Philo of the preservation of hierarchical relationships within the family, and in particular, of the authority of the father over his children. Recourse to execution is only the most extreme form of asserting such authority; it is an option only after the failure of other disciplinary actions such as upbraiding and admonishing him severely, beating and degrading him, and putting him in bonds. Also to be considered is the possibility of disinheritance. None of these are mentioned in the biblical text about the rebellious son, suggesting that they may derive from Greco-Roman law and/or the actual practice in the community.[50]

---

49 Aristotle, *Nicomachean Ethics* 1165a21-27.

50 See Goodenough, *Jurisprudence*, 70-76; Colson, *Philo* 7.629; Isaak Heinemann, ed., *Die Werke Philos von Alexandria*, vol. 2 (Breslau: M. and H. Marcus, 1910) 173; idem, *Philons griechische und jüdische Bildung* (Breslau: M. and H. Marcus, 1932) 234.

b. Implications for the study of the Jewish family in Alexandria

The fact that Philo spends so much time on this topic implies that the discipline of children, particularly male children, was a problematic issue for him (*Spec.* 2.232, 234, 240-248). Philo himself blames the permissiveness of parents in allowing their children every luxury with the result that "they run to waste both in body and soul" (*Spec.* 2.240).

Conclusions

Our sampling of Philonic exegesis has yielded one certain result: it is much easier to reconstruct Philo's Jewish family values than it is to discern the actual contours of Jewish family life in first-century Alexandria. If one is willing to live with uncertain conclusions, however, several points may be made. First, careful attention to the relationship between biblical legislation and Philonic exegesis thereof may help to identify the issues about which Philo was most concerned. On the assumption that his concerns may be based on the realities of Jewish family life in his community, some exegetical discussions may yield social-historical results. Most significant for this purpose are the passages in which Philo extends the scope of a biblical law to cover areas not mentioned in the biblical formulation of that law. Also significant may be those passages which he reinterprets in the light of changing social relationships. Second, impressions based on Philo's exegetical strategies must be supplemented by considering the tone, length, and content of a particular comment. A lengthy, detailed, and vehement discussion of a topic related only tangentially to a biblical "tag" may be evidence of a significant issue in Philo's community. Third, "throwaway" comments and references to contemporary events, which often appear in Philo's rationalizations, may provide hints regarding household structures and social norms. On the basis of these considerations, it seems reasonable to conclude that situations like adultery, the death of fathers of unmarried daughters, the "rebelliousness" of male children, and the killing or exposure of infants were not unknown within this community, and required the development of particular legislative or community policy decisions and procedures.

This preliminary study supports the cautious use of Philo's *Exposition* as a source for data on the Jewish family in Alexandria. These exegetical treatises cannot, however, be our sole source. Rather, they must be supplemented, and, where feasible, corroborated or corrected by relevant material in the rest of the Philonic corpus, other Jewish and non-Jewish writings of the time,[51] by inscriptions, and papyri. Finally, the entire enterprise must be informed by a healthy but disciplined historical imagination.

One cannot ignore the methodological pitfalls of a social-historical approach to Philo's *Exposition*, nor those that pertain to the other types of material relevant to the Jewish family in the Diaspora. Despite its inherent uncertainty, however, the endeavor is both interesting and worthwhile. It

---

[51] E.g. Pseudo-Phocylides. For this text and discussion of its dating and provenance, see P. W. van der Horst, *The Sentences of Pseudo-Phocylides* (Leiden, 1978); idem, 'Pseudo-Phocylides Revisited,' *JSP* 3 (1988) 15.

promises to enhance our knowledge of Jewish life in antiquity as well as contribute to the growing field devoted to the social history of the family.

Philo's *Quaestiones et solutiones in Genesim*: A Synoptic Approach

Sze-kar Wan
Andover Newton Theological School

Among the many, largely unresolved critical issues in the study of Philo's enigmatic *Quaestiones et solutiones in Genesim et in Exodum*,[1] the relationship between the *Quaestiones* and the *Allegoriae* remains the least explored.[2] Three recent studies have attempted to address this lacuna. Peder Borgen and Roald Skarsten, on the basis of comparing selected passages from the *Quaestiones in Genesim* to corresponding passages in the *Allegoriae* and *Expositiones* in terms of form,

---

[1] Problems may be broadly categorized into textual and structural. For a history of the Armenian text, Latin translations, and Greek fragments, see the excellent survey by E. Hilgert, "The *Quaestiones*: Texts and Translations," *Both Literal and Allegorical: Studies in Philo of Alexandria's Questions and Answers on Genesis and Exodus* (Hay, ed; Brown Judaic Series 232; Atlanta, GA: Scholars Press, 1991) 1-15. Aucherean's *Philonis Judaei paralipomena armena* (Venice: St. Lazarus, 1826) remains the only published (uncritical) Armenian text to date. As for the structural problems, significant gaps exist in the treatment of Biblical texts in the *Quaestiones*. In addition to the beginning and end of Genesis (ch. 1 and 28:10-50:26), Gen 10:10-15:6, which would have appeared between Books Two and Three, is missing from the *Quaestiones in Genesim*, as are the smaller but no less significant lacunae of Gen 21:1-22:24 and 25:9-18. The *Quaestiones in Exodum* are equally fragmentary: large sections from the beginning and end of Exodus (Exod 1:1-12:1 and 28:35-40:36) are missing from the discussion, as well as a sizable mid-section (Exod 12:24-20:24). This latter section would have occupied the gap between Books One and Two of *Quaestiones in Exodum*. Whether Philo compiled the *Quaestiones* to cover the entire Pentateuch has also been a bone of contention. Arguments on this matter have been collected and evaluated by J. Royse, "The Original Structure of Philo's *Quaestiones*," *SP* 4 (1976-77) 42-44. See also E. Lucchesi, "La division en six livres des «*Quaestiones in Genesim*» de Philon d'Alexandrie," *Muséon* 89 (1976) 383-95; A. Terian, "The Priority of the *Quaestiones* among Philo's Exegetical Commentaries," *Both Literal and Allegorical*, 29-46. Eusebius's account in *H. E.* 2.18.1, 5 raises some questions about the original book division of the *Quaestiones*; for this question see the erudite discussion by Royse, "Original Structure," *passim*.

[2] The importance of such a study has been emphasized by D. Runia, "Further Observations on the Structure of Philo's Allegorical Treatises," *VC* 41 (1984) 113; "Secondary Texts in Philo's *Quaestiones*," *Both Literal and Allegorical*, 70.

introductory formulae, and content, concluded that there was close correspondence between the *Quaestiones* and his other treatises.[3] Valentin Nikiprowetzky, in two studies of Philo's commentaries, went a step further and suggested that *all* of the *Allegoriae* and *Expositiones* had been composed by means of this question-and-answer technique.[4] According to Nikiprowetzky, Philo was not so much a systematic philosopher as a commentator of Scripture for whom the principal structure of organization was the Biblical text and all of Philo's commentaries shared a common trait of using the question-and-answer technique, a technique characteristic of though not unique to the *Quaestiones*. An accurate reading of Philo's treatises, therefore, entails first discovering the underlying *quaestio* of each passage. Most recently, Gregory Sterling observed that the *Quaestiones* and the *Allegoriae* follow essentially the same topical order and that solutions raised in the former are often found in the latter. The *Quaestiones* should therefore be considered "Prolegomena" to the *Allegoriae*.[5]

As important as the question of relationship is, it cannot be answered without making reference to the purpose and intended audience of the *Quaestiones*, which are closely tied to the genre of the work. Why did Philo cast a work that covers essentially the same grounds as his *Allegoriae* in an utterly different genre? In what follows, I will first survey pre-Philonic works of the genre ζητήματα καὶ λύσεις and try to locate Philo's *Quaestiones* in the history of the genre.[6] I will then analyze, necessarily in broad outline, the *Quaestiones* with the *Allegoriae* and, as a case study, Philo's discussion of the second creation of man (Gen 2:4-7; *QG* 1.1-5 par *LA* 1.19-42). My thesis is that the *Quaestiones* are an independently compiled work intended most likely for Alexandrian Jews who had been introduced to the rudiments of Biblical exegesis but whose progress had not yet reached the sophistication of the *Allegoriae*.

---

[3] "*Quaestiones et Solutiones*: Some Observations on the Form of Philo's Exegesis," *SP* 4 (1976-77) 1-15.

[4] This hypothesis, first developed in *Le commentaire de L'Ecriture chez Philon d'Alexandrie* (Leiden: Brill, 1977), was later applied to a pericope-by-pericope analysis of the treatises *De gigantibus* and *Quod Deus immutabilis sit* in "L'exégèse de Philon d'Alexandrie dans le *De gigantibus* et le *Quod Deus*," in D. Winston and J. Dillon, *Two Treatises of Philo Alexandria* (D. Winston, J. Dillon, eds.; BJS 25; Chico: Scholars Press, 1983) 5-75.

[5] Gregory E. Sterling, "Philo's *Quaestiones*: Prolegomena or Afterthought?" *Both Literal and Allegorical*, 99-123. The suggestion was first made by S. Sandmel, "Philo's Environment and Philo's Exegesis," *JBR* 22 (1954) 249: "it is likely that the verse by verse exposition are [*sic*] preliminary notes on the basis of which Philo in part got around to composing connected treatises and in part did not."

[6] For a discussion of the socio-cultural dependency of literary genre, see E. D. Hirsch, *Validity in Interpretation* (New Haven, London: Yale University Press, 1967) 76; and D. Aune, *The New Testament in its Literary Environment* (Philadelphia: Westminster, 1987) 13. For a discussion of the evolution of genre, see C. S. Lewis, *A Preface to Paradise Lost* (Oxford: Oxford Univ. Press, 1942) 27-39; Brooks Otis, *Vergil: A Study in Civilized Poetry* (Oxford: Oxford Univ. Press, 1964); and A. Fowler, "The Life and Death of Literary Forms," *New Literary History* 2 (1971) 199-216.

History of Genre

There has never been any doubt about the literary genre of Philo's *Quaestiones*. Scholars since Eusebius have general agreement that the work belongs to the class of writings known as ζητήματα καὶ λύσεις which flourished during the Hellenistic Period. The major disagreement has to do with what conclusion one might draw regarding the purpose of the work.

Basic to the genre ζητήματα καὶ λύσεις is the use of the question-and-answer technique for the purpose of exploring and probing a subject. The subject under scrutiny could be of any variety (scientific, religious, literary) and the nature of the questions could also be equally far-ranging. After all, raising questions is but a natural mode of human enquiry. A. Gudeman made a distinction between the literary and non-literary uses of the question-and-answer technique, according to which literary zetematic works have to do with textual exegesis and non-literary zetematic works with such diverse subjects as physics, ethics, music, metaphysics, and so on.[7] But such a distinction is based on subject matter and content, not on form. To appreciate the versatility of the technique, compare, e.g., Plutarch's *scientific* question on the octopus's color ("Why does the octopus change its color?" *Quaest. nat.* 916b) to his *literary* question on Plato ("Why does Plato say that speech is a mixture of nouns and verbs [*Soph.* 262c2-7]? For it seems that except for these two [parts of speech] Plato dismissed all the parts [of speech], whereas Homer in his exuberance went so far as to pack all together into a single line..." *Plat. quaest.* 1099b-c). Besides the obvious difference in length and in subject matter, there is no discernible formal difference between these two questions: both preface their questions with διὰ τί and both have to do with some kind of curiosity, albeit one draws from nature and the other from literary sources.

Aristotle appears to have composed the first zetematic work, the title of which has been variously reported as Ἀπορήματα Ὁμηρικά, τὰ Ὁμήρου προβλήματα, or Ὁμηρικὰ ζητήματα. The variability of the title bespeaks the interchangeability of the three terms, ζήτημα, πρόβλημα, and ἀπόρημα, when dealing with this genre. The apparently large work[8] has not survived except for 38 fragments gleaned mostly from Porphyry's Ὁμηρικὰ ζητήματα.[9] Most all the fragments

---

7 "Λύσεις," *RE* 13 (1927) 2511.

8 Variously reported as consisting of 6 books (*D. L.* 5.21; *Vita Arist. Hesych.*, 106) or 10 (*Vita Arist. Hesych.*, 147). R. Pfeiffer, *History of Classical Scholarship* (Oxford: Clarendon, 1968) 69 n. 3, thought the work originally consisted of 6 books.

9 Frgs. 142-79 Rose, pp. 120-37. K. Lehr, *De Aristarchi studiis Homericis* (3d ed; Leipzig, 1882; repr. Hildesheim: G. Olms, 1964) 219f., doubted the authenticity of the work, but scholars today by and large agree with Emil Heitz (*Die verlorenen Schriften des Aristoteles* [Leipzig: Teubner, 1865] 258-79) that these fragments can be traced back to Aristotle. Most recently Pfeiffer (*History*, 70) accepted these as genuine fragments from Aristotle's Ἀπορήματα Ὁμηρικά on account of their uniformity of style. For a summary of the discussion pertaining to the issue of authenticity, see Mitchell Carroll, *Aristotle's Poetics, C. XXV in the Light of the Homeric Scholia* (Baltimore: Murray and Co., 1895) 13-14, n. 6. The uniformity of style and pertinence to well-known Homeric questions strongly support the claim that these citations are from Aristotle's lost Ἀπορήματα Ὁμηρικά. The

include questions introduced with the formulaic διὰ τί.[10] There are fourteen exceptions,[11] of which five do not contain questions or objections at all, only comments;[12] two contain only solutions but no questions;[13] and seven are objections or censures (ἐπιτιμήματα) introduced by other zetematic formulae.[14] In sum, 24 out of the extant 31 questions begin with διὰ τί and seven others use fairly standard zetematic terminology.[15]

Two basic forms are represented in these questions, one long and one short. The short *quaestio*-form consists of a simple question introduced by διὰ τί and posed with no elaboration or further objection.[16] The long *quaestio*-form, on the other hand, begins with διὰ τί followed by either a citation or a paraphrase and, as if for emphasis, reiterates the main problem, offers an explanation, or elabora-

solutiones are even more uniform: of the 38 *solutiones*, 31 are introduced either by φησὶ ὁ 'Αριστοτέλης or some such formula. The most frequent being the stereotypical λύειν, *vel sim.*, which is used 11 times in frgs. 149, 152, 160, 161, 164, 166, 170, 171, 172, 173, and 174. This may reflect the consistent style of the scholia or their sources rather than that of Aristotle, however.

10 The glossators, of course, were responsible for the final forms of these questions. But that these questions are relatively free of Hellenistic terms and that often several solutions by different authors would be collected under the same question would argue for the likelihood that these ζητήματα must have been well-known problems whose forms were established and stabilized relatively early on. See the similar judgment by F. Wehrli, ed., *Die Schule des Aristoteles, Bd.* 7 (2d edn; Basel & Stuttgart: Schwabe, 1969) 121.

11 Frgs. 143, 144, 154, 160, 161, 162, 165, 167, 168, 169, 172, 175, 177, 179.

12 Frgs. 154, 162, 165, 169, 179. Frg. 179 also contains references to the title of the work.

13 Frgs. 168, 177.

14 Frgs. 143, 144, 160, 161, 167, 172, 175: Frg. 143 objects to Odysseus's apparent impropriety when he casts off his cloak in public and dons only his tunic in *Il.* 2.183, complaining that ἀπρεπὲς εἶναι δοκεῖ ("It seems improper. . ."). Frg. 144 introduces the question of Menelaus's sleeping alone (contra *Il.* 2.226) with θαυμάσαι δ' ἄν τις, ("Someone may wonder..."). In frg. 160, the standing of spear shafts on butt-ends (cf. *Il.* 10.153) seems to critics as careless (φαύλη δοκεῖ εἶναι). In frg. 167, Aristotle thinks it incredible that the wound sustained by Hector would have healed after his death (cf. *Il.* 24.420); the objection is simply introduced by παράδοξον. Frg. 175, finally, judges the Achaean "unworthy" (ἀπόβλητον) for their killing of the cattle of Helios (cf. *Od.* 12.128). All these are standard terms of objections and represent no surprise. In addition, frgs. 161, 172 introduce their objections with πῶς. See Gudeman, "Λύσεις," 2515-16 for a standard list of zetematic vocabulary.

15 In addition to the formulae outlined in the last footnote, the verb ζητεῖν is also used in frgs. 171, 172, whereas the question used in frg. 161 is explicitly identified as a ζήτημα.

16 See, e.g., frg. 149 Rose, which tries to resolve a contradiction between two contrary descriptions of Helios. The question is raised and answered with no explanation: "Why, after saying that Helios sees all and hears all (*Il.* 3.277), did he [=Homer] portray him as in need of the tidings of his messenger, 'Swiftly then to Helios Hyperion came Lampetie of the long robes, bearing tidings that we had slain his kine' (*Od.* 12.374-75)?"

tes further objections.[17] In neither form does the citation of text play the kind of role it plays in Philo's *Quaestiones*: the Homeric texts are used only insofar as to clarify the problem or contradiction at hand. In none of the fragments can we document the Philonic form of διὰ τί or τί ἐστι followed by a Biblical lemma.

Heraclides Ponticus (IV BCE), student of Plato but later close associate of Aristotle, wrote a work entitled *Homeric Solutions* in two books (Λύσεων Ὁμηρικῶν α' β').[18] Five fragments, probably all from these two books, have come down to us and all five follow the Aristotelian forms.[19] Four fragments each from the Homeric works of Aristotle's students Dicaearchus (fl. 326-296 BCE)[20] and Demetrius of Phalerum (b. c.350 BCE)[21] have also survived. Neither represents any major formal or methodological departure from their teacher's *magnum opus*. Some of Heraclides's questions are identical to Aristotle's (frg. 171 Wehrli=Arist. frg. 146 Rose; frg. 172 Wehrli=Arist. frg. 147 Rose), strongly suggesting that these questions were entertained and resolved by successive generations of students. For these to be transmitted and collected as they have, there must have been institutional support.

Institutional support may also be reflected in the Ps.-Aristotelian *Problemata*, a Peripatetic compilation of miscellanea that possibly reached its final form only around V CE.[22] Several observations are in order. (1) The work does not show any self-consistent method of organization.[23] (2) Of the 887 questions in the *Problemata*, all but thirteen are introduced by the διὰ τί-formula.[24] In other words, fewer than 1.5% of all extant questions use introductory formulae other than διὰ τί. (3) The solutions are of unequal lengths. Question 30.1, e.g., takes up seven pages in the Loeb edition, while most others typically are but a few

---

17 See, e.g., frg. 146, which also tries to resolve a contradiction between two Homeric texts: "Why does he say here, 'And all they beside that dwelt in Crete of the *hundred cities* (*Il.* 2.649),' whereas in the *Odyssey*, after he says that Crete is 'beautiful,' 'rich,' and 'sea-girt,' he goes on, 'Therein are many men, past counting, and *ninety cities* (*Il.* 19.173-4)?' For to say 'ninety' in one occasion and 'hundred' in another seems to be a contradiction."

18 *D. L.* 5.88.

19 Frgs. 171-75 Wehrli, *Die Schule des Aristoteles* 7 (2d ed.; Basel-Stuttgart: Schwabe, 1969) 51-54. So the judgment of Wehrli (ibid.) and Pfeiffer, *History*, 70.

20 Frgs. 90-93 F. Wehrli, *Die Schule des Aristoteles* 1 (Basel-Stuttgart: Schwabe, 1944) 32. The title of his work is unknown.

21 Frgs. 190-93 F. Wehrli, *Die Schule des Aristoteles* 4 (Basel-Stuttgart: Schwabe, 1949) 41-42. *D. L.* 5.81 reports three works on Homer by Demetrius, Περὶ Ἰλιάδος α' β', Περὶ Ὀδυσσείας α' β' γ' δ', and Ὁμηρικὸς α'.

22 So the judgment of W. S. Hett, ed. & tr., *Aristotle* (LCL 15 & 16; Cambridge, MA: Harvard Univ. Press; London: W. Heinemann, 1936).

23 E.g., Book One contains questions on medicine, Book 15 on mathematics, Book 19 on music, Book 30 on thought and intelligence, and Books 31-38 on anatomy. All other books are also random collections of curiosities, displaying no discernible principle of organization.

24 10.12, 20.7 use the equivalent long form διὰ τίνα αἰτίαν. The thirteen are: 1.30, 31, 32, 33, 34, 37, 2.21, 2.33, 9.6, 10.12, 12.3, 12.10, 15.4, 17.3, 20.7, 26.36.

lines. Some passages contain no solutions at all, only questions; it is as if the questions are more important than the solutions. (4) There are repetitions (e.g., 1.32 and 1.34) and occasional contradictions. (5) Almost all the answers contain multiple solutions. These solutions are sometimes delineated one after another with no transition and sometimes introduced by "Is it because... Or..." (ἢ ὅτι or διότι... ἤ...). Formulae such as these may be editorial devices to add new solutions to an existing series.

No genuine Aristotelian *Problemata* have ever survived, but according to his bibliographers, Aristotle might have compiled similar works of scientific nature after the fashion of his Ἀπορήματα Ὁμηρικά.[25] It is therefore possible that the *Problemata* as they currently stand may contain material going back to Aristotle and to his students at the Lyceum, even if centuries of editing have made it impossible to extract the authentically Aristotelian material. One only has to look for the number of problems (e.g., the ἀπορίαι interspersed in his Φυσική) to see that the collection of questions on various scientific and philosophical issues is most likely a standard practice in the Aristotelian school.[26] These observations and others raise the possibility that the *Problemata* might have been a work collected and compiled over a long period of time and edited by different hands.

After Aristotle, the zetematic activities seem to have been pursued mainly in the learned circles of the Alexandrian Museum. Porphyry related that "in the Alexandrian Museum, it was the custom for questions to be posed and the developed solutions to be written down."[27] His statement was taken at face value by Gudeman, but H. Erbse doubted whether Porphyry could have had an accurate picture of the Alexandrian activities of three centuries earlier, doubts which Fraser also shared.[28] Whether or not Porphyry is to be trusted, however, reports abound to the effect that zetematic discussions of Homer delighted the Ptolemaic kings and Roman emperors but were dismissed by serious grammarians as frivolous games.[29]

---

25 *D. L.* 5.21; Hesychius, *In onomatologo*, s.v. There is a witness, by Alex. Aphr., of a lost work Περί προβλημάτων (*in Top.* 63.11f.). But judging from the lone citation, one might conclude that the work was probably a theoretical discussion on how to classify the different types of problems rather than a collection of problems. See also Rose, 3-22; H. Flashar, *Problemata Physica* (Berlin: Academie Verlag, 1962) 303-16.

26 See F. M. Cornford, *Aristotle: The Physics II* (LCL; Cambridge: Harvard Univ. Press, 1935) 5. Plutarch also seems to have used a version of the *Problemata* as source for his own Αἴτιαι φυσικαί and Συμποσιακὰ προβλήματα.

27 *Schol. Hom. ad Il.* 9.682 (Venetus B)=Schrader, 1.141. Hadrian likewise reports, "apud Alexandreiam in Musaeo multas quaestiones professoribus proposuit et propositas ipse dissolvit" (*Spart. Hadr.* 20). See evaluation by Lehr, *Aristarchi studiis,* 206.

28 Cf. Gudeman, "Λύσεις," 2512-13; Erbse, "Beiträge zur Überlieferung der Iliasscholien," *Zetemata* 24 (1960) 66; Fraser, *Ptolemaic Alexandria* (Oxford: Clarendon, 1972.) 1.317-19; 2.417 n. 86.

29 See Lehr, *Aristarchi studiis,* 206; Pfeiffer, *History,* 70.

Six fragments from the lost works of Demetrius the Alexandrian Jewish historian (fl. III BCE) have survived in Eusebius's *Praeparatio evangelica*.[30] As much as can be inferred from these fragments, Demetrius's works do not belong to the genre ζητήματα καὶ λύσεις proper; they are not compilations of questions and answers, *seriatim*, in the manner of Aristotle's Ἀπορήματα Ὁμηρικά or Philo's *Quaestiones*. The title of one work, *Concerning Judean Kings* (frg. 6=Clement *Strom.* 1.21.141.1-2), tells us little about the genre of the work. In spite of the traditional designation "historian," however, it might be more helpful to view him as an exegete who cast his rereading of Genesis in the form of a historical narrative.[31] In the longest of the fragments, frg. 2 (=Euseb. *P. E.* 9.21.1-19), Demetrius begins his narrative with the flight of Jacob to Haran where he marries Leah and Rachel (Gen 27:41-28:5) and then continues, following closely the text of Genesis. In 9.21.13, in the midst of describing Joseph's fame and fortune in Egypt (Gen 41:46-51),[32] he interrupts his narrative with an explanation:

> But though Joseph had good fortune for nine years, he did not send for his father because he was a shepherd, as were his brothers too, and Egyptians consider it a disgrace to be a shepherd. That this was the reason he did not send for him, Joseph himself declared. For when his kin did come, he told them that if they should be summoned by the king and were asked what they did for a living, they were to say that they were cowherds.[33]

This explanation was clearly prompted not by the Biblical text but by an unexpressed ζήτημα, "Why did Joseph not send for his father and brothers after nine years of prosperity?" The ζήτημα was not cited, probably because Demetrius could assume his readers' familiarity with it.[34]

That Demetrius's exegetical narrative is in some way connected to the *quaestio-et-solutio* technique becomes clear when he solves an explicitly cited ζήτημα in 9.21.14:

---

[30] Thus making Demetrius the earliest known Jewish exegete. For a brief discussion of the scholarly consensus on Demetrius's date, see C. R. Holladay, *Fragments from Hellenistic Jewish Authors, Volume I: Historians* (Chico, CA: Scholars Press, 1983) 51-52. The fragments are edited and translated on pp. 62-79. Cf. also N. Walter, "Fragmente jüdisch-hellenistischer Exegeten: Aristobulos, Demetrios, Aristeas," Kümmel, *et al.*, eds., *Jüdische Schriften aus hellenistisch-römisher Zeit 3.2: Unterweisung in lehrhafter Form* (Gütersloh: Mohn, 1975) 280-92.

[31] Walter, "Fragmente," 281; "Jewish-Greek Literature of the Greek Period," *The Cambridge History of Judaism II* (W. D. Davies, L. Findelstein, eds.; Cambridge: Cambridge Univ. Press, 1989) 387-88, sees Demetrius primarily as an exegete. But Holladay (*Fragments*, 1.51) and H. Attridge ("Jewish Historiography," *Early Judaism and its Modern Interpreters* [R. Kraft and G. W. E. Nickelsburg, eds.; Chico: Scholars Press, 1986] 312) continue to treat Demetrius primarily as a historiographer.

[32] See Walter, "Fragmente," 287 n. 12a-c; Holladay, *Fragments*, 1.84 n. 30 for discussion of this passage.

[33] Tr. Holladay, *Fragments*, 1.70-71.

[34] Other unstated ζητήματα may stand behind frg. 3 (9.29.2-3), and frg. 2 (9.21.3-5). See Walter, "Fragmente," 281; "Jewish-Greek Literature," 388.

Qu.: A crucial question arises as to why (διαπορεῖσθαι δὲ διὰ τί) Joseph gave Benjamin a fivefold portion at the meal even though he would not be able to consume so much meat.

Sol.: He did this because seven sons had been born to his father Leah whereas only two sons had been born to him by Rachel his mother. For this reason, he served up five portions for Benjamin and he himself took two. Thus, there were between them seven portions, that is, as many as all the sons of Leah had taken. (Tr. Holladay)

This question follows Aristotle's short form: it consists of a *quaestio* introduced by διὰ τί, a short paraphrase of the verse in question, and a solution. There was no need for an explanatory clause, since the question could clearly stand on its own.[35] More than two hundred years before Philo, then, we have evidence of Alexandrian Jewish exegesis using zetematic techniques. The brevity of these fragments does not allow one to say with certainty whether results from such exegesis ever existed as separate works or whether Demetrius made use of sources for his writings.

The same phenomenon of incorporating what is normally associated with a zetematic work into an exegetical discussion is observed in the *Anonymous Commentary on Theaetetus* 34.9-35.44, a verse-by-verse commentary on Plato's *Theaetetus*.[36] The structure of the work greatly resembles that of Philo's *Allegoriae*, except that the latter display a propensity for long parenthetical discussions of secondary texts.[37] Arranged schematically, the passage has the following structure:

Citation of text (34.9-14): "And in this way taking every single case in turn up to the root of 17 square feet; but at this point for some reason he came to a halt" [cf. *Theaet.* 147d.5-6].

---

35 Cf. also frg. 5 (=Euseb. *P. E.* 9.29.16), which poses a well-known ἀπορία: How could the supposedly unarmed Israelites have won battle with the powerful Egyptian army so soon after crossing the Red Sea. The question follows Aristotle's long form. *Quaest.*: But someone asked how the Israelites obtained weapons, seeing that they departed from Egypt unarmed. *Explanation*: for they said that after they had gone a three days' journey and had offered a sacrifice, they would return again. *Solutio*: It appears, therefore, that those who did not drown appropriated the weapons of those who did drown" (Tr. Holladay).

36 The work stood in the tradition of the Fourth Academy, one which was heavily influenced by skeptic epistemology. Recently Harold Tarrant dates the document, on internal grounds, to the late first century BCE and suggests strongly the authorship of Eudorus; cf. *Scepticism or Platonism? The Philosophy of the Fourth Academy* (Cambridge: Cambridge Univ. Press, 1985) 67-69; and his own works cited on p. 158 n. 4. Eudorus, in turn, is said to represent the kind of Platonism that influenced Philo; cf. J. Dillon, *The Middle Platonists* (Ithaca: Cornell Univ. Press, 1977) 178.

37 See comparison between these two works in D. Runia, "Further Observations," 114-15.

Qu. (34.33-35): "There are those who inquire why (ζητοῦσιν διὰ τί) he proceeds to 17 square feet"

Sol. (34.35-35.44): "Some say (τινές φασιν) that Theodorus..." (34.35-35.12). "Others (ἔνιοι δή) are of the opinion that... (35.13-21). "Perhaps it would be better to affirm (μήποτε ἄμεινον ἦ λέγειν) that he proceeded to 17 square feet because... (35.21-44).[38]

That this passage is identical in form to Demetrius's question-and-answer units is clear. Like Demetrius's fragments, *Anon. in Theaet.* is not a zetematic work but an exegetical commentary into which is introduced a question purportedly raised by an unnamed inquirer. But unlike Demetrius, the Anonymous Commentator's inclusion of the question-and-answer unit does not interrupt the narrative as it does in Demetrius's frgs. 2 and 6; the question-and-answer unit in *Anon. in Theaet.* is intended as comment proper to the text at hand (*Theaet.* 147d.5-6).

A zetematic work on Greek questions has been discovered in two papyri of independent hands, *P. Oxy.* 2688 and 2689.[39] These two third-century CE papyri at times parallel each other and are witnesses to a collection of ζητήματα καὶ λύσεις, whose lack of any discernible organization recalls the Ps.-Aristotelian *Problemata*. *P. Oxy.* 2688 includes four *quaestiones*, all introduced by διὰ τί, and four answers introduced by ὅτι. All four passages are short, the longest being ten lines.[40] *P. Oxy.* 2689, on the other hand, contains essentially the same type of material. The editor thought that these fragments might possibly have come from Plutarch's lost work αἰτίαι καὶ τόποι (Lamprias no. 160), even though they reflect a flatter and less careful style.[41]

Among Plutarch's writings, two extant works, Αἰτίαι φυσικαί (*Quaestiones naturales*) and Αἰτίαι Ῥωμανικαί (*Quaestiones Romanae*), show a predominant preference for the διὰ τί-form. All 41 questions in the *Quaestiones naturales* begin with διὰ τί, as do the 113 questions in the *Quaestiones Romanae*.[42] Characteristic

---

38 Translation found in Runia, "Further Observations," 131-32.

39 Vol.34 (1968) 26-33.

40 These are: (1) Why in the temple of the Paphian Aphrodite... and... [with] garlands of roses? Because [Cinyras], son of Paphus the citizen of the metropolis, stealing [the image] of the Cyprian Aphrodite, took it away to his house. [The goddess coming] and seeing the young man holding it in his hand approached him for the purpose of sexual relations. He [was deceived] and lay with her as if she were a mortal woman and... (with) garlands of roses (4-13). (2) Why does Hermes [carry] a *caduceus?* Because when he was send to the Titans he saw two snakes... (14-20). (3) Why in Argos [is there] a tomb of silence? Because when Amphiaraus the seer... was encamped... (21-25). (4) Why are the [islanders] near the Pillars of Hercules called "gymnetes"? Because companions of Odysseus after swimming naked.... And when in time they begot (children) they called their sons "gymnetes" (26-32),

41 The editor also gave reference to a catechism on the *Iliad* in Pack[2] 2644; gnomic questions in 2712; and medical questions in 2340-43.

42 The only exception is *Quast. Rom.* 112, which uses the variant διὰ τίνα δ' αἰτίαν. The 59 questions in the Αἰτίαι Ἑλληνικῶν (*Quaestiones Graecae*), on the other hand, use

of the *solutiones* in both works are the frequent references to opinions of others. Each answer in the *Quaestiones naturales* contains several solutions (even more consistently than the *Problemata*), each separated by key words like πότερον and ἤ. The same phenomenon can be observed in the *Quaestiones Romanae*.[43] F. C. Babbitt has noted that, since not all these solutions could be right, "the other explanations will embody the results of Plutarch's researches on the matter or his own quaint speculations."[44] Just as we have seen before, notably in the Ps.-Aristotelian *Problemata*, Plutarch's *Quaestiones* are repositories and compilations of solutions others have proposed.

More than a mere compiler, however, Plutarch was also a redactor with his own *Tendenz*. H. J. Rose, detecting Plutarch's hand in the opinions purportedly coming from others, concluded that these works are "a series of selections from [Plutarch's] reading-notes... by a writer who must have been widely known as what we should call an essayist. Formal regularity of arrangement characterizes none of his works, which seek rather to attract the reader by informality and variety."[45] Furthermore, the enumeration of others' views is consistently used as a technique of preparing for and accentuating the last, presumably Plutarch's own preferred, answer in the series, a tactic also used in the *Anonymous Commentary on Theaetetus* (see above 34.35-35.44). In *Quaest. nat.* 3 (3.912d-f), e.g., the answers of others are first listed and subtly rejected before the third and preferred answer is announced:

Qu.: Why (διὰ τί) do herdsmen put down salt for their animals?

Sol.: Is it (πότερον), as most people think, so that they shall eat plentifully so as to fatten them?.... Or is it rather (ἤ μᾶλλον) for the sake of health and reduction of bulk that they accustom their herds to lick salt?.... Consider,

more varied forms, as, e.g., in "Who (τίνες) were the 'dusty-feet' and the 'directors' in Epidaurus?" (qn. 1; 291e) or "What (τί) is the 'sheep-escaper'?" (qn. 10; 293a). Questions introduced by διὰ τί are the exception rather than the rule; they account for only fifteen of the 59 questions (or 25.4%): Qns. 31 (298b), 36 (299a), 37 (299c), 39 300a), 45 (301f), 46 (302a), 47 (302b), 48 (302c), 49 (302e), 50 (303a), 51 (303a), 52 (303b: τίς ἡ αἰτία, δι᾽ ἥν), 53 (303b), 54 (303c: τίς ἡ αἰτία, δι᾽ ἥν), 58 304c).

43 The sources behind the Αἰτίαι Ἑλληνικῶν (*Quaestiones Graecae*) seem to be of a different sort and, probably as a result, the solutions also appear less multitudinous. W. R. Halliday has argued that the major source for Plutarch's work was probably Aristotle's *Greek Constitutions*; see his *Greek Questions of Plutarch* (Oxford: Clarendon, 1928). If Halliday's theory is right, and it seems to have gained wide support, it would explain the relatively reticence on others' solutions.

44 LCL Plutarch *Moralia* 4.2.

45 H. J. Rose, *The Roman Questions of Plutarch* (Oxford: Clarendon, 1924) 50-51. What Rose, and to a lesser extent Babbitt, claimed for the *Quaestiones Romanae* also applies, *mutatis mutandis*, to the *Quaestiones naturales*. A similar conclusion is reached by H. Cherniss, *Plutarch Moralia* 13.1 (1976) 5, in regard to Plutarch's Πλατωνικὰ ζητήματα.

however (σκόπει δὲ μή),[46] whether they do not become at once more fertile and readier to mate.[47]

In other words, these works are not random collections of notes, organized in preparation for other writings; they are purposeful compilations designed to appeal to an intended audience.[48] Plutarch's Πλατωνικὰ ζητήματα are in some way closest to Philo's *Quaestiones*. A collection of ten ζητήματα καὶ λύσεις on various problems on Plato, they are unconnected to each other and the arrangement does not seem to follow any particular order. The formulae used in the ten questions of varied: τί (used four times), πῶς (three times), διὰ τί (twice), and διαπορήσειεν ἄν τις (once). These questions do not represent radical departure from what one might expect of a zetematic work during this period, though the τί-formula is never used in Aristotle's Ἀπορήματα Ὁμηρικά but is regularly used in Plutarch's Αἴτιαι Ἑλληνικῶν and Philo's *Quaestiones*. And the *solutio*-sections of the Πλατωνικὰ ζητήματα are much lengthier than those of Ἀπορήματα Ὁμη-ρικά, again placing them close to Philo's *Quaestiones*. One reason may be that they often incorporate the views of others, though such multiple solutions are not found with any consistency. The answer of Question 3,[49] e.g., begins with references to anonymous views introduced by δόξει δ' αὐτόθεν ("From this it would appear") and closes by rejecting them.[50]

H. Cherniss suggested that Plutarch's Πλατωνικὰ ζητήματα might have been "notes on Platonic passages that he had written at different times and had found no suitable occasion to incorporate into his other compositions."[51] In support, Cherniss mentioned *De tranquillitate animi* (464f), in which Plutarch responds to a request for exegetical comments on the *Timaeus* by saying, "I have gathered observations on tranquillity from my *notebooks* (ὑπομνήματα) which I happened to have made for myself;" as well as *De defectu oraculorum* 421e-431a, which might well have been an elaboration of such a ζήτημα on *Tim.* 55c7-d6.[52] Such a description might well apply to Plutarch's comment in *De tranq. animi*, but unless there is verbal correspondence, there is little reason to think that the Πλατωνικὰ ζητήματα were intended primarily as private notes. Cherniss is on more solid ground when he suggests that Questions 2 and 4 represent views on the *Timaeus* that Plutarch developed in greater detail in his *De animae procreatione*

---

[46] On the significance of σκόπει δὲ μή, see Rose, *Roman Questions*, 49.

[47] Tr. Hett, LCL *Plutarch Moralia* 11.159-60.

[48] What is said here about Plutarch's *Quaestiones* applies equally to his other works that use the *quaestio-et-solutio* technique, namely his Συμποσιακὰ προβλήματα and Πλατωνικὰζητήματα.

[49] On Plato's division of reality into the intelligible and sense-perceptible (*Rep.* 509d6).

[50] Cf. also Likewise, Question 5, on *Tim.* 53c4-55 and 55d7-56b6 (1003b-c): Someone's view is introduced by "Is it that, as some suppose,..."(πότερον, ὡς ὑπονοοῦσιν ἔνιοι 1003c).

[51] LCL *Plutarch Moralia* 13.1 (Cambridge: Harvard Univ. Press, 1976) 4.

[52] ibid., 4 n. b.

in Timaeo.[53] But to say that both works embody similar interpretations to different degrees of details is not the same as to say that one was intended as a notebook for the other. In any case, these considerations make it plausible that works in the genre ζητήματα καὶ λύσεις by this time were not merely used to resolve difficulties, but were also being developed as independent works.

The use of standard zetematic terminology like διὰ τί and the compilation of discrete question-and-answer units place Philo's *Quaestiones* squarely in the tradition of the genre ζητήματα καὶ λύσεις. In this regard, scholars are correct who view the zetematic exegesis of Homer a distant ancestor of Philo's *Quaestiones.*[54] But beyond this most obvious level, there are also significant differences. In terms of organization the *Quaestiones* follow the text of Genesis verse by verse, in a manner unparalleled by any of the extant works before Philo.[55] The overall organizational principle of Aristotle's Ἀπορήματα Ὁμηρικά, even when the fragmentary nature of the work's preservation is taken into account, is not that of a verse-by-verse commentary. The ten questions in Plutarch's Πλατωνικὰ ζητήματα, likewise, are not systematic comments but notes on isolated problems related to Plato. What pre-Philonic systematic commentaries there were, namely, the *Anon. in Theaet.* and Demetrius's writings, are not zetematic works, even though they make use of *quaestio-et-solutio* techniques.

When one examines the types of questions asked in Philo's *Quaestiones*, one is immediately struck by the preponderance of what might be called "rhetorical" questions, i.e., questions composed of a stereotypical formula (διὰ τί or τί ἐστι) and a Biblical lemma. Questions in Aristotle's Ἀπορήματα Ὁμηρικά show relatively little reliance on citation of text. Both his short and long forms are designed to pose substantial problems on Homer; brief citations are included only insofar as to illustrate problems already clearly stated (in the short form) or to reinforce with an explanatory note (the γάρ-clause in the long form). A lemma never stands alone as the ζήτημα; the latter never takes the form of διὰ τί or τί ἐστι followed by a lemma. Questions in Plutarch's Πλατωνικὰ ζητήματα are lengthier than Aristotle's questions but otherwise show the same sparing use of textual citation.

In Philo's *Quaestiones*, by contrast, the Biblical lemma is frequently stated with little or no elaboration. There is often little attempt in the *quaestio* to define what, if any, the underlying problem might be; explanatory notes and follow-up questions are rare. One has to turn to the *solutio* to gather hints of what is to come. Take, e.g., the *quaestio* of QG 1.2: "What is, 'And God made every verdure of the field before it came about on earth and every grass before it grew on

53 ibid., 5 and n. c.

54 Cf., M. L. Massebieau, "Le classement des œuvres de Philon," *Bibliothèque de l'école des hautes études, Science religieuses* 1 (1889) 1-91, esp. 7 nn. 1, 4; L. Cohn, "Einteilung und Chronologie der Schriften Philos," *Philologus Supplementband* 7 (1899) 387-435, esp. 403; H. Leisegang, "Philon (Alex.)," *RE* 20 (1941) 1-41, esp. 35-36; H. Dörrie and H. Dörries, "Erotapokriseis," *RAC* 6 (1966) 342-70, esp. 344, 347-48; R. Marcus, *Philo Supplement I: Questions and Answers on Genesis* (LCL; Cambridge: Harvard Univ. Press, 1953) ix.

55 As far as can be judged from the extant fragments. Cf. Dörrie and Dörries, "Erotapokriseis," 344: Philo was "an exception" to the aimless tendency of the zetematic literature.

earth' (Gen 2:5)?" which gives no indication what direction in which the ensuing *solutio* is about to take or what problem, if problem there be, might have prompted the question. The only information it provides is that Philo is about to comment on Gen 2:5! In all, of a total of 636 questions in the *Quaestiones in Genesim et in Exodum*, 288 are rhetorical *quaestiones* (i.e., 45.3% of total). Another 52 questions (8.2%) might be call "paraphrastic" questions, in which the lemmata are paraphrased instead of cited. If the rhetorical and paraphrastic questions are considered together—the Armenian translation often blurs the distinction between the two[56]—they account for 340 questions or 53.4% of the total. In other words, *more than half* of the questions do not raise substantial ζητήματα but are little more than markers for the Biblical lemmata. Fewer than half (296 or 46.6%) of the passages contain substantial queries.

There are 21 passages in which the underlying ζητήματα are found not in the *quaestio*-sections but in the *solutio*-sections.[57] In *QG* 4.91, e.g., an allegorical interpretation of Gen 24:8, Philo is concerned with discussing the marriage between reason and the soul. Abraham makes his senior servant swear an oath that the latter would return to his fatherland and find a woman for his Isaac. At the servant's departure, Abraham gives him his blessing: "The Lord, the God of heaven, who took me from my father's house and from the land of my birth... will send his angel before you, and you shall take a wife for my son from there" (Gen 24:7). The *quaestio* of *QG* 4.91 is a rhetorical question but the *solutio* begins with a ζήτημα introduced in classical fashion:

> *Qu.*: What is, "If the woman does not wish to come with you, you will be cleared of this oath; but only you will not return my son there" (Gen 24:8)?

> *Sol.*: Someone may inquire how (διαπορήσαι δ' ἄν τις, πῶς *vel sim.*), after it has been confirmed that the woman would come because the angel of God was to accompany him, he now says as if in doubt, "If the woman does not wish to come with you, you will be cleared of this oath"? Perhaps this is solved by means of a special form of the most natural allegory (οὐκοῦν μήποτε καὶ τοῦτο φυσικωτάτας ἀλληγορίας εἴδῳ λύεται *vel sim.*)? [allegorical interpretation begins]... (my translation).

The operating ζήτημα that evokes the subsequent (allegorical) interpretation is introduced by a formula "Someone may inquire how" (διαπορήσαι δ' ἄν τις, πῶς) that recalls Demetrius, frg. 2 (9.21.14). It has to do with the seeming contradiction between sending the angel of God to accompany the servant on his trip (Gen 24:7), which leads one to be confident of the servant's success, and Abraham's conditional caveat of Gen 24:8, which leaves room to doubt the eventual outcome of the mission.

The *solutio*-sections in Philo's *Quaestiones* are likewise different from the pre-Philonic works surveyed thus far. Solutions in Aristotle's Ἀπορήματα Ὁμηρικά

---

56 It remains an urgent task to study the principles of the Armenian translation. Then and only then will one be able to distinguish with certainty between the verbatim and the paraphrastic.

57 QG 1.3, 36, 93; 2.30, 31, 54, 61, 67; 3.3, 48, 54; 4.51, 90, 91, 141, 152, 168, 175, 230; QE 1.1; 2.45.

more often than not consist of a few pithy sayings and are shorter than the more elaborate questions. In frg. 144 Rose, e.g., the *quaestio* takes up 13 printed lines, while the *solutio* takes up fewer than three.[58] It is almost as if the main concern is to describe the difficulties rather than solve them. Answers in Philo, on the other hand, are much lengthier than Aristotle's; full, expansive notes or comments on Biblical lemmata, they are invariably longer than the questions. This is what one would expect from a commentary in which textual notes are of the primary importance. In this regard the *solutio*-sections of Plutarch's Πλατωνικὰ ζητήματα come closest to the *Quaestiones* if only because of their length and elaboration.

A Philonic innovation, so far as can be judged from the extant works, is the combination of literal and allegorical interpretations in the same *solutio*. Of the 636 total answers, 156 or about a quarter contain both literal and allegorical interpretations, as opposed to 226 (35.5%) that contain only literal interpretations and 188 (29.6%) that contain only allegorical interpretations. There are, in addition, 55 *solutiones* (8.7%) that assume the apophatic form, "The literal meaning being clear, the allegorical meaning is as follows...," and only seven (1.1%) that reject outright the literal meaning of the text before launching an allegorical interpretation.[59] In other words, over 70% of the passages contain some type of allegorical interpretation and the overwhelming majority of these are quite accommodating towards the literal readings of the text; 55 of them, in fact, declare the literal meaning of the texts self-evidently clear. But all these passages, problem-free as they are, are nevertheless formulated as questions and answer. The reason is that they set a platform for Philo's allegorical interpretations. In other words, it is mostly his penchant for allegorization, not any intrinsic difficulties with the text, that motivated Philo to introduce these texts as questions.[60] For Philo, every Biblical lemma is a code that can be decoded only by allegorical interpretation and every text becomes a new type of ἀπορία that must be resolved.[61]

In sum, Philo's rhetorical questions have displaced the substantive, zetematic queries of Aristotle, Demetrius, and Plutarch in prominence. Texts are not just cited to illustrate but in half of the cases have also *replaced* the ζητήματα. Similarly the explanatory γάρ-clause has gradually disappeared in Philo's questions. All this points to a developed stage in the history of the genre in which a formula like διὰ τί has become a technical or stereotypical marker for

---

58 The same proportion can be observed in frgs. 146, 148, 153.

59 These seven are: QG 1.39; 3.33; 4.88; 168, 175, 141; QE 1.16.

60 This is not to deny that Philo could have *allegorical* difficulties with the text or that he could disagree with or criticize his fellow allegorists. But the zetematic works prior to Philo have been confined to the concern of *textual*, not allegorical, difficulties. Not one of Philo's substantial questions, e.g., inquires about the allegorical nature of a verse.

61 In their assessment of Philo's role in the genre of what they called "religious question-and-answer dialogues," Daly and Suchier suggested that Philo contributed not only the allegorical method to later Christian writers but also the *aporia* and question-and-answer method; cf. L. W. Daly and W. Suchier, *Altercatio Hadriani Augusti et Epicteti philosophi* (Urbana: Univ. of Ill. Press, 1939) 26. If my evaluation here is correct, it was Philo's concern for allegory that necessitated the question-and-answer method.

lemma. It seems possible to posit two intellectual if not written sources standing behind Philo's *quaestiones*. Passages introduced by substantial questions, which still account for nearly half of the works, might reflect concrete exegetical problems with which Philo and company were still wrestling, while passages introduced by rhetorical questions might be scholiastic notes cast in question-and-answer form. In the hands of Philo, then, the genre is in danger of losing its zetematic veneer and becoming scholia. The Patristic *quaestiones*, after all, as Daly and Suchier noted,

> are... not much more than scholia provided with questions instead of lemmata. These scholia were dressed out in this attire, one might guess, in order to make them a little more pleasant reading... How superficial this [attire] is, and how easily dispensed with, is to be seen from the way the *quaestiones* finally lose themselves in *florilegia* and *catenae*.[62]

The survey above yields three general characteristics of the genre ζητήματα καὶ λύσεις: apologetic, public, and popular or educative. *The apologetic character of the genre* is readily evident in the earlier works, which often include actual questions raised by critics of Homer. Questions in Aristotle's Ἀπορήματα are all raised as censures of Homer, variously described as "unseemly," "thoughtless," or "objectionable,"[63] because of such perceived problems as grammatical mistakes, strange words or customs, internal contradiction, moral offensiveness, or unworthy behaviors ascribed to the gods and goddesses. These censures belong to the general critical atmosphere of the time. Xenophanes was said to have dismissed Homer for belittling the gods and goddesses by his anthropomorphic depiction, as did the sophists and Protagoras.[64] Plato's opinion of Homer was

---

62 Ibid., 19. G. Bardy, in fact, took the genre ζητήματα καὶ λύσεις as the point of departure for his discussion of the patristic scholia and he began his lengthy study with Philo; cf. Bardy, "La litérature patristique des «quaestiones et Responsiones» sur l'écriture sainte," *RB* 41 (1932) 210-11. Commenting on the writings of Origen and John Chrysostom, Bardy said, "Ceux d'entre eux qui ont écrit des scholies ont trouvé, dans la litérature profane, un genre littéraire particulièrement adapté à leur but: celui des questions et réponses, ζητήματα καὶ λύσεις, et ils n'ont pas hésité à l'employer" (210). Cf. also C. F. G. Heinrici, "Zur patristischen Aporienliteratur," *Abhandl. der K. S. Gesellschaft der Wissenschaften, phil.-hist. Kl.* 27 (1909) 843-60, esp. 853. Bardy's study on patristic scholia can be equally applied to Philo's *Quaestiones*. As has been noted in this chapter, what separates Philo's *Quaestiones* and Aristotle's Ἀπορήματα Ὁμηρικά or for that matter any zetematic work is that Philo followed the Biblical texts faithfully in order. In so doing he as often as not would pose rhetorical questions, questions which, except for the additon of διὰ τί or τί, are indistinguishable from the lemmata in later *scholia*.

63 I.e., ἀπρεπὲς εἶναι δοκεῖ (fr. 143); φαύλη δοκεῖ εἶναι (fr. 160); Ἀπόβλητον ἦν (fr. 175). Other formulae used: θαυμάσαι δ' ἄν τις φησὶν Ἀριστοτέλης (frg. 144); αὐτίκα τῶν παλαιῶν ζητημάτων ὡμολογοῦνται εἶναι τὸ τοιοῦτο, ἐν οἷς φησιν (fr. 161); and πῶς (fr. 172; cf. fr. 173).

64 See Lehr, *Aristarchi studii*, 219; M. Carroll, *Aristotle's Poetics, C. XXV*, 11.

evidently so low that he reportedly banished Homeric studies from the Academy.[65]

The Public Character of the Genre. If the early zetematic works originated with critics, it follows that these questions were of concerns not only to private individuals but also to the reading public. Several times Aristotle himself is said to be the originator of his own questions in the Ἀπορήματα,[66] but this simply means that Aristotle could, and at times did, become the critic.[67] In spite of the ostensibly apologetic concerns, therefore, implicit in Aristotle's Ἀπορήματα is an awareness that problems existed for the contemporary readers of Homer and that only the poetic art could overcome this hermeneutical difficulty.[68] Works in this genre are therefore not private compilations, whose purpose is subordinate to another work, but are compiled as independent works in their own right. Material in a zetematic work could have been, and in fact was, incorporated into another work, as we have seen in Plutarch's own works, but that is not the primary purpose of a zetematic work.

The Popular or Educative Character of the Genre. Two intended audiences may be distinguished here. Works in this genre might be popular writings cast in "a form of literature which, content aside, given a knowledge of reading and writing, even the most unschooled could create."[69] "Popular" in this regard refers to the *reading* public whose educational level might not be that of philosophers but who are nevertheless skilled in reading and writing.[70] Such would be true of the Ps.-

---

65 The most famous among the critics of Homer was a Zoïlos of Amphipolis, whose violent attacks on Homer earned him the title "Scourge of Homer" (Ὁμηρομάστιξ). Two books, now lost, are attributed to Zoïlos: ψόγος Ὁμήρου and κατὰ τῆς Ὁμήρου ποιήσεως λόγοι ἐννέα, which as the titles indicate are meant to censure Homer. See Hans Gärtner, "Zoilos (*Homeromastix*)," *RE Supp* 14 (1978) 1531-43.

66 Frgs. 159, 171, 172. One suspects the number of questions posed by Aristotle might be a great deal higher in the original work.

67 See esp. *Poetica* 25

68 The scholarly attention to Homer in the Lyceum and the popularity of the zetematic literature among Aristotle's students and the peripatetics suggest that the school was the center of such zetematic activities. The evidence is not conclusive, since I have not come across any reference that ties the ζητήματα directly to the school. Bywater's comment that questions were raised mainly in schools and symposia is intriguing but is unfortunately not accompanied by documentation; cf. Bywater, *Aristotle*, 323. From the symposiac literature of this period, there is no evidence that entertaining Homeric problems was a part of the learned discussion. Plato's *Symposium* centers around a philosophical definition of love, while Aristotle's *Symposium*, of which only fragments are extant, deals with the question of drunkenness. Plutarch's Συμποσιακὰ προβλήματα do contain a few questions on Homer, but they came later and are in any case artificial compositions, combining the classical genre symposium and the genre ζητήματα καὶ λύσεις.

69 Daly and Suchier, *Altercatio*, 24.

70 Daly wrote, "By popular I do not mean a Herderian *Volkstümlichkeit*, whereby such works would spring forth panoplied from the breast of the folk. The point in calling them popular at all, is that, by whatever author, whether known or unknown, they were

Aristotelian *Problemata*, Plutarch's *Quaestiones naturales* and *Quaestiones Romanae*.[71] On the other hand, technical and highly exegetical works cast in this question-and-answer form might be intended not for the frivolous but for the serious students.[72] This might be true of Aristotle's Ἀπορήματα Ὁμηρικά, which appear to be associated with the Lyceum, and perhaps also Plutarch's Πλατωνικὰ ζητήματα.

It is in this educative milieu that I propose to locate Philo's *Quaestiones*. The apologetic concerns of the work have by and large receded into the background, though echoes are still heard through the few remaining anti-anthropomorphic passages.[73] The public character does not readily spring to the fore but is assumed throughout the work. References to other exegetes indicate that Philo was evidently in public dialogue with his fellow-exegetes and the results of such discussions might well have been incorporated into the fabrics of the *Quaestiones*.[74] The adoption of the technique of enumerating other people's views in order to set up for one's own,[75] moreover, a technique used by the Anonymous Commentator and Plutarch (see discussion above), points to a well-constructed, tendentious work meant to persuade as well as educate. Given the generally simpler argumentation, as compared to the more discursive *Allegoriae*, it may be reasonable to hypothesize that the *Quaestiones* were intended for Jewish readers who have gone beyond the rudiments of Biblical exegesis but were poised to learn more. The final goal of such an educative endeavor was perhaps the type of allegorical sophistication represented by the *Allegoriae*, but progress towards which would require better command of and greater skills in the art of allegorical interpretation. Such a hypothesis necessitates a closer examination of the relationship between the *Quaestiones* and the *Allegoriae*.

Relationship between the Quaestiones and the Allegoriae

The three recent studies by Nikiprowetzky, Borgen-Skarsten, and Sterling collectively advanced three arguments for positing a relationship between the *Quaestiones* and Philo's other commentaries. First, it is argued that the *Quaestiones* and the *Allegoriae* follow a similar if not identical sequence of *topoi*. In strong support of this is Sterling's contention that some questions raised in the *Quaestiones* are in fact answered in the *Allegoriae*. Second, all three studies make the same observation that the question-and-answer technique is the fundamental building

---

written essentially for popular consumption. I say essentially, because, although in the Middle Ages the circle of readers would be comparatively small, confined to those who had education enough to be at least literate, it was essentially unlearned" (Daly and Suchier, *Altercatio*, 16). Daly's comment is restricted to Medieval works but is nonetheless *à propos* in the present context.

[71] I would also put Plutarch's symposiac literature in this category.

[72] Daly and Suchier, *Altercatio*, 17: "The *aporia* represents the more learned or instructional side of the question-and-answer, and the riddle the more popular."

[73] Only seven such cases remain: QG 1.21, 42, 55, 68, 93; 2.54; 4.24, which are far fewer than either the *Allegoriae* or the *Expositiones*.

[74] Cf. D. M. Hay, "References to other Exegetes," *Both Literal and Allegorical*, 81-97.

[75] I have counted 111 such passages, accounting for 17.5% of the total.

block for all three commentaries. The implication is that the *Allegoriae* draw explicitly cited question-and-answer units directly from the *Quaestiones*. Third, according to both Nikiprowetzky and Sterling, the two-tiered, literal-allegorical pattern is characteristic not only of the *Quaestiones* but also of the *Allegoriae* and *Expositiones*.[76]

The last argument can be readily answered. As shown above, the combination of literal and allegorical interpretations is what makes Philo's *Quaestiones* unique among surviving zetematic works. But it need be reiterated that only a quarter of the *solutiones* take the literal-allegorical form; the presence of two-tiered exegesis, while unique, is hardly overwhelming. The propensity for combining literal and allegorical interpretations outside the *Quaestiones*, on the other hand, is characteristic only of the *Expositiones*. In *De Abrahamo* and *De Iosepho*, e.g., the basic mode of exegesis is that of a literal interpretation followed by an allegorical one.[77] But two-tiered exegeses in the *Allegoriae* are decidedly rarer. Of the twenty-eight passages cited by Sterling to illustrate the two-tiered, literal-allegorical pattern,[78] only two come from the *Allegoriae*: *Conf.* 1-198 and *Mut.* 60-80. In both, the so-called literal portions are of the apologetic variety; they were most likely traditional material developed to refute the charge that the Mosaic Law contains unworthy, mythic elements.

As to the suggestion that the *Allegoriae* might be dependent on the *Quaestiones* for explicitly cited question-and-answer units, there is little evidence. I have identified 130 passages in the allegorical treatises that use zetematic terminology or formulae. Of these, 16 correspond to possible lacunae in the *Quaestiones* and their origins cannot be determined with certainty. Sixty-three of these passages correspond to extant passages in the *Quaestiones* but their counterparts do not use zetematic formulae at all. Of the remaining 48 passages that do find zetematic formulae used in their corresponding passages in the *Quaestiones*, 26 turn out to have different ζητήματα and only 22 seem to share similar ζητήματα in both the *Allegoriae* and *Quaestiones*. A break down of these 22 parallels in terms of problems is as follows:

Anthropomorphism:

Gen 2:8	LA 1.43-45	QG 1.6
Gen 4:9	Det. 57-60	QG 1.68
Gen 6:6a	Deus 20-21, 33	QG 1.93
Gen 6:7	Deus 70	QG 1.95

---

76 See nn. 3-5 above.

77 See, e.g., *Abr.* 60-88, in which 60-67 deals with the literal interpretation and 68-88 deals with the allegorical interpretation. The same structure can be observed in *Abr.* 89-98 (literal) and 99-106 (allegorical); 107-18 (literal) and 119-32 (allegorical); 133-46 (literal) and 147-66 (allegorical); 167-99 (literal) and 200-204 (allegorical); 208-16 (literal) and 217-24 (allegorical); 225-35 (literal) and 236-44 (allegorical). In other words, the whole of *De Abrahamo* is structured according to the literal-allegorical pattern. It must be noted, however, the treatise does not follow the Biblical text sequentially but episodically.

78 See Sterling, "Philo's *Quaestiones*," 107.

Impossibility:

Gen 2:17	LA 1.105	QG 1.16
Gen 2:19	LA 2.11-12	QG 1.19
Gen 3:9	LA 3.49-50	QG 1.45

Mythic quality of the Mosaic Law:

Gen 2:21	LA 2.20-22	QG 1.25

Worthiness of the patriarch:

Gen 17:17	Mut. 177	QG 3.56

Contradiction, Consistency, etc.:

Gen 2:4-5	LA 1.24	QG 1.2
Gen 2:17	LA 1.101-4	QG 1.15
Gen 3:17	LA 3.246-7	QG 1.50
	Cher. 125	QG 1.58
Gen 4:2	Sac. 11-14	QG 1.59
Gen 4:3	Sac. 52	QG 1.60
Gen 6:8	Deus 86, 104-8	QG 1.96
Gen 9:25ff	Sobr. 31-33	QG 2.77, 65

No Intrinsic Difficulty:

Gen 2:7	LA 1.33-35	QG 1.5
Gen 3:24b	Cher. 21-30	QG 1.57
Gen 15:8	Her. 215	QG 3.5
Gen 15:15	Her. 277-83	QG 3.11
Gen 15:16	Her. 300-6	QG 3.13
Gen 17:18	Mut. 202	QG 3.57

Without entering into a detailed discussion, suffice it to say for now that these parallels are not unambiguous. All except the last category deal with such traditional difficulties as anthropomorphism, impossibility, contradiction, etc.; these parallels are at least as likely dependent on common traditional material as they are on each other. In other words, of the 130 uses of zetematic formulae in the *Allegoriae*, only six case (less than 5%) might be eligible to claim dependence on the *Quaestiones*.[79] Evidence does not favor the hypothesis that the *Allegoriae* might have derived explicitly constructed questions-and-answers units from the *Quaestiones*.

---

[79] It should also be pointed out that there is no verbal convergence in any of the six parallels.

Case Study: The Second Creation of Man (Gen 2:4-QG 1.1-5 par LA 1.19-42)

A response to the first argument, that the *Allegoriae* and the *Quaestiones* follow the same sequence of *topoi*, involves a systematic examination of these two series of commentaries in terms of *implicit* or *unexpressed* questions and answers.[80] Space does not permit such an undertaking here, but a case study comparing the treatment of the second creation of man (Gen 2:4-7) in *QG* 1.1-5 and *LA* 1.19-42 would give some indication what a thorough synoptic study could hope to demonstrate. The choice of these parallels is motivated in part by the Sterling's selection of them for his argument[81] and in part by the relatively straightforward, linear progression of *LA* 1.19-42. There is no parenthetical discussion of secondary texts and every *topos* seems to correspond neatly to a passage in the *Quaestiones*. For this to be a meaningful comparison, however, it has to be based on the working assumption that an implicit *quaestio-et-solutio* unit might underlie every *topos*, an assumption that has been partially justified by the works of Nikprowetzky and Sterling.[82] This comparison aims at determining whether and to what extent we can detect dependency, intellectual or literary. The following schematic synopsis will facilitate my discussion:

QG 1.1 *(Gen 2:4)*	LA 1.19-20 *(Gen 2:4)*	
Q: Time of creation?	Q: What is "book"?	*same*
S: Undetermined and uncircum-scribed.	S: Book=Logos	*diff*
Q: What is "book"?	Q: Time of creation?	*same*
S: Contains the creation of the world.	S: Unobserved, undescried	*same*

QG 1.2 *(Gen 2:5a)*	LA 1.21-24 *(Gen 2:4b-5a)*	
Q: Why God made verdures before they came into being?	Q: Why the repetition of "field"?	*similar*
S: Incorporeal ideas	S: Incorporeal ideas	*similar*
	LA 1.25-27 *(Gen 2:5b)*	*no para*
	Q: [citation of lemma]	
	S: Allegorical interpretation of "rain"	

QG 1.3 *(Gen 2:6)*	LA 1.28-30 *(Gen 2:6)*
Q: How is it poss. to water the whole earth?	
S: "Spring" a collective term.	

---

80 See Runia, "Further Observations," 113, for discussion of comparing these two series of commentary.

81 Sterling, "Philo's *Quaestiones*," 113-14.

82 Cf. Nikiprowetzky, "L'exégèse de Philon d'Alexandrie," *passim*, in his study of *De gigantibus* and *Quod Deus immutabilis sit*; Sterling, "Philo's *Quaestiones*," *passim*.

Q: What is "face"?	Q: What is "face"?	similar
S: Face=ruling part	S: Face=senses; spring=mind.	diff
QG 1.4 (Gen 2:7a)	LA 1.31-32 (Gen 2:7)	
Q: Who is the molded man and how is he diff. from the acc-to-image man?	Q: [citation of lemma]	similar
S: Molded man=sense-perceptible; man acc. to image=noetic.	S: Earthly man=mixture; heavenly man=incorruptible	similar
	LA 1.33-35 (Gen 2:7)	no para
	Q: Why God deemed the earthly mind worthy of divine breath?	
	S: God loves even the imperfect	
	LA 1.36-38 (Gen 2:7)	no para
	Q: What does "breathed into" mean?	
	S: It means "besouled the soulless"	
QG 1.5 (Gen 2:7b)	LA 1.39-41 (Gen 2:7)	
Q: Why did God breathe "in the face"?	Q: What does "into the face" mean?	similar
S: Face is principal part of body	S: Face is where the senses are	similar
S: Man is of the rational order	S: Face dominant part of body.	diff
	LA 1.42 (Gen 2:7)	no para
	Q: Why he uses "breath" not "spirit"?	
	S: because there is a difference	

Significant gaps exist: of the nine *topoi* delineated in *Legum allegoriae,* four have no parallel discussion in the *Quaestiones.* The last three, *LA* 1.33-35, 36-38, and 42, are especially troubling because they are explicitly introduced by zetematic formulae. On the other hand, the synopsis shows general agreement in the order of *topoi* between the two works. This, however, could be misleading, since the two works more or less follow the Genesis story and the order of presentation might simply be dictated by the text.

QG 1.1 par LA 1.19-20 (Gen 2:4a)

QG 1.1: Why, when reflecting[83] on the creation of the world, does Moses[84] say, "This is the book of the generation of heaven and earth, when they came about"?

"When they came about" apparently indicates undetermined time.[85] And this is an argument that puts to shame those who summed up a number of years during which the world came to be.

LA 1.19-20: [citation of Gen 2:4]

This perfect λόγος, moving in accord with the number 7, is the primal origin both of mind ordering itself after the original patterns and of sense-perception in the domain of mind... ordering itself after those originals. "Book" is Moses' name for the λόγος of God, in which have been inscribed and engraved the formation of all else.

---

83 My translation. Marcus translated ըն միտ ածելով եւ հաշուելով as "considers and reflects," evidently neglecting the possibility of its being a doublet; Ch. Mercier, *Quaestiones et Solutiones in Genesim I et II e versione armeniaca* (Les œuvres de Philon d'Alexandrie 34A; Paris: Cerf, 1979) 63, followed the Greek and restored it to "réfléchit." On the Greek fragment of *Qu. in Gen.* 1.1 and the Armenian text, see J. C. M. van Winden, "The First Fragment of Philo's *Quaestiones in Genesim*," *VC* 33 (1979) 313-18.

84 "Moses" is missing in the Armenian but is found in the Greek fragment.

85 The Greek fragment, Τὸ μὲν ὅτε ἐγένετο ἀόριστον ἔοικε χρόνον ἐμφαίνειν. ("'When it came about' apparently indicates indetermined time."), differs slightly from the Armenian, which has Հյորժամ եղեն անորոշելի եւ անչափորոյն, որպէս երեւեցաւ, զժամանակն գուցանէլ: The Armenian variant որպէս երեւեցաւ (=ὡς ἔοικε) might have misled Marcus, who rendered the Armenian as "The expression 'when they came into being,' which is undetermined and uncircumscribed, apparently indicates time."

But "this book of generation" is either indicative of a supposed book which contains the creation of the world or a correspondence of things said about the creation of the world to what in fact came to be.[86]

But that you may not suppose that the Deity makes anything in definite periods of time, but may know that to mortal kind the process of creation is unobserved, undescried, incomprehensible, he adds, "when it came into being," not defining "when" by a determining limit, for the things that come into being under the hand of the First Cause come into being with no determining limit. There is an end, the, of the notion that the universe came into being in six days (tr. Whitaker).

Even though both passages seem intent on dealing with the same lemmata, there are differences. The superficial differences are easy to isolate and relatively minor. Formally, *LA* 1.19-20 is not cast in *quaestio-et-solutio* form; it unceremoniously begins with a citation of Gen 2:4. Structurally, the two lemmata, αὕτη ἡ βίβλος γενέσεως and ὅτε ἐγένετο, are transposed in the discussions of the two works. Stylistically, the prose of *LA* 1.19-20 is richer and smoother than the economic and sparse language of *QG* 1.1.

More significant are the exegetical disagreements between these two discussions. Both agree that the first lemma, ὅτε ἐγένετο, refers to an indefinite period of time and both construe this interpretation as a refutation of the attempt (by the unnamed "others") at allotting a delimited period of time for creation. Since both passages allude to and reject an outside opinion, there is no need to appeal to literary dependency. The two passages disagree on the second lemma, αὕτη ἡ βίβλος γενέσεως. In *QG* 1.1, Philo suggests two possibilities: it is either "a supposed book"(Genesis?) or a "correspondence of things said about the creation of the world to what in fact came to be." The second suggestion seems to be based on a distinction between "things said about the creation of the world" (τῶν εἰρημένων περὶ τῆς κοσμοποιίας) and "what in fact came to be" (τὰ ἐπ' ἀληθείας γεγονότα), but what these "things" are remains vague. It is possible that it refers to the archetypal ideas and particulars, but it can only remain a guess in lieu of further elaboration. In *LA* 1.19, on the other hand, Philo identi-

86 Following the Greek, Τὸ δὲ αὕτη ἡ βίβλος γενέσεως ἤτοι δεικτικόν ἐστιν τοῦ ὑποκειμένου τεύχους ὁ τὴν κοσμοποιίαν περιέχει ἢ ἀναφορὰ τῶν εἰρημένων περὶ τῆς κοσμοποιίας πρὸς τὰ ἐπ' ἀληθείας γεγονότα, which is considerably different from the Armenian, Բայց այս գիր լինելութեան, կամ ցուցական այսր ի ներքոյ եղելոյ գրոյս է, որ զաշխարհարարութիւնն պարունակէ, ի նա ակնարկութիւն ասացելոցն յաղագս աշխարհարարութեան առ ճշմարտութեանն եղեալ: The translator apparently mistook ἤ as ᾗ and rendered it as ի նա. Mercier, on balance, seems to have the better translation, "«Ceci (est) le livre de la genèse» désigne en vérité le livre que voici, lequel contient la création du monde ou le rapport entre le récit de la création du monde et ce qui s'est réellement produit."

fies "book" with the Logos of God and, in so doing, interprets it in a Middle-Platonic framework. It contains the archetypal patterns of all things and is "the primal origin" (ἀρχὴ γενέσεως) of mind and sense-perception; it is the Logos that is responsible for the creation of the domains of mind and sense-perception.[87] This disagreement has to be evaluated in the context of the next parallel.

QG 1.2 par LA 1.21-24 (Gen 2:4b-5a)

Exactly why Philo identifies "book" as the creative Logos in *Legum allegoriae* becomes clear in the following passage (§§21-24):

> Above he has called this day a book, for he delineates the creation of heaven and earth as wrought in both [i.e., "book" and "day"]: for by His own supremely manifest and far-shining Logos God makes both of them, both the ideas of the mind, which in symbolic language he calls "heaven," and the ideas of sense-perception, to which by a figure he gave the name of "earth."

> And he compares the idea of the mind and the idea of sense-perception to two fields; for they bear fruit, the mind all that is done in thinking, sense-perception all that is done in perceiving. What he means is something of this sort. As before the particular and individual mind there subsists a certain idea as an archetype and pattern of it, and again before the particular sense-perception, a certain idea of sense-perception related to the particular as a seal making impression is to the form which it makes; just so, before the individual objects of intellectual perception came into being, there was existing as a genus the "intellectually-perceptible" itself, by participation in which the name has been given to the members of the genus; and before the individual objects of sense-perception came into existence, there was existing as a genus the "sense-perceptible" itself, by sharing in whose being all other objects of sense have become such.

> "*Green of the field*," then, *is what he terms the* "*intellectually-perceptible*" *of the mind*; for as in a field the green things spring up and bloom, even so the "intellectually-perceptible" is a growth springing from the mind. Before, then, the particular "intellectually-perceptible" came into being, the Creator produces the solely abstract "intellectually-perceptible," as a generic existence. This he rightly calls "all," for the particular "intellectually-perceptible," being a fragment, is not all, but the generic is so, being a full whole.

> "And all the grass of the field," he says, "before it sprang up," that is to say, before the particular objects of sense sprang up, there existed by the Maker's forethought the generic "sense-perceptible," and that it is that he again calls

---

87 G. H. Whitaker in a footnote speculated that the identification was based on the double meanings of λόγος as "word" and "reason" (*LCL Philo* 1.158 n. a.). This etymological connection is possible but unnecessary; it is at least equally possible that Philo's identification is motivated by a parallelism between Logos, *viz.* the repository of all the patterns of creation, and Genesis, *viz.* the book containing all the creation narratives.

"all." Natural enough is his comparison of the "sense-perceptible" to grass. For as grass is the food of a creature devoid of reason, so has the "sense-perceptible" been assigned to the unreasoning part of the soul. Else why, after saying before "green of the field," does he go on to say "and all grass," as if it were impossible for green of the field to come up as grass? The fact is, "the green of the field" is the "intellectually-perceptible," an outgrowth of the mind, but the "grass" is the "sense-perceptible," it in turn being a growth of the unreasoning part of the soul (Tr. Whitaker).

The Biblical lemma under discussion comes from Gen 2:4b-5: "In that day God made heaven and earth and every verdure of the field before it came about on earth and every grass before it grew." "In the day" (ἡμέρᾳ), in the dative, enables Philo to assert that it is "by the supreme manifest and far-shining *Logos*" (τῷ περιφανεστάτῳ καὶ τηλαυγεστάτῳ ἑαυτοῦ λόγῳ) that God made "heaven" and "earth," which Philo immediately identifies as mind and sense-perception. The lemma is different from that of *QG* 1.2 which omits the reference to "heaven and earth." Difference in citation is ordinarily insignificant in commentarial writings, since an abbreviated lemma often stands for the whole verse. But in this case, the inclusion of "heaven and the earth" is crucial for Philo's exegesis; it is on this very phrase that Philo builds his modified Middle-Platonic platform. Philo identifies, symbolically, "heaven" with the *ideas* of the mind (αἱ ἰδέαι τοῦ νοῦ) and "earth" with the *ideas* of sense-perception (αἱ ἰδέαι τῆς αἰσθήσεως). Similarly, the "green of the field," corresponding to heaven, symbolizes "noetic ideas," whereas the "grass of the field," corresponding to earth, symbolizes "sense-perceptible ideas."

To postulate the existence of "ideas" for sense-perception is strange for Platonism, according to which sense-perception is by definition outside the realm of forms. But it is nevertheless consistent with the interpretive strategy taken right from the beginning of *Legum allegoriae*, where Philo, commenting on division between the two creation accounts, draws a distinction between the completion of the generic ideas in Genesis 1 and the creation of the particulars in Genesis 2.

> He had already told of the creation of mind and sense-perception; he now fully sets forth the consummation of both. He does not say that either the individual mind or the particular sense-perception have reached completion, but that the *ideas have done so, that of mind and that of sense-perception.* For using symbolical language *he calls the mind heaven,* since heaven is the abode of natures discerned only by mind, but *sense-perception he calls earth,* because sense-perception possesses a composition of a more earthly and body-like sort (*LA* 1.1).

In other words, Philo devised this modified Middle-Platonic world view in response to the exegetical difficulty made necessary by the two creation accounts, the division between them located at Gen 2:4-5.[88]

The interpretation of *QG* 1.2, by contrast, pays no attention to "heaven and earth" but focuses on the distinction between the ideal and the particular.

---

88 See discussion by Tobin, *Creation of Man,* 59-60, 142.

What is, "And God made every verdure of the field before it came about[89] on earth and every grass before it grew on earth"[90] (Gen 2:5)?

Through these [words] it alludes to incorporeal ideas. Because "before it came about" [Scripture] alludes to the completion of every verdure and grass, plants and trees, and "before it grew on earth" [Scripture] says that he made verdure and grass and the rest. It is evident that as incorporeal [ideas?][91] he also created specific idea[92] in accordance with the intelligible nature of which the sense-perceptible things that are on earth are intended as imitators. (my translation)

The underlying problem here is one of chronology, prompted one by the LXX text "before it came about": How could God have made the plants and grass *before* they came about? Its solution leads Philo to posit a distinction between the creation of ideas (Genesis 1) and the creation of their corresponding particulars in Genesis 2, but not a distinction between heaven and earth. The same interpretation is found in *Op.* 129-30. The problem here is not unlike the one Philo tries to resolve in *Legum allegoriae*, where the same phrase is taken seriously ("'before it sprang up,' that is to say, before the particular objects of sense sprang up, there existed by the Maker's forethought the generic 'sense-perceptible'" *LA* 1.24), but there it is subsumed under the broader distinction between heaven and earth, i.e., the distinction between intelligible *ideas* and sense-perceptible *ideas*.

The metaphysical structure as reflected in *QG* 1.2 is relatively simple and more orthodox Middle-Platonic, while that reflected in *LA* 1.21-24 is more complex and represents a Philonic modification. The difference between these two interpretations may be schematized as follows:

QG 1.2:

Genesis 1:	Intelligible ideas
Genesis 2:	Sense-perceptible particulars

---

89 The LXX has πρὸ τοῦ γενέσθαι.

90 In including "on earth," I am following B and Mercier, *Quaestiones*, 63. This reading is also included in the citation in ensuing *solutio*.

91 The difficulty of this phrase, "he also . . . incorporeal," revolves around the obscure Armenian ɡⁿ֊ɡⱳɥⱳ␣ɢ, "evident, demonstrative." Marcus has "He made incorporeal and intelligible ideas." Mercier renders it as "modèle" (δεικτικός): "il créa aussi les idées modèles comme les (idées) incorporelles" (63-65).

92 "As incorporeal ... idea": ␣ɲɲⁿ֊ ɋⱳ␣ɢ␣ⱳⱳⱳ␣ɢ, ␣␣ ɡⁿ֊ɡⱳɥⱳ␣ɢ ␣␣ⱳ␣␣ⱳ` ␣ⱳ␣ (ὡς ἀσώμαται καὶ δεικτικὴ ἰδέα ἐποίησεν *vel sim.*), which Mercier translated as "aussi les idées modèles comme les (idées) incorporelles...." Marcus ignored the conjunction ␣ɲɲⁿ֊ (ὡς) and took both adjectives as modifying idea: "He made incorporeal and intelligible ideas...."

LA 1.21-24:

	Intelligible ideas	Sense-perceptible ideas
Genesis 1:	Intelligible ideas	Sense-perceptible ideas
Genesis 2:	Intelligible particulars	Sense-perceptible particulars

That *LA* 1.21-24 represents a more developed stage in the history of interpretation of Gen 2:4-5 seems clear, but far from clear is whether it is dependent on *QG* 1.2 for its exegetical material. The *topos* generated by the two creation accounts is traditional, as is apparently the metaphysical solution of *QG* 1.1-2, especially since it is found also in *Op.* 129-30. T. Tobin thinks that Philo devised this schema to accommodate his interpretation of man as mind and woman as sense-perception and the shift from creation of the two *men* into creation of two *mind*. If so, it is at this crucial point where the *Allegoriae* and the *Quaestiones* part company.[93] Given the larger hermeneutical strategy of equating heaven with intelligible ideas and earth with sense-perceptible ideas, it seems easier to envision *LA* 1.21-24 as Philo's own development of a traditional piece of exegesis. There is no compelling evidence for literary dependency.

QG 1.3 par LA 1.28-30 (Gen 2:6)

The *solutio*-section of *QG* 1.3 contains two ζητήματα, one explicitly stated, the other implied. The explicitly stated question-and-answer unit, which has no parallel in the *Legum allegoriae*, is as follows:

How is it possible to water the whole earth from one spring, not only because of its size but also because of the unevenness of the hillocks and plains? May it not be that, just as the whole royal cavalry is called "horse," thus also all the earth's veins, which gush forth like spring when producing drinking water, are called "spring"?

The second ζήτημα can be inferred from the discussion, namely, Why does it say the spring watered the *face* of the earth?

But it is good that it says not "all" but its "face" was watered, which is the ruler and director[94] among living beings. For the earth's good, fertile, and principal part capable of fruit-bearing is that which in need of watery help. (My translation)

The parallel discussion in *LA* 1.28-30 also seizes on the peculiarity of the expression "face" but subjects it to a thoroughly allegorical interpretation. "The spring of the earth" is the mind, its "face" is senses, and "watering" is allegorized

---

93 *Creation of Man* (CBQMS 14; Washington: Catholic Biblical Association, 1983) 142-43.

94 Possibly զզիխաւորն զառաջնորդականն doublet in apposition with զղեմս? Cf. Mercier, 65, "Mais il est très bien de dire également qu'elle abreuvait non «toute» (la terre), mais la «face» de la terre, comme dans l'être vivant la partie principale et directrice."

as the mind's grasping the impression which external objects emit to sense-perception. The interpretation in *QG* 1.2 is of course completely literal or metaphorical; it does not resort to allegory to smooth the text. It is difficult to see how these discussions are materially related to each other.

QG 1.4 par LA 1.31-32 (Gen 2:7)

QG 1.4: Who is the "molded" man and how is he distinguished from him who is "according to the image?"

The "molded one" is the sense-perceptible man and is a likeness of the noetic model, whereas the "according-to-the-image one," noetic and incorporeal, is the likeness of the archetype and is himself the form of the most original seal.[95] And it is the Logos of God, the first principle, the archetypal idea, the primary measure of all things. The molded one, therefore, was formed as regards the body as if from a potter by means of clay and earth and he obtained as his lot a soul[96] when God breathed life onto his face. And the mixture of his nature is a mixture of corruptibility and incorruptibility. But he who is according to the form is incorruptible and un-mixed, of an invisible nature, of simplicity, and of light. (My tr.)

LA 1.31-32: *Citation of Gen 2:7*

There are two types of men; the one a heavenly man, the other an earthly. The heavenly man, being made after the image of God, is altogether without part or lot in corruptible and terrestrial substance; but the earthly one was compacted out of the matter scattered here and there, which Moses calls "clay." For this reason he says that the heavenly man has not been molded but stamped with the image of God; while the earthly is a moulded work of the Artificer, but not His offspring. We must account the man made out of the earth to be mind mingling with, but not yet blended with, body. But this earthlike mind is in reality also corruptible, were not God to breathe into it a power of real life; when He does so, it does not any more undergo moulding, but becomes a soul, not an inefficient and imperfectly formed soul, but one endowed with mind and actually alive; for he says, "man became a living soul."[97]

The discussion in *LA* 1.31-32 bears material resemblance to the *solutio* of *QG* 1.4. Both passages distinguish the two men of Gen 1:27 and 2:7a, but the designations are different: the "molded man" (ստեղծեալ մարդն=ὁ πλασθεὶς

---

95 "And is himself the form of the most original seal" is a somewhat confusing phrase: եւ կերպարան է սա սկզբնատպագունի կնքոյն. Marcus left the reference of the pronoun նա ("he") ambiguous and translated the phrase as "He is a copy of the original seal." Both Aucherean and Mercier take "he" to be the "according-to-the-image man," a judgment I here follow.

96 հոգւոյ հասաւ (probably translating ψυχῆς ἔτυχε *vel sim.*), which Aucherian translated as "animam autem sortitus est." Marcus has "he obtained a spirit," while Mercier rendered the idiom more closely (with Aucherean) as "il reçut en partage une âme."

97 Modified from Whitaker's PLCL translation.

ἄνθρωπος *vel sim.*) of *QG* 1.4 is never called such in *LA* 1.31-32, where "the earthly man" (ὁ δὲ γήϊνος ἄνθρωπος) is used instead. Likewise, the "according-to-the-image one" (ա յ ß np ρսա կերպարանին=ὁ κατ᾽ εἰκόνα *vel sim.*) of *QG* 1.4 is called "the heavenly man" (ὁ οὐράνιος ἄνθρωπος) in *LA* 1.31ff. In spite of the different nomenclatures, both passages attribute more or less similar characteristics to the two men. The "molded man" is a mixture of the corruptible and the incorruptible, according to *QG* 1.4; in *LA* 1.31-32, the mind of "earthly man" penetrates into his body, implying roughly the same idea. The "according-to-the-image man," according to *QG* 1.4, is incorruptible and unmixed; according to *LA* 1.31-32, the "heavenly man" has no part in corruptible, earthly matters.

The resemblance between these two passages, however, stops here; the *Tendenzen* of the two passages are different. The aim of *QG* 1.4 is at delineating the characteristics of the two men without special emphasis on one over against the other. The *solutio*-section, in fact, ends with extolling the virtues of the "according-to-the-image man." In *LA* 1.31-32, on the other hand, Philo's discussion is governed by the exegesis of the text, which has to do not with the "heavenly man" but with the "earthly man." The "heavenly man" is brought in almost as an aside to provide relief for the "earthly man."

The controlling Biblical lemma of *LA* 1.31-32 is the full text of Gen 2:7, whereas the text in *QG* 1.4 extends only to the breathing of the spirit onto the man's face, omitting Gen 2:7b, "The man became a living soul" (καὶ ἐγένετο ὁ ἄνθρωπος εἰς ψυχὴν ζῶσαν). The lemma, the main subject of *LA* 1.31-32, triggers a terminological distinction among three terms of creation: ποιεῖν, πλάττειν, and γίνεσθαι. Ποιεῖν is used exclusively in connection with the heavenly man created in accordance with the image of God (Gen 1:27), an act which Philo in turn rephrases "stamped according to the image of God" (κατ᾽ εἰκόνα δὲ τετυπῶσθαι θεοῦ) in *LA* 1.31. Πλάττειν is applied only to the creation of the earthly man (Gen 2:7a). But once God breathed onto the earthly man, Philo maintains, the mixture of earthly mind and body is then said "to become" (γίνεσθαι) a living soul (Gen 2:7b).

The underlying ζητήματα of the two passages, consequently, are also different. The ζήτημα of *QG* 1.4 is stated at the outset: "Who is the 'molded' man and how is he distinguished from him who is 'according to the image'?" The ensuing *solutio* bears out the centrality of the question. *LA* 1.31-32, on the other hand, appears to be expository and not controlled by any underlying ζήτημα. If anything, it may have to do with the different terms of creation (i.e., ποιεῖν, πλάττειν, γίνεσθαι) that Philo so carefully distinguishes. The real ζητήματα appear in *LA* 1.33-42:

> Someone may ask (Ζητήσαι δ᾽ ἄν τις), why (διὰ τί) God deemed the earthly and body-loving mind worthy of divine breath at all, but not the mind which had been created after the original, and after His own image.

> Secondly, what (τί ἐστι) "breathed in" means.

> Thirdly, why (διὰ τί) the breathing is "into the face."

Fourthly, why (διὰ τί), though he shows his knowledge of the word "spirit" when he says "and the Spirit of God was borne above the water, he now says "breath" not "spirit"

The *solutiones* for these ζητήματα take up the next nine sections (§§34-42), only one of which (§§39-41) finds a parallel in *QG* 1.5. One suspects that the distinction between the two men was a standard *topos* related to the passage; it is included in *LA* 1.31-32 in order to provide background for these four questions. Resemblance between *QG* 1.4 and *LA* 1.31-32 is therefore more likely attributable to a standard discussion of the creation of man that Philo and his contemporaries shared.[98]

QG 1.5 par LA 1.39-41 (Gen 2:7)

QG 1.5: Why is he said to breathe life into his face?

First of all, because it is the principal (part) of the body, for the rest (of the body) is like a base, while it [face], like a bust, sits firmly on top. The fountain of the animal species is sense-perception, and sense-perception is in the face.

Secondly, man has received a part not only of animal but also of rational animal, and the head is the temple of the mind, as some have said.

LA 1.39-41: "Breathing into the face" has to be understood physically and ethically.

Physically, because it is in the face that He set the senses; for this part of the body is beyond other parts endowed with soul.

[Ethically,] as the face is the dominant element in the body, so is the mind the dominant element of the soul: into this only does God breathe, whereas He does not see fit to do so with the other parts, whether senses or organs of utterance and of reproduction; for these are secondary in capacity...

The center of attention in both passages is, again, "face," which is said to have received life. As we saw in the discussion of *QG* 1.3 par *LA* 1.28-30 above, the peculiarity of the LXX expression is most likely responsible for the question. But the answers are different. "Face" in *QG* 1.5 is by and large taken as the equivalent to head, the localization of sense-perception and mind. The interpretation is a literal or physical one. In *LA* 1.39-40, on the other hand, a literal and an allegorical interpretation are offered. The literal takes "face" as the physical repository of senses; the allegorical or "ethical" takes it to be a reference to the dominant element of the soul, namely the mind. Literary dependency is possible but the topic of discussion is perhaps too commonplace to permit one to decide definitively.[99]

---

98 See Thomas Tobin, *Creation of Man*, 164, thinks that all four question-and-answer units are tradition.

99 See last note.

The strength of the suggestion that the *Quaestiones* were intended as "prolegomena" to the supposedly later *Allegoriae* consists in the structural and topical similarities between the *Quaestiones* and the *Allegoriae* and not on any verbatim correspondence. Since both the *Quaestiones* and the *Allegoriae* follow a similar list of *topoi*, the argument goes, there is reason to posit some relationship, intellectual if not literary, between these two works. To evaluate this claim, it may be helpful to distinguish three levels of correspondence: the *quaestio*-level, the *solutio*-level, and the literary or formal level. At the *quaestio*-level, difficulties, censures, or mere questions on a text could have been, and most likely were, raised by exegetes before Philo or by Philo himself. Correspondence at this level tells us that Philo was dependent on his predecessors. Thus, two works by the same author commenting on the same text sharing the same questions ought not be surprising, least of all when Philo is known to have been dependent on traditional material. This is in fact what we have observed in the our case study. At the *solutio*-level, evidence does not lead to the conclusion that Philo gave the same answers to the same questions. In all five parallels which afford some type of comparison, similarities between the two series of commentaries turn out to be rather banal. They can be traced either to the Biblical text, traditional material, or commonplaces. The innovation of *LA* 1.19-42 is the introduction of the intelligible and sense-perceptible *ideas*, which is part and parcel of Philo's effort at reinterpreting the two created *men* into two *mind* and to fit them into his allegory of the soul. To the extent that *QG* 1.1-5 has contributed very little to this overarching theme, one has to dismiss any kind of intellectual connection between these works. There is even less connection at the literary or formal level of correspondence. Explicitly cited question-and-answer units in the *Allegoriae* cannot be traced back to the *Quaestiones*; we hear at best faint echoes. There is not one documented case in which Philo could be shown to have copied his material from another work. What correspondence between the *Allegoriae* and the *Quaestiones* there is, therefore, is restricted to traditional zetematic materials; there appears to be little mutual influence between the two works otherwise.

Summary and Conclusion

This study began by posing the question whether and to what extent Philo's *Quaestiones et solutiones in Genesim et in Exodum* are related to his *Allegoriae*. The assumption that such was a meaningful comparison was confirmed by the observation that both works display the same tendency of following the Biblical text in broad outline. In contradistinction to the *Expositiones*, in which subject matters are arranged topically, both the *Quaestiones* and, to a lesser extent, the *Allegoriae* let the text determine their order of presentation. In this regard, both works can rightly be called "commentary" in the modern, technical sense as independent works set alongside the original text, providing discussion and exegetical notes on the text. The historical survey of the genre ζητήματα καὶ λύσεις has provided ample examples of independent zetematic works compiled on a variety of subject matters and intended for a wide range of audiences. The use of this genre for literary questions was especially prevalent. Authors long predating Philo as well as his contemporaries composed similar works, though Philo's *Quaestiones* appear to be the earliest extant literary zetematic work whose compositional principle was based on a continuous text.

To corroborate results obtained from the external comparison, the synoptic comparison, confined mainly to the *Quaestiones* and the *Allegoriae*, has shown that the *Quaestiones* were composed not as preliminary notes to, but as a work independent of, the more complex *Allegoriae*. The wide application of explicit question-and-answer units in the *Allegoriae* had been seen as supportive of some kind of literary relationship with the *Quaestiones*, but the overwhelming majority of these units have no parallels in the *Quaestiones*. Either the question-and-answer technique of exegesis was a favorite exegetical method of Philo's or these units, if they came from a source at all, owe their existence to a source other than the *Quaestiones*. There is little reason to suggest that the *Quaestiones* were intended as preliminary notes for the *Allegoriae*.

It seems reasonable to conclude, then, that the *Allegoriae* and *Quaestiones* are independent of each other and that the similar questions assumed by both are traditional. Why would Philo undertake to write a series of comments covering essentially the same grounds as the *Allegoriae* but in a different genre? Departing from the bounds of traditional zetematic literature, which had been attentive to isolated problems and questions, the *Quaestiones* reflect a systematic application of the question-and-answer technique to a continuous commentary on the Biblical text. In so doing, Philo transformed the question-and-answer technique into a rhetorical device, so much so that at times it became necessary to pose real difficulties in the *solutio*-sections. In this regard, the *Quaestiones* resemble the *Anon. in Theaet.* and Philo's own *Allegoriae* in that all three works follow the text lemma by lemma and provide continuous comments on the text. But unlike the other two, the *Quaestiones* cast the comments exclusively in question-and-answer forms. The reason for this strategy is perhaps the public and educative appeal associated with the genre. The format provided the general (Jewish) students relatively easy access to allegorical interpretations of greater complexity. The consistently less sophisticated interpretation and the relative prominence given to the literal interpretation all point to such a general audience. It is no accident that so few answers in the *Quaestiones* actually reject the literal interpretation of a verse. The *Quaestiones* are therefore "preparatory" or "preliminary" only in the sense that they were intended as general introduction to the more advanced writings represented by the *Allegoriae*. Whether the *Quaestiones* should be seen as catechetical, however, can only be hypothesized. To the extent that zetematic literature was sometimes thought to be school documents, it might be reasonable to suggest that Philo's *Quaestiones* also functioned in a similar capacity in the Alexandrian synagogue.

The Place of Judaism in Philo's Thought: Israel, Jews, and Proselytes*

Ellen Birnbaum
Harvard University

An intriguing question in Philo's thought, but a question he himself does not directly address, is the relationship between being a Jew and being able to "see" God. For Philo, seeing God is the height of happiness, the goal of the philosopher's quest. Concerning this experience, he writes,

> Now the sight of the eyes is the most excellent of all the senses, since by it alone we apprehend the most excellent of existing things, the sun and the moon and the whole heaven and world; but the sight of the mind, the dominant element in the soul, surpasses all the other faculties of the mind, and this is wisdom which is the sight of the understanding. But he to whom it is given not only to apprehend by means of knowledge all else that nature has to shew, but also to see the Father and Maker of all, may rest assured that he is advanced to the crowning point of happiness; for nothing is higher than God, and whoso has stretched the eyesight of the soul to reach Him should pray that he may there abide and stand firm . . . (*Abr.* 57-58)[1]

Here and elsewhere, Philo emphasizes that one sees God not with the eyes of the body but with the eyes of the mind or soul. Seeing God then is an internal experience, one that is separate and individual. Theoretically, it would seem that anyone—Jew or non-Jew—might strive toward this ultimate spiritual goal.

At the same time, however, it is obvious that Philo is extremely devoted to the Jewish people and that he deeply values their Scriptures, beliefs, and practices. Indeed most of his works are Biblical commentaries in which he explains not only the text but also the Jewish way of life. Philo's dedication to

---

* This paper summarizes in broad outline many of the findings discussed in my dissertation by the same title (Columbia University, 1992), to be published next year by Scholars Press. References provided here are representative, not comprehensive. Further documentation, detailed analyses, and discussion of other aspects of the topic can be found in the dissertation.

1 Unless otherwise indicated, all translations are taken from F. H. Colson, G. H. Whitaker, and Ralph Marcus, trans., *Philo in Ten Volumes (and Two Supplementary Volumes)*, 12 vols., The Loeb Classical Library (Cambridge: Harvard University Press, 1929-62), (hereafter cited as PLCL).

his people, moreover, extends beyond study and writing to political involvement, as exemplified by his participation in a delegation to the Emperor Caligula to plead on behalf of his suffering compatriots.

Taking all this into consideration, one might well ask what connection, if any, Philo might draw between being a Jew and attaining the highest spiritual goal. To state the matter another way, perhaps, does an individual's particular identity as a Jew provide, according to Philo, any advantage in the potentially universal striving to see God?

Although scholars have long debated the extent to which Philo is influenced by Greek or Jewish sources, never has anyone thoroughly examined the tension in his thinking between particularism and universalism. For years writers have argued about whether Philo is more fundamentally a Greek or a Jew, comparing his works with other earlier, contemporary, and later manifestations of Judaism; earlier, contemporary, and later philosophical schools; pagan mystery religions; Gnosticism; and Christianity. Scholars have also examined Philo as—among other things—a philosopher, a mystic, a Jew, a Biblical interpreter, and a rhetorician. Most certainly, these approaches have contributed impressively to understanding the writings of this first century Alexandrian Jew. While recognizing his manifold dimensions, however, the authors of these various studies address only tangentially the basic question of how Philo himself evaluates his Jewish identity in relation to other elements in his thought.

In 1971, Samuel Sandmel published a work whose title epitomizes one of the approaches just described; it is called *Philo's Place in Judaism*.[2] Sandmel compares Philo's portrayals of Abraham with those found in rabbinic literature and concludes that Philo represents a Judaism quite different from that of the Rabbis. The title of the present study, "The Place of Judaism in Philo's Thought," is a deliberate reworking of Sandmel's title. The shift in words is meant to signal the shift in focus from the question of whether Philo is more fundamentally Greek or Jewish to the question of how he himself assesses the significance of being a Jew.[3]

To approach this question, I have selected an issue which enables us to see how Philo balances his particular Jewish loyalties and his universal spiritual strivings. Even though he himself does not explicitly address this issue, namely how being a Jew is related to seeing God, he does provide us with a term that combines both the particular and the universal aspects of the question. This term is "Israel."

As Philo frequently explains, "Israel" means "the one that sees God" (ὁρῶν θεόν).[4] Theoretically the quest to see God and the goal of seeing Him are potentially universal, since anyone may strive to see God. "Israel" therefore may denote anyone who succeeds in achieving this spiritual goal. At the same time, however, "Israel" is also the name used in the Bible for the nation

---

[2] Samuel Sandmel, *Philo's Place in Judaism: A Study of Conceptions of Abraham in Jewish Literature*, augmented ed. (New York: Ktav, 1971).

[3] It should be noted that Philo himself never mentions the term "Judaism" ('Ιουδαϊσμός) though it is in use during his time. See 2 Macc. 2:21, 8:1, 14:38; 4 Macc. 4:26; and Gal. 1:13-14.

[4] E.g., *Abr.* 57, *Legat.* 4. For discussion of this etymology, see my dissertation, 114-27.

of Philo's ancestors and for the Jews themselves before and during his time. Moreover, according to the Bible, Israel is the nation that God selects to be His own people and to serve Him in a covenantal relationship. In Philo's writings then—both in Scriptural quotations and in his interpretations—"Israel" may potentially represent one who sees God, the Biblical nation and its Jewish descendants, or both. Because we do not know precisely who is included in Philo's "Israel," I shall use the term in quotation marks to indicate that its meaning is uncertain.

Philo's blend of associations with "Israel" gives rise to several questions. Does he, for example, equate "Israel" only with the historical Biblical nation and its Jewish descendants? If so, does he think that only they can see God? Conversely, does he redefine "Israel" to mean only those who see God, regardless of their ancestry? If so, what relationship does Philo's understanding of "Israel" as "the one that sees God" have with the Biblical nation Israel or with any contemporary social group, particularly his fellow Jews?

"Israel" and the Jews

Because of the ambiguities that result from the way Philo understands "Israel," a key question in this study is how he uses the terms "Israel" and "Jew" in relation to each other. Indeed my pivotal argument is that one may in fact distinguish in his work between "Israel," a rather loosely defined entity that sees God, and the Jews, the real nation that believes in and worships God. Accordingly, "Israel" is not a clearly identifiable social group but instead may be similar to what we speak of today as an "intellectual elite." In contrast, the Jews are a precisely defined group whose members—by birth or choice—are easily identified. Although "Israel" and the Jews may overlap or may indeed be the same, Philo discusses them as two distinct entities.

To support this argument, I offer and shall elaborate upon the following observations:

1. Philo generally speaks about "Israel" and the Jews in different series of works, which are probably intended for different, though perhaps overlapping, audiences.
2. To describe "Israel" and the Jews as collectivities, Philo uses different words with different connotations.
3. Philo describes the relationship between God and each entity in different ways.
4. "Membership requirements" for belonging to "Israel" and the Jews appear to be different.

The observations listed above are based upon careful study of all Philo's extant writings, particularly those where he discusses "seeing God" and where he mentions "Israel" and "Jews," explicitly by name or implicitly without name. Included then are his three exegetical series—the *Allegory*, the *Exposition*, and *Questions and Answers on Genesis and Exodus* (*QGE*). Among the non-exegetical writings, the most relevant for our present purposes are Philo's two political treatises, *Flacc.* and *Legat.*, where he recounts the political travails of his Jewish contemporaries.[5]

An important assumption behind this study is that Philo's different writings are intended for persons with different spiritual sensibilities and different levels of familiarity with Jewish beliefs, practices, and people. Although much has been written concerning Philo's intended readers, he himself rarely tells us whom he is addressing. At best one can only attempt to make intelligent guesses about who these various readers are. Since the assumption that Philo's works are aimed at somewhat different audiences is particularly relevant to my first observation, I shall present my speculation about these audiences further below. Let us turn now to consider each of the above observations more closely.

1. *Philo generally speaks of "Israel" and the Jews in different series of works, which are probably intended for different, though perhaps overlapping, audiences.* Most striking, perhaps, is that Philo uses the terms "Israel" ('Ισραήλ) and "Jew" ('Ιουδαῖος) together in the same treatise only once, in *Legat.* No other treatise—either exegetical or non-exegetical—mentions both "Israel" and the Jews in the same individual work. Also noteworthy is that we can discern a pattern among the works in which each word does or does not appear. Among the three exegetical series, for example, Philo mentions "Israel" most frequently in the *Allegory*, occasionally in *QGE*, and only twice in the *Exposition*. In the non-exegetical works, "Israel" appears only once, namely in *Legat.* 4. As for where Philo mentions the Jews, he speaks of them by name only in one exegetical series, the *Exposition*, and in the non-exegetical works. Generally speaking, then, the works that mention the Jews do not mention "Israel" and the works that mention "Israel" do not mention the Jews.[6]

Philo's separate use of the terms "Israel" and "Jew" in his writings is particularly salient when one considers his two treatises on Moses, which form part of the *Exposition*. In these works, although Philo narrates the history, during Moses' time, of the nation the Bible calls "Israel," he himself never uses the word "Israel." Instead he calls them "Hebrews" ('Εβραῖοι), or else simply "the nation" (τὸ ἔθνος), or "the people" (ὁ λαός). Even when

---

[5] Also relevant but not discussed in this summary are the fragmentary Apology for the Jews (*Hypoth.*), where Philo refers to the Biblical nation, his Jewish contemporaries, and the Essene sect; and *Contempl.*, where Philo describes the life of the Therapeutae—another contemporary sect—and where he briefly refers to the Biblical nation.

[6] The term "Israel" appears over seventy times in the *Allegory* and four times in *QGE*. Occasionally, instead of using "Israel" in these two series, Philo substitutes a periphrastic expression like the etymology ὁρῶν θεόν, "the one that sees God," or the phrase ὁρατικὸν γένος, "the race/class that can see." In *QGE* especially, he seems to prefer the phrase ὁρατικὸν γένος as a substitute for "Israel" (see, e.g., *QE* 1.21, *QE* 2.46). This phrase is discussed below. When speaking about the Biblical nation and his Jewish contemporaries, Philo does not always use a proper noun (e.g., "Hebrews" or "Jews") nor even a common noun, (e.g., "the nation" or "the people"), but sometimes uses only pronouns (see e.g., *Hypoth.*). This summary reports only on Philo's explicit references to "Israel," the Jews, or the Hebrews. The evidence where he speaks implicitly of these three entities, however—i.e., where he does not use proper nouns to name them—supports the observations presented here.

paraphrasing Scriptural quotations where the word "Israel" appears, Philo changes this term to "Hebrews"![7]

This feature—namely, the non-use of "Israel" to describe the Biblical nation in the treatises on Moses—suggests that for Philo the word "Israel" may hold a specialized meaning that may or may not include the entire Biblical nation. If, as I maintain, "Israel" does indeed signify a loosely defined entity comprising those who can see God, then theoretically this entity could include some or all members of the Biblical nation, some or all descendants of the Biblical nation—namely Jews—and also some non-Jews.

Whatever the composition of Philo's "Israel" may be, one may infer from his separate use of the terms "Israel" and "Jew" that these terms may have different, though perhaps overlapping, meanings. Based upon the pattern that occurs among the various works in which each term does or does not appear, I would also propose that Philo may use these two terms for somewhat different audiences, for whom he writes with somewhat different aims. Let us now briefly consider who and what these audiences and aims might be.

Philo's Audiences and Aims. Certain characteristics of Philo's three exegetical series suggest that these series are directed towards different readers and composed with different purposes. The *Allegory*, for example, presupposes an audience with a sophisticated knowledge of both Scripture and philosophy. In form, this series consists of treatises that, for the most part, provide a running commentary on the Bible. Often Philo expresses his preference for allegorical interpretations, whose dominant concern is the journey of the soul, its struggle against the passions, and its quest for God. "Israel," for example, often symbolizes the mind or soul that sees God (e.g., *Leg.* 3.186; *Somn.* 2.173). Most likely, Philo's readers in this series are Jews like himself, who may look to the *Allegory* as a guide to reading the Bible so that it will reveal to them its secrets about the soul's quest.

Philo's audience in *QGE* is probably also quite knowledgeable about both Scripture and philosophy, but this series, which includes a broader spectrum of interpretations than the *Allegory*, may be intended for a wider Jewish audience. In contrast to the treatises of the *Allegory*, *QGE* is written atomistically, presenting separate questions and answers on individual verses or parts of verses. Since the answers in *QGE* often include without criticism a wider variety of exegeses than we find in the *Allegory* for each verse, this series may be intended as a collation or digest of interpretations reflecting the opinions of a broader community of Alexandrian Jews than just those who share Philo's interest in allegory and the journey of the soul. Perhaps, in fact, *QGE* may function as a sourcebook or even a textbook for this community.

Unlike the *Allegory* and *QGE*, Philo's other exegetical series, the *Exposition*, does not necessarily assume any familiarity with Scripture at all. Instead his presentation here—in the form of treatises on Biblical themes and figures, like Creation, Abraham, Moses, or the Decalogue—might serve equally well for people at different levels of knowledge about the Bible. In addition, since Philo resorts much less frequently to allegorical exegesis and since his discussions are, in some ways, less philosophically complex than those in his other

---

[7] See, e.g., *Mos.* 1.278, 284, 289.

Biblical commentaries,[8] he may also be addressing people with a varied range of familiarity with philosophy. More to the point, Philo's occasional exhortations about disloyal Jews, apologetic remarks defending the Jews and their practices, and welcoming attitude toward proselytes suggest that the *Exposition* is probably aimed primarily at Jews and non-Jews—whether hostile or friendly—who know little about Jewish beliefs and practices. Philo may have several aims in mind here: to reclaim the alienated Jews, educate the less knowledgeable ones, assuage non-Jews who may be hostile, and appeal to those who may be interested.

If we return to consider where Philo speaks of "Israel" and the Jews in his exegetical works, we see that he mentions "Israel" most frequently in the *Allegory*, occasionally in *QGE*, and almost never in the *Exposition*. Thus Philo may confine his discussion of "Israel" to the *Allegory* and, to a lesser extent, to *QGE* in order to address people like himself who understand the goal of seeing God and who strive toward it. Moreover, since the term "Israel" would be more meaningful for Jews familiar with the Bible and Jewish tradition than it would be for people less knowledgeable about these sources, those more familiar with the term would associate it with their own heritage and take pride in the identification of "Israel" with the goal of seeing God.

At the same time, Philo may avoid speaking of "Israel" in the *Exposition* where his readers may be philosophically unsophisticated Jews and non-Jews who have yet to acquire the spiritual sensibility to appreciate what "Israel" represents. It is important to note, however, that although Philo mentions "Israel" only twice in the *Exposition*, he does not completely omit speaking about it nor about seeing God. This suggests that he is not deliberately trying to hide something about "Israel" from his readers but instead may be adapting his discussion to suit their needs and interests.

As for the observation that Philo mentions the Jews only in the *Exposition*, we might reasonably expect him to discuss the Jews in a series aimed primarily at people not well acquainted with Jewish history, beliefs, and practices. At the same time, he would have no need to speak about the Jews and their ways to his more knowledgeable readers in the *Allegory* and *QGE*.

With respect to the non-exegetical treatises, *Flacc.* and *Legat.*, both works recount the sufferings of the Jews—especially the Alexandrian Jews—in the latter part of the fourth decade C.E. In these works, Philo's apparent purpose is to show that God watches over this people when they are in trouble. These treatises may be directed toward both Jews and non-Jews, regardless of their familiarity with the Bible or their philosophical and religious sensibilities. By emphasizing divine providence, Philo may, on the one hand, wish to bolster the spirits of his fellow Jews during a time of suffering; on the other hand, he may also wish to sound a warning to Gentiles to stop their maltreatment of his people.

"Israel" and the Jews in *Legat*. Of special interest, of course, is *Legat.*, since this is the one non-exegetical treatise in which Philo mentions "Israel" and the only treatise of any type in which he speaks of both "Israel" and the Jews in the same work. The term "Israel" appears only in the introductory section

---

8 An exception to this observation is the treatise *Opif*. See my dissertation, 29-30 and 145.

(*Legat.* 1-7). One of Philo's chief aims here is to argue that God extends providence to all people and especially toward the Jews. Declaring that current events should convince even those who have lost faith in divine providence, Philo writes,

> And yet the present time and the many important questions decided in it are strong enough to convince even those who have come to disbelieve that the Deity takes thought for men, and particularly for the [suppliants' race/class which has been allotted or has allotted itself to] the Father and King of the Universe and the Source of all things. Now this [race/class] is called in the Hebrew tongue Israel, but expressed in [Greek], the word is 'he that sees God' and to see Him seems to me of all possessions, public or private, the most precious.[9]

It is interesting that although Philo mentions the Jews explicitly throughout the treatise he does not mention them by name in this introductory section. While he does not directly say then that the Jews are "Israel, the one that sees God," the association between "Israel" and the Jews is nevertheless implicit since the rest of the work is about the Jews.

Why would Philo wish to equate "Israel" with all Jews in this political treatise, when he does not do so anywhere else? Perhaps he is guided here by a polemical purpose. In this treatise, after all, Philo presents for everyone the story of his persecuted nation. Presumably he hopes to elicit sympathy, outrage, and finally admiration for them. Not only should these victims be spared such heinous treatment, they are worthy only of the best consideration! To underscore this point, perhaps, Philo chooses to portray the Jews here as those who have attained the very highest philosophical ideal.

2. *To describe "Israel" and the Jews as collectivities, Philo uses different words with different connotations.* Philo most frequently calls "Israel" a γένος, but the Jews and their forbears, the Hebrews, either an ἔθνος (nation) or a λαός (people) and occasionally a πολιτεία or a γένος. In contrast, he never directly calls Israel an ἔθνος, λαός, or πολιτεία.[10]

When Philo describes the Jews or Hebrews as an ἔθνος or λαός it is always clear that he is speaking of them as a nation or people, i.e., as an easily identifiable social or political group. Even when he calls them a γένος (*Virt.* 206, *Legat.* 178), a term which, as we shall see, can be understood in a variety of ways, it is still evident from the context that he means a race defined by birth and perhaps too a social or political entity.

Philo's use of πολιτεία in relation to the Jews is somewhat more complicated, since the word πολιτεία carries several meanings. It can signify a constitution of laws, a form of government, political life in general, the

---

9 Bracketed sections are my own adaptations to the PLCL translation. My translation of γένος as race/class is discussed below. For detailed analyses of this passage, see my dissertation, 184-87, 321-26.

10 Philo uses the word ἔθνος in connection with "Israel" five times (*Her.* 279; *Abr.* 57; *QG* 3.49; *Deus* 145 [see 148]; *QE* 2.30). Whether or not "Israel" is a nation, however, is beside the point of these passages, each of which focuses upon other issues. In the first three citations given here, for example, Philo notes that the nation is called "Israel," and he develops the significance of the name.

political life of a specific community, citizenship, or the people themselves
who live under a common form of government. To be sure, occasionally
more than one meaning may obtain. When Philo talks specifically about the
πολιτεία of the Jews (*Virt.* 108, *Legat.* 194), he most likely wishes to emphasize
that they are a group of people with a shared constitution of laws. Sometimes it
is unclear whether he is speaking about the people themselves or their form of
government. Whichever meaning he intends, however, the ambiguity of
πολιτεία does not affect our understanding of the Jews or their forbears as a
group that lives under a common set of laws.

While the various words Philo uses for the Hebrews and Jews may
emphasize different aspects of the same group—be it, for example, their
common descent (as with γένος), or their shared laws (as with πολιτεία)—his
use of γένος to characterize "Israel" is ambiguous, making it possible for this
entity to be understood in more than one way. Although γένος can refer to a
race defined by birth, the term can also denote a class distinguished by
shared characteristics, a genus as opposed to an individual species, an abstract
nature or kind, or an ideal as opposed to a real entity.

Most often, for example, Philo describes "Israel" as the ὁρατικὸν (able to
see)γένος. Certainly when he uses ὁρατικόν here, he has in mind the spiritual,
not physical, capacity to "see."[11] Less certain, however, is what Philo means
by γένος. Is "Israel" a race into which one is born, a race with the genetic
ability to "see"? Is it a class defined only by its ability to see, whether this
ability be inherited or acquired? Is "Israel" meant to represent the abstract
quality of seeing? Or, does Philo intend "Israel" to encompass a little bit of all
these things? Indeed when Philo uses the word "Israel," the etymology ὁρῶν
θεόν, or the phrase ὁρατικὸν γένος in allegorical interpretations, ambiguities
like these are only compounded![12] Because it most often appears that the γένος
"Israel" should be understood either as a race with common ancestry or as a
class defined by shared qualities, I translate γένος as "race/class" to indicate
the ambiguity.

Lest anyone remain unconvinced about the significance of Philo's choice
of γένος to characterize "Israel," I would like to call attention briefly to *Sacr.* 6-7,
where he presents γένος as superior to λαός. In this passage, which interprets
Gen. 35:29, Philo notices that this verse mentioning Isaac's death has one
word that is different from the verses that mention the deaths of Abraham
(Gen. 25:8) and Jacob (Gen. 49:33). In the Masoretic text, all three expressions
have the same Hebrew wording, "And he was gathered to his people (עמיו)."
The Greek Bible, however, translates the word for "people" as λαός in both
verses about Abraham and Jacob but renders the noun as γένος in the verse
about Isaac. In the Bible, both Greek words appear to mean the same thing,
namely a people. Philo, however, understands γένος here in a philosophical

---

11 The phrase ὁρατικὸν γένος appears to be an adaptation of the etymology ὁρῶν θεόν to
characterize "Israel" as a collectivity. In this adaptation, the ability to see as expressed by
the singular participle ὁρῶν is extended to a larger group or γένος. In addition, "God" as
the object seen drops out, so that while the ability to see is explicitly ascribed to "Israel,"
the ability to see God per se remains unexpressed in this phrase, becoming, perhaps,
implicit.

12 See, e.g., *Leg.* 3.186; *Conf.* 56; *Migr.* 18.

sense and his interpretation echoes statements he makes elsewhere about the relationship between genus and species.

In *Sacr.* 6-7, Philo takes advantage of the discrepancy in wording among the three verses to expand upon the differences between Abraham and Jacob, on the one hand, and Isaac, on the other. According to a paradigm commonplace in his writings, all three patriarchs symbolize virtue acquired in different ways: Abraham symbolizes virtue acquired by learning; Isaac, virtue acquired by nature; and Jacob, virtue gained through practice. In this passage, Philo explains that Isaac is distinguished from the other two patriarchs because natural or inherent virtue is superior to that acquired by learning or practice. Isaac's superiority is highlighted by the fact that he is added to a γένος, while Abraham and Jacob are gathered to a λαός.

In presenting this interpretation, then, Philo juxtaposes the philosophical sense γένος or genus with the literal sense of λαός or people to underscore Isaac's superiority to the other patriarchs as well as the superiority of γένος to λαός. One can hardly fail to notice that γένος—the term Philo uses most frequently to describe "Israel" as a collectivity—carries for him significant nuances.

3. *Philo speaks differently about the relationship between God and "Israel," on the one hand, and between God and the Jews, on the other.*

Basing himself upon its etymology, ὁρῶν θεόν, Philo associates "Israel" with seeing God and the ability to see Him. Although he occasionally speaks of "Israel" as worshipping God (*Sacr.* 120, *Plant.* 60), this characterization is rare and he never specifies how "Israel" worships Him. Indeed while Philo sometimes mentions other qualities of "Israel" in relation to God, the ability to see Him is by far the most predominant characteristic. Moreover, this characteristic pertains to both sides of the relationship: For its part, "Israel" sees God. At the same time, God grants "Israel" the very ability to see Him (*Abr.* 57-59, *Praem.* 40-46).

With regard to the Jews, in contrast, Philo never specifically talks about them as seeing God.[13] Instead he writes that they believe in God and are the only ones who serve Him by following specific laws and customs (*Spec.* 2.165-67; *Legat.* 115-18). In this capacity, they also serve as priestly intermediaries for the whole world (*Mos.* 1.149; *Spec.* 1.97), which errs in its various forms of false worship (*Spec.* 2.162-67). Philo in fact denounces all these forms of false worship, including worship of nature, animals, idols, mythic gods, and even reason (*Decal.* 52-80, *Spec.* 1.327-45).

It is important to remember that these denunciations are not concerned with false worship in theory alone but are directed at real beliefs held and rituals practiced within Philo's environment. Moreover, for Philo, Judaism represents the only monotheistic religion; indeed, he gives no evidence of knowing about the beginnings of Christianity.

The relationship between God and the Jews, then, is characterized by their faith in and service to Him, a feature which distinguishes them from all other peoples. In addition, perhaps in return for service and devotion, the Jews also

---

13 In *Legat.* 4, discussed briefly above, it is only by association that Philo implies the Jews are "Israel, the one that sees God."

benefit specially from God's πρόνοια or protective concern (*Spec.* 4.179-81, *Flacc.* 170).[14]

4. *"Membership requirements" for belonging to "Israel" and the Jews appear to be different.*

Unlike the other three observations, this one is necessarily speculative, since Philo himself never addresses the issue of what one must do to become part of "Israel" or the Jews. To help us consider this issue, however, we may draw upon some of the previous discussions, particularly concerning the relationship between God and each entity.

What chiefly characterizes God's relationship with "Israel," for example, is its ability to see Him. We have noted that Philo describes seeing God as an intellectual or spiritual activity; one perceives Him with the eye of the mind or soul. Beyond this, Philo's portrayal of the phenomenon is imprecise. Indeed, he depicts seeing God in such different ways that he seems at times to be describing a general belief in or awareness of God—i.e., seeing that God is—while at other times, he seems to be describing a specific experience, a mystical transport. Philo also portrays seeing God as an ability or an achievement. Some of these variations may correspond to different spiritual capacities of the seers. Accordingly, people may strive to develop their capacity to see Him, may attain different kinds of vision, and may achieve vision of Him in different ways. Occasionally, however, Philo also emphasizes that no one can see God without His help.

In contrast to the vision of God with which "Israel" is associated, Jewish worship of God is not an achievement or reward but consists of very specific practices. Philo speaks, for example, about Jewish prayers, festivals, first fruit offerings, laws, and customs. Not only do Jews believe in and serve God, then, they serve Him in particular ways, and their practices reinforce their belief in Him. Unlike the vision of God—which may be an ability, achievement, or reward—Jewish worship and belief are rooted in a deliberate commitment and the choice to live a certain kind of life.

Philo himself does not explicitly draw a connection between the vision of God and Jewish worship of Him. We may speculate, however, that it is possible that seeing God *may* lead one to worship Him in the Jewish way and worshipping God in the Jewish way *may* lead one to be able to "see" Him. Thus, people who see God may also worship Him through Jewish practices, while Jewish worshippers of God may also "see" Him. "Israel" and the Jews then may be one and the same or they may overlap. It is important to remember, however, that the vision of God and Jewish worship of Him are not *necessarily* connected. We therefore cannot determine precisely the relationship between those who see God—"Israel"—and those who worship Him in the Jewish way—the Jews. Instead the connection between the two entities remains ambiguous.

---

14 I have also identified other features that characterize the relationship between God and the Jews according to Philo, namely that the Jews are allotted or have allotted themselves to God and that they are God-beloved or God-loving. These features, however, are not relevant to the present summary. For a full discussion of the relationship between God and the Jews, see Chapter Five of my dissertation.

If we turn now to the question of membership requirements for "Israel" and the Jews, it would seem that "Israel"—as the ὁρῶν θεόν, the one that sees God, or the ὁρατικὸν γένος, the race/class that can see—might include anyone who sees God, whether Jewish or not. The experience of seeing God, however, is by its very nature an elusive ideal. As something to strive for, it appears difficult to maintain and impossible to achieve without God's help. If "Israel" is indeed the entity that sees God or the race/class that can see, not only would one become a member of "Israel" by virtue of spiritual ability or divine will, but the composition of "Israel" itself may be constantly fluctuating. Thus one would not "convert" to "Israel"; rather one would strive both to belong to and remain among those who can see.

The Jews, on the other hand, are a political and social group. One becomes a member of the Jewish people by being born a Jew. Although one can reject his or her heritage, it seems nevertheless that he or she remains a Jew. At the same time, however, Philo describes the relationship between God and the Jews in such a way as to suggest that it may be available to anyone who wishes to participate, regardless of birth. For example, the Jews worship God by following specific laws and practices. The adoption of these laws and practices is the result of choice, not ability or divine will, as in the case of seeing God. Philo notes in fact that even some of his non-Jewish contemporaries choose to honor Jewish practices (*Mos.* 2.17-24).

Proselytes. Philo's discussion of proselytes reinforces some of the observations described above, specifically regarding "membership requirements" and generally regarding the features that distinguish "Israel" and the Jews. If one examines what Philo says about proselytes in relation to each of the four observations presented here, it becomes obvious that proselytes are to be associated with the Jews, though not necessarily with "Israel." In other words, if we consider 1) the writings in which Philo discusses proselytes, 2) the way he characterizes the collectivity which they join, 3) the relationship proselytes have with God, and finally, 4) what they do to join a new group, we find that proselytes correspond more closely to the Jews than to "Israel."

With respect to the writings in which Philo discusses proselytes, we can see that among the exegetical works he speaks of them as real people, i.e., not as symbolic figures, only in the *Exposition*.[15] The *Exposition*, moreover, is the only exegetical series where Philo discusses the Jews by name, mentioning "Israel" only twice. Philo does not mention proselytes at all in his non-exegetical works. Since he speaks of proselytes and Jews, but not "Israel" in the same treatises, it stands to reason that he sees proselytes as coming over to the Jews but not necessarily to "Israel." It is also worth recalling that the *Exposition* expresses a welcoming attitude towards proselytes and may, in part, be directed toward potential newcomers.

---

[15] *Mos.* 1.7, 147; *Spec.* 1.51-53, 308-9; *Spec.* 2.116-19; *Spec.* 4.176-78; *Virt.* 102-4, 180-82, 212-19; *Praem.* 152. Compare these references from the *Exposition* to those in the *Allegory* (*Somn.* 1.160-62, *Somn.* 2.272-73), where proselytes are symbols in allegorical interpretations. Similarly, in *QE* 2.2, the proselyte is important only as an exegetical figure. For extensive discussion of proselytes in Philo's works, see Chapter Six of my dissertation.

As for his characterization of the collectivity that proselytes join, Philo never directly says that they become members of the Jews nor of "Israel," nor does he state that they enter a new ἔθνος, λαός, or γένος. He does, however, write that they come over to a new πολιτεία (*Spec.* 1.51; *Virt.* 219; cf. *Virt.* 175). Since he uses this word in connection with the Jews but not with "Israel," we may logically assume that he views proselytes as joining the πολιτεία of the Jews, i.e., the community of people who live according to the constitution of Moses.

Concerning the relationship between proselytes and God, Philo writes that they abandon false beliefs and worship to adopt belief in and worship of the one God (*Spec.* 1.51-53; *Virt.* 102-4). In return, proselytes enjoy God's πρόνοια or protective concern (*Spec.* 1.308-9; *Spec.* 4.176-78). It is noteworthy that Philo does not say that proselytes acquire a vision of God nor that they gain the ability to see Him. Since Philo observes that the Jews are the ones who believe in and worship God and that they too benefit from divine concern, it is clear that what he says about the relationship between proselytes and God corresponds more closely to what he says about the Jews than to what he says about "Israel."

Finally, as to their fulfillment of "membership requirements," proselytes are characterized by their activity of leaving behind their religious and social backgrounds to adopt new beliefs and worship and a new community or πολιτεία (*Spec.* 1.51-53; *Virt.* 219). That is, they abandon their belief in and worship of many gods for belief in and worship of the one God, and they leave behind their social network of family and friends to join a new group of people. Again, Philo does not comment about whether or not proselytes also become able to see God as a result of their new way of life. As with the other areas just reviewed, then, here too, Philo's comments about proselytes lend support to a distinction between "Israel" and the Jews and place proselytes closer to the Jews than to "Israel."

The Membership of "Israel"

Having now considered the factors that distinguish "Israel" and the Jews in Philo's writings, let us recall that the argument that Philo uses these terms quite separately is presented here to help us determine the relationship in his thought between being a Jew and being able to see God. If those who see God are equated with "Israel," and if "Israel" may not always be exactly the same as all the Jews, as the evidence suggests, whom then might Philo have in mind when he speaks about "Israel"? Who, in other words, sees God? The following four groups suggest themselves as possibilities:

1) all respected philosophers, or philosophically-minded people, whether they are Jews or not;
2) a subset of the Jews who are philosophically-minded;
3) all Jews; or

4) all Jews, whether philosophers or not, and all respected non-Jewish philosophers.[16]

Of these possibilities, I believe the first to be the most likely. For one thing, Philo emphasizes again and again how difficult it is to see God and how few are able to achieve this vision (see, e.g., *Post.* 13-21; *Migr.* 46; *Praem.* 43). Although he may believe that Judaism embodies the best way of life through its beliefs and practices, he occasionally speaks disparagingly of other Jews who interpret the Scriptures literally. This suggests that he does not view all Jews as equally sophisticated and therefore may not regard them all as equally worthy of belonging to the elite who can "see." In addition, if Philo does believe that all Jews can see God, it is surprising that he never mentions this in the *Exposition* where he talks at length about this nation. The elitist nature of his discussion about seeing God, then, seems to rule out the last two choices suggested above which would include all Jews.

As to the second suggestion that "Israel" is comprised of an elite group of Jews alone, although this is certainly possible, nothing that Philo says about seeing God necessitates that one *must* be a Jew to achieve this vision. Even though he may speak about the God who is seen as the God whom the Jews honor and worship, this God is still the Father and Maker *of all*, not simply the God of the Jews. In addition, although the Jews believe in and worship God, Philo speaks about "seeing" Him in different, more philosophical terms. Believing in God and worshipping Him then are not necessarily the same as "seeing" Him. Thus it would appear that Philo's concept of "Israel" allows for the possibility that both Jews and non-Jews who are spiritually capable may belong.

Philo's Estimation of Non-Jewish Philosophers. Should one deduce from the above observation that Philo esteems non-Jewish philosophers on a par with the Jews? On this matter we can find different positions among his works. In at least one passage, *Virt.* 65, for example, he does seem to view the two groups equally. There he writes that " . . . what the disciples of the most excellent philosophy gain from its teaching, the Jews gain from their customs and laws, that is to know the highest, the most ancient Cause of all things and reject the delusion of created gods."[17]

Another perspective, however, can be found in *Legat.* 1-7, discussed briefly above, where Philo seems to place the Jewish way of life above philosophy, implying that philosophy—or reason—alone is not enough to attain the vision of God. In this introductory passage, in which Philo also mentions "Israel," he comments as follows about the inadequacy of reason: "For reason cannot attain to ascend to God, who nowhere can be touched or handled, but [reason] subsides and ebbs away unable to find the proper words by which it may approach [explanation of], I do not say the God who IS, . . . [but even His] attendant powers" (*Legat.* 6).

---

16 I am grateful to Prof. Alan Mendelson for pointing out that Philo would not wish to include a thinker like Epicurus in the company of "Israel." I have therefore qualified my suggestions that non-Jewish philosophers might be part of Philo's "Israel" by speaking only of *respected* non-Jewish philosophers.

17 Other passages in which Philo highly praises non-Jewish sages include *Prob.* 74 and *Spec.* 2.44-48.

In this section too, Philo calls "Israel"—and by association, the Jews—"the suppliants' γένος which has been allotted or has allotted itself (προσκεκλήρωται)" to God (*Legat.* 3, my translation). The phrase "suppliants' γένος" suggests a group that worships God[18] and that may also serve an intercessory role with him, since supplication may be on behalf of other people. This description accords with what Philo writes elsewhere about the relationship between God and the Jews, namely that the Jews worship God and serve as priestly intermediaries for all humankind. Moreover, we are also reminded of the mutual bond that exists between God and the Jews when Philo writes that they "have been allotted or have allotted themselves" to God—a phrase he uses elsewhere to describe the Jews.[19]

As the "suppliants' γένος which has been allotted or has allotted itself" to God, "Israel" or the Jews, then, exemplify something greater than philosophy, namely, worship of God through observance of His special laws. Philo argues, moreover, that these suppliants receive God's special protection (*Legat.* 3). Taking all these remarks into consideration, one might understand that Philo is implicitly placing the Jewish way of life above the philosophical.[20]

It is reasonable to contend, of course, that Philo's differing positions can be explained by the contexts in which each appears. His equation of Jews and non-Jewish philosophers in *Virt.* 65, for example, occurs in the *Exposition*, where he apparently wishes to present Jews and their way of life in the best light in order to impress favorably those who may be interested in or hostile toward them. Accordingly, one might maintain that Philo equates Jews and philosophers in this passage not because he necessarily regards them as equal, but because he wants to show that Judaism incorporates the best that philosophy has to offer. Similarly, one could also argue that in *Legat.*, Philo may wish to portray his suffering compatriots as superior even to philosophers in order to highlight ever more sharply the outrage of the persecution of the Jews. Indeed since one can find rationales for either point of view—that Philo esteems Jews and non-Jewish philosophers equally or that he regards Jews more highly—any firm conclusion about what he really thinks on this issue eludes us.

Some Further Reflections

Finally, although this highly condensed presentation has focused upon the relationship in Philo's thought between "Israel" and the Jews, I would like to reflect briefly upon two larger issues which relate to this study: first, Philo's

---

18 Philo often links together suppliants and worshippers of God (see, e.g., *Spec.* 1.309; *Virt.* 185).

19 *Spec.* 4.159, 180; *Virt.* 34. Because the verb προσκληρόω always appears in the middle voice in these passages, it remains unclear whether the Jews have allotted themselves to God or God has allotted them to Himself. See my dissertation, 295-98, 323-26.

20 For another passage in which Philo holds the Jewish way of life superior to that of philosophers, see *Contempl.* 57-64, where he derisively compares the banquets described by Xenophon and Plato with the banquets of the Therapeutae, who live in contemplation of the truths of nature "following the truly sacred instructions of the prophet Moses." Strictly speaking, however, Philo's comparison here is between the philosophers and the Therapeutae, not all Jews.

balance (or non-balance) of particularism and universalism, and second, as indicated by the title of this study, the place of Judaism in Philo's thought.

As to the first issue, one's assessment of Philo as a universalist or a particularist will most certainly depend upon one's understanding of these terms. I would argue that Philo presents a universalist vision of both "Israel" and the Jews, in the sense that both groups are potentially open to all people. Here, then, I understand "universalism" to signify an openness to everyone, a potential inclusiveness of all people. Accordingly, Philo's "Israel" may embrace any and all people who see God, regardless of their ancestry. Belonging to "Israel" would appear to be a matter of spiritual capacity, not birth. At the same time, the Jews, as Philo understands them, stand ready to welcome anyone who is prepared to believe in and worship the one God and to join the Jewish πολιτεία. If one is not born a Jew, then, one can become a Jew through conscious choice and commitment to the Jewish way of life.

It is important to note, however, that Philo's universalist vision of "Israel" and the Jews does not embrace all people as they are. One must also keep in mind that he speaks quite disparagingly of polytheists, idolaters, and atheists, that is, people who believe in many gods, created gods, or no god (*Spec.* 1.327-44). For Philo to embrace such individuals as part of "Israel" or the Jews, they would first have to relinquish their wrong beliefs and adopt the monotheist premise. After all, in order to be able to see God—to be part of "Israel"—one must also believe He exists. Similarly, to worship God—as the Jews do—one again must believe He exists.

Philo's attitude toward those who do not believe in the one God, then, tempers his universalist stance. In short, Philo might well appear to be a universalist to a non-Jewish sage—who, because of his philosophical understanding, could be part of "Israel"—but he certainly would not appear so to an idolater—who, because of his wrong beliefs, would be excluded from both "Israel" and the Jews!

As to the second issue, the place of Judaism in Philo's thought, one must take into account that Philo represents Judaism to a great extent as a kind of philosophy. As such, Judaism presents one approach, indeed probably the best approach to belief in the one God. Judaism, however, is not the only path to this supremely important doctrine. To be sure, as the above summary suggests, Philo probably believes that even non-Jews may belong to "Israel," that they too might attain a vision of God.

Despite this observation, however, it is clear from Philo's works that for him being a Jew is not only a matter of believing in a certain philosophy; it also involves a way of life embodied by a very particular community. To him, the Jewish πολιτεία refers both to the laws of this community and to the community itself. Thus "Judaism"—as a philosophy and a way of life—is only one component in the experience of being a Jew. While this experience certainly involves adherence to the philosophical and legal aspects of Judaism, it also involves being a member of the Jewish people. Philo's political treatises *Flacc.* and *Legat.* provide ample evidence of how deeply committed he is to protecting the welfare of his people. More than in his other works, he speaks here in the first person, expressing his anguish about the plight of the Jews and describing his own role in the delegation sent to the emperor to plead on their behalf.

Philo's thought, then, can provide only a partial impression of how and why being a Jew is important to him. For a complete understanding, one must also consider his life.

Divine Power in the Apocalypse to John: Revelation 4-5 in Process Hermeneutic

Ron Farmer
Cincinnati, Ohio

The last few decades have witnessed a small but growing number of scholars attempting to bridge the long-standing gulf separating process thought and biblical studies. One of the most promising endeavors is the development of a "process hermeneutic"—a theory of interpretation based upon Alfred North Whitehead's understanding of language. The purpose of this paper is twofold: to sketch the contours of a process hermeneutic and to apply that hermeneutic to the issue of divine power in the Apocalypse, with special attention to Revelation 4-5.

A Process Hermeneutic

Due to space limitations only the most distinctive and important concepts of a process hermeneutic will be discussed. These include: methodological inclusiveness, Whitehead's theory of perception. Whitehead's theory of language, the nature of texts, and validity in interpretation and theological norms. (A brief overview of Whitehead's metaphysical system is appended to the paper.)

Methodological Inclusiveness

Occasionally, a new hermeneutical model will develop new exegetical methods (e.g., structuralism). Generally, however, existing methods are used from a new hermeneutical perspective. The process hermeneutic has not developed any new exegetical methods; consequently, its distinctiveness lies in its new perspective rather than any new "process" exegetical tools.

Most of the current hermeneutical options are reductionistic or exclusive when it comes to the act of interpretation. For example, some use structuralist methods whereas others use historical-critical methods; some focus on sociological data whereas others focus on ideas; some locate meaning in the internal world of the text whereas others locate meaning in the external reality to which it refers, or in the author's intention, or in the reader's response. Of course, every hermeneutic is exclusive in *practice*, but the process hermeneutic is not reductionistic in its *theory* of interpretation. Consequently, a process hermeneutic is open to all existing methods of exegesis with the conviction that when carried far enough the various methods will illuminate one another. This "methodological inclusiveness" is not *ad hoc* but rather is derived from its theory of perception-as-interpretation.[1]

Whitehead's Theory of Perception

According to Whitehead, the fundamental error of Western epistemology lies in its identification of sense-data as the basis of all perception.[2] Whitehead affirmed the soundness of Western philosophy's foundational principles: that philosophical generalizations must be based upon the primary elements in actual experience, and that all knowledge is grounded in perception. He disagreed, however, with the traditional analysis of perception. Ordinary human perception (sense perception) occurs at the level of conscious experience. But because consciousness arises only in the fourth phase of concrescence, it can illuminate the more primitive aspects of experience—i.e., prehensions in earlier phases—only in so far as they are elements in the integrations of later phases. Thus,

> those elements of our experience which stand out clearly and distinctly in our consciousness are not its basic facts . . . The consequences of the neglect of this law, that the late derivative elements are more clearly illuminated by consciousness than the primitive elements, have been fatal to the proper analysis of an experient occasion. In fact, most of the difficulties of philosophy are produced by it. Experience has been explained in a thoroughly topsy-turvy fashion, the wrong end first.[3]

Ordinary human perception—which Whitehead termed "perception in the mode of *symbolic reference*"—is actually a mixed or composite mode of perception. Careful analysis of symbolic reference reveals that it is composed of two more primitive modes: "perception in the mode of *causal efficacy*" and "perception in the mode of *presentational immediacy*." According to Whitehead, the traditional analysis of perception errs in that this composite nature is not discerned, especially the mode of causal efficacy.

Perception in the mode of causal efficacy is a primal awareness of one's relationship to the causal nexus in which one exists. This type of perception is not restricted to humans and other higher levels of actuality, but rather is an ubiquitous feature of all reality. The character of causal efficacy is inheritance from the past or derivation or continuity (physical prehension). As evidence of this "non-sensuous" mode of perception, Whitehead pointed to two aspects of

---

1 David J. Lull, "What is 'Process Hermeneutics'?" *Process Studies* 13 (1983) 189-90; and Kent Harold Richards, "Beyond Bruxism," in *Society of Biblical Literature 1976 Seminar Papers* (Missoula: Scholars Press, 1976), 469, quoting William A. Beardslee, "Notes on a Whiteheadian Hermeneutic" (unpublished paper).

2 Alfred North Whitehead, *Process and Reality: An Essay in Cosmology*, corrected ed., ed. David Ray Griffin and Donald W. Sherburne (New York: Free Press, 1978), 130-84, and *Adventures of Ideas* (New York: Macmillan, 1933; New York: Free Press, 1967), 175-90.

3 Whitehead, *Process and Reality*, 162. Similarly, in *Symbolism: Its Meaning and Effect* [(New York: Macmillan, 1927; New York: Fordham UP, 1985), 52] Whitehead noted that Western philosophy has assumed that "presentational immediacy is primitive, and that causal efficacy is the sophisticated derivative. This is a complete inversion of the evidence." The assumption that presentational immediacy is foundational has led to the explanation of causal efficacy as a habit of thought (Hume) or a category of thought (Kant). ("Presentational immediacy" and "causal efficacy" are explained immediately below.)

human experience: memory of one's own immediate past state of consciousness—"that portion of our past lying between a tenth of a second and a half a second ago. It is gone, and yet it is here"—and a vague awareness of one's own body as part of a causal nexus moving from past to present to future.[4] In general, however, causal efficacy is largely unconscious in human experience due to the dominance of perception in the mode of presentational immediacy.

Whereas causal efficacy arises in the first phase of the concrescence of an actual entity, presentational immediacy is a product of later phases of concrescence. As a result, "presentational immediacy is an important factor in the experience of only a few high-grade organisms, . . . for the others it is embryonic or entirely negligible."[5] Whereas causal efficacy is vague, direct, massive, inarticulate, and produces a sense of derivation from the past and of passage to the future, presentational immediacy is clear, indirect, sophisticated, articulate, and produces a sense of immediate enjoyment. Causal efficacy is the objectification of the past external world; presentational immediacy is the objectification of "a contemporary region of space as illustrating specific geometrical, extensive relationships."[6]

The ability to distinguish one contemporary spatial region from any other contemporary region rests on the perception of an eternal object (or objects)— such as the color "gray"—residing in that contemporary spatial region. At this point it is imperative to note that contemporary actual entities are causally independent of each other; that is, whereas an actual entity prehends past actual entities, it cannot prehend contemporary actual entities. The immediate present[7] is perceived as an extensive continuum potentially divisible into regions, but the actual entities occupying these regions cannot be prehended. Thus, the eternal object—such as "gray"—is not actually prehended from the contemporary region; rather, it is prehended from the past actual world perceived in the mode of causal efficacy and "projected"[8] onto the contemporary spatial region. Perception in the mode of presentational immediacy results in a flashing awareness of "gray-there"; the contemporary spatial region is "illustrated" by the medium of the eternal object "gray."

Presentational immediacy alone obviously does not describe ordinary human perception; on the contrary, it describes classical empiricism's (e.g., Hume's) idea of sense perception. In presentational immediacy there is clear, distinct consciousness of the extensive relations of the world, but because there is an absence of connections with the past, the regions of the world thus perceived are isolated, cut off, self-contained temporally. There is no information as to the past

---

4 Whitehead, *Adventures of Ideas*, 180-4, and *Process and Reality*, 176-8.

5 Whitehead, *Symbolism*, 23.

6 Donald Sherburne, ed., *A Key to Whitehead's Process and Reality* (Chicago: Chicago UP, 1966), 99.

7 The notion of the immediate present will be examined in more detail below in relation to the term "presented duration."

8 As Whitehead (*Process and Reality* 172-3) noted, this terminology is misleading. Both the eternal object and the location in the immediate present are derived from causal efficacy. Presentational immediacy, which occurs in a supplemental phase of concrescence, is simply the enhancement of the relationship between the eternal object and the location vaguely perceived in the first phase of concrescence.

or the future; this mode merely defines a barren cross-section of the universe. To describe ordinary perception, the two primitive modes must be combined in the mixed mode of symbolic reference. Whereas presentational immediacy merely presupposes causal efficacy, symbolic reference integrates the two modes so that there is both clear location in a contemporary region (presentational immediacy) and the power of continuity with the past and an efficacy for the future (causal efficacy). This is Whitehead's description of ordinary human perception of an enduring object, such as a "gray stone." The word "stone" has a reference to the past, for a stone has a history and probably a future as well. Thus, the mixed mode of symbolic reference perceives the "stone" both as clearly located in a contemporary region of space, illustrated by the eternal object "gray," and also as an enduring entity with a past and an efficacy for the future. Because symbolic reference takes place without conscious effort or reflection, its composite nature is not normally noticed in human experience, and the fundamental error of Western epistemology arises.

The integration of causal efficacy and presentational immediacy in symbolic reference (which occurs in a late phase of concrescence) is possible due to two elements of common ground the more primitive modes of perception share. One common element is the *presented duration* or presented locus (location), that duration which conforms to the common-sense notion of "the immediate present condition of the world at some epoch"[9]. Although the past actual worlds of the perceiving occasion and its contemporaries are not identical, they are practically identical. Thus, in the mode of causal efficacy the perceiving occasion *directly* perceives those past occasions which are causally efficacious for both itself and the occasions forming its presented duration. This amounts to an *indirect* perception of the presented duration itself. In the mode of presentational immediacy there is an inversion of what is perceived directly and indirectly: The presented duration is *directly* illustrated by the eternal objects; while the causal past, the causal future, and the other contemporary events, are only *indirectly* perceived by means of their extensive relations to the presented duration.[10] Thus, the presented duration supplies one element of common ground enabling perception in the mode of symbolic reference to occur; it is perceived directly and distinctly in the mode of presentational immediacy and indirectly and indistinctly in the mode of causal efficacy.

The second element shared by causal efficacy and presentational immediacy is a common ingredient eternal object. The eternal object "projected" upon the presented duration in presentational immediacy is derived from the earlier mode of perception, causal efficacy. Thus, the identical eternal object ingredient in both primitive modes of perception supplies a second element of common ground allowing perception in the mode of symbolic reference to occur.

A deeper appreciation of symbolic reference can be gained by means of a brief examination of Whitehead's general notion of symbolism.[11] Symbolic

---

9 Whitehead, *Process and Reality*, 125.

10 Whitehead, *Process and Reality*, 169 (emphasis added).

11 William A. Beardslee ["Recent Hermeneutics and Process Thought," *Process Studies* 12 (1982) 69, 71] noted that Whitehead "separated what in other schools is broadly the topic of symbolism into two parts: his theory of symbols, which deals with important aspects of perception, and his theory of propositions, which deals with the use of perception in the total act of self-realization or self-creation. . . . The imaginative and creative dimensions of 'symbolism' appear in

functioning occurs whenever one set of components of a subject's experience elicit another set of components of its experience; the first set are the "symbols" and the second set are the "meanings" of the symbols. The first set elicits the second because the two sets share some "common ground." The subject determines which set of components will function as symbols and which set will serve as meanings for the symbols. Generally stated, then, "'symbolic reference' is the process of transference from a symbol to its meaning."[12] Relating this understanding of symbolic reference to the modes of perception, "presentational immediacy *refers to* causal efficacy; the latter places the former in a context of meaning."[13]

Now to say that one is aware of being internally related to a larger causal nexus—perception in the mode of causal efficacy—is to affirm that one's perceptions are *based upon* data external to oneself. One is aware of a causal past distinct from one's immediate subjectivity. Yet the Whiteheadian understanding of perception also makes it clear that no experience can take place apart from the appropriation of causal forces *in terms of* one's own subjective immediacy which defines their meanings. Because one perceives data only in relation to the significance the data have for oneself, *perception is always perspectival.* (The prehension of past occasions involves negative prehensions—the elimination of data—as well as positive prehensions; moreover, these positive prehensions are clothed with subjective forms which are to some degree unique to the prehending occasion.) Thus, perception implies a world of real causal relations which is experienced through subjective participation and valuation.[14]

Although symbolic reference produces a sense of the external world, it is not infallible. One must acknowledge the possibility of error in relating perception in the mode of causal efficacy and perception in the mode of presentational immediacy—e.g., common human sense perception errors. Perception in the mode of presentational immediacy is essentially the projection onto the presented duration of eternal objects the percipient inherited from the past actual world. But it is possible that the occasions occupying the presented duration did not inherit these eternal objects (i.e., these eternal objects were negatively prehended by the occasions occupying the presented duration). Consequently, the perception of these eternal objects as ingredient in the presented duration is erroneous. Moreover, because the perceiver does not prehend the contemporary world but rather projects the immediate past world onto the present, the greater the distance between the perceiver and the nexus being observed, the greater the chance for error. For example, one can observe the light of a star that perished millions of years ago. Furthermore, ordinary human perception is dependent upon the state of the body in general and the

---

Whitehead's thought under the rubric of the theory of propositions, in contrast to symbols which appear in the context of prehension." (Whitehead's theory of propositions is set forth below.)

12 Michael L. Harrington, "Whitehead's Theory of Propositions," (Unpublished Ph.D. dissertation, Emory University, 1972), 177. See Whitehead, *Symbolism,* 7-13.

13 Russell Pregeant, *Christology Beyond Dogma: Matthew's Christ in Process Hermeneutic* (Missoula: Scholars Press; Philadelphia: Fortress Press, 1978), 34.

14 Valuation is the subjective form of conceptual feelings. This is the most primitive type of creative response open to an entity: valuation up or down.

brain in particular. Numerous factors can affect bodily functioning; for example, drugs can cause hallucinations, color blindness can prevent the perception of certain colors, and optical illusions such as those produced by mirrors can deceive the sense organs. Yet in spite of the possibility that error can occur, real knowledge of external data is possible because the two modes of perception share a common eternal object as well as a common present duration. Therefore, contrary to the idealism of Kant, one can know about the world as it is, in spite of the contributions of one's mind in shaping one's perception; contrary to the skeptical empiricism of Hume, the notion of cause and effect can be restored; and contrary to the rationalism of Descartes, knowledge begins with experience rather than innate ideas.[15]

Whitehead's theory of perception as presented thus far can be described as a complex, integrated process of *interpretation* of data from the past, actual world and *projection* onto the contemporary world. For the purpose at hand, one more aspect of perception must be discussed. Perception in its broadest sense also includes the process of interpretation of "*propositions*" about the past, actual world germane to its possible future states.

One of Whitehead's most significant contributions to modern thought is his understanding of propositions, entities he also termed "concrete possibilities," "theories," or "proposals." The rise of a proposition occurs in the following manner: an actual entity or nexus—the logical subject of the proposition—is abstracted from experience to the point of being a mere "it," and some eternal object (or group of eternal objects)—the predicate of the proposition—is predicated of it. A proposition, then, is a proposal, a predication of an abstract possibility upon an actual entity or nexus already known in a subject's experience. Moreover, because the eternal object predicated of the logical subject may differ to some degree from that which is actually ingredient in the logical subject (the technical explanation of which would take us far afield), an important function of propositions is to serve as "the indispensable vehicle of imagination which reaches out from that which has already been experienced toward possibilities as yet unrealized."[16] In fact, "transformation of 'the way things *are*,' for better or worse, depends on entertaining proposals about 'how things *could be*.'"[17]

Whitehead adopted the term "proposition" from logic; to avoid possible misunderstandings of his use of the term, three points should be noted. 1) Most propositions do not function at the conscious level. Consciousness is the subjective form of intellectual feelings which arise in the fourth phase of concrescence. Because propositional feelings arise in the third phase of concrescence, only those which function as component feelings in the more complex intellectual feelings enter into consciousness. 2) Because propositions arise in the third phase of concrescence, they are prelinguistic. Only those which become component feelings in intellectual feelings are capable of linguistic expression. 3) According to Whitehead, it is more important that propositions be

---

15 See, Pregeant, *Christology Beyond Dogma*, 35, and William A. Beardslee, "Whitehead and Hermeneutic," *JAAR* 47 (1979) 32-3.

16 William A. Beardslee, "Whitehead and Hermeneutic," 34. This is Whitehead's explanation of creative imagination.

17 Lull, 190 (emphasis added).

interesting than that they be true; the importance of truth is that it tends to add to interest.[18]

What, then, is the primary function of a proposition? A proposition is a datum for feeling that awaits a subject to feel it. Therefore, the primary function of a proposition is to serve as a "lure for feeling"; that is, a proposition lures the subject to feel a past datum in a particular way in the subject's process of self-creation. A given proposition can be felt by many subjects and in many ways, i.e., the subjective form varies from subject to subject (e.g., it can be felt as hopeful or dreadful, interesting or dull, attractive or repulsive, true or false, and so forth). The main point to observe is that propositions grow out of the past, actual world (because of the logical subject) and pave the way for the advance into novelty as lures for creative emergence in the future (because of the predicate). Thus, propositions combine "imaginative freedom with grounding in reality."[19]

The logical subject of a particular proposition may not lie in the actual world of a particular actual entity; when this is the case that proposition is non-existent for that actual entity. For example, the proposition "the airplane is silver"[20] did not exist until this century; for such a proposition to exist, it had to await the emergence of its logical subject. Thus, not only do propositions pave the way for the advance into novelty in the future; new propositions themselves come into existence with the creative advance of the world.[21]

In summary, whereas symbolic reference focuses on the external world in its pastness or actuality—i.e., symbolic reference focuses on the *receptive* aspect of perception—propositional feelings focus on a future or potential world as well as a past, actual one—i.e., propositional feelings focus on the *imaginative* and *creative* aspects of perception. Perception, then, "is a complex process of interpretation of 'data from the real [past] world' as well as of 'proposals' about the past, actual world germane to its possible future states."[22] Thus, *perception is interpretation.*

Whitehead's Theory of Language

Language is nothing more than a set of definite sounds or marks on paper. A unit of language becomes meaningful only when it is associated with some particular thing; expressed in terms of symbolic reference, the unit of language is the "symbol" and the thing associated, the "meaning" of that symbol. Thus, language is humankind's "most obvious and elaborate symbolic system."[23]

Expressed in terms of process metaphysics, what language does is: 1) to arouse in a thinking subject a physical prehension of those entities which are "meanings" and are to be logical subjects for the emerging proposition; 2) to promote the development of a conceptual prehension of the eternal objects which are to be the predicate for the emerging proposition; and 3) to encourage the integration of the physical and conceptual prehensions into a propositional prehension whose datum is the proposition. "Words and phrases are thus

---

[18] Whitehead, *Process and Reality*, 259.

[19] Beardslee, "Recent Hermeneutics and Process Thought," 72.

[20] The notion of a proposition should not be equated with a sentence. (See below.)

[21] Whitehead, *Process and Reality*, 188.

[22] Lull, 191.

[23] Beardslee, "Whitehead and Hermeneutic," 33.

efficacious in indicating to a thinker which actual entities and eternal objects should be prehended, so that a propositional prehension can be originated involving the proposition expressed by the sentence."[24]

Language, then, is a tool facilitating the recall and communication of propositions. But it is by no means a perfect tool. Whitehead called attention to the fact that "every proposition refers to a universe exhibiting some general systematic metaphysical character"; and he further noted the "impossibility of tearing a proposition from its systematic context in the actual world."[25] The reason for this is that the logical subjects of a proposition are actual entities. Now each actual entity has a definite internal bond (either positive or negative) with every actuality in its universe; the entire universe is ingredient in the actual entity. Therefore, a proposition cannot be abstracted from this set of complex and dynamic relationships. But language attempts to do just that; it attempts to express a proposition without reference to its system of relations, its "concrete connectedness." The fallacy of misplaced concreteness is mistaking the clear and distinct impressions which arise in the conscious phase of concrescence for the most concrete and basic elements of experience. But as Gerald Janzen noted, "we experience more than we know, and we know more than we can think; and we think more than we can say; and language therefore lags behind the intuitions of immediate experience."[26] Consequently, Whitehead asserted that "it is merely credulous to accept verbal phrases as adequate statements of propositions."[27] Language can only approximate the full meaning of a proposition; language is always incomplete and fragmentary.

Process metaphysics of necessity, then, understands language to be analogical, indeterminate, imprecise, and value-laden. Because reality is a fluid environment composed of myriads of internally-related causal nexuses rather than a world of discrete objects, it is obvious that words can never be understood in a univocal sense, as if they referred to absolutely definite and discrete objects. The application of a name to an object requires that *some* aspects of an actuality be lifted out of the complex and dynamic set of relationships within which it occurs (its concrete connectedness) and that *other* aspects of the actuality be ignored. Consequently, language is always abstract[28]—an imprecise, incomplete, and indeterminate representation of concrete actuality. Moreover, "the process of abstraction necessary for the formation of a word is anything but a cold and unfeeling activity. It takes place only because a *felt value* is already at work in the

---

24 Harrington, 179.

25 Whitehead, *Process and Reality*, 11.

26 Gerald J. Janzen, "The Old Testament in 'Process' Perspective: Proposal for a Way Forward in Biblical Theology," in *MAGNALIA DEI: The Mighty Acts of God. Essays on the Bible and Archaeology in Memory of G. Ernest Wright*, ed. Frank Moore Cross, Werner E. Lemke, and Patrick D. Miller, Jr. (Garden City: Doubleday, 1976), 492. Similarly, Bernard E. Meland ["Response to Paper by Professor Beardslee," *Encounter* 36 (1975) 340] noted that "we live more deeply than we can think . . . There are vast dimensions of experienced reality which must remain unavailable to conceptual formulation which, nevertheless, have important bearing upon our thinking."

27 Whitehead, *Process and Reality*, 11.

28 "The essence of language is that it utilizes those elements in experience most easily abstracted for conscious entertainment, and most easily reproduced in experience" [Alfred North Whitehead, *Modes of Thought* (New York: Macmillan, 1938; New York: Free Press, 1968), 34].

very act of discriminating an object for naming."[29] Thus, the act of naming—both on the part of a speaker/author and a hearer/reader—involves an element of creativity.

The plurisignificant nature of language so conceived is obvious. Due to the "elliptical" character of language, each word is potentially capable of designating a whole host of things; no word can indicate precisely one singular and individual thing. A sentence, therefore, is capable of eliciting an indefinite number of related propositions which fit its verbal form; each of these propositions becomes a possible meaning for the sentence. Moreover, no sentence or similar verbal unit merely *enunciates* a proposition. Inherent in all statements, written as well as oral, is some *incitement* for entertaining a proposition in a given way. For example, the tone of voice, the choice of words, and even the book (e.g., an "authoritative" book such as the Bible or a text book) in which the words occur can convey particular incitement.[30]

Whitehead was aware that people often ignore the fact that words are analogical, imprecise, and value-laden, and treat the objects so designated as if they were self-contained, self-defined, valueless entities. As Janzen remarked:

> The language of the special sciences, logic, mathematics, and rational philosophy have as their ideal the development of terms that are univalent, conceptually focused, precisely defined. These languages—examples of what Philip Wheelwright calls *steno-languages*—are enormously useful for the formulation of rational explanations, and for exercising control over the world for specific purposes. But these 'definitive' languages constitute a high abstraction from, and therefore a quite limited representation of, the concrete totality of the world as experienced.[31]

Therefore, to assume that steno-language is the most adequate language for the attempt to understand and report empirical reality is to commit the fallacy of misplaced concreteness because the assumption arises from a failure to acknowledge the degree of abstraction involved in the formation of words. However much elements of steno-language "be stabilized as technicalities, they remain metaphors mutely appealing for an imaginative leap."[32]

For Whitehead, "the deeper truths must be adumbrated by myths" and poetry[33]—what Wheelwright called *tensive language*. "Employing multivalent words laden with innumerable associational and valuational and emotional ligatures, this mode of language conveys the essential connectedness and concrete particularity of things." These features render tensive language incapable of serving the *limited* functional purposes of the special sciences, but these same features "enable it to report the empirical world most richly and concretely for human understanding. And indeed, such language not only

---

29 Pregeant, *Christology Beyond Dogma*, 37 (emphasis added).

30 Harrington, 180-181, 184.

31 Janzen, 492-3. Janzen referred to Philip Wheelwright, *The Burning Fountain: A Study in the Language of Symbolism*, rev. ed. (Bloomington: Indiana UP, 1968). See also Wheelwright's *Metaphor and Reality* (Bloomington: Indiana UP, 1962).

32 Whitehead, *Process and Reality* 4.

33 Whitehead, *Modes of Thought* 10.

reports, but in some sense conveys, or re-enacts, what it reports." Thus, contrary to common assumption, "the most concretely historical mode of language is the poetic, while the definitive languages of the sciences, including that of historical scholarship, are, for all their enormous utility, only in a secondary and abstract sense historical."[34]

If one may describe steno-language as the language of rational discourse, and tensive language as the language of empirical expression, then "it can readily be appreciated that, for Whitehead's rational empiricism, neither mode has exclusive, or even preponderant, claims to credence."[35] Rather, each is indispensable. The two forms of language merely differ with respect to the degree of indeterminacy each possesses. All language is relatively (in)determinate; each instance of language can be located on a spectrum ranging from one hypothetical extreme—completely determinate—to the other hypothetical extreme—completely indeterminate.

Whitehead's understanding of language means that religious language (and other manifestations of tensive language) can be valued positively. "Because words never refer to absolutely definite and discrete objects, but point analogically to elements abstracted from a continuous flow of experience, every assertion ultimately presupposes and points toward a larger whole, an encompassing process that embraces all experience." To be sure, religious language is subjective and value-laden, but the same is also true in some measure of all language—even that which claims the highest objectivity. But the unique value of religious language is that it, like metaphysical language, makes "explicit what is merely implicit in all other modes of speech: an understanding of and a commitment to a particular vision of the ultimate nature of things."[36]

As with all types of language, religious language can be misleading. The problem occurs when an interpreter takes any form of language to be literal rather than analogical. With respect to religious language, this occurs when an interpreter understands religious statements "as dogmas, as denoting the content of faith in a direct, precise, literal fashion . . . Properly understood, religious statements (like all statements) are primarily lures for feeling."[37] Moreover, whereas the *descriptive* and *metonymic* views of language understand religious language as objective assertions about the world of nature and the transcendent realm (respectively) which are to be grasped by an externally-related subject (i.e., subject and object are distinct from one another), the *Whiteheadian* view of language understands religious language as donations of propositions for feeling in the self-creation of an internally-related subject (i.e., subject and object are inseparable).

The Nature of Texts

In light of the preceding discussion, it is apparent that all texts are proposals, clusters of propositions. As lures for feeling, propositions grow out of objective events in the actual world (including events in the personal experience of the author and events to which his or her writing refers) and concern possibilities for

34 Janzen, 493.

35 Janzen, 493.

36 Pregeant, *Christology Beyond Dogma*, 38.

37 Pregeant, *Christology Beyond Dogma*, 39.

the future (the future of subsequent as well as the original readers). This view of the text relates it to historical events on the one hand and to creative, alternative ways of constituting one's self with regard to those past events on the other.[38]

Three observations should be noted: 1) a text is always the partial, inexact expression of an author's original vision of propositions; 2) a text will of necessity evoke propositions not entertained by the author; and 3) the propositions entertained by one reader will never be exactly the same as those felt by another reader.[39] There are at least three reasons for this "evolutionary nature"[40] of texts. First, the imprecision of language affects both authorial expression and reader interpretation. Words cannot express exhaustively or precisely that which they seek to convey. Not only do words merely approximate a given proposition, but they also evoke an indefinite number of related propositions. Second, even if the same proposition is felt by the author and a reader, or by two different readers, or by one reader at two different times, the proposition will not be felt the same way. The subjective forms of the feelings will differ to some degree. A third reason for the evolutionary nature of texts is that a proposition presupposes a general nexus which includes not only that nexus of actual entities forming the logical subject of the proposition, but also that nexus of entities which, as prehending subjects, can entertain that proposition. Now it is apparent that the perspectives and actual worlds of author and reader—or of two different readers, or of the same reader at two different times—differ. Consequently, these differences change the range of propositions which may be entertained by a reader and evoked by a text. Thus, "new propositions come into being with the creative advance of the world."[41]

Most hermeneutical models have assumed that the present meaning of a text must be expressed in terms similar to what it meant when it was composed. In the eyes of many interpreters, "what the text historically meant has become an essence from which its present meaning can only deviate within narrow confines." But if the text inevitably evokes new propositions during the course of time, "what the text might come to mean can theoretically be more important than anything the text has meant in the past." One could say that "potential meanings of the text remain encoded in its total capacity to elicit lures for feeling until the kairotic moment arrives." At the opportune moment, the givenness of a particular past, the contingencies of a particular present, and the possibilities for the future converge in the reading of a text, and a new meaning emerges.[42] Thus, according to a process hermeneutical model the meaning of a text consists

---

[38] Barry A. Woodbridge, "An Assessment and Prospectus for a Process Hermeneutic," *JAAR* 47 (1979) 123.

[39] Yet the fact that some of the same propositions entertained by the author are felt by the original and subsequent readers supplies the continuity needed to justify saying that the author, the original readers, and subsequent readers all have to do with "the same text." [See Barry A. Woodbridge, "Process Hermeneutic: An Approach to Biblical Texts," in *Society of Biblical Literature 1977 Seminar Papers* (Missoula: Scholars Press, 1977), 79-82.]

[40] Woodbridge, "An Assessment and Prospectus for a Process Hermeneutic," 124.

[41] Whitehead, *Process and Reality*, 259.

[42] Woodbridge, "An Assessment and Prospectus for a Process Hermeneutic," 124. Because these new meanings stand in genetic continuity with past meanings, it is possible to trace the history of the transmission and development of a particular tradition. This will be discussed in some detail below in connection with "historic routes of living occasions."

of the totality of propositions it can evoke. The meaning of a text is open-ended, evolving with the creative advance of the world.

Interpreting a text from the standpoint of a process hermeneutic requires what Russell Pregeant called "a bifocal approach to the text." First, because language is analogical, imprecise, and value-laden, "the interpreter must work through the discursive implications of the text back to the complex of feelings toward which it lures the reader."[43] In this way the interpreter identifies the major lures (propositions) at work in the text. Second, it was noted above that all language "ultimately presupposes and points toward a larger whole, an encompassing process that embraces all experience." Moreover, the unique value of religious language was said to be that it, like metaphysical language, makes "explicit what is merely implicit in all other modes of speech: an understanding of and a commitment to a particular vision of the ultimate nature of things."[44] Therefore, the biblical interpreter must trace "the broadest presuppositions of the address embodied in the text" to arrive at *the basal lures* underlying the other lures at work in the text. These basal lures reveal "a fundamental disposition toward reality itself," the presupposed metaphysical commitments of the language of the text.[45]

Pregeant referred to this search for basal lures as "metaphysical criticism." Being sensitive to the metaphysical implications of the text does not mean that the interpreter "must begin with rigid metaphysical commitments."[46] On the contrary, since all language is incomplete and fragmentary, a final, univocally-understood metaphysic is impossible. Moreover, "metaphysical reflection is not, for Whitehead, the construction of a system closed to new insights; metaphysics itself, and hence any critical method based upon it, must be seen as ongoing activities which are themselves checks upon subjectivity." Thus, metaphysical criticism should not be understood as "the imposition of a foreign ideology on the text but rather as an open-ended process by which certain fundamental metaphysical insights are employed in the working out of a standpoint from which the text can be clarified."[47]

Metaphysical criticism so conceived results in viewing the understanding of reality implicit in the text as a proposition, a proposal, a possible way to understand existence. And it is important to note that this implicit metaphysical understanding may function in a manner quite at odds with a univocal reading of language of the text; in such instances one may speak of this basal lure as an "undercurrent."[48]

---

43 Pregeant, *Christology Beyond Dogma*, 44.

44 Pregeant, *Christology Beyond Dogma*, 38.

45 Pregeant, *Christology Beyond Dogma*, 44.

46 Pregeant, *Christology Beyond Dogma*, 44. Pregeant ("Where Is the Meaning? Metaphysical Criticism and the Problem of Indeterminacy." *JR* 63 [1983] 116) acknowledged that "the traditional wariness, on the part of both literary and biblical scholars, of metaphysically oriented interpretations is well-founded. The process of reading a text through the eyes of a system can easily suppress tensive elements which are the sources of evocative power, strip a text of all its concreteness, and even turn a text completely against itself."

47 Pregeant, "Where Is the Meaning?" 116-17.

48 The importance of detecting "undercurrents" will be illustrated in the analysis of Revelation 4-5. See also Russell Pregeant, "The Matthean Undercurrent: Process Hermeneutic and the 'Parable of the Last Judgment,'" in *Society of Biblical Literature 1975 Seminar Papers* (Missoula:

Validity in Interpretation and Theological Norms

According to a process hermeneutic, novel meanings of a text are to be anticipated not rejected *a priori* as if only the original meaning were valid. This feature of a process hermeneutic obviously raises questions concerning validity in interpretation and theological norms.

The emphasis on texts as proposals could lead one to assume that the cluster of propositions in a biblical text is what is normative for theology.[49] David Lull noted three problems with this approach to theological norms, however. First, "the propositions in question are not simply properties of a *text*; text *and* interpretation participate in the creation of a given proposition, so that it is as much 'in *interpretation*' as it is 'in *Scripture.*'" Thus, propositions are found in Scripture-as-interpreted. Second,

> the term 'proposition' itself does not set material limits to what belongs to its general class. It therefore neither states nor implies the criterion/ criteria by which a proposal can be judged appropriate to Christian theology. For appropriateness entails a judgment *about* a certain text-as-interpreted, within which 'propositions' reside; it is not a judgment made *in* the interpretation of a text.[50]

Third, a proposition has no "force" in and of itself. The subjective form (*how* the proposition is felt) is supplied by the interpreter. Thus, although a process hermeneutic proposes that an interpreter attend to the propositions evoked by a text, this does not answer the questions: What constitutes a valid interpretation? and What is normative for theology?

Process interpreters approach these important questions primarily through two Whiteheadian concepts: *historic routes of living occasions* and God's work of *creative transformation*. A distinctive understanding of the authority of the Bible emerges from these concepts. A third notion relevant to these questions is the role of "the community of interpretation," a feature not unique to a process hermeneutic.

Historic Routes of Living Occasions

An actual occasion prehends all of the occasions in its past actual world either "immediately" (those in the immediate past) or "mediately" (those in the more distant past). But although the becoming occasion inherits from all past occasions, certain of these occasions are more important with respect to what the concrescing occasion becomes. When these more important occasions exhibit serial order, they are termed "an historic route of occasions." Because the becoming occasion's inheritance from these occasions is especially important to its self-creation, it may be said to belong to that route. The occasion then transmits what it inherited from this historic route to succeeding occasions; it also transmits some element of novelty due to its creative response to the past.

Scholars Press, 1975), 143-59, and "Matthew's 'Undercurrent' and Ogden's Christology," *Process Studies* 6 (1976) 181-94.

[49] E.g., David H. Kelsey, "The Theological Use of Scripture in Process Hermeneutics," *Process Studies* 13 (1983) 181-8.

[50] Lull, 194.

Now if this route of occasions contains living occasions, then it is termed an historic route of living occasions; and with living occasions the note of novelty is heightened considerably.

When Whitehead's notion of an historic route of living occasions is applied to the interpretation of texts, one notices a striking similarity to what Hans Georg Gadamer called "effective history." Contrary to most hermeneuticians, Gadamer did not view the temporal distance between interpreter and text as an empty chasm needing to be bridged. This temporal distance "is not a yawning abyss, but is filled with the continuity of custom and tradition, in the light of which all that is handed down presents itself to us."[51] The term effective history refers to the effect a text has upon generation after generation as the text is interpreted in light of new events and new events are interpreted in light of the text. Thus, the present interpreter does not encounter the text alone, but the text and its effective history. In process terminology, the interpreter, as a member of this historic route, is internally related not only to the text but also to the tradition of interpretation associated with the text. For example, Augustine's interpretation influenced Luther's; Augustine's and Luther's interpretations influenced Schleiermacher's; and so on down to the present interpreter. This does not mean that the present interpreter has "no immediate access to the lures elicited by reading the text itself," but it does mean that the kind of lures the interpreter feels "have been socially conditioned by prior feelings of the text's lures."[52]

Similarities also exist between Whitehead's concept of an historic route of living occasions and James Robinson's call to replace the term "tradition"—in the sense of the *transmission* of traditions—with "trajectory."[53] For Robinson, "tradition" defines the continuity involved in the process of transmission too much by the *content* of what is transmitted. The more important level of *existential meaning* is not conveyed by the term. In spite of the similarities between Whitehead's concept and that of Robinson, John Cobb enumerated four important differences—differences which actually clarify and strengthen the point Robinson was making.[54]

1) Robinson's trajectory image suggests that individual trajectories "are so formed by the initiating impetus and the situational field that they can be described in mutual independence of one another as quite distinct and discrete entities." It is important to note that this was not Robinson's intention. In an historic route of occasions, however, the individual historic routes "influence one another by constituting part of the situational field for one another"; consequently, "their distinctness is a matter of emphasis or degree." Cobb noted that "in some cases the extent to which one event is shaped by a particular series of past events is so dominant that it may be considered as a member of that series

51 Hans Georg Gadamer, *Truth and Method*, trans. by Garrett Barden and John Comming (New York: Seabury Press, 1975), 264.

52 Woodbridge, "Process Hermeneutic: An Approach to Biblical Texts," 84-85. See also Clark M. Williamson, "Process Hermeneutics and Christianity's Post-Holocaust Reinterpretation of Itself," *Process Studies* 12 (1982) 79-82. The point made in this paragraph will be expanded below in relation to "creative transformation" and "the community of interpretation."

53 James M. Robinson, "Introduction: The Dismantling and Reassembling of the Categories of New Testament Scholarship," in *Trajectories through Early Christianity*, with Helmut Koester (Philadelphia: Fortress Press, 1971), 1-19.

54 John B. Cobb, Jr., "Trajectories and Historic Routes," *Semeia* 24 (1982) 92-93.

and as relatively separable from other factors in its environment. But more commonly an event is shaped by multiple factors such that it can be viewed as a member of more than one historic route."

2) Another inadequacy of Robinson's trajectory image is that it "fails to highlight the elements of creative novelty in the events that make up the trajectory." Because trajectories are usually bits of matter, it is all too easy "to think of the trajectory as determined exhaustively by the impetus of the past and the force of the field through which the entity passes." But the historic routes Robinson is concerned to trace "are self-determining as well as externally caused."

3) "Normally in a trajectory the direct cause of the locus at any given point is found in the impetus transmitted by the preceding point on the trajectory together with the new field which has been entered." But in religious trajectories a major factor in each event is the "reencountering of the originating events, that is, the reading of sacred texts, the proclamation of their meaning, and the reenactment of sacred rites. Hence, in addition to the originating impetus of those events, their conscious reconsideration is an important factor in forming the trajectory." This conscious reconsideration of originating events is better depicted by an historic route of living occasions since each occasion in the route "takes account not only of immediate past members of the route but also, in memory, of more distant ones."

4) In contrast to the trajectory image, the image of an historic route "does not conjure up so strongly the image of a single all-decisive originative impetus." Rather, "it allows for the recognition that several streams of events may have flowed together to constitute the route and that, however important a particular past event was as a distinctive impetus, it was itself part of an historic route and not its absolute beginning."

A most important feature of applying Whitehead's historic route of living occasions to the interpretation of religious texts is that it does not promote the idea of a self-identical "essence" of a religion. That is, the unity of the historic route is not found in a common essence at all points along the route. Instead, the unity is a causal continuity which allows for change. What happens in later occasions of the route is deeply affected by what happened in earlier occasions, but it is not simply repetitive. No feature of earlier occasions need be repeated unchanged in later occasions. What is distinctive about life is novelty. Identity through time for living occasions is not achieved by the endless repetition of a particular form; in fact, identity achieved through endless repetition is a form of decay because intensity of feeling and zest continually diminish from the levels present in earlier occasions of the route. On the contrary, for living occasions "identity through time is maintained when successors include, transform, and build upon what they have received. . . . The past is more resource for new and creative response to opportunities and challenges than pattern to be reiterated or preserved." Thus, the identity of an historic route of living occasions is found "more in the form of its change than in its unchanged preservation of particular forms."[55]

In considerations of validity in interpretation and theological norms, therefore, what is needed is a way of discerning when change is the appropriate

---

[55] Cobb, "Trajectories and Historic Routes," 94-5.

novel expression continuing an historic route and when it is betrayal breaking away from an historic route. Cobb stated the criteria as follows:

> Change is appropriate development or healthy growth when central elements in the historic route encourage the emergence of novel forms capable at once of enlivening much of the content of that route and of appropriating potential contributions from other sources. Change is betrayal when, for the sake of appropriating elements foreign to the historic route, the continuing contribution of that route is curtailed or blocked.[56]

Creative Transformation

In order to appreciate fully this discussion of change verses repetition, one must view it in light of Whitehead's understanding of God's work of "creative transformation." In process thought, God is not simply the foundation of order but also the goad toward novelty. Order and novelty are instruments in God's overall aim of creating intensity of harmonious feeling in the universe.

Growth—on the microcosmic or macrocosmic level—is not achieved simply by adding together the various discordant elements in the actual world of a concrescing subject. Discordant elements cannot be united in a single experience simply by addition. The easiest way to achieve a new synthesis is by blocking out the discordant elements (by means of negative prehensions). The trivial harmony which results lacks intensity of feeling, however. Whitehead labeled this approach "anaesthesia."[57] There is another approach. Although the various discordant elements cannot be brought into harmony as they stand, there may be a larger, more inclusive novel pattern which can contain the discordant elements in such a manner that the contrast[58] between them contributes to the intensity of the whole. This new pattern is not part of the world; rather, it comes from God (the initial aim). To the extent that the subject appropriates this new pattern, it experiences creative transformation.[59]

---

56 Cobb, "Trajectories and Historic Routes", 95. It should be noted that the process understanding of historical development differs from both traditional Protestant and modern Catholic understandings. Protestants have tended to view the historical development of Christianity as a perversion of or a deviation from the normative essence, i.e., the first expression of Christianity. In an effort to avoid this negative evaluation of historical development, Catholics have viewed development as the unfolding of what is implicit in the normative essence; the full meaning of the first expression of Christianity becomes clear only through later development (e.g., later developments are read back into the New Testament as implied meanings). The Protestant understanding denigrates development, and the Catholic understanding robs the past of its ability to encounter the present as something foreign (past and present have been assimilated).

57 Whitehead, *Adventures of Ideas*, 256, 259, 275.

58 A contrast is the unity had by the many components in a complex datum (e.g., holding many colors in a unified pattern, as in a kaleidoscope, as opposed to a single color). Contrast is the opposite of incompatibility, for incompatibility results in the exclusion of one or more elements to achieve a (more trivial) harmony. The more a subject holds the items of its experience in contrasts and contrasts of contrasts, the more it elicits depth and intensity of experience.

59 See John B. Cobb, Jr. and David Ray Griffin, *Process Theology: An Introductory Exposition* (Philadelphia: Westminster Press, 1969), 99.

Because God works in the world through the process of creative transformation, the process interpreter will pay special attention to the way in which the Bible contributes toward this end. The propositions in Scripture-as-interpreted—that is, proposals of how events or reality might be viewed—are set alongside alternative propositions, from the Bible and from other sources. But instead of immediately choosing between the disparate propositions, the process interpreter will seek to create a harmonious contrast of the propositions through a novel, more inclusive pattern, and thereby experience creative transformation.[60] Because creative transformation is the theological norm, Christians can be open to insights from other historic routes without breaking away from their own. This theological norm encourages interpreters to seek inclusion, to attempt to shed new light on old propositions by relating them to new propositions, to explore the possibility that propositions once experienced as (or assumed to be) incompatible actually complement one another. A process hermeneutic does not presuppose that *all* propositions can be brought into harmonious contrasts. Nor does it presuppose that every transformation is creative; for transformation to be creative it must manifest openness toward other sources of meaning without abandoning previous sources, thereby resulting in an enlargement of perspective. Nevertheless, a process hermeneutic clearly aims at a goal quite different from that of most hermeneutical models.[61]

As Barry Woodbridge observed, interpreters may not sense the arrival of a kairotic moment for creative transformation of a text if they have not attended to its history of interpretation. "This is not to suggest that only historical scholars of scripture will be attuned to its new possibilities for feeling. But it may be that those who have attended to its function in the community where it is read and proclaimed find themselves in a better position to feel its relevance for the present hour."[62]

Yet one may ask why process theologians bother with the Bible. Process theology can stand on its own without biblical warrant. In fact, one can even argue that the Bible is not necessary for Christian existence.[63] Christian existence is genetically indebted to the events of its emergence in the first century C.E., but it is not dependent upon conscious knowledge of those events or conscious beliefs about them. "The indebtedness of a particular mode of existence to the past is largely on a preconscious level; thus, while knowledge and conscious beliefs about the Christian past are important, they are not all-controlling."[64]

---

[60] The experience of creative transformation in the process of interpreting a text is similar to Gadamer's fusion of horizons. See Williamson, "Process Hermeneutics and Christianity's Post-Holocaust Reinterpretation of Itself," 82-85 for a comparison.

[61] David Lull ("What Is 'Process Hermeneutics'?" 194-6) has argued persuasively that the process notion of "creative transformation" is central to the biblical witness to the reality of God and to the uses of tradition within the Bible.

[62] Woodbridge, "An Assessment and Prospectus for a Process Hermeneutic" 124-5.

[63] As Augustine (*On Christian Doctrine*, 1.39.43) noted, a person "supported by faith, hope, and charity, with an unshaken hold upon them, does not need the Scriptures except for the instruction of others. And many live by these three things in solitude without books."

[64] Lull, "What Is 'Process Hermeneutics'?" 197.

Nevertheless, if one's theology is to *remain* Christian, i.e., is to maintain continuity with the Christian tradition, one must attend to the Bible. Conscious knowledge and beliefs do increase the effectiveness of the past in shaping one's present existence; consequently, attention to the Bible is important since the Bible records and interprets those events surrounding the first appearance of Christian existence. That this does not mean the mere repetition of some "essence" should, by now, be obvious. As John Cobb wrote:

> Rather than seeking an essential form of faith identical with that witnessed to in Scriptures, we must seek to discern the present movement of the spirit that is continuous with a movement begun in primitive Christianity.

> Even so the Bible remains authoritative. We can discriminate the process of faith within the present only as a trajectory whose early states are already discernible in the New Testament. Without attention to the origins, we cannot make reliable judgments in the present.[65]

This "process view" of biblical authority enables one to live from the past, in the present, toward the future.[66] That this description parallels the concrescence of an actual occasion is significant.

The Community of Interpretation

As was noted above, a process hermeneutic attributes a great deal of importance to the history of a religious tradition and the influence of the community upon the individual interpreter. Of course, other hermeneutical systems acknowledge the importance of this "community of interpretation"; but because process thought asserts that interpreters are internally related to their environment, the significance of the community is heightened. Thus, the community to which an interpreter belongs—e.g., a particular faith group or the scholarly guild—determines to some degree what he or she "sees" in a text.

But the significance of the community goes beyond simply influencing what the interpreter sees in a text. The individual's interpretation finds its confirmation *in part* within the community. The individual's interpretation may either enhance the growth of the community or contribute to its decay. For a process hermeneutic, then, one criterion for a valid interpretation is that it promote the community's growth.[67]

Divine Power in the Apocalypse

The process hermeneutic formulated above will undergird the following study of divine power in the Apocalypse to John. In order to set the stage for this

---

65 Cobb, "The Authority of the Bible," 201.

66 See Norman Pittenger, *The Christian Church as Social Process* (Philadelphia: Westminster Press, 1971).

67 Woodbridge, "Process Hermeneutic: An Approach to Biblical Texts," 85, and Woodbridge, "An Assessment and Prospectus for a Process Hermeneutic," 126-7. In the words of Lyman T. Lundeen ("The Authority of the Word in a Process Perspective," *Encounter* 36 [1975] 298), "Interpretations are . . . proposals for testing in experience."

adventure in interpretation, two conceptions of power will be distinguished and certain recent developments in the study of the Apocalypse will be noted.

Two Conceptions of Power

The view of God expressed in classical theism[68] has dominated the Western world. Two aspects of this portrait are important for understanding what has become the dominant conception of divine power. First, God is viewed as omnipotent in the sense of determining or controlling all that happens. All talk of genuine creaturely freedom or decision making is double-talk.[69] Second, God is completely impassive, incapable of feeling the feelings of others. God influences all things, but nothing influences God; God's power is unilateral. To be sure, God is viewed as a God of love, but the word love is emptied of a most essential element, the element of sympathy, of feeling the feelings of others. Thus, divine love—frequently termed agape—is merely beneficence, totally unmoved by creaturely sufferings or joy.

Process thinkers have criticized the classical view of divine power on several points. First, this definition of divine power results in the notoriously insoluble problem of evil. Second, this understanding of omnipotence is not asserted unambiguously by either Greek philosophy or the Judeo-Christian scriptures. And third, process metaphysics suggests a different understanding of divine power, one which is also found in Greek philosophy and the Bible. For the purpose at hand, the process conception of power can be divided into two aspects.

The first aspect of the process definition is that divine power is persuasive and all-influencing rather than coercive and all-controlling. God does influence every actual occasion, but this operation of divine power is not determinative. God seeks to lure or persuade each actual occasion toward the optimum mode for its development, but each occasion is genuinely free[70] to choose the degree to which it follows the divine aim in its concrescence. Thus, rather than God's power being coercive and all-controlling, it is persuasive and all-influencing.

The second aspect of the process definition is that divine power is relational rather than unilateral. Upon completion of its concrescence, each actual occasion is prehended or felt by God in the consequent nature. This feeling is then integrated with God's feelings of the entire world within the primordial nature of harmonized possibilities; thus, what each actual occasion becomes influences the divine concrescence. Therefore, if unilateral power is the ability to produce effects in others and is essentially one-directional in its workings—that is, the capacity to influence others without being influenced—and if relational power is the ability both to produce and to undergo an effect—that is, the

---

68 "Classical theism" refers to medieval scholarship (and its present day remnants) which Charles Hartshorne characterized as "a compromise between a not-very-well-understood Greek philosophy and a not-very-scholarly interpretation of sacred writings" [*Omnipotence and other Theological Mistakes* (Albany: SUNY Press, 1984), 43].

69 Of course, classical theologians speak of human free will, but such talk is misleading. Hartshorne (11-12) simply labeled it "double-talk": God decides that a person shall perform a certain act, but the divine decision is that the act shall be performed "freely."

70 In process thought, there are degrees of freedom ranging from negligible (e.g., sub-atomic particles) to considerable (e.g., human beings).

capacity to influence others and to be influenced by others[71]—then it is obvious that according to the process model God's power is relational not unilateral.

Because the initial aim of God is for the welfare of the actual occasion, and because the power of God is relational, one might be tempted to refer to the process understanding of divine power as "love." Caution must be exercised at this point, however. Because classical theism views God as completely impassive, incapable of feeling the feelings of others, it therefore understands God's love—agape—to be unilateral. According to the process model, however, God's love is not only creative (influencing others), it is also responsive (capable of being influenced). Consequently, process theologians John Cobb and David Griffin use the phrase "creative-responsive love" to refer to God's power;[72] process-feminist theologian Rita Nakashima Brock prefers the expression "erotic power."[73]

In light of the preceding discussion of two conceptions of power, doubtless many will think that I have chosen to apply a process hermeneutic to one of the least promising genres of biblical literature. After all, many New Testament scholars quote with approval D. H. Lawrence's estimation of the Apocalypse to John. He felt there were two kinds of Christianity: one focused on Jesus and the love command, and the other focused on the Apocalypse with its sanctification of the will-to-power and envy. Thus for him, Revelation is the "Judas" of the New Testament.[74] Whitehead himself called the Apocalypse "barbaric" in that its notion of "the absolute despot" leads to "the undoing of Christian intuition" (i.e., the doctrine of grace).[75] Yet two factors make sense of my choice of text. First, the process hermeneutic formulated above is applicable to all texts, not just those which evoke propositions compatible with process thought. Second, recent developments in the study of early Christian apocalyptic literature have made possible new understandings of the Apocalypse to John.

Recent Developments in the Study of the Apocalypse

Recently several scholars[76] have argued that early Christian apocalypticism is an expression of early Christian prophecy. This proposal significantly affects one's understanding of Revelation's portrayal of divine power. Like prophecy, process thought views the future as organically growing out of the past by means of the lure of God; the divine lure does not cancel out genuine creaturely freedom. Process thought differs sharply with thorough-going apocalyptic

---

71 Cf. Bernard Loomer, "Two Conceptions of Power," *Process Studies* 6 (1976) 5-21.

72 Cobb and Griffin 41-62.

73 Rita Nakashima Brock, *Journeys by Heart: A Christology of Erotic Power* (New York: Crossroad, 1988).

74 D. H. Lawrence, *Apocalypse* (Penguin Books, 1974), 14-15.

75 Whitehead, *Adventures of Ideas,* 170.

76 For example, Elisabeth Schüssler Fiorenza, "The Phenomenon of Early Christian Apocalyptic," in *Apocalypticism in the Mediterranean World and the Near East,* ed. by David Hellholm (Tübingen: J. C. B. Mohr, 1983), 300; and "Apokalypsis and Propheteia: The Book of Revelation in the Context of Early Christian Prophecy," in *L'Apocalypse johannique et l'Apocalyptique dans le Nouveau Testament,* ed. by J. Lambrecht (Leuven: Leuven University Press, 1980). See also M. Eugene Boring, "The Theology of Revelation: 'The Lord Our God the Almighty Reigns'" *Int* 40 (1986) 257-69, especially n. 9.

expectation because such expectation is based upon divine determinism and cataclysmic interruption.[77]

Recent socio-historical studies[78] have cast doubt on the widely held hypothesis that the crisis which occasioned the book was government-sponsored persecution. Christians were, however, a despised minority, so from time to time individual Christians were accused and brought to trial by hostile Gentile or Jewish neighbors. Faced with this crisis in which their opponents' power was clearly coercive, controlling, and unilateral, Christian leaders proposed two quite different responses.[79] One group of leaders—represented in Revelation by the Nicolaitans, the Balaamites, and Jezebel—advocated participation in civic life to counter the antipathy Christians experienced. Such a solution amounted to embracing their opponents' conception of power. The other group of Christian leaders—represented by John—called for a Christian communal life of social radicalism; no accommodation was allowed. As will be demonstrated below, John's solution necessitated a rejection of their opponents' conception of power in favor of a radically different understanding of power.

The function of Revelation's mythopoetic language has also been the subject of recent study. Numerous scholars understand the symbolic universe of the Apocalypse to be an alternative to the social world of everyday life—an ephemeral world John and his readers participate in "so as to experience momentarily the reality of their hopes, to gain strength and courage to face social oppression, and to resolve tensions experienced between their faith and their social experience." Themes such as hope, salvation, and vindication "function as compensations for Christians who feel deprived in their social situation."[80] Thus, John's symbolism evokes an "emotional catharsis," a release of pent-up, disquieting emotions such as fear, powerlessness, and aggression by projecting them onto a cosmic drama.[81]

In contrast to viewing Revelation's symbolic universe as an alternative, ephemeral world separate from the "real social world," a few scholars have proposed that John's symbolic world is a comprehensive and coherent replication of reality—"comprehensive in that John offers his symbolic structure as an all-inclusive world embracing the whole of Christian existence including social, political exchanges in everyday life," and "coherent in that, if appropriated, it integrates human experience and makes Christian existence whole." Thus, conflict in the Apocalypse is not between elements of Christian existence (e.g., faith versus sociopolitical realities) but between two comprehensive and coherent worlds or interpretations of reality, one set forth by

---

[77] See Lewis S. Ford, *The Lure of God: A Biblical Background for Process Theism* (Philadelphia: Fortress Press, 1978), 24, 31.

[78] For example, Adela Yarbro Collins, *Crisis & Catharsis: The Power of the Apocalypse* (Philadelphia: Westminster Press, 1984), and Leonard Thompson, "A Sociological Analysis of Tribulation in the Apocalypse of John," *Semeia* 36 (1986) 147-74.

[79] David Barr ["The Apocalypse of John as Oral Enactment," *Int* 40 (1986) 243-56] labeled this "a struggle between prophets." As Boring (261-2) noted, a prophet's ministry is hermeneutical in nature: a prophet interprets history, especially the contemporary historical situation which has produced "a crisis of meaning."

[80] Thompson, 163-7.

[81] See especially Yarbro Collins, *Crisis & Catharsis*, chapter five.

John and one embodied in the Roman Empire, which John judged to be false.[82] Moreover, myth is not just pretend; it transforms reality. As the readers accept John's myth, they are transformed.

> This is no ephemeral experience. The hearers are decisively changed. . . . Persecution does not shock them back to reality. They live in a new reality.

> They no longer suffer helplessly at the hands of Rome; they are now in charge of their own destiny and by their voluntary suffering they participate in the overthrow of evil and the establishment of God's kingdom.[83]

Understanding the function of John's mythopoetic language in this manner has a profound metaphysical implication.

An Analysis of Revelation 4-5

Commentators frequently identify the issue of power as one of the deepest theological concerns of Revelation. The drama, set forth in what to modern readers is bizarre symbolism, can be characterized as a clash of powers. The Dragon (Satan), working through his henchman the Beast (the Roman government), wages war against the people of God. The power the Beast exercises is clearly coercive, controlling, and unilateral. That God overcomes the Beast and the Dragon is clear. What many interpreters have failed to perceive, however, is the manner in which God conquers. The question to be answered in the course of this brief analysis is, What is the nature of God's power?

The main title for God in the Book of Revelation is *pantokrator*, a term variously translated "almighty," "all-powerful," "omnipotent," and "ruler of all things."[84] Although many commentators tone down the classical understanding of omnipotence, they find it difficult to abandon altogether, as the "classic" statement by R. H. Charles illustrates:

> But though omnipotent, His [God's] omnipotence is ethically and not metaphysically conceived. It is not unconditioned force. *That He possesses such absolute power is an axiom of the Christian faith,* but He will not use it, since such use of it would compel the recognition of His sovereignty, not win it, would enslave man, not make him free.[85]

Many commentators have correctly noted that chapters four and five are pivotal to the understanding of the book as a whole and the issue of power in particular. Nevertheless, their inability to abandon the classical definition of omnipotence has blinded them to the significance of certain lures within these crucial chapters.

---

82 Thompson, 166-9.

83 David Barr, "The Apocalypse as a Symbolic Transformation of the World: A Literary Analysis," *Int* 38 (1984) 48-50.

84 Of the ten occurrences of the term in the NT, nine are found in Revelation (1:8; 4:8; 11:17; 15:3; 16:7, 14; 19:6, 15; 21:22). In the Septuagint the term frequently translates Sebaoth (Hosts) and Shaddai (Almighty).

85 R. H. Charles, "A Critical and Exegetical Commentary on The Revelation of St. John," 2 vols., in *The International Critical Commentary,* ed. by S. R. Driver, A. Plummer, C. A. Briggs (Edinburgh: T. & T. Clark, 1920), 1:cx, (emphasis added).

In a manner reminiscent of the Old Testament prophets, John is invited to observe the heavenly council where the purpose of God is revealed.[86] In keeping with this prophetic motif, John is admitted to the heavenly throne room in order that he may subsequently reveal to God's people the divine purpose and what part they are to play in implementing it.

Dominating chapter four—indeed, dominating the entire book—is the recurring symbol of the heavenly throne, a symbol of divine sovereignty.[87] Unlike his probable source (Ezek 1:26-28), John refrains from an anthropomorphic description of the one occupying the throne (with the exception of 5:1). Rather, "with evocative language he hints at what is beyond description. Yet the whole chapter is numinous with the divine presence."[88] Clearly the vision depicts God as Creator, the one who is worthy of worship. Moreover, God's holiness, power, eternity, and creative work form the basis for John's assurance of the ultimate triumph of righteousness.[89] What comfort this vision of the heavenly throne must have brought to those who lived under the shadow of another throne!

Chapter five opens with a scroll lying on the right[90] palm of the one sitting upon the throne. Although other interpretations have been proposed, most commentators are in general agreement with G. B. Caird: "the scroll is God's redemptive plan, . . . by which he means to assert his sovereignty over a sinful world and so to achieve the purpose of creation."[91] The scroll is sealed (perfect passive participle) with seven seals; hence, the scroll is *securely* sealed. Although the scroll rests in God's open hand, its opening awaits the emergence of a human agent[92] willing and worthy to break the seals, thereby revealing and implementing the content of the scroll. The revelation that no one in all creation—in heaven, on earth, or under the earth—was found worthy to open the scroll moves John to uncontrollable weeping. Will God's purpose fail to be revealed and enacted for lack of a worthy agent?

At this point it is instructive to observe the significance of the word "worthy." Whereas the term "throne" is central to chapter four, the word "worthy" is central to chapter five. Many commentators have understood the use of *axios* in this passage to be "the inner ethical presupposition of the ability . . . to open the Book,"[93] but few have dealt with the question *why* a certain worthiness is indispensable if one is to open the scroll. After surveying numerous Hellenistic, Jewish, and Christian parallels involving the entrusting of holy books, mysteries, or revelations to worthy people, W. C. van Unnik concluded that "'worthiness' is

---

[86] 1 Kgs 22:19-23; Amos 3:7; Jer 23:18.

[87] Forty-seven of the 62 NT occurrences of the word *thronos* are in Revelation, 14 of which are found in chapter four.

[88] G. B. Caird, "A Commentary on the Revelation of St. John the Divine," in *Harper's New Testament Commentaries*, ed. by Henry Chadwick (New York: Harper & Row, Publishers, 1966), 63.

[89] Cf. Charles, 1:127, 133-4.

[90] God's right hand is the hand of power (Exod 15:6; Ps 44:3) and salvation (Isa 41:10; Ps 138:7).

[91] Caird, 72.

[92] Examples of God's salvation being contingent upon a human agent include Rom 5:11-21 and Heb 2:5-18.

[93] Charles, 1:139.

not a quality that as such entitles a man to something divine, but it is the right inner attitude, shown forth by deeds which enable him to receive this gift. A severe test has brought this to light."[94]

Thus, anyone who wanted to open the divine scroll must be worthy, must through testing manifest that there is nothing in his or her life to hinder receiving the scroll. That not a single person was found worthy sets in bold relief the announcement of the elder that "the Lion of the Tribe of Judah, the Root of David," has conquered (aorist tense) so that he can open the scroll. That the announcement is couched in the traditional messianic imagery of the Old Testament is noted by all commentators.[95] Less frequently noted is the "martial ring"[96] of both expressions.

In reading Revelation, one is wise to examine the dialectical relationship between what John hears and what he sees. Auditions and visions explain one another. An unfortunate paragraph break between verses five and six in most Greek editions and English translations can cause the reader to miss the full impact of two contrasting images. John looks for the Lion of the audition but sees instead a Lamb. The vision in verse six of a Lamb bearing the marks of sacrificial slaughter stands in stark contrast to the militant messianic audition of verse five.

The most frequent symbol referring to Jesus the Christ in the Apocalypse is the Lamb. Of the 30 New Testament occurrences of the word *arnion*, 29 are in Revelation.[97] Originally the diminutive of *aren* with the significance of "little lamb," *arnion* had lost this force by the first century. The meaning of the term in Revelation is disputed, however. Some commentators argue that in the Apocalypse the term should be translated "ram" due to the depiction of the wrath (6:16-17), and victorious warfare (17:14; cf. 19:11-21) of the *arnion*. Moreover, the *arnion* is depicted with seven horns (5:6) leading some scholars to explain the *arnion* in terms of the ram of the zodiac. Other commentators, however, point out that passages such as Dan 8:3; 1 Enoch 89:42-49; 90:9-16 (cf. T. Joseph 19:8, especially Armenian); and Zech 4:10 could easily account for the seven horns. In any case, "the philological justification of the translation 'ram' is highly doubtful."[98] In Jewish usage—the Septuagint, the Psalms of Solomon, and Josephus, for example—the only significance is "lamb." Indeed, Josephus distinguished between *arnion*, lamb, and *krios*, ram.[99] The only New Testament occurrence of *arnion* outside Revelation, John 21:15, clearly used the term to mean lamb. Moreover, the fact that the *arnion* is depicted as slain[100] (cf. Jer

---

94 W. C. van Unnik, "'Worthy is the Lamb': The Background of Apoc 5," in *Mélanges Bibliques* (Gembloux: J. Duculot, 1970), 457-8.

95 Gen 49:9-10; Isa 11:1-10.

96 Caird, 73.

97 Twenty-eight times *arnion* refers to Jesus the Christ; once (13:11) it refers to the Earth Beast, a parody of the Christ.

98 *TDNT*, s.v. "arnion," by J. Jeremias.

99 *Ant.* 3.221.251.

100 Although *sphazō* can be used for slaughtering one's enemies, its main LXX usage is in sacrificial settings. The sacrificial sense is frequently found in secular Greek as well (*TDNT*, s.v. "sphazō, sphage," by Otto Michel.). Sphazō is also used of the deaths of Christians in Rev 6:9 and 18:24 thus transforming their murders into sacrifices.

11:19; Isa 53:7, 10-12) indicates that the symbol should not be separated from the early Christian depiction of Jesus as the sacrificial lamb who suffers patiently, innocently, and representatively (John 1:29, 36; Acts 8:22; 1 Pet 1:19[101]).

The Lamb is described *"standing as* having been slain" because in the vision the Lamb is very much alive. The perfect passive participle pictures the sacrifice as having been accomplished, with the marks of slaughter still visible.

Returning to the audition/vision dialectic, the audition (Lion of Judah/Root of David) explains the vision (slain Lamb): the death of Jesus is not weakness and defeat but power and victory. Likewise, the vision explains the audition: God's power and victory lie in suffering, redemptive love. This contrasts sharply with Satan's power: in 13:11, the Earth Beast *looks* like a lamb but *speaks* like a dragon! The Earth Beast is a deliberate parody of the Lamb. Christ's only power is that of the sword which issues from his mouth (1:16; 2:12, 16; 19:15), words which pierce people's souls.[102] The paradox resulting from this dialectical relationship between seeing and hearing is the key both to John's interpretation of the Old Testament and to the symbolism of his apocalypse. God's victory is achieved only through suffering, redemptive love.[103]

In addition to the marks of slaughter, the Lamb has two other striking characteristics: seven horns and seven eyes.[104] Horns frequently symbolize power in Jewish literature. The presence of seven horns indicates that the Lamb is perfect in power. Thus, John asserts that suffering, redemptive love is the most powerful force in the universe. Eyes frequently symbolize wisdom or knowledge; consequently, seven eyes means that the Lamb is perfect in wisdom.[105]

Caird was undoubtedly correct when he stated that by means of this symbolism John redefined omnipotence. In fact, Caird came close to the process definition of divine power when he asserted, "Omnipotence is not to be understood as the power of unlimited coercion, but as the power of infinite persuasion, the invincible power of self-negating, self-sacrificing love."[106] The first portion of his statement clearly indicates that he viewed God's power as persuasive and all-influencing rather than coercive and all-controlling. However, the last part of his statement—"self-negating, self-sacrificing love"—reflects classical theism's understanding of God's love. Recently process, liberationist, African-American, and especially feminist theologians have called attention to

---

[101] The term *amnos* occurs in these passages.

[102] Cf. Heb 4:12. As Barr ("Symbolic Transformation," 42) noted, this is a complex symbol. The enemies of God are vanquished by the word of Jesus, which is both "the Word of God" (a title for Christ 19:13) and "the word of his testimony." This latter expression has two referents in Revelation: Jesus' own faithful testimony, which is his sacrificial death, and faithful testimony about Jesus (1:2, 5, 9; 2:10, 13; 3:14; 6:9; 11:7; 12:11, 17; 17:14; 19:10-11; 20:4).

[103] The expression "suffering, redemptive love" includes both the sacrifice of the Lamb and faithful testimony to that act of love by the Lamb's followers (see below).

[104] Seven horns (power) corresponds to the Lion of Judah (Gen 49:9-10); seven eyes (wisdom), to the Root of David (Isa 11:1-2).

[105] Cf. 1 Cor 1:23-24, "Christ crucified, . . . the power of God and the wisdom of God."

[106] Caird, 75. Cf. Barr ("Symbolic Transformation," 41), "a more complete reversal of value would be hard to imagine"; and Boring (266), "as profound a 'rebirth of images' and redefinition of the meaning of 'power' as anything in the history of theology."

the fact that a self-negating or "no-self" theology—characteristic of patriarchy and paternalism—is destructive to personality, especially for the oppressed and marginalized. Redemptive suffering,[107] which recognizes the interconnectedness of existence, is to be distinguished from self-centeredness and its alter ego self-negation, both of which deny the interconnectedness of existence. Thus, missing from Caird's definition is the relational versus unilateral aspect of God's power. The relational aspect can be discerned in chapter five (and throughout Revelation), however, as the remainder of this analysis will demonstrate.

John goes on to state that the horns and the eyes of the Lamb are "the seven spirits of God sent out into all the earth." The Spirit of God in all its fullness ("*seven* spirits") can be sent out only as the horns and eyes of the Lamb. Apparently John has interpreted Isaiah 11 by Zech 3:8-4:10 where seven lamps are "the eyes of the Lord which range through the whole earth," and the point is, "Not by might, nor by power, but by my Spirit." The earlier symbolism of the seven churches as seven lampstands (1:12, 20) would have prepared John's readers to understand the seven flaming spirits of God (1:4; 4:5), which are the manifold energies of the Spirit of God, in terms of their own mission and witness.[108] Thus, John asserts that the continued activity of God in the world is contingent on the followers of the Lamb acting as the horns and eyes of the Lamb.[109]

In verse seven the Lamb takes the scroll from the hand of God, and in 6:1 begins opening the seals.[110] Thus, the Lamb becomes the agent through whom God implements the divine purpose. Upon the Lamb's receiving the scroll, the heavenly worship of chapter four is resumed; however, the celebration has changed its focus from creation to redemption.[111] Throughout Revelation, heavenly hymns serve to interpret visions; the hymn of 5:9-14 is no exception. In ever enlarging circles—beginning with the four living creatures and the twenty-four elders and expanding to every creature in heaven, on the earth, under the earth, and in the sea—the Lamb is proclaimed worthy to open the scroll because by his sacrificial death he redeemed to God people from every tribe, tongue, people, and nation. As the hymn indicates, the redeemed are liberated to serve as priests (5:10), with the goal of unifying the cosmos in the worship of God and the Lamb (5:13).

---

107 The Apocalypse's call for suffering, redemptive love is comparable to Beardslee's and Cobb's notion of self-transcending existence fulfilled in love. See Jack Boozer and William Beardslee, *Faith to Act: An Essay on the Meaning of Christian Existence* (New York/Nashville: Abingdon Press, 1967) and John B. Cobb, Jr., *The Structure of Christian Existence* (Philadelphia: Westminster Press, 1967).

108 Cf. John 20:21-22, "As the Father has sent me, even so I send you. . . . Receive the Holy Spirit."

109 Cf. Eph 3:10, "that through the church the manifold wisdom of God might now be made known to the principalities and powers in the heavenly places."

110 It should be noted that the Lamb opens the seals in conjunction with the prayers of the saints (5:8; 6:10; 8:3-5), another example of relational rather than unilateral power.

111 The new song (5:9-10) is a song of redemption (cf. 14:2-3; 15:2-4; Ps 33:3; 40:3; 98:1).

At this point, it is important to refer to the literary structure of Revelation. Several structural analyses[112] have noted that the visions of destruction (6-20) are bracketed by the vision of God the Creator and Redeemer (4-5) who makes all things new (21:1-22:5). Moreover, the whole drama (4:1-22:5) is itself bracketed by exhortations to faithfulness addressed to the readers (1-3 and 22:6-21). Now if chapters 6-20 stood alone, it would be hard to see them as anything other than a cry for vengeance arising from anger, hatred, and envy—"an attitude poles apart from the love for enemies which Jesus taught"—and a gruesome portrait of divine coercive power. Reading chapters 6-20 in light of this bracketing, however, significantly alters the interpretation of the passage. The wrath and victory of the Lamb (6-20) is to be understood in light of the slain Lamb who redeemed a people to serve as priests with the task of unifying the cosmos in the worship of God (5:1-14). Moreover, the nations and their kings, the victims of the destructions of 6-20, will walk by the light of the New Jerusalem's lamp, which is the Lamb (21:23-27), and the leaves of the tree which grows in the city's street are for the healing of the nations (22:1-3). But this New Creation (21:1) is not accomplished by divine fiat. The whole drama (4:1-22:5) is itself bracketed by exhortations to faithfulness addressed to the readers (1-3; and 22:6-21). For the Word of God to accomplish the New Creation, the followers of the Lamb must bear faithful testimony.[113] Thus, the testimony of the Lamb's followers is not merely *witness* to the reality and nature of God's power; their testimony is also the *instrument* through which the divine power accomplishes its purposes.

An often overlooked aspect of Revelation lends additional support to this interpretation suggested by the bracketing structure: God's ability to implement the divine purpose is contingent upon finding a worthy human agent. An axiom of process thought is that God works with what is to bring about what can be. The failure of a becoming occasion to follow the initial aim influences the nature of the initial aim God is able to supply for the next moment of concrescence. Conversely, the degree to which a becoming occasion actualizes the initial aim influences the nature of the succeeding initial aim. Furthermore, because everything influences everything else in a process universe, the initial aim God is able to supply to one occasion is somewhat dependent upon all other occasions. A similar idea is presented in the Apocalypse. When John wrote that Jesus' sacrificial death enabled God to do what could not be done before—i.e., open the scroll—he indicated that God's power is relational not unilateral. The implementation of God's will is contingent upon the response of a human agent.

But John did not limit this interdependent relationship to God and Jesus. In the Apocalypse, the scene continually shifts from earth to heaven and back. As J. P. M. Sweet noted, in heaven are found "both the origin and the reflection of earthly events, . . . [Moreover,] heaven's will waits on earth's response." Sweet further noted that in worship "the heavenly will is communicated and becomes fruitful in earthly doing and suffering; [then] the earthly victory is registered . . . and becomes effective in new heavenly dispositions."[114] Yet not only are good

---

112   For example, J. P. M. Sweet, "Revelation," in *Westminster Pelican Commentaries*, ed. D. E. Nineham (Philadelphia: Westminster Press, 1979), 13, 47, 51, 126, and David Barr "Symbolic Transformation," 46, and "Oral Enactment," 252-6.

113   Sweet, 13, 126.

114   Sweet, 113-4.

earthly deeds reflected in heaven—deeds in which the divine will has been accomplished—but also deeds resulting from neglecting the divine will in varying degrees.[115] These bad deeds also are registered and affect new heavenly dispositions. Throughout the Apocalypse, John exhorts his readers to conquer *in the same fashion* as Jesus conquered.[116] Jesus' sacrificial death may have enabled God to inaugurate the divine purpose, but the *continued* implementation of God's purpose is contingent upon the followers of Jesus making his lifestyle their lifestyle. Obviously, this requires a radically new understanding of reality, one in which a slain Lamb conquers and faithful testimony—accompanied by voluntary, redemptive suffering—result in the overthrow of evil and the establishment of the rule of God.

Hermeneutical Reflections on John's "Undercurrent"

The preceding analysis of Revelation 4-5 has uncovered a cluster of basal lures in which John provides his readers a new perspective on power, both divine and human. The power which will triumph—that is, which will result in God's purpose—is persuasive not coercive, influencing not controlling, relational not unilateral. Surprisingly, then, there is an aspect of the Apocalypse, this "undercurrent," which is compatible with process theology in that it portrays ultimate power as the power of creative-responsive love.

But even if this analysis has proven convincing, undoubtedly some will insist, and rightly so, that the undercurrent is not the whole picture. That the dominant imagery of the Apocalypse (the surface lures) presents God's power as coercive, all-controlling, and unilateral seems undeniable. Interpreters throughout the ages have felt that the major textual lures operate in this deterministic fashion. As was noted above, propositions are lures for feeling, *suggestions* for the way things might be appropriated in the interpreter's process of self-creation. But suggestions are not demands; they may be adopted as they are, or modified, or even rejected. In the course of Christian history, many people have adopted the view of God's power suggested by these deterministic lures; as was noted earlier, classical theism has been the dominant mode of conceptualizing God in the West. But other interpreters have felt compelled to modify this understanding of God, as the quotation from R. H. Charles testifies. And some, D. H. Lawrence for example, have rejected it all together.

Now clearly this deterministic view of divine power is incompatible with process theology. But unlike other hermeneutical models, a process hermeneutic does not excise propositions incompatible with its world view; on the contrary, it encourages special attention to those dimensions of a text. The entertainment of lures foreign to the interpreter's sensibilities may result in the emergence of a novel pattern large enough to include both the foreign and the familiar in a harmonious contrast. When this occurs, the interpreter experiences creative transformation. How might this occur with respect to the discordant propositions at hand: that God's power be viewed as coercive, all-controlling, and unilateral

---

115   Examples of evil being reflected in heaven include the sea (4:6), the martyrs under the altar (6:9-11), and the war in heaven (12:7-12).

116   See the promise to those who "conquer" at the end of each of the seven letters in chapters 2-3; see also 12:11 and 20:4, 6.

(the surface lures) and that God's power be viewed as persuasive, all-influencing, and relational (the basal lures)?

As was stated above, the basal lures uncovered by a process hermeneutic may at times operate in a manner quite at odds with the dominant textual lures. Of course, it is a matter of conjecture as to how aware John was of the tension he created by means of this undercurrent. Being a child of the first-century may have prevented him from perceiving what is obvious—obvious at least in light of the preceding analysis—to present-day readers operating with a radically different world view. Thus, it is possible that John was unaware of the problem he created with 1) his insistence on the necessity of a worthy human agent to reveal and implement God's purpose for creation, 2) his image of the slain Lamb as the wisdom and power of God, 3) his call for the Lamb's followers to adopt the Lamb's lifestyle, rather than the lifestyle of the Beast, so that the continuance of God's aim is insured, and 4) his portrayal of earthly events as not only reflected in heaven but also affecting heavenly dispositions. But whether John created this "undercurrent" intentionally or inadvertently, these basal lures nevertheless stand in tension with the deterministic world view implied by the "surface" lures.

Whether John viewed the deterministic language of the surface lures univocally or imaginatively is also a matter of conjecture. But even if John intended it to be understood univocally, present-day readers may view it imaginatively because all language, especially mythopoetic language, is relatively indeterminate. Moreover, a process hermeneutic proposes that when the basal lures of the text function as an undercurrent to the surface lures, then the surface lures should be read imaginatively rather than univocally. The reason for this hermeneutical proposal is that the basal lures form the deepest metaphysical assumptions undergirding the text as a whole (and thus are the most important lures), even if these implied assumptions were not consciously entertained by the author.

Therefore, when held in the unity of a contrast with the basal lures, John's deterministic language can evoke non-deterministic lures. The deterministic language of the surface lures can evoke the firm conviction that God and God's people will eventually overcome evil, while the non-deterministic language of the undercurrent can evoke the manner: suffering, redemptive love (the basal lure) will eventually triumph (the surface lure); creative-responsive love (the basal lure) is the most powerful force in the universe (the surface lure). Thus, a process hermeneutic enables the Apocalypse to speak powerfully and relevantly to today's reader.

Appendix: The Process Metaphysic

According to the process world view developed by Alfred North Whitehead, what is real is what happens; that is, ultimate reality is composed of events rather than substances. People tend to think of an event as happening to "something" that exists before and after the event. In order to promote a new perspective on events, Whitehead developed a specialized and somewhat difficult terminology. The purpose of this appendix is to introduce those aspects of a process world view and the Whiteheadian terminology which are necessary to undergird the development of a process hermeneutic.

Viewing ultimate reality in terms of events rather than substances means that experiences, not tiny bits of matter, are the building blocks of the universe.[117] These energy-events or occasions of experience Whitehead labeled "*actual entities*" or "*actual occasions.*" Under certain circumstances, groups of actual entities, termed "*societies,*" can impinge upon the human sense organs as data in such a manner that they are perceived as the physical objects of ordinary human experience (e.g., rocks, trees, animals, and people).[118] Individual actual entities are detectable only by means of scientific instruments or intense introspection; they are not observable through ordinary conscious human experience.

Although there are differences between actual entities, one thing that all entities have in common is that they transmit energy from preceding actual entities to succeeding actual entities. In some instances that which is inherited from preceding entities is transmitted to succeeding entities virtually unaltered; in other instances what is inherited is significantly modified before being transmitted. The former occurs in low-grade entities which characterize phenomena typically labeled inorganic; the latter occurs in high-grade entities which characterize phenomena associated with life and consciousness.

The process by which these brief occasion of experience come into being Whitehead labeled "*concrescence,*" a growing together of a diverse "many" into a unified "one."[119] Each becoming occasion inherits, or appropriates as its own, energy or data from past actual occasions. This process of appropriating or grasping a datum from a past actual occasion is termed a "*prehension*" or a "*feeling*";[120] each feeling is clothed with a "*subjective form*" which is "how" the becoming occasion feels that datum, the tone of the feeling (examples in human occasions of experience include consciousness, joy, and anger). Clearly, then, the data of the past largely determine what the becoming occasion will be since the past requires of the becoming occasion that it somehow conform to or reenact the past. Yet this determination is never complete, for every actual occasion also exercises some degree of self-determination in its concrescence. What an occasion must prehend is determined, but how the occasion prehends it is not. In high-grade occasions, such as animal or human experience, this self-determination may properly be termed freedom; in low-grade occasions, such as electronic or molecular experience, one should speak rather of indeterminacy in that this term does not imply consciousness and the freedom exercised by low-

---

117 The term "experience" can be misleading. Although Whitehead derived the term from human experience, he did not mean that the building blocks of the universe were exactly like human experience. Most occasions of experience lack such things as sense perception, consciousness, and imagination (the term experience does not necessarily imply these things, however; for example, people do speak of unconscious experience).

118 Any group of actual occasions interrelated to one another in any way Whitehead termed a "nexus." A society is a nexus of actual occasions in which members of the nexus depend upon other members for common inherited characteristics.

119 A discussion of the stages of concrescence is beyond the scope of this appendix.

120 Technically, only "positive prehensions"—prehensions in which there is the definite inclusion of a datum into positive contribution to the becoming occasion's internal constitution—are referred to as feelings. "Negative prehensions" are the definite exclusion of a datum from positive contribution.

grade occasions is negligible.[121] Thus, a becoming occasion selects, harmonizes, and supplements the data of the past, integrating and reintegrating the "many" feelings into "one" final, unified, complex feeling called the "*satisfaction*" of the actual occasion. This concrescence of feelings is guided by the occasion's "*subjective aim*" which is a feeling of what the occasion may become. This subjective aim always takes into account 1) the givenness of past occasions, 2) the goal of achieving the greatest intensity of feeling in the becoming occasion, and 3) the goal of the becoming occasion contributing maximally to relevant future occasions.

In its moment of concrescence, every actual entity is a subject, though usually an unconscious one. As a subject, each actual entity presides over its own immediacy of becoming. But upon attaining satisfaction, this subjective immediacy passes over into objectivity in the sense of being a datum for prehension by succeeding entities. This aspect of being an object conditioning all concrescences beyond itself as something given is termed the entity's "*objective immortality*"; it lives on in the finite world through its effect on (or its prehension by) succeeding actual entities.[122] Thus, according to the process world view, the "many" occasions of the past are unified in the "one" becoming occasion; but upon attaining satisfaction, the "one" becomes part of a new "many" which requires unification in a succeeding occasion. This dynamic rhythm of the many and the one is the continuing rhythm of process.

Now if reality is viewed in terms of individual momentary events, how is one to understand the existence of enduring objects[123] such as rocks, trees, animals, and people? As was noted above, large societies of actual occasions sometimes impinge upon the human sense organs in such a fashion that the perception of the physical objects of ordinary human experience occurs: a common pattern of inheritance is perceived over a period of time among a group of actual occasions. Historically, the perception of many "things" as manifesting the same characteristic has been attributed to the notion that the many things all correspond to the same idea or form or universal (as in Platonism). For example, all particular instances of gray are manifestations of the idea gray. Although Whitehead agreed with many of the notions of these idealistic philosophies, he disagreed with others. For example, there is a tendency in such philosophies to consider these unchanging ideas or universals to be more real than the

---

121 By means of the notion of the self-determination of actual occasions Whitehead accounted for both human freedom and the indeterminacy revealed in modern physics.

122 Whitehead overcame one of the destructive dualisms of modern thought: the subject-object split. The subjective and the objective are not opposing realities, as in dualistic thought, nor is either of them unreal, as in materialism and idealism. On the contrary, both are alternating aspects of each actual occasion.

123 Although "enduring object" is an technical term for Whitehead, it is used here in a non-technical sense. As a technical term, an enduring object is a series of occasions, only one of which exists at a time, and each of which inherits its data primarily, though not exclusively, from the immediately preceding occasion in the series (thus, an enduring object is a serially ordered society). In enduring objects repetition of the past, rather than novelty, predominates resulting in stability (e.g., an electron is a series of electronic occasions each of which largely repeats the experience of the preceding occasion). An enduring object in the non-technical sense (e.g., a rock) is a collection of enduring objects in the technical sense. Whitehead called enduring objects in the non-technical sense "corpuscular societies" because they are composed of numerous "strands" of enduring objects.

particular temporal manifestations. But for Whitehead, there is nothing more real (i.e., more actual) than the particular entities manifesting these ideas; consequently, he avoided the traditional terminology and referred to these ideas or universals as "*eternal objects*." Eternal objects are defined as "pure possibilities" which indicate how something might be actual. As "potentialities of definiteness" they are capable of specifying the character of any actual entity, but in themselves they refer to no particular actual entity.

A becoming occasion prehends or feels a past occasion by means of one of the past occasion's own prehensions or feelings (for this reason one can speak of the rhythm of process as a "flow of feelings"). Ingredient in each component prehension of the past actual occasion is at least one eternal object. Thus, the becoming occasion's prehension of the past occasion by one of its own prehensions results in the two occasions sharing an eternal object. Although the same eternal object has "*ingression*"[124] in both actual occasions, how the eternal object is felt by the two occasions will not be identical; that is, the subjective forms of the two feelings will differ to some degree ranging from negligible to considerable. Because most actual entities transmit—without significant alteration—to succeeding entities the data they have inherited from past entities (i.e., the same eternal object has ingression throughout the series), there is order, repetition, and continuity in the universe. Large groups or societies of these low-grade occasions account for the enduring objects of human sense perception.

But if occasions become what they become simply by inheritance from the past, how is one to account for instances of genuine novelty instead of only slight variations within an endless pattern of repetition? Granted, most enduring objects exhibit change—and slight change at that—only over a long period of time (e.g., molecules and rocks), but in the case of animals and human beings change can be both rapid and dramatic. The occurrence of genuine novelty means that new possibilities have been actualized. Therefore, eternal objects which were not ingredient in any past occasion must somehow be available to new becoming occasions. One could attempt to explain this simply by asserting that the "realm" of eternal objects is available to becoming occasions. A problem immediately arises with this explanation, however. For a novel concrescence to occur, the infinite multiplicity of eternal objects must be ordered in such a manner that certain eternal objects which have not been realized in past actual occasions become relevant to the situation of the concrescing occasion.[125] The past actual world of the becoming occasion determines which "*pure possibilities*" are relevant, i.e., which pure possibilities are "*real possibilities*" for actualization given that situation. (For example, one hundred years ago flying to Rio was a pure possibility; today it is a real possibility, at least for those who can afford to purchase an airline ticket.) But how is the vast realm of eternal objects ordered or graded so that certain unrealized eternal objects become relevant to each new concrescing actual entity? As with many thinkers, Whitehead felt that only what is

---

124 Other equivalent expressions are realization, participation, exemplification, and illustration.

125 That is, a "graded relevance" must be established in which unrealized eternal objects are graded on a scale from very relevant to not relevant at all. See below on the initial aim.

actual has agency.[126] Eternal objects in themselves are abstract not concrete, possibilities not actualities; consequently, agency cannot be attributed to eternal objects in themselves. The eternal objects realized in the past are available to becoming occasions through the agency of past actual occasions; in like manner, eternal objects unrealized in the past must be made available through the agency of some actuality. Thus, because novelty exists there must be an actual entity that so orders the realm of eternal objects with respect to each becoming occasion that certain unrealized eternal objects become relevant to each individual concrescence.

Obviously this entity must differ in certain respects from all other actual entities. 1) Whereas actual occasions in the mode of objective immortality are available only to those occasions that succeed them, this entity must be universally available to all becoming occasions. There can be no occasions which do not prehend it. Furthermore, whereas actual occasions have their moment of subjective immediacy and then perish, this entity must be an everlasting[127] entity (the justification for this statement will become evident below). 2) Although an actual occasion is the realization of only a limited number of eternal objects, this entity must envisage the entire realm of eternal objects, for apart from their envisagement in one actuality eternal objects would not be available for ingression in other actual entities. 3) For particular, finite actualities to exist there must be some limitation on possibility; because it orders the realm of eternal objects with respect to each becoming occasion, this entity serves as the necessary "principle of limitation." 4) Moreover, the very existence of particular, finite actualities requires that this envisagement of the realm of eternal objects be primordial in nature. Unless this act were primordial, there could be no particular actualities, absolutely none. Thus, the ordered envisagement of the realm of eternal objects by this entity is prior to and presupposed by all other actual entities.

Whitehead named this entity "*God*"; the primordial envisagement of the realm of eternal objects, the "*primordial nature*" of God; and the ordering of possibilities offered to each becoming occasion, the "*initial aim*".[128] The initial aim God supplies each becoming occasion is the initial phase of the development of that occasion's subjective aim. Although the initial aim contains that possibility which is the optimum way to unify the many into a novel one—i.e., if adopted it will guide the concrescence in such a way as to result in the richest, most intense unification of feelings possible in light of the past and the relevant future—the occasion is not bound to implement that possibility. Because the initial aim offers

---

[126] Whitehead labeled this "the ontological principle." This principle can also be expressed, "everything must be 'somewhere' and somewhere means some actual entity." Thus, unrealized eternal objects or new possibilities cannot come to a becoming occasion out of "nowhere."

[127] Everlasting, not eternal, is the appropriate term to describe this entity for if the entity were eternal it would be totally separate from time. As the following discussion reveals, this entity is related to all finite, temporal actual entities. Frequently Whitehead referred to this entity as non-temporal, but this expression is misleading since it applies to only one aspect of this entity (see the discussion of the primordial nature below).

[128] One should note that Whitehead's introduction of God was not religiously motivated; he introduced God in order to give a philosophical explanation of the world.

a graded relevance of possibilities,[129] there is room for the becoming occasion to accept, modify, or reject the optimum possibility in the development of the subjective aim which will guide its concrescence. According to the process world view, then, God's power is persuasive rather than coercive. God seeks to lure each occasion toward that ideal way of becoming which is in keeping with God's own subjective aim of promoting intensity of harmonious feeling in the world.

Although God's primordial nature is timeless and thus in this respect God can be described as a non-temporal actual entity, God is an actual entity and so must meet the basic requirements for actuality. In a manner similar to the way in which every occasion of experience influences succeeding occasions and is influenced by preceding occasions, God also both influences and is influenced by the temporal world. Thus, God cannot be described as non-temporal without qualification. Although the primordial envisagement of the realm of eternal objects was unconditioned by any preceding actualities and thus is timeless, every subsequent act of divine concrescence is influenced by whatever actualities have come into being. With respect to God, the rhythm of process may be summarized as follows. God supplies the initial aim to "begin" each new actual occasion. After the occasion achieves its satisfaction God prehends it in its totality, saving everlastingly what has been accomplished in the divine *"consequent nature."*[130] What has been accomplished in the temporal world (preserved everlastingly in the consequent nature) is then integrated with the divine envisagement of eternal objects (the primordial nature) in such a way that the divine satisfaction results in relevant initial aims for prehension by the next generation of occasions. According to the process world view, then, temporal actualities matter; they matter both to succeeding temporal occasions of experience and to the divine experience.

---

129 The initial aim is the envisagement of a set of related, relevant possibilities for actualization; the becoming occasion "chooses" from among them.

130 Whitehead's description of God in terms of the primordial and consequent natures should not be understood as implying that God can be "divided" into two natures in the usual sense of the term. Rather, these expressions refer to two functions of one reality. The primordial nature is the aspect or dimension of God typically discussed in Western philosophies (God as eternal, unchanging, infinite, and so forth). It is to Whitehead's credit that he also emphasized the neglected dimension of God.

The Apocalypse as Utopia:
Ancient and Modern Subjectivity

Randall C. Webber
Salvation Army, Louisville, KY

The interplay between objective and subjective components enriches, and possibly also plagues, both academic and other readings of the Apocalypse. This interplay creates overlap in the sets of issues with which all readers must grapple. That the text is a first century Christian composition and that most of its readers have lived long since the text was written are beyond doubt. In other words, the author and earliest recipients, on the one hand, and most subsequent readers, on the other, represent different cultural milieux.

The most questionable fundamentalists and the most respectable academicians share the recognition that the great cultural divide influences their understandings of the Apocalypse substantially; they differ simply in their ways of bridging the gulf. For example, H. Lindsay and C. C. Carlson read the Apocalypse as a prediction of future events (1975), while L. Thompson reads it as a symbolic depiction of the dichotomies which its author saw in his communities' *Sitze im Leben* (1990:174 ff.). These authors represent opposite tendencies in interpretive method but share the goal of rendering the Apocalypse informative to their twentieth century audiences.

This observation suggests that subjective elements are inevitable in any reading of the Apocalypse. Since the modern reader lacks direct access to the composition in its earliest milieu, s/he must determine which assumptions and heuristic models will influence his/her reading of the Apocalypse.

Objective elements, in contrast, are optional for some readers. Each modern reader decides for him/herself the extent, if any, to which s/he should grapple with any theories regarding the authorial intention or probable early reader responses associated with the Apocalypse. To return to the previous example, Lindsay and Thompson share a twentieth century, North American vantage point but base their works on opposite propositions regarding the importance of the text's earliest cultural milieu for the development of a modern reader's understanding. These propositions define their respective positions on the objective-subjective continuum.

This essay lays the groundwork for a hybrid socio-literary strategy which emphasizes the seemingly contradictory subjective and objective aspects of a consciously cross-cultural reading of the Apocalypse. The essay begins with an exposition of a theory of genre which proposes the interpretation of written materials in terms of subjective, socially influenced understandings. The suggestion of a cross-cultural generic type and the classification of the

Apocalypse as an example of this type ensue. The essay concludes by describing the benefits and limitations of a particular type of political reading of the Apocalypse, a strategy based on the assumption that the earliest historical situations and social locations in which the text was read, as well as the words of the text, constitute important data for a worthwhile twentieth century reading. In this respect, the essay's social location is in the European and North American academic tradition of the past two centuries, exemplified by the work of Thompson in the example cited above.

An Eclectic Theory of Genre

What factors should a twentieth century reader take into account in order to produce a coherent, meaningful interpretation of the Apocalypse? The answer to this question constitutes a proposed genre for the Apocalypse, at least in broad, descriptive terms. The question itself, however, presupposes another, more basic issue: How is reading accomplished? In other words, before one may determine the genre of a particular work, s/he must produce a working definition of genre in general. This observation suggests a deductive format for the current essay. The current section describes the concept of genre, the next proposes a specific generic classification for the Apocalypse, and the final one discusses the ways in which the classification may inform the methodology used in the political analysis of the Apocalypse.

The concept of genre articulated here is based on five assumptions regarding reading strategy. The validity of these assumptions in combination is asserted and explained rather than argued; each one has its defenders among critics, but the combination produces a proposal which may not conform to any accepted literary model. The contribution of the assumptions to a model of genre construction which can be used beneficially to analyse the Apocalypse determines the viability of the assumptions and the model of which they are components; in other words, the test of the theory is the utility or lack thereof of its application to the Apocalypse.

The series of assumptions begins with the hypothesis that the relationship between a reader and an author, mediated by a text, includes both adversarial and cooperative aspects. W. Iser's view of the reader and the text as opposite poles in the process of literary communication (1978:ix) may be modified beneficially by the assertion of polarity between the author, rather than the text, and the reader. The text, then, becomes the medium of communication, the common element with which both the author and the reader must grapple. In the case of the Apocalypse, the spoken words of oral performances probably comprised a second layer of communication, modifying the text itself (1:3) for early audiences and allowing the reader to join the author as a creator of communication (cf. Aune's description of the copyist's role, 1991:143). However, this layer, unlike the written text and its history of transmission, is not accessible to modern audiences.

A text has the potential both to elucidate and to obscure its own interpretation. This internal polarity may be attributed primarily to the author's techniques. For example, an author may use plain narrative, discourse, logic, and a variety of other techniques to communicate his/her intentions clearly. Likewise, an author may conceal his/her intentions or suggest polyvalent interpretations of a text by using veiled references, circumlocutions, unusual imagery, and figures of speech. The frequent use of this second set of techniques in the Apocalypse promotes a diversity of interpretations.

A reader must respond to the cues which the author places in a text. When an author uses a relatively straightforward style, the reader may follow the cues easily and allow the text to lead him/her to the author's desired conclusion. When the author uses more confusing or polyvalent imagery, the reader must put forth a greater analytical effort to pry a defensible interpretation out of the text. In the first case, the relationship between author and reader is cooperative, with each party to the textual communication doing his/her part to bring about a desired outcome without a struggle. In the second, the relationship is more adversarial, since the reader must disassemble, see through, or resist the author's language in order to produce a coherent or reasonable interpretation. Of course, what constitutes a coherent or reasonable interpretation is determined by the standards of the reader and his/her peers, an entirely subjective process.

Many texts include a variety of smaller literary units. The gospels' constituent forms have been analyzed repeatedly (e.g., Bultmann, 1963), and the Apocalypse has been identified as a hybrid genre which includes differing constituent units (e.g., Linton, 1991:173-179). The variety of literary forms and conventions, including both epistolary and visionary frameworks and a number of prophecies, formulaic sayings, and other materials in the case of the Apocalypse, suggests that adversarial and cooperative reading strategies cannot be separated easily, with one or the other used in the reading of any given text; they must be used in conjunction to produce coherent interpretations of entire texts.

The determination of reading strategy by the author's use of language brings into play the second hypothesis regarding reading strategy. The author sets the ground rules for the game of reading, but the reader has the final word on interpretation. F. Jameson notes that "as texts free themselves more and more from an immediate performance situation, it becomes ever more difficult to enforce a given generic rule on their readers" and identifies the exclusion of undesirable responses as an important aspect of writing (1981:106-107). E. D. Hirsch, Jr. identifies the author's ground rules as the primary factors which identify any given response as valid or invalid (1967:200). His argument, however, assumes that a reader can identify the author's ground rules and use those rules to exclude undesirable responses.

The success with which an author communicates his/her intended degree of clarity or confusion depends substantially on the nature of the reader. A shared language, culture, perspective, and series of literary conventions increases the probability of a close correspondence between authorial intention and reader response. The lack of common elements, conversely, increases the probability of discrepancy between authorial intention and reader response.

The dissemination of a text entails the author's surrender of control over interpretation. Once a text enters the public domain, any reader is free to perform his/her own analysis and draw his/her own conclusions. A living author's opportunity to interpret his/her text is roughly equivalent to any other reader's opportunity to interpret the same text; for example, R. Crosman cites E. Pound's suggestion in 1916 of three possible interpretations of a short poem which he had written in 1914 (1980:150-151). The limitations on interpretation include the author's intention only when it is known and then only when the reader is a constituent of a community which values authorial intention as a vital criterion for acceptable interpretation.

The influence of the reader's community on the standards of acceptable interpretation suggests a third hypothesis regarding reading strategy. Even when reading is a silent and solitary activity, as it is currently (a point of dissimilarity between the first and the twentieth centuries [Achtemeier, 1990:3-27]), interpretation is a social endeavor. A reader draws conclusions in light of his/her community's body of common knowledge and standard practices. J. Leenhardt's comparison of the reading strategies used by a French and a Hungarian group for the same novels, one from each country, indicates that both groups interpreted the foreign novel in light of their own "national patterns of literary perception" and "unifying cultural schemes" (1980:223; cf. 214-219).

Whenever a particular reader's conclusions depart markedly from the accepted standards, either of the following processes of reconciliation may ensue: (1) the community exerts pressure, subtle or otherwise, on the reader to suppress his/her unusual interpretation or to conform to accepted standards, or (2) the community ultimately accepts the new interpretation and incorporates it into a new *status quo*. This characterization of interpretation could be incorporated into either T. Parsons' conservative (1977:5-7) or G. Theissen's conflict-oriented (1983:passim) view of social development.

The didactic method used by D. Bleich in his English literature classes illustrates the influence of social factors on interpretation. Bleich defends the primacy of subjective elements in interpretation and uses social control rather than his individual authority to limit the extent of controversial interpretations among his students, who are inexperienced, or at least young, readers. He bases his method on J. Piaget's theory regarding social control over the development of intelligence in general:

> The social group . . . plays the same role that the "population" does in genetics and consequently in instinct. In this sense, society is the supreme unit, and the individual can only achieve his own inventions and intellectual constructions insofar as he is the seat of collective interactions that are naturally dependent, in level and value, on society as a whole.
>
> (Piaget, 1971:369, as quoted in Bleich, 1978:29)

Bleich's process begins, of course, with readings of the assigned works. Such readings are followed by response statements from the students, and the negotiability of the response statements is determined by the needs of the class (1978:188-189). This process results in the development of accepted interpretations, possibly amenable to characterization as authoritative for the purposes of the class, by means of consensus. "Determining the negotiability of response statements is part of the communal definition of its purposes and part of the delineation of individual responsibility within the group" (1978:189). The revision of individual class members' responses to particular works, in light of social influences, is inherent in the learning process. The effect of encouragement to analyze authorial background and intention on one student's respose to a work by W. Joyce illustrates both the social aspects of interpretation and the reader's responsibility for the use of any criterion, including that of of authorial intention or original setting (Bleich, 1978:238-263).

The majority of the examples in Bleich's book convey the impression that Bleich's students are encouraged to emphasize the individual, psychological ramifications of their readings. This orientation is not normally associated with the academic analysis of ancient texts, but the hypothesis of social control over interpretation is applicable to such writings. Academic analysis occurs in accordance with a socially defined paradigm, as is discussed below, and social pressures influenced the development of texts of interest to scholars of several religious traditions. For example, both the development of the Christian canon, a process which nearly excluded the Apocalypse, and the Qumran community's composition of its own texts and deviant interpretation of well-known texts from its Jewish heritage may be understood as conscious, explicit social efforts to determine the limits of two religious communities' acceptable interpretations of their writings (cf. Thompson's concept of "public knowledge" vs. "deviant knowledge," 1990:181-185). The development of a corpus of legal literature by schools of thought descended from the pharisaic tradition, a process encompassing several centuries and culminating with the Babylonian Talmud, may be viewed as an especially long-lived and narrowly focused example of the development of a written corpus in terms of a socially defined paradigm.

The social influence on the development of guidelines for writing and interpretation suggests a fourth hypothesis of reading strategy. Interpretation depends largely on socially approved classification schemata. As described above, an author may or may not propose clear literary conventions to guide readers in the selection of appropriate criteria for interpretation (cf. Linton, 1991:165-166). However an author handles this matter, though, the reader, influenced by his/her social norms and peers, makes the final selection. The selection of heuristic criteria constitutes a *de facto* classification of the work; to paraphrase Linton, the construction of a generic identity allows a reader to interpret a text in terms of its similarities with selected other texts (1991:161, 166-167). Thus, genre is a social as well as a literary concept. The mutual influence of interpretation and conditions within a reader's group of peers suggest that *genre may be defined as the comparison of written works on the basis of socially validated criteria.*

In a relatively clear situation, F. Jameson's forensic, metaphorical description of genre summarizes the social dimensions of the literary comparison. According to this description, "genres are essentially literary *institutions*, or social contracts between a writer and a specified public, whose function is to specify the proper use of a particular cultural artifact" (1981:106, emphasis in original). To extend this metaphor in a different direction, however, the analogy of a social contract may be fraught with difficulties when a work lacks clear indications of literary convention or is read by a public which differs markedly from the one specified. To use literary jargon,

Jameson's dsecription of genre assumes that the actual reader is similar in key respects to some ideal or implied reader.

The interpretation of a text depends partially on the reader's decision regarding its genre, that is, the reader's selection of other works with which it should be compared. The author's intention regarding genre is important data which should inform the reader's interpretive method; this is the major point of Hirsch's influential work (1967:passim). However, in the absence of especially clear criteria, whatever is known of the author's intention is likely to provide no more than an indication of which possible genres are defensible and which are indefensible. A reader is responsible for his/her interpretation of any given text and must acknowledge the influence both of his/her own background and social location and of the available information about the author on that interpretation. This responsibility is particularly salient in the case of texts which are relatively "writerly" (Barthes, 1974:4-5) or "open" (Eco, 1979:49-50).

The fifth hypothesis of reading strategy is that a reader's generic assumptions regarding a particular text may be arranged hierarchically. To push T. L. Kent's journalistic example (1986:16-19) in a different direction, the following generic identifications, ranging from the most widely to the most narrowly focused, would be defensible for an editorial cartoon: a given number of newspaper column inches; a line drawing; a cartoon; an editorial cartoon; a statement of opinion; an interpretation of newsworthy events, institutions, or persons; and an interpretation of the newsworthy in the form of political satire, household hints, policy advocacy, or some other such category. Each of these types of comparison would meet the test of pragmatism, but each would push the reader towards a different basis of comparison and thus towards a different perspective from which to interpret the work. The hierarchical level at which the term "genre" becomes appropriate and the necessity of considering content, form, and function in the classification of literature as apocalyptic are discussed at length in D. Hellholm's essay (1986:14-33). D. Aune suggests that the otherwise problemmatical concept of a mixed genre might be a necessary factor in the comparison of seemingly apocalyptic texts which are smaller, self-contained units of larger written works (1986:79).

The variety of plausible generic identifications for any given text suggests that genre should be characterized in a manner analogous to taxonomy in the natural sciences. This observation suggests a cautionary note for a reader's formulation of generic assumptions. Living organisms are classified into families, phyla, genera, and species, with each grouping narrower than its predecessor; the nature of each grouping is determined by the number of types of organisms and the extent of the differences among organisms which it can include by definition. An organism belongs to a family, a genus, a phylum, and a species simultaneously, but a zoologist is likely to derive the most coherent conclusions by studying it only in terms of one level of comparison at a time. Hellholm proposes his "conceptual hierarchicalization," in contrast with taxonomy, to analyze smaller units within a text diachronically; within the context of his method, his caveat of the smaller literary units' sequence and interdependence (i.e., synchronic considerations) as major factors in the identification of the larger unit is salutary (1986:16).

In summary, genre, from a reader's perspective, is a system of literary classification in accordance with or reaction to accepted social standards. Objective factors, such as the nominal meaning of the words, whatever is known of the author's intention, and the earliest settings in which the text was read, are weighted in accordance with the reader's socially informed criteria. Genre, therefore, is a highly subjective concept; the viability of any given generic construction is determined by the utility of that construction for its proponents and the peers to whom they are accountable.

A Generic Identification of the Apocalypse

The Apocalypse is notable for its complex arrangement and unusual imagery. These factors, along with the previously mentioned cultural distance between the author/earliest readers and modern readers, pose obstacles for modern readings which strive toward a standard of consistency with probable authorial intention or early reader response. Such a standard is valued by academic readers, as exemplified by the favorable response to Hirsch's defense of the objective paradigm (1967). The selection of this type of paradigm over any other, of course, exemplifies the subjective elements which pervade interpretive decisions.

Within the context of academic concerns for interpretive authenticity, several points of departure are defensible. The Apocalypse includes a variety of cultic, economic, mythic, political, visionary, and other elements, any of which might be defensible as primary categories for a reading strategy. Among modern academic interpreters, T. Pippin (1987), A. Yarbro Collins (1985), E. Schüssler Fiorenza (1985), and L. Thompson (1990), to name only a few, have emphasized political aspects of the Apocalypse. In addition, the group for which this working paper is intended has requested a session on political readings of the Apocalypse for 1993. There is little doubt that the Apocalypse is susceptible to political readings within the constraints of academically rigorous interpretive paradigms and that attempts to formulate such readings enjoy a degree of social validation within the academic religious studies community.

The following analysis is cursory, suggestive, and hopefully informative for forthcoming political analyses of the Apocalypse. In accordance with the theory of genre articulated above, it is based on the following assumptions: (1) The Apocalypse is characterized by a potential for unclear and polyvalent responses; thus, adversarial elements are prominent in interpretive efforts. (2) Due to the differences between the first century liturgical and the twentieth century academic milieux, there is no implied contract between the author and modern readers regarding the proper use of the Apocalypse. The author is dead, so modern readers have sole responsibility for negotiating a new contract in accordance with their interpretive paradigms. Since authenticity is a major component of academic paradigms, all available data about probable authorial intention or early reader response is relevant to the new contract. (3) The selection of interpretive paradigms and the acceptance, modification, or rejection of proposed readings are artefacts of social pressure from the reader's peers, in this case, from other academic readers. (4) Any interpretation of the Apocalypse is influenced by the proposed classification of the work (cf. Rosmarin, 1985:23 ff.). This theoretical perspective clarifies the circularity and reductionism inherent in a political reading. The interpreter classifies the Apocalypse as a political treatise, emphasizes political elements in his/her reading, draws political conclusions from the reading, and, finally, includes political elements in any proposed generic description of the Apocalypse. (5) Generic descriptions of the Apocalypse can be arranged hierarchically. Any political reading leads to a generic description which neither excludes non-political readings nor necessitates the inclusion of political criteria in all levels of generic description.

The seer of the Apocalypse narrates the entire work from a consistent political perspective. After a brief introduction in which he identifies himself and the circumstances of his composition, he begins the Apocalypse proper with a narration of his first encounter with a being who is majestic beyond the scope of earthly reality (1:12-16). After the seer prostrates himself (1:17a), a traditional ritual of oriental courts, the being identifies himself as the risen one who lives forever (1:17b-18), that is, as the risen Christ since a Christian perspective is specified (1:4-5, 9-10). This initial characterization of the risen Christ as an oriental despot colors the politics of the entire Apocalypse.

After the letters to the seven churches of Asia Minor, the portrayal of the risen Christ as an oriental despot is carried out systematically. In a more comprehensive vision of the throne room, he is provided with 24 elders and four unusual living creatures as retainers, all of which prostrate themselves and acknowledge his honor (4:8-11). The imagery of a sea of glass, white clothes, golden crowns, incense, and sound effects provides additional material to aid the reader's visualization of an oriental throne room. The possibility of astronomic connotations for much of this imagery (Malina, 1992:45-48) both heightens the portrayal of the risen Christ's majesty (a political concept) and demonstrates the polyvalence of much of the imagery in the Apocalypse.

The throne room becomes the setting for the entire work. The despot's retainers reinforce his power by means of obeisance throughout the Apocalypse. Ascriptions of honor and power (e.g., 5:9-12, 7:10, 12:10-12, 15:3-4, 16,5-7) and songs of praise and thanksgiving (e.g., 5:13, 7:12, 11:17-18) are scattered throughout the work. These acclamations culminate with the songs of gloating over the fall of Babylon in chs. 18-19.

The seer describes the risen Christ as an oriental despot, not only in terms of physical trappings but also in terms of behavior. The risen Christ initiates conversation with the seer, orders him to send an account of his visions to seven churches in Asia Minor (1:10-11), and has an angel instruct him to conceal certain matters (10:8-11). The brief introductory letters themselves assume a form possibly recognizable as that of royal or imperial edicts with *praescriptiones, narrationes, dispositiones*, and, finally, *sanctiones* (Aune, 1990:204). The angels who initiate the numbered series of seven seals, trumpets, and vials, perform their responsibilities from the throne room and as agents of the risen Christ; the description of the effects of these curses on the earth and its inhabitants obscures this perspective only slightly.

The portrayal of the risen Christ as an oriental despot culminates with the destruction of "Babylon." He is portrayed as a brutally effective general, even to the point of denying his slain enemies proper burial, in 19:11-21. Finally, he renders judgement from a great white throne, vindicating his followers and consigning his enemies to the lake of fire on the basis of their inclusion in or exclusion from the book of life, the citizenship roll of his kingdom (21:11-15).

The despotism of Christ is identified with the Christian cultus throughout the Apocalypse. The acclamations mentioned above have connotations not only of political obeisance but also of worship. The incense in the throne room scene of chs. 4-5 is a metaphor for the prayers of the saints (5:8). As the fifth seal is opened, those executed for their political allegiance to the seer's version of Christianity are described as souls under the altar (6:9-11).

Cultic imagery from the Christian community's Jewish heritage identifies the despot and his supporters as the rightful successors to that particular religious tradition. The "servants of God" with the despot's brand on their foreheads are identified with the traditional twelve tribes of Israel (7:1-8). The measurement of the Jerusalem temple and the activity, murder, and vindication of the two cultic prophets (11:1-18) clear the way for the succeeding acts of the political power struggle (Kraft, 1974:160). The city itself is identified as the one in which their lord was crucified, named figuratively Sodom and Egypt (11:8), and given over to the heathen (11:2). After this episode, the temple of God in heaven is opened and the ark of the covenant appears to supplant the cultic center in Jerusalem.

The establishment of the new Jerusalem marks the complete merger of politics and cultus: "I saw no temple in her, for the Lord God almighty is her temple, and also the lamb" (21:22). In this respect, the seer's view of the unity of church and state typifies the common orientation of hellenistic culture. The privileges of sacrifice and worship corresponded to political status in many Greek city-states (Detienne, 1989:3-4). The concentric arrangement of the Jerusalem temple premises necessitated the validation of a cultic hierarchy which paralleled and reinforced the political hierarchy. The Qumran community established its conventicle, a dissident political entity, in order to legitimate a cultus which differed from that in Jerusalem (Webber, 1989:106-110). Pliny the Younger's forensic use of the imperial cultus constituted a political loyalty test for accused Christians in Bithynia about thirty years after the Apocalypse was written in an adjacent province (*Ep.* 2:287-289). This integrated view is similar to that of the seer, who identified Pergamum, the seat of the imperial cultus in Asia Minor, as the location of Satan's throne (2:13). Twentieth century American readers should remember that the first amendment was an innovation and that the seer's unitary view of politics and cultus is more typical both of ancient and of modern thought in Europe and the Middle East.

The Apocalypse attributes a coherent, thorough political program to its protagonist. Specifically, the seer ascribes the status of ruler of the entire cosmos to the deity. The antagonists, however, are described as multiple layers of opposition. The letters to the seven churches condemn the troublesome Jews in Smyrna and Philadelphia as the "synagogue of Satan" (2:9, 3:9), threaten internal discipline for Christians in Pergamum and

Thyatira (2:14-16, 2:20-25), refer eliptically to the imperial cultus in Pergamum (2:13), and mention one lynching or execution in the same verse. Ch. 13 seems to ridicule the imperial cultus, and chs. 17-19 parody the vast influence of the Roman economic system. The numbered seals, trumpets, and vials mark the beginning of generalized anathemata for the entire inhabited world, presumably identified as the Roman Empire and some adjacent regions. Chs. 12 and 20, in particular, are susceptible to interpretation in terms of myth (e.g., Yarbro Collins, 1976), and one commentator has noted not only political but also mythic elements in ch. 13 (Kraft, 1974:173-185). The lack of a unified polemic accords well with the conclusion of Yarbro Collins that Domitian did not instigate any systematic persecution of Christians in Asia Minor (1984:104), and with that of Thompson that Domitian did not demand an increase in the divine honors which the previously existing imperial cult was obligated to render (1990:107).

The opposition of the new Jerusalem to "Babylon" is sharpened to the point of a close analogy only in chs. 16-21 to bring the Apocalypse to the desired conclusion (Deutsch, 1987:123). The Apocalypse vilifies several opponents (or straw men?) but does not identify a single enemy as the focus of a sustained polemic. This technique allows the seer to use vilification selectively to reinforce the positive political program of the Apocalypse without assuming a life of its own.

The conclusion of the Apocalypse illustrates an explicit but equivocal approach to the concept of limited good (described in Malina, 1978). On one level, the struggle between the oriental despot and his enemies is a zero-sum game. The seer visualizes only total victory and total defeat as possible outcomes of the struggle depicted in his visions. On another level, however, the concept of limited good is abrogated. After the despot's total victory, the new heaven, earth, and Jerusalem are characterized as the sites of unlimited good for the victorious party. The city is of especially large dimensions and arranged symetrically—12,000 stadia high, long, and wide (21:15-16). The twelve traditional tribes of Israel and the twelve apostles are given prominent places in the city's public architecture (21:12-14). The foundations of the city walls are made of gemstones (21:19-21). The river and tree of life provide both reliable sustenance and a varied diet throughout the year (22:1-2). Most importantly, death itself is eliminated (21:4).

The preceding overview of the Apocalypse's setting and plot may be summarized as follows: The seer appeals to Christian audiences within a first century, eastern Mediterranean cultural milieu by describing their ultimate destiny in terms of a political model well-known from the behavior of Roman client kings throughout the region, despots in adjacent areas, and the reputations of their indigenous predecessors. He describes this model in terms of implementation which is successful beyond the scope of earthly possibility, with highly favorable consequences for the subjects of the new, figurative entity. The opposition, in contrast, is described in a less consistent fashion with the result that it functions as a foil to sharpen the description of the protagonist's political program.

The scope of the protagonist's program and the presence of thinly veiled political satire (e.g., chs. 13, 17) may suggest the imperial cultus and Roman economic policies as imperfect comparisons which intensify the depiction of perfection in the risen Christ's kingdom. To be sure, much of the anti-Roman material presents the empire as a parody of the kingdom (Webber, 1988:139-140). The comparisons are inadequate to be considered systematic but too obvious to be considered coincidental.

In summary, the Apocalypse narrates the establishment of the perfect political structure and the destruction of all others. This polity is described in terms of a culturally specific model which was familiar to first century audiences in Asia Minor. Thus, a reader with a political agenda must base his/her generic description of the Apocalypse on a comparison of that work with others concerned primarily with an ideal or perfect polity. Such works frequently are described as utopias, descriptions of "no place" or a "good place." As discussed below, utopian literature has a long history.

The Apocalypse as a Utopia

The generic identification of the Apocalypse as a utopia raises a host of troubling issues, all of which are related to the need or lack thereof for cultural specificity in literary theory. The term utopia, the title of a work by T. More, entered the language as a generic term after other political works were compared with that of More; in this respect, its history is comparable to that of the generic term apocalypse. However, by using a generic descriptor from the English Renaissance to classify a text from the Roman imperial era, we define the utopian genre broadly by comparing subject matter and approach with little regard for the cultural compatability of the texts under consideration. The social sciences can appeal either to cross-cultural application or to cultural specificity to validate their heuristic models. Obviously, literary theory can appeal to cultural specificity; this tendency is a prominent component of all academically rigorous attempts to define the apocalyptic genre (e.g., Bousset's definition, 1906:3). Whether or not literary theory can appeal to cross-cultural application to create generic definitions narrow enough to be useful is uncertain.

One may validate the utopia as a cross-cultural generic model by arguing that both literary and political theory are sub-categories of social theory. As discussed above, a utopia is a concrete proposal for a new political *status quo,* so it can be realized or rejected only in a political arena on some level. In other words, a utopia is a work of political propaganda. Politics, of course, is the maintenance of prescribed social relationships among concentrations of people; such activity assumes culturally specific forms (cf. Lenski, 1984, Weber, 1978) but occurs whenever and wherever humans congregate. Thus, one may perform political analysis either from culturally specific or from cross-cultural perspectives, depending on the desired type of information and level of abstraction.

If one reads the Apocalypse as a utopia, s/he must compare it to literature in a long, culturally diverse tradition. The reader might start with Plato's *Republic,* continue with Virgil's *Aeneid* (admittedly, a conservative distortion of the utopian comparison) and fourth Eclogue, skip to More's *Utopia,* look at the European utopias of the eighteenth and nineteenth centuries, and complete the survey with Orwell's dystopias. Such an analysis might clarify the position and techniques of the seer as utopist (cf. Bleich, 1984:31), facilitate the development of a general model of political rhetoric, and thus emphasize the unique aspects of each of the utopias mentioned above. In other words, the utopia is defined primarily in terms of function and secondarily in terms of form.

The comparative method described above is notable for its avoidance of Jewish and Christian works from the same chronological period as the Apocalypse. Such works, to be accounted for in a second level of comparison, might include the Hebrew scriptures cited frequently in the Apocalypse (especially Daniel, Ezekiel, and Isaiah), the apocalypses analysed in Semeia 14 and 36, IQM and IQS, and Aune's culture as intertext (1991:142). This level of comparison would facilitate the analysis of the Apocalypse's political program within the context of its own cultural milieu and might provide a suitable framework for a commentary which builds upon Malina's work by analysing the contribution of the astronomical perspective to the promulgation of the Apocalypse's political program; Malina's commentary hints at such a possibility (1992:4). The anthropological theories which SBL social sciences group popularized during the 1980s are useful as checks on the potential excesses of cross-cultural analysis. In other words, culturally specific investigation is a necessary adjunct to cross-cultural comparison for a utopia. One level of comparison facilitates macro-analysis, and the other micro-analysis.

The Apocalypse is a product of a culture familiar with metaphysical dualism but without a clear concept of the distant future (Malina, 1992:15-16). Thus, its political proposal was as specific and this-worldly to its audience as were those of A. Smith and of K. Marx and F. Engels to nineteenth century audiences. Both of the latter utopias, were implemented internationally with the result that they currently are regarded as *faits accomplis*.

One may accept K. Mannheim's definition of utopian thought, which emphasizes its discontinuity with the *status quo* (1936:40), or Jameson's critique, which emphasizes the roots of utopian thought in class solidarity (1981:281-299). In the case of the Apocalypse, the text is both a political proposal for a break with the status quo and a circular letter from a writer to a group of churches from which he expected some degree of loyalty. The letters to the seven churches are simultaneously edicts from the risen Christ (the ruler of the proposed utopian kingdom) and circular letters from an absent elder to actual churches. The way in which the reader sets up the generic comparison necessarily influences the conclusions which s/he makes regarding the polity advocated in the Apocalypse.

In conclusion, the Apocalypse may be read as a utopia not because it belongs naturally in that category but because modern academic readers may find the comparison informative. Utopia, like apocalyptic, is a modern generic construction (cf. Schüssler Fiorenza, 1985:150) and is useful for the comparison of ideal and worst-case political states ranging from the proposals of Plato to those of Orwell. Thus, culturally specific models must serve as a check on the potential excesses of a cross-cultural generic construction. This proposal is presented as a working paper rather than as a polished article with the intention of stimulating further discussion of the types of comparison best suited to advance the analysis of the political perspective of the Apocalypse.

Works Cited

Achtemeier, P. (1990). "*Omne Verbum Sonat:* The New Testament and the Oral Environment of Late Western Antiquity." *JBL*, 109/1, 3-27.

Aune, D. E. (1986). "The Apocalypse of John and the Problem of Genre." *Semeia: An Experimental Journal for Biblical Criticism*, 36, 65-96.

_____ (1990). "The Form and Function of the Proclamations to the Seven Churches," *NTS*, 36, 182-204.

_____ (1991). "Intertextuality and the Genre of the Apocalypse." SBLSP 30, 142-160.

Barthes, R. (1974). *S/Z*, tr. R. Miller. New York: Hill & Wang.

Bleich, D. (1978). *Subjective Criticism.* Baltimore/London: Johns Hopkins Univ.

_____ (1984). *Utopia: The Psychology of a Cultural Fantasy.* Studies in Speculative Fiction 5; Ann Arbor, MI: University Microfilms International Research Press.

Boussett, W. (1906). *Die Offenbarung Johannis*, 6. aufl., Kritische-exegetischer Kommentar über das Neue Testament; Göttingen: Vandenhoeck & Ruprecht.

Bultman, R. K. (1963). *History of the Synoptic Tradition*, tr. J. Marsh. New York/Hagerstown/San Francisco/London: Harper & Row.

Crosman, R. (1980). "Do Readers Make Meaning?" S. R. Suleiman & I. Crosman, eds. *The Reader in the Text: Essays on Audience and Interpretation.* Princeton, NJ: Princeton Univ., pp. 149-164.

Detienne, M. (1986). "Culinary Practices and the Spirit of Sacrifice." M. Detienne & J.-P. Vernant, eds. *The Cuisine of Sacrifice among the Greeks*, tr. P. Wissing. Chicago: Univ. of Chicago, pp. 1-20.

Deutsch, C. (1987). "Transformation of Symbols: The New Jerusalem in Rv 21:1-22:5," *ZNW* 78, 106-126.

Eco, U. (1979). "The Poetics of the Open Work," in *The Role of the Reader: Explorations in the Semiotics of Texts.* Bloomington, IN: Indiana Univ.

Gager, J. (1975). *Kingdom and Community: The Social World of Early Christianity.* Englewood Cliffs, NJ: Prentice-Hall.

Hellholm, D. (1986). "The Problem of Apocalyptic Genre and the Apocalypse of John." *Semeia: An Experimental Journal for Biblical Criticism*, 36, 13-64.

Hirsch, E. D., Jr. (1967). *Validity in Interpretation.* New York/London: Yale Univ.

Iser, W. (1978). *The Act of Reading: A Theory of Aesthetic Response.* Baltimore/London: Johns Hopkins.

Jameson, F. (1981). *The Political Unconscious: Narrative as a Socially Symbolic Act.* Ithaca, NY: Cornell Univ.

Kent, T. L. (1986). *Interpretation and Genre: The Role of Generic Perception in the Study of Narrative Texts.* Lewisburg, PA: Bucknell Univ.

Kraft, H. (1974). *Die Offenbarung des Johannes.* HNT; Tübingen: J. C. B. Mohr (Paul Siebeck).

Leenhardt, J. (1980). "Towards a Sociology of Reading," tr. B. Navelet & S. R. Suleiman. *The Reader in the Text: Essays on Audience and Interpretation,* ed. S. R. Suleiman & I. Crosman. Princeton, NJ: Princeton Univ.

Lenski, G. (1984). *Power and Privilege: A Theory of Social Stratification.* Chapel Hill, NC: Univ. of North Carolina.

Lindsey, H. & Carlson, C. C. (1970). *The Late Great Planet Earth.* Grand Rapids, MI: Zondervan.

Linton, G. (1991). "Reading the Apocalypse as an Apocalypse." SBLSP 30, 161-186.

Malina, B. J. (1978). "Limited Good and the Social World of Early Christianity." *BTB* 8/4, 162-176.

_____ (1992). *A Commentary on the Book of Revelation: Astral Prophecy.* Copyrighted material released on floppy disk; pagination variable based on computer formatting.

Mannheim, K. (1936). *Ideology and Utopia: An Introduction to the Sociology of Knowledge,* tr. L. Wirth & E. Shils. San Diego/New York/London: Harcourt Brace Jovanovich.

Parsons, T. (1977). *The Evolution of Societies,* ed. J. Toby. Englewood Cliffs, NJ: Prentice-Hall.

Piaget, J. (1971). *Biology and Knowledge,* tr. B. Walsh. Edinburgh: Edinburgh Univ., 1971.

Pippin, T. (1987). "Political Reality and the Liberating Vision: The Context of the Book of Revelation." Ph.D. diss., Southern Baptist Theological Seminary, Lousiville, KY.

Rosmarin, A. (1985). *The Power of Genre.* Minneapolis, MN: Univ. of Minnesota.

Schüssler Fiorenza, E. (1985). *The Book of Revelation: Justice and Judgement.* Philadelphia: Fortress.

Theissen, G. (1983). "Theoretische Probleme religions- soziologischer Forschung und die Analyse des Urchristentums." Studien zur Soziologie des Urchristentums, 2. aufl. WUNT; Tübingen: J. C. B. Mohr (Paul Siebeck), pp. 55-76.

Thompson, L. L. (1990). *The Book of Revelation: Apocalypse and Empire.* New York/Oxford: Oxford Univ.

Webber, R. C. (1988). "Group Solidarity in the Revelation of John." SBLSP 27, 132-140.

_____ (1989). "An Analysis of Power in the Jerusalem Church in Acts." Ph.D. diss., Southern Baptist Theological Seminary, Louisville, KY.

Weber, M. (1968). *Economy and Society: An Outline of Interpretive Sociology,* tr. E. Fischoff, H. Gerth, A. M. Henderson, T. Parsons, et al. Berkeley/Los Angeles/London: Univ. of California, 2 vols.

Yarbro Collins, A. (1976). *The Combat Myth in the Book of Revelation.* Harvard Dissertations in Religion 9; Missoula, MT: Scholars.

_____ (1984). *Crisis and Catharsis: The Power of the Apocalypse.* Philadelphia: Westminster.

_____ (1985). "Insiders and Outsiders in the Book of Revelation and Its Social Context." *"To See Ourselves as Others See Us": Christians, Jews, "Others" in Late Antiquity,* ed. J. Neusner & E. S. Frerichs. Scholars Press Studies in the Humanities; Chico, CA: Scholars.

Help for Interpreting Jesus' Exorcisms

Paul W. Hollenbach
Iowa State University

Introduction

When I first began to study Jesus' exorcisms over a decade ago, I was surprised in several ways: 1) Most startling was the meager attention scholars had given to the exorcism stories. In the six most popular works on Jesus one gave one page, three gave three pages, and two gave 18 and 25 pages to exorcisms, while none made any effort to integrate Jesus' exorcisms into his whole career. This situation still reigns for the most part. The new Anchor Bible Dictionary has only a short article on demons, nothing on demoniacs, or exorcists, and only a tiny bit on Jesus' exorcisms. It seems beliefs, ideas are much more important than persons and actions. 2) Until very recently biblical scholars made little or no use of anthropological studies of illness and healing, including possession and exorcism, in indigenous cultures, despite the insights these studies provide for situations such as ancient Palestine. This medical anthropology not only helps us to focus on the persons involved, but shows us the larger cultural context including the familial and political settings. This source of insight also helps us to cure two of the diseases of modern scholarship: ethnocentrism, expressed, e.g., in the focus on the problem of the miraculous, and logocentrism, expressed, e.g., in the focus on beliefs about demons.

Since the N.T. and especially Jesus, came out of ancient Middle Eastern culture, we need to become at home in that culture as much as possible so as to avoid ethnocentrism and achieve the best possible interpretation of the texts. The following ways are suggestions for reaching these goals.

If we haven't already, we need to experience culture shock ("shock of the other," Maybury-Lewis, *Millennium*) at least once in our lives so as to become existentially aware of cultural differences. Some ways to achieve this are: 1) read non-scientific books that express, or provide a basis for culture shock. Examples: Sue Bender, *Plain and Simple* (Amish); Bapsi Sidhwa, *The Bride* (Pakistani mountain people). 2) See movies or videos for this purpose. Examples: Zorba the Greek (Mediterranean village life). Bono Medicines (traditional medicine in Ghana). 3) Visit other cultures, even in one's own country or neighborhood. Examples: ethnic communities, Jewish, Hispanic, etc. 4) Live in other cultures for a while, preferably of course in Middle Eastern areas such as Israel, Jordan, Syria, etc. Examples: Chilean economist,

Manfred A. Max-Neef, deep personal crisis; Kenneth E. Bailey, gradual intellectual "conversion."

These first or second hand experiences should prepare one existentially for more formal routes to an alien culture provided by social sciences, especially anthropology. Examples: Ted C. Lewellen, *Political Anthropology: An Introduction* (Bergin and Garvey, 1983); Peter Farb and George Armelagos, *Consuming Passions: The Anthropology of Eating* (Houghton Mifflin, 1980); David D. Gilmore, "Anthropology of the Mediterranean Area" (*Ann. Rev. Anthropol.* 1982, 11:175-205); Gilmore, ed. *Honor and Shame and the Unity of the Mediterranean* (American Anth. Assn. No. 22, 1987); the movie, *Kypseli* (Greek village life).

Then one can begin to use these studies for understanding the "strange new world of the Bible." The classic in this area is Bruce J. Malina's, *The New Testament World: Insights from Cultural Anthropology* (John Knox, 1981). Some more recent examples: Jerome H. Neyrey, ed., *The Social World of Luke-Acts* (Hendrickson, 1992); Carolyn Osiek, *What are they Saying About the Social Setting of the New Testament* (rev. ed.; Paulist, 1992), and Kenneth E. Bailey, *Finding the Lost: Cultural Keys to Luke 15* (Concordia, 1992).

Finally, we can use more specific studies of illness and healing, in which area possession and exorcism fall. There are some films such as *Legacy of the Spirits, The Spirit Possession of Alejandro Mamani*, and the film mentioned above, *Bono Medicines*. There are many anthropological studies such as Peter Worsley, "Non-Western Medical Systems," *Ann. Rev. of Anth.* 1982: 11:315-48, and Allen Young, "The Anthropology of Illness and Sickness," *Ann. Rev. of Anth.* 1982: 11:257-85. See also the articles by John Pilch listed in *The Social World of Luke-Acts*, with their bibliographies. His 1985 article, "Healing in Mark: A Social Scientific Analysis," *Bib. Theol. Bul.* XV: 142-150 is especially helpful.

Anthropology focuses on the cultural dimension of human life. As in all social sciences there are differences and disagreements among anthropologists as to methods of study and terminology. However, most would agree that the first and basic aim is to produce as unbiased *descriptions* of cultures as possible, *ethnography*, with the emphasis on *-graphy*. The aim is to let the "natives' point of view" emerge as authentically as possible, so that "otherness" rules. The second aim is understanding as deeply and comprehensively as possible particular cultures and culture in general using our Western cultural categories of *explanation, ethnology*, with the emphasis on *logy*. The aim is to provide as comprehensive rational explanations as possible so that a science of humanity may be developed. In this connection it may be appropriate to warn against a too direct use of the term "explanation" in describing non-Western cultures. What to us may appear as an explanation (e.g., of creation) most likely is simply an expression or narrative description. Explanation is predominantly a Western cultural category.

Some anthropologists would include in this science the "natural science" of neurobiology in order to find a genetic neurobiological basis of such culture phenomena as possession, etc. I myself find such efforts of little *social* scientific significance and will not include them in this essay.

I. The Contribution of Anthropology

Most important is that medical anthropology indicates that in ancient Mediterranean culture there was no focus or scientific accounts of illness. Indeed, there were no diseases in the modern biomedical sense. There were only what we may call "illnesses" seen in the setting of family and the larger society, i.e., the political realm. All aspects of life were subsumed under these two social institutions.

Ethnography of Demoniacs

We will focus here mainly on demon possession, not on other forms of possession such as ecstasy and trance in individual or social forms. Demon possession takes place within the context of the cosmology of good and evil spirits familiar to most Bible readers. Now what is the situation of those possessed by evil spirits, i.e., demons? To try to answer this question we can use our own observations of demoniacs in the New Testament and other contemporary literature as well as the relevant descriptions provided by cultural anthropologists. In all of our efforts we should notice and remember the social reality of demoniacs as so wonderfully expressed by a character in Faulkner's novel, *As I Lay Dying*: "It's like it ain't so much what a fellow does, but it's the way the majority of folks is looking at him when he does it."

Thus, illness could occur when family members or social leaders recognize another "self" in a person different from his/her usual self. In cultures where angels and demons are a part of the ideology, this other self could be seen as the presence (invasion) of either an angel or a demon (a good or evil spirit) in that "possessed" person. If the person involved were politically significant, i.e., had an impact on the larger society, he/she could be seen as possessed by either a good or evil spirit. Both John the Baptizer and Jesus were such persons and both were accused of being possessed by demons because from the point of view of the authorities their new character was seen as threatening.

So how is a demoniac identified, singled out, in the N.T.?" First of all he/she has a radically divided selfhood. There is a conflict of minds in most demoniacs. Thus, the demoniac at Capernaum refers to himself as both "us" and "I" (Mark 1:24; cf. 5:17-13). The demons are both separate from but also the self of a person. This new dimension of a person's self is also manifested in the separation of a demoniac from his normal social relations as seen so graphically in the Gerasene demoniac. The new self exists in a new social relationship, one of ostracism.

Secondly, the fundamental social character of demon possession leads to another basis of identity. The strange behaviors of the Gerasene (extreme strength, howling, etc.) apparently defined him for his community as not normal or "sane." Any even mildly different behavior can indicate the presence of demons. While the Gerasene is an extreme case, other less extreme behaviors lead to seeing the presence of demons. Josephus says that King Saul was overcome by strange disorders and demons which brought suffocation and strangling upon him (*Ant.* VI: 166). Even following a different diet such as John the Baptizer did (no bread or wine) can elicit accusations of demon possession. Other manifestations of demons were loss of speech (Matt 9:32; Mark 9:17), sight (Matt 12:22), or hearing (Mark 9:25). So, to put Faulkner's works into more academic style: whether or not a person is demon-possessed "depends on the degree to which his behavior is disturbed, and the attitudes of the members of his social group towards deviant behavior" (Rosen: 90).

This conclusion leads to several other observations with regard to identifying demoniacs. Hardly ever is a reason or cause given for demon possession. It seems simply to have been accepted or not even thought about. Also, similar behaviors can be seen as the presence of demons or not connected to demons at all, or even caused by God. Thus muteness at one time is seen as a demon (Luke 11:14) but at another even as the presence of God (Luke 1:20, 22, 64). Jesus heals both a blind demoniac (Matt 12:22) and other blind people who apparently are not seen as demon possessed (Luke 7:21, 22). It can be said however that generally the more active illnesses such as shrieking, convulsing, foaming, etc. are directly attributed to demons, while the more passive illness such as barrenness, blindness, fever, paralysis, etc. are not connected with demons.

The life situation of demoniacs has already begun to be noted. Basic is that we are looking at a "socialist," i.e., communitarian society, not an individualistic one as in our modern world. This means that always other people are involved with the demoniac. This is especially prominent in the case of the Gerasene who was ostracized by, yet continued to draw the involvement of the citizens of his home city. A demoniac's family would be most directly concerned so that they often continued to live at home under the care of family members (Mark 7:24-30; 9:14-29, 1:32). This was also a class stratified society so that wealthy demoniacs received better professional care (Luke 8:3; Rosen: 64, 89) than the poverty stricken (Luke 8:27 Rosen: 98, 125-35). Sometimes the latter were regarded with fear, contempt,. ridicule, scorn, abuse, and very little compassion (Rosen: 88). Also, less obnoxious demoniacs were present in public places such as synagogues (Rosen: 64: Mark 1:21-23, Philo, *Contra Flaccum*, 36-39).

It is easy to imagine how in this situation there was a widespread, often desperate search for successful healers (e.g., Mark 1:32-34; 3:7-12), for failure was common (Mark 9:18, *Ant.* VIII:47). And there were numerous healers (Mark 9:38-41; Matt. 12:27; *Ant.* VI: 166; Rosen: 68), some of whom were itinerants, Jesus among them (Mark 1:39; Luke 9:1-6; Acts 19:13). They practiced and taught arts of healing (*Ant.* VIII: 45-49; Rosen: 69; Böcher 168-82; Mark 6:7). Among them were sorcery (Matt. 9:34), magic (*Jewish War* VII: 185), spells (*Ant. VIII*:45, 47), and the use of names (Mark 9:38). In this way the exorcist uses a variety of powerful forces (including colors and smells) and begins to gain control over, and command the demons. There was also competition between healers (Mark 9:38-41). The exorcism itself was very dramatic, a terrifying struggle between opponents (Mark 1:24, 26; 9:20, 26).

Understandable reactions to exorcisms were observers' amazement (Mark 1:27), and the exorcised persons' attachment to the healer (Mark 5:18; Luke 8:2). That exorcists should sometimes be feared and rejected is surprising

(Mark 5:17; 6:10-11). This of course was the case with Jesus who was slandered by the scribes and Pharisees (Mark 3:22).

What happened to demoniacs? One of two things: 1) They were generally excluded from family and the larger society. This happened to the Gerasene demoniac who was expelled from town and forced to live in a cemetery. It also happened to John and Jesus who were both hounded by the authorities and finally eliminated, i.e., assassinated. 2) The other possibility is that the demoniacs were healed, i.e., restored to their old self, by a healer, i.e., an exorcist. This exorcist had power over demons and could control them in various ways. Their basic power was to expel the demon from the possessed person. This act was seen by those related to the exorcised person with wonder and gratitude. This reaction was characteristic in the case of Jesus' exorcisms, except on the part of the authorities. Their hostile reaction calls for special notice and explanation. We can move to this explanation by noting next how anthropologists understand possession in certain social settings, in particular the situation of oppressive colonization, a situation very similar to first century Palestine.

Ethnology of Demoniacs and Exorcists

There are personal as well as social dimensions to possession and exorcism; however social tensions are most apparent. Social class antagonisms, the eroding of traditions where conflicts of interpretation appear, and colonial domination and resistance are some examples (Lewis: 35, ch. 3; Kiev: 25, 135-7, 204-5, 236, 248, 262-3, 339, 343, 364-83, 433, 445-6, 456-8; Bourguignon: ch. 3, and 53-4). The conflict between Jesus and the social authorities, and the demons(s) named "Legion," would be examples in Jesus' life.

Possession is often a form of oblique protest against, or escape from oppressions. The man possessed by "Legion" is such an example. Anthropologists have noted this mode of adjustment in widely diverse communities. In Muslim countries economically depressed women use shaman-led possession as a "means of insinuating their interests and demands in the face of male constraint" (Lewis: 79). This kind of "oblique redressive strategy"(88) does not disturb the social system. Especially "in a rigid social structure, where individuals have little . . . control over their daily activities, possession . . . is more likely to occur" (Bourguignon: 31). This was the case in Haiti where possession "protest cults" were very likely to occur, since there was a sharp "differentiation between a small elite and the masses" (32). Some call this form "salvation by possession" and "a weapon against humiliation and despair" (Wallace: 143-4; J. P. Sartre, in Fanon: 19).

If this form of possession is a strategy of the weak masses of society for finding some, to be sure, circuitous sense of self, then the other side of this coin are accusations of demon possession and witchcraft by the elite against the many as a means of social control. While the weak seek "salvation by possession," the strong seek "salvation by ostracism," especially again in times of social unrest (Bourguignon: 53; Rosen: 5-17). "Witchcraft and sorcery accusations . . ., representing . . . more drastic and direct lines of attack, often seek to sunder unbearably tense relationships . . . For witchcraft accusations represent a distancing strategy which seeks to discredit, sever, and deny links. . ." (Lewis: 121). Leading shamans (exorcists) are often "singled out for attacks and denunciation as witches," especially those "who in assuming a positive, active, and above all, militant role are indeed in danger of exceeding the bounds of tolerance. . . They are held in check by accusations of witchcraft which seem designed to discredit them and to diminish their status" (Lewis: 122).

II. Jesus the Exorcist: Christography

Jesus was a zealous exorcist. He not only practiced exorcism himself but he organized a team of exorcists. His repeated exorcisms exposed the situation of oppression because so many cases of possession were passive forms of accommodation to oppression acceptable to the elites. So when Jesus destroyed these accommodations via exorcism, he brought out into public consciousness and expression what everyone knew about but was afraid to face up to.

This is classically expressed in the case of the Gerasene demoniac.

In the first place, I believe he represents demon possession as an "oblique aggressive strategy" (Lewis:32), as "a regression in the service of the self" (Bourguignon:34), i.e., as at once both an illness and a cure (Fanon:290). For this demoniac is able to "give the Romans the devil" by identifying their legions, probably the most visible Roman presence to him, with demons (Brown:78-79). However, he is able to do that only obliquely, through madness. It is likely that the tension between his hatred for his oppressors and the necessity to repress this hatred in order to avoid dire recrimination drove him mad. But his very madness permitted him to do in a relatively socially acceptable manner what he could not do as sane, namely, express his total hostility to the Romans; he did this by identifying the Roman legions with demons. His possession was thus at once both the result of oppression and an expression of his resistance to it. He retreated to an inner world where he could symbolically resist Roman domination.

In the next place, we note that his accommodation was accepted by his community, within certain limits, of course. His violence, reflecting perhaps the militaristic context of his illness, had to be dealt with. Thus, he was at first bound, but when that failed he was ostracized to the inhospitable cemetery. In all respects the status quo was preserved by the demoniac's community authorities—until Jesus came along and disturbed it by healing the man.

Jesus' disruption of the prevailing accommodation is indicated especially by one of the more puzzling aspects of the story, namely, the fear of some of the townspeople, which is manifested in their request to Jesus that he get out of their neighborhood. Perhaps we can account for this response, which seems not to be directly connected to the loss of the 2,000 swine (or is this another slur on the legions? "They are swine!"), by suggesting that Jesus' healing of the demoniac brought the man's and the neighborhood's hatred of the Romans out into the open, where the result could be disaster for the community. The man had been transformed by Jesus from a passive "Uncle Tom" into a threatening "John Brown." Jesus appears as an outside troublemaker whom the locals wish would get out of town and never show up again.

Now, is it possible that Jesus' exorcising activity as a whole can be understood in terms of this pattern? This appears to be the case, since he is said to come into conflict with the two most important Galilean authorities (the Pharisees and Herod) in connection with his exorcising activity. That the Pharisees take particular notice of Jesus as an exorciser is indicated by their accusation that as an exorciser he practices witchcraft and is himself a demoniac (Mark 3:22).

However, there seem to be other reasons as well for the authorities' hostility to Jesus. First, Jesus *interpreted* exorcisms differently from the Pharisees and was thus regarded as a deviant. Jesus not only explicitly stated that exorcisms are the central act of God in the world (Luke 11:20), but he also sent out his followers on an exorcising mission (Mark 3:14-15), which also indicates the central importance he attached to exorcisms. Jesus' interpretation constituted a radical transformation of the values held by the Pharisees. They were conservatives who focused narrowly on doing God's will in everyday life. This permitted them to escape confronting directly the terrifying social conditions and issues of their day. They were ready to pay not only taxes but total allegiance to Caesar in exchange for maintaining their privileged place in Galilean society. They were willing, naturally, to practice a kind of genteel medicine that included intermittent exorcising. But to focus on exorcising (and as well as other kinds of healing) as a major form of action was not within their purview, probably because they recognized, even if they refused to face up to, the connection between the illnesses of their time and the unjust colonial social system of which they were an integral, privileged part. Thus, Jesus' exorcising activity must have appeared to them as an independent countercultural move which would ultimately be a threat to their social position. If a fair number of healed demoniacs were like the Gerasene demoniac, this would have exacerbated the relation between Jesus and the Pharisees. So they moved against him.

The other important Galilean authority with whom Jesus came into conflict in connection with exorcising was Herod Antipas (Luke 13:31-33). Jesus' response to the news that Herod wanted to kill him ("Behold, I cast out demons and perform cures today and tomorrow") shows both that exorcising continued to be Jesus' central activity and that it was because of this specific kind of activity that Herod moved against Jesus. It is significant, too, that some (apparently friendly) Pharisees were the ones who warned Jesus about Herod's threat. The preceding argument has shown that they were vitally concerned with Jesus as an exorcist. On the part of those hostile to Jesus, that concern could very well have spilled over to Herod. At that moment, however, some Pharisees friendly to Jesus deserted their normal stance and warned Jesus of the plot against him. The involvement of Herod was probably stimulated by the expansion of Jesus' movement into political significance, known as the "mission of the twelve" (Mark 3:13-15). The disciples spread out through Galilee, doing and preaching the same things as Jesus. This activity appeared to Herod and others to be similar to John the Baptizer's movement and to be, similarly, a threat to Herod's position and security (Mark 6:14-16).

Thus, once again we find a public authority responding hostilely to Jesus specifically in connection with his exorcising activity because that activity threatened to upset the social and political status quo in relation to demoniacs and other debased persons. It was all right to have numerous demoniacs of various kinds filling various niches of the social system, and it was all right for professional exorcists to ply their art; but it was not all right for an unauthorized exorcist to make so much over demon possession and demoniacs that he identified their healing with God's saving presence and led a widespread exorcising mission that attracted a large following, thereby challenging the prevailing social system and its underlying value system. If Josephus' description of Palestine during Jesus' time is correct—that it was relatively free of public disturbances—this condition would make Jesus' movement all the more exceptional, visible, and threatening. Such a challenge had to be met head on and its leader liquidated. Thus it was that Jesus as an exorcist struck out directly into the vortex of the social tensions of his day and before long became a public figure of sufficient stature that at first local, and finally national, authorities had to take account of his movement. Jesus' movement would threaten to effect the release of the smoldering discontent which appeared more and more until its final explosion in 66-70 C.E. In this way, then, Jesus' first exorcism led inevitably to his crucifixion.

Conclusion

Through the use of various kinds of modern social-scientific studies especially anthropology, it has been possible to suggest a more indigenous description of Jesus' exorcisms, and to propose a solution to the problem of Jesus' conflict with public authorities over his exorcising activities. Because demon possession and exorcism were integral parts of the social structure and manifested in important ways its dominant value of *social stability*, when Jesus disrupted this structure by countering it through his exorcisms with his own dominant value of *social healing*, conflict between Jesus and the public authorities was inevitable. Jesus became a militant exorcist, or in biblical terms, an activist prophetic disturber of the peace. (Rosen: 59-64).

Selected Bibliography

Böcher, Otto.

   1976   *Dämonenfurcht und Dämonenabwehr: Ein Beitrag zur Vorgeschichte der christlichen Taufe* (Beiträge zur Wissenschaft vom Alten und Neuen Testament, Fünfte Folge, Heft 10). Stuttgart: Kohlhammer.

Bourguignon, Erika.

   1976   *Possession.* San Francisco: Chandler and Sharp.

Brown, John P.

1976 "Techniques of Imperial Control: The Background of the Gospel Event." In Gottwald, 1976:73-83.

Case, Shirley J.

 1923 "Art of Healing in Early Christian Times." *Journal of Religion* 3:238-55.

Crossan, John Dominic.

 1991 *The Historical Jesus: The Life of a Mediterranean Jewish Peasant.* Harper.

Fanon, Frantz.

 1963 *The Wretched of the Earth.* New York: Ballantine.

Geertz, Clifford.

 1976 *The Religion of Java.* Chicago: University of Chicago Press.

Gilmore, David D., ed.

 1987 *Honor and Shame and the Unity of the Mediterranean.* American Authr. Assn. no. 22.

Gorkin, Michael.

 1991 *Days of Honey, Days of Onion: The Story of a Palestian Family in Israel.* Beacon.

Gottwald, Norman, ed.

 1976 *The Bible and Liberation: Political and Social Hermeneutics.* San Francisco: Community for Religious Research and Education.

Kee, Howard Clark.

 1986 *Medicine, Miracle and Magic in New Testament Times.* Cambridge.

Kiev, Ari, ed.

 1964 *Magic, Faith, and Healing: Studies in Primitive Psychiatry Today.* New York: Free Press.

Lewellen, Ted C.

 1983 *Political Anthropology: An Introduction.* Bergin & Garvey.

Lewis, I. M.

 1971 *Ecstatic Religion: An Anthropological Study of Spirit Possession and Shamanism.* Baltimore: Penguin.

Maybury-Lewis, David.

 1992 *Millennium: Tribal Wisdom and the Modern World.* Viking.

Neyrey, Jerome, ed.

 1991 *The Social World of Luke-Acts.* Hendrickson.

Oesterreich, T. K.

1966 *Possession: Demoniacal and Other Among Primitive Races, in Antiquity, the Middle Ages, and Modern Times.* New Hyde Park: University Books.

Rosen, George.

1968 *Madness in Society: Chapters in the Historical Sociology of Mental Illness.* University of Chicago Press.

Sidhwa, Bapsi.

1983 *The Bride.* St. Martins.

Ward, Colleen A., & Beaubrun, Michael H.

1980 "Psychodynamics of Demon Possession." *Journal for the Scientific Study of Religion* 19/2:201-7.

Jesus, an Exorcist of a Kind

John J. Rousseau
University of California, Berkeley

The purpose of this paper is to situate Jesus in the world of exorcism and by comparison to attempt to determine the kind of exorcist he was and what his purpose and his understanding of himself were when he was practicing this craft. As a brief survey of ancient exorcism unfolds and certain of its aspects are treated, questions are raised regarding Jesus' attitude and method in connection with each aspect. At the end of the paper all the questions are collected and tentative answers are suggested which will help to understand the personality of Jesus in his social-historical context.

The subject is treated according to the following plan:

    I.   Origins and perenniality of exorcism.
    II. Exorcism in the time of Jesus.
    III. Exorcism by Jesus.
    IV. The originality of Jesus as an exorcist and his purpose.

I. Origin and Perenniality of Exorcism

Anthropology and the study of religions have revealed that civilizations recognize or create gods and demons which express their fears and hopes. The Asian nomadic hunters, with their shamans (an ancient Tongus word transmitted to us through Russian) attempted to find the logic of the gods and the causes of human misery. Shepherding and agricultural peoples called with offerings and sacrifices the protection and favors of the gods and genies. The Iranian demonology which influenced Judeo-Christian religions appeared as a salvation doctrine, its aim being to place humans on the side of the good god in its struggle against the evil spirits. How does exorcism find its place within these broad strata of cultures?

In Central Asia, Mongolia and Siberia, shamanism has been in existence since prehistorical times. Possession or ecstatic trance was purposely caused by the shaman himself in order to unite his flesh and blood with the spirits he evoked; they were literally entering his body. While in a state of trance, he was able to guide his people; his role and techniques presented some analogies with those of the bands of prophets of Israel in the times of the Judges and early monarchy. The shaman was not a passive agent, he was a professional of possession, he caused it and, pre-exorcising himself, he remained in control and came out of it at will. Shamanism occurrences have been observed in Alaska, Tibet, Greenland, Indonesia, in the Pacific Islands and among

129

native Americans. Different from the magician and medicine-man, the shaman is a technician of ecstasis, but he can be also a magician, healer, an exorcist. His soul is supposed to leave his body, to ascend to heaven or to visit hell. With the knowledge acquired during his journeys, he comes back with powers he can use against evil spirits.

Exorcism becomes a more specific form of activity in shepherding and agricultural civilizations. There, in return for the offerings and worship of the believers, the gods must provide rain, productivity of the earth and fecundity of the flocks and herds. On a ritualistic vase dating from about 3,000 BCE found at Warka, Eastern Mesopotamia, a long procession of naked men carrying offerings walk toward the entrance of the sanctuary of the goddess *Innim* who is going to have her annual hierogamic union with the god *Dumuzi* and bring fertility to the earth. But hostile forces try to annihilate the benefits brought by the divine union; they are the invisible demonic powers of drought, storm, diseases and sterility which ruin the fields and decimate the animals.

By repeated incantations, the exorcist overcame the powers of destruction coming from "below," and cut off their links with earthly things or beings. The incantations were said over rocks, resin, the ground of quays, asphalt, animal hides, in order to "charge" them with a prophylactic divine power. The Assyrian exorcists were officials of the temple, they operated in ritualistic costumes, like the priests of *En-ki*, the Sumeriam god of medicine and magic; they would wear tunics of scales and miters shaped like that of the god. They might use magical circles drawn on the ground (Honi the Circle Drawer did not innovate!). The practice was very ancient, and one of the names given to the Babylonian magician was *sahiru*, (the one who surrounds); the name is preserved in the Arabic *sahir* (magician).

During the Exile, the Jews became acquainted with Babylonian-Iranian beliefs: Supremacy of the Most High God, *Ahura-Mazda*, creator of both the good spirit, *Spenta Mainyu*, and the evil spirit, *Angra Mainyu*; cosmic struggle between *Angra Mainyu* and his progeny, the *daevas* opposing *Spenta Mainyu* who would eventually prevail; existence of heaven, place of eternal reward, and hell, place of eternal punishment. Exorcism called on the power of *Spenta Mainyu* to subdue *Angra Mainyu* and his hordes of *daevas*. These beliefs, adapted by the Jews, were at the origin of the Judeo-Christian demonology and angelology.

WHAT KIND OF EXORCIST WAS JESUS? A SHAMAN? A PRIEST? A MAGICIAN? AN INITIATE?

This brief overview of the origins of exorcism gives already some idea of its universality and perenniality; archaeology revealed their extent. Two remarkable examples are the cuneiform tablets of the dead of Mesopotamia and the stele of Bakhtan. In 1983, Jean Bottéro made an analysis of the tablets in his article, "Les morts et l'au-delà dans les rituels en accadien contre l'action des revenants" (in *Zeitschrift für Assyriologie und Vorderanatische Archäologie*, 73). He retrieved the concepts of exorcism as they were in the Lower Mesopotamia of the third millennium BCE. The underlying religious and cosmogonic ideas were already quite elaborate: It was thought that after death, individuals kept their identities and names; they continued to exist in their bones (*esemtu*) and ghosts or "shadows" or "spirits" or "souls" (*etemmu*).

In all the cases studied by Bottéro, the dead were the invisible hostile entities to be exorcised, dead strangers were seen as the most dangerous. They were those whose bodies were abandoned in the desert or battle fields, those who had died of starvation or thirst, burnt in a fire, or who had been executed after judgment. Their anger came from lack of posthumous care, which prevented them from reaching their final abode. But an unknown *etemmu* could be adopted and called upon for help against another one, for instance, by picking up a skull in a ditch and addressing it as recorded in one of the tablets:

> You are the ghost of an unknown one, nobody buried you and closed your grave. Nobody knows your name, only *Šamaš* knows it . . . Whoever you are, man, woman . . ., since in the presence of *Šamaš* . . . and of the manes of my departed you received a gift from me, listen to my request. Whoever the evil ghost who attacked me is, seize him, lock him up and keep him so that he will never come back. (translation mine).

DOES THIS RECOURSE TO AN *ETEMMU* TO EXORCISE ANOTHER ONE INVALIDATE JESUS' ARGUMENT IN MARK 3:23-26 AND PARALLELS?

The stele of Bakhtan is of great interest because it connects ancient Mesopotamia with Ptolemaic Egypt. It was described and interpreted by Paul Tresson (*Revue Biblique* 42 [1933] 57-78). It is a stone slab shaped like a vertical rectangle crowned with a semi-circular arch. Hyppolite Rosellini found it in 1829 in the ruins of a small Ptolemaic building near the temple of *Khonsu* erected by Rames III, 200 meters south of Karnak. The text was copied by Champollion, which allowed for an accurate reading even after some lines were damaged on the original. The stele was carried to France in 1844 and is now kept in the Louvre. Lines 8-9, 11-12, 18-20 treat of the illness and healing of princess Bint-neshit, (also, Benit-resh) who suffered from the attacks of an evil spirit who acts as an equal of the god and accepts to leave the princess only when certain conditions are met. It is a forgery committed some time between 323 BCE (death of Alexander III) and 246 BCE (death of Ptolemy II). The priests of *Khonsu* produced the fake stele with the intention to rekindle the fervor of their congregation. They took an old popular tale and adapted it to their concepts of ritual and beliefs. They gave such details of royal protocol, dates, liturgy, etc., that egyptologists were misled until 1883 when surprising errors in the hieroglyphs revealed to Adolph Earmann that the stele was a fake. Nevertheless, it remains an important witness giving precious information on popular beliefs about evil spirits and possession in the third century BCE.

Here follows an abbreviated translation of the story:

> As his Majesty the Pharaoh was in Neharina (Mesopotamia), he received precious offerings from all the high dignitaries. The prince of Bakhtan sent his older daughter at the head of his present bearers. She was so beautiful that the Pharaoh married her and gave her the title of Nefu-Ré (Beauty of Ré, the sun-god). When the Pharaoh was back to Thebes, the prince of Bakhtan sent a messenger with many presents (and this message:) "Your sister-in-law is possessed by an evil spirit, please send a magician to her." The Pharaoh sent a wise scribe who found her possessed by a spirit so strong that he could not fight it. Then, the prince of Bakhtan

sent another message: "Please, gracious sovereign, send a god." The Pharaoh addressed *Khonsu* residing in Thebes, Perfect Tranquility (K1) for his help. The statue of the god was drawn to that of *Khonsu* Master of Destinies, Exorciser of Evil Spirits (K2). By nodding toward K2, K1 instructed the former to go to Bakhtan. The statue of K2 was taken to a ship escorted by five others carrying a chariot and horses. K2 went to Benitresh and made a magic sign. The evil spirit said to him, "I will return where I came from if you order a great feast where I shall be a guest as well as the prince of Bakhtan." K2 agreed by nodding toward his prophet-priest and added, "Ascertain that the prince of Bakhtan will make a large offering to this spirit." So it was done and the evil spirit left the princess and went where he wanted. The prince of Bakhtan was so happy that he exclaimed, "May this god become the property of Bakhtan, I will not allow him to return to Egypt." So K2 stayed three years and nine months in Bakhtan, after which he returned with quantities of precious presents which he offered to K1 "without keeping anything in his own sanctuary."

It is impossible to say whether the prophets—priests of *Khonsu* really believed in the exorcisms they performed either in person or through the intervention of the status of their god. Whatever the case may be, they certainly knew how to use exorcisms as a means of domination and manipulation of people.

DID JESUS ENCOUNTER AN EVIL SPIRIT WHICH WAS HIS EQUAL?
WHAT WAS JESUS' MOTIVATION FOR PERFORMING EXORCISMS?

The Akkadian incantations used against the *etemmu* developed in formulas woven with long strings of powerful names. McCasland quotes a few, two of which I reproduce here. The first one comes from Babylon and invokes the gods Marduck and Shamash.

> In my body do not dwell,
> On my body do not press.
> By Shamash the Mighty, be exorcised.
> By Marduk, chief exorciser of gods, be exorcised.
> By the fire god who burns you, be exorcised.
> From my body, be taken away . . . (*By the Finger of God*, 97)

The old sun-god *Šamaš* of Akkad had been appropriated by the Babylonians and associated with their own Most High God, *Marduk*, chief exorciser. The other incantation was used to control the female vampire, *Lamashtu*, also an Akkadian import. But this time, *Lamastu*, the name of a male demon, has been attributed to her; and, probably because of the phonetic similarity, she was associated with Ishtar. It was a strange semantic shift since *Ishtar* was originally the Mesopotamian goddess of fertility, the *Isis* of the Egyptians. By association, she could also be called *Anat*, the fertility goddess of Ras Shamra and by other derived names. In Greek mythology, *Lamashtu* became *lamia*, a category of female infernal creatures as in Philostratus (*Life Apo.* IV. 25):

> (By) the names of *Anu* and *Anto*, of *Enlil* and *Ninil,*
> of gates and entrances, of swords and seed plough,
> of *Ezibu* and his son, I cause you to swear,
> if you return to his house [and] come hard on the little one,

sit on the seat where he sits,
lift to your lap the babe which I lift to my lap,
O *Ishtar,* [that you] hold back the mouths of your whelps.
May the sleeper, who has laid down upon a bed not awake
until the sun sheds its rays at dawn. (*By the Finger of God,* 98; both
quotations borrowed from S. M. Langdon, *Semitic Mythology,* 366-378).

This last incantation was used to calm or heal infants whose sleep was
disturbed at night. In *Enlil* and *Nilil* we recognize *lilû, lilitû* and *aradat lili* of the
cuneiform tablets who became the *Lilith* of rabbinic literature, the "night hag"
or harpy of Isa 34:14. She was seen as the leader of the evil beings attacking
women and children at night. Similarly, *Aeshma-Daeva/Asmodeus* became the
Asmedai of the Talmud where he is represented as ruling over all demons.
These phenomena of appropriation, transference, assimilation, are attested
throughout the millennia and eventually ancient names of past divinities
became associated with the name of YHWH (under different forms) and
Jesus, as will be seen below. The Judeo-Christian traditions of exorcism can
trace back their common origins to the Iranians-Aryans through Early
Judaism, Persia, Babylon, Assyria, Sumer and Akkad. In the course of time,
Egyptian and Greek traditions added their own contributions.

BY WHAT POWERS OR IN WHAT NAMES DID JESUS EXORCISE?

We must now complete our study of methods and techniques of exorcism
with music, noise, and magical objects. David's harp had a soothing effect on
Saul who was truly possessed and who was truly exorcised (1 Samuel 16:14-
23). The evil spirit would return, however, but this was seen as the will of God.
In order to drive demons out of the sick, some tribal peoples beat drums or tree
trunks and emit strange sounds. Elaborate forms of musical exorcism exist in
Central Africa where every spirit is identified by its own tune (McCasland, p.
101). In Buddhist temples, a gong is banged before worship services to drive
away the evil spirits which might occupy or surround the place. Magical
objects such as rings, bracelets, amulets and phylacteries are used to this day,
as well as the crucifix in Roman Catholic exorcism. Mély-Ruelle, in *Les
Lapidaires de l'Antiquité et du Moyen-Age* gives a collection of lapidary and
magical lore called *Kyriamides*. He reports the directions given for making a
ring having magical virtues: The stone is to be *nemesites,* that is chipped from
an altar of Nemesis made of hard stone. A figure of Nemesis is carved on the
stone—a maiden resting her foot on a wheel, symbol of changing fortune—
with a cubit rule in her left hand and a twig in the right. According to Pliny,
Nemesis was invoked for protection against the evil eye (*Nat. Hist.* 28.22).
Cambell Bonner, in his article, "The Techniques of Exorcism" (*Harvard
Theological Review* [1943] 39-49) drew on the work of Mély-Ruelle to report that
an exorcism was not completed if the demon had not been compelled to do
one or more of three things: speak to the exorcist, tell its name or at least
describe its nature or activities, and give tangible proof that it had left the body
of its victim (usually, some violent action).

WHAT METHODS AND TECHNIQUES DID JESUS USE IN HIS EXORCISMS?

One point remains to elucidate: How did one become an exorcist? In the
societies of nomadic hunters, when religion had not yet become an
establishment with hierarchies and codes, any one could become a shaman.

The shaman was a "deranged" and solitary person who had gone through and survived an initiation by the god itself, under the form of an illness with fever and hallucinations. He could have been previously recognized by the shaman of the tribe and prepared to go through the dangerous test, but it was not a requirement. In shepherding and agricultural societies, exorcism became the monopoly of the priestly caste; but outsiders, magicians, claimed that they had the power to cast out evil spirits and perform other acts of healing. Then, the question becomes, "How does one acquire the status of priest or magician?" Different answers were given in different societies, the common attitude being that the monopoly was to be kept by the same group and the secrets jealously guarded. However, lay individuals would continue to come forward, saying that they had obtained the secret of the art from a qualified practitioner or directly from some deity. But they were dubbed charlatans or magicians by the religious establishment.
HOW DID JESUS BECOME AN EXORCIST?
HOW WAS HE CONSIDERED BY THE RELIGIOUS ESTABLISHMENT?

II. Exorcism in the Time of Jesus

Palestine belonged to two worlds: Near- and Mid-East, and Eastern Mediterranean. The Judaism of Jesus' time had been influenced by Babylonian and Persian cultures, by Egyptian civilization and by Hellenism. It is in this broad context that the exorcism of Jesus must be studied.

The popular theological background of the Jews of first century Palestine included beliefs in one god, in angels, in demons or evil spirits led by Satan, master of this world, in a final judgment, in the resurrection of the dead, in eternal reward or punishment. Certain groups like the Qumranites and the Baptist's adepts believed in the imminence of God's judgment with or without a cosmic battle between the armies of God and the forces of evil, with or without the destruction of the Temple and the disappearance of the corrupt priesthood. One or two messiahs were expected to introduce the reign of God, and in family tombs, believers collected the bones of their dead in ossuaries so they would be raised and easily identified when the messiah came. The old Iranian belief that demons could possess individuals and cause diseases had gained wide acceptance and techniques of exorcism were used for the treatment of illnesses. However, a distinction was made between exorcism and healing as will be seen below. For the Sadducees, most of these beliefs were pure heresy, but they had little influence, if any, on the mind of the people. The Pharisees who were the most influential group and the Qumranites practiced exorcism as well as some priests.

Josephus wrote about Solomon, his knowledge of exorcism, and how his methods were still practiced in the Palestine of the first century CE.

> God also enabled him to learn that skill which expels demons . . . And he left behind him the manner of using exorcism by which they drive away demons so that they will never return, and this method of cure is of great force unto this day, for I have seen a certain man of my own country . . . Eleazar, releasing people that were demonical in the presence of Vespasian . . . He put a ring with a root of those sorts mentioned by

Solomon to the nostrils of the demoniac, after which he drew the demon through his nostrils; and when the man fell down immediately, he abjured him to return to him no more, making still mention of Solomon and reciting the incantations which he composed . . . He set a little way off a cup full of water and commanded the demon, as he went out of the man to overturn it; and when this was done, the skills and wisdom of Solomon were shown very manifestly. (*Antiq.* VIII, 2, 5, W. Whiston's translation.)

Certain aspects of Jewish exorcisms are perfectly in line with the ancient Mesopotamia practices: use of a ring, root of some plant, use of an incantation, collapse of the patient, command to the demon not to return and to show a sign of his departure. The perenniality of the exorcism tradition is well demonstrated here, it was probably more than 2,000 years old in Solomon's time when he endorsed it, and was revered as his 1,000 years later.

WAS JESUS ACQUAINTED WITH SOLOMON'S TRADITION AND SECRETS?

Lucian of Samosata, the Northern Syrian satirist of the second century, describes a typical case of exorcism in *Lovers of Lies.*

Every one knows about the Syrian from Palestine, the adept, (and) how many he takes in hand who fall down in the light of the moon and roll their eyes, and fill their mouths with foam; he restores them to health and send them away normal in mind, delivering them from their suffering for a large fee. When he stands beside them as they lie down, he asks, "From where did you come in this body?" The patient himself is silent but the spirit answers in Greek or in the language of whatever country he comes from, telling where he came from and how he entered in the man; whereupon, by adjuring the spirit, and if he does not obey, by threatening him, he drives him out. Indeed, I actually saw one coming out, all black and smoky. (From A. M. Harmon, Loeb Classical library.)

The profession of exorcist could be very lucrative. Here the patient is suffering from epilepsy; the "light of the moon" points to Selene and the "Sacred Disease," and there are typical symptoms, rolling of the eyes and foaming mouth. The exorcist asks questions that the demon answers, commands the spirit to leave the patient, and if necessary, threatens him. Lucian also reports exorcisms performed by an Arab (*L. of L.* 17) and a Babylonian (*L. of L.* 11), hereby testifying to a well spread practice.

DID JESUS RECEIVE MONEY OR OTHER COMPENSATION FOR HIS EXORCISMS?

Normally, Jewish exorcism implied the use of magical devices like amulets, as attested by archaeological finds, and herbs, roots, stones, odors; but the rabbinic literature has recorded one remarkable exception in the first century CE, an exorcism by command performed by Hanina ben Dosa *circa* 70 CE.

One should not go out alone at night on Wednesdays and Sabbath because Agrath bath Machlath goes out with eighteen myriads of destroying angels, each of them having by itself power to destroy. Originally, they were encountered in daytime, but when rabbi Hanina ben Dosa met her, she said to him, "If it had not been said in heaven about you, 'Beware of Hanina ben Dosa and his knowledge of the Torah,' I would have harmed you." He told her, "If I enjoy such reputation in heaven, I charge you never to prowl again in inhabited land." She said to him, "I beg you to leave me some room." Then he allowed her the nights of Sabbath and Wednesdays. (Talmud of Babylon. Peshim 114).

This is obviously the legendary etiology of a popular superstition but it reveals an unusual method of exorcism practiced by a rabbi in the first century CE. The power of Hanina ben Dosa resided in his knowledge of the Torah, consequently, it came from God. He was then able to command the evil spirit without the help of the traditional techniques. Nevertheless, he listened to Agrath's supplication and gave her some leeway. It is to be noted that the demonic female with her "myriads of destroying angels" resembles the Hecate of the Greeks with her dogs (S. H. Langdon, 369) and the Diana of the Romans with her horde of dead women's souls.

DID JESUS NEGOTIATE WITH OR MAKE CONCESSIONS TO THE DEMONS HE EXORCISED?

Besides Jesus' exorcisms, the New Testament refers to demon possession and Jewish practices of magic and exorcism in his time:

Mark 9:38/Luke 9:49	Man casting out demons.
Q 11:19	Sons casting out demons.
Acts 13:6,8	Bar Jesus/Elymas.
Acts 16:16-18	The slave girl.
Acts 19:13-16	Itinerant Jewish exorcists.
	Sons of the high priest Sceva.
Acts 19:19	Magical books burnt.

The first instance indicates that Jesus was not the only one to cast out demons in Galilee, and according to both versions, the unknown exorcist was already using Jesus' name to threaten evil spirits, which tends to demonstrate that Jesus' special power was already recognized. In the Q recording of the Beelzebul controversy, it is clear that the "Pharisees" (Matthew) or some in the crowd (Luke) or their sons engaged in exorcism; we may assume that they were following the tradition of Solomon. In Acts 16:6-8, Paul and Barnabas, while in Paphos, on the island of Cyprus, came upon "a certain magician, a Jewish false prophet, named Bar Jesus" (Elymas). In Philippi of Macedonia, where there was a Roman colony, a slave girl who had "a spirit of divination," followed them day after day until Paul ordered the spirit out of her "in the name of Jesus Christ." At Ephesus, it seems that there were many itinerant Jewish exorcists since (only) "some" of them began to pronounce the name of the Lord Jesus over those who had evil spirits. Among them, the seven sons of Sceva were operating this way but were not recognized by the evil spirit and had to flee, beaten up and naked; as a result of their failure, many new converts confessed that they practiced magic, brought their magical books together and burnt them publicly. And there must have been a large quantity of these books for their total value was estimated at 50,000 pieces of silver. It would appear, then, that in the Greco-Roman world, exorcism and magic were a common practice and a specialty of the Jews. Even members of priestly families were exorcists, which is in agreement with Q 11:19.

Other New Testament texts reinforce the impression that the people of Jesus' time believed they were living in the invisible company of demons and spirits: I Cor. 10:20-21 (sacrifices to demons-false gods), I Cor. 12:10 (ability to distinguish between spirits), II Cor. 4:4 (the god of this world), II Cor. 12:7 (a messenger of Satan), Eph. 1:21 (rule, authority, power, dominion), Eph. 2:2 (the prince of the power of the air), Eph. 6:12 (principalities, powers, spiritual hosts of wickedness), Eph. 6:16 (flaming darts of the evil one).

BY CASTING OUT DEMONS, DID JESUS DO ANYTHING UNUSUAL?

The work of Philostratus, *Life of Apollonius of Tyana*, came rather late to be considered as an irrefutable witness, he was born *cira* 172 and his work was completed in the third century. But his sources seem reliable and his work is supported by the apology of another writer, Hierocles, a provincial governor under Diocletian (284-305). He wrote a treatise to promote Apollonius, Eusebius responded immediately by denouncing the sage as a charlatan and a magician. Nevertheless, it remains that, to some extent, Apollonius was a figure comparable to Jesus, and that he performed healings and probably some exorcisms as they were understood at the time. It is worthwhile to study at least one of them, the exorcising of a demon by stoning its physical form: There was a devastating plague at Ephesus and the people called on Apollonius for help.

> He led the entire population to the theater where the image of the Adverting God (Hercules) had been set up. There he saw what seemed an old mendicant artfully blinking his eyes as if blind . . . Apollonius ranged the Ephesians around him and said, "Pick up as many stones as you can and hurl them at this enemy of the gods." The Ephesians were shocked at the idea of murdering such a miserable stranger . . . Nevertheless Apollonius insisted . . . As soon as they hit him with their stones, the beggar who had seemed to blink and be blind, gave them all a sudden glance and his eyes were full of fire . . . They stoned him so thoroughly that their stones were heaped into a great cairn around him . . . [When] they removed the stones . . . they found that he had disappeared, and instead of him there was a hound . . . (as large as) the largest lion. And Ephesus was purged of the plague. (*L. of Apo.* IV, 10)

This is the "beat-the-hell-out-of-him" method that Jesus is not reported to have used. Apollonius did not throw stones himself, the people of Ephesus did all the dirty work. We may speculate, for the sake of comparison, that such a drastic method was used because the evil was devastating a whole city. By contrast, in a difficult case, Jesus recommended that his disciples use prayer (Mark 9:29).

Much more significant, since they come directly from Jesus' time or immediately before, are four well preserved texts on exorcism and incantations in some of the Dead Sea Scrolls. Two exorcisms have been studied by Dupont-Sommer, and Emile Puech reconstructed two incantations. Josephus had already indicated that the Essenes were expert healers of souls and bodies. "They also take great pains in studying the writings of the ancients, and choose out of them what is most advantageous for their souls and bodies, and they enquire of such roots and medicinal stones as may cure their illness." (*Wars* II, 8, 6, 136). As G. Vermes pointed out in his article, "Essenes and Therapeutai," (*Revue de Qumran*, 12, 495-504), according to Philo, "essene" signifies "healer" (Aramaic root *'asyâ*), that is to say, a person who heals "the wounds of wickedness and extirpates the seeds of evil, and offers to

God truly spiritual worship." For Philo, the Essenes of Palestine and the Therapeutai of Egypt were two religious societies inspired by the same ideal, but the Essenes thought to fulfill it by "active life" [in expectation of the final cosmic war] and the Therapeutae by contemplation (*De Vita Contemplativa*, 2). Thus, says Vermes, "The Essenes were therapeutai, worshipers of God, because they offered him the true worship of their spiritual healing." Consequently, because of their concern for the healing of the soul, it was only natural that they were practitioners of exorcism which was, besides, a normal activity of the time as we have already established.

A. Dupont-Sommer, in "Exorcisms et guérisons dans les écrits de Qumran,"(*Supplement to Vetus Testamentum*, V. 7, Congress Volume, [Oxford, 1959], 241-261) studies two texts: The Aramaic scroll *Genesis Apocriphon* from Cave I published by N. Avigad and Y. Yadin in 1956, and the fragments of another Aramaic scroll form Cave IV called The *Prayer of Nabonidus* published by J. T. Milik in 1956 (Revue Biblique 43, 407-411, 415).

1. *Genesis Apocryphon.* It is a midrash on Gen, 12:10-20, it covers two columns of the scroll from XX, 11 to XX, 32 with the story of the exorcism in XX, 12-29. I give an abridged translation of the exorcism story which in the text is in the first person (Abram is speaking).

> Pharaoh just took the wife of Abram and he prays to God for justice. God hears his prayer and sends an "evil spirit" to Pharaoh which strikes him with a disease as well as everybody else in the palace. The condition is getting worse and Pharaoh sends for all the sages of Egypt and physicians and sayers of incantations to eliminate both the disease and the "evil spirit." But they cannot perform the healing and they too get the illness. Horqanosh then asks Abram to intervene by praying for Pharaoh and by imposing his hands on him. But Lot reveals to Horqanosh that Sarai is in fact Abram's wife, Pharaoh must first return her to her husband, which is immediately done. Abram prays and imposes his hands on Pharaoh who heals at once.

The complete rendering of the resulting healing is: "and the plague was removed from him and the evil [spirit] was expelled and he lived." Thus, it is truly an exorcism, the evil spirit is the agent of the disease with which he is identified. The Assyrian-Babylonian concept of demon-disease had fully penetrated Judaism. In the text, the evil spirit is more specifically called *ruâh sehlânayyâ* (spirit of pustules), from the root *SHL* (flow, run, drip), probably the same infectious disease as in Ex. 9:11.

DID JESUS LEARN EXORCISM TECHNIQUES FROM THE ESSENES?
DID JESUS BELIEVE THAT HE WAS EXORCISING DEMONS BY HIS OWN POWER?

2. *Nabonidus' prayer.* After corrections and fillings made by Dupont-Sommer, the fragments read as follows (in my translation):

> The words of the prayer of Nabunai, the king of Babylon, the [great] king [when he was struck] by a malignant inflammation by the order of the [Most High God] at Teiman . . . (The king is speaking) . . . "I was struck during seven years and [my face] was no longer like that [of a son of man]. But I prayed the Most High God and an exorcist forgave my sins. He was a Jew, one of the [exiles and he said to me}, "Tell and write to

render homage, praise [and glory] to the name of the [Most High God."
And I wrote this:] I was struck with a malignant inflammation at Teiman
[and my face] was no longer like that of a son of man. For seven years [I]
prayed [all] the gods of silver and gold, [bronze and iron], wood, stone and
clay, because [I thought] they were gods . . . and] was healed without
them . . . How much you look like [Daniel?]!

It was probably the same disease, *sehî râ* as in Deut, 28:35 and Job 2:7,
"loathsome sores from the sole of his foot to the crown of his head." The
prayer was of a common type in Assyrian-Babylonian literature and in
penitents' psalms like Ps. 35:3-8 by which the sick person asks at the same
time healing and forgiveness of sins because sin was the cause of the disease
(Dupont-Sommer's rendering is the literal translation of the original Aramaic,
contrary to J. T. Milik's interpretation). Although in Nabonidus' case, there
was no exorcism, I brought it up here because there is an interesting
conjunction: intervention by prayer, and a Jewish "exorcist" who could
forgive sins.

DID JESUS BELIEVE THAT HE WAS FORGIVING SINS WHEN EXORCISING DEMONS
OR HEALING PEOPLE?

Emile Puech translated scroll 11QPs Ap[a] in "Un rituel d'exorcisms. Essai
de reconstruction" (*Revue de Qumran* 55 [January 1990] 377-403). The original
document is a leather manuscript from Cave XI. It was published by the Royal
Academy of Netherlands with Fr. Van der Ploeg as editor. It contains four
psalms in the following order: (a) Ps. 91, (b) Third Davidic psalm, (c) Second
Davidic psalm, (d) First Davidic psalm. Psalm (b), (c) and (d) are explicit
incantations. As (d) is too fragmentary and does not add anything of
significance to the rest, I translated only the texts of (b) and (c).

(b) From/to/of David: Regarding words of incantation in the name of
YHWH.
At all time invoke heaven.
When Belial comes to you, say to him:
"Who are you, cursed among men and among the race of the saints?
Your face is a face of vanity
And your horns are horns of illusion.
You are darkness, not light, Injustice and not justice.
The Prince of Hosts is against you,
YHWH will imprison you in the infernal sheol
And he will close the two gates
And will lock you up with the two [doors?]
Through which light does not go
And through which the sun does not shine,
Whose [light] will rise upon the just
In order to illuminate his face."
And you will say to him:
"Is not there an angel with the just
When he enters into judgment
Because Satan mistreated him?"
And the Spirit of truth will deliver him
from darkness for justice is in his favor

To keep it in judgment.
And YHWH will cause to perish forever
All the sons of Belial. Amen. Amen. Selah.

The incantation is made in the name of YHWH, "Belial" is a name of Satan typical of Qumranite literature, "horns" were symbols of power. The opposition Darkness/Light is characteristic of the Qumranite beliefs.

(c) From/to/of David:
Regarding the words of incantation in the name of YHWH.
. . . according to Solomon's deeds
And he will invite in the name of YHWH
So that he will deliver from any plague, spirits and demons,
Liliths, owls and wild cats.
These are demons and the prince of hostility is Belial
[....]
And in order to magnify the God of gods
[....]
The sons of his people achieve healing.
And invoke heaven
And trust in the guardian of Israel.
Rely on YHWH, God of Gods,
Who made heaven and earth and all that is in it,
Who separated light from darkness,
[....]
And the angels of YHWH will bound Belial forever.

Our old Akkadian acquaintance, *lilitû*, has now many descendants, the liliths, probably as numerous as the owls and wild cats which too are demons. Here again the power resides in YHWH. According to Puech, the scroll is written in Herodian script which dates it from *circa* 50 BCE to 68 CE, date of the destruction of Qumran by the Romans. As a manuscript of exorcism ritual, it is referred to in other manuscripts of Cave XI.

Most likely, these documents describe methods and incantations used by the Qumranites. Dupont-Sommer suggests that the Qumranites, because they were healers and exorcists, attributed their methods to two great figures of the past, Abram and Daniel, (playing the role of recreated Hebrew Hippocrates, their own patrons and masters), pictured as healing two great pagan kings. By this choice of two powerful patients, they would demonstrate the superiority of their God and methods, and probably their own. As Philo commented on the Therapeutae, they "profess the art of healing better than that practiced in their cities, this heals only the bodies, whereas theirs heals also souls oppressed with grievous and almost incurable disease inflicted by pleasure, grief and fear, covetousness, folly and injustice, and the countless multitude of the other passions and evils" (*De Vita* 2). The isolated reference to Solomon, cut from its context, may indicate that they would consider him also as one of their patrons and masters although it seems they did not use his secret formulas, at least in exorcisms.

DID JESUS FOLLOW THE METHODS OF A GREAT MASTER OF THE PAST?

The crux of the matter is now before us. Since, in the time of Jesus, exorcism was seen as a form of struggle against the evil spirits and their master, Satan, two important questions arise: What were the popular beliefs regarding the role of the Messiah in the termination of Satan's reign? And, was exorcism seen as a function of the Messiah? If the answer to the second question is positive, then an exorcist could be considered as a messianic candidate.

To answer the first question, there is no doubt that, for a number of Jews of the first century, one of the most important tasks of the Messiah was to destroy Satan and his kingdom. This statement is supported by the Qumranite literature, especially the War Scroll, and by apocalytic writings: I Enoch 53:3-5; 54:4-6; Test. Levi 18:12; Jubilees 23-29; Test. Judah 25:3, etc. When the design of God is fulfilled, Satan shall be no more (Assumption of Moses 10:1, Qumran literature, etc. It will be as in the time of Joseph in Egypt when Satan was unknown (Jubiles 40:9; 46:2). Early rabbinic literature supports also this view: According to Midrash Pesikta Rabbat 31, ¶1, God has put the light under his throne of glory. Satan asks for whom was this done. God answers that it was for the one who will turn him back and confound him utterly. Satan asks God to see such a one and God shows him. Satan says in amazement, "Surely, this is the Messiah who will cause me and all the counterparts in heaven of the princes of the earth's nations to be swallowed up in Gehenna . . . (as quoted by John Bowman in *Exorcism and Baptism*).

Let us now turn to the second question, "Was exorcism seen as an attribute of the Messiah?" At first, one is tempted to give a negative answer for apparently good reasons: There was a plethora of exorcists in the first century CE, as well established, and many of them were not Jews and could not be messiahs. Furthermore, it is not reported that any of the would-be messiahs known before 165 CE performed exorcism. Bar Kokhbah himself, although he was recognized as the Messiah by Rabbi Akiva who died with him, was certainly not an exorcist. From the opposite point of view, it may be argued that all these pretenders were seeking only worldly power and that exorcists not seeking an earthly kingdom for themselves used the old techniques akin to magic (with the exception of Apollonius and Hanina ben Dosa, in later instances which may have been inspired by Jesus' stories). The Qumranites, however, constitute a different group and may provide a positive answer, as far as they were concern. As we have seen, their procedures and incantations expressly called on the name of YHWH, and they may have expected that one (or two) of them would be the Messiah(s) since they were seeing themselves as the only true remnant of Israel.

DID JESUS THE EXORCIST THINK THAT HE WAS GOING TO BE VICTORIOUS OVER SATAN?

III. Exorcisms by Jesus

There is little doubt that Jesus performed exorcisms as they were understood in his time. It was just a natural thing to do for an itinerant charismatic healer and teacher in his social-historical environment; and he was not the only one to do it as is abundantly documented. There is quasi-unanimity on this point among New Testament scholars, and when the proposition, "Jesus exorcised what were thought to be demons," was submitted to the Fellows of the Jesus Seminar, only 5% disagreed.

In the activities of Jesus, what is to be considered "exorcism" as opposed to "healing"? The distinction is not self-evident since demons were seen as the cause of many ailments: dumbness, lameness, epilepsy, infirmity, blindness, madness, hysteria, fever, paralysis and other. But some New Testament passages cite together exorcisms and healings, which indicates that the writers made a distinction between the two (Mark 1:32-33; 3:10-11; 6:13; Luke 18-19; 7:21; 13:32); the second ending of Mark lists separately "cast out demons," . . . and . . . "lay their hands on the sick . . ." (Mark 16:17-18).

The distinction between exorcism and healing becomes more apparent if we consider that exorcism is the expulsion of a demon which occupies (possesses) the body of its victim. In diseases caused by a demon, the evil spirit may or may not occupy the body. If he does, there is exorcism concomitant with healing, if he does not, there is only healing. But there can be some confusion as in the case of the healing of Peter's mother-in-law. Mark and Matthew present it as a simple healing (Mark 1:30-31; Matt. 8:14-15) while Luke uses the term "rebuke the fever" (4:38-39). Fever was believed to be caused by demons and "rebuke" was used for the expelling of a demon. Thus, Luke implies that the demon was possessing the body of the patient, which neither Peter or Luke specifies. In this particular case, we would prefer Mark's version on the ground that it may be the most ancient.

Besides general statements that Jesus performed exorcisms, the gospels record a few instances in which his action can be recognized without ambiguity as exorcism. They will be examined, as will other passages of the gospels where Jesus is accused of being possessed, where he delegates his power and where Satan is involved.

1. The Beelzebul Controversy

Mark 3:20-35; Matt. 12:22-50; Luke 11:14-21

Mark 3:21: "And when his friends heard it, they went out to seize him for they said, 'he is beside himself.'" This is probably an authentic account in consideration of the criterion of "embarrassment." Seen in the historical perspective of exorcism, this accusation of madness could indicate that Jesus was behaving as a shaman.

Mark 3:22: "And the scribes who came down from Jerusalem said, 'he is possessed by Beelzebul, and by the prince of demons he casts out demons.'" Here again, the probability of authenticity is high by virtue of the same criterion of "embarrassment." Jesus' activity was noticeable enough to justify an investigation by the religious establishment. The delegation did not deny that Jesus performed exorcisms but claimed that he was possessed by Beelzebul, not by the Holy Spirit.

Matt. 12:27, Luke 11:19: It is implied that persons in scribal or priestly families performed exorcisms, which is confirmed by Acts 19:14-16. This is highly probable in the general context of the time and in consideration of historical precedents.

2. Jesus is possessed

Mark 3:30; John 7:19-20; 8:39-52; 10:21.

Mark 3:30 must be read in connection with Mark 3:29, "But whoever blasphemes against the Holy Spirit never has forgiveness, but he is guilty of an eternal sin—for they had said, 'He has an unclean spirit.'" (The other logia from John only confirm that Jesus was thought of by some as being possessed by demons, but they may bring a second independent attestation). According to Mark, Jesus seems to have said that the accusation of his opponents was a blasphemy against the Holy Spirit because he was possessed by it, not by Beelzebul. This interpretation has at least the advantage of giving a logical explanation in the socio-historical context of the time for the juxtaposition of the two sayings. Once more, we are faced with the possibility that Jesus was a shaman.

3. Jesus tested by Satan

Mark 1:12-13; Matt. 4:11; Luke 4:1-13

Jesus, "driven by the Spirit" (of God) is tested by the devil. Neither possession nor exorcism is mentioned. However, if we look back to the long history of exorcism, we must ask a few questions, even if the answers elude us. Was Jesus already possessed by the Holy Spirit, or on his way to be possessed by it? (He just had some kind of religious experience at his baptism). Did he have visions or hallucinations in which Satan appeared to him? Was he going through the painful initiation of a shaman? Some characteristic pointers are here: Withdrawal, isolation for a long period, intense struggle. WAS JESUS A SHAMAN POSSESSED BY THE HOLY SPIRIT, PERHAPS LIKE THE PROPHETS OF OLD?

4. Exorcism in the Capernaum Synagogue

Mark 1:21-28; Luke 4:31-37; Matt. 7:28-29

The story reported by Mark and Luke is a typical case of exorcism. The demon speaks. Jesus commands him to leave the victim, the demon obeys and convulses the patient (but does not resist Jesus' command), the demon comes out of the victim in the midst of the congregation but does him "no harm." Luke or his source knew that, when forced to leave his victim, the demon could injure or kill him as an act of revenge, according to popular belief. Some features are to be noted:

(1) The demon identifies Jesus,

(2) The demon fears to be destroyed, not merely expelled, with all his congeners ("us").

(3) The demon acknowledges that Jesus is the "Holy One of God," probably the Messiah who is expected to destroy Satan and his hosts.

(4) Jesus operates by a simple injunction which is immediately obeyed by the demon.

5. Simon's Mother-in-Law

Mark 1:29-31; Matt. 8:14-15; Luke 4:38-39

This healing probably does not involve an exorcism *stricto sensu*.

6. Evening Exorcisms

Mark 1:32-34; Matt. 8:16; Luke 4:40-41

In the exorcisms which happened that night, we see three characteristics, two similar to (3) and (4) of case #4, and a new one:

(3) The demons acknowledge that Jesus is the "Son of God" or the "Christ."
(4) Jesus casts out the spirits/demons with "a word" (a simple injunction) and they offer no resistance.
(5) He enjoins the demons to keep silent (Mark 1:34: Luke 4:41.

7. Galilean Exorcisms

Mark 1:39; Matt. 4:23-25
No specifics are given; this is a confirmation that Jesus casts out demons as an itinerant exorcist.

8. Crowds are cured

Mark 3:7-12; Matt. 12:15-16; Luke 6:17-19
Two of the previously found characteristics exist, (3) and (5) and two new ones appear:

(3) The demons acknowledge that Jesus is the "Son of God" before whom they fall down (Mark 3:11),
(5) Jesus enjoins the demons to keep silent (Mark 3:12; Matt. 15:16),
(6) Jesus' fame as an exorcist and healer expands abroad,
(7) Jesus exercises a great charismatic attraction on the crowds, people rush in mass to touch him at the risk of crushing him for "power came out of him" (Luke 6:19).

9. The disciples receive authority to exorcise

Mark 3:13-15; Matt. 10:1, 8; Mark 6:7, 13; Luke 9:1, 6; 10:19
Another characteristic appears:

(8) Jesus can delegate his power to exorcise and those who receive it are successful most of the time, (Mark 9:18 and parallels).

10. The Gerasene Demoniac

Mark 5:1-20; Matt. 8:28-34; Luke 8:26-39
The man from Geresa (location unknown) suffered from an extreme case of possession because there were many demons in him. The procedure of exorcism is typical of what was standard. It involved a possessed person persecuted psychologically and physically by demons, an injunction by the exorcist (but no other techniques), a dialogue between the demon and the exorcist. In this instance, the demon recognizes Jesus as the "Son of the Most High" and as his "tormentor." Jesus asks his name and the demon answers, adding a supplication, Jesus grants the request, the demons leave and by a physical demonstration show that they have come out of the man. The exorcism is perfected, the man returns "to his right mind." This case is somewhat similar to that of the Bakhtan stele, except that the Gerasene demons do not impose a condition as if they were Jesus' equals; they make a supplication for a favor which is granted to them: They are allowed to stay in the country. The story, however, contains two very usual features:

1. It is said that the demons were "legion" (a Roman legion counted from 3,000 to 6,000 men) while, according to ancient Mesopotamian

beliefs, multiple possession would not involve more than seven hostile spirits—a tradition preserved in the story of Mary Magdalene and in Q 11:24-26. In the latter instance, the end result was eight evil spirits, but seven were more evil than the first one who presented probably only a mild case of possession (he needed rest and left on his own initiative!).

2. The legion of demons, now lodged in the swine, plunged in the water while it was believed that evil spirits were afraid of water. This was another ancient Mesopotamian tradition preserved in "he passes through waterless places seeking rest" (Q 11:24). In his article, "Jewish Liturgical Exorcism" (*Harvard Theological Review* [July, 1938] 191-203), W. L. Knox reports that the ancients believed that demons were powerless against water as testified by Apuleius' *Metamorphosis*, (I, 19.62) and Talmud Sanhedrin 67b. In his *Dictionnaire d'Archéologie Chrétienne*, (I, 1808), Leclerq reports the use of a Christian charm by which a demon was banished over the Jordan which he could not cross back.

In consideration of this evidence, I am convinced that the initial account was embellished in 66 CE when told to Jewish insurgents just after the legions of Vespasian landed at Ptolemais. That was a double hit! Legionnaires assimilated to pigs and pushed back to the water—and drowned! The story teller-evangelist certainly got attention.

The story presents features we have already encountered, and a few new ones:
(1) The demons identify the exorcist as Jesus;
(2) The demons fear to be tormented;
(3) The demons acknowledge that Jesus is the Son of the Most High God;
(4) Jesus operates by a simple injunction;
(4a) which is not opposed but not answered immediately;
(9) Jesus asks for the demon's name and the demon answers;
(10) The demons ask for a favor which is granted;
(11) The demons give physical evidence that they have left the body of the possessed man;
(12) Contrary to feature (5), Jesus asks the healed man to tell around him "how much the Lord had done for him" (Mark 5:19).

The last five features (4a to 12) are new and support the theory that the legion and swine incident is a timely creation added to what was probably an authentic instance of exorcism.

11. The Daughter of the Syrophoenician Woman

Mark 7:24-30; Matt. 15:21-28
Many elements are missing in this story of an instant "tele-exorcism;" the story deals mainly with the mission of Jesus vis-à-vis Jews and Gentiles. However, two new elements appear, faith and exorcism at a distance.
(6) Jesus' fame has indeed reached the territory of Tyre and Sidon, "he could not be hid" . . . "a woman heard of him" (Mark 7:24-24).
(13) The mother's faith is presented as the determinant factor of the exorcism-healing,
(14) Jesus does not see the victim but obtains instant results.

12. The Epileptic Boy

Mark 9:14-29; Matt. 17:14-20; Luke 9:37-43

Here too, the faith of a parent is a determinant factor. Of the three versions, Matthew, which presents the boy as epileptic is probably the one describing more closely the symptoms and the exorcism. The appearance of a "dumb spirit" or "dumb and deaf" one must be due to a conflation with a different story as noted for instance by Latourelle (*The Miracles of Jesus*, 1988, p. 151). According to Matthew, the disciples could not perform the exorcism because of "their little faith;" but the "faithless and perverse generation" as a whole may be responsible too for the lack of wellness and healing (in all three versions). Mark and Luke do not mention the disciples' lack of faith, but they are part of the "faithless generation." Mark tempers the implied accusation by having Jesus say, "This kind cannot be driven out by anything but prayer" (Mark 9:29).

Three features previously recognized exist in the basic story:

(4) Jesus operates by a simple injunction and the demon obeys immediately.

(8) Jesus can delegate his power to exorcise, but those who receive it are not always successful.

(13) Faith (of the disciples, father and people) is a determinant factor, and a new one is added:

(15) Prayer is a powerful method of exorcism.

14. Mary Magdalene

Mark 16:9; Luke 8:2

We have here only incidental remarks about Mary Magdalene who had been possessed by seven demons which Jesus had exorcised. Nothing else can be said except for the observation on the number of demons.

15. The Disciples receive power to exorcise

Mark 16:17; Luke 10:17-20

These are mere references to powers already delegated.

16. Tell Herod

Luke 13:32

"I cast out demons," this statement of Jesus indicates a deliberate intention to perform exorcisms.

17. The Fall of Satan

Luke 10:18; John 12:31; John 14:30

Here are three references to the ultimate exorcism, the fall of Satan, or the end of his reign or the end of his power over Jesus. They are in harmony with the Qumranite concept of the final victory over Belial.

WHAT WAS THE INFLUENCE OF QUMRAN, IF ANY, ON JESUS' VIEW OF ESCHA-TOLOGY AND ON HIS UNDERSTANDING OF HIMSELF IN HIS ROLE AGAINST SATAN?

A surprising observation results from the above review of all the references pertaining to Jesus' exorcisms and related statements as recorded in the four canonical gospels: While a very large number of exorcisms is implied, only in six instances are they described to some extent.

-Exorcism in the Capernaum Synagogue	Mark 1:21-28+L//
-Evening exorcisms	Mark 1:32-34+//s
-Crowds are cured	Mark 3:7-12+//s
-The Gerasene demoniac	Mark 5:1-20+//s
-The Syrophoenician woman's daughter	Mark 7:24-30+Mt//
-The epileptic boy	Mark 9:14-29+//s

Mark is the common denominator of these few instances. Matthew and Luke may add, modify or ignore some details; but it remains that the six accounts are based on single attestations and their authenticity can be doubted.

In the course of our review, fifteen features of Jesus' exorcisms have been recognized:

(1) Demons identify Jesus by name	2 cases
(2) Demons fear to be destroyed or tormented by Jesus	3 cases
(3) Demons acknowledge that Jesus is the "Holy One" or "Son of God"	4 cases
(4) Jesus operates by a simple injunction	4 cases
(5) Jesus enjoins the demons to keep silent	2 cases
(6) Jesus' fame as an exorcist expands abroad	2 case
(7) Jesus exercises a great charismatic attraction upon the crowds	1 case
(8) Jesus can delegate his power to exorcise	2 cases
(9) Jesus asks for the demon's name	1 case
(10) A demon asks a favor which is granted	1 case
(11) Demons give physical evidence of their departure	1 case
(12) Jesus asks the healed person to testify	1 case
(13) Faith is a determinant factor of success	2 cases
(14) Jesus can exorcise at a distance	1 case
(15) Prayer is a powerful method of exorcism	1 case

Only three of these features are recurring three or more times:

(2) Demons fear to be destroyed or tormented	3 times
(3) Demons acknowledge that Jesus is the "Holy One" or "Son of God"	4 times
(4) Jesus operates by a simple injunction	4 times

They show that, in their context, the exorcisms of Jesus are part of a wider battle against Satan whose total destruction or final banishment is in process. Jesus is convinced of the immediacy of the coming of God's reign and acts as if he had a certain role in the battle against Satan and his demons. On Q 11:19-20, the opinions of the Fellows of the Jesus Seminar were divided as follows: *Red* 29%, *Pink* 50%, *Grey* 4%, *Black* 17%, for a final rating of *Pink*, which means that, in their opinion, the historical Jesus probably said, "If it is by the finger/power of God that I cast out demons, then the reign of God has come upon you." On Luke 10:18 they expressed their opinion as *Red* 25%, *Pink* 58%, *Grey* 9%, *Black* 8%, for a final rating of *Pink*. They think that Jesus probably said, "I saw Satan fall like lighting from heaven." This gives support to the conclusion of this chapter: Jesus was conscious that, by exorcising, he was playing a certain role in the eschatological battle against Satan . . . But what role?

DID JESUS BELIEVE THAT HE WAS THE MESSIAH?

IV. The originality of Jesus as an exorcist and his purpose

An observation imposes itself once Jesus the exorcist is placed in perspective in the world of exorcism: While his predecessors, contemporaries and successors used complex, lengthy procedures involving ingredients, herbs, magical objects, oral formulas, amulets and other methods, he came empty-handed, uttered simple irresistible commands immediately obeyed by the demons. In only one instance, probably embellished by the storyteller, did he ask the demon's name and granted him and his co-squatters their request (the Gerasene demoniac). He is even said to have performed an exorcism at a distance (the Syrophoenician woman's daughter). This unprecedented power which even ancient gods did not have (Khonsu) attracted crowds to him. People came from neighboring countries to seek his services and his opponents, either among his contemporaries or those from later times, did not deny it. All they could do was to explain it by satanic origin, by sorcery or by fraudulent obtention of the divine secrets.

The specifics of Jesus' exorcism seems well established. But what was it which gave him and the first Christians operating in his name their extraordinary powers? The one answer which comes to mind is, "the Holy Spirit" with which they were filled. Jesus had discovered the secrets of the ancient Asian shamans or, somehow, they had been revealed to him. It is a phenomenon which is foreign to our civilization which has polluted its invisible environment with an infinite number of electromagnetic, sonic and ultrasonic emissions, cutting us off from the etheral vibrations that some of our ancestors had learned to recognize and use. I agree with Marcus Borg's observations:

> . . . what can be known about Jesus is a vivid witness to the reality of the Spirit. Most generations have not needed to hear this, simply because most generations took the reality of the Spirit for granted. We do not. . . because of the pervasive effect of the modern image of reality upon the psyches of believers and unbelievers alike. (*Jesus, A New Vision*, p. 190).

One thing is certain, the Old Testament, especially in connection with the prophets, the gospels, the Book of Acts and the epistles, all mention the Holy Spirit as if it was a familiar phenomenon, a simple fact of observation, a reality of life.

Can we learn more about Jesus and his exorcisms by having placed him, in space and time, in the world of exorcism? Let us review the questions raised and statements made in the course of this study.

1. *What Kind of Exorcist was Jesus? A Shaman? A Priest? A Magician? An Initiate?*

It is certain that Jesus was not a priest for he was not of the tribe of Levi. Contrary to Morton Smith's thesis, I do not think that he was a magician since it is not reported that he used any of the magical devices and techniques which were known in his time. He may have been an initiate of the Therapeutae-Essene category or a shaman of the Old Testament ecstatic prophet type.

2. *Does the recourse of an* etemmu *to exorcise another one invalidate Jesus' argument in Mark 3:23-26 and parallels?*

Originally, the *etemmus* were ghosts of the dead, it is only later that they were included among the infernal spirits. Like the living, they were supposed to have different personalities and interests, presumably, they could oppose each other. They were not part of a hierarchical order under the authority of a "Prince of Demons." But in Jesus' time, it could have been inconceivable that a demon would disobey its superiors. Jesus' argument is most likely valid in the demonologic context of his time.

3. *Did Jesus encounter an evil spirit which was his equal?*

In the ancient Mesopotamian concept of two equal powers, one good, one evil, opposing each other, it could happen that an exorcist would encounter an evil power equal or even stronger than himself as illustrated by the story of Benit-resh. But nothing like this is reported in connection with Jesus' exorcisms, the evil spirits always submitted to him.

4. *What was Jesus' motivation?*

This question was raised when the craftiness of the priests of Khonsu appeared obvious, they used their art as a means of domination and manipulation of people. It is possible that Jesus used exorcism (and healing) as a means to develop his popularity and attract large audiences in order to spread his message about the imminent coming of God's Reign. But it was not for his own satisfaction and glory, and the very fact that he spent a great amount of his time in healing people shows that he was also motivated by compassion. Effective "public relations" work did not require so much involvement in relieving people from their misery.

5. *By what power or in what name did Jesus exorcise?*

Jesus did not use any of the "powerful names" which were the stock-in-trade of the profession (e.g., Šamaš, Marduck, Anat, Enlil, Lilitu), not even the name of Solomon or the "camouflaged" names of YHWH (Iael, Yahe, Iaeo, etc.). He operated, as it seems directly from the power which was in him and which his followers called the Holy Spirit.

6. *What methods and techniques did Jesus use in his exorcisms?*

Jesus did not use any of the techniques and methods of the exorcists of his time or of the past. He operated only by injunctions and obtained quick results.

7. *How did Jesus become an exorcist?*

Only a few possibilities exist: Formal training and initiation in a group like the Therapeutae or Essenes-Qumranites, training by an unknown isolated master, ecstatic experience and revelation like the shamans.

8. *How was Jesus considered by the religious establishment of his time?*

He appeared as another charismatic figure (just after John the Baptist) who needed to be examined according to the prescriptions of the Torah (Deut. 13; 18:15-22). Since he was not stoned, although he may have been threatened with stoning, or banished immediately, there must have been some factors in his favor, even if he was perceived as an unorthodox and dangerous opponent. He was probably more acceptable to the Pharisees than to the Sadducees.

9. *Was Jesus acquainted with Solomon's tradition and secret?*

There is a possibility that he was, although he did not invoke Solomon's name or seal or use any of his techniques. It is to be noticed that the Qumranites did not use Solomon's name either in their exorcisms. However, some of those who called him "Son of David" in connection with healings and exorcisms may have considered him as a reincarnation or a disciple of Solomon (cf. Matt. 12:23; 9:27; 14:22[a pagan woman could not have meant "Messiah"]; Mark 10:47,48 and parallels).

10. *Did Jesus receive money or other compensation for his exorcisms?*

It is most likely that Jesus received a compensation for his exorcisms and healings although indirectly, Judas was the purser, according to John 13:29, and money had to come from somewhere. Also, some women whom he had healed supported the group (Luke 8:3). To compensate the healer or exorcist was a natural thing to do and often a requirement of the practitioner.

11. *Did Jesus negotiate with, or make concessions to the demons he exorcised?*

Only in one reported instance (the Gerasene demoniac) did he allow the demons to express a request which he granted. But this was not to be seen as a condition of their departure. However, the story of the demons possessing the pigs is only an addition to the original story and cannot be authentic.

12. *By casting out demons, did Jesus do anything unusual?*

Jesus fits perfectly in a long tradition of exorcism which continues to this day. In his time many other exorcists were operating.

13. *Did Jesus learn exorcism from the Essenes?*

That he learned from the Essenes is a strong possibility in consideration of the geographical proximity of Jesus' baptismal site, desert retreat and Qumran. There is also a common trait of simplicity in Jesus' and the Qumranites' exorcisms.

14. *Did Jesus believe that he was exorcisinq demons by his own power?*

If he did, he would have seen himself as the equal of God, which is not supported by the Synoptics. His unity with the Father is a Johannine concept which came late and, anyway, does not necessarily mean equality with God. He was most probably seeing himself as under the power of the Holy Spirit as suggested by the Beelzebul controversy and expressed in Luke 4:18.

15. *Did Jesus believe that he was forgiving sins when exorcising demons and healing people?*

Two premises have to be considered in order to answer this question: a) It was believed that misfortune, diseases and possession were caused by sin; b) A Qumranite text explicitly indicates, "an exorcist forgave my sins" (Nabonidus' prayer) and many other texts, biblical or extra biblical, specify or infer that healing and forgiveness are obtained only when the sinful situation ceases and hereby tie together forgiveness and healing.

If the Nabonidus text reflects a Qumranite belief retrojected into an old story, I think that Jesus might very well have shared the same belief.

16. *Did Jesus follow the methods of a great master of the past?*

He certainly did not follow the magical methods of Solomon. If he was acquainted with the Qumranite writings, he could have considered Abram or Daniel as his masters.

17. *Did Jesus believe he was going to be victorious over Satan?*

In consideration of his decision to participate in the religious campaign of John the Baptist and then to start his own, considering also the sense of urgency in his actions and message, we may infer that he was expecting the final defeat of Satan. In fact, Satan was not defeated and Jesus may have come to a point where he realized his failure when his enemy did not "fall like lighting."

18. *Was Jesus a shaman possessed by the Holy Spirit?*

I alluded to this possibility in answering question 1, and Morton Smith considered it, although he equates shaman with magician in his reasoning (*Jesus the Magician*, p. 104). In consideration of the accusation of insanity by his friends, which I take as authentic by virtue of the criterion of "embarrassment" (Mark 3:21,31); in consideration of the accusation of possession by a demon, of his habit of withdrawals, of the Old Testament precedent of ecstatic prophets, Jesus may indeed be considered as a shaman possessed by the Holy Spirit.

19. *What was the influence of Qumran if any on Jesus' understanding of himself as an exorcist?*

The Qumranites saw themselves as the righteous remnant of Israel and as the eschatological warriors of God on earth. They expected the coming of the Messiah(s) who would lead the final battle of God's hosts against Belial and the sons of darkness. One way to prepare for the cosmic battle was to exorcise and send away from the earth as many demons as possible. By analogy, Jesus may have had similar ideas and seen himself as the harbinger of the Messiah and rule of God on earth as he was expelling demons.

20. *Did Jesus see himself as the Messiah?*

That is the question! The big and final question. Scholarship is divided on the subject. From what we have seen about the implication of doing exorcism in a time of eschatological expectation, Jesus probably believed that he was, at least, working for the coming of the reign of God on earth, and of the Messiah, since the Messiah was supposed to introduce it. There was also the belief that the Messiah was going to destroy Satan. But we cannot conclude that Jesus believed that he himself was the Messiah simply because he was doing exorcisms. He may have perceived himself as only an advanced "detachment" preparing the terrain and people's minds for the final battle. There was also the belief that the Messiah would be revealed at the last moment, if he was to be a human being, and would not know his role before the time.

Conclusion

In the wide and turbulent stream of exorcism which flows to us from the most ancient times, from the steppes of Mongolia and Siberia through Mesopotamia and Egypt, Jesus appears as an isolated case, a man who could operate by a simple command and obtain immediate results. He transmitted his extraordinary power to his disciples, but it was lost after a few generations. There is little doubt that he was a spiritual force and had the knowledge or experience of some invisible power that people call God. In agreement with the eschatological beliefs of his time, he thought he had a certain role to play in the final struggle against Satan, and accordingly, went about exorcising demons. As his hopes did not materialize, he made a last "suicidal mission" to Jerusalem, perhaps a last attempt to change his world. But at this point of our knowledge, it is impossible to affirm that he saw himself as the Messiah.

Selected Bibliography

Bonner, Campbell. "The Techniques of Exorcism." *Harvard Theological Review* (1943) 39-49.

Borg, Marcus. *Jesus. A New Vision.* (San Francisco: Harper and Row, 1987) 23-75, 150-171.

Bottéro, Jean. "Les morts et l'au-delà dans les rituels en Accadien contre l'action des revenants." *Zeitschrift für Assyriologie und Vorderanatische Archäologie* 73 (1983) 153-203.

Dupont-Sommer, A. "Exorcism et guérisons dans les écrits de Qumran", Supplement, *Vestus Testamentum* (Congress Volume: Oxford, 1959-1960) 7.246-261.

Edelstein, Ludwig. *Ancient Medicine.* (Baltimore: Johns Hopkins, Eds. O. and C. L. Temkin. 1967, paperback 1987).

Eliade, M. *Shamanism.* Pantheon Books (Bollingen Series 76), 1964.

Goldstein, Morris. *Jesus in the Jewish Tradition.* (New York: Macmillan, 1950).

Grmk, Mirko D. *Diseases in the Ancient Greek World.* (Baltimore: Johns Hopkins, 1989, First edition 1983).

Howard, J. K. "New Testament: Exorcism and its Significance Today." *Expository Times*, Edinburgh. 96 (1984-1985).

Kee, H. C. "Short Studies: The Terminology of Mark's Exorcism Stories." *New Testament Studies* 14 (1967-1968) 232-246.

_____. *Miracles in the Early Christian World.* (New Haven: Yale University Press, 1983).

_____. *Medicine, Miracles and Magic in New Testament Times.* (Cambridge: Cambridge University Press, 1983).

Kirchschlager, Walter. "Exorcisms in Qumran." *Kairos* 18 (1976) 135-135.

Knox, W. L. "Jewish Liturgical Exorcism." *Harvard Theological Review* 21.3 191-203.

Langdon, S. H. *Semitic (Mythology).* (The Mythology of all Races Series: Norwood, 1931).

Latourelle, Réné. *The Miracles of Jesus and the Theology of Miracles.* (New York: Paulist Press, 1988).

Leeper, Elizabeth A. "From Alexandria to Rome: The Valentinian Connection to the Incorporation of Exorcism as a Pre-Baptismal Rite." *Vigilae Christianae* 44 (1990) 6-24.

McCasland, S. Vernon. *By the Finger of God: Demon Possession and Exorcism in Early Christianity in the Light of Modern Views of Mental Illness.* New York: Macmillan, 1951).

Neusner, J. *The Rabbinic Tradition about the Pharisees before 70.* (3 Volumes. Leiden: Brill, 1971).

Philostratus. *The Life of Apollonius of Tyana.* trans., F. C. Conybearer. (Loeb Classical Library, Cambridge, MA, 1912, repr. 1960).

Puech, Emile. "XIQ Ps Ap[a]: Un rituel d'exorcismes. Essay de reconstruction." *Revue de Qumran* 14 (1990) 377-408.

Sabourin, L. S. J. "The Miracles of Jesus, 2. Jesus and the Evil Powers." *Biblical Theology Bulletin* 4, (1974) 115-175.

Smith, Morton. *Jesus the Magician* (Wellingborough: The Aquarian Press, paperback 1985. First edition 1978).

Tamborino, Julius. "De antiquorum deomonismo." *Religionsges. Versuchen u. Vrarbeier* 7.3 (1909) (Giessen: Topelmann).

Theissen, Gerd. *The Miracles Stories of the Early Christian Tradition.* (Philadelphia: Fortress Press, 1983). (German edition 1974).

Tresson, Paul. "Mélanges. I. Un curieux cas d'exorcisme dans l'Antiquité. La Stèle égyptienne de Bakhtan." *Revue Biblique* 42 (1933) 57-78.

Vermes, G. "The Etymology of 'Essenes.'" *Revue de Qumran* 2.7 (June, 1960) 427-443.

"Essenes, Therapeutai, Qumran." *Durham University Journal* (June, 1961) 97-115.

"Essenes and Therapeutai." *Revue de Qumran* 3.12 (October, 1962) 495-504.

Insights and Models for Understanding the Healing Activity of the Historical Jesus

John J. Pilch
Georgetown University

Introduction

The "moonstruck" were one category of people Jesus healed (Matt 4:24; 17:15). Plutarch described the effects of moonlight upon human beings in this way:

> Nurses are exceedingly careful to avoid exposing young children to the moon, for, being full of moisture like green wood, they are thrown into spasms and convulsions. And we see that those who have gone asleep in the light of the moon are hardly able to rise again, like men with senses stunned or doped, for the moisture poured through them by the moon makes their bodies heavy. (*Quaes. Conviv.* 658E-F)

Some translators of the gospels render the Greek word for "moonstruck" by the English word "epileptic." This translation is an interpretation that illustrates medicocentrism (Pfifferling), a species of ethnocentrism that chooses to view texts from the ancient Middle East about sickness and healing in a Western biomedical perspective. Historians of medicine are as guilty of medicocentrism as exegetes and theologians (Scarborough 1969).

Medical anthropologists would identify the human experience of being "moonstruck" as a "culture-bound syndrome" similar to *phii pob* in rural Thailand (Simons and Hughes, 489) or *gila babi* in rural Malaysia (481). The sickness that results from the "evil eye" belongs to this same category (487; Herzfeld). Since all illness is culturally constructed, a more accurate term would be "folk conceptualized disorders," but "culture-bound" is still commonly used. No medical anthropologist identifies such human problems as misconceptions or superstitions.

This essay sketches a basic introduction to medical anthropology for those interested in understanding the healing activity of the historical Jesus respectfully and appropriately in its cultural context. It presents select literature, leading experts, fundamental concepts, and insights and models of particular interest to biblical specialists.

Arthur Kleinman is universally respected as one of the most knowledgeable and influential medical anthropologists who along with various collaborators has shaped and contributed to the growth and development of the field. By reading just the works he has authored (e.g.,

1988), co-authored (e.g., Csordas and Kleinman; Hahn and Kleinman), or edited (Eisenberg and Kleinman), a researcher can learn the entire field in all its complexity.

For those interested in a broader grasp of medical anthropology, Wellin surveys the five or six decades of research leading up to 1978 and highlights the major conceptual models. The extensive bibliography in Johnson and Sargent (1990) can serve as a master list for additional references on any topic mentioned in this essay. It can be supplemented with the resource lists in Hill (1985) and Logan and Hunt (1978).

Situating the Discipline

Medical anthropology is one of five subdisciplines of anthropology (McElroy and Townsend 13-17):

1. *Physical anthropology*, also called biological anthropology or human biology, is the study of the physical origins and variations of the human species. The study of origins focuses on the fossil record and on the behavior of living nonhuman primates. Investigation of variations compares contemporary human groups on the basis of skin color, blood type, hair form, bone structure, and stature.

Subdisciplines include: anthropometry or surface measurements; biomedical anthropology: growth and nutrition; health and physique; disease.

2. *Prehistoric archaeology* works without benefit of documents such as those used by classical archaeology. It focuses on artifacts and other material remains, including skeletons. This subdiscipline demonstrates how health, culture, and environment are related.

3. *Anthropological linguistics*, also called sociolinguistics, analyzes sound systems and grammars. Its contribution to medical anthropology is the methodology called ethnobioscience or ethnosemantics that seeks to learn how participants in a given culture categorize their experience. Such research helps construct "semantic illness networks" (Good; Good and Good) that highlight the culturally significant categories natives or insiders use to describe a human condition of misfortune called sickness. Technically, this is called the "emic" perspective.

4. *Cultural Anthropology* studies the way of life that a particular group of people follows. Foster and Anderson identify three roots of medical anthropology in the earlier work of cultural anthropology: studies of witchcraft, magic and primitive medicine; studies of personality and mental health in diverse cultures; and, particularly after World War II, studies in international public health.

Of special interest to Historical Jesus research is the sub-discipline of *Mediterranean anthropology*, which provides medical anthropology with knowledge about distinctive cultural values, beliefs, and behaviors that illuminate the understanding of health, sickness, and healing in the circum-Mediterranean area (Gilmore; Murdock; Gaines and Farmer; Harwood; Henderson; Henderson and Primeaux; McGoldrick et al.; Palgi; Saunders; Spiegel).

5. *Medical anthropology* currently is one of the most highly developed areas of anthropology, benefiting from the knowledge base already provided by

other subdisciplines. Those who seek to dissociate this discipline further from scientific Western medicine prefer to call the field *Ethnomedicine* (Seymour-Smith 187; Hughes), but medical anthropologists prefer to reserve this latter term for the study of healing rituals.

One of the aims of medical anthropology is to disentangle "the closely interwoven natural-environmental, human-biological, and socio-cultural threads forming the behavioral and conceptual network of human responses to the experience of illness" (Unschuld 1988: 179). To this end, medical anthropology has developed its own methodological and topical specialties. A sample is presented in the following table:

Table 1: *Subfields and Specialties of Medical Anthropology* (McElroy and Townsend 17)

Biomedical Studies of Adaptation	Ethnomedical Studies of Health and Healing	Social Problems and Interventions
genetics and disease	culture-bound syndromes	mental health
medical ecology	folk therapies	clinical anthropology
evolution of diseases	healing roles	addictions
social epidemiology	medical pluralism	family violence
nutrition	ethnopharmacology	birthing studies
demography	ethnoscience	disabilities
paleopathology	midwifery	public health

The columns in this Table should be read vertically; there is no horizontal correlation. Each column identifies a subfield and approach in medical anthropology, under which are listed topical specialties. The research results and insights produced by each subfield make medical anthropology a particularly rich science.

Medical Anthropology's Challenge

Biomedicine is as much ideology as science (Kleinman 1980: 301). It is guided by Western cultural assumptions and thoroughly permeated with a particular theoretical and value orientation (Kleinman 1980: 18).

Biomedical specialists tend to ignore the sick person's account of the experience and prefer to rely on laboratory tests for the "truth." This approach has no means for taking into serious account alternative therapies offered by other healing systems (ancient; primitive; traditional non-Western; folk; popular; modern; Kleinman 1980: 18; 28)

Medical anthropology grew out of the spread of Western medicine to other cultures, especially after World War II (Whyte in van der Geest and Whyte, 10). The encounter highlighted just how deeply biomedicine is afflicted with ethnocentrism and biomedical reductionism. Critics believe that this posture continues to be the conventional wisdom of that profession.

One must ask why should a discipline whose roots are so deeply planted in Western culture, whose major figures are almost entirely

European and North American, and whose data base is largely limited to the mainstream population in Western societies, why should so strongly Western-oriented a discipline regard cross-cultural research among the more than 80 percent of the world's people who inhabit non-Western societies as marginal? (Kleinman 1988: xi-xii)

Kleinman's observations on biomedicine, echoed by most if not all medical anthropologists (see Worsley), propose an analogous challenge for biblical studies as well. Why are cross-cultural, social-scientific approaches to studying the ancient Mediterranean world so strenuously resisted by European and North American researchers?

Medical Anthropology's Fresh Approach

Kleinman (1988) lists three ways to investigate and write about sickness and healing across cultures:

1. Borrow concepts originally intended to study other domains of human experience and use them to describe health care beliefs and practices. Thus, results from anthropological investigations of witchcraft, magic, symbol, and the like are transferred to human health questions. This is a useful method in structurally simple, kinship based societies, particularly if they are anti-introspective. The body is a "black box," so people concentrate instead on the social and symbolic conditions of sickness.

2. Borrow concepts from medical sociology (Turner). This works best in research on industrial societies, but like sociology it is not very helpful for studying pre-industrial societies (Fabrega 1971).

3. Develop an evolving conceptual system centered on the social and experiential peculiarities of sickness and healing. There are two equally important elements in healing: efficacy (see below) and meaning. Biomedicine focuses exclusively on efficacy, especially as viewed in a narrow biomedical perspective. The ordinary human person is interested in an outcome, but the most important outcome frequently is restoration of lost meaning or discovery of new meaning in life. Medical anthropology is particularly interested in meaning or the hermeneutic dimension of healing.

Medical anthropology has elected this latter method as the most appropriate for its interests. Its practitioners prefer to develop and advance its own ethnomedical paradigm as an alternative to the biomedical paradigm. The science needs an autonomous theoretical frame that is more suitable than any other for describing and interpreting the human experience of health, sickness, and healing (Kleinman 1980: 377)

Importance of Medical Anthropology

The researcher who has devoted a career to studying the historical Jesus should be encouraged to look to other, supplementary methodologies by this comment from Simons (and Hughes 29) in the study of culture-bound syndromes:

the approach advocated here is problem centered rather than discipline centered. Too often discipline-centered approaches have included subtle and sometimes not so subtle attempts to restrict relevances to Those in which I am Certified Expert (or, more charitably, to Those I am Competent to Discuss). In reality, relevant data may lie within many disciplines. And these data can seldom be organized hierarchically. Every set of human behaviors exists in a complex matrix of biological, social, psychological, and cultural facts which shape each other. How any portion of this set of facts shapes specific aspects of behavior or experience is a matter which must be discovered empirically, and an accurate analogy is not a layer cake but a marble cake.

Interdisciplinary specialists point out that the best interdisciplinary co-operation is often that carried out in the mind of a single researcher, an expert in one field who borrows eclectically from other disciplines and creatively integrates the insights.

Some Basic Terms and Definitions

Kleinman's definitions (1980; Kleinman et al. 1978) are generally and widely shared in medical anthropology (Caplan et al.; Cassell; Eisenberg; Engelhardt 1981; 1986; Fitzpatrick; Landy; Ohnuki-Tierney) even if sometimes modified (Young):

Health is very difficult to define. It is never clear what is lost when one has lost "good health." In generally any definition of health is a descriptive and often culturally normative concept that plays a defining role in a given society.

In the United States where a major cultural value is achievement and self-sufficiency, health might be defined as "the ability to perform those functions which allow the organism to maintain itself, all other things being equal, in the range of activity open to most other members of the species (e.g., within two standard deviations from the norm) and which are conducive toward the maintenance of its species" (Engelhardt, Jr. 1981: 32).

The classic definition offered by the World Health Organization "state of complete physical, mental, and social well-being and not merely the absence of disease and infirmity" is routinely challenged by Western specialists because of its focus on health as a "state." Non-Western populations, however, find the definition very meaningful since their cultural values place a high priority on well-being from a variety of perspectives.

Thus, from a general, medical anthropological perspective, health is best understood as a condition of well-being proposed as such by a given culture.

Sickness is a blanket term used to label real human experiences of disease and/or illness. This is the proper domain of medical anthropology, though special attention is paid mainly to illness (Twaddle).

Disease is not a reality but rather an explanatory concept that describes abnormalities in the structure and/or the function of human organs and organ systems. This includes pathological states even if they are not culturally recognized (Foster). Disease is the arena of biomedicine and the biomedical model (Kleinman 1980; Grmek; Lipowski).

The concept of disease attempts to correlate constellations of signs and symptoms for the purpose of explanation, prediction and control (Engelhardt,

Jr. 1981: 39). The biomedical jargon for these strategies is diagnoses, prognosis, and therapy, and these concepts lead into the field of power and politics (Glick; Pilch 1991a; 1992a and b).

Illness, too, is not a reality but an explanatory concept that describes the human perception, experience, and interpretation of certain socially disvalued states including but not limited to disease (see Worsley, 327). Illness is both a personal and social reality and therefore in large part a cultural construct (Kleinman 1974b; Lewis). Culture dictates what to perceive, value, express, and then how to live illness (Kleinman 1980: 417-418; Ohnuki-Tierney 1981; 1984; Weidman 1988; Kaplan).

Curing is the anticipated outcome relative to **disease,** that is, the attempt is made to take effective control of disordered biological and/or psychological processes.

Healing is directed toward **illness,** that is, the attempt is made to provide personal and social meaning for the life problems created by sickness. Treatment, of course, can be concerned with one or the other aspect of a human problem (disease or illness), and either or both can be successfully treated. The complaint against modern biomedicine is that it is concerned only with "curing the disease" while the patient is searching for "healing of the illness." This dichotomy separates what nearly all human societies view as essential in healing, that is, some combination of symptom reduction along with other behavior or physical transformation that reflects that society's understanding of health and the provision of new or renewed meaning in life for the sick person (Etkin, 300).

Healing is an elemental social function and experience. It is equally basic and fundamental as the gift or the exchange relationship. Healing is one of the primary forms of symbolic action. (Kleinman 1974: 210)

These definitions and their implications offer historical Jesus researchers a fresh perspective on sickness and healing in the first century, Eastern Mediterranean world and a welcome rescue from the tyranny of Western biomedical perspectives.

The Health Care System

In every society, the health care system (Mackintosh) is created by a collective view and shared pattern of usage that operates at a local level and is seen and used somewhat differently by different social groups and individuals (Kleinman 1980: 39). Thus the health care system is a concept, and not an entity. It is a conceptual model held by the researcher. Kleinman constructed a structural model of a health care system (see Figure 1) that he suggested could be used be used to analyze the system in any society or culture (Pilch 1985).

Figure 1: The Health Care System (after Kleinman 1980, 50; Pilch 1985, 144)

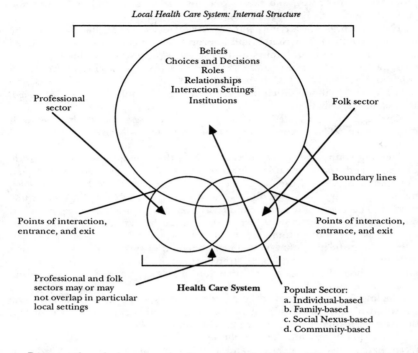

Because the whole system heals, not just the healer (Kleinman 1980: 72), the investigator needs to conduct both a micro and a macro analysis to see how small-scale events within the healing system in its three sectors might relate to large-scale social structure and processes.

Consider the element of power. Glick (1967) proposed that knowing a culture's chief source(s) of power, whether political, social, mythological, religious, technological, etc., will allow the researcher to deduce the beliefs about the causes of illness and how to treat illness. Social reality determines what the power is: witchcraft, exorcism, fortune-telling, surgery, psychotherapy, and symbolic reality lays down the pathways by which the application of power may be effective (see symbolic healing below). In turn, political, socioeconomic, and cultural power determines which view prevails and which outcomes are acceptable. What insight does this offer into the arguments about the source and legitimacy of Jesus' power to heal?

Finally, Kleinman cautions that health care systems are nearly impossible to understand once they are removed from their cultural contexts (1980: 415). All the greater reason for seeking to discover as much about cultural beliefs, values, and behaviors as possible.

Five Major Functions of Health Care Systems

Five elements working together in a given system construct and define both health and illness (Kleinman 1978: 416-471). These elements are also called the "core clinical functions." In this phrase the word "clinical" represents "general health care."

1. *Cultural hierarchies of health values.* Societies construct a hierarchy of health values, and "in small scale, pre-literate societies, as well as in many historical cultures, the fit between health values (needs, expectations, choices and evaluations) and healing (therapeutic approaches and outcomes) can often be very tight" (Kleinman 1978: 417). This is so because the individual internalizes these health values during the socialization process.

The semantic illness networks (see Good and Good) of given societies tend to cluster a variety of values, concepts, and experience. The West seems to prefer metaphors of war: germs "invade," the threatened person "fights" infection, biomedical researchers "wage war" against viruses, etc. On the other hand, the Taiwanese among whom Kleinman has conducted extensive research, talk about being "hit" by ghosts, either purposefully or inadvertently, and thereby becoming ill.

In the Mediterranean cultural world, one must attend to the core values of honor and shame, gender-based division of society, client and patron, sheep and goats (Pilch 1992a and b; Murdock), belief in spirits (Saler), attitudes toward pain (Zborowski; Zola) and many other concepts and values that comprise that distinctive cultural hierarchy of health values.

2. *Experience of illness.* Culture dictates what to perceive, value, express, and how to live illness. Culture also plays a significant role in symptom formation (Pilch 1988b), as well as the various psychophysiological processes in and reactions to illness. Culture's greatest contribution is the meaning given to the illness experience. This is also the first stage of healing because the experience can be acknowledged and recognized as something specific which charts the initial path toward an appropriate response.

3. *Cognitive response: ordering illness by means of labelling, classifying, and explaining.* Culture establishes general criteria to guide the therapeutic process and to evaluate the outcomes. This involves creating structures of relevance: is this experience major or minor? important or negligible? The response involves knowing the hierarchies of resort: family, friends, the village, the herbalist, the prophet, the "professional," etc. (Pilisuk; Romanucci-Ross 1969)

Mary Douglas has convincingly demonstrated that illness and its consequences are intensely social and communal events. They are disruptive and often threaten the most essential values, behavioral norms, and conceptions of order. What is required is restoration of order by placing the threat in its proper framework, by controlling the disruptive effect on the sick person and that person's network, and by making the entire experience personally and socially meaningful.

To explore this dimension further, one needs to investigate "explanatory models" (see below) which differ from sick person to sick person, and also between the sick person and the therapist. The cognitive response to misfortune or sickness forms the core of "symbolic healing" (see below).

4. *Healing Activities.* In actual fact, healing goes on throughout the entire system and in each of these five functions, so one must consider individual healing practices within the *total* context of the system and indeed of society. In other words, healing entails much more than demonstrable empirical efficacy, important as this may be when or whether it actually occurs (Frank).

Strategies include healing and preventive activities per se which range from empirical remedies (see van der Geest et al.) and technological interventions to symbolic therapies like the placebo (Moerman 1983; see also Dow).

5. *Potential outcomes: managing cure or treatment failure, recurrence or chronic illness, permanent impairment, and death.* Anthropologists note that much of "traditional" health care is dedicated to preparing for death and making the experience of dying meaningful. It is especially at this point that health care often overlaps with religion and other cultural systems. In the entire process, of course, constructing a meaningful life is equally important. In this stage, human efforts are focused on answering the question: "now what?"

These five functions provide a fairly comprehensive basis for understanding healing and health care in any given culture and allow for more appropriate cross-cultural comparisons. All attempts to understand illness and treatment can be thought of as explanatory models.

Explanatory Models

"EMs" are more or less formally structured and coherent accounts of reality, in this case, the reality of illness and its treatment. They may be and often are ambiguous and changing and may even contain contradictions and varying degrees of logical development. Social scientists note that all people have multiple belief systems to which they turn when they need help.

EMs are the notions about an episode of sickness and its treatment which are employed by everyone involved in the process (the sick person, family, friends, village, healers). These models are embedded in the larger cognitive systems which in turn are anchored in particular cultural and structural arrangements, i.e., the health care system sectors and sub-sectors. Of great import to the medical anthropologist is not only grasping and understanding the EMs but also observing the interaction (see below) between sick persons and healers. This interaction is a central component of health care, and one learns about it by exploring and recording the EMs involved.

Structurally, there are five questions that EMs seek to explain relative to each illness episode (Kleinman 1980: 105):

1. Etiology, that is, origins and causes
2. Time and onset of symptoms
3. Pathophysiology
4. Course of sickness, including the degree of severity and the type of sick role (acute, chronic, impaired, etc.)
5. Treatment

The healer EMs seek to answer all five questions. The family and sick individual EMs usually answer only salient questions. In contrast to professional EMs, those of the lay person ordinarily disclose the significance of a given health problem for the patient and the family, along with their treatment goals. A review of all the information gathered by the EMs of everyone involved in a given illness episode helps an investigator to realize that efficacy always involves both symptom reduction and restoration of meaning to life.

In practically all of his publications, Kleinman never concludes without suggesting avenues of future research. Here, adapted for historical Jesus specialists, is his list for additional research topics relative to EMs:

– a systematic and holistic study of the local health care system in first century Palestine, emphasizing interaction between different sectors (professional, lay, folk; public and private; male and female; patron-broker-client; etc.) and the relation of health-care functions to their component elements;

– a focus on cognitive and communicative aspects of the healer-client relationships, stressing comparisons of and interactions between EMs in the popular, folk, clinical and "scientific" domains;

– a cross-cultural comparison of psychosocial and psychophysiological aspects of illness experience in first century Palestine, emphasizing mechanisms by which culture molds behavior and biology (e.g., swaddling socializes an infant to control very early in life; loss of control is permitted in possession or in angry rage after which the person is puzzled and repentant about the uncontrolled behavior just experienced; etc.)

– the relationship between meaning (subjective and social) and efficacy in "traditional" and modern health care;

– a study of local medical systems as adaptive responses to specific stress factors in the physical and social environments (e.g. fathers use physical punishment in rearing sons; a son who becomes a violent adult explains violent behavior through possession by a violent spirit; the violence is tamed by casting out the demon).

Transaction: The Interaction With The Healer

While it is the whole system and not just the healer that heals, the transactions between sick people and healers are critical (Mason et al.). All transactions between the sick person and the healer(s) should be considered fundamentally hermeneutic (Good and Good 1981; Pilch 1988b). What takes place in the interaction is interpretation of symbols and signs in terms of very particular interpretive schemata.

The diverse EMs that all the actors in a healing transaction bring to the event influence the interactions and interpretations that take place. The sick person and the healer are best understood as engaging in the interpretation of the context of the encounter which itself is symbolic, and of the symbolic forms that are manipulated by the other during the encounter. Symbols include words, acts, events, and/or gestures. The healing encounter is recognized as a distinctive kind of encounter, and the specific encounter under consideration is either a new form of interaction, or a repetition of a previously known form of encounter. What the encounter produces is "understanding" rather than new "knowledge" or "explanation" (Gaines, 244).

In a recent reflection on these encounters, Kleinman (1988: 115-116) constructed another model for comparing healing systems across cultures. The following summary of its key points omits the detail which is understandably required by Kleinman's interest in contemporary industrialized cultures where biomedical systems prevail as well as the traditional cultures he studies in the Far East.

1. Setting: folk, popular, professional
2. Characteristics of the Interaction
   a. Number of participants
   b. Time character: episodic or continuous, brief or lengthy;
   c. Quality of relationship: formal or informal, authoritarian or dyadic, etc.
3. Characteristics of the healer: personality, training, type of practice, insight into the process, etc.
4. Idioms of Communication
   a. Mode: somatic, religious, moral, social, etc.
   b. Code: nonverbal, verbal, special semiotic system
   c. EM of a particular illness episode, e.g., shared, conflicting, open, tacit, etc.
   d. Rhetorical devices for narratizing illness and negotiating treatment
   e. Interpretation
5. Clinical Reality: sacred or secular; disease-oriented or illness-oriented; focus of treatment: sick person, family, etc.; symbolic and/or instrumental interventions; etc.
6. Therapeutic Stages and Mechanisms: Process; mechanisms of change: catharsis, confession, altered state of consciousness, etc.
7. Extratherapeutic Aspects: social control, political implications, etc.

Kleinman designed the model specifically for examining symbolic healing systems (e.g., forms of religious healing, shamanism, various lay psychotherapies sometimes called ministries). With appropriate modifications and fine tuning, which is standard procedure in the construction and application of models, it can serve well for analyzing healing interactions in the first century world.

Symbolic Healing

Medical anthropologists generally agree that religious healing, shamanism, and Western psychotherapy are versions of one and the same thing: symbolic healing (Dow, 56; Moerman; Kleinman 1988: 131). In symbolic healing, the therapist or healer mediates culture. What is especially important is the metaphorical structure of culture. This is as decisive in effectiveness as any other elements whether physiological, pharmacological, or anything else. Symbolic healing is best understood by examining the four essential structural processes involved in accomplishing it.

Stage 1. Symbolic bridge. It is important to establish a symbolic bridge between personal experience, social relations, and cultural meanings. Every system of symbolic healing is based on a model of experiential reality that is called the *mythic world*. If this world does not derive from society's shared meaning, then it derives from initiation into a particular system of healing such as a psychoanalytic relationship or a Catholic charismatic prayer group.

The particular cultural mythic world contains knowledge that is experientially but not necessarily empirically true. Together, the healer and the sick person agree to particularize a segment of the cultural mythic world for use in a particular case of symbolic healing (Dow, 61).

The mythic world contains the symbols that link the social system to the self system of the sick person. The relationship of these two systems to other systems can be examined in Dow's hierarchy of living systems presented in Table 2. Note the point at which the symbolic bridge between two systems will occur.

Table 2: Hierarchy of Living Systems (Dow 62)

Environment	System	Units
Natural environment	Ecological	Populations
Social environment	Social	Individuals
Individual environment	Self	Somatic systems
Body Cells	Somatic Molecular	Cells, etc.
		Molecules (genes)

The hierarchy of linked systems in this Table is the biopsychocultural basis for healing. For instance, the individual experience (serious loss) is linked with a group's master symbols (the paschal mystery; crucified Christ) which in turn are the deep cultural grammar governing how an individual orients self to others and to the inner world. The cultural grammar is found in the central myths (scripture). Both Dow and Kleinman suggest the associations noted in parentheses that have preceded. Just as illness is expressed at different levels of this hierarchy, so is healing a transformation of these linked systems at various or all levels.

Stage 2. Relating the sick person to the mythic world. A healer activates the symbolic connections for a sick person. The healer persuades the sick person that the problem can be related to some part of the mythic world. For instance, Peter's mother-in-law in the Lucan account suffers from a demon named "Fever" and therefore she can be treated by exorcism (Pilch 1991a; 1992b). In small scale pre-literate societies healer, sick person, and the family usually agree about these core meanings.

Stage 3. Transactional symbols. A healer employs mediating (also called transactional) symbols that are particularized from the general meaning system and guides therapeutic change in the sick person's emotional reactions. The focus on emotion in the self system works an effect by way of hierarchical linkage in the somatic system.

It is not just the healer's rhetorical skill at work here. Rather, the participants in symbolic healing share mutual expectations which shape and name the clinical reality, that is, the illness. Then the healer generalizes the personal experience into the therapeutic meaning system, and the sick person particularizes that symbolic meaning into personal experience.

The sand painting images of Navaho spirits as used with other techniques by Navaho healers are an illustration of such a transactional symbol.

Stage 4. Confirmation. The healer confirms the transformation of the particularized symbolic meaning. Thus, an intrusive spirit, now named, is subjected to specific rituals of exorcism. "In anthropological terms, the healing interaction fosters this transformation as a work of culture: the making over of psychophysiological process into meaningful experience and the affirmation of success" (Kleinman 1988: 134).

Most symbolic healing around the planet takes place in the popular sector, that is the family and community, and the folk sector (Kleinman 1988: 117). Of particular interest is that most healing is not long-term, divorced from every life encounters between participants, psychologically minded, secular, or oriented to the needs and rights of the individual vis-à-vis those of the family and community. The therapeutic relationship is authoritarian in nearly all cultures except the West. This is what one would expect in the sociocentric non-Western cultures as contrasted with egocentric Western culture.

Clearly, interpretation is the core task of healing cross-culturally (Kleinman 1988: 119). Non-Western healing systems (Worsley) ordinarily emphasize sacred reality, illness orientation (that is, they take the sick person's account to be the "real" problem), symbolic intervention, interrogative structure, socio-centric, particularly family-centered locus of control, and rather substantial expectations of change and even cure.

Efficacy

"Do (did) *real* cures *really* happen?" "Do these techniques and strategies *really* work?" Such questions routinely emerge from Western skeptics unaware that they stem from the biomedical reductionism into which natives of Western culture have been socialized for almost a century now.

Efficacy is "the perceived capacity of a given practice to affect sickness in some desirable way" (Young, 277). Actually, efficacy can mean any number of things ranging from total symptom reduction to some physical sign, like fever, emeses, or the like, which can be interpreted as a required *proximate* effect indicating that the *ultimate anticipated outcome* is on the way (Etkin 301-302). From the perspective of medical anthropology, curing is efficacious when biomedical changes take place; healing is efficacious when the people who seek it say it is.

What is crucial to evaluating efficacy is understanding the cultural expectation and the biological outcomes at various stages of the therapeutic processes. Efficacy is always a cultural construct (Kleinman 1974a: 210):

> The healing dialectic has been considered effective when the bonds between the sick individual and the group, weakened by disease, are strengthened, social values reaffirmed, and the notion of social order no longer threatened by illness and death; or when the individual experience of illness has been made meaningful, personal suffering

shared, and the individual leaves the marginal situation of sickness and been reincorporated in health or even death back into the social body.

Medical anthropologists cannot totally explain *how* cultural factors are related to the healing process. There is more here than meets the biomedical eye. The best contemporary hypothesis is that the sick person in a specific context uses the semantic resources available and creates meaning. The meaning may be wholesome (*placebo*) or noxious (*nocebo*).

Moerman (1983) records the traditional wisdom on this point: "meaning mends" and "metaphor can heal." Medical anthropologists note that placebos mend when they are not understood to be that. Metaphors heal best when they are taken literally and their symbolic identity is not recognized. When they are demystified they tend to lose their efficaciousness.

In other words, healing boils down to meaning and the transformation of experience. The change or transformation is created by all participants who effectively enact culturally authorized interpretations. When demons are exorcised, the anxious client believes the cause of the problem is gone. This conviction is affirmed by the healer and encouraged by the social circle. It alters the client's cognitive processes from apprehension to calm.

"What has changed?" The life problems may or may not still be present, but their perception is no longer the same. "Altered meanings exert practical efficacy in the felt experience of the patient" (Kleinman 1988: 134).

Conclusion

Medical anthropologists believe that one advantage of ethnomedical and cross cultural research is that the biomedical practitioner is forced out of a narrow professional orientation and exposed to aspects of the human health that are frequently hidden by the role and social space the practitioner exercises in modern Western culture. Medical anthropology could work the same effect for the similarly specialized historical Jesus researcher.

In traditional cultures it is not always possible to separate medicine from the religious system as is routinely done in the West. Religion can be viewed as a cultural adaptive response to a much wider range of suffering and misfortune, of which human sickness is only a small part.

For this reason, Kleinman (1973: 57) insists that "without first possessing a fairly deep understanding of its cultural setting, it would seem impossible to understand a given system of medicine; this seems to hold as well for systems of scientific knowledge." The historical Jesus researcher would thus move from a study of medical anthropology to the equally important study of Mediterranean anthropology. There is no other way to learn the concepts and values that govern and shape the understanding of healing in the first century Eastern Mediterranean world.

What is the result? Medical anthropology, like all anthropological study, could help the exegete to adopt a transcultural stance, "a perceptual stance and research posture that is detached or 'alienated' but equidistant from two or more cultural units, however they may be defined" (Weidman 1988: 261-262). One of these cultural units is the investigator's own.

From this position, the exegete could choose to become a "culture broker," that is, one who helps others understand cultures other than their own. The next step is to help others adopt a third culture rooted in expanded cross-cultural understanding. The process of developing a third culture entails first knowing one's own culture well, then recognizing the differences of the other culture. After learning to empathize with those differences, the exegete works at creating the common ground necessary for intercultural communication, that is, for answering the question: "what does it mean for us?"

Bibliography

Caplan, Arthur L., H. Tristram Engelhardt, Jr., and James J. McCartney, editors

    1981   *Concepts of Health and Disease: Interdisciplinary Perspective.* Reading, MA: Addison-Wesley Publishing Company.

Cassell, E. J.

    1976   "Illness and Disease." *Hastings Center Report* 6: 27-37.

Chrisman, Noel J. and T. W. Maretzki, editors

    1982   *Clinically Applied Anthropology: Anthropologists in Health Science Settings.* Culture, Illness, and Healing, Volume 5. Dordrecht: D. Reidel Publishing Co.

Csordas, Thomas J. and Arthur Kleinman

    1990   "The Therapeutic Process." Pp. 1-25 in Johnson and Sargent.

Douglas, Mary

    1966   *Purity and Danger.* New York: Praeger.

    1970   "The Healing Rite." *Man* 5: 302-308.

Dow, James

    1986   "Universal Aspects of Symbolic Healing: A Theoretical Synthesis." *American Anthropologist* 88: 56-69.

Draguns, J. and Harry Triandis, Editors

    1980   *Handbook of Cross-Cultural Psychology*, Volume 6: Psychopathology. New Jersey: Allyn and Bacon.

Eisenberg, Leon

    1977   "Disease and Illness: Distinctions between Professional and Popular Ideas of Sickness." *Culture, Medicine and Psychiatry* 1: 9-23.

Eisenberg, Leon, and Arthur Kleinman, Editors
    1981   *The Relevance of Social Science for Medicine.* Dordrecht: D.
                Reidel Publishing Company.

Engelhardt, H. Tristram, Jr.
    1981   "The Concepts of Health and Disease." Pp. 30-35 in Caplan et
                al.
    1986   "The Social Meanings of Illness." *Second Opinion* 1: 26-39.

Etkin, Nina L.
    1988   "Cultural Constructions of Efficacy." Pp. 299-320 in van der
                Geest and Whyte.

Fabrega, Horacio
    1971   "The Study of Medical Problems in Preliterate Settings." *Yale
                Journal of Biology and Medicine* 43: 385-407.
    1974   *Disease and Social Behavior: An Interdisciplinary Perspective.*
                Cambridge and London: MIT Press.

Fitzpatrick, Ray
    1984   "Lay Concepts of Illness." Pp. 11-31 in Ray Fitzpatrick, John
                Hinton, Stanton Newman, Graham Scambler, and James
                Thompson, Editors. *The Experience of Illness.* London and New
                York: Tavistock Publishers.

Foster, George M.
    1976   "Disease Etiologies in Non-Western Medical Systems."
                American Anthropologist 78:773-782.

Foster, George M. and Barbara Anderson
    1978   *Medical Anthropology.* New York: John Wiley.

Frank, Jerome
    1974   *Persuasion and Healing: A Comparative Study of Psychotherapy.*
                New York: Schocken Books.

Gaines, Atwood D.
    1982   "Knowledge and Practice: Anthropological Ideas and Psychi-
                atric Service." Pp. 243-273 in Chrisman and Maretzki.

Gaines, Atwood D, and P. Farmer
    1986   "Visible Saints: Social Cynosures and Dysphoria in the
                Mediterranean Tradition." *Culture, Medicine and Psychiatry* 10:
                295-330.

Gilmore, David D., editor

  1987   *Honor and Shame and the Unity of the Mediterranean.* A Special
          publication of the American Anthropological Association,
          number 22; Washington, D.C.: American Anthropological
          Association.

Gilmore, David D.

  1982   "Anthropology of the Mediterranean Area." *Annual Review of
          Anthropology* 11: 175-205.

Glick, Leonard B.

  1967   "Medicine as an Ethnographic Category: The Gimi of the
          New Guinea Highlands." *Ethnology* 6:31-56.

Good, Byron and Mary Jo DelVecchio Good

  1981   "The Meaning of Symptoms: A Cultural Hermeneutic Model
          of Clinical Practice." Pp. 165-196 in Eisenberg and Kleinman.

Good, Byron J.

  1977   "The Heart of What's the Matter: The Semantics of Illness in
          Iran." *Culture, Medicine and Psychiatry* 1: 25-28.

Grmek, Mirko D.

  1989   *Diseases in the Ancient Greek World.* Translated by Mireille
          Muellner and Leonard Muellner. Baltimore and London:
          The Johns Hopkins University Press.

Hahn, Robert A. and Arthur M. Kleinman

  1983   "Biomedical Practice and Anthropological Theory:
          Frameworks and Directions." *Annual Review of Anthropology*
          12: 305-333.

Harwood, Alan, Editor

  1981   *Ethnicity and Medical Care.* Cambridge, MA and London:
          Harvard University Press.

Henderson, George

  1989   *Understanding Indigenous and Foreign Cultures.* Springfield, IL.:
          Charles C. Thomas, Publisher.

Henderson, George, and Martha Primeaux

  1981   *Transcultural Health Care.* Menlo Park, CA.: Addison-Wesley
          Publishing Co.

Hill, Carole E., Editor
1985   *Training Manual in Medical Anthropology*. Washington, DC: American Anthropological Association.

Herzfeld, Michael
1986   "Closure as Cure: Tropes in the Exploration of Bodily and Social Disorder." *Current Anthropology* 27: 107-120.

Hughes, Charles C.
1968   "Ethnomedicine," *International Encyclopedia of the Social Sciences*. New York: Free Press, 1968.

Johnson, Thomas M. and Carolyn M. Sargent, Editors
1990   *Medical Anthropology: A Handbook of Theory and Method*. New York: Greenwood Press.

Kaplan, Marcie
1983   "A Woman's View of DSM-III." *American Psychologist* July: 786-803.

Kleinman, Arthur M.
1973   "Toward a Comparative Study of Medical Systems: An Integrated Approach to the Study of the Relationship of Medicine and Culture." *Science, Medicine, and Man* 1: 55-65
1974a   "Medicine's Symbolic Reality: On a Central Problem in the Philosophy of Medicine." *Inquiry* 16: 206-213.
1974b   "Cognitive Structures of Traditional Medical Systems: Ordering, Explaining, and Interpreting the Human Experience of Illness." *Ethnomedizin* III: 27-49.
1978   "Problems and Prospects in Comparative Cross-Cultural Medical and Psychiatric Studies." Pp. 407-440 in Kleinman et al., *Culture and Healing in Asian Societies*.
1980   *Patients and Healers in the Context of Culture*. Berkeley: University of California.
1988   *Rethinking Psychiatry: From Cultural Category to Personal Experience*. New York and London: Free Press and Collier Macmillan Publishers.

Kleinman, Arthur M., Peter Kunstadter, E. Russell Alexander, and James L. Gate, editors
1978   *Culture and Healing in Asian Societies: Anthropological, Psychiatric, and Public Health Studies*. Cambridge, MA: Schenkman Publishing Co.

Kleinman, Arthur M. and Lilias H. Sung

    1979   "Why Do Indigenous Practitioners Successfully Heal?" *Social Science & Medicine* 13B: 7-26.

Landy, David, Editor

    1977   *Culture, Disease and Healing.* New York: Macmillan.

Lewis, Gilbert

    1981   "Cultural Influences on Illness Behavior: A Medical Anthropological Approach." Pp. 151-162 in Eisenberg and Kleinman.

Lipowski. Z.

    1969   "Psychosocial aspects of Disease." *Annals of Internal Medicine* 71: 1197-1206.

Logan, Michael H. and Edward E. Hunt, Jr., Editors

    1978   *Health and the Human Condition: Perspectives on Medical Anthropology.* North Scituate, MA.: Duxbury Press, 1978.

Mackintosh, Douglas R.

    1978   *Systems of Health Care.* Boulder, CO: Westview Press.

Mason, Randall C., Jr., Graham Clark, Robert R. Reeves, Jr., S. Bruce Wagner

    1969   "Acceptance and Healing." *Journal of Religion and Health* 8: 123-142.

McElroy, Ann and Patricia K. Townsend

    1989   *Medical Anthropology in Ecological Perspective.* Second Edition. Boulder, San Francisco, and London: Westview Press, reprint of 1979.

McGoldrick, Monica, John K. Pearce, and Joseph Giordano, Editors

    1982   *Ethnicity and Family Therapy.* New York/London: The Guilford Press.

Mitchell, J. C.

    1969   "The Concept and Use of Social Networks." Pp. 1-50 in J.C. Mitchell, *Social Networks in Urban Situations.* Manchester: University Press.

Moerman, Daniel E.

    1979   "Anthropology of Symbolic Healing." *Current Anthropology* 20: 59-80.

    1983   "Physiology and Symbols: The Anthropological Implications of the Placebo Effect." Pp. 156-167 in Romanucci-Ross et al.

Morley, Peter
    1978   "Culture and the Cognitive World of Traditional Medical
            Beliefs: Some Preliminary Considerations." Pp. 1-18 in
            Morley and Wallis.

Morley, Peter and Roy Wallis, Editors
    1978   *Culture and Curing: Anthropological Perspectives on Traditional
            Medical Beliefs and Practices.* Pittsburgh: University of Pitts-
            burgh Press.

Murdock, George Peter
    1980   *Theories of Illness: A World Survey.* Pittsburgh: University of
            Pittsburgh.

Ohnuki-Tierney, Emiko
    1981   *Illness and Healing Among the Sakhalin Ainu: A Symbolic
            Interpretation.* Cambridge: Cambridge University Press.
    1984   *Illness and Culture in Contemporary Japan: An Anthropological
            View.* Cambridge: Cambridge University Press.

Palgi, Phyllis,
    1983   "Mental Health, Traditional Beliefs, and the Moral Order
            among Yemenite Jews in Israel." Pp. 319-335 in Romanucci-
            Ross et al.

Pfifferling, John-Henry
    1981   "A Cultural Prescription for Medicocentrism." Pp. 197-222 in
            Eisenberg and Kleinman.

Pilch, John J.
    1981   "Biblical Leprosy and Body Symbolism." *Biblical Theology
            Bulletin* 11: 119-133.
    1985   "Healing in Mark: A Social Science Analysis." *Biblical
            Theology Bulletin* 15: 142-150.
    1986   "The Health Care System in Matthew: A Social Science
            Analysis." *Biblical Theology Bulletin* 16: 102-106.
    1988a   "Interpreting Scripture: The Social Science Method." *The Bible
            Today* 26: 13-19
    1988b   "Understanding Biblical Healing: Selecting the Appropriate
            Model." *Biblical Theology Bulletin* 18: 60-66.
    1989a   "Sickness and Healing in Luke-Acts." *The Bible Today* 27: 21-
            28.
    1989b   "Reading Matthew Anthropologically: Healing in Cultural
            Perspective." *Listening: Journal of Religion and Culture* 24: 278-289.

1991a   "Sickness and Healing in Luke-Acts." Pp. 181-209 in Jerome H. Neyrey, S.J., Editor, *The Social World of Luke-Acts.* Peabody, MA: Hendrickson Publishers.

1991b   "Health in the New Testament: Did Healings Happen?" *National Outlook* (Australia) 13 (June, #4): 12-14.

1991c   *Introducing the Cultural Context of the New Testament.* New York/Mahwah, NJ: Paulist Press.

1992a   "Separating the Sheep from the Goats." *PACE* (Professional Approaches for Christian Educators) 21 (April, 1992): 215-218.

1992b   "A Spirit Named 'Fever.'" *PACE* (Professional Approaches for Christian Educators) 21 (May, 1992) 253-256.

1992c   "BTB Readers Guide: Understanding Healing in the Social World of Early Christianity." *Biblical Theology Bulletin* 22: 26-33.

Pilisuk, Marc and Susan Hillier Parks

1986   *The Healing Web: Social Networks and Human Survival.* Hanover, N.H.: U. of New England Press.

Romanucci-Ross, Lola

1969   "The hierarchy of resort in curative practices: the Admiralty Islands, Melanesia." *Journal of Health and Social Behavior* 10: 201-209.

1978   "Melanesian Medicine: Beyond Culture to Method." Pp. 115-138 in Morley and Wallis.

Romanucci-Ross, Lola, Daniel E. Moerman, and Laurence R. Tancredi, Editors

1983   *The Anthropology of Medicine: From Culture to Method.* New York: Praeger.

Saler, Benson

1977   "Supernatural as a Western Category." *Ethics* 5: 31-33.

Saunders, Lyle

1954   *Cultural Differences and Medical Care: The Case of Spanish Speaking People of the Southwest.* New York: Sage.

Saunders, Lyle and Gordon Hewes

1969   "Folk Medicine and Medical Practice." Pp. 402-408 in *The Cross-Cultural Approach to Health Behavior.* L. Riddick Lynch, Editor. Rutherford, NJ: Farleigh Dickinson University Press.

Scarborough, John

1969   *Roman Medicine.* Ithaca: Cornell University Press.

1988   "Medicine," Pp. 1227-1248 in Michael Grant and Rachel Kitzinger, Editors. *Civilization of the Ancient Mediterranean.* New York: Charles Scribner's Sons.

Seymour-Smith, Charlotte

1986   "Medical Anthropology," in *Dictionary of Anthropology.* Boston, MA: G. K. Hall & Co.

Simons, Ronald C. and Charles C. Hughes, editors

1985   *The Culture-Bound Syndromes: Folk Illnesses of Psychiatric and Anthropological Interest.* Dordrecht: D. Reidel Publishing Co.

Spiegel, John

1982   "An Ecological Model of Ethnic Families." Pp. 31-51 in McGoldrick et al.

Turner, Bryan S.

1980   "The Body and Religion: Towards an Alliance of Medical Sociology and Sociology of Religion." *The Annual Review of the Social Sciences of Religion* 4: 247-284.

Turner, Edith with William Blodgett, Singleton Kahona, and Fideli Benwa

1992   *Experiencing Ritual: A New Interpretation of African Healing.* Philadelphia: University of Pennsylvania Press.

Twaddle, Andrew C.

1981   "Sickness and the Sickness Career: Some Implications." Pp. 111-133 in Eisenberg and Kleinman.

Unschuld, Paul U.

1976   "Western Medicine and Traditional Healing Systems: Competition, Cooperation or Integration?" *Ethics in Science & Medicine* 3: 1-20.

1980   "The Issue of Structured Coexistence of Scientific and Alternative Medical Systems: A Comparison of East and West German Legislation." *Social Science and Medicine* 14B: 15-24.

1988   "Culture and Pharmaceutics: Some Epistemological Observations on Pharmacological Systems in Ancient Europe and Medieval China" Pp. 179-197 in van der Geest and Whyte.

van der Geest, Sjaak and Susan Reynolds Whyte, Editors

  1988   *The Context of Medicines in Developing Countries: Studies in Pharmaceutical Anthropology.* Dordrecht/Boston/London: Kluwer Academic Publishers.

van der Geest, Sjaak

  1988   "Pharmaceutical Anthropology: Perspectives for Research and Application." Pp. 329-369 in van der Geest and Whyte.

Weidman, Hazel Hitson

  1982   "Research Strategies, Structural Alterations and Clinically Applied Anthropology." Pp. 201-241 in Chrisman and Maretzki.

  1988   "A Transcultural Perspective on Health Behavior," Pp. 261-280 in David S. Gochman, Editor. *Health Behavior: Emerging Research Perspectives.* New York and London: Plenum Press.

Wellin, Edward

  1978   "Theoretical orientation in medical anthropology: change and continuity over the past half-century," pp. 23-51 in Logan and Hunt.

Worsley, Peter

  1982   "Non-Western Medical Systems." *Annual Review of Anthropology* 11: 315-348.

Young, Allan

  1982   "The Anthropology of Illness and Sickness." *Annual Review of Anthropology* 11: 257-285.

Zborowski, Mark

  1952   "Cultural Components in Responses to Pain." *Journal of Social Issues* 8: 16-30.

  1969   *People in Pain.* San Francisco: Jossey-Bass.

Zola, Irving K.

  1966   "Culture and Symptoms: an Analysis of Patients' Presenting Complaints." *American Sociological Review* 31: 615-630.

Some Key Journals

Medical Anthropology Quarterly – International Journal for the Cultural and Social Analysis of Health.

Official journal of the Society for Medical Anthropology, published by the American Anthropological Association.

Medical Anthropology Newsletter to 1984; then succeeded by *Medical Anthropology Quarterly*

Medical Anthropology, Cross-Cultural Studies in Health and Illness

Published by Gordon and Breach Science Publishers.

Social Science and Medicine.

Includes articles by anthropologists, sociologists, geographers, economists, and other social scientists.

Ethnomedizin (Hamburg, Germany)

Culture, Medicine and Psychiatry

Jesus' Healings of Women: Conformity and Non-Conformity to Dominant Cultural Values as Clues for Historical Reconstruction

Joanna Dewey
Episcopal Divinity School

In this paper, I propose to look from a variety of perspectives at the healing narratives involving females in the synoptic tradition. I am concerned with issues of cultural conformity and non-conformity, issues of orality and textuality, and issues of historicity and oral transmission. I focus on the stories involving females first because feminist scholars have often found that using gender as a major category of analysis reveals aspects of texts and tradition hitherto unnoticed; second, because the strictures involving women and men's interaction with men were culturally fairly rigid,[1] so that it should be quite easy to identify counter-culture and culture-conforming elements; and finally, because I am as interested in investigating the women in the reign-of-God movement[2] as I am in investigating the historical Jesus.

Part I of the paper is introductory, looking at issues of conformity and counter-culture as they may interact with oral and textual transmission. Part II addresses classification of miracles, finding Antoinette Wire's system most helpful for identifying possible oral narratives. Part III analyzes the culture-conforming and counter-cultural elements of the six miracles involving females, according to Wire's categories, which results in the most counter-cultural healings being discussed last. The fourth and final part compares the sicknesses of the females in the synoptic healings with the sicknesses commonly listed in the early Christian miracle-record lists.

---

1 See Bruce J. Malina, *The New Testament World: Insights from Cultural Anthropology* (Louisville: John Knox, 1981), pp. 25-70, 94-121; idem, "Dealing with Biblical (Mediterranean) Characters: A Guide for U.S. Consumers," *BTB* 19 (1989) 127-141. It should be noted that sub-dominant groups not only internalize the values and prescriptions of the dominant society but also resist them. See James C. Scott, *Domination and the Arts of Resistance: Hidden Transcripts* (New Haven and London: Yale University, 1990).

2 Mary Rose D'Angelo ("Re-Membering Jesus: Women, Prophecy, and Resistance in the Memory of the Early Churches," *Horizons* 19 [1992] 199-218; esp. pp. 206-209) suggests using reign-of-God movement rather than Jesus movement in order to emphasize all people involved, not just Jesus.

I

Along with many biblical scholars today, I share both the belief that the historical Jesus was a popular healer[3] and the skepticism about our ability to demonstrate that any particular healing goes back to Jesus. Our written sources do not help us with the miracle tradition to the extent they do with the sayings tradition. According to John Dominic Crossan's "Inventory of the Jesus Tradition by Chronological Stratification and Independent Attestation," few miracles go back to the first stratum, and even fewer miracles from any strata have more than a single attestation.[4] None of the miracles involving females is from the first stratum, and none has more than a single attestation. The later attestation of miracles involving females may suggest that the transmission history of stories involving women differed from that involving men.

Unlike sayings material, miracle stories are narratives and are thus easily remembered orally.[5] In a culture as overwhelmingly oral as the first century was in general, and in a social movement as non-elite as the reign-of-God movement, it is not in the least surprising that we find fewer miracles in the first stratum or multiply attested. There is no need to commit to writing stories that are easily remembered and transmitted orally.[6] Miracles may well have been written down only when they become part of longer written narratives describing the whole ministry of Jesus.[7] Thus the task for historical reconstruction of the miracle tradition may consist less of comparing textual variants and textual transmission history than of reconstructing oral performance possibilities. I will consider the miracle form in terms of oral dynamics in part II.

Here I would like to suggest that the existence of counter-cultural elements and a minimum or absence of culture-conforming elements may be clues to oral performance and transmission. A miracle either may serve to uphold the status quo, by, for example, restoring a person to his/her proper role or

---

3 I am not concerned in this paper with the distinction between illness and disease. See John J. Pilch, "Sickness and Healing in Luke-Acts" (*The Social World of Luke-Acts: Models for Interpretation* [Ed. Jerome H. Neyrey; Peabody MA: Hendrickson, 1991] 190-192). John Dominic Crossan, *The Historical Jesus: The Life of a Mediterranean Jewish Peasant* (San Francisco: Harper San Francisco, 1991) 137-167, 303-310. I would argue that first century people understood Jesus to both heal the illness and cure the disease.

4 *The Historical Jesus*, pp. 427-450. I would argue that his database even overstates the early attestation of miracles by classifying miracles found in John and Mark (or secret Mark) as first stratum, double attestation (complexes 127, 129 and 130). If their written source is a miracle collection as Crossan suggests, they have only a single attestation, the miracle collection. The alternative is to view Mark and John both drawing on oral tradition, in which case they would be second stratum, double attestation.

5 See Eric A. Havelock (*Preface to Plato* [Cambridge: Belknap of Harvard University, 1963]); Walter J. Ong, *Orality and Literacy: The Technologizing of the Word* (London and New York: Methuen, 1982).

6 This may explain the relative scarcity of early and multiple attestation for the parables, which are also easy to remember orally.

7 The orality of early Christian culture makes the existence of miracle narrative collections less probable.

function in society, or it may challenge elements of the dominant social structure by, for example, crossing or obliterating purity boundaries or presenting women in non-stereotypical roles. If, as seems probable, the recent reconstructions of Jesus as a social revolutionary are even remotely correct,[8] then we would expect his healings to be counter-cultural. Elements which uphold the dominant culture are more likely to be found in the writings of the few educated men than among the oral stories of peasants or urban artisans existing at the subsistence level.[9] Indeed, radical elements may well have been modified to conform more with the dominant culture as stories were incorporated into manuscripts written by literates, by definition men of higher social classes with more invested in the dominant culture.

Crossan[10] suggests that precisely such modification or damage control has occurred as the oral story of the cleansing of the leper was transmitted into writing in Mark 1:40-45 and the Egerton Gospel 2:1-4.[11] Each narrative presents an anti-temple anti-purity Jesus who heals the leper by declaring him clean, something only priests are authorized to do. Both versions then modify the anti-temple stance by the after-the-fact command to the leper to show himself to the priest—and the Egerton Gospel shows goes on to describe the man as a sinner and commands him to sin no more. Crossan proposes a history as follows "(1) a first stage orally telling how Jesus had ignored purity regulations in healing the leper and was therefore anti-Temple; (2) a second scribal stage in which the story is retold *in writing* precisely to reinterpret it in a pro-Temple direction and to contain the oral versions."[12] These versions both retain a counter-cultural emphasis and reveal some attempt at damage control.

Crossan contrasts this leper story with that of the ten lepers in Luke 17:11-19, which he considers probably a lukan composition:

> it clearly demonstrates how law-observant lepers and healers should interact. To begin with, they 'stand at a distance.' Next, Jesus immediately commands them to observe the legal regulations: 'When he saw

---

8 Crossan, *Historical Jesus*. See also Richard A. Horsley, *Jesus and the Spiral of Violence: Popular Jewish Resistance in Roman Palestine* (San Francisco: Harper & Row, 1987) and Marcus J. Borg, *Conflict, Holiness and Politics in the Teachings of Jesus* (Studies in the Bible and Early Christianity 5. New York and Toronto: Edwin Mellen, 1984) among others.

9 On ancient literacy, see William V. Harris, *Ancient Literacy* (Cambridge and London: Harvard University, 1989). On literacy among early Christians, see Joanna Dewey, "Early Christianity as an Oral Media Movement," *Orality and Textuality in Early Christianity, Semeia*, Forthcoming, 1994.

10 "Orality and The Miracles of the Jesus Tradition," Unpublished paper for the Fall 1992 meeting of the Jesus Seminar. Crossan is arguing against Robert Funk ("The Oral Repertoire: Quoted Speed, Gist, Clichés, and List," Unpublished paper for the Spring 1992 meeting of the Jesus Seminar), asserting that there is a written source underlying both versions.

11 Robert J. Miller, Ed., *The Complete Gospels: Annotated Scholars Version* (Sonoma: Polebridge, 1992) Crossan sites as as GosEg 35-47 in John B. Daniels, "The Egerton Gospel: Its Place in Early Christianity" (Ann Arbor, MI: University Microfilms International, 1990), pp.14, 24-25.

12 Crossan, "Orality," p. 6.

them he said to them, 'Go and show yourselves to the priests.'' Finally,
they are healed *only* as they go."[13]

This version of healing of leprosy, then, conforms basically to the cultural
norms of the society and may have been entirely a textual construct.

Crossan concludes that for the leprosy narratives there was a radical oral
story, modification to conform more to the dominant society in written
versions of the oral story, and another story which totally conforms to the
dominant society which originated in writing. I suggest that the connection
between orality and counter-culture miracles on the one hand, and textuality
and culture-conforming miracles on the other, may well apply to the synoptic
miracle tradition in general. It is worthwhile to investigate all the miracles
from this perspective, and I begin with an analysis of the miracles involving
females in part III.

II

For the purposes of this meeting of the Historical Jesus section of the SBL,
the healings were divided into exorcisms and other healings, that is,
according to the etiology of the sickness—whether or not it was due to evil
powers. For the purposes of looking for oral stories underlying the written
narratives, I do not find the etiological distinction helpful. In the first place, in
regards to the etiology of the sickness, diagnosis in the ancient world was not
fixed. In the synoptic tradition, blindness, muteness, physical deformity and
fever are found attributed to demons (Mt 12:22-24/Lk 11:14-16; Mt 9:32-34; Lk
13:10-17; Lk 4:38-39) and are found *not* attributed to demons (Mt 9:27-31; Mk
8:22-26; Mk 10:46-52 and par.; Mk 7:31-37; Mk 2:1-12 and par.; Mk 3:1-6 and par.;
Mk 1:29-31/Mt 8:14-15). There is no set correspondence between sickness and
diagnosis.

Secondly, in Luke but not in Mark or Matthew there seems to be a
connection between etiology of a sickness and gender, with Luke more likely
to see women than men as objects of demon possession. In Mark and
Matthew, the only exorcism of a female is of the Syrophoenician woman's
daughter, which Luke omits (see below). Luke, unlike Mark and Matthew,
however, attributes Simon's mother-in-law's fever to an evil spirit and adds the
story of the Bent woman on the Sabbath, as spirit possession. Further, Luke
describes the women following Jesus as formerly demon-possessed: "Some
women who had been healed of evil spirits and infirmities: Mary, called
Magdalene, from whom seven demons had gone out, and . . ." (8:2). On the
other hand, he adds no additional references to males possessed of demons,
either in his modification of markan and Q material or in his own special
material. I would argue that this is part of Luke's general pattern of rendering
women visible in his narrative, but at the same time restricting them to
subordinate roles. It is one of his ways of discrediting the authority of
women.[14] Whether the increased attribution of demon possession to females

---

[13] Ibid., p. 5.

[14] For Luke's portrayal of women in restricted roles, see Mary Rose D'Angelo, "Women
in Luke-Acts: A Redactional View," *JBL* 109 (1990) 441-461; and Jane Schaberg, "Luke" in

is an idiosyncracy of Luke, or is characteristic of literate men's views of women is a question that goes far beyond the scope of this paper. The finding in Luke, however, does suggest that the etiology of a sickness is not a helpful approach for trying to establish an oral prehistory for any miracle narrative.

The most useful classification of the miracles for establishing the existence of oral performance versions underlying written texts, I believe, is that of Antoinette Clark Wire, since her interest is precisely in the tellers and hearers of the individual tales.[15] She seeks to understand the function(s) of the miracle stories as individual whole narratives in an oral setting, so she looks at the miracles in terms of the dynamics of oral story-telling. She classifies the miracle tradition according to "the basic interaction that is the organizing center of the whole story . . . the story as a self-organizing and complete unit of communication" as it might have been used by oral story tellers.[16]

Wire discovers four categories or four basic interactions that generate a miracle story. They are exorcism, exposé, provision and demand miracles. First, an *exorcism* is a story in which the basic interaction is the struggle of the healer with demonic forces, such as the healing of the Gerasene Demoniac (Mk 5:1-20 and par.). None of the healings of females, even when evil spirits are involved, is based on this interaction. Indeed none of the synoptic illnesses in which the diagnosis was sometimes portrayed as demonic and sometimes not fits this dynamic.

Second, the *exposé* is a story in which the basic interaction is the contest is between Jesus and the religious authorities, and the miracle serves to break through the laws' restrictions. In these stories the person being healed is usually a passive recipient of the miracle, a person in the right place at the right time. Classifying the exposé stories as a separate form with its own dynamic obviates the usual form-critical debate over whether the story is a miracle or an apothegm. The major examples are of course the sabbath healing narratives.

Third, the *provision* story is based on a interaction in which the healer acts to meet the need of a group or person, which has no expectation of the miracle. The interaction occurs in "situations of hunger, scarcity or oppression where people have lost hope in their ability to provide for themselves"[17] and Jesus intervenes. This group consists primarily of the feeding miracles, but Wire also classifies a few healings here.

The Women's Bible Commentary (Eds., Carol A. Newsom and Sharon H. Ringe; Louisville: Westminster/John Knox, 1992), pp. 275-292.

15 "The Structure of the Gospel Miracle Stories and Their Tellers," *Semeia* 11 (1978) 83-113. For other systems of classification, see Rudolf Bultmann, (1) Exorcisms (2) Healing miracles (3) Raising from the dead (4) Nature miracles (*The History of the Synoptic Tradition* [Tr., John Marsh; Oxford: Basil Blackwell, 1963] pp. 209-245) and Gerd Theissen, (1) Exorcisms (2) Healings (3) Epiphanies (4) Rescue Miracles (5) Gift Miracles (*The Miracle Stories of the Early Christian Tradition* [Tr., Francis McDonagh; Ed., John Riches; Philadelphia: Fortress, 1983] pp. 85-112). Wire follows and develops Theissen's lead in focusing on the interactions of the characters, which she argues he fails to carry through in his analysis ("Structure," pp. 83, 85-86).

16 "Structure," pp. 86, 85.

17 Ibid., p. 84.

Fourth and last, the *demand* story is based on the interaction between someone's demand for healing (for themselves or someone else), some opposition to or by the healer, and the fulfillment of the demand.[18] The demand story is the most common of the synoptic types and has often been used to define the form of the miracle, with the other types being deviations from the true form. Wire stresses the active role of the person demanding healing in this form. Wire writes, "In the demand story the demanding party takes from the beginning an active role in the struggle and overcomes." In retelling the stories, "the teller seeks to draw the hearers into a demanding stance."[19]

> . . . the teller calls the hearer to break out of a closed world and to demand, struggle and realize miracle in human life. . . . Even in the stories where Jesus opposes the demand he is always drawn with respect as one who provokes people in their own cause and leaves them whole and in possession of their own story.[20]

In other words the demand stories, unlike the exposé and provision stories, focus as much on the persons being healed as upon Jesus, and in oral performance, their points of view are likely to be represented.

Wire concludes that the oral miracle stories are counter-cultural or, in her words,

> The narrative tells a marvelous breakthrough in the struggle against oppressive restrictions on human life. . . . This basic structure of the miracle story—the juxtaposition of an accepted oppressive context and an extraordinary breaking out of it . . . indicates the miracle stories had a common function. . . . The stories are structured around an extraordinary rift in a given, closed system. This shows that the teller of the story affirms both a realistic, even tragic view of the human condition and a transforming event that changes the human condition. . . . The kerygma or announcement of such concrete, total change in the common lot is the whole story of the tellers to the hearers.[21]

Her classification according to possible oral dynamics helps to situate the miracle narratives—all four types—as counter-dominant or subversive stories.

III

There are six healings involving females in the synoptic tradition.[22] Listing them in the order of Wire's categories, there is one exposé, the bent

---

18 Ibid., 84, 100. Miracles can also overlap categories. The healing of the paralytic has characteristics of both a demand story and an exposé.

19 Ibid., pp. 100, 106.

20 Ibid., p. 108.

21 Ibid., pp.109, 110.

22 There are no healings of females in John. Since I am including all healings in which a female is a character I should perhaps include the raising of Lazarus in which

woman on the Sabbath (Lk 13:10-17); one provision story, the raising of the widow's son at Nain (Lk 7:11-17); and four demand stories, all from Mark, Simon's Mother-in-Law (Mk 1:29-31/Mt 8:14-15/Lk 4:38-39); Jairus' daughter and the woman with the hemorrhage (Mk 5:21-43/Mt 9:18-26/Lk 8:40-56) and the Syrophoenician's Woman's daughter (Mk 7:24-30/Mt 15:21-28). I shall discuss the six narratives in this order, analyzing for each the counter-cultural and/or conforming aspects of Jesus' behavior and the stereotypically proper or counter-cultural aspects of the women's behavior. Dealing with the stories in the order first of Wire's categories and then in the narrative order of Mark for the last category happens to result in beginning with the strongly culturally-conforming miracles and moving to those which are strongly counter-cultural in regard both to Jesus' and the woman's behavior. Thus we are moving in general from stories portraying conformity to the dominant culture to those which do not.

Exposé Story: The Bent Woman on the Sabbath (Lk 13:10-17).

This miracle is a standard exposé story, and is, as such, counter-cultural, questioning the religious establishment's control of sabbath regulation. Jesus breaks the Sabbath law by touching the woman, which was considered work (v 13). The dialogue, however, presents a Jesus who is law-observant. Jesus cites as legitimate work on the sabbath the untying (*luei*) of an animal to lead it to water; likewise a woman bound to Satan should be untied (*luthēnai*) on the sabbath day. What is at stake is simply correct application of sabbath regulations regarding work, not the principal of sabbath observance.

In an exposé, we would expect the person being healed to have a passive role, and this is what we find. She is presented as a good Jew, attending synagogue on the sabbath; when healed, she responds appropriately by praising God.[23] Jesus refers to the woman as a 'daughter of Abraham,' that is, he recognizes her as a legitimate member of the Jewish community which is characterized by Sabbath observance. Like Luke's story of the healing of the ten lepers, this story shows how law-observant healers and faithful women should behave on the sabbath.

As exposé stories go in the synoptic tradition, this story would have little appeal to oral storytellers. It minimizes the challenge to "standard procedures and exalted egos" and does not set up "a fissure in an otherwise closed legal system."[24] I would suggest that this story is basically a Lukan composition,[25]

Martha and Mary play major roles, but I choose to limit this study to the synoptic miracles.

[23] In exposé stories, the person being healed does not usually speak at all. So the reference to the woman praising God in this story is giving the woman a more active role than the men have in the other exposé stories. I am indebted to Satoko Yamaguchi for this insight.

[24] Wire, "Structure," p. 83.

[25] Contra Joseph A. Fitzmyer (*The Gospel According to Luke X-XXIV* [Anchor Bible; Garden City: Doubleday, 1985] pp. 1010-1011) who attributes the passage to "L," and sees it reflecting a real-life situation of Jesus' own ministry. Elisabeth Schüssler Fiorenza (*But She Said: Feminist Practices of Biblical Interpretation* [Boston: Beacon Press, 1992] p. 199) believes

utilizing the exposé tradition, and rendering a woman visible in the narrative, but in a suitably restricted role.[26]

Provision Story: The Widow's Son at Nain (Lk 7:11-17)

Wire includes this healing as a provision story, a story in which the miracle worker takes the initiative. It is a story meeting dire human need—it remedies the predicament of a widow without sons to support her. This story appears to be almost entirely culture-maintaining. Touching the bier would render Jesus impure, given the degree of contagion corpses were believed to possess,[27] though that offense would have been far less than touching the corpse itself. The miracle is accomplished by word, not by touching the body.

The woman is entirely passive in the narrative. The narrator tell us the son speaks, verifying his resurrection, but the widow is not shown speaking or acting in the narrative at all. The story restores her to her proper cultural role, embedded in male kin. If my hypothesis is correct that stories with counter-cultural elements are more likely to derive from oral tradition, this story may well be a scribal creation. Wire also considers that the story may "be purely a literary creation" on the grounds that it "lack[s] the specific organizing interaction necessary to whole stories,"[28] that is, it is not an oral story-telling whole.[29]

Demand Healings: Simon's Mother-in-Law (Mark 1:29-31 and par.)

This story also contains few counter-cultural elements pertaining either to Jesus or the woman. The location of the story in the markan narrative between the exorcism in the synagogue on the sabbath and the crowd gathering for healing at the door at sundown, the end of the sabbath (1:21-28, 32-34) places the healing on the sabbath, and thus Jesus' act of touching the woman, work breaking the sabbath rest. However, the story itself makes no mention of this being a sabbath healing, and as an independent oral unit, it was not necessarily connected to the sabbath. If the story is not a sabbath healing, Jesus' behavior is not subversive. In Matthew's narrative order, the story does not occur on the sabbath (Mt 8:14-15); in Luke's version, the story is in the same narrative placement as Mark, but Luke treats it as an exorcism, cured by speech, command, which was not considered work on the sabbath. Thus both Matthew and Luke avoid even the inference of sabbath breaking which is present in Mark's narrative.[30]

---

that a miracle story about the woman "can be read independently from the ensuing 'controversy dialogue.'"

[26] See references in note 14.

[27] Bruce J. Malina and Richard L. Rohrbaugh, *Social-Science Commentary on the Synoptic Gospels* (Minneapolis: Fortress, 1992), p. 330.

[28] Wire, "Structure," p. 99.

[29] Its parallels to the raising of the son of a widow of Zarephath by Elijah in 1 Kings 17:8-24 further strengthen the possibility that it may be a literary composition without any oral preexistence.

[30] See also above, on Luke's attribution of women's illnesses to demons.

The woman's role also seems to be conforming. After her cure, the woman then serves (*diēkonei*) the men present (Mk 1:31/Mt 8:15/Lk 4:39). In Mark, the later use of *diakonos* and *diakoneō* in the instruction of the twelve (9:34; 10:43,45) and for the women followers in 15:41 suggests that the woman in Mk 1:29-31 is performing a ministry of service as a disciple.[31] However, given the cultural expectations of women's roles, I would expect that service in the story as an independent oral narrative would be generally construed as referring to women's traditional role in cooking and serving food. The mother-in-law has been restored to her proper role in a peasant patriarchal household. The narrative basically upholds the dominant cultural values. For this story as well, Wire notes that the story lacks the full interaction necessary for oral telling: "there is no intensifying of the demand to make a true demand story."[32] In this story, both Jesus and the woman behave in culture-conforming ways *and* the story does not have the full oral interaction.

Jairus' daughter (Mk 5:21-24, 35-43 and par.)

In this story an elite Jewish man seeks healing on behalf of his daughter. The demand is intensified by the interruption by the woman with the hemorrhage, and then by the news from the ruler's house that the girl is dead. The interchange with the mourners who ridicule Jesus heightens the challenge to Jesus. According to Wire's analysis, the story has the dynamics of a "whole story" suitable for oral telling.

The story contains a curious mixture of mainly culture-conforming elements. It is a resuscitation story, like that of the widow's son, and, as in that case, Jesus offends against official purity understandings by contact with the dead, a powerful source of pollution. In this story, the contagion is greater for Jesus actually touches the corpse: he takes the girl by the hand. Jesus defiles himself, ignoring one of the major purity constraints. On the other hand, Jesus is portrayed as insisting that the daughter is merely sleeping, not dead, which removes the source of impurity. Although the debate over whether the girl is asleep or dead seems to function in the narrative to heighten the drama rather than to show Jesus' conformity to purity rules, it also, from the perspective of Jesus and the narrator, functions to protect Jesus from pollution.

The official, the person making the demand, is shown acting in a counter-cultural way. One would expect a synagogue ruler to seek out a physician, part of the official medical establishment, rather than a traditional healer. Nor would one expect him to fall at Jesus' feet, indicating his social inferiority to Jesus. Finally the girl plays a stereotypical passive female role, remaining silent. The counter-cultural element in this story is not that of Jesus or the female character, but that of Jairus who does not maintain his public honor

---

31 Hisako Kinukawa ("Women Disciples of Jesus" *In God's Image* 11 (1992) 18-19) argues that Mark's use of the imperfect tense of *diakoneō* suggests ongoing ministerial activity. Elaine Mary Wainwright (*Towards a Feminist Critical Reading of the Gospel According to Matthew* [Berlin and New York: Walter de Gruyter, 1991] pp. 178-187) argues that the Matthean version (8:14-15) is an independent vocation or call story.

32 Wire, "Structure," p. 100. Wire suggests that perhaps the connection to Peter may have been sufficient reason for the story to be retold orally.

fitting his status as synagogue leader. This is the story of a man relinquishing status to seek healing for his daughter.

In the four stories so far, we have identified some moderately counter-cultural elements: Jesus bests the synagogue ruler over the proper application of sabbath regulations, and Jesus risks pollution through contact with corpses. But even here, the stories are careful: Jesus touches only the bier, not the corpse of the son; he touches a sleeping not a dead girl. These four stories present no serious challenge to the dominant Jewish purity understandings, and thus no serious threat to the Jewish authorities who maintain and benefit from these understandings. Likewise, in these four healings, the females behave appropriately, conforming to the dominant gender code in which women are passive.

The two healings remaining to be discussed, the woman with the hemorrhage and the Syrophoenician woman's daughter, present a different picture. In both stories, Jesus seriously violates purity boundaries through contact with a Jewish menstruant woman and through contact with a Gentile woman. And in both of these stories, the women behaves aggressively, violating the cultural gender code of appropriate female behavior. Since in these stories, it is the woman who makes the demand, I shall consider first the woman's and then Jesus' behavior.

The Woman with the Hemorrhage (Mk 5:25-34 and par.)[33]

According to both the priestly regulations of Leviticus and the rabbinic rules of the Mishnah, a woman who is menstruating or has an irregular bloody discharge was considered a powerful source of pollution to men. She is unclean. Anyone who touches her or touches anything she has sat or lain on also becomes unclean. The woman is unclean for seven days after the discharge ends. Then she is to bring two turtledoves or pigeons to the priest to make atonement for her before God (Lev 15:25-30).

The purity rules are clear. It is unclear to what extent Galilean peasant women at the time of Jesus observed the laws of menstrual purity. We may conjecture that unless they were the wife of a priest or a strict scribe or Pharisee, they probably did not feel strongly bound by the menstrual regulations.[34] Yet popular culture internalizes much of the value system of the dominant group, including here the understanding of menstruating women, or women with an irregular flow, as unclean. With a disease as severe as a twelve-year nonmenstrual bleeding, almost surely the society and the woman herself would consider her unclean and a source of impurity to

---

[33] See Marla J. Selvidge, "Mark 5:25-34 and Leviticus 15:19-20: A Reaction of Restrictive Purity Regulations" *JBL* 103 (1984) 619-623; eadem, *Woman, Cult, and Miracle Recital: A Redactional Critical Investigation on Mark 5:24-34* (Lewisburg: Bucknell University, 1990); Hisako Kinukawa, "The Interactions between Women and Jesus in Mark's Gospel from a Japanese Feminist Perspective," (D.Min. Dissertation/Project; San Francisco Theological Seminary, 1992), pp. 49-79.

[34] For an excellent discussion of how menstrual purity laws affected Jewish women, see Ross Shepard Kraemer, *Her Share of the Blessings: Women's Religions Among Pagans, Jews, and Christians in the Greco-Roman World* (New York and Oxford: Oxford University, 1992), pp. 99-105, 125-126, 143.

others. If she were maintaining proper "shame" as the dominant male culture understood it, she should have remained secluded.

We find the narrative of a woman more brazen than the leper who approached Jesus (Mk 1:40-45). That story portrays the leper (who should not have approached Jesus) kneeling before Jesus (Mk 1:40/Mt 8:7; "fell on his face" Lk 5:12), politely requesting assistance. This story portrays the woman not requesting but claiming her own healing. She works her way through the crowd (according to the picture created by the narrative, bumping into people and rendering them unclean) and then touches Jesus' garments, rendering him unclean. According to elite prescriptive statements, the woman should not have been out in public at all. She certainly should not have been mingling in a crowd while suffering an irregular flow of blood. But the story places her there.

Further, if the woman was to observe proper female shame, and maintain the honor of the males around her, she should have kept silent, rather than shamelessly telling in public what she has done. (Granted, this would detract from the drama of the story. However, given the silence of women in other narratives, the text could easily have ended "she felt in her body that she was healed of her disease, and she returned home praising God." Indeed Matthew does end his version without any response on the part of the woman, simply Jesus' confirmation of the healing [9:20-22].) The woman behaves shamelessly in seeking and touching Jesus; she behaves shamelessly by publicly confessing what she has done.

Jesus is also shown behaving in a counter-cultural fashion. Rather than rebuking her for her behavior, Jesus compounds the dishonor and disregard of purity rules by ignoring her shameless behavior and welcoming her as kin, as "daughter." She is not called a daughter of Abraham, a member of the Jewish people, but simply, daughter, a woman with a kinship relationship to Jesus. If this story had followed the same pattern of the healing of the leper, we would now expect to find some admonition qualifying the breaking of the purity boundary, perhaps an instruction to make the proper offering to the temple. However, no such modification or damage control is found. What we find is clear rejection of the purity regulations.

This story differs from the ones we have looked at earlier both in the absence of any textual indicators modifying the anti-purity stance and in the counter-cultural rather than stereotypical portrayal of the woman. The two may be connected. The gender asymmetry of the purity codes in regard to bodily fluids functioned to enforce male dominance and control the behavior of women.[35] In this story, we have at the same time the rejection of the purity code as it affected women's bodies *and* Jesus' affirmation of a woman who stepped outside of the dominant male view of the appropriate role for women. This narrative is consistently counter-cultural.

---

[35] Howard Eilberg-Schwartz, *The Savage in Judaism: An Anthropology of Israelite Religion and Ancient Judaism* (Bloomington and Indianapolis: Indiana University, 1990), pp. 177-194. See also Kraemer, *Her Share*, pp. 99-105.

The Syrophoenician Woman (Mk 7:24-30/Mt 15:21-28)[36]

This last healing involving a female—actually two females, the woman and her daughter—is also consistently counter-cultural on the part of the woman and of Jesus. The fundamental social boundary between Jew and Gentile is overridden. The woman violates the dominant view of the appropriate role for women. She is portrayed entering a house where she is not wanted, entering the company of men where she does not belong, and speaking to a male stranger. After Jesus refuses her request, insulting her and her child as "dogs," the woman does not submissively withdraw, but takes up the challenge (as a male might be expected to do) and speaks to Jesus again, cleverly using his response in her retort in order to get her way.

Jesus also is shown ignoring the rules. He enters into debate with a woman as he would with a man who was his equal. Furthermore, he admits that she has won the debate. He praises her teaching (her *logos*), and grants her request, healing her daughter. The narrative portrays Jesus being bested by a woman, and changing his behavior on that account. This is the only instance in the extant tradition of Jesus being taught by someone, and that someone is a woman who should not properly be speaking to him at all. As a result of her speech, Jesus ignores the fundamental boundary between Jew and Gentile.

In terms of first century cultural norms, this is a shocking story, and both Luke and Matthew take steps to deal with it. Luke omits it altogether, along with its surrounding episodes. He presents the overcoming of the Jew/Gentile barrier in Acts, instigated by God through Peter and a relatively elite gentile male. This boundary is only overcome at the explicit direction of God and through male leaders. Matthew drastically rewrites the story in such a way that the boundary of Jew/Gentile is overcome, but the woman is presented much less favorably (Mt 15:21-28). The story takes place outside, with the woman following after Jesus and the disciples, importuning Jesus to help her. Matthew's changes in the story shift its emphasis. In Mark, the stress was on the woman's single speech, her word, that is, her wit or intelligence that convinced Jesus to cure a Gentile. In Matthew, the stress is more on the woman's persistence, and her request is granted because of her faith (v. 28). Matthew's version reminds one of Luke's parable of the wicked judge who finally grants the widow justice in order to get rid of her (Luke 18:1-8). Matthew has transformed the woman from a model of creative intelligence in Mark to that of a persistent or nagging woman - a model more traditional and perhaps less of a threat to patriarchal norms. But even in Matthew's version, the story is counter-cultural, showing Jesus breaking the fundamental social boundary at the instigation of a woman.

Summary of the analysis of healings

Of the six healings involving female characters, three display strong interactions that would function well orally—the stories of Jairus, the woman with the hemorrhage and the Syrophoenician woman. All three also violate cultural norms. In the first—the healing of Jairus' daughter—Jairus dishonors

---

[36] See Kinukawa, "Interactions," pp. 80-103 and the literature cited there.

himself publicly to seek healing for his daughter, while Jesus and the daughter behave appropriately. The latter two—the woman with the hemorrhage and the Syrophoenician woman—stand out as strongly counter to the dominant culture both in Jesus' violation of purity boundaries and in the portrayal of women who violate the prescriptive norms for women's behavior. They are probably the most counter-cultural of all the healings of males or females in the synoptic tradition. In the healings involving female characters, those with the strongest interactions suitable for oral performance are also those which are most strongly counter-cultural. This suggests to me that these stories might well have been told and retold by and among women before they were textualized in Mark.[37] At minimum, my hypothesis that counter-cultural emphases are indicative of orality seems to be borne out.

Excursus on the historicity of the woman with the hemorrhage and the Syrophoenician woman

To say a miracle derives from oral tradition, of course, is not to say that it goes back to the life of Jesus. Scholars who assume the historicity of any miracles often will affirm the general historicity of the healing of a woman with a hemorrhage.[38] The fact that the story focuses on the woman's medical history, how much she spent on doctors and how it made her worse rather than on the religious or purity implications of her illness suggests to me that the story in its oral retelling has been adapted to a gentile audience, for whom menstruation was of no religious significance.[39]

Scholars, however, regularly exclude the story of the Syrophoenician woman from any claim to historicity for two reasons. First, Jesus is located outside of Galilee in the region of Tyre and Sidon, and scholars generally consider the spread of the movement outside of Jewish territory to be a post-Easter movement. Second, as in the cure of the centurion's boy (Mt 8:5-13; Lk 7:1-10), the healing is at a distance; the daughter is not present.

In regard to the first objection, the setting north of Galilee is due to Mark's editorial placement of the story in his narrative. Certainly the only indication of the story's geographical location is in the markan editorial introduction, which Matthew follows. Mark also indicates that the woman is a Syrophoenician by birth,[40] but Matthew describes her simply as a Canaanite. Since there certainly were Gentiles living in towns in Galilee who might well have sought out any successful healer, it is quite possible that oral versions of the story told of a Gentile woman approaching Jesus in Galilee or in some unspecified place, and it is only the textual tradition that locates the

---

[37] So also Dennis Ronald MacDonald, "From Audita to Legenda: Oral and Written Miracle Stories," *Forum* 2 (1986) 15-26.

[38] Crossan (*Historical Jesus*, p. 44), for example, rates this story a "plus" in spite of its second stratum single attestation.

[39] Kraemer, *Her Share*, p. 101.

[40] The indication is part of a double expression, *hellenis, Syrophoinikissa*, which is a common markan characteristic and may indicate markan editing. See Frans Neirynck, *Duality in Mark: Contributions to the Study of the Markan Redaction* (Louvain: Leuven University, 1972). There are also textual variants of Phoenician and Tyrophoenician. Even the geographical introduction varies. UBS[4] prefers the reading "region of Tyre."

story near Tyre. In regard to the second argument about healing at a distance, which of course stresses Jesus' miraculous power, not all Gentile healings are at a distance: Jesus exorcises the Gerasene demoniac in person. So the distance argument cannot really be used to indicate gentile healings are only post-Easter. Given the mixtures of population in Galilee, it would be surprising if gentiles had not sought out Jesus or any successful healer.[41]

There is also a strong reason for considering this miracle authentic. The interaction in the story portrays the triumph of the woman over Jesus. While it is certainly common in oral transmission for a story involving a minor figure to be attributed to the hero, in this instance Jesus, I question if a story with so critical a view of Jesus would have been attributed to him.[42] I suggest we may need to rethink the authenticity of this story.

IV

Currently, scholars are debating the relationship of the early miracle-record lists to the miracle narratives: have the lists generated the narratives, are they summaries of the narratives, or is there a more complex relationship between the two?[43] The lists would seem to be a literate phenomenon, both because lists with a fixed order require writing, and because the miracle lists seem initially to derive from Isaiah 35:5-6, which suggests concern for and explication of written texts. If I am correct that the lists were developed and used by literates—which for practical purposes means men—then I would expect the illnesses represented in the narratives with strong counter-cultural and/or oral elements would be underrepresented or not represented on the lists.

When one compares the illnesses found in the synoptic miracles with the illnesses of the miracle lists, a clear gender bias can be observed. The illnesses of males in the synoptic gospels are found much more frequently on the lists than the illnesses of females in the gospels. Isaiah 35 includes blindness, deafness, lameness, and speech defects. About half of the healings of males in

---

41 The lack of respect for ethnic boundaries in regard to healing is evident in the fact that professional (non-Jewish) magicians included Jesus' name in their repertoires (Elisabeth Schüssler Fiorenza, "Miracles, Mission, and Apologetics: An Introduction" in *Aspects of Religious Propaganda in Judaism and Early Christianity* [eadem, Ed.; Indiana: University of Notre Dame, 1976] p. 13).

42 Wire ("Structure," p. 103) suggests that other demand stories in which the opposition to the miracle comes from the healer may well have been in oral circulation but "were not included in the written collections, lacking the 'redeeming social value' of this argument for gentile mission to make up for the offense of the woman's brazen success."

43 See David T. M. Frankfurther, "The Origin of the Miracle-List Tradition and its Medium of Circulation," in *Society of Biblical Literature 1990 Seminary Papers*. (Ed. David J. Lull; SBLSP 29. Atlanta: Scholars, 1990), pp. 344-374; Julian Hills, *Tradition and Composition in the Epistula Apostolorum* (Harvard Dissertations in Religion 24; Minneapolis: Fortress, 1990), pp. 38-44; idem, "Tradition, Redaction, and Intertextuality: Miracle Lists in Apocryphal Acts as a Test Case," in *Society of Biblical Literature 1990 Seminary Papers*. (Ed. David J. Lull; SBLSP 29. Atlanta: Scholars, 1990), pp. 375-390; John Dominic Crossan, "Lists in Early Christianity: A Response to *Early Christianity, Q and Jesus,*" *Early Christianity, Q and Jesus, Semeia* 55 (1991) 235-243.

the synoptic tradition fit this list: the paralytic (Mk 2:1-12 and par.), the two blind men[44] (Mt 9:27-31), the dumb demoniac (Mt 9:32-34), the blind-dumb demoniac (Mt 12:22-24/Lk 11:14-16), the deaf-mute (Mk 7:31-37), the blind man at Bethsaida (Mk 8:22-26), and blind Bartimaeus (Mk 10:46-52 and par.). In addition, Matthew describes the centurion's servant as paralyzed (Mt 8:6) and Mark describes the epileptic boy as having a dumb spirit (*pneuma alalon*) (Mk 9:17). There are no female healings at all of blindness, deafness or muteness, the most common male categories.[45] The only healing of a female that could possibly fit this list is that of the bent woman, but the emphasis in that story is on her inability to straighten up, not on her lameness, so it should not be considered. This suggests to me that the miracle-record list based on Isaiah has in fact been influential in generating miracle stories about men but not in generating stories about women. Some other source must be sought for the women's stories.

The illnesses of the expanded miracle lists, cleansing lepers, casting out demons and resurrecting the dead,[46] also are found disproportionately among males. There are two cures of leprosy, both male, four exorcisms, three of males in which the dynamic of the story is Jesus' struggle with evil powers, and one female, the Syrophoenician woman, in which story dynamic has nothing to do with exorcism, and two resurrections, one of a son and one of a daughter. Thus out of sixteen male miracles, twelve or seventy-five percent of the illnesses are found on the extended miracle lists, while only one of five (twenty per cent) of the female illnesses is on the miracle lists. I exclude the story of the Syrophoenician woman from the illnesses on the miracle list, since the motif of exorcism could not generate our present story.

The fact that the same gender pattern occurs with the expanded list as with the Isaiah list may be due not to generation of miracles of males to fit the list, but simply to the natural androcentric selection process: the men writing down the lists were probably more likely to remember miracle stories about men.[47] As the miracle lists expand to include miracle narratives, the woman with the hemorrhage does occur on a few lists. Whatever the precise significance of the far greater overlap between the illnesses of the miracle lists and the illnesses in the male healing narratives, it seems safe to conclude that literate men and early textual transmission have affected the healing narratives of males more than the healing narratives of females.[48]

---

[44] The masculine plural of the Greek may of course obscure female presence. As Satoko Yamaguchi pointed out to me, the story may concern a blind man and a blind woman.

[45] Excluding the two resurrection miracles, because of the difficulty over whether to classify them according to the sex of the parent or the child, six of the fifteen male healings (forty percent) are of deafness, blindness or muteness, while none of the four female healings is.

[46] Hill (*Tradition*, pp. 40-44) gives the texts of nineteen lists; Frankfurter ("Miracle-List" pp. 372-374) gives a useful synopsis of a selection of the earliest miracle lists.

[47] On androcentric selection, see Elisabeth Schüssler Fiorenza, *In Memory of Her: A Feminist Theological Reconstruction of Christian Origins* (New York: Crossroad, 1983), pp. 48-53.

[48] The miracle collection that Crossan posits lying behind Mark and John consists entirely of male healings (*Historical Jesus*, p. 429).

Conclusion

As is usually the case when doing historical Jesus research, there is some circularity of argumentation and no firm conclusions can be reached. This exploration of the healings of females in the synoptic tradition suggests to me several tentative conclusions:

(1) In attempting to determine the tradition history of any miracle story, it is necessary to consider *both* the degree of oral interaction characterizing the story and the degree of counter-cultural emphasis. Furthermore, at least among the women's stories, stories with strong counter-cultural elements also tend to have interactions that would make a strong oral story.[49]

(2) Counter-cultural elements are more likely to be found in stories with an oral genesis.

(3) The women's stories in the synoptics, or at least the counter-cultural stories among them, may well stand closer to the oral performance of the miracle narratives than do the men's stories.

Or in other words,

The different overlap with the miracle lists suggests that the male stories have been more influenced by literate men and textual transmission than the synoptic women's stories.

(4) The oral transmission of the women's stories may be significantly different from that of the men's stories, maintaining a higher counter-cultural emphasis because of less interaction with textuality.

(5) Gender differences are significant enough in the healing narratives that gender should be taken into account as an important variable when analyzing the narratives.

In conclusion, since textual transmission of the miracles seems to result in modification and elimination of counter-cultural elements, if we are to advance in our study of the miracle tradition, we need to develop greater knowledge of how oral cultures preserve, adapt, and transmit traditions, and how oral and written cultures interact to affect traditions when literacy is the preserve of a small mostly male elite.

---

[49] A cursory review of the male stories suggests that this would be true for them as well.

From Wrath to Justification: Tradition, Gospel and Audience in the Theology of Romans 1:18–4:25

Andrew T. Lincoln
University of Sheffield

Within the confines of the initial stage of Paul's exposition of his gospel for the Roman Christians in Romans 1:18–4:25 the movement of thought is from wrath (1:18) to justification (4:25). Within the confines of this paper, there can be no hope of doing justice to the weighty theological concepts encountered en route or to the debate surrounding them.[1] While the attempt will be made to trace the main stages of Paul's theological argument, a primary focus will be on the nature of that argument, highlighting some of the ways in which Jewish traditions function within it and exploring its relationship to the letter's rhetorical situation.

1. Orientation to the Argument

To speak of a movement from wrath to justification is misleading, if it is taken to represent how Paul's thought is presented in the letter as a whole. This would be to tear this section loose from its context in the letter and miss the obvious point that Paul has already stated the solution of justification by faith before he begins his depiction of the plight of human sinfulness under the wrath of God.[2] He has already made clear his distinctive understanding of the gospel as "the power of God for salvation to everyone who has faith, to the Jew first and also to the Greek" and provided Scriptural warrant through the words of Hab 2:4—"the one who is righteous by faith shall live." In terms of

---

[1] Indeed chapters 2 and 3 in particular have rapidly become one of the most disputed parts of the letter. See, to name only four recent pertinent titles from one press, G. N. Davies, *Faith and Obedience in Romans: A Study of Romans 1-4* (Sheffield: JSOT Press, 1990); N. Elliott, *The Rhetoric of Romans* (Sheffield: JSOT Press, 1990); B. W. Longenecker, *Eschatology and Covenant: A Comparison of 4 Ezra and Romans 1-11* (Sheffield: JSOT Press, 1991); D. A. Campbell, *The Rhetoric of Righteousness in Romans 3.21-26* (Sheffield: JSOT Press, 1992). Space forbids both the necessary detailed interaction with the positions represented by such monographs and the necessary detailed defence of the more traditional reading offered here.

[2] In this regard, the thought pattern of Romans as a whole is no different from what E. P. Sanders has claimed about Paul's thought in general, cf. *Paul and Palestinian Judaism* (Philadelphia: Fortress, 1977), 442-43.

the rhetorical structure of the argument (following Jewett[3]), the *propositio* has already been stated in 1:16, 17 and what follows is the *probatio*, of which 1:18-4:25 constitutes the initial *confirmatio*. This enables us to see that Paul's thought pattern is one which moves from solution to plight and then back to solution. His claim is that he has a gospel in which the righteousness of God is revealed through faith for all. So now he must show why all need this gospel, why it has to be by faith for all—both Jews and Gentiles, and why it is therefore appropriate to his worldwide mission, in which the Roman Christians have their role to play (cf. 1:5, 6, 13-15; 15:23, 24). This does not yet, however, state his task in the argument accurately enough, for there is a significant element in his thesis statement that has been omitted. The salvation mediated by his gospel comes to all, but it comes "to the Jew first and also to the Greek" (1:16), and so he must also demonstrate how within the universal scope of his gospel there somehow remains a Jewish priority. All of this reinforces the likelihood that, whatever previous understanding of the human plight was part of his Jewish heritage,[4] when he depicts that plight in relation to his presentation of his gospel in this letter, he will do so not only in the light of what he now believes to be the revealed solution but also in a way that will correspond with that solution.

If Paul's own formulation of the gospel is a decisive factor in setting the agenda for his theological argument, so is the other element in the rhetorical situation, namely, his perception of his audience. The apostle needs to demonstrate his thesis about the gospel in dialogue with Roman Christians, whose support as a unified community he wishes to gain for his proposed mission to Spain (cf. 15:22-33). Paul appears to conceive of these Christians as primarily Gentiles, whose "obedience of faith" he also wishes to secure as part of his purpose in writing. But there is an obstacle to be overcome if his wishes are to be fulfilled. As Paul understands their situation, harmony among the Christians in Rome is threatened, because these Gentile Christians are experiencing tensions with Jewish Christians, whom Paul evidently also expects to be among the recipients of the letter (cf. 1:5-7; 14:1-5; 15:7, 14-16).[5] This is, of course, to espouse the view that such tensions are reflected in the exhortations of 14:1-15:13. The self-styled "strong in faith" appear to be *predominantly* the Gentile Christian majority who have dubbed those who are *predominantly* Jewish Christian the "weak in faith."[6] From their name for themselves it appears that the Gentile Christians stressed their faith and the freedom it engendered and despised those who considered it necessary, as part of their obedience to God, to observe food laws and sabbaths and festivals. As a consequence of embracing the gospel they also appear to have adopted an

---

3 R. Jewett, "Following the Argument of Romans," in *The Romans Debate: Revised and Expanded Edition*, ed. K. P. Donfried (Peabody: Hendrickson, 1991), 278-96.

4 On this, see F. Thielman, *From Plight to Solution* (Leiden: E. J. Brill, 1989).

5 Elliott, *Rhetoric*, 69-104, is right in his emphasis on a primarily Gentile Christian audience, but neglects the Jewish Christian element, which he acknowledges to be there (cf. *Rhetoric*, 95-96). Several of the recipients mentioned in chapter 16 appear to be Jewish Christians, e. g. Prisca and Aquila (vv. 3-5a), Andronicus and Junia (v. 7), Herodion (v. 11).

6 The Gentile/Jew categories in 15:7-13, which constitutes the climax of the exhortations, provide very strong support for this interpretation.

arrogance about Jewish unbelief which may have inclined them to believe that any purposes of God for ethnic Israel were now abrogated (cf. esp. 11:20, 25). The Jewish Christian minority condemned the "strong" for what they viewed as the latter's moral laxity, and, quite naturally, would have associated the Gentile Christians' attitudes with Paul's law-free gospel. The disputes in Rome would only have heightened any suspicions about Paul they already had from reports about his distinctive formulation of the gospel and its implications.

Paul begins in 1:18-4:25 the demonstration of the confidence he has asserted in the gospel depicted in 1:16, 17, and, having sketched all too briefly the rhetorical situation, we are now in a position to set out an initial hypothesis about what, it would appear, Paul needs to argue, how he needs to argue it and why the argument takes the form it does. If his gospel proclaims salvation for all who have faith, then Paul is required to demonstrate both that all (both Jews and Gentiles) need his gospel in order to be righteous before God and that the only way for both Jews and Gentiles to be righteous before God is by faith in Christ. He must show that apart from faith in Christ all are unrighteous.[7] In particular, this will entail showing that not only unbelieving Gentiles but also unbelieving Jews, whose membership of the covenant is marked by their circumcision and adherence to the law, are unrighteous. By definition, his gospel of righteousness by faith in Christ will not be able to allow for righteousness through membership in the covenant or through the law.

Paul in fact proceeds to do what is necessary. In 1:18-2:29 and 3:9-20 he argues that the Gentile world is under the wrath of God because of its inexcusable idolatry and immorality, and then claims that those who join in this judgment from the supposed security of their relationship with God through the covenant are ultimately in no different a position. They are one and equal in their thraldom to sin and they too must face the wrath of God. Neither knowing the law nor being circumcised will be of any avail, since God is impartial in his judgment. A considerable amount of space is given in this argument to showing that unbelieving Jews are in the same position of desperate need as unbelieving Gentiles, and the argument is developed by employing viewpoints similar to those found in the Wisdom of Solomon and by beginning with what no Jew would dispute in order then to turn the tables on such a Jewish dialogue partner before concluding with the backing of a catena of Scriptural citations. These factors clearly indicate to which section of his audience Paul is chiefly addressing himself.

This impression is only reinforced by the rest of the argument in these early chapters. The issues treated in 3:1-8 are those that would be raised by a

---

7 This is disputed by Davies, *Faith and Obedience*, 47-112, who holds that Paul is indicting only unrighteous Jews and Gentiles, righteous Jews and Gentiles have always been acceptable to God if they realized that their faith in God precedes and is the basis for their righteous deeds, and all that is required in the new era is the recognition that this faith should now be focused in Christ. This removes the radical edge of Paul's gospel, leaving one wondering why any faithful Jew should be expected to sense any plight from which the gospel provided salvation, why any Jewish Christian should sense any threat to his or her own position from the implications of Paul's law-free gospel for Gentiles, and why Paul would take the whole of 1:18-3:20 to remind Jews of the truism that a righteous God punishes wicked Gentiles and faithless Jews.

Jew in response to what has been said. What advantage has the Jew? What are the implications for the faithfulness and righteousness of God? And is not morality undermined? The formulating of the argument with a particular section of the audience primarily in view does not change even when Paul returns to depict the solution more fully in the light of the plight he has portrayed. Here, in reiterating that his gospel is for all without distinction and that those who are one and equal in sin can be one and equal in receiving by faith God's gift of justification, he in all probability adapts a Jewish Christian formulation of the gospel, is concerned to draw out the implications of this solution for the matters of boasting and law works, and appeals to traditional belief in the oneness of God to drive home his insistence on the universal scope of his gospel. At the same time, Paul feels the need to make clear that, although righteousness is not attained by law, this does not mean that the law is totally done away with or of no account. At various points he is at pains to assert that the law has to be seen as having a different function in God's righteous purposes (cf. 3:19, 20; 4:5), and above all claims that the law witnesses to his gospel (3:21) with its depiction of Abraham's faith as his chief example of this role (4:1-25).

The obvious and age-old question must now be faced. Why, despite Paul's stress that his gospel is for all, is the argument shaped primarily for Jewish Christians, particularly when it is Gentile Christians who make up the majority of his readers?[8] The rhetorical situation suggests some possible answers. First, there is the situation of the writer. What has not yet been mentioned but is plain from 15:22-33 is that Paul, the Jewish Christian who is apostle to the Gentiles, is about to set off for Jerusalem with the collection. As is revealed by his anxiety about whether this offering from the churches of his Gentile mission will be accepted by the Jewish Christian Jerusalem church (cf. 15:30), he is being forced to reflect about the same basic issues of Jewish Christian–Gentile Christian relationships current in Rome but to do so at the level of his whole Gentile mission. For Paul, the Jerusalem church's acceptance of the collection and of those who accompanied it would signal the unity of the Christian movement and the successful completion of his mission in the eastern half of the empire. In pondering the outcome of this critical visit which would also affect his proposed visit to Rome and beyond to Spain in the west, Paul would inevitably be reflecting on the controversy and objections his gospel provoked among Jewish Christians. Because he desires unity, not least for the sake of fulfilling his own calling, he will be intent on making the best possible case for his position in Jerusalem in the face of any charges of apostasy, but he remains unrepentant about his basic proclamation. Hence, as he considers the impending Jerusalem visit and the situation in Rome, he can make the ringing affirmation, "I am not ashamed of the gospel" (1:16a).

Paul knows too that his reflections about the gospel in his immediate situation are precisely what the Roman Christians need to hear in their own circumstances. Sensing that the troubles in Rome have been fuelled by some distortions and misperceptions of his gospel caused in part by Gentile

---

8 Cf. the classic formulation of the "double character" of Romans by W. G. Kümmel, *Introduction to the New Testament* (London: SCM, 1975), 309.

Christian attitudes and views which he would not want to own, Paul is anxious to speak for himself. He wants to be his own advocate for his distinctive gospel in the discussions with Jewish Christians and to address their objections and suspicions himself. Jewish Christians need to be won over if there is to be harmony in Rome and if its Christians are to provide the effective base for the next stage of his mission. The Gentile Christian majority, if it is to help in this process, has a profound need to see how the one whose stress on faith it believes it is promoting himself goes about the task of persuading Jewish Christians who are hesitant to embrace the cause. Paul knows that Gentile Christians will have no problem with the major aspects of his demonstration that there is no distinction between Jews and Gentiles as far as sin and the possibilities for faith are concerned, but he is worried about the implications some of them are drawing from this. So Paul takes the opportunity of rehearsing his gospel for the Roman Christians and of rehearsing it in a way which he hopes will prove persuasive to Jewish Christians.

It should be noted that, in comparison with the direct address of Gentile Christians in 11:13ff., the attempt to persuade Jewish Christians is more indirect. Actual Jews among the recipients are not addressed. Instead, the diatribe style enables Paul to dialogue with an imagined conversation partner or questioner, who, though representative, is addressed in the singular in 2:1-5, 17-23, 25, 27 (the second person plural of 2:24 is part of a Scriptural citation). Paul's imagined dialogue partner is portrayed initially as one who feels morally superior to the unrighteous pagans who have just been described, but, from the attitudes depicted, which, as we shall see, are characteristic of Judaism, and from the explicit address later in 2:17, it is highly likely that such a person is a Jew.[9] The use of the diatribe indicates that Paul is not attacking those he considers opponents but rather setting out his teaching in a way designed to lead its recipients to the truth, sometimes by correcting pretensions and presumptions.[10] Yet it cannot be denied that in terms of the rhetorical situation in the letter, the addressees for whom this dialogue with a Jew would have particular force are Jewish Christians, for whom belief in Jesus as Messiah has been added to earlier beliefs about Israel's privileged covenant status and the necessity of observing the law and who object to the far more radical version of the gospel Paul is preaching in his mission to Gentiles.[11] "In the diatribe there is often little distance between the real audience and the fictitious interlocutor" and "the typical is addressed to the

---

[9] Cf. also e. g. F. Watson, *Paul, Judaism and the Gentiles* (Cambridge: C.U.P., 1986), 109-10; J. D. G. Dunn, *Romans 1-8* (Dallas: Word, 1988), 78-80; *pace* S. K. Stowers, *The Diatribe and Paul's Letter to the Romans* (Chico: Scholars Press, 1981), 112.

[10] Cf. Stowers, *Diatribe*, esp. 75-78.

[11] Whatever its previous history and whatever its wider applicability to Judaism as a whole, the material in 1:18-4:25 functions rhetorically therefore not so much as a "debate with Judaism" as a dialogue with Jewish Christians, cf. J. C. Beker, *Paul the Apostle* (Philadelphia: Fortress, 1980), 83: "Romans 1:18-4:25 . . . is essentially a dialogue with the Jews," by whom he means the Jews among Paul's auditors in Rome. Once the presence of some Jewish Christians is reckoned with as an element in the rhetorical situation, objections about the intelligibility and rhetorical plausibility of this material fall away, *pace* Elliott, *Rhetoric*, esp. 167-223.

particular pedagogical needs of the audience."[12] This view is reinforced when it is noted that the attitude of the one addressed in 2:1 is that of passing judgment on others and this is precisely the characteristic of Jewish Christians in Rome according to the later paraenesis.[13] While the "strong" are depicted as despising the "weak" (14:3a, 10b), the latter are seen as judging the "strong" (14:3b, 4, 10a).

The diatribe style is intended to enable Jewish Christians to see the force of Paul's arguments without being alienated personally. At the same time, as we have said, this letter is addressed to a primarily Gentile Christian audience, whose own understanding of that gospel will be both reinforced and corrected, as they see how Paul treats the very issues they are discussing and disputing with Jewish Christians. If any of them are claiming to be Pauline with their emphasis on faith, then they need to grasp the proper Pauline perspective on the matters under debate. In this way the letter's rhetoric falls into the category of epideictic. It is designed to persuade both sections of the audience to hold a particular viewpoint, which they partially share already, the Gentile Christians somewhat more than the Jewish Christians, but which Paul wants to see prevail and orient their future actions. We should not expect therefore that Paul will be totally even-handed toward the two groups. As apostle to the Gentiles, he is not about to compromise the law-free gospel which he considers integral to his vocation.

Paul's mode of argument makes clear that he remains the *Jewish* apostle to the Gentiles and that one does not need to renounce one's Jewish heritage in order to espouse his controversial gospel. He wants to show that the distinctive elements of his gospel are not only compatible with his Judaism but also provide the best possible way of reshaping the Jewish tradition now that has become necessary because of the implications of what God has done in Christ. In the course of the argument in 1:18-4:25 he attempts to explain that the gospel of justification by faith for all sits comfortably within his Jewish heritage of belief in the one Creator God and his just judgment, in the Scriptures, in being children of Abraham and in God's will expressed in the law. His is not a gospel that undermines the righteousness of God in any way. Instead it takes that righteousness as a given and reinforces it. It is worth asking why it is only in Romans that Paul actually formulates his statement of the gospel in terms of the righteousness of God (1:17). After all, although he had talked about justification and righteousness in relation to believers in Galatians, he had not spoken of the righteousness of God, let alone expressed a crucial statement of his message with this concept.[14] Surely this initial statement is not unrelated to the objections, of which Paul shows he is aware in 3:1-8, that his gospel casts aspersions on God's righteousness both in the sense of his faithfulness to Israel and in the sense of his upholding of justice and

---

12 Stowers, *Diatribe*, 99, 180.

13 The parallel is pointed out by W. A. Meeks, "Judgment and the Brother: Romans 14:1-15:13," *Tradition and Interpretation in the New Testament*, ed. G. F. Hawthorne and O. Betz (Grand Rapids: Eerdmans, 1987), 296, though he interprets its significance differently.

14 Though cf. 2 Cor 5:21.

morality.[15] Already in this initial statement of the salvation offered in his gospel, Paul has hinted strongly that it is not a gospel that calls into question the righteousness of God by entailing that he has now turned his back on Israel. After all, it is "to the Jew first and also to the Greek." It asserts both that there is no distinction between Jew and Gentile and yet that there is still a priority for Israel. The paradox or contradiction (one's choice of terms depends heavily on one's sympathies with the argument and its presuppositions) does not await chapters 9-11 but is embedded in the *propositio* and repeated in 3:1, 2, 9. In terms of Paul's view of God, this is a paradox which lies at the heart of divine righteousness, involving on the one hand God's impartiality and on the other his faithfulness.[16] Clearly the most delicate and difficult of these issues surrounding the relation of the gospel to Judaism, both for Paul, in his own understanding of the gospel as that has been shaped by conflict with both non-Christian and Christian Jews, and for the audience in Rome, is the place of the law, and that issue, as we have noted, runs like an undercurrent through the main argument of these early chapters before Paul gives it more extended treatment later, particularly in chapter 7.

Again, the Jewish Christians among the recipients need to be reassured by Paul's views on these matters but also the Gentile Christian majority is equally in need of hearing such a full explanation and of being induced to a change of attitude by understanding that the gospel is not only by faith but to the Jew first. In this way they may be helped to temper any exaggeration of the gospel's faith aspect, which plays down its relation to its Jewish roots, in their own discussions with fellow Jewish Christians. So in the first four chapters, as throughout the letter, Paul proves himself an apologete for his gospel from within the Jewish tradition. He not only makes the claim that his is a gospel which is for the Jew first but also for the Greek, but he also rehearses the gospel in a way that is for the Jew first and also for the Greek.

2. The Need of Humanity for Paul's Gospel of Righteousness through Faith (1:18-3:20)

Although Paul is convinced that in Christ God has acted decisively to rescue humanity and in this light depicts the sort of plight that required a rescue act of this particular nature, with the exception of what might appear to be an almost incidental reference in 2:16, the name of Christ is not mentioned in his discussion. He makes his case for humanity's universal plight from within the parameters of assumptions his Jewish Christian addressees would already have held as Jews. He begins his demonstration of Jewish inclusion in humanity's sinful plight with an indictment of that plight with which all Jews would agree. In fact, much of the indictment is an adaptation of material from the Wisdom of Solomon 12-14. So this is not so much an indictment that works from specifically Christian maxims as the presuppositions and theology of Hellenistic Judaism being employed in the service of Paul's

---

[15] Cf. also A. J. M. Wedderburn, *The Reasons for Romans* (Edinburgh: T. & T. Clark, 1988), 108-23.

[16] For discussion of these two elements as the theme of Romans, see W. S. Campbell, *Paul's Gospel in an Intercultural Context* (Frankfurt: Peter Lang, 1991), 173-83.

argument for his gospel, a service that will then include being used in the case against Jewish presumption.

It would seem reasonable to attempt to find an exegetically plausible reading of some of the less clear stages in the argument in the light of its clear final goal before either declaring the whole incoherent or resorting to reinterpreting the conclusion on the basis of a particular reading of one of the stages. Recognition of Paul's goals and tactics in 1:18-3:20 helps in accounting for the apparent contradictions in the actual argument pointed out by Sanders and Räisänen among others.[17] At certain points there are some rather optimistic assertions about Jews and Gentiles being able to do what the law requires and thereby gaining justification and life (cf. 2:7, 10, 13-15, 27) and in one place it is said only that some Jews have been unfaithful, not all (3:3). The deductions that Paul eventually draws in 3:9-20 that all people alike are sinful and that justication through the law is impossible appear therefore to be undermined. But in 2:7, 10 Paul is talking about the criterion of God's future judgment and spelling out clearly the Jewish assumption which he will in fact subvert. And talk of law-fulfilling Gentiles (2:13-15, 27) is one of the weapons used in the subversion. But when the situation of Gentiles themselves is directly in view, it is a different story and Paul is quite clear about their need of his gospel because of their being under sin and God's wrath (1:18-32; 3:9). The talk of some Jews being unfaithful in 3:3 is best taken as part of a diatribal question arising from Paul's previous discussion, particularly that of 2:17-24,[18] and it is noticeable that Paul's reply in 3:4 moves back to universal terminology—"although everyone is a liar . . ." Having, as he believes, subverted Jewish presumption from its own premises, Paul himself has no difficulty coming to the conclusion in 3:9-20 that he has wished to reach all along, namely, that apart from faith in Christ *all* Jews and *all* Gentiles are dominated by sin and condemned by the law. While some opt for elements of incoherence, Davies attempts to produce coherence by denying that this is Paul's conclusion. To support his reading of 2:6-16 in terms of righteous Jews and Gentiles receiving salvation before the coming of Christ, he has to reinterpret the clear universal language of 3:9-12, 20 as simply a reference to "the distributive presence of sinfulness . . . across the boundaries of Jew and Gentile."[19]

Not only his formulation of the gospel in 1:17 but also the framework in which he places his indictment of humanity's sinfulness indicate Paul's concern to show how seriously his gospel takes the matter of the righteousness of God. As we shall see, his talk of God's righteousness cannot be divorced from its forensic connotations as God's righteous judgment, so to begin by talking about the wrath of God in 1:18 is not to introduce a totally unrelated topic. The parallelism between ἀποκαλύπτεται γὰρ ὀργὴ θεοῦ and

---

17 E. P. Sanders, *Paul, the Law and the Jewish People* (Philadelphia: Fortress, 1983), 123-32; H. Räisänen, *Paul and the Law* (Tübingen: Mohr, 1983), 99-108.

18 On which, see below.

19 Cf. Davies, *Faith and Obedience*, esp. 96. The earlier attractive presentation of a similar view by K. R. Snodgrass, "Justification by Grace—to the Doers; an Analysis of the Place of Romans 2 in the Theology of Paul," *NTS* 32 (1986) 72-93, appears to founder at the same point by not accounting adequately for the force of 3:9-18 as it leads into the conclusion of 3:19-20.

δικαιοσύνη γὰρ θεοῦ ἐν αὐτῷ ἀποκαλύπτεται should be observed and the γάρ of v.18 given its normal force. God's righteousness has to be revealed in the gospel for faith, because, apart from the gospel, when God's righteousness meets human unrighteousness, his righteous judgment is revealed not as salvation but as wrath.[20] That wrath is the negative side of God's righteous judgment is indicated in the conclusion to the first stage of the argument in 1:32, which speaks of τὸ δικαίωμα τοῦ θεοῦ—"the just requirement of God." It is precisely because of God's righteousness, Paul is claiming, that such a gospel as his is necessary. And in the next section (cf. 2:3, 5) he attempts to demonstrate that it is not his gospel but Jewish Christian objections to it which have not taken seriously enough this aspect of God's righteousness—"Do you imagine ... that you will escape the judgment of God (τὸ κρίμα τοῦ θεοῦ)?"; "You are storing up wrath for yourself on the day of wrath, when God's righteous judgment will be revealed (θησαυρίζεις σεαυτῷ ὀργὴν ἐν ἡμέρᾳ ὀργῆς καὶ ἀποκαλύψεως δικαιοκρισίας τοῦ θεοῦ)." We should be clear then that the notion of "the righteousness of God" is itself a Jewish tradition or axiom. Paul will exploit its two major aspects—the legal or forensic aspect, God's righteous judgment, as seen here with its negative consequence of wrath, and the relational aspect, God's faithfulness to the covenant in bestowing righteousness on humans, which will appear together with the forensic in 3:21-26.[21]

It is widely recognized that Paul's indictment of the situation of ungodliness and unrighteousness that calls forth God's wrath may not only allude to Gen 1-3,[22] but is also similar to the indictment of paganism found in Wisdom 12-14. What is not sufficiently recognized, when attention is drawn to specific parallel texts in Wisdom,[23] is the way in which the themes of Wisdom as a whole provide a most appropriate resource for Paul's discussion in Romans 1 and 2. After all, Paul wishes to deal with God's righteous judgment as it relates to humanity as a whole and to Jews, and this is precisely what can be found in Wisdom. It provides a discussion of the life and destiny of the righteous and the unrighteous and of God's righteous judgment on behalf of the righteous. This discussion is peppered with the concepts of wrath and mercy in the context of God's judgment on pagans and on Israel.[24] Again, God's righteousness involves his righteous judgment —"You are righteous and you order all things righteously, deeming it alien to

---

[20] Wisdom, to which we shall return, is illuminating for the close relationship in Jewish thought between God's righteousness and his wrath. In 5:17-20 righteousness, impartial justice or judgment, holiness and wrath constitute the whole armour put on by God.

[21] The recent tendency has been to play down the forensic aspect in favour of the aspect of either covenant faithfulness, cf. e. g. Dunn, *Romans 1-8*, 41-42, 165-76, or simply salvation, cf. Campbell, *Rhetoric of Righteousness*, 138-65.

[22] Cf. M. D. Hooker, "Adam in Romans 1," *NTS* 6 (1959-60) 297-306 and "A Further Note on Romans 1," *NTS* 13 (1966-67) 181-83; A. J. M. Wedderburn, "Adam in Paul's Letter to the Romans," *Studia Biblica* 3 (1980) 413-30.

[23] Cf. the list of parallels in W. Sanday and A. C. Headlam, *The Epistle to the Romans* (Edinburgh: T. & T. Clark, 1902), 51-52.

[24] On the similar treatment of these topics in the Psalms of Solomon, see M. Seifrid, *Justification by Faith* (Leiden: E. J. Brill, 1992), 117-33.

your power to condemn anyone who does not deserve to be punished" (12:15; cf. also, e.g., 12:12, 13, 18). Occasionally Wisdom speaks of God's sovereignty in his universal mercy ("but you have mercy on all"—11:23; cf. also 12:16), but most characteristic is the frequent juxtaposition and discrimination it makes between pagans' and Israel's experience of God's judgment. Pagans, who are spoken of in terms of the ungodly and unrighteous, the foolish and futile, should have known God from his creation but have refused to do so, and instead their idolatry has led to fornication and a whole catalogue of vices. As a result they will be deservedly punished through the very things by which they sinned and will experience God's wrath. The righteous, however, who know God and are his holy people may experience his discipline as sons but can be assured of his mercy and kindness. Two instances of this characteristic juxtaposition can be cited—". . . although they were being disciplined in mercy, they knew how the ungodly were judged in wrath and tormented. You admonished and tested them as a father, but examined and condemned the ungodly as a severe king" (11:9, 10); ". . . with what care you have judged your own sons, to whose fathers you have given oaths and covenants of good promises! So while chastening us, you scourge our enemies ten thousand times more, so that when we judge, we may meditate on your goodness, and when we are judged, we may expect mercy" (12:21, 22; cf. also 14:31 and 15:1; 16:1, 2; 16:4, 5; 16:9-11; 16:24; 18:19, 20; 18:25 and 19:1). As he writes Romans, Paul appears to be aware of Wisdom,[25] and it is not difficult to see what he does with its treatment of God's righteous judgment. He is going to exploit the notion of the sovereignty of God in his mercy on all later in chapters 9-11, but at this early stage in the letter he wants to show God's righteous judgment on all, and does so by first reinforcing the sort of perspective on paganism found in Wisdom before subverting its theology by arguing that Jews are in fact in the very same position in regard to God's judgment and wrath.

Paul's initial purpose in reinforcing the typical Jewish indictment of the pagan world is to demonstrate that such pagans need his gospel because they are deservedly under God's wrath. Whatever positive aspects of their knowledge of God are mentioned only render them without excuse (1:20), demonstrating that their idolatry is not innocent ignorance but culpable refusal to acknowledge God. They know the truth (particularly about the Creator in relation to the creation) but suppress it in their unrighteousness (1:18). Paul's supporting assertions in 1:19-21 are strong ones. The invisible God is known through the visible creation. God has in fact made plain to people this knowledge of himself. So there is no problem, according to Paul, with the clarity of God's revelation; the problem is with the human response. Humanity has known God but has chosen not to respond appropriately by glorifying and giving thanks to its Creator. In similar fashion Wis 13:1-9 had indicted all people who were ignorant of God for being "unable from the good things that are seen to know the one who exists . . . For from the greatness and

---

25 This is also suggested by material later in the letter, where, for example, 5:12 echoes the language about death coming into the world from Wis 2:24, 9:20-23 in its potter and clay analogy cites Isa 45:9, but then, in its discussion of the uses to which the potter decides different vessels will be put, also reflects Wis 15:7, while Rom 13:1-7 with its view of the state having its authority from God and acting as his servant recalls Wis 6:1-4.

beauty of created things comes a corresponding perception of their Creator." Yet this passage talks about such inability in terms of seeking God and its reason why people should not be pardoned is "if they had the power to know so much that they could investigate the world, how did they fail to find sooner the Lord of these things?" So Paul has intensified the indictment and made it more damning. In traditional categories, whereas Wisdom talks of a failure in natural theology, not having succeeded in reasoning from the creation to the Creator, Paul talks of a failure to respond to natural revelation, suppressing a knowledge of God which has already been given.

But the results of the failure are the same for both Paul and Wisdom— idolatry, fornication and all kinds of evils which in themselves constitute a deserved punishment. In the words of Wisdom—"In return for their foolish and unrighteous thoughts, which led them astray to worship irrational serpents and worthless animals, you sent on them a multitude of irrational creatures to punish them, so that they might learn that one is punished by the very things by which one sins" (11:15, 16; cf. also 12:24-27). "For the devising of idols was the beginning of fornication and the invention of them the corruption of life" (14:12). ". . . they no longer keep either their lives or their marriages pure, but they either treacherously kill one another, or grieve one another by adultery, and all is a raging riot of blood and murder, theft and deceit, corruption, faithlessness, tumult, perjury, confusion over what is good, forgetfulness of favors, defiling of souls, sexual perversion (γενέσεως ἐναλλαγή), disorder in marriages, adultery, and debauchery. For the worship of idols not to be named is the beginning and cause and end of every evil" (14:24-27). For Paul too, Gentiles, who began with knowledge of God, end up with the futility and folly of idolatry (1:21-23), which has the further consequence of sexual impurity (1:24-27). Whereas in this area Wisdom stressed disordered marriages and adultery and mentioned the "exchange of natural sexual roles"[26] in passing, Paul focuses more on what, with other moralists of the time, he sees as the choice of exchanging or giving up natural intercourse for unnatural, and regards this as receiving the due penalty for error (1:27; cf. Wis 12:24-27; 14:30, 31). For him also a whole catalogue of "things that should not be done," which overlaps with Wisdom's in terms of murder, deceit and faithlessness, follows on from humanity's wilful refusal to treat God as God (1:28-31). But Paul broadens out the catalogue to include "every kind of unrighteousness," and lists several more subtle sins than does Wisdom, such as covetousness, envy, gossip, slander, haughtiness, boastfulness, and heartlessness.

There are also differences in the way Paul has formulated his indictment. He is concerned to stress again and again the root sin, which provokes God's judgment and from which all else follows. ". . . they exchanged the glory of the immortal God for images" (1:23); "they exchanged the truth about God for a lie and worshiped and served the creature rather than the Creator" (1:25); and "they did not see fit to acknowledge God" (1:28). Following each of these charges is the refrain "God gave them up. . . ," indicating that Paul is not content only to declare that sin has its own consequences but is convinced that God's activity is to be discerned in those consequences, so that the revealing of

---

26 Cf. D. Winston, *The Wisdom of Solomon* (New York: Doubleday, 1979), 280.

God's wrath within this process consists in giving humans what they choose in all its consequences. To underline this, Paul provides in each case a correspondence between that to which God gave humans up and the sinful attitude to God which produced this judgment. Exchanging the glory (δόξα) of the immortal God for images results in being given up to the dishonoring (ἀτιμάζεσθαι) of their bodies; exchanging (μετήλλαξαν) the truth of God for a lie results in exchanging (μετήλλαξαν) natural intercourse for unnatural; and failing to acknowledge (οὐκ ἐδοκίμασαν) God results in a debased (ἀδόκιμος) mind. Wisdom can assert that the ungodly recognize God when they are punished (12:27), they know that they sin (15:13) and why they are perishing (18:19). In the climax of his indictment Paul takes this further. Not only do the unrighteous know God, they also know his righteous judgment and recognize death as a deserved punishment for their deeds. Yet, despite this, they not only continue in these deeds, which could simply indicate their bondage to a process that has gone beyond their control, but they also applaud others who practise such deeds, which leaves no doubt that they are wilfully flouting and suppressing the ethical insight they have been given (1:32).

The diatribe style makes its first contribution to Paul's argument in 2:1-5. Paul's dialogue with his imaginary partner is designed to show why he holds that being made right with God through faith in Christ and not through law works is the gospel for all and not just for Gentiles and, as we have suggested, enables him indirectly to attempt to puncture presumption about Jewish privilege still harboured by some of the Jewish Christians in Rome. He will attempt the same with Gentile Christian pride later in 11:17-25, employing the same notion of presuming on God's kindness. But for now, for the Gentile Christian majority, the use of the diatribe serves as an invitation to listen in on the way Paul himself sets out the implications of his gospel for Jewish Christian attitudes.

The dialogue proceeds in three main stages in chapter 2. First, Paul tackles the Jewish presumption about the outcome of God's judgment by stressing the impartiality of God's righteous judgment on the basis of human deeds (2:1-16). Then he addresses more directly the issue of reliance on the law, which has already come into the discussion in v. 13 (2:17-24), before turning to the Jewish identity marker of circumcision (2:25-29). Just as Paul has asserted that unrighteous pagans are under God's wrath (1:18) and without excuse (1:20), now he will say exactly the same about those who believe themselves able to judge such evil deeds from a privileged position.[27] They too are deserving of wrath (2:5) and without excuse (2:1). They have no excuse, because, while they agree with the indictment Paul has made, they are doing the very same things and are thereby condemning themselves. The premise on which this argument depends for its effectiveness is that all people, including Jews, are tainted in some way by participation in the evils which have been described in 1:28-31 and Paul's purpose in broadening and refining the list of vices

---

27 The sequence and technique in Rom 1 and 2 is similar to that in Amos 1 and 2, where the prophet begins by indicting the surrounding nations for their war crimes and, having secured his audience's agreement with this condemnation, then turns the indictment back on Israel by proclaiming the same judgment on its social injustices, cf. J. Barton, *Amos's Oracles Against the Nations* (Cambridge: C. U. P., 1980), 3-4, 46-50; cf. also H. Moxnes, *Theology in Conflict* (Leiden: E. J. Brill, 1986), 35.

mentioned can now be seen.[28] His interlocutor has no trouble in agreeing that God's judgment on the perpetrators of such vices is in accord with truth and is just (2:2). Such a person would echo the sentiments of Wis 12:12-15 that no one could plead as an advocate for the unrighteous before God, since God is righteous and his condemnation is just. But, according to Paul, to endorse such sentiments while sharing in the vices is to shut off all escape from experiencing the same judgment of God (2:3).

The dialogue partner's response might well be to appeal to God's kindness, and such an appeal would, as we have seen, correspond precisely with the attitude reflected in Wisdom. This has been the pattern in the past— "Therefore they were deservedly punished through such creatures . . . Instead of this punishment you showed kindness to your people" (16:1, 2; cf. also 11:9) and continues to hold good—". . . the just penalty for those who sin . . . always pursues the transgression of the unrighteous. But you, our God, are kind and true, patient, and ruling all things in mercy. For even if we sin we are yours, knowing your power" (14:31-15:2),[29] so that there can be confidence that "while chastening us, you scourge our enemies ten thousand times more, so that when we judge, we may meditate on your goodness, and when we are judged we may expect mercy" (12:22). But Paul is ready to cut off this escape route also, and does so by playing off against this attitude another aspect of traditional Jewish theology found in Wisdom. To presume on God's kindness in this way, he claims, is in fact to despise that kindness, because God's kindness has always been meant to lead to repentance. This challenge simply reminds the interlocutor of Wisdom's own teaching—"you overlook people's sins so that they might repent (εἰς μετάνοιαν)" (11:23). In regard to the unrighteous this is the case, "judging them little by little you gave them an opportunity to repent" (12:10; cf. also 12:20), and the same is true for the righteous—"you have filled your sons with good hope, because you give repentance for sins" (12:19). So, concludes Paul, to entertain any notion of leniency if one judges sin and yet participates in it oneself is to misunderstand drastically the purpose of God's kindness, to show a hard and impenitent heart and thereby to store up wrath for oneself at the time of the revelation of God's righteous judgment (2:5). Whereas the characteristic attitude of Wisdom is to indulge Israel by pointing to God's kindness and asserting that, in contrast to the ungodly who experience God's wrath without mercy to the end, Israel only tastes God's wrath temporarily and that wrath does not continue to the end (cf. Wis 11:9; 16:4, 5; 18:25; 19:1), Paul asserts

---

28 *Pace* Longenecker, *Eschatology*, 175-81, who argues that Paul's indictment is simply a rhetorical technique typical of ethical denunciation and polemic without any empirical correspondence. But this is not only to leave Paul without any real grounds for his conclusion in 3:9, 19, 20 but also to distort his use of the diatribe, which is pedagogical rather than polemical.

29 To observe correctly that Wis 15:2 continues, "but we will not sin, because we know that you acknowledge us as yours," and to claim that this invalidates appeals to Wisdom as the background to 2:1-5, is to miss the point (*pace* Elliott, *Rhetoric*, 174-82). There is no dispute that Wisdom encourages Israel not to sin. The issue is what happens when Israel does sin, and here the evidence from Wisdom, not just 15:2, is clear. Israel, in contrast to the Gentiles, has a distinctive claim on God's mercy.

uncompromisingly that God's people who act unrighteously can expect to experience wrath on the day of God's wrath.

Paul brooks no compromise because he holds that the criterion on which God's righteous judgment is based is a person's deeds or works (ὅς ἀποδώσει ἑκάστῳ κατὰ τὰ ἔργα αὐτοῦ—2:6). To point to judgment on the basis of works is only to underline in a rigorous fashion another tenet embedded in Jewish thought. Paul cites the formulation found in LXX Ps 61:13—σὺ ἀποδώσεις ἑκάστῳ κατὰ τὰ ἔργα αὐτοῦ and Prov 24:12—ὅς ἀποδίδωσιν ἑκάστῳ κατὰ τὰ ἔργα αὐτοῦ. Again this is a familiar theme in Hellenistic Judaism—"For mercy and wrath are with the Lord . . . Great as his mercy, so also is his chastisement; he judges a person according to one's deeds (κατὰ τὰ ἔργα αὐτοῦ) . . . everyone receives in accordance with one's deeds (κατὰ τὰ ἔργα αὐτοῦ)" (Sir 16:11b-14). Twice Paul elaborates on this basis for judgment, making clear that seeking glory and immortality by the working of good will result in eternal life, while the working of evil in unrighteousness will have wrath and fury as its consequence (2:8-10). There ought to be no confusion at this point. Paul is talking about the principle of judgment. He does not have in view here whether anyone succeeds in gaining eternal life in accordance with this principle. Once that question is raised, however, his answer is overwhelmingly clear, not only in terms of the thrust of the overall argument in 1:18-3:20 but quite explicitly—"there is no one who is righteous . . . there is no one who seeks God . . . there is no one who does good" (3:10-12).[30]

Significantly, Paul adds to both the negative and the positive side of the second elaboration of the principle the phrase "the Jew first and also the Greek." It is not, as might have been assumed on the basis of the theology of Wisdom, the ungodly Greek who will be judged first and then the Jew on a more lenient basis. Just as his gospel is for the Jew first and also the Greek, so Paul insists that God's righteous judgment has the same priority. If anything, then, the Jew with privileged knowledge should expect to be judged more rather than less harshly. But again this is a priority within a basic equality, for what Paul's dialogue partner needs to remember is that in his judgment "God shows no partiality" (2:11). It comes as no surprise to realize that again Paul is, for the sake of his argument, drawing on a classic depiction of Israel's God, which had clear forensic connotations—"For the Lord your God is God of gods and Lord of lords, the great God, mighty and awesome, who is not partial and takes no bribes" (Deut 10:17; cf. also, e.g., 2 Chron 19:7; Jub 5:16; 21:4; 30:16; 33:18; Ps Sol 2:18). Again this axiom would also be familiar from Hellenistic Judaism—"The Lord is judge, and with him there is no partiality" (Sir 35:12). In the hands of Paul it moves beyond any more restricted application to the orphan, the widow and the stranger within Israel (cf. Deut 10:18, 19) and is given a universal application, which both illuminates Paul's purpose in the

---

30 Cf. also U. Wilckens, *Der Brief an die Römer* 1 (Zürich: Benzinger, 1978), 130-31, 145-46, 174-75; D. J. Moo, *Romans 1-8* (Chicago: Moody, 1991), 139-41.

preceding discussion and serves as a thematic foundation for the ensuing elaboration of the argument.[31]

God's impartiality is demonstrated, argues Paul, in that all who sin will perish, whether or not they have the law, though that distinction will be taken into account (2:12). God's impartiality is linked with the principle Paul has already appealed to in 2:6, namely, that his judgment is on the basis of works. This is why it will be of no help to be judged by the law. It is not the hearers but the doers of the law whom God deems righteous (2:13). Again this is a principle embedded in the law itself. Paul does not pause to cite it here, but his key text to underline this principle is Lev 18:5, which he will employ later in 10:5. Instead he underlines that there can be no assumption that having the law and doing the law are identical by claiming that those who do not have the law can still do the law, and he shows that God's impartiality is at work because there is a sense in which these Gentiles will be judged on the same basis of works of the law (2:14-16). The argument is this. The very fact that on occasion Gentiles are by nature, without the benefit of knowledge of the law, able to do what the law requires indicates that the work of the law is for them written in their hearts.[32] This ethical awareness is further witnessed to by their conscience and by their own accusatory or defensive thoughts and provides the law by which they will be judged by God. It is here that Paul adds "according to my gospel through Jesus Christ." The addition is not superfluous. It provides a timely reminder to his Jewish Christian dialogue partner of the point Paul has been making all along, namely, that it is precisely his gospel which takes the righteousness of God in the sense of his righteous judgment seriously and that it is because it takes it seriously that this gospel is necessary for all.

It should be noted that, so far, the main basis for any condemnation of Jews is the same as that for the condemnation of Gentiles—their sinful deeds, their failure to match up to the criterion of judgment according to works. They are not condemned in the first instance because of their views about their covenantal status. Such views obscure the proper evaluation of their sinful deeds, leading them to think that despite these deeds they will be protected from judgment.[33] From this perspective Paul can now drive home the distinction between having the law, with the accompanying attitudes of superiority about the privileges this bestows, and actually doing it. It is frequently observed that the challenges of 2:17-24 will not support the condemnation of all Jews found in 3:9. But this is to misunderstand Paul's argument. The foundation for the conclusion of 3:9 has already been laid in

---

[31] Cf. J. M. Bassler, *Divine Impartiality: Paul and a Theological Axiom* (Chico, CA; Scholars Press, 1982), 121-70, who has shown clearly the ways in which this axiom can be related to Paul's overall argument, though her claims about the pivotal place of 2:11 in the structure of the argument are more debatable.

[32] The Gentiles in view are not Gentile Christians, *pace*, e.g., C. E. B. Cranfield, *A Critical and Exegetical Commentary on the Epistle to the Romans* 1 (Edinburgh: T. & T. Clark, 1977), 155-56; Watson, *Paul*, 121; N. T. Wright, "Romans and the Theology of Paul," *SBL 1992 Seminar Papers* (Atlanta, GA: Scholars Press, 1992), 192 n.12. Cf. also Bassler, *Divine Impartiality*, 141-49; Moo, *Romans 1-8*, 144-47.

[33] *Pace* Longenecker, *Eschatology*, 174-95, who makes ethnocentric covenantalism the sole ground for the condemnation of Jews.

2:1-16. His point here is a more limited one. By stating what cannot be disputed, that is, that some Jews, who know God's will in the law and are therefore in a position to provide teaching and enlightenment for others, in fact break central elements of the law such as the commandments about stealing and adultery,[34] he is able to dispose of the notion that such a privileged position provides a safeguard against God's judgment.[35] Such breaches of the law by the very ones who boast in the law exemplify the distinction between having the law and doing it and lead to the ironic indictment that the God, in whom they also boast (cf. 2:17), is dishonored. The indictment is intensified by Paul's use of Scripture in 2:24. Having the law and not doing it is to be the cause of the sin of blasphemy, since, citing LXX Isa 52:5, "the name of God is blasphemed among the Gentiles because of you."[36]

The axioms of God's impartiality and the necessity of doing the law provide the basis for Paul's reply to the dialogue partner who might still be inclined to contend that if having the law is of no avail, then surely being circumcised and bearing the badge of belonging to God's elect people must count for something in terms of being right in God's eyes. Paul simply pushes the logic through. Circumcision unaccompanied by doing the law is the equivalent of uncircumcision, and if the uncircumcised keep the requirements of the law, this can not only be regarded as circumcision but will also be a condemnation of those who have the law and circumcision but do not keep the law. In making his point, Paul again draws on Scriptural tradition, in fact the same passage from which the axiom of God's impartiality had been taken. Deut 10:16 talked of the circumcizing of the foreskin of the heart (cf. also Jer 4:4) and this circumcision which entails true obedience is the one that counts. These insights produce finally a whole new perspective on who is a Jew. Since being a Jew is not a matter of external, physical identity markers but an inward matter of the heart, the implicit thought is that the way is also open for a Gentile to be considered a Jew.

The significance of Paul's bold case should not be passed over. By this stage of his argument, through the creative use of Jewish Scriptural tradition, Paul has not only attempted to demonstrate to his interlocutor that there is nothing about being a Jew that exempts a person from the consequences of God's righteous judgment and therefore from the need for the gospel he propounds, but he has also asked his interlocutor to rethink radically all the basic categories he or she has been employing for self-identification. The

---

34 As is sometimes observed, the question "Do you rob temples?" may well have had particular and embarrassing connotations for the Jewish community in Rome. The expulsion of Jews by Tiberius in 19 CE, which preceded the most recent expulsion with its disruptive effects for the Christian community, had as its cause the appropriation for their own use by certain Jews, including a teacher, of a contribution to the temple (Josephus, *Ant.* 18. 81-84). Cf. also Watson, *Paul*, 114.

35 Cf. also Dunn, *Romans 1-8*, 113-14.

36 R. B. Hays, *Echoes of Scripture in the Letters of Paul* (New Haven: Yale University Press, 1989), 45-46, argues that the later chapters of Romans show that Paul's misreading of this text as a word of reproach instead of an oracle of promise is only provisional. But whether any of Paul's audience in Rome would have been aware of such a dialectical reading must be doubtful.

progression from "if you call yourself a Jew" (2:17) to the notion of whom God considers a Jew, with its allusion to the Hebrew wordplay (2:29),[37] underlines this. Without being asked to abandon it, Paul's Jewish Christian dialogue partners are being invited to transcend the ethnic identification—and the circumcision and possession of the law integral to this—in which they place such stock and to see themselves and Gentiles with new eyes as ultimately standing with the same possibilities before God. In this way the ground is being prepared for them to accept the proposition that Paul will put to them in chapter 4 that Gentile Christians can lay claim on the same basis as themselves to having Abraham as their father.

In 3:1-8 Paul embarks on the balancing act of explaining that, although there is ultimately no distinction between Jew and Gentile before God, there do remain advantages to being a Jew. This section is vital for Paul's perceptions of Jewish Christian objections to his gospel, but it will have to be passed over rapidly, both for reasons of space and because Paul postpones any detailed reply to these objections until later in the letter. Chapters 9-11 take up the questions of vv. 1-7 and chapter 6 that of v. 8. We pause only to draw attention to the significance of the Scripture citation in the argument. In response to the question of whether God's faithfulness is nullified by Israel's faithlessness Paul cites LXX Ps 50:6—"so that you may be justified in your words, and prevail when you are judged." The background of this text and the introductory assertion—"let God be (proved) true . . ."—is the lawsuit where God is shown to be in the right.[38] The text now functions first of all as a vindication of God's faithfulness when this is brought into question. But its forensic character leads to its shaping of the follow-up question, which is now formulated in terms not of faithlessness and faithfulness but of unrighteousness and righteousness. The text has prompted the thought that human unrighteousness only serves to confirm the righteousness of God, which leads to the further question whether God is unrighteous in inflicting wrath on Israel. Such a question is dismissed as impossible in the light of Israel's axiomatic belief in God as the righteous judge of the world. The issue now has become not so much whether God is unfaithful to his promises to Israel, if wrath is inflicted, as whether he is just in his judgment in doing so. Again, and emerging from within the Jewish tradition itself, it can be seen that both forensic and relational connotations are integral to the meaning of righteousness in Paul's discussion.

Just as later Paul will make use of a catena of Scriptural citations to drive home his exhortation (cf. 15:7-13), so in 3:9-20 a catena of passages, presented back to back with no linking phrases in 3:10-18, function to clinch the main thrust of his argument. The oracles of God (cf. 3:2) now serve to demonstrate human unrighteousness (3:9-20), which in turn is part of the demonstration of the necessity of Paul's gospel. Paul expresses his conclusion through a modification and reapplication of the words of Torah. LXX Ps 13:1-3, which is taken up in 3:10-12, contained a repetition of the clause "there is no one who does good, not even one." Paul, however, changes the wording of the first occurrence to "there is no one who is righteous, not even one," thereby

---

[37] Cf. Gen 29:35; 49:8.

[38] Cf. also H. Ljungman, *Pistis* (Lund: Gleerup, 1964), 21-26.

making it fit more exactly his purposes in the overall argument about attaining righteousness. Whatever were the possibilities left open by the discussion of the criterion of judgment in chapter 2, they are closed off by this first line of the citation which summarizes the force of the whole catena of texts. There is no one who is righteous (3:10). That is why righteousness must be attained some other way. It is not just that people have failed in their search for God, as Wis 13:6-9 put it, but "there is no one who seeks for God" (3:11). This contributes to the recognition that the criterion for a positive judgment that Paul has set out in 2:7, 10—doing good, while seeking glory and honor and immortality—remains unfulfilled. "There is no one who does good, not even one" (3:12). Not only is sin universal but, as LXX Ps 5:10; 139:4; 9:28; Isa 59:7, 8; Ps 35:2 are then enlisted to show by synecdoche, it also affects all of human life—throat, tongue, lips, mouth, feet and eyes. It may well be that the texts in 3:10-18 would not only have been recognized as Scripture but in this particular combination would have been known as a traditional catena already in existence prior to Paul's use.[39] If this were so, the material could have functioned originally either as an indictment of fellow Jews who were considered apostate[40] or as an indictment of Israel's Gentile oppressors. Paul would then be deliberately applying this traditional catena to "all, both Jews and Greeks" (3:9) and in the process again including those who concurred with such an indictment of others in their own indictment.

He anticipates the objection that such texts refer only to the really wicked or those cut off from the covenant and claims that whatever the law says, no matter what the original context or referent,[41] it speaks to those who are "in the law," those who possess these oracles. The Jewish Scriptures themselves are in this way made to provide the universal indictment of humanity, including those to whom the Scriptures were entrusted—the Jews.[42] The picture painted in 3:19b is again a forensic one. Because of the weight of the evidence against them, humans will have nothing to say in their own defence—"so that every mouth may be stopped, and the whole world may be held liable to God's judgment." The modification of LXX Ps 142:2 adds to this picture. The original wording was "Do not enter into judgment with your servant, for no one living will be justified before you." Paul has already

---

[39] Cf. esp. H.-J. van der Minde, *Schrift und Tradition bei Paulus: ihre Bedeutung und Funktion in Römerbrief* (München: F. Schoningh, 1976), 54-58; L. E. Keck, "The Function of Rom 3:10-18—Observations and Suggestions," *God's Christ and His People*, ed. J. Jervell and W. A. Meeks (Oslo: Universitetsforlaget, 1977), 142-51. Among the reasons for supposing the existence of a pre-formed catena are the elaborate structuring of the material and the lack of direct relevance of the central part (vv. 13, 14) to Paul's purposes. For arguments against a pre-Pauline source, see D.-A. Koch, *Die Schrift als Zeuge des Evangeliums* (Tübingen: Mohr, 1986), 179-84.

[40] Cf. the similar material in CD 5. 13-17 and Keck's discussion in "Function," 148-49.

[41] Davies, *Faith and Obedience*, 82-88, provides a useful discussion of the original meaning and context of the citations, but holds that Paul is simply using them to make the same point—that there is no righteousness among the wicked, be they Jew or Gentile (cf. 93). But this is hardly a point that would be under dispute or in need of spelling out.

[42] Cf. Hays, *Echoes of Scripture*, 50—"Those who are entrusted with the oracles of God are thus given the paradoxical privilege of learning from those oracles the truth of their own depravity."

provided the judgment context and so can omit the first line. He changes πᾶς ζῶν το πᾶσα σάρξ and adds before the psalm's wording "by works of the law." In this way 3:20 provides an appropriate summing up of the whole section—a universal indictment of humanity but with special reference to Jews. In the light of the preceding argument it appears highly likely that the mention of "works of the law" by which a person cannot be justified is to be related to the judgment according to works (2:8) and to the principle of doing (2:13). Even if the deeds by which one hopes to be justified are deeds laid down in the law, this fails to alter the universal indictment that no one passes the judgment, no one is righteous.[43] Indeed 3:20—ἐξ ἔργων νόμου οὐ δικαιωθήσεται πᾶσα σάρξ—asserts the reality which provides the counterpart to the principle of 2:13—οἱ ποιηταὶ νόμου δικαιωθήσονται. For Paul the law only serves to show up a person's lack of righteousness, a person's sin (cf. also 7:7-25), and he has just employed the law in its wider sense to do precisely this (3:10-18).

3. Restatement of Paul's Gospel of Righteousness by Faith and its Implications (3:21-31)

Paul is now in a position to restate his gospel in which the righteousness of God is revealed and to do so in the light of his depiction of humanity's plight, which was itself shaped in the light of his earlier formulation of the gospel (1:16, 17). He is also in a position to underline what his depiction of the plight has demonstrated, namely, that the solution offered has to be quite apart from law. The solution indicates that a new era in God's dealings with humanity has been inaugurated and it is marked by the disclosure of his righteousness. As we have seen, Paul's talk of the righteousness of God takes up a Jewish and indeed Scriptural tradition. Paul's treatment here highlights three aspects. In 3:21, and earlier in 1:17, the focus is on God's righteousness as his saving activity, whereby he shows his covenantal faithfulness, and in 3:22 it becomes clear that this activity is one which also bestows his righteousness on all who have faith in Christ, setting them in a right relationship with himself. But God's saving activity cannot be divorced from the character of God himself. It is in accord with who he is as the righteous judge, and so it is not surprising that in 3:25 (cf. also 3:26), and earlier in 3:5, God's righteousness denotes his justice or right judgment. Paul holds that, in acting to provide righteousness by pardoning those who have been declared guilty by his judgment, God retains his own character of righteous judge.[44] In restating his solution in

---

43 For the broad reference of ἐξ ἔργων νόμου, see e.g. Wilckens, *Der Brief an die Römer* 1, 176-77 and "Was heisst bei Paulus: 'Aus Werken des Gesetzes wird kein Mensch gerecht'?" *Rechtfertigung als Freiheit: Paulusstudien* (Neukirchen: Neukirchener, 1974), 77-109; Moo, *Romans 1-8*, 209-18; *contra* the narrow reference in terms of ethnic identity markers suggested by, e.g., Dunn, *Romans 1-8*, 153-55; Longenecker, *Eschatology*, 200-202, 206-7.

44 This topic, of course, deserves a paper in itself. Suffice it here to point to the recent clear overview of the main issues by Moo, *Romans 1-8*, 65-70; 75-86. For a similar interpretation to that sketched above, see P. Stuhlmacher, "The Apostle Paul's View of Righteousness," *Reconciliation, Law, and Righteousness* (Philadelphia: Fortress, 1986), 68-93. In its Scriptural roots, especially in Isaiah, the righteousness of God can be synonymous both with his righteous judgment (e.g., LXX Isa 5:16; 33:5; 59:9; 59:14) and with the

3:21-26, the apostle stays with his picture of the lawcourt from 3:19 not only through his mention of righteousness with its forensic connotations, but also through his assertion that, although righteousness cannot come through the law, both the law and the prophets act as *witnesses* to the righteousness of God which comes through faith in Jesus Christ.[45] In particular, the witness of the law will be provided through his treatment of Gen 15:6, while the witness of the prophets has already been adduced through the use of Hab 2:4 in the *propositio*.

In the new formulation of the solution offered in his gospel Paul may well make use of a Jewish Christian formulation about Christ's sacrificial death and its significance, which already contains a reference to God's righteousness.[46] He connects this formulation with his own emphasis on the justification achieved through Christ's death, adds his own stress on faith in v. 25, and rounds it off with a further statement about the significance of Christ's death for the issue of God's righteousness in v. 26. His rhetoric of persuasion for the Jewish Christian members of his audience is again at work. He takes a statement about Christ's sacrificial death and its relation to God's righteousness with which they would agree, makes it the basis for his own formulation of the role of Christ's death in the solution offered by his gospel, and then extends it a stage further in support of the aspect of his gospel about which they are suspicious. They already believe that God has set forth Christ through his life yielded up in violent death (ἐν τῷ αὐτοῦ αἵματι) as a ἱλαστήριον. They have also already related this sacrificial death to their past sins. When God in his forbearance passed over or remitted Israel's previous sins, this was with a view to his future action in Christ's death, so that his forbearance with Israel is not to be interpreted as indifference to sin. His righteousness is demonstrated because it had been his purpose that the judgment for such sin would be met in Christ's death. Now Paul, in effect, invites his readers to apply this perspective on Christ's death and God's righteousness to the present. He moves from εἰς ἔνδειξιν τῆς δικαιοσύνης αὐτοῦ διὰ τὴν πάρεσιν τῶν προγεγονότων ἁμαρτημάτων to πρὸς τὴν ἔνδειξιν τῆς δικαιοσύνης αὐτοῦ ἐν τῷ νῦν καιρῷ and asserts that it is also because of Christ's sacrificial death that God in justifying the one who has faith in Jesus remains righteous. Jewish Christians should be able to see that their objections to Paul's gospel are ill-founded. In

---

salvation he provides (LXX Isa 46:13; 51:5; 51:8; 62:1), and it is made clear that this salvation is his judgment, the activity of the righteous judge (LXX 63:1; 33:22; 45:21).

45 This is to agree with J. D. G. Dunn, "Once More, ΠΙΣΤΙΣ ΧΡΙΣΤΟΥ," *SBL 1991 Seminar Papers* (Atlanta, GA: Scholars Press, 1991), 730-44 on the force of the genitive construction in 3:22 and 3:26 rather than R. B. Hays, "ΠΙΣΤΙΣ and Pauline Christology: What is at Stake?" *SBL 1991 Seminar Papers* (Atlanta,GA: Scholars Press, 1991), 714-29 or Campbell, *Rhetoric of Righteousness*, 58-69, 214-18.

46 The most convincing version of this view holds that vv. 25-26a contain traditional material; cf. especially K. Wengst, *Christologische Formeln und Lieder des Urchristentums* (Gütersloh: Mohn, 1972), 87-91; B. F. Meyer, "The Pre-Pauline Formula in Rom 3:25-26a," *NTS* 29 (1983), 198-208, though he takes "to show his righteousness" in v. 25 as a Pauline addition; also P. Stuhlmacher, "Recent Exegesis on Romans 3:24-26," *Reconciliation, Law and Righteousness* (Philadelphia: Fortress, 1986), 94-109, esp. 96. For arguments disputing the use of such a formulation, see Campbell, *Rhetoric of Righteousness*, 45-57.

proclaiming that Gentiles can be justified simply by means of faith in Jesus and that any one who has faith in Christ can be set in a right relation with God without obeying the law, he is not abrogating the need for justice or casting aspersions on God's righteousness, because the claim of God's righteousness has been met by the atoning sacrifice God provided in Christ. In this way, Paul claims, God's righteousness, not only in the sense of his saving activity to restore the relationship humanity has ruptured but also in the sense of his righteous judgment, is indeed revealed in his gospel.

Paul's use of the Jewish Christian formulation also enables him to provide a statement of the solution offered in the gospel which matches his depiction of the plight. He has already made clear that just as the plight was universal— all have sinned, so the solution is universal—God's righteousness is available to all who believe in Jesus Christ; and there is no distinction between Jew and Gentile (3:22, 23). But he goes on to stress that the solution has come freely, generously and undeservedly ("by his grace as a gift") and to show that in it each of the main elements of the plight is met. The three types of imagery employed for God's activity in Christ match the three main elements in the situation of human sinfulness. The imagery of the law court predominates through the language of justification. God's righteousness is the power by which those unable to be justified on the criterion of works are set right with him and being set in a right relationship with God involves his judicial verdict of pardon. It is not that people are deemed innocent of the charges in the indictment against them. Their unrighteousness has been clearly depicted in Paul's argument. But he believes the righteous judge has acted ahead of time in history and in his grace has pronounced a pardon on those who have faith in Christ, so that their guilt can no longer be cited against them. God's justification of sinners is "through the redemption that is in Christ Jesus" (3:24). Here the imagery is from the slavemarket, but the concept of redemption also has Scriptural roots in God's acts of liberating his people from slavery in Egypt (cf. Deut 7:8) and in Babylon (cf. Isa 51:11). In the plight depicted in 1:18-3:20 sin had a dual character. Humans were responsible for it; their rebellion against the Creator left them without excuse, guilty. But they also unleashed a situation which they were unable to control; sin became a force to which they were in bondage, imprisoned under its power (3:9). The righteousness of God not only justifies, but it also emancipates, freeing people from this domination of sin. As we have seen, the third kind of imagery employed for the death of Christ is taken from the sacrificial system. His death is regarded not only as an expiatory sacrifice, making amends for sin, but also as a propitiatory sacrifice, averting the wrath of God on account of sin.[47] Paul could not have made clearer that both Gentiles and Jews are deserving of God's condemnation and wrath (1;18; 2:5,

---

[47] The linguistic evidence favors this force for ἱλαστήριον and it is the one most appropriate to the context, cf. e.g., D. Hill, *Greek Words and Hebrew Meanings* (Cambridge: C.U.P., 1967), 23-41; C. E. B. Cranfield, *The Epistle to the Romans* 1 (Edinburgh: T. & T. Clark, 1975), 214-18. In the traditional formulation the term may well have had specific reference to the mercy seat as the place of propititiation, cf. e.g., Stuhlmacher, "Recent Exegesis," 96-104; Meyer, *NTS* 29 (1983) 206; Wilckens, *Der Brief an die Römer* 1, 191-93, but as it now stands is also open to the broader force of "means of propitiation" cf. also Dunn, *Romans 1-8*, 171.

8). Now in the resolution provided by Paul's gospel the imagery of a propitiatory sacrifice makes explicit that in dealing with sin Christ's death also averts God's wrath, and in this formulation it is of course God himself who provides the means of dealing with his own wrath. In this way Paul's solution fits the plight he has depicted. Corresponding to the universal situation of guilt, bondage to sin and condemnation under the wrath of God is a gospel of the righteousness of God, which is available universally to faith and which through Christ's death offers a free and undeserved pardon, liberates into a new life where the tyranny of sin is broken and righteous behaviour becomes possible, and provides satisfaction of God's righteous wrath.

Paul evidently hopes that his use of their understanding of Christ's sacrificial death will enable his Jewish Christian readers to appreciate both the way in which his gospel of justification by faith is the answer to the universal human plight and the way in which it safeguards God's righteous judgment. Taking up the diatribe form again, he now underscores for them two implications. If works of the law cannot produce God's verdict of approval and instead justification is by faith apart from such works, then there is no point in any boasting of a relationship to God based on reliance on the law (3:27, 28). Paul then presses another reason on Jewish Christians for recognizing their equality and unity with Gentile Christians solely through faith in Christ. He appeals to their fundamental belief that God is one, a belief confessed in the Shema (cf. Deut 6:4).[48] Since there is only one God, Paul argues, this God has to be the God of both Jews and Gentiles. From the unity of his relation to all as the one God of all, Paul deduces a unity of principle in this God's saving activity on behalf of both groups. There are not two routes to justification—one involving faith and the law and the other simply involving faith. Instead, the unity of God's relation to both Jews and Gentiles is shown by his justifying the circumcised by faith and the uncircumcised through faith. Again Paul's claim is that so far from involving any abandoning of the basics of the Jewish heritage, his gospel of justification by faith is in fact more appropriate to the universal monotheism of Judaism than is any emphasis on the law. It is precisely its faith aspect which makes his gospel universal in scope and fitted for his world mission, because, unlike an emphasis on law, it places no ethnic limits on participation in a right relationship with the one God.

4. Abraham as the Law's Witness
to Paul's Gospel of Righteousness by Faith (4:1-25)

Both of the main preceding points—justification being by faith not works of the law, thus excluding boasting, and faith as the unifying factor for Jewish Christians and Gentile Christians—are taken up in Paul's treatment of Abraham in 4:1-25. There is also an immediate link with the preceding argument, however, through 3:31. To the objection of Jewish Christians that his formulation about justification means the abrogation of the law, Paul replies that, far from this being the case, he upholds the law and he substantiates this claim by calling on Abraham as his witness from the law

---

[48] See esp. N. A. Dahl, *Studies in Paul* (Minneapolis: Augsburg, 1977), 178-91; Moxnes, *Theology in Conflict*, 78-80.

(cf. 3:21). He realizes he is entering disputed territory and that the view of Abraham as the father of the Jews who showed his faithfulness by keeping the commandments and thus being reckoned as righteous could well be used against him.[49] So Paul anticipates such an objection with a diatribal question in 4:1 and then attempts to secure Abraham for his own position.[50] In so doing, he appears to believe that he is upholding the law in the sense that, when it is read in the light of his gospel, the law can be seen to support that gospel's emphasis on faith. After all, it is the law—Gen 15:6—that says of the patriarch, "Abraham believed God and it was reckoned to him as righteousness," and Paul proceeds to provide a reading of the law in the light of justification by faith. His extended midrashic treatment of this passage allows us to see most clearly what we have been observing all along, namely, the way in which Paul employs tradition familiar to his Jewish Christian readers, here Scriptural tradition, in the service of his rehearsal of the gospel for both Jewish and Gentile Christians in Rome.[51] Having explicitly cited his Scriptural text in v. 3, Paul then elaborates on the significance of one of its major terms, ἐλογίσθη, in vv. 4-8, drawing in Ps 32:1 in the process. He has already discussed δικαιοσύνη in 3:21-26 against the backdrop of 1:18-3:20 and so in vv. 9-21 he can develop the meaning of the other major term in his text, ἐπίστευσεν, weaving in material from Gen 17 and 18 and also citing Gen 15:5, the verse immediately preceding his main text. Finally he returns to this original text in vv. 22-25, making explicit its contemporary application.

In fact, the question of 4:1 is already formulated in such a way as to allude to Scripture and to do so in a manner favorable to Paul's theology. "What then shall we say that Abraham our forefather according to the flesh has found?" is probably meant to recall LXX Gen 18:3 where Abraham says, "If I have found favor (εὗρον χάριν) before you . . ."[52] Through this formulation Paul is already implying what he will make explicit in 4:4, namely, that Abraham's status before God is a matter of grace (cf. also 4:16). If the widespread Jewish understanding of Abraham were right (cf. 1 Macc 2:51, 52—"Remember the works of the fathers, which they did in their generations . . . Was not Abraham found faithful when tested, and it was reckoned to him as righteousness?"; cf. also Sir 44:19-21; CD 3.2; Pr Man 8) and Abraham was justified by works, he would have a cause for boasting. But the preceding demonstration that justification has to be through faith by grace as a gift has ruled this out as a possible stance before God. The question "For what does the Scripture say?" introduces Paul's reading of the law which puts Abraham's relation to God in a different perspective. The fact that the key text which he cites, Gen 15:6, does not talk of works but only mentions faith in Abraham's

---

[49] For one Jewish Christian response to a Pauline "faith not works" slogan which employs the case of Abraham, see Jas 2:18-24.

[50] For the use of an *exemplum* in relation to dialogical exchange in the diatribe, see Stowers, *Diatribe*, 155-74.

[51] I have reflected on Paul's imaginative correlation between Scripture, his gospel and the situation in Rome in an earlier discussion of Romans 4 in "Abraham Goes to Rome: Paul's Treatment of Abraham in Romans 4," *Worship, Theology and Ministry in the Early Church* (Essays in Honor of Ralph P. Martin) eds. M. J. Wilkins and T. Paige (Sheffield: JSOT Press, 1992), 163-79, esp. 176-79.

[52] Cf. also, e.g., Wilckens, *Der Brief an die Römer* 1, 261.

being reckoned righteous enables Paul to press the point that in the case of Abraham there can be no thought of a justification owed him on the basis of a successful performance according to the criterion of judgment according to works (4:4; cf. 2:6, 10). By describing the object of faith as "the one who justifies the ungodly" (4:5), Paul is using language which would confirm the fears of those who believed with some Scriptural support (cf. LXX Exod 23:7— "you will not justify the ungodly") that his gospel undermines the righteousness of God. But he has already attempted to deal with this objection in drawing out the significance of Christ's propitiatory death (3:25, 26). The formulation of 4:5 also by implication places Abraham among the ungodly (cf. 1:18) who deserve only God's wrath and therefore have to receive justification as a gift.[53] So Paul's reflections on the Genesis text not only show Abraham to be a representative of the principles of the apostle's gospel but also open up for Jewish Christians a perception of Abraham, their forefather according to the flesh, and, by extension, themselves as being in exactly the same position as Gentile Christians in regard to receiving justification.

Through the exegetical device of *gezerah shawah*, linking two passages which contain the same term (here the verb λογίζεσθαι, "to reckon"), Paul had drawn LXX Ps 31:1, 2 into his midrash (vv. 6-8). He now goes on to claim in vv 9-12 that the psalm's pronouncement of blessing on the one to whom God reckons righteousness apart from works does not just apply to Jews, as his Jewish Christian readers might well have supposed. It is the Abraham story that enables him to make his point. This time he draws attention to the sequence in the Genesis narrative whereby the statement of Gen 15:6 comes before the account of Abraham's circumcision in Gen 17. So, when Abraham was reckoned righteous by faith, he was uncircumcised (4:9, 10). Again at this point Abraham was in precisely the same position as the Gentile Christian and the Genesis story demonstrates that circumcision is irrelevant to a person's being reckoned righteous by God by means of faith. Abraham's circumcision can be described, therefore, not in the traditional way as a sign of the covenant but as a sign which was the seal of the righteousness he already had by faith (4:11a). Taking the argument a stage further, Paul can now claim that God's purpose in this sequence in the Abraham story was that Abraham's fatherhood should not be restricted to those who are circumcised or who become circumcised as proselytes but should embrace those, who like Abraham himself in Gen. 15, are uncircumcised but have faith. He is to be seen as the father of both uncircumcised believers and circumcised believers, Gentile Christians and Jewish Christians (4:11b, 12).

In 2:17-29 Paul had claimed that neither reliance on the law nor an appeal to circumcision could provide any safeguard in the light of God's impartial judgment. Now his treatment of Abraham reverses the order of topics and attempts to show that neither circumcision nor the law has any role in being reckoned righteous. He makes the point about the law in 4:13-15 by reading the Abraham story in the light of his own contrast between promise and faith on the one hand and law on the other. What Abraham believed when he was reckoned righteous was God's promise that he would have innumerable descendants (cf. Gen 15:5). So, Paul argues, building on his previous point, the

---

53 Cf. also Wilckens, *Der Brief an die Römer* 1, 263; Dunn, *Romans 1-8*, 205.

218 / SBL 1993 Seminar Papers

promise, now extended to inheriting the world (cf. Sir 44:21), did not come through the law; it was believed by Abraham before the law as anticipated in the requirement of circumcision was given. Jewish Christians need to see the law in a new light. So far from it providing a safeguard against God's righteous judgment, as they thought, the situation is quite the reverse—the law in fact brings about God's wrath, it contributes to the universal condemnation depicted in 1:18-3:20, because where there is law, sin becomes conscious violation of the law and all the more deserving of judgment (cf. also 5:13, 20). Paul now asserts that if there is to be any guarantee about inheriting the promise, the whole process has to depend on faith, because only in that way is the principle of grace rather than of law and performance (with their inevitable transgression and failure) brought fully into play (4:16a). The conclusion about Abraham's fatherhood from 4:11, 12 can now be restated in terms of law rather than circumcision. The promise is "guaranteed to *all* his descendants—not only to those of the law [i.e. Jewish Christians who observe the law] but also to those [simply] of the faith of Abraham [i.e. Gentile Christians], for he is the father of us all" (v 16b).[54] In this inclusion of Gentiles in Abraham's family Paul sees the fulfilment of Gen 17:5—"I have made you the father of many nations (πολλῶν ἐθνῶν)."

By now it has become clear that Paul wishes his Jewish Christian readers to reconsider any view of Abraham as simply "our forefather according to the flesh." Exposure to Paul's perspective on Abraham means they have to entertain the notion of accepting Gentile believers as equally children of Abraham solely on the basis of their faith.[55] To see Abraham as "the father of us all" would be quite different from the way they had viewed Gentile proselytes in their synagogues. It appears that proselytes, who were regarded as Abraham's children by adoption, were not permitted to call him "our father." When in the liturgy Jews by birth called the patriarch "our father," proselytes had to say "your father."[56] Previously they would have perceived Abraham primarily as the great dividing point in the history of humanity. Before Abraham there was the history of the nations, but with him began God's particularism in choosing out one nation. But now Paul has made Abraham the great rallying point for all who believe, whether Jews or Gentiles.[57] Gentile Christians, hearing Paul's midrash designed primarily to persuade Jewish Christians of his gospel, are therefore at the same time being invited to see themselves as part of a larger family which can trace its ancestry back to Abraham. They cannot write off Israel's past as of no account. The blessings in which they participate are blessings promised to Abraham

---

54 On any view Paul's wording is difficult and requires filling out. For the view taken here, cf., e.g., E. Käsemann, *Commentary on Romans* (London: SCM, 1980), 121; Wilckens, *Der Brief an die Römer* I, 271-72; Watson, *Paul*, 141, who hold that the adherents of the law are Jewish Christians; *pace*, e.g., Dunn, *Romans*, 216; Moxnes, *Theology in Conflict*, 112 n.18, 250-51, who hold that they are Jews and that Paul is speaking from the perspective of the final eschatological salvation.

55 Cf. also P. Minear, *The Obedience of Faith* (London: SCM, 1971), 53, 55; Watson, *Paul*, 141, who expresses this somewhat differently.

56 Cf. m.Bikkurim 1.4.

57 Cf. A. Nygren, *Commentary on Romans* (Philadelphia: Fortress, 1949), 175, who does not, however, apply this insight to the situation of the readers.

and his descendants. As Paul will remind them later in 15:8, their faith in Christ is faith in the one who has confirmed God's promises to the patriarchs.

Paul's presentation of Abraham and his faith as a symbol of unity has clear implications for the situation of both sections of his audience. Sharing Abraham's justifying faith makes Jewish Christians and Gentile Christians equal members of the one family. Yet, as we have noted, the exhortations of 14:1-15:13 reflect a setting in which faith and its implications had become a divisive issue. The "strong" and the "weak" were despising and judging one another on the basis of their different interpretations of faith. At one point in his exhortation Paul in fact has to tell his readers to stop advertising their faith because of the destructive consequences for community life of such a display (cf. 14:22—"The faith which you have, keep to yourself before God"). Paul's treatment of Abraham should have provided a demonstration that justifying faith is a grounds for unity rather than division in the Christian community. Both groups have Abraham as their father and inherit the promises, because they are reckoned righteous before God and accepted by him on the same basis—faith. When he comes to make his explicit plea for unity in the paraenesis, Paul utilizes this fundamental conviction effectively.[58] He calls first on the strong to accept the weak and then on both groups to accept each other, and his warrant is that God and Christ have first accepted both (cf. 14:1, 3 and 15:7).

In a key insight for the relation between Abraham and the gospel, Paul points out that, in believing the promise that God would make him the father of many nations, Abraham had to believe in a God who gives life to the dead. It was this kind of faith that was reckoned to him as righteousness (4:17b-22). With Gen 17:15-21 and 18:9-15 in view, Paul can talk of Abraham displaying the strong faith that looked at the apparent impossibilities of his situation and yet still trusted completely in God to bring life (Isaac) out of death (his own body as good as dead—νενεκρωμένος—and the deadness—νέκρωσις—of Sarah's womb, cf. 4:19). And in a key insight for the relation between Abraham and the readers, when the apostle describes the quality of Abraham's faith in 4:19, 20, he does so in precisely the terms that are being used in the conflict in Rome—μὴ ἀσθενήσας τῇ πίστει ... ἀλλ' ἐνεδυναμώθη τῇ πίστει, "he did not weaken in faith ... but he grew strong in faith."[59] In the later paraenesis Paul will speak of "we, the strong" (15:1) and will underline his persuasion that nothing is unclean in itself (cf. 14:14, 20). So, in his depiction of Abraham, Paul signals clearly ahead of time where he stands theologically in the debate in Rome. Abraham does not merely exemplify the Pauline gospel as one who is righteous by faith, he is portrayed in such a way as to be aligned with the strong in faith. In his strong faith he is described as displaying the qualities which Paul will later stress as essential in the situation in Rome. He does not doubt. In 14:23 doubt, while eating meat, is a characteristic of the weak, who will be condemned because they are not acting out of their own faith. Similarly, in 4:21 Abraham is said to have been

---

58 Cf. also Minear, *Obedience of Faith*, 55.

59 For a fuller discussion of the links between 4:1-25 and 14:1-15:13, see my "Abraham Goes to Rome," 167-78. On this particular link, cf. also Minear, *Obedience of Faith*, 54; Campbell, *Paul's Gospel*, 32.

"fully convinced," and in 14:5 Paul will argue that whether Roman Christians hold that one day is more important than another or treat all days alike, what matters is that they have the kind of faith that enables them to be "fully convinced" in their own minds, in effect, Abraham's kind of faith. So to share Abraham's justifying faith is also to have strong faith, not to doubt, and to be fully convinced.

Was it not enough that Paul should have asked Jewish Christians to give up their exclusive claim to be Abraham's descendants and to share him as father with Gentile Christians? Depicting Abraham as one of the strong in faith is one way of showing that his distinctive gospel was "to the Jew first, and also the Greek," but does it not add insult to injury? Whatever his readers' response may have been, seen from Paul's point of view, this rhetorical move can still be considered part of his tactics of persuasion. After all, at this stage in the letter he is rehearsing his own perspective on justification by faith and its consequences, knowing this to be controversial. Later in the paraenesis, for the sake of harmony in the community, he will not insist on all its ramifications being accepted and will argue that love and mutual acceptance are more important than being right. But at this point in the argument he would also like to convince the Jewish Christian minority that his interpretation of the gospel is right. He has already asked it to rethink radically the issues of law, circumcision and ethnic identity in 2:17-29. He hopes it will already have been persuaded to think of Abraham in his way as one who was justified by faith. So it is not surprising that he allows his full position to emerge in his midrash on the Abraham story and talks of Abraham as strong in faith. If Jewish Christians can be drawn into reading the Abraham story in Paul's way, they might just be coaxed into seeing not only the basic gospel message but all the issues differently. For, on this reading, to treat all foods as clean and all days as holy need not be thought of as forsaking their election and becoming apostate but as emulating the strength of faith of father Abraham.

Paul's interpretation of Abraham's faith obviously reinforces the views of Gentile Christians at this stage of his argument. But giving them a sense of their own solidarity with Abraham prepares them in two ways for what is to come. By showing them that justification and strong faith are found first in Abraham, Paul provides a needed reminder that the gospel in which they believe is "to the Jew first, and also the Greek" and helps them to empathize with his later assertion that ethnic Israel will not finally miss out on the salvation, which they enjoy at present, because "as regards election they are beloved for the sake of their forefathers" (11:28). And when Paul in the paraenesis asks them to change their attitude and make concessions to Jewish Christians, this portrait of Abraham will have been one of the means of helping them to realize that the request comes from one who clearly shares their basic perspective on faith.

There is one particular aspect of Paul's depiction of Abraham's faith, which, in the light of the later exhortation, will be seen to have force for both groups in Rome. It is with Abraham that Paul introduces for the first time in the letter the theme of hope or confident assurance that will prove significant in the later argument (cf. 5:1-11; 8:18-39). Abraham is said to have "against hope, in hope believed." Paul will complete his paraenesis about mutual acceptance with the aid of Scripture citations, and this, he says, is in order that "by the encouragement of the Scriptures we might have hope" (15:4). His prayer wish which forms the climax is "May the God of hope fill you with all joy and peace in believing, so that by the power of the Holy Spirit you may abound in hope" (15:13). As in the case of Abraham, hope is connected with believing. And just as Abraham's hopeful belief that he would be the father of many nations impelled him to positive action in the present despite the obstacles, so Paul holds that it is the faith which abounds in the hope of the salvation in which Jew and Gentile are one and equal that will provide the motivation for the Roman Christians to accept one another and worship together in unity and equality in Rome despite all obstacles.

This strong and hopeful faith in the creator God and his life-giving power is what was reckoned to Abraham as righteousness (4:22), and this is why, says Paul, as he now makes explicit the correlation that has been at work throughout his midrash, Gen 15:6 was written not only for Abraham but also for Christian believers in the same God who raised Jesus from the dead. Significantly for his attempt to persuade Jewish Christians, in 4:25 Paul's formulation of the gospel, in the light of which he has been reading the Abraham story, employs Jewish Christian traditional material, which interpreted Jesus' death and resurrection on the basis of Isaiah 53.[60] He wants his audience to see Abraham as a type of Christian believers, whose justification is through belief in Christ's resurrection, whereby Christ's vindication in the reversal of the condemnation of death, to which "he was handed over because of our transgressions," also becomes theirs. What is readily apparent from Paul's typological pattern of thinking is that he holds that being placed in a right relationship with God is like Isaac being born despite Abraham being as good as dead and despite the death of Sarah's womb. It involves a radical intervention on God's part to rescue humanity from its situation of death and bring it into the realm of life.[61] This is an appropriate note on which to end our sketch of Paul's thought in 1:18-4:25, since it reminds us that in the letter as a whole justification by faith and the enjoyment of eschatological life go hand in hand. The *propositio* has asserted that "the one who is righteous by faith shall live" (1:17) and the burden of the next stage of the argument, the *exornatio* (5:1-8:39), will be that through sharing in the death and resurrection of Christ believers not only receive the free gift of righteousness but escape from death and reign in life.

5. Paul's Gospel and the Theological Argument of Romans 1:18-4:25

In the letter-opening Paul provides a threefold description of the gospel for which he believes himself to have been set apart. It is a gospel which has God as its source (1:1), which was promised beforehand in the Scriptures (1:2), and which concerns God's Son (1:3). In the *propositio* there is then also the more specific formulation of this gospel as the power of God for salvation for all, the Jew first and also the Greek, because in it the righteousness of God is revealed

---

60 Cf. e. g. Wengst, *Christologische Formeln*, 101-3; van der Minde, *Schrift und Tradition*, 89-99; Wilckens, *Der Brief an die Römer* 1, 279-80.

61 Cf. also Moxnes, *Theology in Conflict*, 275-76; D. Patte, *Paul's Faith and the Power of the Gospel* (Philadelphia: Fortress, 1983), 214-22.

for faith (1:16, 17). All these elements of Paul's gospel are prominent within the argument of 1:18-4:25, and, not surprisingly, they come together especially in 3:21-26 in his restatement and elaboration of his gospel's solution to the human plight.

The theocentric focus of Paul's argument has frequently been noted,[62] and this section of the letter begins with God, a God active in wrath in a world in revolt, and ends with God, a God at work for human justification in the resurrection and death of "Jesus our Lord." The God who is the source of Paul's gospel is clearly Israel's God, the God of Scripture, the God of Abraham, but as such he is also the God of all human beings. Crucial to Paul's argument is that the creator God is related to all his creatures and remains in relation to them even when they fail to acknowledge him. His saving righteousness in the gospel takes place therefore not in a vacuum created by his absence nor simply in the context of human sinfulness but in the context of his own judging righteousness, his wrath. That the disclosure of God's righteousness is at the heart of the solution offered by the gospel (3:21) underlines that for Paul God is not only the gospel's source but his activity is its content. Paul's argument reveals that he is at pains to demonstrate that his gospel in no way impugns the righteousness of God in the sense either of his faithfulness or his moral integrity. But his formulation goes further and involves the claim that in fact it is in his gospel that God's righteousness is most fully displayed. The God who is the righteous judge, impartial in his judgment of both Jews and Gentiles, is shown in Paul's gospel to be the one God who justifies both Jews and Gentiles in the same way—on the basis of Christ's sacrificial death and by means of faith—and who in doing so remains righteous in his judgment and faithful to his promise, in particular his promise to Abraham.

What enables Paul to make such a claim for his gospel in relation to God is of course his conviction that the divine righteousness has now been decisively disclosed in the death and resurrection of Christ. For Paul it is through these events that humans encounter God's saving power, have their sins atoned for in a way that deals with God's wrath, and are liberated from the power of sin. He is also convinced that through these events God has been at work in history inaugurating a new era by effecting justification ahead of the eschaton for those who have faith in Christ, both Gentiles and Jews, and that this makes everything else, including the law as a means of achieving righteousness, part of an old era characterized by unrighteousness, the power of sin and the wrath of God. The formulation of the gospel in 1:16, 17, the forensic motifs throughout 1:18-3:20, the repetition of the language of justification in 3:21-31 and the content of the Abraham midrash make justification by faith the dominant soteriological metaphor in these early chapters. Although the gospel is rehearsed for the Roman Christians in a context of Jewish Christian—Gentile Christian tensions, the importance attached to its formulation in terms of a right relationship with God by faith indicates that this concept is more than a mere *Kampfeslehre* against Judaizers.[63] It is integral to the universal scope of the gospel Paul believes himself called to proclaim as the apostle to the Gentiles. Appreciation of it is essential for both Jewish

---

62 Cf. esp. Moxnes, *Theology in Conflict.*

63 On its indispensability for Paul's gospel, see now Seifrid, *Justification*, esp. 182-270.

Christians and Gentile Christians if they are to see themselves as one and equal before God and if they are to live together as those who can jointly claim Abraham as their father. In his modification of the Jewish Christian tradition in 3:24-26 Paul underscores that justification is by God's grace as a gift and through faith. This makes clear that the new status of both Jews and Gentiles in the one people of God comes freely and undeservedly to them as those who were liable to God's righteous judgment and that all the credit for such a status belongs to the divine initiative and accomplishment.

Although the depictions of humanity's plight and that plight's resolution are mutually illuminating, as the correlation between guilt, bondage and wrath on the one side and justification, redemption and propitiation on the other has shown, it is the logic Paul believes to be inherent in his gospel that has led to the depiction of a universal plight in the first place. His efforts at theological persuasion derive from his belief that in the gospel about the death and resurrection of Christ the power of God is decisively at work. His Abraham midrash indicates that he sees God bringing life out of death and, in particular, raising Jesus from the dead as integral to justification (4:17-25). The righteousness of God revealed in his gospel is this life-giving power at work. So Paul holds that through his gospel and its proclamation both the righteousness and the life of the end-time are being brought into the present. And by defining the gospel as the power of God (1:16), he is linking his own distinctive formulation of the gospel to the earlier more traditional summary in 1:3, 4, which asserted that by the resurrection from the dead Christ became Son of God in power. On the basis of its Christological content Paul is confident then that this powerful justifying and life-giving gospel is the fulfilment of Scriptural tradition and meets supremely human needs. Such confidence lies behind the way in which in this letter his gospel is paramount in shaping his thought and in interpreting both the particular traditions he employs and the specific needs of his audience.

What emerges distinctively in Romans, and in a way that suggests it is not merely part of the contingent argument of the letter, although it certainly fits the rhetorical situation, is that Paul believes that in both the old and the new situation there is a priority in God's dealings with Israel. Paul's gospel itself is for all, but for the Jew first. The gospel of righteousness through faith in Christ and apart from the law or works of the law makes for a paradoxical faithfulness of God to his promises to Israel. Romans 1:18-4:25 with its stress on the impartiality of the divine righteousness in both its judgmental and its saving aspects, just as much as the discussion of Romans 9:1-10:21, prepares the ground for the revelation of 11:25-32 about the unexpected way God will remain faithful to his election of Israel. It helps to remove any notions of presumption about that election and to make clear that God will be faithful in a free and sovereign way—not because Israel as an ethnic entity can make binding claims on him but because in his mercy he will choose to have Israel recognize its Messiah.

The early chapters of Romans show Paul forging a theology based on his gospel through creative interpretation of Jewish and Jewish Christian tradition. He exposes the Scriptural roots integral to the nature of his gospel, but at the same time his employment of such Scriptural notions as God's righteous judgment, his impartiality and his oneness, judgment on the basis of works and circumcision as a matter of the heart, his interaction with Wisdom in 1:18-2:5, his use of the collection of citations in 3:10-18 and his extended midrash in 4:1-25 show him to be not only an exegetical theologian but also a critical Biblical theologian, reading, adapting and correcting Scripture in the form of the LXX in the light of the gospel and in the light of his own and his readers' situation. It is no accident that Scripture features so prominently in these chapters, just as it is no accident that Romans as a whole contains 51 of the 89 citations of Scripture in the undisputed Paulines.[64] Nor is it surprising that Paul should incorporate and adapt Jewish Christian formulations of the gospel at crucial points in his argument in 3:25, 26 and 4:25 (cf. already 1:3, 4). Both phenomena are integral to the pastoral and apologetic purposes of Paul in this letter, as he introduces and applies his gospel to an audience in which a Gentile Christian majority are disputing with a Jewish Christian minority about the implications of that gospel. His stress on their unity and equality in sin and in experiencing justification by faith is what both groups need to hear. But, as we have seen, although it also has force for the Gentile Christians, the formulation of the argument in 1:18-4:25 is designed to persuade the Jewish Christian minority. Hence the choice of subject matter and method of argument and the dominance of interaction with Jewish and Jewish Christian tradition.

At this early stage in the argument it is primarily the Jewish Christians, whom Paul is asking to make the changes in their thinking and attitude. His critique of the views they may hold is therefore balanced within this section not only by affirmation of Jewish priority but also by the continuities he attempts to draw between his position and both Jewish and Jewish Christian traditions. It is also worth remembering that the position, in which Jewish Christians find themselves in relation to Paul's argument in this part of the letter, is the position Gentile Christians will be in later in chapters 9-11. After being able to agree with Paul about God having been true to his purposes in his bringing a new people out of Jew and Gentile, about Christ being the end of the law, and about Israel being a disobedient people, they then have the tables turned on them and their own presumption is attacked. This makes sense tactically in four ways. (i) Paul will already have shown himself to be fully the apostle to the Gentiles before he makes this move. (ii) Having seen the move carried out in dialogue with Jewish Christians, Gentile Christians ought not to be totally unprepared or surprised when it is carried out on them. (iii) The unity and equality of Jew and Gentile in sin and salvation which it has been part of Paul's purpose to stress is reinforced by the even-handedness of his admonition; Jew and Gentile are one and equal in their need to refrain from arrogant presumption. (iv) And by the time Paul comes to his exhortations in 14:1-15:13, the Gentile Christian "strong" will be in a more chastened and humble frame of mind to receive these exhortations about mutual acceptance, which are primarily addressed to them as the majority grouping, and Jewish Christians, while having seen that Paul's gospel does mean abandoning any superior or judgmental attitudes stemming from their belief in Israel's election, will be able to know that acceptance of Gentile

---

[64] According to the list in Koch, *Schrift*, 21-24.

Christians does not mean acceptance of God having abandoned his purposes for Israel.[65]

In the interaction between Paul's gospel and tradition, both Scriptural and Jewish Christian, there is interplay and mutual illumination. The tradition supplies concepts and semantic possibilities within which the gospel can be expressed, most notably the righteousness of God and sacrificial terminology in 3:21-26 and the formulations about the death and resurrection of Christ in 4:25. The Jewish Christian formulations are woven into Paul's overall pattern of thought in the correspondences between plight and solution and between Abraham's belief and Christian belief. But in the end tradition is clearly subordinate to gospel. Whether being exploited to show the universal sinfulness of humanity that is the presupposition for Paul's gospel or modified to demonstrate how God can remain righteous in providing justification for faith or reworked to portray Abraham as having justifying and strong faith independent of circumcision and the law, tradition is in the service of Paul's gospel. Because Paul starts with the gospel, he interprets Abraham as the prototype of Christian faith, but the continuity thereby established between the Abraham story and the gospel means also that Abraham becomes the precedent for the way in which God deals with humanity.[66] Clearly it is important for Paul to find confirmation of his gospel in Scripture and to claim that authentic justifying faith existed before the coming of Christ in the case of Abraham (and David). Yet equally clearly it is beside Paul's point in these chapters to attempt to extrapolate from his argument the outlines of a theology of saving faith before or outside of Christ.[67] Paul's dominant way of thinking from solution to plight, from the new as a whole to the old as a whole, means that however crucial such an issue might be to the concerns of biblical theology, it is simply not his interest in Romans 1:18-4:25.

As we have said, the choice of tradition as the ground on which the gospel is rehearsed is determined largely by the nature of the audience and its needs. And the rehearsal of the gospel is itself geared to those same audience needs, as it is formulated in terms of the unity and equality of Gentile and Jewish Christians in regard to sin and its condemnation and in regard to justification by faith. Yet it is not that the audience is finally determinative for the theology. The Roman Christians are engaged in disruptive disputes, but it is Paul who, in the light of his conception of the gospel, interprets this situation, sees in it the need for unity, and lays down the basis on which the two groups can come together. It is because he conceives of the gospel as for all, both Jews and Gentiles, but for the Jew first, that he can be even-handed in his rebuking of the pride on both sides. In this first part of the letter it is because of his particular conception of the gospel, deriving from his call to

---

65 C. H. Cosgrove, "The Justification of the Other: An Interpretation of Rom 1:18-4:25," *SBL 1992 Seminar Papers* (Atlanta, GA: Scholars Press), 613-34, esp. 616, 631, has rightly and forcefully pressed the issues of the likely success of such tactics in regard to Jewish Christians and whether the sequence of Paul's argument with the changes of attitude it requires from them early in the letter might in fact result in their being unreceptive to his later more clearly positive statements about Israel.

66 Cf. Beker, *Paul the Apostle*, 101, on this element of continuity—Abraham "already constitutes within the old the seed or reality of the new to come."

67 Cf. also Koch, *Schrift*, 311-315; *pace* Davies, *Faith and Obedience, passim.*

Gentile mission, that he pulls no punches in dealing with the obstacles in Jewish Christian thinking to their acceptance of his gospel, asks for a radical re-assessment of some of their cherished views, and even depicts Abraham as one who has seen the full implications of justification by faith.

Given the way in which Paul's exposition of his gospel in these chapters is so closely interwoven with his interaction with particular traditions because of the specific needs of his audience, there is obviously the need for those who wish to engage in a critical appropriation of his message to explore how much and in what ways his thinking about God's disclosure in Christ and about the human condition under God can be exploited for a contemporary theology. Such an appropriation cannot be undertaken here. But, now that Paul's argument has become part of Scriptural tradition, if his interpreters read the Pauline tradition and relate it to contemporary issues in the light of their present understanding of the Christian gospel, they will at least be following the apostle's lead, for, in regard to his own theology in Rom 1:18-4:25, tradition, gospel and audience abide, these three; and the greatest of these is gospel.

The Story of Israel and the Theology of Romans 5-8

Frank Thielman
Beeson Divinity School, Samford University

One of the classic problems in the interpretation of Romans lies in deciding how the second major section of the letter is related to the rest of Paul's argument. The problem is not that the great theme of righteousness is missing, nor that there are insufficient logical links between this section and the others.[1] The problem, simply stated, is that Israel and its scriptures seem to recede from view. Chapters 1-4 and 9-11 engage in vigorous dialogue with Israel: Paul speaks directly to *ho Ioudaios* or to *Israēl* and quotes Scripture fifty-three times.[2] Chapters 5-8, however, never mention Israel, *Ioudaios* never appears, the subject is Christ rather than God, and Paul's biblical quotations shrink to two.[3] The discontinuity seems less drastic if chapter five is placed with chapters 1-4 and if chapter seven is taken as a digression in defense of the Mosaic law and as therefore connected thematically with chapters 1-5; but chapters six and eight still stand apart, and the thematic connections between 5:1-11 and 8:1-39 go unexplained.[4]

Suggestions about how to solve the problem are manifold. Prior to 1980, when chapters 1-8 were widely thought to contain the theological substance of the letter, the problem appeared less acute. Those who believed Romans to be a

---

[1] In chapters 5-8 Paul uses *dikaiosunē* eight times, *dikaioō* six times, *dikaios* and *dikaiōma* three times each, and *dikaiōsis* once. At the beginning of the section, the connective *oun* (5:1) as well as the reappearance of the concepts of boasting (5:2-3, 11), Christ's death for the ungodly (5:6-8), justification by Christ's blood (5:9a), and salvation from God's wrath (5:9b) connect chapters 5-8 with chapters 1-4. At the other end, Paul's question, "Who will bring charges against the elect [people] of God?" in 8:33 points forward to the discussion in chapters 9-11.

[2] Paul uses the term *Ioudaios* 9 times in chapters 1-4 and twice in 9-11. *Israēl* is the term of choice in chapters 9-11 where it appears eleven times. Paul quotes scripture twenty one times in chapters 1-4 and thirty-two times in chapters 9-11. See Robin Scroggs, "Paul as Rhetorician: Two Homilies in Romans 1-11," in *Jews, Greeks and Christians: Religious Cultures in Late Antiquity: Essays in Honor of William David Davies* (Studies in Judaism in Late Antiquity 21; Leiden: E. J. Brill, 1976) 278.

[3] On the *theo*logical orientation of chapters 1-4 and 9-11 and the *christo*logical orientation of chapters 5-8, see Scroggs, "Paul as Rhetorician," 276-77 and Halvor Moxnes, *Theology in Conflict: Studies in Paul's Understanding of God in Romans* (NovTSup 53; Leiden: E. J. Brill, 1980) 29-30.

[4] For these thematic connections, which seem decisive in favor of placing all of chapter 5 with chapters 6-8, see N. A. Dahl, "Two Notes on Romans 5," *ST* 5 (1952) 37-38.

theological compendium viewed Paul's argument in these chapters as a progression from justification in chapters 1-4(5) to sanctification in chapters 5(6)-8. Far from posing a problem, Romans 5-8 contained a necessary exposition of an important step in the *ordo salutis*.[5] The *religionsgeschichtliche Schule* responded to this interpretation with the claim that in chapters 1-5 Paul was thinking primarily as a Jew since he was in dialogue with other Jews but that in chapters 6-8 Paul's real position emerged, a position derived from Hellenistic concepts.[6] Even Albert Schweitzer, who was uncomfortable with both interpretive trends, believed that Paul's initial line of reasoning in chapters 3-5 only represented a rhetorically necessary concession to traditional ways of thinking and that it gave way in 6:1-8:1 to the real center of Paul's thought, "the mystical doctrine of redemption through the being-in-Christ."[7] For virtually everyone the crucial evolution from justification to sanctification, from "fighting doctrine" to "Christian conception," or from "subsidiary" to "main crater" had already taken place by the end of chapter eight. In a rare moment of agreement among all parties, the embarrassment posed by Paul's return to Israel in chapters 9-11 was considered a small price to pay for the organizational and evolutionary beauty of these diverse schemes.[8]

Most recent interpreters, however, believe that this way of reading Romans is artificial. Chapters 9-11, they claim, cannot be an appendix to Paul's argument, for the dialogue with Israel in chapters 1-4 is incomplete without them. The question of how God can be righteous and yet define the covenant so that the gentile condemns the Jew (2:27) reaches a certain urgency at the end of chapter four and is only resolved in chapters 9-11.[9] The problem posed

---

5 Among the reformers, John Calvin believed that chapter 5 made the argument of chapters 1-4 on the righteousness of faith clearer by giving illustrations for it and that in chapter 6 Paul moved to a discussion of sanctification. See his essay "The Theme of the Epistle of Paul to the Romans" in *The Epistles of Paul to the Romans and to the Thessalonians* (Grand Rapids; Eerdmans, 1960) 7. Among more recent commentators see Charles Hodge's *A Commentary on Romans* (Edinburgh: Banner of Truth Trust, 1972; orig. pub. 1835, rev. 1864) 10-11, 191. The scheme has continued to influence commentators in this century. See R. C. H. Lenski, *The Interpretation of St. Paul's Epistle to the Romans* (Columbus, Ohio: Wartburg Press, 1945) 89, 330, 387 and M.-J. Lagrange, *Épitre aux Romains* (3d ed.; Paris: Librairie Victor Lecoffre, 1922) 99. C. E. B. Cranfield, *The Epistle to the Romans* (2 vols.; Edinburgh: T. & T. Clark, 1975-79) 1.295-96 argues that chapters 6-8 explore "the meaning of the believer's sanctification . . .," although he does not believe (2.445-447) that Paul's argument is therefore complete at the end of chapter eight.

6 See, for example, Otto Pfleiderer, *Das Urchristenthum, seine Schriften und Lehren, in geschichtlichem Zusammenhang* (Berlin: Georg Reimer, 1887) 117-127, 258-59 (esp. the note to p. 259).

7 *The Mysticism of Paul the Apostle* (New York: Henry Holt, 1931) 212-226, esp pp. 213 and 225-26. E. P. Sanders, *Paul and Palestinian Judaism: A Comparison of Patterns of Religion* (Philadelphia, Fortress: 1977) 497-502, argues similarly that Paul adopts a traditional description of the human plight in Romans 1-3 for rhetorical reasons but that Paul's real convictions about the human plight appear in Romans 5-6.

8 Cf. the comments of J. Christiaan Beker, *Paul the Apostle: The Triumph of God in Life and Thought* (Philadelphia: Fortress, 1980) 68-69.

9 See, for example, Cranfield, *Romans*, 2.445-46; Ulrich Wilckens, *Der Brief an die Römer* (EKK 6; 2 vols.; Cologne/Neukirchen-Vluyn: Benziger/Neukirchener Verlag, 1980) 2.181-83; Paul Achtemeier, *Romans* (Atlanta: John Knox, 1985) 153-54; James D. G. Dunn, *Romans*

by the interposition of chapters 5-8 between 1-4 and 9-11, therefore, has become especially important in recent years.

Occasionally someone takes the dilemma by the horns and argues boldly that chapters 5-8 are an independent composition, which either Paul or someone else dropped into the epistle at this point for reasons about which we can, at this distance, only speculate.[10] Most recent interpreters, however, opt for less drastic measures. James D. G. Dunn believes that chapters 1-4 state the gospel and that chapters 6-8 and 9-11 apply the gospel in two different situations, chapters 6-8 to the individual and chapters 9-11 to national Israel.[11] Chapter 5 serves as a bridge between the statement of the gospel in chapters 1-4 and these two applications of the gospel in 5-8 and 9-11 respectively.[12] Ulrich Wilckens, similarly, argues that two urgent issues have emerged from chapters 1-5: whether Paul has destroyed the basis for ethics with his claim that one is justified by faith apart from works of the law and whether Paul has cast a shadow of doubt over God's faithfulness to Israel by his polemic against their confidence in the law. Chapters 6-8 are directed to the first issue, says Wilckens, and chapters 9-11 to the second.[13] For both interpreters, therefore, the reason Paul's dialogue with Israel recedes from view in chapters 6-8 is that Paul has intentionally set it aside to deal with the moral conduct of the individual and plans to return to it after he finishes the business at hand.[14]

Nearly all of these explanations of the structure of Romans make valid points. Paul's argument *does* advance from a discussion, in Cranfield's terms, of "the revelation of the righteousness which is from God by faith alone" to an examination of "the life promised for those who are righteous by faith."[15] Paul's language *does* take on a tone appropriate to the individual in chapters 5-8, as the predominance of first person verbs indicates. Paul's concept of dying and rising with Christ *is* difficult to explain in biblical and Jewish terms,

---

9-16 (WBC 38b; Dallas: Word Books, 1988) 519-520; and John Ziesler, *Paul's Letter to the Romans* (London/Philadelphia: SCM/Trinity Press International, 1989) 233-34.

10 Scroggs makes the classic case in "Paul as Rhetorician," 272-98.

11 *Romans 1-8* (WBC 38a; Dallas: Word Books, 1988) 242-44. Chapter eight, in Dunn's view, begins the transition from concern with the individual believer to concern with God's cosmic purposes when, in vv. 14-15, Paul refers to the eschatologically oriented concept of adoption. See pp. 243 and 458-59.

12 *Romans 1-8*, 243.

13 *Römer*, 2.3-5, 181-82.

14 Somewhere between the solutions of Scroggs on one hand and Dunn and Wilckens on the other lie those of Bent Noack, "Current and Backwater in the Epistle to the Romans," *ST* 19 (1965) 154-66, Moxnes, *Theology in Conflict*, 29 and Franz J. Leenhardt, *The Epistle to the Romans: A Commentary* (Cleveland, Ohio: World, 1961) 24. Noack believes that 1:1-7; 3:9-20, 27-31; 4:1-25 and 9:1-11:36 form the "current" of the letter, 5:1-8:39 the backwater. Moxnes contends that in chapters 1-4 and 9-11 Paul addresses Jews whereas in chapters 5-8 he addresses Christians. Leenhardt believes that Paul moves from a statement of the gospel in theological terms to a discussion of its anthropological ramifications. On the significance of the problem together with a survey of some solutions to it see L. E. Keck, "What Makes Romans Tick?" a paper distributed to the Pauline Theology Group of the Society of Biblical Literature (1992) 7-11.

15 See Cranfield's outline of chapters 5-8 in *Romans*, 1.xi.

unlike his sacrificial language in 3:21-26. Nevertheless, many interpreters of
Romans have too readily assumed that the content of chapters 5-8, in the
words of Robin Scroggs, "has nothing to do with the meaning of the history of
Israel."[16] It is true that Paul's explicit citations of the Bible grind nearly to a
halt, that Paul shifts from the third person to the first in 4:24, and that "the
history of Israel," so prominent in the discussion in chapters 1-4, is less
obvious to readers removed by twenty centuries from Paul's context; but the
biblical story of Israel is still present, guiding the discussion and defining its
terms. We do not see it as clearly because we do not appreciate how important
the story of Israel was within the "symbolic universe" of first century Jews.

The Story of Israel and the Symbolic Universe
of First Century Judaism

In their book *The Social Construction of Reality*, Peter L. Berger and Thomas
Luckmann argue that societies overcome the dark, marginal experiences
which threaten their existence by recourse to a "symbolic universe." This
collection of symbols explains terrifying occurrences by asserting a theory of
reality which interprets these experiences in familiar terms and therefore
renders them harmless to the society's cohesiveness. Dreams, for example,
might cause members of a technologically oriented society to wonder
whether the dream world or the world of wakefulness were "real." In
response, the scientific community explains dreams by means of
sophisticated psychological theories. These theories pull the marginal, and
sometimes disquieting, experience of dreaming into the ambit of a wider view
of reality by explaining dreams in the language of waking reality. Science
assures the dreaming person that "reality" resides in the world which one
experiences during waking hours, not in the dream world one experiences
when asleep, and so forestalls a threat to the way the technological society
perceives reality. In other similar ways the symbolic universe of science
prevents both threatening experiences in everyday life and unusual
catastrophes from paralyzing the society which it serves.[17]

The most significant "marginal" experience of Jews during Paul's time
was the Roman domination of Judea and the scattering of the people of God
throughout the world to live under the rule of various foreign powers. This
experience seemed to threaten Israel's very election, the most important of the
various convictions which held the nation together. As a result, most people
looked to the "symbolic universe" which the biblical history of Israel supplied
to pull this disturbing enigma into the boundaries of the society's view of
reality. In the midst of this on-going national crisis the Bible's account of
Israel's history provided assurance that, in allowing Israel to suffer, God was

---

16 "Paul as Rhetorician," 281.

17 *The Social Construction of Reality: A Treatise in the Sociology of Knowledge* (New York:
Doubleday, 1966) 92-104. A society's "symbolic universe," as Berger and Luckmann define
it, bears some similarity to N. T. Wright's description of a society's "worldview" and to
Howard Clark Kee's reference to a society's "life-world." See N. T. Wright, *The New
Testament and the People of God* (Minneapolis: Fortress, 1992) 123 n. 5. and Howard Clark
Kee, *Knowing the Truth: A Sociological Approach to New Testament Interpretation* (Minneapolis:
Fortress, 1989) 105.

only acting within the stipulations of the Sinai covenant. The biblical story of Israel also gave Jews confidence that in spite of Israel's present suffering, their election was still certain and their future bright.[18]

The elements of the story are simple and appear frequently in the Scriptures, especially in the so-called Deuteronomic history and in the prophets. God made a covenant with Israel at Sinai which required them to obey God's commands.[19] The covenant stipulated that blessing would come to Israel if they obeyed, various curses if they disobeyed.[20] Although Israel's history had, with a few exceptions, been marked by disobedience and curse rather than obedience and blessing, God remained faithful to the relationship which he had established with his people and promised that one day he would give them obedient hearts and restore their fortunes.[21]

This interpretation of Israel's history, moreover, was widespread within the Judaism of antiquity. At least from the composition of Deuteronomy, and particularly during the centuries surrounding Paul, ancient Jews appealed to this account of Israel's story in order to explain their suffering. The story is such an important part of the thinking of the author of Tobit, for example, that his tale not only assumes its truth on the national level but raises and answers an important question about it at the individual level: what happens to pious individuals who seem to suffer rather than experience blessing because of their piety?[22] The author of Judith, likewise, registers horror at the thought

---

18 According to Berger and Luckmann, *The Social Construction of Reality*, 65, a society's stories form part of its assumed or "pre-theoretical" knowledge and therefore play an important role in shaping its view of reality. Members of the Pauline Theology seminar have tacitly confirmed this insight when they have found narrative useful in describing Paul's theology. Richard Bevan Hays, "Crucified with Christ: A Synthesis of 1 and 2 Thessalonians, Philemon, Philippians, and Galatians" in David J. Lull, ed. *Society of Biblical Literature 1988 Seminar Papers* (No. 27; Atlanta: Scholars Press, 1988) 318-335 argues that a story beginning with Abraham's obedient faith and ending with Jesus' *parousia* is the map on which Paul plots and directs the progress of his communities. N. T. Wright, *The Climax of the Covenant: Christ and the Law in Pauline Theology* (Edinburgh: T & T Clark, 1991) believes that the place which Paul assigns the Messiah in the story of Israel is critical for understanding Paul's theology. In light of such efforts, Jouette Bassler sounds a note of caution about the usefulness of ferreting out Paul's narrative assumptions in order to describe Paul's theology in "Paul's Theology: Whence and Whither? A Synthesis (of sorts) of the Theology of Philemon, 1 Thessalonians, Philippians, Galatians, and 1 Corinthians" in David J. Lull, ed., *Society of Biblical Literature 1989 Seminar Papers* (No. 28; Atlanta: Scholars Press, 1989) 412-23. Kee, *Knowing the Truth*, 70-106, however, provides a sound rationale for including within any description of a New Testament writer's theology an account of the basic assumptions of his social world.

19 Ex 19:1-24:18; Deut 4:13, 5:1-30:20.

20 Lev 26:3-46; Deut 28:1-30:20; Cf. Isa 1:19-20.

21 The following list is representative: Deut 29:19-30:10; 31:16-32:43; 1 Kings 8:23-53; 2 Chron 6:14-32; Ezra 9:6-15; Neh 9:6-37; Isa 2:2-22, 30:19-33, 42:24-25; 48:18-19; Jer 3:15-18, 4:4, 11:1-13, 22:8-9, 29:10-14, 30:1-33:26; Ezk 5:6, 11:5-21, 16:1-63, 20:5-44, 22:3-23:49, 34:11-31, 36:2-37:28, 39:23-29; Dan 9:4-27.

22 Tob 3:3-5 laments Israel's sin and its consequent exile in terms which show that the biblical story of Israel forms part of the author's symbolic universe. The tale itself, moreover, focusses on two Israelites who, although careful to observe the law, suffer severe hardship. With this complication the author seems to be posing the question of how God can be just and allow the righteous to suffer, in seeming violation of the Deuteronomic promises. The problem is neatly solved by the story's end, however, when both

that God's people might once again compromise with gentile ways and suffer the covenant's curses.[23] Jason of Cyrene's epitomizer tells the story of Israel's oppression and rescue from the Seleucids in order to show that those who keep God's law are victorious and those who break it inevitably suffer defeat.[24] The confessions in Dan 9:4-19, Neh 9:6-37, Bar 1:15-3:8, and *Pr Azr* 3-22, since they were probably used liturgically, demonstrate that this understanding of Israel's history was common not simply among the sophisticated and literate but among all who recited the synagogue's liturgy.[25]

The best illustration of the importance of this motif during Paul's era, however, comes from Josephus. In the *Jewish War* Josephus appeals to the biblical story of Israel again and again to make sense of his people's suffering during and after the great war with Rome. Just as God had used Nebuchadnezzar to punish his people for their sins, he claims, so God is now using Vespasian and Titus to chasten his people for their sins once again (4.370; 5.368; 6.215, 411; cf. *Ant.* 10.139). The destruction of Herod's temple, therefore, stands in parallel to the destruction of Solomon's temple, a correlation strikingly confirmed for Josephus by his belief that the dates on which the two temples burned corresponded exactly (6.250, 268).[26] The history of sin against God's law which had culminated in the burning of the first Temple had continued in Josephus' time with the excesses of the Jewish insurrectionists and had once again culminated in the Temple's destruction.

In his later work on the *Antiquities of the Jews* Josephus elevated the principle of divine retribution, so clearly articulated in the biblical story of Israel, to a description of the way God deals with all people. The principal lesson that the reader of his work should learn, says Josephus, is that

> . . . men who conform to the will of God, and do not venture to transgress laws that have been excellently laid down, prosper in all

---

protagonists recover health and happiness through the intervention of God's messenger. G. W. E. Nicklesburg, *Jewish Literature between the Bible and the Mishnah* (London: SCM, 1981) 33 comments that Tobit's outlook is close to Job's, with one major difference: "Whereas the book of Job confines its treatment to an individual, the fate of the nation is of great concern to the author of Tobit . . . ."

[23] Jdt 5:17-21; 8:18-19.

[24] The law-abiding Judas and his army succeed against great odds (8:24-36) whereas Hellenizers (4:16-17), Israelite idolaters (12:39-42), and errant high priests (13:7-8) suffer and die because of their sins. In addition, the righteous acknowledge that when they have suffered in the past, God has only been mercifully chastening them so that they will not sin more seriously and receive worse punishment (6:12-17; 7:18, 32-33; cf. 10:4).

[25] On the prayer in Nehemiah, see Leon J. Liebreich, "The Impact of Nehemiah 9:5-37 on the Liturgy of the Synagogue," *HUCA* 32 (1961) 227-37. Bar 1:15-3:8 occurs within a liturgical setting and was probably used liturgically after the composition of Baruch. It is modelled on the prayer in Daniel. The popularity of the story of Israel as it is told in Deuteronomy 28-32 among average diaspora Jews of the third century CE is clear from the grave inscriptions which Paul R. Trebilco cites in *Jewish Communities in Asia Minor* (SNTSMS 69; Cambridge: Cambridge University Press, 1991) 60-69.

[26] In his famous speech before the walls of Jerusalem, Josephus takes the correspondence between these two events in Israel's history even further when he compares himself to Jeremiah. See *BJ* 5.391-94.

> things beyond belief, and for their reward are offered by God felicity;
> whereas, in proportion as they depart from the strict observance of these
> laws, things (else) practicable become impracticable, and whatever
> imaginary good thing they strive to do ends in irretrievable disasters
> (1.14).[27]

Although the work runs to twenty volumes in length, Josephus never loses sight of this purpose. From the account of the flood in Genesis (1.72) to the burning of the temple during the war with Rome (20.166), Josephus points out at every opportunity that God blesses those, whether individuals or nations, who keep his laws and punishes all who stray from them. As we might expect, the theme is especially prominent in Josephus' paraphrase of Deuteronomy and the historical books; but he often makes it more explicit than it appears in scripture and on occasion plants it in his sources when he finds it missing from them.[28]

The Deuteronomic interpretation of Israel's story, then, was an important element in the symbolic universe of ancient Judaism and was especially important during Israel's two tragic centuries on either side of Paul's career.[29] If we attempt to enter this symbolic universe and read Romans 5-8 in light of it, not only does the connection between these chapters and Romans 1-4 and 9-11 become clear but the interpreter assumes a better position for resolving some of the classic exegetical difficulties within these chapters as well.

The Function of the Story of Israel
in the Argument of Romans 5-8

Most interpreters of Romans agree that, whatever the exact boundary of the letter's second major section, the purpose of that section is to describe the new, eschatological era of life to which those justified by faith have obtained access.[30] It is seldom recognized, however that Paul draws the language and

---

[27] Here and elsewhere translations of Josephus are from the Loeb edition.

[28] See for example Josephus' retelling of Israel's encounter with the Midianite women in Num 25:1-9 (*Ant.* 4.131-155) and his paraphrase of Judas' short speech to his troops prior to battle with Gorgias in 1 Macc 3:58-60 (*Ant.* 12.302-304).

[29] After arriving at this conclusion independently, I have been heartened to find that others have discovered it also. See Odil Hannes Steck, *Israel und das gewaltsame Geschick der Propheten: Untersuchungen zur Überlieferung des deuteronomistischen Geschichtsbildes im Alten Testament, Spätjudentum und Urchristentum* (WMANT 23; Neukirchen-Vluyn: Neukirchener, 1967); David P. Moessner, *Lord of the Banquet: The Literary and Theological Significance of the Lukan Travel Narrative* (Minneapolis: Fortress, 1989) 82-91; N. T. Wright, *Climax*, 140-141; and James M. Scott, "The Restoration of Israel" in *The Dictionary of Paul and His Letters* (Downers Grove: Inter-Varsity, forthcoming).

[30] Dahl, "Two Notes on Romans 5," 37-40 argues persuasively that the new section begins with 5:1. Ernst Käsemann, *Commentary on Romans* (Grand Rapids: Eerdmans, 1980) has reservations about Dahl's analysis, but nevertheless believes that the primary dividing line between sections comes at the end of chapter 4. See also Karl Barth, *A Shorter Commentary on Romans* (Richmond, Va.: John Knox, 1959) 55; Anders Nygren, *Commentary on Romans* (Philadelphia: Muhlenberg, 1949) 187-89; Cranfield, *Romans*, 1.252-54, who notes the recurrence throughout chapters 5-8 of the phrase "through Jesus Christ our Lord"; and Ziesler *Romans*, 134-35. Calvin, *Romans*, xxxii; Lagrange, *Romains*, 99; Wilckens, *Römer*, 286-88; and Dunn, *Romans 1-8*, 242-44 believe that the new section begins at 6:1. Paul

the theological symbols which he uses to accomplish this purpose in large measure from the biblical story of Israel's disobedience to the law given at Sinai, Israel's punishment in the exile for that disobedience, and Israel's eschatological restoration.[31] The deliberateness with which Paul recalls this story in chapters 5-8 appears most clearly in the first and last chapters of the section; but allusions to it are probably present in the middle two chapters as well.

The Story of Israel in Romans 5 and 8

In a well known study, Nils A. Dahl demonstrated the close thematic relationship between 5:1-11 and 8:1-39.[32] Justification, hope, eschatological glory, patience in suffering, the love of God, the Spirit of God, and the death of Christ all appear in these two sections. The similarity is so striking that Dahl could describe chapters 6 and 7 as digressions which Paul used to anticipate misunderstandings of his negative statement about the law in 5:20. In 8:1, says Dahl, Paul "finds his way back to the general themes of 5:1-11."[33] Although Dahl did not say so, one of those themes is that the people of God, newly defined on the basis of faith, are the recipients of God's promises through the prophets to restore Israel's fortunes and make a new covenant with them.

Chapter 5

Chapter 5 consists of two parts, the first of which (vv. 1-11) is commonly recognized as both transitional and introductory. It both sums up the themes of 1:18-4:25 and introduces the new emphases of 5:12-8:39. The second part of chapter 5 (vv. 12-21) lays the foundation for 6:1-8:39 by exploring the theological significance of the concepts of "life" and "death." These two concepts, as carefully defined in 5:12-21, become the chief subject of the chapters which follow.[34] This much is commonly observed. Less frequently recognized, however, is the role which the biblical story of Israel plays in both

---

Achtemeier, *Romans* (Atlanta: John Knox, 1985) 89-95 divides the argument at 4:23. On the importance of the term "life" in these chapters, see Nygren, *Romans*, 188 and Cranfield, *Romans*, 1.254 n. 1. On the importance of the death-life antithesis see Dunn, *Romans 1-8*, 301-303.

[31] Dunn is an exception. His commentary consistently points out the biblical and covenantal significance of Paul's language.

[32] "Two Notes on Romans 5," 37-42.

[33] "Two Notes on Romans 5," 41.

[34] The statistics on the use of terms related to "death" and "life" in the undisputed pauline epistles show this clearly. In these letters Paul uses the term *apothnēskō* a total of 42 times, 23 of which are in Romans, and 17 of which are in Romans 5-8. The case is similar with *thanatos*: Paul uses it a total of 45 times, 22 of which occur in Romans, and 21 of which occur in Romans 5-8. *Zōē* appears 25 times, 14 of which are in Romans, and 12 of which are in Romans 5-8, and *zō* a total of 51 times, 23 of which belong to Romans, and 12 of which belong to Romans 5-8. If we shape these figures into percentages, 45 percent of the references to "death" in the undisputed letters occur in Romans 5-8 and 32 percent of his references to "life." These are impressive figures for such a narrow slice of the pauline corpus.

parts of chapter 5, and especially in Paul's efforts in 5:12-21 to define the principal terms of his subsequent argument.

5:1-11

Paul begins 5:1-11 by describing the new era which believers have entered as a period of righteousness (5:1, 9), peace (5:1), the outpouring of God's love into believers' hearts through the Holy Spirit (5:5), and reconciliation (5:10-11). Paul's use of these terms together, and his use of them to characterize the eschatological hope of God's people, recall the biblical hope that God's wrath toward a disobedient Israel would one day cease and that the people of God would receive the covenantal promises of blessing. Paul's concern to echo this biblical motif becomes clear when his language and the context in which it occurs are compared to prophetic descriptions of the restored Israel.

Isaiah, Jeremiah, and Ezekiel frequently speak of the period of Israel's restoration as a time of peace characterized by the presence of a new spirit, the remaking of Israel's heart, and the reign of righteousness. Isaiah and Jeremiah depict the period of Israel's disobedience to the covenant as a time when "peace" is absent from Israel (Isa 59:8; Jer 8:11, 15). Not surprisingly, then, in Isaiah and Ezekiel, during the time of restoration God will establish a "covenant of peace" with his people (Isa 54:10; Ezk 34:25, 37:26), and, according to Isaiah, peace will reign during that time because of the presence of righteousness (Isa 32:17-18, 60:17). During this period, God will pour out his spirit on the anointed king (Isa 11:1), on the servant who proclaims the good news of Israel's restoration (Isa 61:1), and on the whole people (Ezk 37:1-14; 39:29).[35] This new spirit, moreover, will re-create Israel's heart to make it "new" (11:19, 18:31, 36:26).[36]

Nowhere does the similarity between Paul's language in 5:1-11 and the biblical interpretation of Israel's history appear stronger, however, than in Isa 32:15-17. Here the prophet says that Israel's punishment will continue

> . . . until a spirit from on high is poured out (*yᶜrh*, LXX, *epelthē*) upon us and the wilderness becomes a fruitful field, and the fruitful field is deemed a forest. Then justice will dwell in the wilderness, and righteousness (*ṣdqh*, LXX, *ta erga tēs dikaiosunēs*) will be peace (*šlôm*, LXX, *eirēnē*) and the result of righteousness (*ṣdqh*, LXX, *dikaiosunē*) quietness and trust forever (NRSV).

The outpouring of God's spirit, the presence of righteousness, and the combination of righteousness with peace are used to describe the eschatological period of hope much in the way that Paul uses these concepts to describe the same period in Rom 5:1-5. Although the resemblance is not so close that we can speak of direct dependence, it is close enough to show that

---

[35] At Ezk 39:29, the LXX has "And I will no longer turn my face away from them since I have poured out my *wrath* upon the house of Israel, says the Lord."

[36] In 11:19 the MT reads "one heart" and the LXX, "another heart." The Aramaic targums and the Peshitta, however, have "new heart."

Paul conceived of the eschatological period to which believers now had access as the final chapter in the biblical story of Israel.[37]

5:12-21

Paul has briefly mentioned the key terms "life" and "death" already in 5:1-11 (v. 10; cf. vv. 6-8); but in 5:12-21 he explores the theological significance of these terms at length in order to define them carefully for the subsequent argument.[38] He does this through referring to the role which death and life play in three interlocking stories–the story of Adam, the story of Christ, and the story of Israel. The first two stories claim most of the scholarly attention given to this passage; but the story of Israel is as important for Paul's purposes in 5:12-21 as the other two. Both rhetorical and theological considerations demonstrate this.

Israel's story first appears in 5:13-14 where Paul interrupts his comparison of Adam and Christ with the statement that although sin is only "reckoned" in the presence of law, death nevertheless reigned over those who had not sinned against a specific command. The rhetorical usefulness of placing this statement at this position in the argument is not entirely clear. Paul's point, after all, is simply that even people who did not violate a specific command of God, as Adam had, nevertheless sinned and so were subject to death.[39] All Paul needed to say in order to make this point was that "death reigned . . . even over those who had not sinned in the likeness of the transgression of Adam" (5:14). But Paul is determined, even at the cost of clouding his immediate argument, to point out the similarity between what happened in Adam's case and what happened in Israel's:

> For until the law sin was in the world, but sin is not reckoned when there is no law; nevertheless, death reigned from Adam until Moses . . . (5:13-14a).[40]

Paul's discourse, therefore, runs ahead of his argument to reveal an important basic assumption: Israel had violated the covenant which God established with them at Sinai and so had received the penalty of death which, according to that covenant, all such violators would suffer.[41] Although mention of the law

---

37 The remarkable parallels between Paul's language in 5:1-11 and the language of the opening prayer in the first introductory letter to Second Maccabees increases the likelihood that Paul's use of the terms "peace," "heart," and "reconciliation" are allusions to the prophetic promises of Israel's restoration. In 2 Macc 1:2-6, as in Rom 5:1-11, the suffering of God's people is in focus (v. 5b), and the expected time of restoration is described using the terms "peace" (v. 4), "heart" (vv. 3-4), and "reconciliation" (v. 5).

38 By mentioning death and life in 5:6-10 Paul is following his usual custom of introducing at the end of one section the key terms which he will use in the next. On this feature of Paul's discourse in Romans see Nils Alstrup Dahl, *Studies in Paul* (Minneapolis: Augsburg, 1977) 82-83.

39 Cranfield, *Romans*, 1.282.

40 For the translation of *alla* as "nevertheless" in 5:14, see BAGD, s.v., 2.

41 J. Paul Sampley comments insightfully that in certain passages Paul opens a window onto his theology by revealing his "primary assumptions." These, Sampley says, are important moments in Paul's letters, for they reveal the basic terms of his theological thinking. See "From Text to Thought World: The Route to Paul's Ways" in *Pauline*

of Moses seriously obfuscated Paul's argument by delaying the conclusion to his statement in 5:12 until 5:18b, the story of Israel's violation of the covenant at Sinai was so close to the surface of Paul's thinking at this point in his discourse that, almost in the manner of a Freudian slip, it broke through.

In 5:20-21 the story of Israel's violation of the covenant with God at Sinai again comes to the surface; but unlike its appearance in 5:13-14, here it is well integrated into the flow of Paul's discourse. After drawing his comparison between Adam and Christ to a close in 5:19, Paul moves to another stage of salvation history, the period of the law's intrusion, to draw a similar comparison between what happened when the law was given to Israel at Sinai and what happened in Christ. At first Paul's reference to the giving of the law looks like a relatively unimportant appendix to an argument which he had made previously and more impressively in 5:12-19 by reference to Adam.[42] Much of 5:12-19, however, is devoted to a series of caveats and clarifications designed to prevent the reader from taking the similarity between Adam and Christ too far (5:13-18a). Once these are removed, Paul's statements about the parallels between Adam and Christ in 5:12, 18b-19 turn out to be nearly as simple as the comparison between Israel and Christ in 5:20-21. In 5:12 and 18b-19 Paul says that the disobedience of Adam sent many on a downward spiral toward death and that the obedience of Christ has, in a similar but opposite way, rectified this situation. In 5:20-21 Paul says that the law given to Israel increased sin by defining it more specifically and that in a similar but opposite way God caused grace to increase "through Jesus Christ our Lord."[43] The fundamental point of Paul's discussion in 5:12-21, then, is that Christ is God's answer to the disasters created by Adam's sin and Israel's violation of the covenant, and the story of Israel's failure to keep the terms of the covenant is parallel to, and on an equal footing with, the story of Adam's failure in this argument.

The conclusion to which these rhetorical observations have led is confirmed by an examination of the theological function of Israel's story in 5:12-21. The theme which holds Romans 5-8 together as a discreet section of Paul's total argument is how God has brought life out of death "through Jesus Christ our Lord." It cannot be denied that this movement from death to life is described in terms which take much of their meaning from the story of Adam's fall, with its result of death for all, and the story of Christ's death and resurrection with its result of life for all. Paul's language of death and life in 5:12-21, and therefore his use of these concepts elsewhere in the section, however, are also indebted to the story of Israel. Paul uses this third story in 5:12-21 to emphasize the depth of the human plight: Adam began the process

---

Theology, vol. 1: *Thessalonians, Philippians, Galatians, Philemon* (ed. Jouette M. Bassler; Minneapolis: Fortress, 1991) 12. See also Kee, *Knowing the Truth*, 103.

[42] Thus Käsemann, *Romans*, 158 regards 5:20-21 as a "digression" which "unexpectedly . . . returns to the question put in v. 13."

[43] The adverb *hou* of 5:20b probably refers to Israel as the place where sin increased. See Cranfield, *Romans*, 1.293 and Wright, *Climax*, 39-40, 196. Wright believes that the *hou* also refers to Christ who, as the Messiah, represented Israel. Sin was concentrated not only onto Israel, therefore, but onto their Messiah who was then able to "condemn sin in the flesh" (8:3).

of disobedience (5:12a), all humanity followed his lead (5:12b, 18a, 19a), and the situation grew worse with the coming of the law and Israel's disobedience to it (5:20). The result has been "death" for all (5:21a), a result which is remedied by the gift of life "through Jesus Christ our Lord" (5:21b).

Paul can assume a connection between violation of the law in Israel and death in 5:20-21, however, only because he shares with his readers a symbolic universe that includes the biblical story of Israel. A prominent part of the story as it is preserved both in the scriptures and in the literature of Paul's day is Israel's toil under the penalty of death which Israel received for violating the covenant. In Deut 30:15-20 (LXX) Moses places *zōē* and *thanatos* before Israel, "life" if they obey the commandments which Moses has spelled out, and "death" if they change their "heart" (*kardia*) and worship other gods. "Life" is used figuratively to refer to numerous descendants and length of days in the land of promise (30:15, 20; cf. Deut 4:1, 32:47); "death" conversely means destruction and exile (28:15-29:29). Ezekiel picks up this theme in his effort to persuade the exilic community that their present suffering is a result of their violation of the Sinaitic covenant (18:1-32; 20:11, 21, 25; 33:10-20) and is designed to lead to their repentance, cleansing, and restoration (20:40-49; 33:29). The prayer of confession in Nehemiah 9 similarly laments Israel's repeated disobedience to God's "ordinances, by the observance of which a person shall live" (9:29).

The reason why the story of Adam, the story of Christ, and the story of Israel are linked together in 5:12-21 now becomes clear. All three protagonists experienced death at the hands of sin, but only two of the three–Israel and Christ–experience life at the hands of God: Christ by means of the resurrection and Israel by means of their eschatological restoration. Israel, then, is the middle term between Adam and Christ, the two great representatives of death and life. God's people form the historical stage on which the consequences of the actions of these two meta-historical figures are played out: like Adam, post-exilic Israel had experienced "death" as the penalty for violating God's commandments, and, like Christ, the eschatological people of God would experience the covenant's blessing of life. Not only the stories of Adam and Christ give theological depth to the critical terms "death" and "life," therefore; but the story of Israel contributes to the definition of these terms as well. Everywhere these two terms appear in chapters 5-8, therefore, part of their meaning comes from the story of Israel's death in the exile and God's promise to restore his people to life.

Chapter 8

When we move from chapter 5 to chapter 8, we find that the story of Israel remains a prominent feature of Paul's argument. Paul again uses the complex of terms so popular among the prophets in describing Israel's restoration to refer to the eschatological era which believers have entered. "Spirit" reappears, as do "peace," "righteousness," "heart," and, of course, "life." Much more frequent in chapter 8 than in chapter 5, however, are references to the law. Having shown in chapter 7 that the law was good and should have been obeyed, Paul now advances the thesis that the eschatological era is one in which the "requirement of the law is fulfilled" in believers (8:4) who, because of the Spirit, are able to submit to it (8:7-9). "For the mind of the flesh is death," he says, "but the mind of the Spirit is life and peace, because the mind of the flesh is at enmity with God, for it does not submit to God's law, nor is it able to do so" (8:6-7). Paul alludes here to the blessings and curses of Deuteronomy 28 and Leviticus 26 to say that the time of warfare and death because of Israel's disobedience to the covenant of life and peace (cf. Mal 2:5) is over, and that the time of God's favor has come.

The allusions to those passages continue in Paul's assertion that God has rescued believers from slavery and fear a few sentences later (8:15). Paul recalls the description of Israel's exile in Deut 28:64-68 where Moses says that if Israel is disobedient to the law the Lord will scatter them among the nations (28:64) where they will have a "trembling heart, failing eyes, and languishing spirit" (28:65). There, we read, Israel will live lives of dread and will sell themselves into slavery (28:66-68). God has rescued the believing community from this plight, Paul tells the Romans, "for you have not received a spirit of slavery again with its consequence of fear but you have received a Spirit of adoption by which we cry, 'Abba, Father!'" (8:15; cf. v. 23).[44] In light of (*gar*, 8:15) this rescue from the plight into which disobedience has plunged God's people, Paul is able to call believers "children of God" (8:14), a term which Deuteronomy uses of God's covenant people (Deut 14:1) and Hosea of their eschatological restoration (Hos 1:10).[45]

He is also able in light of this to end the chapter and this whole section of his argument with a series of rhetorical denials that the kind of suffering which the biblical story of Israel describes as punishment for violation of the law will be able to separate the believer from the love of God demonstrated eschatologically through the sacrifice of Christ (8:32, 35a). The description of this suffering in 8:35b is drawn largely from the portraits of the suffering of God's disobedient people painted in Deuteronomy 28 and Leviticus 26. Deut 28:53, 55, and 57 link together *thlipsis* and *stenochōria* to describe the terrors of famine which will come to Israel if they disobey the law.[46] A few verses earlier Deut 28:48 links *gymnotēs* and *limos* to describe the terrors of military defeat which will come to Israel as a result of disobedience. Lev 26:25 and 33 use *machaira* in a similar way. The suffering which Paul and other believers experience as the people of God, therefore, is strangely analogous to the suffering which the disobedient and unrestored Israel experienced because of

---

44 James M. Scott, *Adoption as Sons of God: An Exegetical Investigation into the Background of HYIOTHESIA in the Pauline Corpus* (WUNT 2.48; Tübingen: J. C. B. Mohr [Paul Siebeck], 1992) 96-117 has demonstrated that Jews of Paul's era understood 2 Sam 7:14a as a reference to God's "adoption" of his people in the period of eschatological restoration. This understanding of the term, Scott argues (pp. 221-66), informs Paul's use of it in 8:15 and 23.

45 Dunn, *Romans 1-8*, 451. In 9:26 Paul will use the phrase "children of God" again but this time in a direct quotation of Hos 1:10 which refers specifically to gentile believers as part of God's eschatologically restored people. Believing Jews are also included according to the quotation of Isa 10:22 in 9:27. On this see Richard Hays, *Echoes of Scripture in the Letters of Paul* (New Haven: Yale University Press, 1989) 66-68.

46 Paul links these words together in 2:9 also. See Dunn, *Romans 1-8*, 88. Here, as in Deuteronomy, the words indicate the punishment which comes "to every person who does evil, the Jew first and also the Greek." Even the idea that the curses of the law apply to gentiles is anticipated in Deuteronomy. See, for example, Deut 8:19-20. If the list of tribulations in 8:35 is indebted to Stoic ideas, as Lagrange, *Romains*, 218 (following Rudolf Bultmann) believes, Paul has nevertheless given it a biblical shape.

their sins. Paul can assert in a rhetorical question that it cannot separate the believing community from the love of Christ; but that it is present at all during the period of eschatological restoration is puzzling.

Perhaps this is why Paul chose in 8:35 to summarize his list of evils with a quotation from Psalm 44 (LXX 43). This Psalm is probably post-exilic (43:12-15) and laments Israel's defeat and suffering at the hands of their enemies during a period when many in the nation believed that they had learned the lesson of disobedience and had diligently tried to keep the law. The experience of suffering within this context, then, retains an enigmatic quality:

> All these things have come upon us; but we have neither forgotten you nor dealt unrighteously with your covenant. Our hearts have not turned back to the former things and you have turned the paths of our lives (*tribous hēmōn*) aside from your way (43:19-20, LXX).

The Psalm recognizes the tension which exists when a restored Israel, whose covenant relationship with God is unbroken, nevertheless suffers. It is precisely this kind of tension which Paul describes when he summarizes the puzzling suffering of the believing community in the words of this Psalm: "For your sake we are being killed all day long; we are accounted as sheep for the slaughter" (8:36; cf. Psa 43:23 [LXX]).

Summary

To those who shared Paul's symbolic universe, therefore, the language which the apostle used to describe the movement of the believing community from death to life in Romans 5 and 8 would have resounded with echoes from the story of Israel's disobedience to the law, subsequent suffering, and eventual restoration. In 5:12-21 Paul refers to the story explicitly and uses it as part of the theological foundation for his discussion of death and life. In 5:1-11 and 8:1-39 Paul uses many of the same terms that the Bible uses to describe Israel's restoration, uses them in contexts similar to the biblical ones, and often links them together in ways reminiscent of their use in the prophets. He even explains the problem of a righteous but suffering community in the words of a Psalm whose subject is the tension which a restored Israel experienced when, despite their restoration to piety, they suffered. Neither Israel nor its scriptures, therefore, have receded from view in Romans 5 and 8. Although explicit references are rare, the story of Israel is still present, filling Paul's language with theological significance and providing Paul's symbols with a theological context.

The Story of Israel in Romans 6 and 7

Echoes of Israel's story do not resound as loudly in chapters 6 and 7, and investigation must proceed cautiously to avoid the exegetical disease which Samuel Sandmel has famously described as "parallelomania."[47] There are,

---

47 ". . . That extravagance among scholars which first overdoes the supposed similarity in passages and then proceeds to describe source and derivation as if implying literary connection flowing in an inevitable or predetermined direction." "Parallelomania," *JBL* 81 (1962) 1. The antidote may be found in Hays, *Échoes*, 29-32.

however, two encouraging indications that the attempt to find the story of Israel in these chapters is not a symptom of that plague. First, we have already seen that these chapters are bounded on either side by clear allusions to the story of Israel. Paul was thinking in these terms as he wrote chapters 5-8, therefore, and so we may reasonably expect allusions to the story of Israel in chapters 6 and 7. Second, if the story of Israel forms the context of Paul's argument, then several difficult texts become easier to understand. We can safely assume that if parallels to Israel's story help to explain problems as difficult as the meaning of 6:17, Paul's abruptness at 7:1, and the antecedent of the *egō* in 7:7-25, then we are in the presence not of parallelomania but its cure.[48]

Chapter 6

To Jews steeped in the Deuteronomic perspective on Israel's history and committed to the premise that what happened to God's people happened through God's foreordination, Paul's claim that the law caused sin and its penalty of death to increase (5:20) may have been less shocking than interpreters commonly suppose. More shocking, perhaps, was Paul's assertion that God's wrath had been removed, peace had come, and reconciliation had taken place not when his chastened people were praying prayers like the one in Nehemiah 9 but while they were still impious sinners (5:6-8, 20). Would this not mean that "we should remain in sin in order that grace might abound?"

Paul tackles this question first in 6:1-11 by speaking of the believer's death with Christ and then in 6:12-23 by using the metaphor of slavery. Echoes of the story of Israel in 6:1-11 are attenuated at best; but in 6:12-23, they resound more clearly. They begin with Paul's provocative statement that sin cannot rule over believers because they are "not under law but under grace" (6:14) and the repetition of the question at issue, "What therefore? Should we sin because we are not under law but under grace?" (6:15). The phrase "under law" in these two verses has been the subject of much debate; but the simplest explanation of it makes its meaning here consistent with the meaning of 5:13-14 and 5:20-21, the two passages in which Paul last referred to the law.[49] There, as we have seen, he traces the history of sin into the period of Moses. During that time, sin became worse because Israel violated the now unambiguously expressed will of God and experienced the penalty of death as a result. If this reading is correct, then "under law" in 6:15 refers to existence under the penalty of death–the curse of the law–which according to the biblical interpretation of Israel's history, came to Israel as a result of their disobedience.[50] By claiming that believers are no longer "under law" Paul is simply saying that they no longer live in the era during which, according to

---

[48] Hays, *Echoes*, 30-31 writes that if, *inter alia*, the proposed echo renders a reading of a passage which is consistent with other themes in Paul and makes sense within its immediate context, then it is probably not a product of the reader's imagination.

[49] On the connection between *hypo nomon* in 6:14 and *nomos de pareisēlthen, hina pleonasē to paraptōma* in 5:20a see Lagrange, *Romains*, 154; Nygren, *Romans*, 248; Dunn, *Romans 1-8*, 339; Ziesler, *Romans*, 165.

[50] Cf. Cranfield, *Romans*, 1.320.

the biblical account of Israel's history, the law pronounced its curse of death upon the disobedient.[51]

This means in turn that Paul's comparison of the believer to a slave in 6:15-23 may also be indebted to the story of Israel. Usually the metaphor is interpreted within the context of the common Greco-Roman institution of slavery, and that is probably the primary context from which Paul's metaphor draws its power.[52] We should not forget, however, that the biblical portrait of God as redeemer, a portrait upon which Paul draws in this letter (3:24, 8:23), depends for its forcefulness upon the assumption that Israel was enslaved either to foreign nations (Deut 7:8; 9:26; Isa 41:14; 43:1, 14; 52:3; 54:5) or to sin (Psa 130:7-8; Isa 44:22). The connection between Israel's enslavement to foreign nations and its sin, moreover, was clear to post-exilic biblical writers. The great prayers of confession in Ezra 9 and Nehemiah 9 both use the imagery of slavery to describe the suffering into which Israel's violation of the law had led them. After confessing that from ancient days Israel had been handed over to captivity for their sins, Ezra comments

> But now for a brief moment favor has been shown by the Lord our God, who has left us a remnant, and given us a stake in his holy place, in order that he may brighten our eyes and grant us a little sustenance in our slavery. For we are slaves; yet our God has not forsaken us in our slavery . . . (9:8-9, NRSV).

Nehemiah, similarly, summarizes the history of Israel's disobedience to the law and then describes the result this way:

> Here we are, slaves to this day–slaves in the land that you gave to our ancestors to enjoy its fruit and its good gifts (9:36, NRSV).

Josephus' paraphrase of Deuteronomy shows us, moreover, that this concept was still alive during Paul's time. Josephus summarizes the message of Deuteronomy in a speech of Moses which emphasizes blessing for obedience to the law and suffering for neglect of it. Moses warns the people that the wealth which they are about to inherit by conquering Canaan should not lead them to neglect their covenant with God,

> For, should ye be carried away by it into a contempt and disdain for virtue, ye will lose even that favor which ye have found of God; and, having made him your enemy, ye will forfeit that land, which ye are to win, beaten in arms and deprived of it by future generations with the grossest ignominy, and, dispersed throughout the habitable world, ye will fill every land and sea with your servitude (*emplēsete kai gēn kai thalassan tēs hautōn douleias, Ant.* 4.190).

---

51 *Contra* Dunn, *Romans 1-8,* 340, who believes that Paul refers to the "social function of the law" here, and Barrett, *Romans,* 129, who believes that the phrase refers to "the upward striving of human religion and morality."

52 See Dale B. Martin, *Slavery as Salvation: The Metaphor of Slavery in Pauline Christianity* (New Haven: Yale University Press, 1990) 61-62 who does, however, recognize biblical influence on Paul's use of the metaphor.

If this imagery lies behind Paul's use of the word here, then he is reminding his readers that they have been delivered from the bondage of "death" in which Israel labored because of their disobedience and subsequent punishment under the curse of the law (6:14-15) and have now become slaves of obedience with the result that they stand in a new covenant relationship with God (*hypakoēs eis dikaiosunēn*, 6:16). They have entered the period of restoration when, according to Isaiah, "righteousness" (*ṣdqh*; LXX, *dikaiosunē*) will be the "taskmaster" (*ngś*; LXX, *episkopos*) of God's people (60:17, cf. Rom 6:18-23).

The new covenant relationship, Paul next says, is marked by obedience from the heart to the type of teaching which the Romans received. The controversy surrounding these words is notorious;[53] but a measure of clarity can be brought to Paul's language by recognizing that here too Paul is using imagery drawn from the biblical story of Israel's turbulent relationship with their God. The words "obedience from the heart" recall the language of Deut 30:14 (LXX) where the commandments are said to be easy to do (*poieō*) because they are in the Israelites' heart and 30:17 where the Israelites are warned not to change their hearts so that they do not obey (*eisakouō*) the commandments. Paul's choice of words in v. 17 also resembles the language of Jer 38:33-34 (LXX) which not only promises a new heart to the covenant people but indicates that the teaching of God will be so indelibly written on their hearts that they will not need to teach it to one another. Ezk 11:19-21 and 36:26-27 likewise speak of a time when God will give to Israel a new heart of flesh after plucking out their heart of stone, with the result that Israel will obey God's precepts and commands. The story of Israel's disobedience together with the hope that God would one day correct their disobedience, therefore, seems to be the context within nearest reach for understanding what Paul means in this otherwise enigmatic verse.

The same is true of v. 19.[54] Here Paul uses a series of terms which recall the biblical language of sanctity prominent in both the law and the prophets.[55] Paul tells his readers,

---

53 Some believe that the words are not Paul's own but an interpolation (for example, Rudolf Bultmann, "Glossen im Römerbrief" in *Exegetica* [Tübingen: J. C. B. Mohr (Paul Siebeck)] 278-84 and Victor Paul Furnish, *Theology and Ethics in Paul* [Nashville: Abingdon, 1968] 196-98). Others believe that Paul is simply being inconsistent in denying the validity of law as an ethical guide and then introducing a new law (C. H. Dodd, *The Epistle of Paul to the Romans* [London: Collins, 1959] 117; John Knox, "The Epistle to the Romans" in *The Interpreter's Bible*, 12 vols. (Nashville: Abingdon, 1954) 9:483-84). Still others believe that Paul does not speak of the handing on of a fixed tradition—of a new moral code—in these verses, but of obedience to "the way of life demanded by the gospel" (Cranfield, *Romans*, 1.324) or of commitment to "something like a baptismal creed" (Käsemann, *Romans*, 181).

54 V. 18 repeats the substance of v. 16, and so what was said in connection with v. 16 is true of v. 18 as well.

55 For God's desire that Israel should be holy, see particularly Lev 11:44-45; 15:31; 18:1-5, 24; 19:2; 20:24-26; and 22:32. For the hope that God would one day restore Israel's violated sanctity see Ezek 20:33-44; 22:15; 36:25, 29, 33; 37:23, 28. For the literary connections between Ezekiel and Leviticus, see in particular Ezk 18:5-9 and the analysis in Walther Zimmerli, *Ezekiel 1: A Commentary on the Book of the Prophet Ezekiel, Chapters 1-24* (Hermeneia; Philadelphia: Fortress, 1979) 379-82.

244 / SBL 1993 Seminar Papers

> For just as you presented your members as slaves to impurity (*akatharsi*) and lawlessness (*anomi*) for the purpose of lawlessness (*eis tēn anomian*), so now present your members as slaves to righteousness for the purpose of sanctification (*eis tēn hagiasmon*).

The terms *akatharsia, anomia,* and *hagiasmos* recall one of the primary functions of Israel's covenant with God–the separation of Israel from other people as a "priestly kingdom and a holy nation" (Ex 19:6).[56] *Akatharsia* is used in the LXX not only to indicate the kind of ritual impurity which every Israelite contracted, but also to refer to the conduct of those who lived outside the law, whether Gentiles (1 Esd 1:49, 2 Esd 9:11) or disobedient Israelites. Ezekiel especially uses the term to describe the flagrant violation of the laws of sanctity which led Israel to experience the curses of the covenant and from which God would eventually deliver his people.[57] If Paul's use of the story of Israel in chapters 5-8 is as prominent as we have argued above, then this word does not refer simply to "immorality" but to immorality as a violation of the sanctity which God requires of his people. The same can be said of *anomia* which, like *akatharsia*, was frequently used simply to mean wickedness but which, by the Hasmonean period, had become a special term for both Gentiles and Jews who, by their violation of the laws of Israel's sanctity, had placed themselves outside Israel's covenant.[58]

Paul intends to say, however, that his readers have moved from outside to inside the circle of blessing created by God's restoration of the covenant with his people. Now, he says, they must present their members as slaves to righteousness "for the purpose of sanctification" (*eis hagiasmon*). The word *hagiasmos* is used infrequently in the LXX and is not used to refer specifically to the people of God; but, when it is used, it refers to the special nature of that which is unique to the people of God, whether God himself (Sir 17:10, 2 Macc 14:36), the temple (3 Macc 2:18), or the sacrifices (Sir 7:31, 2 Macc 2:17). Far more importantly, it participates in the semantic field of the term *hagios*, which in the LXX is the adjective of choice for describing the distinctiveness of God's people.[59]

In 6:19, then, Paul wants to remind his readers that they have crossed the boundary of sanctity from *akatharsia* and *anomia* to *hagiasmos*. This change in status means that they are in a right covenant relationship with God (6:16, 18, 19) and that they have moved from existence under the curse of death (6:21, 23) which the law pronounces upon all who are unclean, lawless, and

---

56 James Barr, *The Semantics of Biblical Language* (Oxford: Oxford University Press, 1961) 263-82 has spoken eloquently and correctly about the fallacy of isolating particular Old Testament words and then claiming that, when New Testament writers use them, they import into the words some special biblical significance. He concedes, however, that "some words become specialized" and that, when this happens, the significance of these words in one context may be transported to another. It is this kind of specialization which the words *akatharsia, anomia,* and *hagiasmos* possess.

57 See Ezek 9:9; 22:15; 24:11; 36:17, 25, 29; 39:24; cf. Micah 2:10 and Lam 1:9.

58 See 1 Macc 3:5-6; 7:5; 9:23, 58, 69; and 11:25 and the comments in Dunn, *Romans 1-8,* lxix-lxx, 206, and 346-47.

59 See, for example, Ex 19:6; Deut 7:6; 26:19; Jer 2:2-3; Lev 17-26; Isa 4:3; 1 Macc 10:39, 44; and Wis 18:9.

unholy, to existence under the blessing of life (6:22-23) which the law promises to all those who live within the ambit of God's covenant.

In summary, if we read Paul's references to the law in 6:14-15 through the lens of his reference to it in 5:20, and if we then take 6:14-15 as a clue to the conceptual world in which Paul is thinking as he constructs his argument in 6:12-23, enigmatic texts appear less strange and we begin to appreciate how deeply indebted the structure of Paul's theology is to the biblical story of Israel: Paul believed his Roman readers to be the purified and restored Israel for which Ezekiel and others had hoped.

Chapter 7

If this understanding of 6:12-23 is correct, then Paul's facile movement into the topic of the law in 7:1-6 should seem less surprising that it usually does to interpreters. Many believe that other than his brief references to the law in 5:20 and 6:14-15, Paul has concentrated on other matters in chapters 5 and 6. It then comes as a surprise that Paul introduces his lengthy discussion of the law in 7:1-25 with the phrase *ē agnoeite*, a phrase which implies that

> if the people addressed really know–the assumption is that they surely must–the truth which is about to be stated (in every case a *hoti* clause follows), then they ought to recognize the truth, or agree with the sentiment, expressed or implicit in something that has been said already (*usually immediately before the formula is introduced*).[60]

Because of their belief that the law has not been central to Paul's argument in chapters 5-6, however, most commentators are obligated to argue that in 7:1 Paul has not followed his usual custom but has instead used the phrase *ē agnoeite* to refer all the way back to his statement about the law in 6:14b.[61] If, on the other hand, the story of Israel's violation of the law, punishment, and restoration has defined the terms of Paul's discussion in 6:12-23, then 7:1 looks perfectly natural.

If Paul's mention of the law in 7:1 should occasion less surprise than it usually does, however, what he says about the law in 7:1-6, should probably occasion more. After hinting in 6:17 that the new covenant of Jer 31 (38):31-34 with its heart-inscribed law has been fulfilled in those who believe in Jesus Christ, Paul now says unequivocally that we "have no more to do with" the law (7:2,6, BAGD, s.v. *katargeō*). Like the husband in Paul's notorious illustration, we "have died to the law through the body of Christ" and so, like the wife, we are free "to belong to another" (7:4). It is not easy to reconcile Paul's positive and negative statements about the law in this letter; but if the story of Israel's disobedience and restoration is as prominent in chapters 5-6 as the argument above indicates, then at least here Paul seems to say in a more complete way what he has already said in 6:14-15–that the eschatological community of believers no longer labors under the curse of the Mosaic law but is subject to a new "law" which Paul identifies with the new covenant of the spirit and of peace about which the prophets so frequently speak. This

---

60 Cranfield, *Romans*, 1.332, my emphasis.

61 Lagrange, *Romains* 160; Dodd, *Romans*, 119; Cranfield, *Romans*, 1.332 all comment on the abruptness with which Paul introduces the law into the discussion at 7:1.

seems to be Paul's meaning in 7:6 when he says that "we have been set free from the law, having died to that by which we used to be suppressed, so that we serve in the newness of the spirit and not in the oldness of the letter."[62]

Such an interpretation of the prophetic passages about God's establishment of a new covenant was not, of course, the typically Jewish one. Jews, whether Christians or not, would probably have understood the prophets to be predicting a restoration of the eternally valid Mosaic covenant. In light of this, Paul must address the objection that he has, in a circuitous way, argued that the law is not good. Just as at the end of chapter 5 Paul had placed a new twist on the old story of Israel and had been compelled to warn against misunderstanding as a result, so here Paul faces a new misunderstanding and produces a lengthy argument against it. Using the same rhetorical signal that he used in 6:1 (*ti oun eroumen*), Paul in 7:7 addresses the question, "Is the law sin?"

Paul's basic answer to the question in 7:7-13 is clear enough: the law, far from being sin, is exonerated from blame because sin took advantage of the law to cause "me" to disobey God. The fault lies with sin, therefore, and not with the holy, righteous, and good law. The details of Paul's argument, however, particularly the identity of the infamous *egō* and the period of time to which the secondary tenses in the passage point, are matters of hot dispute.

It has become increasingly popular for interpreters to see the story of Adam, already recounted in 5:12-21, behind the *egō* and the past tenses of 7:7-12. Since W. G. Kümmel's revolutionary work,[63] most interpreters have been willing to view the *egō* in Romans 7 as figurative rather than as a straightforward reference to Paul himself, and with the door open to a figurative interpretation, Adam has seemed to many to be the most likely candidate for the reality behind the figure. "I was once alive apart from the law" (7:9) appears to be a statement which only a figurative Adam could make, and a reference to Genesis 3 would certainly clarify more sharply than any other context the statement that "sin . . . deceived me" (7:11). Observations such as these eventually led to Ernst Käsemann's famous pronouncement that "there is nothing in the passage which does not fit Adam, and everything fits Adam alone."[64]

This statement is, however, more rhetorically effective than exegetically sound. There are, after all, several aspects of the passage which do not fit Adam alone, and at least one which does not fit him at all. Paul's five-fold use of the words *entolē* and *nomos* and his quotation of the the tenth commandment (7:7) can hardly be described as fitting Adam alone, since the Bible uses them not in connection with Adam but with Israel.[65] Moreover, as Douglas Moo

---

62 Wright, *Climax*, 196-97, 203, perhaps correctly, does not speak of a "new law" in this context but of a "new covenant, whose boundary-marker is Christ and Spirit and not Torah." We do not fundamentally disagree on this point. I am simply taking 8:2 as permission to use the term "law" of the new covenant.

63 *Römer 7 und die Bekehrung des Paulus* (UNT 17; Leipzig: J. C. Hinrichs, 1929).

64 *Romans*, 196. Others who see Adam in the passage include S. Lyonnet, "L'histoire du salut selon le chapitre vii de l'épitre aux Romains," *Bib* 43 (1962) 117-51; Cranfield, *Romans*, 1.344; Dunn, *Romans 1-8*, 399-403; and Ziesler, *Romans*, 182.

65 Josephus, *Ant.* 1.43 uses *entolē* of God's command to Adam; but the Bible does not use the word in this way.

points out, most interpreters of Romans agree that 7:7-12 is an excursus in defense of the law, made necessary by Paul's negative statements about the law in 3:20, 4:15, 5:13, 5:20, 6:14-15, and especially 7:1-6. That law, however, is clearly distinguished in 5:13-14 from the commandment given to Adam. Having distinguished between the period of Adam, an intervening period in which there was no law, and the period after the law came, Paul would now be veiling his argument with confusion if he suddenly used the word "law" to refer to the period of Adam.[66]

In addition to these considerations, one aspect of the passage seems inexplicably inappropriate if the "I" refers exclusively to Adam: Paul says that the commandment's purpose was life (*hē entolē hē eis zōēn*, 7:10), and yet the purpose of the commandment given to Adam is nowhere connected with life. The penalty for not obeying the commandment is, of course, death according to Gen 3:19; but it would be faulty logic to say that the penalty expresses the opposite of the commandment's purpose. Gen 3:22 says that Adam had to be expelled from the garden because he had gained divine knowledge and might eat of the tree of life and live forever; but it is difficult to see how this could express the purpose of the command not to eat of the first tree.[67] The most obvious context for the statement that the purpose of the commandment was life, then, is once again the story of Israel. At Israel's initiation into the covenant, God told his people that he intended the commandments to bring "life" (Deut 6:24; 30:15-20; Lev 18:5), and this claim became Israel's settled conviction (Prov 6:23; Ezk 20:11, 21; Sir 17:11, 45:5; Baruch 3:9).[68] Nevertheless, as we have seen, many Jews believed that Israel had not yet attained life because they had disobeyed the covenant, and many awaited the restoration of Israel when the life promised in the covenant would be theirs.

Some elements of 7:7-13, then, fit Adam and others fit Israel. The most sensible explanation for this is that Paul has mingled elements of both stories in this passage.[69] We have already seen that in chapter 5 Paul viewed the story of Israel as the existential outworking and heightening of the experience of the primal Adam and that the two stories were theologically intertwined. Both violated a specific precept (5:13-14) and Israel's sin caused the sin which Adam had initiated to increase (5:20).[70] If this understanding of chapter 5 is correct, then, it seems natural for Paul in chapter 7 to combine elements of both stories in order to exonerate the command of God from blame for the plight of humanity in general and of Israel in particular.

Beginning with 7:13, however, allusions to Adam seem to be replaced with references to an individual's struggle to keep the law, and discussion of the passage has tended to focus on who this individual is. Does Paul speak of himself, of unbelievers generally, or of believers? If of himself, does he speak as an unbeliever or as a believer?[71] In the tangle of attempts to sort out the best

---

66 Douglas J. Moo, "Israel and Paul in Romans 7.7-12," *NTS* 32 (1986) 124.

67 *Contra* Dunn, *Romans 1-8*, 384.

68 For several of these references I am indebted to Dunn, *Romans 1-8*, 384.

69 See also Wright, *Climax*, 227.

70 See also Wright, *Climax*, 196.

71 The alternatives are presented and debated by Cranfield, *Romans*, 1.344-47 with characteristic thoroughness.

answers to these questions the correlation between what Paul says in 7:13 and in 5:20 is seldom noticed.[72] In 5:20 Paul has identified Israel as the place where sin, because of the giving of the law, increased. In 7:13 Paul uses the first person singular to make much the same statement:

> . . . sin, in order that it might be revealed as sin, worked death in me through what was good, in order that through the commandment sin might become exceedingly sinful.

Whoever the *ego* of 7:13-25 is, he or she functions in a way similar to Israel in Paul's previous argument.

The possibility that the story of Israel lies beneath the struggle of the *ego* in 7:13-25 is strengthened, moreover, by the broad similarity between this passage and the prayers of confession in Ezra 9:5-15, Nehemiah 9:6-37, Daniel 9:4-19, and Baruch 1:15-3:8. Just as Rom 7:13-25 is marked by an anguished awareness of the individual's tendency to disobey the Mosaic law, so the primary characteristic of these prayers is anguish over national Israel's repeated disobedience of the law in spite of God's continuing faithfulness to his people. Ezra is grieved that after the great iniquity of his ancestors, and the great mercy of God in spite of that iniquity, once again he and his people have violated the Mosaic covenant and intermarried with the people of the land. He is so moved by this lack of concern for the covenant that as he prays he not only weeps but throws himself on the ground before the Temple (10:1). The prayer in Nehemiah focusses similarly on Israel's repeated violation of the law in spite of God's merciful patience in withholding punishment (9:16-17, 18, 26, 28-30). Daniel says that Israel has sinned, acted wickedly, turned aside from God's commandments, and refused to listen to God's prophets (9:4-5), and Baruch confesses that "from the day when the Lord led our fathers out of Egypt even until this day we have been disobedient to the Lord our God and careless to disobey his voice" (1:19). Although all of these prayers are in the first person plural rather than the first person singular, Daniel and Baruch recognize the role of the individual in the sins which they confess. Daniel describes his prayer as a confession of "my sin and the sin of my people Israel," and Baruch twice attributes the sins of the nation to the evil intentions of each person's heart (1:22, 2:8).[73]

The similarity between Rom 7:13-25 and these passages does not reach to the level of specific details; nor is there any biblical precedent for Paul's bifurcation of the law and of the self in this passage. But the anguish of the confession, and the origin of that anguish in continued disobedience of the law, open the possibility that as he wrote Paul was thinking not simply of himself but of his people and of the biblical story of their disobedience.

---

[72] Wright, *Climax*, 197-98 and "Romans and the Theology of Paul" in Eugene H. Lovering, Jr., ed., *Society of Biblical Literature 1992 Seminar Papers* (No. 31; Atlanta: Scholars Press, 1992) 200 is a prominent exception.

[73] Bar 1:22 says, *ōchometha ekastos en dianoi kardias autou tēs ponēras*, and 2:8, *kai ouk edēthēmen tou prosōpou kuriou tou apostrepsai hekaston apo tōn noēmatōn tēs kardias autōn tēs ponēras*.

Conclusions

If the story of Israel is as important to the argument of Romans 5-8 as this essay suggests, then the tension which many interpreters have found between these four chapters and chapters 1-4 and 9-11 begins to relax.[74] Because Paul argues in chapters 5-8 that the believing community stands in continuity with the story of Israel as it appears in Leviticus, Deuteronomy, the historical books, and the prophets, these chapters are as important as chapter 4 for supporting Paul's claim that faith establishes rather than nullifies the law (3:31). By his appropriation of the language which these writings use to describe the restoration of Israel, Paul implies that the believing community of Jews and Gentiles in Rome have become the protagonists in the last chapter of Israel's story as it is told in the Bible.

This assumption, however, creates a theological tension which grows in intensity throughout Romans 5-8 until it reaches the boiling point at the end of the section in the rhetorical question "Who will bring charges against the elect of God?" (8:33). How could Paul claim that the ethnically mixed community of believers in Rome were God's elect–the restored Israel–when so many circumcised Jews still lived, in the words of Second Maccabees, "in the time of evil" (2 Macc 1:5)?[75] Paul's reply to this critical difficulty comes, of course, in chapters 9-11. The presence of the story of Israel in chapters 5-8 means, therefore, that Paul's argument is neither complete at the end of chapter 8 as a previous generation of scholarship thought nor, as more recent treatments of Romans sometimes imply, that Israel dives beneath the text at 4:25 to re-surface only at 9:1.

The presence of the story of Israel in Romans 5-8 also means that these chapters are as concerned with the people of God as they are with the individual. Although they certainly use the first person and therefore take on a more personal tone than chapters 1-4 and 9-11, the interpreter should not reduce them only to a discussion of the implications of justification for the individual believer. By using biblical language for the restoration of God's people they constantly situate the individual within the wider community. This is true even of chapter seven where, as we have seen, the first person singular reflects a corporate as well as an individual struggle.[76]

The biblical story of Israel, therefore, forms a pivotal part of the theology of Romans 5-8. Even in these chapters, where Israel never appears by name and Paul quotes scripture only rarely, Paul's theology takes a biblical shape. All of this is substantial evidence that Paul's symbolic universe was Israel's symbolic universe, and that any adequate description of Paul's theology must understand the symbols of that universe as well.

---

74 See also Wright, *Climax*, 194-95.

75 The phrase *en kairō ponērō* may refer to life in the diaspora and therefore under the curse of the broken covenant. See the comments of Solomon Zeitlin in *The Second Book of Maccabees* (ed. Solomon Zeitlin; trans. Sidney Tedesche; New York: Harper Brothers, 1954) 100-101.

76 Cf. Isa 61:10-11 where the prophet uses the first person singular to describe the restored community.

The Function of the Oracles against Babylon in Isaiah 14 and 47

Chris A. Franke
College of St. Catherine

In my study of the function of the satirical lament against Babylon in Second Isaiah,[1] I discussed the pivotal role that this chapter played in the development of Second Isaiah. I showed that the downfall and humiliation of Virgin Daughter Babylon was a foil to the rising and restoration of Virgin Daughter Zion. As Babylon was deposed, was sent from her throne into exile, indeed descended to death, conversely Zion was released from exile, and was elevated once again to a position of honor. While one of the main themes of Isaiah 40-46 was the downtrodden Judah, chapters 48ff. emphasized Zion/Jerusalem reborn.

It is generally agreed that chapters 40-48 of Isaiah form a unit by virtue of several common elements—the emphasis on the importance of Cyrus in 40-48, the theme of Jacob/Israel, a concern with the return to Zion, all of which elements disappear, to be replaced in 49ff. by other motifs. Another feature which is found in 40-48, but not in 49ff. is mention of Babylon/Chaldea.

All references to Babylon/Chaldea in the book of Isaiah occur between chapters 13 and 48 of the book.[2] Furthermore, these references are concentrated within three segments of the book, the Oracles Against Nations (hereafter OAN) in 13-23, the Isaiah/Hezekiah narratives in 36-39, and 40-48, the Jacob/Israel passages. (None are found in the chapters usually considered to be from Isaiah of Jerusalem.) In all, thirteen references to Babylon appear in Isaiah, seven to Chaldea (Chaldeans): 13:1, 19 (Chaldea also in 19); 14:4, 22; 21:9; 23:13 (here, Chaldea); 39:1, 3, 6, 7; 43:14 (also Chaldea); 47:1 (also Chaldea), 5 (also Chaldea); 48:14, 20 (also Chaldea).

The subsection of 13-23, 13-14, is often referred to as "the burden of Babylon."[3] These oracles against Babylon/the Chaldeans speak of the

---

[1] "The Function of the Satiric Lament over Babylon in Second Isaiah (xlvii)," *VT* 41 (1991) 408-418.

[2] See Christopher T. Begg, "Babylon in the Book of Isaiah," *The Book of Isaiah/Le Livre d'Isaïe* ed. J. Vermeylen, 121-125. BETL 81. (Leuven: University Press, 1989), for a discussion of references to Babylon in Isaiah.

[3] See Seth Erlandsson, *The Burden of Babylon: A Study of Isaiah 13:2-14:23* (Lund, Sweden: CWK Gleerup, 1970), and Bernard Gosse, *Isaïe 13,1-14,23: Dans la tradition littéraire du livre d'Isaie et dans la tradition des oracles contre les nations* (Orbis Biblicus et Orientalis 78; Göttingen: Vandenhoek & Ruprecht, 1978) for treatments of this section.

overthrow of Babylon, the downfall of the Babylonian king and the annihilation of his posterity.[4] Commentators have questioned whether the names Babylon/the Chaldeans are integral to the oracles, and suggest they are redactional additions. Another oracle in chapter 22, the oracle concerning the wilderness of the sea, refers to the fall of Babylon in 22:9, in language reminiscent of Amos 5:2—"fallen, fallen is Babylon . . . ." A problematic reference in 23:13—*hn ᵓrṣ. ksdym zh hᶜm lᵓ hyh ᵓšwr* is the last occurrence of the names Babylon/Chaldeans within the OAN segment.

The next group of references to Babylon/the Chaldeans appears in the Isaiah/Hezekiah narratives. Babylon is a far off country; the king of Babylon has sent his enjoys to King Hezekiah. This chapter is an ominous warning of days to come when Babylon will carry off all that belongs to the house of David, including some of the king's own descendants. This section of the book presents Babylon as a threat yet to come, as a power which has not yet realized its full potential against God's people.

The references in Second Isaiah (40-48) return to the theme in the OAN, warnings about the overthrow of Babylon. The Lord promises in 43:14 to break down all the bars of the Babylonians, and to turn the joyful shouting of the Chaldeans to laments.[5] The ironic lament in 47 speaks of the downfall of Virgin Daughter Babylon, daughter Chaldea. The last references in the book of Isaiah in 48 assert that God will accomplish his purpose on Babylon and his arm shall be against the Chaldeans (48:14), and urge the people to go out of Babylon, and flee from Chaldeans (48: 20).

The concentration of these references to Babylon within the three sections of the book of Isaiah bears further investigation. The name Babylon first appears at a crucial point in the development of the book, a point at which most scholars agree that First Isaiah has been left behind. Seitz asserts that Isaiah 13-14, the oracle concerning Babylon, "now works in conjunction with a theology of history embracing the whole book . . . ."[6] It appears again at another pivotal point in the book, in chapter 39, where it bridges the gap between eighth century Isaiah, when Babylon was only a distant threat, and the events of the sixth century where Babylon prevails. It eventually disappears after the fall of Babylon is replaced by the flight from Babylon and the elevation of Zion in chapters 47 and 48. This study will examine the poems on the King of Babylon (hereafter KOB) in Isaiah 14 and Virgin Daughter Babylon (hereafter VDB) in chapter 47 to determine interdependencies between the poems[7] and to see how each chapter relates to

---

4 Though, see R. E. Clements, *Isaiah 1-39* (NCB; Grand Rapids: Wm. B. Eerdmans Publishing Co., 1980), 132, who points out that 13 is entitled oracle "concerning" Babylon, and that the first two utterances are positive toward Babylon, not negative.

5 See John D. Watts, *Isaiah 34-66* (WBC; Waco: Word Books, 1987), 127-28, for the various renderings of the verse.

6 Christopher R. Seitz, "Isaiah 1-66: Making Sense of the Whole," in *Reading and Preaching the Book of Isaiah*, Christopher R. Seitz, ed., (Philadelphia: Fortress Press, 1988), 112.

7 Gosse, *Isaie 13,1-13,23*, pp. 11-12, sees little if any connection between the oracles against Babylon in 13-14 and those in Isaiah 46-47. The latter are not part of a collection of Oracles against Nations, and they are more preoccupied with salvation for Israel, than

the larger sections of the book of Isaiah, with the end in mind to understand their redactional function. The following approaches have been taken with other similar sections of the book of Isaiah.

One of the techniques used in studies on the composition of the book of Isaiah to determine relationships between various segments of the book is to identify certain pivotal chapters which seem to show interrelations in both directions. For instance, Steck identified chapter 35 as the juncture between 1-34 and 40ff.[8] Seitz's study on Isaiah 36-39 discussed these chapters and their function in the redaction of the book of Isaiah.[9]

Another method used in investigating the interdependence between the various parts of the book of Isaiah is the study of parallels between first and Second Isaiah, First and Third Isaiah, etc. An examples of this approach to the question can be seen in the recent study of Christopher R. Seitz on parallels between Isaiah 40:1-11 and 6:1-11.[10] Both of these chapters are considered pivotal in the book of Isaiah.

Interdependence has also been discussed by demonstrating the use of citations or allusions within the book of Isaiah.[11] Textual citation and allusions in one part of the book can be used "as a means for understanding the redactional function of these chapters within the book of Isaiah." Sweeney shows that the author of chapters 24-27 uses other texts from the book of Isaiah to illustrate his own particular hermeneutical perspective.

The mocking songs of taunts against Babylon in Isaiah 14 and 47 have similarities in language, form, and tone. These features of Isaiah 14 will form the basis of the examination of these similarities. The mashal against the king of Babylon is considered to be one of the best examples in the Bible of a prophetic parody of a lament.[12] Yee analyzes this parody by first discussing the features of the lament proper. The six typical features of the lament (according to Yee's analysis of the lament of David over Saul and Jonathan in 2 Samuel 1) are: (1) a rhetorical introduction announcing the death; (2) suppression of the news of the death from enemies; (3) description of the reaction of nature to the person's death; (4) description of the person's life; (5) call to mourners to weep; (6) an expression of the singer's personal grief. In addition, laments are usually written in qinah meter.

---

with chastisement of Babylon. In addition, they do not have the violence, the elevated style, the pretensions that are typical of chapters 13-14.

8 O. J. Steck, *Bereitete Heimkehr: Jesaja 35 als redaktionelle Brücke zwischen dem Ersten und Zweiten Jesaja* (SBS 121; Stuttgart: Katholisches Bibelwerk, 1985).

9 *Zion's Final Destiny: The Development of the Book of Isaiah: A Reassessment of Isaiah 36-39* (Minneapolis: Fortress Press, 1991).

10 "The Divine Council: Temporal Transition and New Prophecy in the Book of Isaiah," *JBL* 109 (1990) 229-247.

11 Marvin A. Sweeney, "Textual Citations in Isaiah 24-27," *JBL* 107 (1988) 39-52.

12 Gale A. Yee, "The Anatomy of Biblical Parody: The Dirge Form in 2 Samuel 1 and Isaiah 14," *CBQ* 50 (1988) 565-86. I am indebted to Yee's analysis of this poem, and follow her outline throughout this section of the paper.

Yee's reading of Isa 14:4b-21 shows that the poet adhered closely to the features of the lament, but altered these features to achieve the parody by reversing the reader's expectations.[13]

(1) There is a *rhetorical introduction* announcing the death which opens with the exclamation *ʾk*, an expression of astonishment at what has happened. The qinah meter is also used.[14]

As in (4) above, the person's *life and achievements* are described—in 14:5-6, the staff and scepter are symbolic descriptions of the KOB's oppressive power. Use of participles, apposition and hyperbole further describe and praise the object of a lament. In this poem they are not used to praise the lamented one, but to accuse him of tyranny (14:6).

In 14:13-14 the description of the person's life is not from the mouth of the singer of the lament, but in the KOB's own boastful words, where he describes his pretensions to glory. Heroic laments commonly have the theme of the "incomparability" of the deceased person to other beings.[15] The tyrant of 14 is far from incomparable; he is weak, just like the other kings who have died before him (14:10).

(3) True laments show *how nature is affected* by the death of the person. In 14:7-8, the whole earth is at rest at the news of the death; trees rejoice at the news, and the underworld itself is aroused by it.

(5) In laments, mourners are *called to weep* or to grieve publicly; in 14:16-17, there is no call to weep. No sympathy is evoked for the deceased. Instead, the crudely exposed corpse of the KOB is an object of scorn to those who pass by and mock it.

(6) True laments contain *expressions of personal grief* over the death of the lamented one. This is often expressed by the use of negatives such as "never again," or "no longer." (See Amos 5:2, "Fallen, no more to rise.") The sadness is due to the fact that the deceased will no longer be present to the mourners. In this parody there is an expression not of grief but of relief, satisfaction and retribution on the occasion of this death (14:18-21), and the negations (e.g., "may descendants nevermore be named") "elicit a sense of relief" that the sufferings are at an end.[16]

Chapter 47, a poem unique in structure,[17] does have some of the characteristic features of mourning and lament. Its overall form has been identified as a taunt song,[18] or mocking song,[19] a triumph song,[20] an oracle

---

13 Yee, 575.

14 See also these same features in the dirge within, in 14:12-15, Yee, pp. 577-79.

15 Yee, 571.

16 Yee, 581.

17 Roy F. Melugin, *The Formation of Isaiah 40-55* (BZAW 141; Berlin: de Gruyter), 135.

18 R. Clifford, *Fair Spoken and Persuading: An Interpretation of Second Isaiah* (New York: Paulist Press, 1984), 135.

19 J. Muilenburg, "The Book of Isaiah: Chapters 40-66," *IB* 5 (New York: Abingdon, 1965), 543.

20 B. Duhm, *Das Buch Jesaia* (4th ed.; HAT III, 1; Göttingen: Vandenboeck & Ruprecht, 1922), 354.

against foreign nations.[21] Most see it as a combination of different formal elements. For instance, Westermann[22] sees evidence of the diction of the prophetic oracle of doom. Melugin sees it as a "taunt to a large extent influenced by the style of the prophetic oracle,"[23] but agrees with Westermann that the chapter is a freely created poem. Whybray[24] sees two different forms of speech—the mocking- or taunt-song, and the funeral-song or dirge over the dead. He shows how the poem has elements of mocking or taunt, but does not discuss which elements he believes are related to the funeral song or dirge.

Using the criteria for the lament as outlined in Yee's article, chapter 47 can be seen to have several but not all of the elements of a lament proper. Comparison with Isaiah 14 will also illustrate the features of lament which are present in this poem.

(1) While there is no *rhetorical announcement* of the death of the individual, the very beginning lines of the poem show the subject of the poem, VDB, descending from her throne to earth. This descent is not just to the ground but to the darkness of the underworld (47:5). The root *yrd* appears only once in Isaiah 47, the very first word in the poem; in Isa 14:4b-21 it occurs three times, each time in connection with the descent to Sheol (14:11, 15, 19). The theme of "descent" is a crucial one in both poems.

The descent in 47:1 is "to the dust . . . to earth," in 47:5 "to darkness." In 14:11 KOB descends more specifically "to Sheol," to the "pit" (14:15). While most scholars interpret the descent of VDB as the change of her status from ruler to slave, comparison with biblical and non-biblical texts demonstrate that a more radical change is meant here. Tromp[25] considers the word pair "earth-dust" to be associated with the thought of the death. Further, he says the expression *yrd ʿpr* means "to go down to the grave/the netherworld."[26]

The thrones of VDB and KOB are prominent features in each poem. VDB sits down "dethroned" (47:1). KOB plans to ascend to the heavens, elevate his throne (14:13), and sit on the mount of assembly. Reference is also made to the thrones of the other leaders of the earth (14:9) who are dwelling in Sheol. An Ugaritic funerary liturgy in KTU 1.161[27] sheds light on Biblical passages dealing with thrones and mourning rites. Mourning rites are often done to express identification with the predicament of the dead.[28] The descent of El

---

21 J. McKenzie, *Second Isaiah* (AB 20; Garden City: Doubleday & Company, Inc., 1967), 91; C. Westermann, *Isaiah 40-66: A Commentary*, translated by D. M. G. Stalker (OTL; Philadelphia: Westminster), 188; R. N. Whybray, *Isaiah 40-66* (NCB; London: Marshall, Morgan & Scott Publications, Ltd., Wm. F. Eerdmans Publishing Company, 1981), 118.

22 189.

23 135.

24 118.

25 N. J. Tromp, *Primitive Conceptions of Death and the Netherworld in the Old Testament* (BibOr 21; Rome, 1969), 23.

26 Tromp, 33. See also Jonah 2:7; Ps 30:10 associates the "pit" with "dust," another connection with the underworld.

27 J. Glen Taylor, "A First and Last Thing to Do in Mourning: *KTU* 1.161 and Some Parallels," 151-177 *Ascribe to the Lord: Biblical and Other Studies* 29 Memorial Craigie (1988).

28 Taylor, 162.

from the throne at the news of Baal's death is usually interpreted to be merely a preliminary to El's sitting on the ground in mourning. But Taylor suggests it could be an act in which El identifies with Baal's loss of his throne by descending from his (El's) own throne.

The interpretation of Isaiah 47 as a lament over the death of VDB is supported by the ideas in these texts. VDB mourns not just because she has to carry out the tasks of a slave. The reference to VDB being "without a throne" means more than loss of rule; it is written in the language of mourning which relates to death.[29] KOB like VDB is also bereft of his throne. Unlike the other rulers of the earth who have died and reside in Sheol, on their thrones, KOB is denied a throne in death—he is to lie on a bed of maggots with worms to cover him (14:11). There is a play on words in v. 9—*mks'wtm* "their thrones," and in v. 11—*mksyk* "your covering." The kings have their thrones, KOB has his covering of worms. Further (v. 20), KOB will not be joined with the kings of the nations in death because of his ill treatment of his own people. For similar reasons, VDB will lose her throne—she has abused God's own people.

Chapter 47, like 14 and the true laments, is written in qinah meter.

(4) The *life and achievements* of the deceased are mentioned, not in praise, but in condemnation (47:6b). The cruelties of KOB in Isaiah 14 include the following: unceasing blows and relentless persecution of nations (14:6), hewing trees (14:8), making the earth into a desert, overthrowing cities, refusing to let prisoners return home (14:17), destruction of his land and people (14:20). The main condemnation against VDB is her merciless treatment of God's inheritance, God's people. VDB placed a heavy yoke upon the aged.

An additional feature unique to all of the descriptions of Babylon in the book of Isaiah, is VDB's lifelong devotion to magic, astrology, and sorcery (vv. 10, 12-13). This lifelong devotion emphasized VDB's folly, rather than the wisdom she claimed to have. In fact, this devotion in the end led to her destruction (v. 10).

Several times throughout the poem VDB speaks of herself in a fashion similar to the boastful pretensions of KOB in Isaiah 14. In the true lament, others sing of the incomparability of the deceased. Here Babylon vaunts herself as incomparable—"I am, and there is no other" (vv. 8, 10). She exalts herself in an exaggerated fashion as "mistress forever" (v. 7). But the reader is well aware, from the beginning of the poem to the end, that these are mistaken pretensions of a defeated power. The speaker challenges VDB to depend on her powers, and suggests mockingly "perhaps you may succeed, perhaps you will inspire awe" (v. 12). VDB's boasts are empty words; this is a parody of the motif of incomparability, a parody of the hyperbole often included in laments.

As VDB proclaims her incomparability, she also seems to be claiming to be impervious to the powers of death. She believes, mistakenly, that she will never grieve the death of husband or children (vv. 8-9). In fact, these two things happen to her suddenly, without warning. She will become a widow, and she will be bereft of her children.

---

29 Taylor, 165.

KOB and his descendants suffer the same fate. Because of his evil deeds, his descendants will not be named. Because of his guilt, his children will be slaughtered (14:20b-21).

(5) There is no *call to mourners to weep* in this poem. In fact, no one mourns VDB's fate. VDB and KOB at one time caused nations to tremble, and inspired awe (47:12, 14:16). Now, VDB will be exposed to humiliation ("your nakedness will be uncovered, your shame will be seen" v. 3); the implication is that anyone seeing the sorry condition of VDB will rejoice rather than grieve over what has happened. One of the features in the lament of David over Saul and Jonathan is the attempt to keep news of the deaths from the enemies so that they could not gloat (2 Sam 1:20). VDB's enemies will have occasion to gloat and taunt as VDB is stripped and exposed before all to see. The fate of KOB was that he would be the object of scorn and derision, as people pondered how this once intimidating and powerful ruler could have been brought so low (14:16-17).

(6) No one *expresses grief* at these occurrences. The underlying tone of mocking and taunt throughout express the sense of retribution at what happens to VDB. The use of negatives to communicate personal grief in true laments has been turned to a very different purpose. "No more shall you be called" by grand titles (vv. 1, 5). The tone of mocking comes from the audience's awareness that VDB is deluded in her belief that these titles were hers in perpetuity. As in the parody in Isaiah 14, the negations ("no one to deliver, no coal for warming, no one to save" in vv. 14-15) here evoke a sense of satisfaction and retribution as the ignominious end of VDB, her helplessness in the face of what is to come, and abandonment by her cohorts are in sight.

The several features of the lament which are taken up in Isaiah 47 do not constitute a full fledged lament, or a parody of a lament as in Isaiah 14. However, the two poems (14 and 47) are similar in many respects, especially since both involve satisfaction at the death of KOB and VDB. The aspect of taunt or mocking is strong is both. The theme of the downfall of a great and arrogant ruler is also an important feature of both poems.

One feature of the lament proper that is exploited in these poems relating the fall of Babylon is that of the contrast between "then" and "now," "life" and "death."[30] The wonder of the past accentuates the agony of loss in the present. A related opposition which is played up in the two poems is that of "up" and "down."[31] In the past ("then"), KOB was the mighty ruler who prevailed over nations, "now" he is powerless, an exposed corpse trodden under foot. VDB in the past was considered to be mistress of kingdoms, she lived in security, relying on her magical powers. Now VDB is dethroned, and has no one to rely on.

The up and down movement of the two poems is integral to the development of both. In Isaiah 14 the tyrant's fall is illustrated in a variety of ways. The hewer does not "come up" to hew trees because he (the tyrant) has

---

[30] Yee, 572-73.

[31] See Robert H. O'Connell, "Isaiah XIV 4b-23: Ironic Reversal Through Concentric Structure and Mythic Allusion," *VT* 38 (1988) 407-418, on the "upward/downward movement."

been "laid low."[32] Sheol wakes up the shades and raises the kings from their throne as the tyrant arrives.[33] Day Star, son of dawn aspired to ascend to the heavens, and set his throne on high. Instead he falls from heaven, cut down to the ground, is brought down to Sheol, to the pit.[34] He wants to reach the far recesses of Mount Zaphon, but instead reaches the far recesses of the pit.

The motif of descending and rising is a unifying element in Isaiah 47. It begins with the first word, a command to Babylon to "go down," and continues with the various commands throughout to "go" into darkness, to "sit down" in the dust. Not only is VDB's descent described, but also the descent of a variety of evils with which she will be punished (vv. 9, 11, 13). Later on in the poem, VDB is commanded to stand up, to arise and stand for judgment. The poem ends with VDB's cohorts, wandering helplessly, without direction.

Both VDB and KOB presume to attain to the status or near status of divinity. KOB says in his heart ($\gic{}mr\ blbb$) "I will ascend to the heavens, . . . to the mount of the assembly . . . I will make myself like the Most High" (14:13-14). VDB says in her heart ($h\gic{}mrh\ blbbh$), "I am and there is no other" (47:8, 10). This is a claim to divinity. Elsewhere in Isaiah 40-48 similar words are spoken by Yahweh (Isa 45:5, 18, 21, 22, 46:9). Both KOB and VDB are brought down, and their claims shown to be without substance.

An obvious connection between the poems is the identify of the addressees. The king of Babylon ($mlk\ bbl$, 14:4a) is the addressee and subject of 14:4b-21, mistress of kingdoms, queen ($gbrt\ mmlkwt$ and $gbrt$) of 47. Both poems address and speak of a royal figure, an imperial power. In the case of chapter 14, the King of Babylon is sometimes identified with a specific ruler of Babylon (Nebuchadnezzar or Nabonidus have been suggested). VDB in chapter 47 is a metaphor for the Babylonian empire, or more specifically, the capital city, Babylon. In this respect the poems are somewhat different. In chapter 47, the figure of VDB acts as a foil to that of Daughter Zion, a pervasive theme of chapters 49-55. As VDB descends, loses power and status, Zion rises from exile, gains power and status.

The same pattern holds true for chapter 14 in that the king of Babylon functions as a foil for the idealized messianic king of Isaiah 11.[35] Clements, for example, sees one of the explanations for the inclusion of the anti-Babylon prophecies of 13-14:23 to be related to a preoccupation with the fate of the Davidic kingship, as well as the temple.[36] Some examples of identical terminology in Isaiah 11 and 14 will help in demonstrating that relationship between the two chapters, and point to the possibility of a third connection, with Isaiah 40-66. A term used to describe the messianic king in Isa 11:1 is $n\?r$, a "branch" from the root of Jesse. The same term is used of KOB in 14:19, but

---

32 Yee, 576.

33 Yee, 577.

34 Yee, 578.

35 Chapter 13, which portrays the destruction of the whole earth, and the return of all nature to chaos, has as its opposite the idyllic portrayal of the days of the messianic king, when nature will return to its state of harmony (11:6-9). Isa 65:25 is a variation on Isa 11:6-9.

36 R. E. Clements, "Isaiah 14,22-27: A Central Passage Reconsidered," in *The Book of Isaiah/Le Livre d'Isaïe*, ed. J. Vermeylen (BETL 81; Leuven: University Press, 1989), p. 262.

the sense is very different. He is referred to as a *nṣr ntʿb*, "a loathsome branch."
In the first instance (11:1), the coming of the messianic ruler is a sign of the
restoration of order, justice.[37] In the case of KOB, he will be known as a
loathsome branch in his death, and will be cast out like a rejected carcass.
The term *nṣr* appears only three times in the book of Isaiah. The last
occurrence is in 60:21, where it is a symbol of God's planting his people once
more in the land. The symbol is used as an image of the ideal davidic
monarch, the defeated Babylonian king, and finally God's people once more
planted in the land from which they had been dispossessed.

This messianic king (11:4) will smite (*hkh*) the earth with the rod (*šbt*) of
his mouth, and will slay the wicked (*ršʿ*). The same terms are used in the
description of the reign and the defeat of the reign of KOB. The staff of the
wicked (*ršʾym*) will be broken by God, as well as the rod (*šbt*) (of the kings who
smote (*mkh*) the nations. The rod or scepter was the sign of the might and
power of KOB.

The terms used in chapter 11 to describe the reign of the messianic king
are used in chapter 14 to describe God's destruction of KOB. If we interpret
these terms in chapter 14 to be allusions to chapter 11, in chapter 14 the role of
the messianic king has been taken over by God who will accomplish those
things that previously were expectations of a now non-existent Davidic ruler.
Furthermore, reading 14:19 and 60:21 as reinterpretations of 11:1, the overall
direction of these allusions can show a development from reliance on the
righteous Davidic ruler ("branch") in the eighth century (or pre-exilic times),
to destruction of the loathsome Babylonian imperial rule, to the
reestablishment of the "branch" in the form of an entire righteous people.

This paper has not discussed the relationship of chapters 24-27 to the satiric
laments against KOB and VDB. But further investigations of the
interrelationships between the contrasts of KOB and the messianic ruler, VDB
and Daughter Zion, and contrasts in this section may prove fruitful. Sweeney
has pointed out a number of allusions in Isaiah 24-27 whereby the author of
this section has reinterpreted other sections of the book of Isaiah to form
striking contrasts thereby demonstrating a unique hermeneutical purpose.[38]
For example, in 26:1-6, the poet develops a contrast between the once lofty
fallen city and the strong city. The inhabitants of the lofty city are brought
low, down to the earth, down to the dust, much like KOB and VDB. Reading
26:1-6 in light of 2:6-21, Sweeney sees the day of the Lord to include Yahweh's
establishment of Jerusalem as well as the downfall of the lofty city. The fall of
VDB in chapter 47 is likewise connected to the flight from Babylon (Isa 48:20)
and the return to Zion.[39]

Sweeney shows a connection between the birth imagery of 26:7-18 and
numerous passages in First, Second and Third Isaiah, but especially

---

[37] P. Ackroyd, "Isaiah 1-12: Presentation of a Prophet," *Studies in the Religious Tradition of
the OT* (London: SCM. 1987), 101, sees this as the climax of the section 9:7-11. He points to
the contrast between the overthrow of the exalted trees in 10:33-34 and the establishment
of the Davidic shoot.

[38] Sweeney (1988).

[39] Sweeney (1988), 49, also shows the theme of the restoration of Israel in Zion to be a
key theme of Isa 27:2-13.

emphasizes the connections between Isa 13:8 and Isa 66:17.[40] The imagery and vocabulary of these verses link major themes—"judgment against Babylon and rebirth for Israel at Zion." While there is no lexical correspondence between Isaiah 47 and these verses, we are reminded of the loss of children of VDB, and the contrasting theme of the fruitfulness of Daughter Zion in chapters 49-55.[41]

The taunting or mocking aspects of the poems against KOB and VDB may be compared to the taunting of Sennacherib in Isa 37:22-29. That there are connections with Second Isaiah Seitz has clearly demonstrated.[42] More specifically, in comparison with Isaiah 47, we note that the taunt song against Sennacherib begins with Virgin Daughter Zion, followed by Daughter Jerusalem, as the one doing the mocking. Isaiah 47 begins with Virgin Daughter Babylon, followed by Daughter Chaldea as the object of the taunt. The despised tyrant in 37:24 reveals his plan to ascend to far recesses of Lebanon, and to hew down the trees, much like KOB in Isaiah 14. A formal analysis of this taunt song may show further interconnections between the three segments of the book of Isaiah which mention Babylon by name. A further study of the relationship between passages which specifically mention Assyria[43] and the references to Babylon may also shed light on the redactional function of references to the imperial power in the book of Isaiah.

---

[40] Sweeney (1988), 48-49.

[41] See Isa 49:20-21, 54:1-4.

[42] Seitz, (1991), 84, 200.

[43] For instance, Isa 23:13, which refers to Chaldeans and Assyria.

On the Question of Divisions Internal to the Book of Isaiah

Christopher R. Seitz
Yale University

The division of Isaiah into thirds has become a commonplace, reinforced by the many commentary series (including the newer ones) that perpetuate, even if for neutral or simply practical reasons, this increasingly time-honored convention.[1] Different sorts of considerations go into the division of other large prophetic books (Jeremiah and Ezekiel), while in the case of Isaiah critical adherence to an old notion of separate Isaianic personalities (Isaiah, Deutero-Isaiah, Trito-Isaiah), even if now giving way to a more strictly literary conception, has led to the convenient partitioning of the book into three blocks (1-39; 40-55; 56-66).[2]

We are, of course, becoming much more aware of the internal relationships across these standard divisions. By this I do not mean the older conception of prophetic disciples carrying on the work of their Isaianic forebears. Rather, in the Book of Isaiah we meet with clear efforts at editorial coordination, however rough or intermittent, running across three sections once deemed relatively independent, the inspired efforts of individuals, schools, or prophets working at three specific, independent moments in time and space. It is true that on this reckoning Isaiah 1-39 was always a difficult block to understand in terms that were too strictly independent, since it appeared to be comprised of material from very different ages, some of these contemporaneous with or post-dating Isaiah 40-55, if not also 56-66. Actually, what now seems striking in retrospect is how little effort it took to view portions of text in First Isaiah acknowledged to be late as totally unrelated to texts in chapters 40-66. Such was the force of the independence model, especially in respect of First and Second Isaiah. I have remarked on this curiosity in more detail in another context.[3] But for our purposes I trust that the

---

[1] This makes the decision of the *Word Biblical Commentary* series to divide at chapters 33/34 appear idiosyncratic, bold, or prophetic. On divisions in prophetic books, see my remarks in the introduction to *Reading and Preaching the Book of Isaiah* (Philadelphia: Fortress, 1988) 13-22.

[2] On the critical distinctions reflected in the various terminologies (First Isaiah, Deutero-Isaiah, Pseudo-Isaiah, etc.), see "Isaiah, Book of (First Isaiah)," *The Anchor Bible Dictionary* (Vol. 3; D. N. Freedman, ed.; New York: Doubleday, 1992) 472-488.

[3] See "Two Independent Isaiahs," in *Zion's Final Destiny* (Minneapolis: Fortress, 1991) 1-35.

history of the discussion of critical work on Isaiah, including its more recent phases, is familiar enough and that my brief summary up to this point is relatively uncontroversial.

The point I wish to emphasize is that a sensitivity to—and indeed an emphasis on—the relationship between texts across sections traditionally partitioned may have little or no effect on the divisions themselves, whether they ought to be retained, re-thought, adjusted, and so forth. I found myself arguing for a wide variety of associations between chapters 1-39 and the other two sections of the book when writing a commentary on First Isaiah, for a series which has adopted the standard division without further ado (*Interpretation*). I anticipate doing the same when writing on chapters 40-66 for the *New Interpreters Bible* series, and the same general tack would commend itself to me were I to write a commentary on 56-66 for *Hermeneia*. But in each of these cases the convention of three divisions would be retained within the framework of the commentary series in question, regardless how compelling the evidence relative to each section for its intended affiliation with the other two. In short, in my experience what we now have is an odd set of circumstances in which the older tripartite convention is retained in order to identify its points of overstatement. On this score, Isaiah work at present has something of the hands of Esau, and the voice of Jacob.

Still, working within the conventional model of division, in a commentary on "First Isaiah," I was able to point out both in the front matter and in the commentary proper why the term still had a certain legitimacy, but also why on occasion it ought to be placed in scare quotes. My argument in favor of a continued division at chapters 39 and 40 is not the traditional one (meaning here "historical-critical"), but neither is it uncontroversial, even given recent trends toward "unitary" readings of Isaiah. Dependent on conclusions reached in an earlier essay, I argued that chapters 40-66 belong to a different—self-consciously different—temporal perspective, one that understands itself within the presentation of the larger Book of Isaiah as looking back on the "former things" as truly former.[4] These include not only the person of Isaiah,[5] but also especially his word regarding the divine destiny of Assyria, Babylonia, and the nations—a message now located in chapters 1-39, but referred to within chapters 40-49 as the "former things."[6] To state the issue negatively: when we confront a first-person voice in chapters 40-66 we confront neither the voice of Isaiah nor a persona constructed to fictively represent that voice. In other words, Isaiah 40-55 does not represent an early reflex toward pseudepigraphy, as this will later emerge in mature form. Yet precisely what is characteristic of chapters 1-39, "First Isaiah," is that the the Isaiah persona—however withdrawn in comparison with Jeremiah or Ezekiel—is nevertheless maintained throughout.[7] This reinforces the sense

---

4 "The Divine Council: Temporal Transition and New Prophecy in the Book of Isaiah," *JBL* 109 (1990) 229-247.

5 In my view, Isaiah's is a voice of the past in Second Isaiah chapters, symbolized in the opening divine council scene by the unknown voice who says "all flesh is grass."

6 See my final chapter in *Zion's Final Destiny*.

7 See my remarks in "Isaiah 1-66: Making Sense of the Whole," in *Reading and Preaching the Book of Isaiah*, especially pp. 116-122.

that one is meant to see a dividing point at chapter 40, between a former period of real Assyrian assault and prophetically foreseen Babylonian world-judgment (for the latter see especially chapters 13-14, 21, 24-27, 39), and the actual fulfillment of that same world-judgment, on whose other side chapters 40-66 stand, looking back on both the proclamation and the person of Isaiah of Jerusalem.

But then there are also scare quotes to be reckoned with, which imply that any undue emphasis on the separatedness of Isaiah 1-39 as "First Isaiah" would be misleading. Here one should also reckon with the possibility that Isaiah's final shape is only penultimately concerned with the presentation of Isaiah the prophet, his extension or non-extension into chapters 40-66, as a key index in understanding the book's final form or divisions relevant within that form. Perhaps a better way to put it is that interest in the prophetic voice of Isaiah is only one index operating in the book, capable of coordination with the former-latter things distinction, represented by chapters 1-39 and 40-66 respectively. Yet my own work on "First Isaiah," precisely at the juncture between these two major sections of the larger book (chapters 33-39) revealed that efforts have also been made to bring the two halves into clear coordination, thus blurring the sharpness of the literary division between them while at the same time ruling out any possible conception of two independent "books," unrelated to one another and to be read as such (I will turn to the question of a Third Isaiah shortly). I will simply summarize my findings here and direct the reader to a fuller treatment in the *Interpretation* volume, especially in the section on chapters 33-35, a portion of which is reproduced below.

Scholars have long seen the connection between chapters 34-35 and so-called Second Isaiah, and one recent interpreter has gone so far as to call chapter 35 a redactional bridge linking the two halves of the book. But why would such a bridge be constructed *before* chaps. 36-39?[8] Steck has his own answer to this question, which I regard as diachronically possible, but extraordinarily *überspitzt* and unnecessarily complex (though probably necessitated by his dense redaction-critical argumentation and logic which involves the whole Isaiah book). My own position bears some slight resemblance to an earlier theory of Torrey.[9] On this view, chapters 34-35 both anticipate themes in Second Isaiah, as numerous commentators note, but they also change our interpretation of intervening chapters (36-39). What once stood, in my judgment, as the culmination of First Isaiah traditions (chaps. 36-38), the narrative vindication of Isaiah's earlier Zion proclamation and Immanuel preaching,[10] has now been incorporated within traditions

---

[8] O. Steck, *Bereitete Heimkehr: Jesaja 35 als redactionelle Brücke zwischen dem Ersten und dem Zweiten Jesaja* (SBS 121; Stuttgart: Katholisches Bibelwerk, 1985).

[9] C. C. Torrey, *The Second Isaiah* (New York: Charles Scribner's Sons, 1928) esp. 98-104. On the significance of a gap between chaps. 33 and 34 in 1Q Isa(a), see also P. Kahle, *Die Hebräischen Handschriften aus der Hoehle* (Stuttgart: Kohlhammer, 1951) 72f.; also, W. H. Brownlee, *The Meaning of the Qumran Scrolls for the Bible With Special Attention to the Book of Isaiah* (New York: Oxford University, 1964) 247-259.

[10] This is essentially the thesis of *Zion's Final Destiny*.

concerning Zion's imminent exaltation following the judgment of Babylon, the return of exiles, and the restoration of that same Zion (chapters 34-35,40-55).

The effect achieved in the present shape of Isaiah is that the very close connection between the account of Zion's dramatic deliverance and prior "First Isaiah" literary traditions has been "loosened," as it were, in order that this dramatic deliverance might serve as a "type" which, in the final form of the book, now foreshadows God's final vindication of Zion after Babylonian assaults.[11] Moving beyond the depiction of chaps. 36-39, these assaults reached even "beyond the neck," to use the earlier idiom describing the onslaughts of "the mighty flood waters of the River, the king of Assyria and all his glory" (8:7-8), which are themselves "types" anticipating later assaults by the great Sea, Babylon (see Isa. 21:1-10). This "sea," like the Assyrian waters before it, will also be rendered impotent (43:2), dried up as once the Red Sea was dried up (43:16), slain as a "dragon in the sea" (27:1), replaced by divine waters (55:1), as once water was given in the wilderness (43:20). These rich themes are now sounded—before the account of Zion's deliverance—in chapters 34-35, thus making the dramatic deliverance which follows a historical example of God's final intentions, a surety or pledge, as it were (compare 7:11 and 38:7). In these chapters it is Edom that stands as the destroyed "No Kingdom," anticipating the fates both of Assyria in chapters 36-38, and Babylonia in chapters 39 and following.[12] Above all it is chapter 35 that resounds with the message of chapters 40-55, promising sight and hearing where once these were forfeited (Isa. 6:10), a rejuvenated creation, and a highway of safe passage to Zion. The deliverance of Zion and faithful king in the chapters immediately following offers a foretaste of the promised weal: a sign unrefused, provided for the reader, bearing witness to the faithfulness of the One who promises and the promises themselves.

As this brief summary is fairly compressed, let me quote at some length from my earlier treatment in *Isaiah 1-39*. This will also allow aspects of my larger conception of Isaiah, especially including chapters 13-27, to come into view.

> In a very general sense, one can see that by prefacing the narratives that tell of Zion's deliverance in 701 B.C. with chapters 34-35, the specific historical instance of Zion's protection in the days of Sennacherib has been placed within a much broader framework of God's ongoing attention and care for his vineyard amidst the nations at large. The wonderous deliverance of 701 B.C. foreshadows Zion's final triumph as God's chosen place of exaltation and return. The Assyrian destroyer about to be destroyed (chap. 33) becomes a type of the nations at large (34:1-4); God's gracious sparing of the old vineyard, after Assyrian waters reached to the very neck, becomes a type of God's total protection of the new vineyard from any and all violation, as promised in 27:2-6. Still, such typology might have been

11 De-historicizing would be too strong a term for this redactional move, since the linkage to 701 events remains. I therefore would prefer the term "typologizing," as this respects both the type's original locus in history and tradition, but also its capacity to engender later associations beyond those first intended.

12 The destruction of Babylon, revealed in a "stern vision" to Isaiah in chapter 21, is there also associated with Edom (21:11-12).

executed equally well with chapters 34-35 *following* the account of Zion's deliverance in chapters 36-39 rather than preceding it.

We would seek the primary explanation for the present location of chapters 34-35 in a slightly different realm, as having to do with the merger of First Isaiah and Second Isaiah chapters into one synthetic presentation whose combined portrayal is greater than the sum of its parts. I have argued in another context for a First Isaiah collection that once ended dramatically with the account of Zion's deliverance in 701 B.C., as the culmination and vindication of the prophet's complex Zion and royal theology. The presentation of chapters 28-33 would have led logically into chapters 36-39 .... The effect of the placement of chapters 34-35 has been to "enclose" this dramatic finale with material from Second Isaiah on either side. Zion's deliverance is no longer an act of historical significance validating Isaiah's preaching; it is that, and more: the Hezekiah narratives in chapters 36-39 point ahead to God's final defense of his new vineyard, with a new and restored Zion at its center. The violators of the new vineyard will come to the same end as the Assyrian destroyer in Isaiah's day.

One other major effect is achieved. The sharpness of the distinction between "First" and "Second" Isaiah is blurred by the placement of chapters 34-35. It is impossible to link these two "halves" of the book neatly with fixed historical periods, one fluctuating around the key date of 701 B.C. and the other around the key date of 587 B.C. Already "First" Isaiah has a major level of tradition under the influence of the events of 587, namely, the nations section (chaps. 13-27). Now those "First" Isaiah chapters most closely connected to historical events in the period of Isaiah's preaching, concerning the deliverance of Jerusalem in "the fourteenth year of King Hezekiah" (36:1), have been enclosed within "Second" Isaiah chapters. To be sure, the final chapter (chap. 39) eases the transition to the "Babylonian" half of the book, with its reference to coming Babylonian assault. But that transition is effected not just by means of prophecy-fulfillment schemes (39:5-7) but also by the present arrangement of chapters 34-39 as such.

Moreover, it is now a striking fact that the first half of the book, strictly speaking (what the Masoretes mark in the margin of the Hebrew text as "midpoint of the book according to verse count"), comes precisely at the twentieth verse of chapter 33, practically where chapter 34 picks up with its vision of the new vineyard's protection. While scholarship may prefer to speak of a division of the Book of Isaiah into two or three sections, marked at chapters 39/40 and 55/56, a more significant division in the final shaping of the tradition may now be found at 33/34, at the halfway point of the sixty-six-chapter full presentation. In a manner of speaking, chapters 34-35 introduce a "second" Isaiah: sustained speech concerned with the aftermath of Babylonian desolation and Zion's restoration (chaps. 40-66). In so doing, they "enclose" the record of Zion's deliverance and royal triumph in the days of Assyrian assault (chaps. 36-39) within a broader framework of God's care for Zion against all assaults of the nations.

One other factor is to be considered in this context, regarding the "merger" of two Isaiahs. In chapters 1-33, texts abound that point to or presuppose the destruction of Jerusalem in 587 B.C. But as was noted above, we have no formal record of that desolation, such as we find in the Books of Jeremiah or Ezekiel. What remains of paramount concern to those who have shaped the present tradition is not Zion's defeat but rather *God's fundamental, abiding concern for Zion's final triumph and permanent fortification against the nations.* Chapters 34-35 speak of that triumph; chapters 36-39 give a concrete example of God's care at one moment in Zion's history; and chapters 40-66 pursue the same line of interest. We do not move from "first" to "second" Isaiah by way of a record of Zion's defeat but, more mysteriously, from the promise of victory amidst the nations (chaps. 34-35), to one miraculous victory in the past (chaps. 36-38), to foreseen exile (chap. 39), and finally to bold words of comfort and forgiveness (chap. 40). First and Second Isaiah are not distinguished merely as preexilic and postexilic blocks of tradition but rather as promised and revealed phases of Zion's ongoing destiny, as God's place of exaltation and Israel's place of return. (*Isaiah 1-39*, 240-42)

One final aspect of the question of internal divisions in Isaiah yet to be discussed is revealed in this lengthy quote. On occasion I have referred above to the second half of Isaiah as comprising chapters 40-55, traditionally called Second Isaiah, or more broadly as 40-66 (in the context of analyzing the function of chaps. 34-39). Here too we touch on the question of the propriety of a further division internal to Isaiah, namely that which marks off Second from Third Isaiah. There is not space to treat the question in detail, so I offer only these few remarks.

1) I remain convinced that the major scholarly reason for separating the material in these chapters was neither temporal nor literary, but geographical. So it was argued: chaps. 40-55 were written in Babylonian exile; 56-66 reflect prophecies back at home, concerning the cult and community membership. What if this distinction is faulty and chaps. 40-55 were to be better understood as Jerusalemite both in orientation (as many have admitted) and in origin (as most have not). The consequence would be that one of the strongest planks in the argument for a distinct "Trito-Isaiah" corpus would be removed.[13]

2) There seems little evidence to me that the material in 40-66 can be separated temporally on the basis of the temple being rebuilt in 56-66, but not in 40-55. This might mean that material in 40-55 is later than some have thought, but also that 56-66 is earlier.

3) Even if arguments for the tight structure and literary organization of 40-55 be granted (with further division between 40-48 and 49-55), this says nothing, in my view, about subsequent shaping, which may have the explicit intention of merging these two sections into one roughly continuous whole. The rubrics provided at 48:22, 57:21, and 66:24, if indeed that is what they are, have divided the entire 27 chapter collection into even thirds (40-48; 49-57; 58-66), obliterating any (possibly original) division at 55/56. And, as suggested above, even this "second" Isaiah (40-66) has been shaped in the final presentation of the book into a yet more obvious second half, marked now by a division at chapter 33, with 34-35 enclosing 36-39 in the manner described above.

In the foregoing my attention has been most closely focused on *Zion* as key to the interpretation of the book as a whole and the divisions that give the book structure and dramatic movement. The one major question that cannot

---

13 See "Isaiah, Book of (Third Isaiah)," *Anchor Bible Dictionary*, 500-510.

be treated here, but which is also affected by one's notions of both divisions and the role of typological editing (and thinking) in the book, involves royal and messianic material in the larger shape of the book as a whole. Are earlier royal promises made by Isaiah transferred to Cyrus in later chapters or to the people as a whole, as many have contended? Or would this represent perhaps a too straightforwardly *linear* conception of Isaiah's final form, understood even on purely synchronic terms?[14] That is, are earlier promises in the final form of the book (esp. those in chapters 9 and 11), whether understood on diachronic or synchronic terms, eclipsed or rendered otiose in later sections of the book, or do they retain their force simply by dint of remaining as yet unfulfilled?[15]

Here is a place where one must acknowledge that moves toward synchronic readings, especially in Isaiah, still require enormous attention to a whole nest of difficult historical-critical and diachronic issues. For the resolution of (especially these) difficult theological issues, synchronic readings will find themselves not avoiding diachronic analysis, but returning to it when all is said and done. There is nothing obvious about the intended redactional structure of a book like Isaiah, taken synchronically, or the way it was meant to be read as it moved from the hand of the "last editor" to that of the "first reader." It is for this reason that the chief question facing modern interpreters is not if but how diachronic analysis should be properly utilized so as to illuminate and make comprehensible the final canonical shape of the Book of Isaiah, which can be read synchronically to be sure, but which has never lost its high degree of historical referentiality. This referentiality has been recast and reconceived in the highly complex final presentation, but in the movement toward textualization and final canonical stabilization it has by no means vanished or become somehow "internalized." The Book of Isaiah is not modern literature, and the fact that it bears the marks of a distinct culture, history, and social matrix cannot be ignored even in (or one might say, especially in) a climate concerned to understand the book's final canonical shape.

---

14 The problem is a major one. To what degree are portions of the text "left behind" as one moves ahead in a more synchronic orientation? See for example David Meade's treatment of the royal theme in his analysis of the final form of the entire Isaiah collection, trading on the work of others (*Pseudonymity and Canon* [WUNT 39; Tübingen: J. C. B. Mohr (Paul Siebeck) 1986]). His reading strikes me as too linear, and insufficiently atuned to the effects of typological editing in the Book of Isaiah. The problem of correct understanding of principles of organization in Isaiah (thematic, chronological, etc.) is a very old one (see the *Anchor Bible Dictionary* essay on First Isaiah cited above).

15 See my discussion in *Isaiah 1-39*, pp. 95-105.

On Multiple Settings in the Book of Isaiah

Marvin A. Sweeney
University of Miami

I

One of the primary achievements of the Isaiah seminar is the recognition of both the synchronic and the diachronic character of the book of Isaiah.[1] Although Isaiah contains blocks of material that were composed, at least in part, in relation to distinct socio-historical settings, the present form of Isaiah constitutes a discreet literary entity in and of itself, rather than a collection of two, three, or more originally independent prophetic compositions. Scholars have come to recognize that although some of these components have a demonstrable compositional history, they can no longer be treated entirely in isolation from the literary context of the book as a whole. Indeed, some scholars have correctly questioned whether blocks such as chapters 1-39 or 56-66 ever existed as independent prophetic compositions.[2]

This recognition has important implications for the interpretation of Isaiah in that it calls into question the standard historical-critical model for writing commentaries on separate parts of Isaiah, such as Isaiah 1-39; 40-55; 56-66; or even 40-66, as if they were separate books. Although the original composition of the individual texts in the book ranges at least from the 8th through the 5th centuries,[3] the emergence of a 66-chapter book of Isaiah presents a new literary context that will necessarily affect the interpretation of all its constituent sub-units. Whether the constituent texts are composed relatively early or relatively late in the book's compositional history, the full literary form of the book will define the framework in which all of the constituent sub-units function as well as the overall interpretational context to which they contribute and which, in turn, will influence their interpretation. Commentators must therefore account for individual texts from the book *both* in relation to the compositional settings in which they were produced *and* in relation to the later literary contexts or settings in which these texts appear.

---

[1] See R. Rendtorff, "The Book of Isaiah: A Complex Unity. Synchronic and Diachronic Reading," *Society of Biblical Literature 1991 Seminar Papers* (ed. E. H. Lovering, Jr.; Atlanta: Scholars Press, 1991) 8-20.

[2] R. Rendtorff, "Zur Komposition des Buches Jesajas," *VT* 34 (1984) 295-320; C. R. Seitz, "Isaiah 1-66: Making Sense of the Whole," *Reading and Preaching the Book of Isaiah* (ed. C. R. Seitz; Philadelphia: Fortress, 1988) 105-126.

[3] M. A. Sweeney, *Isaiah 1-4 and the Post-Exilic Understanding of the Isaianic Tradition* (BZAW 171; Berlin and New York: Walter de Gruyter, 1988).

This brief paper will therefore attempt to examine the role that such multiple settings play in the interpretation of the book of Isaiah. It will first examine recent developments in the conception of setting and its relationship to the interpretation of biblical texts. It will then examine the royal psalm of thanksgiving in Isaiah 9:1-6 in relation to its compositional setting and the subsequent literary settings in which it functions. Isaiah 9:1-6 serves as an example of the impact of multiple settings on the interpretation of texts in Isaiah in that it plays a major role in defining the overall perspectives and expectations of the book throughout the history of its composition and its interpretation is, in turn, influenced by the literary settings in which it appears.

II

Form-critical methodology presupposes an integral relationship between literature and human life so that any discussion of the interpretation of biblical texts must address the question of setting, including both *Sitz im Leben*, the social contexts in which genres function, and situation, the specific circumtances in which texts function. It is not always possible to reconstruct the original compositional setting of a text, but every text is composed in relation to a specific set of social and historical circumstances that play a major role in defining its overall outlook, modes of expression, and concerns. Although the compositional setting of the text does not necessarily determine the meaning of a text after the time of its composition, its form and initial intention is determined in large measure by its author and the setting in which the author composes the text.

The concept of *Sitz im Leben* has undergone some development in the history of form-critical discussion. In his analysis of the history of the concept of *Sitz im Leben*, Martin Buss demonstrates that Hermann Gunkel's conceptualization of *Sitz im Leben* synthesized two major elements: "a concern with genres and a historical focus on originating circumstances."[4] This conceptualization combines a concern with literature, whether oral or written, and the socio-historical circumstances in which it is written and which play a major role in defining its literary form and intention. The interrelationship between literature and its socio-historical setting, whether that of its author or that of its readers, must play a primary role in the interpretation of literature. But Buss points out that Gunkel made an invalid distinction between the authentic "oral" or "life" situations in which a text is composed and its artificial "written" stages.[5] This distinction is undoubtedly rooted in 19th century Romanticist conceptions of the purity and spontaneity of the primitive religious spirit as opposed to the mechanical pedanticism of scribes who did not comprehend the spiritual impulses of the oral literature. Gunkel's emphasis on the "original" circumstances of a text's composition therefore placed undue emphasis on defining the interpretation of a text in relation to

---

[4] M. J. Buss, "The Idea of *Sitz im Leben*—History and Critique," *ZAW* 90 (1978) 157-170, see p. 157.

[5] Buss, "The Idea of *Sitz im Leben*," 157-60

the author's setting and intentions, but he overlooked the setting in which a text is received as a significant element in its interpretation.

More recent methodological discussion of the sociology of language has developed Gunkel's ideas by placing greater emphasis on the interrelationship between texts and the socio-historical settings that generate them.[6] Thus, Steck emphasizes a literary-sociological conception of setting in which literary genres must be defined in relation to both the literary context in which they appear and the socio-cultural conditions and circumstances that produce them.[7] Richter defines three types of settings that define texts, including institutions, the style of an epoch, and literature itself.[8] This last point is particularly important in that it emphasizes the formative role of literature, or the *Sitz in der Literatur*,[9] alongside the more customary *Sitz im Leben* in the composition of texts. In other words, literature itself provides a component of the setting in which literature is created.

But literature also plays a role in defining social reality, and this role must be examined in order to understand fully the interaction between literature and human life. In reference to myth, for example, Knierim points out that myth creates reality ritually in that myth is inseparably related to its ritual setting.[10] Likewise, the studies of oral literature by Parry and Lord demonstrate that each performance of oral literature is a unique social event in that each performance creates a new literary text that is heard for the first time by the audience on hand.[11] In both cases, the performance of ritual or oral literature plays a constitutive role in the creation of social reality in that the performances reinforce social identity by reiterating the world views, mores, social practices, history, and other factors that define the culture.

Both of these examples focus on the performance of oral literature, but written literature can play a similar role in defining social reality. The liturgical reading of Torah, for example, regularly reinforces the social and religious identity of Jewish communities. In the case of Ezra's reading of the Torah upon his return to Jerusalem in the late 5th century, the implementation of the written Torah's stipulations and the authority granted to those stipulations by the history of YHWH's interaction with Israel as presented in the Torah together play a constitutive role in defining the reality of the post-exilic Jewish community. Likewise, Koch demonstrates that Ezra's return to Jerusalem is presented in part as a fulfillment of prophecy in the book of Isaiah, in that Ezra's return is presented as the "second Exodus"

6 Buss, "The Idea of *Sitz im Leben*," 165-170; see esp. R. P. Knierim, "Old Testament Form Criticism Reconsidered," *Int* 27 (1973) 435-468.

7 O. H. Steck, *Exegese des Alten Testaments. Leitfaden der Methodik* (12th edition; Neukirchen-Vluyn: Neukirchener, 1989) 114-119.

8 W. Richter, *Exegese als Literaturwissenschaft. Entwurf einer alttestamentlichen Literatur Theorie und Methodologie* (Göttingen: Vandenhoeck & Ruprecht, 1971) 145-148.

9 Richter, *Exegese als Literaturwissenschaft* 148.

10 Knierim, "Old Testament Form Criticism Reconsidered," 438; cf. M. Eliade, *The Myth of the Eternal Return, or, Cosmos and History* (Bollingen Series, XLVI; Princeton: Princeton University Press, 1954).

11 A. B. Lord, *The Singer of Tales* (New York: Atheneum, 1974).

announced by Second Isaiah that was designed to reestablish the "holy seed" in Jerusalem (Ezra 9:2; cf. Isa 6:13).[12]

Insofar as the post-exilic Jewish community provided an important social context for the composition of Biblical texts, one may note that the interaction of literature and human life results in the creation of both texts and social reality. As canonical critics note, the continued interaction of literature and social reality prompts the creation of more texts, and this in turn results in the reinforcement of existing social realities or the creation of new ones.[13] In sum, literature and human life interact to create and to sustain each other.

III

This interaction between socio-historical and literary setting is particularly important in relation to the book of Isaiah with its long and complex literary history that extends through four centuries or more. The book clearly underwent various redactions during this period in which both socio-historical and literary factors were relevant in the composition of its various editions. My forthcoming commentary on Isaiah 1-39 will argue that the book underwent four major stages of composition.[14] Lack of space precludes a full defense of the details of this model, but it will suffice to demonstrate the principle that the interpretation of a text will be influenced by its setting. The first stage comprises an undefined body of 8th century oracles from Isaiah ben Amoz that appear throughout chapters 1-10; 14-23; and 28-31. The second stage comprises a 7th century Josianic edition of Isaiah in chapters 5-23; 28-33; and 36-37 that was designed to announce and justify King Josiah's program of national restoration. The third stage comprises a late-6th century edition of Isaiah in chapters 2-55; 60-62 that points to the return of Jews to Jerusalem and the rule of Cyrus as a manifestation of YHWH's sovereignty over the world. Finally, the fourth stage comprises a late-5th century edition of the entire book of Isaiah that looks forward to the manifestation of YHWH's world sovereignty following the cleansing of Jerusalem and the world from evil. In light of this compositional history, the interpreter must ask not only about the social setting of the composition of texts within the book, but also about the role that earlier texts play in defining the social realities that result in the composition of later editions and texts within the book. Furthermore, the interpreter must ask whether or how these later literary contexts influence texts that were composed at an earlier time.

Isaiah 9:1-6 plays a particularly important role in the book of Isaiah throughout all the stages of its composition. It is constituted as a royal psalm of

---

12 K. Koch, "Ezra and the Origins of Judaism," *JSS* 19 (1974) 173-197.

13 J. A. Sanders, "Adaptable for Life: The Nature and Function of Canon," *Magnalia Dei— The Might Acts of God: Essays on the Bible and Archaeology in Memory of G. Ernest Wright* (ed. F. M. Cross, Jr., W. E. Lemke, and P. D. Miller, Jr.; Garden City: Doubleday, 1976) 531-560; idem, "Hermeneutics in True and False Prophecy," *Canon and Authority: Essays in Old Testament Religion and Theology* (ed. G. W. Coats and B. O. Long; Philadelphia: Fortress, 1977) 21-41.

14 M. A. Sweeney, *Isaiah 1-39, with an Introduction to Prophetic Literature* (FOTL 16; Grand Rapids: William B. Eerdmans, forthcoming 1995).

thanksgiving[15] that announces the reign of a monarch who will lead the people out of a period of darkness and oppression in order to establish a kingdom of peace, justice, and righteousness guaranteed by YHWH. When considered apart from its literary context, Isaiah 9:1-6 provides no clue as to the identity of the monarch or the historical circumstances of his reign; it only maintains that he will establish "the throne of David" (v. 6) as the basis for his ideal reign. But when it is considered in relation to the literary contexts of the four editions of Isaiah outlined above, Isaiah 9:1-6 provides prophetic justification for specific political and religious policies that relate to the socio-historical settings of each edition of the book. The interpretation of Isaiah 9:1-6 is thereby determined in part by the conceptual outlook and the literary and socio-historical setting of each edition of the book in which it appears.

In the case of the 8th-century oracles of Isaiah ben Amoz, there is no clear evidence that enables scholars to determine the specific literary form of an 8th-century book of Isaiah. Nevertheless, the immediate literary context in Isaiah 8:1-9:6 makes it clear that Isaiah 9:1-6 must be read in relation to the prophet's statements concerning the Syro-Ephraimitic War and the consequences of Tiglath-Pileser's defeat of the northern kingdom of Israel in 734-732 B.C.E. when the Galilee and Trans-Jordan regions were stripped from Israel and incorporated as provinces of the Assyrian empire.[16] Isaiah 8:1-9:6, and especially 8:16-9:6, is constituted as a prophetic disputation that asks the addressees to choose between two positions outlined in v. 23. The first will disparage the loss of the lands of Zebulun and Naphtali and lead to the pessimistic outlook for the land described in vv. 21-22. But the second position will recognize the value of the Assyrian incorporation of these territories as provinces in that it provides the opportunity for the Davidic monarch to reassert Davidic rule over the northern kingdom of Israel. In this setting, Isaiah 9:1-6 is directed to King Ahaz, and it urges him to seize the opportunity presented by the Assyrian victory to reunite the tribes of Israel.[17]

When read in relation to the 7th-century Josianic edition of Isaiah, Isaiah 9:1-6 plays a somewhat similar legitimizing role, albeit in very different literary and socio-historical conditions. Within the literary context of Isaiah 5-12,[18] the passage stands in between an unflattering portrayal in Isaiah 7 of King Ahaz's lack of trust in YHWH's promises of security for Jerusalem and the monarchy as expressed in the Davidic covenant tradition (see esp. Isa 7:9b) and the presentation of the ideal Davidic monarch who will rule following

---

[15] On the generic identification of this psalm, see H. Barth, *Die Jesaja-Worte in der Josiazeit: Israel und Assur als Thema einer produktiven Neuinterpretation der Jesajaüberlieferung* (WMANT 48; Neukirchen-Vluyn: Neukirchener, 1977) 148-151.

[16] For the following understanding of the 8th century context of Isaiah 8:1-9:6, see M. A. Sweeney, "A Philological and Form-Critical Reevaluation of Isaiah 8:16-9:6," *HAR* 13 (1993), forthcoming.

[17] On Isaiah's attitude toward Ahaz and potential Davidic control of the north during the Syro-Ephraimitic War, cf. S. A. Irvine, *Isaiah, Ahaz, and the Syro-Ephramitic Crisis* (SBLDS 123; Atlanta: Scholars Press, 1990) 133-177, 215-233.

[18] For a study of Isaiah 5:1-10:4 as a product of the Josianic redaction of Isaiah, see C. E. L'Hereux, "The Redactional History of Isaiah 5.1-10.4," *In the Shelter of Elyon: Essays on Ancient Palestinian Life and Literature in Honor of G. W. Ahlström* (ed. W. B. Barrick and J. R. Spencer; JSOTSup 31; Sheffield: JSOT Press, 1984) 99-119.

the collapse of the Assyrian king. Both Isaiah 7 and 11 appear to be the products of the Josianic redaction,[19] and it is noteworthy that Isaiah 11 portrays the major elements of Josiah's program, including a child's rule of peace (vv. 5-9) in Zion; the return of the exiles from Assyria, Egypt, and elsewhere (vv. 11-12, 15-16); the reunification of Israel and Judah (v. 13) and their domination of lands that formerly constituted the Davidic empire (v. 14).[20] In this regard, Isaiah 9:1-6 must also be understood as a reference to and legitimization for the coming reign of Josiah, and it would likely play a role in motivating the composition of the Josianic texts that prepare the reader for the reign of the righteous Davidic monarch, including Isaiah 7; 11; and 32.

When read in relation to the late-6th century edition of the book of Isaiah in chapters 2-55; 60-62,[21] Isaiah 9:1-6 again provides legitimization for a specific view of royal power, but in very different political and socio-historical circumstances. The late-6th century sees the rise of the Persian empire of Cyrus the Great and the return of Jews from Babylonian exile so that they might rebuild Jerusalem and the Temple. These events are presupposed throughout the 6th-century edition of the book in which no Davidic monarch is evident in chapters 40-55; 60-62. Rather, Cyrus is explicitly named as YHWH's messiah and temple builder (Isa 44:28; 45:1) and the Davidic promise is applied not to a specific Davidic scion, but to the people of Israel at large (Isa 55:3). In this context, YHWH's plans for the world are identified with and manifested in the establishment of the Persian empire[22] so that the restoration of Zion will point to YHWH as the actual world sovereign, recognized by Israel and the nations (cf. Isaiah 2:2-4; 60-62) who authorizes Cyrus to act. Isaiah 9:1-6 (cf. Isaiah 11; 32) announces righteous Davidic rule, but it lacks reference to a specific Davidic figure. It thereby justifies YHWH's sovereignty exercised through Cyrus as a legitimate expression of the Davidic promise of peaceful and righteous rule from Zion.

Finally, the late-5th century edition of Isaiah anticipates the manifestation of YHWH's world rule from Zion in Isaiah 66, but it presupposes that Jerusalem must first be cleansed of evil (see Isaiah 1; 2-4; 65-66).[23] When read in relation to the political upheaval that racked the Persian empire from the late-6th through the 5th centuries, the final form of the book of Isaiah presents such conflict as the necessary prelude that prepares the world for the manifestation of YHWH's rule of righteousness and peace. Isaiah 9:1-6 therefore points to ultimate goal of peaceful and just kingship in the book, but the absence of reference to a specific king enables it to be read in relation to

[19] See the relevant sections of my *Isaiah 1-39* for full argumentation.

[20] For a full discussion of the Josianic character of Isaiah 11, see my study, "Jesse's New Shoot in Isaiah 11: A Josianic Reading of the Prophet Isaiah," forthcoming in the James A. Sanders *Festschrift*.

[21] For this definition of the 6th-century edition of Isaiah, cf. the model of the "Great Book of Isaiah" (*Grossjesajabuch*) postulated by O. H. Steck, "Tritojesaja im Jesajabuch," *The Book of Isaiah/Le Livre d'Isaïe* (ed. J. Vermeylen; BETL 81; Leuven: Peeters, 1989) 361-406, esp. 373-379; idem, *Bereitete Heimkehr. Jesaja 35 als redaktionelle Brücke zwischen dem Ersten und dem Zweiten Jesaja* (SBS 121; Stuttgart: Katholisches Bibelwerk, 1985) 45-79.

[22] Cf. R. G. Kratz, *Kyros im Deuterojesaja-Buch* (FzAT 1; Tübingen: J. C. B. Mohr [Paul Siebeck], 1991) esp. 175-191.

[23] See Sweeney, *Isaiah 1-4* 96-99, esp. 99 n. 224.

the announcements of YHWH's sovereignty in Isaiah 66 and similar texts from earlier editions of the book (e.g., Isaiah 2:2-4; 32; 60-62). In this regard, Isaiah 9:1-6 justifies a future vision of YHWH's rule, which is again portrayed as the ultimate fulfillment of the Davidic promise.

IV

In conclusion, the above discussion of the function of Isaiah 9:1-6 in the various literary and socio-historical settings of the successive editions of the book of Isaiah demonstrates the constitutive role that setting plays in the interpretation of this text. Because it anticipates the peaceful reign of a righteous Davidic monarch, Isaiah 9:1-6 aids in defining the literary character and in justifying the conceptual outlook of the various editions of the book. But it does so in part because it contains no reference to a specific monarch. This enables the passage to be understood in relation to the very different religio-political agendas and conceptual outlooks that characterize the successive editions of Isaiah in relation to their respective socio-historical settings. This discussion thereby points to the adaptability of this text to various settings. It further demonstrates that the emergence of the final form of the book of Isaiah is due in part to the dynamic character of the prophetic word in that later readers and authors of the book of Isaiah were able to see its applicability to their own socio-historical settings and religio-political agendas.[24] In short, these later readers and authors believed that Isaiah ben Amoz addressed their own situations, and they produced successive editions of the book that presented the fulfillment of Isaiah's oracles in their own times.

---

[24] Cf. C. R. Seitz, *Zion's Final Destiny: The Development of the Book of Isaiah. A Reassessment of Isaiah 36-39* (Minneapolis: Fortress, 1991) esp. 39-45, who points to the fulfillment of Isaiah's positive portrayal of Zion's future as a basis for the continued growth of the book of Isaiah.

The Book of Isaiah as a Human Witness to Revelation within the Religions of Judaism and Christianity

Gerald T. Sheppard
Emmanuel College, University of Toronto

I hope to raise some larger hermeneutical issues here rather than to draw an outline for a commentary on the book. My paper last year in this seminar dealt with several specific problems such as the relation of the presentation of Isaiah to the book as a whole, the central message of the prophet, and the role of Torah. Here I want to argue more generally for the pragmatic possibility of commmmentary on the book of Isaiah that highlights its role as scripture in two religions. My aim is to find a descriptive, hence, pre-theological and pre-midrashic, level of discourse about the book. By using a canonical approach I am trying to secure a perspective on the book of Isaiah as an effective historical text, partly defined by its intertext among other books within a larger Jewish or Christian scripture. This effort to describe a text is inherently text-oriented rather than reader oriented, but presupposes a high degree of correspondence between some late editors who leave traces, modify the context, or give an explicit scope to such a text and the historical community of religious interpreters who claim to interpret it competently.

By a canonical approach, I am less concerned about "canon" as a fixed list of books and more with the awareness that some books are read together as having, at least in theory, a prior claim in terms of their human witness to a central revelation.[1] This revelation is treasured, taught, and ideally practiced by a religion, with political consequences. A canonical approach does not suggest a pious approach, but ought to help us empathetically understand the genius of religious interpretation rather than merely allow us to mock its folly. It acknowledges that this effective text is not the only one historically significant for religious and other purposes. It also admits that even this pragmatically chosen text can be envisioned in a great variety of other ways, all equally valid and requiring a different employment of methods for the illumination of each. While a method, or "criticism," implicitly carries with it a particular pragmatic vision of a text, a canonical approach does not begin

---

[1] Gerald T. Sheppard, "Canon," Vol. 3, 62-69, *The Encyclopedia of Religion* (ed. Mircea Eliade; New York City: Macmillan, 1987). Note Brevard Childs' recent description of "the church's ongoing *search* for the Christian Bible," 67, in his *Biblical Theology of the Old and New Testaments* (London: SCM Press, 1992), 177-179.

with a method but seeks to describe a particular kind of text by using every available method or criticism that proves illuminating of it. It must, nonetheless, be no less rigorously critical in that effort and in its use of modern historical criticisms as aids in doing so. By its very nature and formulation, a canonical approach derives from the left wing of late modern critical inquiry. Though it may seek to understand empathetically pre-modern Jewish and Christian interpretation and may even find some virtues in some historically conservative modern efforts, its very logic turns on a rejection of modern fundamentalist or pietistic claims to represent in the modern period the genius of the older heritage of pre-modern biblical interpretation. Whether robust and constructive modern religious or theological interpretation ought to accompany a canonical approach to biblical commentary belongs to another question not addressed by this essay.

In the last essay for this seminar, I offered several constructive efforts at the end of my paper and one of the most provocative concerned the role of the Torah and Isaiah. I would like to add here two brief additional comments. Sweeney's monograph reminds us of an important role for Torah in Isa 1:10 as part of the introduction to the book, on a subject virtually ignored by Christian commentary. My comments concern the problem of how Isa 1:10 could be heard in terms of the pentateuchal torah, when Isa 56:3, 6-7 (see Isa 14:1 and Esther 9:27) allows for Gentile "joiners" which Ezra's reforms would seem to reject. First, the retention of apparent contradictions between books is no more unusual that the retention of potential contradiction within books. In my view, a lack of harmony in ideas and anachronism are commonplace in religious canons generally. Second, I think Y. Kaufmann's discussion of this tension over the association of outsiders with Jewish monotheism from the time of Deutero-Isaiah and later views of conversion to Judaism is highly suggestive. He argues:

> the answer of Deutero-Isaiah is only an eschatological vision, and he does not solve the juristic problem of new judaizers. Jewry was destined to struggle with this problem for many generations.[2]

Kaufmann recognizes that the pentateuch was not yet the normative torah in the period of Deutero-Isaiah and that in the pentateuch itself religious proselytes "are nowhere mentioned" and have "no legal status," so that, "This confusion, in the time of Zerubbabel, Ezra, and Nehemiah, had far-reaching consequences . . . ."[3] In any case, the question of the relation of the torah/law to Isaiah was in the history of interpretation both a Jewish and Christian concern, with warrants in the scriptural text of Isaiah itself.

The rest of this essay will consider two other matters: the question of the "unity" of Isaiah in commentary and how a canonical approach to commentary on Isaiah might treat messianic interpretation, using as an example the instances of Isa 7:14; 9:1-6[2-7]; 11:1-10.

---

2 Y. Kaufmann, *The Babylonian Captivity and Deutero-Isaiah* (New York City: Union of American Hebrew Congregations, 1970 [an abridged translation from his four volume *Toledot ha-Emunah ha-Yisra'elit* (Jerusalem and Tel Aviv: The Bialik Institute and the Devir Co., Ltd., 1937-1956)]), 167.

3 Kaufmann, *The Babylonian Captivity*, 56.

On the Unity of Isaiah

The first part of my essay for this seminar last year partly addressed my criticism of a tendency to confuse a redaction-historical reconstruction with a canonical approach or as proof of a structural unity. Again, redactional features in biblical books, in my judgment, reflect esoteric, self-conscious rules of poetic beauty and an anxiety of influence as often as they may also serve as strong semantic indicators. An editorial device may trade on a persistent theme in order to wed traditions together without elevating that theme to be "the key" to the larger text's semantic import. So-called "catch word" connections provide just one example. Some larger hermeneutical preunderstanding regarding the nature of the text must be discerned and declared before redactional indicators can be adjudicated for their semantic role within it.

Furthermore, David Carr's recent revision of his 1990 paper for our seminar cogently shows, also, that current evidence of editing alone is insufficient to prove "the literary unity" or the presence of a macrostructural conception inherent in the formation of the book of Isaiah.[4] As Carr recognizes, the alternative to "unity" or even "shape" (which has the liability of sounding like a totalizing metaphor implying balance and harmony) is not mere disunity or a random collection of tradition. For such heavily edited texts, pre-modern metaphors of a territory of land or the anatomy of a human body perhaps better conveys the sense of such a text as disciplined chaos, to use a recent scientific category. A territory of land still has scope, compass directions, and presents us with a boundaried set of limitations and possibilities for whatever we may try to do with it. A body has a head, not as a hierarchical dimension, but as a sign of its intentionality despite the disproportion or a disability inherent in its limbs, torso, and other dimensions.

John Barton's recent *Oracles of God* considers this question of unity in his effort to describe "Perceptions of Ancient Prophecy in Israel After the Exile." On the canonical "Torah" he concludes,

> As a matter of historical fact such a genre never existed, in the sense that anyone had sat down to write 'a Torah'; it was the adventitious product of a long and chaotic process of redaction, in which originally separate sources and fragments were woven together into a shapeless collection. But no one knew that. Consequently the Torah was read with an assumption of coherence (though indeed little attention was actually paid to its whole sweep—it tended to be heard piecemeal), in rather the way we are urged to read it by Brevard Childs in his proposals for a 'canonical' reading of the Old Testament.[5]

What is not so clear in Barton's backhanded compliment is whether he thinks the "assumption of coherence" is purely a figment of their imagination or if there are *some* supports for it in the Torah itself. On the prophets, Barton applies a similar pejorative assessment. "Prophecy" in early

---

4 David Carr, "Reaching for Unity in Isaiah," *JSOT* 57 (1993) 61-80.

5 John Barton, *Oracles of God: Perceptions of Prophecy in Israel After the Exile* (New York City: Oxford University Press, 1986), 145.

post-exilic Jewish interpretation, he observes, "was not seen only as the defining characteristic of a particular sort of *person*, it was also the name of a type of *literature*." Consequently,

> Once a book is classified as a 'Prophet', then anything it contains can easily come to be thought characteristic of 'prophecy': if the book of the Prophet Isaiah includes narratives about the history of Israel, then this will tend to imply that writing historical narratives is a 'prophetic' task; for the modern distinction between the prophet Isaiah as the hero of the book and the prophet Isaiah as its author is not drawn. Conversely, once 'Prophet' comes to be used as a generic classification for a particular group of books, it will be asssumed that their authors were all 'prophets', that is, figures who stand in the succession that runs back through Jeremiah, Amos, Elijah, and Nathan, all the way to Moses himself. *And this will lead to a whole string of assumptions about the character and inspiration of those authors quite remote from anything a modern student of the Bible will be likely to say about them* (my italics).[6]

In New Testament times, Barton assures us, "the image of the prophet for them was much more likely to conform to just the picture which modern Old Testament study has been at pains to correct. In brief, *"Revelation* is the key word here: through prophets one could obtain secret information which was unknowable apart from revelation."[7] I would acknowledge that canonical presentation of torah, prophecy, and wisdom in scripture and the relation of scripture to revelation becomes obvious only from a larger perspective within the intertext of Jewish scripture itself, warranted by only modest but noteworthy redactional clues to that effect. But a canonical approach, in contrast to Barton's comments, seeks to appreciate how just such possibilities of interpretation arise as competent rather than incompetent responses to scripture. The question of whether modern Jews or Christians can today hold similar views involves religious and theological questions not solved by such descriptions alone, but certainly dependent upon them.

Jewish and Christian Messianic Interpretation of Isa 7:14; 9:1-6[2-7]; 11:1-10: A Text-Oriented, Canonical Approach

A canonical approach can think in terms of a common Jewish and Christian understanding only by honoring fully the hermeneutical differences between them.[8] If much of Jewish interpretation can be called "midrash," Qumran exegesis is better defined as "pesher" and interpretation by the Jesus and New Testament writers runs the gamut between current first century options. A change occurs in Christian interpretation after the formation and recognition of a "New Testament" in the mid-second century

---

6 Barton, *Oracles of God*, 7.

7 Barton, *Oracles of God*, 132.

8 See Rolf Rendtorff, "Toward a Common Jewish-Christian Reading of the Hebrew Bible," 89-108, in *Hebrew Bible or Old Testament: Studying the Bible in Judaism and Christianity* (ed. by Roger Brooks and John J. Collins; Notre Dame: University of Notre Dame Press, 1990).

C.E. Not only is the semantic character of Jewish scripture partly altered by its appropriation as "Old Testament" within a literary horizon including a New Testament, but from Irenaeus on doctrinal interpretation became in theory based upon the "literal sense," discerned within the church and protected by the rule of faith.[9] In the same period when the Mishnah (Oral Torah) is codified, rabbinic Judaism put emphasis on midrash and Torah, while by adding another canon to Jewish scripture, Christianity became predisposed toward its own peculiar version of literal sense (or peshat) and emphasis on the Gospel. The prophets played a less significant role than Torah in rabbinic Judaism and wisdom literature still less. In Christianity, prophecy and wisdom became major resources for finding fulfillment or further revelation in the Gospel, while torah/law became a much more debated issue. Futhermore, if the Apostle Paul was the first to use "tupos" as phenomenal prophecy without any full hermeneutical program, Tertullian was apparently the first to use "figura" in the same sense as part of the literal sense of Christian scripture.[10] At a minimum, if we are to understand how Jewish and Christian interpreters confronted the text of Isaiah we need to have some of these distinctions in mind.

What does all this have to do with a commentary on Isaiah and the subject of messianic prophecy in Isa 7:14; 9:1-6[2-7]; 11:1-10? For Barton, apparently nothing, since he thinks Justin in his Dialogue with Trypho simply rejected Trypho's proposal that the child in Isa 7:14 is Hezekiah as a ploy to reject any obvious "surface meaning" of the text in order to find a more cryptic messianic reference to Christ.[11] However, a canonical approach must ask how Isa 7:14 and the promise of the child named Immanuel related to the other references to Immanuel that follow and the other promises of a king in the line of David in 9:1-6[2-7] and 11:1-10. S. Talmon thinks the child is likely Hezekiah in 7:14 but also aknowledges that the passage in context serves as "a prolepsis of the Davidic visions assembled in the ensuing chapters." Talmon concludes,

> the structurally not directly connected but nevertheless consecutive three Isaiah oracles reflect in their juxtaposition the posited three stages in the development of the biblical *mashiah* theme: historicity (Isa 7:14-16); ideation (Isa 9:5-6); idealization (Isa 11:1-10).[12]

In a related manner, I have argued in my own commentary on these texts that the later editorial interpretations of the child from Isa 7:14 in exilic additions in 7:21-15 and in chapter 8 point in the direction of messianic hope. Similarly, Isaiah 9:1-6[2-7] is contextually presented as a response to

---

[9] See the lucid discussion of these historical issues in chapters 2-6 in Frances Young, *Virtuoso Theology: The Bible and Interpretation* (Cleveland: The Pilgrim Press, 1993).

[10] Erich Auerbach, "Figura," in *Scenes from the Drama of European Literature: Six Essays by Erich Auerbach* (Gloucester: Peter Smith, 1977), 11-76.

[11] Barton, *Oracles of God*, 187, 295, n. 10.

[12] S. Talmon, "The Concept of Mashiah and Messianism in Early Judaism," in *The Messiah: Developments in Earliest Judaism and Christianity* (ed. James H. Charlesworth; Minneapolis: Fortress Press, 1992), 97.

circumstances of the exile in 8:19-22.[13] Without rehearsing these details here, I want to mention Paul Wegner's recently published dissertation, done under Ronald Clements, which argues similarly. Using what he calls "the Literary/Redactional Analysis," Wegner shows how the editorial levels have shifted the semantic import of older tradition toward post-exilic messianic interpretation.[14]

For rabbinic Judaism, the Mishnah and Talmud did not give much attention to the Messiah beyond the role of a teacher of Torah, though popular Jewish messianism drawing partly on these Isaiah texts thrived throughout the centuries. Christian interpretation similarly relied on these Isaiah texts and sought to defend their messianic import by appeal to their literal sense. In 1886 Charles Briggs' *Messianic Prophecies* illustrated an informed modern Christian response to recent criticism on Isa 7:14. First, he argues contextually that the name Immanuel means "God with us," and that no child by that name actually appears elsewhere in the book. On the basis of the "in that day" oracles that follow in Isa 7:21-25 and without anticipating later redactional attribution of these to a later period, he states,

> The deliverance was not to be wrought at the birth of the child, for the infancy was to pass in hardship. He would be compelled to live upon curds and honey, the products of a land that had become a wilderness, a place for shepherds and their flocks. The affliction of the land was to continue until the maturity of Immanuel. This pledge was given in a period of impending distress. It remained a predicted pledge until the birth of the Messiah.[15]

Briggs further defends his interpretation by appeal to the larger context of 9:1-6[2-7] and 11:1-10.

After this argument, Briggs concedes that "the child" may have been originally a promise made only to Ahaz, providing a tangible sign to the king of Judah that God would indeed deliver him from his present enemies, Syria and northern Israel. The "young woman" might have been someone Ahaz knew or even Isaiah's own wife, "the prophetess" (Isa 8:3). To that possibilty, Briggs replies,

> If however, anyone should prefer to think that a child of the prophet or the royal house bore this name as a sign, the prediction would then become typical and cease to be direct prediction, but the Messsianic idea would not be lost. This Immanuel would be a type of the great Immanuel, just as David and Moses and Solomon and other have been such types of the Messsiah.[16]

---

[13] Gerald T. Sheppard, "Isaiah 1-39," *Harper's Bible Commentary* (New York: Harper & Row, 1988), 555-556.

[14] Paul D. Wegner, *An Examination of Kingship and Messianic Expectation in Isaiah 1-35* (Lewiston, NY: Mellen Biblical Press, 1992), 303.

[15] Charles Briggs, *Messianic Prophecies*, (2nd ed.; New York City: Scribner's Sons, 1893), 196.

[16] Briggs, *Messianic Prophecies*, 197.

My point by this illustration is to show that a description of the canonical context ought to help us understand what it is about a scriptural text that elicits such interpretation in Judaism and in Christianity. For example, it sheds light on Briggs' effort to distinguish within the literal sense verbal from phenomenal prophecy (typology) in Christian interpretation.

With the late modern understanding of the redactional history and better attention to the canonical context of Isaiah, we may discover that some ancient interpretations had, in fact, an astoundingly rich intuitive sense for a biblical text which some of our own modern criticism has tempted us to ignore completely or neglect. At the same time, I am not suggesting that a commentary on the scriptural contours of Isaiah ought to neglect any level of inquiry into the book's pre-history and redaction history, but that there are some good pragmatic reasons, interest in Jewish and Christian interpretation for one, to seek to describe the canonical context. Moreover, I do not think the canonical context is a static final text, but concur with Childs' recent emphasis on the scriptural text in its changing historical character as a *witness* to a revelation of reality rather than merely a *source* for reconstructing a biblical pre-history.[17] An acknowledgement of the retention of the biblical pre-history here and there in the canonical context is not the same as a reading of the Bible in terms of its redactional history. While the latter critical task ought to be heuristically helpful to the former, the former presupposes an understanding regarding the nature of scripture and its own critique of history from a very different hermeneutical perspective. Finally, I would simply add that the political and social consequences for reading a scripture scripturally are potentially no less radical that a pious or humanistic reading of "the facts" of modern history itself.

---

[17] Childs, *Biblical Theology*, 98, 104.

"With the Power of the Spirit": Plotting the Program and Parallels of Luke 4:14–37 in Luke-Acts

Jeffrey L. Staley
University of Notre Dame

Inasmuch as many others have undertaken the task of writing on the topic of Jesus' opening sermon in the Nazareth synagogue, it seemed somewhat ostentatious for me also, having not investigated absolutely everything from the very first, to do the same thing.[1] Nevertheless, since I have been in conversation for some time with "οἱ αὐτόπται καὶ ὑπηρέται τοῦ λόγου" who apply social and cultural anthropological insights to the study of the New Testament, it seemed fitting to pursue this conversation further, over a common text and in a more public forum.[2]

---

[1] The placement of the first footnote reference in a published piece is a clue to its genre and the perceived quality of its author's research. In a survey of recent, major English language journals of biblical studies, I found that the average placement of first footnotes is after 1.6 sentences in *JBL* articles and after 2.9 sentences in *CBQ* articles.

"To write as a scholar is scrupulously to keep track of one's debt to the 'fathers' of one's discipline and to their less illustrious sons and daughters," say Janice C. Anderson and Stephen D. Moore (*Mark and Method New Approaches in Biblical Studies* [Minneapolis: Fortress, 1992] 10), and consequently, footnotes often reflect the dis-ease of our scholarship. They are fungi growing at our extremities, computer viruses infecting ever larger portions of our professional, bionic bodies. We seem to have the academic's equivalent of athlete's foot, itching to find that one elusive source overlooked by all previous scholarship, scratching the skin to the bare bone for fear that someone will discover the rottenness beneath our thinning epidermis. No longer free to roam footloose and fancy free, the footnote reflects the contemporary scholar's good posture and elite training. We know who we are by the neat feet we keep. Not coincidentally, feminist criticism has been especially helpful in uncovering the foot (note especially feminist interpretations of Ruth 3:4, 7-8; cf., Ex 24:4-6; Jdg 3:24; 1 Sam 24:3; Isa 7:20) in the face of androcentric biblical exegesis.

As an ancient mariner once crooned, "The ocean is a desert with its life underground, and the perfect disguise above." Our footnotes are the scavenging, cephalopodic monsters roaming beneath that wavy-worded surface.

[2] Most of the material for this paper has been robbed from work I originally prepared for another, now defunct project. It has been sitting on my desk for three years now, gathering dust and crayon scribblings from my eagle-eyed children in search of scratch paper and nesting material, and so I am only too happy to clean it off and share it with a more sophisticated (implied) audience. R. Rohrbaugh (who is working on this same text from a social world perspective) and I were both participants in that former project, and have had the opportunity to discuss much of this material previously.

A few years ago, Robert Tannehill argued that Jesus' opening sermon in the Nazareth synagogue "interprets his ministry as a whole and . . . anticipates his later rejection."[3] After setting out the structure of Luke 4-10,[4] this paper expands upon Tannehill's idea, showing how the setting of the sermon and its consequences (i.e., its emplotment) lead naturally[5] to viewing Jesus' additional sermons in this narrative sequence[6] as descriptive for the narrative sections that follow them. Drawing upon these resources, I will conclude by discussing the ideological implications of Jesus' sermons (and actions) for the oft noted Peter and Paul parallels.[7]

---

[3] *The Narrative Unity of Luke-Acts: A Literary Interpretation* (Philadelphia: Fortress, 1986) 1:61, cf., 63-73. See also his earlier "The Mission of Jesus according to Luke iv 16-30," in *Jesus in Nazareth* (ed. W. Eltester; Berlin/New York: de Gruyter, 1972) 51-75. For a more comprehensive bibliography on the programmatic quality of the text, see B.-J. Koet, "'Today this Scripture has been fulfilled in your ears'. Jesus' Explanation of Scripture in Luke 4,16-30," *Bijdragen* 47 (1986) 368-394; Judette M. Kolasny, "An Example of Rhetorical Criticism: Luke 4:16-30," in *New Views on Luke and Acts* (ed. Earl Richard; Collegeville, MN: Liturgical, 1990) 67-77; and more recently, Jeffrey S. Siker, "'First to the Gentiles': A Literary Analysis of Luke 4:16-30," *JBL* 111 (1992) 73-90. Older important studies are those of Hugh Anderson, "Broadening Horizons: The Rejection at Nazareth Pericope of Luke 4:16-30 in Light of Recent Critical Trends," *Int* 18 (1964) 259-275; and Larrimore C. Crockett, "Luke 4:25-27 and Jewish-Gentile Relations in Luke-Acts," *JBL* 88 (1969) 177-183. So much for the father's footprints.

[4] I can't believe that I just used the expression "*the* structure of Luke 4-10!" Saying that is kind of like writing a book entitled *The Historical Jesus: The Life of a Mediterranean Peasant* (J. Dominic Crossan; San Francisco: Harper and Row, 1992), or *The Literary Guide to the Bible* (eds. Frank Kermode and Robert Alter; Cambridge: Harvard University, 1987), or *The Poetics of Biblical Narrative: Ideological Literature and the Drama of Reading* (Meir Sternberg; Bloomington: Indiana University, 1985). Each one of these "thes" has been roundly criticized (see for example, Danna Fewell and David Gunn, "Tipping the Balance: Sternberg's Reader and the Rape of Dinah," *JBL* 110 (1991) 193-212; and Sternberg's rejoinder, "Biblical Poetics and Sexual Politics: From Reading to Counterreading," *JBL* 111 (1992) 463-488, esp. 464). So why haven't we put this sort of formalist, essentialist, absolutist talk behind us by now? Surely I'm only presenting another one of a myriad possible ways of structuring these chapters of Luke (see, for example, Fearghus O'Fearghail, *The Introduction to Luke-Acts: A Study of Lk 1,1-4,44 in the Composition of Luke's Two-Volume Work* AB 126 [Rome: Pontifical Biblical Institute, 1991]). My particular way of reading this section is no more obvious nor more objectively verifiable than any other, is it? My "the" here must be just a rhetorical sleight of hand, solely intended to give the reader a false sense of my control and mastery over the text. It's probably OK to ignore all my "thes."

[5] "Naturally" is an interesting choice of words here. Today I know better than to use such an obviously loaded rhetorical term, since it betrays what is no doubt precisely the opposite: a grossly unnatural reading of the text. Beware of the "it goes without saying" kinds of expressions. If my reading of Lk 4-10 is so "natural," then why do I spend so much time developing and defending it? Shouldn't a "natural" reading be "obvious?"

[6] Traditionally these have been called the "Sermon on the Plain" (6:20-49; "Sermon on the what?," the sleepy student asks. "The Sermon on the Plain! You know, 'Da plane! Da plane!'" "Oh, now I get it," the student replies.), "The Parable of the Sower" (8:4-21), and "The Mission of the Seventy -Two" (10:2-16).

[7] Tannehill hints at this with his numerous cross-references to Acts, *Narrative Unity*, 1:71-73; see also Siker, 89-90.

The Plot Sequence of the Third Gospel

The plot of the third gospel falls fairly easily into four major sequences.[8] The introductory sequence, made up of non-Markan material, focuses upon events surrounding the births of Jesus and John in Judea, and their initial appearances in the public realm. The second sequence, which largely follows Mark's structure, focuses upon Jesus' Galilean ministry, with a particular interest in Jesus' miracles. The third sequence is the "travel section" where Jesus is on his way to Jerusalem. It is dominated by non-Markan teaching traditions, highlights a growing opposition to Jesus, and emphasizes Jesus' own resoluteness in living out his prescribed purpose. The fourth and final sequence, which parallels Mark's gospel more closely, focuses upon Jesus' prophetic activities in Jerusalem, his consequent martyrdom, and God's vindication of him.

Although there is a common consensus about Luke's general plot structure, there is little agreement about the precise demarcation of these four sequences.[9] This is not at all unusual, since an individual scholar's own particular theological interests, social world models, source-critical theories, or literary inclinations will influence the refinements of any consensus. Moreover, the nature of narrative itself often works against critical attempts to sharply separate the interweaving of plot, metaphor, and ideology.[10] Therefore, since I see Luke 4:14 as the beginning of the second major plot sequence in the gospel—a point of progammatic change that has implications for subsequent plot developments and parallel structures in the book—it will be helpful to spend a little bit of time investigating my reasons for beginning my discussion where I do.

---

8 Charles H. Talbert, for example, divides it into "Prophecies of Future Greatness" (1:5-4:15); "Anointed with the Holy Spirit" (4:16-9:50); "Guidance on the Way" (9:51-19:44); and "Martyrdom and Vindication" (19:45-24:53) (*Reading Luke: A Literary and Theological Commentary on the Third Gospel* [New York: Crossroad, 1989] vii-viii); while O'Fearghail distinguishes 1:5-4:44, 5:1-9:50, 9:51-19:48, and 20:1-24:53 as four separate narrative units (3-5; 9-10, 40-43, 48-54, 61-63). Even Joseph A. Fitzmyer's Anchor Bible Commentary, not particularly noted for its literary sensitivies, is not far from these. He has eight narrative divisions in the gospel (including the prologue), separating out the passion and resurrection narratives (22:1-23:56a; 23:56b-24:53) from Jesus' ministry in Jerusalem (19:28-21:38), and dividing 1:5-4:13 into two parts: "The Infancy Narrative" (1:5-2:52) and "The Preparation for the Public Ministry of Jesus" (3:1-4:13) (*The Gospel According to Luke I-IX* [Garden City: Doubleday, 1981] 134).

9 For example, does the Lukan passion narrative begin at 18:15 when Luke picks up the Markan source once again, after having abandoned it in 9:50; or at 18:35 with the mention of Jericho, the first explicit geographical reference to Jesus' location since 9:10? Perhaps it should begin at 19:29, with the triumphal entry to Jerusalem; at 19:41, when he sees the city and weeps over it; or at 19:45 when he enters the temple (O'Fearghail, 48-51).

10 A mildly deconstructionist voice in me wants to say "the nature of narrative *always* works against critical attempts to sharply separate" these issues, but since most of this project was written in the more formalist stage of my career, I will stifle that urge.

The Plot Sequence of Luke 1:5-9:62

I believe that Luke 1:5-4:13 represents the first major plot sequence of the gospel. After a general prologue (1:1-5) the story proper begins, and it is set off from what follows in 4:14ff. in two important ways. First, there is a geographical change between these sequences. Almost all of the action in 1:5-4:13 takes place in Jerusalem or Judea (1:26-38 is the only exception), whereas all the stories of 4:14-18:35 take place outside of Judea. Secondly, although Jesus will become the main character in the gospel, he is only a passive character at the beginning—even when he is clearly the focus of attention (2:41-52; 3:21-4:13). However, in 4:14ff. Jesus' public ministry begins to be the focus of attention as he becomes an active participant in fulfilling his own divine purpose.[11]

In the opening narrative sequence, Jesus is the subject of songs and prophecies, the object of his parent's frantic three day search, the person baptized, the beginning point of a genealogy, and the person "led by the Spirit, tempted by the devil." His only original lines in the entire opening sequence are the two questions he asks of his parents in 2:49, and in 4:4-13 he simply quotes scripture in a defensive posturing with the devil.[12] In this opening sequence it is minor characters like the angel Gabriel, Zechariah and Elizabeth, Simeon, Anna, Mary, and John, who are much more active participants in the plotted events than Jesus.

Moreover, the opening sequence is easily divided into three parts, each of which is composed of two carefully paralleled sub-units It consists almost entirely of non-Markan material (only Lk 3:3-4, 16, 19-22; 4:2 is from Mark), most of which is unique to Luke (only Lk 3:7-9, 17; 4:3-13 is Q material). Finally, just prior to Jesus' decision to go to Jerusalem, the reader will find a cluster of scenes similar to those encountered toward the end of this plot sequence. Prayer (3:21; 9:18, 28), the disclosing of divine status (3:22; 9:20, 35), and the multiplication of loaves (4:3-5; 9:12-17) will all reappear, as if to

---

11 Mark McVann ties Lk 3:1-4:30 together as "a narrative and a ritual transition . . . which narrates the transformation of Jesus from private person at Nazareth to public prophet in Israel" ("Rituals of Status Transformation in Luke-Acts: The Case of Jesus the Prophet," in *The Social World of Luke-Acts: Models for Interpretation* [ed. Jerome Neyrey; Peabody, MA: Hendrickson, 1991] 341). Curiously, however, the genealogical "aside" of Jesus (345) plays no role in his description. It seems to me that the concern for Jesus' sonship, which is the focus of that genealogy (3:38; cf., 3:22, 4:3, 9), is more central to 3:1-4:13 than his prophetic office (350) which begins to dominate only after 4:14.

Similarly, O'Fearghail ties all of 4:14-44 together under the subtitle "Anticipation of Jesus' Ministry" (24-25), seeing "a type of syncrisis in 1,5-4,44 [which is intended] to show the superiority of Jesus" to John, much like that found in the classical encomium (35). Thus, "[t]he unit 4:14-44 does not narrate the "beginning' of Jesus' ministry but represents an anticipation of that ministry which does not stand in a chronological relationship with what follows" (38). For O'Fearghail, the decisive shift in plot comes at 5:1 with the call of the first disciples, whose role will be that of eyewitnesses (36-37).

12 As McVann notes, Jesus' quoting of Scripture is not inconsequential, since "in his career as prophet, Jesus will herald God's word" (347). My argument is only that at this early juncture Jesus pointedly is not a herald, but is rather more a parrot of God's word.

confirm the proximity of a new turn in the narrative's plot. Thus, its overall structure can be outlined as follows:[13]

> A. Appearances by an angel of the Lord 1:5-56
> 1. Announcement of the prophet's birth 1:5-25
> 2. Announcement of the savior's birth 1:26-56
> B. First fulfillments of the angel's messages 1:57-2:52
> 1. Birth of the prophet and his early life 1:57-80
> 2. Birth of the savior and his early life 2:1-52
> C. Second fulfillments of the angel's messages 3:1-4:13
> 1. Historical introduction 3:1-2
> 2. Threefold confirmation of John as a prophet 3:3-20
> 3. Threefold confirmation of Jesus as God's son 3:21-4:13

From the beginning of Jesus' public prophetic activity in Galilee (4:14) until its conclusion in Jerusalem, the plot of the gospel centers upon Jesus' proclamation of God's good news, the expansion of his prophetic reputation and ministry, and the consequent controversy that they arouse. In the opening summary of Jesus' activity, the narrator is careful to note that the main character begins his mission in the cities and synagogues of Israel (Galilee and Judea; 4:14-15; cf., 43-44; 5:17; 6:17; 7:9, 17; cf., Acts 13:13-52),[14] before moving outward to village and countryside (Lk 8:1; 37; 9:6).[15] As Jesus' popularity grows, he selects and empowers twelve men out of a group of many disciples (6:12-16) to share in his work (9:1-6, 10-17), and people of status and social position begin to acknowledge his power (7:2; 8:3; 9:7-9). When he senses antagonism and opposition to his prophetic activity (6:8; 7:9; 8:11-15; 9:21-22, 41, 43-45), he attempts to move to non-Jewish regions (8:26-39; 9:52-56), but is rebuffed.[16] Finally, during the latter stages of his Galilean ministry (8:1-

---

13 Outlines have a way of looking very convincing on paper, but when one puts them up against the text they are intended to bring order to, they often begin to fall apart. That is patently not true in this case. I've worked hard on this outline and it makes sense, believe me. It is pure exegesis.

14 O'Fearghail also observes this, but does not recognize its significance for the chronological emplotment of Jesus' ministry (24-25).

15 For a helpful socio-economic analysis of Luke's use of "countryside" language, see Douglas Oakman, "The Countryside in Luke-Acts," in *The Social World of Luke-Acts*, 151-179. I believe his conclusions about the Lukan narrative world are correct, that "[w]hile Luke views the countryside in a positive way in his two-volume work, his rural traditions have not spoken so much for rural interests as for Luke's argument to the powerful and wealthy of his own community . . ." (178; see also Vernon K. Robbins, "The Social Location of the Implied Author of Luke-Acts," in *The Social World of Luke-Acts*, 304-332, esp. 331-332).

16 While Tannehill, Koet, and Siker may be right to emphasize the focus on the inclusion of Gentiles in Jesus' programmatic Nazareth sermon ("Mission of Jesus," 62; Koet, 391; Siker, 85), the point still remains that from the perspective of Luke's plot sequence, Jesus turns toward Gentile territory only after facing opposition from his fellow Jews (note Luke's well-known omission of Mark's Gentile stories, Mk 7:24-8:10). However, unlike Paul who has great success with his Gentile mission after being rejected by diaspora Jews, Jesus essentially has little positive response in Gentile territories (compare the author's reworking of Mk 5:17-20 in Lk 8:37-39; cf., Tannehill, "Rejection by Jews and Turning to Gentiles: The Pattern of Paul's Mission in Acts," in *Luke-Acts and the Jewish*

9:62), the reader hears for the first time that Jesus will die at the hands of the elders, chief priests, and scribes (9:22; see also 9:44), and that his "departure" from this world will take place in Jerusalem (9:31; 9:51).

If Luke's first major plot sequence ends at 4:13, the second major plot sequence of the gospel seems to end at 9:62.[17] Similarly to 4:16, the author has Jesus open the third major plot sequence with a programmatic proclamation, this time addressed to the seventy-two who foreshadow the Gentile mission. Having "set his face to go to Jerusalem" (9:51), and having been refused admittance into Samaritan territory (9:52-56), Jesus then prolongs his Galilean ministry on his way to Jerusalem. In contrast to 4:14-9:62, the geographical references throughout Jesus' Jerusalem journey become more vague and less frequent. Yet it is quite evident that the conversations in 9:18-22, 30-31, 43-45 and Jesus' decision in 9:51 undergird and define this third major plot sequence.

Below I have subdivided Luke's second major plot sequence (4:14-9:62) into three units which, coincidentally, roughly parallel Luke's use of sources. Each subsequence can be distinguished from the others by the ways in which it develops Jesus' prophetic activity in new directions.[18] As the outline below shows, I have simply called these plot subdivisions three "phases" of Jesus' early prophetic activity.

  A. First phase of Jesus' prophetic activity 4:14-6:11
      Jesus proclaims the good news of God's rule in "Israel"
      (primarily in the synagogues of "Israel's" cities);
      the report of his mighty deeds spreads to villages
      1. Introduction 4:14-15
      2. Proclamation of the Lord's acceptable year 4:16-30
         (Jesus speaks about Elijah and Elisha, speaks with a παραβολή)
      3. The power of Jesus' words 4:31-5:16
         (first in Capernaum)
         (Jesus attracts his first followers)
      4. His words arouse controversy 5:17-6:11
         (the Pharisees discuss "what they might do to Jesus")
  B. Second phase of Jesus' prophetic activity 6:12-7:50
      the report of Jesus' mighty deeds reaches Gentiles (a centurion);
      and Gentile territories (Tyre and Sidon)
      1. Introduction 6:12-16
         (Jesus chooses twelve apostles)
      2. Proclamation of the blessings of God's rule 6:17-49
         (Jesus speaks with a παραβολή)
      3. The power of Jesus' words 7:1-17
         (first in Capernaum)
         (Jesus performs miracles like Elijah and Elisha)

People: Eight Critical Perspectives [ed. Joseph B. Tyson; Minneapolis: Augsburg, 1988] 83-101; see also Tannehill, *Narrative Unity*, 1:114).

17 I realize that this flies in the face of most scholarly opinion which, following source-critical analysis, argues for placing the second major plot division at 9:51 (O'Fearghail, 48).

18 Perhaps it is just this kind of "order" the author has in mind by using the word in the prologue (1:3; cf., O'Fearghail, 102-110).

4. Jesus' words raise questions regarding his status 7:18-50
   (a Pharisee doubts whether "this man is a prophet")
C. Third phase of Jesus' prophetic activity 8:1-9:62
   Jesus' activity is rebuffed in territories outside of "Israel"
   (Gerasa and Samaria); his ministry spreads from city to village
   and countryside; his reputation reaches centers of political power
   (Herod Antipas's household)
   1. Introduction 8:1-3
   2. Proclamation of the secrets of God's rule to the disciples 8:4-21
      (Jesus speaks with a παραβολή)
   3. The power of Jesus' words revealed to the disciples 8:22-56
   4. Jesus' words are entrusted to the disciples 9:1-62
      (but they fail to understand them)
      (Jesus is identified as Elijah and appears with him, but refuses
      to act in judgment like Elijah once did)

As this outline reveals, each plot subsequence opens with a brief summary
of Jesus' prophetic activity. This is followed by a proclamation of God's rule
(though the word βασιλεία is not always explicitly used). As I shall show
below, each proclamation is programmatic of the plot subsequence it
introduces, just as Jesus' opening sermon in Nazareth is programmatic of
Jesus' entire ministry. Each proclamation is then followed by stories which
emphasize the miraculous power of Jesus' words, and finally, these are
followed by controversy stories that emphasize issues which the proclamation
and the miraculous demonstrations of power have raised. It is not
insignificant that all but one of the challenging Son of Man sayings are found
in these concluding collections (6:22 is the only exception), along with all
references to Jesus' prophetic predecessor, John the Baptizer.

Some Programmatic Elements in Jesus' Proclamation of

the Lord's Acceptable Year, Lk 4:16-30

Fresh from his victory over the devil, and with a reputation that precedes
him, Jesus returns to the city of Nazareth where he spent his childhood (Lk
4:16; cf., 1:26; 2:4, 39, 51).[19] There he teaches in its synagogue. Paul, a later
follower of Jesus, will mimic Jesus' prophetic ministry by beginning his own
missionary activity in the synagogues of Asia's cities, his own native territory
(Acts 13:14-44; 14:1).

Peter's Pentecost sermon in Acts 2:14-36 is often viewed as the closest
parallel to Jesus' Nazareth sermon.[20] Both proclamations are placed within the

---

19 Contrary to Rohrbaugh and Oakman, I do not believe that "Luke applies the word
[πόλις] indiscriminately" or "inconsistently" (Oakman, 170; and Rohrbaugh, "The Pre-
Industrial City in Luke-Acts: Urban Social Relations," in *The Social World of Luke-Acts*, 126).
More likely, the term πόλις functions rhetorically in Luke's narrative world. Bethlehem
and Nazareth have to be cities here because Jesus, a more important person than Paul, is
from them (just as Paul is from Tarsus, "an important city" (Acts 21:39); cf., Neyrey,
"Josephus' *Vita* as Encomium: A Native Model of Personality," *Journal of Jewish Studies*
[forthcoming]). Likewise, Bethsaida, Capernaum, Chorazin, and Nain are cities precisely
because Jesus ministers there (just as Paul ministers in cities [e.g., Acts 13:50; 14:19]).

20 Tannehill notes the many parallels (2:28-29, 49-50), but mentions no parallels
between Acts 7 and Luke 4:16-30 (*Narrative Unity*, 2:84-101).

context of the Holy Spirit's mighty power (Lk 4:1-2, 14-15; Acts 2:1-13), both emphasize the fulfillment of scripture (Lk 4:21; Acts 2:16, 23, 30-33), and both thrust their respective speakers into more public arenas. But in reality, Stephen's sermon in Acts 7 more closely parallels Jesus' sermon in Lk 4:16-30. Unlike Peter's Pentecost sermon, these both speak of God's liberation of the oppressed[21] and reflect a common theme of rejection (illustrating it with examples from Israel's past [Lk 4:24-27; Acts 7:35, 39, 42, 51-53]). But more importantly, they both share the same strident tone and function in a similar fashion with respect to plot. In both instances the strong negative tone of the sermons (Lk 4:24; Acts 7:51-53) cause equally negative reactions in their hearers (ἐξέβαλον/ἐκβαλόντες, Lk 4:29; Acts 7:58), forcing the proclamation of "the word" (λόγος, Lk 4:32, 36; Acts 8:4, 14; 11:19) to extend beyond the pale of the speakers' home territories (Lk 4:31-37; Acts 8:1, 5-8; 11:19). Like Jesus, Stephen is full of grace, power, and the Holy Spirit (Lk 4:1, 14, 22; Acts 6:5, 8); and as with Jesus, the audience "gazes" at Stephen (ἀτενίζοντες/ἀτενίσαντες, Lk 4:20; Acts 6:15), surprised and stunned at his words in their "ears" (Lk 4:21; Acts 7:51, 57; cf., Lk 8:8; 9:44; Acts 28:27).[22]

As many scholars have noted, Jesus' Sabbath reading from Isaiah, his subsequent comments, and the audience's reaction capture in a dramatic fashion the full scope of his year-long ministry. My purpose, however, is not to repeat those significant programmatic elements mentioned in other places, but rather to focus upon some rarely recognized threads that are woven into the fabric of the narrative at later points.

After the reading of Isaiah 61:1-2,[23] Jesus rolls up the scroll, hands it back to the attendant, and sits down.[24] He then begins his sermon by saying "Today this scripture is fulfilled in your ears."[25] But at this point the narrator hastily

---

21 Jesus, quoting a text from Isaiah 61, describes this as a present reality (Lk 4:18), whereas Stephen illustrates it from Israel's past (Acts 7:34, 36).

22 Koet is one of the few scholars to recognize that Jesus' opening sermon in Nazareth most closely parallels Stephen's sermon in Acts 7, but does not discuss their similar plot functions (380).

23 The opening words, "The Spirit of the Lord is upon me," recall Gabriel's announcement to Mary "the Holy Spirit will come upon you" (1:22) and Jesus' baptism when the Holy Spirit descended upon him "in bodily form" (3:22). Just as those manifestations of the Spirit had visible, physical effects, so also will the message of good news which Jesus is now beginning to preach. Jesus will indeed preach good news to the poor (4:43; 6:20; 7:22; cf., 14:13, 21), the blind will receive their sight (Lk 7:22; 18:35-43; cf., Acts 9:8-9, 17-18), and those who are oppressed and captive will be set at liberty (Lk 5:17-26; 7:36-50; 8:26-39, 43-48; 13:10- 17; cf., Acts 8:7-8; 16:19-34).

24 In a reversal of the Lukan narrator's activity, who "writes" (γράψαι, 1:3) about events "fulfilled" among his audience (πεπληροφορημένων, 1:1), things which had been "handed on" παρέδοσαν, 1:2) by "servants" (ὑπηρέται, 1:2) of the "word" (λόγου, λόγον, 1:2, 4); Jesus now "hands over" something (ἀποδούς, 4:20) to an attendant (ὑπηρέτῃ, 4:20). He then proclaims "fulfillment" (πεπλήρωται, 4:21; cf., 24:44) of the "writing" (γραφή, 4:21), which causes amazement at his "words" (λόγοις, 4:22).

25 Notice the organs of sensory perception mentioned here: eyes, ears, and mouth. Ears are important for the Reformed sounding, professorial narrator of Luke (Koet, 380), whose Jesus "often reads when he is speaking" (Jacques Derrida, *The Ear of the Other: Otobiography, Transference, Translation* [trans. Avital Ronell, Lincoln: University of Nebraska, 1988] 36).

intrudes to give the reader the audience's reaction to Jesus' opening statement ("all spoke well of him, and wondered at the words of favor [τοῖς λόγοις τῆς χάριτος] which proceeded out of his mouth" [4:22]). A week or two later, when Jesus enters a Capernaum synagogue, the audience is "astonished at his teaching, for his word [λόγος] was with authority" (4:32; cf., Mk 1:22 which omits λόγος), and after he exorcises a demon there, "They were all amazed and said to one another, 'What is this word [ὁ λόγος]? For with authority and power he commands the unclean spirits and they come out'" (4:36; cf., Mk 1:27 which omits λόγος).[26] Only in Luke's gospel does Jesus "rebuke" the fever which Simon's mother-in-law had (4:39 [cf., 4:41]; cf., Mk 1:31; 3:11-12; Mt 8:15), thereby dispelling it.[27] Again, when Jesus is beside the lake of Gennesaret, "the crowd presses upon him to hear the word of God" (τὸν λόγον τοῦ θεοῦ, 5:1). And when he gets into Simon's boat,[28] Simon lets down his nets at Jesus' word (ῥήματι, 5:5).[29] Afterwards, "the report" went abroad concerning him (ὁ λόγος, 5:15).[30]

Clearly, the repetition of λόγος in these opening scenes reflects the author's intent to project the authoritative voice of Jesus above the buzzing conversations of ordinary folk. Unlike common speech—or even the extraordinary prophetic utterances of Mary, Zechariah, Simeon, or John—Jesus' words will

However, one should not neglect the broader range of Lukan epistomalogy (see Stephen Moore, *Mark and Luke in Poststructuralist Perspective: Jesus Begins to Write* [New Haven: Yale University, 1992] 111-158). Indeed, in Derridean-like fashion, the quintessential λόγος of Luke's Jesus is much more closely related to writing than to speech. The writing "fulfilled in [their] ears" (4:21) becomes only secondarily "words of favor proceeding out of his mouth" for his audience (4:22). But curiously, the λόγοι/γραφαί do not actually exist in the one "place" which Jesus has found and read (4:17), for his (ex)citation is a unique combination of Is 61:1-2 and 58:6 (cf., Koet, 372-373; Darrell L. Bock, *Proclamation from Prophecy and Pattern: Lucan Old Testament Christology* JSNTSupp Ser 12 [Sheffield: JSOT Press, 1987] 104-111). Thus Jesus, the ideal reader in Luke's gospel, has surreptitiously and problematically scripted himself into the scroll (note the peculiar Lukan concern for reading and writing in Lk 1:1-4; 6:3; 10:25-26; 24:25-26, 44-47; Acts 1:1; 8:29-35; 15:20-21, 30-31; 17:10-11; 25:26-27; 28:21; cf., Moore, 125-126; Gary Phillips, "'What is Written? How are You Reading?' Gospel, Intertextuality and Doing Lukewise: A Writerly Reading of Lk 10:25-37 (and 38-42)," *SBLSP* 31 [1992] 266-301). Except in the case of the lately resurrected Jesus and the castrated Ethiopian, these scripts, which intend light and life, provoke only blindness and death.

26 On the connection between teaching and miracles in Luke, Paul J. Achtemeier writes, "both teaching . . . and miracle-working . . . are examples of Jesus' activity *en exousia*" ("The Lucan Perspective on the Miracles of Jesus: A Preliminary Sketch," *JBL* 94 [1975] 550).

27 I wish, however, that the narrator had added τῷ λόγῳ at this point.

28 Parallel to his action in the Nazareth synagogue, Jesus "stands" beside the lake of Gennesaret, and after he gets in the boat he "sits" to teach (Lk 4:16, 20; 5:1, 3). I do not believe he ever sits down again, although he will often recline at meals.

29 Ῥήματι reflects a poor choice of words by the narrator. τῷ λόγῳ would have been much better, and would have added weight to my argument.

30 Tannehill recognizes the significance of λόγος here, but does not relate it to the narrator's earlier use of the word when commenting upon the hometown reaction to Jesus' opening proclamation (4:22; Tannehill, *Narrative Unity*, 1:84-85). See also my discussion below of Lk 7:1-10.

be the very means through which the liberating power of God is activated in human experience. Jesus' λόγοι will be words that can heal (4:38-41)—even from a great distance (7:1-10); they will be like sown seed (σπόρος), worming its way into people's lives (8:11-15); they will be words that must be acted upon, forming a firm foundation for living and reflective of new social relationships (6:47; 8:21; 11:28); they will be words that "will not pass away," even though heaven and earth may disappear (21:33); words that will eventually find their fulfillment in his own death and resurrection (24:44-47). In Acts λόγοι become even more active, appearing 66 times to the Gospel's 33 occurrences.

After the narrator's brief interruption, Jesus' words continue with the quoting of a proverb (παραβολή) which seems to reflect his audience's mood ("Physician, heal yourself," 4:23), and which is juxtaposed to another proverb, "No prophet is acceptable in his own country" (4:24). In this gospel, Jesus will become the speaker of παραβολαί par excellence (5:36; 6:39; 8:4-18; 10:29-38; 15:1-16:10; 18:1-14; et al.). And the ironic and tragic contrast between "proclaiming the good news" (4:18; cf., 19) and not being "acceptable in [one's] own country" will be reflected in his last publicly spoken parable (the parable of the vineyard and the tenants, 20:1-18), after which the scribes and chief priests will try to "lay hands upon him" (20:19; cf., 4:28-30). At the mid-point of Jesus' ministry the second proverb ironically will be turned into a lament as Jesus cries "O Jerusalem, Jerusalem, killing the prophets and stoning those who are sent to you!" (13:34); while in slightly different form, the first proverb will come back to haunt him in his final hours. It will be thrown back in his face as he hangs on the cross, "He saved others, let him save himself . . ." (23:36, 39).

Jesus concludes his inaugural proclamation with two examples from scripture of prophets who were sent beyond the physical boundaries of Israel to "set at liberty those who were oppressed" (4:25-27). Like Elijah and Elisha, Jesus is a Spirit-filled prophet who will occasionally step beyond the borders of Israel to help those in need (8:26-39). But also like them, the greater part of his prophetic activity will occur within Israel—not so much among the elite as among those who are outside the established channels of power and honor. It will be primarily through the activity of the later Christian community that those outside the physical boundaries of Israel come to hear the message of liberation (Acts 8:4ff.; esp., 10:34-43). Finally, like Elijah and Elisha, Jesus will one day come to the aid of a widow bereft of her only son (7:11-17), a leper (5:12-16), and a foreign military officer (7:1-10).[31]

In light of Simeon's previous dark prophecy (2:34) and John's earlier imprisonment (3:18-20), the Nazareth synagogue's reaction to Jesus' words are predictable (4:28-30). Every true prophet faces trials and persecutions (13:33-34; Acts 7:52; 13:13-52), and Jesus will not be the exception. But this time he

---

[31] Many people have written about these parallels (see most recently Koet, 385-391; Siker, 86-89; and Thomas L. Brodie, "Luke-Acts as an Imitation and Emulation of the Elijah-Elisha Narrative," in *New Views on Luke and Acts* [ed. Earl Richard; Collegeville, MN: Liturgical] 78-85; and their respective bibliographies). What has not been noted is that just as Jesus mimics the activity of Elijah and Elisha in back-to-back stories (Lk 7:1-16), so does Peter (Acts 9:36-10:43).

escapes from the mob, mysteriously "passing through the midst of them" before they are able to dispose of him (4:30).[32] In spite of the fact that Jesus will never again return to his childhood home, the rejection he finds in Nazareth will stalk him throughout his journeys—whether it be to the lakeside cities of Chorazin, Bethsaida, and Capernaum (10:13-15; cf., 4:23, 31-41); Galilee at large (13:31), Samaria (9:52-55), or Judea, where it finally culminates in his arrest, trial, and death (22:47-23:56). Yet even a Jerusalem tomb will not be able to hold this Christ of God (9:20; 24:26, 46)—much less an angry hometown mob.

Jesus' Nazareth proclamation of the "acceptable year of the Lord" (4:19) is, indeed, programmatic. It not only introduces the reader to the major motifs of Jesus' year-long ministry (releasing the powerless from their oppression, including Gentiles in God's benefaction, with a striking ambivalence to the implications of these for his own reputation); but it also gives the reader clues as to the manner in which Jesus will speak (with words of favor and with perplexing παραβολαί), and to the response that his message will engender (initial favor, ultimate rejection).[33] Finally, this early phase of Jesus' ministry, which opens with two synagogue stories, emphasizes that Jesus' activity centers in synagogues and encompasses all of Jewish territory (Lk 4:44; cf., 6:17; 7:17; 23:5; Acts 10:37), and closes with two more Sabbath stories (Lk 6:1-11).

Some Programmatic Elements in the Opening Scene of Jesus' Second Phase of Prophetic Activity, Lk 6:12-49

Jesus chooses twelve apostles from his group of disciples and so opens the second phase of his Galilean ministry (Lk 6:12-7:50).[34] The narrator has used the word μαθηταί twice already to describe Jesus' followers (5:30; 6:1), but the word ἀπόστολοι is new (6:13). The term μαθηταί can be used to describe anyone who chooses to follow Jesus (14:25-33; Acts 6:1-2; 9:10; 11:26; 13:52; 14:20; 16:1; 19:1; 21:15),[35] and as the word implies, Jesus' followers are portrayed as learners (Lk 6:40; 11:1-4)—albeit sometimes bewildered learners (9:33, 45-54). The term ἀπόστολοι, however, will be reserved almost exclusively for the twelve chosen here, for they will have a special role to play as witnesses to and for the unfolding of God's promised salvation (9:1-2, 10; 11:48-49; 22:14, 28-30; 24:48; Acts 1:6-8, 22, 25; cf., Lk 4:43).[36] In Luke-Acts, the only other persons ever favored with the designation ἀπόστολοι are Matthias, who one day will be chosen to replace the traitor Judas (Lk 6:16; Acts 1:15-17;

---

[32] For a discussion of the variety of ways in which this curious text has been understood, see T. Baarda, "'The Flying Jesus,' Luke 4:29 in the Syriac Diatessaron," *Vigiliae Christianae* 40 (1986) 313-341; esp. 332-336.

[33] Kolasny, 71-72.

[34] The Lukan author seems to follow Mark's sequence rather slavishly at this point, since the twelve play no special role in the narrative's plot until the next phase of Jesus' ministry (Lk 8:1-9:62).

[35] Dennis M. Sweetland, "Following Jesus: Discipleship in Luke-Acts," in *New Views on Luke and Acts* (ed. Earl Richard; Collegeville, MN: Liturgical, 1990) 109-123, esp. 111.

[36] O'Fearghail calls this the "eyewitness-ship" role of the apostles, 36.

20-26), and Paul and Barnabas whom the narrator so describes when they are in Iconium (14:4, 14).[37] Following Jesus' example, the apostles and their associates will also pray before they choose their helpers and successors (1:23-26; 6:3-6; 13:1-4).

In contrast to his first sermon, where he stood up to read in his hometown synagogue then sat down to speak, here Jesus stands in the open to deliver his message (Lk 6:17-19; cf., Mt 5:1).[38] From here until his entry into Jerusalem (Lk 19:45-48), the vast majority of Jesus' teaching will take place in the open

---

[37] These two texts from Acts 14 create problems for me. Time and again the author of Luke-Acts seems intent on separating Paul from the apostles, yet here, twice in the same chapter, Paul and Barnabas are called ἀπόστολοι. Only in Luke-Acts does Jesus tell his disciples/apostles to "stay here in the city until you have been clothed with power from on high" (Lk 24:49; Acts 1:4), thus ensuring that all resurrection appearances will occur in and around Jerusalem within a forty day period (Acts 1:3). In Acts, however, Paul himself and the narrator are careful to say that he merely saw a light from heaven on the road to Damascus (Acts 9:3-5; 22:6-11; 26:12-19; but see Tannehill for the symbolic significance of "light" in Paul's call stories, *Narrative Unity*, 2:324). Thus, like Stephen, whose death he witnessed, Paul seems to have seen the Lord Jesus in heaven as the exalted Son of Man (7:55-56, 59; cf., 2:36, and Ananias' and Barnabas' statements that Paul saw the *Lord* Jesus, 9:17, 27; cf., 22:10; 26:15). Finally, apostleship is reserved for twelve men who had to have been with Jesus from his baptism to his resurrection (1:15-26). But compare this with Paul S. Minear's perspective which is that "in Luke's eyes Paul was an apostle" *To Heal and to Reveal: The Prophetic Vocation According to Luke* (New York: Seabury, 1976) 144.

According to the author of Luke-Acts, then, Paul fails to qualify for apostleship on four counts: 1) he was not with Jesus from his baptism to his resurrection; 2) the Holy Spirit had already designated a replacement for Judas, thus maintaining the significance of the number twelve for the apostolic office; 3) Paul's call occurred long after Jesus' ascension and far from Jerusalem; 4) Paul never saw the resurrected Jesus on earth, instead saw a light from heaven and heard a voice.

I suppose that I could opt for a redaction-critical solution to the problem of Paul's apostolic designation in Acts 14, and say that in Acts 13-14 we have a new source, an "Antioch source" that has not been perfectly worked into the author's point of view (e.g., Jacques Dupont, *The Sources of Acts: The Present Position* [trans. Kathleen Pond; London: Darton, Longman and Todd, 1964] 62-72; cf., Ernst Haenchen, *The Acts of the Apostles: A Commentary* [trans. Bernard Noble and Gerald Shinn; Philadelphia: Westminster, 1971] 420 n. 10, 428 n. 5; Hans Conzelmann, *Acts of the Apostles*, [trans. by James Limburg, A. Thomas Kraabel, and Donald H. Juel; edited by Eldon Jay Epp with Christopher Matthews; Philadelphia: Fortress, 1987] 108). Or perhaps the narrator is surreptitiously elevating Paul and Barnabas to the status of apostle in view of their role in the upcoming Jerusalem Council (15:1-35). The other option, of course, is just to say that these two texts represent the rupture in my interpretive rapture; the thorn in my flesh; the deconstructive edge in my carefully cultivated plot of words and narrative worlds. Maybe I should be more wary of the perfect fit, the foolproof composition, than of the occasional miscue.

As Stephen Moore wisely notes, "[t]he more one is willing to home in on the crevices and the interstices that result in the Gospels (the Synoptic Gospels in particular) from the conflation of source marterial, the more bizarre the authorial intention one will need to hypothesize to fill in those widened cracks" (*Literary Criticism and the Gospels: The Theoretical Challenge* [New Haven: Yale University, 1989] 33-34; see also Fewell and Gunn, 194; and Sternberg's response, "Biblical Poetics and Sexual Politics," 465-467).

[38] The Lukan narrator is particularly fond of "standing" language (ἱστάναι), and often uses the word to connote the quality of witnessing to or proclaiming God's good news (Lk 1:11; 5:1; 6:8; 9:27, 47; 21:36; 23:10, 49; 24:36; Acts 1:11-12, 23; 2:14; 4:7, 14; 5:20, 27; 6:6, 13; 7:55-56, 60; 10:30-31; 16:9; 17:22; 21:40; 22:30; 24:20-21; 25:10, 18; 26:6, 16, 22).

countryside or in houses (13:10-17 is the rare exception). The narrator also notes that Jesus' proclamation has drawn a large number of disciples to him and that people are coming from the Gentile areas of Tyre and Sidon (6:17).[39] Not coincidentally, Jesus will encounter a Gentile for the first time in this phase of his ministry (7:1-10), and some of those seeking to touch him (6:19) will find themselves scandalized by his touch (7:14, 39; 8:44-47).

This, the second of Jesus' programmatic proclamations, begins with a fourfold blessing and a fourfold curse. The fourth blessing and woe each end with a reference to prophets, a word which had been important in Jesus' first proclamation (4:24), and in this phase of Jesus' ministry the prophet motif will become particularly significant (7:16, 26, 28, 39). Furthermore, all the blessings which Jesus pronounces over his followers will have a degree of fulfillment in this story. The poor will receive recognition and praise (21:1-4); those who hunger, will be filled (9:12-17); those who weep, will be consoled (7:11-17, 36-50);[40] and those who face rejection, will rejoice (10:10-11, 17-20; Acts 5:41-42; 16:19-25). But of the woes, only the one pronounced over the rich will find any sort of immediate fulfillment (Lk 18:18-23; Acts 5:1-11).

Other unusual language in the proclamation is that of "lending/creditor" ($\delta\alpha\nu\epsilon\acute{\iota}\zeta\epsilon\iota\nu/\delta\alpha\nu\epsilon\iota\sigma\tau\acute{\eta}s$, 6:34-35; 7:41), which otherwise occurs in Luke-Acts only in the confrontation between Jesus and the Pharisee, the final story of this narrative subsequence (7:41). There it is contrasted with the rather rare Lukan language of "judging" ($\kappa\rho\acute{\iota}\nu\epsilon\iota\nu$, 6:37; 7:43), "sinner" ($\dot{\alpha}\mu\alpha\rho\tau\omega\lambda\acute{o}s$, 6:32, 34; 7:37, 39), "loving" ($\dot{\alpha}\gamma\alpha\pi\hat{\alpha}\nu$, 6:32; 7:42, 47), and "credit/showing favor" ($\chi\acute{\alpha}\rho\iota s/\chi\alpha\rho\acute{\iota}\zeta\epsilon\sigma\theta\alpha\iota$, 6:32-34; 7:42, 43). Finally, the command to forgive, found in 6:37 ($\dot{\alpha}\pi o\lambda\acute{\upsilon}\epsilon\tau\epsilon$) is the central point of the concluding dialogue between Jesus and the Pharisee ($\dot{\alpha}\phi\iota\acute{\epsilon}\nu\alpha\iota$, 7:47, 48, 49), and it reemphasizes one of the major concerns of Jesus' ministry (4:18; 5:20-24; et al.). Jesus' proclamation ends with a parable admonishing his listeners to act upon what they have heard (6:48-49), and although the example of the wise and foolish builders is not called a $\pi\alpha\rho\alpha\beta o\lambda\acute{\eta}$, parables do play an important role in each of Jesus' first three proclamations (cf., 4:23-24; 6:39-42; 8:4-15).

Like the first miracle story which followed Jesus' proclamation of the "Lord's acceptable year" (4:31-37), the healing of the centurion's slave directly follows Jesus' second proclamation (6:17-49) and also occurs in Capernaum.[41] Moreover, the synagogue mentioned in 4:33 is alluded to in 7:5. On Jesus' first appearance in that synagogue, the congregation had been astonished at the authority of Jesus' teaching. Now, outside that same synagogue, it is Jesus' turn to marvel. With an echo of Elijah's and Elisha's mighty deeds which the reader cannot fail to miss, Jesus marvels at a level of trust not even found in Israel (7:9; cf., 4:25, 27).

---

39 Tannehill, *Narrative Unity*, 1:145.

40 The motif of weeping (connected with mourning and dying) is especially important in this narrative subsequence, connecting all its major scenes: the healing of the centurion's slave (7:2), the miraculous resuscitation (7:12-14), Jesus' remarks about John (7:32), and the woman in the Pharisee's house (7:38, 44). Outside of these two chapters, the verb "to weep" ($\kappa\lambda\alpha\acute{\iota}\epsilon\iota\nu$) is found only six times in the gospel, all of them in later chapters.

41 Siker, 87-88.

Like the miracles in 4:31-5:16, this miracle (as well as the one following it), illustrates and confirms for the reader the power of Jesus' words spoken so authoritatively in the proclamation of kingdom blessings (7:7-8, 14). For as in Jesus' concluding example of the solid foundation (6:46-49), the centurion is a builder (οἰκοδομοῦντι, 6:48-49; ᾠκοδόμησεν, 7:5) who calls Jesus "Lord" (κύριε, 6:46; 7:6) and understands the authority of Jesus' words (λόγον, 6:47; λόγῳ, 7:7).[42] But in an unusual twist to the typical miracle story form, Jesus never says the words which the man requests or which the reader expects to hear (e.g., "Go; be it done for you as you have believed," Mt 8:13; Jn 4:50; cf., Luke 4:35, 39; 5:13, 24; 7:14).[43] By omitting the words which effect the miracle and expanding the centurion's verbal response, the author moves the climax of the story away from the expected miracle and instead, dramatically places it upon Jesus' exclamation of the centurion's trust. As a result of these two miracles, the "report" (λόγος, 7:17) of Jesus' prophetic deeds spreads more broadly throughout Jewish territory and the surrounding region.

Thus, like Jesus' opening proclamation in Nazareth, his second proclamation is also programmatic of the second phase of his ministry. Moreover, the miracles that immediately follow it reflect the narrator's concern for illustrating the powerful effect of Jesus' authoritative words, similar to the emphasis found in the first two miracles of Jesus (4:31-41).

Some Programmatic Elements in the Opening Scene of Jesus' Third Phase of Prophetic Activity, Lk 8:1-9:62

The third phase of Jesus' ministry begins with a brief introduction (Lk 8:1-3). However, in spite of its limited length, the narrator's opening summary gives a remarkable number of clues regarding the new directions which Jesus' ministry will take. For the first time in the story the narrator mentions that Jesus' ministry takes him to villages as well as cities. Indeed, villages and countryside are highlighted in these two chapters (κώμη, 8:1; 9:6, 12, 52, 56; but only 7 more times in Luke-Acts); "countryside" (χώρα, 8:26; ἀγρός, 8:34; 9:12; περίχωρος, 8:37).

The narrator also mentions that "the twelve were with him" (8:1), and the reader is not surprised to find that they play a much more significant role in this phase of Jesus' ministry than they had earlier. The twelve disciples are given the secrets of the kingdom of God (8:9), they are with him when he calms the storm (8:22-26), and when he miraculously heals (8:45, 51; 9:37, 40). He sends them out on their own mission (9:1-6), and they help him in

---

42 David R. Catchpole is the only writer I've found who hints at a possible connection between Lk 6:46 and the healing of the centurion's slave, and he sees this connection only at the level of Q. Catchpole speaks of the "ποιεῖν theme continuing to be given prominence in the next Q unit, the healing of the centurion's servant (Mt 8.5-10, 13/Lk 7.1, 2, 6-10)" ("Jesus and the Community of Israel—the Inaugural Discourse in Q," *BJRL* 68 [1986] 296-316). However, he also sees dissimilarity at the level of Q, in the centurion's addressing Jesus as Lord. This is because he sees the "Lord" mentioned in 6:46 as Q's future coming one, the Son of Man (302).

43 Achtemeier hints at this carefully crafted twist in the miracle story form when he says, "the 'solution' [to the miracle] has, in fact, been omitted" (549).

specific ways (9:12-18, 51-56). They are also with Jesus on the mountain when his appearance is changed (9:28-36), and he trusts them with the mystery of his identity and destiny (9:18-27, 43-45).

Finally, the narrator mentions a number of women who are with Jesus. What is important from the perspective of plot development is not only the fact that women are now in his company, but also the particular kinds of women that are mentioned. Mary, called Magdalene, is one "from whom seven demons had gone out," and it is not insignificant that the reader will find the most dramatic exorcisms in this phase of Jesus' ministry (8:26-39; 9:37-43), and two miracles involving women (8:40-56). Since Joanna is described as "the wife of Chuza, who was the manager of Herod's estate,"[44] Jesus' message must be beginning to reach the elite and powerful. Not coincidentally, the reader will discover later in this phase of Jesus' ministry that Herod the tetrarch is perplexed by the accounts of the disciples' and Jesus' ministry, and wishes to see Jesus, having heard of "all that was done" by him (9:7-9; cf., 13:31-33). Herod's cameo appearance does not foreshadow good, for he claims to have beheaded John (9:9; cf., 3:18-20). Herod will, of course, eventually meet Jesus, but he will not be impressed by him (23:6-12). Finally, the fact that the women provide for Jesus and his followers is further evidence of the growing importance of his prophetic ministry.[45]

After this brief, programmatic introduction, the author opens the third phase of Jesus' ministry by once again casting Jesus' proclamation of God's reign in sermon-like form.[46] However, this time, Jesus begins with a parable ($\pi \alpha \rho \alpha \beta o \lambda \acute{\eta}$, cf., 4:23; 5:36; 6:39) addressed to a "great crowd," which he then privately interprets for his disciples (8:12-15).[47] This interpretation is followed by an additional parable (8:16) and interpretation (8:17-18) which further elaborate his earlier quotation from Isaiah 6:9-10 (8:9-10). The proclamation concludes with the arrival of his mother and brothers (8:19) who provoke his aphoristic response "My mother and brothers are those who hear the word of God and do it" (8:20; cf., 6:46-49).

Jesus finishes this opening parable of the sown seed with a plea to the crowd to "hear" ($\dot{\alpha} \kappa o \acute{\nu} \epsilon \iota \nu$, 8:8; found 8 times in this proclamation). The importance of rightly hearing the word of God will become particularly

---

44 See Fitzmyer's discussion of $\dot{\epsilon} \pi \iota \tau \rho \acute{o} \pi o \nu$ (1:698).

45 Tannehill, *Narrative Unity*, 1:138.

46 Although this 35 line unit of Jesus' teaching is rarely called a "sermon" (due in part to its shorter length when compared to its Markan and Matthean parallels), and is only half the length of the "Sermon on the Plain" (73 lines), it is still longer than Jesus' opening sermon in Nazareth (22 lines). So I think I can get away with calling it a "sermon" or a "programmatic proclamation." But I must confess that its length still bothers me. If the author had Mark as a model, why not make this "sermon" at least as obvious as the Markan collection of parables and the two preceding sermons in Luke? That is what I would have done. Furthermore, if I call these 35 lines a sermon, why shouldn't Jesus' 30 line response to John the Baptizer's disciples (7:22-35) also be called a sermon? Doubtless, the answer to these troubling questions is as plain as the nose on my face. If only the text were a mirror, then I would be able to see things more clearly.

47 For the growing importance of the crowds ($\ddot{o} \chi \lambda o \iota$) in this phase of Jesus' ministry, see Tannehill, *Narrative Unity*, 1:145-148.

crucial for the disciples in this phase of his ministry as they begin to share Jesus' mission in a more direct way (8:22-26, 45, 51; 9:1-6, 10, 12-36, 37, 40, 43-50, 54-56). It is not unusual, then, to find that most of the remaining sermon is directed toward his disciples, and that Jesus' own interpretation of the parable will focus upon how various people "receive" or hear the word (8:13, cf., 8:10, 18). Interestingly, the verb "receive" (δέχεσθαι) is also found in Jesus' commissioning of the twelve (9:5), in his reprimand of the disciples (9:48, four times), and in the narrator's description of the the the crowds' response (ἀποδέχεσθαι, 8:40; 9:11)[48] and the Samaritans' response (9:53). It is used only nine other times in the book, four of which occur in the parable of the unjust steward (16:1-9).

At the conclusion of the parable, Jesus' disciples emerge as a group with a specific concern for the first time (8:9). In response to their request for its meaning, Jesus begins to speak of the "secrets of the kingdom of God." This is the fourth time Jesus has used the expression "kingdom of God" (see also 4:43; 6:20; 7:28), and it is the only time in the book that the phrase is used to qualify another word. Here, the secrets Jesus reveals are contrasted with parables, things which do not necessarily lead to insight. Jesus will go on to tell many more parables, and the narrator uses the word to describe Jesus' sayings on a number of occasions. But the only other time in the book that Jesus uses the word is in his opening sermon in Nazareth (4:16-30). For that scurrilous hometown audience he had quoted a proverb (4:23), to which he then had added a comment. The meaning was so readily apparent that Jesus' own life was immediately threatened because of it (4:28-29).

For "the others," then, parables do not reveal anything about God or humans; they are neither words of hope nor admonitions (cf., 8:17-18). Without an explanation or injunction (e.g., 10:30) they accomplish nothing. In the final phrase, Jesus alludes to Isaiah 6:9, a text which Paul will one day find occasion to quote. For Paul, and ultimately for the author, the Isaiah text reflects the mystery and paradox of Israel's failure to recognize the presence of God's salvation in Jesus, and the eventual turning of that very same God toward the Gentiles (Acts 28:25-28).[49]

The interpretation which Jesus gives to the parable seems especially well suited to the disciples who soon will be sent out on their own mission (9:1-11). Its focus is centered upon the various responses to "the word of God" (ὁ λόγος τοῦ θεοῦ, 8:11), and its language is evoked in a number of the subsequent pericopes. Particularly significant is the phrase "trust and be saved" (πιστεύσαντες/σωθῶσιν, 8:12). After Jesus stills the storm (8:22-24), he asks the disciples exasperatingly, "Where is your trust?" (πίστις, 8:25). The witnesses to Jesus' exorcism of the Gerasene demoniac announce how "he was well" (ἐσώθη, 8:36), and Jesus says to the woman with a hemorrhage, "Daughter, your trust has made you well," (πίστις/σέσωκεν, 8:48). He encourages Jairus with the words, "Just trust and she shall be well" (πίστευσον/σωθήσεται, 8:50), and he admonishes his disciples, "For those who want to save their life, will

48 Tannehill, Narrative Unity, 1:146.

49 Tannehill, "Rejection by Jews and Turning to Gentiles," 97-101; Narrative Unity, 2:344-357.

lose it and those who lose their life for my sake will save it" ($\sigma\hat{\omega}\sigma\alpha\iota/\sigma\hat{\omega}\sigma\epsilon\iota$, 9:24).[50]

If positive responses to Jesus' words are expressed with $\sigma\hat{\omega}\zeta\epsilon\iota\nu$, $\pi\iota\sigma\tau\epsilon\acute{u}\epsilon\iota\nu$, and their cognates, the various-rooted words express the opposite. Jesus has said that like thorns, the cares, riches, and pleasures of life can grow up and "choke" his words ($\dot{\alpha}\pi\acute{\epsilon}\pi\nu\iota\xi\alpha\nu$, 8:7; $\sigma\nu\mu\pi\nu\acute{\iota}\gamma\nu\tau\alpha\iota$, 8:14). And the stories that follow his interpretation of the parable graphically illustrate this possibility. First, the disciples nearly perish in a storm-tossed lake (8:22-25);[51] next the Gerasene livelihood, their swine, "drown" in the lake ($\dot{\alpha}\pi\epsilon\pi\nu\acute{\iota}\gamma\eta$, 8:33). Finally, when Jesus returns to the other side of the lake and is "welcomed" by the needy crowds ($\dot{\alpha}\pi\epsilon\delta\acute{\epsilon}\xi\alpha\tau\o$, 8:40; cf., 8:13) he is "crushed" by them ($\sigma\nu\nu\acute{\epsilon}\pi\nu\iota\gamma\nu$, 8:42) and nearly prevented from completing his appointed tasks.

In the first miracle of his second phase of ministry, Jesus marveled at the depth of a foreigner's trust (7:9). But here, in marked contrast, Jesus seems exasperated at his own disciples' lack of it (8:25). Furthermore, the disciples' two-fold repetition of the word "master" ($\dot{\epsilon}\pi\iota\sigma\tau\acute{\alpha}\tau\alpha$, 8:24) accentuates their limited trust, their anxiety, and their fear.[52] The disciples use the term "master" ($\dot{\epsilon}\pi\iota\sigma\tau\acute{\alpha}\tau\eta\varsigma$) fairly consistently throughout this phase of Jesus' ministry (8:24, 45; 9:33, 49; found elsewhere only at 5:5; 17:13), and the only time they use the more common word "Lord" ($\kappa\acute{u}\rho\iota\omicron\varsigma$, 9:55), Jesus strongly rebukes them. From these numerous examples it is evident that Jesus' third proclamation of God's rule is also programmatic of the phase of Jesus' ministry which follows it.

This third phase of Jesus' Galilean ministry (8:1-9:62), the concluding part of the second major narrative sequence in the gospel of Luke (4:14-9:62), approaches its conclusion with the narrative of Jesus' transfiguration (9:28-36). At a moment of prayer, just prior to the beginning of his Galilean ministry, a heavenly voice confirmed Jesus as God's son (3:21-22). Now, just before his momentous decision to go to Jerusalem, he is again in prayer. Once more the heavenly voice is heard; but this time its message is directed toward the twelve disciples rather than toward Jesus (9:32-36).

As if to reassure both the reader and the disciples that Jesus is indeed the person whom God has destined him to be (in spite of his recent prediction of death), the author expands the prayer scene with an account of the divine unveiling of Jesus' glory. To this he adds the conversation of Jesus with Elijah and Moses, the two central prophets from Israel's ancient past. This translucent transformation of Jesus will send a shock wave rolling toward the future. Flowing just below the surface of his journey to Jerusalem, its themes

---

50 But it would have been even more helpful for my argument if the Lukan narrator had followed Matthew's lead at this point and had the woman healed at precisely the moment Jesus speaks these words.

51 This would have been an appropriate place for the narrator to use the verb $\dot{\alpha}\pi\omicron\pi\nu\acute{\iota}\gamma\epsilon\iota\nu$, but for some reason he does not. This failure on the part of the Lukan narrator disturbs me, since it would have made my argument for the significance of the word and its connection to the preceding episode much stronger.

52 Tannehill, *Narrative Unity*, 1:213.

and motifs[53] will finally break into the open once again in the account of Jesus' final hours with his disciples (22:7-46) and in the story of his resurrection (24:1-53). Perhaps even Moses and Elijah, who are on this mountain discussing with him his ἔξοδος, will reappear, incognito, at his tomb (24:4) and at his ascension (Acts 1:10).[54]

The transfiguration brings the early period of Jesus' ministry to a climax by disclosing for the first time the particular place where Jesus' goals will be "fulfilled" or "completed" (πληροῦν, Lk 9:31; cf., 1:1). This period of ministry opened with Jesus' proclamation that God's promises were beginning to be fulfilled (4:21), and that theme is now reiterated and projected toward Jerusalem, far beyond the present moment of the reader. But the scene not only gives the reader a vista from which to determine the future direction of the story; it also highlights the central revelatory experiences recorded earlier.

The sleepy-eyed disciples see Jesus' glory (9:32) and hear the voice from the overshadowing cloud (9:34) which virtually repeats what Jesus heard privately at his baptism (3:22). The reference to "glory" recalls the "glory of the Lord" that shone around the shepherds when they were told, "to you is born . . . a savior, who is Christ, the Lord" (2:9); while the "overshadowing" cloud recalls Gabriel's words to Mary, "the power of the Most High will overshadow you; therefore the child to be born will be called . . . the Son of God" (1:25). For both the reader and Jesus, then, the scene reaffirms Jesus' mission outlined so long ago. Yet the command, "listen to him" (9:35), coupled with Peter's lack of understanding (9:33), shows that the disciples have not fully grasped the significance of the transfiguration. The use of the verb ἀκούειν (9:35) reemphasizes the import of Jesus' proclamation of the kingdom's secrets (8:8, 10, 18, 21) and sets up the reader for the irony of the disciples' future failures (9:40, 45, 46, 49-50, 54-56).

The third major division of the narrative closely follows upon Jesus' decision to go to Jerusalem (9:51), and it opens with the sending out of the

---

53 See, for example, 9:51-53; 11:53-54; 13:31-35; 17:24-25; 18:31-34; 19:47-48; 24:26.

54 Tannehill wishes to call these two white-clothed men (ἄνδρες) "angels" (*Narrative Unity*, 1:278; 2:18), but surely this is wrong. The Lukan narrator knows the word ἄγγελος and uses it when appropriate (e.g., Lk 1:11, 13, 18-19, 26, 30, 34-35, 38; 2:9-10; Acts 5:19; 8:26; 10:3, 7, 22; 12:7-11; 27:23).

Haenchen credits Wellhausen with being the first to make the Moses/Elijah identification in these two additional scenes, but then quickly dismisses the possibility (150, n. 4). But Wellhausen's conjecture demands further reflection. While it is true that the two Emmaus-bound disciples speak of a "vision of angels" (ὀπτασίαν ἀγγέλων, 24:23; cf., 1:22) that the women saw at the tomb, these disciples are clearly repeating second hand nonsense (λῆρος, 24:11, 22). Thus, their construal should not be taken as seriously as the narrator's description of the characters as men.

In support of Wellhausen's thesis, it should be noted that the three episodes are initially connected by the common expression καὶ ἰδοὺ ἄνδρες δύο (9:30; 24:4; Acts 1:10). Secondly, the transfiguration and ascension are united by the narrator's repetition of the motif of an overshadowing cloud and white clothing, while the transfiguration and resurrection are joined by the added adjective "dazzling"(ἐξαστράπτων, 9:29; ἀστραπτούσῃ, 24:4). Finally, the resurrection and ascension are connected by the repetition of the noun ἐσθής (24:4; Acts 1:10; cf., Brodie's discussion of the Elijah/Elisha motif in the Lukan resurrection/ascension narratives, 83-84).

seventy-two. While it has obvious parallels with Jesus' sending out of the twelve disciples (9:1-6), there are significant new developments in this pericope which mark it as a major turning point of the plot. As many have noted, the number seventy-two probably symbolizes the number of Gentile nations thought to exist (Gen 10:2-31), and foreshadows Paul's missionary journeys to the Gentiles (Acts 13-14, 16-20). Indeed, just as Jesus sends out the seventy-two "two by two" (Lk 10:1), so also Paul will be paired either with Barnabas (Acts 13:1-3) or Silas (15:36- 41). And when Pisidian Antioch rejects the message of Paul and Barnabas, they will shake the dust off their feet (13:51: cf., 18:6), reminiscent of Jesus' words to the seventy-two to wipe any unreceptive city's dust off their feet (Lk 10:11; cf., 9:5). Finally, in an echo of Jesus' admonition to the seventy-two (10:3; cf., 11:32-34), Paul will warn the Ephesian elders of "fierce wolves" who will enter the community, "not sparing the flock" (Acts 20:29).

As many others have noted, and as I have hinted at in this paper at various places, it seems that Jesus becomes the model for Paul's ministry later in the book of Acts. But in fact, I think that the mechanics of the parallels were developed in precisely the opposite direction: that is to say, I believe that it was actually the Lukan author's idealized model of Paul's evangelistic program that was read back into his plotting of the Jesus story (see below).[55] This is why, in spite of the more episodic character of the gospel of Luke,[56] there is an important progressive development in Jesus' Galilean ministry, a particular "order" ($\kappa\alpha\theta\epsilon\xi\hat{\eta}s$) that moves from city to countryside, from Jew to Gentile, and ultimately, from Jerusalem to Rome. This order is constructed largely to parallel the author's conception of Paul's missionary activity.[57] However, in the process of drawing out the parallels between Jesus and Paul, the author also takes pains to separate Paul from Peter as representative of Jesus' twelve apostles.[58] Here the ideological concerns of the Lukan author radically

---

55 And now am I in the brain of an original flesh-and-blood author? I think not. I'm just playing the game of classic fiction, acting like an omniscient narrator who inhabits the body of one of his or her characters. Here, the character I've invented is "the Lukan author." Beware of taking the rhetoric of academic fictions too seriously.

56 See Tannehill, for example, who says that "the bulk of Luke, like the other Synoptic Gospels, is episodic. A causal continuity among successive scenes is the exception rather than the rule. If there are narrative continuities, they inhere more in the characters and the general roles they play than in a causal connection of events" (*Narrative Unity*, 2:5; cf., 6-7).

57 This is particularly evident in Acts 19:11-23, where Paul confronts the seven sons of Sceva who are using the name of Jesus to cast out demons (19:11-20). This scene is then immediately followed by Paul's decision to go to Jerusalem, where he sends helpers on ahead of him (19:21-22). Interestingly, precisely the same topics and order are found in the author's juxtapositioning of Mk 9:38-40 (Lk 9:49-50), his own editorial seam (9:51), and "special L material" (9:52).

I can't believe that I've resorted to redaction criticism to explain this peculiarity. Somebody help me! Exorcise the recalcitrant demon! Get me back on a literary path.

58 Ronald D. Witherup has recently shown how "the redundancy in Acts 9,22 and 26 [and 22:1-16; 26:12-19] is part of the purposeful characterization of Paul growing in stature as a witness to the gospel to the ends of the earth" ("Functional Redundancy in the Acts of the Apostles: A Case Study," *JSNT* 48 [1992] 67-87; 70). While this is indeed true, what

overshadow his structuring of the plot, for it seems to me that the author is implicitly delineating three periods—or better, three generations of Christian experience and work. So although there are significant "historical" differences between Peter (as representative of the twelve apostles) and Paul's relationship to Jesus, there is a remarkable unity in the way the Spirit of God works in each of them and in the life of their Lord; a unity that transcends time and place.

The following columns are an attempt to portray some of those major similarities and important differences between Jesus, Peter, and Paul in Luke-Acts.

Differences between the religious experiences of Jesus, Peter, and Paul

Jesus	Peter	Paul
God's messiah	apostle who walked with Jesus	one who never saw Jesus
	sees Jesus perform miracles	sees neither Jesus' nor Peter's miracles
born in a Judean city	from a Galilean city a Pharisee, educated in Jerusalem	born in a Cilician city
completely faithful to God	denies having known Jesus	persecutor of Christians
conceived of Holy Spirit	filled with Holy Spirit at Pentecost with signs by unimportant disciple	received Holy Spirit from laying on of hands
transfigured	sees transfigured Jesus	sees a light, hears the voice
resurrected	sees resurrected Christ	of the exalted Lord Christ
in Jerusalem	in Jerusalem before the ascension	near Damascus much later

Similarities between the ministries of Jesus, Peter, and Paul

Jesus	Peter	Paul
proclaims God's salvation	proclaims God's salvation	proclaims God's salvation
in cities	in cities	in cities
has a vision	has a vision	has a vision
contacts with a centurion	contacts with a centurion	contacts with a centurion
performs miracles	performs miracles	performs miracles
heals the lame	heals the lame	heals the lame
raises the dead	raises the dead	raises the dead
heals by his clothes	heals by his shadow	heals by kerchief
exorcises demons	exorcises demons	exorcises demons
before the Jewish Council	before the Jewish Council	before the Jewish Council
questioned by a Herod	imprisoned by a Herod	questioned by a Herod
tried by Roman prefect	tried by Roman prefect	

Witherup doesn't note is how these very same repetitions of Paul's call also emphatically separate him from Peter and the other apostles who saw the resurrected Christ within the forty day period prior to his ascension (Lk 24:34-49; Acts 1:3-11, 21-26; cf., Tannehill, *Narrative Unity*, 2:24, 119-120; Minear, 148-166). Although Tannehill wants to argue that Paul also saw the resurrected Christ, I believe it would be more accurate to say that what Paul saw was Christ as the exalted Lord (ibid., 280-281; cf., Acts 22:14; 26:15-16).

| killed by Romans | imprisoned by Jewish Council | imprisoned by Romans[59] |

Conclusions

As I noted at the beginning of this paper, the gospel of Luke seems to fall into four major plot sequences. The introductory sequence centers upon events surrounding the births of Jesus and John in Judea, and their initial appearances in the public arena. The second sequence centers upon Jesus' Galilean ministry. The third sequence is the "travel section" where Jesus is on his way to Jerusalem, and the fourth sequence centers on Jesus' Jerusalem ministry and his passion.

In focusing my attention upon the second of these major plot sequences (4:13-9:62), I have attempted to show how Jesus' programmatic proclamation in Nazareth generates a tripartite narrative subsequence (4:13-6:11; 6:12-7:50; 8:1-9:62), each of which begins with a proclamation of Jesus. The first of the three proclamations is a purely Lukan construction (4:16-30), the second is formed from Q material (6:20-49), and the third is a shortened version of Mark 4 (8:4-21). These three proclamations and their introductory frames (4:13-15; 6:12-19; 8:1-3) summarize plot developments for their narrative sequences with respect to Jesus' expanding ministry and the new emphases in his activity—plot developments which also will eventually be paralleled by Paul in Acts. To a lesser extent, then, the two additional Galilean proclamations are also programmatic. Finally, I have tried to show the interconnectedness of Jesus' three proclamations with the miracles following them by tracing the ways in which the authoritative λόγοι of Jesus bear immediate fruit in his powerful deeds.

Toward a Dialogue Between Methods

So in what ways might New Testament literary criticism interact with social world criticism? While we cannot expect most New Testament literary critics to become experts in social theory and cultural anthropology, nor can we expect social world critics to become experts in literary theory, it is important to converse with one another. We both claim to be reading the same texts, and both perspectives are increasingly sensitive to the implicit ideologies motivating contemporary and ancient readers. Furthermore, both approaches claim to be methodologically explicit and synchronic.

From my perspective, one of the values of a literary critical perspective is that it reveals how language functions rhetorically within a narrative world such as the one created by the author of Luke-Acts.[60] This is not to negate the

---

59 This list is not intended to be complete. For additional parallels, see Charles H. Talbert, *Literary Patterns, Theological Themes, and the Genre of Luke-Acts* (Missoula, MT: Scholars, 1974) 16-18, 23-24; and more recently, Susan M. Praeder, "Jesus-Paul, Peter-Paul, and Jesus-Peter Parallelisms in Luke-Acts: A History of Reader Response," *SBLSP* 24 (1984) 23-39.

60 Or perhaps I should say, literary criticism gives me a professionally acceptable grammar and an arena for showing how language can function within an ancient

broader social world outside Luke-Acts, but rather points out that Luke-Acts' world is also an artifice, an imaginative, artificial construct which may have its own peculiar ways of using language. Literary theory and narrative poetics may offer additional insights into this world and the foundations upon which it is constructed.[61]

Social world people tell us that the literature we have from the ancient world represents perhaps the elite 5%, and so we might expect the values of that 5% to be represented in Luke-Acts as well.[62] But here a cautionary note is in order. The common charge of elitism, anachronism, and ethnocentrism directed at non-social, non-anthropological methods betrays precisely the type of positivist underpinnings which many New Testament literary critics found disconcerting in the traditional historical-critical approaches, and from which they are seeking to liberate themselves. Most literary critics today are seriously engaged with questions about the reader "in front of the text," and the political and ideological implications of "canonical" readings. Insofar as both approaches attempt to challenge these readers and readings (whether it be from the perspective of the ancient elite or the contemporary elite), we are on common turf; but insofar as one approach or the other seeks to claim a kind of primordial presence for itself, I think we are headed in wrong directions.

Finally, on a more personal note, I have gained much from my conversations with the strange ethnological birds perched among us. Having grown up in a cross-cultural environment on the Navajo Reservation and having married into an Asian-American subculture, I have learned as much about myself from these emic and etic dialogues as about the Mediterranean world itself. And to the extent that cultural-anthropological work on the Bible illuminates the narrative worlds of ancient texts, I find it helpful for my own literary work. At the same time, I believe that a recognition from the social world people of narrative, its components and poetics, can illuminate their work and keep them from the positivist, one-dimensional types of problems evident in earlier historical-critical work.

---

narrative world. Of course, it also gives me a grammar and a critical perspective for deconstructing that narrative world and all other worlds. But that is a different story, another writing, and another reading.

[61] And, I might add, it offers the seeds for its deconstruction.

[62] Oakman and Robbins are particularly good at making this distinction.

Narrative Outline of the Composition of Luke According to the Two Gospel Hypothesis

Lamar Cope, Carroll College, Waukesha, WI
David L. Dungan, University of Tennessee, Knoxville
William R. Farmer, University of Dallas
Allan J. McNicol, Inst. for Christian Studies, Austin, TX
David B. Peabody, Nebraska Wesleyan University
Philip L. Shuler, McMurry University

Preface

This paper is part of a continuing analysis of the composition of Luke according to the Two Gospel Hypothesis. Our earlier work on Luke may be found in Lamar Cope et al., "Narrative Outline of the Composition of Luke according to the Two Gospel Hypothesis" in *Society of Biblical Literature 1992 Seminar Papers,* SBLSP 31 (ed. Eugene H. Lovering, Jr.; Atlanta, GA: Society of Biblical Literature, 1992) 98-120. This earlier paper dealt with Lk 3:1-7:10 and was divided into two parts—"Part Two: The New Era of Salvation Announced by John and Jesus. Lk 3:1-4:13" and "Part Three: The Inauguration of Jesus' Ministry in Nazareth, Capernaum and throughout Galilee. Lk 4:14-7:10."

Philip L. Shuler's analysis of "Luke 1-2" in that same 1992 collection of SBL Seminar Papers (pages 82-97) dealt with "Part One: A Prologue, the Birth and Infancy Narratives of John and Jesus, and a Concluding Narrative of Jesus' Youth. Lk 1:1-2:52."

This paper takes up where the earlier co-authored paper concluded and deals with "Part Four: Jesus the Prophet Does Mighty Deeds Throughout Galilee Lk 7:11-9:50."

A discussion of the format and a table of abbreviations we have adopted for this continuing analysis of Luke may be found in the 1992 SBL Seminar paper on pages 99-100.

Part Four:
Jesus the Prophet Does Mighty Deeds Throughout Galilee Lk 7:11-9:50

Introduction

According to Luke, Jesus has appeared in Nazareth (Lk 4:16) and announced the fulfillment of Isaiah's prophecy (Lk 4:21, cf. Lk 4:18-19/Isa 61:1-2 LXX). Following Jesus' inaugural sermon in Luke's gospel (Lk 4:16-30),

Jesus' initial mission tour began and ended in Capernaum (Lk 4:31-7:10; cf. the geographical references to Capernaum at Lk 4:32 and 7:1). The essential message of the mission of Jesus, given at the outset of his ministry in Nazareth (Lk 4:16-30), was reaffirmed in the Sermon on the Plain (Lk 6:20-7:1a). Between these two blocks of teaching (Lk 4:16-30 and Lk 6:20-7:1a), Luke narrates the early Galilean ministry as a series of actions (Lk 4:31-6:19) validating Jesus' inaugural sermon (Lk 4:16-30). An expanded account of the teaching of Jesus will also be set out in the section on the Way to Jerusalem (Lk 9:51-19:44).

Lk 7:11-9:50 has a similar structure to that found in the earlier unit (Lk 4:31-6:19). With the exception of Lk 8:4-18 (Luke's version of the parable complex of Mt 13:1-53), the material in Lk 7:11-9:50 consists of the narration of a series of episodes in Jesus' ministry as he moves through Galilee (Lk 7:11, in the city of Nain; 8:1, 4, going city by city and village by village; 8:22, crossing the lake [of Galilee]; 8:26, in region of the Gerasenes across from Galilee; 8:40 returning [to Galilee]; 9:10, in the city of Bethsaida; 9:28, on a mountain; 9:37, coming down from the same mountain; 9:51, Jesus sets his face to go to Jerusalem).

For Lk 7:1-10, Luke utilized Mt 8:5-13. From Mt 8:13, Luke continued to follow Mt and, since he had utilized Mt 8:14-17 earlier at Lk 4:38-41, Luke arrived at Mt 8:18. There in Mt, Luke would read that Jesus left Capernaum (ἀπελθεῖν εἰς τὸ πέραν, Mt 8:18, cf. Mt 8:5). Luke uses this information from Mt to say that Jesus is beginning a second journey within his adult ministry through the cities of Galilee (Lk 7:11-12; 8:1, 4, 27, 34, 39; 9:5-6, 10, 12 [See also Lk 23:49, where the women mentioned there, looking back to Lk 8:1-4, are said to have followed Jesus from Galilee]; cf. Mt 9:1, 9:35 and 11:1). Luke apparently uses the Stichwörter πόλις (Lk 7:11) and κώμη (Lk 9:52, 56) to form an inclusio around this second tour of Jesus' Galilean ministry (Lk 7:11-9:50; Note that Tischendorf reads πόλιν Σαμαριτῶν at Lk 9:52 for the Nestle-Aland κώμην Σαμαριτῶν). Thus, the first half of Jesus' Galilean ministry consists of a tour going from Capernaum and returning to Capernaum (Lk 4:31-7:10; cf. 4:32 and 7:1); the second half consists of a tour going from city to city (Lk 7:11-9:50; cf. Mt 9:35-10:5[11:1?]).

In Lk 7:11-8:21 we learn from the narrative that Jesus was confessed as a great prophet in Nain (Lk 7:16) Contrast Lk 4:24 where Jesus was rejected as a prophet (Lk 4:24, 28-29) in Nazareth (Lk 4:16), in his own country (Lk 4:23), even as Elijah and Elisha worked outside their own country (Lk 4:25-27). And contrast the implicit denial of Jesus as a prophet by Simon the Pharisee at Lk 7:39, following Jesus' own affirmation that his kinsperson, John the Baptist, was "more than a prophet" (Lk 7:26).

In Lk 8:22-9:6 Jesus gives further demonstrations of power (Lk 8:22-56) and finally transmits this same power to the Twelve whom he commissions to follow his example (Lk 9:1-6). These demonstrations of power sometimes elicit faith (Lk 8:39, 48, 56); but more often they produce fear or ridicule (Lk 8:25, 34-37, 47, 50). As deeds of power, they provide a fitting parallel to the astonishing deeds recounted in Lk 7:11-22 which opened the unit.

Lk 7:11-17 Restoring to Life the Son of the Widow at Nain

Continuing to invoke images of the work of the great earlier prophets, Elijah and Elisha, Jesus brings a widow's son back to life. The healing takes place amidst exclamations that a prophet like them has emerged once again. God has once again visited his people for healing.

[After narrating an account of a healing of a servant near death (Lk 7:1-10; cf. ἤμελλεν τελευτᾶν at Lk 7:2) Luke appends an even more impressive account, a resuscitation from death itself (cf. τεθνηκώς in Lk 7:12) of a widow's only son (Lk 7:11-17). Luke may be balancing two similar stories here, one dealing with the dying son of a man (Lk 7:1-10) and one dealing with the dead son of a woman (Lk 7:11-17). But there is also a contrasting balance between the Gentile man of power, a Centurion, and the Jewish powerless widow whose only son had died. • This story may have been taken from another source (διήγησις?) to which Luke had access (cf. Lk 1:1-4), since it is not found in Matthew. • The account also reflects an implicit Elijah-Elisha motif that was made explicit by Luke at Lk 4:25-27. The account of the healing of the centurion's servant (Lk 7:1-10) also had many formal similarities to the account of Elisha's healing of Naaman the leper in 2 Kings 5:1-14 to which Luke had made explicit reference in Lk 4:27. Although Lk 7:11-17 has certain verbal similarities to the Elijah story in 1 Kings 17, the similarities are not numerous enough to lead one to the conclusion that Luke has composed this account solely on the basis of 1 Kings 17:17-24 (pace Goulder). • καὶ ἐγένετο to open a new unit (Lk 7:11) is a certain linguistic usage of Luke [Collison, 43], as is the use of πορεύομαι followed by εἰς [Collison, 61]. Other Lukan usages that may be found within this unit would include 'the articular participle of καλέω used as an appositive usually to a proper noun' [Collison, 80], ὡς [Collison, 121], ὡς δὲ ἤγγισεν [Collison, 228], Μὴ κλαῖε [Collison, 231], ἐδόξαζον τὸν θεόν [Collison, 46], λαός [Collison, 173-174], περὶ αὐτοῦ of Jesus [Collison, 140], περίχωρος [Collison, 175], the collocation of καί + a verb meaning 'to go out' with ἦχος/φήμη/λόγος + ὅλος/πᾶς + περὶ αὐτοῦ + περίχωρος [Collison, 214].]

Mt 11:2-19 ===> Lk 7:18-35 The Messengers From John the Baptist

Continuing the theme of Jesus as the newly risen prophet (Lk 7:16), Luke inserts a lengthy account depicting John the Baptist explicitly requesting confirmation from Jesus that Jesus is the eschatological prophet promised by Isaiah. Jesus' reply (Lk 7:22-23) repeats some elements from Jesus' programmatic sermon in Nazareth (Lk 4:16-27). "The blind see" and "the poor are evangelized" (Lk 4:18/Lk 7:22). Having seen all these things (Lk 7:18) John's disciples are then exhorted to tell John what they have *seen* and *heard* (Lk 7:22). Jesus' ministry, as it is depicted from Lk 4:18 through Lk 7:23 is the fulfillment of promises given to Israel.

Lk 7:18-35 ends with Jesus' retrospective soliloquy on John the Baptist (Lk 7:24-35). As prophet of the most high (Lk 1:76) and as the forerunner of the dawning messianic age (Lk 7:27), John is said to be "more than a prophet" (Lk 7:26). Later in Lk and presumably in dependence upon Mt 11:13, Jesus will be depicted as saying that John and his ministry concluded the period of "the Law and the Prophets" (Mt 11:13/Lk 16:16 cf. Lk 7:30-31). Jesus points out that the Pharisees and the lawyers rejected the purposes of God in not accepting John's baptism (Lk 7:30). But in accepting John, the people and the tax gatherers recognized his message was a display of God's righteousness (cf. Lk 7:29 which is retrospective within the text of Luke to Lk 3:10-14). Jesus, the Spirit-anointed prophet (Lk 3:22, 4:1, 18) has appeared and has manifested the purpose of God (Lk 7:34-35).

[Having left Mt at Mt 8:13/Lk 7:10 in order to insert the story of the raising of widow's son at Nain (Lk 7:11-17), Luke now resumes his use of the text of Mt at Mt 11:2/Lk 7:18. Luke has moved forward within the text of Mt from Mt 8:13/Lk 7:10 to Mt 11:2/Lk 7:18 to continue comparing John, the prophet, who is not the anointed one (Lk 1:76, 3:15, 7:26), with Jesus, the prophet, who is the anointed one (Lk 4:18, 24, 7:16). Luke's move forward from Matthew 8:13 to 11:2 may also have been influenced by the "marker verses" in Mt 7:28 and 11:1.

⟨7:28⟩ Καὶ ἐγένετο ὅτε ἐτέλεσεν ὁ Ἰησοῦς τοὺς λόγους τούτους, . . .
⟨11:1⟩ Καὶ ἐγένετο ὅτε ἐτέλεσεν ὁ Ἰησοῦς διατάσσων τοῖς δώδεκα μαθηταῖς αὐτοῦ, . . .

• Consistent with his use of comparison in Lk 1-2, Luke brings John to the forefront of his narrative here (Lk 7:18-35) with a question : "Are *you* He who is to come or should we await another?" (Lk 7:19/Mt 11:3; cf. Lk 7:20 where the question is repeated in a "dualistic" fashion) • Luke follows Mt closely in this unit (Mt 11:2-19/Lk 7:18-35). However, congruent with his theological agenda there are several places where Luke modifies Mt (Lk 7:18), adds to Mt (Lk 7:21, 29-30) or omits from Mt (Mt 11:8b, 12, 14-15). • In Lk 7:18 Luke claims that John sent two disciples to Jesus. This is characteristic of Lukan delegations (Lk 10:1; 19:29; 22:8; Acts 23:23). • The strikingly forced addition of Lk 7:21, "and on many that were blind he bestowed sight," is designed to fill out the summary of the ministry of Jesus, so that it will be more in keeping with Jesus' explicit announcement of the fulfillment of Isa 62 at Lk 4:18-21: "He has anointed me to bring good news to the poor. He has sent me to proclaim. . . recovery of sight to the blind" (Lk 4:18/Lk 7:22). Luke has not mentioned Jesus' healing a blind person up to this point in his gospel (Lk 7:21/Mt 11:5; but cf. the healing summaries in Lk 4:40 and 6:18-19), even though such a healing did precede this context in Mt (Mt 9:27-31). On the Two Gospel Hypothesis, had Luke not moved forward from Mt 8:13/Lk 7:10 to Mt 11:2/Lk 7:18, thereby passing over Mt 9:27-31, Luke would not have needed to rush to include a reference to the healing of the blind (Lk 7:21) prior to Jesus' summary of his activities at Lk 7:22/Mt 11:5. • Most of the activities that Jesus lists in his response to John at Lk 7:22 seem to reflect roots in a particular understanding of the prophecies of Isaiah. "The blind receive their sight" (cf. Lk 4:18, 7:21-22/Isa 61:1-2 LXX; Isa 29:18 and 35:5). "The lame walk" (cf. Lk 5:17-26,

7:22/Isa 35:6). "The deaf hear" (cf. Lk 5:12-16, 7:22/Isa 29:18, 35:5). "The poor have the good news preached to them" (Lk 4:18, 6:20/Isa 29:19) The balance of the activities to which Jesus makes reference in this Lukan literary context (Lk 7:22) that do not seem to have their roots in a particular understanding of Isaiah (i.e., "the lepers are cleansed" and "the dead are raised") seem to unite Jesus' actions rather directly with those of the prophets, Elisha ("the lepers are cleansed" cf. Lk 4:27/2 Kings 5) and Elijah ("the dead are raised" cf. Lk 4:25-26/1 Kings 17:17-24) to whom Luke, in contrast to Matthew, made explicit reference in Jesus' inaugural sermon (Lk 4:16-30). • The appearance of σκανδαλίζειν in the text of Luke (Lk 7:23/ Mt 11:6) indicates Luke's literary dependence on the text of Mt. The word, σκανδαλίζειν, is a frequently reoccurring literary feature of the gospel of Matthew. It is found in Lk only twice, always in contexts parallel to Mt where there is evidence of copying. Mt 17:26/No parallel context in either Mk or Lk; Mt 18:6/Mk 9:42/Lk 17:2; Mt 18:7 (three uses)/cf. Mk 9:42 No Parallel/Lk 17:2 (one usage); Mt 18:8/Mt 5:30/Mk 9:43, 45/No Parallel Context in Lk; Mt 18:9/Mt 5:29/Mk 9:47/No Parallel Context in Lk; Mt 11:6/Lk 7:23; Mt 13:21/Mk 4:17; Mt 13:57/Mk 6:3; Mt 15:12NP; Mt 17:27NP; Mt 24:10/Mk 14:27; Mt 26:31/Mk14:29; Mt 26:33NP complete the usages of σκανδαλίζω within the Synoptic gospels. • Luke omits a key saying ("For all the prophets and the law prophesied until John came," Mt 11:13) from Mt 11:12-14 at this point in his narrative for two reasons. First, although Luke was careful to claim that John was a great prophet (Lk 7:26-28), he was not, in Luke's view, in contrast to Matthew, the "Elijah who is to come" (Mt 11:14; cf. Mt 17:9-13, also omitted by Luke). Second, Luke will use a modified form of Mt 11:13 later in Lk 16:16, as part of a series of teachings condemning the Pharisees who "justify themselves before men," in contrast with those who "eagerly seize the Kingdom of God" (Lk 16:14-16). • The addition of the parenthetical statement in Lk 7:29-30 is a Lukan composition, perhaps created on the basis of Mt 11:19c (Lukan linguistic characteristics in Lk 7:29-30 include ἅπας/πᾶς ὁ λαός [Collison, 174], βαπτίζω [Collison, 42] and νομικός [Collison, 174-175]). This statement is intended to provide a contrast between the Pharisees and the lawyers, on the one hand, and the people and the tax-collectors, on the other. The tax-collectors (Lk 3:12) and the people (Lk 3:21) had responded to John with baptism and, thus, merited retrospective praise from Jesus at Lk 7:29. The Pharisees and the lawyers, however, did not submit to John's baptism (cf. Lk 3:3-22) and thus were said by Jesus at Lk 7:30 to have rejected God's βουλήν. The word, βουλή occurs ten times in Lk-Acts, but never in Mt. • Lk 7:29-30 sets the stage for Luke to move on to a discussion of another set of contrasting responses, i.e., those made by "this generation 'of children'" to John, on the one hand, and to Jesus, on the other (Lk 7:31-35/Mt 11:16-19). Assuming that "the Son of Man" is to be identified with Jesus in this context (Lk 7:34; see Acts 7:55-56 where this identification is explicitly affirmed) Luke takes one more opportunity to compare Jesus with John the Baptist (cf. Lk 1:5-3:21; 5:27-39; 7:18-30).

• This unit in Luke (Lk 7:18-35) ends with the Lukan version of the saying about Wisdom, who is "justified" (ἐδικαιώθη; Lk 7:35) by *all* her *children*," in contrast to Mt which says that "Wisdom is justified by her *works*." For Luke, wisdom's children are presumably the people and the tax-collectors who were said by Luke also to have "justified God" (ἐδικαίωσαν τὸν θεόν) in Luke's parenthetical comment at Lk 7:29-30. Note that τελῶναι is complemented in Lk 7:34 by the addition of "sinners" (καὶ ἁμαρτωλῶν; cf. Mt 11:19, See also Mt 21:31-32, another Matthean context dealing with John the Baptist, where the similar phrase, τελῶναι καὶ πόρναι, is found). • The use of "sinners" at Lk 7:34 helps Luke unite this story with the next one in Luke which is about a woman whom Luke describes as a "sinner" (cf. Lk 7:34 and Lk 7:37, 39, cf. Lk 7:47, 48, 49). Thus, the text of Luke contains at least three themes that connect this story in Luke (Lk 7:18-35) with the next one in sequence within his gospel (Lk 7:36-50); "eating," (cf. Lk 7:34 and 7:36), "Pharisees who reject the Wisdom of God" (cf. Lk 7:30 and 7:36, 39) and "sinners" (cf. Lk 7:34 and Lk 7:37, 39, cf. Lk 7:47, 48, 49).]

(Mt 26:6-13) Lk 7:36-50 The Forgiveness of a Sinful Woman

Luke next recounts a banquet scene in which Jesus' actions are condemned by his host, a Pharisee. A local woman, known to be a sinner, came in, undoubtedly uninvited, and began to cry, wetting Jesus' feet with her tears. Drying his feet with her unbound hair, she poured expensive myrrh on his feet and kissed them. At this, Simon the Pharisee decides that Jesus is no *prophet* because of his failure to send away the sinful woman. Jesus understands the thoughts of Simon and, in Luke's view, demonstrates his prophetic character by pronouncing the woman's sins forgiven because of the love (Lk 7:47) and faith (Lk 7:50) demonstrated by her actions. The vignette ends on a note of irony when those sitting in the Pharisee's house ask themselves, "Who can forgive sins?" Readers of Luke know that scribes and Pharisees themselves had already said at Lk 5:11 that "God alone can forgive sins." The final word of Jesus (Lk 7:50) echoes a major Lukan theme: "Your faith has saved you" (cf. Lk 8:48 within the story of the woman with the flow of blood, which, like Jesus' words in Lk 7:50 also continues with the phrase, "go in peace"; Lk 17:19 within the story of the ten lepers; and Lk 18:42 within the story of the healing of the blind man).

[Jesus has been described in Lk 7:34 as one who comes eating and drinking, a friend of tax gatherers and sinners. Luke goes on with a story about a sinful woman (Lk 7:36-50). • The history of the transmission of this particular story is difficult to determine. In its present form, Lk 7:36-50 has some striking parallels with Mt 26:6-13 (e.g., a setting in the home of a man named Simon and a visit from a woman with an alabaster flask of ointment). On the other hand, there are many differences in detail as well. The fact that a similar account is found in Jn 12:1-8, where the woman is named Mary, adds to the complexity of the tradition-history of this unit. • Note the verbal similarities between Luke 5:20-21 and 7:48 [Collison, 216]. Given these verbal similarities, we may be in touch with Lukan redaction and the irony to which we called attention above was probably in Luke's mind when he composed, or edited, these two literary contexts.

Luke 5:20-21

‹5:20› καὶ ἰδὼν τὴν πίστιν αὐτῶν
εἶπεν, Ἄνθρωπε,
ἀφέωνταί σοι αἱ ἁμαρτίαι σου. ‹5:21›
καὶ ἤρξαντο διαλογίζεσθαι
οἱ γραμματεῖς καὶ οἱ Φαρισαῖοι
λέγοντες,
Τίς ἐστιν οὗτος
ὃς λαλεῖ βλασφημίας;
τίς δύναται
ἁμαρτίας ἀφεῖναι
εἰ μὴ μόνος ὁ θεός;

Luke 7:48-49

‹7:48› εἶπεν δὲ αὐτῇ,
Ἀφέωνταί σου αἱ ἁμαρτίαι.
‹7:49› καὶ ἤρξαντο
οἱ συνανακείμενοι
λέγειν ἐν ἑαυτοῖς,
Τίς οὗτός ἐστιν
ὃς καὶ
ἁμαρτίας ἀφίησιν;

(Mt 9:35, 11:1 ; 27:55-56)   Lk 8:1-3 Women Who Have Faith in Jesus

Jesus and the Twelve are now joined by certain women. Some are those who were healed and became followers, such as Mary of Magdala. Others are wealthy and help to support Jesus' mission, such as Joanna, Susanna, and many others. All of the women evidently manifest *faith* in Jesus, as did the sinful woman in the story just recounted (Lk 7:50).

[On the principle of association with the previous story about a woman who showed faith (Lk 7:36-50), Luke now includes a brief reference to other women who respond to Jesus in faith and service (Lk 8:1-3). • The name of Mary of Magdala may have come to Luke from Mt 27:56/Lk 8:2. The reference to "service" in Mt 27:55 may also be reflected in Lk 8:3. • To the name, Mary of Magdala in Galilee, that Luke may have borrowed from Mt, Luke adds the name of Joanna, who will appear later in Luke's accounts of the post-resurrection appearances of Jesus (Lk 24:10). • Joanna's identity as "the wife of Chuza, Herod's steward," and the name, "Susanna," are details that Luke could not have gotten from extant text(s) of Mt. Luke had first introduced Herod Antipas to his readers at Lk 3:1 and included a reference to Herod's arrest of John the Baptist at Lk 3:18-20. After this oblique reference in Lk 8:3, the next reference to Herod is to his curiosity about Jesus (Lk 9:7-9). After Jesus "sets his face to go to Jerusalem" (after Lk 9:51), the Pharisees suggest that Herod wants to kill Jesus (Lk 13:31). Some subsequent references to Herod in Lk (Lk 23:7bis, 8, 11 12, 15) only confirm Herod's pleasure at finally fulfilling his long-time desire to see Jesus, about whom he had heard reports (Lk 23:7bis, 8 cf. Lk 9:7-9). and his irritation at Jesus' silence when Pilate sent him to him (Lk 23:11-12). Apart from hearsay words on the lips of the Pharisees at Lk 13:31, there is nothing in Luke's gospel which would suggest that Herod wished to see Jesus dead and Luke's Pilate confirms this (Lk 23:13-16). Joanna's identity both as a wealthy supporter and follower of Jesus and as a member of Herod's household may also serve in Luke's gospel to relieve Herod of whatever responsibility he may have had in the death of Jesus. Luke, however, is not reluctant to affirm Herod's responsibility for the death of John, Jesus' kinsman (Lk 9:9). Of course, Luke may be depicting Herod and Pilate as Josephus treated the Romans. The truth about Herod's response to Jesus may be better represented by Lk 13:31 and 23:11-12 than by other Lukan contexts. But even in these two most negative contexts, Herod's responsibility for the death of Jesus is tempered by the voices of Jewish Pharisees (Lk 13:31) or Jewish chief priests and scribes (Lk 23:10). • Luke is careful to remind the reader that Jesus is on a tour, "city by city and village by village" (Lk 8:1). Lk 8:1 may echo Mt 11:1 and Mt 9:35, the verses which serve to open and close Matthew's Missionary Discourse (Mt 9:35-11:1).

Matt 9:35	Luke 8:1	Matt 11:1
Καὶ περιῆγεν	Καὶ ἐγένετο	Καὶ ἐγένετο
ὁ Ἰησοῦς	ἐν τῷ καθεξῆς	ὅτε ἐτέλεσεν ὁ Ἰησοῦς
	καὶ αὐτὸς διώδευεν	διατάσσων
		τοῖς δώδεκα μαθηταῖς αὐτοῦ,
τὰς πόλεις πάσας	κατὰ πόλιν	μετέβη ἐκεῖθεν
καὶ τὰς κώμας	καὶ κώμην	
διδάσκων		τοῦ διδάσκειν
ἐν ταῖς συναγωγαῖς αὐτῶν		
καὶ κηρύσσων	κηρύσσων καὶ	καὶ κηρύσσειν
		ἐν ταῖς πόλεσιν αὐτῶν.
τὸ εὐαγγέλιον	εὐαγγελιζόμενος	
τῆς βασιλείας	τὴν βασιλείαν τοῦ θεοῦ καὶ οἱ	
	δώδεκα σὺν αὐτῷ,	
καὶ θεραπεύων		
πᾶσαν νόσον		
καὶ πᾶσαν μαλακίαν.		

Mt 9:35 and 11:1 are the verses in Matthew's gospel that frame the unit just prior to the one that Luke, on the Two Gospel Hypothesis, was just using (Lk 7:18-35/Mt 11:2-19). • Collison [220] lists "an imperfect plus a prepositional phrase with κατά plus two participles" as a collocation that appears three times within the gospel of Luke (Lk 8:1, 9:6, and 13:22). Other Lukan linguistic characteristics that appear within Lk 8:1-3 include καὶ αὐτός of Jesus [Collison, 194], εὐαγγελίζομαι [Collison, 51], ἡ βασιλείαν τοῦ θεοῦ [Collison, 169-170], οἱ δώδεκα [Collison, 168], ὅς + εἶναι + participle [Collison, 226], θεραπεύω ἀπό [Collison, 124], the collocation of a person ἀφ᾽ οὗ/ἧς + δαιμόνιον and ἐξερχόμαι [Collison, 219], articular participle of καλέω used as an appositive, usually to a proper noun [Collison, 80], δαιμόνιον [Collison, 171], ἀπό with verbs of healing [Collison, 124], ἕτερος [Collison, 184], and ὅστις in a demonstrative sense [Collison, 208].]

(Mt 5:15, 10:26)   Mt 13:1-23 ===> Lk 8:4-18   (cf. Lk 11:33; 12:2-3)
Lessons on Faith: the Parable of the Sower and the Lamp

Luke now portrays Jesus giving a deeper insight to all those who seek to follow him in a life of faith (Lk 8:12-13). The parable of the sower urges his listeners to trust in God. Those who sow are not responsible for the mysterious results (Lk 8:4-8). Although the disciples are given the secrets of the Kingdom of God, others do not see, hear, or understand (Lk 8:9-10). The parable of the sower is interpreted to emphasize the mystery of those who receive that which is sown, which, for Luke, is "the Word of God" (Lk 8:11). The first grouping which includes three soils ("by the ὁδόν"; "on the rock"; and "among the thorns"; Lk 8:11-14) are those who have initially heard, or received the word, but fell away. The second grouping includes only those "in the good earth" (Lk 8:15) "with a good heart," like the disciples, who "hear the word, hold fast, and bear fruit in abundance." Jesus then goes on to say that all who *hear* are like a lamp on a stand that enables all who enter the house to "*see the light*" (Lk 8:16; cf. Lk 8:10 on *seeing* and *hearing*). For everything hidden will be made manifest. On the other hand, even the disciples must watch how they hear. For, those who only seem to have seen and heard will have even that apparent possession taken from them (Lk 8:18).

[The opening verse, with its reference to those who came to Jesus from each city (Lk 8:4, τῶν κατὰ πόλιν ἐπιπορευομένων πρὸς αὐτόν), ties this story (Lk 8:4-18) to the immediately preceding account in Luke of the women who followed Jesus as he went from city to city, κατὰ πόλιν (Lk 8:1-3, esp. Lk 8:1) • The attachment of the saying on the lamp (Lk 8:16-17) to the interpretation of the Parable of the Sower (Lk 8:11-15) augments the themes of "seeing" (Lk 8:10, 16, 18) and "hearing" (Lk 8:10, 12, 13, 14, 15, 18) that Luke found already in Matthew's version of Jesus' parable discourse (Mt 13:9/Lk 8:8, Mt 13:13/Lk 8:10, Mt 13:14-15, Mt 13:16-17/(Lk 10:23-24), Mt 13:18, Mt 13:19/Lk 8:12, Mt 13:20/Lk 8:13, Mt 13:22/Lk 8:14, Mt 13:23/Lk 8:15, Lk 8:16,18). • The references to the "heart" at Lk 8:12 and 15 reflect Mt. 13:15bis and13:19. The note about the heart in Mt 13:19 is surely grounded, for Matthew, in the reference to the "heart" in the Isaiah passage (Isa 6:9-10) Matthew quoted in Mt 13:15. Although Luke does not quote this passage from Isaiah in his parallel to Mt, he has fragmentarily preserved this Matthean theme by including references to "the heart" in his parallel to Mt 13 at Lk 8:12 and 15. This constitutes good evidence of Luke's literary dependence upon the text of Matthew within this literary context. • Luke's collection of sayings in Lk 8:16-18a appears to be a conflation of logia found in Luke in two later contexts, Lk 11:33 and Lk 12:2-3.

Luke 11:33	Luke 8:16-18a	Luke 12:2-3
33 Οὐδεὶς λύχνον ἄψας	16 Οὐδεὶς δὲ λύχνον ἄψας	
εἰς κρύπτην	καλύπτει αὐτὸν σκεύει	
τίθησιν		
οὐδὲ ὑπὸ τὸν μόδιον		
ἢ ὑποκάτω κλίνης		
τίθησαν,		
ἀλλ' ἐπὶ τὴν λυχνίαν,	ἀλλ' ἐπὶ λυχνίας	
	τίθησιν,	
ἵνα οἱ εἰσπορευόμενοι	ἵνα οἱ εἰσπορευόμενοι	
τὸ φῶς		
βλέπωσιν.	βλέπωσιν	
	τὸ φῶς.	
	17 οὐ γάρ	2 οὐδὲν δὲ
	ἐστιν κρυπτὸν	συγκεκαλυμμένον ἐστὶν
	ὃ οὐ φανερὸν γενήσεται,	ὃ οὐκ ἀποκαλυφθήσεται,
	οὐδὲ ἀπόκρυφον	καὶ κρυπτὸν
	ὃ οὐ μὴ γνωσθῇ	ὃ οὐ γνωσθήσεται.
		3 ἀνθ' ὧν ὅσα ἐν τῇ σκοτίᾳ
	καὶ εἰς φανερὸν ἔλθῃ.	εἴπατε ἐν τῷ φωτὶ
	18 βλέπετε οὖν πῶς	
	ἀκούετε·. .	ἀκουσθήσεται,
		καὶ ὃ πρὸς τὸ οὖς
		ἐλαλήσατε
		ἐν τοῖς ταμείοις
		κηρυχθήσεται
		ἐπὶ τῶν δωμάτων.

• Further, Lk 8:16, in wording similar to Lk 11:33, notes that "those who go in should see the light." Luke may have united these two sayings about "the lamp" and "the light revealing all things" within this context to emphasize "coming to see the light" as a metaphor for "faith." Luke has been discussing the theme of "faith" within the larger literary context at least since Lk 7:1-10. • The interpretation of the parable of the sower deals with "hearing." Luke also emphasizes "seeing" as another metaphor for the response of faith (cf. Lk 8:16, 18, 20). • All of these themes—seeing, hearing, understanding and "the heart"—are also motifs in the parallel context of Mt 13:13-16. • The main parallel to Matthew's version of the saying about the lamp set on a lamp stand (Mt 5:15) is Lk 11:33 and the main parallel to Lk 12:2-3 is Mt 10:26-27. That is, Luke seems to have chosen to use these teachings of Jesus from Mt's Sermon on the Mount (Mt 4:23-7:29) and Mt's Missionary Discourse (Mt 9:35-11:1) within his Central Section/Travel Narrative (Lk 9:52-19:44). Perhaps it seemed to Luke to be "more orderly" to present much of Jesus' teaching in one very long central section (Lk 9:52-19:44) rather than in five rather long speeches of Jesus, as Matthew had done (Mt 4:23-7:29, 9:35-11:1, 13:1-53, 18:1-19:1 and 24:1-26:1). Although Luke did plan to use these materials later in his gospel, he seems to have thought it appropriate to utilize teachings similar to Lk 11:33/Mt 5:15 and Lk 12:2-3/Mt 10:26-27 within this earlier Lukan context also (Lk 8:16-17). By anticipating teachings he would recount later in his gospel (Lk 8:16-17), Luke would add emphasis to them when they appeared later (Lk 11:33, 12:2-3). However, in order not to be verbally redundant, Luke modified the wording of both Mt 5:15 and Mt

10:26 for use in Lk 8:16-18, reserving the wording that is closer to Mt for use later in his Central Section. The materials from Mt 5:14-16 and 10:26-27 have been included by Luke within this context because they both contain references to "light" (τό φῶς, Mt 5:14, 16 and 10:27), which is emphasized by Lukan redaction at Lk 8:16 (cf. Lk 11:33).]

Mt 12:46-50 ===> Lk 8:19-21 Jesus' Mother and Brothers

Continuing with the theme of "hearing the Word of God and doing it" (Lk 8:21, cf. esp. Lk 8:11-15) Luke next recounts the brief exchange concerning Jesus' mother and brothers wanting to see him.

[While focusing on teachings that related to those who "hear and do the word of God," a theme which reached its peak and culmination with the Interpretation of the Parable of the Sower (Lk 8:11-15) and the Sayings about the Lamp and Light (Lk 8:16-18), Luke here concludes a unit with a story that affirms Jesus' true relatives are "those who hear the Word of God and do it" (for "Word of God" in Lk cf. Lk 5:1; 8:11, 21; 11:28). • Two units in Matthew's gospel that include references to Jesus' family (Mt 12:46-50 and Mt 13:54-58) frame Matthew's parable chapter (Mt 13:1-53). In utilizing material from Matthew, Luke reversed the order of two of these units, thus placing Luke's version of the Parables Discourse *before* his unit on Jesus' family (Lk 8:4-15/Mt 13:1-23[53] and Lk 8:19-21/Mt 12:46-50). But Luke may have been influenced in making this change in order by the fact that Mt 13:54-58, which also contains references to Jesus' family, does follow Matthew's parable chapter immediately and Luke had already utilized Mt 13:54-58 at Lk 4:16-30. • The preceding series of vignettes, including a number of stories about women, exhibits a literary finesse which cannot be seen in synopses arranged according to the priority of Mark. • Luke's use of παραγίνεσθαι with πρός (Lk 8:19) may be Lukan (Collison, 96-97). The use of τυγχάνειν (Lk 8:19: six times in Luke-Acts, but never in Mt or Mk) may be Lukan composition [Goulder 1, 419]. Ακούειν τὸν λόγον τοῦ θεοῦ (Lk 8:21) and εἶπεν with the preposition are characteristic Lukan expressions [Goulder 1, 419]. Lukan literary characteristics tend to distinguish Luke's version of the response of Jesus' family to his mission from Matthew's version.]

Mt 8:18, 23-27 ===> Lk 8:22-25 The Stilling of the Storm

Setting off on another "tour"—this time to the other side of the Sea of Galilee—the disciples are quickly put to the test as a violent storm arises, threatening to swamp the boat. In panic, they beseech Jesus to do something. He immediately calms the storm, asking them "Where is your faith?" (Lk 8:25; cf. Mt 8:26 where the disciples are described as ὀλιγόπιστοι). The disciples, who will continue to see great displays of Jesus' powers, should not have succumbed to panic.

[At Lk 8:22, Luke begins to construct a brief side tour that ends at Lk 8:40. This side tour includes four deeds of power by Jesus, the stilling of the storm (Lk 8:22-25), the healing of the Gerasene Demoniac (Lk 8:26-39), the healing of Jairus' Daughter (Lk 8:40-42a, 49-56) and the healing of the woman with the issue of blood (Lk 8:42b-48). Luke's move forward from Mt 8:34 to Mt 9:18 in composing this side tour is explained by the fact that Luke had already utilized all of the material in Mt that intervenes between Mt 8:34 and 9:18 earlier in his gospel (cf. Lk 5:17-39/Mt 9:1-17). • The introductory, transitional and temporal reference in Lk 8:22 accords with Luke's style, ('Εγένετο δὲ ἐν μιᾷ τῶν ἡμερῶν cf. Lk 5:17 and Collison, 132-133, 214) • Lk 8:22 echoes Mt 8:18 with the use of εἰς τὸ πέραν. Note that Mt 8:18 is where Luke stopped utilizing Mt at Lk 7:10, prior to introducing his story of the raising of the Widow's Son at Nain from his special material (Lk 7:11-17) and moving forward to Mt 11:2 for the subsequent unit, Lk 7:18-35/Mt 11:2-19. Luke now returns precisely to Mt 8:18 to begin composing this miracle story unit from Matthew's first collection of miracle stories within Mt 8-9. • Although Lk 8:22 does echo Mt 8:18 (εἰς τὸ πέραν), Lk 8:22 also shares a number of features with Mt 8:23.

Mt 8:23 καὶ ἐμβάντι αὐτῷ εἰς τὸ πλοῖον. . . οἱ μαθηταὶ αὐτοῦ
Lk 8:22 καὶ ἐνέβη   εἰς   πλοῖον καὶ οἱ μαθηταὶ αὐτοῦ

The appearance of verbal parallels in Lk 8:22 both to Mt 8:18 and to Mt 8:23 provides some evidence of Luke's omission here of material within the text of Matthew that intervenes between these verbal parallels. This intervening material from Mt 8:19-22 will be utilized by Luke later as the first unit within Luke's Central Section (Lk 9:57-62/Mt 8:19-22) following Luke's transitional and introductory story (Lk 9:51-56). • Within the story of the stilling of the storm, Matthew has Jesus rebuke his disciples *before* Jesus calms the storm, but Luke records that Jesus questioned the *faith* of his disciples *after* the storm has been calmed. The emphasis on the faith of the disciples in Lk 8:25 probably derives from the appearance of ὀλιγόπιστοι at Mt 8:26 and ὀλιγόπιστοι is one of Matthew's literary characteristics [Tevis, Table 105] • Luke emphasizes the disciples' fear, followed by their amazement (cf. Mt 8:25). Lk 8:25 should be translated, "having been afraid, they now marveled," presumably at the *power* of Jesus to calm the storm. • Compare the verbal agreements between Lk 8:25 and 4:36 [Collison, 216] • Luke, more correctly, refers to the "lake" (λίμνη) of Galilee (e.g., Lk 8:22-23), rather than to the "sea" (θάλασσα) of Galilee, as does Matthew typically (e.g., Mt 8:24, 26, 27, cf. Collison, 182). • Luke changes Mt's primitive form of address to Jesus from κύριος to ἐπιστάτα (Lk 8:24; Collison, 181). • Other Lukan linguistic characteristics within this literary context include πρὸς ἀλλήλους [Collison, 201-202] and "the inferential ἄρα following the interrogative pronoun" [Collison, 101-102] • Other significant Lukan parallels with the text of Mt also appear in this story (cf. Mt 8:25/Lk 8:24; Mt 8:27/Lk 8:25). • The action from Lk 8:22 through Lk 9:5 seems to take place in one great day of Jesus' demonstrations of *power* that concludes with the sending out of the twelve (Lk 9:6).]

Mt 8:28-34 ===> Lk 8:26-39 The Salvation of the Gerasene Demoniac

Having demonstrated great power over creation, Jesus now encounters the demonic world directly. Jesus' power is awesome. At his appearance, the demons beg him not to be sent into the abyss (Lk 8:31). Nevertheless, ultimately, they are drowned (Lk 8:33). Luke narrates that the herdsmen went into the city and told everybody how the demoniac had been healed. People came to see the healed demoniac and found the man completely healed, and reacted with intense fear (Lk 8:37), begging Jesus to leave. The concluding scene of the man who had been healed sitting παρὰ τοὺς πόδας τοῦ Ἰησοῦ (Lk 8:35) is a picture of ideal discipleship, especially since Jesus sends him out to proclaim to the whole city what *God* had done for him and the former demoniac proclaims, rather, what *Jesus* had done for him (Lk 8:39).

[Luke continues to follow Mt's order for this Lukan miracle story collection and side tour, but turns this healing story in Mt into an account of ideal discipleship, as we can see from Luke's additions to Matthew's version. • The phrase παρὰ τοὺς πόδας τοῦ Ἰησοῦ (Lk 8:35; cf. προσέπεσεν, Lk 8:28) is a characteristic Lukan description of the ideal disciple (cf. Lk 7:38; 8:35, 41; 17:16; cf. Lk 10:39). • The demoniac's confession of Jesus as "Son of the Most High God" (Lk 8:28, cf. Mt 8:29, simply "Son of God") is probably intended by Luke to be a reminiscence of Lk 1:32 where the angel, Gabriel, announces to Mary that the child in her womb "will be called the Son of the Most High" (cf. Lk 2:14). But note that Jesus' disciples, according to Luke's Sermon on the Plain, are also to receive this same title, "sons of the most high," (Lk 6:35), perhaps after they are "clothed with power from on High" (Lk 24:49). This event would come sometime following the ascension of Jesus (Lk 24:50-52), probably at the next Pentecost festival (Acts 2:1ff.). • Lk 8:29, an addition to Mt, provides reasons why "no one was strong enough to pass through the way" inhabited by the two demoniacs (Mt 8:28). • Lk 8:30, also an elaboration of Mt, may be an attempt by Luke to harmonize his story of one man with Matthew's story of two demoniacs. While Luke discusses only one demoniac, he does say that this one man had "many demons." Hence, the one man's name has a corporate meaning, "Legion" (Lk 8:30). • Luke omits Matthew's note that the swine were "far off," since Luke has no need to preserve Jewish sensibilities for his more Gentile readers. (Mt 8:30/Lk 8:32). • Again, Luke changes Matthew's references to the "sea" of Galilee (Mt 8:32) into a reference to a "lake" (Lk 8:32; cf. Lk 5:1-2, cf. Mt 4:18bis; Lk 8:22-23, cf. Mt 8:27; see also Mt 13:1, 14:25, 15:29). • Others of Luke's changes in the text of Mt are necessitated by his basic change from the two demoniacs in Mt to the one in his own version (e.g., Lk 8:27, ἀνήρ τις, Lk 8:28, ἐμοί instead of ἡμῖν and με instead of ἡμᾶς, cf. Mt 8:29).]

Mt 9:18-26 ===> Lk 8:40-56 The Healing/Raising of Two Women

Here, in his final demonstrations of power within this section (Lk 8:22-9:5), Jesus shows his control over sickness and death. We also have yet another example of a woman showing great faith which "saves" her. Immediately after the salvation of the woman with the issue of blood, Jesus exhorts those who report that the synagogue ruler's daughter has died "not to fear, but to believe and she will be well." Despite cries of derision (Lk 8:53) and the absence of faith (Lk 8:50), Jesus raises the ruler's daughter from death (Lk 8:54-55).

[Luke, still following the Matthean order as he composes this miracle story complex (Lk 8:22-56/Mt 8:18-34, 9:18-26), narrates the account of the dramatic saving of two women (Lk 8:40-56). This miracle story unit culminates in the account of the raising of Jairus' daughter. • This composition fits well with Luke's use of the text of Mt. Luke is at the end of Mt 8 (i.e., Mt 8:34). Luke has already utilized material found in Mt 9:1-17 (Lk 5:17-26). The very next unit in Mt is Mt 9:18-26 and this is precisely where Luke resumes his composition. • Again, Lk 8:40-56 is an expansion of Mt (See, especially, Lk 8:43b, 44b, 45-47, 49-50c, 51b-52a, 53b, 54b-56). • Goulder [1, 424-425] has noted two examples of unusual phraseology from Mt echoed in Luke. See ἄρχων εἶς from Mt 9:18 echoed in Lk 8:41 and τοῦ κρασπέδου τοῦ ἱματίου αὐτοῦ from Mt 9:20 repeated in Lk 8:44. • The concluding admonition of Jesus to the parents, μηδενὶ εἰπεῖν τὸ γεγονός (Lk 8:56), stands in opposition to the ending of this particular story in Mt 9:26, καὶ ἐξῆλθεν ἡ φήμη αὕτη εἰς ὅλην τὴν γῆν ἐκείνην. But Luke seems to have utilized Mt 9:26 already at Lk 4:14. • It also contrasts with the conclusion of the previous story where Jesus explicitly instructs the healed demoniac to return home and "proclaim what God has done for" him (Lk 8:39). What seems to be involved in this particular case, is not a fragment of the so-called "Messianic Secret" in Lk. Instead, it is to be explained as part of the noteworthy Lukan aversion to reports of resurrection as a basis for faith in God. See, for instance, the conclusion to the parable of the rich man and Lazarus, found only in Luke among the canonical gospels (Lk 16:19-31), and Herod's curt reference to John the Baptist's resurrection from the dead at Lk 9:7/Mt 14:2; cf. Acts 20:9-10.].

Mt 9:35-10:16, 11:1 =====> Lk 9:1-6 Sending out of the Twelve

Jesus, who has just modeled casting out of demons (Lk 8:26-39, cf. 4:41), healing diseases (Lk 4:40, 5:15, 6:18 and 7:21) and preaching the good news of the Kingdom of God (Lk 4:44, 6:20-7:1 and 8:1), now sends the Twelve disciples out with authority to do the same (Lk 9:1-2, 6). The emphasis on traveling light assumes they will be well-received (Lk 9:3-5; cf. Lk 10:1-12; Contrast Lk 22:35-38). They are not to tarry; but to travel swiftly, proclaiming the Kingdom to the houses, cities, and villages round about (Lk 9:4-6).

[For now, Luke passes over The Healing of Two Blind Men (Mt 9:27-31) which he will use in a modified form later in Lk 18:35-43 (but cf. Mt 20:29-34). He then omits The Healing of a Dumb Demoniac altogether (Mt 9:32-34). These omissions from Mt (Mt 9:27-34) within this Lukan literary context (Lk 8-9) bring Luke to the Sending of the Twelve in Mt 9:35-10:15. For the moment, Luke passes over the bulk of Mt's missionary discourse (Mt 9:35-11:1), just as he once passed over the material within the Sermon on the Mount (Mt 4:23-7:28, cf. Lk 4:32). And just as Luke chose to recount an abbreviated version of the Sermon on the Mount (Mt 5:2-7:28) in a later literary context within his gospel (Lk 6:20-7:1), so Luke will also use portions of Matthew's missionary discourse (Mt 9:35-11:1, cf. Lk 9:1) in later Lukan literary contexts (cf. Mt 9:35-10:16, cf. Lk 10:1-12; Mt 10:17-25, cf. Lk 21:12-19; Mt 10:26-33, cf. Lk 12:2-9; Mt 10:34-36, cf. Lk 12:51-53; Mt 10:37-11:1, cf. Lk 14:26-27). The majority of the material that Luke will use from Mt's Missionary Discourse, Luke moves to three or four alternative literary contexts (Lk 10, 12 and 14) within his Central Section (Lk 9:51-19:44). The balance of what Luke uses from Matthew's Missionary Discourse finds a place in Luke's version of Jesus' last eschatological discourse within Lk 21. [See Allan J. McNicol, W. R. Farmer, David L. Dungan, J. Bernard Orchard, David B. Peabody, "The Two-Gospel Hypothesis Textual Discussion. The Composition of the Synoptic Eschatological Discourse," in *The Interrelations of the Gospels. A Symposium led by M.-É. Boismard - W. R. Farmer - F. Neirynck. Jerusalem 1984*, Bibliotheca Ephemeridum Theologicarum Lovaniensium 95 (ed. David L. Dungan; Leuven: Leuven University Press/Uitgeverij Peeters, 1990)156-200. In this same volume, also see "Appendix. Synopsis. The Eschatological Discourse," 615-28]. • Lk 9:1-2 contains a fragmentary preservation of a major Matthean literary characteristic (See Mt 4:23, 9:35 and 10:1; cf. Lk 9:1, νόσους θεραπεύειν, and Lk 9:2, κηηρύσσειν τὴν βαλισείαν and τούς ἀσθενεῖς (reading τούς ἀσθενεῖς with א A D L alii). Some of these literary characteristics seem to have come to Matthew from one of the prophetic texts that the first Evangelist uses so often to shape his narrative (See Mt 8:17/Isa 53:4 Αὐτὸς τὰς ἀσθενείας ἡμῶν ἔλαβεν καὶ τὰς νόσους ἐβάστασεν; cf. Mt 10:8). • Luke gave the names of twelve of the disciples (Mt 10:2-4), whom Luke distinctively also designates as "apostles," already at Lk 6:13-16. Luke, therefore, does not need repeat this list of names here (Lk 9:2ff.) when he comes to the later literary context in Mt where the list appears for the first time (Mt 9:35-10:4). This omission of the list of the twelve names from Mt 10:1-4 brings Luke to Mt 10:5 where Matthew says that Jesus sent these Twelve out. Lk 9:2 says simply, by way of abbreviation, that "he sent them." Unlike Mt, Luke has divided the call of the twelve (Mt 10:1-4/Lk 6:12-16) from their commissioning (Mt 10:5-16/Lk 9:1-6). • And unlike Mt, Luke has a commissioning not only of twelve "apostles" (Lk 9:1-6), but also of seventy(-two) other "disciples" (Lk 10:1-12). It would appear that Luke has utilized materials from Mt 9:35-10:16 in composing his two commissionings of "apostles" and "disciples." Luke has divided some of the materials from Mt 9:35-10:16

between his two different literary contexts (Mt 10:1/Lk 9:1; Mt 10:7-8/Lk 9:2b; Mt 9:35-38/Lk 10:1-2; Mt 10:13/Lk 10:6-9; Mt 10:15-16/Lk 10:12) and duplicated a few details from Mt in both Lukan contexts (Mt 10:5/Lk 9:2a/Lk 10:3; Mt 10:9-11/Lk 9:3-4/Lk 10:4-5; Mt 10:14/Lk 9:5-6/Lk 10:10-11) • That Lk 9:1-6 is a revision of an early Jewish-Christian missionary tradition, like that found in Mt 10, is evident from Luke's omission of key concepts, vis-à-vis Mt, such as "worthy" (ἄξιος, Mt 10:10, 11, 13bis, but cf. ἄξιος at Lk 10:7) and "peace" (*shalom*, Mt 10:13bis, but cf. Lk 10:5, 6bis). Luke's editing of Mt makes the Jewish background of the material in Mt 10 disappear in Lk 9, but Luke's editing of Mt 10 also makes Lk 9 more appropriate for a Greco-Roman, Gentile, reader. "Shake the dust off your feet" was a standard Jewish way of leaving a Gentile area behind. Matthew did not explain this Jewish practice and implied curse, but Luke offers an explanatory addition (cf. Lk 9:5, εἰς μαρτύριον ἐπ' αὐτούς and David L. Dungan, *The Sayings of Jesus in the Churches of Paul. The Use of the Synoptic Tradition in the Regulation of Early Church Life* [Oxford: Basil Blackwell, 1971] esp. Part 1. Chapter 3, "The Mission Instructions in the Synoptic Gospels," pp. 41-80). (See St.-Bill., I, 571.) • Goulder argues that the phrase, ἐξερχόμενοι ἀπὸ τῆς πόλεως ἐκείνης τόν κονιορτόν. . . ἀποτινάσσετε, at Lk 9:5, is triply characteristic of Matthew ([1] the participle, ἐξερχόμενοι; [2] two locations joined by "or" such as "town or village," and [3] a phrase beginning with an article and ending with ἐκεῖνος, such as τῆς πόλεως ἐκείνης). Lk 9:5 reflects all three of these Matthean literary characteristics according to Goulder [Goulder, 1, 431]. • Lk 9:1-2 and 6 seem to reflect both the opening of Matthew's Missionary Discourse (Mt 9:35) and its ending (Mt 11:1).]

Mt 9:35	Lk 9:6, 1-2	Mt 11:1
35 Καὶ περιῆγεν	6 ἐξερχόμενοι δὲ διήρχοντο	1 Καὶ ἐγένετο ὅτε ἐτέλεσεν
ὁ Ἰησοῦς		ὁ Ἰησοῦς διατάσσων τοῖς δώδεκα μαθηταῖς αὐτοῦ, μετέβη ἐκεῖθεν
τὰς πόλεις πάσας καὶ τὰς κώμας, διδάσκων	κατὰ τάς κώμας	τοῦ διδάσκειν καὶ κηρύσσειν
ἐν ταῖς συναγωγαῖς αὐτῶν καὶ κηρύσσων τὸ εὐαγγέλιον τῆς βασιλείας,	εὐαγγελιζόμενοι	ἐν ταῖς πόλεσιν αὐτῶν
	καὶ θεραπεύοντες πανταχοῦ.	

```
                          1 Συγκαλεσάμενος δὲ
                          τοὺς δώδεκα
                          ἔδωκεν αὐτοῖς
                          δύναμιν
                          καὶ ἐξουσίαν
                          ἐπὶ πάντα τὰ δαιμόνια
καὶ θεραπεύων           καὶ νόσους
πᾶσαν νόσον             θεραπεύειν,
καὶ                       2 καὶ ἀπέστειλεν αὐτοὺς
                          κηρύσσειν
                          τὴν βασιλείαν τοῦ θεοῦ
                          καὶ ἰᾶσθαι
πᾶσαν μαλακίαν.          τοὺς ἀσθενεῖς,
```

Luke 9:6 may also constitute the closing member of an inclusio in Luke that opened at Lk 8:1

Luke 8:1

<8:1> Καὶ ἐγένετο ἐν τῷ καθεξῆς
καὶ αὐτὸς διώδευεν
κατὰ πόλιν καὶ κώμην
κηρύσσων
καὶ εὐαγγελιζόμενος
τὴν βασιλείαν τοῦ θεοῦ
καὶ οἱ δώδεκα σὺν αὐτῷ,

Luke 9:6

<9:6> ἐξερχόμενοι δὲ
διήρχοντο
κατὰ τὰς κώμας

εὐαγγελιζόμενοι

καὶ θεραπεύοντες πανταχοῦ.

Mt 14:1-2 ====> Lk 9:7-9 Herod's Comment on Jesus

While the disciples are away on their mission (between Lk 9:6 and Lk 9:10), Luke changes the scene (Lk 9:7-9) and reports Herod the tetrarch's wonder at the reports that John the Baptist had been raised (ἠγέρθη) from the dead, that Elijah had appeared (ἐφάνη), or that a certain one of the prophets of old had been raised (ἀνέστη). To these reports Herod responds, "I beheaded John (Lk 9:9, cf. Mt 14:10), but who is this concerning whom I hear such things?" These reports motivate Herod to seek to see Jesus (Lk 9:9, cf. the retrospective reference back to Lk 9:9 at Lk 23:8).

[We noted evidence above that Luke was aware of the compositional framework of Mt. Lk 9:1-2 and 6 follow the wording of both Mt 9:35 and 11:1, the verses that frame Matthew's "Missionary Discourse." Luke passes over the teaching material in Mt 11-13 within this Lukan literary context (Lk 9:7-9) because he has used some of this material from Mt already and because he plans to use more of it within his Central Section. Luke has already used some of Mt 11-13 in the following earlier Lukan literary contexts (Mt 11:2-19/Lk 7:18-35; Mt 12:1-14/Lk 6:1-11; Mt 12:33-37/Lk 6:43-45; Lk 12:46-50/Lk 8:19-21; Mt 13:1-23/Lk 8:4-15, Mt 13:54-58/Lk 4:16-30). Luke will use more of this material in the following later Lukan literary contexts (Mt 11:20-30/Lk 10:13-22; Mt 12:22-32/Lk 11:14-23; Mt 12:38-45/Lk 11:24-32). Luke used much of the parable material from Mt 13:1-53 within his version of the parable chapter already in Lk 8 (Mt 13:1-23/Lk 8:4-15). Luke will use a bit more of Mt 13 at Lk 10:23-24/Mt 13:16-17 and Lk 13:18-21/Mt 13:31-32. • The concluding verse of Matthew's parable chapter is Mt 13:53 which, like Mt 11:1 (the literary context parallel to Lk 9:6), includes a formula with which Matthew characteristically concludes each of the five major discourses of Jesus within his gospel (cf. Mt 7:28-29, 11:1, 13:53, 19:1, 26:1 and Tevis, Table 1). It may be that Luke simply moved forward in Mt's text at this point (Lk 9:6/Mt 11:1) from one "marker verse" in Mt 11:1 to what follows the next "marker verse" in Mt (Mt 13:53). It may also be that Jesus' reference to the rejection his disciples might experience while on their mission (Mt 10:14/Lk 9:5) also led Luke forward within the text of Matthew to the story of Jesus' own rejection (Mt 13:54-58). But Luke had already used some of the material from Mt 13:54-58 earlier in his gospel, when he was composing his version of Jesus' inaugural sermon (Lk 4:16-30). Skipping over Mt 13:54-58 would bring Luke to Mt 14:1-2. And Mt 14:1-2 is precisely where Luke next makes use of Matthew's text (Lk 9:6/Mt 11:1, Lk 9:7-9/Mt 14:1-2). • Matthew uses these reports to Herod about Jesus as a transitional introduction for his story of the execution of John by Herod (Mt 14:3-12). Luke already alluded to John's imprisonment at Lk 3:18-20, so he could omit most of this story from Mt within this later Lukan literary context (Mt 14:3-12; cf. Lk 9:9-10). The allusion to John's beheading in Lk 9:9/Mt 14:10 is the major reminiscence of Mt 14:3-12 within Lk 9. • The vignette about Herod in Lk 9:7-9/Mt 14:1-2 functions in several ways in Luke's gospel. First, it provides for the literary passage of time between the sending out of the apostles (Lk 9:6) and their return (Lk 9:10). Luke's text, at this point, is an improvement over the text of Matthew because Matthew fails to mention the return of the disciples from their mission at all (contrast Mt 14:13 with Lk 9:10). Second, it may be noted that the reports to Herod about who Jesus is (Lk 9:7-9) are similar to the reports the disciples give to Jesus himself when he questions them about who others report him to be (Lk 9:18-19). These similar reports about who Jesus is (Lk 9:7-9 and Lk 9:18-19) serve to frame Luke's version of the Feeding of the Five Thousand (Lk 9:10-17). Third, this vignette may also serve to foreshadow the interrogation of Jesus by Herod Antipas later in Luke's gospel. The scene in Lk 23:6-12 is a unique feature of Luke's gospel when compared with the gospels of Matthew and Mark. • Luke revises Mt's account (Mt 14:1-2) to reject Herod's identification of Jesus with John the Baptist (Mt 14:2). • Luke seems to have combined the tradition about "Who do men say that I am?" (Mt 16:13-16/Lk 9:18-20) with this scene about Herod where several *prophets* are said to have reappeared (Lk 9:7-9; cf. Mt 16:13-16/Lk 9:18-20) The following may be taken as evidence that Luke is working with both Mt 14:1-12 and Mt 16:13-16 in composing Lk 9:7-9: (1) The appearance of διὰ τὸ λέγεσθαι ὑπό τινων ὅτι in Lk 9:7 and ὑπό τινων δὲ ὅτι in Lk 9:8 seem to reflect Τίνα με λέγουσιν οἱ ἄνθρωποι εἶναι τὸν υἱὸν τοῦ ἀνθρώπου; in Mt 16:13 (cf. Lk 9:18) more than anything in Mt 14:1-12 (Contrast καὶ εἶπεν τοῖς παισὶν αὐτοῦ in Mt 14:2), (2) The name, "Elijah," in Lk 9:8, which does not appear at all in Mt 14:1-12, does appear in Mt 16:14 (cf. Lk 9:18). Luke's interest in comparing Jesus and Elijah appears at least at early as Jesus' inaugural sermon in Lk 4:16-30, esp. Lk 4:25-26. (3) The wording, ὅτι προφήτης τις τῶν ἀρχαίων ἀνέστη, in Lk 9:8, may be the result of Lukan redaction (cf. Lk 9:19), but the reference to "a certain one of the prophets" probably comes from Mt 16:14 rather than from Mt 14:1-12. (But see the reference to John as a prophet in Mt 14:5 which may provide a clue to Luke's joining of materials from Mt 14:1-12 and Mt 16:13-16 as he composed Lk 9:7-9.) • On Herod's question, "Who is this about whom I hear such things?" (Lk 9:9, cf. Lk 4:36 and 8:25) see Fitzmyer, 1, 779.]

Mt 14:12-14====> Lk 9:10-11 The Return of the Disciples and Gathering of Crowds

The apostles, having been commissioned at Lk 9:1 and having gone out on their commission at Lk 9:6, are now carefully said by Luke to have returned at Lk 9:10. Upon their return, the apostles report everything they did on their mission to Jesus. Along with these newly returned apostles, Jesus withdraws into a city called Bethsaida. There, having attracted a crowd, Jesus speaks to them concerning the Kingdom of God and heals all of those having need of healing. Luke uses this scene to set the stage for his version of the Feeding of the Five Thousand.

[At Lk 9:10, Luke inserts a note about the disciples' return into the context of Mt 14:13. This verse in Mt describes Jesus' "withdrawing in a boat to a desert place privately" because of Herod's reaction to the reports of Jesus' activities. Matthew, unlike Luke, just recounted the story of John's execution by Herod in some detail (Mt 14:1-12). Luke omits the reference to the desert at this point, but does mention Jesus' withdrawal. However, Lk says that Jesus' "withdrawal" was "to a city called Bethsaida." This seemingly unmotivated reference to Bethsaida is to be explained by Luke's concern to prepare the grounds for the curse on Bethsaida which will come in Lk 10:13 (cf. Mt 11:21). As the rich number of variants in the manuscript tradition indicates, however, this reference to Bethsaida introduced serious strains in Luke's account. Under the influence of Mt's version, the disciples next say that they are "in a desert place" (cf. Mt 14:13, 15), and the people are told to "go get food from villages" round about (cf. Mt 14:15) despite the fact that in the world of Luke's text, they were still in the city of Bethsaida. • Although Luke picks up the "withdrawal of Jesus" theme from Mt 14:13 (cf. Lk 9:10), he misses the point of Matthew's carefully nuanced story of the threat of Herod. In Matthew, far from forgetting that John was "long dead" [cf. Rudolf Bultmann, *The History of the Synoptic Tradition* (tr. John Marsh; N.Y.: Harper & Row, 1963) 351-352] Jesus reacts to the word that Herod is comparing him to John by withdrawal to a desert place. Since Herod is not viewed as a threat to Jesus by Luke, Luke has Jesus receive the returning disciples' report in the city of Bethsaida. • That Matthew's story lies behind Luke's version, however, is demonstrated by the appearance of several Matthean literary characteristics within the parallel text of Luke. See, for instance, Luke's use of ὑπεχώρησεν (cf. the Matthean ἀνεχώρησεν at Mt 14:13; Tevis, Tables 13 and 15), κατ ' ἰδίαν (Mt 14:13/Lk 9:10; cf. Tevis, Table 28), the Matthean phrase, οἱ ὄχλοι ἠκολούθησαν αὐτῷ (cf. Mt 14:13; Tevis, Table 4; and Boismard, "Introduction au Premier Récit de la Multiplication des Pains [Mt 14:13-14; Mc 6:30-34; Lc 9:10-11] in *The Interrelations of the Gospels. A Symposium led by M. É. Boismard - W. R. Farmer, - F. Neirynck Jerusalem 1984* [ed. David L. Dungan; Leuven: Leuven University Press/Uitgeverij Peeters, 1990]: 244-258, esp. 245-246), and θεραπεία (cf. the Matthean verb, ἐθεράπευσεν, at Mt 14:14, cf. Tevis, Tables 5 and 8). Some of Luke's modifications of Mt are also characteristic of Luke: ὑποστρέφω [Collison, 169-170], the absolute use of οἱ ἀπόστολοι [Collison, 168], the participle of κάλεω [Collison, 179] • Luke 9:11c, "he spoke to them of the Kingdom of God" is a typical Lukan addition. (Collison, 169-170) • The "report" of the "apostles" [of Jesus] in Lk 9:10 does not refer to the story of the death of John, as the "report" of the "disciples" [of John?] does in Mt 14:12, but rather to the report of the apostles' ministry, i.e., "as many things as they had done." [cf. L. Cope, "The Death of John the Baptist in the Gospel of Matthew; or, the Case of the Confusing Conjunction," *CBQ* 38 (1976) 515-519].]

Mt 14:15-21====>Lk 9:12-17 The Feeding of the Five Thousand

Now Luke relates the story of the Feeding of the 5,000. The story highlights the role of Jesus as the prophet. In keeping with the major theme of Jesus as the great prophet that Luke has been developing through this whole unit (Lk 7:11-9:50, see esp. Lk 7:16 and 9:8), Jesus recapitulates the actions of Moses and Elisha by feeding a large group of people with few provisions (cf. Ex 16:4-36; 2 Kings 4:42-44; cf. the explicit reference to the immediately following section of 2 Kings, i.e., 2 Kings 5:1-14 in Lk 4:27).

[Since Luke has changed the locale of the feeding to the city of Bethsaida (Lk 9:10, cf. Mt 14:13), he creates a major difficulty by having the disciples remark in Lk 9:12 that they were in "a desert place." This is another indication of Luke's use of Mt. Mt 14:13 and 14:15 indicate that Jesus was in an ἔρημον τόπον for the feeding and Luke has incorporated this detail at Lk 9:12, thus creating a tension within the text of Luke between Luke's urban (Lk 9:10) and desert (Lk 9:12; cf. Mt 14:13, 15) locale for the feeding. • Lk 9:14b, "Make them sit down in companies, about 50 each," appears to be a storyteller's touch, added by Luke. • Again, a number of the literary features that distinguish the text of Luke from the text of Matthew turn out to be literary characteristics of Luke, πορεύομαι [Collison, 60-61], ἅπας/πᾶς ὁ λαός [Collison, 174], ὡσεί, especially with numerals and with the noun preceding the numeral [Collison, 112], and the collocation of οὕτως and ποιέω [Collison, 230, cf. οὕτως, Collison, 160].]

Mt 14:22-23, 16:13-20   ====> Lk 9:18-21 Peter's Confession

The move from the feeding story (Mt 14:15-21/Lk 9:12-17) to Peter's Confession (Mt 16:13-20/Lk 9:18-21) is an intriguing one. It appears that Luke has conflated two stories about Peter in his mind, thereby jumping from Mt 14:23 to Mt 16:13. That is, Luke 9:18 begins with Jesus "praying alone," as in Mt 14:23. In Matthew, this situation indicator sets up the story of the walking on the water and its dramatic dialogue with Peter (Mt 14:24-33). Luke, however, blends the story into Peter's confession by having the disciples with Jesus in prayer alone (Lk 9:18a). Luke uses that circumstance to introduce Jesus' dialogue, first, with his disciples (Lk 9:18b-20a) and, then with Peter. The scene culminates with Peter's confession that Jesus is "The Christ of God" (Lk 9:20b).

[This transition from the end of the feeding of the five thousand (Mt 14:22-23/Lk 9:18a) to Peter's Confession (Mt 16:13ff/Lk 9:18b ff.) is no more difficult for the Two Gospel hypothesis than for the Two Document hypothesis since, on both hypotheses, some explanation of Luke's great omission (Mk 6:45-8:26/Mt 14:24-16:12) is needed. • Luke's Bethsaida location (Lk 9:10) may help explain Mark's odd geography at this point (Bethsaida [Mk 6:45], Dalmanutha? [Mk 8:10], Bethsaida [Mk 8:22], Caesarea Philippi [Mk 8:27]). • If Luke changed "you are the Messiah, the Son of the Living God," (Mt 16:16) to "the Christ of God," Τὸν Χριστὸν τοῦ θεοῦ. (Lk 9:20) the phrasing, though perhaps odd, is paralleled by χριστὸν κυρίου at Lk 2:26.
• For Luke's introduction to this unit, in Lk 9:18a, cf. esp. Lk 11:1 and Collison, 218]
Lk ⟨9:18⟩ Καὶ ἐγένετο ἐν τῷ εἶναι αὐτὸν   προσευχόμενον
Lk ⟨11:1⟩ Καὶ ἐγένετο ἐν τῷ εἶναι αὐτὸν ἐν τόπῳ τινὶ προσευχόμενον,
• Comments on the verbal agreements between Lk 9:19 and 9:8 may be found in the discussion of Lk 9:7-9 above.]

Mt 16:20-23 ====> Lk 9:21-22 The First Prediction of the Passion

After Jesus charges his disciples not to tell anyone about Peter's confession that Jesus is "The Christ of God" (Lk 9:21), Jesus goes on to predict his suffering, death and resurrection "on the third day" for the first time in Luke (Lk 9:22).

[The wording of this first passion prediction in Luke (Lk 9:21) is particularly close to the wording of another passion prediction passage at Lk 17:25 [Collison, 217]. • For a detailed discussion of the passion prediction passages within the Synoptic Gospels and how the literary evidence within them provides support for the Two Gospel Hypothesis, cf. William R. Farmer, "The Passion Prediction Passages and the Synoptic Problem: A Test Case," NTS 36 (1990) 558-570. • Following this first passion prediction (Lk 9:21-22/Mt 16:20-21), Luke omits the rebuke of Peter (Mt 16:22-23), as he usually omits anything unflattering to Peter [cf. Fitzmyer, Luke, 1, 777]. • Lukan literary characteristics within this unit include παραγγέλλω [Collison, 59] and οἱ ἀρχιερεῖς καὶ οἱ γραμματεῖς [Collison, 168-169].]

Mt 16:24-28 ====> Lk 9:23-27 The Costs of Discipleship

This section of teachings that includes the requirement of bearing the cross appropriately follows Jesus' first passion prediction in Lk, as it does in the parallel in Mt. One of the major differences between Lk and Mt within this literary unit is that Lk addresses these teachings to "everyone" whereas Mt addresses them only to Jesus' "disciples." Another difference is that Luke's text specifically requires bearing of the cross "daily." A teaching similar to Lk 9:26 is also found at Lk 12:9.

[Lk 9:23-27 follows these teachings from Mt 16:24-28 very closely. Such minor differences as exist between Mt and Lk can often be explained on the basis of Lukan redaction. Lukan literary characteristics within this context would include ἔλεγεν δέ [Collison, 56], καθ᾽ ἡμέραν [Collison, 137], the anaphoric use of οὗτος [Collison, 202-203], the collocation of the interrogative pronoun τίς with the inferential particles/conjunctions ἄρα, γάρ, and οὖν [Collison, 210], λέγω δὲ ὑμῖν [Collison, 57]; cf. λέγω δὲ ὑμῖν ἀληθῶς [Collison, 225], βασιλεία τοῦ θεοῦ [Collison, 170] Also note Luke's classical usage of αὐτοῦ as a substitute for ὧδε. • On the prophetic saying in Lk 9:27 and how it and all similar prophetic sayings within the Synoptic tradition might provide evidence for solving the synoptic problem, see David B. Peabody, "A Pre-Markan Prophetic Sayings Tradition and the Synoptic Problem," *Journal of Biblical Literature* 97/3 (1978) 391-409.]

Mt 17:1-13 ====> Lk 9:28-36 Jesus in Glory

About eight days after the disciples had heard that "the Son of Man would come in his glory, in the glory of the Father, and in the glory of God's holy messengers" (Lk 9:26, cf. Mt 16:27), Jesus took Peter, James, and John onto the mountain, where this promise is fulfilled (Lk 9:29-31). While praying (Lk 9:28-29), the appearance of Jesus' face (τοῦ προσώπου αὐτοῦ) became different (ἕτερον, Lk 9:29). Moses and Elijah, two of God's holy messengers, appear in glory and converse with Jesus, "the Son of Man, in glory," just as Jesus had foretold it in Lk 9:26 (Lk 9:30-31). Moses and Elijah discussed Jesus' departure (τὴν ἔξοδον) which "he was about to fulfill in Jerusalem" (Lk 9:31, cf. Mt 16:21 and Lk 9:51-53). God's kingly power, or the divine glory, would be made manifest definitively in the death, resurrection and ascension of Jesus (Lk 19:45ff.).

Awakening from sleep, the three disciples who had accompanied Jesus to the mountain also become privy to this momentous event (Lk 9:32-33). Probably still half asleep (and not knowing what else to say), Peter suggests building a tent for Jesus, Moses and Elijah, before the latter two get away (Lk 9:33). But Peter's suggestion is interrupted by a cloud that envelops them all. Naturally, the disciples are afraid when they go into the cloud (Lk 9:34), but a voice from the cloud assures the disciples of what had already been revealed at Jesus' baptism. Jesus is not only a prophet on the level of Moses and Elijah. He is also the "elected" Son of God. The disciples are commanded to "hear him" (Lk 9:35). With the proclamation of the voice from the cloud, Jesus is found alone, but the disciples themselves keep silent and report to no one what they had seen in those days (Lk 9:36).

[At Lk 9:28, Luke begins with a redactional introduction (ἐγένετο δὲ μετὰ τοὺς λόγους τούτους, cf. Collison, 42-43) that refers his readers back to the words of Jesus in Lk 9:23-27. • Also in Lk 9:28 there is a temporal reference to "after . . . about eight days." The parallel passage in Mt 17:1 has "and after six days." In early Christian tradition there is a linkage between the eighth day and the final manifestation of Jesus in his glory (cf. Jn 20:26; Epistle of Barnabas 15). By the use of ὀκτώ Luke makes a link between the event on "*the* mountain" (Lk 9:28) and the events that will take place shortly in Jerusalem (Lk 19:45ff.). • Lk 9:28-29 depict Jesus engaging in prayer before a momentous event in his ministry, as is typical of Jesus in Luke's gospel (cf. Lk 3:21, 5:16, 6:12; 9:18; 9:28-29, 11:1, 22:40, 45-46). • The reference to the alteration of Jesus' face (τοῦ προσώπου αὐτοῦ) is probably intended to be reminiscent of the quotation from Mal 3:1, which was applied to John the Baptist at Lk 7:27, Ἰδοὺ ἀποστέλλω τὸν ἄγγελόν μου πρὸ προσώπου σου, ὃς κατασκευάσει τὴν ὁδόν σου ἔμπροσθέν σου. This language also anticipates Luke's introduction to his Central Section (Lk 9:51-19:44).
9:51> Ἐγένετο δὲ ἐν τῷ συμπληροῦσθαι τὰς ἡμέρας τῆς ἀναλήμψεως αὐτοῦ καὶ αὐτὸς τὸ πρόσωπον ἐστήρισεν τοῦ πορεύεσθαι εἰς Ἰερουσαλήμ. <9:52> καὶ ἀπέστειλεν ἀγγέλους πρὸ προσώπου αὐτοῦ.
It is also language that characterizes the commissioning of the seventy (-two) disciples, early in the Lukan Central Section.
<10:1> Μετὰ δὲ ταῦτα ἀνέδειξεν ὁ κύριος ἑτέρους ἑβδομήκοντα [δύο] καὶ ἀπέστειλεν αὐτοὺς ἀνὰ δύο [δύο] πρὸ προσώπου αὐτοῦ εἰς πᾶσαν πόλιν καὶ τόπον οὗ ἤμελλεν αὐτὸς ἔρχεσθαι.
First, John the Baptist, and then the seventy (-two), are to go before the face/presence of Jesus in preparing his way. • Luke's use of ἤμελλεν in Lk 9:31 probably anticipates the use of ἤμελλεν in Lk 10:1. Luke's use of ἤμελλεν πληροῦν ἐν Ἰερουσαλήμ in Lk 9:31 also probably anticipates what Luke will write in introducing his Central Section.
<9:51> Ἐγένετο δὲ ἐν τῷ συμπληροῦσθαι τὰς ἡμέρας τῆς ἀναλήμψεως αὐτοῦ καὶ αὐτὸς τὸ πρόσωπον ἐστήρισεν τοῦ πορεύεσθαι εἰς Ἰερουσαλήμ. <9:52> καὶ ἀπέστειλεν ἀγγέλους πρὸ προσώπου αὐτοῦ. καὶ πορευθέντες εἰσῆλθον εἰς κώμην Σαμαριτῶν ὡς ἑτοιμάσαι αὐτῷ· <9:53> καὶ οὐκ ἐδέξαντο αὐτόν, ὅτι τὸ πρόσωπον αὐτοῦ ἦν πορευόμενον εἰς Ἰερουσαλήμ.
• In parallel with the earlier theophanies to Moses and Elijah, Luke accentuates the factor of divine revelation. Both in the description of the change of Jesus' appearance (Lk 9:29) and in the Lukan additions to Mt (Lk 9:31-33), Luke has numerous references to the LXX accounts of these earlier theophanies (Moessner, *Lord of the Banquet*, 60-70). But, for Luke,

the definitive theophany is in the death and resurrection of Jesus. Jesus, God's prophet of the new era, elected Son, and anointed one, is the mediator of the divine purpose. • With his additional references to the sleepiness of the disciples, Luke may be suggesting that this story had its genesis in the dreams of the disciples. • Earlier, Luke had omitted Mt's references to the church being built on Peter (Mt 16:17-19, cf. Lk 9:20) and the rebuke of Peter (Mt 16:22-23, cf. Lk 9:22). In place of these omissions Luke now stresses that Peter, James and John see Jesus in the glory that is to be manifested in his death and resurrection (9:31-32). • As earlier, here again we see Luke modifying Mt's primitive address to Jesus as "Lord" (Mt 17:4) to his own preferred ἐπιστάτης (Lk 9:33, cf. Lk 5:5, 8:24bis, 8:45; See also Lk 9:49 and Collison, 181) • Luke's addition to Peter's suggestion in Mt 17:4 that they build three tents (i.e., that "Peter didn't know what to say," Lk 9:33) may indicate that Luke either didn't recognize or didn't affirm Peter's parallel statement in Mt as an allusion to Sukkoth. • Unlike Mt 17:6-7, where the disciples are said to be in mysterious fear after the statement comes from the voice from the cloud, Luke says that the disciples have a natural fear when they are enveloped by the cloud (Lk 9:34). • Luke's change of "beloved son" in Mt 17:5 to "elected" son in Lk 9:35 anticipates Luke's affirmation of Jesus as "the elected Christ of God" in Lk 23:35. Luke's change of wording here, in combination with his preservation of wording similar to Mt 3:17 at Lk 3:22 reveals Luke's literary dependence upon the text of Mt. Matthew quotes a Greek text of Isa 42:1-4 extensively at Mt 12:18-21. Within this quotation from Isaiah, introduced by a typical fulfillment of prophecy formula in Mt (Mt 12:17), God's son/servant is referred to as "beloved." Presumably, this passage from Isa influenced Matthew's wording of the voice from the cloud both at Jesus' baptism (Mt 3:17) and at Jesus' transfiguration (Mt 17:5). Luke preserves the wording "beloved son" once, in the words from the voice from heaven at Jesus' baptism (Lk 3:22), and alters the wording once, in the words from the voice from heaven at Jesus' "transfiguration" (Lk 9:35). This constitutes evidence of fragmentary preservation within the text of Luke of phrasing characteristic of the text of Matthew. The case for Luke's literary dependence upon the text of Mt, in this instance, is strengthened by the fact that Luke does not preserve within his gospel the quotation from Isa 41 that provides the background for these words from heaven in Mt. • As usual, Lukan literary characteristics tend to distinguish Luke's account from that at Mt. See, for instance, ὡσεί with numerals (Collison, 112), προσεύχομαι of Jesus (Collison, 63), ἕτερος (Collison, 184), ἀνήρ (Collison, 167), ὅστις as an implied demonstrative (Collison, 208), the imperfect of μέλλω (Collison, 58), the periphrastic pluperfect (Collison, 73), καὶ ἐγένετο (Collison, 42), the genitive absolute (Collison, 77-78), ἐπιστάτης (Collison, 181], ἐν with the articular infinitive of verbs implying motion (Collison, 229), καὶ αὐτοί emphatic (Collison, 196), σιγάω (Collison, 64), the collocation of ἐν with ἡμέρα and ἐκεῖνος (Collison, 225), double negatives (Collison, 164-165), ὅς with the attraction of the antecedent (Collison, 205-206).]

Mt 17:14-23 ====> *Lk 9:37-45 The Healing of the Demon Possessed Boy and The Second Prediction of the Passion*

Following the transfiguration ("on the eighth day") on the mountain, Jesus and those with him descend the mountain and are confronted by a great crowd. With Lk 9:38, Luke has signaled his omission of Matthew's identification of the coming of Elijah with John the Baptist (Mt 17:10-13) and moved on to Mt 17:14 where the ὄχλος is present. Here, Jesus receives a man who says a spirit/demon has seized his only son (Lk 9:42). As in Mt's account, the disciples were not able to aid the man (Lk 9:40/Mt 17:16). This occasions Jesus' rebuke of his disciples as part of a "faithless and perverse generation" (Mt 17:17/Lk 9:41). In contrast with Matthew's emphasis on the cure, Luke's interpretation of this cleansing exorcism is a theological reflection upon the relation of the cleansed man and God: i.e., compare Lk 9:42b where the boy is given "to his father" (ἀπέδωκεν αὐτὸν τῷ πατρὶ αὐτοῦ cf. Lk 7:15) with Lk 9:43 where the response is to "the majesty of God" (ἐπὶ τῇ μεγαλειότητι τοῦ θεοῦ). It is in this majestic context that Luke attempts to confront his disciples with the announcement of the necessity of the Son of Man's impending death (Lk 9:44), but they were unable to understand (Lk 9:45), just as they were unable to exorcise the demon possessed son (Lk 9:40).

[Luke 9:37 follows Mt 17:9, the setting for Matthew's discussion of the coming of Elijah that was otherwise omitted by Luke (Mt 17:10-13), by bringing Jesus and his disciples down from the mountain (κατελθόντων αὐτῶν ἀπὸ τοῦ ὄρους). • Luke's use of the aorist participle in the genitive absolute (Lk 9:37) is explained by the presence of the aorist participle in Mt 17:14. Since a first prediction of Jesus' resurrection already appeared in Lk 9:22 and since a prediction of what is about to happen to the "Son of Man" will again appear at Lk 9:44, Luke loses little by the omission of Lk 17:10-13. In addition, the note at Mt 17:13 could identify John the Baptist with Elijah (Mt 17:12a-b) or with "the Son of Man" (Mt 17:12c). Therefore, Luke omits the ambiguous note. • Luke moves beyond Mt with his use of δέομαι (Lk 9:38) in comparison with Mt's ἐλέησον (Mt 17:15). The man now appeals to Jesus directly (δέομαι) even as he had earlier appealed to Jesus' disciples (ἐδεήθην, Lk 9:40). • Luke retains Mt's record of Jesus' answer to the man (Mt 17:17/Lk 9:41). • Goulder has noted the similarity and parallelism of Luke's use of "only begotten" in Lk 9:38 and in Lk 7:12. The "only begotten" healed son of a widow in Lk 7:12 is paralleled by the "only begotten" healed son of a father in Lk 9:42. The son of the widow in Nain is "returned to his mother" in Lk 7:15 while the "only begotten son in Lk 9:42 is "returned to his father" (Goulder, I:445).]

328 / SBL 1993 Seminar Papers

Mt 17:24-27 The Temple Tax =====> Omitted by Luke
Mt 18:1-5 (Mt 17:9-21; Mt 10:42) ====> Lk 9:46-48
The Debate Over "Who Is Greatest?"

Luke's introduction to his version of Jesus' discussion of True Greatness with his disciples is vague. "A dialogue came in among them. Who might be greatest of them?" (Luke 9:46; cf. Luke 22:24).

Matthew introduces his literary unit on True Greatness, immediately following his unique story of the Temple Tax (Mt 17:24-27), with a similarly vague situation indicator and a question on the lips of the disciples, "In that hour the disciples came to Jesus saying, 'Who then is greatest in the Kingdom of the heavens?'" (Mt 18:1).

In Mt 18:4, Jesus provides an answer to this question, in wording similar to the original question. The question and the answer in Mt focus not simply on "Who is greatest?" but more specifically on "Who is greatest *in the kingdom of Heaven?*" This question and answer structure provides an inclusio around the opening pericope of Matthew 18 (Matt 18:1-4).

Matt 18:1 Τίς ἄρα   μείζων ἐστιν ἐν τῇ βασιλείᾳ τῶν οὐρανῶν;
Matt 18:4 οὗτός ἐστιν ὁ μείζων   ἐν τῇ βασιλείᾳ τῶν οὐρανῶν.

Note that Matt 18:3 fits beautifully into this section of Matthew (Mt 18:1-5), concerned as it is, both with "the kingdom of the Heavens" (cf. Mt 18:1, 3 and 4) and "children" (cf. Mt 18:2, 3, 4, and 5).

A section relating to "one of these little ones" (Mt 18:6-10, esp. 18:6, 10, and 14) immediately follows this unit concerned with "children" in Mt (Mt 18:1-5).

That a question and answer structure characterizes the parallel to Mt 18:1-5 in Lk 9:46-48 provides good support for a theory of direct literary dependence between Luke and Mt within this context.

Luke 9:46 Εἰσῆλθεν δὲ διαλογισμὸς ἐν αὐτοῖς, τὸ   τίς ἂν εἴη   μείζων αὐτῶν.
Luke 9:48 ὁ γὰρ μικρότερος ἐν πᾶσιν ὑμῖν ὑπάρχων, οὗτός ἐστιν μέγας.

Both Matthew and Luke frame their parallel literary units with a question from the disciples (Matt 18:1/Luke 9:46) and an answer from Jesus in language similar to the original question (Matt 18:4/Luke 9:48). On the Two Source theory such evidence constitutes a significant minor agreement of Matthew and Luke against Mark in literary structure.

In Mt, the disciples openly question Jesus about "Who is the greatest in the Kingdom of Heaven?"

In Lk, however, the disciples seem to question one another rather than Jesus directly about this matter. And Luke seems to imply that the dialogue was not open. Jesus, in Lk, is able to discern this dialogue in the hearts of his disciples.

Matthew begins chapter 18 of his gospel by having Jesus call and stand a child in the midst of the disciples as part of Jesus' answer to the disciples' initial question about "Who is greatest in the kingdom of Heaven?" With the child as a visual aid, Jesus then gives three admonitions. First, he says that those who do not turn and become like *children* really won't enter *the Kingdom of Heaven.* Second, whoever will humble himself, like this *child,* this one is the greatest in *the Kingdom of Heaven.* This statement answers the disciples' initiating question. Third, whoever receives one such *child in the name of Jesus* is said to receive Jesus.

Matthew has Jesus conclude his speech prior to the entry of Peter at Mt 18:21 with the statement that "Where two or three are gathered together *in the name of Jesus*, there is Jesus in the midst of them." This statement repeats two earlier themes from the larger literary context of Mt 18:1-20, namely, the theme of Jesus/the child "in the midst" of his disciples (cf. Mt 18:2 and 20) and the theme of receiving/gathering "in the name" of Jesus (cf. Mt 18:5 and 20).

Luke shares Mt's earlier reference to receiving a child "in Jesus name" (Mt 18:5/Lk 9:48), but Luke does not share the latter reference to "Jesus' name" (Mt 18:20). Luke can be seen to have fragmentarily preserved a literary structure traceable to Matthew within his parallel literary context and such constitutes further evidence of literary dependence of Luke upon the text of Matthew.

Following this initial unit in Mt 18 (Mt 18:1-5) in which a child is used to illustrate three teachings of Jesus (Mt 18:3, 18:4 and 18:5), comes a section in Mt (Mt 18:6-14) that deals with the consequences of "scandalizing" (Mt 18:6, 7 [3 Xs], 8, 9) "the little ones" (Mt 18:6, 10, 14).

Already included in Matthew's story of the Temple Tax, which Luke passed over, is an anticipatory reference to "scandals" (Mt 17:27), the theme that characterizes this immediately following material in Mt (Mt 18:1-9, esp. 18:6, 7, 8, 9).

Luke records some, but not all, of the references to "scandals/scandalizing" in his text parallel to Mt 17:24-18:9. The appearance of the verb σκανδαλίζω and the noun, σκάνδαλον, in Lk supports the literary dependence of Luke upon the text of Matthew.

The phrase, "one of the(se) little ones" (A Form of εἶς + τῶν μικρῶν τούτων), is a literary characteristic of Matthew's text. The phrase reoccurs within the Gospel of Matthew and appears elsewhere in the New Testament only in one Synoptic parallel to Mt where there is evidence of copying (Mt 18:6/Mk 9:42/Lk 17:2; See also Mt 10:42NP; Mt 18:10NP; Mt 18:14NP). Based upon the method for making linguistic characteristics of service in solving the Synoptic Problem as developed by Eduard Zeller, the evidence provided by the appearance of "A Form of εἶς + τῶν μικρῶν τούτων" within the Synoptic Gospels also suggests the literary dependence of Luke upon the text of Matthew.

Let us look briefly at the Matthean literary context in Mt 10 (Mt 10:40-42) in which Mt 10:42 is found. It is a context that features several "reception sayings" and includes numerous other similarities in language and content to Mt 18:5-14.

Mt 18:5-6, 10a, 14

καὶ ὃς ἐὰν δέξηται
ἕν παιδίον τοιοῦτο
ἐπὶ τῷ ὀνόματὶ μου,
ἐμὲ δέχεται.

Mt 10:40-42

a Ὁ δεχόμενος
b ὑμᾶς
c
de ἐμὲ δέχεται,

ab καὶ ὁ ἐμὲ δεχόμενος
d δέχεται
e τὸν ἀποστείλαντά με.
a ὁ δεχόμενος
b προφήτην
c εἰς ὄνομα προφήτου
f μισθὸν προφήτου
  λήμψεται,
a καὶ ὁ δεχόμενος
b δίκαιον
c εἰς ὄνομα δικαίου
f μισθὸν δικαὶου
  λήμψεται.

Ὃς δ' ἂν σκανδαλίσῃ   a καὶ ὃς ἂν ποτίσῃ
ἕνα τῶν μικρῶν τούτων   b ἕνα τῶν μικρῶν τούτων
τῶν πιστευόντων

                     ποτήριον ψυχροῦ μόνον
εἰς ἐμέ,   c εἰς ὄνομα μαθητοῦ
                     ἀμὴν λέγω ὑμῖν,
συμφέρει αὐτῷ ἵνα κρεμασθῇ   b οὐ μὴ ἀπόληται
μύλος ὀνικὸς   f ὁ μισθὸς αὐτοῦ
περὶ τὸν τράχηλον αὐτοῦ
καὶ καταποντισθῇ
ἐν τῷ πελάγει τῆς θαλάσσης.
Ὁρᾶτε μὴ καταφρονήσητε
ἑνὸς τῶν μικρῶν τούτων
οὕτως οὐκ ἔστιν θέλημα
ἔμπροσθεν τοῦ πατρὸς ὑμῶν
τοῦ ἐν οὐρανοῖς
ἵνα ἀπόληται
ἓν τῶν μικρῶν τούτων.

One section of Matthew's Missionary Discourse (Mt 9:35-11:1) is marked off by similar formulas which introduce two parts of that Discourse. The first part (Mt 10:14-39) deals with conditions to be faced by the disciples and by those who "do not receive" the disciples (Mt 10:14).

The second part (Mt 10:40-11:1) deals with the rewards of those who "do receive" the disciples.

Mt 10:14 καὶ ὃς ἂν μὴ δέξηται ὑμᾶς. . .
Mt 10:40 Ὁ   δεχόμενος ὑμᾶς. . .

The second of these two parallel parts opens with the affirmation that the one who receives the disciples receives Jesus and further affirms that he who receives Jesus also receives the one who sent Jesus (Mt 10:40). Next follow two examples of rewards that are forthcoming from certain types of reception.

"The one who <u>receives</u> a prophet <u>in the name</u> of a prophet will receive <u>a reward</u> of a prophet" (Mt 10:41a).

"The one who <u>receives</u> a righteous man <u>in the name</u> of a righteous man will receive <u>a reward</u> of a righteous man" (Mt 10:41b).

The teaching of this part of Mt closes with the affirmation that "whoever should give a drink of cold water to <u>one of these little ones</u> only <u>in the name</u> of a disciple. . . surely his <u>reward</u> is not lost" (Mt 10:42).

This last logion (Mt 10:42) is tied to the two previous logia by the *Stichwörter,* "in the name" (εἰς ὄνομα) and "reward" (μισθόν).

The idea of "receiving in the name" links the first two examples of reward in Matt 10:41 with the similar teaching found in Matt 18:5, "And whoever <u>receives</u> one such child <u>in my name</u> receives me."

The subsequent verses in these two Matthean contexts, (Mt 10:42 and 18:6) may also be connected in the mind of a careful reader of Matthew's gospel by their common concern for εἰς τῶν μικρῶν τούτων. It would not be difficult to imagine a reader of Matthew's gospel seeing a connection between the literary context at Mt 10:40-42 and that at Mt 18:1-6 since they are united by the common themes of (1) receiving Jesus (Mt 10:40 and 18:5) (2) receiving in the name (Mt 10:41, 18:5, cf. Mt 10:42, 18:6 and 18:20) and (3) concern for "one of these little ones" (Mt 10:42, 18:6, 10, 14).

If one were to compare the teachings on reception within these two literary contexts (Mt 10:40-42 and 18:1-6), one might reason as follows. Mt 10:40 teaches that he who receives the disciples, receives Jesus. Mt 18:5 teaches that the one who receives a child in Jesus' name also receives Jesus. Mt 10:40 further teaches that the one who receives Jesus receives the one who sent Jesus. If the one who receives Jesus may be either someone who receives a child in Jesus' name (Mt 18:5) or someone who receives a disciple (Mt 10:40), one could change Mt 10:40 from "The one who receives you (i.e., a disciple) receives me, and the one who receives me, receives the one who sent me" to an equivalent saying, "One who receives a child in my name receives me, and the one who receives me, receives the one who sent me."

This, in fact, is precisely what the text of Luke says at Lk 9:48, namely, "Whoever receives this child in my name, receives me, and whoever receives me, receives the one who sent me."

These statements in Mt 10 and 18 dealing with "reception" develop logically from the text of Matthew to the text of Luke. There is nothing in the text of Luke that cannot be derived from the two contexts in Matthew, but the development cannot be reversed. Not all of Mt can be derived from Lk.

What appears to be a development from Mt to Lk on the basis of logic may be confirmed by literary criticism. In fact, the text of Luke 9:48b-c appears to be a conflation of Mt 10:40 with Mt 18:5.

Mt 10:40	Lk 9:48b-c	Mt 18:5
Ὁ δεχόμενος	Ὃς ἐὰν δέξηται	καὶ ὃς ἐὰν δέξηται
ὑμᾶς	τοῦτο τὸ παιδίον	ἓν παιδίον τοιοῦτο
	ἐπὶ τῷ ὀνόματί μου,	ἐπὶ τῷ ὀνόματί μου,
ἐμὲ δέχεται	ἐμὲ δέχεται·	ἐμὲ δέχεται·
καὶ ὁ ἐμὲ δεχόμενος	καὶ ὃς ἂν ἐμὲ δέξηται,	
δέχεται	δέχεται	
τὸν ἀποστείλαντά με.	τὸν ἀποστείλαντά με.	

When Luke comes to Mt 18:6-9, he chooses to move logia just prior to Matthew's section on "Moral Surgery" (Mt 18:8-9) to his Central Section (Lk 17:1-2/Mt 18:6-7). The origin of this material now at Lk 17:1-2 in Mt 18:6-7 is indicated by the appearances in Lk 17 of the following literary characteristics of Matthew: the verb σκανδαλίζω (Lk 17:2/Mt 18:6, 8, 9), the noun σκάνδαλον (Lk 17:1/Mt 18:7 [three times]), and the phrase "one of the little ones" (Lk 17:2/Mt 18:6, 10, 14; cf. Mt 10:42).

The literary unit in Mt 17:24-18:35/Lk 9:46-50 is followed immediately in Matthew by a unit on family matters: sex, marriage, divorce, children, celibacy, etc. (Mt 19:1-15).

The immediately following verse in Lk (Lk 9:51) begins his Central Section with its focus on Jesus' going up to Jerusalem (See especially Lk 9:51, 53, 17:11, 18:31 [and 19:11?]). Luke shares only part of the material in Mt 19:1-15 with Matthew and only toward the conclusion of his Central Section (cf. Lk 18:15-17/Mt 19:13-15). On the Two Gospel Hypothesis it was between Mt 18:35 and Mt 19:1 (another marker verse in Mt, like Mt 7:28-29, 11:1, 13:53 and 26:1) that Luke chose to open up his gospel and insert most of his Central Section (Lk 9:51-19:44).

It may be noted that Luke moves the logion found in Mt 18:3 (See Lk 18:17; cf. Lk 9:47-48 omit) in spite of the fact that Mt 18:3 fits beautifully into that section of Mt (Mt 18:1-5), concerned as it is, both with "the kingdom of the Heavens" (cf. Mt 18:1, 3 and 4) and "children" (cf. Mt 18:2, 3, 4, and 5).

Again, if one is looking for an explanation, on the Two Gospel Hypothesis, for why Luke would have moved Mt 18:3 to an alternate literary context, the answer would seem to lie in the similarity between Mt 18:3 and Mt 19:14, the immediately preceding verse for the parallels to Mt 18:3 in the new context of Lk (Lk 18:15-17).

Mt 18:3	Mt 19:14
καὶ <u>εἶπεν,</u>	ὁ δὲ Ἰησοῦς <u>εἶπεν,</u>
Ἀμὴν λέγω ὑμῖν,	
ἐὰν μὴ στραφῆτε	
καὶ γενήσθε	Ἄφετε
ὡς <u>τὰ παιδία,</u>	<u>τὰ παιδία</u>
	καὶ μὴ κωλύετε αὐτὰ
	ἐλθεῖν πρός με,
οὐ μὴ εἰσέλθητε	τῶν γὰρ τοιούτων ἐστιν
εἰς <u>τὴν βασιλείαν</u>	<u>ἡ βασιλείαν</u>
<u>τῶν οὐρανῶν.</u>	<u>τῶν οὐρανῶν.</u>

The literary unit in Mt 19:13-14, as noted above, is concerned with "children" (Mt 19:13-14). Mt 18:3 also deals with "children" (Note the plural). The parallel in Lk 18:15-17 to Mt 19:13-14, toward the close of Luke's Central Section (Lk 9:51-19:44) contains the plural of children once (Lk 18:16) and the variants, "child" (Lk 18:17, same word but different number) and "infants" (Lk 18:15, different word but same number) otherwise. This evidence also could be construed as the fragmentary preservation of literary characteristics of Matthew in the parallel text of Luke and, therefore as evidence of Luke's direct literary dependence upon Mt.

Luke's parallels in this context to Matthew's Jewish locution, "the kingdom of the Heavens" is, as always, "the kingdom of God" (Mt 18:3, cf. Lk 18:17). On the Two Document Hypothesis, this is understood as an example of Matthew's "rejudaizing tendency." This explanation is as convincing here as it is wherever it is invoked by those who do not accept the priority of Matthew.

Lk 9:49 Whoever is Not Against Us is For Us

This is one of the most interesting linkages in the gospels. Following Matthew 18:1-5, Luke relates the dispute about greatness. He extends it, however, by "John answered," Lk 9:49, with a story about another exorcist. Even Mark has recognized Luke's linkage here and has separated the two stories (John does not "answer" in Mk, but introduces a new subject.).

What prompted Luke to make this connection? One plausible explanation is a formal one. The saying in Luke 9:48 is a set of "whoever" (ὄς) clauses. Luke is led to combine them with another "whoever" saying from his own special material, "Whoever is not against you is for you" (Lk 9:50b). That the two sayings are only tangentially related in content, at best, does not seem to disturb Luke, although he may be thinking that these sayings illustrate Jesus' wide acceptance of people; i.e., children and 'unknown' allies.

Betwixt and Between:
The Samaritans in the Hasmonean Period

Lester L. Grabbe
University of Hull

The aim of this paper is to make a contribution to research on the sociology of the Second Temple period. The Samaritan community, with its cult on Mt. Gerizim, is one of the most important religious communities in Palestine besides the Jews, not least because it has continued to exist even to the present. To get at the sociology of the community is not a simple matter, and we must begin with the basics: What are the sources? What are the problems with extracting their data? What do they tell us about the history of the community? Only then can we ask sociological questions.

Unless otherwise qualified, the term "Samaritan(s)" will be used of the community whose religious center was the cult on Mt. Gerizim and which produced the community still in existence. How large and extensive that community was, and whether it embraced most of the population in the old region of Samaria, has yet to be determined. This paper makes no *a priori* assumptions about them.

1 The Sources and their Data

1.1 Books of Maccabees

There is nothing in 1 Maccabees which clearly bears on the question of the Samaritans.[1] 2 Maccabees may have been written at a time when relations between Jews and Samaritans were deteriorating. Yet even if this was so, two passages give information not necessarily detrimental to the Samaritans:

> And he [Antiochus IV] left governors to afflict the people: at Jerusalem, Philip . . .; and at Gerizim, Andronicus; and besides these Menelaus, who lorded it over his fellow citizens worse than the others did. (2 Macc 5:22-23, RSV)

---

[1] 1 Macc 3:10 says that Apollonius "gathered the Gentiles and a large force from Samaria to fight against Israel." If Apollonius was governor of Samaria (so Josephus, *Ant.* 12.5.5 §261; 12.7.1 §287), he would have had a military force at his disposal, no doubt in part recruited locally. Since this need not imply that the Samaritans as a nation or community sided with Apollonius against the Jews, the incident has no clear bearing on our question.

The context and wording indicate that the Samaritans were put under the same restrictions, even religious persecution, which affected the Jews. Another passage supports and supplements this:

> Not long after this, the king sent an Athenian senator to compel the Jews to forsake the laws of their fathers, . . . and also to pollute the temple in Jerusalem and call it the temple of Olympian Zeus, and to call the one in Gerizim the temple of Zeus the Friend of Strangers, as did the people who dwelt in that place. (2 Macc 6:1-2, RSV)

What are the implications of this? Did the Samaritans accept the Hellenization of their cult? Some translations suggest that the Samaritans themselves requested that their temple be given a Greek name.[2] The little information in the context does not require that conclusion, but the question will be considered further at 1.3 below.

1.2 Statements of Josephus

Josephus is clearly prejudiced against the Samaritans.[3] When he mentions them, he often takes the opportunity to disparage the Samaritan community. Neverthelesss, in some instances he may have had useful sources even if he has turned them to his own purposes. (One of these is the alleged letter from the Shechemites to Antiochus IV discussed below at 1.3.) In one of his more notorious statements, he claims (*Ant.* 9.14.3 §291, translation from LCL 6.153, 155; similarly, 11.8.6 §341):

> . . . they alter their attitude according to circumstance and, when they see the Jews prospering, call them their kinsmen, on the ground that they are descended from Joseph and are related to them through their origin from him, but, when they see the Jews in trouble, they say that they have nothing whatever in common with them nor do these have any claim of friendship or race, and they declare themselves to be aliens of another race.

This may strike one initially as only another expression of prejudice. Undoubtedly, Josephus intended no less, but in fact the statement may describe a genuine state of affairs. Those who have had the experience of sectarian infighting know well that a group may emphasize or disavow resemblances to other groups, depending on the circumstances. It would hardly be surprising if the Samaritans did the same.

---

2 The problem is the final phrase: καθὼς ἐτύγχανον οἱ τὸν τόπον οἰκοῦντες, Διὸς Ξενίου. Some take it to refer to the practice of the community, i.e., to be hospitable. Others interpret it to mean that the inhabitants requested that their temple be renamed. The former interpretation seems more likely. See R. Pummer, "Antisamaritanische Polemik in jüdischen Schriften aus der intertestamentarischen Zeit," *BZ* 26 (1982) 224-42, specifically 238-39; R. Doran, "2 Maccabees 6:2 and the Samaritan Question," *HTR* 76 (1983) 481-85.

3 This seems plain from many passages, despite R. Egger, *Josephus Flavius und die Samaritaner: Eine terminologische Untersuchung zur Identitätsklärung der Samaritaner* (NTOA 4; Freiburg: Universitätsverlag; Göttingen: Vandenhoeck & Ruprecht, 1986) esp. 310-13. She may well be right that there are passages where his approach is more neutral, but a quite few simply cannot be explained away.

Josephus relates another incident on the Samaritans in *Ant.* 12.4.1 §156 (translation from LCL 7.81, 83):

> At this time the Samaritans [Σαμαρεῖs], who were flourishing, did much mischief to the Jews by laying waste their land and carrying off slaves; and this happened in the highpriesthood of Onias.

The first question is when this took place. It is dated to the time of Ptolemy V Epiphanes (204-180 BCE) and the high priest Onias, son of Simon the Just. This Simon the Just is often identified with Simon II who lived around 200 BCE and is mentioned in Ben Sira 50:1-24. That would date the event to the early 2nd century. Yet various other episodes in this context, mainly those relating to the Tobiads, are misdated and should be put earlier.[4] Therefore, we cannot be confident that Josephus has correctly placed the incident.

Secondly, who were those doing the enslaving? Although Josephus is not consistent in his terminology, the term *Samareis* is often used generally for the inhabitants of the region of Samaria.[5] We do not know if his source understood the raiders to be members of the community on Mt. Gerizim, and Josephus does not make this specific identification. They could have been inhabitants of Samaria who had nothing to do with the Gerizim cult, but neither can we rule this possibility out. Therefore, the relevance of this event to the main question is uncertain.

1.3 Shechemite Letter to Antiochus IV

Josephus quotes a letter, allegedly written at the time of Antiochus IV, as follows (*Ant.* 12.5.5 §§258-61, quotation from LCL 7.133-35):

> To King Antiochus Theos Epiphanes, a memorial from the Sidonians in Shechem. Our forefathers because of certain droughts in their country, and following a certain ancient superstition, made it a custom to observe the day which is called the Sabbath by the Jews, and they erected a temple without a name on the mountain called Garizein, and there offered the appropriate sacrifices. Now you have dealt with the Jews as their wickedness deserves, but the king's officers, in the belief that we follow the same practices as they through kinship with them, are involving us in similar charges, whereas we are Sidonians by origin, as is evident from our state documents. We therefore petition you as our benefactor and saviour to command Apollonius, the governor of the district, and Nicanor, the royal agent, not to molest us in any way by attaching to us the charges of which the Jews are guilty, since we are distinct from them both in race and in customs, and we ask that the temple without be known as that of Zeus Hellenios. For if

---

4 The activities of Joseph Tobiad could have taken place only during Ptolemaic rule over Palestine; therefore, their dating to the reign of Ptolemy V must be mistaken. Ptolemy III (246-221 BCE) is more likely the person intended, though Josephus may have misunderstood his source.

5 The main study on Josephus' terminology is Egger, *Josephus Flavius und die Samaritaner*; however, she argues for a theoretical consistency on Josephus' part which is not borne out by the data. See the review by R. Pummer in *JBL* 107 (1988) 768-72.

this be done, we shall cease to be molested, and by applying ourselves to our work in security, we shall make your revenues greater.

Antiochus' reply is given as follows (*Ant.* 12.5.5 §§262-64, quotation from LCL 7.135-37):

> King Antiochus to Nicanor. The Sidonians in Shechem have submitted a memorial which has been filed. Now since the men sent by them have represented to us sitting in council with our friends that they are in no way concerned in the complaints brought against the Jews, but choose to live in accordance with Greek customs, we acquit them of these charges, and permit their temple to be known as that of Zeus Hellenios, as they have petitioned.

The first question is whether these two documents are authentic. Although the question was widely debated in the past, with eminent names on both sides of the argument, most writers have accepted authenticity since Bickerman's study.[6] Both the alleged petition and its reply bear the characteristics expected of Seleucid documents from the period. Just as persuasive is the argument that no clear reason can be found as to why a Jewish forger would have written the documents in their present form.[7] Also in the surrounding context, Josephus makes statements which are contradicted by the documents (e.g., origin of the Samaritans as colonists from the Medes and Persians). The one difficulty which Bickerman did not deal with is whether we might have original documents which have nevertheless been tampered with in some way.[8] Such documents are likely to be found elsewhere in Josephus and, despite Bickerman, it seems that this possibility cannot be ruled out here.[9]

If authentic, this letter and the Seleucid response give an important message about the Samaritans, especially when read in the light of 2 Maccabees 6.1-2 (1.1 above). Should we conclude, as many have, that the

---

6 E. J. Bickerman, "Un document relatif à la persécution d'Antiochos IV Epiphane," *Studies in Jewish and Christian History* (AGAJU 9; Leiden: Brill, 1980) 2.105-35 (originally published in *RHR* 115 [1937]). Studies which have more or less accepted Bickerman's conclusions include A. Schalit, "Die Denkschrift der Samaritaner an König Antiochos Epiphanes zu Beginn der Großen Verfolgung der jüdischen Religion im Jahre 167 v. Chr. (Josephus, *AJ* XII, §§258-264)," *ASTI* 8 (1970-71) 131-83; Egger, *Josephus Flavius und die Samaritaner,* 280-81.

7 Bickerman, 129-31.

8 Also noted by R. J. Coggins (*Samaritans and Jews: The Origins of Samaritanism Reconsidered* [Growing Points in Theology; Oxford: Blackwell; Atlanta: John Knox, 1975] 98-99), G. Alon ("The Origin of the Samaritans in the Halakhic Tradition," *Jews, Judaism and the Classical World: Studies in Jewish History in the Times of the Second Temple and Talmud* [Jerusalem: Magnes, 1977] 354-73, specifically 369), and R. Pummer ("Antisamaritanische Polemik," 239 n. 94).

9 This is very probably the case with the alleged decree of Claudius in *Ant.* 19.5.2 §§280-85. Although much of the document could well be genuine, the final conclusion is contrary to that of a known decree of Claudius, published in V. A. Tcherikover, A. Fuks, and M. Stern, *Corpus Papyrorum Judaicarum* (3 vols.; Cambridge, MA: Harvard; Jerusalem: Magnes, 1957-64) 2.36-55 (text #153).

Samaritans gave themselves over to allow their cult to be Hellenized? A closer inspection does not lead to this conclusion. The actual religious practices of the Jews and Samaritans were very similar: the same Sabbath observance, the same food laws, much the same purity laws, the same requirement of circumcision. The primary distinction between them was the question of God's chosen place for his temple. To an outsider, especially, they must have looked indistinguishable. Antiochus' order suppressing Jewish worship must therefore have delivered the same blow to the Shechemites as to the Jews. The religion to which they adhered with equal fervor was about to be abolished. But they had done nothing to anger Antiochus or to attract this abolition; it was simply a side effect of the Jewish situation. Therefore, it would hardly be surprising if the community of Shechem attempted by diplomacy to have the decree lifted with regard to themselves. But in so doing, they do not deny keeping the Sabbath; instead, they emphasize an origin which might sound rational to a Greek and also appear on a different basis from that of the Jews. This does not suggest they are abandoning the Sabbath but rather are intending to continue observing it. As another means of defense, they could also put stress on an ethnic origin different from the Jews. Although the precise significance of the phrase, "Sidonians of Shechem," is still not clear, it had a useful function in attempting to distance the community from the Jews.[10] None of this suggests an intent to change their cult. On the contrary, it would be a useful means of defending it.[11]

1.4 Other Early Jewish Literature

Various scholars of the past and present have claimed to find anti-Samaritan polemic in a number of early Jewish writings. For the most part

---

[10] Bickerman ("Document," 2.118-23) took the phrase as a synonym for "Phoenician" which, in turn, was only the Greek term for "Canaanite." Schalit ("Denkschrift," 149-56) seems to agree, though his position is not completely clear. But this view is based on assumptions about the origins of the Samaritans which no longer stand up. There is no reason to think that the Samaritans would have any more willingly identified themselves as Canaanites than the Jews. The term Sidonians is known for a group in the Hellenistic Edomite city of Marissa, and it has been proposed that there was a Sidonian colony at Shechem who wrote this letter: M. Delcor ("Vom Sichem der hellenistischen Epoche zum Sychar des Neuen Testamentes," *ZDPV* 78 [1962] 34-48); followed by Pummer ("Genesis 34 in Jewish Writings of the Hellenistic and Roman Periods," *HTR* 76 [1982] 177-88, especially 184-86), Egger (*Samaritaner*, 266-80), and a number of others. This is unlikely. One can hardly expect a Phoenician colony to be Sabbath keepers, and the explanation that they had picked up some practices from the Samaritan community or were loosely associated with its cult is merely an attempt to explain away a difficulty. Pummer correctly notes (pp. 184-86) that nothing is said about circumcision, implying that it was being kept; if so, this says little for their being a Sidonian colony but much for the Samaritan community. The best explanation to me is that the Samaritan community itself wrote the letter and that, whatever the origin of the designation, it was trying to distance itself from the Jews.

[11] Bickerman, "Document," 126-28, 131-35; K. Bringmann, *Hellenistische Reform und Religionsverfolgung in Judäa* (AAWG, Phil.hist. Klasse, 3. Folge, Nr. 132; Göttingen: Vandenhoeck & Ruprecht, 1983) 142-43.

these do not stand up.[12] Although Genesis 34, with its massacre of the inhabitants of Shechem by Jacob's sons, is treated by several documents, Jubilees and Judith are not clearly anti-Samaritan. The author of Testament of Levi 5-7 is plainly polemicizing against the Shechemites of his own time; however, the date and provenance of the Greek writing are disputed.[13]

Similarly, Ben Sira 50:25-26 derides the "senseless folk that live at Shechem."[14] There is some question, however, as to whether these verses were written by Ben Sira himself or were from another source, whether before his time or a later insertion.[15] They do not fit well into the context. The sentiment expressed seems clear, but how early it arose is more problematic. Purvis has attempted to suggest a historical background for the statement, but the evidence offered is extremely scanty.[16] Nevertheless, the statement in Ben Sira is likely to have originated no later than the 2nd century BCE since it is found in the Greek translation of Ben Sira's grandson, about 132 BCE.

1.5 Samaritan Writings in Greek

Pseudo-Eupolemus is the name given to two fragments preserved among the Fragmentary Jewish Greek writers.[17] One of these is preserved in the

---

[12] See especially the studies of R. Pummer, "The Book of Jubilees and the Samaritans," Eglise et Théologie 10 (1979) 147-78; "Antisamaritanische Polemik"; "Genesis 34 in Jewish Writings of the Hellenistic and Roman Periods."

[13] The main debate about the Testaments of the Twelve Patriarchs is whether these are Christian documents which make use of Jewish material or are Jewish writings with Christian intervention. Some Aramaic fragments of T.Levi are known from the Cairo Genizah and Qumran. One of the Genizah fragments (Cambridge T-S 16.94) seems to contain a version of the story in Genesis 34, though it does not correspond to the extant Greek text of T.Levi. See J. C. Greenfield and M. E. Stone, "Remarks on the Aramaic Testament of Levi from the Geniza," RB 86 (1979) 214-30. For discussion of recent scholarship, see E. Schürer, The Jewish People in the Age of Jesus Christ (revised G. Vermes, et al.; 3 vols. in 4; Edinburgh: T & T Clarke, 1973-87) 3.767-81; J. J. Collins, Between Athens and Jerusalem: Jewish Identity in the Hellenistic Diaspora (New York: Crossroad, 1986) 154-62; "Testaments" in M. E. Stone (ed.), Jewish Writings of the Second Temple Period (CRINT 2/2; Assen: Van Gorcum; Philadelphia: Fortress, 1984) 325-55.

[14] NEB. Although the Hebrew and Greek texts differ slightly in these two verses, this phrase is essentially the same.

[15] Cf. Coggins, Samaritans and Jews, 83-86; Pummer, "Antisamaritanische Polemik," 232 plus n. 45; Egger, Samaritaner, 85-93.

[16] The only data he seems to offer are Ant. 12.4.1 §156 and the scholia of the Megillat Taanit. The first is problematic because its dating is very uncertain, and it does not necessarily have anything to do with Shechem (see the discussion at 1.2 above). His use of the scholia of the Megillat Taanit is surprising since these are commonly acknowledged to be post-Talmudic in origin, not like the Megillat Taanit itself which is commonly dated to the 1st or 2nd century CE. (On this writing and the scholia, see H. L. Strack and G. Stemberger: Introduction to the Talmud and Midrash [Minneapolis: Fortress; London: SCM, 1991] 39-40.) We can have no confidence that the scholia are likely to contain any reliable information for the 2nd or 3rd century BCE.

[17] For an edition and translation, with a summary of scholarship up to the time of writing, see C. A. Holladay, Fragments from Hellenistic Jewish Authors, Volume I: Historians (TT 20, Pseudepigrapha Series 10; Atlanta: Scholars, 1983) 157-87. One should add to this Collins, Between Athens and Jerusalem, 38-39. R. Doran ("Pseudo-Eupolemus," in J. H. Charlesworth [ed.], Old Testament Pseudepigrapha [2 vols.; Garden City, NY: Doubleday, 1983-85] 2.873-82) suggests the first fragment is from Eupolemus himself.

name of Eupolemus, the other as "anonymous"; the consensus of scholarship is that they are both by an anonymous Samaritan who wrote sometime during the 3rd or 2nd centuries BCE. Among the Fragmentary Writers is also Theodotus. He has also often been identified as a Samaritan, but the weight of evidence seems against it; he is more likely a Jewish writer.[18]

Even with the small amount of preserved text, Pseudo-Eupolemus tells several things. He evidently had a good Greek education, showing that such opportunities were available for Samaritans as well as other Orientals. Pseudo-Eupolemus was quite happy to interpret biblical tradition in the light of Greek mythology. Sometimes this is called "syncretism" but inaccurately. Pseudo-Eupolemus gives no indication of diluting the Samaritan cult or other aspects of the religion with pagan elements; rather, the biblical tradition is only put in the Greek context, showing how the native tradition fits in with Greek legend and myth. Far from engaging in compromise Pseudo-Eupolemus is actually strengthening his people's tradition by showing that the Greeks have a memory of it, if perhaps only a dim and inaccurate one. He is using his Greek knowledge for apologetic purposes, with the aim not of diminishing his own tradition but of defending it.

Pseudo-Eupolemus is thus very much like contemporary Jewish writers in Greek. These, too, made use of Greek knowledge and literary techniques to extend, update, interpret, and defend their religious tradition. But to do so required a knowledge of Greek language, literature, and culture. This shows that such knowledge was available and that a Samaritan could gain a Greek education but also remain loyal to his native people.

1.6 Samaritan Chronicles

The relevant Samaritan Chronicles are Chronicle 2,[19] the Tolidah (Chronicle 3),[20] the Shalshalah (Chronicle 5),[21] Abu 'l-Fath (Chronicle 6),[22]

---

18 See the summary of the arguments and earlier literature in Holladay, *Fragments*, 2.51-68. Add to it Pummer ("Antisamaritanische Polemik," 234-36). F. Fallon ("Theodotus" in *OTP*, 2.785-93) sees no clear evidence to decide the matter. D. Mendels (*The Land of Israel as a Political Concept in Hasmonean Literature* [TSAJ 15; Tübingen: Mohr(Siebeck), 1987] 110-16, however, argues that Theodotus was Samaritan.

19 The section on the Hasmonean period has not been published. For a summary of the entire contents, see J. Macdonald, "Samaritans," *EJ* 14.728-32. From his description, the contents sound very similar to Abu 'l-Fath.

20 A. Neubauer, "Chronique samaritaine, suivie d'un appendice contenant de courtes notices sur quelques autres ouvrages samaritains," *Journal Asiatique* 14 (1869) 385-470 (text and French translation); M. Heidenheim, "Die samaritan. Chronik des Hohenpriesters Elasar," *Vierteljahrsschrift für deutsch- und englisch-theologische Forschung und Kritik* 4 (1971) 347-89 (German translation only); J. Bowman, *Transcript of the Original Text of the Samaritan Chronicle Tolidah* (University of Leeds, 1954) (text only, using a different manuscript from Neubauer).

21 M. Gaster, "The Chain of Samaritan High Priests," *Studies and Texts* (London: Maggs, 1925-28) 1.483-502 (English translation), 3.131-8 (text).

22 English translation in P. Stenhouse, *The Kitāb al-Tarīkh of Abū 'l-Fath, Translated into English with Notes* (Mandelbaum Studies in Judaica 1; Sydney University Press, 1985), though Stenhouse's own critical text of the Arabic original is still unpublished; partial translation in J. Bowman, *Samaritan Documents Relating to their History, Religion and Life* (Pittsburgh Original Texts and Translations 2; Pittsburgh: Pickwick, 1977) 114-213.

and the Adler Chronicle (Chronicle 7).[23] The Chronicles are a mine field of problems. On the one hand, they claim to trace the Samaritan religion back to Moses and to give an account of their history independently (at least, in part) of the OT. On the other hand, all the Chronicles are late, some of them from the 19th or even 20th century in their present form. Study of them is not far advanced, and Samaritan specialists have reached no consensus on their interrelationships.[24]

Where the Chronicles relate Samaritan history to external events, there is often confusion. In addition, some of the events which Jewish literature recounts with reference to the Jews is claimed for the Samaritans by the Chronicles. For example, where Josephus and other Jewish sources have Alexander the Great doing obeisance to the Jewish high priest, the Chronicles (Adler; Tolidah; Abu 'l-Fatḥ; Chronicle 2, *apud* Macdonald) make him do it to the Samaritan high priest.[25] For the Hasmonean period, the only event mentioned is the reign of "King John," evidently John Hyrcanus though possibly Alexander Janneus.[26] According to their version, however, John destroys Samaria but not Shechem. Eventually, he acknowledges its claim and attempts to go on a pilgrim to Gerizim! The source of this account is uncertain, though it seems remarkably close to that of Josephus; one could argue that it is his version with a deliberate twist.

Another account is more problematic. It concerns a king of the Jews named Simeon and his son ʿArqiah (Abu 'l-Fatḥ) or Ḥilqiyah (Adler). This sounds very much like Simon Maccabee and his son (John) Hyrcanus, but the episode is dated to the Persian period, and their reigns are followed by a captivity of the Jews. Simeon is said to have caused great hostility between the Jews and Samaritans because the Jews persecuted the Samaritans and forbade them to worship. Finally, the Samaritans called their diaspora brethren from Babylon and attacked Jerusalem, destroying it and the temple, though Simeon got away. King Darius heard of this and supported the Jews, whereupon many Samaritans emigrated while those left again had their religion proscribed. Under ʿArqiah/Ḥilqiyah a quarrel arose between "the sons of Ithamar and the sons of Manasseh," appears to be an inner-Samaritan quarrel. After that "the nations" besieged Jerusalem and exiled the Jews, allowing the Samaritans to return with thanks and praise to God.

---

[23] E. N. Adler and M. Seligsohn, "Une nouvelle chronique samaritaine," *REJ* 44 (1902) 188-222; 45 (1902) 70-98, 223-54; 46 (1903) 123-46.

[24] It seems that each specialist prefers a different Chronicle as the most basic. Bowman thinks Tolidah is earliest. P. Stenhouse concentrates on Abu 'l-Fath ("Samaritan Chronicles," in A. D. Crown [ed.], *The Samaritans* [Tübingen: Mohr (Siebeck), 1989] 218-65). A. D. Crown ("New Light on the Inter-relationships of Samaritan Chronicles from Some Manuscripts in the John Rylands Library," *BJRL* 54 [1971-72] 282-313; 55 [1972-73] 86-111) argues that the basis of all the Chronicles is the Samaritan Book of Joshua (Chronicle 4) and a Sefer ha-Yamim (of which the Adler Chronicle and Chronicle 2 are late examples), with the former being incorporated into the latter at some point.

[25] For a discussion of this event, its sources and historicity, see my article, "Josephus and the Reconstruction of the Judean Restoration," *JBL* 106 (1987) 231-46.

[26] The story is found in Abu 'l-Fath (Stenhouse, *Tarikh*, pp. 140-42; Bowman, *Documents*, pp. 134-35) and apparently also in Chronicle 2 (so Macdonald in his summary).

Can anything of historical value be gleaned from these accounts? This seems doubtful in the present state of knowledge. The most one can say is that Josephus' account of the destruction of the Gerizim temple has no memory in the Samaritan sources.[27]

1.7 Samaritan Pentateuch

It is widely accepted that the Samaritan Pentateuch is a community (sectarian) recension of a previously existing nonsectarian text-type, sometimes referred to as the proto-Samaritan.[28] If we accept this position, the question remains: When did this sectarian recension take place? Purvis has argued that it followed shortly after Hyrcanus' destruction of Samaria and Shechem in the late 2nd century.[29] This suggestion is plausible, but is there actual evidence? Purvis argues primarily from the script and orthography which he claims indicate an origin in the Hasmonean period. None of his arguments seem to preclude a recension as much as two or three centuries after 100 BCE, however.[30] Indeed, a recension before 100 BCE cannot be excluded, though it is not attested. Thus, the Samaritan scriptures do not provide us with any certain data on when or whether a major break occurred between the Jewish and Samaritan communities.

1.8 Archeology

Until recently it was thought that the general picture of Josephus had been confirmed archeologically. Excavations in the 1950s and 1960s had, it was believed, confirmed the building of the Samaritan temple at the end of the Persian or beginning of Greek period.[31] More recent archeological work has

---

[27] Bowman makes the surprising claim that both these events confirm the accounts of Josephus (see the notes to his translation). If the incident relating to "King John" is borrowed from Josephus, it has no independent value; if not, it specifically denies the destruction of Shechem by Hyrcanus. Similarly, the quarrel between the sons of Ithamar and the sons of Manasseh cannot be dated (is it the Persian period or the time of Hyrcanus?) nor does it make any allusion to the supposed defection of Manasseh, a son of the high priest, to Gerizim. On this last event and its historicity, see my "Josephus and the Reconstruction of the Judean Restoration."

[28] For a summary of the current consensus with discussion of earlier studies, see E. Tov, "Proto-Samaritan Texts and the Samaritan Pentateuch," in Crown (ed.), *The Samaritans*, 397-407; *Textual Criticism of the Hebrew Bible* (Assen/Maastricht: Van Gorcum; Minneapolis: Fortress, 1992) 80-100.

[29] J. D. Purvis, *The Samaritan Pentateuch and the Origin of the Samaritan Sect* (HSM 2; Cambridge: Harvard University Press, 1968). At this point, I would like to acknowledge a debt to Professor Purvis. Many years ago he kindly loaned me a number of books and texts relating to Samaritan studies which were unavailable to me.

[30] See, for example, the doubts expressed by Z. Ben-Hayyim in his review of Purvis in *Biblica* 52 (1971) 253-55: "Yet the question which is raised upon the reading of this interesting book is: can one really come to an important historical and social conclusion such as the time of the formation of the Samaritan sect according to the orthographic form and the script of its Holy Writ?"

[31] *Ant.* 11.8.1-6 §§304-45. R. J. Bull, "er-Ras, Tell (Mount Gerizim)," *Encyclopedia of Archaeological Excavations in the Holy Land* (ed. E. Stern; Jerusalem: Israel Exploration Society, 1978) 4.1015-22.

now thrown the question up into the air.[32] What was originally thought to be evidence of a Hellenistic structure (identified as a temple by some but otherwise by others) on Tell er-Ras is now found to have been misdated by intruded Hellenistic pottery from a fill. Whether there was a temple and when it was built cannot be said at present.

The destruction of Shechem by John Hyrcanus shortly before 200 BCE was also thought to be confirmed archeologically.[33] So far, no new information seems to have been forthcoming. In the light of present data, though, the final destruction of the city could have come during the reign of Alexander Janneus rather than of John Hyrcanus.

2 Analysis of Data

As with so much Samaritan history, we have very little information. There is considerable danger of over interpreting the data that we do have, and it seems to me that this has often been done. The desire to know more is understandable, but we must recognize the fragility of many hypotheses. Indeed, in many cases they are little more than guesses.

The source which seems to give the most information is in many ways also our most problematic one: Josephus. In most passages, if perhaps not in all, he is openly prejudiced against the dwellers of Shechem. This does not mean that he does not give us historical data, but sorting it out of the negative polemic is not easy. Further, his terminology is not always consistent or clear. Sometimes he explicitly refers to the cult on Gerizim and its adherents, but at other times he may have had inhabitants of the entire region of Samaria in mind, and we cannot be sure that they necessarily had anything to do with the Gerizim cult and community. One has to proceed with a good deal of caution and skepticism.

For the origins of the Gerizim cult, Josephus gives two contradictory answers. First, he says that they were foreigners brought in from elsewhere in the ancient Near East (Mesopotamia, Media, Persia). Secondly, he claims they were made up of defected priests and Jews who left the Jerusalem cult for various nefarious reasons. Both claims have a polemical intent; neither is necessary. For my purposes, however, there is no need to settle the matter of origins of the cult, and I shall proceed on the basis that the cult was Yahwistic,

---

[32] Unfortunately, the information is available only in preliminary form. See the summary in R. Pummer, "Samaritan Material Remains and Archaeology," in Crown (ed.), *The Samaritans*, 166-75. Not available to me were Y. Magen, "A Fortified City from the Hellenistic Period on Mount Gerizim," *Qadmoniot* 19 (1986) 91-101; "Mount Gerizim—A Temple-City," *Qadmoniot* 23 (1991-92) 70-96.

[33] *Ant.* 13.9.1 §§255-56. For a report on the excavations, see G. E. Wright, "The Samaritans at Shechem," *HTR* 55 (1962) 357-66; *Shechem: The Biography of a Biblical City* (New York-Toronto: McGraw-Hill, 1964) 170-84. For a complete bibliography of excavations to 1987, see E. K. Vogel, "Bibliography of Holy Land Sites: Part I," *HUCA* 42 (1971) 1-96; "Bibliography of Holy Land Sites: Part II," *HUCA* 52 (1981) 1-92; "Bibliography of Holy Land Sites: Part III, 1981-1987," *HUCA* 58 (1987) 1-63. Most studies focus on the pre-exilic period while the few which discuss the Hellenistic strata unfortunately do not clearly distinguish archeological data from interpretation.

with no more foreign elements than contemporary Judaism—indeed, that in most respects it was very similar to the worship in Jerusalem at the time.[34]

The first and perhaps most difficult area to investigate is that of Jewish and Samaritan relations. The animosity between the Samaritan and Jewish communities has often been taken for granted, though there has been debate over when it began. Yet we do not have to assume a severe breach before the first century CE and perhaps not even then. The episode in which Samaritans scattered bones in the Jerusalem temple (*Ant.* 18.2.2 §30), the attack on Jewish pilgrims from Galilee and the counter charge of Jewish attacks on Samaritan villages (*War* 2.12.3-6 §§232-44; *Ant.* 20.6.1-3 §§118-36), and the statement in John 4:9 all suggest major barriers between Jews and Samaritans. The first example suggests individuals who were hostile to the Jerusalem temple; the second is less clear but could also show religious hostility; the third definitely has differences of worship in mind. But these all relate to the first century CE. Counter to this are many examples showing contact between Jews and individuals from the region of Samaria: Herod's relations (*Ant.* 14.15.3 §408; 14.15.4 §413; 14.15.14 §467; 17.1.3 §20; 17.4.2 §69); joint delegation to complain against Archelaus (*Ant.* 17.13.2 §342); loan to Agrippa from a Samaritan freedman (*Ant.* 18.6.4 §167); Josephus' Samaritan friends (*Life* 52 §269). All of these can be explained away, but they indicate the matter is not straightforward.

If the two religious communities had little to do with each other in the first century, this situation could have had its roots in earlier periods. The enmity between Nehemiah and Sanballat might have been a foreshadow, but the text shows that many Jews did not agree with Nehemiah (Neh 6:17-19; 13:4-7). The Tobiads, who were intermarried with the high priestly Oniad family, also seem to have had relations with and even relatives in Samaria, whether the city or the region (*Ant.* 12.4.3 §168). The Samaritan decision to protect their temple by disavowing the Jews may not have helped inter-community relations (1.3), but it need not have created a permanent breach. Hyrcanus' conquest of Samaria and Shechem could have strained relations seriously— and some scholars see this as the incident which closed the communities off from one another—but we cannot be sure of that. Hyrcanus also forcibly converted the Idumeans, and most of them remained Jewish in their religion according to the later references to them.

The archeology has yet to be clarified. The latest data still seem to bear up a destruction of the city in the time of Hyrcanus or Janneus (1.8). If the temple (assuming there was one) and cult were also destroyed at this time, it could have created great hostility. But destruction of the city does not require destruction of the cult. Against the interpretation that Shechem's conquest was the decisive point is the absence of polemic in Jewish literature until the first

---

[34] I am not aware of significant arguments against the idea that the cult was ultimately descended from the Yahwistic worship of the northern kingdom, which would explain its similarity to Second Temple Judaism but would also recognize a certain independence. Cf. Coggins (*Jews and Samaritans*, 162-65) and the later view of Purvis ("The Samaritan Problem: A Case Study in Jewish Sectarianism in the Roman Era," in B. Halpern and J. D. Levenson [ed.], *Traditions in Transformation: Turning Points in Biblical Faith* [Winona Lake, IN: Eisenbrauns, 1981] 323-50, specifically 337). Nevertheless, for present purposes it is not necessary to take a position on the question of origins.

century. The only probable earlier example is Ben Sira (1.4). If the Samaritans were the ones to sever relations, Jewish writers as members of the dominant ethnic group may not have been interested in polemicizing against the Samaritans; that is, the Samaritans may not have been of sufficient interest to warrant attention. On the other hand, it is not necessary to assume a breach before the first century, and the literature would bear this out. The argument that the Samaritan Pentateuch shows redaction in the decades after the destruction of Shechem is based on too many uncertainties (1.7). Neither would such a redaction even require the assumption that the two communities had ceased to communicate.

The question of Hellenization has exercised a number of researchers on the Samaritans, often with unfortunate results. Part of the problem is that the situation in Jerusalem is misunderstood and then a false analogy imported to Shechem. The process of Hellenization was complex, but both the Jews and Samaritans were affected by it the same as other Near Eastern peoples.[35] Therefore, it is hardly surprising to find works in Greek which seem to be by Samaritan authors (1.5). If the situation in Judea is anything to go by, there was likely a variety of attitudes toward Hellenistic culture within the Gerizim community. Those who propose a "Hellenistic" party among the Samaritans have plausibility on their side.

Where the misconception lies is assuming a dichotomy of a "Hellenistic" party on one side versus a "loyal, pious" group on the other. The authors of the Hellenistic reform in Jerusalem were also loyal, pious individuals—many of them priests—who did not attempt to compromise the traditional temple cult.[36]

Similarly, there is no reason to think that any Hellenistic party in Samaria would have done so there. As has already been noted (1.3), the evidence available does not indicate that those who wrote to Antiochus IV were seeking a change to their traditional cult. Postulating that this letter was written by a "Hellenistic party" at Shechem is, therefore, irrelevant to the question.

3 Conclusions and Social Implications

Our investigation has turned up both positive and negative aspects of the question. We must first accept that there is a lot we do not know with regard to Samaritan history in the Hasmonean period. But sometimes even negative conclusions have their positive implications, so both sides of the question will be considered, both what we know and what we do not:

---

[35] The question, with supporting data, is discussed at length in ch. 3 of my book, *Judaism from Cyrus to Hadrian* (2 vols.; Minneapolis: Fortress, 1992), including interaction with such classic works as M. Hengel, *Judaism and Hellenism* (Philadelphia: Fortress, 1974) and V. A. Tcherikover, *Hellenistic Civilization and the Jews* (New York: Jewish Publication Society, 1959).

[36] For a discussion, see ch. 5 of my book, *Judaism from Cyrus to Hadrian*. The Jewish cult and religion were, of course, eventually compromised and suppressed at the order of Antiochus IV, and some Jews seem to have had a hand in it. But there is no evidence that the authors of the Hellenistic reform, led by Jason, were involved. When opposition developed, it was not against Jason's Hellenistic reform (which had already been aborted by Menelaus) but against the alleged sale of temple vessels.

1. The origins of the community and cult are still uncertain. The origins according to interpretations of 2 Kings 17 (pagan foreigners brought in) and Josephus (dissident Jerusalem priests) are the product of considerable bias and cannot be taken at face value.

2. Likewise, the ethnic diversity of Samaria is unknown. One could no doubt argue that ethnic outsiders were brought in at various times,[37] producing some ethnic mixing, but whether the older identity was preserved is unknown. But if so, there is little evidence that such mixing had a significant impact on the Samaritan religion. If there were pagan groups in the region of Samaria, this may have created antagonism between them and the Samaritan community, just as between the latter and the Jews. Also, if there were other groups, some of the references to "Samaritans" may have nothing to do with the Gerizim community.

3. We often do not know precisely who is being referred to when the sources speak of "Samaritans" and the like.[38] Was it the community with worship centered on the Gerizim cult or was it some other group in the region of Samaria, perhaps with no connection to the Samaritan community of concern to us? The problem may even be more acute when no names are used, and we are left guessing from the context (cf. 1.5).

4. If or when major Samaritan/Jewish hostility arose is uncertain. At least until about 100 BCE there was communication between the Jewish and Samaritan communities. Exactly when friction developed between them is unknown, though some friction could go back to an early time, as early as the time of Nehemiah or even pre-exilic times. But the existence of strained relations does not preclude communication and even good relations between some parts of the community. Evidently, these were best between the upper classes, such as the Tobiad family.[39]

5. The Samaritans were evidently as affected by Hellenization as the Jews. As argued elsewhere, the dichotomy of "Hellenized" versus "faithful" Jews is a false one. Similarly, the idea that the Samaritans were more "syncretistic" than the Jews is equally a caricature. Hellenization was a cultural phenomenon of the entire ancient Near East. No people was immune to it, though different peoples and different individuals may have responded in different ways. One response was what has been called apologetic historiography, the interpretation of the native history in such a way that it

---

37 T. L. Thompson (*Early History of the Israelite People From the Written and Archaeological Sources* [Studies in the History of the Ancient Near East 4; Leiden-New York-Köln: Brill, 1992], especially 412-21) argues this. It seems to me that he exaggerates the amount of ethnic mixing since the deportation of peoples often involved a minority of the population. Also, where communities were deported, they frequently kept their identity in their new habitation, sometimes even for centuries.

38 Despite Egger's arguments, Josephus does not use his terminology consistently, leaving us uncertain at least some of the time.

39 As already noted, Joseph Tobiad borrowed money from friends in Samaria to fund his initial venture into Ptolemaic politics (*Ant.* 12.4.3 §168). This may well have been a continuation of contacts going back at least to the time time of Nehemiah (Neh 4:7; 6:1). Cf. B. Mazar, "The Tobiads," *IEJ* 7 (1957) 137-45, 229-38 (revision of articles in *Tarbiz* 12 [1941] 109-23, and *EI* 4 [1956] 24951).

would commend itself to Greek readers.[40] A good example of this is the "Anonymous Samaritan" or Pseudo-Eupolemus who combines Samaritan tradition with material from Greek mythology.

6. The history of the Samaritan community seems similar to that of Jews but in miniature, since the Gerizim community was apparently smaller than that of the Jews. They had much the same basic customs, with the main difference being the appropriate place for God's temple. They both had a Diaspora population.[41] They both suffered religious suppression or persecution, the Samaritans suffering also at the hands of the Jews and possibly vice versa.

One final point is really little more than speculation, but it has sociological implications:

7. There is some small evidence of intermarriage between the Jewish and Samaritan communities. What few data we have concern the upper classes: Joseph Tobiad who had friends in Samaria who loaned him money; Herod, who married a wife from there; perhaps even Josephus himself who admits to having friends in Samaria. Except for Herod, who may have married for diplomatic reasons, no explicit reference is made to relatives. Yet our sources may have been somewhat coy to admit actual intermarriage. If there was intermarriage, it illustrates a common sociological phenomenon in which the upper classes have a different standard from those at the bottom end of the scale.[42]

---

40 On the concept, see especially G. E. Sterling, *Historiography and Self-Definition: Josephus, Luke-Acts and Apologetic Historiography* (NovTSup 64; Leiden: Brill, 1992). This was a common phenomenon of nationalism among nations under Greek and then Roman rule; see D. Mendels, *The Rise and Fall of Jewish National* (Anchor Reference Library; New York: Doubleday, 1993) 35-54.

41 For a summary of information on this, see A. D. Crown, "The Samaritan Diaspora" in Crown (ed.), *The Samaritans*, 195-217. Much of the information on the early history of this Diaspora is, unfortunately, semi-legendary. According to Josephus, Samaritans were taken to Egypt and even held a dispute with Jews there (*Ant.* 12.1.1 §§7, 10; 13.3.4 §§74-79). The Samaritan Chronicles have a version of this dispute and also refer to a large Diaspora in Babylonia (1.6). Two inscriptions from Delos from the 3rd to 1st centuries BCE also seem to be a Samaritan product (see A. T. Kraabel, "New Evidence of the Samaritan Diaspora Has Been Found on Delos," *BA* 47 [1984] 44-47). The "Israelites in Delos" here use the Greek form Argarizein for Mt. Gerizim which often, though not always, is evidence of Samaritan ethnicity (see R. Pummer, "Ἀργαριζιν: A Criterion for Samaritan Provenance?" *JSJ* 18 [1987] 18-25).

42 I wish to express my thanks to the British Academy for a travel grant which has helped toward the costs of presenting this paper.

What Do We Mean by "First-Century Jewish Monotheism"?[1]

Larry W. Hurtado
University of Manitoba

I

The nature of first-century Jewish religion is an obviously important question both for the history of Judaism and for Christian Origins. In recent years especially, there has been a lot of attention given to the monotheism of first-century Jewish religion, especially (but not exclusively) among scholars discussing the emergence of "high christology" and the reverence given to Jesus in early Christianity. In my 1988 book, *One God, One Lord: Early Christian Devotion and Ancient Jewish Monotheism*, I urged that first-century Jewish religious commitment to the uniqueness of God was the crucial context in which to approach early Christian devotion to Christ. I emphasized two characteristics of ancient Jewish religiousness: (1) a remarkable ability to combine a genuine concern for God's uniqueness together with an interest in other figures of transcendent attributes described in the most exalted terms, likening them to God in some cases; and (2) an exhibition of monotheistic scruples particularly and most distinctively in cultic/liturgical behavior.

In this paper I wish to return to the question of "ancient Jewish monotheism," engaging some others who have written on the subject recently, and offering some further reflections and additional evidence on the nature of first-century Jewish religion. I wish to argue that first-century Jewish religion characteristically exhibited a monotheistic scruple. I also wish to make the methodological point that our understanding of ancient Jewish monotheism needs to be inductively formed and sufficiently sophisticated to take account of the variety, flexibility and changes in the way it was manifested in the Greco-Roman world.

II

Before we look at the evidence of ancient Jewish religion, I want to offer some critical reflections on some recent studies alluded to above in which the question of Jewish monotheism plays a major role. There are significant differences distinguishing them from one another, but for our purposes they

[1] I gratefully acknowledge a research grant from the Social Sciences and Humanities Research Council of Canada.

can be classified into two major groups. One group portrays first-century Jewish religion as monotheistic, and the other group questions the validity of doing so. I tend to support those who attribute monotheistic scruples to first-century Jewish religion, but I think that studies on both sides of the issue reflect the need for more careful thinking about the data and how we deal with them.

In his 1982 study *Jesus and the Constraints of History*, A. E. Harvey devoted a chapter to "The Constraint of Monotheism." Harvey's discussion of Jewish monotheism here is, however, in fact quite limited. I mention his study more on account of the importance he attached to Jewish monotheism than for the contribution he made to understanding it. He did address the honorific language used to describe figures other than God, insisting, for example, that reference to Moses as "divine" (*theios*) in Josephus (e.g., *Ant.* 3.180; 8.34, 187; 10.35) and Philo (e.g., *Vita Mos.* 1.158) "is not so much a religious as a linguistic phenomenon" indicating "the exceptional nature of his gifts" but never intended or taken as qualifying "in any way the unique divinity of the Creator of the world."[2]

But for Harvey, Jewish "monotheism" was more a premise than his subject. Having posited as the controlling influence upon early Christian thought about Jesus a firm Jewish monotheism manifested essentially in a refusal to attribute real divinity to figures other than God, Harvey then sought to use this to determine what the christological thought of the NT could have allowed. His stated as his aim "to show that there is no unambiguous evidence that the constraint of monotheism was effectively broken by any New Testament writer," insisting that the NT documents "show no tendency to describe Jesus in terms of divinity . . ."[3] In Harvey's view, it is not until Ignatius of Antioch that we have the "first unambiguous instances" of Jesus being described as divine.

> It was not until the new religion had spread well beyond the confines of its parent Judaism that it became possible to break the constraint and describe Jesus as divine . . .[4]

Both in his description of ancient Jewish monotheism and in his portrayal of the reverence for Christ reflected in the NT Harvey is subject to criticism. Our interest here, however, is the former matter. I single out two things in particular about his view of Jewish monotheism. First, he refers to it consistently as a "constraint" that might or might not be "broken," giving the impression of a fixed doctrinal system with little adaptive capacity. Second, Harvey focuses on conceptual and linguistic phenomena, giving insufficient attention to the critical importance of cultic/liturgical practices emphasized by ancient Jews as boundary-markers that distinguished the true God from other divine beings, and that set apart right devotion from its idolatrous counterfeit.

---

2 A. E. Harvey, *Jesus and the Constraints of History* (Philadelphia: Westminster Press, 1982), 157.

3 Ibid.

4 Ibid.

In Maurice Casey's recently published Cadbury lectures we have another study of the development of NT christology that employs Jewish monotheism in a manner similar to Harvey's treatment.[5] As does Harvey, Casey invokes a Jewish monotheism that limited and restrained reverence for Jesus so long as early Christianity was dominated by this mindset, making it impossible for Jesus to have been regarded as divine. In Casey's view, however, the restraint was effectively (and lamentably) removed earlier than Harvey thought, within the Johannine community after 70 C.E., when Gentiles came to dominate the community ensuring that "Jesus was hailed as God," a second deity alongside the God of the Bible.[6] At the risk of some oversimplification, they let the Gentiles move into the Johannine community and there went the neighborhood! Casey's programmatic portrayal of the development of NT christology requires more attention than I can give it here.[7] I restrict myself to a few comments about his references to Jewish monotheism.

As with Harvey, Casey is mainly concerned to offer an analysis of NT christology, and he postulates a firm Jewish monotheism primarily as the crucial device which allows him to determine the possible limits of early Christian reverence for Jesus so long as the Christian movement was mainly Jewish in makeup. In other words, as with Harvey, Casey's view of Jewish monotheism drives his exegesis of NT christological texts. Postulating a Jewish monotheism with fixed and powerful restraints, Casey is then able to insist in case after case that pre-Johannine NT passages that might at first appear to reflect a reverence for Jesus as divine cannot in fact be taken that way. It is handy way of doing exegesis, though not always persuasive, in my view at least.

Casey's discussion of Jewish monotheism is mainly in chapter six, where he analyzes the place of messianic and intermediary figures in second Temple Jewish religion, granting that they are given an "unusually elevated status" in various ancient Jewish sources, but insisting that it was impossible for any such figure to be really regarded as divine within Jewish monotheism.[8] Though he describes the impressive roles given to divine agents in various Jewish texts, I am not sure that he has adequately presented

---

5 P. M. Casey, *From Jewish Prophet to Gentile God: The Origins and Development of New Testament Christology* (Louisville: Westminster Press/John Knox Press; Cambridge: James Clarke & Co., 1991).

6 Ibid., 36. And see, e.g., 138, 144, 156.

7 For a critique, see J. D. G. Dunn, "The Making of Christology—Evolution or Unfolding?" in the forthcoming *Festschrift* for I. H. Marshall edited by M. M. B. Turner. I limit myself here to observing that Casey's attempt to explain the development of christology purely on the basis of the changing social makeup of early Christianity rests too heavily upon two dubious notions. (1) He assumes that Gentile Christians were automatically less concerned about monotheistic commitment, an assumption Casey could have avoided by studying the literature of second-century Gentile Christians, who often seem more concerned about monotheism than christology. (2) His claim that a Gentile-dominated new religious movement would have had to deify its identification-figure (in this case, Jesus) in order to provide sufficient cohesiveness for itself, is refuted by the example of Islam, which felt no need to deify its central revealer-figure, yet quickly acquired a quite adequate cohesion!

8 Ibid., 85.

the rather flexible ability of ancient Jewish monotheism to incorporate a plurality in the operation of the sovereignty of the one God. Like Harvey, he sees the restraining force of Jewish monotheism manifested primarily in the way God was conceptually distinguished from other honorific figures, that is, in the language used to describe God and other figures. But I am not sure that the rhetorical distinctions were quite as firm as Casey claims. Also, he gives scant attention to the importance of cultic practice in understanding Jewish religion. Further, in consistently posing the question as to whether Jews or Christians thought of any figure as a second deity fully distinguished from the God of Israel, he shows a disappointingly simplistic and wooden grasp of the complexities and possibilities of ancient Jewish and Christian beliefs.

In several publications J. D. G. Dunn also has invoked Jewish monotheism as crucial in his effort to analyze early Christian reverence for Jesus. In a 1982 essay Dunn poses two main questions: (1) Was pre-Christian Jewish monotheism "threatened" by beliefs about "heavenly redeemer figures and intermediary beings"? (2) Did earliest christology constitute a threat to or departure from Jewish monotheism?[9] Both questions he essentially answers in the negative, but we are concerned here primarily with the way he deals with the first question. It is interesting to note the subtle shifts and developments (of a positive nature, in my judgment) in his views over the past decade or so.[10]

Though the general drift of Dunn's analysis is that there was no significant threat to Jewish monotheism in pre-Christian Jewish conceptions of redeemer and/or intermediary figures, he seems to allow for development and change in Jewish traditions of the Greco-Roman period, implying more than Harvey or Casey a flexible Jewish monotheism able to stretch and bend a good deal without breaking.[11] In his 1982 essay he granted potential threats to Jewish monotheism in the vivid language of personification of divine attributes (such as Wisdom and Logos), and, more seriously, in "one strand of esoteric mysticism" involving a human-like figure, a principal angel and/or patriarch described as bearing the divine name and/or glory.[12] In the pre-Christian period the former was "kept under control and would not have been perceived as a threat" to monotheism.[13] Dunn initially saw speculations about a second figure like God becoming a danger to Jewish monotheism in the early second century,[14] but more recently has emphasized "strains" from

---

[9] J. D. G. Dunn, "Was Christianity a Monotheistic Faith from the Beginning?" *SJT* 35(1982), 303-36. The two questions are posed on p. 307.

[10] See J. D. G. Dunn, *Christology in the Making: An Inquiry into the Origins of the Doctrine of the Incarnation* (London: SCM; Philadelphia: Westminster Press, 1980); *id.*, "Foreword to the Second Edition," *Christology in the Making* (2nd ed.; London: SCM, 1989), where Dunn explicitly indicates how his views have been shaped in the years since 1980. And see also *id.*, *The Partings of the Ways between Christianity and Judaism and their Significance for the Character of Christianity* (London: SCM, 1991), esp. chaps. 9-11.

[11] E.g., Dunn, "Was Christianity a Monotheistic Faith," 321-22.

[12] Cf. ibid., 322; *id.*, "Foreword," xxiv, xxviii-xxix.

[13] Dunn, "Was Christianity a Monotheistic Faith," 322.

[14] Ibid.

various speculations about principal agent figures becoming apparent by the end of the first century.[15] His suggestion that the "high" christology of Hebrews, the Gospel of John and Revelation may be one strand of a larger number of speculations about the divine in Jewish groups of the late first century that distended or threatened monotheism is worth further consideration.

There are also slight shifts in the way Dunn approaches Jewish monotheism. In his earlier comments on the significance of secondary figures in Jewish monotheism, Dunn dwelt entirely on the descriptions of them and the concepts held about them.[16] More recently, he has also taken some account of the importance of cultic practices (worship) as indicators of religious scruples, both in Jewish and Christian circles.[17]

Over against the view that first-century Jewish religion was strongly monotheistic, there are recent claims directly to the contrary by Peter Hayman and Margaret Barker especially.[18] There are striking similarities in their views, along with distinguishing features also. Although both could be subjected to strong criticisms, the claims both advance encompass such a breadth of material that it is not possible here to offer a detailed examination. It will have to suffice for this essay to give some limited critical observations.

Taking as his subject "the pattern of Jewish beliefs about God from the Exile to the Middle Ages," Peter Hayman states as his aim "to assess whether or not it is truly monistic."[19] Hayman claims that down to the Middle Ages Jewish religion retained a "dualistic pattern" from the ancient Canaanite background and that "functionally Jews believed in the existence of two

---

15 Dunn, "Foreword," xxviii-xxix. See also Dunn, *Partings*, 223-25 and 228, where he locates problematic developments in Jewish monotheism from mystical and apocalyptic groups within the period 70-132 C.E. Dunn takes the rabbinic criticisms of "two powers" heretics as evidence that such developments were perceived as unacceptable "strains" in monotheism.

16 This emphasis is evident in *Christology in the Making* (1980) and in his 1982 essay, "Was Christianity a Monotheistic Faith."

17 See Dunn, *Partings*, 219-20, where he notes that the "clear and uninhibited worship of the Lamb" in Revelation 5 represents a significant abandonment of typical monotheistic "inhibitions" and, along with the theophanic portrayal of Christ in the visions of Revelation, shows that the "constraints of monotheism previously observed were being challenged". In chapter 10 of *Partings* (204-6), Dunn interacts with my argument that such cultic veneration of Jesus was the decisive Christian innovation in Jewish monotheistic religion, granting that the worship of Jesus was significant but questioning whether it developed as early and as quickly as I have suggested. Cf. L. W. Hurtado, *One God, One Lord*, esp. chap. 5 (93-124). Though I agree that there was likely growth in the intensity of cultic/liturgical devotion offered to Jesus in the early Christian groups, I think that the initial steps in the cultic veneration of Jesus were more significant than Dunn appears to grant, and more rapidly constituted a significant innovation in Jewish monotheistic practice. In a critique of Casey, Dunn affirms my emphasis on the early origins of devotion to Christ as important ("The Making of Christology: Evolution or Unfolding?" forthcoming in the *Festschrift* for I. H. Marshall edited by Max Turner).

18 Peter Hayman, "Monotheism—A Misused Word in Jewish Studies?" *JJS* 42(1991) 1-15; Margaret Barker, *The Great Angel: A Study of Israel's Second God* (London: SPCK, 1992).

19 Hayman, 2.

gods."[20] He invokes five things in support of his case: (1) indications that a doctrine of creation *ex nihilo* is not found until well into the Middle Ages; (2) references to the possibility of mystical unity with God and to ideas of metamorphosis of human figures (e.g., Enoch) into heavenly/angelic beings;[21] (3) the prominence of angels in ancient Jewish texts, and prohibitions against worshipping them; (4) evidence of Jewish practice of magic involving the invocation of a variety of heavenly figures (usually named angels) along with God as sources of magical power; (5) the alleged survival of a divine consort of Yahweh in post-exilic references to Wisdom and Logos. Hayman illustrates that ancient Jews were not unitarians, but it is not clear that his data shows them to be di-theistic.

Barker gives a book-length case for a somewhat similar point of view. Ranging over "an enormous amount of material from ancient Canaan to mediaeval Kabbalah,"[22] Barker's discussion is certainly provocative. It is also frequently infuriating in its almost cavalier handling of ancient evidence and modern scholarship. Her view seems to be that Greco-Roman Jewish religion included both a monotheistic strain (the heirs of the Deuteronomistic reformers) and, as a kind of underground theology, another strain or line of religious tradition which resisted the reforming, purging efforts of the Deuteronomistic school and its heirs, and in which there were always two deities. Unfortunately, the wide range of Barker's discussion results in a wide range of dubious claims.[23]

Moreover, it is clear that Barker's real aim in alleging a di-theistic Judaism in the first century is to provide a ready explanation for the rapid ease with which Jesus was treated as divine in first-century Christian groups.[24] According to Barker, Jesus was quickly and easily regarded as divine by Jewish Christians because they were well accustomed to thinking in terms of two deities. But I confess to wondering if Barker's sharply polemical purpose has controlled too much her handling of the Jewish and Christian evidence.[25]

---

20 Hayman, 14.

21 This is emphasized also by C. R. A. Morray-Jones, "Transformational Mysticism in the Apocalyptic-Merkabah Tradition," *JJS* 43(1992) 1-31; *id.*, "The Body of Glory: *Shiur Qomah* and Transformational Mysticism in the Epistle to the Ephesians," unpublished paper presented at the 1992 meeting of the SBL Consultation on Mediator Figures in Greco-Roman Jewish and Christian Religion. I am grateful for his discussions but not always persuaded by his attempts to push for very early dating of the traditions and by the inferences in the direction of di-theism he sometimes draws from the evidence.

22 Barker, xiii.

23 I have expressed some more specific criticisms in a brief review of Barker's book forthcoming in *Theology*. Of course, Morton Smith had sketched a case for a survival of pre-Exilic "syncretistic" Israelite religion into the post-Exilic period, but he seems to have thought that it had essentially waned by the first century C.E., except for possible traces in Jewish magical materials (Smith, *Palestinian Parties and Politics that Shaped the Old Testament* [London: SCM, 1987 reprint of the 1971 edition], esp. chap. 4).

24 Barker, 1-3.

25 Barker refers to a "hidden agenda" and "an alliance between Jewish and Protestant scholars" whose purpose is "to emphasize the humanness of Jesus and to show that his 'divinity' was a later development and an unfortunate one at that," which she sets out to refute (p. 1). Hayman says, "The fact that functionally Jews believed in the existence of two

In any case, though Barker's discussion is longer than Hayman's, it basically elaborates a very similar position, and I therefore treat their views together.[26]

I suggest that on both sides of the issue (to varying degrees among the individual studies) there has been a tendency to proceed deductively from *a priori* presumptions of what monotheism must mean, instead of building up a view inductively from the evidence of how monotheism actually operated in the thought and practice of ancient Jews. There seems to be an implicit agreement on both sides that more than one transcendent being of any significance complicates or constitutes a weakening of or threat to monotheism. Those who see first-century Jewish religion as monotheistic tend, therefore, to downplay the significance and attributes given by ancient Jews to any transcendent beings other than God. For these scholars often, ancient Jewish monotheism must mean that the descriptions of such beings are largely rhetorical. Though I am convinced regarding some examples, I am not sure that the descriptions are always purely rhetoric, as we shall see later in this paper.

Those on the other side of the issue tend to emphasize the honorific ways in which transcendent beings other than God are described and the prominent positions they occupy in the religious conceptions reflected in ancient Jewish texts, alleging that first-century Jews were not really monotheists after all. It is clear that ancient Jews were not characteristically monists or unitarians, but does this mean that they were not monotheists? That is, on both sides there is a tendency to proceed as if we can know in advance what "monotheism" must mean, which turns out to be a very modern, monistic form of monotheism, and can accordingly evaluate ancient Jewish texts and beliefs as to whether or how closely they meet an *a priori* standard of "pure" monotheism. Interestingly, Hayman disavows any such intention, but it seems to me that he in fact winds up doing this very thing.[27]

In place of this rather Aristotelian approach, I urge us to work more inductively, gathering what "monotheism" is on the ground, so to speak, from the evidence of what self-professed monotheists believe and practice. In

---

gods explains the speed with which Christianity developed so fast in the first century towards the divinization of Jesus" (14), but does not have the same stridently polemical tone and his discussion does seem so driven by this view.

26 In this limited survey, I have not dealt with the suggestion of Christopher Rowland that in second-Temple Jewish tradition there had developed a speculation about a bifurcation of the divine involving God and his personified glory. Fossum seems to take a somewhat similar view. Traditions about the divine glory (and the divine name) are certainly important, but I do not find Rowland's or Fossum's case for a bifurcation of God convincing. See my discussion of their views in *One God, One Lord*, 85-90. On the divine glory, see now esp. Carey C. Newman, *Paul's Glory-Christology: Tradition and Rhetoric* (NovTSup, 69; Leiden: Brill, 1992).

27 Early in his essay Hayman says, "I do not intend to proceed here by setting up a model definition of monotheism and then assessing the Jewish tradition against this yardstick." But then he proceeds to do exactly this in my judgment, in imposing such things as a doctrine of *creatio ex nihilo* as a requirement of true monotheism (3-4), and in making the question turn on whether ancient Jews were "truly monistic" (2).

fact, I suggest that for historical investigation our policy should be to take people as monotheistic if that is how they describe themselves, in spite of what we might be inclined to regard at first as anomalies in their beliefs. Such "anomalies," I suggest in fact are extremely valuable data in shaping our understanding of monotheism out of the actual beliefs of actual people and traditions who describe themselves in monotheistic language.

Moreover, with a few exceptions, scholars on both sides (but perhaps especially those who have portrayed ancient Jewish religion as strongly monotheistic) have tended to give insufficient allowance to the flexibility and variety in forms of monotheistic religion. In previous work I have emphasized how early Christians such as Paul were quite able to refer to their beliefs in monotheistic language while accommodating devotion to Christ in terms and actions characteristically deemed appropriate for God (e.g., 1 Cor. 8:4-6). Though I have not found another fully analogous example of quite such a robust and programmatic binitarian monotheistic devotion in first-century Jewish tradition, with other scholars I have illustrated the sometimes astonishingly exalted ways divine agents can be described in Jewish texts which exhibit a strong monotheistic orientation.[28] In particular, we should note the cases where a principal angel is given God's name (e.g., Yahoel) and is visually described in theophanic language, sometimes causing the human who encounters the angel to confuse the angel initially with God.[29] These data illustrate the variety and flexibility in ancient Jewish monotheistic tradition, especially the ability to accommodate "divine" figures in addition to the God of Israel in the belief structure and religious outlook.

In addition to variety, we should allow for change and development. In his proposal that Jewish monotheism may have undergone some significant changes and developments in the late first and early second century, whether or not one finds his proposal persuasive in all specifics, Dunn seems commendably to allow for a more flexible and dynamic Jewish monotheism than many other scholars on either side of the debate I have been surveying.

As a final observation in this section reviewing recent statements about ancient Jewish monotheism, I wish to criticize the tendency among scholars to focus on describing concepts and doctrines, with inadequate attention given to religious practices, especially cultic and liturgical practices and related behavior. Thus, for example, scholars argue largely about whether ancient Jews conceived of more than one figure as divine, and seek to answer the question almost entirely on the basis of semantic arguments, without studying adequately how ancient Jews practiced their faith.

I suggest that, for ancient Jews, Christians and pagans, the primary exhibitions of what we would call their religiousness were in cultic and liturgical behavior, and that Jewish and Christian monotheistic commitment was exhibited most sharply in scruples about worship (as I shall argue more extensively later in this paper). Consequently, if we wish to understand ancient Jewish and Christian monotheism, if we wish to measure its

---

28 Hurtado, *One God, One Lord*, passim.

29 Ibid., chap. 4. See R. Bauckham's study of this motif of confusing angels with God: "The Worship of Jesus in Apocalyptic Christianity," *NTS* 27(1980-81) 322-41.

intensity, if we wish to know how it operated and what it meant "on the ground" in the lives of adherents, we should pay considerable attention to the way their commitment to the uniqueness of one God was exhibited in their practice with regard to granting cultic veneration to other beings or figures.

As I have argued in *One God, One Lord*, and as I shall reiterate again below, it is precisely with reference to worship that ancient Jewish religious tradition most clearly distinguished the unique one God from other beings, even those described as "divine" and clothed with god-like attributes. And I add in passing here that this makes the early readiness of monotheistic Christians to accommodate public cultic veneration of Jesus the most striking evidence that Christian devotion quickly constituted a significant innovation in Jewish exclusivist monotheism.

III

I have suggested for a working principle that we should take as "monotheism" the religious beliefs and practices of people who describe themselves as monotheistic. Otherwise, we implicitly import a definition from the sphere of theological polemics in an attempt to do historical analysis. Protestants, for example, might find some forms of Roman Catholic or Orthodox piety involving the saints and the Virgin problematic forms of monotheism, and this might constitute a fully valid *theological* issue to be explored. But scholars interested in historical analysis, I suggest, should take the various Protestant, Roman Catholic and Orthodox traditions as representing varying forms of Christian monotheism. If we are to avoid *a priori* definitions and the imposition of our own theological judgments, we have no choice but to accept as monotheism the religion of those who profess to be monotheists, however much their religion varies and may seem "complicated" with other beings in addition to the one God.

With reference to first-century Jewish tradition, then, two initial questions naturally arise. Did Jews of the period characteristically profess their religious commitment in monotheistic terms? What was the monotheistic rhetoric they used? Fortunately, these are rather easy questions to answer, on account of the work of several other scholars who have given quite detailed attention to these matters. I shall, therefore, restrict my discussion here to a few illustrations of ancient Jewish monotheistic rhetoric and point the reader to the studies in question for more full presentations of the evidence.

I note in passing that monotheistic rhetoric, e.g., the use of *heis* and *monos* formulae in references to the divine, can be found in non-Jewish sources of the Greco-Roman period as well, as Erik Peterson has shown.[30] But in religious practice, this pagan "monotheism" amounted to the recognition of all gods as expressions of one common divine essence or as valid second-order

---

[30] Erik A. G. Peterson, *Heis Theos: Epigraphische, formgeschichtliche und religionsgeschichtliche Untersuchungen* (FRLANT, 24; Göttingen: Vandenhoeck & Ruprecht, 1926). Morton Smith has drawn attention to the same sort of honorific rhetoric, exalting one deity above all others and even calling one deity the "only" god, across the ancient period of the Near East in "The Common Theology of the Ancient Near East," *JBL* 71(1952) 135-47.

gods under a (often unknowable) high god, and, as such, as worthy of worship. This was categorically different from the exclusivist monotheism of Jews who rejected the worship of beings other than the one God of the Bible.[31] That is, apparently "monotheistic" rhetoric may represent quite different conceptions and may be employed by people with quite different commitments and patterns of religious behavior. We have here a dramatic example of the necessity of complimenting a study of religious rhetoric and concepts with adequate attention to religious practice in taking the measure of a religion. But, before we turn to key religious practices of ancient Jews, we may consider evidence that they did express their faith emphatically in monotheistic rhetoric.

In a lengthy article from 1955, Samuel Cohon surveyed references both in ancient Jewish and non-Jewish texts illustrating Jewish self-affirmation and their identification by others in clearly monotheistic rhetoric.[32] Of non-Jewish writers, we may note Tacitus as an example: "the Jews acknowledge one God only, and conceive of Him by the mind alone,"[33] reflecting Jewish monotheism and rejection of cult images. Among non-rabbinic texts of Jewish provenance, Cohon surveys affirmations of God's uniqueness in *Sibylline Oracles* (3.11-12, 545-61; cf. 4.27-32; 5.172-76, 493-500), *Aristeas* (132-38), *Wisdom of Solomon* (13-15), and references in Philo (e.g., *Quest.Gen.* 4:8; *Vit.Mos.* 1:75; *Decal.* 52-81; *Spec.Leg.* 1:1-52; *Leg.Alleg.* 3:97-99, 436-38) and Josephus (e.g., *Ant.* 2.12:4; *Apion* 2:33ff.).[34]

We may also cite Ralph Marcus' frequently overlooked but very valuable compilation of theological vocabulary from Jewish Hellenistic texts (excluding Josephus and with only illustrative citations from Philo).[35] Marcus' main point was to indicate the degree to which Greek-speaking Jews maintained traditional expressions for God and the degree to which they adopted religious and philosophical vocabulary of Greek literature. Marcus listed some 470 expressions, attributing about twenty-five percent as borrowed from Greek literary tradition, the remaining, overwhelming majority coming from the Greek Bible.[36] Marcus' summary of the theological themes

---

31 See, e.g., my brief discussion of the question and references to other literature in *One God, One Lord*, 129-30; Yehoshua Amir, "Die Begegnung des biblischen und des philosophischen Monotheismus als Grundthema des jüdischen Hellenismus," *Evangelische Theologie* 38(1978) 2-19. See also Erik Peterson's discussion of the interaction between pagan, Jewish and Christian forms of monotheistic conceptions and political ideas in the ancient world, in *Der Monotheismus als politisches Problem: Ein Beitrag zur Geschichte der politischen Theologie im Imperium Romanum* (Leipzig: Jakob Hegner, 1935). For a general introduction to pagan and Jewish conceptions of the divine, see R. M. Grant, *Gods and the One God* (Philadelphia: Westminster Press, 1986).

32 Samuel S. Cohon, "The Unity of God: A Study in Hellenistic and Rabbinic Theology," *HUCA* 26(1955) 425-79.

33 Tacitus, *Histories* 5.3, cited in Cohon, 429.

34 Ibid., esp. 428-38.

35 Ralph Marcus, "Divine Names and Attributes in Hellenistic Jewish Literature," *Proceedings of the American Academy for Jewish Research 1931-32*, 43-120.

36 Ibid., esp. 47-48.

reflected in these expressions shows the strongly monotheistic nature of concept of God they reflect.

> God is variously represented as one and unique, as creator, ruler and king, residing in heaven, all-powerful, all-seeing, omniscient, as father of Israel, as savior, as judge, as righteous, terrible, merciful, benevolent and forbearing.[37]

Marcus left Josephus out of his study because Schlatter had earlier devoted two publications to an in-depth analysis of Josephus' language and conception of God, showing Josephus' indebtedness and fidelity to the Jewish emphases on the uniqueness and sovereignty of the God of Israel.[38] Schlatter's studies were supplemented by Shutt in an article investigating whether Josephus' ways of referring to and describing God "show any appreciable influence of Greek language and culture."[39] Though he concedes that Josephus' expressions show the influence upon him of non-Jewish terms and ideas (e.g., references to "Fate" and "Fortune"), Shutt concludes that "fundamental theological principles of Judaism" remained dominant in Josephus' writings, including the belief in the sovereignty of the God of Israel over all.[40]

H. J. Wicks conducted a still valuable study covering Jewish apocryphal and apocalyptic literature of the second-Temple period, analyzing the language and doctrine of God reflected therein. He gave persuasive evidence of strong monotheistic beliefs throughout the period and of a lively religious sense of God's sovereignty and accessibility.[41]

Surely the most wide-ranging analysis of second-Temple Jewish monotheistic rhetoric, however, is in the recent dissertation by Paul Rainbow.[42] Working from a database of 200 passages where he finds monotheistic expressions (including about twenty-five passages from the NT), Rainbow offers some sophisticated linguistic analysis of the "ten forms of explicit monotheistic speech" characteristic of Greco-Roman Jewish texts.[43] These are: (1) phrases linking a divine title with adjectives such as "one," "only," sole, alone, etc.; (2) God pictured as monarch over all; (3) a divine title linked with "living" and/or "true"; (4) positive confessional formula,

---

[37] Ibid., 48.

[38] Adolf Schlatter, *Wie sprach Josephus von Gott?* (BFCT, 1/14; Gütersloh: Bertelsmann, 1910); *id., Die Theologie des Judentums nach dem Bericht des Josefus* (BFCT, 2/26; Gütersloh: Bertelsmann, 1932).

[39] R. J. H. Shutt, "The Concept of God in the works of Flavius Josephus," *JJS* 31(1980), 171-87. The quotation is from p. 172.

[40] Ibid., 185-86.

[41] Henry J. Wicks, *The Doctrine of God in the Jewish Apocryphal and Apocalyptic Literature* (London: Hunter & Longhurst, 1915).

[42] Paul A. Rainbow, "Monotheism and Christology in 1 Corinthians 8:4-6," (Oxford, D.Phil. diss., 1987). See also *id.,* "Jewish Monotheism as the Matrix for New Testament Christology: A Review Article," *NovT* 33(1991) 78-91, esp. 81-83 for an abbreviated citation of evidence from his dissertation.

[43] Ibid., esp. chap. 4. The 200 passages are listed in Appendix 1 (228-86). They include some from the OT and NT, but are mainly drawn from extra-canonical Jewish documents, with only token citations of Philo and Josephus.

"Yahweh is God" etc.; (5) explicit denials of other gods; (6) the glory of God not transferrable; (7) God described as without rival; (8) God referred to as incomparable; (9) scriptural passages used as expressions of monotheism, e.g., the Shema; (10) restrictions of worship to the one God.

As the studies I have cited here lay out the data in considerable detail and can be consulted, it would be tedious to burden this discussion with a host of additional references to the primary texts. I submit that the religious rhetoric of Greco-Roman Jewish texts indicates that Jews saw themselves as monotheists. If their willingness to include other heavenly beings in their beliefs may cause problems for modern monistic or unitarian definitions of monotheism (as Hayman and Barker complain), the problem is in imposing such definitions. If we follow the principle I advocate of taking people as monotheists who proclaim such a commitment, then ancient Jews must be seen as characteristically monotheists.

I suggest that there are two major themes or concerns that seem to come through in this monotheistic rhetoric. I emphasize these two concerns here because I think that recognizing them helps us to get inside the rhetoric, so to speak, and also will help us in understanding better the significance of developments in Jewish monotheistic rhetoric toward the end of the period we are concerned with in this essay.[44]

First, there is a concern to assert God's universal *sovereignty*. This is reflected with particular frequency in statements insisting that the one God created everything and rules over all, even nations that do not acknowledge this God. Even where spiritual powers of evil are pictured as opposing God, as is often the case in apocalyptic writings, their opposition is characteristically described as temporary, ultimately futile. Satan/Beliel/Mastema figures are rebellious servants of God, whose attempts to thwart God's will only serve it by exposing the wicked (who cooperate with evil) and by testing and proving the righteous (who oppose evil and remain true to God).

Second, there is a concern to assert God's *uniqueness*, which is characteristically expressed by contrasting God with the other deities familiar to ancient Jews in the larger religious environment. The classic ridicule of other gods and of the practice of worshipping images in Deutero-Isaiah (e.g., 40:18-20; 41:21-24; 45:20-21; 46:5-7) is echoed in texts of the Hellenistic and Roman periods (e.g., Wis., 13-15). We may take Philo's comment in his discussion of the first commandment as representative of conscientious Jews of his time:

> Let us, then, engrave deep in our hearts this as the first and most sacred of commandments; to acknowledge and honour one God who is above all, and let the idea that gods are many never even reach the ears of the man whose rule of life is to seek for truth in purity and guilelessness.[45]

---

44 For a recent discussion of Jewish monotheistic commitment, see E. P. Sanders, *Judaism: Practice and Belief 63 BCE–66 CE* (London: SCM; Philadelphia: Trinity Press International, 1992), esp. 241-51.

45 Philo, *Decal.*, 65. On Philo, see now Folker Siegert, *Philon von Alexandrien: Über Gottesbezeichnung "wohltätig verzehrendes Feuer"* (WUNT, 46; Tübingen: Mohr-Siebeck, 1988),

It is important to note that this concern for God's uniqueness also comes to expression in a contrast or distinction between God and his loyal heavenly retinue, the angels.[46] For example, angels can be distinguished as created beings from God who is uncreated. In general, God is distinguished from the angels rhetorically by emphasizing that he is superior to them and is their master. Even when we have a principal angel such as Yahoel who bears the divine name within him and in some sense may be taken thereby as "divine," as special vehicle of God's attributes (*Apoc.Abr.* 10:3-4, 8-17), the angel acts at the pleasure of God, and is finally a minister of God, an extension of the sovereignty of the one God.

IV

These two concerns, for God's sovereignty and uniqueness, are also manifested in the cultic/liturgical and larger devotional behavior of practicing Jews in the Greco-Roman era. Indeed, these concerns come to most visible and characteristic expression in this area of religious practice, and it is here that Jewish (and Christian) religiousness was most sharply distinguished from other forms which may also have used "monotheistic"-sounding rhetoric.[47] In our definition of first-century Jewish monotheism, I argue, we must go beyond religious rhetoric and attempts to define theological concepts, and recognize the importance of religious practice.

We may begin by pointing to an obvious datum about which I assume there will be no controversy: at least in the Greek and Roman eras, Jerusalem Temple sacrifice was offered exclusively to the one God of Israel. In other words, this central Jewish religious institution by its cultic practice reflects a

---

who offers a fresh study of a less well used text from Philo. In line 57 of the text, Philo describes the God of Israel as the basis of all existence ("*autos monos estin*").

[46] See now Michael Mach, *Entwicklungsstadien des jüdischen Engelglaubens in vorrabinischer Zeit* (TSAJ, 34; Tübingen: Mohr-Siebeck, 1992) for an analysis of material from biblical texts through Josephus and other Greco-Roman evidence. I have not yet had a chance to examine Saul M. Olyan's, *A Thousand Thousands Served Him: Exegesis and the Naming of Angels in Ancient Judaism* (TSAJ, 36; Tübingen: Mohr-Siebeck, 1993), in which he emphasizes the Jewish creative exegetical use of the OT as a source for naming and ranking of God's angelic entourage.

[47] This point is made persuasively by Amir, "Die Begegnung," (note 31 above). "In diesem Sinne möchte ich die Monolatrie nicht nur, wie üblich, als eine Vorstufe, sondern geradezu als den eigentlichen religösen Kern des biblischen Monotheismus bezeichnen" (4). On Jewish devotional practice in general, see now E. P. Sanders, esp. 195-209. Older studies include Adolf Büchler, *Types of Jewish-Palestinian Piety from 70 B.C.E. to 70 C.E.: The Ancient Pious Men* (Jews College Publications, 8; London: Jews College, 1922), whose rather uncritical handling of rabbinic traditions will now be questioned, but whose study is still worth noting, esp. for his discussion of the piety of the Psalms of Solomon (128-95). Schlatter, *Die Theologie des Judentums nach dem Bericht des Josefus*, includes a lengthy chapter on "Die Frommigkeit" reflected in Josephus (96-158).

strongly monotheistic orientation.[48] For all the lofty ways patriarchs and angels were described in contemporary Jewish texts, there was no cultus to them, no evidence of them receiving liturgical honors in the Temple services.

The Qumran texts show an apparent dissent from the administration of the Jerusalem Temple, but reflect no different orientation of religious devotion. The hymns (1QH) are sung to the one God. The prayers are offered to the one God. The *Angel Liturgy* shows an interest in the worship offered by the heavenly court, with the angels' worship as a pattern and inspiration for the earthly elect, but the angels are not objects of worship.[49]

As to the nature of synagogue services, though recent studies caution us about reading too much of later material into the pre-70 C.E. period and suggest greater variety and flexibility than was later the case, nevertheless all available evidence points to synagogue religious devotion focused on the one God and his Torah.[50] The Nash Papyrus (second century BCE) gives evidence of the Decalogue and *Shema*, key traditional expressions of God's uniqueness, being used for instructional and/or liturgical purposes.[51] Other texts suggest daily recitations of the *Shema* by at least some pious Jews of the Greco-Roman period, and there are wider indications of the impact of this classic monotheistic text on the devotional practices of Jews as shown in the use of *tefillin* and *mezuzot* and the custom of daily prayers (e.g., Josephus, *Ant.* 4.212).[52]

We have a good deal of material with which to form impressions of the patterns of Jewish prayer in the second-Temple period, as Charlesworth and Flusser have shown in helpful inventories of the evidence.[53] Though the prayers recorded in the surviving texts may well be more rhetorically sophisticated than most spontaneous prayers of ordinary Jews of the time, it is likely that the basic pattern and themes are representative. Jewish readers were likely expected to see in these literary prayers only more eloquent expressions of the piety they shared with the authors.

In his study of the doctrine of God in non-canonical second-Temple texts, Wicks included special attention to the prayers of these writings. Somewhat

48 As I have elsewhere pointed out, whatever the pattern of cultic devotion at Elephantine, the material is hardly characteristic of the Jewish population of the Greco-Roman period and is in any case too early to be of direct relevance. See my *One God, One Lord*, 144 n. 83.

49 Carol Newsom, *Songs of the Sabbath Sacrifice: A Critical Edition* (HSS, 27; Atlanta: Scholars Press, 1985). And see my comments and references to additional literature in *One God, One Lord*, 84-85.

50 For a helpful review of recent scholarship on the early synagogue service, see now Paul Bradshaw, *The Search for the Origins of Christian Worship* (London: SPCK, 1992), 1-29.

51 See W. F. Albright, "A Biblical Fragment of the Maccabean Age: The Nash Papyrus," *JBL* 56(1937) 145-76.

52 See Sanders, 196-97, for further discussion and for additional references.

53 James H. Charlesworth, "A Prolegomena to a New Study of the Jewish Background of the Hymns and Prayers in the New Testament," *JJS* 33(1982) 265-85; *id.*, "Jewish Hymns, Odes, and Prayers (ca. 167 B.C.E.–135 C.E.)," in R. A. Kraft & G. W. E. Nickelsburg, eds., *Early Judaism and its Modern Interpreters* (Atlanta: Scholars Press, 1986), 411-36. See also David Flusser, "Psalms, Hymns and Prayers," in M. E. Stone, ed., *Jewish Writings of the Second Temple Period* (Assen: Van Gorcum; Philadelphia: Fortress Press, 1984), 551-77.

later, N. B. Johnson devoted a monograph to the prayers in these texts. Both demonstrated that all the prayers in these writings are offered to the God of Israel alone. Though angels may serve as bearers of prayers and as intercessors for humans (e.g., *Tob.* 12:11-15), God is the object of prayers by humans and angels alike.[54] As I have pointed out elsewhere, in those texts where angels figure prominently in the operation of God's sovereignty, God is the recipient of worship and the object of the prayers.[55] We may also note Bauckham's study of apocalyptic passages in which a human recipient of a revelation initially mistakes for God the angel who delivers it and starts to offer the being worship, but is forbidden by the angel to proceed.[56]

In the 1992 meeting of the SBL, Clinton Arnold presented a study of epigraphical evidence in an effort to determine the pattern of Jewish piety reflected in it, especially concerned with the role of angels.[57] He grants that angels "figure prominently in the belief system" of the Jewish individuals or circles from which the inscriptions derive, and that angels are invoked for protection in an apotropaic manner. But he emphasizes that the evidence does not indicate any organized devotional pattern in which Jews "gather regularly to adore, pray to, and worship angels."[58] The inclusion of angels in rabbinic lists of prohibited objects of worship may be directed in part against such apotropaic invocations and against Jewish syncretistic dabbling in magical practices, as Mach suggests.[59] These prohibitions, however, hardly prove an actual Jewish angel cultus in operation.[60]

In references to *One God, One Lord*, several scholars have demurred from my position that there is no evidence of organized devotion to angels or other figures among groups of devout Jews. Andrew Chester has recently alluded to the *Life of Adam and Eve* (13-16) and *Joseph and Asenath* (15:11-12) as possible references to such practices.[61] But I find neither text persuasive. The scene in

---

54 Wicks, esp. 122-29; N. B. Johnson, *Prayer in the Apocrypha and Pseudepigrapha: A Study of the Jewish Concept of God* (SBLMS, 2; Philadelphia: Society of Biblical Literature, 1948). In light of the renewed interest in extra-canonical texts in recent decades, the availability of fresh translations, analyses and studies of them, and the increase in available materials since Wicks and Johnson (e.g., the Qumran texts), it is high time for a fresh and full-scale analysis of the prayers in Jewish second-Temple writings. Agneta Enermalm-Ogawa, *Un langage de prière juif en grec: Le témoinage des deux premiers livres des Maccabées* (ConBib, NT 17; Uppsala: Almquist & Wiksell, 1987), studies the prayers in 1-2 Maccabees, arguing that they witness early developments in synagogue prayers.

55 *One God, One Lord*, esp. 24-27.

56 Bauckham, "The Worship of Jesus," (n. 29 above). The key texts are *Apoc.Zeph.* 6:15; *Ascen.Isa.* 7:21-22; Rev. 19:10; 22:8-9.

57 Clinton E. Arnold, "Mediator Figures in Asia Minor: Epigraphic Evidence," unpublished paper presented at the SBL Consultation on Jewish and Christian Mediator Figures in Greco-Roman Antiquity, San Francisco, November 1992.

58 Ibid., 21. See also his conclusions, 26-27.

59 Mach, 291-300.

60 See my discussion of these prohibitions in *One God, One Lord*, 31-32. Whatever one makes of the rabbinic passages, their late date makes them questionable evidence for first-century Jewish religion.

61 Andrew Chester, "Jewish Messianic Expectations and Mediatorial Figures and Pauline Christology," in *Paulus und das antike Judentum*, eds. M. Hengel, U. Heckel

Adam and Eve is surely laden with theological meaning, specifically the idea that humans are God's most favored creature, superior to the angels (cf. 1 Cor. 6:3), and that Satan's hostility to humans is rebellion against God. But this etiological story of God's demand that the angels acknowledge the superior honor of the human creature as God's "image" hardly constitutes evidence that Jews actually offered worship to Adam.[62] Chester's allusion to *Joseph and Asenath*, appears to ignore my observation that the mysterious angel who appears to Asenath in fact refuses to cooperate with her desire to offer him worship, which suggests that her request is to be taken as a misguided pagan response corrected by the angel.[63]

Rainbow has pointed to *Pseudo-Philo* 13:6 (where God says, "The feast of Trumpets will be an offering for your watchers") as a possible hint of angel worship, but this is not the more plausible way to take the passage, as the translator in the Charlesworth edition indicates.[64] Moreover, 34:2 makes it clear that the author regards sacrificing to (disobedient) angels as a forbidden practice of gentile magicians.[65] Nor is there in fact any cogent evidence from Philo of prayer or worship being offered to figures other than God.[66]

In short, the data largely represent faithful Jews expressing their scruples about worship and prayer to figures other than God.[67] We may have hints

---

(WUNT, 58; Tübingen: Mohr-Siebeck, 1991), 17-89, esp. 64. Chester does not give the exact passages but I presume these are the ones which he intended.

[62] Cf. David Steenberg, "The Worship of Adam and Christ as the Image of God," *JSNT* 39(1990), 77-93. Steenberg proposes that the idea of Adam being/bearing the image of God could have been taken as justifying worship of Adam, but admits that there is no evidence that Jews reached this conclusion and actually practiced such devotion to Adam.

[63] See *One God, One Lord*, 81, 84.

[64] Rainbow, "Jewish Monotheism as the Matrix," 83. Cf. Charlesworth, *Old Testament Pseudepigrapha*, 2:321 n. "e", at *Pseudo-Philo* 13:6.

[65] The Midianite magician works miracles by the aid of fallen angels "for he had been sacrificing to them for a long time" (*Pseudo-Philo* 34:2). This tells us how the author explained the feats of gentile magicians but is hardly evidence of a *Jewish* devotion to angels!

[66] Cf. F. Gerald Downing's curious claim that in *de Somn.* 1.163-64 "Philo clearly takes [Abraham's appeal in Gen. 28:21] as 'prayer', addressed to the Word . . ." has no basis in this passage (cf. "Ontological Asymmetry in Philo and Christological Realism in Paul, Hebrews and John," *JTS* 41[1990] 440 n. 28). The Logos is not even mentioned here. Philo takes Abraham as requesting God to be to him "bestower of kindness" and not merely "ruler." Philo's deliberately rhetorical invocation of the "Sacred Guide" (*hierophanta*) in *de Somn.* 164 is not addressed to the Logos, but may allude to Moses in his role as great teacher of true religion who works through his sacred writings. Downing's citation of *de Abr.* 127 and *Gig.* 54 are likewise puzzling. Neither in fact offers any historical evidence for worship directed to any being but God. Philo merely makes distinctions between inferior and superior understandings of the nature of God, and, in somewhat elitist sounding language, claims that few of humankind achieve a higher perception of God.

[67] Sanders (245-46) discusses Josephus' reference to Essene prayer practices connected with the rising sun (*War* 2:128, 148), concluding that "the Essenes really offered prayer to the sun". Solar symbolism was certainly widespread in both non-Jewish and Jewish religion, but I doubt that Josephus is to be taken as Sanders does. On Christian appropriation of solar symbolism, see the classic study by Franz J. Dölger, *Sol Salutis: Gebet und Gesang im christlichen Altertum, mit besonderer Rücksicht auf die Ostung in Gebet und Liturgie*

here of a concern that some Jews were not sufficiently faithful in maintaining a sharp distinction between the unique God of Israel and other figures, whether pagan gods or servants of the true God (a concern explicitly expressed in rabbinic criticism of "two powers" heretics).[68] We certainly have evidence of faithful Jews attempting to maintain and strengthen a distinction between their monotheistic devotional pattern and the polytheistic pattern of the larger Greco-Roman world. But we hardly have evidence of Jewish religious groups in which cultic/liturgical devotion to angels or patriarchs formed part of their open religious practice.

The point I wish to emphasize is that all these data show how important cultic/liturgical practice was as an expression of monotheistic scruples. Jews were quite willing to imagine beings who bear the divine name within them and can be referred to by one or more of God's titles (e.g., Yahoel or Melchizedek as *elohim* or, later, Metatron as *yahweh ha-katon*), beings so endowed with divine attributes as to be difficult to distinguish them descriptively from God, beings who are very direct personal extensions of God's powers and sovereignty. About this, there is clear evidence. This clothing of servants of God with God's attributes and even his name will seem "theologically very confusing" if we go looking for a "strict monotheism" of relatively modern distinctions of "ontological status" between God and these figures, and expect such distinctions to be expressed in terms of "attributes and functions." By such definitions of the term, Greco-Roman Jews seem to have been quite ready to accommodate various divine beings.[69] The evidence we have surveyed here shows that it is in fact in the area of worship that we find "the decisive criterion" by which Jews maintained the uniqueness of God over against both idols and God's own deputies. I may also add that the characteristic willingness of Greco-Roman Jews to endure the opprobrium of non-Jews over their refusal to worship the other deities, even to the point of martyrdom, seems to me to constitute a fairly "strict monotheism."[70] Their strictness, however, was expressed more in cultic scruples rather than in a theological monism or the kind verbal and of conceptual distinctions modern scholars might more readily appreciate.

(Münster: Aschendorffschen Verlagbuchhandlung, 1925). On the use of solar images (and other motifs) in ancient Jewish synagogues, see Elias Bickerman, "Symbolism in the Dura Synagogue," in *Studies in Jewish and Christian History: Part Three* (Leiden: Brill, 1986), 225-44 (critical of Goodenough's interpretation); and now Rachel Hachlili, *Ancient Jewish Art and Archaeology in the Land of Israel* (Handbuch der Orientalistik; Leiden: Brill, 1988).

68 See Alan F. Segal, *Two Powers in Heaven: Early Rabbinic Reports about Christianity and Gnosticism* (SJLA, 25; Leiden: Brill, 1977).

69 Part of the problem in estimating what Jews made of heavenly beings other than God "ontologically" is that scholars tend to employ distinctions and assumptions formed by Christian theological/philosophical tradition. For a helpful critique of such anachronism and an illustration of the much wider and more complex semantic field represented by "divine" and "god" in ancient Greek, see S. R. F. Price, "Gods and Emperors: The Greek Language of the Roman Imperial Cult," *Journal of Hellenic Studies* 104(1984), 79-95.

70 In this paragraph, I lift phrasing from Chester, 64-65, whose otherwise very helpful essay shows here a failure to appreciate these points adequately.

To summarize this point, God's sovereignty was imagined as including many figures, some of them in quite prominent roles. There was a plurality in the operation of the divine as characteristically described by ancient Jews. God was distinguished from other beings most clearly in this: It is required to offer God worship; it is inappropriate to offer worship to any other.

V

I propose that Jewish monotheism can be taken as constituting a distinctive version of the commonly-attested belief structure described by Nilsson as involving a "high god" who presides over other deities.[71] The God of Israel presides over a court of heavenly beings who are likened to him (as is reflected in, e.g., the OT term for them "sons of God"). In pagan versions, too, the high god can be described as father and source of the other divine beings, and as utterly superior to them.[72] In this sense, Jewish (and Christian) monotheism, whatever its distinctives, shows its historical links with the larger religious environment of the ancient world.

There are distinctives of the Jewish version, however, both in beliefs and, even more emphatically in religious practice. As Nilsson has shown, in pagan versions often the high god is posited but not really known. Indeed, in some cases (particularly in Greek philosophical traditions), it is emphasized that the high god cannot be known. Accordingly, often one does not expect to relate directly to the high god or address this deity directly in worship or petition.[73] In Greco-Roman Jewish belief, the high god is known as the God of Israel, whose ways and nature are revealed in the Scriptures of Israel. Also, as the evidence of Jewish prayer and cultic practice surveyed above shows, Jews characteristically expected, indeed felt obliged, to address their high God directly in prayer and worship.

Moreover, in pagan versions, beliefs about a high god were not characteristically taken as demanding or justifying a cultic neglect of the other divine beings. In Jewish religious practice, worship characteristically is restricted to the high God alone. This is not simply a religious preference; it is taken as an obligation, and failure to observe this obligation is idolatry. Philo, for example, urges his readers to avoid confusing the "satraps" with "the Great King" (*Decal.* 61-65), when it comes to worship.

These constitute chief distinctives of the ancient Jewish understanding of the nature of the divine. In basic structure, their view of the divine involved a principal deity distinguished from all other divine/heavenly beings, but characteristically accompanied by them, a "high-god" or "monarchial" theology not completely unlike other high-god beliefs of the ancient world. But in the identification of the high god specifically as the God revealed in the Bible, and, even more emphatically, in their characteristic reservation of worship to this one God, their religion demonstrates what we can call

---

[71] M. P. Nilsson, "The High God and the Mediator," *HTR* 56(1963) 101-20.

[72] Smith, "The Common Theology of the Ancient Near East," shows that such conceptions and rhetoric are quite old and widespread.

[73] Nilsson, 110-11, 115-16.

"exclusivist monotheism." Both in theology and in practice, Greco-Roman Jews demonstrate concerns for God's supremacy and uniqueness to an intensity and with a solidarity that seem to go far beyond anything else previous in the Greco-Roman world.

Quite a lot could be accommodated in Jewish speculations about God's retinue of heavenly beings, provided that God's sovereignty and uniqueness were maintained. I think that we may take it as likely that the glorious beings such as principal angels who attend God in ancient Jewish apocalyptic and mystical texts were intended by the authors very much as indicating God's splendor and majesty, and not as threatening or diminishing God in any way. The greater and more glorious the high king, the greater and more glorious his ministers, particularly those charged with administering his kingdom.

God's sovereignty was expressed and protected by portraying all spheres creation and all the heavenly beings, even those temporarily "disobedient" (Satan/Beliel, demons, fallen angels) as inferior and subservient to God, ultimately within God's power. God's uniqueness was characteristically manifested and protected in religious practice, by directing prayer (especially in the cultic/liturgical setting) and worship to God alone, withholding such devotion from any other heavenly being, including God's closest ministers and agents.

In his study of rabbinic criticisms of "two powers" heresies, Alan Segal has identified two types of heresies attacked, and has suggested that one type was Jewish Christian reverence of Jesus and the other was gnostic speculation about a Demiurge creator-god.[74] I think Segal is correct, and that the two developments in question were considered heretical because they were seen to challenge the two fundamental concerns of Jewish monotheism. Gnostic speculations attributing the creation to a divine being other than the high god were likely taken as constituting a severe diminishing of the universal sovereignty of God, removing from God's purposes and control the sensory world and human history. Jewish-Christian reverence of the exalted Jesus in terms and actions characteristically reserved for God, as described in *One God, One Lord*,[75] though it was initially a "mutation" within Jewish monotheistic tradition, was a sufficiently distinctive variant form to have been seen by many non-Christian Jews as compromising the uniqueness of God in the important sphere of cultic action. Whether there were other versions of such heresies that developed within the Jewish monotheistic tradition of the late first or early second century remains an intriguing but thus far debatable possibility.

The reactions against the known "heresies" the rabbis had in mind, Jewish Christianity and Gnostic groups, may well have produced a hardening of rabbinic monotheism in the direction away from the more inclusive and monarchial monotheism and toward a more monistic or unitarian character in some rabbinic circles, as Dunn has suggested. But, as Mach has recently argued, we should probably also allow for other (e.g.,

---

74 Segal, *Two Powers in Heaven* (see n. 68 above).

75 *One God, One Lord*, esp. chap. 5, "The Early Christian Mutation."

political) factors, in accounting for rabbinic unease with angel speculations.[76] We should also recognize that interest in angels, including principal angels likened to God and closely associated with God, may have declined in some circles and in some periods, but was active in some devout Jewish circles after the first century, as evidenced in 3 Enoch and other texts. There were reactions against Christian and Gnostic developments, but it is not clear whether these reactions produced a significantly and widely-embraced modification of the fundamental shape of Jewish monotheistic belief and practice. It does seem, however, that reaction against the Jewish Christian form of binitarian monotheism, involving devotion to God and to the exalted Christ, may have had the effect of making any other such programmatic binitarian development unacceptable thereafter.

VI

We may summarize this discussion of first-century Jewish monotheism in the following points.

(1) Definitions of monotheism must be formed on the basis of the beliefs and practices of those who describe themselves in monotheistic terms. This means that there will likely be varieties within and among monotheistic traditions, and that it is inappropriate for historical purposes to impose one definition or to use one definition as a standard of "strict" or "pure" monotheism in a facile manner.

(2) "First-century Jewish monotheism" represents the religious commitment to the universal sovereignty and uniqueness of the one God of Israel, a commitment widely expressed in religious rhetoric of Jewish texts of the entire second-Temple period and reflected also in the NT.

(3) This commitment to the one God of Israel accommodated a large retinue of heavenly beings distinguished from God more in degree than kind as to their attributes, some of these beings portrayed as in fact sharing quite directly in God's powers and even his name. The monotheism of ancient Jews was thus characteristically "monarchial" and may be seen as a significant adaptation of the "high god" belief structure of the ancient world. Among God's entourage, there is often a particular principal agent or vizier, who can be likened to God in appearance, name and attributes/functions. This too was not apparently seen as a problem, for the principal agent was not characteristically given cultic devotion. Early Christian cultic devotion to Christ alongside God, though indebted conceptually to pre-Christian Jewish traditions of principal agent figures, apparently represents an extraordinary adaptation of Jewish monotheistic tradition.[77] In their own eyes, early

---

[76] Mach, esp. 300-32.

[77] Rainbow ("Jewish Monotheism as the Matrix," 88 n. 22) seems to me to overestimate the ease with which cultic devotion to a divine agent figure could be seen as logical and acceptable in the Greco-Roman Jewish tradition. The arrival of a hoped-for figure would not so readily produce cultic devotion to him. Rainbow's larger problem lying behind his argument is the view that there can in fact be no such thing as religious innovation, a notion falsified by the history of religions (cf. Rainbow, "Jewish Monotheism as the Matrix," 86-87).

Christians offered cultic devotion to Christ in obedience to the one God and saw their binitarian devotion as legitimate, indeed, required. As, however, rabbinic authorities sought to consolidate Judaism in the post-70 C.E. period, they succeeded more effectively in identifying the Jewish-Christian binitarian adaptation as an unacceptable form of Jewish monotheistic tradition.

(5) There are distinguishing features of Greco-Roman Jewish monotheism, over against the more prevalent religious structures of the ancient world. There are theological distinctives: The high god has in fact revealed himself in Scripture, is known and can be characterized, and can and must be approached quite directly in prayer and worship. There are additional important distinctives in scruples about religious practice: Worship is restricted to the one God and it is forbidden to offer devotion to other beings, even God's own glorious angelic ministers. First-century Jewish monotheism was, thus, an exclusivist, monarchial view of God, manifested particuarly in "orthopraxy" in cultic/liturgical matters.

". . . you teach all the Jews . . . to forsake Moses, telling them not to . . . observe the customs" (Acts 21:21; cf. 6:14)

David L. Balch
Brite Divinity School,
Texas Christian University

I begin with three assumptions, the first of which I have argued before,[1] that is, that the two-volume work Luke-Acts is historiography. The thesis needs some modification, but for the purposes of this paper, I assume that the two volume work Luke-Acts owes much more to Greco-Roman historiography than to the genres of biography or novel.[2]

I am tempted to overstate my second assumption and say that Acts 21-28 has really nothing to do with the person of Paul.[3] The concluding section of this two-volume work narrates events in the life of Paul, but the real subject is not the historical Paul or a defense of him to Rome or to the church. The 1987 conference on "Paul and the Legacies of Paul," hosted at SMU by Professor Victor Paul Furnish, convincingly demonstrated that no one in the early church had to defend Paul, only to interpret him.[4] That has been conclusively argued by both Ernst Dassmann and Andreas Lindemann.[5]

---

[1] David L. Balch, "Comments on the Genre and a Political Theme of Luke-Acts: A Preliminary Comparison of Two Hellenistic Historians," *SBL 1989 Seminar Papers* 28 (1989) 343-61 and "The Genre of Luke-Acts: Individual Biography, Adventure Novel, or Political History?" *Southwestern Journal of Theology* 33/1 (1990) 5-19.

[2] Compare Gregory E. Sterling, *Historiography and Self-Definition: Josephus, Luke-Acts and Apologetic Historiography* (SupNT 64; Leiden: E. J. Brill, 1992) and Eckhard Plümacher, "Die Missionsreden der Apostelgeschichte und Dionys von Halikarnass," *NTS* 39/2 (1993) 161-77. Contrast Richard A. Burridge, *What Are the Gospels? A Comparison with Graeco-Roman Biography* (SNTS 70; Cambridge: Cambridge, 1992). My review of Burridge will appear in *JAAR*.

[3] *Pace* C. K. Barrett, "The Acts-of Paul," *New Testament Essays* (London: SPCK, 1972) 86-100, esp. 92, and William R. Long, The Paulusbild in the Trial of Paul in Acts," *SBL 1983 Seminar Papers*, ed. K. H. Richards (Chico, Scholars, 1983) 87-105, esp. 104-05.

[4] *Paul and the Legacies of Paul*, ed. William S. Babcock (Dallas: Southern Methodist University, 1990).

[5] Ernst Dassmann, *Der Stachel im Fleisch: Paulus in der frühchristlichen Literatur bis Irenäus* (Münster: Aschendorff, 1979). Andreas Lindemann, *Paulus im ältesten Christentum: Das Bild des Apostels und die Rezeption der paulinischen Theologie in der frühchristlichen Literatur bis Marcion* (Beiträge zur historischen Theologie 58, hrsg. J. Wallmann; Tübingen: J.C.B. Mohr [Paul Siebeck], 1979).

My third assumption, the thesis I will develop in this paper, is simple: the topic of Acts chapters 22-28 in which Paul gives several defense speeches, is closely related to the accusation against him in the previous chapter (Acts 21:21).[6] The brethren in Jerusalem tell Paul,

> You see, brother, how many thousands there are among the Jews of those who have believed; they are all zealous for the law, and they have been told about you that you teach all the Jews who are among the Gentiles to forsake Moses (ἀποστασίαν . . . ἀπὸ Μωϋσέως), telling them not to circumcise their children or observe the customs (μηδὲ τοῖς ἔθεσιν περιπατεῖν).

This, of course, recalls the accusation against Stephen in chapter 6, and, as has been repeatedly argued, Luke emphasizes this accusation by narrating it twice, so that we cannot fail to see how important it is. In Acts 6:11, 13-14,[7] false witnesses accuse Stephen with these same words:

> We have heard him speak blasphemous words against Moses and God (βλάσφημα εἰς Μωϋσῆν καὶ τὸν θεόν). . . . This man never ceases to speak words against this holy place and the law (κατὰ . . . νόμου); for we have heard him say that this Jesus of Nazareth will destroy this place, and will change the customs which Moses delivered to us (καταλύσει τὸν τόπον τοῦτον καὶ ἀλλάξει τὰ ἔθη ἃ παρέδωκεν ἡμῖν Μωϋσῆς).

What exactly the author would like to prove is stated clearly in 21:24. James and the brothers encourage Paul to take a temporary Nazarite vow,

> thus all will know that there is nothing in what they have been told about you but that you yourself live in observance of the law (φυλάσσων τὸν νόμον).

For anyone who has been reading Greco-Roman historiography, certain key terms in these accusations almost jump out of the text. The most important ones are the noun "custom" (τὸ ἔθος) and the verbal roots referring, on the one hand, to "observing/guarding" (φυλάσσω) the law and, on the other, to "changing" (ἀλλάσσω) it. What follows is a discussion of seven points about what Greco-Roman persons thought in relation to guarding or changing customs. Since I assume that the historiographical tradition informs Luke-Acts I have employed the *Thesaurus Linguae Graecae* to see what the Jewish historian Josephus and the earlier Greek historian of Rome, Dionysius of Halicarnassus, narrate about "customs." I will make seven points:

First, Josephus wrote a "History of the Jewish War against the Romans," and in the preface, he surveys his coming narrative. The story will concern, he writes, the invasion by Titus, the plan of the temple, certain festival customs (ἔθη), the seven degrees of purity, etc. (*War* 1.25, trans. Thackeray in LCL) In the preface to his history Josephus lets us know that he will treat certain customs of the Jews, precisely the term used in the accusations made in Acts against Stephen and Paul.

---

6 Cf. Paul Schubert, "The Final Cycle of Speeches in the Book of Acts," *JBL* 87 (1968) 1-15, at p. 5.

7 Sterling, *Historiography* 335-36 argues from this text to the unity of Luke-Acts.

The same is true of Dionysius' history of Rome. In the preface he writes,

I begin my history then with the most ancient legends. . . . I relate all the foreign wars. . ., the internal seditions. . . . I give an account also of all the forms of government Rome used. . . . I describe the best customs (ἔθη) and the most remarkable laws; and in short, I show the whole life of the ancient Romans (Dionysius, *Ant. Rom.* 1.8.2, trans. Cary in LCL)

The first point in support of my thesis is that these histories, Dionysius' history of Rome, Josephus' history of the Jewish war, and this final section of Acts, explicitly treat the "customs" of the peoples whose history is being narrated.

Second, one key custom concerns how people treat aliens. Immediately after telling us that his history will detail certain customs, Josephus promises to describe the revolutionaries' brutal treatment of their fellow-countrymen (ὁμοφύλους) and the clemency of the Romans towards an alien race (ἀλλοφύλους) (*War* 1.27). One aspect of Josephus' history will concern how members of one people treat each other and how they treat aliens.

And indeed, when Josephus narrates the beginning of the war against Rome, he gives the cause of the hostilities in the following words:

Eleazar, son of Ananias the high-priest, a very daring youth, then holding the position of captain, persuaded those who officiated in the Temple services to accept no gift or sacrifice from a foreigner (ἀλλοτρίου). This action laid the foundation of the war with the Romans; for the sacrifices offered on behalf of that nation and the emperor were in consequence rejected. The chief priests and the notables earnestly besought them not to abandon the customary (ἔθος) offering for their rulers. . . . (*War* 2.409-10)

The leading citizens, chief priests, and Pharisees argue the opposite:

Their forefathers, they said had adorned the sanctuary mainly at the expense of aliens (ἀλλοφύλων) and had always accepted the gifts of foreign nations; . . .they had never taken the sacrilegious step of forbidding (διακεκωλυκέναι) anyone to offer sacrifice. . . . But now here were these men, who were provoking the arms of the Romans and courting a war with them, introducing a strange innovation (καινοτομεῖν . . . ξένην) into their religion, and besides endangering the city, laying it open to the charge of impiety, if Jews henceforth were to be the only people to allow no alien (ἀλλότριος) the right of sacrifice or worship. Should such a law be introduced in the case of any private individual, they would be indignant at so inhuman (ἀπανθρωπίας) a decree; yet they made light of putting the Romans and Caesar outside the pale (*War* 2.412-15)

A similar debate is found in Dionysius. This historian stages a debate between the Greek Alban Fufetius and the Roman king Tullus. Alba is the mother city who sent out colonists to Rome, but Fufetius accuses Rome as follows:

You have corrupted the purity of your body politic by admitting Tyrrhenians, Sabines, and some others who were homeless, vagabonds and barbarians, and that in great numbers too, so that the true-born element among you that went out from our midst is become small, or rather a tiny fraction, in comparison with those who have been brought in and are of an alien race (ἀλλοφύλου; Dionysius, *Ant. Rom.* 3.10.4).

Tullus notes the charge that Rome has been corrupted by mixing with aliens (ἀλλοφύλου; 3.11.3), but asserts that Rome is not ashamed of the policy of making the privileges of Rome free to all, but rather proud of it (cf. the apologetic in 1.89-90 and 2.15-17). Emilio Gabba places his discussion of this debate at a climactic point in the conclusion of his book interpreting Dionysius' history.[8]

Similarly, the climax of Luke-Acts, or at least one of them, is Acts 10,[9] the story of Cornelius. When Peter arrives in Caesarea, Cornelius is expecting him and has invited friends. Peter goes in to the gathering and says, "You yourselves know how unlawful it is for a Jew to associate with or to visit any one of another nation" (ἀθέμιτόν ἐστιν ἀνδρὶ 'Ιουδαίῳ κολλᾶσθαι ἢ προσέρχεσθαι ἀλλοφύλῳ; Acts 10:28). The words that the Christian Peter says are analogous to the position of Eleazar, who succeeded in getting the priests in the temple not to accept the sacrifice of a foreigner according to Josephus. Neither Josephus, Dionysius, nor the author of Acts want their main subjects to appear misanthropic.[10] In other words, one of the primary tensions in the narratives of Dionysius and Josephus is also a central concern in Luke-Acts: in his history Luke must narrate how one practicing the customs of Moses relates to aliens, persons of another ethnic group, and all agree that philanthropic relationships are best. I note specifically that this is a debate within Judaism and Christianity, as the narratives in Josephus and Acts show, not merely a debate between Jews and Christians.[11]

A related, third point is that the narration of a people's customs in the Greco-Roman world occurs in an international context. In detailing the debate in Jerusalem, Josephus has the leading citizens reflect whether "Jews henceforth were to be the only people to allow no alien (ἀλλότριος) the right of sacrifice or worship" (*War* 2.414). This sort of thought about one's own customs in light of other people's customs is typical in both Josephus and Dionysius. Immediately before narrating the decision to go to war with the Romans, Josephus presents Agrippa's long speech (*War* 2.345-401) opposing the revolution against Rome; through seven pages of Greek he compares the Jews with numerous other cities and nations (Athens, Sparta, Macedon. . . .), before he comes to Sabbath customs (ἔθη; 392) of the Jews and their interest in preserving the institutions of their

---

8 E. Gabba, *Dionysius and the History of Archaic Rome* (Berkeley: University of California, 1991) 209. Other relevant texts concerning natives and foreigners: Josephus, *War* 4.136; *Ant.* 4.136-37; 5.90; 15.267; 16.1; 20.39, 47 (Izates); Dionysius, *Ant. Rom.* 2.17.1; 2.19.5.

9 Martin Dibelius, "Speeches in Acts and Ancient Historiography," *Studies in the Acts of the Apostles* (1956) 161-62: Luke "has made a great composition out of the story of Cornelius, which, as an elaborated narrative, has no equal in the whole book." Cf. Dibelius, "The Conversion of Cornelius," *Studies*, 115, 117-19. Contrast Luke Timothy Johnson, *The Acts of the Apostles* (Sacra Pagina 5; Collegeville: Liturgical, 1992) 14, who sees the climax in Acts 1-7. See the combined force of the observations in nn. 18, 20, and 31.

10 Josephus, *War* 2.411 presents the Pharisees as philanthropic; Acts 15:1, 5 presents the same group as misanthropic.

11 Cf. Joseph B. Tyson, *Images of Judaism in Luke-Acts* (Columbia: University of South Carolina, 1992).

fathers. The debate about excluding the sacrifices of aliens is made in this international environment.

This international context may also result in accusations of misanthropic behavior and beliefs. After Josephus narrates Israel's receiving the Torah in *Antiquities* 3, he tells the story of Balaam's advice to the Midianites about defeating Israel. Their young girls were to seduce Hebrew boys, and after they had fallen in love, to make the following demands:

> Seeing then, said the [Midianite] maidens, that you agree to these conditions, and that you have customs and a mode of life wholly alien to all mankind (ἔθεσι καὶ τῷ βίῳ πρὸς ἄπαντας ἀλλοτριώτατα), insomuch that your food is of a peculiar sort and your drink is distinct from that of other men, it behooves you if you would live with us, also to revere our gods (*Ant.* 4.137, trans. Thackeray in LCL).

Also, when Josephus is retelling the story of Esther, of Haman's hatred of Mordecai and the Jews, he writes:

> [Haman] went to the king and brought a charge (κατηγόρει), saying that there was a certain wicked nation scattered throughout the habitable land ruled by him, which was unfriendly and unsocial (ἄμικτον ἀσύμφυλον) and neither had the same religion nor practiced the same laws as others, but both by its customs (ἔθεσι) and practices it is the enemy of your people and of all mankind (ἐχθρὸν ... ἅπασιν ἀνθρώποις; *Ant.* 11.212; cf. 217).

These are false charges and slanders (275), slanders and accusations (276); the Jews are not evil doers (279), but are to be permitted to live in peace under their own laws (281), Josephus' argues. These examples show that the international environment stimulated comparison, that each nation valued its own particular customs, but at the same time it was socially, politically, and religiously imperative to avoid being seen as misanthropic.[12]

Luke-Acts exhibits tensions similar to those seen in Dionysius and Josephus. Over against the misanthropic position ascribed to some Christians in 10:28, 11:3, and 15:1, Luke argues that "God shows no partiality" (Acts 10:34; cf. the inclusion in vs. 43).[13] That this salvation is for "all people" is a prominent Lukan theme (also e.g. Luke 2:31-32; 3:6; 4:25-29; 24:47; Acts 2:39;13:46-48; 15:19; 17:30; 22:21; 26:17-18, 20, 23; 28:30).

---

12 Other examples of the international context: Josephus, *War* 3.472; *Ant.* 15.328; 16.46, 176-78; Dionysius, *Ant. Rom.* 1.41.1; 60.2; *Letter to Gnaeus Pompeius* 1.6.5 (in Loeb, "Critical Essays," 2.394): ". . .who will not admit that it is necessary for students of philosophic rhetoric to acquire a thorough knowledge of the many customs (ἔθη) of the barbarians and the Greeks, to hear about various laws and forms of government, the lives of their men and their exploits (πράξεις), their deaths and their fortunes?" This contradicts the often quoted argument of C. K. Barrett, *Luke the Historian in Recent Study* (London: Epworth, 1961) 63: "No Roman official would ever have filtered out so much of what to him would be theological and ecclesiastical rubbish in order to reach so tiny a grain of relevant apology." Cf. Otto Hiltbrunner, "Warum wollten sie nicht ΦΙΛΑΝΘΡΟΠΟΙ heissen? *JAC* 33 (1990) 7-20.

13 Ulrich Wilckens,"Kerygma und Evangelium bei Lukas (Beobachtungen zu Acta 10:34-43)," *ZNTW* 49 (1958) 223-37 demonstrates that this speech is Lukan.

I have argued that Dionysius, Josephus, and Luke-Acts are all histories concerned with their people's customs, that one of prominent questions concerns how they customarily treat aliens, and that the whole discussion occurs in a comparative, international atmosphere in which a people would be judged to be either philanthropic or misanthropic. Fourth, I observe that official Roman policy not only tolerated but promoted each nation keeping their own customs, while some other rulers were intolerant. Tiberius Alexander, the Jewish procurator, did not interfere with the customs of Judea so kept the nation at peace (Josephus, *War* 2.220). Similarly, in 41 CE Claudius, perhaps influenced by king Agrippa I, sent an edict to Alexandria and Syria, remembering that "Augustus did not prevent (μὴ κεκωλυκέναι) the continued appointment of ethnarchs, desiring that the several subject nations should abide by their own customs (ἰδίοις ἔθεσιν) and not be compelled to violate the religion of their fathers" (*Ant.* 19.283). And Claudius himself decrees:

> It is right, therefore, that the Jews throughout the whole world under our sway should also observe the customs of their fathers without let or hindrance (τὰ πάτρια ἔθη ἀνεπικωλύτως φυλάσσειν). I enjoin upon them also by these presents to avail themselves of this kindness in a more reasonable spirit, and not to set at nought the beliefs about the gods held by other peoples but to keep their own laws. It is my will that the ruling bodies (ἄρχοντας) of the cities and colonies and municipia in Italy and outside Italy, and the kings and other authorities through their own ambassadors, shall cause this edit of mine to be inscribed. . . . (*Ant.* 19.290-91; also 305-06. Cf. 310-11)[14]

I conclude that Roman official policy was not only to avoid interference in subject peoples' customs, but to promote them as a means of reducing urban conflict. However, there were examples of such interference and intolerance of traditional customs on all sides.[15]

The quotations above have already introduced my fifth point, which concerns the meaning of the concluding word of Luke-Acts: ἀκωλύτως, "unhindered" (Acts 28:31).[16] It comes close to the powerful German prohibition, "(nicht) verboten!"

---

14 Cited by W. C. van Unnik, "Die Anklage gegen die Apostel in Philippi, Apostelgeschichte xvi 20 f.," now in his *Sparsa Collecta: The Collected Essays of W. C. van Unnik* (NovTSup 29; Leiden: E. J. Brill, 1973, orig. pub. 1964) Part One, 374-85, at p. 381, n. 2.

15 Other examples of tolerance: Josephus, *War* 4.99; 4.182-84; 5:397, 402; *Ant.* 16.176-78. Examples of intolerance: Josephus, *Ant.* 1.166 (Egyptians); 12.255 (Antiochus Epiphanes); 13.397 (Alexander Jannaeus); 15.254 (Hyrcanus); 15.267 (Herod); 15.281; 16.225; *Apion* 1.224-25, 272. Intolerance stimulates persecution of Jews in *Apion* 2.282.

16 Gerhard Delling, "Das Letzte Wort der Apostelgeschichte," *NT* 15 (1973) 193-204. D. L. Mealand, "The Close of Acts and its Hellenistic Greek Vocabulary," *NTS* 36 (1990) 583-97. I am astounded that Mealand used the *Thesaurus Linguae Graecae* without discovering more. His conclusions are twofold and confused: "In Acts 28:31 the primary and strongest element in the force of ἀκωλύτως is that of the unhindered exercise of religious liberty by one who had been accused of a criminal offense, had made some kind of appeal, and who was now being permitted to proclaim his message openly without hindrance. . . . But the word is, in addition to all that, the normal word used in Greek papyri for the unhindered access to rented property. . . . This evidence suggests an inference about the historical circumstances of Paul's time in Rome. . . . My inference is this. Paul did, as Acts suggests, rent accommodation during his time in Rome. When the author of Acts inquired about Paul's activity during this period that fact was remembered.

or to the French "(non) interdit!" It does not have to be argued that the conclusions of ancient or modern works give us clues about the meaning of the whole.[17] I have shown above that the prefaces of Josephus' and Dionysius' histories state their concern with "customs." Not only the accusation in Acts 21:21 but also the concluding word of Luke-Acts, which together bracket the whole final section, show that these two volumes also have an apologetic, historiographical concern about the practice of Christian customs. When I searched the *Thesaurus Linguae Graecae* for texts on "customs" in Dionysius and Josephus, I repeatedly saw the concluding word of Luke-Acts, and I have become convinced that was not accidental. I have already quoted Josephus, *Ant.* 19.283 and 290,[18] the decrees of Augustus and Claudius that the practice of Jewish customs not be "hindered," not be forbidden. There are more significant texts.

According to Josephus, Julius Caesar wrote to the people of Parium as follows:

> The Jews in Delos and some of the neighboring Jews . . . have appealed to me and declared that you are preventing (κωλύετε) them by statute from observing their national customs (πατρίοις ἔθεσι) and sacred rites. Now it displeases me that such statues should be made against our friends and allies and that they should be forbidden (κωλύεσθαι) to live in accordance with their customs (ἔθη). . . . for this they are not forbidden (μηδ '. . . κεκωλυμένων) to do even in Rome. For example, Gaius Caesar, our consular praetor, by edict forbade (κωλύων) religious societies to assemble in the city, but these people alone he did not forbid (οὐκ ἐκώλυσεν) to do so. . . . Similarly do I forbid (κωλύων) other religious societies but permit these people alone to assemble and feast in accordance with their native customs (κατὰ τὰ πάτρια ἔθη) and ordinances (*Ant.* 14.213-14, 216; the verb occurs six times).

Galba writes Miletus similarly:

> . . .contrary to our expressed wish you are attacking the Jews and forbid (κωλύειν) them to observe their Sabbaths, perform their native rites or manage their produce in accordance with their custom (καθὼς ἔθος). . . . I have decided that the Jews are not to be forbidden (κωλύεσθαι) to follow their customs (ἔθεσι) (*Ant.* 14.245-46).

Perhaps the author even visited the location. . . ." (p. 590) Mealand assumes that Luke has a biographical interest in the historical Paul, but this misunderstands Acts. See J. Roloff, "Die Paulus-Darstellung des Lukas: Ihre geschichtlichen Voraussetzungen und ihr theologisches Ziel," *EvTh* 39 (1979) 510-31, at p. 512: "sie ist ihrer ganzen Anlage nach überhaupt nicht als Biographie gemeint. . . ."

[17] Mikeal C. Parsons, *The Departure of Jesus in Luke-Acts: the Ascension Narratives in Context* (Sheffield: JSOT, 1987). See W. C. van Unnik, "Luke's Second Book and the Rules of Hellenistic Historiography," in *Les Actes des Apotres: Tradition, rédaction, théologie*, ed. J. Kremer (BETL 48; Leuven; University, 1979) 37-60.

[18] The second of these is cited by Delling, "Das letzte Wort," 200. Further, under the second point above, I quoted Josephus, *War* 2.413: the chief priests and Pharisees argue against Eleazar that they have never "forbidden" foreigners to sacrifice in the temple, an historical analogy to Luke's conclusion that Romans did "not forbid" Christians to practice their customs in Rome. Note that in this text in Josephus, the terms "custom," "alien," and "forbid" are connected and debated, as they are in Acts.

The final example in Josephus is the most important for understanding the situation presupposed in the Pauline section of Acts. The historian narrates the meeting of Herod I with Marcus Agrippa in Ionia in 14 BCE. Herod's beneficence set the stage for many Jews speaking to Agrippa about the mistreatment (*Ant.* 16.27) they suffered in not being allowed to observe their own laws. Herod asked Agrippa to listen as they pleaded their cause, and he assigned Nicolas of Damascus to speak "in behalf of the Jews" (30-57). He begins by appealing to Agrippa for all those in distress, who seek the protection of those able to end their mistreatment (31). Some are opposing the Jews (34).

> And if someone should ask them which of these two things they would rather have taken from them, life or their country's customs (τὰ πάτρια ἔθη), including the processions, sacrifices and festivals which they observe in honour of the gods in whom they believe, I know very well that they would rather suffer all manner of things than violate any of their country's customs (καταλῦσαί τι τῶν πατρίων). . . . And the happiness that the whole human race now enjoys, thanks to you, we measure by the fact that it is possible for people in every country to live and prosper while respecting their own (traditions). And what our opponents would not choose to suffer themselves, this they forcibly try to do to others, as if they were not acting just as impiously in violating the sacred traditions of others as they would in neglecting their own sacred duties to their own gods. . . . Those who deprive others of the privileges that you have given them leave themselves no security either. . . . (*Ant.* 16.35-39)

> . . .it is through you that we, in common with all men, prosper. The only thing which we have asked to share with others is the right to preserve our ancestral religion without interference (ἀκωλύτως τὴν πάτριον εὐσέβειαν διαφυλάττειν). . . . There is nothing hostile to mankind in our customs (ἐθῶν ... ἀπάνθρωπον ... οὐδέν), but they are all pious and consecrated with saving righteousness. Nor do we make a secret of the precepts that we use as guides in religion and in human relations. . . . Our customs are . . . ancient (παλαιά). . . . It is these customs which they would outrageously deprive us of . . . by imposing taxes upon us, and by taking us to court and other public places of business even on holy days, not because this is called for by legal agreements but in order to outrage our religion, toward which they feel a hatred (μῖσος) which . . . is undeserved. . . . (*Ant.* 16.41-45;[19] cf. 166)

> We therefore ask, great Agrippa, that we may not suffer this mistreatment, that we be not outraged, that we be not prevented from observing our own customs (μὴ κακῶς πάσχειν μηδ' ἐπηρεάζεσθαι μηδὲ κωλύεσθαι τοῖς ἔθεσι) and that we be not deprived of our present rights nor have forced upon us by these opponents what we do not force upon them. . . . (*Ant.* 16.47)

---

[19] Cited first by van Unnik, "Die Anklage gegen die Apostel in Philippi," 380, then by Delling, "Das letzte Wort," 200.

To these remarks of Nicolas there was no counter statement from the Greeks, for the Jews were not arguing about specific points as if in a court of law (ὡς ἐν δικαστηρίῳ) but only petitioning for relief from violence. And their opponents did not defend themselves (ἀπολογία . . . οὐδεμία) by denying that they had done these things but gave the excuse that by merely spreading over their country the Jews were now doing them all kinds of harm. But the Jews proved that they were natives and that even by honouring their own customs they caused no distress to others in living there. (*Ant.* 16.58-59)

Thereupon Agrippa, who perceived that they had been subjected to violence, . . . was ready to grant the Jews all they might ask for . . . provided, of course, that it did not cause the Roman government any trouble. . . . He would confirm their right to continue to observe their own customs (e[qesin) without suffering mistreatment (*Ant.* 16.60).

Josephus explains his purpose in citing these decrees to show that Jews were treated with respect, not prevented by rulers from practicing their ancestral customs (οὐδὲν τῶν πατρίων ἐκωλύθημεν), but rather experienced cooperation in preserving their religion and way of honoring God (*Ant.* 16.174).[20] His purpose is to reconcile other nations and to remove causes for hatred (μίσους αἰτίας), for "there is no nation which always follows the same customs" (175). "We therefore have a right to expect this same attitude from them, for one should not consider foreignness (τὸ ἀλλότριον) a matter of differences in practice, but of whether there is a proper attitude to goodness" (178).

In many of the local cities of Asia Minor, then, Jews had been mistreated and persecuted; Gentiles in the city came to hate them and prevented them from living according to their "customs." This hatred might come either officially by statutes or popularly by requiring a Jew to appear in court or to conduct business on the Sabbath or by hassling them with taxes. The response is not a trial in a court of law, but an appeal for relief from violence, all in an international context assuming that Romans protect the right of each group to live according to their own customs, as long as they do not interfere with others' similar rights or cause trouble to the Roman government.

Dionysius often uses the verb "forbid" in similar contexts, but I will quote only one text. In a crucial excursus (*Ant. Rom.* 7.70-73), he argues that Romans were not originally barbarians, but Greeks who have preserved down to his own time ancient customs, laws, and institutions (ἔθη καὶ νόμιμα καὶ ἐπιτηδεύματα παλαιά) just as they received them from their ancestors (70.2).[21] They have made

---

[20] Cited by Delling, "Das letzte Wort," 200. Again in this text Josephus connects the terms "custom," "alien," and the question about what rulers "forbid" (cf. n. 18). See Sterling, *Historiography* 295, 302 on Josephus' addition of these *acta* to his history and the key role they played in fulfilling his purpose: "overtly then the *acta* address Greeks throughout the diaspora in an effort to persuade them to allow Jews to practice their ancestral customs. . . . Attitudes rather than individual cases are at the heart of his appeal." (303).

[21] Paradoxically, Dionysius inserts this excursus claiming that Romans have always kept their ancient customs at the conclusion of book 7 just after he has narrated a strike of the plebeians that successfully changed the constitution and founded the new office of tribunes. He also inconsistently observes that "the Romans have often deliberated whether they should repeal this institution [custom] or preserve (καταλῦσαι . . . ἢ φυλάττειν) it as they received it from their

no innovation because of their fear of divine anger (70.3), and no nation exchanges their institutions for those of their conquerors (70.4).

Nothing could have hindered (ἐκώλυσεν) the whole Greek world, which is now subject to the Romans for already the seventh generation, from being barbarized if the Romans had indeed been barbarians (70.5).[22]

As ruler of the world, Rome has functioned to "hinder" Greeks from becoming barbarians, just as according to Josephus they hindered Greeks from destroying Jewish customs.

Not dissimilarly, Jesus had prophesied a time of persecution that Luke's churches were seeing fulfilled:

> But before all this they will lay their hands on you and persecute you, delivering you up to the synagogues and prisons, and you will be brought before kings and governors for my name's sake. . . . You will be hated by all (ἔσεσθε μισούμενοι ὑπὸ πάντων) for my name's sake. (Luke 21:12, 17. Cf. 12:11-12; Josephus, *Ant.* 16.175)

Luke was not able not cite official decrees as Josephus could, but he does narrate related accusations against Stephen and Paul, followed by the "trials" of Paul. He could report the outcome hoped for both by Nicolas of Damascus and by Christians in Luke's churches: they could practice the customs of Moses as they interpreted them ἀκωλύτως. Nicolas' non-judicial[23] speech is a rhetorical form that could be employed not only before Romans of the stature of Marcus Agrippa, but before any appropriate urban magistrate, including those in the cities of Luke's churches where the kind of popular opposition to the church was occurring that both Josephus and Luke picture, e.g. in Acts 16:11-40. In Philippi the "rulers" of the city hear the charge: "These men are Jews and they are disturbing our city. They advocate customs which it is not lawful (ἔθη ἃ οὐκ ἔξεστιν) for us Romans to accept or practice" (Acts 16:20b-21).[24] The kinds of appeal that "Paul" makes in Acts 22, 24, and 26 would be relevant to such a local, popular, urban situation, and the Christians could argue that "even in Rome" (cf. Josephus, *Ant.* 14.214) Paul had practiced such customs "unhindered."[25] By this interpretation, in other words, I am not assuming that Luke wrote an apologetic for a judicial defense to the Roman government, but rather that popular, local opposition to Christians occurred and that some leaders in the church would find themselves before their local rulers in cities like Philippi needing to make a

---

ancestors, but have never come to any final decision. If I am to express an opinion myself [rare in Dionysius!]. . . ." (*Ant. Rom.* 7.65.3; cf. 2.6.1-2; 2.14.3; 10.55.5; 19.16.5 and perhaps Acts 10:13-15?) Contrast the more typical Roman attitude against changing customs discussed by van Unnik, "Die Anklage gegen die Apostel in Philippi," 382-83, an attitude analogous to Paul's as Luke portrays him in Acts 21-18. See P. Vielhauer, "On the 'Paulinism' of Acts," in *The Writings of St. Paul*, ed. Wayne A. Meeks (New York: W. W. Norton, 1972) 166-75, esp. p. 170: "Acts portrays the Gentile missionary Paul as a Jewish Christian who is utterly loyal to the law."

22 See also Polybius 12.6b.7; 22.8.3; Dionysius of Halicarnassus, *Ant. Rom.* 2.15.2; 3.71.2; 4.9.9; 4.42.5; 5.5.1, 2; 6.78.3; 7.16.1; 8.71.6; 8.81.3; 9.5.1; Josephus, *Apion* 2.267; *War* 2.413, 416; 6.335.

23 Schubert, "The Final Cycle," 4, 11 interprets the defense speeches in Acts as judicial.

24 Cf. van Unnik, "Die Anklage gegen die Apostel in Philippi."

25 From this point of view it is understandable that Luke did not report Paul's martyrdom, although 20:38 shows he knew of it.

plea that they not be forbidden to continue practicing their philanthropic customs.[26]

Just as Luke writes 12:11-12 and 21:12 for Christian readers to reassure them in their trials, so he writes the narratives of Paul's trials for the same audience. Their customs are not secret (cf. Josephus, *Ant.* 16.43; 1.11) but are to be proclaimed as Paul had done. Dibelius suggests that by sketching these scenes "the author wants . . . to commend to the Christians of his day the use of such themes in their own defense."[27] There was an intense interest in ethnography, in cross-cultural anthropology in that world, and Josephus wrote for that audience as Gregory Sterling has explicated.[28] Although Luke expected rulers, authorities, kings, and governors (Luke 12:11; 21:12) to listen to Paul and the Christians who followed him in giving their defense, he seems not to have written his apologetic history for them.[29]

Sixth, in Acts 22:3-21, "Paul" defends the Christian custom of admitting Gentiles as philanthropic, a custom opposed by some other Christians (Acts 10:28; 11:3; 15:1-2). Similarly, within Judaism according to Josephus and within Rome according to Dionysius, there were also intense debates about how open they should be towards outsiders, including outsiders who wanted to become insiders. My second point above recalls Josephus' assertion that rejection of aliens was the foundation of the disastrous war against Rome and recalls Dionysius' construction of a debate between an Alban and a Roman king concerning whether aliens should become citizens. Romans did admit aliens as citizens:

> When I compare the customs (ἔθη) of the Greeks with these [of Rome], I can find no reason to extol either those of the Lacedaemonians or of the Thebans or of the Athenians. . .; all of whom, jealous of their noble birth and granting citizenship to none or to very few (I say nothing of the fact that some even expelled foreigners [ξενηλατοῦντες]), not only received no advantage from this haughty attitude, but actually suffered the greatest harm because of it. . . . (Dionysius, *Ant. Rom.* 2.17.1)

Rome, on the contrary, is the most hospitable and philanthropic of all cities (κοινοτάτην τε πόλεων καὶ φιλανθρωποτάτην) (1.89.1) because it admits innumerable citizens from other nations. Their ancestor Hercules had already taught men who "lived in the manner of savages" (ἀνημέρῳ διαίτῃ) "humane and sociable modes of life" (βίων ἔθη φιλάνθρωπα καὶ κοινοπαθῆ). "He mingled barbarians with Greeks, and inhabitants of the inland with dwellers on the sea coast, groups which hitherto had been distrustful and unsocial (ἀπίστους καὶ ἀσυναλλάκτους) in their dealing with each other" (1.41.1). Rome "received"

---

26 R. Maddox, *The Purpose of Luke-Acts* (Edinburgh: T. & T. Clark, 1982) 116 argues that Luke's church looked back on these persecutions, but the final section of Acts suggests otherwise. See esp. David P. Moessner, "Paul in Acts: Preacher of Eschatological Repentance to Israel," *NTS* 34 (1988) 96-104, at pp. 98-101.

27 M. Dibelius, "Paul in the Acts of the Apostles," *Studies in the Acts of the Apostles* (1956) 207-14, at p. 213. Cf. F. F. Bruce, "Paul's Apologetic and the Purpose of Acts," *BJRL* 69 (1987) 379-93, at pp. 389-92.

28 See Sterling, *Historiography* 298-308 as well as n. 12 above.

29 Sterling, *Historiography* 375, 385-86. Still, "the concern . . . was the social and political standing of the group within the empire" (387).

(some form of [ὑπο-] δέχεσθαι) many foreign nations as citizens (*Ant. Rom.* 1.57.4, 60.3, 63.2; 66.2, 89.3; cf. Acts 2:41; 11:1); with these "additions" (προστιθέντες) Rome became inferior in numbers to none of the other nations (*Ant. Rom.* 2.16.3; cf. Acts 2:41, 47 etc.). Dionysius gives lists of the nations received (1.60.3 and 1.89.2-3), just as does Acts 2:9-11.

But there was great dispute about these "additions" as the debate between Fufetius and Tullus (quoted above under point two) illustrates. Further, Rome allowed not only foreigners but also slaves to become citizens. When Romans freed their slaves, these also become Roman citizens, a policy which, however, is severely criticized. This dispute is so basic to Dionysius that it is one of the few times in his 20 volumes that he writes in the first person singular (4.24).

> . . .I think it is necessary to give an account of the customs which at that a time prevailed among the Romans with regard to slaves (δούλους ἔθη), in order that no one may accuse either the king who first undertook to make citizens of those who had been slaves, or the Romans who accepted the law, of recklessly abandoning their noble traditions. The Romans acquired slaves by the most just means. . . . So that neither Tullius, who established this custom, nor those who received and maintained it thought they were doing anything dishonourable. . . . Most of these slaves obtained their liberty as a free gift because of meritorious conduct, and this was the best kind of discharge from their masters; but a few paid a ransom raised by lawful and honest labour. (*Ant. Rom.* 4.24.1-4)

> This, however, is not the case in our day, but . . . some who have made a fortune by robbery, housebreaking, prostitution and every other base means, purchase their freedom with the money so acquired and straightway are Romans. Others, who have been confidants and accomplices of their masters in poisonings, murders. . . . (4.24.4-5)

> Most people, nevertheless, as they look upon these stains that can scarce be washed away from the city, are grieved and condemn the custom, looking upon it as unseemly that a dominant city which aspires to rule the whole world should make such men citizens (4.24.6)

Similarly, there are different attitudes in the Judaism Josephus describes about how to become a member of the community, as the case of Izates illustrates (*Ant.* 20.34-48, esp. 41 and 44).[30] I conclude that in Rome as described by Dionysius, in Judaism as described by Josephus, and in earliest Christianity as described by Luke-Acts, there were significant disputes about who might be received into the group and how.

But in the international Roman empire, there would be social and political consequences if a people appeared misanthropic, if the entrance requirements

---

30 A student at Brite, John Brillo, points out to me that κωλύω also occurs in Mark 10:14, "Let the children come to me; do not hinder them." Peter Müller, *In der Mitte der Gemeinde: Kinder im Neuen Testament* (Neukirchen-Vluyn: Neukirchener, 1992) correctly argues (42-80, 260, 287-94) that the key debate concerns whether children may be received into the community as full members. "Die Grundfrage, um die es dann geht, ist: Wer gehört dazu und wer nicht–zur Gemeinde und damit letzlich zur Basileia. . .?" (p. 77) This is a key tension in Dionysius, Josephus, and Luke-Acts.

were so narrow that one appeared to hate other humans. I recall the story of Balaam's advice to Midianite young women that they charge their Hebrew lovers with having "customs and a mode of life wholly alien to all mankind, insomuch that your food is of a peculiar sort," as well as Haman's charge that Jews are the enemies of all mankind, not so different from the misanthropic misunderstanding that Luke puts in the mouth of the Christian leader, Peter (Acts 10:28), an interpretation of Torah corrected by visions from God in chapter 10 and proclaimed by Paul as the concluding, climactic thought in two of his defense speeches (22:21 and 26:17-18, 23). Precisely the philanthropic God of the temple in Jerusalem (22:17; cf. Luke 2:31-32)[31] sends Paul to the Gentiles, an inclusive, philanthropic custom opposed by some who still misunderstand Torah. Acts 26:17 comes after 26:3 has claimed that Paul's defense concerns "the customs [ἐθῶν] and controversies of the Jews," just as in 28:17 Paul again claims that "I had done nothing against the people or the customs (ἔθεσι) of our fathers. . . ." Earlier in his history, Luke has argued by citing scripture that philanthropy is the ancient custom (e.g. Luke 2:31-32 [Isa 42:6; 49:6]; 3:6 [Isa 40:5]; Acts 13:46-48 [Isa 49:6], etc.) In one way or another, all three historians promote a more open, philanthropic policy of membership than some others in their own people.[32] Discussing point three above, I observe that attitudes toward foreigners are compared in an international environment; now I add that these historians all want their subjects to appear philanthropic in granting membership to aliens, the primary point in Paul's first apologetic speech in Acts 22, repeated at the end of the third and final apologetic speech in 26.

Seventh, one of the most prominent disputes in these historians concerns customs towards the gods. It is, of course, anachronistic to separate politics and religion: all three historians criticize certain ideas and practices in relationship to the divine and promote others. Very briefly, Dionysius criticizes Greek "mythology" in contrast to the "theology" of the Romans (*Ant. Rom.* 2.20.1-2), while Josephus ridicules Egyptian animal gods (Apion 2.139). And it hardly needs to be stated that in the Greco-Roman world, traditional worship of the gods is imperative (Dionysius, *Ant. Rom.* 7.70-73; Josephus, *Ant.* 5.101, 113; 8.190; 9.95, 137; 12.126, 271). Paul too insists that he is proclaiming the law of the "God of the fathers" (Acts 22:14; 24:14; 26: 6; cf. 22:3, 12, 17; 26:5, 22). He wants and politically and religiously must prove to king Agrippa II exactly what James and

---

31 The similarity between the climax of the final, apologetic speeches in Acts (22:21 and 26:17-18, 23) and the conclusion of the Nunc Dimittis (Luke 2:31-32), the final canticle in the birth narrative, corresponds to the observation of Raymond E. Brown, *The Birth of the Messiah: A Commentary on the Infancy Narratives in Matthew and Luke* (Garden City: Doubleday, 1977) 347 (cf. 363, n. 70): "In some ways the Lucan canticles resemble the speeches in the Book of Acts." God appears to Simeon and Paul in the *temple* commanding philanthropy towards aliens, which counters the accusation in Acts 6:13-14. As a historian Luke interpreted the narrative by canticles and speeches. Cf. Dibelius, "The Speeches in Acts and Ancient Historiography," *Studies in the Acts of the Apostles* (SCM, 1956) 138-91, at pp. 139-43.

32 The Roman centurion keeping Paul prisoner treats him philanthropically (Acts 27:3), as do the "barbarians" on Melita (28:2). Luke contrasts this Roman and barbarian philanthropy with the reception given Paul by the Jewish leaders of Rome (Johnson, *Acts of the Apostles* 465-67).

the brothers suggest to him in 21:24, that he himself lives in observance of the ancient law given by the "God of our fathers."[33]

As Vielhauer[34] observes, Paul himself in his authentic epistles differs from this orthopraxic Paul of Acts (contrast esp. 1 Cor 10:25, 27 with Acts 21:21).[35] But although the authentic and the Lucan Paul differ in practice, they had the same goal, the salvation and inclusion of Gentiles (compare Gal 2:3, 7-9, 11-16; Rom 9:30-10:4 with my paper above). Paul himself rejected the positive theological significance of physical circumcision (Gal 5:2-4; Rom 2:25-29) partially because[36] that would exclude Gentiles like Titus from first class status in the community. But if Luke assumed an audience for his history like those of Dionysius and Josephus, these readers would be suspicious of changing or abolishing ancient customs, as Paul indeed had done. Luke's primary concern (or at least one of them) is to claim that the ancient Torah (Abraham, Moses, David, and Isaiah) and Jesus philanthropically promise salvation to Gentiles (e.g., Luke 2:31-32; 24:47; Acts 3:25; 13:47; 28:29), and for this disputed claim to be valid, Luke's characters including Paul must not change but observe other ancient traditions as well, e.g. circumcision (Acts 16:1-3), purity (21:24, 26), and holy days (20:16). If the accusations were true that Stephen and Paul changed or did not observe the ancient customs, Luke's case to Greco-Roman, Gentile Christian readers for the legitimacy of their own inclusion in the people of God (cf. Acts 15:14) would collapse, as would the case of Christians called to defend themselves before the Jewish people (21:39), a local governor (24:1), or a king who "knows the customs and controversies of the Jews" (26:3).[37]

In conclusion, I have argued seven points about how "customs" are narrated in Greco-Roman history, in Dionysius, Josephus, and Luke-Acts:

1. The prefaces of Dionysius, *Roman History*, and Josephus, *War*, observe that these historians will narrate customs of Rome and of the Jews, and since Luke and Acts are also history, they concern "the customs and controversies of the Jews" (Acts 26:3).

2. One of the customs narrated concerns how the people treat aliens, the climax of Luke-Acts (Acts 10-15).

3. Customs are compared in an international context, a comparison that results in a claim that they are philanthropic, often also in a denial that they are misanthropic.

4. Official Roman policy promoted each nation preserving its own, ancient customs and allowing other people to practice theirs.

---

33 The conclusion of Christoph Burchard, "Paulus in der Apostelgeschichte," *ThLZ* 100/12 (1975) 882-95, at p. 891, "Nun hat nach diesem Schluss der Acta in 28,23-28 Paulus sehr wohl auch mit der Ablösung des Christentums vom Judentum zu tun. . ." thus does *not* follow.

34 Cf. n. 20 and Ernst Käsemann, "Ephesians and Acts," *Studies in Luke-Acts: Essays Presented in Honor of Paul Schubert,*" ed. Leander E. Keck and J. Louis Martyn (Nashville: Abingdon, 1966) 288-97

35 Cf. C. K. Barrett, "Things Sacrificed to Idols," *NTS* 11 (1964-65) 138-53.

36 I am not discussing Paul's basic Christological reason (Gal 3:10-14).

37 I discuss how Matthew addressed this dilemma in "The Greek Political Topos Περὶ νόμων and Matthew 5:17, 19, and 16:19," in *Social History of the Matthean Community: Cross-Disciplinary Approaches,* ed. Balch (Minneapolis: Fortress, 1991) 68-84.

5. The final word of Luke-Acts proclaims that even in Rome, Christian customs were ἀκωλύτως, not forbidden, the author's final evaluation of the accusation in Acts 21:21, so that the whole concluding section of the two volume work concerns whether Christians preserve the ancient, legitimate, philanthropic customs of Moses.

6. Rome opposed any group living as unsocial "savages," and promoted friendly relations between groups and nations, and in this political context ethnic groups became more open to receiving outsiders as citizens or members.

7. These three historians were also concerned with theological customs, with the identity and will of the "God(s) of the fathers," as Paul is in Acts.

The Seed of Abraham and the People of God: A Study of Two Pauls

J. Bradley Chance
William Jewell College

Introduction

The following paper will explore the theme of the "seed of Abraham" and other closely related issues in the writings of Paul and the Lukan corpus. In Part One Paul will be the focus of examination. In Part Two, Luke-Acts will be given a careful reading in relation to this issue. The Conclusion will offer some correlations between the two sections. It will be apparent as well that the paper was written with an eye to "how [the paper's] method or methods contribute to the description of the location of Luke-Acts."[1]

The Seed of Abraham in Paul

It is almost axiomatic to say that in Paul "the seed of Abraham" are to be equated with the people of faith (cf. Rom 4.11-12, 16; Gal 3.7, 29). In exploring this notion focus shall be given to the two chapters in Paul's correspondence which make the argument: Rom 4 and Gal 3. On first reading, the two chapters have much in common—so much so that J. C. Beker has stated that among interpreters it seems to have been assumed that "Galatians might just as well have been sent to Rome or Romans to Galatia."[2] In this section of the paper I will 1) explore the different nuances of Paul's arguments regarding the seed of Abraham in Gal and Rom and the differing *Sitze im Leben* of the two communities which account for Paul's differently nuanced arguments, and 2) argue that gentile legitimation vis-à-vis descent from Abraham was not for Paul or his gentile followers an intrinsically significant means of legitimation. Rather, it was primarily an argument of response directed at Jewish messianists for whom the issue of descent from Abraham was a significant factor.

It is a fact that the two chapters of Gal 3 and Rom 4 do offer quite a bit of overlap in subject matter. Abraham, who is of little interest to Paul elsewhere, is certainly the central figure in these two chapters.[3] One finds in both

---

[1] Quoted from the letter of David Moessner and David Tiede, describing the agenda of the seminar. Dated February 12, 1991.

[2] *Paul the Apostle: The Triumph of God in Life and Thought* (Philadelphia: Fortress, 1982) 37.

[3] In the Pauline corpus, one finds 19 references to Abraham. All but four of them (Rom 9.7; 11.1; 2 Cor 11.22; Gal 4.22) are found in Rom 4 or Gal 3. It is perhaps significant

384

chapters a discussion of faith,[4] righteousness/justification,[5] works,[6] law,[7] seed,[8] and nations/gentiles.[9] It would seem apparent that in both chapters Paul is concerned to show that the people of faith are the descendants of Abraham. Both chapters seem to share the assumption that, somehow, being a descendant of Abraham is a mark of one's legitimacy, making one an heir of a promise[10] or the recipient of a blessing.[11] A quick reading allows the rather straightforward summary: "The heirs of God's promises and recipients of God's blessings are Abraham's descendants; Abraham's descendants are the people of faith." A closer reading of each of the chapters will show some interesting differences, however.[12]

Paul's argument to the Galatians. Paul begins his discussion in Gal 3 by setting up some clear, dualistic, contrasts (Gal 3.1-5). Spirit is opposed to flesh (3.3); faith is opposed to works of the law (vv. 2, 5). The rather abrupt introduction of the Spirit may indicate that Paul assumes the reality of the Spirit (manifested in miracles? [v 5]) among the Galatians and, more importantly from a rhetorical perspective, assumes that they assume the reality of it.

In vv. 6-9 Paul quickly introduces numerous issues: Abraham, faith, descendants of Abraham, gentiles, justification, and blessing. He begins by quoting Gen 15.6 and then quickly wants to move to the seemingly logical conclusion (γινώσκετε ἄρα)[13] that people of faith are the children of Abraham. In fact, it does not follow that because Abraham was reckoned as righteous by faith that all people of faith are children of Abraham. Walter Hansen has argued that Gal 3.6-7 "taken together form an argument by

---

as well that all but one reference (2 Cor 11.22) are found in either Rom or Gal. Abraham was not a common topic in Paul's letters.

[4] One finds 17 references to πίστις or its cognates in each of the chapters under discussion.

[5] One finds 11 references to δικαι- stems in Rom 4; six references in Gal 3.

[6] Four references to ἔργα in Rom 4; three in Gal 3.

[7] Rom 4 has five references to νόμος; Gal 3 has 15.

[8] Three references in each chapter.

[9] Two references in each chapter.

[10] This is also an important theme in each chapter. Rom 4 offers four references; Gal 3 offers eight.

[11] Paul uses a different word for blessing in Rom and Gal. In Rom 4.7-9 he uses μακάριος; in Gal 3.8, 9, 14 Paul employs εὐλογία and cognates. As the discussion will show below, he defines "blessing" differently as well.

[12] The following discussion will show its indebtedness to the many previous readers who have informed my reading. I would note as especially influential Beker, *Paul the Apostle,* 37-108; Francis Watson, *Paul, Judaism and the Gentiles: A Sociological Approach* SNTSMS 56 (Cambridge: Cambridge University Press, 1986) 49-87; T. L. Donaldson, "The 'Curse of the Law' and the Inclusion of the Gentiles: Galatians 3:13-14," *NTS* 32 (1986) 94-112; J. D. G. Dunn, "Works of the Law and Curse of the Law (Gal 3.10-14), *Journal of Law and Religion* 31 (1985) 523-42; David T. Gordon, "The Problem at Galatia," *Interpretation* 41 (1987) 32-43. G. Walter Hansen, *Abraham in Galatians: Epistolary and Rhetorical Contexts* JSNTSS 29 (Sheffield: JSOT, 1989); Klaus Berger, "Abraham in den paulinischen Hauptbriefen," *MTR* 17 (1966) 47-59.

[13] BAG, s.v. ἄρα.

enthymeme."[14] This form of argument draws conclusions, though perhaps unexpected, from an agreed upon premise, shared by the author (speaker) and reader (hearer). In the case of Gal 3.6-7, "the conclusion (ἄρα) in v. 7 is derived from the implicit premise that as God dealt with Abraham, so he will deal with all men (*sic*)."[15] The conclusion that Paul draws, however, is unexpected. The conclusion one might expect would be that if God treats all like he treats Abraham, then all are made righteous by faith—not all people of faith are his descendants. Perhaps something is happening in the Galatian churches that is compelling Paul to draw certain conclusions from his reading of Gen.

Paul cites another text in v. 8 (Gen 18.18; cf. 12.3): "in you [Abraham] shall all the gentiles [ἔθνη] be blessed." Paul draws another seemingly premature conclusion in v. 9: "with the result [ὥστε] that those who are of faith are blessed along with the faith of Abraham." Again, it is not clear how Gen 18.18 allows the conclusion that *those of faith* will be blessed with the faith of Abraham. Apparently, Paul has merged Gen 15.6, which speaks of Abraham's righteousness by faith, and Gen 18.18 which speaks of the gentiles being blessed in Abraham. That Paul allows himself this merger is clear from v. 8, where he refers explicitly to God's justification of "the gentiles by faith" (v. 8a) whence he moves directly to the quotation of Gen 18.18 in 8b. What is clear from this maneuver is that Paul is not all that interested in *Abraham's* faith; he is really interested in affirming that by faith the gentiles are the children of Abraham (v. 7) and made righteous (v. 8a), that is to say, "blessed" (v. 8b). The lack of tight logic raises the question whether something other than scriptural interpretation is driving Paul's argument here. He simply appears to move too quickly to his assertion of gentile blessing through faith and descent from Abraham based on faith.[16]

In vv. 10-14 Paul again offers some dualistic contrasts. On one side are works of the law and curse; on the other are faith and righteousness/ justification. Christ is introduced on the side of faith and righteousness, with his relationship to curse and law being offered only in negative terms: by dying on the tree, and thereby being cursed by the statement of the law (Deut 21.23), he redeems humanity from the curse of the law. Though Paul has failed to articulate how Christ's becoming the curse redeems from the curse, the conclusion he wishes to draw is clear: that in Christ—and implicitly only in Christ—can the blessing of Abraham occur for the gentiles (v. 14a).[17] V.

---

14 *Abraham in Galatians*, 112.

15 Ibid.

16 E. P. Sanders, *Paul, the Law, and the Jewish People* (Philadelphia: Fortress, 1983), states that Paul selects his quotations for Gal with his conclusion in mind. "It depends on finding proof texts for the view that *Gentiles* are *righteoused* by *faith*. These three words are crucial, and Paul is able to link Gentiles to "righteousness by faith" through the Abraham story" (21). I would only add that for Paul "Abraham" is also a crucial term, for, as many interpreters have noted (including Sanders [*ibid.*, 18]) Paul's opponents at Galatia viewed descent from Abraham as crucial for gentile legitimation, with circumcision serving as the requisite entrance requirement.

17 See Donaldson, "The 'Curse of the Law' and the Inclusion of the Gentiles" *NTS* 32 (1986) 94-112 for an interesting interpretation of Paul's argument. He argues that those

14b now makes clear what this blessing is: the promise of the Spirit, to be received by faith. Hence, Paul has returned to the beginning point of his argument, the Galatians' experience of the Spirit (vv. 1-5). His point in vv. 10-14 is that it is only in the sphere of faith and in connection with the redeeming work of Christ that the promise of the Spirit can be made effective.

It should be noted that Paul has again made an apparently premature move. Gen 18.18 (v. 8) indicated that it was *in Abraham* that the gentiles were to find blessing. Paul has declared in v. 14a that it is *in Christ* that the gentiles find blessing. Paul's logic is partially explained in the following paragraph (vv. 15-18). By a *tour de force* he argues that "the promises (note the plural, but presumably the Spirit is among the promises) were made to Abraham and to his offspring." Paul exploits the singular here and declares the "seed" to be Christ—and only Christ, though it is by assertion and not argumentation.[18] The narrow focus of the promise to only Abraham and Christ apparently allows Paul to understand that the promise to Abraham in Gen 18.18 that *in him* the gentiles would be blessed, refers ultimately to Christ.

But Paul has another concern in vv. 15-18. He wishes to drive a wedge between the promise (the first covenant) and the law (vv. 17-18). Paul will push the wedge more deeply between promise and law in vv. 19-25. Regardless of the precise understanding one might offer for the reason for the law ("because of transgressions"),[19] one thing is quite clear: the law is

---

freed from the curse of the law are the Jews. This liberation of the Jews then opens up the way for gentiles to be saved. The Jewish curse of being under the law served as a concrete example of the plight of all humanity being under the curse of the elemental spirits (cf. Gal 4.3). The purpose of the law, therefore, was to increase the transgression of the Jew and seal the curse (Donaldson brings in Rom 4.15 and 5.14 to complete his case). It makes for an interesting reading, but it is not clear to me why Paul, wishing to convince gentile readers that they need not submit to the demand of circumcision would find this a particularly useful line of argument or, for that matter, how Paul would expect his gentile readers to be able to understand this line of argument. If Donaldson's reading is valid, it appears to me to be valid to uncover some of the deeper assumptions of Paul's thinking–not to elucidate Paul's strategy for convincing his gentile Galatian readers to abandon their thoughts of circumcision. For more on the Galatian situation, see below.

18 Max Wilcox, "The Promise of the 'Seed' in the New Testament and the Targumim," *JSNT* 5 (1979) 2-20 finds evidence in the Hebrew Bible and the Targumim of a connection between the promise to Abraham of a "seed" and statements made concerning David's seed. He notes, e.g., Jer 33.22 where the formula used in the promise to Abraham (the abundance of sand and stars) is applied to a promise concerning the seed of David. He notes also the Targum to Ps 89.4. Whereas the Ps in the Hebrew Bible makes no reference to Abraham, but only David, the Targum states: "I made a covenant for Abraham my chosen one" (the Hebrew Bible does not identify Abraham), I swore to David my servant . . . I shall establish your seed forever." Such a connection between the seed of Abraham and the seed of David (whom Jewish messianists would identify with Jesus Messiah) would allow believers to see allusions to the seed of David (Jesus) in biblical references to the seed of Abraham. Such a reading unveils, perhaps, for us the deeper logic of Paul's argument; but I suspect it would have been lost on his gentile readers.

19 Debate centers on whether it means "to increase the trespass" (along the lines of Rom 5.20; 7.7-13 (so e.g., Donaldson, "The 'Curse of the Law," *NTS* 32: 94-112). This reading might be confirmed by appeal to Gal 3.22-23 where scripture and the law are said to "imprison" humanity under the power of sin. Some argue that it means to deal with, or to curtail, transgressions. See David J. Lull, "The Law Was Our Pedagogue," *JBL* 105/3

something temporary, added only "until the seed to whom it was promised should come" (v. 19). The only positive thing Paul says about the law is that is not against the promises of God (v. 21). The rest is negative: the law is temporary (v. 19b, 23, 25); offering ordinances through angels by the hand of a mediator (v. 19 [hardly comparable to the promise made directly to Abraham by God]); it confines (v. 23); it imprisons under sin (vv. 22-23); it plays the role, usually assigned to a slave, of the one who keeps the boys in line, but only until they grow up (παιδαγωγός, vv. 24-25).

But the temporary era of the law is now over, for now faith has come; Christ has come. In these last few verses Paul ties up the loose ends noted in the earlier part of his argument; specifically, how it is that *faith* makes one a child of Abraham. First, Paul links faith exclusively with Christ: the coming of faith and the coming of Christ are synonymous. Second, the faith of the human being links one with Christ. Once Paul speaks of becoming a child of God through faith in Christ Jesus (v. 26), the language of attachment to and inclusion in Christ continues through the remainder of vv. 27-29. Given that Christ is *the* seed of Abraham, the one to whom the promise had been made, attachment to Christ offers one inclusion within the seed and renders one an heir to the promise. Hence, though the argument is not tight, the assertions of vv. 6-9, that those who are of faith are the children of Abraham is argued at the conclusion of the chapter. The people of faith are the "seed" of Abraham because it is faith that attaches one to *the* seed of Abraham which is Christ.

By linking one's status as a child of Abraham so exclusively with Christ, Paul shows forth another agenda. That is to make one's status as a descendant of Abraham mutually exclusive from "works of the law." The dualistic manner in which Paul contrasts works and faith (vv. 1-5) and curse/law vs. blessing/faith (vv. 10-14) and the manner in which Paul associates Christ with faith and blessing, hence against law and curse, and the way that Paul asserts that with the coming of Christ/faith the era of the law is over all serve to lead the reader to one conclusion: faith in Christ and works of the law are mutually exclusive alternatives. Thus, if descent from Abraham is linked exclusively with Christ and faith, then law and works have absolutely nothing to do with being a child of Abraham.

The wide wedge which Paul attempts to drive between law and Christ is undoubtedly rooted in polemics against real opponents: opponents who were insisting that Paul's gentile believers had to be circumcised if they wished to be a part of God's people (cf. 5.2-3). *This* is what was driving Paul's reading of the Hebrew scriptures. Reconstructions of the opponents' line of argument abound, so I need only summarize the results.[20] It would appear that Jewish

---

(1986) 481-98; a reading which seems to be confirmed by Paul's comparing of the law to a παιδαγωγός.

20 See esp. Hansen, *Abraham in Galatians*, 167-74 for a clear and concise reconstruction of the opponents' arguments. A very differently nuanced view is offered by Helmut Koester, "ΓΝΩΜΑΙ ΔΙΑΦΟΡΟΙ: The Origins and Nature of Diversification in the History of Early Christianity," *HTR* 58 (1965) 307-310. Koester argues that Paul's response to his opponents "shows a mythologizing of Old Testament covenant theology . . ." understanding the present time ". . . as the renewal of the covenant (now in its cosmic dimensions) . . ." (300). It was Paul, in his refutation of the Galatian opponents, who removed the covenantal

messianists had entered the Pauline communities of Galatia and attempted to persuade the gentile believers that circumcision, perhaps even conversion to Judaism, was necessary to be a part of the covenant people. After all, Gen 17 indicates quite clearly that God had made a promise to Abraham and his seed that he would be the God of Abraham and his seed (Gen 17.7). But that same text made equally clear that Abraham and his seed must be circumcised. Failure to obey this command would result in being cut off from the people, for such a one has broken the covenant (Gen 17.9-14).

Paul must convince his *gentile* readers that they are indeed legitimate participants in the covenant, while at the same time undermining his opponents' claim that participation in the covenant depends upon being a circumcised child of Abraham. His line of attack is absolute: he must undermine the validity of the law completely, show it to be mutually exclusive to faith in Christ, and something only added on to the original covenant made between God and Abraham—something that has now passed away with the coming of Christ. In short, discontinuity between law and gospel is the primary emphasis.[21] The promise of Gen 17, as Paul interprets it in Gal 3, completely bypasses historic Israel, being offered only to Abraham and his seed, which is Christ. Being a child of Abraham has nothing to do with law and it has nothing to do, presumably, with being Jewish or a part of ethnic Israel.[22] This point is accentuated by the focus Paul gives to Gen 18.18 in Gal 3.8: "the pre-preached gospel declared to Abraham, 'In you shall all the gentiles be blessed.'" The whole focus of the declarations and promises to Abraham was the gentiles, the non-Jews. Having made this argument, Paul can present his gentile readers with the uncompromising conclusion: "if you receive circumcision, Christ will be of no advantage to you. . . . You are severed from Christ, you who would be justified by the law; you have fallen away from grace" (5.2, 4).

Paul's argument to the Romans. This rather absolutist line of argument, severing law from faith and Jew from gentile believer, disappears from Paul's

---

thinking from the cosmic speculations and linked it with the historical figure of Abraham. Koester's reconstruction is plausible assuming a proto-gnostic starting point (which he does, vis à vis Schmithals). Such a context, however, is not demonstrable, nor is it necessary. Paul's attention to the Jerusalem church and James (Gal 1-2) would perhaps make a more "orthodox Jewish" (Koester's phrase, 303) context more plausible.

[21] See Beker, *Paul the Apostle*, 49-52. In his summary of the logic of Paul's argument about Abraham he notes that "the element of discontinuity dominates" (51).

[22] The comment of H. Boers is apropos. "Christians, thus, have no direct relationship to Abraham. Their relationship to him is dependent on their belonging to Christ (3:29). . . . [E]verything that happened between the announcement of the promise and its pre-envisioned fulfillment is understood to have no essential relationship. . . ." "The Significance of Abraham for the Christian Faith." In *Theology Out of the Ghetto: A New Testament Exegetical Study Concerning Religious Exclusiveness* (Leiden: E. J. Brill, 1971) 81.

discussion of Abraham, faith, and descendants in Rom 4.[23] To be sure, Paul is interested in legitimating the gentiles' status as descendants of Abraham based on faith and it is precisely this similarity that can so easily cover over the different rhetorical thrust of Rom 4 compared with Gal 3. However, some important differences should be noted.

First to be noted is the greater focus given to the faith of Abraham himself in Rom 4. Whereas he is mentioned several times in Gal 3, and reference is even made to his faith (Gal 3.6, 9), the focus in Gal quickly turns to the children of Abraham and *their* faith—a faith which is very christocentric. In Rom, however, Paul speaks much of *Abraham's* faith (4.3, 11, 12, 13, 16, 17, 18, 19, 20, 22). What is more, "faith" in Rom 4 is *not* christocentric. Christ is not even mentioned until the end of the chapter and then faith is still *theocentric*: "[Righteousness] will be reckoned to us who believe in him that raised from the dead Jesus our Lord" (Rom 4.24).

Second, in Rom Paul offers a differently nuanced discussion of "righteousness," as compared to Gal. In Gal, righteousness and justification of the gentiles are synonymous with the gentiles being "blessed" in Abraham (Gal 3.8). This "blessing" is later defined in v. 14 as the receipt of the "promise of Spirit." In Rom Paul's focus is on the "reckoning" of righteousness,[24] which he defines not as the blessing of the promised Spirit, but as the blessing of forgiveness, the covering of sin, and God's decision not to reckon one's sin against the sinner (Rom 4.7-8, quoting Ps 31.1-2 [LXX]).[25] This definition of righteousness is tied very closely to Rom 4.5, where reference is made to God's justification of the ungodly. Paul apparently is using Abraham as a corporate example of the ungodly (ἀσεβῆ) person justified (forgiven) by God.[26] That would be most appropriate, given Paul's emphasis in Rom 1-3 on the ungodliness of all humanity, both gentile and Jew. In fact, Paul introduces his long discussion of human sin in Rom 1-3 with "the wrath of God is revealed from heaven against all ungodliness (ἀσέβειαν) and wickedness of men . . . "(1.18).[27]

Third, Paul's emphasis on the common plight of ungodliness and sin of both Jew and gentile and his use of Abraham as an example of the ungodly person, Jew or gentile, justified by faith, offers a common link between Jew

---

23 My reading of Rom 4 has been influenced by the following: Boers, "Significance of Abraham"; Watson, *Paul, Judaism and the Gentiles*, 88-176, esp 135-42; W. Baird, "Abraham in the New Testament: Tradition and the New Identity," *Interpretation* 42 (1988) 367-79; A. J. Guerra, "Romans 4 as Apologetic Theology," *HTR* 81:3 (1988) 251-70; Beker, *Paul the Apostle* 59-93.

24 Paul uses the word for "reckon" 11 times in Rom 4; it appears in Gal only in the quotation of Gen 15.6.

25 Paul does not use the same word for blessing in the respective chapters, making for even less similarity between the two. He uses εὐλογ⁻ and cognates in Gal; μακαρ⁻ and cognates in Rom 4.

26 So Baird, "Abraham in the New Testament," *Inter* 42: 375-76.

27 'Ασέβεια and cognates are found within the indisputably Pauline letters only in Rom (see Rom 1.18; 4.5; 5.6; 11.26). It clearly is a theme particularly relevant to the Roman situation only.

and gentile not found in Gal: both are under the power of sin (Rom 3.9).[28] This association of condemnation between the two groups lays a foundation for a close association of justification. Note the thrust of Paul's argument of Rom 4.9-12. He begins by asking the question, "Is the blessing [of forgiveness] pronounced only upon the circumcised, or also upon the uncircumcised?" Paul goes on to answer that it is pronounced on *both* Jew and gentile who follow the example of Abraham's faith. Abraham serves as "the ancestor of all who believe without being circumcised . . . and likewise the ancestor of the circumcised who are not merely circumcised but also follow the example of faith which *our* ancestor Abraham had before he was circumcised" (Rom 4.11-12). To be sure, like Galatians, it is faith that makes one a child of Abraham. But whereas Gal focuses exclusively on the status of gentiles as the descendants of Abraham by faith, with salvation history passing right over the Jews and the law serving only as one large parenthesis, Rom gives equal attention to the status of gentiles and Jews as Abraham's descendants.

Fourth, one finds no traces of Paul's rather forced argument of Gal 3.16 that the promise was only to Abraham and his singular seed of Christ. To be sure, Christ is the "seed of David" and the gospel concerning him was promised in the scriptures (Rom 1.2-3). But there is no attempt to by-pass historic Israel and to make its history and its law a parenthetical pause in the salvation history of God. In Rom 4.13 Paul speaks of the promise made to Abraham and his seed. The promise is defined not as the receipt of the Spirit but as the inheritance of the world. He goes on to state that "those who are of law" (presumably non-messianist Jews) are not the heirs of this promise (v. 14). But in v. 16 a confusing element is found. Paul speaks again of the promise (of inheriting the world) guaranteed "to all the seed—not only to the one who is of law but also to the one who is of the faith of Abraham." Read strictly, Paul is contradicting himself, for v. 16 asserts that *both* the person of the law *and* the person who follows the faith of Abraham are of his seed and heirs of the promise, whereas in v. 14 he has asserted that those who are of law are not the heirs. Even if we clarify and paraphrase Paul's language and contend that what he really means to say in v. 16 is something like "not only the Jewish believer but the gentile believer as well,"[29] the conclusion appears inescapable that Paul's muddled language is rooted in his desire to argue that the seed of Abraham consists of *both* Jews and gentiles who have faith, "for Abraham is the ancestor of us all, as it is written, 'I have made you the ancestor of many ἐθνῶν'" (vv. 16b-17 [quoting Gen 17.5]). It was clear in Gal that when Paul quoted Gen 18.18 he intended the reference to ἔθνη to be a reference to non-Jews. Yet the way that Paul has set up this quotation of Gen 17.5 in Rom makes

---

28 If one follows Donaldson's reading of Gal (see above, n. 17) then in Gal both Jew and gentile share the fate of being cursed under the power of the elemental spirits, of which the law is a concrete example. Still, Rom, much more than Gal, emphasizes the common plight of Jew and gentile under the power of sin.

29 So, e.g., C. E. B. Cranfield, *The Epistle to the Romans*, 2 vols, ICC (Edinburgh: T & T Clark, 1975) 1:242-43.

clear that he does not use ἔθνη to designate non-Jews but all *nations,* Jewish or gentile.[30]

Paul concludes his argument of Rom 4 by focusing on the theocentric faith of Abraham, which he defines as Abraham's being "fully convinced that God was able to do what he had promised" (v. 21). Vv 23-25 portray Abraham's faith as a type of the faith which is demonstrated in Paul's day by those who, like Abraham, believe in God, though, to be sure, specifically the God who raised Jesus from the dead. Still, the reader of Rom 4 is not left with the impression, as is the reader of Gal 3, that only with the coming of Christ did faith come into the world and present itself as a possibility. The emphasis on Abraham's faith in God, and the non-christocentric definition of faith offered in v. 21 as trusting God to keep his promises, allows for the conclusion that faith has always been a possibility and the basis of the righteous relationship between God and his people.[31] This, combined with Paul's emphasis on the unity of gentiles and Jews of faith, would not lead the reader to conclude, as in Gal, that God's sole concern in offering a promise to Abraham was the justification (= blessing = promise of Spirit) of the gentiles, but rather the unity of faithful Jews and gentiles in the seed of Abraham who, though once equally condemned before God, are now equally forgiven. Finally, the reader does not detect the radical polemic against the law that is found in Gal. To be sure, "those who are (only) of law" are not heirs to the promises (assuming Paul does not really mean what he says in Rom 4.16b). But "being of law" is not presented as an option mutually exclusive to "being of faith." The very example of Abraham shows that being circumcised *and* being a person of faith can mutually co-exist—hardly a conclusion which the reader of Gal would obtain.

Unlike Gal, what the reader finds in Rom is a line of argument emphasizing *continuity* between law and gospel and Jew and gentile.[32] What accounts for this different line of argument? As with Gal, one must look to the situation. The situation at Rome is not as clearly defined as that of Galatia. As Karl Donfried states, "Current research concerning the purpose of Romans is

---

[30] So Cranfield, *ibid.,* 243; John Ziesler, *Paul's Letter to the Romans* (Philadelphia: Trinity Press International, 1989) 131.

[31] Boers, "Significance of Abraham," finds Paul piercing "his own system of thought in Rom 4, even if he probably did not intend to do so . . ." (101). Boers, of course, is trying to get Christian theology out of the ghetto and sees here an opening. The usefulness of Rom 4 for such a discussion does show how different Paul's discussion of faith here is from Gal.

[32] See Guerra, "Romans 4 as Apologetic Theology," *HTR* 81/3 (1988) 251-70. A key theme of Paul's apologetic here is to show continuity and consistency in his actions. "Christian apologetics affirms that God acts 'now' in the Christ event and that this act is consistent with God's past acts in history" (263). See also Richard B. Hays, "'Have We Found Abraham to be Our Forefather According to the Flesh?' A Reconstruction of Rom 4:1," *NovTest* 27/1 (1985) 76-98.

in a state of confusion."[33] Is the primary audience Jewish messianist,[34] gentile believers,[35] or, rhetorically at least, Jews?[36]

The introduction of Abraham in Rom 4.1 may shed some light on the issue. Paul introduces Abraham with the statement, τί οὖν ἐροῦμεν εὑρηκέναι Ἀβραὰμ τὸν προπάτορα ἡμῶν κατὰ σάρκα;[37] Some suggest that Paul introduces Abraham as "our forefather according to the flesh" to refer to Abraham "as the forefather of all Christians," perhaps in anticipation of his forthcoming argument.[38] But the phrase, κατὰ σάρκα seems out of place if Paul has gentiles in mind. Watson sees the speaker of 4.1, rhetorically at least, as the Jewish messianists. "The Roman Jewish Christians appeal to 'Abraham, our forefather according to the flesh' (v. 1), perhaps in response to Paul's setting of Jews and Gentiles on the same level (Rom 3)."[39] Richard Hays offers a most intriguing translation and interpretation arguing that one should translate Rom 4.1, "What then shall we say? Have we found Abraham (to be) our forefather according to the flesh?"[40]

According to Hays, the question serves to introduce the argument of chap 4 and is a continuation of the argument of chap 3. An important point of chap 3 has been to argue that God is one and, hence, the God of all persons, Jew or gentile. Consequently, God justifies both Jews and gentiles in the same manner—by faith. Paul introduces Abraham in order to continue this line of argument and to refute an understanding of Abraham which Paul views as inappropriately ethnocentric:

> Paul is going to argue that Judaism itself, rightly understood, claims its relation to Abraham not by virtue of physical descent from him (κατὰ σάρκα) but by virtue of sharing his trust in the God who made the promises. In that sense, the Gospel, which invites all people, including Gentiles, into right relation with God through faith, confirms the Law; it is consistent with the real substance of the Law's teaching. This is the

---

33 Karl P. Donfried, "False Presuppositions in the Study of Romans," in *The Romans Debate*, ed. Donfried, rev. and expanded (Peabody, MA: Hendrickson, 1991) 102.

34 So, e.g., A. J. M. Wedderburn, *The Reason for Romans* (Edinburgh: T & T Clark, 1988) and "The Purpose and Occasions of Romans Again," in Donfried, *Romans Debate*, 194-202; Peter Stuhlmacher, "The Purpose of Romans," in Donfried, ibid., 231-42; Francis Watson, *Paul, Judaism, and the Gentiles*, 88-105.

35 Wolfgang Wiefel, "The Jewish Community in Ancient Rome and the Origins of Roman Christianity," in Donfried, *ibid.*, 85-101. He states, "Although we were able to show that the first Christians in Rome unquestionably originated from the synagogues, all attempts to define the addressees of the Roman letter as Jewish Christians are unconvincing" (93).

36 Beker, *Paul the Apostle*, esp. 89-91.

37 There is textual confusion, particularly revolving around the presence of εὑρηκέναι. We have followed the reading of Nestle 26, what most commentators consider the more difficult and "authentic" reading.

38 Ziesler, *Romans*, 122.

39 *Paul, Judaism and the Gentiles*, 139.

40 "'Have We Found Abraham to be Our Forefather According to the Flesh?'" *NovTest* 27: 81.

proposition that Paul now sets out to demonstrate, beginning in Rom 4:3, through his exposition of Genesis.

This reading of the text will appear odd only if we are committed to the presupposition that Paul is expounding a message which stands in an antithetical relation to Judaism. If we do not hold this view *a priori*, it will be clear enough that Paul means precisely what he says: the gospel confirms the Torah. Only a narrowly ethnocentric form of Judaism would claim that God is the God of the Jews only or that Abraham is the progenitor of God's people "according to the flesh," i.e., by virtue of natural physical descent. For the purpose of his argument, Paul associates these (evidently false) claims with the (disputed) claim that Gentile Christians must come under the Law. Paul, speaking from within the Jewish tradition, contends that the Torah itself provides the warrant for a more universally inclusive theology which affirms that the one God is the God of Gentiles as well as Jews and that Abraham is the forefather of more than those who happen to be his physical descendants. . . . This is the case to be made in Chap. 4.[41]

Hays' reading is provocative and, to me, persuasive. It complements nicely the larger context of Paul's concerns in Romans: the righteousness of God understood very specifically as "the problem of God's saving righteousness *in relation to Israel.*"[42] What kind of real life situation would seem to fit best the rhetorical situation of Romans—a situation concerned to demonstrate the gentiles' place in God's saving righteousness "in relation to Israel" and which argues "from within the Jewish tradition . . . that the Torah itself provides the warrant for a more universally inclusive theology which affirms that the one God is the God of Gentiles as well as Jews"?

Francis Watson has offered a reconstruction worth exploring.[43] Paul's focused readers of Rom were messianist Jews who were reluctant to be fully inclusive of gentile believers. In short, whereas Paul is trying to convince gentile believers in Gal not to submit to "works of the law," he is trying to convince Jewish believers in Rom to recognize the complete legitimacy of the gentile believers. Read from this proposed situation the climactic texts of Rom 15.7-13 make excellent sense. A Jewish messianist reluctant to embrace the gentile believer might not be persuaded by, but surely would feel the rhetorical sting of statements such as "For I tell you that Christ became a servant to the circumcised to show God's truthfulness, in order to confirm the promises given to the patriarchs, *and in order that the Gentiles might glorify God for his mercy.* As it is written . . . 'Rejoice, O Gentiles, *with his people.*'" (Rom 15.8-9a, 10).

The recognition that Paul is concerned to persuade Jewish messianists to embrace gentiles gives rationale to Paul's emphasis on the continuity between law and Israel and the gospel. It would have been rhetorically disastrous to try

---

41 Ibid., 87-88.

42 Richard B. Hays, *Echoes of Scripture in the Letters of Paul* (New Haven: Yale University Press, 1989) 34; emphasis mine.

43 *Paul, Judaism and the Gentiles,* esp. ch 5.

to persuade Jewish messianists to embrace the gentiles by presenting the law as a now irrelevant stop-gap measure or by presenting the promises God made to Abraham as made only to him and his singular seed Christ with an eye exclusively on the gentiles all along. By arguing for the close association of Jew and gentile, both in condemnation as sinners and justification as the seed of Abraham, Paul could hope to persuade Jewish messianists of the equal status of gentile believers and thereby bring to realization the scripture: "'Praise the Lord, all Gentiles, and let all the peoples [Jews] praise him'" (Rom 15.11 [quoting Ps 117.1]).

Descent from Abraham: A Jewish Messianist Concern. I have tried to show, clearly influenced by readings of Paul offered by other readers, that the contingencies of Paul's immediate situation very much influenced the way that Paul shaped his argument. There emerges a coherent element within Paul's discussion, namely that faith is what makes one a child of Abraham and, thus, an heir of God's promises of blessing (however that blessing might be defined).[44] But I would like to present for discussion one other element which links Gal 3 and Rom 4—namely that it was a *Jewish* concern for legitimacy which sparked the debate about Abraham and his seed. Put another way, the legitimization of gentiles as God's people by showing them to be of the seed of Abraham was not an intrinsic concern to the gentiles, or even to Paul. It was a concern *only* to Jewish messianists and it was only because Paul had to respond to Jewish messianists or gentiles who listened to them that it presents itself as a dominant theme of the Pauline corpus.

One observes, on the one hand, that outside of Paul's discussions of Gal 3 and Rom 4, Paul makes only four references to Abraham. In two of the texts (Gal 4.22 and Rom 9.7) Paul is offering further elaboration and nuancing of arguments he has already developed in response to Jewish messianist claims concerning the lack of gentile legitimacy. One suspects that had Gal 3 and Rom 4 and the Jewish messianist objections that gave rise to these chapters not been present, neither would Gal 4.22 and Rom 9.7. In the other two references, Rom 11.1 and 2 Cor 11.22, Paul is clearly using the reference "seed of Abraham" in a traditional sense to mean "Jew." This shows that the phrase does not always have the specially nuanced meaning that one would suspect from reading Rom 4 and Gal 3. Paul can use the term as would any Jew as a way of referring to Jews. It is important to note, however, that even in these latter two texts the argumentative context with Jewish messianists is still to be assumed: Rom 11.1 as a continuation of the argument of the whole of Rom and 2 Cor 11.22 as a statement against "false apostles" who are Jewish messianists of some sort.[45] The issue of descent from Abraham always arises from within a framework where, in some manner, Jewish messianists are

---

44 See Sanders, *Paul, the Law and the Jewish People,* 148-49 for a good summary of what the two chapters have in common.

45 "Are they Hebrews? So am I. Are they Israelites? So am I. Are they descendants of Abraham? So am I. Are they ministers of Christ? I am talking like a madman–I am a better one" (2 Cor 11.22-23a). That we are to take these descriptions to conclude that Paul's opponents are Jewish appears beyond serious dispute. See C. K. Barrett, *The Second Epistle to the Corinthians,* HNTC (New York: Harper and Row, 1973) 293-95.

initiating the conversation. It was, apparently, not a burning issue to Paul or his gentile readers.

On the other hand, abundant evidence exists that the issue of descent from Abraham and circumcision was of immense importance for Jews.[46] First, "the seed of Abraham is synonymous with the word Jew," as Sandmel so succinctly puts it.[47] The notion is deeply rooted in the biblical tradition (Ps 105.6; Isa 41.8) and is simply assumed in literature of the second temple period and beyond (e.g., 4 Macc 6.22; 18.1). Second, it was to Abraham's seed, the Jews, that the promises of God had been made. "You made an everlasting covenant with him [Abraham], and promised him that you would never forsake his descendants; and you gave him Isaac, and to Isaac you gave Jacob and Esau" (2 Esdr 3.16; cf. also Sir 44.21). Third, closely connected with the notion of being Abraham's seed and the heirs of the promise is the issue of law and obedience.[48] This indissoluble connection between God's chosen people and obedience to God's law is expressed most clearly in the Hebrew scriptures in Deuteronomy, which "provides the classic statement of Jewish covenant theology."[49] This connection was only more firmly made in the post-Exilic era as testimony from the spectrum of Jewish literature demonstrates.[50]

Being a Jew, a descendant of Abraham, and being obedient to the Torah were indissolubly connected. It was obedience to the Torah which marked a Jew as Jew—as one of God's people to whom the promises had been given. And it is in this framework that one must understand the importance of circumcision. Gen 17 made clear to many Jews of the second temple period and beyond that circumcision was *the* distinctive rite which confirmed the covenant made between God and Abraham and his descendants: "Everyone who is born, the flesh of whose foreskin is not circumcised on the eighth day, belongs not to the children of the covenant which the Lord made with

---

[46] Helpful bibliography includes Jeffrey Siker, "Abraham in Graeco-Roman Paganism," *JStJud* 18 (1987) 188-208; J. D. Cohen, "Crossing the Boundary and Becoming a Jew," *HTR* 82/1 (1989) 13-33; William Braude, *Jewish Proselytizing in the First Five Centuries of the Common Era: The Age of the Tannaim and Amoraim* (Providence: Brown University, 1940); Samuel Sandmel, *Philo's Place in Judaism: A Study of Conceptions of Abraham in Jewish Literature* (New York: KTAV, 1971); D. Harrington, "Abraham Traditions in the Testament of Abraham and in the 'Rewritten Bible' of the Intertestamental Period," in *Studies in the Testament of Abraham*, ed. G. W. Nickelsburg, Jr. (Missoula: Scholars Press, 1976); R. Ward, "Abraham Traditions in Early Christianity," *SBL Septuagint and Cognate Studies* 2 (1972) 165-79; J. D. G. Dunn, "What was the Issue between Paul and 'Those of the Circumcision'?" in *Paulus und das antike Judentum*, hrsg. Martin Hengel und Ulrich Heckel (Tübingen: J. C. B. Mohr [Paul Siebeck], 1991) 295-317.

[47] *Philo's Place*, 37.

[48] The short hand term to denote this relationship between God's covenantal promises and the obedience to Torah as Israel's means of remaining within the covenant is covenantal nomism, coined by E. P. Sanders, *Paul and Palestinian Judaism: A Comparison of Patterns of Religion* (Philadelphia: Fortress, 1977) and *Paul, the Law, and the Jewish People*. See Dunn's article (n 46) for a good summary and application of this thesis to the issue at hand.

[49] Dunn, "What Was the Issue?" 298.

[50] *Ibid*, 299.

Abraham, but to the children of destruction" (*Jub* 15.26). During the crisis of the Maccabean era, circumcision "became the test of covenant loyalty" (1 Macc 1.48, 60-61).[51] Even Philo, who insisted that the Mosaic law was but a copy of the higher law of nature insisted that literal obedience to the commandment of circumcision was necessary (*Mig* 89-94, esp 92).

It follows that gentiles who wished to become part of the covenant people would have to be circumcised. For gentiles who sympathized with Judaism it might be possible to be a part of God's people on the day of judgment, but for the present the gentile must accept circumcision if he wished to join the Jewish community.[52] Even then, the exact status of the proselyte was ambiguous. While Philo appealed to the Abraham narrative to legitimate the inclusion of the gentile into the Jewish community (*Virt.* 219), he also declared the proselyte to be inferior in nature (*Life of Moses* 1.27 § 147).[53] It was even debated among the rabbis whether proselytes could truly claim as their "fathers" the ancestors of Israel.[54]

There was no immediate reason for messianist Jews to assume that the coming of Jesus Messiah nullified the whole of their entire covenantal heritage.[55] Understanding this covenantal heritage allows one to understand why such messianist Jews would not believe that gentiles who were not circumcised could truly claim to be part of God's covenant people. A religious disposition which viewed circumcision as the sign of covenantal loyalty and which, in some circles, was inclined not to be fully inclusive even of the proselyte could very easily reject any claims that uncircumcised gentiles (non-Jews) were heirs of any kind of salvation which had to do with promises made in the Hebrew scriptures. They would see such claims to salvation as having to be realized in the context of the promises made to Abraham and his seed. It would be *they* who would raise objections to Paul's inclusive gospel and insist on circumcision to legitimate the status of the gentile believers.

The thesis of this portion of the paper, therefore, is quite simple. While Paul was capable of legitimating the status of gentile believers by showing them to be descendants of Abraham, this was not to him or his gentile followers an intrinsically significant argument for such legitimation. It became an issue to the gentile believers of Galatia only after Jewish messianists brought this particular understanding of the covenantal tradition to their attention. It was an issue in Rome only because Jewish messianists were reluctant to be fully

---

51 *Ibid*, 304.

52 Cohen, "Crossing the Boundary," *HTR* 82: 27.

53 Here Philo refers to certain pilgrims of the Exodus as "children of Egyptian women by Hebrew fathers." He describes this lot as a "promiscuous, non-descript and menial crowd, a bastard host." LCL trans.

54 Braude, *Jewish Proselytizing*, 80-81.

55 For some good and empathetic discussions of what may very well have motivated the "Judaizers" to insist on circumcision of the gentiles see Heikki Räisänen, *Paul and the Law* (Philadelphia: Fortress, 1986) 183-84 and E. P. Sanders, *Paul* (New York: Oxford University Press, 1991) 49-64.

inclusive of gentile believers. For the gentiles themselves other phenomena served to legitimate their existence, among which would be the Spirit.[56]

The Seed of Abraham in Luke-Acts

The method for comparing Luke-Acts with Paul on the issue of descent from Abraham as a means of legitimating gentile believers will be first, to examine the data, noting who speaks of Abraham and the ancestors and their descendants, the speakers' audiences in the story, and about whom the speaker speaks as he or she refers to Abraham's (and the ancestors') descendants. The discussion shall regularly have an eye to question, "Does Luke-Acts think of gentile believers as descendants of Abraham?" Second, I shall offer some discussion concerning what the agenda of the implied author appears to be in relation to this issue. Third, I shall offer some suggestions concerning the implied reader and the social location of this reader

In examining the motif of descent from Abraham in the Paul of Luke-Acts, I shall not begin with the scenes where Paul plays a role. Paul does not appear as a character until about a third of the way through Acts, by which time the reader has already encountered much relating to descent from Abraham— textual information likely to shape how she or he understands what the character Paul has to say about the issue. Thus, I shall begin at the beginning of the narrative.

The Data. The reader first hears of Abraham and his descendants through the voice of Mary (Lk 1.54-55). The reader may conclude that she is Jewish, for she is said to be engaged to a man from the house of David (1.27), to be related to Elizabeth (1.36), who is from a priestly family (1.5), and clearly her God is the God of the Jews (1.30-33). This Jewish woman, speaking in the hearing of another Jewish woman, Elizabeth (1.39-46a), makes reference to "our ancestors, to Abraham and his seed." Reference to God's "servant Israel" in 1.54a offers clear definition of who is meant by the ancestors, consisting of both Abraham and his seed: Israel. The speaker is Jewish. The audience is Jewish. The referent is the Jews (Israel).

The Jewish priest Zechariah, speaking in the context of the Jewish circumcision ceremony of his son (1.59) which is attended by his neighbors (1.65) who are presumably Jews, makes reference both to "our ancestors" (1.72a) and "Abraham our ancestor" and the promise and covenant which God had made with them. This promise is now finding fulfillment for "the

---

[56] It would be far beyond the scope of this paper to move into this issue. But it is interesting that Paul refers to the Spirit as the ἀρραβών (guarantee) of the believer's salvation (2 Cor 1.22, 5.5) and seems to assume in many of his letters that he can refer to the reality of the Spirit as the basis for developing arguments (cf. Rom 8.9ff.; 1 Cor 12-14). Even in Gal 3, Paul *begins* the argument by appealing to what is apparently an agreed upon criterion of legitimation: the Spirit. Further, he continues to move the Abraham argument along this same pneumatic track, trying to convince the Galatians that the Spirit they know they have received is the real fulfillment of the promise that God made to Abraham. See Sam K. Williams, "*Promise* in Galatians: A Reading of Paul's Reading of Scripture," *JBL* 107/4 (1988) 709-20.

Lord God of Israel . . . has looked favorably on his people and redeemed them" (1.68). The speaker is Jewish. The audience is Jewish. The referent is the Jews.

John, son of the Jewish priest Zechariah, is the next character to make reference to Abraham and his children (3.7-9). His audience is the crowds who had come out to be baptized by him. This crowd consists of persons who, John can assume, claim descent from Abraham (3.8). Given what the reader knows to this point that means that John's audience consists of Jews. What exactly is meant by John's statement that God can raise up from stones children to Abraham is not made clear. What is made clear is that merely being a child of Abraham is not sufficient to escape "the imminently coming wrath" (1.7); one must "produce fruits worthy of repentance" (1.8). The speaker is Jewish. The audience is Jewish. The referent is the Jews, though the reader hears for the first time that being Jewish does not ensure salvation from God's judgment.

In 3.34 the narrator for the first and only time speaks with his own voice in reference to Abraham. The context is Jesus' genealogy. Jesus is a descendant of Abraham, though Luke clearly does not specify the point with the clarity that Matthew does (Matt 1.1). It cannot at this point be determined whether the speaker (narrator) and audience (reader) are Jewish. The referent (Jesus) is clearly Jewish; something the reader already knew simply given the whole thrust of Lk 1-2.

In the remainder of the gospel only Jesus and characters who speak in stories he is narrating will speak of Abraham, the ancestors, and his or their descendants. The first reference is found in Lk 6.23, 26. Jesus' audience consists most immediately of his disciples (6.20). Readers have no reason not to assume that they are Jewish, an assumption which is never challenged in the subsequent narrative. The indirect audience consists of "a great multitude of people from all Judea, Jerusalem, and the coast of Tyre and Sidon" (1.17). The reader has no reason not to conclude that the people from Judea and Jerusalem are Jewish. S/he might not be clear about those from the coast lands. The phrase in 7.1 ("the hearing of the people" [λαός]) indicates that the implied author is thinking primarily of Jews as Jesus' secondary audience, given that he consistently uses λαός to denote Jewish people.[57] Hence, one can conclude that Jesus is speaking to Jews.

In the context of this discourse, he makes reference not to "your ancestors" but to "their ancestors" (6.23, 26). In both instances he is speaking of the ancestors of those who hate you on account of the Son of Man (v. 22) or speak well of you who are rich, full, and laughing (vv. 24-26). These ancestors are described as having treated badly "the prophets" (v. 23) and well "the false prophets" (v. 26). Whoever these ancestors were precisely, Jesus is making reference to persons who live in the Jewish scriptures, as their treatment of true and false prophets indicates. Jesus is indicating to his Jewish listeners that there exists a group who will persecute his followers who find their ancestors among those persons of the scriptures who dealt unjustly with the prophets. Might this imply that *within* the broader circle of the ancestors of the Jews

---

57 Many have made this observation. See, e.g., my discussion in *Jerusalem, the Temple, and the New Age in Luke-Acts* (Macon: Mercer University Press, 1988) 61.

there exists a smaller circle of persons who are the ancestors of those who persecute followers of Jesus? Subsequent texts will bear this out. In this passage the speaker and the audience are Jewish. The exact referent of "their ancestors" is not known—but these "ancestors" live in the Jewish scriptures as persecutors of Israel's prophets. This implies that they too are Israelites.

The next reference which Jesus makes to "ancestors" is 11.47-48. His audience is Jewish, specifically Pharisees (v. 42) and "lawyers" (v. 45), with the latter denoting his immediate audience. It is to this audience that Jesus makes reference to "your ancestors." These ancestors are described as those who killed the prophets (11.47-48), linking this saying with that of 6.23, 26. These lawyers and Pharisees are clearly Jewish, hence are descendants of Abraham. The reader suspects that they are of that lot of whom John the Baptist spoke: those who will not escape the wrath of God.[58] Yet these characters also find their ancestry in a sub-group of Israel's ancestors: the group which killed the prophets.

Lk 13.16 offers Jesus' first explicit reference to Abraham. Here Jesus addresses a Jewish audience—note the synagogue setting (13.10) and, most especially, the leader of the synagogue (vv. 14-15). Jesus refers to the woman whom he has healed as a "daughter of Abraham" (v. 16). There is no hint that she is not Jewish.

Later in chap 13 Jesus again refers to Abraham, and adds Isaac and Jacob as well as all the prophets (13.22-30 [esp v. 28]). He is addressing an anonymous audience, the inhabitants of various cities and villages (13.22) through which he passes on the way to Jerusalem. Jesus has only recently (in terms of reading time) left the synagogue and Pharisees are introduced as being on the scene in the very next pericope (within an hour in terms of story time). All of this implies a Jewish setting and audience for the pericope in question. In this context Jesus speaks of the ancestors who will participate in the kingdom and of those of his hearers who will be cast out. Reference is made to others who will take their place at the table. As to whether these others are Jewish or gentile is not immediately clear. Later in Acts, the reader learns that those "who are far off" can refer to gentiles (cf. Acts 22.21), and this retrospect might inform this passage. But these persons who come from the four corners of the earth are *not* described as descendants of Abraham in this pericope.

In Lk 16.24-31 Jesus offers several references to Abraham and his children, all through the voice of the character of the rich man, traditionally named Dives. Jesus' audience is Jewish, the Pharisees (16.14). Dives' audience is Abraham himself. Dives is Jewish, as indicated by his continued appeal to Abraham as his father (16.24, 27, 30). Abraham does not reject the appellation, for he refers to Dives as "child" (τέκνον [v 25]). Readers unarmed with concordances might not know with certainty that in only one other place thus far have τέκνον and Abraham occurred in the same context: John the Baptist's declaration that not all children of Abraham will escape the wrath of God, but only those who bear fruits worthy of repentance (3.7-14). Still, attentive

---

58 This seems particularly likely given the encounter between Jesus and the Pharisees chap 7, esp. 7.29-30, 36-50.

readers, even without such precise knowledge, should recall the Baptist's warning. In the context of the Baptist's warning, Dives serves as an example of a Jew, a child of Abraham, who suffers punishment for failure to bear fruits of repentance. The Dives text makes clear that in the Lukan story world one who is judged by God—sentenced even to Hades—can be thought of as a child of Abraham. "Descendant of Abraham" is not a term reserved for "the saved." To this point in the story at least, it is a term reserved for Jews—saved or damned.

Jesus' last reference to a "son of Abraham" is found in 19.9. Jesus' audience is not specifically identified, beyond the assumption that it is the residents of Jericho (18.35; 19.1). However, in 18.43 Luke has made reference to the λαός, implying a Jewish audience. There is nothing in the story to imply that Zacchaeus is not Jewish. The reader has already met persons who were designated as "children of Abraham" who were also tax collectors (Lk 3.12-13). In fact this story, like that of Dives, harks back to the Baptist's preaching. Whereas Dives represents a child of Abraham destined for judgment, as an example of one who had food and refused to share with the one who had none (cf. Lk 3.11; 16.19-21), Zacchaeus represents a child of Abraham who repents, specifically who, henceforth, will collect no more taxes than the lawful amount (cf. Lk 3.12). This is a child of Abraham who will experience salvation.

In the book of Acts, the reader first encounters Abraham and the ancestors in Peter's speech of 3.12-26, specifically in 3.13 and 25. In the first reference Peter speaks of the God of Abraham, Isaac, Jacob, and our ancestors. In the latter text Peter refers to his audience as "the children (υἱοί) of the prophets and the covenant which God made with your [59] ancestors saying to Abraham, 'And in your seed all the families of the earth shall be blessed.'" Peter's audience is Jewish, as indicated by his salutation in v. 12: ἄνδρες Ισραηλῖται. Peter, of course, is Jewish. The ancestors of whom he speaks are the ancestors of a Jewish group; the seed of these ancestors through whom all the families will be blessed (v. 25) is Jewish as well, whether one understands this seed to be the Jew Jesus or the Jews as a people.[60]

In Acts 5.30 Peter makes a second reference to "the God of our ancestors." His audience is the council (v. 27) which consisted of the high priest and the whole body of the elders of Israel (v. 21). Is Peter intending to exclude his

---

59 There is a textual problem here, with some mss. saying "our ancestors" (see Nestle-Aland 26). The use of "your" here should not raise the suspicion that Peter is referring to that subset of ancestors who killed the prophets (cf. Lk 6.23,26; 11.47-48). There no pejorative connotation as in other instances of "your ancestors," a number of which references are yet to come. The immediate context makes clear that in this text "your ancestors" are represented by Abraham.

60 Interpreters debate this issue. E.g., Donald Juel understands the "seed" to refer to Christ. See *Messianic Exegesis: Christological Interpretation of the Old Testament in Early Christianity* (Philadelphia: Fortress, 1988) 82-85. Others view the seed of Abraham as a reference to the Jewish people. See, e.g., Jacob Jervell, *Luke and the People of God: A New Look at Luke-Acts* (Minneapolis: Augsburg, 1972) 58-60 and J. Dupont, "Salvation of the Gentiles," in *The Salvation of the Gentiles: Essays in the Acts of the Apostles*, trans John R. Keating (New York: Paulist, 1979) 23.

listeners from the "our" of "our ancestors," implying that these Jewish leaders who oppose the followers of Jesus cannot claim the patriarchs as their ancestors? That is, does Peter mean by "*our* ancestors" the "true Jews' ancestors"—the ancestors of those who follow Jesus (cf. Acts 3.23)? If that is his point, we can only conclude that the narrator is extremely subtle. But even if this point is conceded, Peter is only *excluding* the Jewish leadership from the seed of the ancestors—he is not *including* any gentiles.

The Stephen speech is by far the richest in reference to Abraham and the ancestors, with the phrase "our ancestors" occurring seven times (7.11, 12, 15, 38, 38, 44, 45). Though there is some debate as to whether Stephen and the other Hellenist leaders were Jewish or gentile believers, the consensus of readers sees them as Jewish.[61] Stephen's accusers are clearly Jewish, being described as belonging to the synagogue of the Freedmen (6.9) and, a bit later in the narrative, "the people and the elders and the scribes" and even "the council" (6.12). Finally, Stephen refers to his audience as ἄνδρες ἀδελφοὶ καὶ πατέρες (7.1). Given Stephen's salutation, it strains the reading of the text to conclude that Stephen would *not* be including in the "our" of "our ancestors" his listeners—even though they are clearly not believers. The point, quite simply, is that Stephen can assume that Jews—be they messianist Jews or not—can view the patriarchs as their ancestors. Quite clearly, there is no hint that Stephen is including gentiles of any sort, believers or non-believers, among the descendants of the patriarchs—gentiles are simply not in view when Stephen speaks of the ancestors. Jews are the descendants of the patriarchs, the ones to whom the covenant of circumcision had been given (7.8); the ones who rejected Joseph (v. 9); the ones who did not obey Moses (v. 39). This speech is most telling in that it indicates that neither "the ancestors" nor their "seed" are code words to denote the truly faithful within Israel. It is a term, a neutral term, to denote the ethnic progenitors of Stephen's Jewish audience.

Toward the end of the speech there is a significant shift of pronoun. Stephen makes reference to "your ancestors" (7.51-52). These ancestors are said to have persecuted and killed the prophets. This immediately reminds readers of Lk 6.23, 26 and 11.47-48, where reference was made to "their" or "your ancestors" who persecuted and killed prophets. The descendants of this sub-group of Israelites of old are those who in Luke's story time persecute and kill Jesus and his followers. In Luke, and again here in Acts, these descendants are Jews. Among the Israelites of old and contemporaneous with the characters of Luke-Acts there are those who persecute and kill God's people. This does not preclude them from being included in the descendants of Abraham or the ancestors. But they clearly form a special group within this larger group called Israel.

---

[61]E.g., Martin Hengel, *Acts and the History of Earliest Christianity*, trans John Bowden (Philadelphia: Fortress, 1980) 71-80; Hans Conzelmann, *Die Apostelgeschichte* (Tübingen: J. C. B. Mohr, 1963) 43. The notable exception, of course, is H. J. Cadbury, "The Hellenists," in *BC*, ed. Jackson and Lake (repr., Grand Rapids: Baker, 1979; original date: 1932) 5: 59-74.

Before turning our attention to Paul in Acts I shall summarize the results thus far. To this point in the narrative, the reader understands a descendant of Abraham or the ancestors to be one of the people of Israel—a Jew. The reader also has learned that being Jewish as such does not spare one from the coming wrath of God; one must bear fruits of repentance as aptly illustrated negatively by Dives and positively by Zacchaeus. The reader has also learned of another group of ancestors who have their own descendants: those who killed the prophets of the Jewish scriptures. The descendants of these ancestors are those who in Luke's story persecute and kill the followers of Jesus (Lk 6.23; Acts 7.54-8.1) and even Jesus himself (Acts 7.52). Specific representatives of this group are the Pharisees and lawyers (11.47-48), though one learns explicitly from the Stephen episode that any Jew can be a descendant of this sub-group of persecuting ancestors (see Acts 6.12; 7.51-53). Further, thus far the reader has encountered nothing of Paul's argument that persons other than Jews can be called "descendants of Abraham" on the basis of their faith. Perhaps John's statement concerning God's ability to raise up children of Abraham from stones raised an expectation that another group, perhaps non-Jewish, would arise to become "children of Abraham." Thus far, nothing in the story satisfies this expectation. Perhaps, if ever raised in the first place, this expectation is already forgotten by this point. If not, the reader will continue to look for the satisfaction of this expectation in the remainder of Acts.

Paul first makes reference to Abraham and the ancestors in his speech of Antioch of Pisidia (Acts 13.17-41). One reads, "Men, Israelites and those who fear God, listen: The God of this people Israel chose our ancestors and exalted the people . . . " (13.16b-17a). One reads later in the speech a similar statement. "Men, brothers, sons of the kindred (γένους) of Abraham and (?) those among you who fear God, to you the word of this salvation has been sent" (13.26). The antecedent of "our ancestors" in 13.16b-17a is clearly ʾΙσραηλῖται καὶ οἱ φοβούμενοι. The question is whether ʾΙσραηλῖται καὶ οἱ φοβούμενοι form two groups or one, i.e., is the καί copulative or epexegetical? If the latter then "those who fear God" further defines the Israelites. If the former then those who fear God are apparently non-Israelites who can be included in the "our" of "our ancestors." The issue cannot be resolved without appeal to 13.26. Here Paul refers to "men, brothers, sons of the kindred of Abraham (= the ancestors of 13.16b) καὶ οἱ ἐν ὑμῖν φοβούμενοι τὸν θεόν. The omission of the καί in some mss (p[45], B) would render the impression that "those among you who fear God" do not refer to a different group than "sons of the kindred of Abraham." Even the inclusion of the καί could still render such a reading if the καί is understood epexegetically. If the καί is understood copulatively "those among you who fear God" would be a group in addition to the "sons of the kindred of Abraham."

To my way of thinking the "among you" would give favor to the copulative reading. Unless the implied author wishes to make the subtle distinction between "the sons of the kindred of Abraham" and a sub-group "among [them] who (actually) fear God," it seems easiest to read the "God-fearers" as a group closely related to the "sons of the kindred of Abraham" but not identical to them. If this is the case, then it is clear that Paul speaks of two groups in v. 26: "sons of the kindred of Abraham" and "those who fear God."

That would imply that those whom Paul is addressing in 13.16b would also be two groups: "Israelites and those who fear God." Interestingly, however, Paul appears to include both groups when he makes reference to "our ancestors" in v. 17, in tension with v. 26 which clearly distinguishes between the "sons of the kindred of Abraham" and "those who fear God." By the time the reader gets to 13.32-33 any distinction between the Israelites and those who fear God seems forgotten. "And we preach to you the promise made to the ancestors, that this [promise] God fulfilled to the children, to us, having resurrected Jesus . . ." (13.32-33a). Here the reader would perhaps again assume that "the children, us" includes Paul's whole audience, the Israelites and those who fear God.

The crux, of course, is whether the Paul of Acts can include among the descendants of Abraham and the ancestors persons other than Israelites. The following observations are relevant with respect to this text. One, Paul (and, implicitly, his authorial creator) does not appear to be aiming at precision. In one text he appears to include "those who fear God" among the descendants of the ancestors (16b-17a) while in another he does not (13.26). Then again, near the conclusion of the speech, he once again appears to include "those who fear God" among "the children." Two, Paul is not portrayed as being interested in making any profound point concerning the relationship of "those who fear God" to Abraham and the ancestors. The issue of this speech is not the status of "those who fear God" in relation to Abraham—it is about God keeping his promise to the ancestors and their children. Finally, at the end of the story explicit reference is made to gentiles who come to believe Paul's message (13.48). Absolutely nothing is said by either Paul or the narrator concerning the relationship of these gentiles to the ancestors of Israel.

The point in summation is this: this speech of Paul's is the closest thing the reader has thus far observed which implies that persons other than Jews can be included among the descendants of Abraham. Perhaps it is significant that it is found on the lips of Paul, the character inspired by the historical Paul who really did include gentiles in the seed of Abraham. Yet the evidence in Acts is not all that clear. The very lack of precision indicates that no argument is being made to legitimate non-Jewish believers by incorporating them into the seed of Abraham. I suspect that a reader, conditioned to this point in the narrative to understand talk of the ancestors and their descendants as talk about Israelites of old and Jews of story world of Luke-Acts, might not even pause to the degree that this critical reader has. The barest hint that I, through close critical reading, have detected of the inclusion of non-Jewish "God-fearers" among the descendants of Abraham is probably the result of critical over-kill. To the more casual, even if attentive, reader no point, I suspect, would be made regarding the relationship of non-Jewish people to Abraham and the other ancestors.

With the exception of Acts 15.10, all other references to Abraham and/or the ancestors come from Paul. In Acts 15.10, however, Peter offers one last word. All the characters at this Jerusalem meeting are Jewish—Jewish messianists to be sure, but Jewish nonetheless. The topic of discussion is the legitimacy of the gentile believers. Must they be circumcised and follow the law of Moses (Acts 15.5)? That is, must they become Jews? The Jewish messianists who take this position do not relate their demands to the explicit incorporation of the gentile believers into the seed of Abraham. Perhaps one could conclude that *de jure* such persons would, indeed, become children of Abraham. But the advocates for circumcision and Torah observance are not the least bit interested in bolstering their case by any explicit appeal to the covenant of circumcision which God made with the ancestors and demanded of the ancestors' seed. It is only Peter who refers to "our ancestors" (15.10) and he does so quite casually as a way of referring to the ancestors of himself and his Jewish (messianist) audience. In short, no one is the least bit interested in explicitly incorporating the gentile believers into the seed of Abraham.

In 22.3 and 14 Paul makes reference to the ancestors. His audience is clearly Jewish (21.40; 22.1). It is to this audience that Paul makes reference to "the ancestral law" (τοῦ πατρῴου νόμου) (22.3). Within this speech Paul offers a narrative about Ananias, described by Paul as a "devout man according to the law." This devout Jew, according to Paul's narration, is said to have spoken to Paul about "the God of our ancestors" (22.14). The speakers (Paul in Luke's narrative and Ananias in Luke's narrative of Paul's narrative) and the audiences (the Jewish masses and Paul) are all Jewish. It is Jews talking to Jews who speak of the ancestors.

In the context of two further defense speeches Paul again makes reference to "our ancestors." In the first, the immediate audience is Felix (24.14). It is clear from the context that by "our" Paul means himself and his Jewish accusers—not Felix. In the other defense speech Paul is speaking to Agrippa. Paul speaks of Agrippa as one "familiar with all the customs and controversies of the Jews" (26.3), though whether Paul assumes Agrippa to be a Jew is not clear.[62] Given that Paul makes reference to "our religion"(26.5), "our ancestors" (26.6) and "the twelve tribes" (26.7) in the context of speaking about charges Jews have made against him, it is easiest to understand the "our" again as referring to Paul and his accusers—specifically identified as "the Jews" (26.4).

Paul's final references to the "ancestors" occurs in his final words addressed to the leadership of the Jewish community of Rome. In 28.17 Paul speaks of the "customs of the ancestors." Paul's final reference offers an ominous note when he says to his Jewish audience, "The Holy Spirit was right in saying to your ancestors through the prophet Isaiah. . . " (28.25). What follows are the sharp words condemning the people's inability to understand, hear, and see. Paul does not speak of "our ancestors" but of "your ancestors." We have seen elsewhere in Luke-Acts[63] that when this distinction is made, reference is being made to that sub-group of ancient Israelites who represent

---

62 Paul's comment about Agrippa's being well versed in Judaism would not be challenged by informed readers familiar with Agrippa's reputation. He was known as one who dialogued with the Rabbis, required circumcision of his brothers-in-law, and watched closely over temple procedures (this even to the priests' chagrin). See Schürer, rev. ed., 1: 471-83. Within the story world of Acts, Paul's comment does not seem to imply the assumption that Agrippa is Jewish, however. A practitioner of a religion is generally not described by a fellow practitioner as one "familiar with the customs . . . of the Jews."

63 Excepting Acts 3.25.

the persecutors and killers of God's prophets—the ancestors of those who reject and kill Jesus and his followers. These rebellious ancestors are those with whom the concluding words of Acts associate the Jews.

The conclusion is clear: Paul blends in with the other characters and offers no distinctive point of view with reference to Abraham and the ancestors; they denote the ancestors of the Jews, the Jews are the ancestors' seed. It is in Luke-Acts a way almost *exclusively* for Jews to talk to and about other Jews and their ethnic ancestors, the only exceptions being in Paul's defense speeches before Felix and possibly Agrippa. To be sure, to be a descendant of Abraham and the ancestors does not ensure salvation from God's wrath—one must bear fruits worthy of repentance. In Acts that translates into believing in Jesus (e.g., Acts 2.38; 3.19-23). Save for the possible exception of Acts 13.16-17, no character in Luke-Acts nor the narrator when speaking in his own voice refer to gentiles as children, seed, descendants, sons, daughters, or any other similar term of Abraham or any of the other ancestors of Israel. The seed of Abraham is the Jewish people. The gentiles are simply not in view. Any possible expectation regarding gentile inclusion into Abraham's seed raised by the Baptist's declaration that God could raise up children to Abraham from stones is now dissipated. Whatever the Baptist meant, it was directed at Jews. It offered no word on gentile identity.

The agenda of the implied author. This is not to say that our implied author is not interested in legitimating the gentile believers as God's *people*. Acts 15 is especially concerned with this issue (see esp. 15.14). Here James refers back to Peter's immediately preceded speech (15.7-11). In Peter's short speech he summarized the two legitimating criteria of the gentiles emphasized by the narrative of Acts 10-11. One, God has given the Holy Spirit to the gentiles (15.8; cf. 10.44-47; 11.15-17); two, God has "cleansed" the gentiles, making no distinction between them and the Jews (15.9; cf. 10.15, 28; 11.9). No attempt is made, however, in these texts to argue for the legitimation of the gentiles by appeal to their descent from Abraham or the ancestors.

The Jewish messianist characters of Acts 15.1-6 are reminiscent of the Jewish messianists with whom Paul had to deal in Galatians and Romans. In the case of both, gentile legitimation came with circumcision and Torah observance. In Acts, however, the Jewish messianists make no reference to the Abraham connection, an important element of the historical Paul's Jewish messianist opponents. Luke creates a story world which implies that he is aware of attempts to demand gentile legitimation vis-à-vis proselytism to Judaism. It is clear that our implied author rejects any attempt to legitimate gentiles by requiring them to become Jews. This point of view is espoused in his story by only minor, anonymous characters who are not portrayed all that sympathetically—especially since they are identified with Pharisees.[64] However, Luke's story world implies no awareness of attempts to legitimate gentiles vis-à-vis descent from Abraham.

---

[64] I find John Darr's characterization of the Pharisees a persuasive reading. See *On Character Building: The Reader and the Rhetoric of Characterization in Luke-Acts* (Louisville: Westminster/John Knox, 1992) 85-126.

Major, sympathetic, and credible characters, Peter and James in Acts 10, 11, and 15, legitimate the gentiles by other means: by declaring what God has done (Peter) and by interpreting scripture in view of what God as done (James). They, too, make no attempt to offer gentile legitimation vis-à-vis descent from Abraham.

In short, our implied author speaks of a world where 1) Jews, be they headed for salvation or damnation, are thought of as descendants of Abraham; 2) gentiles are legitimated as God's people vis-à-vis the Spirit and cleansing offered by God; 3) Jewish messianists wish to legitimate gentiles vis-à-vis circumcision and law observance, presumably "conversion to Judaism"; 4) no characters on any side of the gentile debate are concerned to legitimate gentiles vis-à-vis descent from Abraham. What does this imply about his social location and reading audience?

The implied audience of Luke-Acts. For this section of the essay I shall appeal to the work of other readers and interpreters, most especially the contributors to Neyrey's volume and Joseph Tyson.[65]

The former offer a view of Luke's social location by focusing on a model of reading which Neyrey calls the scenario model. This model assumes that meaning in texts is formulated within a broad social framework in which "a full and verifiable grasp of how the world works" is operative.[66] It is quite similar to what Darr refers to as the "extratext" that informs readers—in this case the extratext of "original" readers.[67]

Two essays in the Neyrey volume are particularly apropos to this study, one by Neyrey and another by Vernon Robbins.[68] Neyrey's essay on the symbolic universe of Luke-Acts detects a concern by the text of Luke-Acts to address the objection that the Jewish world was being subverted by "Christian" (*sic*) missionaries. He notes in Luke-Acts an awareness of and familiarity with *Jewish* systems of purity and ordering of the world, including people, places, and even the body. Luke-Acts offers a new definition of such models of purity and order, yet within a framework in conversation with traditional Jewish understandings of such. One quotation illustrates well Neyrey's observations:

> Nevertheless, two radically different perspectives existed on the way the universe was ordered. The impulse to order was strong in both cases. It should be noted that Luke and the early Christians in one sense affirmed the basic elements of Israel's system of order and purity, namely, faith in the God of Israel and belief in God's scriptures. The different perceptions both of God and the scriptures account for the

---

65 Jerome H. Neyrey, ed. *The Social World of Luke-Acts: Models for Interpretation* (Peabody, MA: Hendrickson, 1991). Joseph B. Tyson, *Images of Judaism in Luke-Acts* (Columbia: University of South Carolina Press, 1992).

66 Bruce Malina, "Reading Theory Perspective: Reading Luke-Acts," in *Social World*, 15.

67 *Character Building*, esp. 20-23.

68 J. Neyrey, "The Symbolic Universe of Luke-Acts: 'They Turn the World Upside Down,'" *Social World*, 271-304; V. Robbins, "The Social Location of the Implied Author of Luke-Acts," *Social World*, 305-332.

different configuration of lines, boundaries, and classifications. Observant Jews labelled them as revolutionaries, while Christians claimed to be authentic reformers. The decisive conflict centered around the "correct" interpretation of the tradition.[69]

In short, Luke-Acts operates from within a social context which stands very close to traditional Judaism, though not identical with it.

Observations offered by Robbins place the social context of the implied author of Luke-Acts in a similar sphere. He makes three conclusions which are particularly pertinent.[70] One, "the cultural achievement represented by Luke-Acts reflects a Jewish sphere of society using the Greek language, the lingua franca of the Mediterranean world." Two, "the presence of foreign affairs has created a view that the affairs of Israelites, Jews, and Christians, are 'foreign' to the dominant population in the Mediterranean world." Three, "in the arena of belief systems and ideologies, the thought of the implied author appears to challenge the dominant Jewish purity system at its center. The thought in Luke-Acts celebrates diversity and claims that God has 'cleansed' it. In this way, the thought of the implied author claims to be an authentic part of the heterogeneous population of the Roman Empire."

These conclusions point to a social location which cannot think of itself in categories foreign to Judaism and its traditions. Yet the implied social location clearly appears to reach beyond the boundaries of traditional Judaism, wishing to be more fully integrated into the larger Roman culture, but not yet there.

Joseph Tyson's study in quest of the implied reader points us, I believe, to a similar social location. He concludes an early portion of his study by stating that "the most significant aspect of this profile is the claim that the implied reader is familiar with the Hebrew Scriptures and knowledgeable about some fundamental Jewish concepts but is probably not to be identified as Jewish. . . . In major respects, this reader is similar to those characters in Acts that are called 'God-fearers.'"[71] Tyson defines such a person as "a Gentile who is positively attracted to Judaism but has not made a total commitment by accepting circumcision and the obligations of Torah."[72]

While Tyson is quite hesitant to offer too firm a conclusion about real authorial intent, he does say that "some judgment can be made about the probable purpose of the implied author and the probable effect of Luke-Acts on the implied reader."[73] Luke shows the reader "that what is good about Judaism may be found in Christianity without the burden of circumcision and full Torah obedience."[74] "[W]e may say that the purpose of Luke-Acts is to

---

69 "Symbolic Universe," 299.

70 "Implied Author," all quotations are from p. 332.

71 *Images of Judaism*, 36.

72 *Ibid.*, 181.

73 *Ibid.*, 181-82.

74 *Ibid.*, 182.

persuade God-fearers to accept the Christian message about Jesus rather than accepting Judaism."[75]

Tyson's reading of "social location" of the implied reader appears to square with than of Neyrey and Robbins: a reader closely associated with Judaism, but who does not identify totally with it. That is, a gentile who is a Jewish sympathizer and who, thus, very much understands his or her world in the context of Jewish ways of thinking. This reader, however, has a larger vision of the boundaries of his or her world. Jewish categories are meaningful, but not exhaustive for self- and world-definition.

Conclusion: Correlations

How does our implied author compare with Paul on the issue of gentile legitimation? Perhaps it is significant that the only text in Luke-Acts which even hints at the inclusion of some group other than Jews being thought of as descendants of Abraham is found on Paul's lips (Acts 13.16-17). But save for this questionable exception, the Paul of Acts shares the same point of view as the other characters of Acts: only Jews are descendants of Abraham. On the surface, this offers a perspective clearly different from that of the Paul of the authentic epistles. In Gal and Rom this Paul argues that gentile believers are the seed of Abraham, though with nuances.

Beneath the surface, however, the two show more in common. I argued above that Paul's arguments to legitimate the gentiles vis-à-vis descent from Abraham were in *response* to Jewish messianist claims that gentiles be so legitimated. It was not a matter of intrinsic concern either to Paul or his gentile followers. In Acts Paul nor anyone else argues that gentiles are descendants of Abraham. But also in Acts no Jewish messianist argues that gentiles need to be so legitimated. Unlike the situation of the epistolary Paul, the issue is never raised by the Jewish messianist characters of Acts. Keeping in mind that such Jewish messianist characters are creations of our author, this implies that for the author of Luke-Acts gentile legitimation vis-à-vis descent from Abraham is an issue about which he is either unaware or unconcerned. If Luke is simply unaware of or unconcerned with this specific argument of gentile legitimation, what does this imply about his social location and reading audience?

Luke's understanding of Jews as the descendants of Abraham combined with his apparent ignorance of or lack of interest in legitimizing gentiles (including gentiles sympathetic with Judaism) vis-à-vis their descent from Abraham, complements the conclusions regarding the social location of Luke's readers offered by the above interpreters. If our reading of the epistolary Paul and his situation is valid, we may conclude that neither Paul nor gentiles were intrinsically interested in legitimizing gentiles vis-à-vis their descent from Abraham. Other phenomena legitimized Paul's readers, the Spirit being a primary mark of legitimacy. We note the same in Luke-Acts: descent from Abraham as a mark of gentile legitimacy is not our author's concern; other phenomena, the Spirit being most important, legitimate the gentiles.

---

[75] *Ibid.*

Paul was capable of arguing for the descent of gentile believers from Abraham when it was necessary for him to do so because Jewish messianists argued against gentile legitimacy. What might it imply about Luke's social situation that gentile legitimacy was not conceived of, even by minor antagonistic characters, in terms of descent from Abraham? First, and most obviously, Luke's social context is not that of the Jewish messianists whom Paul opposed. Luke clearly does not advocate gentile legitimacy vis-à-vis descent from Abraham. Second, Luke's social context seems removed from Jewish messianists who made such arguments. Was Luke so removed because Jewish messianist opponents such as those Paul faced a generation earlier had simply disappeared from the scene? Or were they still present but only so marginally related to the Lukan situation that no response to them was necessary? Or were they present in Luke's time but so thoroughly marginalized from Luke's situation that he was unaware of them? The conclusion seems the same regardless of how one might address the questions specifically: Jewish messianist insistence on gentile descent from Abraham is a non-issue in Luke's context. Jewish messianists of the like with whom Paul had to deal a generation earlier are not Luke's primary audience nor do they appear to be his primary antagonists.

Descendants of Abraham are the Jews in Luke's world. No particular salvific status is associated with such descent as the Baptist's opening words make clear and as the subsequent narrative of Luke-Acts demonstrates. In Luke's world, it is important to be one of God's people and it is important to know that the story of Jesus and his followers fulfills God's promises made to the ancestors of the Jews in the Jewish scriptures. But is not important that Abraham be one's ancestor. This would appear to complement an audience similar to that described by Tyson. Luke's reader finds significance in having his or her identity confirmed by Jewish scriptures, including promises made to the Jewish ancestors in these scriptures. That points to a reader *sympathetic* with Judaism. But Luke's reader apparently has no interest in *being* a descendant of Abraham. If our study of Paul sheds any light, this could very well point to a *gentile* audience, for we saw there that Paul's gentile readers were not all that intrinsically interested in being children of Abraham—it was Jewish messianists who raised this concern. Luke's reader's lack of concern with being a child of Abraham may point, therefore, to a gentile reader who, like most gentiles of his time, knew there was a connection between the Jews and Abraham[76] but like the gentiles of his time, did not think it important to be such a descendant. Hence, a gentile sympathetic with

---

[76] According to J. Siker, "Abraham in Graeco-Roman Paganism," *JStJud* 18 (1987) 188-208, the non-Jewish, non-Christian writers whom he surveyed assumed a connection between Abraham and the Jews. In his words, Abraham was seen as "an ancestor of some kind" of the Jews (208). However, "Abraham was not so closely identified with the Jews or Israel that the pagan criticism of the Jews ever rubbed off on him" (*ibid.*). This describes what the reader finds in Luke-Acts. Increasing criticism of the Jews as the narrative progresses never rubs off onto Abraham. Our author understands the Jews to be Abraham's descendants. Surely he finds more significance in this than the "pagan" writers surveyed by Siker. This is due to his sympathies with Judaism. Still, our author, like pagan writers, viewed Abraham primarily as the ancestor of the Jews.

Judaism might very well describe the reader implied by this narrative. Tyson, taking his cue from Luke himself, defines such a person as a "God fearer."[77] This paper would agree.

---

[77] Cohen's essay, "Crossing the Boundary," *HTR* 82:13-33 is helpful here. One might get the impression from Acts, which speaks of "God-fearers," that we are dealing with something of a well defined, homogeneous group. Cohen suggests the term "sympathizer" to cover the wide range and degrees of respect for and attachment to Judaism which gentiles could demonstrate. These included: 1) admiration of some features of Judaism, 2) acknowledging the power of the Jewish God, 3) being a benefactor to Jews and their causes, 4) practicing selected Jewish rituals, 5) worshipping only the Jewish God, 6) joining the Jewish community, 7) converting to Judaism. I find this discussion helpful for it encourages us to avoid the reductionistic conclusion that Luke's reference to "God-fearers" is a reference to a monolithic block without diversity.

Historical Jesus the Healer: Cultural Interpretations of the Healing Cults of the Graeco-Roman World as the Basis for Jesus Movements

Ralph J. Coffman
Fitchburg State College, MA

Healing cults within the Graeco-Roman world prior to Constantine, both pagan and Christian, addressed shared "first order" concerns that were intimately connected with the bases of life of the common person.[1] Healing was of pre-eminent importance because the perceived universe was in decay and dissolution—physically, politically and spiritually. It was for this reason that some paganisms were rejected and some survived alongside Christianity.

In response to social and physical anxieties created by this general cultural malaise, cults of healers developed, most prominently among which were those of Asklepios and Jesus, both historical healers who generated a lineage of disciples with an unbroken continuity of transmission. At some point in the development of their cults, the founders were divinized, symbolized by dual divine-human parental lineages. Transformation from human healer to divine-human savior-healer was a powerful response to the rampant social and physical anxieties of perceived decay, dissolution and imminent disaster. The healer could address physical disease, but the savior could address spiritual dissolution, and people aspired to healings of saviors precisely because they were theandric, both physical and spiritual.

We shall see that just as Asklepios cults slowly transformed and replaced earlier mother goddess healing cults from the fifth century B.C. to the second century A.D., Jesus cults slowly transformed and replaced Asklepios cults from the first through the sixth centuries A.D. Both transformations lasted centuries and were indicative of processes in the deep structure of society. Both Asklepios' and Jesus' healing cults were able to co-exist, develop and diffuse because they addressed "first order" concerns of the people and shared a common, popular. fluid religiosity in Roman Palestine and Syria, Asia Minor and Greece, and Rome.

A pervasive pagan supernaturalism in the cults of Asklepios prepared the way for emerging popular local cults of Jesus, or Jesus Movements, with which they co-existed in eclectic tension in popular religious *practice* for three centuries after the *pax christiana*. Physical disease and spiritual dissolution in late antique society were addressed by Asklepios and Jesus cults, side-by-side,

---

[1] Eric Wolf, *Peasants* (Englewood Cliffs, N.J.: Prentice-Hall, 1966), pp. 1-21.

in tension and harmony, and this helps explain the enigmatic phenomenon of pagan survivals in the early medieval Christian world. Islam and not the Theodosian formula of 380 provoked *theoretical*, doctrinal, and second order concerns of religious institutionalization.

1. Asklepios, Savior-Healer

The pre-eminent healer in the Graeco-Roman world was Asklepios, a fifth century B.C. historical physician from Epidauros, who balanced spirituality with empirical medicine, and who displayed miraculous healing powers. His cult was introduced to Athens shortly before 419/8 B.C. by Telemachos, a private citizen from Epidauros. The socio-political reason why Asklepios' cult was introduced to Athens is suggested by Aristophanes' *Wasps,* produced in 422 B.C. during the Pelopponesian war, which indicated that since Athenians who had been ravaged by disease and bloodshed during the war had been prevented from journeying to the Asklepieion at Epidauros because it was in enemy territory,[2] a new Asklepieion at Athens was eagerly sought.[3] In *ca.* 420 B.C., the Meidias Painter, a mannerist-style potter,[4] portrayed the bringing of Asklepios' to Athens in a commemorative nativity plate.[5]Asklepios is in the midst of an adoring trinity of Goddesses: Eudaimonia (inspiration of healing and of poetry), Epidauros (his hometown goddess of mid-wifery holding him as the fruit of his virgin mother, Koronis), and Eukleia (goddess of healing), all framed in a laurel wreath, suggesting how a male savior-healer originated from and was nutured by pre-Indo-European mother-goddesses devoted to healing.

An Asklepieion shrine was erected on the Acropolis, the cult was awarded state patronage in *ca.* 400 B.C., and by 300 B.C. Asklepios became one of the first foreign gods given legal status in Rome. By the fourth century A.D. the cult had diffused throughout the Empire to over four hundred locations.[6] In the process, Asklepios evolved from mortal physician, to cult hero, to divine son of god Apollo and human son of Koronis, and finally to healing god of Athens and Rome, a process that resembles the divinization of Jesus and the diffusion of the various Jesus Movements.[7]

Diffusion of the cult of Asklepios followed ancient paths of transmission. Healing mythologies of ancient pre-Indo-European goddesses were transformed and their healing sanctuaries throughout the ancient world were

---

[2] Aristophanes, *Wasps* 121-3; F.R. Walton, "A Problem in the *Ichneutai* of Sophocles," *Harvard Studies in Classical Philology,* 46(1935):167-189.

[3] Lucilla Burn, *The Meidias Painter* (Oxford: Clarendon Press, 1987), p. 71.

[4] *Ibid.*, pp. 97-119: "Catalogue of Vases Attributed to the Meidias Painter and His Associates."

[5] D. Cramers, *Aison en de Meidias-Schilder* (Ph.D. Dissertation, Catholic University of Leuven, 1980), pp. 67-73.

[6] Emma and Ludwig Edelstein, *Asclepius: A Collection and Interpretation of Testimonies.* (2 vols.; New York: Arno Press,1975), 2:71-2

[7] W. A. Jayne, *The Healing Gods of Ancient Civilizations* (New Haven: Yale University Press, 1925).

renovated into Asklepieia. In the Homeric poems Asklepios had been identified as the mortal founder of a Mycenaean healing cult at Trikke who had transmitted his powers to two sons Podaleiros and Machaon.[8] By demythologizing Homer using archaeology, we now know that Trikke and the terraced sanctuaries of Ithame and Oichalia were actually pre-Indo-European sanctuaries of Minoan and Maltese Mother Goddesses.[9] The uroboric Mother Goddess, as snake mistress of the underworld, had her child attached to her and who finally emerged as the human Madonna and the human-divine child.[10] The snake was identified with the chthonic Earth Mother, the Minoan moon goddess (later Hecate) and the mother goddess of rebirth, Demeter. Later, the Gnostic Ophites identified Christ with the serpent.[11]

In Malta, the sick and ailing underwent "incubation" in sacred tomb-like menhir structures, evocative of subterranean caves of the Earth Mother, from which the patient would emerge after a curative sleep, resurrected to new life, a scene depicted on a Knossos sealstone of the 15th-12th centuries B.C.[12] and in the Sleeping Lady Statuette from the Hal Saflieni Hypogeum. This female patient was clothed from the waist down in a tiered, fringed skirt, characteristic of Minoan snake priestess figurines and symbolic of the healing powers of subterranean mineral springs. She was depicted in a curative sleep, reclining on a couch, head on a pillow, as water spirals and snakes danced on the ceiling and walls.[13]

In Athens this healing mother goddess was chthonic Demeter, and her mysteries of rebirth and resurrection transpired in her cave-like shrine, the Eleusinion. When Asklepios first arrived in Athens he shared his shrine with Demeter to give the cult prestige,[14] but Asklepios emerged as the primary deity,[15] remaining a savior-healer near to earth, his mother Koronis, and the pre-Indo-European Titans.[16]

Wherever the Askelpios cult was transferred, tangible reality of the deity's physical presence was made explicit in the form of a human actor, an animal

---

[8] *Iliad*, 2.728-33, trans. Richmond Lattimore (Chicago: University of Chicago Press, 1951).

[9] Nanno Marinatos, *Minoan Religion* (1992), pp. 3-34.

[10] Erich Neumann, *The Origins and History of Consciousness*, trans. R. F. C. Hull (Princeton: Princeton University Press, 1954), p. 49.

[11] Carl G. Jung, *Dreams*, trans. R. F. C.Hull (Princeton: Princeton University Press, 1974), p. 218.

[12] Erich Neumann, *The Great Mother, An Analysis of the Archetype* (Princeton: Princeton University Press, 1963), p. 292; Peter Warren, *Minoan Religion as Ritual Action* (Studies in Mediterranean Archaeology and Literature, pocket-book 72; Partille, Sweden: Astrom, 1986), p. 17, fig. 9.

[13] Neumann, *Op. cit.*, pl. 3; J. D. Evans, *Malta* (London: Thames and Hudson, 1959), p. 163, pl. 57.

[14] *IG* II 2 4960a: BM 8821.

[15] George Roebuck , *Introducing New Gods* (New York, 1951), pp. 153-4.

[16] Jane Ellen Harrison, *Themis: A Study of the Social Origins of Greek Religion* (New York: World Publishing Co., 1962), p. 384.

form (the snake), or a cult statue. His daughter, Hygieia, always accompanied him, since Greeks, with dual Minoan-Mycenaean heritage, required an androgynous healing divinity. Hygieia's presence was made explicit by a lioness, her theriomorphic form, or her cult-animal. Thus, Telemachos transported a snake and a lioness to the Eleusinion in his chariot. A wooden archway, emulating the Lion Gate at Mycenae was constructed in Athens, proclaiming the triumph of the cult of Asklepios-Hygieia.[17] Although other healing deities existed in Attica, none surpassed Asklepios[18] in the first century A.D. Pausanias described how he participated in the celebration of Asklepios' nativity called the Epidaurea;[19] Lucian referred to the Asklepieion as a popular meeting place;[20] Philostratos indicated that the Athenians had a special relationship with Asklepios;[21] and Socrates related how Crito was about to sacrifice his famous "cock for Asklepios" in Athens.[22]

The institution of the Asklepieion was intimately linked with civic administration. In 343/2 B.C. the cult came under the administrative control of the Athenian *demos* when the annual rotation of priesthood as a magistrate's office was inaugurated. Between 25 B.C. and *ca*. 10 A.D. the priesthood was to a religious office, *dia biou,* and could be held only by an Athenian citizen.

The process of healing in the Asklepieion followed a prescribed order. Upon arriving in the *temenos*, the patient was purified by baths, lodged in a guest house, and while lying wrapped in linen shrouds on a cot in the *abaton* would meditate awaiting the god who would come in a nocturnal dream or vision, comparable to the incubation of Lazarus in the tomb at Bethany, as we shall see.

Asklepios' popularity is attested by the bronze coins of him struck in the second and third centuries, making him one of the few deities besides Athena to enjoy this honor.[23] His temple was renovated in the second century A.D. and remained active into the fifth century A.D. when Proclus, the neoplatonist, was living near the Asklepieion *ca*. 431 A.D. where he would pray for one young afflicted girl, Asklepiegenia, who was successfully healed[24] by a process that was typical: "All who came to him sick with festering sores, or with limbs wounded by shiny bronze or by far-hurled stones, or with bodies that were wasting from the scorching summer or chilly winter, he loosed and delivered from their assorted aches and pains, attending some with soothing spells, making others drink comforting potions, or

---

17 L. Beschi, "Il Monumento di Telemachos, Fondatore dell'Asklepion Atheniese," *Annuario della Sculia Archeologica di Atene* 29/30 (1967/8): 381-436.

18 F. Kutsche, *Attische Heilgötter und Heilheroen* (Giessen, 1913).

19 Pausanias, 2.26.8.

20 Lucian, *Pisc.* 42.

21 Philostratos, *Ep.* 8.

22 Plato, *Phaedrus*, 118A.

23 J. N. Svornos, *Les Monnaies d'Athènes* (Munich, 1923-1926), pl. 98.1-10.; A. S. Walker, *A Chronological Study of the Greek Imperial Coinage of Athens* (Ph.D. diss, University of Pennsylvania, 1980), pp. 18, 214-216.

24 Marinus, *Vita Procli*, ed. J. F. Boissonade (Leipzig, 1814). sec. 29.

wrapping their limbs all round in bandages, or setting them back on their feet through surgery."[25]

Mother Goddess healing power was so threatening to Indo-Europeans that Asklepios and his mother, Koronis, were killed by Zeus, Koronis because she had sought a mortal husband to legitimize the birth of their son and Asklepios because he could resurrect the dead and thus liberate humans from mortality.[26] Chiron a man-bull, was chosen to rear and train Asklepios. The historical fact underlying the myth was that Mycenaeans destroyed the civilization of Koronis and substituted their patriarchal mentor, the Mycenean man-bull, Chiron. Both Pindar and Sophocles defended Chiron as the replacement of Asklepios' real mother by claiming Chiron was "the hero who warded off sickness of every kind."[27] Thus, a new myth of resurrection was born: Father God replaced Mother Goddess; Asklepios was depicted as a bearded Zeus. Hygieia was seated on a throne above the snake Gaia, wrapped around an omphalos, the earth's center, the site of the holy tree, resembling, in the late Jesus Movement, the cross on the hill of Calgary. The omphalos is plainly evident on the Ninnion *pinax* at Eleusis and on coins at Pergamon.[28]

Asklepios' healing cult arrived in Rome shortly after a plague in 293 B.C. Just as in the case of Athens, Asklepios came directly from his nativity in Epidauros. Livy described the plague as a scorching wildfire with heaps of corpses piled high, destroyed by the wrath of Apollo, echoing Homer's earlier description: "He shot an arrow with a dreadful twang from his silver bow, attacked the mules first and the nimble dogs; then he aimed his sharp arrows at the men, and struck again and again. Day and night innumerable fires consumed the dead."[29] Such apocalyptic imagery accorded well with the sense that the true savior would come in the *eschaton*. The god who kills, purifies from sin and heals. Both redemption and healing were closely linked in the oracle "The wounder heals."[30]

When Asklepios arrived in Rome, he was memorialized by a sculpted travertine marble sun-ship dedicated to Apollo on the southern tip of the Tiber Island.[31] At the rear mid-ships on the gunwale a bust of Asklepios (Asculapius in Latin) with his snake and staff was carved in bas relief.[32] Pausanias, the Greek traveler revealed in ca. 150 A.D. the "temple secret" of Asklepios' original shrine in Epidauros. When he asked why no water was brought to the temple to clean the ivory on Asklepios' statue, priests told him that there was plenty of water concealed in the sacred spring over which the statue had

---

[25] Pindar, *Pythian Ode* 3, 47-53.

[26] A. David Napier, *Masks, Transformation and Paradox* (Berkeley: University of California Press, 1986), p. 79.

[27] Pindar, *Pythian Ode* 3.7.

[28] Harrison, *Op. cit.*, p. 384.

[29] Livy X, 47.

[30] E. Leutsch and F. G. Schneidewin, eds., *Corpus paroemiographorum graecorum* (Goettingen, 1839-51), 2:pt. 3, 1139.

[31] Codex Vaticanus 3439, fol. 42.

[32] Giovanni Battista Piranesi (1707-1778), "The Tiber Island in Rome," British Museum.

been erected to protect it.[33] As sites for early churches were sought, Asklepios' sacred springs were highly revered for their healing powers, and Asklepieia were renovated into Christian chapels. Thus, in the early fourth-century church of San Bartolomeo on the Tiber Island in Rome, Asklepios' holy spring was concealed under steps leading to the presbytery.[34]

Renovation of Asklepieia into churches was accompanied by destruction or removal of cult objects and statuary. The process, however, was delayed since the Christian and pagan rites co-existed in harmony until the advent of Islam. The statue of Asklepios from the Tiber Island sun-ship was removed but not until the sixth century A.D.,[35] when the *temenos* was renovated into a church and hospital and Jesus iconography silently replaced that of Asklepios: just as Asklepios had used his *digitus medicinalis* or healing finger, to touch diseased parts of an incubant's body, so too Jesus the Healer was depicted as touching or pointing to the afflicted part of the human anatomy.

The cult of Asklepios was promulgated by testimonials of successful healings. Many of these testimonial dedications and accompanying inventories of gifts are extant. The Athenian Asklepieion has records of 908 dedicants between 350 to 25 B.C. from varied economic and social backgrounds. Those who were not Athenian citizens for whom only an inventory exists were probably of lower social and economic status, if we can assume that the monetary worth of the dedication was a measure of wealth and that the use of a title with a name was of little significance in identifying higher status. What mattered most was the size of the monumental plaques and their associated architectural edifices. Athenian citizens can be classified socially according to this index.

Only eight of those dedicants who engaged in other civic activities were affiliated with other cults.[36] They are associated with cults of Athena, Plouto, Themis, Dionysios, Olympia and Isis. This suggests that a variety of healing cults were being consolidated into the Asklepios cult from the period of the founding of the cult in Athens to the second century when it became pre-eminent among healing cults of the Empire.

Families of dedicants also engaged in a variety of other civic activities. The Asklepieion on the south slope of the Acropolis attracted a wide following from diverse economic and social backgrounds, much like the diffusion of the Jesus Movements. Ritual testimonials of faithful adherents of Asklepios regularly recorded healings. Testimonials were accompanied by gifts ranging from less than one drachma to 500 drachmas, and these gifts are assumed to correspond to the economic resources of the dedicants.

---

33 Pausanias, 5:11:11.

34 C. Kerenyi, *Asklepios* (New York: Pantheon/Bollingen Foundation, 1959), p. 4.

35 Martin, *Op. cit.*, p. 51.

36 These are 1) Egesias, tamias of Athena cult, 349/8 B.C.: *IG* II2 1436.7, 2822.92) Purros, cult of Plouto, 330-320 B.C.,*IG* II2 1933.8; 3) Gulon, archetheoros, *IG* II2 668.30-31; 4) unknown priestess of Themis; 5) Theogenes, epimeletes of the pompe; 266/5 B.C., *IG* II2668.30-31; 6) Gaios, agonothetes of the Dionysia, *ca.* 100 A.D., *IG* II2 4511.2-3; 7) Aurelia, priestess of Ge Olympia, *ca.* 150 A.D., *IG* II24521a; 8) Eukarpos, zakaros and hagiaphoros of Isis, 118-138 A.D., *IG* II2 4772.

At Athens equality of access to priesthood in the cult of Asklepios was insured by the Constitution, and male citizens, their wives and daughters participated in the cult as a family tradition through twelve and more generations. The same Athenian families contributed priests and priestesses from the third century B.C. to the fourth century A.D. For instance, Ammonios was priest ca. 190-170 B.C., of a family active in Athens and on Delos. Ammonios II rose to become the gymnisarch of Delos in 155/4 B.C. and was victorious in the Panathenian games.[37] A descendant, Pambotades, was priest of Apollo on Delos in 103/2 B.C. and was honored by a statue of him. He was also a participant in the Pythian games and was honored as the theodokos of the Delia when he was proxenos of Tenos. In the Roman period the Athenian Askelpieion continued to be a center of healing. Hegias I of Pompeii in the period 192-200 A.D. was a hoplite general, agonthetes of the Olympieia, gymnasiarch and priest of Zeus Olympios. He married Gellia Dionysia who was a dedicant of Asklepios at Athens.[38] The Theodorikos family has one of the most impressive lines of priestly involvement from 430 B.C. beginning with Kallikrates, a rare pronomen, to his descendants in 50 A.D. Dedicants to Asklepios were often dedicants to Hygieia as well, as one Archon, Syndromou of 63/2 B.C., typifies.[39]

Separation of laity and priesthood had already transpired by the mid-first century A.D., since cultic financial responsibilities demanded more economic resources than selection by lot would allow. Thus, priests were supplied by certain families who had long-standing ties with the cult and higher social and economic status. The Asklepieion priesthood by 50 A.D. was becoming a life profession, having once been a yearly appointment, and hierophants in Attica avoided secular careers and were forbidden to hold other sacred offices.

By the beginning of the Christian era, other healing cults were consolidating with the cult of Asklepios. This collapse of diversity would prove to be especially climacteric for the Jesus Movement as it began to compete with the Asklepios cult. Tertullian in *ca.* 190 A.D. revealed with Christian anxiety that Athenians sacrificed to Asklepios, to his *mother*, and to their own ancestral spirits.[40] Tertullian's misidentification of Asklepios' daughter (not *mother*) Hygieia suggests that Tertullian identified Hygieia with Mary and that the worship of Jesus and his mother Mary was in direct competition with the Hellenistic rite.

2. Hygieia, Savior-Healer

Kronos' relegation to a secondary role in Asklepios' birth presented the notion that the pre-Indo-Europeans had nothing to offer their Mycenaean conquerors. The same gender/culture revolution is evident in the treatment of

---

[37] Sara Aleshire, *Asklepios at Athens: Epigraphic and Prosopographic Essays on the Athenian Healing Cults* (Amsterdam: J. C. Gieben, 1991), p. 83; *IG* II2 2317.

[38] *Ibid.*, p. 125.

[39] *Ibid.*, p. 134.

[40] Tertullian, *ad Nat.* 2.14.

Hygieia, Asklepios' daughter, originally a pre-Mycenaean earth goddess. She was also associated with healing ritual in a chthonic setting as a 15th-12th century B.C. Knossos sealstone clearly depicts: a naked woman clasps a stone (omphalos) in a ritual posture of incubation within a cave sanctuary.[41] When Indo-Europeans invaded Greece and Crete, Hygieia became associated with Athena, and the dual goddess was shown seated on an omphalos, the symbolic connection of the human and the subterranean regions. Omphalos stones are found in the central courts of Crete palaces such as Mallia, dated to 1450 B.C.[42]The dual goddess Athena-Hygieia was still operative in 420 B.C. when the cult of Asklepios was introduced in Athens.[43] For instance, in the mid-fifth century B.C. Perikles healed an injured workman on instructions from Athena-Hygieia and set up a dedication near her altar on the southeast corner of the Propylaia, where her statue base has been recovered.[44] Similarly, the Meidias Painter shortly after *ca.* 420 B.C. depicted newly-ensconced Hygieia holding a scepter in the Garden of the Hesperides beside Attic heroes associated with the healing serpent of Asklepios.[45]

The lioness, Hygieia's pre-Mycenaean protectress theriomorph, was her favorite heraldic animal, the lone mother who raised her children in a matrifocal pride. Two examples of her theriomorph, flanking a Minoan column, are preserved on the renown lintel of the Gate of Mycenae, now ensconced within the fortress wall. The original sacred stele which probably had the Goddess standing on top of the Minoan column was set within the precinct of an earlier sanctuary. The "mother of the Mountains" seal from Knossos clearly indicates this iconography.[46] The incorporation or rather imprisonment of the goddess stele in the Mycenaean wall with the goddess missing may indicate that she was ritually destroyed, but in any case it demonstrates how completely the conquerors triumphed over Hygieia's matrifocal civilization.

Further patriarchalization of the Minoan religion is recorded iconographically by gem seals from Crete and Greece. An early Minoan Goddess of the Mountains found at Menidi shows her holding the chthonic emblem, the snake, symbol of rebirth.[47] On Crete from the cave of Psychro, the Goddess has snakes as a crown, flanked by the two lionesses.[48] In Mycenae the goddess has become a demon standing between two seated lions.[49] This demonization of the Goddess has the same misogynist intent that

---

41 Warren, *Op. cit.*, p. 17, fig. 9.

42 *Ibid.*, p. 19, fig. 10.

43 H. A. Shapiro, *Personification of Abstract Concepts in Greek Art and Literature to the End of the Fifth Century B.C.* (Ph. D. Dissertation, Princeton University, 1977), 242-245.

44 Plutarch, *Perikles* 13.8; Pliny, *Hist. Nat.* 22.44; *Inscriptiones Graecae* I, 2nd. ed. (Berlin, 1924), 395.; herinafter abbreviated as *IG* I2.

45 British Museum, London, Cat. no. E224 (M5); Shapiro, *Op. cit.*, p. 243.

46 Martin P. Nilsson, *The Minoan Mycenaean Religion and its Survival in Greek Religion* (2nd. ed.; Lund: C. W. K. Gleerup, 1950), p. 353, fig. 162.

47 *Ibid.*, p. 363, fig. 164.

48 *Ibid.*, p. 361, fig. 173.

49 *Ibid.*, p. 359, fig. 171.

accompanied the demonization of Eve in the creation story beginning in Genesis 2:4. The Garden of Eden was made into a Hell inhabited by infernal creatures, a mirror of the fallen state of humanity on earth. The chthonic Babylonian deity was challenged by the Enuma Elish Babylonian cult just as Edenic serpent was challenged by the Yahwistic Jewish patriarchs.[50] The trajectory in both cases, however, amounts to the same. Woman became the devil incarnate and man became ruler over all, first the beasts, then one man over another, and finally over all creation through a male god. Mycenaeans accomplished this transformation, as did the established church under Augustine: by the laws of nature, man was commanded by the male deity to preserve subjection of nature, women and other men.[51]

Yet, memory of goddess' power lingered on the periphery of the Indo-European stronghold of Greece. Hygieia is the only other member of the Asklepian circle who shared his exhaltation as savior (*soter*) of the world. Hygieia preceded Asklepios in Epidauros, which was less affected by the Mycenization of Greece than was Athens. When she accompanied Asklepios to Athens as a female savior-healer,[52] the persistence of her healing cult was implicit, and it lasted into the third century B.C., when dedications were made to her by many including two potters, Euphronios and Kallis[53] and by others in Rome.

3. Jesus, Savior-Healer

Jesus the savior-healer was a product of two worlds, Jewish and Graeco-Roman. The Jewish world associated Jesus with Elisha, the messianic healer of disease[54] and raiser of the dead,[55] and with Moses, the magician who was able to make the water of new life flow from dry rock with his magic wand. The Graeco-Roman world associated Jesus with Asklepios, the savior-healer who cured illnesses with miraculous water in subterranean caves or tomb-like chambers. Both performed miracles to minister to the symptoms of generalized physical, spiritual and cultural disintegration.

Profound consequences resulted from the fluidity between Graeco-Roman and Jewish historical savior-healers, like Asklepios and Jesus. Popular religion in the first three centuries was mainly concerned with miracle working and supernatural healing not doctrinal orthodoxy. Cults were less competitors than correlatives which ministered to popular anxieties by offering renewed life and reintegration, spiritually, bodily and communally.

The first radical shift in Jewish concepts of healing that later impacted the Jesus Movements regarded physicians as proponents rather than opponents of

---

50 Tivka Frymer-Kensky, *In the Wake of the Goddess: Women, Culture, and the Biblical Transformation of Pagan Myth* (New York: Free Press, 1992), pp. 74-75.

51 Augustine, *De Civitate Dei*, 19.15. See Elaine Pagels, *Adam, Eve and the Serpent* (New York: Vintage Books, 1988), p. 114.

52 *Inscriptiones Graecae* I, 3rd. ed. (Berlin, 1980), 414.2. Hereinafter abbreviated *IG* I3.

53 *IG* I2, 516 .

54 2Kg 5; cf. Mk 1.40-45.

55 2Kg 4:18-37; cf. Lk 7.11-17.

Yahweh. Prior to the Babylonian Captivity physicians had been regarded as magicians in league with Satan. Saul had consulted the witch of Endor and Manasseh had practiced prophecy and augury, and the whole nation was punished by being taken captive and deported to Babylon.[56] The shift occurred when Sirach proclaimed[57] that natural cures were even made by Moses when he sweetened Marah's bitter water by adding juices of a tree that Yahweh had shown him.[58] The godly physician was created to administer medicines made from Yahweh's nature which should be utilized by those with common sense.[59] Thus, the Jewish physician became an agent of Yahweh in Hellenistic times, and healing by Jesus followed Sirach's model.

Jewish concepts of healing and salvation were intimately connected. *Soter* simultaneously signified savior and healer. While illness was not equated with divine retribution for sin,[60] power over disease was related to forgiveness of sin.[61] Healing by Jesus was reported as messianic, a portent of the conquest of Satan, the deluder of Saul and Manasseh.[62]

The proverb "Physician, heal thyself!"[63] was associated by Jesus with the proverb that the true prophet was never accepted in his home town.[64] Three types of healers existed in the Graeco-Roman world. The first, known as an *iatros* or physician, was appointed by the local town,[65] served at public baths and used empirical techniques.[66] The second, known as an exorcist, worked only with incantations, such as the Jewish doctors at Ephesos (Acts 19:13), had no automatic tenure and was subject to the town's review. Jesus related the two

---

[56] I Sam 28; II Kings 17:16-18; 21:9-15; II Chron 33:1-13.

[57] Sirach 38:1-15.

[58] Ex 15:23-5.

[59] Howard Clark Kee, *Medicine, Miracle & Magic in New Testament Times* (New York: Cambridge University Press, 1986), p. 19.

[60] Lk 13:1-5; Jn 9:1-3.

[61] Mk 2:1-2.

[62] Mt 11:4; Lk 7:22.

[63] Lk 4: 23.

[64] Matt 13:57-58: "But Jesus said to them, 'A prophet is not without honor except in his own country and in his own house.' And he did not do many works there because of their unbelief." Mk 6:4-6: "And Jesus said to them, 'A prophet is not without honor except in hs own country, and among his own kin and in his own house.' And he could do no mighty work there, except that he haid his hands upon a few sick people and healed them."
Lk 4:23-24: ". . . and they said, 'Is not this Joseph's son?' And he said to them, 'Doubtless you will quote to me this proverb, "Physician heal thyself; what we have heard you did at Capernaum, do here also in your own country."' And he said, 'Truly, I say to you, no prophet is acceptable in his own country.'"
POxy 1.31: "Jesus said, 'No prophet is acceptable in his own country; no physician heals those who know him.'"
GThom 31: "Jesus said, 'No prophet is accepted in his own village; no physician heals those who know him.'"

[65] V. Nutton, *PBSR* 45 (1977):197-226

[66] J. and L. Robert, *Hellenica* 9 (1950):25-27, print the inscription on a tombstone from Thyatira, "Helios, archiatros of the entire athletic association, here I lie. Hail!"

proverbs to indicate that the civically appointed *iatros* and the Jewish exorcist, the empiricist and the spiritualist were equally ineffectual.

The third type of healer in the Graeco-Roman world as both a physician and prophet, an *iatros* and an instructing priest of a religious cult, like that of Asklepios.[67] These physicians were noted for their successful healings. They were not solely empiricists who diagnosed scientifically, accepted payments but often failed to cure ailments, like those who had failed to treat the woman with the flow of menstrual blood.[68] This "physician" failed because he did not invoke divine inspiration[69] and was disparaged six of the seven times he was mentioned in the New Testament. Neither were the solely spiritualist healers, like the Jewish exorcists, effective, for they relied on magic.

The third type of healer, also called an *iatros*, mentioned only once in the New Testament had both the empirical knowledge of a physician and the spiritual inspiration of a prophet. This combined technique (*techne*) was associated with that of an accomplished craftsperson (*technikos*), the term that was translated as "carpenter." The reference to Jesus as the "carpenter's son" in Mt 13:56 may indicate that Jesus' father, Joseph, was himself one of these healers. This would make sense since the practice of healing in the Graeco-Roman world was often transmitted in family lineages, as we have seen in the Asklepios cult in Athens.

An early third-century variant of the dual proverb reveals the nature of the diffusion of healing cults: "Jesus said, 'No prophet is acceptable in his own country and no physician performs cures on those that know him'."[70] For Jesus, the imperative to hate one's biological family meant to love the spiritual family of God.[71] Similarly, for Asklepios, this meant forsaking Epidauros his home for new cities converting to his cult. For both Asklepios and Jesus, the forsaking of family and friends marked the beginning of their missionary enterprise.

One correlative of this act of voluntarily forsaking one's biological family and geographical home is preserved in the Gospel of Thomas: "Whoever does not hate his father and his mother as I do cannot become a disciple to Me. And whoever does [not] love his father and his mother as I do cannot become a [disciple] to Me. For My mother [gave me falsehood], but [My] true [Mother] gave me life."[72] The intention here seems to be referring to the Mother Goddess Sophia, the source of life, and this relates to the connection between Mary, Jesus' biological mother, and Sophia the Earth Mother. In the

---

[67] In an early third-century inscription from an altar from Koloe in Lydia (*IGRR* 4:1383) one *iatros*, Artemidoros, of the cult of Artemis, is both physician and instructing priest. Nearly 100 attestations of the use of *iatros* are found in Karia (V. Nutton, *PBSR* 45 (1977):197-226.) Often, healers' names were taken from the cult divinity. The same process can be seen in the Jesus movement where practitioners took *christianoi* from Christos.

[68] Mk 5:26 = Lk 8:43.

[69] Sir 38:14; Geza Vermes, *Jesus the Jew* (New York: Macmillan, 1973), p. 61.

[70] *P.Oxy.* 1:11.

[71] Mt 1037; Lk 14:26; GThom 55:1-2a; 101.

[72] GThom 101.

Asklepian myth, Koronis was similarly the Earth Mother from whom the savior-healer was born.

Thus, tension between empirical medicine and prophetic healing penetrated Judaism, the Jesus Movement and Graeco-Roman healing cults. Prayer and meditation invoked by the priest through the sequence of complaint, petition, cure and thanksgiving was used in conjunction with empirical medicine.[73] First-century Hellenistic-Jewish physicians valued empirical medicine[74] as well as prophetic power.[75] Ben Sira advised that physicians relied on "medicines" the Lord had "created out of the earth" and that "a prudent man will have no aversion to them."[76] In addition to medicine, prayer and meditation were regarded by Hellenistic Jews to play a determinative role.[77] Those who, like Asa, resorted only to physicians rather than to priestly healers were admonished.[78] However, strict interpreters of the Torah like the Essenes regarded all illness as Satan's bondage and all healing as solely within the spiritual domain of the priest.[79]

Luke, Mark and Matthew all indicated that Jesus healed the sick[80] by touching them or laying on of hands[81] which may be interpreted in the empirical sense,[82] but they accented spiritual power through the *logos* or word. Casting out of demons often resulted in violent struggle,[83] which may be interpreted in this sense.

Central to Jesus' healing was the ritual of baptism. Mark indicated that it was in baptism at the hands of John the Baptist that the Spirit came to Jesus[84] and that this empowered him to perform healings and exorcisms.[85] The probable function of the pre-Markan collections was that they responded to claims of competing healing cults like that of Asklepios in which divine legitimation was given for the proclamation of the healer's powers. This same intention was operative in Mark when he used miracle stories to demonstrate that Jesus is an agent of supernatural power.[86]

Jesus' healing techniques were transmitted to his disciples through teaching, revelatory authority and baptism. Mark designated Jesus as teacher twelve times and rabbi three, an emphasis characteristic of healing cults. Revelatory authority, stemming from the healing cult founder, originally

---

[73] Ps. 6; 16.10; 38; 107.17ff.

[74] Sir. 38; Is: 3.7; Jer. 8:22.

[75] Sir. 19:2-3.

[76] Ecclus. 38:4.

[77] Lev. 38:13-14.

[78] 2 Chr. 16:12.

[79] Lev. 13:49ff.

[80] Lk. 7:21ff., Mk. 3:10; Mt. 12:15.

[81] Mk. 1:31, 41; 5:28.

[82] Mk. 7:33; Jms. 5:14.

[83] Lk. 4:40-1; Mk. 3:10-11.

[84] Mk 1:10.

[85] Mk 3:22-30.

[86] Mk 4:35-41; 5:25-34; 6:47-52.

was inherited since these holy men were considered sons of the gods, and therefore Jesus was depicted as the son of God who leaves the audience breathless.[87] Through teaching and baptism by Jesus the disciples then became the practitioners of his healing power.

Mark devoted about forty percent of his Gospel to teaching, mentioning disciples and students forty-six times.[88] After Jesus' death and resurrection, succeeding followers had to be content with the transmission of special powers through baptism and teaching by those in the hierarchy. Transmission by teaching applied to Graeco-Roman healing cults as well Jesus' disciples.[89] Technique (*techne*) and godly devotion were equally crucial for the true healer: if faith was weak cures were ineffectual.[90]

Promulgation of healing cults was primarily though accounts by disciples. Mark's accounts, comprising about a quarter of his Gospel, are similar to those of Asklepians' testimonials[91] who became disciples.[92] Luke-Acts present six exorcisms and eighteen healings in the manner and style advised by Lucian,[93] Herodotus,[94] Dionysios,[95] and Josephus.[96] Miracles were presented by both Christians and pagans in variant versions with a dash of skepticism and a *caveat emptor*, like Luke and Acts variants of miracles,[97] Paul's conversion[98] and the ascension.[99]

Aretalogies or miraculous healing by apostles, literally "messengers," were an important means of promulgating a cult and these were invoked by Asklepians as well as early Christian. The *Apocryphal Acts*, a series of popular codex parchments written between 175 and 225 A.D.,[100] present Paul, Peter, Thomas, Andrew and John as itinerant apostles of the Cynic model without family or home,[101] who demonstrated spiritual clairvoyance,[102] and who confronted rivals.[103] *The Acts of John*, for instance, written in Greek *ca.* 150

---

87 Mk 1:22,27; 10:24; 12:17; 12:34; Mt 22:33,46; Lk 20:39-40.

88 G. Fowden, "The Pagan Holy Man in Late Antique Society," *Journal of Hellenic Studies* 102 (1982):33-59.

89 Acts 5:16; Peter in Acts 3:1ff; Philip in Acts 8:7; Paul in Acts 28:8-9.

90 Lk. 4:23; Mk. 6:5; Mt. 17:14ff.

91 Mk 1:45; 2:2; 3:7-8; 5:27; 6:13-14; 7:25.

92 Mk 1:45; 5:17-20; 10:52.

93 Lucian, *History* 60.

94 Herodotus 2.123; 3:3; 4:11; 5:45.

95 Dionysius 1.48:1.

96 Josephus (*Ant.* 1.108; 2:348; 3:81).

97 Lk 4:40-41; 6:17-19; 7:21; Acts 2:43-47; 5:12-16; 19:11-12.

98 Acts 9:1-22; 22:4-16; 26:9-18.

99 Lk 24:44-53; Acts 1:6-11.

100 All references are to the *New Testament Apocrypha*, ed. Wilhelm Schneemelcher, tr. by R. McL. Wilson *et al.*, (2 vols.; Philadelphia: Westminster Press, 1966).

101 Acts Jn 113; Acts Thom 20, 96, 139.

102 Acts Pt 2; Acts Paul 11.1; Acts Jn 46.56f.

103 Peter Brown, "The Rise and Function of the Holy Man in Late Antiquity," *Journal of Religious Studies* 61 (1971):80-101.

A.D., related how, after preaching his first sermon to the Ephesian assembly, John healed Cleopatra and a group of old women, resurrected four people from the dead, including Cleopatra's husband and a priest (of Asklepios ?), and then delegated apostle healers.[104] He was reported to have destroyed the temple of Artemis in the process which was closely associated with the Asklepieion and its healing priests. Peter, similarly, resurrected a widow's son and senator Nicostratus for whom Simon had been an ineffectual healer, and then he healed a group of blind old women.[105] Thomas freed a woman from demonic possession[106] as did Andrew. These healing miracles[107] and the rites of baptism and the eucharist[108] prompted accusations of magic by rivals.

As the Jesus Movements diffused with Graeco-Roman healing cults, ancient healing places were acculturated, first in the Galilee, then in the Decapolis (Gerasa), Jerusalem (Bethesda Pools), Syria (Mark's locus as well as the important *domus ecclesia* at Dura Europos), Asia Minor (especially Ephesus and the nearby city of Sardis), Greece (Epidauros, Athens and Corinth), Italy (Rome), Gaul (Lyons) and Britannicum (Luddingstone). Ancient sites of Demeter (the Eleusinia), of Artemis (the Artemesia) and Asklepios (the Asklepieia), were engulfed, claimed, renamed and Christianized through healing miracles performed by or in association with the name of Jesus. This dynamic of growth, diffusion, appropriation and renovation explains how the Jesus Movements were able to penetrate the Graeco-Roman world so imperceptibly yet so thoroughly before Christianity was given legal status.

4. Convergences: Asklepios and Jesus, Demeter and Mary, Hygieia and the Holy Spirit

The Epidaurian Mysteries, the Eleusinian Mysteries and the Jesus Movement were subtly interconnected in the public mind as savior-healing cults. We shall now present some convergences of these cults.

The Epidaurian Festival of Asklepios was celebrated jointly with the festival of the Eleusinian Mysteries.[109] Although the Epidauria was a festival sacred to Asklepios, Eleusinian priestesses and priests officiated at the ritual.[110] It was recorded that Asklepios was initiated into the Mysteries of Demeter and Persephone on his arrival in Athens, and he was housed in the Eleusinion for a period afterwards.[111] This connection is graphically confirmed in the mid-fourth century B.C. relief from the Asklepieion depicting Asklepios with Demeter and Kore.[112]

---

104 Acts Jn 19-25, 30-37, 46-47, 51, 75, 80, 82f.

105 Acts Pet 27, 28, 21-22.

106 Acts Thom 42-49.

107 Acts Andr 10.11-40; Acts Pet 16-29.

108 Acts Thom 152.

109 L. Deubner, *Attische Feste* (Berlin, 1932), pp. 72-73, 78.

110 K. Clinton, *American Journal of Archaeology* 92 (1988):240.

111 *Supplementum Epigraphicum Graecum* (Leiden-Amsterdam, 1923).

112 P. Girard, *L'Asclépieion d'Athènes au deuxieme et au troisieme siècle* (Paris, 1976), pl. 2.

Demeter was the Olympian Goddess of rebirth and resurrection. In her cultic rite of initiation a sacred libation was used to induce health and new life. This libation involved a psychotropic drug derived from ergot, a communal meal paralleled by the Seder and the eucharist. The Eleusinian potion (*kykeon*), was dispensed in a vessel (*angol*) by priestesses in a ceremony in an initiation hall (*telesterion*). In an inner chamber (*anaktoron*), "the lord's dwelling," where only the priestesses and priests were allowed to enter, the theriomorphs of Demeter and Dionysios, the god of wine, were ritually present.[113] The sacred libation of Demeter and Dionysios' sacred wine were correlative: initiates who raised the holy chalice in their initatory rite raised them for both deities. Asklepios was incorporated into these proceedings beginning in the fifth century B.C. when his cult was first set up in the *telesterion*, and special chalices or *paterae* were fashioned by artists for him: Asklepios and Demeter were associated as savior-healers.

The transformation of the Eleusinion into Asklepios' shrine was indicative of the transformation from a mother goddess to a father god and has been attributed to an origin in Thessaly, also the home of Asklepios, where Eumopolos, the first celebrant of the Mysteries, originated,[114] and where a Homeric sanctuary of Demeter at Pyrasos was located.[115] This dual rite of resurrection and rebirth co-existed with the development of Christianity: in the second half of the fourth century A.D. a large marble relief (2.86m. x 1.15 m.) shows both receiving Athenian physicians.[116] Demeter and Asklepios, Jesus and Mary paralleled each other's healing powers. As in the Telemachos Monument, names of dedicators were prominently displayed within olive wreaths, commemorating honors paid to these apostles for having donated this sanctuary. Demeter waits to receive these six physicians paying homage to Asklepios, their savior-healer. On the left stands Persephone holding two torches to guide the way to salvation while Demeter is seated on a round omphalos, the connection making her the great Earth Mother. To the right of Demeter, Asklepios stands to receive the visitors, who are noticeably diminutive before the divinities. This scene reveals how the Asklepios cult in Athens was established with active cooperation of Eleusinian priestesses, assimilating coordinate functions as the needs of the community changed. Priestesses and priests, apostles and disciples of healing miracles finally succumbed to Christianization in the fifth century when most if not all of their ancient sanctuaries were converted into churches.[117]

Similarly, the Eleusinian Mysteries merged with Christianity. There were two classes of initiates who paralleled the two classes of initiates in the Jesus Movement: those *telete* who spent only one night in the *telesterion* and those *epoptai* who spent two nights and who took part in the sacred meal. In

---

[113] R. Gordon Wasson, Carl A. P. Ruck, Albert Hofmann, *The Road to Eleusis: Unveiling the Secret of the Mysteries* (London: Harcourt Brace Jovanovich, 1978), pp. 78-81.

[114] Pausanias, I,38,2-3; George E. Mylonas, *Eleusis and the Eleusinian Mysteries* (Princeton: Princeton University Press, 1961), p. 19.

[115] *Iliad*, 2.695.

[116] National Museum, Athens, cat. no. 1332.

[117] Martin, *Op. cit.*, p. 51.

like manner, the Christian church built near the Eleusinian sanctuary had two classes of converts, those who were catechumens who were asked to leave the church after the celebration of the Mass where the confessed Christians remained to partake of the eucharist.[118]

Demeter had one well-known daughter, Persephone, around whom the Eleusinian Mystery of death and rebirth revolved. Another daughter was revealed in the fifth century B.C., Artemis, the Amazonian Moon-Goddess connected with the pre-Indo-European agricultural chthonic deity. She represented the queens of a matrifocal society in which men were peripheral to the family and often beheaded after they served their purpose of fathering children. Artemis, as a pre-Indo-European deity, was originally from Lydia in the form "Artimis," and was named Mistress of the Wild Beasts (*potnia theron*), the huntress mother and protectress who lived apart from the male.[119] Her priestesses selected a sacrificial king for their queen with whom she had sexual intercourse. After the queen was impregnated the king ventured into nearby woods, where, dressed as a stag the theriomorphic form of Actaeon, the male Horned God, he was slain by trained hunting dogs (*alani*).[120] Artemis' groves extended from Sweden to Scythia and were known as deer gardens (*Tiergarten*), places of medieval venison feasts.

After the Mycenaean conquest of Greece, the king was no longer slain, and Artemis was ritually propitiated with drops of blood drawn from a man's neck using a symbolic sword, perhaps the same ritual swords that show the ritual hunting of the lioness. In Sparta, she was called Artamis, the butcher, in consequence of the Dorian destruction of the pre-Indo-European matrifocal society. Male victims were replaced with bulls, and the Goddess became slayer of bulls, *tauropolos*. The bull-fight literally reenacted the triumph of the male (matador) Indo-Europeans over the ancient Mother Goddess, whose horns were the sublime bull-like incarnation of the female reproductive system.[121]

Artemis was considered as being both virgin and mother, and in this dual aspect she gradually conformed to the evolving mythic image of Mary. She was the enemy of sexual love and the protagonist of life and healing. Statues and statuettes of her depict the fullness of her power as the fecund theriomorphic Queen bee, laden with egg sacks (sometimes wrongly viewed as breasts), worshipped by theriomorphic male drones and female honey bees. The Artemis cult provided another healing ritual that actively competed with the Jesus Movement and merged with it.

Artemis was paradoxically virgin goddess and mother goddess. Euripides had her declare contempt for Aphrodite,[122] while Herodotus reported that

---

118 Mylonas, *Op. cit.*, p. 274.

119 *Iliad*, 21.

120 Robert Graves, *Greek Myths* (2 vols.; New York: Penguin Books, 1955), I:85.

121 Marija Gimbutas, *The Language of the Goddess* (New York: Harper and Row, 1989), p. 265.

122 *Hippolytus*, l. 1301.

428 / SBL 1993 Seminar Papers

Aeschylus regarded her as the daughter of Demeter, Persephone's sister.[123] In Crete she was Britomartis, in Thrace Cybele and in Cappadocia Ma.

The mysterious paradox of being both mother and virgin was viewed by the Jesus Movement as evidence of her similarity to Mary, the virgin mother. The concept of the virgin birth began to develop as patriarchalism began to assert itself in the Jesus Movement. As Mary and Artemis merged some saw the new religion as threatening male empowerment. When Saul of Tarsus confronted the Artemis cult in Ephesus he confronted this problem which had originated in Jewish restrictions on women in the worship of Yahweh. While domestic duties excused women from participation in the Law, this liberty became the basis of exclusion from public religious leadership. Among the non-Jewish women, however, the cult at the Artemision in Ephesus provided an outlet that Jewish women did not have. Within the house-church of Ephesus women from Graeco-Roman backgrounds commingled with Jewish women. To live and worship as a Jew one had to abide by gender restrictions. Was the same going to be true of the Jesus Movement?

The Artemis cult consecrated the month of Artemision (March-April) as a spring festival, Ephesia. During this period tourists from throughout the empire gathered to participate in her athletic, musical and dramatic contests. The drama as recorded by Xenophon of Ephesus in the second century involved hundreds of priestesses, called *melissae* (theriomorphic honey bees), in a holy procession serving Artemis as the many egg-bearing queen mother bee (a bee was engraved at her feet). In this theriomorphic guise Artemis need recognize no male as her master and could fulfill motherhood as a true parthenoi,[124] unmarried yet not virginal.[125] Her male priests, *megabyzi*, were castrated eunuchs who were considered as theriomorphic drones ritually sacrificing their lives for the their queen, a modification of the earlier practice of ritual slaying of the king. Some sources called these *megabyzi*, Essenes, an ascetic monastic order perhaps linked with the Jewish Essenes of the Dead Sea.[126] It is unknown to what extent these priests actually owed their identification with the puritanical Jewish sect, but it does indicate the extent to which Jewish religious ideas of ascetic monasticism infiltrated the Hellenistic world of Asia Minor, an association which Saul of Tarsus would have known. Like their Jewish counterparts, the chief of these male Essenes was at the top of the temple hierarchy, a further example of Mycenization, but Artemis in her theriomorphic form as the queen bee took symbolic precedence over all.[127] Her mural crown, the emblem of the city's defensive turreted walls, was

---

[123] Herodotus, 2.156.

[124] *Theological Dictionary of the New Testament* (10 vols., ed. by Gerhard Kittel and Gerhard Friedrich. tr. Geoffrey Bromiley; Grand Rapids: William B. Eerdmans, 1964-1974), 5:827.

[125] H. G. Liddell, and R. A. Scott, *Greek-English Lexicon* (9th ed., rev. by H. S. Jones and R. McKenzie; Oxford: At the Clarendon Press, 1940), p. 1339.

[126] Robert Fleischer, "Artemis Ephesia und Aphrodite von Aphrodisias" In *Die orientalischen Religionen im Poemerreich* (ed. Maarten J. Vermaseren; Leiden: E. J. Brill, 1981), pp. 298-315.

[127] Lewis Richard Farnell, *The Cults of the Greek States* (5 vols.; New Rochelle, N.Y.: Caratzas Brothers, 1904).

symbolic of her protection of the hive. Worship of her took precedence over even that of the emperor.[128]

As the annual processional approached the Artemision, *melissae* and *megabyzes* held forth gold, silver and ivory images of the goddess, while the bystanding crowds did likewise. Saul of Tarsus in the audience with his strong Jewish aversion for images of the divine was contemptuous of these devotees. When he chastised the sculptors of cultic votive statues, their guild was understandably upset since it was one of the major industries of the city. The success of Paul's mission in Ephesus provoked a predictable reaction from the city's silversmiths who regularly manufactured statuettes of Artemis for the tourist trade.[129]

Inside the Artemision sacred ritual dramas promised triumph over bodily afflictions and immortality in the hereafter. The dramas and rituals were transcribed, interpreted and recited by another group of adherents of temple officials (*theologici*), who maintained the sacred legends. The temple employed hymnists and musicians. A boys' choir performed for the celebrants. Presbyters handled the temple's finances and functioned as its bank. Indentured servants were attendants and custodians.[130] The temple was the center of the city's business. It was natural to come to Ephesus in the sacred month if one wished to gain the attention of a large cosmopolitan audience. Saul of Tarsus had chosen well.

In Ephesus Paul argued in the synagogue[131] returning there over a three-month period before retreating to the hall of Tyrannus because of Jewish opposition to him .[132] Luke records[133] that seven sons of a high priestly family of Sceva were itinerant Jewish exorcists who performed their rites of healing by using the name of Jesus in their incantations.[134] It is possible that these men were actually in the employ of the Jewish temple[135] and that Jews of Ephesus had become involved in this endeavor in order to counter the popularity and attention of both the worshippers of Artemis and of Jesus. In the theater where Paul was attacked, Alexander, an Ephesian Jew, accepted the spokesmanship for the Jewish community to argue against Paul. He endeavored to distinguish the Jews from the Christians, but when the Greek audience realized he was a Jewish advocate they did not want to listen any further because he was obviously not a worshipper of Artemis. The worshippers of Artemis shouted their cultic cry at both Paul and Alexander for

---

128 Camden M. Coburn, *The New Archaeological Discoveries* (9th ed.; New York: Funk and Wagnalls Company, 1929), p. 464.

129 Acts 19:23-41.

130 Ferguson, John. *The Religions of the Roman Empire* (Ithaca, N.Y.: Cornell University Press, 1970), p. 21.

131 Acts 18:19.

132 Acts 19:8-9.

133 Acts 19: 11-17.

134 Lk. 11:19; Luther H. Martin, *Hellenistic Religions: An Introduction* (New York: Oxford University Press, 1987), pp. 405-412.

135 M. Verus Israel Simon, *A Study of the Relations between Christians and Jews in the Roman Empire (135-425 A.D.).* (Oxford: Oxford University Press, 1986), pp. 339-368.

two hours: Jews as well as Christians were seen as challenging the city's religion. Later, these same Ephesian Jews (identified because they recognized one Trophimus who had recently been in Ephesus) saw Paul in the Jerusalem Temple and incited the crowd, charging him with attacking the fundamentals of Jewish identity, the Torah, the Temple and the congregation. Paul's paramount act of defilement was bringing Greeks into the Temple.

Greeks, Jews and the Jesus Movement struggled to assert the supremacy and normative value of their healing cults, but only the Jesus Movement sought to establish its uniqueness.[136] Wandering Jewish charismatic healers, like the Scaevean brothers, threatened normative monocultural Jewish Torah. Charismatic priests and priestesses Asklepios and Artemis challenged emergent, normative Christianity after 313 A.D.

The diffusion of Jesus Movements was gradual, subtle, pervasive, and transformative. As normative Christianity slowly triumphed over the cult of Artemis, she was made into a Christian Saint, Artemidos, and in some traditions was transformed from female to male and prayed to as a holy man.[137] This represents a further extension of the process begun by Indo-Europeanization.

Theodotos was the first of the "adoptionist" interpreters who sought to portray Jesus as a mere man (*psilanthropos*) upon whom God's spirit had descended in baptism. He was a Byzantine leather merchant who arrived in Rome *ca.* 190 A.D., at precisely the time when Asklepians had reached the zenith of cultic activity. Theodotos was scandalized by Christian historians Epiphanius and Eusebius for maintaining that Jesus was supremely virtuous but not essentially divine. Jesus was, Theodotos maintained, like Asklepios, born of a divine father and a mortal mother, but his essence was mortal. It was only after the spirit or Christ (christos = messiah) descended upon him that he could work miraculous healings.[138]

Theodotus and his adoptianist followers interpreted Jesus' healing in the spiritual-rational mode of the philosophical physician Galen.[139] In the second century A.D. Galen acquired an eminence and prestige that no healer had enjoyed before.[140] Galen was not merely a proponent of scientific diagnosis, as some have maintained.[141] When he was sixteen he was apprenticed by his father to the Asklepieion at Pergamon where he was exposed to both the scientific tradition derivative of Hippocrates and the religious savior-healer

---

136 Martin Hengel, *Between Jesus and Paul. Studies in the Earliest History of Christianity* London: SCM, 1983), pp. 105-106.

137 Homer Smith, *Man and His Gods* (Boston: Little, Brown & Co., 1952), p. 227.

138 Lk 1:35; Hippolytus, ret. 7, 35.

139 Epiphanius, *Haer.* 54, 1, 7; Eusebius, *Hist Eccl.* 5,28, 13-17.

140 Glenn W. Bowersock, *Greek Sophists in the Roman World* (Oxford: Clarendon Press, 1969), pp. 59-60.

141 Luis Garcia Ballester, "Galen as a Medical Practitioner: Problems in Diagnosis," in Vivian Nutton, ed., *Galen: Problems and Prospects* (London: Wellcome Institute of the History of Medicine, 1981), p. 35.

Asklepios.[142] It was a period of great popular interest in Asklepios as a personal savior and as a patron of physicians. After having contracted a near fatal disease, Galen petitioned Asklepios, credited him with having saved his life, became his servant, dedicated an essay on anatomy to him, and expressed the opinion that medical science must be accompanied by spiritual inspiration to cure ailments successfully.[143] Human nature had been corrupted by passion and therefore must be healed by the spirit before true curing can occur.[144]

For Galen, Hermes, a disciple of Asklepios, was the source of this wisdom preserved in manual, *Asklepios, The Perfect Teaching* found with the Nag Hammadi Codices. It is a dialogue between an initiate, Asklepios, and the mystagogue Tresmesgisitus, *alias* Hermes. Humans become immortal through wisdom, a view consistent with Theodotus' adoptionism, Galen's savior-healing, and the Asklepios cult. This tractate indicates Asklepios' cult and Gnosticism interpenetrated one another.[145] Wisdom, or Sophia, the cornerstone of healing in gnosticism, was parallel to Asklepios' *techne*, but its positive view of nature was more consistent with Asklepios than with the Gnosticism.

The massive following of Asklepios led Eusebius, the church historian, to regard him as a serious challenger to Jesus. At Aegae in Cilicia Eusebius noted "thousands were excited over Asklepios as a savior and as a physician who was sometimes manifest to sleepers and sometimes healed the diseases of those who were ill." Eusebius did not doubt the healings, but he also rejoiced when Constantine destroyed the Asklepieion.[146] The cult of Asklepios was not eradicated by Constantine, however, since there were still dedicants from Aegae at Epidauros in 355 A.D. who called themselves "hierophants and priests of the Savior."[147]

In cryptic and clandestine ways adherents to ancient savior-healers remained associated with the renovated cultic sites long after their supposed Christianization. Although Theodotus had been excommunicated by Pope Victor (186-198 A.D.), Theodotus' healing cult was not discontinued. Another healing disciple took the name of Theodotus II, a Roman Jewish banker with high social and economic connections[148] who developed an elaborate theology based on Melchizedek, whom he regarded as the supreme mediator between God and man, and therefore the spiritual son of God from whom Jesus received the spirit at baptism.[149] Joining him were two confrères, who

---

[142] Wesley D. Smith, *The Hippocratic Tradition* (Ithaca, NY: Cornell University Press, 1979), p. 63.

[143] Edelstein, *Op. cit.*, I:473.

[144] Howard Clark Kee, *Medicine, Miracle and Magic in New Testament Times* (Cambridge, Eng.: Cambridge University Press, 1986), pp. 59-60.

[145] James M. Robinson, *The Nag Hammadi Library* (2nd. ed.; San Francisco: Harper-Collins, 1990), pp. 330-338.

[146] Eusebius, *Vita Constantine*, 3.56; Sozomen, *Ecclesiatical History* 2.5; E. and L. Edelstein, *Op. cit.*, I:419-20.

[147] *IG* I.2.438.

[148] Eusebius, *Op. cit.* 5, 28, 103).

[149] Hippolytus, ref. 7, 36.

took their names Asclepiodotus and Artemas from the two largest healing cults of the age.

Adoptionists have been regarded as isolated and unrepresentative of gentile Christianity, but their following was large and threatening to the emerging male establishment, since they provided an empowering role for women and paved the way for Christian healing by developing a dualistic version of Jesus' healing miracles. Led by Paul of Samosata, they were condemned at the synod of Antioch in 268 A.D. Their major opposition were the Origenists who stressed that Jesus was *homoousios* or the same divine substance as God but a real person distinct from Him.[150] This apparently technical issue really was designed to relegate Asklepios to a secondary position. By the end of the third century, the Christological trajectory had shifted subtly from Jesus as a human-divine healer-savior to divine-human savior-healer, indicative of growing tension within the pre-Nicene church to maintain a claim of uniqueness based on divine substance in order to distinguish and elevate Jesus above other divinities of the Graeco-Roman world who were merely adopted by the divine.

5. Transformations and Renovations: Asklepieia into Christian Chapels

The act of cleansing both physically and spiritually in holy water was an important component of healing sanctuaries. Mineral waters were deemed especially miraculous, and sites of shrines to Asklepios were located where baths could make use of mineral waters. Ritual cleansing in the Greek world was wide-spread, and the medium varied from mineral waters to the blood of a bull or ram (*taurobolium*). In any case the action was meant to provide new life for the communicant through special properties of the medium after the well had been properly consecrated. The Jewish world, and the Islamic world later, held ritual cleansing in high esteem, and forms of immersion in holy water (*mikveh*) such as those at Qumran, Bethesda or the Jordan delineated the bounds of the sacred world: by immersion one stepped from the profane into the holy.

A bearded Askelpios crowned with olive branches and bare-chested in a toga stood before Hygieia seated on a throne flanked by a lioness, her symbolic animal of protection. Forceps and other surgical instruments hang on the wall, a unique feature obviously used by a human physician, Asklepios, in the intermediate stage between hero and god who saved the life of Telemachos the dedicator of this monument.

Mystery and medicine, spirituality and surgery, were complimentary aspects of healing mind and body, *psyche* and *sarx* mirrored by a monotheistic tendency in late antique paganism. In a statue fragment from the Piraeus now in the National Museum, a calm and composed Asklepios is shown nude to the waist with up-turned eyes gazing on the power of heaven, Theos Hypsios, God Almighty.[151] Asklepios was both venerated and venerable, and as Jesus

---

150 Epiphanius, *Haer.* 73, 12.

151 Athens, Greece, National Museum cat. no. 258.

competed with his cult he took on more the role of the savior sent by Theos. Asklepios became god's agent, assuming more and more the role of the divine-human mediator, as Graeco-Roman cults, in general, became more and more monotheistic in their competition with Christianity.

The afflicted would spend the night in "incubation" with the *therapeutae* or Asklepian priest within in the *abaton* or inner sanctuary, where the god would appear in a dream or vision, touch the afflicted part of the body and render a miraculous cure:

> A man whose fingers, with the exception of one, were paralyzed, came as a suppliant to the god. While looking at the tablets in the temple he expressed incredulity regarding the cures and scoffed at the inscriptions. But in his sleep he saw a vision. It seemed to him that, as he was playing at dice below the Temple and was about to cast the dice, the god appeared, sprang upon his hand, and stretched out his [paralyzed] fingers. When the god had stepped aside it seemed to him that he bent his hand and stretched his fingers one by one. When he had straightened them all, the god asked if he would still be incredulous of the inscriptions on the tablets in the Temple. he answered that he would not. "Since, then, formerly you were incredulous of the cures, though they were not incredible, for the future," he said, "your name shall be 'Incredulous'. "When the day dawned he walked out sound.[152]

These incubation practices continued with the Jesus Movement. First, Jesus was recorded as a healer and then, later, a healing god.[153]

The Lazarium Renovation. The best example of this description of incubation in the Jesus Movement is found in the story of Lazarus being raised from the dead by Jesus at Bethany preserved in the Secret Gospel of Mark, antedating all others and presenting Jesus as healer in the tradition of Asklepios:

> Jesus being angered, went with [Lazarus' mother] into the garden where the tomb was. And immediately a great voice was heard from the tomb. And Jesus, drawing near, rolled away the stone from the entrance to the tomb. And immediately, going in where the young man was, he stretched out (his) hand and raised him, grasping his hand. And the young man, looking at Jesus, loved him and began to beseech him that he might be with him. And as they came out of the tomb, they went into the house of the young man, for he was rich. . . . And after six days Jesus gave him an order; and when the evening had come, the young man went to him, dressed with a linen cloth over his

---

152 *Inscriptiones Graecae,* IV,1, nos. 121-2; Edelstein I:230 Testimony 423, 3.

153 Mary Hamilton, *Incubation or the Cure of Disease in Pagan Temples and Christian Churches* (St. Andrews, Scotland: W. C. Henderson and Sons, 1906).

naked body. And he remained with him that night, because Jesus taught him the mystery of the kingdom of God.[154]

The site of the "tomb" of Lazarus in Bethany about two miles from Jerusalem on the Road to Jericho was known in the first three centuries as a cave "and a stone lay upon it,"[155] similar to the ancient healing sites of chthonic deities in Crete. In 330 A.D. Eusebius recorded that "the place of [the tomb of] Lazarus is still pointed out even until now" a phrase used to indicate that the site was of great antiquity.[156] This grotto was an ancient Asklepieion, and Eusebius was especially interested in the cult of Asklepios as we know from his investigations into the sanctuary at Aegae in Cilicia.[157] When Aetheria visited Jerusalem in 381-4 A.D. she referred to a church that had been built on the site and the town was now called by the same name, "Lazarium." Jerome, revising Eusebius' description in 390 A.D. confirmed Aetheria's report that a church had been constructed on the site.[158]

In 1950 the evidence that enabled the connection between the church and the Asklepieion was unearthed: an ancient tomb on the western edge of the village was discovered about 400 meters from the church called the Lazarium. The entrance led to a single central pillar (the ancient symbol of the mother goddess) with a subterranean sanctuary (5.4 x 4 x 3m.) where ancient Asklepios' healing rituals had taken place. Graffiti on the north wall indicated that the "Lord God who raised Lazarus from the dead, remember your servant Asklepios and Chionioy, your female servant."[159] Jesus' healing was associated with Asklepios' healing by Christians who partook of both cults. Subterranean and secluded, the afflicted prayed and meditated. Awaiting the epiphany of their god, Jesus came! Asklepian-Christian pilgrims incubated as Asklepios taught but prayed for healing as Jesus taught, through remission of sin, the cause of affliction, as another graffiti makes clear: "God of Christians, have mercy on Anamos and take away his sins. Amen."[160] Asklepios, embraced by the Jesus Movement, was transformed to meet needs of a new age and a new savior.

The Bethesda Renovation. The Pool of Bethesda has special significance for the story of Asklepieia being converted into churches. In ancient Aramaic "Bethesda" means "house of the poured-out waters." A fourth century story related how Jesus remarked to the Pharisee that he had washed "in these

---

154 Helmut Koester, *Ancient Christian Gospels: Their History and Development* (Philadelphia: Trinity Press International, 1990), p. 296.

155 Jn 11:38.

156 Eusebius, *Onomasticon*, ed. Erich Klostermann *Die grieschen christlichen Schritsteller der ersten drei Jahrhundert* (Berlin, 1950), p. 58.

157 Eusebius, *Vita Constantine*, 3.56.

158 Eusebius, *Onomasticon*, p. 59.

159 Jack Finegan *The Archaeology of the New Testament: The Life of Jesus and the Beginning of the Early Church.* (rev. ed.; Princeton: Princeton University Press, 1992), p. 157.

160 *Ibid.*, p. 157.

poured-out waters."161 An Old Syriac version gave the name as *Byt hsd*, meaning "house of mercy," appropriate for a healing site. The Qumran Copper Scroll, *ca.* 25-68 A.D., identified two pools at Beth Bshaydathayinin.162 The Bordeaux Pilgrim called these twin pools, *piscinae gemellares*, with five porticoes, Bethsaida, indicated that "There were those who have been sick for many years who are now cured, because the pools contain water which is wine-red when turbid," *in modum coccini turbatam*, in seasons of higher rainfall. This echoes the miracle of water made wine-red: "For an angel went down to the pool in the spring and made the waters flow with great turbulence, and whosoever stepped into the pool then was made whole of whatsoever disease he had." The pools in the turbid period were higher in mineral content, especially iron, which colored the waters from yellow to red. This provided the empirical basis of healing while spiritual prescience provided the miracle: "Jesus, seeing this man lying there and knowing that much time had passed, says to him, 'Do you want to become whole again?' The man answered, 'Sir, I have no one to help put me into the water when it is turbulent. Jesus said to him, 'Rise take up your mattress and walk.' And immediately the man became whole again and took up his mattress and walked."163

The 5000 sq. yd. area of these two pools was made *ca.* 220-195 B.C. in the reign of the high priest Simon II whose medicinal spirituality based on Sirach 38164 conformed architecturally and medically to the Asklepios' cult. East of the twin pools a natural grotto with man-made vaulted chambers, basins and canals had been hewn from bedrock. In the Roman period the site was renovated into an Asklepieion with paintings and mosaics decorating walls, and statues of Asklepios positioned in the *abaton* in which was found an inscription "Pompeia Lucilia dedicated this" as her votive gift of healing.165 The Asklepieion of Bethesda was known to the Jews simply as the house of mercy (Aramaic: "Bethesda"), and for the lame man it became efficacious by the command of Jesus.166 Thus, Jesus knew and utilized common ancient healing sites as localities for his healing ministry.

During the third century the Pools were rededicated, and Christians bearing crosses would come to be healed, leaving their crosses behind as votive offerings. These crosses were discovered buried underneath the church in the Asklepieion renovated as a baptistery, and date the church's construction prior to 427 A.D. when Theodosius forbade crosses in

---

161 *Oxyrhynchus Papyri*, ed. Bernard P. Grenfell and Arthur S. Hunt (London: Egyptian Exploration Fund, 1898), p. 840 lines 25, 32-33; Jack Finegan, *Hidden Records of the Life of Jesus* (Philadelphia: United Church Press, 1969), sec. 222.

162 3Q15, cols., 12-13; *Discoveries in the Judaean Desert* (Oxford: At the Clarendon Press, 1965), III p. 297. The double ending ("inin") indicates there were two pools and that "poured-out water" was synonymous for pool.

163 Jn 5.1-8. My translation.

164 Ecclus. 50:1-3; Richard M. Mackowski, *Jerusalem, City of Jesus: An Exploration of the Traditions, Writings and Remains of the Holy City from the Time of Christ* (Grand Rapids, Mich.: Eerdmans, 1980), p. 79In.

165 L.-Hugues Vincent and F. M. Abel, *Jérusalem récherches de topographie, d'archéologie et d'histoire* (2 vols.; Paris: Librarie Lecoffre, 1914-1926), 2:694-695.

166 Finegan, *Op. cit.*, p. 232.

churches.[167] By 451 A.D. a three-hall basilica (18m x 45m) of the Lame Man had been built on the spot according to Peter the Iberian.[168] Thus, holy sanctuaries of the Jesus Movement in the first three centuries were placed on or near Asklepios' sacred pools and grottos and later renovated into distinctively Christian architectures.

The Gerasa, Decapolis, Renovation. This structural arrangement of an ancient pre-Christian sacred healing site adjacent to an early church site is replicated by others of a pre-Constantinian origin. For instance, the Decapolis, noted for its Hellenistic syncretistism was mentioned in the Gospels only three times and only once did Jesus actually visit there.[169] The Cathedral at Gerasa is in the Gilead mountains on the Chrysorhoas stream, a tributary of the Jabbok River. The town was built on the Graeco-Roman plan of colonnaded streets, spaced 51.6m (175 *pedes*) apart intersected by north-south tetrapylons on the main cardo. Enclosed by a town wall, with theaters, private habitations, and a forum, it had temples to Zeus, Artemis and Asklepios dating to the mid-first century.

The temple of Artemis was located originally fronting the main cardo, Antonine Street, was 122m wide and was part of an earlier street layout.[170] The northernmost bridge, of which the base is extant, led across the wadi from the east side of the city to the original temple by the Sacred Way. The extant temple was relocated north of its present location and is slightly out of alignment with this Sacred Way.

Inside the existing cathedral we can see the remains of the early house-church that renovated the Artemesion's healing-bath as a baptistry in the first century. Steps descended into a baptismal pool from the north and south. At the east was a semi-circular apse with a bench and three body-sized depressions for immersion. A cistern behind the baptistry was connected to mineral springs via earthenware piping which opened into the font. On either side of the baptistry were large rooms with mosaic floors, perhaps original rooms of the house-church before it was renovated. The Fountain Court was supplied with sacred water by a lead pipe from the northwest corner and was drained into the northeast corner. On the west side a patch of second-century Roman mosaic is at the level of the court.

The Gerasa church was formally renovated before 375 A.D., when Epiphanius noted that every year on the anniversary of the Cana miracle which coincided with the Feast of the Ephiphany, a sacred spring at the

---

167 J.-M. Rousée and R. de Vaux, *Révue Biblique,* 64 (1957):226-228 ; J.-M. Rousée, *Révue Biblique* 69 (1962):107-109; Asher Ovadiah, "Supplementum to the Corpus of the Byzantine Churches in the Holy Land," *Levant* 13 (1981):223-224.

168 As the Curetonian Syriac version of Jn 5:2 makes clear. Joachim Jeremias, *The Rediscovery of Bethesda, New Testament Archaeology* Monographs, no. 1 (Louisville, Kentucky: Southern Baptist Theological Seminary, 1966), pp. 33-34.

169 Mt 4:25; Mk 5:20; 7:21.

170 Roberto Parapetti, "The Architectural Significance of the Sanctuary of Artemis at Gerasa," *Studies in the History and Archaeology of Jordan,* 1 (1982): 255-260.

matyrium in Gerasa ran with "wine,"[171] indicative of mineral waters rendered red by iron oxide. Arabic inscriptions indicate that the site was sacred to Dusares, "god of Arabia," who was associated with a miracle of transforming water into wine. Hellenistic Greeks viewed the sacred well as a sacred spring, either for Asklepios or for Dionysios since it seasonally poured forth in the sacred color of Dionysios' wine. The Cana miracle was an extension of this ancient holy epiphany.

The Fountain Court provides a glimpse of how earlier ancient healing sanctuaries were identified in terms of later religious beliefs and how the knowledge of the previous use was totally obliterated by successive adherents.[172] This silent process transformed an ancient Arabian site into a Graeco-Roman shrine and, finally, into a Christian church.

The Dura Europos Renovation. The Syrian *domus ecclesia* at Dura Europos provides a glimpse of another process of renovation. Captured and destroyed by attacking Sassanians in 256 A.D., the ruins of the city preserved a most important pre-Constantinian church structure when a house-church was discovered in block 17 next to the city wall in 1932.

Eighteen prayer graffiti were found, six of which were apotropaic chants possibly used for Asklepian healing rituals. Another group of four graffiti were Christian: "One God in heaven." "Christ with you! Remember Siseon the humble." "Christ Jesus be with you. Remember Proclus." "May Dorotheos be remembered. Anno Domini 232-3."[173] The last graffito establishes the *terminus ad quem* of the *domus ecclesia* and was found under the last plaster layer. These prayers offered here were an innovation in that they are addressed to deceased members of the congregation in a benediction using the accusative case, whereas God or Christ was usually the subject of the verb "remember." This personalized theologizing suggests that this group acted and behaved as an extended family with intimate social relationships, similar to those we have noted in the Asklepios' cult. Apotropaic healing invocations and benedictions to Christ on behalf of the special dead were combined in prayer in a syncretistic milieu. Far from being doctrinally rigid belief systems interpenetrated each other.

Sociological evidence helps us understand who these congregants were . About 55% of the domestic houses at Dura conform to the Mesopotamian central-court type house surrounded by rooms accessible from the street level through a foyer which offered privacy.[174] Four classes of central court-type houses can be identified: 1) central court with rooms on one side; 2) with rooms on two sides; 3) with rooms on three sides; 4) with rooms on four sides. If we accept the ethnoarchaeological assumption that surface area of dwelling

---

171 Epiphanius *Pan. haer.* 51.30, 1-2, *Die grieschen christlichen Schritsteller der ersten drei Jahrhundert* (Berlin, 1950), II:301.

172 J. W. Crowfoot, *Palestine Exploration Fund Quarterly Statement* (Jerusalem, 1929), pp. 31-35; *Ibid.*, (Jerusalem , 1931), pp. 153-154.

173 Graydon Snyder, *Ante Pacem* (Mercer University Press, 1989), pp. 147-148.

174 P. Delougaz, H. D. Hill, S. Lloyd, *Private Houses and Graves from the Diyala Region* (Chicago: Oriental Institute Press, 1967); L. Wolley and M. Mallowan, *The Old Babylonian Period, Ur Excavations* (London, 1975); C. Preusser, *Die Wohnhaueser in Assur* (Berlin, 1954).

roughly corresponds to economic status, a basic social structure of Dura can be attempted.[175]

At the time of the Sasanian siege in 256 A.D., at least 100 houses were occupied. The smallest dwellings comprised less than 100 sq. m. and accounted for 9% of the 114 dwellings. In this group we find a central court with rooms on one side or two sides only. The next size house covered from 100 to 400 sq. m. and accounted for 72% of the dwellings. For this size of house 21% are type 2, 40% are type 3, and 22% are type 4. The third group of houses covered from 400 to 100 sq. m. and accounting for 10%. Most of the third group were either type 3 or type 4. The fourth group covered more than 1000 sq. m., all had four-sided central gardens, and had particular prestige.[176]

This analysis correlating surface area with economic status is corroborated by the economic value of archaeological artifacts recovered in the four types of dwellings. Only 25% of the houses less than 100 sq. m. contained valuable structural or movable objects. Of houses with areas between 100 to 400 sq. m., 32% contained valuable objects. Of those between 400 and 1000 sq. m. 66% have valuable architectural structures and 55% have valuable movable objects. All the dwellings over 1000 sq. m. have structurally valuable objects, and 55% have valuable movable objects, since they were probably the first to be looted.[177]

The placement of these houses in the general plan of the city is sociologically apposite to the *domus*. In the southeastern district[178] and in the Roman Camp in the north central type four houses of the wealthy are present.[179] Type three houses are also present in adjacent areas for officials such as the commandant and the city magistrates.[180] In the Wall Street and in the Agora districts the biggest houses are type four but they are very few; palatial houses of type three are more common, but the most common dwelling is 100-400 sq. m. with a court surrounded by rooms on only one or two sides. These were dwellings of people of lower economic means.

The *domus* is located in this last area of lower economic dwellings, even though it is type three. This indicates that the leadership in the second and third centuries of the Jesus Movement in Dura Europos was held by the rising class of more wealthy individuals who nonetheless lived in a section of the city where the majority of inhabitants were of the lower economic order. It is important that they were physically removed from the socially prominent officials of the town.

---

175 See C. Kramer, "An Archaeological View of a Contemporary Kurdish Village: Domestic Architecture, household size and Wealth," in *Ethnoarchaeology* (New York, 1980), p. 158; P. J. Watson, *Archaeological Ethnography in Western Iran* (Tucson: University of Arizona, 1979), p. 292.

176 Anny Allara, "Domestic Architecture at Dura Europos," *Mesopotamia* 22 (1987):71.

177 *Ibid.*, p. 72.

178 Redoubt Area D1.

179 Precinct E4.

180 Precincts J1, C3 and D5.

By comparing the architectural structures of the *domus ecclesia* and the synagogue in Dura Europos we can assess the process of socialization of Jewish Christianity within the Graeco-Roman world.

As has been previously indicated, the members of the congregation in the *domus* regarded themselves as an extended family. They also were operating in a hostile environment. This is proven from structural remains that were exposed archaeologically. Three stages of architectural development indicate the nature of renovation from an earlier dwelling to a private eight-room house to a six-room house-church. The second stage, the private house was built in an unexceptional Graeco-Roman plan with a central courtyard, totaling nearly 18 sq.m. and 5.2m high. The entrance was on the northeast via a vestibule. A partition wall forced one to turn west to enter the central courtyard. Opposite the entrance to the courtyard were three rooms created by walls continuing the courtyard boundaries. To the west of the courtyard (room 1) were rooms 5 and 6 that were the living areas for the women of the house. Rooms 4a and b were living quarters for men. Room 6 in the northwest did not follow the partitions found on the south side, and, being adjacent to the latrine that it fronted, was the least desirable room in the house, and probably housed the sleeping quarters for servants. The east end of the latrine area joined a stairwell to the roof.

When the house was transformed into a house-church, the exterior of the building did not change. Alterations were made within the confines of the existing space. The central courtyard became the meeting hall and room 6 became the baptistry adjacent to the plumbing in the latrine area. This internal reorganization and failure to alter external appearances suggests that the community was clandestine, meeting in secret, without notice of the official authorities. It also indicates why this is a unique find in the history of Christian archaeology, since lack of detection was the goal of the communities of the Jesus Movement under the Severi and prior to the so-called Edict of Milan in 313 when the legality of Christian churches and the equality of all religions was decreed by Constantine and Licinius. However, Christians did adapt private dwellings with obscure renovations that could be easily concealed from the authorities. Should a Roman have walked even into the vestibule of the *domus ecclesia* he would not have noticed the baptistery, so cleverly concealed from his view from the street. It certainly appears from the remains of Dura Europos that the cosmopolitan pluralism of Judaism and the Graeco-Roman religions represented confirms their legal equality (except for the Jesus Movement which remained secretive) in 256 when Dura Europos was sacked.

The architecture of the Dura synagogue compared with that of the domus ecclesia is striking, for the Jewish community was probably double that of the Jesus Movement. Jewish worship was inside a private house, but this house was part of a larger complex of interrelated non-religious buildings. The synagogue area reserved for worship exhibits deliberate architectural planning not found in the domus. Although the surrounding buildings have the same characteristic Graeco-Roman layout as the domus (inner courtyard surrounded by rooms), part of the synagogue was separated from the rest by a blind wall. The synagogue was, therefore, technically a house-synagogue comprised of a courtyard with three porticoes behind which is a large assembly room connected by one central door for men and a side door for women to enter. On the rear wall was the recess (*ciborium*) where the Torah was placed. Around this room was a bench for the congregants. This ciborium resembles the baptistery in the *domus*. Architecturally the Jewish and the Christian houses of worship were identical except for this distinguishing feature and the fact that no permanent walled bench was found in the domus.

In the domus, iconography of the savior-healer converged with the iconography of Jesus the Good Shepherd. In the only room of the *domus* to be decorated with paintings, the baptistery, we find frescoes of baptism as a remission from sin and therefore as healing rite. On the east wall two registers separate a Galilean scene which depicts Jesus and Peter walking on the sea, while amazed fishermen in a one masted boat, similar to the one excavated at Kinneret, look on. This scene is remarkable in that it is nautically accurate as far as the vessel is depicted, so that one might surmise that the painter had access at least to descriptions of vessels on the Sea of Galilee from which to fashion his illustration. Below this scene, separated by a blue, yellow and red horizontal stripe, a second register illustrates a procession of three women entering the tomb of Jesus on Easter morning. All have their heads covered and they wear himation or chiton robes symbolizing their sacred ritual, the same robes used in the Eleusinian Mysteries and in the Artemision cult. They carry torches in their right hands as they would also have in their sacred nocturnal mission, since baptism was usually reserved for Easter eve.[181]

The three Marys, like the three figures on the Leiden Plate depicting the goddesses accompanying the infant Asklepios, are the chief priestesses in this Christian rite of baptism, a practice within the Jesus Movement before its patriarchalization, before the mantles of women had been exchanged for the tonsures of men. One only has to compare the relative predominance of men in frescoes and the separation of the sexes by male and female entrance doors of the Dura synagogue to appreciate the extent of patriarchalism within the Jewish community. Iconographically, women were accorded at least an equal if not superior role in the domus ecclesia.

The three priestesses stand between two great white sarcophagi. The one to the south was draped and closed shut, indicating Jesus in the tomb. The one to the north was open and empty, vines symbolizing new life draped the lintel. The sequence of the two registers becomes obvious now. The top register indicated scenes from Jesus' life beginning with the gathering of the disciples at the Sea of Galilee (other scenes are lost). The lower register continued the story beginning in the south and continuing north, boustrophedon style, from the closed to the empty tomb with the three discoverers of the risen Christ between the two tombs. Women shared in their master's blessings and powers, including that of healing.

---

181 Jean Danielou, "Baptism before the Middle Ages," in R. P. C. Harrison, *The Pelican Guide to Modern Theology* (Baltimore, 1969), pp. 157-170.

The Good Shepherd who lays down his life for his flock[182] is depicted in the lunette above the baptismal font on the north wall of the baptistery. Yet, here we also have the theme of healing repeated, for he carries a ewe as the flock frolics. He is youthful, clothed in a chiton and holding a shepherd's staff. Below him was the stone-built baptismal font shaped like a sarcophagus, large enough to hold a person, since baptism was by immersion. Above the lunette of the Good Shepherd was a ciborium resting on two azure columns painted in water chevrons like the columns supporting the ciborium of the Torah in the nearby house-synagogue. The columns support a heavenly vault painted in bright azure and spangled with stars, for this is the divine mystery of baptism, the healing of the soul and the forgiveness of sins. Appropriately, in the lower left corner of the Good Shepherd tympanum, a diminutive, naked Adam and Eve stand in shame covering their bodies. The old Adam sinned, the new Adam redeems.

Another scene depicts the healing of the man with the mattress at the Bethesda Pools in Jerusalem. Here in a crude rendering two scenes are painted. The first is one of the man in his linen shrouds beside the pool which is painted in the color of the turbulent water, red, signifying the sacred, tinged mineral waters. Jesus stands over him. To the left, the man has taken up his mattress and has begun to walk. Simce the Bethesda Pools were a prominent site of Asklepian activity at the time the Dura artist was recording the scenes perhaps from life. The connection between Asklepios and Jesus could not have been missed by these members of the *domus ecclesia.*

The Athenian Renovation. Sometime after 485 A.D. the Athenian Asklepieion was dissolved and about one hundred years later, coincident with the rise of Islam and after the termination of the schools of philosophy by Justinian, buildings in the sanctuary were sacked by Christians.[183] On the site was built a Christian basilica incorporating the foundations of the former Doric and Augustan stoas before the end of the fifth century.[184] The original church site appears to have been built over the round Spring House of Asklepios' holy water, covering the grotto in the Acropolis rock which was now approached through a concealed tunnel from the back wall on the east side of the short axis of the stoa. In the courtyard between the two stoas are foundations of a very small temple and an altar. [185] This middle terrace and its Spring House had been built in the sixth century B.C. and the two small temples to Themis and Isis were seen by Pausanias in *ca.* 150 A.D.[186] The

---

[182] Jn 10.14.

[183] A. Franz, *Late Antiquity: A.D. 267-700, The Athenian Agora,* vol. xxiv (Princeton: Princeton University Press, 1988), pp. 44, 70-71.

[184] T. E. Gregory, "The Survival of Paganism," *American Journal of Philology* 107 (1986), 238.

[185] J. M. Mack. Camp II, *The Water Supply of Ancient Athens from 3000 to 86 BC* (Ph.D. diss., Princeton University, 1977), pp. 112-116; J. M. Wickens, *The Archaeology of Cave Use in Attica, Greece, from Prehistory through Late Roman Times* (2 vols.; Ph.D. Diss., University of Indiana, 1986), II:329-335.

[186] Pausanias, 1.22.1.

basilica engulfed not only the site of the temple to Asklepios but also the stoa of incubation, the sacred spring and the *katagogoein* of the sanctuary.[187]

6. Consolidations: Theos Hypsistos and Theos Sabazios

This approach to the iconography of Jesus as Healer helps resolves a long-standing debate on the interpretation of Jewish and Jewish-Christian iconography. Carl Kraeling, one of the original excavators of Dura Europos in 1928, was of the opinion that the key to the Jewish and Jewish-Christian iconography in Dura Europos lay in the Talmud, Midrash, ancillary Jewish writings and the New Testament. Erwin Goodenough examined the iconography, the architecture and graffiti in the larger Graeco-Roman context. The present study follows the lead of Goodenough by viewing the Jesus Movement within the cultural context. It appears certain that the Jesus Movement was syncretistic, and that part of its vitality lay in its ability to build on the institutions of the past. Isolation from the Graeco-Roman religions of the day was not desirable, indeed it was not possible.

Although the figures of Asklepios and Hygieia were thought of as foremost healing saviors, they were not identified as omnipotent deities. Theos Hypsistos, however, was used to indicate omnipotence and was evidently prompted by the success of the Christian mission which claimed universality of a god that the Graeco-Roman local deities had seemed to lack.

Concurrently with this new Graeco-Roman theological strategy, Jewish communities, especially in Asia Minor, began to accept non-circumcised Gentiles into the synagogue as Theosebees, Greek "God worshippers." Judaism was undergoing a challenge of identity. Judaism was thoroughly Hellenized in communities of Asia Minor where customs were both diverse and local.

Two simultaneous trajectories within Judaism and the Graeco-Roman religions of the first three centuries converged in confrontation. Graeco-Roman cults began to claim monotheistic status by viewing deities as different aspects of Theos Hypsistos, Almightly God, irrespective of their ancient and divergent mythic trajectories. Even Zeus the most exalted of the Gods was given the epithet "Hypsistos." This usage was probably borrowed from the *LXX* where the term is used 110 times in a variety of forms meaning "the most high" or "almighty." It was obvious that Graeco-Roman religions, Judaism and Christianity were in competition. An example was preserved in the graffiti of the *domus* at Dura Europos. Conversely, Jewish communities began to assume the opposite tendency of becoming more local and identified with their constituent Greek and Roman neighbors, allowing these "God Worshippers" to attend Temple and partake of the holy Law even though they were not technically proselytes and had no intention of being circumcised.

That these were in fact two trajectories with a history and not just spurious developments can be proven by a literary examination of these titles. In the *LXX* of the third century B.C. Theosebees was used only seven times describing the people of Israel as an ethic and religious entity, a practice

---

187 Gregory, *loc. cit.*

which Josephus follows. Jewish inscriptions in Asia Minor use the title for Gentiles, like the ones on the stele found in 1987 at Aphrodisias where Theosebees is used for fifty-two Gentile "God Worshippers."[188]

The cults of Asklepios and Jesus the pre-eminent savior-healers of late antiquity ministered to people of many cultures and similar anxieties. Jews actively participated in festivals and socialized with Christians as potential synagogue attendees, and Graeco-Roman religious cults did the same. People did not establish doctrinal positions to adhere blindly to them. Popular religion and healing cults addressed immediate problems of the age: the decay and dissolution of the institutions, the unforseen consequences of plague and the uncertainty of survival.

The quest for healing penetrated different ethnic and religious groups, homes of ordinary and exceptional citizens, the infirm of body and spirit. Romans, whether Hellene, Jew or Christian, were dismayed by corruption, nostalgic for moral commitment, and desirous to render mutual assistance. They were not timid to experiment, and their anxiety for security never thwarted inventiveness. They renovated houses, experimented with synagogues, Asklepeia and domus ecclesiae. Theirs was a world rife with illness and social disintegration. New dangers lurked in the recesses of the Empire, and Romans recognized the need for a new collegia, a new family with new ideas and new values.

One man attracted attention of the multitudes, brought forth from these old familiar places, a new faith, a new healing. Throughout the countryside and the cities, the dioceses and the empire, wherever he and his successors made house calls, old sanctuaries were renovated with new significance and a universal religion was born.

---

[188] J. M. Reynolds, and R. Tannenbaum, *Jews and God Fearers in Aphrodisias. Greek Inscriptions with Commentary* (Cambridge: Cambridge Philological Society, 1987).

Jesus' Table Practice: Dining with "Tax Collectors and Sinners," including Women

Kathleen E. Corley
University of Wisconsin, Oshkosh

Many New Testament scholars have considered the tradition that Jesus was known for eating with "tax collectors and sinners" to be significant for reconstructions of the "Historical Jesus." Although a few have questioned the historical reliability of this tradition, such voices are still in the minority.[1] Recent reconstructions of the Historical Jesus, most notably that of Dominic Crossan, have also suggested on the basis of such traditions that Jesus was known for some kind of "open commensality." Crossan further suggests that such openness would have extended to women, and that given the social identification of such women, Jesus would have been accused of eating with "whores."[2] As this is precisely the implication of this tradition which I had suggested previously,[3] I would like to further buttress such suggestions by examining the implications of shifts in Greco-Roman meal practice for determining the presence of women at meals with Jesus. It is notable that certain Jesus traditions do imply that Jesus was known for dining with women. This would further imply that one aspect of Jesus' "open" dining practice was that he, like other members of various social, religious and philosophical groups of his time, not only gathered with friends and

---

[1] For a relatively recent review of scholarship on this question, see Dennis Smith, "The Historical Jesus at Table," in *SBL 1989 Seminar Papers*, ed. David J. Lull (Atlanta, GA: Scholars Press, 1989) 466-486. Smith argues that the association of Jesus at meals is a literary motif and presupposes enough of a social formation to render it inauthentic. Dominic Crossan's more recent book makes "table fellowship" central to his reconstruction of the historical Jesus (*The Historical Jesus. The Life of a Mediterranean Jewish Peasant* [San Francisco: HarperCollins, 1991]).

[2] Crossan, *Historical Jesus*, 261-264; 335.

[3] Kathleen E. Corley, "Were the Women Around Jesus Really Prostitutes? Women in the Context of Greco-Roman Meals," *SBL 1989 Seminar Papers*, ed. David J. Lull (Atlanta, GA: Scholars Press, 1989) 487-521; and now in *Private Women, Public Meals: Social Conflict and Women in the Synoptic Tradition* (Peabody, MA: Hendrickson, forthcoming Fall, 1993), chs. 2 and 3. As page numbers are not set at this date, citations will be by chapter and section.

associates for communal meals[4] but welcomed women to his table. In this paper I intend to argue that: 1) the accusation that Jesus ate with "tax collectors and sinners" was in part criticism for dining with women, 2) these women were being accused of "promiscuous" behavior for appearing at public meals with men, 3) these women were not peasants, as the accusation itself betrays Hellenistic expectations held by higher classes for women of higher economic status, and finally 4) this has implications for our understanding of the social environment of Jesus and his associates.

Women and Meal Innovations

The appearance of women at communal meals is characteristic of the period of Greco-Roman history in which the historical Jesus lived. That means that gender inclusive meals, although noteworthy, were not unique in the social world of Jesus. I have suggested that such gender inclusive meals, which were characteristic of Christian groups generally, show that early Christians were participants in the innovative culture of their times, but would not have set them apart from their Hellenistic environment. Such gender inclusive meals were thus not distinctively Christian, but were rather the result of an Empire-wide social innovation beginning in the Late Republican era, whereby free women began having increased access to the "public" sphere of men, and began attending public meals. This innovation in meal practice of Greco-Roman women was met with strong resistance, as such an innovation undermined the social and gender based hierarchy of Greco-Roman society. As such behavior had long been associated with the less restricted habits of lower class women, slave women, prostitutes and courtesans, women who ventured out into public in this manner or attended public meals with men were labeled "slaves," "courtesans" or "prostitutes," regardless of their actual social status, occupation or social position. This fluctuation in Greco-Roman meal etiquette may be found throughout the Hellenized Mediterranean world, even in Palestine.[5] Thus, it is notable that it can be shown that one aspect of the slander against Jesus' table practice implies that he is eating with "promiscuous" women.

Jesus as an Advocate for Open Table Practice–
Meals with "Tax Collectors and Sinners"

The notion that Jesus ate with "tax collectors and sinners" meets the standard criterion of multiple attestation, and for this reason is usually

---

4 Dennis E. Smith, "Social Obligation in the Context of Communal Meals: A Study of the Christian Meal in 1 Corinthians in Comparison with Graeco-Roman Communal Meals," (Th.D. Dissertation, Harvard Divinity School, 1980); and with Hal Taussig, *Many Tables: The Eucharist in the New Testament and Liturgy Today* (London: SCM Press; Philadelphia: Trinity International Press, 1990).

5 Corley, *Private Women, Public Meals*, ch. 2, part 4. Even the community at Qumran followed standard Greco-Roman meal conventions. The Passover Seder liturgy, as well as following standard meal conventions, required that women recline next to their husbands for the meal. In Egypt, Jewish women monastics reclined with men for communal meals in the Therapeutic society described by Philo.

considered to be historical in some sense. This tradition is found in both Mark and Q, and the theme of the open table or banquet can be found in various literary genres of the gospel tradition.[6] Such a characterization of Jesus is therefore early and pervasive throughout the Gospel tradition.

In Mark 2:14-17 Jesus is described as joining a tax collector and his friends for a private banquet. Although the scene has long been recognized as Markan composition, it is a scene probably expanded from an earlier chreia which contained the criticism of Jesus for "eating and drinking with tax collectors and sinners."[7] In Q 7:34 Jesus is similarly slandered for his table practice, one that features "wine bibbing and gluttony." He is also accused of being a "friend of tax collectors and sinners." The idea of "friendship" would include eating with them as well, as "friendship" is a common banquet theme.[8]

The history of literature on the identity of Jesus' banquet companions and reasons behind the scandalous implications of eating with such individuals is immense, and need not be repeated here.[9] Suffice it to say that attempts to clearly identify literal "tax collectors and sinners" in first century Palestine have remained inconclusive and unsatisfactory.[10] In the context of my own research, such characterizations of Jesus reflect typical depictions of those known for banqueting with "promiscuous" women and pimps.[11] For example, tax collectors were often linked in antiquity to prostitution. In ancient Greece, state revenue was collected by special tax gatherers known as *pornotelōnai* who kept lists of licensed harlots. Prostitutes were not taxed during the Roman period until the reign of Caligula (37-41 CE), but were still required to register to ply their trade. However, tax collecting and keeping a brothel were still two trades that remained linked in Hellenistic literature. As a despicable set of occupations, tax collecting and brothel keeping were also taken up by rhetoricians as a means to slander groups of individuals. Thus Plutarch remarks that the Spartans slight the Athenians for collecting taxes and keeping brothels,[12] and Dio Chrysostom remarks of rulers, "Is it not plain to see that many who are called kings (*basileis*) are only traders, tax collectors (*telōnai*) and keepers of brothels (*pornoboskoi*)?"[13]

Not only was the term "tax collector" associated with those who kept company with promiscuous women and pimps, but the term "sinner"

---

[6] The most obviously related gospel traditions would be the Feast parable (Lk 14:15-24; Mt 22:1-13; Thomas 64) as well as the tradition that Jesus "feasts" whereas John "fasts" (Mk 2:18-20; Mt 9:14-17; Lk 5:33-39).

[7] Burton L. Mack, *A Myth of Innocence* (Philadelphia: Fortress Press, 1988), 183; Smith, "Historical Jesus at Table," 475-476.

[8] Smith, "Historical Jesus at Table," 477-478; Dennis E. Smith, "Table Fellowship as a Literary Motif in the Gospel of Luke," *SBL* 106 (1987) 613-638; esp. 634.

[9] Smith, "Historical Jesus at Table," 480-484; Corley, *Private Women, Public Meals*, ch. 3, part 3.

[10] See for example Richard Horsley's assessment of the situation in *Jesus and the Spiral of Violence. Popular Jewish Resistance in Roman Palestine* (Minneapolis: Fortress Press, 1987), 212-228.

[11] Corley, *Private Women, Public Meals*, ch. 3, part 3.

[12] *Mor.* 236C.

[13] *Or.* 4.98.

likewise held connotations of sexual impropriety. Certain typical bad behavior identified Hellenistic persons as "sinners," particularly those who participated in sexual misconduct, such as drunkards, male prostitutes, men who chased women, and adulterers.[14] In Hellenistic literature *hamartōlos* usually had to do with either a person's lack of education or moral failure of some kind, and as such appears in Hellenistic catalogues of virtues and vices.[15] Plutarch uses it in the first sense to slander his Stoic opponents.[16] Luke uses the term to designate a "woman of the city" (i.e., a "prostitute") who anoints Jesus at a meal (Lk 7:37).

This background confirms the recent suggestion that the term "sinners" (*hamartōloi*) is best understood in the context of Jewish sectarianism and philosophical debate, where it is used as rhetorical slander to denounce other Jews outside the boundaries of a particular sect.[17] Dennis Smith has suggested that not only "sinners" but "tax collectors" should likewise be viewed in this manner. Thus, the entire phrase, "tax collectors and sinners" should be categorized as a *topos* in Greco-Roman Jewish polemic.[18] The connection between these two terms and their use as slander against Jesus or his followers' table practice is apt, as tax collectors are connected in Greco-Roman literature to those who trafficked in prostitution and slavery, particularly to brothel keepers and pimps, those most responsible for supplying women and slaves for banquets.[19] Moreover, demeaning descriptions of individuals often included an accusation against their dining behavior. For example, when Cicero is trying to malign Verres, he paints a rhetorical picture of his degenerate behavior at banquets with lewd women.[20] It is therefore not surprising to find *telōnai* combined with *pornai* (Mt 21:31), nor surprising that Luke chooses a prostitute at a meal to fill in his narrative about Jesus' attitude toward "sinners" (Lk 7:37ff.). Where one found tax collectors and brothel keepers, one would expect to find prostitutes as well. Eventually, however, such language functioned as traditional slander, and as such would not serve to identify actual tax collectors, sinners or prostitutes within a particular group, nor characterize a group's actual behavior at meals. The accusation that Jesus

---

14 Ronald F. Hock, "The Will of God and Sexual Morality: 1 Thessalonians 4:3-8 in its Social and Intellectual Context," paper presented at the Annual Meeting of the SBL, New York, 1982, p. 35.

15 K. H. Rengsdorf, "hamartōlos, ktl," TDNT, v. 1, ed. G. Kittel (Grand Rapids, MI: Eerdmans, 1968), 317-8; A. Deismann, *Light from the Ancient Near East* (London: Hodder and Stoughton, 1927), 113-115.

16 *Aud. Poet.* 7 [ii, 25C]; Rengsdorf, 319.

17 James G. Dunn, "Pharisees, Sinners and Jesus," in *The Social World of Formative Christianity and Judaism*, ed. J. Neusner, et al. (Philadelphia: Fortress Press, 1988), 274-80, esp. 276-280; followed by Smith, "Historical Jesus at Table," 482, 484; and by myself, *Private Women, Public Meals*, ch. 2, part 3; ch. 3, part 3. See also Luke T. Johnson, "The New Testament's Anti-Jewish Slander and the Conventions of Ancient Polemic, *JBL* 108 (1989) 419-441, esp. 438-439.

18 Smith, "Historical Jesus at Table," 482.

19 Corley, *Private Women, Public Meals*, ch. 2, part 2.

20 *Verr.* II.3.68.159-160; II.5.12.30-13.31; II.5.13.34; II.5.32.83; II.5.36.94.

associated at meals with "tax collectors and sinners" thus in one sense serves to identify Jesus or his followers as opponents.[21]

However, given the link between "tax collectors" and prostitution, the link between "sinners" and sexual promiscuity, and the link between banqueting and consorting with lewd women at banquets, such slander also suggests that Jesus is here being accused of eating with "promiscuous" women. Hellenistic women were often accused of promiscuity for public behavior generally, particularly when they participated in unorthodox table etiquette, or engaged in free association with men in public situations.[22] In fact, the accusation of prostitution is also found in the context of philosophical repartee, in particular as a term bandied about by groups in the habit of slandering one another when debating the relative merits of one another's philosophical systems.[23] The use of this kind of slander reveals the presence of women in certain philosophical groups, rather than actual prostitutes.[24] The Cynic school in particular was notable for its inclusion of women like Hipparchia and for their defense of women's ability to study philosophy and achieve moral virtue.[25] As having a philosophical education was a characteristic traditionally associated with ancient Greek courtesans,[26] women in these groups were called "prostitutes" by rival philosophical sects. What this means is that the term "prostitute," then, as well as an accusation of sexual promiscuity on the part of women in a group, can be seen as one of the standard charges of Hellenistic rhetoric, and not necessarily indicative of the actual occupation or behavior of the women so labeled.[27]

Thus, the accusation that Jesus dined with "tax collectors and sinners" reflects typical characterizations of those known for banqueting not only with disreputable tax collectors and pimps, but implies the presence of their women as well. The very imagery of disreputable banquet behavior, replete with "wine bibbing and gluttony" calls to mind the presence of lewd women, slaves and courtesans, the kind of women present in a typical Hellenistic banquet scene. Thus, both Mark and Q imply that Jesus was slandered for eating with women, and was thus a participant in the social progressivism of his day, as were Cynics and others who allowed women to attend

---

21 Smith, "Historical Jesus at Table," 482.

22 Corley, *Private Women, Public Meals*, ch. 2; "Were the Women Around Jesus Really Prostitutes?"

23 Corley, *Private Women, Public Meals*, ch. 2, part 3; Johnson, "Anti-Jewish Slander," 431.

24 Corley, *Private Women, Public Meals*, ch. 2, part 2; "Were the Women Around Jesus Really Prostitutes?," 519-520.

25 The *Cynic Epistles*, esp. the "Letters of Crates" addressed to Hipparchia, illustrate non-traditional Cynic ideas on women's roles. In Lucian's *Fugitivi*, a woman Cynic leaves her husband and runs away with two slaves. See F. Gerald Downing, *Jesus and the Threat of Freedom* (London: SCM Press, 1987) 115-17; idem, *Christ and the Cynics: Jesus and other Radical Preachers in First Century Tradition* (JSOT Manuals 4; Sheffield: Sheffield Academic Press, 1988), 1-5.

26 For example, chreiai attributed to courtesans are quite numerous. See Athenaeus, *Deipn.* 13.584a and *Deipn.* 13, passim; Corley, *Private Women, Public Meals*, ch. 2, part 1.

27 Corley, *Private Women, Public Meals*, ch. 2, part 3; "Were the Women Around Jesus Really Prostitutes?," 519-521.

philosophical symposia or other public meals. Moreover, it is notable that both Luke and Matthew interpret the group called "sinners" from Mark and Q to include women, and interpret the tradition that Jesus ate with "sinners" to mean that Jesus had women present with him for meals.[28]

Jesus, John, the Courtesans and Q

In light of this discussion, it is notable that Q may have included a reference to "tax collectors and prostitutes" as numbering among those who accepted the messages of Jesus and John. In Luke, we find a comparison of those who accept Jesus and John with those who reject them:

"I tell you, among those born among women no one is greater than John; yet the least in the kingdom of God is greater than he." (And all the people who heard this, including the tax collectors, acknowledged the justice of God, because they had been baptized with John's baptism. But, by refusing to be baptized by him, the Pharisees and the lawyers rejected God's purposes for themselves) (7:29-30, NRSV).

There is, however an intriguing parallel to this is in Matthew 21:31-32:

Jesus said to the them, "I tell you the truth, the tax collectors and the courtesans (*pornai*) are entering the Kingdom of God ahead of you. For John came to you to show you the way of righteousness, and you did not believe him, but the tax collectors and courtesans did. And even after you saw this, you did not repent and believe him." (NRSV with emendations).

There are several reasons for arguing that some form of this pericope might have been present in Q, arguments that I have made elsewhere and for the sake of brevity will not repeat here.[29] It is notable, however, that William Arnal, the member of the International Q Project reconstructing this section of Q 7, now suggests that "tax collectors and prostitutes" could very well have been named in Q 7 as numbering among those who responded positively to John, and subsequently, to Jesus.[30] If this kind of slander leveled against the followers of John and Jesus were present in Q, it would further connect Jesus and John at the level of philosophical sectarianism, particularly the argument that they were both perceived as Cynics of some kind.[31] Moreover, as Cynics were among those groups known for their inclusion of women, and as women in Cynic groups were also characterized as "whores," such sectarian slander would reveal that Jesus not only inherited disciples from John the

---

28 Corley, *Private Women, Public Meals*, chs. 4-5.

29 Kathleen E. Corley, "Jesus, Egalitarian Meals and Q," paper presented to the Q Section of the SBL at the Annual Meeting, San Francisco, November, 1992; also in *Private Women, Public Meals*, ch. 5, part 2.

30 "Reconstruction of Q 7:29-30," unpublished paper to be presented to the International Q Project members this summer (1993). The International Q Project has yet to vote on this section officially. Arnal rates his decision with a {C}.

31 Ron Cameron, "What Have You Come Out to See? Characterizations of John and Jesus in the Gospels," *Semeia* 49 (1990) 35-69.

Baptist, but that some of these followers were women. The scandalous characterization of Jesus' women followers as "prostitutes" would certainly cohere with the tradition that Jesus was accused of dining with promiscuous women and pimps or "tax collectors and sinners," which would have included women.

It seems clear that the banquet imagery under girding the rhetoric and slander that Jesus was accused of eating with "tax collectors and sinners" reveals the presence of women at meals with Jesus. If the tradition that Jesus practiced some kind of "open" or "egalitarian commensality" is to be considered historical, then the participation of women in that "open commensality" must also be assumed to be equally historical.[32] The nature of the accusation itself requires this conclusion. However, just as it is unlikely that Jesus dined with real "tax collectors," it is also unlikely that Jesus dined with real practicing "prostitutes." Who then were these women? What was their real social class?

Crossan, in his most recent work, assumes that the egalitarian ethic of Jesus has its roots in a peasant mentality.[33] One would assume that if Jesus was a peasant, then the women he associated with would likewise have been peasants. However, in light of the Hellenistic evidence, the accusation that Jesus dined with "tax collectors and sinners" does not evoke the image of one dining with members of a lower class, such as peasants, or even outsiders or social expendables.

Social Science Models of Agrarian Societies

Many biblical scholars now use social science models to aid in their understanding of Greco-Roman society and ancient Palestine.[34]

Scholars of sociology and anthropology consider the society current in first century Palestine an agrarian society, which would have certain common features.[35] Following the cross cultural analysis of Gerhard Lenski, the population in Galilee would be divided into eight classes apart from the *ruler*, there being a great economic gulf between the four elite classes and the four lower classes. Assisting the ruler would be the *governing class*, no more than one to two percent of the population. The ruler and the governing class together would have shared between them no less than half of the national income.[36] In service to the aristocracy would be the *retainer class*, who aided the elite, such as bureaucrats, personal retainers, soldiers, servants, petty officials, tax collectors and the like. On account of their service to the elite,

---

32 So Crossan. See *Historical Jesus*, 263; 335.

33 Crossan, *Historical Jesus*, 263.

34 Crossan, for example, is very dependent on Lenski's model (*Historical Jesus*, 43-71). See also the recent collection of articles utilizing social science models in biblical interpretation done by the Context Group, Jerome H. Neyrey, ed. *The Social World of Luke-Acts. Models for Interpretation* (Peabody, MA: Hendrickson, 1991).

35 Throughout the next section of this paper, I am dependent on the cross cultural analysis of social stratification by Gerhard E. Lenski, *Power and Privilege. A Theory of Social Stratification* (New York; St. Louis; San Francisco: McGraw-Hill, 1966).

36 Lenski, *Power and Privilege*, 210-242.

such individuals would have been elevated above the mass of the common people, and to a limited degree would have shared in the economic surplus. Members of this class would account for around five percent of the population.[37] Although the ruler and the governing class controlled much of a nation's wealth, in virtually all agrarian societies there evolved from the lower classes a *merchant class,* who were often able to acquire both economic and political power. Probably numbering around three to four percent of the population, this was a group always eager to emulate the life of their betters; they often sought to marry into noble families and to be accepted by them as equals. Of course, not all merchants were rich, and many remained quite poor.[38] The fourth group among the privileged was the *priestly class,* which would have included not only the leaders of organized religion, but all religious leaders such as monks, rabbis, religious teachers and the like who were dependent on the religious system for their status. Certain members of the priestly class were among the wealthiest in an agrarian society, and often enjoyed the favor of the elite. However, as well as contributing to the stability of social inequities or *status quo* by legitimizing the rule of the political elite, on many occasions members of this class have also opposed tyranny and injustice, and have provided the ideological undergirding for revolutionary movements.[39] According to Lenski's analysis, priests and retainers together would have made up a small percentage of the population, about seven or eight percent.[40]

Economically far below these four elite classes would have been the bulk of the population, particularly the *peasant class.* Peasants carried the burden of supporting the state and the privileged classes, given the extent of the taxes and other obligations which they owed. Although practices have varied from place to place and century to century, peasants have at various times owed anywhere from 30-70% of their income in land taxes, rent, or crops. According to Lenski, throughout history, "the great majority of peasant farmers had little more than the bare necessities of life" and lived very simply, although peasants were by no means all reduced to the same level. The peasant class could be anywhere from sixty to seventy percent of the total population.[41] Close in status to the peasants were members of the *artisan class,* about five to seven percent of the population, which in most agrarian societies came from the ranks of dispossessed peasants. Although there was a great degree of overlap in wealth and income between peasants and artisans, many artisans were poorer than most peasants. Many artisans organized into guilds, particularly in urban areas.[42] In some agrarian societies, below artisans were the *unclean and degraded classes,* who had to resort to culturally offensive occupations, and often had only their bodies or physical energy to sell. Another five percent of the population, these would include those who performed the tasks of pack animals, as well as tanners, miners and low class

---

37 Lenski, *Power and Privilege,* 243-248.
38 Lenski, *Power and Privilege,* 248-256.
39 Lenski, *Power and Privilege,* 256-266.
40 Lenski, *Power and Privilege,* 284.
41 Lenski, *Power and Privilege,* 266-278, esp. 270.
42 Lenski, *Power and Privilege,* 278-280.

prostitutes.[43] Finally, at the bottom of the agrarian class system would be the *expendables*, the five to ten percent of the population for whom society had little or no need, such as petty criminals, beggars, or underemployed itinerant workers.[44] Of the entire population, only about three to eight percent would have lived in urban areas, the rest in rural areas and small villages. However, urbanites would have dominated rural society "politically, economically, religiously and culturally."[45]

The Social Class of Jesus' Table Associates and the Lives of Peasant Women

Given Lenski's stratification of agrarian societies, when Jesus is accused of eating with "tax collectors and sinners," he is being criticized for dining with disreputable members of the retainer class and their women. If Jesus had earned such a criticism by members of the peasant class, it would imply that he was betraying his class by socializing with those who exacted anywhere from 30-70% of a peasant's income.[46] However, there is no evidence that Jesus earned the criticism of the lower classes. Rather, such an accusation presupposes a criticism from a more upper class perspective, from at least that of the priestly, retainer or merchant classes, who would have imbibed much more of the cultural expectations of the rich – the social "wannabees," as it were.[47] Not only does the evidence I have gathered suggest this, but the gospels themselves place this accusation on the lips of members of just such a higher class, Pharisees or scribes, who would have been members of the privileged priestly class, not peasants.[48] From this more elite perspective, then, Jesus is accused of running about with disreputable members of society and promiscuous, "lower class" women. This betrays a more elitist or urban perspective, and as such assumes a certain interest in the improper behavior of the women around Jesus. It is not clear at all, however, that members of a privileged class would have had such expectations of *peasant* women.

---

43 Lenski, *Power and Privilege*, 280-281.

44 Lenski, *Power and Privilege*, 281-284.

45 Lenski, *Power and Privilege*, 200.

46 Lenski, *Power and Privilege*, 267-68.

47 See discussion by Lenski, particularly that of the merchant class (*Power and Privilege*, 248-256). Freedmen and women who became wealthy merchants in the ancient world would fit nicely into this category. See *Private Women, Public Meals*, ch. 2, part 1, n. 46; ch. 4, part 4.

48 Mark 2:14-17, par.; Q 7:34. Even if first century Pharisees were not local religious leaders of some sort, they would at least have had some kind of education, and thus would still fit into the "priestly class" of an agrarian society. For a recent appraisal of the identity of first century Pharisees, see Burton L. Mack, *The Lost Gospel. The Book of Q and Christian Origins* (San Francisco: HarperCollins, 1993), 60. On the priestly class, see Lenski, *Power and Privilege*, 256-266. There could, however, also be what Lenski terms a "lower clergy," who would live in a manner similar to the peasants (258-259). The Pharisees, at least as portrayed in the gospels, do not seem to be on the level of medieval rural parish priests. Unfortunately, we know very little about rural religious leaders in first century Galilee (Mack, *Lost Gospel*, 60).

Cross-cultural studies have shown that peasant women have been generally far less restricted in their activities than women of the upper classes. This particularly true for rural women, who even have more freedom than their counterparts among the urban poor. By virtue of necessity, peasant women no doubt crowded the streets of the ancient world, selling household produce, buying household goods or going for water.[49] Peasant women from small villages are characteristically even more likely to have contact with life outside a village or town than peasant men, as the men spend much of their time in the fields.[50] In peasant homes, support for the family is raised by any means possible, and peasant women in ancient Palestine, like all peasant women, probably hired themselves out as day laborers, both as domestics and as agricultural workers.[51] For these reasons, peasant women in Jesus' day probably would have had not only more mobility, but also more actual control over household finances and their own income than many women in the higher classes of similar agrarian societies.[52] Their greater mobility would have allowed these women to be key participants in peasant social life, even though peasant societies remain essentially patriarchal. In such societies women serve as key links in an intricate system of social relations that allows them to have great influence in both the domestic and political realm.[53] Their greater mobility and increased involvement in meeting the economic needs of their families may account for the characteristic participation of peasant women in public riots during times of peasant uprising (which in fact occurred in 1st century Palestine), particularly when the concern of the populace was with subsistence issues.[54] Thus, the social organizational pattern

---

[49] Henry Habib Ayrout, *The Egyptian Peasant* (Boston: Beacon Press, 1963), 78-79; 108; 121-122; Nathan J. Brown, *Peasant Politics in Modern Egypt. The Struggle Against the State* (New Haven and London: Yale University Press), 34-35; Carmen Diana Deere, *Household and Class Relations. Peasants and Landlords in Northern Peru* (Berkeley; Los Angeles; Oxford: University of California Press, 1990), 109-110; 208-209; 284; Eric R. Wolf, *Peasants* (Englewood Cliffs, NJ: Prentice Hall, 1966), 46-47;

[50] Ayrout, *The Egyptian Peasant*, 82-83; 121-122.

[51] Deere, *Household and Class Relations*, 96-97; 208-09; 226-227; 284-87; Brown, *Peasant Politics*, 34-35

[52] The poorer the peasant family, the more this is the case. See Deere, *Household and Class Relations*, 110-11; 199-202; 287.

[53] Susan Carol Rogers, "Female Forms of Power and the Myth of Male Dominance: A Model of Female/Male Interaction in Peasant Society," *American Ethnologist* 2 (1975) 727-756; Joyce F. Riegelhaupt, "Saloio Women: An Analysis of Informal and Formal Political and Economic Roles of Portuguese Peasant Women," *Anthropological Quarterly* 40 (1967) 109-125. Rogers and Riegelhaupt repeat many of the generalizations about the lives of peasant women that can be made on the basis of cross-cultural study, such as their role in agriculture, trade, the marketplace, domestic service for the upperclasses, etc. Also on the status of women in the Middle East generally, see Sondra Hale, "The Politics of Gender in the Middle East," in *Gender and Anthropology. Critical Reviews for Research and Teaching*, ed. S. Morgan (Washington DC: American Anthropological Association, 1989), 246-267; Cynthia Nelson, "Public and Private Politics: Women in the Middle Eastern World," in *Gender in Cross-Cultural Perspective*, eds. C. Brettell and C. Sargent (Englewood Cliffs, NJ: Prentice Hall, 1993), 94-106.

[54] Josephus, *Antiquities*. 18.263, 269; *Jewish War*, 2.192-193; Philo, *Embassy to Gaius*, 222-225. On the characteristic participation of women in peasant revolts, see Ayrout, *The Egyptian Peasant*, 111; Michael Beames, *Peasants and Power. The Whiteboy Movements and Their Control in*

of peasant societies is perceived by certain ethnographers as being much more "egalitarian" in spite of the gendered nature of much of their division of labor.[55]

However, meal customs characteristic of peasant societies still reflect gender inequalities. In meal contexts peasant women have characteristically prepared and served food for the household, are rarely described as leaving the room during meals, and in some peasant societies were assumed to need fewer calories than men, in spite of the equal labor which they performed.[56] However, when men dine together in large groups, peasant women characteristically do not join their husbands at the table, and at times even eat after the men are finished.[57] Gender segregated seating characterizes large formal meals of peasants, such as those held at religious festivals or weddings.[58] This makes the requirement found in the ancient Passover liturgy that directs even lower class housewives as well as women of status to recline for the Passover Seder next to their husbands all the more notable.[59]

It is therefore unwise to use general cross-cultural observations about the greater freedom and mobility of peasant women in a way that obscures the great limitations of their lives. Likewise, it is unwise to idealize the kind of poverty characteristically experienced by the bulk of peasant populations. Moreover, women in peasant societies are discriminated against to the same degree that they are in most societies. For example, peasant women often only work outside of the home as a last resort; when they do their work is devalued and they still receive lower wages for it.[60] They are still greatly limited on account of their role in reproduction, and the decisions they have the most influence in are those made about marriage arrangements, although they are

---

Pre-Famine Ireland (Sussex: Harvesters Press; New York: St. Martin's Press, 1983), 59; Yves-Marie Bercé, *Revolt and Revolution in Early Modern Europe. An Essay on the History of Political Violence* (New York: St. Martin's Press, 1987), 81-84; 107-109; Brown, *Peasant Politics*, 116-117; Frader, *Peasants and Protest*, 123; 154-157; Joan B. Landes, *Women and the Public Sphere in the Age of the French Revolution* (Ithaca and New York: Cornell University Press, 1988), has an entire chapter on "Women and the Revolution," 93-151; Darlene Gay Levy and Harriet B. Applewhite, "Women of the Popular Classes in Revolutionary Paris, 1789-1795," in *Women, War and Revolution*, ed. C. Berkin and C. Lovett (New York: Holmes and Meier, 1980), 9-35. My thanks to UW-O colleague Howard Brown for bringing to my attention these references on the role of common women in revolutionary France.

[55] Rogers, "Myth of Male Dominance," passim; Riegelhaupt, "Saloio Women," passim.

[56] Ayrout, *The Egyptian Peasant*, 82-83; Deere, *Household and Class Relations*, 285; Laura Levine Frader, *Peasants and Protest. Agricultural Workers, Politics, and Unions in the Aude, 1850-1914* (Berkeley; Los Angeles; Oxford: University of California Press, 1991), 32-34.

[57] Frader, *Peasants and Protest*, 82-83; Rogers, "Myth of Male Dominance," 740-41.

[58] Nicholas S. Hopkins, "Clan and Class in Two Arab Villages," in *Peasants and Politics in the Modern Middle East*, eds. F. Kazemi and John Waterbury (Miami: Florida International University Press, 1991), 252-276; esp. 260-261; Rogers, "Myth of Male Dominance," 740-41.

[59] Corley, *Private Women, Public Meals*, ch. 2, part 4.

[60] Brown, *Peasant Politics*, 34-35; Deere, *Household and Class Relations*, 96-98; 109-110; 199-202; 227-28; 286-87; 291; Frader, *Peasants and Protest*, 82-83; 87-89; 117-118.

also by means of manipulation able to influence village politics.[61] In fact, certain studies show that the discrimination against peasant women in great part contributes to the overall poverty of the entire peasant class which is so dependent on the labor of all members of the family.[62] Furthermore, even rural peasant women, in spite of their greater mobility, have still operated under the larger cultural constraints of dominant societies, particularly when it comes to sexual morality and "ideal" feminine behavior, such as not speaking to men in public.[63] In fact, in a peasant context, it is precisely the correct behavior of the women (particularly proper sexual behavior) which upholds the "honor" of the entire community.[64] Peasant women may be poor, but there is no suggestion that they are characteristically more "promiscuous." It is probably for this reason that in peasant societies the "myth" of male dominance is strictly maintained by both men and women, in spite of the actual control over their lives and households that peasant women practiced.[65] Although peasant women indeed characteristically do more (and no doubt did more in ancient Palestine as well), they are also in the least position to actually challenge traditional female roles by taking credit for their own achievements. Rather, credit for their success goes to the family and to the male head of the household, a sleight of hand which in turn really serves to reinforce ideal gender roles, not challenge them.[66] Moreover, the kind of political power exercised by peasant women is still ultimately

---

61 Stephen G. Bunker, *Peasants Against the State. The Politics of Market Control in Bugisu, Uganda, 1900-1983* (Urbana and Chicago: University of Illinois Press, 1987), 34; 41; 66-67; 94-96; 126; Frader, *Peasants and Protest*, 85-86; Rogers, "Myth of Male Dominance," 743.

62 Deere, *Household and Class Relations*, 109-110; 291. See also comments by Nathan Brown, "The Ignorance and Inscrutability of the Egyptian Peasant," in *Peasants and Politics in the Modern Middle East*, eds. F. Kazemi and J. Waterbury (Miami: Florida International University Press, 1991), 203-221; esp. 213, where he discusses findings of demographic studies showing the relationship between rural poverty and peasant ignorance. Such a hard life of struggle for mere survival effectively cripples their intellectual and spiritual growth, leaving them no energy for other matters. The results are ignorance, poverty, overreproduction, the low status of women, lack of sanitation, and loss of mental ability.

63 Ayrout, *The Egyptian Peasant*, 122-123

64 Ayrout, *The Egyptian Peasant*, 122-123. See also Crossan, *Historical Jesus*, 13-15, who cites an article by Jane Schneider, "Of Vigilance and Virgins: Honor, Shame and Access to Resources in Mediterranean Societies, " *Ethnology* 9 (1971) 1-24 (unavailable to me at time of writing). Another recent article on general expectations of Mediterranean women is Jerome H. Neyrey, "Mary, Mediterranean Maid and Mother," *BTB* 20 (1990) 65-76.

65 Rogers argues that men are not in fact in control of peasant societies due to the equal participation and power of peasant women ("Myth of Male Dominance").

66 Rogers, "Myth of Male Dominance," 740; 746-7 and passim. Here I simply disagree with Rogers' analysis. Peasant women do not challenge the ideology of gender present in the society because to do so would be too threatening. This silent agreement between the men and the women in peasant society merely allows the equal participation of women in that society which occurs in fact to continue without disrupting the social order. As soon as the society becomes less domestic-centered, or if the economic situation of the society evolves to the point that the income derived from women's labor and participation is no longer essential for family survival, the equal participation of the women in that society diminishes and disappears (Rogers, "Myth of Male Dominance," 749). Myths are powerful forces, and thus male dominance in appearance is easily transformed into male dominance in fact.

derivative in nature and a matter of influence, rather than direct control.[67] For these reasons it seems unwise to romanticize the "egalitarian" nature of peasant life. "Egalitarianism" among peasants has more to do with the reality of limited resources, in that each member of a peasant society has a stake in making sure that such resources are equally shared, and little to do with some sort of altruistic ideology.[68] Thus, given the pervasiveness of Hellenistic culture in Palestine, and the tremendous influence of urban sensibilities in Galilee,[69] peasant women in first century Palestine would still have been culturally constrained by the common moral expectations for Hellenistic women generally in spite of their greater mobility, their access to "public" spheres like the marketplace and their positions as domestic servants in wealthier households. Furthermore, it seems unlikely that the motivation for Jesus' socially inclusive meals can be explained on the basis of a peasant "mentality" or "egalitarianism," as the more equal distribution of labor and resources among peasants has little to do with such altruism, and peasant meal patterns still characteristically reflect gender divisions and inequities.

It seems more likely then, that the motivation behind the inclusion of women and others at meals in the Jesus movement is better explained by larger social changes that were affecting all Hellenistic society, even Hellenized Jewish society in Palestine. On the level of elite rhetoric, accusations against women who participated in freer Greco-Roman behavior, particularly at meals, were in part accusations that such women were behaving in a manner beneath their station. Lower class women would still have been present for meals, particularly as women often serve food in poorer homes, as well as in their jobs as domestics in homes of the wealthy. Wealthy women at public meals showed themselves to be "lower class" or "slavish," as participation in banquets and public meals was still behavior associated in the popular imagination with women of the lower classes, particularly with slaves.[70] Thus, implied in the criticism of the women who joined Jesus for meals would be a similar accusation of "slavish," or "lower class" behavior. However, if the women around Jesus were really peasant women, why would they be criticized for behaving in a freer manner expected of their class? Rather, as slander stereotypical of this period generally, and as slander directed against Jesus by members of a wealthier

---

[67] In spite of the arguments of Rogers and Riegelhaupt, this remains hard to deny. See Rogers, "Myth of Male Dominance," passim and Riegelhaupt, "Saloio Women," passim. Riegelhaupt's analysis is more realistic overall.

[68] See esp. Lenski, *Power and Privilege*, 216; but also Rogers, "Myth of Dominance," 731-32 and Riegelhaupt, "Saloio Women," 123 who discuss the peasant interest in equality.

[69] For a recent discussion of the extent of hellenization and urban influence in Galilee in the first century, see Crossan, *Historical Jesus*, 17-19 and his references there; See also Mack, *Myth of Innocence*, 65-66 and now in *Lost Gospel*, 51-68; To their discussions I would only add the nicely illustrated book by Richard A. Batey, *Jesus and the Forgotten City: New Light on Sepphoris and the Urban World of Jesus* (Grand Rapids, MI: Baker Book House, 1991). There are dissenters in this discussion. For a recent defense of Galilee as an isolated, rural area, see John P. Meier, *A Marginal Jew. Rethinking the Historical Jesus* (New York and London: Doubleday, 1991), 278-285.

[70] Corley, *Private Women, Public Meals*, ch. 2; "Were the Women Around Jesus Really Prostitutes?" passim.

class rather than the lower classes, this accusation leveled against the women around Jesus fits better within the context of similar accusations leveled against wealthier women who were accused of acting "promiscuously" by attending public meals with men. This suggests that Jesus' movement attracted women from higher segments of society than simple peasants, as Luke implies (Lk 8:1-3). Luke suggests that many women followers of Jesus were wealthy enough to give Jesus his primary financial support. For example, Luke names one woman follower to be Joanna, the wife of Herod's steward, who would have been a member of the retainer class according to Lenski's social model.

Thus, implicit in the accusation that Jesus associated with women at meals is the assumption that these were women members at least of the retainer, priestly or perhaps merchant classes whose social peers would have objected to their being present for communal meals at all. As members of a priestly class, social groups such as Pharisees and scribes would have expected peasant women to serve and be present for meals, or for slavewomen and prostitutes to join men at dinner. They would not have expected women from their own class to participate in meals in this manner, except perhaps at Passover.[71] It is therefore doubtful that the women implicitly criticized by the image of "tax collectors and sinners/prostitutes" were peasants, slavewomen, real prostitutes or "street women." The accusation itself betrays elitist expectations for women of wealthier means and seems best understood in the context of a larger Hellenistic concern for ideal women's roles and in the context of philosophical sectarianism. It seems therefore more likely that the two epithets "tax collectors" and "sinners" are derogatory designations for members of similar social means, and it may well be that they were understood to represent groups of the two sexes: men accused of behaving like "tax collectors" and women behaving like "sinners" (i.e. "prostitutes" or "courtesans"). Neither would be a way to slander members of the peasant class.

In light of these observations, perhaps the various depictions of women throughout the gospels needs renewed attention. Do all of the women in the gospel narratives really act like peasant women? They seem mobile, yes, but where are their children? Could peasant women really leave their homes and farms for long periods of time in order to follow Jesus? Consider the story of the Syro-Phoenician woman. In spite of her daughter's illness, which might make her mother by association "unclean,"[72] Mark implies that this woman

---

71 The Passover Seder liturgy, as well as following Greco-Roman meal conventions generally, requires that the meal be taken reclining, and that women, particularly women with status, recline next to their husbands for the meal. See G. H. R. Horsley, "Reclining at the Passover Meal," *New Documents Illustrating Early Christianity* 2 (MacQuarie University, Australia: The Ancient History Documentary Research Centre, 1982), 75; and Corley, *Private Women, Public Meals*, ch. 2, part 4.

72 Richard Rohrbaugh, "The Social Location of the Markan Community," unpublished paper presented to the Context Group, March, 1993, 15 (To appear in a future issue of *Interpretation*).

has a higher social status than has usually been assumed.[73] Moreover, she walks right up to Jesus, and speaks to him in a manner that can only be described as assertive, and wins the argument to boot. Would a peasant woman behave in this manner? Although it is true that peasant women are talkative and assertive,[74] they are only talkative and assertive with other peasant women, never with men, and are particularly not so with *peasant* men.[75] Another story to reconsider is the story of the woman who anoints Jesus at a meal. In the basic story underlying all accounts, Jesus is anointed at a meal by a woman, and those present object to her action. If she is a slave, or a lower class hireling, what is objectionable about her performing a deed commonly done by such women in such contexts? Perhaps in this instance the omission of her name is a significant indication of her status. In Hellenistic society, it was impolite to mention the name of a respectable woman in public.[76] Thus, although some of Jesus' followers may have been free poor, such as fishermen and the like, the slander of Jesus' table practice indicates that Jesus may have also attracted at least a few women followers to his circle from higher social stations. Moreover, allowing their presence at meals earned him a degree of social criticism. This is not that surprising, as early strands of the gospel tradition like Q characterize the Jesus movement as a community of voluntary poverty. Obviously, some of those joining had to have some wealth to "sell and give to the poor."[77]

The Social Environment of Jesus

The background I am suggesting as the best context in which to understand the accusation that Jesus dined with "tax collectors and sinners" raises many questions about the social environment of Jesus and his associates. If historical, and many New Testament scholars believe that it is, this tradition reveals the presence of women among Jesus' close associates and dining companions. However, not only does this tradition reveal the presence of women among Jesus' dining companions, it further reinforces the characterization of Jesus as one at least familiar with a more urban, Hellenistic environment[78] and may place Jesus in the context of Jewish philosophical sectarianism or debate.[79] This is particularly the case in the way it

---

[73] Mark 7:24-31, par. Gerd Theissen, "Lokal-und Sozialkolorit in der Geschichte von der syrophönikischen Frau (Mk 7:24-30) *ZNW* 75 (1984) 202-25. See also my discussion in *Private Women, Public Meals*, ch. 3, part 5.

[74] Rogers, "Myth of Male Dominance," passim.

[75] Peasant women do not even speak at dinner when their husband is the only man present. Rogers, "Myth of Male Dominance," 740-41; 748.

[76] See Corley, *Private Women, Public Meals*, ch. 3, part 6 for a discussion of the anointing scene in Mark; ch. 2, part 2 on Cicero's invective against the women around Verres; and David Schaps, The Women Least Mentioned: Etiquette and Women's Names," *Classical Quarterly* 27 (1977) 323-30.

[77] That Jesus may have socialized with members of the upper classes is not a new idea. See the discussion (and rebuttal) by Meier, *A Marginal Jew*, 283; 313, n. 168.

[78] See above, and Batey, *Jesus and the Forgotten City*.

[79] It is for this very reason that Smith argues that the tradition that Jesus ate with "tax collectors and sinners" should be abandoned as unhistorical.

characterizes the women around Jesus, in that it assumes a more elitist Hellenistic attitude toward the behavior of Jesus' female associates.

What this means is that the women criticized by this slander do not fit within the social class that many scholars have assumed Jesus came from, attracted and supported. It is possible that the line between the retainer or merchant classes and the peasant class may not have been as rigid as has been supposed. However, if Jesus attracted members of the retainer or merchant classes, this also calls into question suggestions that his movement was some kind of "revolution" against the elite.[80] Rather than characterizing Jesus as an advocate for "peasant egalitarianism," the slander that Jesus ate and drank with "tax collectors and sinners" betrays that Jesus was perceived by his opponents as having more in common with more urbane groups like Hellenistic Cynics, whose social behavior at meals implied a critique (rather than a revolution)[81] of Hellenistic society and challenged Greco-Roman social hierarchy by their inclusion of women at formal meals.[82]

---

[80] So Crossan, Horsley.

[81] Mack, *Lost Gospel*, 120.

[82] I would like to thank my UW-Oshkosh colleagues in Anthropology, Jim Provinzano and Kathleen Dahl, for their insights on peasant societies and women as well as their help with bibliography. Furthermore, my friend Diana Bailey proved to be an excellent discussion partner throughout the writing of this paper.

From Public Ministry to the Passion:
Can a Link Be Found between the (Galilean)
Life and the (Judean) Death of Jesus?

Craig A. Evans
Trinity Western University

The death of Jesus is problematic. How is the historian to account for the crucifixion of an itinerant teacher and miracle worker? To answer this question two important problems must be addressed: (1) how to account for Jesus' execution in Judea at the hands of the Romans and (2) determining what relationship, if any, that execution had to Jesus' earlier Galilean ministry. In his recent and controversial book, *A Myth of Innocence: Mark and Christian Origins*, Burton L. Mack argues that the factors that led to Jesus' execution are unclear[1] and that the Marcan evangelist's linkage of Jesus' public teachings to the story of his death is a narrative fiction.[2] Impressed by Mack's analysis, David Seeley asserts that "Mark concocted the Jewish conspiracy against Jesus for his own, redactional reasons," adding that "the death itself was probably just a mistake."[3]

On the face of it, logic alone suggests the strong probability of a relationship between (a) the execution of a man as "king of the Jews" and (b) well attested traditions that this man had been saying things about a kingdom. That Mark's theological interests played an important role in telling the story of Jesus' death cannot, of course, be denied. But have the evangelist's contributions so completely obscured the chain of events that we cannot say with probability what led to Jesus' death? Is the "Jewish conspiracy against

---

[1] B. L. Mack, *A Myth of Innocence: Mark and Christian Origins* (Philadelphia: Fortress, 1988) 88-89.

[2] Mack, *Myth of Innocence*, 282.

[3] D. Seeley, "Was Jesus like a Philosopher? The Evidence of Martyrological and Wisdom Motifs in Q, Pre-Pauline Traditions, and Mark," *SBLSP* 28 (1989) 540-49, here p. 548. When Seeley says "mistake," I suspect what he really means is *accident*. "Mistake" implies that the Romans either crucified the wrong person or handed down the wrong sentence. "Accident" implies what I think Mack is proposing, namely, that Jesus inadvertently got caught up in a riot (which had nothing to do with his teaching or plans) and was, along with others, summarily executed. Seen in this light, Jesus' death may have had little or nothing to do with his public activities. But from the Roman point of view, Jesus' death was no "mistake."

Jesus" nothing more than a Marcan concoction? Was the death of Jesus nothing more than an accident?

Although I suspect that not too many scholars who engage in Jesus research will be unduly troubled by the views of Mack and Seeley, the problem that they have identified is one that has historically proven nettlesome. The diversity of conclusions bears this out. There are those who have argued that the Jews were principally responsible for Jesus' execution,[4] though advocates of this view are scarce these days. There are those who have argued that the Romans were principally responsible.[5] Some have even argued that the Romans alone were responsible.[6] This diversity notwithstanding, something of a consensus has emerged in which most scholars agree that Jesus was executed by the Roman authorities, in collaboration with a few Jewish persons of influence.[7]

One encounters greater diversity of opinion with regard to the question of what charge was brought against Jesus. It has been argued that Jesus and his followers attempted to overthrow the government in Jerusalem and assume command of the Temple Mount. The coup failed and Jesus was executed.[8] Another study concludes that Jesus provoked deadly opposition because of his charismatic ministry, as Elijah had in his time.[9] Still another contends that Jesus was condemned as a "rebellious elder," for refusing to answer the questions of the ruling priests.[10] One scholar thinks that Jesus was formally charged as a deceiver of the people.[11] Another thinks Jesus' radical views of

---

[4] J. Blinzler, *Der Prozess Jesu: Das jüdische und das römische Gerichtsverfahren gegen Jesus Christus auf Grund der ältesten Zeugnisse dargestellt und beurteilt* (Bibelwissenschaftliche Reihe 4; Stuttgart: Katholisches Bibelwerk, 1951; 4th ed., Regensburg: Pustet, 1969); ET: *The Trial of Jesus* (Westminster, MD: Newman, 1959).

[5] S. Zeitlin, *Who Crucified Jesus?* (New York: Harper & Row, 1942); J. D. M. Derrett, *An Oriental Lawyer Looks at the Trial of Jesus and the Doctrine of Redemption* (London: School of Oriental and African Studies, 1966); P. Lapide, *Wer war schuld an Jesu Tod?* (Gütersloh: Mohn, 1987).

[6] H. Lietzmann, "Der Prozess Jesu," *Sitzungsberichte der Preussischen Akademie der Wissenschaften in Berlin* 14 (1931) 313-22; P. Winter, *On the Trial of Jesus* (Studia Judaica: Forschungen zur Wissenschaft des Judentums 1; Berlin: de Gruyter, 1961; 2nd ed., rev. and ed. by T. A. Burkill and G. Vermes); H. Cohn, *Reflections on the Trial and Death of Jesus* (Jerusalem: Israel Law Review Association, 1967); idem, *The Trial and Death of Jesus* (New York: Harper & Row, 1971).

[7] E. Lohse, *Geschichte des Leidens und Sterbens Jesu Christi* (Gütersloh: Mohn, 1964); W. Koch, *Der Prozess Jesu: Versuch eines Tatsachenberichtes* (Berlin und Köln: Kiepenheuer und Witsch, 1969); O. Betz, "Probleme des Prozesses Jesu," *ANRW* 2.25.1 (1982) 565-647; H. Ritt, "'Wer war schuld am Tod Jesu?' Zeitgeschichte, Recht und theologische Deutung," *BZ* 31 (1987) 165-75; R. A. Horsley, *Jesus and the Spiral of Violence: Popular Jewish Resistance in Roman Palestine* (San Francisco: Harper & Row, 1987).

[8] S. G. F. Brandon, *Jesus and the Zealots: A Study of the Political Factor in Primitive Christianity* (Manchester: Manchester University Press; New York: Scribner's, 1967). Similar views had earlier been articulated by Joseph Klausner and Robert Eisler.

[9] G. Vermes, *Jesus the Jew* (London: Collins, 1973).

[10] J. Bowker, *Jesus and the Pharisees* (New York: Cambridge University Press, 1973)

[11] D. Hill, "Jesus before the Sanhedrin—On What Charge?" *IBS* 7 (1985) 174-86.

finding a place for Gentiles in Israel's faith was enough to get him killed.[12] E. P. Sanders has concluded that it was his specific threat to destroy and replace the Temple that provoked the authorities to eliminate Jesus.[13] Faulting this conclusion, B. D. Chilton suspects that Jesus' arrest and execution were the result of a controversial teaching regarding what constituted appropriate sacrifice.[14] I have argued that Jesus was seized for having condemned high-priestly polity and having predicted the destruction of the Temple.[15]

Leaving aside the specific question of what precise charge, if any, Jewish authorities may have brought against Jesus, the present paper will show that there is considerable evidence of linkage between Jesus' public activities and his crucifixion at the hands of the Romans. This significant evidence, minimized or ignored by Mack and Seeley, primarily consists of two elements: (1) Jesus' proclamation of the Kingdom of God and his subsequent crucifixion as "King of the Jews"; and (2) the appearance of similar, yet independent, linkages in the Fourth Gospel and in the *Testimonium Flavianum.*

The evidence suggests that the Marcan narrative, which admittedly has been edited and arranged to promote distinctive features of Marcan theology, provides a plausible link between Jesus' Galilean activities and his subsequent execution in Jerusalem. In short, Jesus made statements about the Kingdom of God and came to be understood as the Anointed King of this Kingdom. When this teaching was promoted in Jerusalem, during the Passover Feast, Jewish and Roman authorities seized Jesus and put him to death. Jesus' death was not simply a misadventure (and so unrelated to his public activities in Galilee), nor did the Marcan evangelist concoct a Jewish conspiracy. The seizure and execution of Jesus constituted, rather, an inevitable result of and reaction to his proclamation and activities.

Jesus' Proclamation of the Kingdom of God

Proclamation

A suggestive indication of linkage between Jesus' Galilean ministry and his Judean death is his proclamation of the Kingdom of God. This proclamation manifests itself in four areas: (1) parables, (2) prayers and promises, (3) miracles, and (4) politics.

1. Parables and the Kingdom. The most promising place to begin is the kingdom theme in the parables. In the parables, the "bedrock" of the dominical tradition,[16] we hear over and over again the opening words of

---

12 Harvey Falk, *Jesus the Pharisee: A New Look at the Jewishness of Jesus* (New York: Paulist, 1985).

13 E. P. Sanders, *Jesus and Judaism* (London: SCM; Philadelphia: Fortress, 1985)

14 B. D. Chilton, *The Temple of Jesus: His Sacrificial Program Within a Cultural History of Sacrifice* (University Park, PA: Penn State University Press, 1992).

15 C. A. Evans, "Jesus and the 'Cave of Robbers': Towards a Jewish Context for the Temple Action," *Bulletin for Biblical Research* 3 (1993) forthcoming; idem, "Jesus' Action in the Temple: Cleansing or Portent of Destruction?" *CBQ* 51 (1989) 237-70.

16 One recalls J. Jeremias' famous dictum (*The Parables of Jesus* [rev. ed., New York: Scribner's, 1963] 11): "The Parables are a fragment of the original rock of tradition." Recent studies have confirmed this positive assessment; cf. J. D. Crossan, *In Parables: The*

comparison: "The Kingdom of God is like . . ." Several kingdom parables are widely recognized as authentic sayings of Jesus. From Q we have the Parable of the Leaven: "To what shall I compare the kingdom of God? It is like leaven which a woman took and hid in three measures, till it was all leavened" (Luke 13:20-21 = Matt 13:33; cf. *Gos. Thom.* §96).[17] Other promising examples include the Parable of the Treasure (Matt 13:44; cf. *Gos. Thom.* §109),[18] the Parable of the Pearl (Matt 13:45-46; cf. *Gos. Thom.* §76),[19] and the Parable of the Mustard Seed (Mark 4:30-32; cf. Luke 13:18-19; *Gos. Thom.* §20).[20] Crossan rightly concludes: "If, therefore, one precise form of the 'Kingdom' phrase goes back to Jesus, it is most likely 'Kingdom of God.'"[21]

Challenge of the Historical Jesus (San Francisco: Harper & Row, 1973); P. B. Payne, "The Authenticity of the Parables of Jesus," in R. T. France and D. Wenham, eds., *Studies of History and Tradition in the Four Gospels* (Gospel Perspectives 2; Sheffield: JSOT, 1980) 329-44; B. B. Scott, "Essaying the Rock: The Authenticity of the Jesus Parable Tradition," *Forum* 2/3 (1986) 3-53.

[17] Crossan, *In Parables*, 38; idem, *The Historical Jesus: The Life of a Mediterranean Jewish Peasant* (San Francisco: HarperSanFrancisco, 1992) 280-81; D. C. Allison and W. D. Davies, *The Gospel According to Saint Matthew* (2 vols., ICC; Edinburgh: T. & T. Clark, 1988-91) 2.421. According to the "Red Letter" edition of the parables, the Jesus Seminar gives Matthew's version of the parable a "red" rating and *Thomas*' version a "pink" rating; cf. R. W. Funk et al., *The Parables of Jesus: Red Letter Edition* (Sonoma, CA: Polebridge, 1988) 29.

[18] Crossan, *In Parables*, 34, 54-55, 83; idem, *Historical Jesus*, 281-82; B. B. Scott, *Hear Then the Parable: A Commentary on the Parables of Jesus* (Minneapolis: Fortress, 1989) 395; Allison and Davies, *Matthew*, 2.435. The Jesus Seminar gives "pink" ratings to Matthew and to *Thomas*; cf. Funk et al., *Parables*, 37.

[19] Crossan, *In Parables*, 34; idem, *Historical Jesus*, 281; Allison and Davies, *Matthew*, 2.437. The Jesus Seminar gives "pink" ratings to Matthew and to *Thomas*; cf. Funk et al., *Parables*, 46.

[20] Crossan, *In Parables*, 45-51; idem, *Historical Jesus*, 276-79; Scott, *Hear Then the Parable*, 386; R. A. Guelich, *Mark 1-8:26* (WBC 34A; Dallas: Word, 1989) 247. According to the "Red Letter" edition of Mark, the Jesus Seminar gives Mark's version of the parable a "pink" rating and *Thomas*' version a "red" rating; cf. R. W. Funk, *The Gospel of Mark: Red Letter Edition* (with M. H. Smith; Sonoma, CA: Polebridge, 1991) 101. Most scholars think that the Lucan version of the parable (cf. 13:18-19) is derived from Q, not from Mark; cf. J. S. Kloppenborg, *Q Parallels* (Sonoma, CA: Polebridge, 1988) 148-50; R. H. Gundry, *Mark: A Commentary on His Apology for the Cross* (Grand Rapids: Eerdmans, 1993) 226.

[21] Crossan, *In Parables*, 38; idem, *Historical Jesus*, 284. The phrase, "kingdom of God," is very rare in pre-Christian sources. Outside of the LXX (cf. Wis 10:10 [βασιλεία θεοῦ] and *Pss. Sol.* 17:4 [ἡ βασιλεία τοῦ θεοῦ ἡμῶν]), the phrase does not occur in the Old Testament. No clear example of the phrase has yet been found among the Dead Sea Scrolls, which could be significant, given the frequency of the word "kingdom," especially in the texts found in cave 4. At least two examples have been proposed. 1QSb 3:5 breaks off after *twklm*. Some suppose that the line read "kingdom of God (or heaven)," but that is far from certain. R. H. Eisenman and M. Wise (*The Dead Sea Scrolls Uncovered* [Rockport, MA: Element, 1992] 174) restore 4Q525 4 v 3 to read μyhwla tw[klm] ("[the kingd]om of God"), but the restoration is risky (see plate 12). Although the expression was not coined by Jesus, its frequent appearance in the dominical tradition suggests that it was a distinctive feature in his diction; cf. B. F. Meyer, *The Aims of Jesus* (London: SCM, 1979) 129. B. D. Chilton (*The Glory of Israel: The Theology and Provenience of the Isaiah Targum* [JSOTSup 23; Sheffield: JSOT, 1982] 77-81; *A Galilean Rabbi and His Bible: Jesus' Use of the Interpreted Scripture of His Time* [GNS 8; Wilmington, DE: Glazier, 1984] 58-63) has argued that Jesus' use of this expression probably indicates acquaintance with targumic diction, in which this relatively rare expression (*ahlad atwklm*) also occurs (e.g., *Tg. Isa* 24:23; 31:4; 40:9; 52:7; *Tg. Obad* 21b;

2. *Prayers and Promises of the Kingdom.* There is also well attested tradition in which Jesus prays for and promises to his disciples the kingdom of God. Q contains several relevant items. There is the promise that is associated with the Sermon on the Mount and is presented as part of a beatitude: The marginalized of Jewish society are told, "Yours is the Kingdom of God" (Luke 6:20 = Matt 5:3; cf. *Gos. Thom.* §54).[22] Crossan's interpretation of "poor" has implications for kingdom and politics, which will be considered below. In what is probably a related saying, Jesus tells his followers to "Seek His Kingdom" (Luke 12:31 = Matt 6:33) and then expect God to provide for their needs.[23] In the Lord's Prayer, parts of which probably do derive from Jesus, Jesus tells his disciples to pray, "Thy Kingdom come!" (Luke 11:2 = Matt 6:10; cf. *Did.* 8:2).[24] This prayer accurately reflects "Jesus' invocation of the kingdom of God," to quote Crossan in another context, "not as an apocalyptic event in the imminent future but as a mode of life in the immediate present."[25] Again, there are political implications which will have to be taken into account. Finally, Jesus' beatitude that "many prophets and kings desired to see what you see" (Luke 10:23b-24 = Matt 13:16-17) implies the presence of the kingdom.[26]

3. *Miracles and the Kingdom.* There are indications that Jesus' exorcisms and healing miracles related in various ways to his ideas of the kingdom of God. "But if it is by the finger of God that I cast out demons, then the Kingdom of God has come upon you" (Luke 11:20 = Matt 12:28). If this saying goes back to Jesus, and its oddity counts against its invention by the early church,[27] and if

---

Tg. Mic 4:7-8; *Tg. Zech* 14:9). Crossan's conclusion, cited above, is corroborated by Chilton's targumic research: "'The kingdom of God' was the fundamental element in Jesus' preaching" (Chilton, *The Isaiah Targum* [ArBib 11; Wilmington, DE: Glazier, 1987] xxvii).

22 Crossan, *Historical Jesus*, 270-74; Allison and Davies, *Matthew*, 1.436-39. J. A. Fitzmyer (*The Gospel According to Luke I-IX* [AB 28; Garden City: Doubleday, 1981] 632) concludes that Matthew's third-person form of the beatitude is closer to the original. R. H. Gundry (*Matthew: A Commentary on His Literary and Theological Art* [Grand Rapids: Eerdmans, 1982] 67-68) thinks that Luke's second-person form is original.

23 Cf. Meyer, *The Aims of Jesus*, 167. The authenticity of much of Matt 6:25-33 is to some extent corroborated by 1 Cor 9:14 ("the Lord commanded that those who proclaim the gospel should get their living by the gospel"); cf. J. Jeremias, *New Testament Theology: The Proclamation of Jesus* (New York: Scribner's, 1971) 236; Sanders, *Jesus and Judaism*, 105; Allison and Davies, *Matthew*, 1.660. Allison and Davies note that the phrase, "to seek the kingdom," has no precise Jewish parallel.

24 J. A. Fitzmyer, *The Gospel According to Luke X-XXIV* (28A; Garden City: Doubleday, 1985) 898-901; Allison and Davies, *Matthew*, 1.592-93, 604. Crossan (*Historical Jesus*, 293-95) does not think that the prayer, in either Matthean or Lucan form, goes back to Jesus, though it does reflect his views.

25 Crossan, *Historical Jesus*, 304.

26 As is rightly argued by J. D. G. Dunn, "Matthew 12:28/Luke 11:20—A Word of Jesus?" in W. H. Gloer (ed.), *Eschatology and the New Testament* (Peabody, MA: Hendrickson, 1988) 29-49, esp. 45. Dunn's interpretation is to be preferred over Sanders (*Jesus and Judaism*, 148-49) who argues that the disciples are blessed for having witnessed the appearance of one (i.e., Jesus) who announces the coming of the kingdom.

27 R. Bultmann, *History of the Synoptic Tradition* (Oxford: Blackwell, 1972) 162; N. Perrin, *Rediscovering the Teaching of Jesus* (New York: Harper & Row, 1976) 65: "The saying clearly implies a *Sitz im Leben Jesu.*" Allison and Davies (*Matthew*, 2.339) also accept the

we understand it, Jesus apparently understood his power as an exorcist as evidence of the presence and power of the kingdom. Two paragraphs later, in what probably was material grouped together in Q,[28] Jesus asserts that "Something greater than Solomon is here" (Luke 11:31 = Matt 12:42). If this saying goes back to Jesus,[29] it may have been related to Jesus' exorcisms. (The Matthean evangelist clearly believes that there is a connection; cf. Matt 12:22-45.)[30] According to Josephus, it was in the name of Solomon that a certain Eleazar was able to exorcize demons (*Ant.* 8.2.5 §46-49).[31] Accordingly, in healing the demonized, Jesus may have been understood as a Solomon-like figure and, as such, as a "son of David."[32] In one healing miracle, Jesus is actually addressed as "son of David" (Mark 10:47-48).[33] If Jesus were in fact addressed in this manner, messianic connotations are very probable.[34] Jesus'

authenticity of the saying. See also Meyer, *Aims of Jesus*, 154-58; Dunn, "Matthew 12:28/Luke 11:20," 29-49.

[28] J. S. Kloppenborg, *The Formation of Q: Trajectories in Ancient Wisdom Collections* (Studies in Antiquity & Christianity; Philadelphia: Fortress, 1987) 121-34.

[29] Perrin (*Rediscovering the Teaching of Jesus*, 195) and Allison and Davies (Allison and Davies, *Matthew*, 2.357) lean toward authentitiy.

[30] The charges and countercharges in Matt 12:22-45 revolve around Jesus' exorcisms. Matthean contextualization of course does not prove that the saying about one "greater than Solomon" originally belonged in a context of controversy over exorcisms, but given the coherence and symmetry of the bitter exchanges (which are examples of "deviance labeling" common to first-century Palestine; cf. B. J. Malina and R. L. Rohrbaugh, *Social-Science Commentary on the Synoptic Gospels* [Minneapolis: Fortress, 1992] 97-99) it does provide a plausible setting.

[31] Origen (*Comm. Matt.* 33 [on Matt 26:63]) refers to those who attempted exorcisms according to spells composed by Solomon. The pseudepigraphal *Testament of Solomon*, probably written by a Greek-speaking Christian in the second or third century, is wholly dedicated to this theme. Solomon as master exorcist probably arose as part of the legend of his knowledge of plants and proverbs (1 Kgs 4:29-34; Wis 7:17-21).

[32] Note the reading in *T. Sol.* 20:1: "King Solomon, son of David, have mercy on me." On "son of David" as miracle worker, see K. Berger, "Die königlichen Messiastraditionen des Neuen Testaments," *NTS* 20 (1973-74) 1-44, esp. 3-9; E. Lövestam, "Jésus Fils de David chez les Synoptiques," *ST* 28 (1974) 97-109, esp. 100-107; B. D. Chilton, "Jesus ben David: Reflections on the Davidssohnfrage," *JSNT* 14 (1982) 88-112, esp. 92-96. For criticisms, see Gundry, *Mark*, 600.

[33] The Jesus Seminar has given a "black" rating to the conversation between Jesus and blind Bartimaeus; cf. Funk, *Mark*, 169-70. Even if the conversation should be viewed as the creation of the early Church, the episode itself, including the blind man's cry, "Son of David," may well be authentic; cf. Jeremias, *New Testament Theology*, 90. Fitzmyer (*Luke X-XXIV*, 1213) questions the assumption that Mark 10:46-52 is a "community creation." Several scholars have concluded that a core of authentic tradition lies behind the narrative; cf. J. Schmid, *Das Evangelium nach Markus* (RNT 2; Regensburg: Pustet, 1958) 203; C. F. D. Moule, *The Gospel According to Mark* (Cambridge: Cambridge University, 1965) 85; V. Taylor, *The Gospel According to St. Mark* (2nd ed., London: Macmillan, 1966) 446-49; C. E. B. Cranfield, *The Gospel According to Saint Mark* (Cambridge: Cambridge University, 1977) 344-45; E. S. Johnson, "Mark 10:46-52: Blind Bartimaeus," *CBQ* 40 (1978) 191-204; R. Pesch, *Das Markusevangelium* (HTKNT 2.1-2; Freiburg: Herder, 1989-91) 2.169-71; W. Kirchschläger, "Bartimäus – Paradigma einer Wundererzählung (Mk 10,46-52 par)," in F. Van Segbroeck et al. (eds.), *The Four Gospels 1992* (F. Neirynck Festschrift; 3 vols., BETL 100; Leuven: Peeters, 1992) 2.1105-23; Gundry, *Mark*, 596-603.

statement that the "kingdom of God is in your midst" (Luke 17:20-21; cf. *P.Oxy.* 654 §3; *Gos. Thom.* §3, §113)[35] could be related to his exorcisms.

   4. Politics and the Kingdom. There are political and social aspects to Jesus' sayings and actions that relate to his proclamation of the kingdom. The comparison that Jesus makes between himself and David in Mark 2:23-26 may be authentic, especially if it is viewed as originally separate from 2:27-28.[36] Jesus' question ("Have you never read what David did?") and answer (cf. 1 Sam 21:2-7) probably implied that he was acting in the role of the awaited Davidide.[37] The Triumphal Entry (Mark 11:1-10), if a core of genuine history does indeed lie behind this narrative, would probably have been understood in a royal sense. One is reminded of Solomon, mounted on a donkey, anointed, and proclaimed king (1 Kgs 1:32-40). Mules were ridden by Mephibosheth (2 Sam 18:9) and Absalom (2 Sam 19:26) in unsuccessful bids to gain the throne. When Jehu was anointed and proclaimed king, garments were placed on the steps before him (2 Kgs 9:12-13). One thinks also of the singing crowds and the waving of palm branches that greeted Simon as he entered Jerusalem (1 Macc 13:51). The kingly dimension becomes overt in the crowd's shout: "Blessed be the kingdom of our father David" (Mark 11:10).[38] The anointing of Jesus (Mark 14:3-9), which in the light of the subsequent Passion came to be related to Jesus' death and burial, originally could very well have been a messianic anointing.[39]

---

[34] O. Betz, "Die Frage nach dem messianischen Bewußtsein Jesu," *NovT* 6 (1963) 20-48, esp. 41.

[35] The Jesus Seminar has given "pink" ratings to Luke 17:20-21 and *Gos. Thom.* §113, but "gray" ratings to the parallels in *P.Oxy.* 654 §3 and *Gos. Thom.* §3; cf. Funk, *Mark*, 200-201. See also Crossan, *Historical Jesus*, 282-83.

[36] Bultmann, *History of the Synoptic Tradition*, 16; J. Gnilka, *Das Evangelium nach Markus* (EKKNT 2.1-2; Zurich: Benziger, 1978) 119-20; R. Pesch, *Das Markusevangelium*, 1.179-80; Gundry, *Mark*, 148-49. Though in the final calculation it rated Mark 2:25-26 "black," the Jesus Seminar was sharply divided, with six scholars rating the passage "red" and 25 rating it "pink" (as opposed to the 69 who rated it either "gray" or "black"); cf. Funk, *Mark*, 76-77. Evidently members of the Seminar felt that the point of the passage focused on Jesus' disciples and so reflected early community concerns. But is it really probable that early Christians were challenged by Pharisees for picking grain on the sabbath and so found it necessary, by way of reply, to create a dominical saying? cf. E. Haenchen, *Der Weg Jesu* (Berlin: de Gruyter, 1968) 122. It is more likely that the episode derives from the *Sitz im Leben Jesu*. The allusion to the passage from 1 Samuel, especially the problematic reference to Abiathar (which is locative, not temporal; cf. Gundry, *Mark*, 141-42), is not typical of Christian usage of the Old Testament, which normally involves formal quotation. Jesus' challenge, "Have you never read what David did?" (2:25), seems to be characteristic, even distinctive, of his use of Scripture; cf. J. A. T. Robinson, "Did Jesus Have a Distinctive Use of Scripture?" in R. F. Berkey and S. A. Edwards (eds.), *Christological Perspectives* (H. K. McArthur Festschrift; New York: Pilgrim, 1982) 49-57, esp. 53-57.

[37] Betz, "Die Frage nach dem messianischen Bewußtsein Jesu," 41-43.

[38] For arguments in favor of the authenticity of Mark 11:9-10, see Gundry, *Mark*, 631-34. Gundry comments: "The non-quotation of Zech 9:9 in Mark 11:9-10 supports the historicity of the Triumphal Procession, for derivation of the story from Zech 9:9 would probably have left quoted phrases, perhaps quoted statements as well. But we find none" (p. 632).

[39] The word χρίειν (for מָשִׁיחַ) does not appear. In transforming the story into a passion vignette, the deletion of such an overt (and from the Roman point of view treasonable) messianic act should not occasion surprise. That the anointing was originally messianic,

Although precisely what the original point was is debated, the question about scribal messianic ideas ("How do the scribes say that the Messiah is the son of David?" [Mark 12:35-37]), if authentic,[40] may provide additional evidence that Jesus publicly discussed messianic and, by implication, kingly ideas. The fruit of the vine saying ("I shall not drink again of the fruit of the vine until that day when I drink it new in the Kingdom of God" [Mark 14:25])[41] clearly implies that Jesus expected the appearance of the kingdom. Consistent with this saying is Jesus' promise to his disciples that they "will sit on twelve thrones, judging the twelve tribes of Israel" (Luke 22:30 = Matt 19:28).[42] It is probable that the request of James and John ("Grant us to sit, one at your right hand and one at your left, in your glory" [Mark 10:37]) is closely related to this promise.[43] Jesus' admission that he does not possess the authority to grant such a petition surely argues for authenticity.[44]

Besides the possible identification of Jesus with David, there are indications that Jesus anticipated (and promoted) significant social as well as political changes. Statements such as "Blessed are you poor" (Luke 6:20), "Woe to you who are rich" (Luke 6:24), and "How hard it will be for those who have riches to enter the kingdom of God" (Mark 10:23-27; cf. *Herm. Sim.* 9.20.2b-3; *Gos. Naz.* §16) very probably derive from Jesus and reflect his criticism of a wealthy and oppressive establishment of his day.[45] His startling statement that he brings "not peace but a sword" (Matt 10:34-36 = Luke 12:51-53; cf. Luke 12:49) implies that the kingdom that he envisions will divide Jewish society (and not simply families, as might be inferred from the wording of Mic 7:6).[46] Jesus' proverbial statement that "the last will be first, and the first last" (Matt 20:16; cf.

---

see J. K. Elliott, "The Anointing of Jesus," *ExpTim* 85 (1974) 105-7; E. E. Platt, "The Ministry of Mary of Bethany," *TToday* 34 (1977) 29-39. However, Pesch (*Markusevangelium*, 2.332) disagrees.

[40] The Jesus Seminar has given a "black" rating to the saying; cf. Funk, *Mark*, 187-88. For arguments in favor of the authenticity of Mark 12:35-37, see Gundry, *Mark*, 720-24. Gundry does not think that in this utterance Jesus intended to deny his Davidic descent.

[41] The Jesus Seminar has given a "gray" rating to the saying; cf. Funk, *Mark*, 212.

[42] A saying about the Twelve sitting on thrones would not in all probability be invented by the early Church, given the defection of Judas; cf. Meyer, *Aims of Jesus*, 154; Sanders, *Jesus and Judaism*, 98-106.

[43] Gundry, *Mark*, 583: "The request of James and John seems to rest on Jesus' promise that the Twelve 'will sit on thrones judging the Twelve tribes of Israel'" (Matt 19:28 = Luke 22:30).

[44] The Jesus Seminar gives a "black" rating to the whole dialogue; cf. Funk, *Mark*, 167-68. However, if vv 38b-39, which might be a Christian insertion, are deleted, what remains could very well derive from the *Sitz im Leben Jesu*: "You do not know what you are asking. To sit at my right hand or at my left is not mine to grant, but it is for those for whom it has been prepared" (vv 38a + 40). See C. A. Evans, "In What Sense 'Blasphemy'? Jesus before Caiaphas in Mark 14:61-64," *SBLSP* 30 (1991) 215-34, esp. 227-30.

[45] Crossan, *Historical Jesus*, 270-76. The Jesus Seminar gives "pink" ratings to vv 23 and 25; cf. Funk, *Mark*, 162.

[46] Meyer (*Aims of Jesus*, 213), Crossan (*Historical Jesus*, 299-300), Allison and Davies (Allison and Davies, *Matthew*, 2.217), and others regard this saying as authentic. On the meaning suggested here, see M. Black, "'Not peace but a sword': Matt 10:34ff; Luke 12:51ff," in E. Bammel and C. F. D. Moule (eds.), *Jesus and the Politics of His Day* (Cambridge: Cambridge University, 1984) 287-94.

P.Oxy. 654 §4; *Gos. Thom.* §4)[47] presupposes such a reordering of society. It is probable, moreover, that the sayings about receiving the kingdom as children (Mark 10:14-15; cf. *Gos. Thom.* §22)[48] were originally related to this theme. Probably also related is Jesus' declaration that "among those born of women none is greater than John; yet the least in the Kingdom of God is greater than he" (Luke 7:28 = Matt 11:11; cf. *Gos. Thom.* §46).[49] Jesus' saying, "The Kingdom suffers violence" (Matt 11:12 = Luke 16:16; cf. *Gos. Naz.* §8), is probably a comment on the fate of John.[50] The implication is that Jesus viewed the ruling powers of his day as actively suppressing the kingdom which John had proclaimed and which he (Jesus) had declared was present.

When Jesus tells his disciples that they are not to "lord it over" their followers, as do the Gentiles and rulers of their country (Mark 10:42-44),[51] his egalitarian principles become transparently clear. These principles constituted an important dimension in his understanding of the kingdom of God and had much to do with his death in Jerusalem.[52] Horsley has concluded that "the [the Synoptic Gospels] indicate rather clearly Jesus had threatened the Temple, that he was understood as an annointed [*sic*] king, and that he had 'stirred up' the people."[53] Crossan agrees, arguing quite plausibly that Jesus' criticism of the "nonegalitarian, patronal, and even oppressive" Temple establishment, particularly as publicly demonstrated in the Temple precincts,

---

[47] The Jesus Seminar has given Matt 20:16 and reversed form of the saying in *P.Oxy.* 654 §4 "pink" ratings. The Marcan (10:31) and Lucan (13:30) forms are rated "gray"; cf. Funk, *Mark*, 164-65.

[48] Crossan (*Historical Jesus*, 266-69) and Gundry (*Mark*, 547) argue for authenticity. The Jesus Seminar gives Matt 19:14 = Mark 10:14 = Luke 18:16 a "pink" rating, but gives Mark 10:15 = Luke 18:17 a "gray" rating; cf. Funk, *Mark*, 158. Crossan's earlier view of Mark 10:13-14 (cf. *In Fragments*, 315-18) is problematic.

[49] Crossan (*Historical Jesus*, 237-38) argues for the authenticity of both halves of the saying. There is the distinct possibility that the qualification in v 11b ("yet the least in the kingdom of God is greater than [John]") is not original. The Hebrew Shem-Tob version reads: "Truly I say to you, among all those born of women none has risen greater than John the Baptizer." A similar version is found in Ps.-Clement, *Recognitions* 1.60.1-3. See the discussion in G. Howard, "A Note on Shem-Tob's Hebrew Matthew and the Gospel of John," *JSNT* 47 (1992) 117-26, esp. 124-25. If this reading is original, then the case for its authenticity is strengthened, for it is difficult to imagine the early Church coining such a statement. If v 11b is a later gloss, then the original point of the saying may have had more to do with Jesus' unqualified endorsement of John's preaching, which was highly critical of the establishment. For Shem-Tob's Hebrew text of Matt 11:11, see G. Howard, *The Gospel of Matthew according to a Primitive Hebrew Text* (Macon, GA: Mercer University; Leuven: Peeters, 1987) 48.

[50] For arguments favoring authenticity, see Jeremias, *Theology*, 46-47; Allison and Davies, *Matthew*, 2.254. On the interpretation taken here, see Fitzmyer, *Luke X-XXIV*, 1117-18.

[51] The Jesus Seminar has given Mark 10:42-44 a "gray" rating, concluding that these verses "probably vaguely reflect something Jesus might have said"; cf. Funk, *Mark*, 168. For more confident expressions of authenticity, see Fitzmyer, *Luke X-XXIV*, 1414; Horsley, *Jesus and the Spiral of Violence*, 244-45.

[52] Cf. Horsley, *Jesus and the Spiral of Violence*, 190-208.

[53] Horsley, *Jesus and the Spiral of Violence*, 163; see also idem, "The Death of Jesus," in B. D. Chilton and C. A. Evans (eds.), *Studying the Historical Jesus: Evaluations of the State of Current Research* (NTTS; Leiden: Brill) forthcoming.

"could easily have led to arrest and execution."[54] In short, the backdrop to Jesus' arrest and execution was his proclamation and advocacy of a radical change in society; while the specific event that precipitated the arrest itself was the action in the Temple.[55]

Death

According to the Gospels Jesus, the proclaimer of the Kingdom of God, was crucified in Jerusalem as "the King of the Jews." All four Gospels agree in this, though with some variation:

Matt 27:37: οὗτός ἐστιν Ἰησοῦς ὁ βασιλεὺς τῶν Ἰουδαίων
Mark 15:26: ὁ βασιλεὺς τῶν Ἰουδαίων
Luke 23:38: ὁ βασιλεὺς τῶν Ἰουδαίων οὗτος
John 19:19: Ἰησοῦς ὁ Ναζωραῖος ὁ βασιλεὺς τῶν Ἰουδαίων[56]

Common to all four are the words ὁ βασιλεὺς τῶν Ἰουδαίων. According to the Gospels these words, which summarized Jesus' crime, were inscribed on a placard or *titulus* placed over his head. There is literary evidence of such posting of an inscription that refers to the crime and/or the name of the victim. According to Dio Cassius, an unfortunate slave who had been caught up in a plot against Augustus (22 BCE) was led "through the midst of the Forum with an inscription [γράμματα] making known the reason why [ἡ αἰτία] he was to be put to death, and afterwards they crucified [σταυροῦν] him" (*Roman History* 54.3.7). Although not crucified, a slave was, by order of Caligula, "led about among the guests, preceded by a placard [*titulus*] giving the reason for his punishment [*causa poenae*]" (Suetonius, *Caligula* 32.2). In response to a taunt, Domitian had a man "dragged from his seat and thrown into the arena to dogs, with this placard [*titulus*]: 'a favorer of the Thracians who spoke impiously'" (Suetonius, *Domitian* 10.1). According to Eusebius one of the Christian martyrs was led around an amphitheatre carrying a placard "on which was written in Latin [Ῥωμαϊστί], 'This is Attalus, the Christian'" (*Hist. eccl.* 5.1.44).

The fourth evangelist calls the inscription a τίτλος (John 19:19-20), which is a transliteration of the Latin *titulus*. The Marcan and Lucan evangelists call it an ἐπιγραφή (Mark 15:26; Luke 23:38), which is an approximate translation. The Marcan and Matthean evangelists refer to the inscription as stating the reason (αἰτία = *causa poenae*) for Jesus' execution (Mark 15:26; Matt 27:37). The fourth evangelist also states that the inscription "was written in Hebrew, Latin

---

54 Crossan, *Historical Jesus*, 360.

55 Evans, "Jesus' Action in the Temple," 246.

56 The form of the inscription in the *Gos. Pet.* 4.11 (οὗτός ἐστιν ὁ βασιλεὺς τοῦ Ἰσραήλ) is a secondary reformulation based on Matthew that replaces the ethnic designation "of the Jews" to the more theologically acceptable "of Israel." Josephus routinely refers to Herod the Great as "king of the Jews" (*Ant.* 15.10.5 §373; 15.11.4 §409; 16.9.3 §291; 16.10.2 §311). The title as such may have originated with Antony when he gave Herod a kingdom (cf. *J.W.* 1.14.4 §282). The suggestion made by G. M. Lee ("The Inscription on the Cross," *PEQ* 100 [1968] 144) that the variations among the Gospels are due to independent translations of the Latin and Hebrew portions of the inscription (cf. John 19:20) is as implausible as it is unnecessary.

['Ρωμαϊστί], and Greek" (19:20). All of this is completely in step with Roman practice.

Although some scholars have reservations about the historicity of the *titulus*,[57] most accept it,[58] with some regarding it as "historically unimpeachable."[59] Fitzmyer's reasoning is cogent: "If [the inscription] were invented by Christians, they would have used *Christos*, for early Christians would scarcely have called their Lord 'the king of the Jews.'"[60]

Linkage in Independent Sources

The Fourth Gospel

According to Mack, "Mark's fabrication of the narrative theme . . . was to provide a narrative theme to link the Jesus traditions with the account of his death."[61] Since this link also appears in the fourth Gospel, Mack believes that the fourth evangelist drew upon Mark. "John's use of just this narrative design apart from knowledge of Mark would constitute a coincidence of fantastic proportions."[62]

It is, of course, possible that the fourth evangelist knew and made use of Mark (and/or the other Synoptic Gospels), and some Johannine scholars argue this position.[63] Others, however, believe that the fourth Gospel is not dependent on Mark or on any of the Synoptic Gospels.[64] If the latter position is correct, then Mack's conclusion that John's "narrative design" is derived from Mark collapses. Nevertheless, even if for the sake of argument we assume that the fourth evangelist was acquainted with one or more of the synoptic Gospels, it is not at all obvious that the Marcan link between Jesus' miracles and the Jewish leaders' decision to have Jesus arrested underlies the Johannine plot.

---

57 D. R. Catchpole, "The 'Triumphal' Entry," in Bammel and Moule (eds.), *Jesus and the Politics of His Day*, 319-34, here 328.

58 Winter, *On the Trial of Jesus*, 108; E. Dinkler, *Signum Crucis* (Tübingen: Mohr [Siebeck], 1967) 306; N. A. Dahl, "The Crucified Messiah," in Dahl, *The Crucified Messiah and Other Essays* (Minneapolis: Augsburg, 1974) 1-36; Meyer, *The Aims of Jesus*, 176-78; E. Bammel, "The *titulus*," in Bammel and Moule (eds.), *Jesus and the Politics of His Day*, 353-64.

59 G. Schneider, "The Political Charge against Jesus (Luke 23:2)," in Bammel and Moule (eds.), *Jesus and the Politics of His Day*, 403-14, here 404.

60 Fitzmyer, *Luke I-IX*, 773.

61 Mack, *A Myth of Innocence*, 282.

62 Mack, *A Myth of Innocence*, 225 n. 12.

63 Perhaps the ablest proponent of this position is F. Neirynck, *Jean et les Synoptiques* (BETL 49; Leuven: Peeters, 1979); idem, "John and the Synoptics: 1975-1990," in A. Denaux (ed.), *John and the Synoptics* (BETL 101; Leuven: Peeters, 1992) 3-61.

64 C. H. Dodd, *Historical Tradition in the Fourth Gospel* (Cambridge: Cambridge University, 1963) 349; R. Bultmann, *The Gospel of John* (Philadelphia: Westminster, 1971); J. M. Robinson, "On the Gattung of Mark (and John)," in D. G. Buttrick and J. M. Bald (eds.), *Jesus and Man's Hope* (Pittsburgh: Pittsburgh Theological Seminary, 1970) 99-129; D. M. Smith, "John and the Synoptics: Some Dimensions of the Problem," NTS 26 (1980) 425-44; P. Borgen, "The Independence of the Gospel of John: Some Observations," in F. Van Segbroeck et al (eds.), *The Four Gospels 1992* (F. Neirynck Festschrift; BETL 100; 3 vols., Leuven: Peeters, 1992) 3.1815-33.

The Testimonium Flavianum

The historicity of Mark's and John's common narrative design, including the linkage between ministry and execution, receives a measure of indirect support from Josephus. A brief account of the ministry and death of Jesus is given in the famous *Testimonium Flavianum* (*Ant.* 18.3.3 §63-64). Stripped of its obvious Christian interpolations and embellishments, the original form of the text probably read as follows:

> At this time there appeared Jesus, a wise man. For he was a doer of startling deeds, a teacher of people who receive the truth with pleasure. And he gained a following both among many Jews and among man of Greek origin. And when Pilate, because of an accusation made by the leading men among us, condemned him to the cross, those who had loved him previously did not cease to do so. And up until this very day the tribe of Christians (named after him) has not died out.[65]

According to Josephus, Jesus was a παραδόξων ἔργων ποιητής ("doer of startling deeds")[66] and a διδάσκαλος ἀνθρώπων ("teacher of people"), whom Pilate condemned to be crucified, having been accused by τῶν πρώτων ἀνδρῶν ("the leading [Jewish] men"). In this brief passage Josephus does not explain on what grounds Jesus was accused, nor does he explain on what grounds Pilate condemned him to the cross. But he does describe Jesus as a teacher and wonderworker who was crucified at the instigation of the Jewish leaders. Thus, Josephus provides us with an early and independent account which coheres in a significant way with the narrative design common to Mark and John. We need not conclude that this parallel linkage of teachings/miracles to execution constitutes a fantastic coincidence; rather, it reflects history.

Other Jewish figures from first-century Palestine also provide helpful points of comparison. Josephus, with an obvious critical bias, tells us of the various prophetic claimants who promised their respective contemporaries signs from heaven: "Deceivers and impostors, under the pretence of divine inspiration fostering revolutionary changes . . . led them out into the desert under the belief that God would there give them signs of salvation" (*J.W.* 2.13.4 §259). At least two of these would-be deliverers promised Joshua-like signs. During the administration of Governor Fadus (44–46 C.E.) a man named Theudas declared that at his command the Jordan River would be parted, permitting the prophet and his following to cross (*Ant.* 20.5.1 §97-98; cf. Acts 5:36). Although Josephus does not say, this sign would probably have been understood as the inauguration of a new conquest of the promised land. Evidently the Romans understood it that way, for Fadus sent a squadron of

---

65 J. P. Meier, *A Marginal Jew: Rethinking the Historical Jesus. Volume One: The Roots of the Problem and the Person* (ABRL; New York: Doubleday, 1991) 61. For competent assessments of the *Testimonium Flavianum*, see Meier, *Marginal Jew*, 56-88; idem, "Jesus in Josephus: A Modest Proposal," *CBQ* 52 (1990) 76-103; L. H. Feldman, "The *Testimonium Flavianum*: The State of the Question," in Berkey and Edwards (eds.), *Christological Perspectives*, 179-99.

66 In *m. Sota* 9:15 Hanina ben Dosa is described as one of the אַנְשֵׁי מַעֲשֶׂה ("men of deeds"). "Deeds" here probably should be understood as mighty deeds or miracles; cf. M. Jastrow, *A Dictionary of the Targumim, the Talmud Babli and Yerushalmi, and the Midrashic Literature* (2 vols.; London: Putnam, 1895-1903; repr. New York: Pardes, 1950) 1.820; G. Vermes, *Jesus the Jew: A Historian's Reading of the the Gospels* (London: Collins, 1973) 79.

cavalry against them, killing Theudas and many of his followers. Another would-be prophet, a Jew from Egypt (c. 56 C.E.), led a large number of people to the Mount of Olives in order to demonstrate that at his command the walls of Jerusalem would fall down, enabling him and his followers to gain entry into the city (*Ant.* 20.8.6 §169-170; cf. Acts 21:38). Again Josephus does not say so, but it is quite clear that this Joshua-like sign was meant to overthrow the establishment and inaugurate a new order. And, like Fadus before him, Felix the Roman governor sent troops against the Egyptian and his following.

Although we are told very little about Theudas and the Egyptian Jew, it is quite probable that the Roman attacks against these men were directly in response to their public teachings and activities. Would anyone in all seriousness claim that the death of Theudas was "probably just a mistake" and that it had nothing specifically to do with his prior activities? So it was in the case of Jesus of Nazareth. He too had proclaimed an imminent change in the social and political order and the powers of his day responded with deadly force.

Conclusion

Evidence and logic strongly suggest that Jesus' death at the hands of the Roman authorities in Judea was the result of his teaching and activities. The inscription, "the king of the Jews," provides a firm link between Jesus' death and his proclamation of the kingdom of God. Furthermore, this inscription provides an important link between Jesus' ministry and the subsequent emergence of New Testament christology, in that while the Romans would have referred to Jesus as "king of the Jews," early Christians would have applied to him the more theologically charged title, "messiah." To be sure, Mark has interpreted many aspects of Jesus' ministry in the light of the passion and the Easter proclamation, but the basic link between Jesus' Galilean life and his Judean death cannot be reduced to nothing more than a narrative strategy.

"Where No One Had Yet Been Laid": The Shame of Jesus' Burial

Byron R. McCane
Washington and Lee University

Recent scholarship has raised interesting questions about the historical circumstances of Jesus' burial. In particular, a steady stream of books and articles has increasingly raised the possibility that the body of Jesus might have been disposed of in shame and dishonor.[1] Most recently, Raymond E. Brown has argued that the historical Jesus was interred in a criminal's grave, while John Dominic Crossan has concluded that no one really knew what became of the body.[2] In this paper I will draw upon both archaeological and literary evidence to argue that Jesus was indeed most likely buried in disgrace in a rock-cut criminal's tomb. In keeping with well-developed Jewish law and custom, members of the Sanhedrin arranged for a culturally appropriate—and thus dishonorable—interment. From an early date the Christian tradition tried to conceal this unpleasant fact, but the best evidence clearly shows that the historical Jesus was buried in shame.

1

The burial customs of first-century Jews in Palestine are well-known: hundreds of tombs have been excavated, and many texts—from Josephus, the Mishnah and the tractate *Semaḥot*[3]—explicitly discuss the care of the dead.

[1] Josef Blinzler, "Die Grablegung Jesus in historischer Sicht," in *Ressurexit* (E. Dhanis, ed.; Vatican City: Editrice Vaticana, 1974), 56-107. F. M. Braun, "La sépulture de Jesus," *RB* 45 (1936) 34-52, 184-200, 346-363. A. Buchler, "L'enterrement des criminels d'après le Talmud et le Midrasch" *REJ* 46 (1903) 74-88. H. Cousin, "Sépulture criminelle et sépulture prophétique" *RB* 81 (1974) 375-393. D. Daube, *The New Testament and Rabbinic Judaism* (London: Athlone, 1956), 310-311. E. Dhanis, "L'ensevelissement de Jésus et la visite au tombeau dans l'évangile de saint Marc (xv,40-xvi,8)" *Gregorianum* 39 (1958) 367-410. R. H. Fuller, *The Formation of the Resurrection Narratives* (2nd ed.; Philadelphia: Fortress, 1980), 52-57. J. Schreiber, "Die Bestattung Jesu" *ZNW* 72 (1981) 141-177.

[2] Raymond E. Brown, "The Burial of Jesus (Mark 15:42-47)," *CBQ* 50 (1988) 233-245. John Dominic Crossan, *The Historical Jesus* (San Francisco: Harper, 1991), 391-394.

[3] The tractate *Semaḥot* (literally, "Rejoicings," certainly a euphemistic title) dates from the third century CE; for this date and a discussion of the evidence, cf. *The Tractate "Mourning" (Semaḥot)* (Dov Zlotnick, trans. and intro.; New Haven: Yale, 1966), 1-9. In this paper, English and Hebrew citations from *Semaḥot* are from Zlotnick. For the evidence showing that *Semaḥot* and other tannaitic sources accurately reflect first-century Jewish burial practices in Palestine, cf. Eric M. Meyers, "The Use of Archaeology in

Indeed, the archaeological and literary evidence presents a remarkably complete picture, and the following portrait of a typical Jewish funeral is based on the combined witness of texts and tombs.[4]

The Jews of Early Roman Palestine buried their dead promptly, as soon as possible after death and almost always on the same day.[5] As soon as death occurred, preparations began: the eyes of the deceased were closed, the corpse was washed with perfumes and oils, its bodily orifices were stopped, and strips of cloth were wrapped tightly around the body—binding the jaw closed, holding the hands to the sides, and tying the feet together.[6] Thus prepared, the corpse was placed on a bier or in a coffin and carried out of town in a procession to the family tomb, usually a small rock-cut cave entered through a narrow opening that could be covered with a stone.[7] Upon arriving at the tomb, eulogies were spoken and the corpse was placed inside, either in a niche or on a shelf, along with items of jewelry or other personal effects of the deceased.[8] Expressions of condolence continued as the procession returned to

Understanding Rabbinic Materials," *Texts and Responses* (M. A. Fishbane and P. R. Flohr, eds.; Leiden: E. J. Brill, 1975), 28-42; and L. Y. Rahmani, "Ancient Jerusalem's Funerary Customs and Tombs, Part Three," *BA* 44 (1981) 43-53.

[4] For a catalogue of Jewish tombs from Roman Palestine, delineating the architectural features of each tomb and the burial practices found therein, cf. B. R. McCane, "Jews, Christians, and Burial in Roman Palestine" (Ph.D. diss., Duke University, 1992). Other studies include: P. Figueras, *Decorated Jewish Ossuaries* (Leiden: Brill, 1985). R. Hachlili, *Ancient Jewish Art and Archaeology in the Land of Israel* (Leiden: Brill, 1988). S. Klein, *Tod und Begräbnis in Palästina zur Zeit der Tannaiten* (Berlin, Itzowski, 1908). E. M. Meyers, *Jewish Ossuaries: Reburial and Rebirth* (Rome: Pontifical Biblical Institute, 1971). L. Y. Rahmani, "Ancient Jerusalem's Funerary Customs and Tombs, Part Three," *BA* 44 (1981) 43-45. S. Safrai, "Home and Family," in *The Jewish People in the First Century* (S. Safrai and M. Stern, eds.; Amsterdam: van Gorcum, 1976), 2.773-787. David Goldenberg, "Halakhah in Josephus and in Tannaitic Literature: A Comparative Study." (Ph.D. Diss., Dropsie University, 1978).

[5] *Semaḥot* 1.5; *m.Sanh.* 6.5. According to these texts, corpses could be kept overnight if necessary in order to prepare the coffin or burial cloths.

[6] *Semaḥot* 1.2-5, 12.10; *m.Sanh.* 23.5. One prominent rabbi, R. Gamaliel, is said to have disapproved of overly ostentatious preparations for burial, and to have ordered his body to be wrapped in flax rather than linen (BT *Ketuboth* 86, par. BT *Moed Qatan* 27b). Such sentiments are common in the social anthropology of death ritual: Solon, Plato, and Cicero are all said to have urged limitations on funerary expense and display according to class (Plut. *Sol.* 21.5; Cicero, *De Leg.* ii.23.59, ii.24.60). Cf. also Walter Burkert, *Greek Religion* (Cambridge: Harvard, 1985), 194. Donna C. Kurtz and John Boardman, *Greek Burial Customs* (Ithaca: Cornell, 1971), 201-202. J. M. C. Toynbee, *Death and Burial in the Roman World* (Ithaca: Cornell, 1971), 54.

[7] *m. Baba Bathra* 2.9 stipulates that graves may not be located within fifty cubits of a town, and archaeology confirms that tombs were customarily located outside the city limits; for a map plotting tomb locations around first-century Jerusalem, cf. Amos Kloner, *The Necropolis of Jerusalem* (Ph.D. Diss., Hebrew University, 1980) (Hebrew).

[8] *Semaḥot* 8.2-7. Two kinds of burial niches characterize early Jewish tombs in Palestine: (1) the *kokh* or loculus, a deep, narrow slot in the wall of the tomb, and (2) the *arcosolium*, a broad, arch-shaped recess along the wall of the tomb. A typical loculus cave may have 5-8 niches (cf. L. Y. Rahmani, "A Jewish Tomb on Shahin Hill, Jerusalem" *IEJ* 8 (1958) 101-105), while a typical arcosolium cave has only three (cf. L. Y. Rahmani, "The Mahanayim Tomb" *'Atiqot* 3 (1961) 91-120).

the family home until, at the bidding of the family, friends and mourners dispersed.[9] The funeral was thus conducted without delay, and in most cases the body had been interred by sunset on the day of death.

But in early Jewish culture, the rituals of death did not end with this first— or primary—burial. A lengthy period of mourning followed, lasting for a full year and ending only with the rite of secondary burial, i.e., reburial of the bones after the flesh had rotted away. In other words, the Jews of first-century Palestine buried their dead *twice*: first on the day of death, and then again a year later, after a twelve-month period of mourning. The first stage of mourning was a week of intense grieving, called *shiv'ah*, during which relatives of the deceased "stayed away from work, sitting at home upon low couches, heads covered, receiving the condolences of relatives and friends."[10] For the first three days, family members would leave home only to visit the tomb, either to grieve there or to ensure that their loved one was truly dead.[11] Following *shiv'ah* came thirty days of less severe mourning (*shloshim*), during which family members still could not leave town, cut their hair, or attend social gatherings. After *shloshim* almost all aspects of normal life resumed, except that mourners still continued to recite the mourner's blessing each time they visited the synagogue, until a year had passed. In the case of a parent's death, other observances also lasted for up to a year.[12]

It was the rite of secondary burial which brought all the rituals of death to a close.[13] The custom of reburying human bones, which appears in many cultures and which had a long history among Jews even before the first-century CE,[14] was extremely popular during the time of Jesus. In my sample

---

[9] Some texts describe a ceremony in which the mourners arranged themselves in rows to receive condolences, but others seem to imply that the public stood in rows while the mourners passed by (*m.Moed Qatan* 3.7, *m.Meg.* 4.3, *m.Ber.* 3.2, and Safrai, "Home and Family," 782).

[10] L. Y. Rahmani, "Ancient Jerusalem's Funerary Customs and Tombs, Part One" *BA* 44 (1981) 175. Josephus mentions that Archelaus "kept the seven days of mourning" for his father Herod the Great, calling it "a Jewish custom" (*War* II.1; *Ant.* XVII.199-200).

[11] *Semaḥot* 8.1: "One may go out to the cemetery for three days to inspect the dead for a sign of life, without fear that this smacks of heathen practice. For it happened that a man was inspected after three days, and he went on to live twenty-five years; still another went on to have five children and died later." A few manuscripts have "thirty" instead of "three," perhaps a result of confusion with the mourning period of *shloshim*. Some other rabbinic texts (*Semaḥot* 6.1) also refer to a practice of "inverting the bed," which may indicate abstinence from sexual activity during the period of mourning

[12] *Semaḥot* 9.15: "While in mourning for any other dead, he (i.e., the mourner) may not go to any banquet until the *shloshim* have been completed for him; in the case of his father and mother, not for twelve whole months, unless it is to celebrate a religious occasion."

[13] *Semaḥot* 12.4 explains that in no case was mourning to extend beyond the day of secondary burial: "In the case of ossilegium, mourning must be observed for only one day. As a consequence, the bones are gathered only near nightfall. If while gathering them all that day, night falls, a man is released from the obligation of mourning on the very next day."

[14] Robert Hertz, *Death and the Right Hand* (Rodney and Claudia Needham, trans.; New York: Free Press, 1960). Eric M. Meyers, *Jewish Ossuaries: Reburial and Rebirth* (Rome: Biblical Institute Press, 1971), 3-11. Elisabeth Bloch-Smith, *Judahite Burial Practices and*

of two hundred Jewish tombs from this region and period, for example, fully 92% of them held the remains of secondary burials.[15] The most frequent pattern in the first century was ossuary burial, in which bones were collected in small stone chests, or ossuaries. A typical tomb found in Talpioth in 1947 contained nine ossuaries, with two of them in the same burial niche, and similar finds have been located in many other Jewish tombs, including sites at French Hill, Rehov Ruppin, and Beth Guvrin.[16] Even the headline-making "Caiaphas" tomb contained 16 ossuaries,[17] confirming beyond any reasonable doubt that among Jews in first-century Palestine, secondary burial was the burial practice of choice.

Several rabbinic texts shed further light on this practice by discussing such issues as when, how, and by whom the bones of the dead were to be gathered. In so doing, some texts are quite vividly specific, as for example *Semaḥot* 12.7:

> The bones of a corpse should not be taken apart, nor the tendons severed, unless the bones had fallen apart of themselves and the tendons of themselves had been severed. Rabbi Akiba says: "The bones may not be gathered until the flesh has wasted away; once it has, the features are no longer recognizable in the skeleton."

Other texts connect the ceremony of bone-gathering with the closest relatives of the deceased. *Semaḥot* 12.5, for example, debates the problem of potential conflicts between secondary burial and important social events like weddings and ceremonies of circumcision; and while bone-gathering does rank last of the three obligations (after all, it could always be delayed for a day), the text at least shows that secondary burial was one of the more important events in the life of a pious Jewish family.[18] *Semaḥot* 12.9 also connects secondary burial with close family ties:

> Rabbi Eleazar bar Zadok said: "Thus spoke father at the time of his death: 'My son, bury me at first in a fosse.[19] In the course of time, collect my bones and put them in an ossuary; but do not gather them with your own hands.' And thus did I attend him: Johanan entered, collected the bones, and spread a sheet over them. I then came in, rent

---

Beliefs About the Dead (JSOT Supp. 123; Sheffield: JSOT, 1992). In some academic discussions, secondary burial is referred to by the technical term, "ossilegium"; the rabbinic term is *liyqqut etzamoth*, "to gather bones."

[15] B. R. McCane, "Jews, Christians, and Burial in Roman Palestine," Appendix One.

[16] E. L. Sukenik, "The Earliest Records of Christianity," *American Journal of Archaeology* 51 (1947) 351-365. James F. Strange, "Late Hellenistic and Herodian Ossuary Tombs at French Hill, Jerusalem," *BASOR* 219 (1975) 39-67. L. Y. Rahmani, "Jewish Rock-Cut Tombs in Jerusalem," *'Atiqot* 3 (1961) 91-120. Eliezer D. Oren and Uriel Rappaport, "The Necropolis of Maresha—Beth Guvrin," *IEJ* 34 (1984) 114-153.

[17] Z. Greenhut, "The Caiaphas Tomb in North Talpiyot, Jerusalem," *'Atiqot* 21 (1992) Table 1.

[18] Figueras, *Decorated Jewish Ossuaries*, 9.

[19] The phrase "in a fosse" (Heb., **byg'h**) is extremely difficult, but may designate a temporary grave, either a loculus or the floor depression found in many tombs. For discussion, cf. Zlotnick, 158n1.

my clothes for them, and sprinkled dried herbs over them. Just as he attended his father, so I attended him.

Here responsibility rests squarely upon the son of the deceased: he is not to touch the bones himself, but he must see that they are reburied and must be present for the ceremony.

Taken together, this material and textual evidence presents a clear picture of honorable Jewish burial in first-century Palestine. Beginning with primary interment on the day of death, and extending through secondary burial after a year of mourning, Jewish death rituals were clear and well-developed. Two specific characteristics stand out. First, *Jewish death rituals were closely linked to ties of kinship and family.* Several significant practices are directly connected to bonds of family, including funeral processions which typically originated in the family home, as well as rituals of mourning and secondary burial which were performed by near relatives. An archaeological datum can be added here as well: inscriptions show that most Jewish tombs in this region and period were used by single family groups. The parade example is the "Goliath" tomb from Jericho, where inscriptions allowed excavators to reconstruct three generations of the family tree.[20] Even in the Beth She'arim catacombs, an extremely large cemetery complex, inscriptions show that single family groups purchased and used individual burial rooms within the larger catacomb.[21] Group burial in small caves had deep local roots in Syro-Palestine, going back at least to the eighth century BCE,[22] so it is not surprising that the ancient local custom was alive and well in the first century. For the Jews of Early Roman Palestine, then, honorable burial was a traditional family value: the dead were customarily laid to rest with—or by—their nearest relatives.

Second, *Jewish death rituals also addressed the social impact of death.* The rituals of mourning are particularly significant in this regard. For, as social anthropologists have discovered, death hardly "confines itself to ending the visible daily life of an individual"[23]—certainly it does that, but it also tears a hole in the fabric of a society, slashing at the bonds which tie individuals, families, and communities together and knocking the social equilibrium off

---

20 Rachel Hachlili, "The Goliath Family in Jericho: Funerary Inscriptions from a First Century AD Jewish Monumental Tomb," *BASOR* 235 (1979) 31-65. Rachel Hachlili and Patricia Smith, "The Geneology of the Goliath Family," *BASOR* 235 (1979) 67-70. At Meiron, it was analysis of skeletal remains which showed that "the individuals buried in the cave were an endogamous group and that the burial chamber probably belonged to one family" (Joe Zias and Patricia Smith in Meyers, Strange, and Meyers, *Excavations at Ancient Meiron* (Durham: Duke, 1981), 118).

21 Moshe Schwabe and Baruch Lifshitz, *Beth She'arim, Vol. II: The Greek Inscriptions* (New Brunswick, NJ: Rutgers University Press, 1974), 223.

22 E. M. Meyers, "Tomb" in *The Interpreter's Dictionary of the Bible, Supplementary Volume* (Keith Crim, ed.; Nashville: Abingdon, 1976), 905-908. Elizabeth Bloch-Smith, "Burials: Israelite" in *The Anchor Bible Dictionary* (D. N. Freedman, ed.; New York: Doubleday, 1992), I.785-789.

23 Robert Hertz, *Death and the Right Hand*, 77.

balance.[24] Death forcibly and sometimes violently removes a member of the social network: how will family, friends, and community recover and survive? Death rituals—especially customs of mourning—are social constructs which enable life to go on, by providing the time and the orderly means by which a society's wound can be healed.[25] Thus when the loss of a relative or neighbor disrupted a Jewish family and community, practices like *shiv'ah*, *shloshim*, and *liyqqut etzamoth* were their way of putting life back together again. Secondary burial played an especially important role: Jews reassembled the pieces of life by gathering the bones of the dead. Lengthy rituals of mourning, ending with secondary burial, enabled them to cope successfully with the painful fact that their society had lost a significant member.

But among the Jews of Early Roman Palestine there was also another set of burial customs, quite different from those we have been discussing. Both literary and archaeological sources indicate that in the days of Jesus the bodies of some people—specifically, those who had been condemned to death by a Jewish court—were intentionally treated with dishonor and shame. Burial in disgrace is known from earlier periods of Jewish history, as for example when the bodies of some prophets and kings of Israel suffered ignominious treatment after their deaths, so the Jewish culture of Roman Palestine was simply preserving and adapting an ancient tradition.[26] By the first century CE, burial in shame had come to mean, first of all, that *family ties were deliberately severed*. Condemned criminals were buried promptly, to be sure—after all, the Torah specifically commanded as much[27]—but their bodies were never placed in family tombs. The Mishnah reports that criminals condemned by a Jewish court were interred in separate places kept by the court specifically for that purpose.[28] Their remains were moved to

---

[24] Peter Metcalf and Richard Huntington, *Celebrations of Death: The Anthropology of Mortuary Ritual* (2nd ed.; Cambridge: University Press, 1991), 79-85. Maurice Bloch and Jonathan Parry, eds. *Death and the Regeneration of Life* (New York: Cambridge, 1982). Mary Douglas, *Purity and Danger* (London: Routledge, 1966). For further examples, cf. Robert Hertz, *Death and the Right Hand*. For a history of socio-anthropological theories of death, cf. Robert Chapman and Klavs Randsborg, "Approaches to the Archaeology of Death," in *The Archaeology of Death* (R. Chapman, I. Kinnes, K. Randsborg, eds.; Cambridge: Cambridge Univ. Press, 1981), 1-24.

[25] As Bloch and Parry aptly put it, "the last word must be with life" (*Death and the Regeneration of Life*, 17). For an elaboration of the view that death rituals celebrate a culture's most valued constructs of life, with interesting examples from Madagascar and America, cf. Metcalf and Huntington, *Celebrations of Death*, 108-133, 191-214.

[26] Daube, *The NT and Rabbinic Judaism*, 310. Cousin, "Sépulture criminelle et sépulture prophétique," 382. Brown, "The Burial of Jesus," 237.

[27] Dt. 21:22-23: "And if a man has committed a crime punishable by death and he put to death, and you hang him on a tree, his body shall not remain all night upon the tree, but you shall bury him the same day, for a hanged man is accursed by God; you shall not defile your land which the LORD your God gives you for an inheritance." Cf. also *m.Sanh.* 6.4.

[28] *M. Sanh.* 6:5 reads: "They used not to bury him (i.e., one who had been condemned) in the burying-place of his fathers, but two burying-places were kept in readiness by the

family tombs only at the time of secondary burial, after decomposition of the flesh was complete.[29] According to the Babylonian Talmud, decay of the flesh served to atone for the sins of the condemned, so that after twelve months the stain of their guilt would have been removed.[30] There is archaeological confirmation of these practices in the famous case of Yehoḥanan, the crucified man from Givat ha-Mivtar, whose bones—complete with the nail which had pierced his ankle—were found in his family tomb in an ossuary.[31]

In addition, dishonorable first-century Jewish burial also meant that public rituals of mourning were not observed. According to *Semaḥot* 2.6, 2.9 and *m.Sanh.* 6.6, relatives of persons condemned by a Jewish court were neither to sit *shivʿah* nor to keep the thirty days of *shloshim*.[32] On the contrary, they were expected to agree with the verdict of the court, and to confine their grieving to the privacy of their own hearts. By forbidding public ritual mourning for its condemned criminals, early Jewish society made a strong statement about the social impact of their deaths. Specifically, *the deaths of condemned criminals were not treated as a loss to society.* Unlike an honorable death, the execution of a criminal did not damage the social order or tear the social fabric. Far from it: since these criminals died by the verdict of a Jewish court, their deaths were the will of society, not a wound to it. The judgment of the court expressed important ideals and values of Jewish culture—in the words of the Mishnah, the court rendered "the judgment of truth." The social order was preserved and strengthened, not threatened, by such deaths. From a sociological point of

---

court, one for them that were beheaded or strangled, and one for them that were stoned or burnt."

[29] *M. Sanh.* 6.6: "When the flesh had wasted away they gathered together the bones and buried them in their own place (the family tomb)." Thus, as Brown has correctly pointed out ("The Burial of Jesus," 237), the separate burial places for condemned criminals must not be thought of as charnel houses in which bodies were indiscriminately piled together. Rather, they were probably rock-cut tombs with niches in which individual bodies could be laid, and from which bones could later be recovered.

[30] BT Kidd. 31b. Cf. also P. Figueras, "Jewish Ossuaries and Secondary Burial: Their Significance for Early Christianity," *Immanuel* 19 (1984-85) 49.

[31] V. Tzaferis, "Jewish Tombs at and near Givʿat ha-Mivtar, Jerusalem" *IEJ* 20 (1970) 18-32. For two differing analyses of the skeletal remains—and two reconstructions of crucifixion—cf. N. Haas, "Anthropological Observations on the Skeletal Remains from Givʿat ha-Mivtar," *IEJ* 20 (1970) 38-59; and J. Zias and E. Sekeles, "The Crucified Man from Givʿat ha-Mivtar: A Reappraisal," *IEJ* 35 (1985) 22-27. E. M. Meyers was the first to note the significance of the fact that Jehohanan's bones lay in an ossuary (Meyers, *Jewish Ossuaries*, 89-91).

[32] *Semaḥot* 2.6 reads: "For those executed by the court (Heb., **beth din**), no rites whatsoever should be observed. Their brothers and relatives should come and greet the witnesses and the judges, as if to say, "We bear you no ill will, for you have rendered a true judgment." They may not mourn but may grieve, the latter signifying grieving in silence." According to *Semaḥot* 2.9, this prohibition applies only to persons executed by the **beth din:** "No rites whatsoever should be denied those who were executed by the state." *M.Sanh.* 6.6: "After he was put to death, the kinsmen came and greeted the judges and the witnesses as if to say, 'We have naught against you in our hearts, for you have judged the judgement of truth.' And they used not to make open lamentation but they went mourning, for mourning has place in the heart alone."

view, public rituals of mourning for condemned criminals would be both inappropriate and unnecessary.

Thus the Jews of Early Roman Palestine knew of both honor and shame in burial of the dead. Prompt primary burial in rock-cut family tombs was the norm, followed by twelve months of mourning ending with secondary burial, often in ossuaries. Criminals condemned by Jewish courts, however, were treated differently: they were placed in separate burial places kept specifically for that purpose, and no rites of mourning were observed. Only at secondary burial were their remains moved to family tombs.

2

The accounts of Jesus' burial pose many historical problems, not the least of which is their conspicuous tendency toward embellishment and glamorization. Because Jesus held a dear place in the hearts of the early Christians, their stories of his burial quite understandably seek to refine, polish and beautify the reported circumstances of his interment. A few bottles of ointment might suffice for washing an ordinary corpse, but for Jesus, no less than one hundred pounds will do.[33] Reading such narratives for historical purposes is difficult, but the cultural background of first-century Jewish burial practices—especially their distinctions between honor and shame—can be very helpful.

Honor and shame are relevant categories here because, as several scholars have correctly pointed out, the Christian narratives increasingly tend to portray Jesus' burial as honorable.[34] Each stage of the tradition adds details which lend dignity and remove shame. In the very earliest traditions there are hints that Jesus was buried by the same Jewish leaders who engineered his condemnation and crucifixion. In Acts 13:29b, for example, Paul tells the congregation at the synagogue in Antioch of Pisidia that "those who live in Jerusalem and their leaders" took Jesus down from the cross and laid him in a tomb (*ethekan eis mnēmeion*).[35] Under such circumstances we would certainly

---

[33] Cf. Jn. 19:39b, where Nicodemus brings "about a hundred pounds" (*hos litras hekaton*) of perfumes to the tomb of Jesus. Interpreters have speculated that this exorbitant quantity might symbolize Jesus' kingship (F. F. Bruce, L. Morris), or perhaps Nicodemus' respect for Jesus (Schnackenburg, Bultmann) or even his lack of faith in Jesus (J. Schreiber, D. Sylva). More likely, however, it is an embellishment of the sort which commonly appears in early Jewish narratives about the burial of prominent persons (cf. Life of Adam and Eve 40; Josephus, *War*, I.670; *Ant.* XVII.199). For background on the spindle and piriform perfume bottles typically found in first-century Jewish tombs, cf. P. Kahane, "Pottery Types from the Jewish Ossuary Tombs around Jerusalem," *IEJ* 2 (1952) 125-139, 176-182; and *IEJ* 3 (1953) 48-54. Cf. also M. Dayagi-Mendels, *Perfumes and Cosmetics in the Ancient World* (Tel Aviv: Sabinsky, 1989).

[34] Blinzler, "Die Grablegung Jesu," 74. Brown, "The Burial of Jesus," 242-243. Crossan, *The Historical Jesus*, 393-394. Daube, *The NT and Rabbinic Judaism*, 311. R. Pesch, *Das Markusevangelium* (Freiburg: Herder, 1977), II.516. J. A. Fitzmyer, *The Gospel according to Saint Luke* (Garden City: Doubleday, 1981), II.1523-1525. R. Schnackenburg, *Das Johannesevangelium* (Freiburg: Herder, 1977), II.346.

[35] If one is convinced by Crossan's reconstruction of the "Cross Gospel," it can be counted here as well, since G.Pet. 6.21 states that "the Jews drew the nails from the hands of the

expect that Jesus was buried in shame, i.e., laid in the criminals' tomb without any public rites of mourning.[36] Similarly, Mark's narrative—in which Joseph of Arimathea, a member of the Council, wraps Jesus' body in linen and seals it in a tomb—can be interpreted as a dishonorable burial at the hands of a Torah-abiding Sanhedrist: in keeping with prevailing custom and written law, the body is promptly placed in the criminals' burial cave.[37] Later on, women come to the tomb with perfumes, but not to mourn: they intend only to wash the corpse (*hina elthousai aleipsōsin auton*; Mk. 16:1). In depictions like these, the aroma of dishonor is very strong. As the tradition develops, however, possible traces of shame are slowly and steadily expunged from the record: Joseph of Arimathea evolves into a secret disciple of Jesus,[38] the tomb becomes new and is located in a garden,[39] and the body is wrapped in clean linens and bathed in vast quantities of perfume.[40] By the time of the Gospel of

---

Lord and laid him on the earth." Similar traditions also appear in some later texts, including Justin, *Dial.* 97.1, *Epistula Apostolorum* 9a, and Lactantius, *Divine Institutes* 4.19.

[36] J. Blinzler has argued that the syntax of Acts 13:29b does not necessarily imply that the Jewish leaders buried Jesus dishonorably: "Man wird also in Apg. 13,29b eine Brachylogie annehmen und das Subjekt des Satzes unbestimmt fassen mussen: "Man hat ihn vom Holze herabgennomen und ins Grab gelegt.'" (Blinzler, "Die Grablegung Jesu," 96).

[37] R. E. Brown, "The Burial of Jesus." Brown's argument is extremely interesting, but perhaps might be modified slightly, with the following correction: it may not be entirely correct to conclude, on the basis of the story about R. Gamaliel in BT *Ketuboth* 86 and BT *Moed Qatan* 27b, that "we are not sure what constituted honorable burial at the time of Jesus . . . since a change in burial style is reported to have been introduced between then and the time of the Mishnah" (242). R. Gamaliel, of course, did not introduce a change in Jewish burial practices; he only argued for more economical materials, i.e., flax vs. linen (cf. note 6 above). We know rather clearly what honorable Jewish burial was like—it included washing and wrapping the body, sealing it in a rock-cut family tomb, keeping the rituals of mourning, and gathering the bones a year later.

[38] Matthew, Luke, John, and Peter all improve on Mark's rather ambiguous portrait of Joseph: Luke by calling him *agathos kai dikaios*, and stipulating that he did not consent to the action against Jesus (23:51); Matthew and John by stating that Joseph was a disciple (Mt. 27:57; Jn. 19:38), and Peter by calling him *"philos* of the Lord" (2:3). Peter even has Joseph ask for the body *before* the crucifixion (2:3).

[39] Mark describes the tomb as rock-cut (15:46), and implies that it had a rolling stone (15:46), but does not specify either its owner or location. Mt. 27:60 and Lk. 23:53 also specify that the tomb was rock-cut, while Mt. 27:60 and Gos.Pet. 6:24 assert that it was Joseph's own tomb, thereby clearly distinguishing it from the criminals' burial place. Jn. 19:41 and Gos.Pet. 6:24 locate the tomb in a garden; for the connotation of honor which may implied by a garden, cf. 2 Kings 21:18,26. Finally, Mt. 27:60, Lk.23:53, and Jn. 19:41 all assert that the tomb was new, never having been used before, further differentiating it from the criminals' burial ground. The tendency of the tradition is thus to make it increasingly clear that the body of Jesus was not laid in the criminals' grave.

All the Gospels except John describe the movement of the sealing stone with a form of the verb *kuliō* (Mk. 15:46; Mt. 27:60; Lk. 24:2; Gos.Pet. 8:32), terms which connote "rolling" and may suggest a large rolling stone, such as those which blocked the entrance to Herod's Tomb and the Tomb of the Kings. Rolling stones are most often associated with the tombs of the wealthy, so this detail may also reflect an attempt to enhance the dignity of Jesus' burial.

[40] The Synoptics and Gos.Pet. report that Jesus' body was wrapped (Mk. 15:46; GPt. 6:24; Mt. 27:59, Lk. 23:53) in "linen cloth" (*sindoni*, Mk. 15:46par; Gos.Pet. 6:24), but John 19:40

Peter, Christians are asserting that Jesus had been buried in the tomb of a wealthy and powerful family, and that his death had been properly mourned. The tendency of the tradition to enhance the dignity of Jesus' interment is unmistakable.

In view of this tendency, one characteristic of the burial narratives is extremely significant: *the early stages of the tradition do not deny that Jesus' burial was shameful.* The story is steadily enhanced, to be sure, but the two defining marks of shame remain plainly visible—in these stories, Jesus is not buried in a family tomb, and public rites of mourning are not observed. A detail added by Matthew, Luke, and John is particularly revealing in this regard. The tomb of Jesus, they say, was new, "where no one had yet been laid" (Mt. 27:60; Lk. 23:53; Jn. 19:43). This remark clearly differentiates Jesus' resting place from the criminals' burial cave, but—as both David Daube and Josef Blinzler have pointed out—a new tomb would still be a shameful place of interment.[41] In fact a new tomb, never before used by sinner or saint, would be the only culturally acceptable alternative to the criminals' burial place, for it would be the only other way to preserve the boundary of shame which separated Jesus from his people—at least until his guilt could be expiated by decomposition of his flesh. By putting Jesus alone in a new tomb, then, Matthew, Luke, and John do not deny the shame of Jesus' burial: they merely spare him the disgrace of being placed in the criminals' tomb. A residue of shame still clings to him as an executed convict. In addition, these documents also avoid explicit depiction of public rites of mourning for Jesus. When he dies, no one sits *shivʿah*: a few women merely note the location of the tomb, and later visit it after the sabbath.[42] They go there, however, not to grieve or to ensure that Jesus is truly dead, but to anoint the body (Mk. 16:1; Lk. 24:1) or "to see the tomb" (*theōrēsai ton taphon*; Mt. 28:1). In each of these stories, then, the defining marks of shame stubbornly persist. Despite their clear interest in dignifying Jesus'

---

says the body was bound with "strips of linen" (*othoniois*). Do John (*othoniois*; pl.) and the Synoptics (*sindōn*; sing.) disagree over the number of linens in which Jesus' body was wrapped? J. Blinzler thinks not, arguing that the Synoptics use the singular in order to emphasize the material from which the grave wrappings were made ("Die Grablegung Jesu," 78). R. E. Brown proposes the opposite, i.e., that John uses the plural to emphasize the material (R. E. Brown, *The Gospel according to John* (Garden City: Doubleday, 1977), 941-42). Certainly the Jews of Roman Palestine did attribute significance to the material in which corpses were bound: R. Gamaliel requested a simple burial in wrappings of flax rather than linen (cf. note 6 above). Thus simplicity of burial could be expressed by flax wrappings, and elegance by linen, but even R. Gamaliel's simple burial involved many wrappings. Thus Blinzler's proposal is more likely to be correct; cf. also J. Blinzler, "*Sindōn* in evangeliis," *VD* 34 (1956) 112-113; and *Der Prozess Jesu* (Regensburg: Pustet, 1969), 396-397. Matthew adds that the linen was "clean" (*en sindoni kathara*; Mt. 27:59), while Gos.Pet. is the first to specifically note the washing of the body (6.24).

41 Daube, *The NT and Rabbinic Judaism*, 311. J. Blinzler, "Die Grablegung Jesu," 101-102.

42 Each of these gospels includes specific descriptions of mourning in relation to other deaths: in the stories of Jairus' daughter, the beginnings of mourning and the funeral procession are depicted (Mk. 5:21-43par), while in Mt. 8:21-22, a son cannot follow Jesus because he is apparently still observing the thirty days of *shloshim* for his father. In the Lazarus narrative (Jn. 11:1-44), Mary and Martha are observing the ritual of *shivʿah* when Jesus arrives. The absence of such depictions from the narratives of Jesus' burial is thus a significant omission.

burial, the early stories do not deny the dishonor of it. They make Jesus' burial as honorable as possible, but the taint of shame lingers.

Jewish practices of dishonorable burial are, however, directly violated by the Gospel of Peter, which both places Jesus in a family tomb and depicts rituals of mourning. According to Gos.Pet. 6.22, for example, Joseph of Arimathea washed the body of Jesus, wrapped it linen and placed in "his own tomb"—nothing about newness here—which was called "Joseph's Garden." Later, the women come to the tomb with the stated intention of performing the customary rites of mourning for the dead (*ha eiōthesan poiein*; Gos.Pet. 12:52). True, the Jews are said to have prevented such mourning on the day of Jesus' crucifixion, but the women resolutely intend to do so after the sabbath (*kai nun epi tou mnēmatos autou poiēsōmen tauta*; Gos.Pet. 12:53). They determine not to confine their grieving to the privacy of their own hearts: they will do "what ought to be done" (*ta opheilomena*; Gos.Pet. 12:54). With these depictions the tradition of Jesus' burial has turned a significant corner, for the boundary of Jewish custom has been broken, and the burial of Jesus has been made honorable.

In the early stages of the tradition, then, culturally appropriate efforts were made to dignify the burial of Jesus. To that end the early Christians told stories about a member of the Sanhedrin named Joseph of Arimathea, a new tomb, clean linen, and large amounts of perfume. Specific mention of either the criminals' burial place or the forbidden rites of mourning was, however, discreetly avoided. Not until the Gospel of Peter were these stories embellished to the point that they erased what had been—for an earlier generation of Christians—an undeniable fact: the tomb of the historical Jesus was a place of shame.

3

E. P. Sanders, in attempting to reconstruct the course of events at Jesus' trial, has pointed out that probably no single individual was in a position to know fully the exact course of events on that fateful night.[43] Recently John Dominic Crossan has expressed similar skepticism about the burial of Jesus as well: "*Nobody knew what had happened to Jesus' body* . . . With regard to the body of Jesus, by Easter Sunday morning, those who cared did not know, and those who knew did not care."[44] There are good reasons to agree with this sobering assessment. Certainly few—if any—followers of Jesus directly witnessed his death and burial, and the glamorized Christian stories of his interment can hardly be trusted to describe *wie es eigentlich war*. Yet there are good reasons to stop short of complete skepticism about the fate of Jesus' body. Indeed, the evidence adduced here coheres around a single positive conclusion. The trajectory of the early Christian tradition points directly back to the criminals' burial cave, and the archaeological and literary sources for first-century Jewish burial customs point to the same place. As Jewish culture demanded,

---

43 E. P. Sanders, *Jesus and Judaism* (Philadelphia: Fortress, 1985), 300.

44 Crossan, *The Historical Jesus*, 394 (emphasis his).

and as Christian texts tacitly admitted, the historical Jesus was buried in shame in a rock-cut criminals' burial cave.

On the basis of the evidence, in fact, the following scenario emerges as a plausible account of the disposition of Jesus' body: late on the day of his death, one or more of the Jewish leaders in Jerusalem—later personified by Christian tradition as Joseph of Arimathea—requested custody of the body of Jesus for purposes of dishonorable burial. These leaders, having collaborated with the Romans in the condemnation of Jesus, had both the motive and the means to bury him in shame: motive, in Jewish law and custom; and means, in their access to the Roman authority.[45] Pilate did not hesitate to grant dishonorable burial for one of their own condemned criminals.[46] Only the most rudimentary burial preparations were administered—the body was wrapped and taken directly to the tomb, without a funeral procession, eulogies, or the deposition of any personal effects. By sunset on the day of his death, the body of Jesus lay in a niche or on a shelf within a burial cave reserved for criminals condemned by Jewish courts. No one mourned.

The dishonor of Jesus' burial is not only consistent with the available literary and material evidence, but the taint of shame also explains a fact which has long been puzzling to historians of early Christianity: why did the primitive church not venerate the tomb of Jesus? Joachim Jeremias, for one, found it inconceivable (*undenkbar*) that the primitive community would have let the grave of Jesus sink into oblivion.[47] Yet the first indications of Christian veneration of Jesus' tomb do not surface until at least the third century CE.[48] It is a striking fact—and not at all unthinkable—that the tomb of Jesus was not venerated until it was no longer remembered as a place of shame.

---

[45] Crossan's discussion (*The Historical Jesus*, 391-394) appears to overlook the Jewish authorities' motive for burying Jesus. Contrasting the thousands of victims crucified by Varus outside Jerusalem in 4 BCE (*Ant.* XVII.295), as well as the hundreds crucified daily by Titus in 70 CE (*War* V.450), with the lone victim ever found in the archaeological record, Crossan concludes that "what must have happened normally was that the soldiers who executed the crucifixion guarded the cross until death and made sure it was over by burying the crucified one themselves" (392). The difference between the other victims and Jesus, however, is that they were not condemned by a Jewish court. The customs of dishonorable burial did not apply to them. The Jewish authorities had no obligation to bury the victims of Varus' or Titus' judgment: they did have the responsibility to dispose of the victims of their own.

[46] Brown, "The Burial of Jesus," 241.

[47] J. Jeremias, *Heilegengräber in Jesu Umwelt* (Göttingen: Vandenhoeck & Ruprecht, 1958), 145.

[48] Eusebius, *Vita Constantini* III.25-32.

Principal Orientations on the Relations between the Apocryphal Acts (*Acts of Paul* and *Acts of John*; *Acts of Peter* and *Acts of John*)

F. Stanley Jones
California State University, Long Beach

> *La question des rapports entre les Actes apocryphes est un casse-tête. Il faut souhaiter que les études en préparation fournissent des éléments de nature à la rendre moins floue.*
> (Junod and Kaestli, *Acta Iohannis*, 695)

Contents:

I. Introduction
II. On the History of Research
III. Principal Problems in the Current Debate
   A. The Juggling Act: The Multifarious Nature of the Debate
   B. Attributions of the Works
   C. How One Should Imagine These Authors at Work
      1. Oral Influence/Legends
      2. Ancient Publication
   D. Some Criteria for Establishing Relationships
      (Especially Polymorphism)
IV. Inventory of Relevant Passages
   A. *Acts of Paul* and *Acts of John*
   B. *Acts of Peter* and *Acts of John*
V. Conclusion

I. Introduction

A 1981 article by J.-D. Kaestli entitled "Les principales orientations de la recherche sur les actes apocryphes des apôtres"[1] provided welcome guidance for current scientific investigation of the apocryphal acts. It reviewed

---

[1] In François Bovon et al., *Les actes apocryphes des apôtres: Christianisme et monde païen*, Publications de la Faculté de Théologie de l'Université de Genève 4 (Geneva: Labor et Fides, 1981), 49-67.

modern research starting with approximately the last quarter of the nineteenth century and, along the way, identified the tasks that have arisen from the progression of the investigations. Larger historical perspective on this research is found in the same volume in G. Poupon's important contribution "Les actes apocryphes des apôtres de Lefèvre à Fabricius."[2] In the spirit of such studies, the present article seeks to locate principal foci in research on the relations between the apocryphal acts of the apostles; since it has become apparent that unresolved larger issues are often seriously affecting how the texts and problems are viewed,[3] the article also searches for these undercurrents tugging at the debates; finally, this article looks for the vistas that are opening up as the discussion proceeds. By thus contributing to keep the discussion sufficiently anchored in the development of past research, the article hopes to enable the true nature and import of any new ideas to be more easily disclosed and to allow steps to be more easily retraced in efforts to verify or modify results.

It is all the more pressing to capture an accurate picture of the past at this time if Robert Morgan is correct in identifying a transformation *eis allo genos* in biblical scholarship: "the emergence of the United States as trend-setter in place of Germany."[4] One of the most exciting aspects in the study of apocryphal writings at this time is that in the United States the stage is now set for the two traditionally distinct theological disciplines of New Testament and Church History to be bridged by these "marginal writings" and thus for the old disciplines to be deconstructed. In Morgan's view, the new secular university setting of departments of Religious Studies is also perforce opening new possibilities for collaboration with scholars of literature, ancient history, and the social sciences;[5] thus, larger scale restructuring would be under way, too.

II. On the History of Research

For understanding the apocryphal acts, the question of the relations among these acts is approximately as pressing as the Synoptic Problem is for understanding the canonical gospels: it is crucial. As important and central as this issue is, there has been very little discussion of the problem this century. The study of this problem has fallen to the wayside along with the study of the apocrypha generally.

---

2 Ibid., 25-47.

3 Particularly the question of the orality of the texts has surfaced over the last few years in the debates of the Seminar on Intertextuality in Christian Apocrypha. For an example of another way in which unresolved larger issues impinge on the question of intertextuality, see my first printed contribution to the Seminar, "The Martyrdom of James in Hegesippus, Clement of Alexandria, and Christian Apocrypha, Including Nag Hammadi: A Study of the Textual Relations," in *Society of Biblical Literature 1990 Seminar Papers*, ed. David J. Lull, Society of Biblical Literature Seminar Papers Series 29 (Atlanta, GA: Scholars Press, 1990), 322-35.

4 Robert Morgan with John Barton, *Biblical Interpretation*, Oxford Bible Series (New York: Oxford University Press, 1988), 138. Along these lines, compare the conception behind the "Lives of Jesus Series" edited by L. Keck.

5 *Biblical Interpretation*, 138.

One way to deal with this situation is to start completely anew, just to ignore the earlier critical work of the previous century/ies; after all, that work was performed virtually in another era and oftentimes on a quite antiquated textual basis. Such a procedure seems to be fostered by the tradition of Hennecke-Schneemelcher with its meager introductions ever since the accompanying *Handbook* was disbanded.[6]

Though this temptation to ignore the past is considerable, especially in the current age of constant systematic revisionism,[7] such a procedure deprives contemporary historical science of the few educated discussion partners it has when facing the problems. The following is an attempt to round up the partners into a forum. By tracing the genesis of arguments, this article simultaneously attempts to sort out the partners for the discussion: Ideas about the relationships between the acts have often been handed on from one scholar to the next; the "concise" tradition of Hennecke-Schneemelcher has continued in this vein so that (1) the bases for the opinions have become obscured and (2) the opinions themselves have often acquired an irreal appearance of being much more assured than they actually are.

[6] Reference is being made to Edgar Hennecke, ed., *Handbuch zu den Neutestamentlichen Apokryphen* (Tübingen: J. C. B. Mohr [Paul Siebeck], 1904). The disbandment of this *Handbook* is discussed in the Preface of Edgar Hennecke, ed., *Neutestamentliche Apokryphen*, 2nd ed., rev. and exp. (Tübingen: J. C. B. Mohr [Paul Siebeck], 1924), IV.

M. R. James's collection (Montague Rhodes James, trans., *The Apocryphal New Testament: Being the Apocryphal Gospels, Acts, Epistles, and Apocalypses with Other Narratives and Fragments*, corrected ed. [Oxford: Clarendon Press, 1953]) appeared in the same year as the second edition of Hennecke (1924) and strikingly set about the same standard for the English reader as Hennecke's collection without the *Handbook*.

W. Schneemelcher seems to be correct in stating that the Italian collections stand in the tradition of Hennecke-Schneemelcher (see Wilhelm Schneemelcher, ed., *Neutestamentliche Apokryphen in deutscher Übersetzung*, 5th ed., 2 vols. [Tübingen: J. C. B. Mohr (Paul Siebeck), 1987-89], 1:60, in reference to Mario Erbetta, *Gli apocrifi del Nuovo Testamento*, 1st and 2nd eds., 3 vols. [Casale Monferrato: Marietti, 1969-81] and Luigi Moraldi, *Apocrifi del Nuovo Testamento*, 2nd ed., 2 vols. [Turin, 1986]).

In my view, this state of affairs reflects the general disintegration of New Testament studies that began at about the outbreak of World War I, became consummate after World War II (Bultmann and his students), and with the assimilation of the contribution of Bultmann's school is hopefully going to be overcome. The new editions of the texts and studies being published by the Association pour l'étude de la littérature apocryphe chrétienne are some concrete evidence that the fundamental tasks are being taken up anew (if I remember correctly, Pierre Geoltrain [Paris] told me in June 1990 that the impetus for the new work of this Association came after the realization that it would be scientifically irresponsible simply to translate the third edition of Hennecke-Schneemelcher into French). Further evidence is James H. Charlesworth with James R. Mueller, *The New Testament Apocrypha and Pseudepigrapha: A Guide to Publications, with Excursuses on Apocalypses*, ATLA Bibliography Series 17 (Metuchen, NJ, and London: The American Theological Library Association and the Scarecrow Press, 1987), Maurice Geerard, *Clavis Apocryphorum Novi Testamenti*, Corpus Christianorum (Turnhout: Brepols, 1992), the work of the current Seminar, and the projected publication of a *New Testament Apocrypha* by Polebridge Press.

[7] The faster revisionists arise, the shorter the reign of each lasts (in my own thought this notion crystallizes around a complaint of Franz Overbeck against A. Ritschl found in Overbeck's *Christentum und Kultur: Gedanken und Anmerkungen zur modernen Theologie*, ed. Carl Albrecht Bernoulli [Basel: Benno Schwabe, 1919], 160).

The modern starting point for study of the relations between the apocryphal acts, as well as for many, if not most, issues relevant to the interpretation of ancient Christian texts, is the comprehensive research of Theodor Zahn and, following and reacting to him, Adolf Harnack. R. A. Lipsius's collection and detailed investigations of the apocryphal acts provided the raw material for these systematic presentations.[8]

A foundational element of the modern discussion of relations between the *Acts of Paul* (AP), the *Acts of Peter* (APt), and the *Acts of John* (AJ) is Lipsius and Zahn's judgment that AJ and APt were written by the same person.[9] The arguments for this view—highly relevant to the issue of intertextuality among the acts—were supplemented by M. R. James.[10]

As regards the relationship of AP to APt/AJ, Zahn in 1892 expressed his view that AP is catholic and that it is uncertain if AP used APt.[11] By 1899 Zahn had become more certain that the catholic AP borrowed some concepts

---

8 From studies before that time there are some important lessons to be learned, yet for lack of immediate access to the publications I cannot attempt to rehearse these. For a limited overview, see the study by Gérard Poupon mentioned above. There is an unfortunate gap of around 150 years between where Poupon leaves off and where J.-D. Kaestli begins in his survey. Some of this literature is mentioned in Hennecke, *Neutestamentliche Apokryphen*, 1st ed., 24*-26*, and in Hennecke, *Handbuch zu den Neutestamentlichen Apokryphen*, 7-9. Until there is a revolution in the way older publications are available, it must remain the task of the European colleagues to work through the older literature; the United States simply never has possessed, and does not now, a library that can compare even remotely with the European collections of the older literature.

9 Richard Adelbert Lipsius, *Die apokryphen Apostelgeschichten und Apostellegenden: Ein Beitrag zur altchristlichen Literaturgeschichte*, vol. 2, 2 halves (Braunschweig: C. A. Schwetschke und Sohn [Wiegandt & Appelhans; M. Bruhn], 1884-87), 2.1:266, 272 (the basis for Lipsius's identification of authors was the two lists of predicates in APt 20 and AJ 98); Theodor Zahn, *Geschichte des Neutestamentlichen Kanons*, 2 vols. (Erlangen and Leipzig: A. Deichert, 1888-92), 2:839-41 (according to Zahn, the two acts are from the same author or from two colleagues who stood in perfect agreement with each other; Zahn mentioned the following common elements: [1] the same speculation about the cross, [2] the same pan-Christism, [3] the same notion that this is secret tradition, but no polemic against the biblical and ecclesiastical tradition, [4] celebration of the eucharist with water, [5] same strong recommendation of sexual asceticism [see below for references to the relevant passages]); Zahn had earlier distinguished between the two writings and denied Leucianic authorship to APt: *Acta Joannis* (Erlangen: A. Deichert, 1880), LXXVIII).

10 Montague Rhodes James, ed., *Apocrypha Anecdota Second Series*, Texts and Studies 5.1 (Cambridge: University Press, 1897), listed the parallels on pp. xxv-xxviii (see below for references to the passages). Zahn listed observations to this effect also in his "Die Wanderungen des Apostels Johannes," *Neue kirchliche Zeitschrift* 10 (1899):191-218. By 1924, however, James had changed his opinion and wrote that APt used AJ (*The Apocryphal New Testament*, 300).

11 *Geschichte des Neutestamentlichen Kanons*, 2:890.

and names from APt and AJ.[12] Very much in the shadow of Lipsius,[13] Zahn assumed the schema of a historical development from gnostic to catholic (as will be seen, this schema is still a factor in the discussion of interrelationships).

Zahn's view was then attacked by Adolf Harnack insofar as Harnack denied the gnostic character of APt; he listed nine elements to demonstrate the catholic character of APt and to date it no earlier than the middle of the third century.[14] Harnack was hesitant to pronounce on AJ since Bonnet's edition had not yet appeared; nothing he had seen of AJ forced him to date it later than the second century.[15] By this process (and continuing the notion of a development from gnostic to catholic), AJ is left behind as older than APt.[16]

Soon thereafter, Schmidt followed Harnack's lead and now provided actual arguments against the view that AJ and APt were written by the same author. With Zahn, he thought AP imitated AJ, while APt, which he dated to the reign of Septimius Severus, used both AJ and AP.[17] Absolutely no details were provided regarding the presumed relationship between AP and AJ.

Working at about the same time for the first edition of the *Neutestamentliche Apokryphen*, Gerhard Ficker was not impressed with the arguments for direct literary dependency among these three acts; he thought they all just derived from the same theological school and ecclesiastical atmosphere.[18] The editor

---

[12] "Die Wanderungen des Apostels Johannes," 216-17. Zahn mentioned here the passages in which Christ appears in the form of the leading apostle (AJ 87, APTh 21), which he considered more at home in the gnostic AJ, the names Eubula (APt 17, APHamb. 2-5) and Cleobius (AJ 18-19, 25, 59; APCor. 1.2), and the story of the prefect Agrippa (APt 25-26, John Chrysostomus as supposed witness to AP).

[13] Richard Adelbert Lipsius, *Die apokryphen Apostelgeschichten und Apostellegenden: Ein Beitrag zur altchristlichen Literaturgeschichte*, vol. 1 (Braunschweig: C. A. Schwetschke und Sohn, 1883), 4-8. See Kaestli, "Les principales orientations," 53-55.

[14] *Geschichte der altchristlichen Literatur bis Eusebius*, 2nd ed., exp., 2 pts. (Leipzig: J. C. Hinrichs, 1958), 2.1:553-59.

[15] Ibid., 541-42.

[16] In 1904 Harnack (after reading C. Schmidt's investigation) spoke of the use of AJ by APt (*Geschichte der altchristlichen Literatur*, 2.2:170, 174).

[17] Carl Schmidt, *Die alten Petrusakten im Zusammenhang der apokryphen Apostelliteratur nebst einem neuentdeckten Fragment*, Texte und Untersuchungen zur Geschichte der altchristlichen Literatur, n.s., vol. 9, fasc. 1 (Leipzig: J. C. Hinrichs, 1903), 99-102. The notion that AJ inaugurated the series of apocryphal acts is also found in Carl Schmidt, *Gespräche Jesu mit seinen Jüngern nach der Auferstehung: Ein katholisch-apostolisches Sendschreiben des 2. Jahrhunderts*, Texte und Untersuchungen zur Geschichte der altchristlichen Literatur, n.s., 43 (Leipzig: J. C. Hinrich, 1919), 366.

Schmidt, *Die alten Petrusakten*, 93-95, mentioned the following considerations that led to the view that APt used AJ: (1) the clouded docetic statements in APt 20 are best explainable as having been derived from a source, and AJ seem to fit the bill insofar as AJ 109 and 98 have a similar list of predicates for Christ and have the modalistic point of the passage still intact; (2) the statement about writing scriptures to the degree that is humanly possible (APt 20) seems to be a weak reflection of AJ 88; (3) the speculation on the cross.

[18] "Petrusakten," in Hennecke, *Neutestamentliche Apokryphen*, 1st ed., 383-423, p. 386. Compare Gerhard Ficker, *Die Petrusakten: Beiträge zu ihrem Verständnis* (Leipzig: Johann Ambrosius Barth, 1903), 45. J. Flamion, "Les actes apocryphes de Pierre," *Revue d'Histoire Ecclésiastique* 9 (1908): 233-54, p. 250, n. 1, noted that E. von Dobschütz also disagreed with Schmidt's view that APt used AJ.

E. Hennecke, to the contrary, immediately started to canonize Schmidt's views; he considered it "certain" that none of the acts is from the same author and wrote that the dependency of APt on AJ was "personally very enlightening."[19] The editor made sure that the next edition of his collection reflected this opinion: he pulled AJ to the opening position in the presentation of the apocryphal acts and himself presented the case for this being the first of all the acts; AP followed; then came APt. The prior placement of AJ remained through the fourth edition of the work, though with Schmidt's change in views on the relationship between AP and APt (1930)[20] the third and fourth editions reversed the order of these two works.[21] This "canonized" view found broader acceptance with very little modification.[22]

There was a shift in the Hennecke-tradition when K. Schäferdiek took over responsibility for presenting AJ. He started to date AJ to the first half of the third century,[23] and this led Schneemelcher initially to question the dependency of APt on AJ and eventually to abandon it.[24]

---

[19] *Handbuch zu den Neutestamentlichen Apokryphen*, 356. Brief hints by Hennecke that APt is dependent on AJ are already found in *Neutestamentliche Apokryphen*, 1st ed., 355. Hennecke's remarks in the prefaces to *Neutestamentliche Apokryphen*, V, and the *Handbuch zu den Neutestamentlichen Apokryphen*, V, make it clear that the publication of the Handbook *followed* the publication of the collection.

[20] "Zur Datierung der alten Petrusakten," *Zeitschrift für die neutestamentliche Wissenschaft* 29 (1930):150-55, p. 152.

[21] The fifth edition adopts an alphabetical order for the acts, as is found also in the Bovon et al., *Les actes apocryphes des apôtres*, 289-305.

[22] In 1913 Léon Vouaux simply assumed (compare Schmidt) the priority of AJ over AP; he thought AJ furnished AP with no more than the idea of composing such a writing (*Les actes de Paul et ses lettres apocryphes: Introduction, textes, traduction et commentaire*, Les Apocryphes du Nouveau Testament [Paris: Librairie Letouzey et Ané, 1913], 132). In 1922 Vouaux consolidated the discussion of the relations between AJ and APt; he considered the dependency of APt on AJ to be evident in (1) the Christological statements in AJ 88-90 and APt 20, 10, (2) the list of names for Jesus in AJ 98, 109 and APt 20, and (3) statements on the cross in AJ 103 and APt 39. Vouaux saw APt correcting AJ in an orthodox direction in each of these passages (*Les actes de Pierre: Introduction, textes, traduction et commentaire*, Les Apocryphes du Nouveau Testament [Paris: Librairie Letouzey et Ané, 1922], 49-52). Essentially the same three points are mentioned by Hennecke, *Neutestamentliche Apokryphen*, 2nd ed., 171.

As noted above, in 1924 M. R. James wrote that APt used AJ (*The Apocryphal New Testament*, 300). M. Erbetta, *Gli Apocrifi del Nuovo Testamento*, 2:139, also spoke of APt imitating the language of AJ.

[23] Knut Schäferdiek, "The Acts of John," in Edgar Hennecke, *New Testament Apocrypha*, ed. Wilhelm Schneemelcher, trans. ed. R. McL. Wilson, 2 vols. (Philadelphia: Westminster Press, 1963-65), 2:188-258, pp. 214-15, and Knut Schäferdiek, "Johannesakten," in Wilhelm Schneemelcher, ed., *Neutestamentliche Apokryphen in deutscher Übersetzung*, vol. 2: *Apostolische Apokalypsen und Verwandtes*, 5th ed. (Tübingen: J. C. B. Mohr [Paul Siebeck], 1989), 138-93, p. 155.

[24] Wilhelm Schneemelcher, "The Acts of Peter," in Edgar Hennecke, *New Testament Apocrypha*, ed. Wilhelm Schneemelcher, trans. ed. R. McL. Wilson, 2 vols. (Philadelphia: Westminster Press, 1963-65), 2:259-322, pp. 263-65, and Wilhelm Schneemelcher,"Petrusakten," in idem, ed. *Neutestamentliche Apokryphen in deutscher Übersetzung*, vol. 2: *Apostolische Apokalypsen und Verwandtes*, 5th ed. (Tübingen: J. C. B. Mohr [Paul Siebeck], 1989), 243-89, pp. 247-48. Compare Philipp Vielhauer, *Geschichte der urchristlichen Literatur: Einleitung in das Neue Testament, die Apokryphen und die Apostolischen*

More recently, E. Junod and J.-D. Kaestli casually noted the many points of contact between AJ and the other acts and made some evaluative comments throughout their commentary on AJ. Instead of offering a systematic evaluation of the parallels, however, they essentially rested their case on the treatment of the theme of polymorphy in the acts, reverting to the position that the fuller treatment of the topic must be the original: AJ is the only acts to use the motif in both a discourse of the leading apostle and a romantic deliverance, and AJ employs the theme in the most thoughtful manner, underlining its theological significance.[25]

The above summarized work seems to build the true partner for any renewed discussion of the relations between these apocryphal acts. Three possible explanations of the relations among the acts have been articulated: (1) common authorship (Lipsius, Zahn, James), (2) literary dependency (Harnack and Schmidt), and (3) common milieu (Ficker). After mounting a critique of possibility 1, possibility 2 was immediately canonized in the tradition of Hennecke. Possibility 3 was never really explored and seems to be making something of a comeback. In retrospect, it is on a few pages of Schmidt's book from 1903 that the presumption against the previously assumed identity of the authors of AJ and APt rests.[26] AJ moved into the position of priority not so much by straightforward argument for dependence of the other acts on it but by Harnack's late dating of APt, which left AJ behind as older acts. The Christological statements in AJ did soon provide a locus for reasoning to the effect that AJ must be prior.

III. Principal Problems in the Current Debate

With this much said about the specific history of research (and intending to return to the particular passages that have been isolated as important for the debate), attention may now be directed toward finding issues that seem to be strong undercurrents in the present situation. When these undercurrents are isolated, some vistas will hopefully open out from past research and point the way for the debate to proceed. Consideration of the larger history of research can at least lead to the identification of various sets of evidence for specific problems. Such identification then encourages the separation of the issues, which can foster purer and clearer arguments that resist being vitiated by external concerns.

A. *The Juggling Act: The Multifarious Nature of the Debate*

One reason for the lack of clarity with respect to the relations between the acts is that in dealing with one particular question of relationship, the entire

---

Väter, De Gruyter Lehrbuch, 1975, rev. reprint (Berlin and New York: De Gruyter, 1978), 696, who stated that APt is the oldest of the apocryphal acts (i.e., older than AJ), and Eckhard Plümacher, "Apokryphen Apostelakten," *Paulys Realencyclopädie der classischen Altertumswissenschaft*, supp. vol. 15, cols. 11-70, who does not presuppose the priority of the AJ.

[25] Eric Junod and Jean-Daniel Kaestli, eds., *Acta Iohannis*, Corpus Christianorum Series Apocryphorum 1-2, 2 vols. (Turnhout: Brepols, 1983), 698-700.

[26] Schmidt, *Die alten Petrusakten*, 90-99.

larger question of the relations with the other (three or more) acts is perforce involved; this complicates the situation to almost mind-boggling proportions, especially as language barriers are crossed in the transmission of the various acts. This situation partially explains why there has been so little discussion of the entire problem.

The way to deal with the multifarious nature of the debate seems to be to get all the possibilities out on the table in a creative and orderly way; it is perhaps less necessary to proceed from the mathematical computation of all possible variants than from the various positions defended in past research.

In the particular case of the relationship between AP and AJ, for example, the question of the relations with other acts can be highly relevant. It has been suggested that AP is dependent on APt, ATh, and possibly AA.[27] Particularly if the passages on the polymorphous appearances of Christ are derived from ATh,[28] arguments about relations between AP and AJ are affected.

B. Attributions of the Works

The debate at the turn of the century was dominated by the figure "Leucius." It seems to have been assumed that if it could be determined which of the apocryphal acts Leucius wrote, the dependency of the other acts would be demonstrated. The debate about Leucius has since fizzled, but the priority assigned to AJ, which Zahn and others settled on as the true product of Leucius, has remained.

Another figure who has often played a role in discussions of relations among the acts is Tertullian's "presbyter in Asia" who supposedly wrote AP. If the work can be attributed to an identifiable Asian presbyter, this seems to change modern perceptions of the work more than is often imagined; scholars have been less likely to attribute "imitation" to some identifiable church figure. Along these lines, Junod and Kaestli open their discussion of the relations between the acts by an extended argument against AP having been written by this presbyter.[29]

Examination of these traditions about the Asian presbyter[30] and Leucius should continue. Yet it does not seem logical to assign extraordinary

---

27 Jean-Marc Prieur, ed., *Acta Andreae*, Corpus Christianorum Series Apocryphorum 5-6 (Turnhout: Brepols, 1989), 388-89 (others of this opinion are mentioned there on p. 386).

28 So Erik Peterson, "Einige Bemerkungen zum Hamburger Papyrus-Fragment der Acta Pauli," in idem, *Frühkirche, Judentum und Gnosis: Studien und Untersuchungen* (Rome, Freiburg, and Vienna: Herder, 1959), 183-208, pp. 199-200; see also Prieur, *Acta Andreae*, 388. The reverse relationship is defended by Paul Devos, "Actes de Thomas et actes de Paul," *Analecta Bollandiana* 69 (1951):119-30.

29 *Acta Iohannis*, 696. The problem for them is, however, less the attribution itself than the early date that this text could establish for AP.

30 The attribution of AP to the Asian presbyter by Tertullian is generally accepted as reliable without much debate (see, e.g., Prieur, *Acta Andreae*, 385). Some attention was devoted to this issue in *The Apocryphal Acts of Apostles*, ed. Dennis Ronald MacDonald, Semeia 38 (Decatur, GA: Scholars Press, 1986), yet I am puzzled that one question has not been addressed: Does not this entire type of comment derive from ancient invective of the standard heresiological variety: any "heretical" opinion can be attributed to one isolated person who went awry (cf. Tertullian, *de praes.* 6; an example of a fictitious heretical founder is "Ebion" of *de praes.* 33; the motif of the heretic repenting is paralleled in *de praes.* 30 where it is reported that Marcion professed repentance)?

creativity to either one of these figures simply because they are identifiable. The other acts were also written by specific people.

However one decides on these attributions, the issue is best seen as a separate and independent building block for arguments about dependency. Indeed, this block does not seem very well suited to arguments about dependencies at all; it relies rather on the lack of knowledge about the authors of the other works and thereby illicitly allows them to slip into the nebulous category of "imitators." This observation leads to the next issue.

C. How One Should Imagine These Authors at Work

1. Oral Influence/Legends

The issue of whether oral stories lie behind the apocryphal acts has been raised again in recent times above all by D. R. MacDonald's *The Legend and the Apostle*.[31] V. Burrus provided a most helpful inaugural history of research that sets the debate in the context of the work by E. Rohde, E. von Dobschütz, R. Reitzenstein, L. Radermacher, K. Kerényi, and R. Söder (canonized in the Hennecke-Schneemelcher tradition).[32] Burrus's survey is centered perhaps too much on the relation of the apocryphal acts to the ancient novels, and thus some important opinions are not reported.[33] The framework of the debate perhaps needs to be redetermined.

One figure not mentioned by Burrus, C. Schmidt, was strictly opposed to the view that AP was written on the basis of any traditions beyond the canonical Acts and the letters of Paul.[34] As Schmidt's comments in reaction to W. Schubart reveal, the older debate was connected with the concept "legend." R. A. Lipsius had already spoken of the origin of much of the material in local tales and localized legends.[35] The whole concept of ancient Christian legends and hagiography doubtless needs to be reviewed critically. Within the New Testament, the center of attention with respect to apostolic "legends" has traditionally been the Acts of the Apostles. By joining onto studies of the canonical Acts, studies of the apocryphal acts need to clarify both the concept of "legend" and the existence of such in the ancient church. Furthermore, a comprehensive presentation of the reception of the canonical Acts in the apocryphal acts is now overdue.

While it is not possible to carry out this work here, one element that definitely should be kept in mind alongside the question of relations among

---

[31] Dennis Ronald MacDonald, *The Legend and the Apostle: The Battle for Paul in Story and Canon* (Philadelphia: Westminster Press, 1983), esp. pp. 17-33.

[32] Virginia Burrus, *Chastity as Autonomy: Women in the Stories of Apocryphal Acts*, Studies in Women and Religion 23 (Lewiston and Queenston: Edwin Mellen Press, 1987), 7-30.

[33] Even with respect to the genre of the apocryphal acts there seems to be more material. See, for example, the discussion by F. Pfister, "Zusammenhang mit der antiken Literatur," in Hennecke, *Neutestamentliche Apokryphen*, 2nd ed., 163-67, and the literature mentioned there.

[34] *Acta Pauli: Übersetzung, Untersuchungen und koptischer Text*, 2nd ed., exp. (Leipzig: J. C. Hinrichs, 1905), XIV-XIX, 198-217; *Praxeis Paulou: Acta Pauli nach dem Papyrus der Hamburger Staats-und Universitäts-Bibliothek*, Veröffentlichungen aus der Hamburger Staats- und Universitäts-Bibliothek 2 (Glückstadt and Hamburg: J. J. Augustin, 1936), 111.

[35] *Die apokryphen Apostelgeschichten*, 1:10.

the apocryphal acts is that current opinion on oral influence on these works still varies from one extreme to the other. One end of the debate has recently been formulated by E. Junod.[36] In his view, the literary unity of each acts does not allow literary analysis to isolate traditional elements.[37] Only external witnesses can do so. On this basis, Junod concludes that the episodes in the acts are largely free creations of the authors, though known traditions could not be contradicted by the works.[38]

The opposite extreme is represented, on the one hand, by W. Schneemelcher and, on the other hand, by the renewed school of oral influence. Schneemelcher relies again on the concept of personal and local legends to describe the material available to the authors of the acts.[39] The other trajectory, of MacDonald and Burrus, has been extended by Christine Thomas, who addresses some objections raised by J.-D. Kaestli and E. Junod: she employs redaction-criticism and source-criticism to identify sources in APt, and she argues for oral origin on the basis of variant versions of recognizably the same story. Thomas immediately points to the relevance of her remarks for the discussion of intertextuality among the apocryphal acts; she suggests that an oral relationship may be the best for explaining the common material.[40] Jean-Marc Prieur similarly refers to the concept of "topoi" to explain some resemblances among the acts.[41] This is, of course, also where Richard Valantasis's distinctive contribution to the Seminar fits in.[42]

Work on the possible oral origin of some of the material in the acts will hopefully continue; it is a problem in itself that has proven fruitful for the broader discussion, too. Questions of relations among the acts, however, should receive their principal orientation not from this larger problem but from the parallel texts themselves, for which explanations based on orality need to be considered.

---

[36] "Créations romanesques et traditions ecclésiastiques dans les actes apocryphes des apôtres," *Augustinianum* 23 (1983):271-83.

[37] Ibid., 274-75.

[38] Ibid., 280-83. A critique of the methodology of MacDonald and Burrus in isolating oral traditions is found in J.-D. Kaestli, "Fiction littéraire et réalité sociale: Que peut-on savoir de la place des femmes dans le milieu de production des actes apocryphes des apôtres?" *Apocrypha* 1 (1990):279-302, pp. 284-90.

[39] *Neutestamentliche Apokryphen*, 5th ed., 2:79. The concept was already prominent in the first edition in the title of the section on apocryphal acts, p. 346.

[40] "Word and Deed: The *Acts of Peter* and Orality," *Apocrypha* 3 (1992):125-164. In this article Thomas refers to J.-D. Kaestli's "Response to 'Chastity as Autonomy: Women in the Stories of the Apocryphal Acts,' by Virginia Burrus," in *The Apocryphal Acts of the Apostles*, ed. Dennis Ronald MacDonald, Semeia 38 (Decatur, GA: Scholars Press, 1986), 119-31, but she was apparently not yet able to draw upon Kaestli's further presentation in "Fiction littéraire et réalité sociale."

[41] *Acta Andreae*, 387.

[42] "Narrative Strategies and Synoptic Quandaries: A Response to Dennis MacDonald's Reading of *Acts of Paul* and *Acts of Peter*," in *Society of Biblical Literature 1992 Seminar Papers*, ed. Eugene H. Lovering, Jr., Society of Biblical Literature Seminar Paper Series 31 (Atlanta, GA: Scholars Press, 1992), 234-39.

2. Ancient Publication

A strong undercurrent in the present understanding of the apocrypha is the great uncertainty about the way in which early Christian writings circulated in antiquity. In the course of my own work, some specialists of the ancient near east were somewhat startled that I could even imagine an early fifth-century Latin translator in Italy to be working from essentially the same Greek text as a late fourth-century Syriac translator somewhere in Syria. Yet the two translations of the lost Greek Pseudo-Clementine *Recognitions* make it clear that this is indeed the case,[43] and for those acquainted with the documents of ancient church history this would not be considered an extraordinary situation at all. Rather, these scholars are constantly assuming that church writers had read reliable copies of many other church writings from before their time[44] (for the New Testament the use of a couple of textual forms can be traced[45]).

The issue of how early Christian writings actually circulated seems to be having an enormous (unstated) impact on thought about the genesis and relations of the apocryphal acts. In order for this issue to be approached, several preliminary remarks are necessary: First, the importance of the issue and the magnitude of the uncertainty need to be realized. Particularly because the apocrypha lie in the unclaimed land between the New Testament and traditional "church history," the uncertainty seems magnified by both sides. Second, it needs to be recognized that there is actually a rather large gap in current science when it comes to imagining how early Christian writings circulated. Historical research of the nineteenth century did not solve this issue. For the twentieth century it was not "existentially" relevant enough. The problem has thus devolved upon the current generation. Third, the process of sorting through the material unearthed by the great expeditions that began in the nineteenth century—the material (especially papyri and other manuscripts) shipped in trunks back to the museums of the mother European countries—*has* indeed largely been carried out in a preliminary way this century and has provided a wealth of new information pertinent to the ancient world and particularly to ancient writings. This raw data needs to be integrated into the study of ancient Christianity. Fourth, it is becoming apparent that ancient Christianity as a whole was thoroughly part of the ancient world: there was neither a primitive period that was somehow

---

[43] See my article "Evaluating the Latin and Syriac Translations of the Pseudo-Clementine *Recognitions*," *Apocrypha* 3 (1992):237-57.

[44] Modern studies seem to rest here largely on the assumptions of source-criticism of the nineteenth century such as Richard Adelbert Lipsius, *Zur Quellenkritik des Epiphanios* (Vienna: Wilhelm Braumüller, 1865); see Adolf Harnack's praise for this "epoch-making book" in "Zur Quellenkritik der Geschichte des Gnosticismus," *Zeitschrift für die historische Theologie* 44 (1874):143-83, p. 143. For a modern representative, see, e.g., Gérard Vallée, *A Study in Anti-Gnostic Polemics: Irenaeus, Hippolytus, and Epiphanius*, Studies in Christianity and Judaism 1 (Waterloo: Wilfrid Laurier University Press, 1981), 5f., n. 1.

[45] Eldon Jay Epp, "A Continuing Interlude in New Testament Textual Criticism?" *Harvard Theological Review* 73 (1980):131-51, pp. 138-51, and others have properly pleaded for further investigation of these forms.

exempt,[46] nor did the church develop in a world of its own (some sort of vacuum of truth that was regularly assailed from the outside by people pretending to be Christians [so-called heretics[47]]). The phenomenon of Ancient Christianity is emerging as the study of church history is being brought out of its traditional parochial theological setting.

With these four considerations in mind, we may start to ask more directly about the circulation of ancient Christian writings. In the course of the Seminar I once mentioned the concept of "publication" in connection with Christian apocrypha. Since there was at least one spoken reaction of bewilderment over the use of such a "modern" concept when speaking of ancient works (it was stated that the only known "publication" in antiquity was when some upper class Romans read their finished work aloud to friends in their home[48]), this is an opportunity to provide the requested references to such activities in antiquity and to pose the question of whether any of the Christian apocrypha were published.

The classic treatment of the phenomenon of ancient books is Theodor Birt's *Das antike Buchwesen*,[49] which holds its position in much the same way that E. Rohde's *Der griechische Roman* or Strack-Billerbeck do (i.e., flawed in interpretation, but still indispensable collection). Chapter 7, "The Edition" (pp. 342-70), is particularly relevant to the issue at hand: it discusses what happened to the autograph, how it was copied, how many copies were made in an edition, proofreading, publishers, prices, honoraria, bookshops, booksellers, libraries and book-buyers, private collections, the book-trade in general, and other related issues. Birt has been taken to task for adding too much color; for example, while Birt imagined the production of editions to lie in the range of 500 to 1,000,[50] B. A. van Groningen has suggested 20 to 30.[51]

---

46 See in this regard on the one hand the protest of Hans Dieter Betz, review of *Reallexikon für Antike und Christentum, vol. 10, Gnomon* 55 (1983):744-46, p. 746, and some details from the history of the problem in his "Neues Testament und griechisch-hellenistische Überlieferung," in *Loyalitätskonflikte in der Religionsgeschichte: Festschrift für Carsten Colpe*, ed. Christoph Elsas and Hans G. Kippenberg (Würzburg: Königshausen & Neumann, 1990), 225-31, and on the other hand the sketch by Kurt Rudolph, "Early Christianity as a Religious-Historical Phenomenon," in *The Future of Early Christianity: Essays in Honor of Helmut Koester*, ed. Birger A. Pearson (Minneapolis: Fortress Press, 1991), 9-19.

47 For some details on the early Christian development of the notion of "heresy," see Alain Le Boulluec, *La notion d'hérésie dans la littérature grecque IIe-IIIe siècles*, 2 vols. (Paris: Études Augustiniennes, 1985). For the contemporary challenge, see Charles Kannengiesser, "The Future of Patristics," *Theological Studies* 52 (1991):128-39.

48 See Tönnes Kleberg, *Buchhandel und Verlagswesen in der Antike*, trans. Ernst Zunker (Darmstadt: Wissenschaftliche Buchgesellschaft, 1967), 25-26, on this type of activity. He remarks, p. 26, that the first century of the Common Era saw a strong growth in such literary activity.

49 *Das antike Buchwesen in seinem Verhältniss zur Litteratur mit Beiträgen zur Textgeschichte des Theokrit, Catull, Properz und anderer Autoren* (Berlin: W. Hertz, 1882).

50 *Das antike Buchwesen*, 351.

51 *Traité d'histoire et de critique des textes grecs*, Akademie van Wetenschappen, Afd. Letterkunde, n.s., vol. 70, no. 2 (Amsterdam: Noord-hollandsche Uitgevers Maatschappij, 1963), 24.

Nevertheless, H. Marrou's argument against any sort of mass production[52] has (properly) not been able to hold the field.[53]

> With a certain amount of justice one may speak of a relatively homogenous literary public throughout larger parts of the Roman empire in the second century C.E. The borders of nationalities and cultures have fallen. With Rome as its center, the Roman Empire also formed a literary unity. . . . Soon one could buy the works of Latin and Greek authors in the bookstores of present-day France as well as in North Africa, in Spain as well as in the hellenized Orient.[54]

Given the existence of such a book-trade, a quite pressing question for studies of ancient Christian literature is how ancient Christian writings stood with respect to this business. The period in question lies before the time when monastic institutions assumed responsibility for the preservation of the Christian heritage. For the fourth and fifth centuries the involvement with the book-trade is clear, particularly for hagiographical accounts.[55] More uncertainty lies in the earlier period. Recently, some attention has been focused on the writings of the New Testament: the question of *editions* of Paul's letters has properly been raised.[56]

In a study of ancient Christian manuscripts from Egypt, Colin H. Roberts identifies products of the book-trade in Christian books first towards the end of

---

52 "La technique de l'édition à l'époque patristique," *Vigiliae Christianae* 3 (1949):208-24.

53 See especially the refutation by H. L. M. van der Valk, "On the Edition of Books in Antiquity," *Vigiliae Christianae* 11 (1957):1-10. Richard Sommer's study of Atticus as Cicero's editor is something of a classic: "T. Pomponius Atticus und die Verbreitung von Ciceros Werken," *Hermes* 61 (1926):389-422. Other works that reflect this consensus and that cover roughly the same ground as Birt include Wilhelm Schubart, *Das Buch bei den Griechen und Römern*, ed. Eberhard Paul, 3rd ed. (Heidelberg: Lambert Schneider, 1961), Kleberg, *Buchhandel und Verlagswesen in der Antike*, and A.-G. Hamman, *L'épopée du livre: La transmission des textes anciens, du scribe à l'imprimerie*, Collection Pour L'Histoire (Paris: Librairie Académique Perrin, 1985). The theory of mass production through dictation to a group of slaves (found in Birt, *Das antike Buchwesen*, 362) has survived to a much lesser extent; see particularly T. C. Skeat, "The Use of Dictation in Ancient Book-Production," *Proceedings of the British Academy* (1956):179-208.

Other literature on the codex is listed and surveyed in Colin H. Roberts and T. C. Skeat, *The Birth of the Codex* (London: Oxford University Press, 1983), 1-3. See furthermore, Alain Blanchard, ed. *Les débuts du codex: Actes de la journée d'étude organisée à Paris les 3 et 4 juillet 1985 par l'Institut de Papyrologie de la Sorbonne et l'Institut de Recherche et d'Historie des Textes*, Bibliologia: Elementa ad Librorum Studia Pertinentia 9 (Turnhout: Brepols, 1989).

54 Kleberg, *Buchhandel und Verlagswesen in der Antike*, 44-45.

55 See, e.g., the collection of evidence in V. Burr, "Editionstechnik," *Reallexikon für Antike und Christentum* 2:597-610, cols. 605-607.

56 See, e.g., the recent works of John J. Clabeaux, *A Lost Edition of the Letters of Paul: A Reassessment of the Text of the Pauline Corpus Attested by Marcion*, The Catholic Biblical Quarterly Monograph Series 21 (Washington, DC: The Catholic Biblical Association of America, 1989), and David Trobisch, *Die Entstehung der Paulusbriefsammlung: Studien zu den Anfängen christlicher Publizistik*, Novum Testamentum et Orbis Antiquus 10 (Freiburg: Universitätsverlag; Göttingen: Vandenhoeck & Ruprecht, 1989) (see here the discussion of research from Zahn forward on pp. 2-10). Of earlier work, Günther Zuntz, *The Text of the Epistles: A Disquisition upon the Corpus Paulinum*, Schweich Lectures 1946 (London: Oxford University Press, 1953), is a particularly stimulating study.

the third century (pocket codices);[57] earlier manuscripts he describes as
"books privately published for a secret society" (p. 12). The second-century
Christian hands are "not trained in calligraphy and so not accustomed to
writing books," but they are also "not personal or private hands" (p. 14).
Roberts describes these hands as "reformed documentary" (p. 14), writing
essentially books intended for church use (pp. 15, 22). He nevertheless
considers it not unlikely that there was a second or third century scriptorium
for Christian books at Oxyrhynchos (p. 24), and he identifies some late second
century Christian manuscripts as literary in style (pp. 22-23).

Roberts's study will not remain the last word on these subjects, yet his
work does mark some noteworthy advances. Above all, the previously
dominant notion that early Christian writings were spread only through
private transcriptions[58] has received a significant new aspect: the earliest
manuscripts were written not by private or personal hands but were rather
produced for use and distribution in the new society of Christians. With
regard to the Christian apocryphal writings, it is noteworthy that as early as
the end of the third century pocket codices *in the book-trade* already contain
Christian apocryphal acts (p. 11 mentions AJ, APt, and APTh). At some early
point the transmission of the acts thus began to intersect with the general
ancient book-trade; there was doubtless some sort of relationship even at the
beginning (e.g., an imitation in the form of book distribution for a religious
society). There is striking evidence that by the second century Christians
were quite conscious of producing distinctive sorts of books: they were clear
precursors of the revolution from the roll to the codex.[59] Given these
circumstances, it seems only natural for aspiring Christian writers
consciously to compose (apocryphal acts)[60] for distribution in their religious
society, similar to what the early heresiologists were doing. In any event,
these considerations should serve to balance the picture of the apocryphal acts
as loosely organized composites of possibly orally transmitted legends.

D. Some Criteria for Establishing Relationships
(Especially Polymorphism)

The History of Research above discloses that the dates scholars assign to
the acts (on internal grounds) have somewhat surprisingly played a decisive
role in the question of interrelationships. Thus, when Harnack argued for a
late date of APt, AJ was left in the position of priority; with Schäferdiek's late
dating of AJ, Schneemelcher started to abandon the entire notion of the
dependency of APt on AJ. When the literature on the dates of the acts is
reviewed, it seems that further progress might be made in the dating of the
acts, particularly as the history of Christianity in the second century becomes
more of a bridge (and less of a gap) between the traditional disciplines of New

---

57 *Manuscript, Society and Belief in Early Christian Egypt*, Schweich Lectures 1977 (London:
Oxford University Press, 1979), 10.

58 See, for example, the categorical statement of this position by Burr, "Editionstechnik," col. 604.

59 See Roberts and Skeat, *The Birth of the Codex*, 38-61.

60 The question of why the genre "apocryphal acts" arose at this time is a somewhat
separate issue and cannot be treated here.

Testament Studies and Church History. Greater appreciation is accumulating for the diversity of thought (e.g., Christological) and life in ancient Christianity, and the stark opposition of orthodoxy and heresy (e.g., "gnosticism"), which has dominated both disciplines, is properly being discarded as largely anachronistic. Under these circumstances, it might indeed be possible to come up with more convincing dates for the apocryphal acts.[61]

Other criteria that have been invoked to argue for dependencies among the acts often deal with the notion of primitiveness. Thus, E. Hennecke argued that AJ is more primitive than AP because the tendency toward asceticism is not as consequent in AJ as in AP.[62] Again, Robert Stoops pointed to the increased focus on the leading apostle as a possible indication of the lateness of AP in comparison with APt.[63] Similarly, Julian Hills essentially argued that since AP uses Mark, whereas APt uses Matthew, AP might be more ancient.[64] Each of these criteria presumes a development of ideas that needs to be charted before the criterion can be scientifically useful.

One such criterion in need of charting is the motif of polymorphism. The theory that AJ presents a version of polymorphous Christology more original than what is found in APt was first propounded by C. Schmidt and then picked up by E. Hennecke.[65] In his 1961 dissertation on docetism, Peter Weigandt ascribed the origin of this motif in the apocryphal acts to AJ.[66] This ascription was based to a large extent on Weigandt's prior assumption that AJ is the first apocryphal acts; here he seems to have just relied on the dominant view of the time.[67]

Weigandt presented an extended argument for the origin of the motif of polymorphism in Egypt (sun-cult)[68] and drew attention to differences in the polymorphisms in the apocryphal acts.[69] Though Weigandt did not strictly

---

[61] Notwithstanding the warning of Junod and Kaestli, *Acta Iohannis*, 694, there is reason for hope.

[62] *Neutestamentliche Apokryphen*, 2nd ed., 171. This is an advance over the first edition (p. 424) where Hennecke was silent about the relation with AP.

[63] Robert F. Stoops, Jr., "Peter, Paul, and Priority in the Apocryphal Acts," in *Society of Biblical Literature 1992 Seminar Papers*, ed. Eugene H. Lovering, Jr., Society of Biblical Literature Seminar Paper Series 31 (Atlanta, GA: Scholars Press, 1992), 225-33, p. 232.

[64] Julian V. Hills, "Scripture and the Divine in the Petrine and Pauline Acts: Explorations in Method," paper distributed for the Seminar on Intertextuality in Christian Apocrypha, November 1992.

[65] See the references above in the History of Research.

[66] *Der Doketismus im Urchristentum und in der theologischen Entwicklung des zweiten Jahrhunderts* (Evangelical Theological diss., Universität Heidelberg, 1961), 52.

[67] Witnessed in Hennecke's opinion in *Neutestamentliche Apokryphen*, 2nd ed., 171. This assumption is expressed in Weigandt, *Doketismus*, 52.

[68] Here he followed the work of Adolf Iacoby, "Altheidnisch-Aegyptisches im Christentum," *Sphinx* 7 (1903):107-17 (largely just copied [almost verbatim] by Ernst Hammerschmidt, "Altägyptische Elemente im koptischen Christentum," *Ostkirchliche Studien* 6 [1957]:233-50, pp. 238-42). It was on the basis of Weigandt's work that Junod and Kaestli placed the origin of AJ in Egypt (*Acta Iohannis*, 692).

[69] See Weigandt, *Doketismus*, 45, where he points out that among the apocryphal acts only in AJ is polymorphy applied to the earthly Jesus. Compare some work in this direction in David R. Cartlidge, "Transfigurations of Metamorphosis Traditions in the

argue that the statements in AJ are necessarily closer to the Egyptian sun-cult than are the remarks in the other acts, his approach of asking about the origin of this motif and classifying aspects of it seems to open a door for further work. Such study of the exact historical origin and precise development of polymorphism and docetism[70] (the two are not correlate[71]) could perhaps disclose if AJ has the more original form or rather just a later, expanded form. Until then, particular attention must be given to how the motif is understood as a whole and subdivided, for this is where certain spurious facile conclusions seem to sneak in. Weigandt let texts about the Egyptian sun-cult provide the three subdivisions into which he ordered the passages from the apocryphal acts;[72] there should be little wonder that he concluded that the polymorphism of the apocryphal acts is rooted in the cult of the Egyptian sun-god.[73] Junod and Kaestli, on the other hand, distinguish two principal uses of the motif of polymorphism in the apocryphal acts: in the teaching of an apostle and in

---

Acts of John, Thomas, and Peter," in *The Apocryphal Acts of the Apostles*, ed. Dennis Ronald MacDonald, Semeia 38 (Decatur, GA: Scholars Press, 1986), 53-66, Gregory J. Riley, "Thomas Tradition and the *Acts of Thomas*," in *Society of Biblical Literature 1991 Seminar Papers*, ed. Eugene H. Lovering, Jr., Society of Biblical Literature Seminar Paper Series 30 (Atlanta, GA: Scholars Press, 1991), 533-42, esp. pp. 538-41, and Paul G. Schneider, *The Mystery of the Acts of John: An Interpretation of the Hymn and the Dance in Light of the Acts' Theology*, Distinguished Dissertations Series 10 (San Francisco: Mellen Research University Press, 1991), 57-67, 98-112.

[70] Broader work on the background in the history of religions may considerably help such study, but it will not be sufficient; the texts and the history of ancient Christianity must be thoroughly engaged. Current literature on docetism includes: J. G. Davies, "The Origins of Docetism," in *Studia Patristica Vol. VI: Papers Presented to the Third International Conference on Patristic Studies Held at Christ Church, Oxford, 1959*, pt 4: *Theologica, Augustiniana*, ed. F. L. Cross, Texte und Untersuchungen zur Geschichte der altchristlichen Literatur 81 (Berlin: Akademie-Verlag, 1962), 13-35, Antonio Orbe, *Cristología gnóstica: Introducción a la soteriología de los siglos II y III*, Biblioteca de Autores Cristianos 384-85, 2 vols. (Madrid: Biblioteca de Autores Cristianos, 1976), 1:380-412, Karl Wolfgang Tröger, "Doketistische Christologie in Nag-Hammadi-Texten: Ein Beitrag zum Doketismus in frühchristlicher Zeit," *Kairos* 19 (1977):45-52, Michael Slusser, "Docetism: A Historical Definition," *The Second Century* 1 (1981):163-72, Kurt Rudolph, *Gnosis: The Nature and History of Gnosticism*, trans. and ed. Robert McLachlan Wilson (San Francisco: Harper & Row, 1983), 167-71, Norbert Brox, "'Doketismus'--eine Problemanzeige," *Zeitschrift für Kirchengeschichte* 95 (1984):301-14, Udo Schnelle, *Antidocetic Christology in the Gospel of John: An Investigation of the Place of the Fourth Gospel in the Johannine School*, trans. Linda M. Maloney (Minneapolis: Fortress Press, 1992), 63-70, Georg Strecker, "Chiliasmus und Doketismus in der Johanneischen Schule," *Kerygma und Dogma* 38 (1992):30-46.

[71] See Weigandt, *Doketismus*, 83-84. On pp. 40-41, 48, Weigandt reviews a few opinions on the origin of the motif of polymorphism. See, furthermore, Jacques E. Ménard, "Transfiguration et polymorphie chez Origène," in *Epektasis: Mélanges patristiques offerts au Cardinal Jean Daniélou*, ed. Jacques Fontaine and Charles Kannengiesser (Paris: Beauchesne, 1972), 367-72, Gedaliahu G. Stroumsa, "Polymorphie divine et transformations d'un mythologème: 'L'Apocryphon de Jean' et ses sources," *Vigiliae Christianae* 35 (1981):412-34, and Eric Junod, "Polymorphie du dieu sauveur," in *Gnosticisme et monde hellénistique: Actes du Colloque de Louvain-la-Neuve (11-14 mars 1980)*, ed. Julien Ries, Publications de l'Institut Orientaliste de Louvain 27 (Louvain-la-Neuve: Université Catholique de Louvain, Institut Orientaliste, 1982), 38-46.

[72] *Doketismus*, 49-50.

[73] Ibid., 51.

romantic episodes. Since only AJ uses the motif in both ways, AJ begins to appear to them to be more original.[74] Again, D. R. MacDonald (in this volume) implies that the polymorphism in APt and AJ derives from the tradition of the transfiguration; that is a theory about the origin and original shape of this tradition that should be verified on a larger scale.

If an exact history of the motif of polymorphism could be drawn up, one caveat is still in order: It cannot be excluded (though this would be less likely) that a more original form of polymorphism entered the literary tradition of the apocryphal acts only after a less original form was present.[75]

IV. Inventory of Relevant Passages

The final section of this paper will attempt to draw up inventories of passages that should be taken into consideration when the relations between AP and AJ and between APt and AJ are addressed. These are largely just the passages that have been dealt with in previous research.

A. Acts of Paul and Acts of John

Points of possible dependency or relationship between AP and AJ include:[76]

1) mention of brothers accompanying the apostle and of people being sad because the apostle was leaving (AJ 18, 58-59; APHeid. 35);

---

[74] *Acta Iohannis*, 698-99.

[75] This caveat should be kept in mind for all arguments of priority that rest on the identification of primitiveness (which include the criteria mentioned above). It might be worth recalling at this point that the Two-source Theory on the synoptic gospels employs this caveat to discount the view that the most Jewish-Christian gospel (Matthew) should be considered the earliest.

One further general comment is in order here: arguments relating to literary dependency can virtually always be turned on their head to become counter-arguments with usually approximately the same force. This is a truth of which many New Testament scholars are intuitively aware, for the New Testament has been in part a particularly well-plowed field, where many arguments and counter-arguments have been tested. Nevertheless, I cannot remember ever seeing this principle stated straightforwardly. Statements such as the last one are precarious, and they are perhaps only an indication of a weak memory or limited reading, but introductory methods books, in any event, present the old "literary criticism" together with redaction criticism in such a way that the positive, clear results of the methods are emphasized rather than the new difficulties they raise. In these books, the inverse case might sometimes be briefly mentioned, but the implication always is that this case is flawed in some rather obvious ways. This seems to be something of a deception arising from simplification. That is why it seems to be imperative to add at the advanced level the methodological principle that the researcher should actually think out (perhaps even state) what would be the inverse argument. If the job is performed well, she or he will be confronted with something like an exact mirror image of the argument initially developed. It is at this point that an even more refined method needs to be developed to enable differentiation between the two images: which is the right way around, and which is just an inverse (though otherwise perfect) image? Only rarely does an argument stick in one direction.

[76] The following draws on Junod and Kaestli, *Acta Iohannis*, 698.

According to Junod and Kaestli, this motif would appear more original in AJ because in AP Paul goes to places where there are already Christians, whereas John does not.[77]

2) scenes in the theatre (AJ 31-36; APHeid. 38, AP Bodmer Coptic end, APHamb. 1.3-23);

Junod and Kaestli note similar arguments in the two speeches in Ephesus;[78] there is similar mention of error and unquenchable fire and similar polemic against drunkenness, gold, jewels, and adultery.

3) destruction of half of a temple (AJ 42; APHeid. 38);

Junod and Kaestli remark that these are the only places they have found where *half* of a temple falls down;[79] they note that in AP only half of the temple is destroyed because Paul and his companions are in the other half; in AJ half is destroyed supposedly so that the rest of the people could proclaim the mercy of God.[80] While the motivation is clear in AP, it is at most implicit in AJ.

4) a person to be healed left at the door of where the apostle was (AJ 46; APHeid. 33);[81]

5) polymorphous appearances of Christ;
   a) in the form of the leading apostle: Drusiana sees Christ in the form of John (AJ 87); Thekla sees Christ in the form of Paul (APTh 21);[82]
   b) in the form of a youth;[83]
      a *smiling, good-looking* youth (AJ 73, 76; APHamb. 3.13-14, 4.2);

6) common name of Cleobius (AJ 18-19, 25, 59; APCor 1.2);[84]

7) mention of magic and poison (AJ 43; APHamb. 4.35-36);

8) the acclamation "one God" (AJ 42; APHamb. 1.17 [reconstruction]).

From this list two complexes seem to be particularly in need of further investigation: (1) the conversion speeches in Ephesus that are found in both acts and (2) the entire question of the "youth" that appears in both works.[85]

B. Acts of Peter and Acts of John

---

[77] Junod and Kaestli, *Acta Iohannis*, 78f., n. 3.

[78] Junod and Kaestli, *Acta Iohannis*, 459, n. 1.

[79] *Acta Iohannis*, 506, n. 1.

[80] *Acta Iohannis*, 498 with n. 3.

[81] See Junod and Kaestli, *Acta Iohannis*, 227, n.

[82] See Zahn, "Die Wanderungen des Apostels Johannes," 216, n. 2, who lists parallels in the other acts.

[83] It is not at all certain that AP witnesses a double appearance of Christ as the leading apostle *and* a youth at the same time, as in AJ 87. The passage in APHamb. 3.28 is simply too fragmentary to allow the reconstruction required for this parallel (Junod and Kaestli, *Acta Iohannis*, 473, are slightly too definite in this regard).

[84] Zahn, "Die Wanderungen des Apostels Johannes," 217. Simon and Cleobius are mentioned together in Hegesippus (Eusebius *Ecclesiastical History* 4.22.5); in 1905 C. Schmidt was of the opinion that AP got the two from Hegesippus and took this as evidence that AP derives from after 180 C.E. (*Acta Pauli*, 180); for him the Cleobius of AJ was just a fictitious name (*Die alten Petrusakten*, 36).

[85] See especially Peterson, "Acta Pauli," 191-99.

For APt and AJ, T. Zahn pointed to the following correspondences:[86]

(1) the same speculation about the cross, especially the cross being called the Word (AJ 97-101; APt 37, 38);
(2) the same pan-Christism, with the same designations of Christ (AJ 109, 95, 98; APt 20, 39);[87]
(3) the same notion that this is secret tradition, but no polemic against the biblical and ecclesiastical tradition (no particular passage in AJ mentioned; APt 38);
(4) very strong recommendation of sexual asceticism (no particular passage mentioned from AJ; APt 33-34);
(5) celebration of the eucharist with water (AJ 109; APt 2, 5).[88]
The correspondence here lies in the mention only of bread.

The set of verbal parallels listed by M. R. James in support of his view of common authorship should all be evaluated. Here is a list of them:[89]

1) the phrase "having been established in the faith" (AJ 87; APt 3, 4, 10, 30);
   This is perhaps just a common phrase, but it is worth considering.
2) mention of "powers, rulers, activities, devils, Satan" (AJ 98; APt 5, 6, 7);
   This is not a compelling parallel.
3) mention of the great deeds and miracles of Christ (AJ 93; APt 6, 17);
   This is a common idea and phrase.
4) "threats" (AJ 98; APt 8);
   This is probably a common idea, but early Christian usage is worth checking.
5) the statement that those whom Jesus chose have not understood/believed him (AJ 92; APt 10);
6) the notion of the "root" of evil (AJ 98; APt 15);
7) the notion of worshipping the Christ who is with the Christians and is willing to hear them (AJ 103; APt 18);
8) the notion of imparting to each as each was able (AJ 88; APt 20);
9) the account of the transfiguration (AJ 90; APt 20);
10) "a light such as no human can describe" (AJ 90; APt 21);
11) miracles connected with eating (AJ 93; APt 20);
12) descriptions of Christ as large and small, beautiful and ugly, young and old (AJ 88-90; APt 20);
13) a series of epithets of Christ (AJ 98; APt 20);
14) the notion of "bearing steadfastly" (AJ 87; APt 21);
15) the appearance of Christ as a young man (AJ 87, 89; APt 21);
16) the apostle "addressing" others (AJ 88; APt 30);
17) the concept of separating off the human or of the nature of the human not being able to be separated from God (AJ 101; APt 37);

---

86 *Geschichte des Neutestamentlichen Kanons*, 2:839-40.

87 See also Hennecke, *Neutestamentliche Apokryphen*, 2nd ed., 171.

88 Zahn still noted that there was no sign of the eucharist being connected with a meal in AJ, in distinction to APt 5.

89 James, *Apocrypha Anecdota Second Series*, xxv-xxviii, cited passages only from the new piece of AJ that he edited (chpts. 87-105).

18) the notion that there is a cross other than the visible one (AJ 99; APt 37);

19) the concept of the limited abilities of the ears (AJ 88; APt 37);

20) the expression "being hung up" (AJ 97; APt 38);

21) the "conversion" of humans (AJ 102; APt 38);

22) the name "logos" used by the apostle (AJ 98; APt 39);

23) giving thanks to Christ or worshipping him not through (a list of) various physical organs (AJ 103; APt 39);

24) refuge in God (AJ 104; APt 39).

Junod and Kaestli mention the following points of contact:[90]

1) descriptions of the transfiguration (AJ 90-91; APt 20);

2) the cross and its names (AJ 98, 109; APt 20, 38);
    Junod and Kaestli state that the similarities may be due to just a common tradition.[91]

3) last chance for conversion offered to an impious person on the principle, "don't render evil for evil" (AJ 81; APt 28);

4) the conception of death (AJ 24, 115; APt 40);

5) testing of virginity (AJ 113; APt Coptic);
    This scene is merely postulated for the beginning of AJ and thus cannot provide solid information.[92]

6) the threat of quickly falling away into error (AJ 25; APt 4, 6, 10, 32);

7) the phrase "not having anyone to encourage them" (AJ 58; APt 4).

From this list it seems that particularly a study of the speculation on the cross could aid the discussion of intertextuality.

V. Conclusion

Doubtless these last inventories of passages for consideration with regard to the question of the interrelationships between the AP and AJ and APt and AJ are incomplete. The same must apply to the "principal orientations on the relations between the apocryphal acts." Nevertheless, a first attempt to chart the waters has been made, and the need for complete inventories and for broader orientation on the issues at stake surely has been demonstrated.[93] During this period of renewal in the investigation of the apocryphal acts, it could be argued that complete inventories presented in an objective format are more important than the presentation of a solution to the problem of interrelationships that is "compelling" given the current state of knowledge. Such work can, in any event, help to ensure that new syntheses on the problem of the relations among the apocryphal acts at least carry with them all the benefits of past research. This paper was written in the hope of helping

---

90 *Acta Iohannis,* 697.

91 *Acta Iohannis,* 660; cf. also pp. 612-14.

92 See *Acta Iohannis,* 82-84.

93 I welcome corrections and additions.

to anchor the work of the Seminar on Intertextuality in Christian Apocrypha in the past and in the future.[94]

---

[94] I heartily thank the officers of the Inter-Library Loan at the University Library of California State University, Long Beach, for their skilled efforts to track down literature otherwise inaccessible to me.

The Acts of Paul and The Acts of John: Which Came First?

Dennis R. MacDonald
Iliff School of Theology

The SBL Seminar on Intertextuality in Christian Apocrypha has had as one of its primary objectives the creation of a scholarly discourse concerning the problem of the synoptic Acts, the mapping of intertextual contacts among the Acts of apostles, apocryphal and canonical. At this time, no single map of their literary relationships was won general consensus. Last year the Seminar analyzed the relationships between *The Acts of Paul* and *The Acts of Peter*, and although most participants seemed to have favored the priority of *The Acts of Paul*, at least one member favored the priority of *The Acts of Peter* and another preferred a less directly literary relationship.[1] In my initial paper for that session I articulated three criteria for assessing the direction of dependence among these Acts. I repeat them here insofar as they pertain also to this paper on the priority of *The Acts of Paul* or *The Acts of John* and to another that appears later in this volume on the priority of *The Acts of Peter* or *The Acts of John*.

1. The criterion of generative external traditions. When parallel passages exist, one of them may display reliance on antecedent literature or on oral tradition which may sufficiently account for its genesis, voiding the necessity of positing reliance on the other Acts. If the parallel in the other Acts retains no such reliance on external tradition, it may well have derived from the Acts that did.

2. The criterion of internal consistency. Frequently two Acts share episodes that must be genetically related, but neither of them can be traced to external traditions. In such cases, one can at times determine which is the earlier by assessing which provides the episode its more native environment. This assessment may be based on motifs, characterizations, plot sequence, even vocabulary. Conversely, one can often detect scars caused by an author artlessly grafting foreign materials into the story from the other Acts.

3. The criterion of secondary improvement. Sometimes one of the texts seems to repair its parallel in the other Acts. For example, one document may contain a

---

1 See Dennis R. MacDonald, "*The Acts of Paul* and *The Acts of Peter*: Which Came First?" 214–24, Robert F. Stoops, Jr., "Peter, Paul, and Priority in the Apocryphal Acts," 225–33, and Richard Valantasis, "Narrative Strategies and Synoptic Quandries: A Response to Dennis MacDonald's Reading of *Acts of Paul* and *Acts of Peter*," 234–39 in *Society of Biblical Literature 1992 Seminar Papers*, ed. Eugene H. Lovering, Jr. (Atlanta: Scholars Press, 1992).

theologically objectionable concept which becomes more palatable in the other. More often, one of the two Acts presents an apostle in a less than favorable light and the other does not. Insofar as tradition generally improved apostolic public relations, in such cases one can rather confidently monitor the direction of dependence.

The three criteria are not exhaustive, but they do provide some basis for assessing the direction of dependence among the apocryphal Acts and between *The Acts of Paul* and *The Acts of John*, the particular focus of this paper.

Eric Junod and Jean-Daniel Kaestli, who champion the priority of *The Acts of John*,[2] base their judgment primarily on the motif of Jesus' polymorphism, his post-resurrection appearances in various guises. *The Acts of John* and *The Acts of Paul* contain similar stories involving polymorphism; *The Acts of John* and *The Acts of Peter* contain similar discourse on Jesus' protean presence. Thus Junod and Kaestli ask:

> Did *The Acts of John* borrow from *The Acts of Peter* the notion of a discourse on polymorphism by the Lord and from *The Acts of Paul* . . . the idea of a *scénario romanesque?* Or rather was it the origin of this double usage of polymorphism? The question is open. We obviously incline toward the second possibility. Of all the Acts, our text (viz. *The Acts of John*) is the one that demonstrates, far and away, the most concern in using and in underlining the theological importance of this motif.[3]

The Acts of John unquestionably gives more significance to Jesus' polymorphism than *The Acts of Peter* or *The Acts of Paul*, but this of itself is no guarantee that John's Acts came first. One could also argue that the seeds of polymorphism planted already in the other Acts here came to full bloom. One must determine the direction of intertextual dependence by comparing *all* of the passage they have in common, not just those concerning polymorphism.

Unfortunately, textual disrepair impedes comparison. Both *The Acts of Peter* and *The Acts of John* narrate the destruction of a pagan temple. The text of *the Acts of John* is secure, but the parallel passage in *The Acts of Paul* now exists only in a badly damaged Coptic manuscript (*Pap. Heidelberg*). Both apostles, accompanied by other believers, debate religion with pagans in a temple: Paul in the temple of Apollo of the Sidonians; John in that of Artemis of the Ephesians. Both apostles state that their God is more powerful than the god of the shrine, and both threaten their audiences with destruction. Both apostles then pray, and after their prayers, one half of each temple collapses.

Acts of Paul 5 (*Pap. Heid.* 37)	*Acts of John* 42
[Someone says:] "<u>Apollo the god of the Sidonians is fallen</u> [viz. his statue fell]	At those very words <u>the altar of Artemis</u> immediately shattered into fragments, and all the dedicatory objects in the temple suddenly <u>pitched to the ground</u>,

---

[2] *Acta Iohannis*, Corpus Christianorum. Series Apocryphorum 1–2 (Turnhout: Brepols, 1983, 694–700. "We are convinced . . . that the peculiar christology of our text, its silence with regard to Scripture, and its distance from the institution and rites of the church plead for a dating as early as possible" (695).

[3] Ibid., 699.

more than <u>seven statues were</u>
<u>split</u> and their bows broken. <u>A</u>
and half of his temple!"   <u>good half of the shrine collapsed</u>
(ⲦⲠⲈ̄ⲰⲈ ⲘⲠⲈⲩⲢⲠⲈⲈ).[4]   (τὸ τοῦ ναοῦ ἥμισυ κατέπεσεν).[5]

In *The Acts of Paul* the crowds respond with grief and fear; in *The Acts of John* they convert on the spot. If more of the text of *The Acts of Paul* had survived, one might be able to assess with confidence which Acts relied on the other, but even from the little that survives, the nod for priority must go to *The Acts of Paul*. Both stories of the destruction of the temple speak of half of the temple collapsing, but only in Paul's Acts can one understand why only one half was destroyed: believers had been incarcerated in the half left standing.

In another parallel episode it is the text of *The Acts of John* that fails us. A large gap exits between chapters 36 and 87,[6] in which a woman named Drusiana converted and thereafter repelled the sexual advances of her husband Andronicus. According to chapter 63, he "enclosed her in a tomb, asserting, 'Either be to me the wife you once were, or die!' In fact, she preferred to die."[7] Eventually and miraculously, Drusiana escaped from the tomb and Andronicus converted. Even though the episode of Drusiana in the tomb no longer exists, she herself indicates, after the fact, what happened while she was there. Here the story overlaps with motifs from the Artemilla story of *The Acts of Paul*.

Acts of Paul 7 (*Pap. Hamburg* 3)	*Acts of John* 87
[T]he matron left and the blessed	The Lord appeared to me
Paul with [. . .] darkness. . . .	when I was in the tomb.
<u>A youth</u> (νεανίσκος)	He <u>resembled John</u> and resembled
<u>similar to</u> [. . .] <u>of Paul</u>.	<u>a youth</u> (νεανίσκος).

Both passages pertain to women in a prison or a tomb. In *The Acts of Paul* a young man (νεανίσκος) takes on the appearance of Paul; in *The Acts of John* it is Jesus who takes on the appearance of John and a young man (νεανίσκος).

Taken in isolation, these parallels prove little, insofar as this *puer speciosus* pops up frequently in early Christian literature. He appears again later in *The Acts of John*, but in this case, we are not dealing with an isolated motif but with extensive parallels between it and the story of Paul, Artemilla, and the baptized lion. Here at last the texts of the two Acts are sufficiently preserved to permit detailed comparison.

Paul is shackled in an Ephesian jail where Artemilla and her friend Eubula come to him. In *The Acts of John*, Drusiana is in an Ephesian tomb—again!—this time dead. John and Andronicus come to the tomb wanting to get in, but they cannot find the key. Paul wants to get out of prison but he cannot

---

4 For the most part, I use the translation of *The Acts of Paul* prepared by Philip Sellew for the Polebridge collection of AAA.

5 Usually I follow Richard Pervo's translation of *The Acts of John* prepared for Polebridge.

6 Chapters 37-86 exist, but they belong elsewhere in the Acts.

7 Cf. *The Manichaean Psalm-Book* (Allberry) 143.11–12, and 192.32–193.1.

unlock his chains. In spite of these obstacles, neither apostle wants a locksmith.

Acts of Paul 7 (*Pap. Hamb.* 3)
The women said to Paul:
"Do you want us to bring
a smithy, so that once freed
you might baptize us in the sea?"
Paul said (καὶ εἶπεν Παῦλος)
"No, I do not want that,
since I trust in God, who saved
the whole world from chains."

... As Paul was making his plea
in this way,

a very attractive boy
(παῖς λίαν εὐειδὴς ἐν χάριτι)
came in and loosed Paul's bonds,
and with a smile (μειδιάσαντος)
the boy
immediately withdrew.

Acts of John 72-73
When, despite a search that had
begun at the outset,
the keys could not be located,

John said (ὁ δὲ Ἰωάννης εἶπε)
to Andronicus, "They are quite
likely lost because Drusiana is not
in the tomb. Nevertheless,
let us go ahead, so that you may
not lapse. The doors will open
on their own, just as the Lord
has provided many other things
for us."
When we reached the tomb, the
doors came open at John's
command, and they saw
an attractive smiling youth
(τινα εὔμορφον νεανίσκον μειδιῶντα)
by Drusiana's grave.

... After saying this, the beautiful
one ascended into the heavens
as we looked on.

Later in both episodes the young man reappears, this time luminously. (The passage in the column on the right is spoken by a lad raised back to life.)

Acts of Paul 7 (*Pap. Hamb.* 3-4)
A youth (νεανίσκος) [similar ...]
of Paul,

shining (φαίν[ων]) not by a
lamp (λύχνῳ) but by the
chastity of the body (ἀπὸ τῆς
τοῦ σώ[ματος ἁγιω]σύν[η]ς)
led them forth.

Acts of John 76
"I ... found an attractive young man
(τινα νεανίσκον εὔμορφον) shielding
her [Drusiana's corpse) with
his cloak. Rays of light
(λαμπηδόνες φωτός)
leapt from his face (ἀπὸ τῆς
ὄψεως) onto hers."

Later both women are raised from death.

Acts of Paul 7 (*Pap. Hamb.* 4)
Once again the youth smiled
(μειδιάσαντος τοῦ νεανίσκου),
and the matron breathed again.

Acts of John 80
... John said, "Drusiana arise."

Then and there she arose
and left the grave.

These two episodes share too much in common to attribute to happenstance or to oral tradition. Our task now is to assess which account borrowed from the other. *The Acts of Paul* seems to be the earlier.

The women's offer to fetch Paul a locksmith makes perfect sense in light of the apostle's incarceration. Furthermore, Paul's response fits their offer: if God delivered the whole world, God could deliver him from his chains. On the other hand, the entire business about the misplaced keys in *The Acts of John* taxes the reader's credulity. John and Andronicus should have seen to the keys before going to the tomb. Worse is John's theologizing: "They are quite likely lost because Drusiana is not in the tomb," which surely means that God hid them in order to symbolize her soul's departure. Undeterred by divine symbolism, John commanded the doors to open. *The Acts of Paul*, therefore, seems to have met the criterion of internal consistencey insofar as the motifs it shares with *The Acts of John* appear in their more likely native environment.

Furthermore, the beautiful young man plays a far more central role in the plot of *The Acts of Paul* than he does in *The Acts of John*. It was he, after all, who released Paul from his chains, his radiance allowed Paul and his entourage to travel to and from the sea at night without the need of a lamp, and it was he, not Paul, who raised Artemilla back to life. By comparison, the youth in *The Acts of John* was nearly unemployed. He had nothing to do with the opening of the doors to the tomb; John accomplished that with a word. The youth merely notifies the apostle that he was there to help Drusiana. And big help he was! He covered her nakedness with his cloak. Like the young man in *The Acts of Paul*, he radiated light, but the light did not help anybody go anywhere or see anything, except for serendipitously illuminating the face of the corpse. Whereas the youth in *The Acts of Paul* raised Artemilla back to life, it was John who raised Drusiana. Surely it is more likely that divine power was shifted from the heavenly youth to the apostle in *The Acts of John* than that it was shifted from the apostle to the youth in *The Acts of Paul*. John's Acts, demonstrating signs of secondary improvement, meets another of our three criteria.

Notice also that Artemilla plays a role similar to that played earlier by Thecla, whose story probably derived from oral tradition.[8] Like Thecla, Artemilla refused to sleep with her would-be lover who then sought to destroy the apostle. Just as chaste Thecla had been thrown into an arena to face wild beasts, because of Artemilla's chasity Paul was thrown into an arena to face a lion. The episode in the arena approriates the oral tale of Androcles and the lion, an appropriation quite possibly made in Pauline circles prior to *The Acts of Paul*.[9] Be that as it may, one might reasonably conjecture that the author found inspiration for the story of Artemilla, Paul, and the baptized lion from traditional stories. If this were indeed the case, one need not posit dependence also on *The Acts of John*. On the other hand, the absence of independent external attestation to Drusiana—let alone the complexity and sophisticated integration of her story in John's Acts—make it less likely that the author was dependent on a traditional legend. In other words, *The Acts of Paul* also satisfies our criterion of generative external traditions.

---

8 See my discussion in *The Legend and the Apostle: The Battle for Paul in Story and Canon* (Philadelphia: Westminster Press, 1983), 17-33.

9 *Ibid.*

Luke's Paul as the Legacy of Paul

J. Christiaan Beker
Princeton Theological Seminary

I. Introduction

The history of research has made it abundantly clear that the attempt to harmonize the historical Paul with the Paul of Luke-Acts has come to a radical end. This attempt was basically motivated by canonical considerations, in order to establish the unity of the apostolic proclamation in the canon. Thus Irenaeus influenced subsequent generations in both patristic and modern times by claiming that Luke was a "sector Pauli" and "has written down in a book the gospel preached by Paul." In fact, according to Irenaeus, II Tim. 4:10 and Col. 4:14 prove the inseparable connection of Luke and Paul (*Adv. Haer.* 1.1.1.14.1).

However, it is interesting to observe that similar canonical concerns influenced the historical-critical proponents of Luke-Acts, who insisted on the radical discrepancy between the Paul of the authentic letters and Luke's Paul. In the course of their research the place of Luke-Acts within the canon became here the occasion for exacerbating the difference between the genuine Paul and the Lucan Paul to such an extent that Luke's theology was deemed to be the first manifestation of "early Catholicism" in the New Testament.

However, it has become clear that the relation of Luke's Paul to the authentic Paul cannot be decided on a priori theological grounds, but must be ascertained on purely exegetical grounds. For neither the harmonization of the two Pauls, nor the denigration of the one over the other does justice to the theological construals of either Paul or Luke. Indeed, theological prejudgments have not only dominated the charge of early Catholicism, but also the various forms of *Tendenz*-criticism which, since the great work of F. C. Baer, have dominated Luke's portrayal of Paul in Acts.

To be sure, major progress has been made once attention became directed toward a compositional analysis of Luke-Acts. I will here not rehearse the fruits of this new direction in the study of Luke-Acts. It is sufficient to point here to the work of M. Dibelius, H. Cadbury, E. Haenchen, H. Conzelmann, among many others.

The essays by U. Wilckens[1] and W. G. Kümmel[2] were especially interesting to me, since they uncovered so clearly the theological prejudgments of many scholars who are engaged in the study of Acts.

Since I have not discovered any recent work on the relation of the authentic Paul to the Lucan Paul, I may be accused of kicking in open doors when I attempt in the following pages to build on the recent analysis of the compositional structure of Acts: its narrative style, its contingent features, and its theological purpose.

II. The Search for an Adequate Method

As the title of this essay indicates, I will concentrate on Paul's legacy as portrayed by Luke.

In my recent book, *The Heirs of Paul*,[3] I adopted a dual method in order to appraise the achievement of the post-Pauline authors to shape their own distinct theological identity in relation to the Pauline tradition. The dual method meant to satisfy the claims of both Paul's authentic gospel (*the traditum*) and of the manner in which the post-Pauline authors adapted Paul's gospel so that it could serve as a living and relevant voice to the new historical situation with its fresh challenges which they had to face (*the traditio*).

However relevant this dual method may have been in relation to post-Pauline writings which were written in the name of Paul and which claimed Paul as their exclusive hero (cf. Eph., Col., 2 Thess., the Pastoral Epistles), the application of such a dual method to Luke-Acts is inappropriate. For we must realize that an exclusive focus on the comparative method involves us in an a-historical and docetic conception of both the authentic and Lucan Paul.

For such a focus disregards the church's necessity to adapt the tradition in accordance with the demands and needs of its particular location in history. While my dual method attempted to balance its comparative and traditional historical components in investigating the pseudonymous post-Pauline letters, its application to Luke-Acts is not only, as I said, inappropriate, but also destructive of any appreciation of Luke's unique portrait of Paul.

The comparative method delineating the Paul of the authentic letters and the Paul of Acts can only do justice to illuminate the stature and theology of the historical Paul. Indeed, from a Lucan perspective, the comparative method can only result in a distortion of Luke's portrait of Paul.

Such an a-historical and docetic comparison of the authentic and Lucan Paul can be documented throughout the literature of Luke-Acts. I myself characterized Paul's adaptation by Luke as "a grandiose rewriting of Pauline

---

[1] U. Wilckens, "Interpreting Acts in a Period of Existentialist Theology" in *Studies in Luke-Acts: Essays Presented in Honor of Paul Schubert* (Nashville: Abingdon Press, 1966), pp. 60-83.

[2] W. G. Kümmel, "Lukas in der Auflage der heutigen Theologie" in *Das Lukas-Evangelium* (ed. G. Braumann; Darmstadt: Wissenschaftliche Buchgesellschaft, 1974), pp. 416-436.

[3] J. C. Beker, *The Heirs of Paul: Paul's Legacy in the New Testament and in the Church Today* (Minneapolis: Augsburg-Fortress Press, 1991).

tradition" and as "a misguided attempt to refashion Paul to conform him to Luke's ideological presupposition" (*Heirs*, 114). The magisterial essay of P. Vielhauer[4] has influenced this comparative trend to a great extent. Vielhauer lists four basic points which show the deep divide between Luke's and Paul's theology:

1) Luke's use of a stoic-natural theology in Paul's speech on the Areopagus, which serves as a *preparatio evangelii*, whereas in sharp contrast to this the historical Paul employs the same stoic theology to indict all people.

2) Luke portrays Paul as a Jewish Christian who is utterly loyal to the law and thus has no understanding of Paul's polemic against the Torah.

3) Luke's omission of the center of Paul's Christology, i.e., the soteriological significance of the cross of Christ.

4) Luke's displacement of Paul's eschatology to the periphery of his work in favor of a salvation history which has its progressive fulfillment in the history of the church.

Vielhauer concludes his essay as follows: "With the presuppositions of his historiography he [Luke] no longer stands within earliest Christianity, but in the nascent early Catholic Church (*in der werdenden frükatholischen kirche*). This concept of history and his view of earliest Christianity are the same as theirs" (p. 49).

Subsequently E. Käsemann placed Luke-Acts squarely within the category of *"Frühkatholizismus."* "Das lukanische Werk ist im ganzen gar nicht begreiflich, wenn man nicht sieht, dass man nur im Strom der apostolischen Tradition auch zur Una Sancta als dem irdischen Raum des Heils gehört."[5]

In studies such as those of Vielhauer and Käsemann, the comparative method has led to a denigration of Luke-Acts, and especially of his portrait of Paul. Too little attention has been paid to the process of tradition and to the very different historical location of the historical Paul and Luke.

Moreover, it seems clear that the designation of Luke as belonging to "early Catholicism" is motivated more by theological than traditio-historical considerations.

Therefore, my focus in this essay will be on the traditio-historical method. The fact that such a focus entails a high appreciation for the variety in the New Testament canon is self-evident.

The issue whether a theological unity can be discovered in the canon without resorting to a "canon within the canon" is a topic which can only be addressed once the specific function and role of Paul in Luke's overall scheme has been assessed.

III. Paul Within the Context of Luke's Program in Acts

Luke's portrait of Paul must be seen within the context of the overall purpose of his two-volume work. Robert Tannehill correctly points to the

---

4 P. Vielhauer, "On the Paulinism of Acts," in *Studies in Luke-Acts* (ed. L. E. Keck and J. L. Martyn; Nashville: Abingdon Press, 1966), pp. 33-50.

5 E. Käsemann, "Paulus und der Frühkatholizismus," in *Exegetische Versuche und Besinnungen* (Göttingen: Vandenhoeck und Ruprecht, II), p. 249.

narrative unity of Luke-Acts: "Change and development are expected in such a narrative, yet unity is maintained because the scenes and characters contribute to a longer story that determines the significance of each part . . . Luke-Acts is a unified narrative because the chief human characters (John the Baptist, Jesus, the apostles, Paul) share in a mission which expresses a single controlling purpose—the purpose of God."[6] Indeed, Luke highlights God's purpose in his narrative by regularly using the phrases "the purpose of God" (*boulè tou theou*) and "it was/is necessary" (*dei*) [*boulè tou theou*: Luke 7:30; Acts 2:23; 4:28, 5:38, 39; 13:36; 20:27; *dei*: Luke 24:7, 26, 44; Acts 9:16; 14:22; 17:3; 19:21; 23:11; 27:24.]

S. Schulz has pointed out the extent to which Luke has used as the Roman-Fatum ideology in his salvation-historical theology.[7] In this context, Schulz selects from the remarkably many composites with *pro-* (2:23/3:20/13:24/22:14/26:16) two prominent texts: 4:28 (*pro-orizein*) and 10:41 (*pro-cheirotonein*). These texts are, he claims, symptomatic for Luke's central notion of the divine plan, "der das ewige göttliche Konzept der gesamten Vorsehungsgeschichte ist, diese faktisch gestaltet und verwirklicht" (104).

"Weitere herrorragende Indizien dieses Vorstellungskreises sind dei und mellein, die bei Lukas promiscue gebraucht werden und die Planmäßigkeit der Vorsehungs-geschichtlicher Ereignisse kennzeichnen, vor allein die Planmäßigkeit der Passion Jesu" (107). "Die universale Vorsehungsgeschichte verläuft planmäßig trotz und durch alle menschlichen Widerstände. Im engsten Zusammenhang damit steht natürlich der starre Chevakter der Lukanischen Konzeption der Vorsehungs geschichte als eines geschlossenen, kausal gegliederten Geschehensablaufes" (108).

I quote Schulz extensively because he has unmasked a central motif in Luke's conception of salvation-history, although I am not convinced that—as Schulz claims—Luke has displaced Israel's election history with a hellenistic Roman fatum-ideology (Schulz, 111, 112).

It is indeed "Göttes Vorsehungsratschluß" (Schulz, 106), that establishes the continuity within the movement of Luke's salvation-history—a movement which travels from Israel via the ministry of Jesus to the church of the Gentiles.

Luke's narrative, dominated by the plan of God as a single controlling purpose (cf. Tannehill) unfolds its salvation-historical theme in terms of three interrelated subthemes. Those sub-themes determine to a great extent Luke's portrait of Paul; they demonstrate why Luke describes Paul's legacy in the way he does.

1) The theme of the unity of the church, which also prompts Luke's antiheretical stance.

2) The theme of the political innocence of the church, which must demonstrate its inoffensiveness with respect to the Roman state and which motivates Luke's pro-Roman attitude; and

3) The theme of the theological legitimacy of the church, which stresses

---

6 R. C. Tannehill, *The Narrative Unity of Luke-Acts: A Literary Interpretation* (Philadelphia: Fortress Press, 1986, I), xiii.

7 S. Schulz, "Göttes Vorsehung bei Lukas," *ZNW* 54 (1963) 104-116.

the coninuity between the church and Israel. These themes are designed to meet the problems that Luke's church faces at the end of the first century A.D.

The first theme portrays the church of the apostolic past as the *Una Sancta Apostolica*, which in its unity, harmony, and peace serves as the model for Luke's present church. This idealized picture of the apostolic beginnings of the church, which is a mixture of historical memory and Luke's own literary purpose, emphasizes the purity and unity of the beginnings of the church and thus gives Luke a powerful weapon against the threat of heresy in his time.

And so Luke describes Paul in his farewell address to the elders of Ephesus in Miletus as the one who issues a stern warning against imminent heresy: "Keep watch over yourselves and over all the flock of which the Holy Spirit has made you overseers (*episkopous*) to shepherd the church of God that he obtained with the blood of his own Son (*dia tou haimatos tou idiou*). I know that after I have gone (*meta ten aphixin mou*), savage wolves will come in among you, not sparing the flock. Some even from your own group will come distorting the truth (*lalountes diestrammena*) in order to entice the disciples to follow them. Therefore be alert (*dio gregoreite*), remembering that for three years I did not cease night or day to warn everyone with tears" (20:28-31).

Here Paul contemplates the future and addresses the danger the church faces at the time of Luke. The heretical danger is twofold: There is an imminent threat not only from "savage wolves" (v. 29) who will invade the church from the outside, but also from heretics who will arise within the church with their claim to present the gospel in a truer and more effective fashion. And so Luke combats them by stressing the public, non-secretive character of Paul's gospel (v. 20) and his proclamation of "the whole purpose of God" (v. 27).

Paul's farewell address in 20:17-35 demonstrates that Luke's anti-heretical stance underscores not only the theme of the unity of the church, but also the theme of the continuity of the gospel tradition. In other words, Paul is here portrayed as the one who is faithful to the tradition, who since he guards the continuity between past and present, serves as the bridge between the past and the present.

Indeed, Paul's farewell address occupies a unique place among the speeches of Acts: 1) it carries the weight of a last will and testament; 2) it is the only speech of Paul that is addressed to Christians; 3) it is the only speech that is not a response to a specific urgent local problem. Moreover, 4) it is the only speech in which the person of Paul himself is the focus and in which he presents to the church a synopsis of past, present, and future issues. Thus, the speech portrays Paul as the one who guards the continuity of the one apostolic tradition in the face of disruptive heresies.

The second theme which runs like a red thread through Acts deals with the political innocence of the church and its irenic disposition toward Rome. Luke's positive attitude toward the Roman Empire and its officals is remarkable, especially when we compare it with the radical stance of the Revelation of John against Imperial Rome or with the more cautious attitude of the Pastoral Epistles.

One is tempted to characterize Luke as the initiator of the apologetic literature which will flower in the second century A.D. For instance, Justin

Martyr claims that Christians are the emperor's best allies in the cause of peace and good order (*Apol.* I 11:1-12:1), while Tertullian posits Christianity as the soul of the empire (*Apol.* I. 25-33).

However, the decisive difference between Luke and the Apologists is that Luke addresses Christians, not emperors, and he intends his book to be an edifying treatise. Nevertheless, Luke intimates strongly that when Christians behave properly they have nothing to fear from the state. The extent to which Luke articulates the political inoffensiveness of Christianity and its favorable reception by Roman officials is indeed remarkable. Just as the procurator Pilate pronounces Jesus innocent (and that three times: Luke 23:4, 14, 22), so the procurator Fustus and King Agrippa declare Paul innocent of the charges of the Jews (26:32; cf. also 23:9/24:16-20/25:8, 11, 25). Moreover, the proconsul of Achaia, Gallio, refuses to hear Jewish accusations against Paul (18:12-15); a Roman centurion and tribunes guarantee Paul's safety during a riot in Jerusalem (21:22.36/23:22); another Roman centurion prevents his soldiers from killing Paul during a shipwreck off Malta (27:43). Indeed, Paul proudly proclaims twice that he is a born Roman citizen (21:39; 22:27.28)—a fact which allows Paul to appeal to Caesar (25:10) and which makes it possible for him to go to Rome.

Because of this circumstance, Paul—albeit as a prisoner—fulfills the mandate of the risen Jesus to be the Lord's witness "to the ends of the earth" (1:8), i.e., to Rome.

Although this mandate is given to all the apostles in Jerusalem (1:8), it is only Paul who fulfills it (13:47; cf. 9:15, 16).

Luke's pro-Roman attitude is even more manifest in the face of the continuous and politically effective accusations of the Jews: "These people [Paul and Silas] who have been turning the world upside down have come here also—they are all acting contrary to the decrees of the emperor saying that there is another king named Jesus" (17:6-7; cf. 16:21). These pro-Roman features in Luke's narrative serve to discredit the Roman charge of the subversive and revolutionary character of early Christianity. They are motivated by Luke's attempt to protect the church against threats of persecution, illegality, and social ostracism by the Roman state.

In fact, this may well be one of the reasons why Luke does not choose to narrate Paul's death at the hands of the Romans in chapter 28.

Finally, Luke's third theme focuses on the theological legitimacy of the church—a theme which preoccupies him probably more deeply than the other themes. Indeed, Luke's basic problem concerns the theological status of Christianity as a "third race" (*tertium genus*). For what will be the status of this "third race" now that it is no longer a part of either Judaism or pagan society? (Cf., for instance, the charge against the a-social behavior of Christians in 16:16-22 and 19:23-40.)

It is especially an acute problem for the many recent Gentile converts to Christianity, who as "God fearers" (*phoboumenoi/sebomenoi*) were formerly associated with the synagogue. For what does constitute henceforth their religious identity?

In other words, how can the church claim a legitimate identity, when it professes a Jewish messiah as its Lord, while the Jews themselves explicitly have rejected this "Christian" messiah? And how can the church claim as its Scriptures the Old Testament which is the keystone of Judaism? Moreover, how can the church claim to be "the true Israel" of God (Luke 24:44) when it breaks down the very heart of Judaism, i.e., the covenant, the Torah, and circumcision? And if Christianity is no longer committed to the Torah and to its Jewish heritage, how can it dismiss the Roman charge that it is simply another "*nova superstitio*," i.e., a new mystery religion—a charge which, for instance, the Athenians level against Paul: "He [Paul] seems to be a proclaimer of foreign divinities (*xenon daimonion*); "May we know what this new teaching is (*kaine didache*) that you are presenting?" (17:18, 19).

Therefore, Luke addresses the issue of the church's theological legitimacy by emphasizing the continuity of the church with Israel, i.e., the continuity of God's salvation history which, beginning in Israel, found its fulfillment in Jesus and is after his resurrection extended throughout the world by the preaching of his witnesses.

And so Luke's long section on "the trial of Paul" (chapters 21-28) must demonstrate that Christianity is the fulfillment of Judaism rather than its abrogation.

Luke points out that, whereas the rejection of the gospel by the Jews must be attributed to their ignorance and evil stubbornness (28:26-27), Paul himself stands squarely within the Jewish tradition. Therefore, the church is not a new mystery religion or a new philosophical sect (17:21), but instead constitutes the true people of God, i.e., "the true Israel."

IV. The Uniqueness of Paul in Luke-Acts

Within the overall perspective of Luke's salvation-history and the problems he needs to address, his portrayal of Paul becomes intelligible.

(i) Paul seems to be Luke's exclusive hero, since he occupies center stage from chapter 13 to the end of the book. One receives the impression that there were no fellow missionaries besides him, as if Paul alone were responsible for carrying the gospel to the nations and finally to Rome, the heart of the Roman Empire. Paul's prominence in chapters 13-28 is matched by that of Peter in chapters 2-12.

However, notwithstanding the prominence of Peter and Paul in Acts, Luke does not intend to thematize his book in terms of biographical perspectives. Rather, his basic theme is announced in 1:18: "But you will receive power when the Holy Spirit has come upon you; and you will be my witnesses in Jerusalem, in all Judea and Samaria and to the ends of the earth." It has been suggested that because of this basic theme Luke is interested in geographical rather than biographical perspectives.

However, Luke's real purpose is neither biographical nor geographical. Rather, it is God's sovereign plan and salvation-historical purpose which dominates Luke's narrative. Thus, since God alone initiates and directs the worldwide mission of the church, it is in no way the initiative and work of human agents, such as Peter or Paul.

Indeed, the mission to the Gentiles is not the fruit of human planning but solely due to God's providential guidance. Luke's essential theme, then, is *confusione hominum – Dei providentia.*

And so it is important to understand that Paul is not cast as a hero, but rather as a person who is subordinate to God's own iniative and plan. Paul then is from Luke's perspective "a chosen instrument" (9:15) and a "witness" (22:15), who from the time of his call is totally dependent on the guidance of the Spirit (1:8). Just as the Spirit commands Peter to baptize the Roman centurion Cornelius (11:12, 15), so the Holy Spirit calls Barnabas and Paul to the Gentile mission (13:2-4); compels Paul to go where he does not want to go (16:6-7); guides his missionary plans (19:21); predicts his forthcoming suffering (20:23/21:11-14) and inspires his interpretation of the Scriptures (28:15).

Thus, notwithstanding Paul's prominent role in Acts and notwithstanding the fact that he alone fulfills Jesus' mandate to the apostles to be his witnesses "to the ends of the earth" (1:8; 13:47), he is cast by Luke basically as God's instrument in the divine salvation-historical plan.

(ii) Much has been made of the fact that Luke denies Paul the title apostle as attested by Peter's speech in 10:40-41 and Paul's own sermon in 13:30-31.

It may seem peculiar that Paul, the foremost witness to Christ among the Gentiles (22:14, 21) does not qualify as an apostle.

However, as Chr. Burchard[8] has shown, Luke designates Paul as "the 13th witness" and does not intend to make Paul a subordinate delegate to the apostles in Jerusalem. In fact, Luke's conception of the "basic solidity" of salvation-history (Luke 1:4) makes it imperative that the gosepl has a firm historical foundation and is based on a reliable transmission of the gospel tradition. Therefore, Luke must limit the apostolate to those who were not only witnesses to Jesus' life and work, but also to his bodily resurrection and ascension (1:3-9).

(iii) Thus from Luke's perspective Paul fulfills his appointed role as God's witness in the salvation-historical movement of the gospel to the ends of the earth.

Moreover, Paul's portrait as the great ecumenical missionary must serve Luke's primary themes of the unity and the legitimacy of the church. And so Paul is sketched not only as the one whose message is in harmonious *unity* with that of the Jerusalem apostles, but also as the one who safeguards the basic *continuity* of salvation-history.

In order to understand these Lucan emphases properly, and not simply as a distortion of Paul's theology, it is necessary to be aware of two important facts:

1) Luke writes at a time which must confront its own problems and establish the legitimacy of the church in a situation which is radically different from Paul's time. Moreover, Luke is not acquainted with Paul's letters since no collection of those letters has occurred or was available to him.

2) Even more important is the fact that as W. Eltester[9] stresses, Luke could not even understand the Pauline dialectic between law and grace, faith and

---

8 Chr. Burchard, *Der dreizehnte Zeuge* (Göttingen: Vandenhoeck und Ruprecht), 1970.

9 W. Eltester, "Lukas und Paulus," in *Eranion* (H. Hommel Festschrift; Tübingen, 1961), pp. 1-17.

work, or the relation between present Christian existence and the imminent expectation of the eschatological end. "Wir haben in ihm das erste entwickelte Zeugnis dafür vor uns, wie ein Grieche das Christentum aufgenommen hat und wie er dies unter den veränderten Verhältnissen seiner nachapostolischen Zeit tun mußte" (9). The new post-apostolic situation, which Luke faces makes as well intelligible the peculiar relation of Paul to Judaism in Acts which is dramatically opposed to the historical Paul's own confrontation with Judaism.

Luke portrays the disciples and Paul as pious Jews and people who are obedient to the law. Especially in 19:21-28:31 (the section where Paul "the missionary" becomes Paul "the accused"), Paul is redesigned as the faithful Jew. Far from rejecting the law and circumcision, he observes the Torah and its ritual demands (21:21-27): he circumcises Timothy (16:3); announces that he is still a Pharisee (23:6), and that he believes "everything laid down according to the law or written in the prophets" (24:14, cf. also 26:4-8).

This pro-Jewish portrait of Paul by Luke has drawn heavy criticism by scholars, such as Haenchen, Vielhauer, and Käsemann, notwithstanding their overall positive appreciation of Luke's program.

However, this criticism bypasses Luke's intent. Since Luke views the church as the Israel of the promise, the church is the fulfillment of the biblical promises. And so he defines Christianity as the Israel, which confesses Christ as the one prophesied in Scripture. Thus the pro-Jewish description of Paul, along with the other witnesses, must answer an inner-ecclesial need, i.e., the legitimacy of the church in claiming the Old Testament as its holy scripture.

V. Conclusion

Paul's portrait in Acts, then, must be seen within the larger context of Luke's overall purpose and the problems of his time.

Although my description of this portrait has not exhausted all the features of Luke's portrayal of Paul (e.g., the theme of Paul's suffering which is strangely juxtaposed to the picture of Paul's missionary successes), I have intended to emphasize a method in describing the Lucan Paul, which has too often been contaminated by students of Luke-Acts.

Indeed, a method which balances both a comparative and traditional-historical approach must lead to a distorted portrayal of Paul in Luke-Acts.

Therefore, I have suggested that only a radical application of the traditional-historical method can do justice to the unique description of Paul by Luke. And, as I mentioned earlier, the *theological* issue of how the diverse portraits of the historical and the Lucan Paul must be resolved in terms of the unity of the New Testament canon can only be addressed once the specific *historical location* of Luke's portrait of Paul is clarified and honored.

The Social Dimensions of *Sōtēria* in Luke-Acts and Paul

Luke Timothy Johnson
Candler School of Theology, Emory University

What do New Testament writers mean when they speak of salvation? My inability to answer so basic a question has bothered me more in recent years as I worked through two NT compositions (Luke-Acts and James) where salvation language figures prominently. It is easier to state the importance of the language than to define its significance.

The Question

Part of my discomfort—perhaps shared by my readers—derives from my increased awareness of the complexity of such a question and the difficulty of carrying out proper inquiry into it. Soteriologies are complex systems of meaning, which often show only a part of themselves publicly. Statements about salvation bear with them an implicit cosmology, anthropology, and eschatology, but it is not always easy to tease these implicit dimensions into visibility. And the accurate delineation of any soteriology is hampered by an assumption that the system as a whole is already understood even as we examine its parts.

The assumption is often wrong. My inherited Catholic Christianity, for example, leads me to assume that the NT's language about salvation concerns the future blessedness of the individual human soul in heaven. Using such a code, I can deal easily with passages such as James 1:21, which encourages its readers to accept with meekness the implanted word "which is able to save your souls." Likewise, I imagine that I understand what Luke means by those who seek to "save their souls" only to end up losing them (Luke 9:21). My assumptive soteriological code makes good (even if erroneous) sense of statements about individual persons in relation to God.

But I have a harder time supplying sense to Paul's statement, "Thus all Israel will be saved" (Rom 11:26). Can Israel be saved the way souls are saved? What might that mean? Does this passage demand consideration, as many New Testament Theologies suppose, under the rubric of final and universal salvation?[1] The adequacy of my assumed code is challenged. I must scramble

---

[1] See, e.g., D. E. H. Whitely, *The Theology of St Paul* (Philadelphia: Fortress, 1966) 273; E. Stauffer, *New Testament Theology* trans. J. Marsh (London: SCM Press, 1955) 223; G. E. Ladd,

520

for meaning the way Irenaeus was required to when Gnostics read Paul's language of "flesh and spirit" cosmologically rather than morally.[2]

Any attempt to deal seriously with NT soteriology first must pay close attention to the system implied by explicit statements, and second, must question the assumption that the code for understanding the system is already in possession. The third thing any such analysis must do is resist the impulse to harmonize the divergent witnesses precipitously.

Fresh impetus has recently been given to a reexamination of NT soteriology(ies) by the publication of N. T. Wright's *The New Testament and the People of God*.[3] Wright surveys Jewish apocalyptic literature of the first century and concludes that "the hope of Israel" had nothing to do with a world-ending cataclysm but rather with a this-worldly restoration of God's people.[4] On that basis, he further questions widespread assumptions about the NT's "Apocalyptic worldview." He suggests that there is little evidence either for a fervent expectation of the end of the world associated with the parousia, or for a great crisis created by the "delay of the parousia."[5] Wright suggests that the NT writers also may well have viewed salvation as a restoration of God's people here on earth.[6] It is not necessary to deny future or individual or spiritual dimensions of Christian hope, in order to reconsider, as Wright invites us, a this-worldly, socially defined understanding of salvation in early Christianity. It is a good hyothesis.[7] How can it be tested?

Comparative Method

One way to begin to test the hypothesis is through the careful comparison of two NT writers for whom salvation is a major theme. Comparison between bodies of literature is difficult to execute properly. But it is of considerable benefit. Comparison sharpens our perception of each writing, and enables the generation of more encompassing theories.[8] If the examination of salvation language within two sets of NT writings for whom it is most centrally a concern should reveal—despite all the expected dissimilarities—a deep level of fundamental agreement, then a general theory concerning the early Christian conception of salvation is at least one step closer to being demonstrated. Such a comparison, of course, must move beyond the mere

---

A Theology of the New Testament (Grand Rapids: Eerdmans, 1974) 521; W. G. Kümmel, *The Theology of the New Testament* trans. J. Seeley (Nashville: Abingdon, 1973) 238.

[2] Irenaeus, *Adversus Haereses* I, 3; I, 8, 2-5; I, 20, 2.

[3] (London: SPCK, 1992). As he explains in his preface (xiii-xix), this is the first of a projected five-volume study on "Christian Origins and the Question of God."

[4] Wright, 300 and especially 334-338. On this point as on many others in his reconstruction of Judaism (whose main fault is its almost exclusive focus on the Palestinian variety), Wright credits his conversation with E. P. Sanders; see *Judaism: Practice and Belief, 63BCE-66CE* (London: SCM Press, 1992) 278, 298.

[5] Wright, 459-64.

[6] Wright, 400 and 458.

[7] And this is how Wright identifies his own effort, p. 464.

[8] See J. Z. Smith, *Drudgery Divine. On the Comparison of Early Christianities and the Religions of Late Antiquity* (Chicago: University of Chicago Press, 1990) 46.

lining up of "parallels" to deal with dissimilarities as well as similarities, and the functions of each within the respective compositions.

Luke-Acts and Paul's letters offer themselves as good candidates for comparison on the question of salvation. First, we are dealing with the the most substantial bodies of literature in the NT attributable to individual authors. Second, the theme of salvation plays a distinctively important role in each author's writings. In support of this last assertion, a few statistics: a) the Gospel of Luke uses *sōzein* 17 times (compare Mt 14, Mk 13, Jn 6), and Acts uses *sōzein* 13 times; these 30 instances match the 28 uses of the verb by Paul (21 if the Pastorals are excluded). Apart from the Gospel passages already mentioned, *sōzein* is used otherwise in the NT 11 times; in sum, Luke and Paul uses the verb 58 of its 102 occurrences. b) The noun *sōtēria* is found 10 times in Luke-Acts and 17 times in Paul (15 outside the Pastorals). c) The term *sōtērion* is used in the NT only the three instances found in Luke-Acts (Luke 2:30; 3:6; Acts 28:28), and the one case of Eph 6:17. d) The title *sōtēr* appears four times in Luke-Acts (Luke 1:47; 2:11; Acts 5:31; 13:23), and twelve times in Paul (but only twice—Phil 3:20 and Eph 5:23—if we exclude the ten instances in the Pastorals). e) Finally, the adjective *sōtērios* is found in the NT only in Tit 2:11. Third, these statistics show that compared to other NT writings, these authors are not only fond of salvation language, but that the various terms are proportionately distributed in each case. We are not in a position of trying to compare a minor theme in one author to a major theme in the other.

Such an even-handed approach has not always been the rule when comparisons have been made between Luke-Acts and Paul. More often, what has been called comparison has turned out to be a measuring of Luke-Acts against a Pauline standard to Luke-Acts' disadvantage. The approach is classically illustrated by Vielhauer's classic essay on "The Paulinism of Acts,"[9] and is perpetuated by any number of studies that propose to compare the "image of Paul" in the undisputed letters and in Luke-Acts[10] or that consider some theme thought to be "central" to Paul but regrettably deficient in Luke-Acts.[11]

Because of the assumed connections between "Paul" and "Luke," and because "Paul" appears as a character in both sets of writings, it has proven extraordinarily difficult to disentangle a genuine comparison between the compositions from notions of dependence, derivation, development, and distortion.[12] But precisely such a dispassionate and even-handed comparison

---

9 In *Studies in Luke-Acts* ed. L. E. Keck and J. L. Martyn (Philadelphia: Fortress, 1966) 33-50.

10 See, e.g., P.-G. Mueller, "Der 'Paulinismus' in der Apostelgeschichte: Ein Forschungsgeschichtlicher Überblick," *Paulus in den neutestamentlichen Spaetschriften* ed. K. Kertelge (Quaestiones Disputatae 89; Freiberg: Herder, 1981) 157-201, and K. Loening, "Paulinismus in der Apostelgeschichte," *ibid.*, 202-232.

11 See, e.g., the discussion of "salvation" in S. G. Wilson's *Luke and the Pastoral Epistles* (London: SPCK, 1979), which reads the evidence consistently to show that Luke and the Pastorals not only agree on major aspects of this theme but do so in consistent disagreement with Paul. Unfortunately, the argument is based on faulty method; see my review in *JBL* 101 (1982) 459-460.

12 For a very recent example, see J. C. Beker, *Heirs of Paul: Paul's Legacy in the New Testament and in the Church Today* (Minneapolis: Fortress Press, 1991). Despite the use of a

is what is desired if we are to make headway concerning the role of salvation language in each set of compositions. To make the point emphatically, I turn first to the writings of Luke before considering those of Paul.

Criteria for Comparison

For such a comparison to be adequate, several criteria need meeting. First, all of the relevant data should be included. Ideally, this would include all references to redemption and liberation (among others) as well as terms for "salvation." That ideal will certainly not be met in the present essay which aims at suggestion rather than demonstration. On the other hand, it is important as well to isolate specific "language games" to see how they work on their own terms (if they do) before invoking language from another "game" to explicate them.[13] Second, the literary character of the respective writings must be taken into account. Although Paul's letters do not lack some narrative character,[14] the implicit story undergirding his argument requires reconstruction. The analysis of salvation in Luke-Acts must take narrative structure much more directly into account.[15] Third, the ways in which each writer appropriates earlier traditions has some significance for the analysis: Paul obviously makes use of creedal formulae and scriptural texts (Rom 9:10; 10:13),[16] but in addition to citing scripture (Acts 2:21), Luke also takes over and modifies the salvation language already embedded in his Markan gospel source.

Finally, proper comparison demands a consistent set of questions that can appropriately put to both authors' works. The full range of questions concerning salvation would include: who does the saving; what is salvation from; what aids or impedes salvation; how is salvation accomplished; when does salvation take place; what is the *telos* of salvation; where is salvation accomplished; and finally, *who* is saved? Neither Luke nor Paul fills out the survey completely. The questions they most fully and directly respond to are the ones most useful for comparison. Fortunately for the sake of this exercise, the compositions enable us to work toward some answer to our opening question: do these writers conceive of salvation primarily in terms of when, or where? Are they thinking mainly about the individual, or a social group?

"comparative method" (ch.3) and despite protestations of sympathy for the difficulties facing Paul's "adapters," Beker must conclude, "Therefore we can only consider Luke's adaptation of Paul an acute deformation and distortion of the historical Paul" (p. 92).

[13] See the helpful discussion in E. Boring, "The Language of Universal Salvation in Paul," *SBL* 105 (1986) 274-275; also, J. C. Beker, *Paul the Apostle: The Triumph of God in Life and Thought* (Philadelphia: Fortress, 1980) 256-60, in conversation with G. Theissen, "Soteriologische Symbolik in den paulinischen Schriften," *Kerygma und Dogma* 20 (1974) 282-304.

[14] See the seminal work by R. B. Hays, *The Faith of Jesus Christ* (SBLDS 56; Chico, Ca.: Scholars Press, 1983).

[15] See now W. S. Kurz, *Reading Luke-Acts: Dynamics of Biblical Narrative* (Louisville: Westminster/John Knox Press, 1993).

[16] For intertextual connections in Romans 9-11, see R. B. Hays, *Echoes of Scripture in the Letters of Paul* (New Haven: Yale University Press, 1989) 73-83.

The Social Character of Salvation in Luke-Acts

The most appropriate procedure would be to work through Luke-Acts in its narrative order, since that is clearly the way Luke himself wishes to make his argument.[17] Although constraints of space demand here a more efficient approach, the literary unity of the two volumes and their narrative progression must be kept in mind.[18]

To assess the social dimension of salvation in Luke-Acts, I will deal with the verb *sōzein*, which is primarily embedded in specific stories and pronouncements, and then the use of the substantives *sōtēria* and *sōtērion*, which more frequently occur in programmatic announcements.[19] Narrative sequence is observed only by considering each volume's combined data in turn.

The Gospel

By far the hardest material to evaluate is that involving *sōzein*. One difficulty is presented by the fact that Luke takes over some instances from Mark (6:9=Mk 3:4; 8:48-50=Mk 5:23-24; 9:24=Mk 8:35; 18:26= Mk 10:26; 18:42= Mk 10:52; 23:35-37= Mk 15:30-31), while also eliminating Mark's use of *sōzein* in other passages (the healing summary of Mk 6:56 and the eschatological declarations in 13:13, 30), and lavishly increasing the use of the verb in still other places (Lk 7:50; 8:12; 8:36; 9:56; 13:23; 17:19; 19:10; 23:39). Luke's practice can usefully be contrasted to that of Matthew, who adds *sōzein* to his Markan source twice (Mt 8:25; 14:30), and otherwise amplifies the language about salvation only by adding the programmatic statement in the infancy account, "for he will save his people from their sins" (Mt 1:21). Another difficulty is that the *sōzein* is found frequently in healing stories, where the verb obviously bears the straightforward meaning of "being rescued/healed" from some specific physical or spiritual ailment, and *individuals* rather than groups are affected (see Luke 7:50; 8:36; 8:48; 17:19; 18:42). Conclusions about a thematic signifiance of *sōzein* or about any "social dimensions" of salvation must be derived from such passages by inference.

---

17 See L. T. Johnson, *The Gospel of Luke* (Sacra Pagina 3; Collegeville: Liturgical Press, 1991) 1-24.

18 In *Luke: Historian and Theologian* (Exeter: Paternoster Press, 1970), I. H. Marshall declared that "the central theme in the writings of Luke is that Jesus offers salvation to men," (116), and he devoted half his book (pp. 77-215) to developing that theme. Marshall did not yet have the advantage of the work done on the theme of "the people of God" in Luke-Acts by N. Dahl, "The Story of Abraham in Luke-Acts," *Studies in Luke-Acts* ed. L. E. Keck and J. L. Martyn (Philadelphia: Fortress, 1966) 139-158, or J. Jervell, *Luke and the People of God* (Minneapolis: Augsburg, 1972), and he failed to integrate the theme of salvation into that of the shaping of God's people. In this respect, R. F. O'Toole, *The Unity of Luke's Theology* (Good News Studies 9; Wilmington: Michael Glazier, 1984), which also takes salvation as a central Lukan theme, is an advance. But far more attention is given to the playing out of the theme in narrative terms by R. C. Tannehill, *The Narrative Unity of Luke-Acts: A Literary Interpretation* Vol 1 (Philadelphia: Fortress Press, 1986), Vol 2 (Minneapolis: Fortress Press, 1990); see esp. 1:15-44 and 1:103-139.

19 For the similar treatment of Lukan strands, see L. T. Johnson, *The Literary Function of Possessions in Luke-Acts* (SBLDS 39; Missoula: Scholars Press, 1977) 127-139.

In fact, however, the passages do support some such inferences. We note first that Luke, taking the lead from his Markan source, makes the term of healing not only "salvation" from a physical sickness but a "restoration" to human society (see Lk 4:39; 5:14; 5:25; 6:9; 7:10; 8:39; 8:48-56; 14:4; 17:19). Indeed, Luke emphasizes this aspect of *sōzein* by having Jesus return the resuscitated son of Nain to his mother (7:15) and the pacified epileptic to his father (13:10-17). And although the language of "salvation" is not explicitly used, such also is the obvious point of Jesus' three parables of the "lost and found" in 15:3-32, the last of which (15:11-32) restores lost son to father in illustration of Jesus' mission to the outcast of Israel represented by "tax-collectors and sinners" (15:1-2). The coalescence of these ideas is suggested as well by the synonymous character of two declarations by Jesus. In 9:24, he states that "the Son of Man came not to destroy lives but to save (*sōzein*) them," and in 19:10, he says that "the Son of Man came to search out (*zētēsai*) and save (*sōzein*) that which was lost."

That Luke signified something more than physical recovery by his healing stories is also indicated by his expansion of the theme of *faith* beyond trust shown toward Jesus the healer (see 7:50; 8:48-50; 17:19; 18:42), to the message of Good News proclaimed by this prophetic Messiah to the poor and outcast of the people (4:16-32; 6:20). Luke combines deeds of healing with "the good news proclaimed to the poor" (7:22-23), and matches the faith shown toward Jesus the healer with the "faith in order to be saved" that is directed to "the word of God" (8:12). As I stated in my recent commentary on Luke, "By combining physical healings with the proclamation of the good news, furthermore, Luke continues to make the point noted earlier, that the ministry of healing involves most of all the 'healing' or the 'restoration' of the people of God."[20]

The two previous observations are joined by the theoretical question, unique to Luke's Gospel, posed to Jesus as he progresses on his journey to Jerusalem. Luke structures this journey in order to show how, as the prophet Jesus heads toward his death, he is already gathering a people around himself.[21] The question is motivated, therefore, by the events taking place within the narrative itself: "Lord, are those who are being saved few in number?" (*kyrie ei oligoi sōzomenoi*, 13:23). Notice the present progressive sense of the participle. Both the question and Jesus' answer make most sense when "salvation" is understood precisely in terms of inclusion within God's people. Included in the kingdom of God are Abraham and Isaac and Jacob and "all the prophets," as well as those (we note) who will come from the east and west and north and south to recline in the kingdom of God. Excluded are those who do not enter by the narrow gate (Lk 13:24-30). It is surely not by accident that Luke has placed this question so close to the healing of the bent woman who is designated as a "daughter of Abraham" (13:10-17).[22] As the ministry of

---

20 Johnson, *The Gospel of Luke* 125.

21 See Johnson, *The Gospel of Luke* 163-165; and, with a different emphasis, D. P. Moessner, *Lord of the Banquet: The Literary and Theological Significance of the Lukan Travel Narrative* (Minneapolis: Fortress Press, 1989).

22 See M. Dennis Hamm, *This Sign of Healing, Acts 3:1-10: A Study in Lucan Theology* (Ph.D. Dissertation, St. Louis University, 1975) 64-73.

healing is continuous with the the prophetic proclamation of the good news to the poor, so is "saving" of the sick continuous with that "rescuing of the lost" that leads to the restoration of God's people.

The story of Zacchaeus makes the point conclusively. It comes at the climax of Jesus' progression toward Jerusalem. Zacchaeus is the paradigmatic "sinner and tax-collector" who when visited by the prophet responds to him in faith (as is shown by the disposition of his possessions).[23] Jesus' declaration that "the Son of Man has come to search out and save (*sōzein*) that which was lost"(19:10) is here used to support Jesus' pronouncement that "today salvation (*sōtēria*) has come to this house, because he too is a child of Abraham" (19:9).

As the declaration concerning Zacchaeus shows, Luke's language of *sōtēria/sōtērion* corresponds to that of *sōzein*. The statement that *sōtēria* had "come" (or "happened:" *egeneto*) to the house of Zacchaeus (19:9) is the first use of this substantive since the *Benedictus*, where it occurs three times: Zechariah says that God has "raised up a horn of salvation (*sōtēria*) for us (*hēmin*)" in 1:69; that this is understood as a salvation (*sōtēria*) from "our enemies" is stated in 1:71; and that the prophet John would give "knowledge of salvation" (*sōtēria*) to his people (*tō laō autou*) in 1:77. These statements join that in 19:9 concerning Zacchaeus to frame Luke's use of *sōzein*, and move in the same direction. Who saves? God. Through what agency? The visitation of God's prophets. Who is saved? The people Israel. What is the sign of salvation? Negatively, freedom from enemies and freedom from sin (1:75, 77); positively, the freedom to worship God in holiness and righteousness (1:74-75). Salvation "means," then, leading a life before God as a member of God's people.

Mary's designation of God as "my savior" (*sōtēr*) obviously conforms to this understanding, for the entire structure of the *Magnificat* demonstrates how the "raising up" of this lowly servant is emblematic of the "raising up" of the people Israel (1:46-55),[24] in fulfillment of the promises to Abraham. The angelic announcement of Jesus as a "savior born for you who is Lord Messiah" (2:11) fits in the same framework, as does Simeon's declaration upon receiving the child Jesus that "my eyes have seen your salvation" (*sōtērion*, 2:30), which he then elaborates as a "glory of your people Israel" as well as a "light of revelation to the Gentiles" (2:32), a proleptic note of universality sounded also by Luke's inclusion of Isa 40:5 in the citation of 3:6, "and all flesh will see the salvation (*sōtērion*) of God."

In the gospel section of his narrative, then, Luke uses salvation language with reference to the restoration of God's people in response to prophetic visitation. This conclusion is supported negatively by the fact that Luke does *not* use salvation language in other contexts where it might have been expected. Luke avoids using salvation for the resting of Lazarus in Abraham's bosom, for example (16:32), or for the reception of the good thief into paradise (23:42-43)—an ommission the more striking for failing to match the set-up provided by 23:39, "Save yourself, and us." Finally, Luke does not use salvation language with reference to the disciples' future experience of the parousia. I have noted already his omission of *sōzein* as found in Mark's

---

23 For discussion, see D. Hamm, "Luke 19:8 Once More: Does Zaccheus Defend or Resolve?" *JBL* 107 (1988) 431-437; and Johnson, *The Gospel of Luke* 283-288.

24 Johnson, *Gospel of Luke* 43-44.

eschatological discourse (Mk 13:13, 20). In speaking of the parousia in 17:33, Luke uses the language of "losing and gaining" one's life, rather than the language of "losing and saving" (in contrast to 9:24). And in 21:28, those who persevere to the end will find their *apolytrōsis* to be near at hand, rather than their *sōtēria*.

In his efforts to describe the normative story that shapes the world-view of Judaism and early Christianity, Wright makes judicious use of the "actantial model" of narrative analysis associated with A. J. Greimas.[25] Since I have entered into conversation with Wright, it may be helpful to display my findings concerning Luke's salvation-language in the gospel in the form of the model he himself has adopted from Greimas. The basic model looks like this:

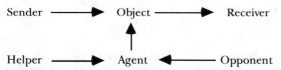

Like Wright, I find the model useful most of all for the way it enables complex data to be organized. My findings with respect to salvation language in the Gospel of Luke fit perfectly into this model:

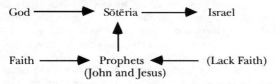

To spell this out: God sent salvation to his people Israel through the agency of his prophets John and Jesus. It could be received by faith and (by implication) impeded by lack of faith. What the model does *not* make clear is that "salvation" has meant precisely to *be* part of this people by faith.

Acts

This discussion of salvation language in Acts will bracket from the start the two cases of *sōzein* in 27:20 and 27:31 as well as the declaration, "this will turn out for your salvation (*sōtēria*)" in 27:34. In the context of Paul's sea voyage and shipwreck, these terms bear the obvious meaning of "rescue and survival." It is possible that they might be read for deeper narrative significance, but they need not be.[26]

Otherwise, the salvation language in Acts develops the theme established by Luke's gospel. Indeed, two of Luke's programmatic statements flesh out the actantial model sketched above. In his recital of Israelite history, Luke has Stephen declare that in Moses' first visitation of the people, God wanted "to give salvation (*sōtēria*) to them through his hand" (Acts 7:25). And in Paul's

---

25 Wright, 69-77; it has also been used effectively by Hays, *Faith of Jesus Christ* 92-125.

26 See L. T. Johnson, *The Acts of the Apostles* (Sacra Pagina 5; Collegeville: Liturgical Press, 1992) 456-459.

proclamation in the Synagogue at Antioch of Pisidia, he states that of David's seed "according to the promise, he sent Jesus as a savior (*sōtēr*) to Israel" (13:23), and concludes to his Jewish audience, "to us the message of this salvation (*logon tēs sōtērias tautēs*) has been sent (*exapestale*)" (23:26). This is the point also of Peter's declaration in 5:31 to the council that "God has raised to his right hand this one as pioneer and savior (*sōtēr*) in order to give repentance (*metanoia*) and forgiveness of sins to Israel (*tō Israēl*)."

On the basis of these texts, the model now looks like this:

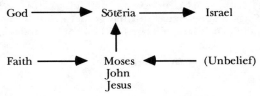

The receiver of salvation, in other words, remains Israel. This social understanding is entirely consistent with Luke's use of *sōzein* in the first part of Acts. In Peter's Pentecost speech, after announcing on the basis of Joel 3:5 that "everyone who calls on the name of the Lord will be saved" (2:21), Peter says in response to those who ask him, "what shall we do?" to "be saved [or: save yourselves, *sōthēte*] from this twisted generation" (2:40). Salvation appears here *precisely* as the formation of a remnant people out of the larger faithless population, which, by being baptized and repenting, receives the gift of the Holy Spirit (2:38), which Luke has Peter interpret as the "promise to you and to your children" (2:39).[27] It is not surprising, therefore, to see those who join this people being referred to as "those being saved" (*hoi sōzomenoi*). In context, the term means virtually the same thing as "being in community" (*epi to auto*, 2:47) and "those who were believing" (*hoi pisteuontes* 2:44).

As the healing of the bent woman in Luke 13:10-17 and as the reception of Zacchaeus in Luke 19:1-10 symbolized the restoration of Israel, so does the healing of the lame man at the gate in Acts 3:1-10, as has been shown so well by Dennis Hamm.[28] Peter makes this clear in his speech to the council following the healing, when he declares the man to have been "saved" (4:9), and connects his healing/salvation to the restoration of Israel through the prophet Jesus: "this is the stone that was rejected by you the builders which has become a cornerstone, and there is not in any other the salvation (*sōtēria*), for neither is another name given among humans under heaven in which we must be saved (*dei sōthēnai hēmas*, 4:12). It is, furthermore, undoubtedly this symbolic function of the healing that helps acount for the awkward inclusion of "faith" as the other active agent of healing in 3:16.[29]

---

27 For the language of "remnant" for believing Jews in Luke-Acts, see also D. P. Moessner, "Paul in Acts: Preacher of Eschatological Repentance to Israel," *New Testament Studies* 34 (1988) 102.

28 D. Hamm, "Acts 3:1-10: The Healing of the Temple Beggar as Lukan Theology," *Biblica* 67 (1988) 305-319.

29 Johnson, *The Acts of the Apostles* 68.

As the proclamation of the word moves into the Gentile world, Luke continues to use salvation language in precisely the same social sense. Cornelius is told by the angel to send for Peter, who will "speak words to you by which you will be saved, you and all your household" (11:15). In still a third symbolic healing, the lame man of Lystra is perceived by Paul to possess "such faith as to be saved" (14:9). This healing by faith symbolizes the spread of the movement among Gentiles through the ministry of Paul, in fulfillment of the programmatic prophecy announced by him at the end of his synagogue speech at Antioch of Pisidia: "I have made you a light to the nations, so that you will be for salvation (*sōtēria*) to the end of the earth" (Acts 13:47; see Isa 49:6). The narrative model for Luke's story of salvation can therefore be expanded still further, both with reference to the "receivers" of salvation and with reference to the "agent:"

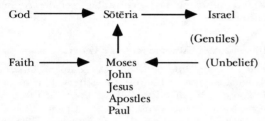

Although the receiver is expanded and the agents multiplied, it remains the same story: God sends salvation to his people through his prophets, and salvation means precisely to be part of that people.

That Luke continues to work with such a fundamentally social understanding of salvation is shown above all by the conflict at Antioch and the Jerusalem Council in Acts 15. Those telling the Gentile believers "you cannot be saved unless you are circumcised according to the custom of Moses" (15:1) are not stating something about a future life with God but something about status within the restored people of God. For them, to be a part of this people demands the practice of the customary circumcision. The same logic attends the statement of the Pharisaic party that the law of Moses must be kept (15:5). But Peter responds by recounting his experience of God's work among the Gentiles, concluding that "through the gift that is the Lord Jesus, we are believing in order to be saved, in the same way that they are" (15:11).[30] He asserts that membership in the people is exactly the same for both Jews and Gentiles. Thus also James speaks of the Gentile mission in terms of the "raising up of the fallen tent of David" (15:16) by which God "has made visitation to take from the Gentiles a people for his name" (15:14).[31]

This decision once made, the message moves even more rapidly into the gentile world through the work of Paul. The Pythian spirit in Philippi announces to the crowd that "these people are announcing to you (*hymin*) a way of salvation (*sōtēria*, 16:17). When the frightened jailor in that city asks

---

30 For this translation, see Johnson, *Acts of the Apostles* 263.

31 See N. A. Dahl, "'A People for His Name' (Acts 15:14)," *New Testament Studies* 4 (1957-58) 319-327.

"what must I do in order to be saved" (16:30), Paul's response is in terms of faith and of the group: "believe in the Lord Jesus and you will be saved, you and your household" (16:31). The upshot is that his entire household is baptized (16:34). The extension of the people of God among Gentiles is solemnly enunicated at the end of Acts. Corresponding to Paul's statement in 13:26 that "*to us* was sent (*exapestalē*) the message of this salvation" is his final prophecy in 28:28, "to the Gentiles this salvation (*sōtērion*) has been sent (*apestalē*). And they will listen."

Luke's use of salvation language is utterly consistent. It has to do with God's restoration on earth of a people drawn from the Jews and Gentiles alike, a people that responds in faith to the prophetic proclamation of good news. Salvation for Luke involves healing and rescue, but its term is present and social rather than future and individual. Salvation means belonging to a certain community, with faith signifying in behavioral terms the commitment that makes that inclusion actual.

The Social Dimension of Salvation in Paul's Letters

The problems of method here are different if no less complex. First, the distribution of salvation language is uneven across the letters. It is missing entirely in Colossians, Philemon and (surprisingly) Galatians. At the other extreme, Romans uses *sōzein* 8 times and *sōtēria* 5 times. 1 Cor uses *sōzein* 8 times but *sōtēria* not at all. 2 Cor uses *sōzein* once and *sōtēria* 3 times. 1 Thess uses *sōzein* once and *sōtēria* twice; 2 Thess uses *sōzein* once and *sōtēria* once. Philippians does not use *sōzein* but has *sōtēria* three times and *sōtēr* once. Ephesians has *sōzein* twice, *sōtēria* once, *sōtērion* once and *sōtēr* once. The obvious conclusion is that the language is not equally central to every letter, and is configured somewhat differently wherever it occurs. A second problem is what to do with the Pastorals. On one hand, their use of salvation language is extravagant, including *sōzein* (1 Tim 1:15; 2:4; 2:15; 4:16; 2 Tim 1:9; 4:18; Tit 3:5), *sōtēria* (2 Tim 2:10; 3:15), *sōtēr* (1 Tim 1:1; 2:3; 4:10; 2 Tim 1:11; Tit 1:3; 1:4; 2:10; 2:13; 3:4; 3:6), and *sōtērios* (Tit 2:11). On the other hand, the data from the Pastorals is so complex and the questioning of their authorship so widespread that including them in this discussion could prove both distending and distracting.[32]

It is sensible method, therefore, to begin with Romans, where the language is most attested and plays the most central thematic role; then compare the other undisputed letters with Romans for consistency; then bracket the data from the Pastorals for another occasion.[33]

---

[32] I adopt this procedure with some regret and only for efficiency; the more the Pastorals are systematically excluded from such analyses, the more stereotypical views of them can prevail. For my own position concerning authenticity, see L. T. Johnson, *Writings of the New Testament: An Interpretation* (Minneapolis: Fortress Press, 1986) 255-257, 381-389.

[33] Although it must exist somewhere, my limited research has yet to uncover a study that proceeds this way. More often, the subject of "salvation" is treated without specific attention to the language of *sōtēria*; J. C. Beker, *Paul the Apostle*, for example, pays close attention to the communal concerns of Paul (309), and in particular to the connection of Church to Israel (316), but without reference to *sōtēria*; E. P. Sanders, *Paul and Palestinian*

Romans

Read on its own terms, Paul's salvation language in Romans also appears to tell a story of how God was revealing through the good news about Jesus a "power for salvation (*eis sōtērian*) to all who believe, Jews first and Gentiles" (1:16). As we all now recognize, that is the "thesis" of Paul's diatribal argument.[34] But it is also the "story-line" in whose plot Paul conceives his mission to be playing a critical role. God's plan for salvation, according to Paul's argument, is not directed first of all at scattered individuals but at social groups, at peoples. This becomes clear in the midrashic argument of chapters 9-11, where the bulk of Romans' salvation language is located.

The first suggestion that *sōtēria* is communal is found in Paul's citation of Isa 10:22, which states that "the remnant will be saved" (*to hypoleimma sōthēsetai*, 9:27). Paul then declares that his prayer is for "them" (*autōn*) — meaning his fellow Jews—"for salvation" (*eis sōtērian*, 10:1). In context, this clearly means that his fellow Jews are not presently part of the remnant people constituted by faith, since their acknowledged zeal for God is not accompanied by "recognition" (10:2).

The tight cluster of statements in 10:9-13 serves to clarify what "recognition" Paul sees as necessary for "salvation," that is, inclusion in the remnant people of God. The confessional language of 10:9-10 deserves especially close attention. How does a person become part of the remnant people? First, there is the verbal profession that "Jesus is Lord" (10:9a). This, says Paul, is *eis sōtērian* (10:10b). He means it has the effect of "recognizing" the claim of the messianic community concerning Jesus (see 1 Cor 12:1-3). This recognition signifies membership in the messianic community. But the verbal profession must be accompanied by "believing in your heart that God raised him from the dead" (10:9b). Such faith establishes one as "sharing the faith of Abraham" (4:16-25) *eis dikaiosynēn* (unto righteousness, 10:10a) and therefore as part of that "remnant chosen by grace in the present time" (11:5). Consequently it issues in, "you will be saved" (10:9b). The faith from the heart defines the right relationship with God, but the confession with the mouth

---

Judaism: A Comparison of Patterns of Religion (Philadelphia: Fortress 1977) similarly has several of the pieces but treats them separately; likewise, L. Cerfaux, *The Church in the Theology of St. Paul* trans. G. Webb and A. Walker (NY: Herder and Herder, 1959). But at least these are aware of the social dimension. More often, salvation in Paul is treated almost entirely in terms of its temporal dimension and in terms of the individual's destiny: The comment by W. Foerster is classic: "In Paul *sōzō* and *sōtēria* are obviously limited quite intentionally to the relation between man and God," in *Sōzō*, ktl. *TDNT* 7:992. See also J. Bonsirven, *Theology of the New Testament* trans. S. F. L. Tye (Westminster: Newman, 1963) 271-272; E. Stauffer, *New Testament Theology* trans. J. Marsh (London: SCM Press, 1955) 223; W. G. Kümmel, *The Theology of the New Testament* trans. J. Seeley (Nashville: Abingdon, 1973) 145-50, 186, 238. R. Bultmann's *Theology of the New Testament* I (NY: Charles Scribner's Sons, 1951) simply equates salvation with righteousness (I:271), and pays no attention to *sōtēria* as social; not suprisingly, Bultmann has no discussion at all of Rom 9-11! The best treatment of *sōtēria* in social terms that I have yet found is F. Amiot, *The Key Concepts of St. Paul* trans. J. Dingle (Freiburg: Herder, 1962), esp. 148, 173.

[34] J. D. G. Dunn, *Romans 1-8* (Word Biblical Commentary 38; Dallas: Word Books, 1988) 37-49.

defines entrance into the "salvation people" (10:10).[35] That Paul is thinking of salvation in terms of membership in the remnant people is shown further by his iteration of the principle of God's impartiality (10:12) and citation from Joel 3:5, "For everyone who should call on the name of the Lord shall be saved" (10:13; compare Acts 2:21). This reading makes good sense of the next three statements involving salvation. In 11:11, Paul asserts that Israel did not stumble so as utterly to fall. God has not rejected his *laos* (11:1). Rather, their "false step" (*paraptōma*) has meant *sōtēria tois ethnesin*. This can only make sense in the historical context of the early Christian mission, including that of Paul, which progressed to the Gentiles largely because of Jewish rejection. Acceptance by the Gentiles of the Good News in "the present season" means "salvation for them," that is, their inclusion in God's *hypoleimma*. Paul also adverts to the deeper game God is playing. The Gentiles are included to *parazēlōsai autous*, that is, stimulate his fellow-Jews to emulation (11:11). Such, indeed, was the motivation for Paul's own work among the Gentiles: he "magnifies his ministry" so that *parazēlōsō mou tēn sarka* ("cause my kins-people to emulate") which he spells out "and I might save some from among them" (*kai sōsō tinas ex autōn*, 11:14).

In these passages, salvation cannot mean anything other than inclusion of the Jews in the restored Israel according to the promise by faith. That Paul expected his mission to have just that effect is expressed in 11:25-26: "Blindness has come upon a part of Israel until the full number of Gentiles come in, and thus all Israel will be saved" (*kai houtōs pas Israēl sōthēsetai*).

Paul's thesis statement in 1:16 and his elaboration of it in chs 9-11 support the suggestion that *sōtēria* means inclusion in God's restored *laos* (see Rom 9:25, 26; 10:21; 11:1, 2; 15:10-11). It should be emphasized that Paul has *not* used salvation with reference to the individual person's spiritual dilemma or as opposed by life according to the flesh or sold under sin. Nor has it been used for an individual's future life before or with God.

This reading enables us to understand 13:11 in the same context of Paul's ministry. The community is encouraged to pay special attention to the commandment of love, "since you also know the season, that the hour [is here] for you already to rise from sleep, for now (*nyn*) our salvation (*sōtēria*) is closer than when we came to believe." In the context of the argument from 9-11, the *sōtēria* Paul has in mind is the inclusion of Jews as well as Gentiles in the people rescued from the *orgē tou theou*. The Gentiles need particularly in "this season" to show that love which is the "fulfillment of the other law" by being its summary (13:8), and by thus demonstrating the "righteous demand of the law" (8:4), cause the Jews to emulate them and turn to Jesus as the *telos tou nomou* (10:4).

The three remaining texts in Romans might be thought to challenge this "horizontal" reading of salvation. In 5:9-10, Paul celebrates the restored relationship between God and humans (5:1) enabled by "this gift in which we

---

35 It is striking to find a consistent tradition of interpretation that simply equates *dikaiosynē* and *sōtēria* in 10:10, clearly because the social implication of verbal profession have not been thought through: see e.g. R. Bultmann, *Theology of the New Testament* I: 271; H. Conzelmann, *Grundriss der Theologie des Neuen Testament* (München: Chr. Kaiser Verlag, 1967) 224; L. Goppelt, *Theology of the New Testament* trans. J. Roloff (Grand Rapids: Eerdmans, 1982) 2:136.

stand" (5:2) by declaring: "How much more therefore, now having been put in right relationship by his blood, shall we be saved through him from the wrath. For if when we were enemies we were reconciled to God through the death of his son, how much more, once reconciled, shall we be saved by his life." We notice at once that the contrast in these sentences establishes a rhetorical rather than a real temporal sequence. The contrast posits "salvation" as a condition distinguishable from "righteousness" (as in 10:9-10). But no more than there should salvation be read here as an entirely future reality: first, the *orgē* is not only future in Romans (2:5, 8); it is also past and present as well (1:18; 3:5; 4:15; 9:22; 12:19; 13:4-5). Second, there is no question that, for Paul, the gift of Jesus' "life" (*zōē*) is already shared by those who "live by faith" (1:17; see 5:17-18; 6:4; 8:2, 10). In these statements, therefore, *sōtēria* is not only clearly communal (referring to all those who "now have peace with God", 5:1), but is at the very least also incipient in those who, justified and reconciled, now live by the Spirit of Jesus. The same temporal tension is expressed by 8:23-24: "ourselves having the first-fruits of the Spirit, we also groan within ourselves as we await the *apolytrōsis tou sōmatos hēmōn*; for we have been saved (*esōthēmen*) in hope." Here, salvation is grammatically past and the redemption of the body (by resurrection?) is future. But as the plurals suggest, the experience of being in the restored people ("salvation") is proleptic of the future and full realization of redemption/reconciliation by God.

In Romans, therefore, salvation has to do with inclusion within God's remnant people. Negatively, it denotes rescue from the *orgē* that is God's judgment on sinful humanity. Positively, it signifies right relationship and reconciliation with God through recognition of the gift given by the faith of Jesus expressed in his sacrificial death (3:21-26).[36] Apart from 10:9-10, 13, which define the terms of inclusion in this people, salvation language in Romans is entirely social in character. It would not distort the "story-line" of Romans, I think, to display it this way:

The major difference from the "story-line" of Luke-Acts involves the major role played by the *orgē tou theou* in Romans, and the dialectical character of Jewish/Gentile roles in God's plan, only a portion of which appears in Acts.

Corinthian Correspondence

Paul's use of salvation language in 1 Corinthians is almost entirely consistent with that in Romans. The Corinthians are "being saved" (notice the plural present progressive, *sōzesthe*) through the Gospel preached by Paul (15:2); the message of the cross is said to be *dynamis tou theou* for those who "are

---

36 On this, see L. T. Johnson, "Romans 3:21-26 and the Faith of Jesus," *Catholic Biblical Quarterly* 44 (1982) 77-90.

being saved" (*tous sōzōmenous*, 1:18), and through its foolishness, God has been pleased to "save those who are believing" (*sōsai tous pisteuontes*, 1:21). That these statements fit within Paul's Roman understanding of "joining the remnant community" is shown further by the marked resemblance to Rom 11:14 in Paul's declaration that he becomes all things to all people *hina pantōs tinas sōsō* (9:22), as well as his assertion in 10:33 that he seeks the good of the many *hina sōthōsin*.

Such a "social" understanding of salvation gives an edge to Paul's cautionary comment to husbands and wives of unbelievers. He asks each in turn, "how do you know that you will save your husband/wife" (7:16)? In context, this surely does not mean, "How do you know you will influence them for eternal life," but rather, "How do you know whether you can draw them into the community/remnant people?"

Two of the statements in 1 Corinthians seem not to fit this framework. In his discussion of the work of himself and Apollos, Paul says that "the day" will make clear how builders of the house have done their work, "for it is revealed in fire." The one whose house is burnt up will "suffer loss but himself be saved (*sōthēsetai*), but thus, as though through fire" (3:12). Here the future judgment of the individual seems to be the clear focus for salvation language. And with reference to the sexually deviant member of the church in 1 Cor 5:1-5, Paul expresses the desire that the *olethron tēs sarkos* (destruction of "his" flesh, or destruction of his "fleshly lusts"?) will have an effect: " *hina to pneuma* (his spirit? that spirit operative in the community?) *sōthē* on the day of the Lord." Once more, future judgment is in view for the individual person. But even in these two texts, we notice, the fate of the individual is very much related to that social reality that is the community (the "house"/the "gathering").

Turning to 2 Corinthians, the use of *hoi sōzomenoi* in 2:15 has exactly the same valence as in 1 Cor 1:18. In 2 Cor 6:2, the citation of Isaiah 49:2, "In an acceptable season I heard you, on a day of salvation I have helped you," is applied by Paul to the community's present circumstances: "Behold, now is the acceptable season; behold, now is the day of salvation," and used as part of the presentation of his ministry as one that "avoids giving offense" (6:3); the combination reminds us of Rom 13:11-14. The precise meaning of 2 Cor 1:6 is harder to pin down: "If we are afflicted it is for your encouragement and *sōtēria*," as is that of 7:10: "sorrow according to God works repentance without regret *eis sōtērian*, but the sorrow of the world works death." There is no doubt, however, that the context in both cases is social rather than individual, present rather than future.

Thessalonian Correspondence

If 1 Thess 2:16 is not an interpolation—as I believe it is not—then the statement concerning the Jews who "are preventing us from speaking to the Gentiles *hina sōthōsin*" corresponds exactly with the missionary language employed by Paul in Rom 11:11-14. Likewise, the two statements in 5:8-9 make sense precisely when understood in application to life in the present time within the messianic remnant community: "But let us who are of the day be alert, having put on the breastplate of faith and love and the hope of salvation as a helmet. Because (*hoti*) God has not destined us for wrath (*orgē*) but for the possession of salvation (*sōtēria*) through our Lord Jesus Christ."

When 2 Thess 2:10 characterizes those who "are being destroyed" (*tous apollymenous*; compare 1 Cor 1:18; 2 Cor 2:15) as those who by deception "do not accept the truth *eis to sōthēnai autous*," the salvation language functions straightforwardly to designate those who belong to the community and those who do not.[37] This can be seen even more clearly when placed next to the sequel in 2:13: they are to thank God, "because God chose you to be the first fruits unto salvation (*aparchēn tēs sōtērias*) in holiness of Spirit and fidelity to truth." Note in passing that "first fruits unto salvation" echoes the language of Rom 11:16 concerning the remnant people.

Captivity Correspondence

The usage in Philippians is more mixed. In 1:27-28, the language of salvation suggests just the sort of insider/outsider distinction found in the Corinthian and Thessalonian correspondence. The Philippians' living according to the good news and not being intimidated by "those who are opposing" is "proof of your salvation" (*sōtēria*) as it is also for those opposing "proof of their destruction" (*endeixis apōleias*; compare 1 Cor 1:18; 2 Cor 2:15; 2 Thess 2:10). Likewise, Paul's instruction in 2:12 to "work out your own salvation (*tēn heautōn sōtērian*) in fear and trembling," when addressed to all "my beloved," suggests that they live out their community identity according to the "mind of Christ" in mutual service (Phil 2:1-12a). In contrast, the expectation from heaven of the Lord Jesus Christ as *sōtēr*, while communal, is certainly oriented to the future. And in 1:19, Paul's assertion that Christ's being preached in whatever circumstances "will turn out to me *eis sōtērian*" has his individual future as its obvious point of reference, especially since this is what is developed by the verses following in 1:20-26.

The salvation language in Ephesians is virtually identical to Romans, no surprise in light of the overall resemblance between these letters.[38] In 2:5 and 2:8, the statements *chariti este sesōsmenoi* and *tē gar chariti este sesōsmenoi dia pisteōs* refer precisely to the inclusion of the Gentiles with the Jews in the one people being shaped by God. Likewise in the opening blessing, the *euangelion tēs sōtērias* (1:13) is mentioned with reference to the Gentiles (*kai hymeis*) who by faith have become heirs of the promise. In contrast to Philippians, Ephesians' designation of Jesus as *sōtēr* fits within this present and social context: he is "head of the church, himself *sōtēr* of the body" (5:23). Finally, the exhortation to "accept the helmet of salvation and the sword of the Spirit which is the word of God" is addressed to the community and has the same sense of 1 Thess 5:8, namely, to live out their identity as God's remnant people even in the face of spiritual opposition.

Such is the evidence in Paul's letters, absent the complicating data from the Pastorals. We have found that Paul's most deliberate use of salvation language is in Romans, and that with some few exceptions, his usage elsewhere fits comfortably within its framework. Salvation language is used more consis-

---

37 For salvation language used in defining insiders and outsiders, see Boring, "The Language of Universal Salvation in Paul," 276-277.

38 See A. Van Roon, *The Authenticity of Ephesians* (NovTSupp 39; Leiden: Brill, 1974).

tently of present circumstances rather than future. It almost entirely has a social rather than an individual application. It seems to mean primarily belonging to a remnant people chosen in the present time by God (by grace and through faith), a people which itself escapes the wrath that is God's judgment turned even now toward the world of sinful humanity, and yet also lives in hope of a future in which the remant will be filled out (Rom 11:12) by Paul's fellow Jews, whose joining of the remnant people, Paul thinks, will mean "all Israel will be saved" (Rom 11:26) and as well, "the resurrection of the dead" (Rom 11:15).

Conclusions

This essay began as an effort to test Wright's hypothesis concerning the conception of salvation in early Christianity by carrying out a careful comparison of salvation language in two NT writers. The sketchy comparison of Luke-Acts and Paul's Letters suggest the following conclusions:

1. The use of *sōtēria/sōzein* language in both writers serves to identify present social realities more than the future destiny of individuals.

2. Both writers share the same basic story and world-view: salvation means belonging to the remnant people God is creating out of Jews and Gentiles in the present season. For Luke and Paul, *extra ecclesiam nulla salus* would not only be true but tautologous.

3. Comparison on the basis of this deliberately limited set of data tends to support the view that at least these two important NT writers shared the overall story and world-view that Wright has described as that of Jewish apocalyptic. Yet by defining the remnant people in terms of grace and faith and spiritual transformation, that story was given a decisive turn and that world-view a definitive new shaping.[39]

4. If doing comparisons adequately is so arduous, it is no wonder that it is also done so rarely.

---

[39] In this respect, Wright's consideration of the ways in which the messianists reshaped Jewish symbols in light of the experience of Jesus (365-70), and redefined hope in light of the continuing presence of Jesus (459-464), is a more adequate account than Bultmann's flat, "what for the Jews is a *matter of hope* is for Paul a *present reality*—or better is also a present reality," *Theology of the New Testament* I:279 (underscoring original).

Who's Characterizing Whom and the Difference This Makes: Locating and Centering Paul

Stephen E. Fowl
Loyola College, Baltimore

Introduction

One way to approach this paper is to read it as a preliminary experiment in comparative characterization. That is to say, I will examine and compare some specific examples of the ways that the character Paul is portrayed in both Acts and in Paul's epistles. Of course, comparisons between the Paul of Acts and the Paul of the epistles is not a new exercise. There is a large body of literature devoted to just this task.[1] The vast majority of scholars undertaking this work have used this comparison as a way of making historical judgments about the nature of earliest Christianity, about the biographical details of the historical Paul, and about the historical author of Acts and that person's relationship to the historical Paul.[2] It is not my intention to say much, if anything, about this work. Without commenting on the particular results of such work, using Acts and the epistles as resources for historical judgments certainly seems to be a valid intellectual enterprise. My interests in this paper simply lie elsewhere—in matters of character and characterization.

This particular task raises a whole host of issues and problems. The first concerns the scope and nature of the material to be compared. Any comparison, if it is to do much useful work, if it is to illuminate interesting differences and similarities, must avoid comparing apples and oranges. In my case it may, ultimately, be impossible to avoid this problem completely in the light of the fact that Acts is a narrative and epistles are occasional discourse, directed to specific people, places and situations. Given this fairly substantial difference between Acts and the epistles, it may be a good idea to try to narrow this generic gap somewhat. With that aim in mind, I will not examine every time the character Saul/Paul appears or is spoken of in Acts. Neither will I take up

---

[1] As I thumbed through the SBL Seminar Papers as part of my research for this paper it became clear that a group much like this one had addressed just this issue exactly 10 years ago.

[2] A paradigmatic example of these interests can be found in Philipp Vielhauer's 1950 essay "zum 'Paulinismus' der Apostelgeschichte" a translation of this can be found in *Studies in Luke-Acts* ed. Leander Keck and J. Louis Martyn (Nashville: Abingdon, 1966), pp. 33-50.

every isolated comment the apostle makes about himself in the epistles.[3] Instead, I will focus my remarks on those four passages in Acts (20:17ff.; 22:2ff.; 24:10ff. 26:4ff.) where the character Paul characterizes himself. I will compare these passages with the sustained accounts Paul gives of himself in Gal.1:10ff and Phil.3:2ff. Examining these texts will allow me both to point to some consistent differences in the way Luke's Paul characterizes himself from the way the Paul of Galatians and Philippians characterizes himself. I will also, however, try to make some general points about the practice of characterization which may help further discussions of this matter.

Having defined a body of material to examine, there are also some conceptual matters about character and characterization in regard to comparisons between Acts and the epistles which I should try to clarify. As John Darr has recently reminded us, matters of characterization are largely literary topics.[4] Darr has also noted that despite a burgeoning of literary readings of Luke/Acts, relatively little attention has been devoted to character and characterization. In addressing this lack, Darr's work largely focuses on Luke rather than Acts and does not touch on Paul. I, too, am interested in the literary and rhetorical renderings of characters. In this respect, my comments here on the character of Paul in Acts may be seen as supplemental to Darr's work.[5]

It strikes me, however, particularly regarding the epistles, but also in relation to Acts, that standard literary questions of characterization are not sufficient. Most literary accounts of characterization are focused on rendering a particular character by compiling and synthesizing a series of direct observations and inferences about a character. These observations and inferences are based on what that character says and does, and on what others say about that character.[6] In the course of doing this, it is also common to note the literary techniques used to render characters. This seems to be a relatively uncontroversial way of going about literary characterization. In the case of Paul's characterizations of himself in Acts, Galatians and Philippians, however, there are several other matters which should also be addressed.

It must be noted that none of the texts we will look at are strictly (auto)biographical.[7] That is, Paul does not render an account of himself for its own

---

3 Having said this, I do not think that the results of my examinations are radically discontinuous from Acts as a whole or from the rest of the pauline corpus.

4 See *On Building Character: The Reader and the Rhetoric of Characterization in Luke Acts* (Louisville: Westminster/John Knox, 1992).

5 See also Robert Brawley's "Paul in Acts: Aspects of Structure and Characterization" *SBL 1988 Seminar Papers* ed. David J. Lull (Atlanta: Scholars Press, 1988), pp. 96-103. Brawley notes that, like this essay, his is an experimental essay.

6 See also the definition of characterization used by Adele Berlin in *Poetics and Interpretation of Biblical Narrative* (Sheffield: Almond Press, 1983) "The reader reconstructs a character from the information provided to him in the discourse; he is told by the statements and evaluations of the narrator and other characters, and he infers from the speech and action of the character himself" (p. 34).

7 The term autobiography is clearly anachronistic when applied to Paul. The term "Autobiographical remark" may be a more accurate designation for the self references found in ancient literature. In regard to pauline autobiography both B. R. Gaventa, "Galatians 1 and 2: Autobiography as Paradigm," *NovT.* 28 (1986) 322-326 and George Lyons, *Pauline Autobiography: Toward a New Understanding* (Atlanta: Scholars Press, 1985),

sake. Hence, simply noting what Paul says about himself and how Paul says it will not be sufficient. In the case of Acts, there is a larger story being told, the story of God's action in the maintenance and spread of the gospel. How one tells that story shapes and is shaped by the ways in which Paul's account of himself fits into that larger story about God. Hence, questions about how Luke tells this larger story will be important for understanding the ways in which Luke's Paul characterizes himself and how that character is related to the story of God's activity.

Galatians and Philippians are not narratives. They do, however, presume a larger story.[8] Paul presumes that he and his audience share a story about God's activity in Christ and how they are related to that activity. How Paul understands that story is crucial for the ways in which he characterizes himself. Further, Paul's characterizations of himself in the epistles are required to do moral and theological work in relation to that larger story. In both Galatians and Philippians (though in different ways) Paul's Paul is to be exemplary for the faith and practice of Paul's audience. Hence, some understanding of the relationship Paul desires his audience to have to that larger, largely unnarrated, story will help one understand what is at stake for Paul when he tells his story in one way in Galatians and in another way in Philippians.

Simply noting the literary and rhetorical renderings of Paul in these texts one will be able to point out differences of detail and technique. Such an examination would not, however, touch on the moral and theological significance of Paul's characterization of himself in Galatians and Philippians (and to a lesser degree in Acts). An examination of the moral and theological issues involved in characterization will need to recognize literary and rhetorical matters without simply stopping there. By asking questions about how Paul's characterizations of himself shape and are shaped by the larger narratives of which those characterizations form a part and by noting what is at stake in telling Paul's story one way rather than another, I hope to be able to make a more substantial comparison between Luke's Paul's Paul and Paul's Paul. I will begin by discussing Acts.

---

chapter 1, comment on autobiography in antiquity. While Lyons' is a more comprehensive account of autobiography, he focuses too heavily on literature that is not easily comparable to pauline epistles. Alternatively, Gaventa shows that the closest parallels to Paul's practice can be found in the autobiographical comments found in the letters of Seneca and Pliny who use self references for didactic or paraenetic purposes. While Gaventa's comments are helpful here, it ought also be noted that Paul, like Augustine, is "less interested in telling the reader about himself than he is in narrating how his life has been located in the story of God." For further comments like this on autobiography see L. G. Jones, "For All the Saints: Autobiography in Christian Theology" *Asbury Theological Journal* 47 (1992) 27-42. The quote here is from p. 34.

8 Richard Hays has persuasively demonstrated the presence of a "narrative substructure" in Galatians in *The Faith of Jesus Christ* (Chico: Scholars Press, 1983). I have tried to demonstrate the importance of the story of Christ for the Paul's argument in Philippians in *The Story of Christ in the Ethics of Paul* (Sheffield: JSOT Press, 1991).

Luke's Paul's Paul

The first time Paul gives a substantial account of himself in Acts is in his farewell speech to the Ephesian elders in 20:17 ff. This passage has the most in common with Paul's epistolary characterizations of himself. In both cases Paul is addressing fellow believers. Like Galatians and Philippians, and unlike other places in Acts, Paul is known to his audience. He is not introducing or defending himself before strangers. Acts 20:17ff. is occasioned by the fact that Paul is soon to be permanently separated from the Ephesians. In addition to saying good-bye and to foreshadowing his impending imprisonment, he wishes to leave them with an account of his ministry that will be a resource to them in the future.[9]

As Paul begins his testamentary address to the Ephesian elders he reminds them of his persistence and boldness in proclaiming the gospel to them (20:20). As the plot of Acts has unfolded we have seen the unrelenting progress of the gospel, spreading out from Jerusalem and soon to reach Rome. It has conquered all comers. Indeed, as opposition has grown more violent, the message and the messengers have grown more resilient. The plots (ἐπιβουλαί) of the Jews (20:18) cannot thwart the plan (ἡ βουλή) of God which Paul both boldly proclaimed to the Ephesians (20:27) and in which Paul willingly participates.[10]

Just as Paul has faced persecution and trials, he will continue to face them in the future (20:22).[11] He is bound by the Spirit and he must finish the course of his ministry (20:24). Paul characterizes his sufferings and the opposition he faces as road blocks that threaten to derail his pursuit of the course of his ministry. This perspective on the tribulations of a witness is consistent with the perspective Luke takes in Acts more generally. Paul, like Peter, Stephen and others, has been made a witness to the work of God and God has providentially overseen the success of that testimony by means of visions and auditions, miraculous escapes and the aid of various sympathizers. Paul's subjection to various persecutions and trials neither raises questions about his apostleship nor does it serve to validate his message. Instead, they provide both tests for his ministry and occasions for the providential work of God.[12]

Although Paul characterizes his message in a variety of ways here ["repentance towards God and faith toward our Lord Jesus" (20:21); "the gospel of God's grace" (20:24); "the kingdom" (20:25); "the whole purpose of God"

---

9 See Robert Tannehill, *The Narrative Unity of Luke-Acts* (Minneapolis: Augsburg Fortress, 1990) vol. 2, p. 253. All of my citations of Tannehill are from volume 2. In the future I will simply cite page numbers.

10 For a recent discussion of the centrality of the "plan of God" to Luke-Acts see, John T. Squires, *The Plan of God in Luke-Acts* (Cambridge: C.U.P, 1993).

11 Richard Pervo in *Profit with Delight: The Literary Genre of the Acts of the Apostles* (Minneapolis: Augsburg Fortress, 1987), p. 68 feels that up until now, Paul has suffered relatively little. Instead he has known astonishing success. He claims that here Luke simply desires to create a sense of pathos. Pervo's claim obscures the fact that Paul could suffer personally [cf. 13:50; 14:19; (the characterization of the Jerusalem council in) 15:26; 16:22ff. etc.] without really compromising the success of his mission.

12 Further evidence of God's providential care of believers is the raising up of these very elders as overseers of God's flock (20:28).

(20:27); "the word of God's grace" (20:32)], he is primarily interested in characterizing the manner in which he proclaimed his message to the Ephesians.[13] Beyond this, however, there is little defense or elaboration of the content of the message.[14] Paul does, however, portray his life among the Ephesians as a way of supporting the truth of his message. He recalls for them the fact that he was not a financial burden on the Ephesians (20:33). He did not preach good news to them for a living. His preaching had no ulterior motives.[15] In addition, Paul's support of himself allowed resources to be given to those in need (v. 35). As the Ephesians face a future in which savage wolves will attack the flock of God by distorting the truth, Paul characterizes his own ministry among them as a standard against which they can both measure their own ministry of service and measure the faithfulness of future teachers.

From Paul's characterization of himself here, it is clear that there is no easy way to separate the truth of the message from the character of the messenger. Paul characterizes his life with an eye toward forming the Ephesians to be faithful followers of his own life and teaching in his absence.[16]

The other occasions on which Luke's Paul gives an account of himself are all situations in which Paul is defending himself before authorities. While there are obvious differences between these passages, they are not substantial enough for my purposes to warrant individual treatments of chapters 22, 24 and 26.

Paul describes his speech in Acts 22 as an ἀπολογία (v. 1); in chapter 24 he uses the verb ἀπολογοῦμαι (v. 10); in 26:2 we find ἀπολογεῖσθαι. While the Roman authorities are the ones who ultimately sit in judgment, the accusers are Jews. Paul's characterization of himself is framed by Jewish accusations, particularly in chapters 22 and 26. As a result, Paul goes to great lengths to characterize himself as a faithful and loyal Jew (cf. 22:3-5; 26:4-11).[17] Even when he characterizes himself before Felix in chapter 24 Paul asserts that he "worships the God of our ancestors," believing in the things written in the law, the prophets and the writings (24:14). He aims "to keep a clear conscience

---

13 This may be what Ernst Haenchen means when he claims that the speech does not aim to convey theology at all [see *The Acts of the Apostles* (Philadelphia: Westminster, 1971), p. 597].

14 Paul's defensive comment in v. 26 that he is innocent of the blood of anyone is based on the fact that he declared the "whole purpose of God" to the Ephesians. If Tannehill is right the whole purpose is reflected in the fact that Paul proclaimed a message to both Jews and Greeks. By including all he is innocent of the blood of some. See Tannehill, p. 257.

15 There seem to be numerous parallels here to the way Paul characterizes his ministry in 1 Thess.2:1-12.

16 While Tannehill (p. 259) notes numerous echoes here between Paul's impending fate in Jerusalem and Jesus' passion announcements in Luke, Paul does not draw these parallels himself. He characterizes himself, not Jesus as an example for the Ephesians (see also Haenchen, p. 596, and Brawley, p. 104 for this same point). For further accounts of the parallels between Paul and other characters in Luke-Acts see D. Moessner, "Paul and the Pattern of the Prophet Like Moses" and Glenn R. Jacobson, "Paul in Luke-Acts: The Savior is Present" both in *Society of Biblical Literature 1983 Seminar Papers*, ed. K. H. Richards (Chico, Scholars Press, 1983) pp. 203-212 and 131-146 respectively.

17 See the comments of Beverly Gaventa in *From Darkness to Light: Aspects of Conversion in the New Testament* (Philadelphia: Fortress, 1986), chapter 2. See also Tannehill, pp. 270ff.

before God" (24:16). Although couched in terms an educated non-Jew would understand, Paul is asserting his faithfulness to Judaism. One of the ways Paul uses to portray his faithfulness is to note that he was a persecutor of Christians (22:4 ff., 26:9 ff.). Paul portrays this aspect of his life in a rather matter of fact way. He does not express remorse. Rather, it is a badge of his diligent adherence to the truth of God as he then saw it.

Paul's characterization of himself here in these three defensive contexts seems to have a dual rhetorical aim. On the one hand he wishes to make it clear that he was and still is a faithful Jew. He has broken neither Roman nor Jewish law. Hence, the charges brought against him are baseless.[18] On the other hand, he also wants to convince his audience that the only way to account for his transformation from persecutor to witness is by assenting to his claims about the resurrected Christ. As Tannehill notes,

> The old Paul and his audience are alike in their understanding of what loyalty to the God of Israel implies. Because of this common beginning point, Paul's autobiography is particularly relevant to the audience he is addressing. Paul's narration of the radical change that took place in his life is an invitation to present persecutors to reevaluate Paul and Jesus and thereby be changed themselves. (p. 279)

This point is not lost on King Agrippa, nor does Paul deny that this is his ultimate aim (26:28 ff.).

Paul portrays himself as a faithful defender of the truth of God, devoted to the law and the prophets and more committed than most of his contemporaries. This commitment and devotion is channelled in a new direction when he encounters the resurrected Christ. Prior to his conversion Paul characterizes himself as an independent, though faithful agent. He controls his own actions. From the time he encounters the resurrected Christ on the road to Damascus Paul presents himself as someone who is called and acted upon.[19] First, Ananias restores Paul's sight for him. Then we find out that God has set aside things for him to do (22:10). Rather than be a defender of the truth, he is to become a witness of it (22:14-15, 18; 26:16, 22). As Paul tells it, he has been incorporated into God's story, a story which he now sees as having a basis in the history of the people of Israel, which has its climax in the death and resurrection of Jesus and which is leading to the incorporation of the Gentiles into the people of God (22:15, 21; 26:22 ff.). Without question Paul sees himself as having a significant role to play in this divine drama. By characterizing his life as he does in these chapters, however, Paul makes it

---

18 It seems odd to deny that there is some apologetic element in these speeches. The real issue is how this function fits in with other ways in which these speeches function. For a recent statements of the apologetic function of these speeches see Jerome Neyrey "The Forensic Defense Speech and Paul's Trial Speeches in Acts 22-26: Form and Function" in *Luke-Acts: New Perspectives from the Society of Biblical Literature Seminar,* ed. Charles H. Talbert (New York: Crossroad, 1984, 210-224; John T. Carroll, "Literary and Social Dimensions of Luke's Apology for Paul" *Society of Biblical Literature 1988 Seminar Papers,* ed. David J. Lull (Atlanta: Scholars Press, 1988), pp.106-118.

19 Gaventa, *From Darkness to Light,* p. 76, accounts for the differences between the story of Paul's conversion in chapter 22 from the account in chapter 9 in this way: "Instead of the 'overthrow of the enemy' we have in Acts 22 'the call of the faithful Jew'."

clear that it is not a role he could have anticipated, nor is it a role he could have chosen himself. He had to be acted upon by God. Even then, his opportunities to be a witness are the result of divine aid (26:22).

Luke's Paul characterizes himself as one who initially found his direction and coherence by participating in a story of conquest which moved in a seemingly irresistible path from Jerusalem towards Damascus. Paul's participation in this story is terminated by his experience of the resurrected Christ. In this respect Luke's Paul's Paul puts much more explicit emphasis on the Damascus road experience than the Paul of the epistles.[20] This experience transformed Paul. After his encounter with Christ Paul's life found its direction and coherence as part of a new story of conquest, albeit of a very different sort. Paul is transformed by the place and role he is given to occupy in the unfolding story of the gospel. The manner in which this larger story is told shapes and is shaped by the way Luke's Paul characterizes himself.[21]

For example, Paul characterizes himself in a manner that fits within one of the central movements of the plot of Acts, the triumphant expansion of the gospel from Jerusalem to Rome. While the character Paul has a definite particularity, he is also a cog in a larger machine. Indeed, in all of Paul's accounts of himself he notes the fact that he is part of a larger plan which God initiated and continues to oversee. Neither Jewish opposition, nor Roman bureaucracy and corruption, nor even forces of nature can stand in his way once he has set his face toward Rome. Paul must end up in Rome. We have been told this by Paul himself in 19:21. It is reconfirmed by a heavenly vision in 23:11 and it is where the narrative comes to its end in chapter 28.

Because Paul's story of himself in Acts is told as a part of Luke's story of the movement of the gospel, Luke's Paul's Paul has a very different view of his sufferings and the opposition he faces from the view we will find in Galatians and Philippians. Luke generally, and Luke's Paul in particular, has an unfailing confidence in God's providence. Paul's imprisonment, persecutions, arrest, and shipwreck are simply seen as hurdles placed by Satan in the way of the gospel which are to be overcome. Paul is forewarned of the rejection he will face in Jerusalem (20:23; 21:11). When this actually happens, it does not raise questions about Paul's message and mission. Instead the Lord informs Paul (and us) that this is all part of the divine plan to get the gospel to Rome (23:11). There is no sense in which Paul has to address questions about his status or his message based on the fact that he suffers persecution and opposition. The Maltese quickly judge him to be a malefactor when he is bitten by a viper. Within the space of a verse, however, they are convinced he is a god when he shows no ill effects from his bite (28:5-6). Paul's appeal to the emperor, which initially saves him from a plot by the Jews, keeps him in prison when he should be set free. Even this is not seen as a problem. It

---

20 See Gaventa's comments on this difference on p. 92 of *From Darkness to Light.*

21 I agree with Brawley, p. 96, that one should avoid reducing character to plot. I think, however, he goes too far when he claims, "the individuated Paul transcends the narrative as if he existed independently from it" (p.103). As Paul characterizes himself in Acts it is clear that after encountering the resurrected Christ he has no self without the narrative of God's actions provided by Acts.

provides both opportunity for authorities to proclaim Paul's innocence (26:30) and the mechanism to get Paul on his way to Rome.

It is not simply the case that Luke's Paul has an unshakable confidence in God's providential care. Because of the aims of the narrative and Paul's place in it, Luke's Paul does not have to address seriously those who would see the opposition and persecution Paul faces as signs of the unworthiness of Paul and his message. Luke's narrative of God's providential oversight of the Christian mission not only gives direction and coherence to the narrative's paradigmatic missionary, Paul, it also provides a particular perspective from which Paul can characterize his own persecutions and tribulations. The way Luke tells the larger story of God's maintenance and spread of the gospel provides a particular perspective from which Luke's Paul can characterize his own tribulations. It is Luke's construction of this perspective that provides one of the most striking differences between Luke's Paul's Paul and Paul's Paul.

Paul's Paul: Gal.1:10-2:21

In the course of his epistles Paul comments on himself and his work at numerous points. The two most substantial presentations of Paul's Paul are Gal.1:10 ff. and Phil.3:2ff. I will look at each of these in turn.

It is tempting to read Paul's account of himself in Gal.1:10ff. as part of an overall apologetic strategy. On such a reading Paul, like the Paul of Acts 22-26, renders his character in a primarily defensive context. Instead of the more formal legal atmosphere of Acts, Paul in Galatians is defending his apostleship against opponents who do not recognize him (or his message) as the equal of someone like Peter.[22]

In a recent essay, however, Beverly Gaventa has challenged this way of reading Gal 1-2.[23] The thrust of her challenge against the apologetic reading of these chapters is that reading them in this light largely divorces them from the theological argument of the rest of the epistle.[24] As a result of being cut loose from the rhetorical unity of the epistle, these chapters have largely been mined for information about the earliest stages of the Christian movement.[25]

As an alternative Gaventa proposes a reading of these chapters in which the autobiographical comments of Gal.1-2 can be seen as the implicit basis for the theological argument which follows. "Paul employs events out of his past, events that have to do with the exclusive nature of the gospel's claim on his own life, to urge that same exclusive claim on the Christians in Galatia."[26]

---

[22] Lyons devotes an entire chapter to reviewing and rejecting the reasons for this view.

[23] See "Galatians 1 and 2: Autobiography as Paradigm." Although Gaventa's work and Lyons work are contemporaneous, and although Lyons work is more substantial in terms of length and material covered, I find Gaventa's constructive proposal for reading Galatians more persuasive. I find that the real merit of Lyons' work lies in the scholarly consensus which he upsets rather than his own constructive account.

[24] Although Lyons does not accept the view that Galatians 1-2 is apologetic, he is not particularly interested in relating chapters 1-2 to chapters 3-4 other than to note that it sounds the call to imitate Paul in 4:12-20.

[25] See Gaventa, "Galatians 1 and 2," pp. 311-12.

[26] Gaventa, "Galatians 1 and 2," p. 313.

Based on Gaventa's reading of the passage, I think one can develop some important insights into Paul's pattern of characterizing himself.

From the opening paragraphs of the epistle, it is clear that Paul is committed to the notion that there is only one gospel (1:6-7). Nothing Paul might say subsequently, nothing said by an angel from heaven, can alter this state of affairs.[27] It is this notion of a singular gospel which Paul both proclaims and to which he subjects himself (1:8) that drives Paul's argument against those who are not simply preaching another gospel, but are perverting the one gospel of Christ (1:7).[28]

Having said this, Paul wants to be sure that the Galatians understand that the gospel he proclaims is not *his* gospel. Rather, it has been given to him by God. Paul presents himself to the Galatians as one whose self has been de-centered by God. This theological claim works rhetorically to allow the divine origin of Paul's gospel to shine through with all of its clarity. In 2:20 he goes so far as to say that, because he has been crucified with Christ, he no longer lives; rather Christ lives in him (cf. 6:14). This comes as no surprise when it is remembered that from conception God set Paul, like Isaiah (Isa. 49:1) and Jeremiah (Jer. 1:5), apart for a special task (1:15). Paul's de-centered self is thus able to view his gospel and his mission as a gift (2:9) rather than his own construction. Like the Paul we find in Luke, the Paul of Galatians wants to be seen, at least in part as an instrument of God's gracious activity. Indeed, as Paul relates it, this is the view of Paul held by those in Judea who had not seen him but had heard that "the one who formerly was persecuting us is now proclaiming the faith he once tried to destroy" (1:23). God, not Paul, receives the glory for this transformation (1:24).[29]

A self which has been de-centered by God in this way cannot simply be characterized in the service of autobiographical ends. Rather, Paul characterizes himself in ways that primarily say something about God. In fact one can go further and say that Paul's characterization of himself here presupposes a narrative about God's activity in Christ in which he presumes both he and the Galatians participate. Without the presumption of this narrative a phrase like "I have been crucified with Christ" is unintelligible.[30] In characterizing himself in a particular way here Paul is implicitly fitting the story of his life into the larger story of the crucified and risen Christ in such a way that this story is seen to be the center of Paul's self.

A de-centered self, however, is not a self devoid of particularity. On the contrary, it is only because Paul's self is now located in a narrative of God's action in Christ, that he can characterize the particular details of his past as he does. This particularity is crucial to Paul's character. Paul was the most zealous

---

27 See John Howard Schütz, *Paul and the Anatomy of Apostolic Authority* (Cambridge: C.U.P., 1975), p. 118 ff.; Gaventa, "Galatians 1 and 2," p. 314.

28 This is against Lyons, p. 128, who does not think Paul is as concerned with the possibility of another gospel as with characterizing those proclaiming this "other" gospel and "troublemakers" etc.

29 See Schütz, p. 136, who quotes Chrysostom as noting that Paul does not say that "they marveled at me, they praised me, they were struck with admiration of me, but he attributes all to grace."

30 Hays, pp. 5ff. makes similar comments about Paul's claims in Galatians.

of Jews. He notes his persecution of the Church as a mark of his unparalleled advancement in Judaism (1:13). With no obvious transition, Paul then goes on to relate that God revealed his son to him so that Paul might evangelize the Gentiles. This dramatic reversal transforms Paul's past into a "negative mission directed against rather than for the Church."[31] What remains consistent in Paul's portrayal of himself is his zeal. It is now, however, rightly directed.[32]

It is important to note, however, that although Paul plays on the temporal distinction between his past and his present in 1:10-2:21,[33] Paul's characterization of himself is not simply a juxtaposition of before and after snapshots. Paul's view of his past is also transformed. Indeed, the very ability to talk in terms of a definable point before which Paul can talk about a former time radically distinct from his present is only enabled by the transformation of his past. Further, some of Paul's characterizations of his past are only possible from the perspective of his transforming experience of Christ. For example, prior to his encounter with the resurrected Christ he could not have characterized his actions as "persecuting the church of God" (1:13).[34] Instead, perhaps, he would have said that he was punishing blasphemers.

As Paul moves on from that transforming experience of the resurrected Christ in 1:18ff. he characterizes himself largely through accounts of how others recognized and responded to the life and message of the persecutor turned proclaimer. As 1:24 makes clear, it is still God who is glorified as the source of Paul's transformation. There is, however, also the emphasis on the fact that Paul himself—in the particularity of his life and mission—is recognized as a faithful proclaimer of the one gospel. Indeed, Paul is at pains to stress his independence from the apostles in Jerusalem. At the same time, citing the fact that the "pillars" of the Jerusalem church approved of his message and mission certainly supports Paul's claim to be an expositor of the one true gospel.

In 2:11ff. Paul continues to characterize himself in terms of his relations to others. This time, however, it is in the context of his confrontation with Peter in Antioch. Coming immediately after Paul has recounted his reception by the Jerusalem apostles, this passage further emphasizes Paul's personal integrity and consistency as a proclaimer of the one gospel in contrast to Peter (and Barnabas). It is important to remember that the primary accusation against Peter here is not bad theology, but hypocrisy (2:13). Peter and the others are "not walking along the straight path of the truth of the gospel" (2:14). As Schütz notes, by phrasing the issue in this way the conflict is not between two conflicting apostles, but about whether or not Peter will submit to

---

[31] Schütz, p. 133.

[32] Presumably Paul could have characterized his past as he characterizes other Jews in Rom. 10:2 as "having zeal for God, but without knowledge."

[33] Lyons, pp. 146-152, nicely displays the "formerly-now" contrast in Galatians. He does not, however, recognize that Paul's account of former things has also been transformed through his encounter with Christ.

[34] While Paul could not have said certain things about his past apart from his transforming experience of Christ, I think it distorts Paul's discourse to try to reduce it to an explication of his Damascus Road experience as Seyoon Kim does in *The Origin of Paul's Gospel* (Grand Rapids: Eerdmans, 1981).

the independent authority of the gospel as Paul has done.[35] In characterizing Peter in this way Paul is indirectly characterizing himself as one who maintains the singularity of the gospel in word and deed. This passage nicely points out a dual focus in Paul's characterization of himself here in Galatians. On the one hand, he is a selfless, servant of God, subject to the truth of the gospel. On the other hand, the particularities of this situation and Paul's specific response to it are to be instructive for the Galatians. I will mention more about this dual focus in a moment.

As Paul's characterization of himself has moved from Galatians 1 into chapter 2 there is a subtle shift of emphasis from Paul's characterization of himself to a characterization of his message. As presented in Galatians (in contrast perhaps to Phil.1:15-17), there is no clear distinction to be made between Paul's character and the gospel he proclaims. "In a sense all that the apostle does is a reflection of what the gospel does; all that he is, is a reflection of what the gospel is."[36] This blurring of the differences between Paul and his message is in part accomplished by Paul characterizing himself as one whose self has been de-centered by God. By presenting himself as an example of what God graciously has done, Paul blurs his personal particularities in a way that makes him an instrument for God's use, a messenger who is subjected to the message.

At the same time, however, Paul wants the Galatians to "become as I am" (4:12). Paul wants the Galatians to see him as an example of what the one true gospel can do, and what that gospel demands.[37] Their zeal for the law ought to be transformed into zeal for God's grace in the same way that Paul's life has been transformed. "To become as Paul is means to allow Christ to live in oneself (cf. 2:20) to the exclusion of the Law or any other tradition or category."[38] This demand requires the particular account that Paul has given of himself. For the demand to "become as I am" to have any bite at all requires a specific "I" (Paul), an "I" which has had a particular experience of God and which stands in a certain relationship to other specific characters, a character who can characterize himself as Paul does. In other words, for the Galatians to become as Paul is they will both have to consider the narrative of Christ's work which is to occupy the center of their selves, and they will have to fit their particular stories into Christ's story in a manner analogous to the way Paul has embedded his particular story into Christ's in such a way that he no longer lives, but Christ lives in him.

As Paul characterizes himself in Gal.1-2 he seeks to balance two potentially competing interests. On the one hand, he is unwilling to say anything about himself which would compromise his conviction that he is who he now is solely on the basis of God's grace, a grace operative in his life from conception. It is this notion which leads him to claim "it is no longer I who

---

35 "The charge of hypocrisy leveled at Peter accuses him of acting inconsistently, out of accord with an authority he himself means to recognize" Schütz, p. 152. See also Bengt Holmberg, *Paul and Power* (Philadelphia: Fortress, 1975), p. 32.

36 Schütz, p. 232; see also Gaventa, "Galatians 1 and 2" p. 317.

37 See Gaventa, "Galatians 1 and 2" pp. 314, 319ff; also Lyons, pp. 164-168.

38 Gaventa, "Galatians 1 and 2" p. 322; see also Richard Hays, "Christology and Ethics in Galatians: The Law of Christ" *CBQ* 49 (1987), pp. 280ff.

live but Christ who lives in me" (2:20). On the other hand, in seeking to persuade the Galatians to change certain aspects of their faith and practice, he portrays the specificities of his own life as exemplary for the Galatians. To weight one side of this balance too heavily is to risk obliterating Paul's self, thus robbing it of its moral and theological force as an exemplar. To put too much weight on the other side is to risk the view that Paul's transformation and, hence, his gospel, is the work of his own zeal and self-discipline. This would, of course, undermine his claims about his apostleship, about the singularity of his gospel, and his characterization of himself as one who pleases God rather than humans. Achievement of such a balance is, of course, always precarious. Nevertheless, given the ends for which Paul portrays himself in Galatians it would seem that for Paul, it is not simply a literary and rhetorical, but also a moral and theological, achievement to be able persuasively to characterize oneself in this way.[39]

Paul's Paul: Phil.3:2-17

When Paul comes to characterize himself to the Philippians, he moves away from this attempt at striking a balance between grace and the exemplary particularity of his own life. Instead he adopts a much more ironic tone. In the early part of the epistle Paul has presented a sustained argument of how the Philippians are to "live in a manner worthy of the gospel of Christ" (1:27) in the face of opposition. This manner of life will entail suffering for the Philippians (1:28). Remaining united in their faith in the gospel and their self-giving love for each other will, however, result in their salvation. This argument is given its direction and force from the narrative about the suffering and exalted Christ presented in 2:6-11.[40] As chapter 3 begins Paul launches a polemical attack against those who would propose a different view of how the Philippians should respond to their situation. Those proposing this alternative way of life do not accept (among other things) Paul's notion that walking in a manner worthy of the gospel of Christ may entail suffering. Paul ultimately comes to call these people enemies of the cross of Christ (3:18).[41]

Paul begins his attack in 3:2 with some strong invective against his opponents. He calls them dogs, malicious workers and mutilators of the flesh. All of these seem to be designed to belittle claims to virtue made by Paul's opponents.[42] In short, "Their glory is their shame" (3:19). These opponents seem to have been Jewish Christian missionaries (ἐργάται) who boasted of

---

[39] Of course, we do not know whether and to what extent Paul actually persuaded the churches in Galatia. It would seem, however, that Augustine saw his Confessions as engaged in a similar sort of balancing act.

[40] See Fowl, chapters 3-4 for comments on the exegetical details of these passages.

[41] It is interesting to note that in Philippians the issue concerns the implications of the gospel. Paul does not need to fight any battles over the singularity of the gospel as in Galatians.

[42] See, for example, Andrew Lincoln's discussion of these terms in *Paradise Now and Not Yet* (Cambridge: C.U.P., 1981), p. 89.

spiritual attainments as in 2 Corinthians.[43] From Paul's comments in vv. 4 ff. it seems that the opponents' claim to spiritual superiority came from keeping the Law to perfection. Their aim would have been for the Philippians to strive after similar spiritual superiority through rigorous adherence to the law, and thus avoid or transcend persecution.

Against this background, Paul characterizes his own life in 3:4ff. As in Galatians, Paul begins by recounting his zeal and incomparable achievement as a Jew. Again, persecution of the Church is seen as a mark of Paul's devotion to God. The achievements in Judaism, of which Paul's opponents boast, are matched and superseded by Paul's own life.

While Acts repeatedly expounds an account of Paul's vision of the resurrected Christ, and Galatians at least touches on this event, it is omitted entirely in Paul's characterization of himself here in Philippians. Rather than a transforming experience of the resurrected Christ, what is crucial for Paul here is a transformation in his perceptions about the ends toward which he should order his life. Presumably this was not a transformation that can be as easily identified with a single event. What is crucial here in Philippians is how Paul considers (see the various occurrences of ἡγέομαι in vv. 7-8) his past and his present direction (λογίζομαι is used in v. 13).[44] What he used to consider to be the manner of life worthy of a follower of God is now rubbish. What he previously considered worthy of persecution now provides the *telos* of his life. Clearly, this new *telos* is not simply a mental ideal. Paul's new perspective is not simply an internal state. It both demands action and provides a standard for shaping one's life so that one "can live in a manner worthy of the gospel of Christ." Ironically, however, the manner of life issuing from this new perspective involves suffering. As Paul explains it, this *telos* provides him with power and a place in the eschatological resurrection of the dead, but, most immediately, it also entails a fellowship with Christ's sufferings (3:11).

Here we have a sharp contrast between Luke's Paul's Paul and the Paul rendered in Philippians. In Acts Paul encounters persecution and various trials. This Paul, however, is able to fit them and himself into an ongoing story of God's providential supervision of the gospel. In Acts Paul never gives any hint that his tribulations are anything more than Satan's futile attempts to inhibit the triumph of the gospel.[45] In Philippians Paul views suffering, and his suffering in particular, as an ironic byproduct of "knowing Christ and the

---

43 See Helmut Koester "The Purpose of the Polemic of a Pauline Fragment" *NTS* 8 (1961-62), p. 321.

44 It seems to me now that there are more connections here both to Paul's demand to φρονεῖτε in a particular way in 2:5 and the manner in which Christ considered (ἡγήσατο) his position ἐν μορφῇ Θεοῦ than I indicated in my criticisms of Morna Hooker's work on this passage [See *The Story of Christ in the Ethics of Paul* (p. 77 n. 1)]. I am still convinced that these connections, however, are not the ones Hooker mentions.

45 Pervo, repeatedly describes this pattern, sometimes calling it a theology of glory (see pp. 24, 27, 74, 137-138). Tannehill, p. 271, takes issue with Pervo but not in a convincing way. I think if Pervo had been less flippant about matters related to Paul's sufferings and tribulations it would have largely mitigated Tannehill's criticisms without blunting Pervo's main point, which seems uncontroversial.

power of his resurrection" (3:10).[46] The humiliations suffered in this life are real, and the threat they pose to the Christians in Philippi are serious; they will, however, be transformed at some future point when all things are subjected to Christ (3:21). In more traditional terms, the Paul of Acts fits himself into a theology of glory; the Paul of Philippians now considers his life from the viewpoint of a theology of the cross. This cruciform perspective allows Paul the ironic distance he needs to view his early achievements as "rubbish" and his present sufferings as part of faithful participation in Christ's resurrection, a participation which is ongoing, awaiting completion (3:12).[47]

As with Galatians, Paul presents himself, and the transformation of perspective he has achieved, as exemplary for the Philippians (3:17ff.). Unlike in Galatians, Paul does not go to such great pains to present him self as one who has been de-centered by God. Without question, Paul recognizes that he is who he is by God's grace. In 3:12 he notes that his transformed perspective, his new *telos* is the result of Christ's prior work. Paul can only make this perspective his own (καταλάβω) because Christ first made Paul his own (κατελήμφθη). Nevertheless, in Philippians Paul does not persistently de-center himself at the same time that he tries to provides a character substantial and particular enough to be exemplary.[48] Instead he presents himself as one who has had his perspective on himself and the world transformed through his knowledge of Christ. It is this transformation which he hopes the Philippians will also attain. Such a perspective will allow them, like Paul, to have the ironic distance needed to view both "fleshly" achievements and temporal sufferings as insignificant in the light of the glory that awaits them.[49]

Summary of Differences and Points of Continuity

Like those who have read these passages for historical information, I have noted several differences between Paul's characterizations of himself in Acts and Paul's characterizations of himself in these two epistles. These are differences of a different sort, however. By way of summary I will note some of the differences I found to be most significant as well as some more general comments about the practice of characterizing. First, Paul's characterizations of himself in Acts are not ultimately Paul's. Paul is simply one character rendered by Luke in his narrative. In Acts Paul characterizes himself in a manner consistent with the aims of the larger narrative. This results in a Paul who stresses his role in the ongoing story of God's dealings with the people of Israel. Given the boundless confidence in God's providence prominent in Acts, it is not surprising that Paul characterizes himself, and the trials he

---

[46] Paul does not directly characterize his sufferings in Gal.1-2, but when he does note them in 6:11ff., he also adopts an ironic perspective, "boasting in the cross of Christ."

[47] This ironic perspective is both clearer and more pointedly polemical in 2Cor.11.

[48] This may be due to the more heated nature of his relationship with the churches in Galatia, as Gaventa proposes, p. 322.

[49] An ironic perspective is not all they will need. Paul also grounds his demands for a manner of life worthy of the gospel of Christ on a very particular narration of the Christ event in 2:6-11.

encounters, in the light of this providence. Finally, Paul's characterization of himself in Acts is primarily apologetic. It is designed to convince friend and foe alike that he is not a threat to the established order, that he is a trustworthy messenger of the gospel and that God will continue to see to the triumphal spread of that gospel.

Paul's characterization of himself in Galatians and Philippians is not part of a literary narrative as in Acts. As such it is not constrained by larger considerations of plot and relationships to other characters and events in the narrative. On the other hand, Paul presumes that both he and his audience participate in a narrative of God's activity in Christ. In Philippians this narrative comes to expression in 2:6-11 but is also presupposed elsewhere (e.g., 3:10-11). In Galatians this narrative can be inferred from the argument of epistle. While neither of these narratives is available to us in anything like the detail of Acts, we have enough detail to see that Luke and Paul are telling the story of God's activity differently. Luke's narrative is one of providentially guided success. Paul's narrative stresses the cross of Christ and the demands implicit in being a disciple of the crucified one. Because all of these texts characterize Paul in ways that fit Paul into these larger narratives, they inevitably characterize Paul differently.

This difference is most sharply seen by comparing Luke's Paul's perspective on his own sufferings and the perspective of the Paul of Philippians. The Paul rendered in Philippians, and to a lesser degree in Galatians, has a much more ironic perspective on past achievements and on his present sufferings than the Paul of Acts. Paul's commitment in Philippians to viewing his past, present and future from the perspective of one who not only participates in the power of the resurrected Christ, but also shares in Christ's sufferings, cannot treat sufferings as small barriers before the juggernaut of the gospel. Rather, they represent real humiliations which are to be transformed. From the perspective of the cross, what Paul had considered achievements are ironically seen as rubbish. Even in the context of Galatians, it is only the fact that Paul's self has been de-centered in favor of participation in Christ that he can characterize his past as he does.

Another relative difference between Acts and the epistles is related to the fact that in Galatians and Philippians Paul is at pains to characterize himself in certain specific ways so that his convictions, perspectives and practices can be exemplary for his audience.[50] A narrowly conceived literary or rhetorical approach to characterization can tend either to gloss or leave undeveloped the moral importance attached to Paul's characterization of himself in the epistles. Simply noting what Paul says about himself and how he says it will fail to account for what is at stake morally and theologically in characterizing oneself one way rather than another.

Given these differences one may be tempted to ask which of these characters (if any) is the "real" Paul? We may be tempted to privilege the Paul

---

[50] The obvious exception here is Acts 20:35. This hardly matches the scope of either Galatians of Philippians. Further, one might claim that Acts 26:29 presents Paul as a sort of exemplar for Agrippa, Bernice and even Festus. The chief difference between Acts and the epistles in this respect is that the Galatians and the Philippians already have responded to the gospel. For them, Paul is an example internal to the body of Christ in a way he cannot be for Agrippa and the others.

of the epistles on the grounds that these are really Paul's accounts of himself rather than accounts that are ultimately dependent on Luke. This is a temptation we should resist. There is no *a priori* reason for preferring the account one gives of oneself to the accounts others might give. In fact, human tendencies to self-deception being what they are might lead one to tilt the scale in favor of an outsider's account. To fall prey to this question of the "real Paul" no matter how one answers it, however, is a mistake. The question presumes that there is something essential and unchanging about Paul (or anybody else) that can be separated from the contingent accounts we have of Paul, some essential core of Paul which can be distilled from the specific narratives of Paul's life which we have looked at. To engage in this quest for the real Paul is to fail to note that character can only be adequately rendered narratively.[51]

Characterizing a person is a narrative achievement. That is, to render a character, one must fit that character into a narrative sequence of actions.[52] This is not to say that one cannot characterize someone or oneself in a single, non-narrative remark. Think, for example, of the characterization "Paul is an apostle." This remark, while not a narrative in itself, presupposes a narratable sequence of events which both display what an apostle is and which involve this character Paul in ways that result in the non-narrative judgment that Paul is an apostle. Failure to provide such a narrative when required would lead one to consider this characterization of Paul unintelligible, incorrect or the result of devious motives. (Of course, all of these judgments would require narrative display as well.)

In addition, the claim that the practice of characterization presupposes the ability to narrate is not to say that the narrative always stays the same. Clearly, in all of the cases I have examined Paul is an excellent example of someone who revises the narrative he tells about himself. No matter how revisable or unstable the narrative, an intelligible character can only adequately result from narration.[53]

Further, to recognize that characterization is a narrative achievement is also to recognize that characterization is always a contestable practice. To order events in a particular way, to endow them with specific significance, to begin at a certain place and end in another, to embed the life of a character within a larger story all reflect decisions which could be made otherwise.[54] All of this is to say that one may be able to articulate standards by which one characterization is seen to be better than another, but there is no intelligible way to claim that one characterization captures the "real" Paul.

---

[51] This point is not original to me. Alasdair MacIntyre, Charles Taylor and Stanley Hauerwas have all made similar claims. For my remarks here I will rely on MacIntyre's account in *After Virtue*, 2nd ed. (Notre Dame: U. of Notre Dame Press, 1984).

[52] This is also true of the characterizations I have given of Paul's characterizations of himself.

[53] So MacIntyre, pp. 216ff.

[54] This is a point MacIntyre makes in *After Virtue*, pp. 212-213. In this section MacIntyre is attacking historians like Louis Mink who seek to deny the epistemological importance of narrative for historiography. See, for example, Mink's "History and Fiction as Modes of Comprehension" *New Literary History* 1 (1970), pp. 541-558.

In that sense, discussions of character inevitably invite, and, when possible, require an exercise of comparative characterization. Further, I have suggested, at least in the case of Paul, that such an exercise is not only a literary and enterprise. It is also moral and theological.[55]

---

[55] I have greatly benefitted from the comments and suggestions of my colleagues Greg Jones and Jim Buckley.

Sexual Practice and the Structure of Prestige: The Case of the Disputed Concubines

Ken Stone
Vanderbilt University

Sex, Culture, and Biblical Interpretation

In recent years, there has been an increasing interest in the variable meanings that have been attributed to sexual activity. This interest has manifested itself in a variety of disciplines, including social history, anthropology, sociology, and literary criticism. In the field of Classics alone, one can speak of a new subspecialty focused upon ancient attitudes toward sexual matters (e.g., Dover 1978; Halperin 1990; Halperin et al., 1990; Keuls 1985; Winkler 1990; the work of Foucault [1978; 1985; 1986] has been an important, if controversial, stimulus to this discussion). There is even a new peer review journal titled *Journal of the History of Sexuality*, published by the University of Chicago Press, the existence of which is surely an indication of a certain academic respectability for a topic once passed over in silence.

The effects of these projects are only beginning to be recognized. However, one can already speak of shifts in the ways that sexual activity is conceptualized as an object of academic analysis. It is possible to detect the emergence of a new discourse in which "culture" has replaced "nature" as the rubric under which sexual practice is analyzed. While it was once thought that phenomena such as sexual activity, gender identity, and sexual desire were matters primarily for psychology and biology, this assumption has come under attack by those who argue that culture, society, and history are the primary matrices for the production of human subjects as sexual subjects.

Within biblical studies, issues such as these have received far less attention. There are a few studies which are both interesting and insightful, particularly in regard to the legal texts of the Hebrew Bible (e.g., Frymer-Kensky 1989; Eilberg-Schwartz 1990:141-94). These studies have tried to go beyond a simple paraphrase of the "sex laws" to uncover the system of beliefs which generated these laws. Nonetheless, the topic of sexual activity has not produced as many results in biblical studies as it has in some other disciplines.

It would be interesting to consider at length some of the factors clouding our perception of biblical attitudes toward sexual matters. There is, for example, the widely held assumption that there exists a "Judeo-Christian tradition" of sexual ethics, which can be differentiated clearly from other traditions, and which has existed with only minor modifications from the Iron Age to the present. There is the influence of religious institutions, generally conservative on sexual matters, upon biblical scholarship. Concerning the Hebrew Bible, there are the characterizations of "Canaanite fertility religion" as something close to an orgy, over against which Yahwism is supposed to have defined itself. This latter theme has played a significant role in the discourse on sex among biblical scholars, who have emphasized a link between sexual activity and "pagan" religions. The details of this picture are now coming under attack from several directions (see Lemche 1991; Hillers 1985; Oden 1987:131-53; Frymer-Kensky 1992), but it remains to be seen whether a new picture of ancient attitudes toward sexual practice will emerge.

There are also methodological problems, some of which concern literary genre. The clearest statements about sexual activity in the Hebrew Bible are found in the collections of laws. These laws make statements about sexual practice that are formulated primarily in terms of proscription and prescription: Israelites are forbidden to do this, and allowed to do that. The proscriptions are more abundant than the prescriptions, a fact which is important for evaluating the subsequent *effects* of biblical texts upon attitudes toward sex. This legal discourse has influenced the ways in which other instances of sexual language or imagery in the Hebrew Bible are explained. Biblical attitudes toward sexual activity are conceptualized by biblical scholars primarily in terms of forbidden and permitted behavior. Biblical narratives in which sexual scenes occur are sometimes treated as if they intended to illustrate the "proscriptive/prescriptive" attitude toward sexual practice which finds expression in the legal texts. One character's sexual actions are explained on the basis of this law, another character's sexual actions are explained on the basis of that law.

Yet the sex laws may have only a limited relevance for the interpretation of a particular biblical narrative. Although it is important to know that a particular act is forbidden or permitted by the religious authorities of a culture, the *meaning* of sex cannot be reduced to the question of the specific proscriptions and prescriptions which build up around it. It is not enough to know that a particular act is forbidden. One must also ask to whom it is forbidden, and by whom, and why, and under what circumstances, and with what exceptions, and what range of symbolic associations might be triggered by its commission. A host of variables can determine the meaning of a sexual act in any particular context. The meaning of sex is *multi-dimensional*, and goes far beyond "ethics" as traditionally understood.

Of course, it is one thing to acknowledge the multiple meanings which sexual practice can trigger. It is quite another thing to suggest, in reference to any particular text, a plausible interpretation of the sexual events that take place. We have relatively little evidence about the range of attitudes which were actually held in ancient Israel on sexual matters. Even the laws may have more to do with the purity concerns of priests than with conventional assumptions about sexual practice.

The remainder of this paper will consider the network of assumptions within which certain biblical narratives dealing with sexual matters seem to make sense. I will focus upon one particular sort of story, which I have called "the case of the disputed concubines." I do not assume that the results of my analysis are applicable to all other biblical texts that deal with sexual practice. However, I do believe that the sorts of questions which I will raise are relevant to a wider range of texts than those upon which I shall concentrate.

The approach that I will utilize here might be called an "anthropological reading." Such an approach joins two terms which appear most frequently in different sorts of projects within contemporary biblical criticism. "Reading" is a term associated with currents of literary criticism. "Anthropology" is associated with approaches to the history of Israel that integrate models and insights from the social sciences. Several scholars have argued that an exploration of the relations between these two approaches remains one of the most important tasks facing biblical scholarship (e.g. Gottwald 1985; Jobling 1991). I will not attempt to "solve" this problem here. However, I suggest that an emphasis upon "reading" as the site of the production of a text's meaning does not rule out the use of anthropological discourse by biblical scholars. On the contrary, it is precisely by focusing upon reading procedures that we can come to a better assessment of the ways in which anthropology might inform our work on biblical literature (see also Wilson 1984:1-8).

As biblical scholars are generally aware, meaning can only be determined in relation to some sort of context. But the context in terms of which a text is read is itself always the result of a prior reading, an interpretation of particular data deemed relevant by the interpreter. There are as many contexts as there are readers. Thus, a "context" is never simply there as a given, but is instead a construct with which we "frame" a text to produce a reading (see Culler 1988). The notion of "framing" is useful since it acknowledges that the contextualizing gesture is the result of our own interpretive practice. If literary scholars can acknowledge this fact about modern texts, it ought to be obvious that the situation applies even more radically to readers of ancient texts. Much of our evidence for the "context" of biblical literature comes from the very texts that the context is supposed to illuminate. Yet these texts often give little explicit information about the assumptions in terms of which they were written.

Anthropological discourse is useful for the scholar of ancient literature when it is used as a tool in the contextualizing process. By framing the text with particular insights derived from anthropology, we are able to generate meaning from the text. The issue here is not one of framing the text with anthropology versus simply reading what is on the page. On the contrary, framing is inevitable. Where stories with sexual scenes are concerned, it is only too apparent that readers have been willing to frame the texts in terms provided by their own definitions of sexual morality. However, a careful use of anthropological concepts can help us to construct and continually reassess our frames in a way that at least mitigates our tendency toward ethnocentric reading. Anthropological concepts, used judiciously, can help us to tease out certain implicit premises of the texts that we are trying to read. Since the use of anthropological discourse frequently causes us to distance ourselves from at least part of what passes as "common sense" in our own culture, such a procedure might help us to develop a reading practice which is concerned to highlight, rather than gloss over, the cultural differences between our society and that in which the biblical texts emerged. Where sexual matters are concerned, such a recognition of difference seems to be a useful, and potentially radical, enterprise.

The Case of the Disputed Concubines

The two texts which I will examine recount brief scenes in the book of 2 Samuel. Both incidents occur at moments in the narrative when Israel's kingship is in dispute. In the first case, 2 Samuel 3:6-11, David is struggling to become Saul's successor. He is opposed by Saul's surviving son, Ishbaal (cf. McCarter 1984:85-6), who in turn is aided by the military leader Abner. In the second case, 2 Samuel 16:20-22, David's kingship is itself being challenged by his own son, Absalom. Absalom is aided by Ahithophel, David's former counselor. The two stories are embedded in narratives about kingship and the public struggle for power between men. Yet in both cases, at a crucial moment in the narrative, sexual acts figure in the plot. Thus, the two texts are instances of a type of story in which sexual practice plays a role in struggles for power between male characters (Schwartz 1992; Linafelt 1992). In these two instances, the acts involve one of the male characters and a concubine, or concubines, of a king.

For my purposes, it is irrelevant whether these characters were "real" persons; or whether, if they were real persons, they actually acted in the manner described. The important point is rather that these characters, these actions, and the relations between them were capable of being conceptualized. They were "thinkable" (Bal 1988b:33), and hence, compatible on some level with someone's ideological assumptions about sexual practice. This attitude toward the historical existence of these characters is emphatically not an "ahistorical" attitude. The motivation behind my analysis is precisely the insight that beliefs about sex can be historicized. It is the ideas and premises about sexual activity whose possible historical existence interests me here.

In 2 Samuel 3, the name of the concubine is Rizpah, and she is identified as a concubine of Saul. Saul, however, is no longer alive, and the plot of 2 Samuel revolves at this point around the question, Who will take Saul's place? We are not actually told in the Masoretic text that Abner has sexual relations with Rizpah. Rather, it is Ishbaal who mentions the sexual contact in a question put to Abner in verse 7: "Why have you gone in to the concubine of my father?" We infer, retrospectively, that sexual contact has taken place. While sexual activity plays a role here, it is not in itself of great interest. Rather, its role in the narrative seems to derive from its impact upon the two men, Abner and Ishbaal, who actually appear upon the narrative stage. Rizpah does not appear at all in this section of 2 Samuel except in the discourse of Ishbaal. The narrator does not tell us about the sexual relation, but only about the conflict between two men which the sexual relation produces.

Ishbaal's question sounds more like an accusation than an expression of curiosity. Abner interprets the question this way, for he responds to it angrily. Abner points out that he has been loyal to the house of Saul, preventing it from falling to the house of David. However, now that he has been accused of a misdeed, he will change his loyalty. As a result, YHWH's promise to give the throne to David will be fulfilled. Ishbaal, afraid, does not pursue the matter further. But Abner does make a covenant with David in the wake of Ishbaal's question.

In order to make sense of this exchange, it is necessary to argue that Ishbaal makes some sort of interpretation of Abner's actions. Ishbaal has accused Abner of an offence. But if Ishbaal interprets Abner's sexual contact, then Abner's sexual activity must be seen as potentially a semiotic act, a sign of some sort for which Ishbaal has supplied a content. The problem for the modern reader is that we are uncertain about the range of meanings which might have been attributed to such a sign in ancient Israel. Although Abner's actions have a meaning for Ishbaal, this meaning is never specified and therefore must be supplied by the reader.

Biblical scholars have long recognized that assumptions about the possible functions of sexual practice are presupposed by this story. With varying degrees of success, hypotheses about these assumptions have been articulated. These hypotheses generally posit the existence of a custom whereby a successor to the throne takes as his own the harem of a previous king. The custom is supposed to explain not only this text, but also that in 2 Samuel 16:20-22, as well as 2 Samuel 12:8 and I Kings 2:13-25. A corollary of the hypothetical custom supplies a specific content for Ishbaal's accusation: if a new king takes for himself the harem of a previous king, then a man who takes the harem of a living king might in effect be claiming the throne for himself (see variously Levenson 1978:27; Levenson and Halpern 1980:508; Tsevat 1958; Ishida 1977:74; Hertzberg 1964:257; Schwartz 1992:52). Thus, Abner's act can be interpreted by Ishbaal as evidence that Abner desires the throne for himself.

This custom is not actually stated in the Hebrew Bible. It is a reading hypothesis, used by scholars to frame the texts in question so that a plausible interpretation of narrated events can be produced. Scholars who utilize this frame recognize that a knowledge of conventional premises about sex seems to have been assumed by the author(s) of these texts. They also recognize that sex has political functions in these narratives. However, it is not entirely clear, in the discourse of the commentators, why sexual relations might be considered significant for political relations. The symbolic associations involved usually remain vague.

So far as the specific interpretation of 2 Samuel 3 is concerned, the value of the hypothesis is limited by the fact that Abner does not actually seem to be aspiring to the throne. It is Abner who has made Ishbaal king over Israel (2 Sam. 2:9). To be sure, Abner's ability to do so demonstates that he is the more powerful man of the two. Abner's strength and Ishbaal's weakness are both apparent in the story. Nonetheless, when Abner is challenged by Ishbaal he does not decide to claim the throne for himself, as well he might had he been interested in doing so. On the contrary, Abner is aware that YHWH wishes to give the throne to David, and Abner decides that he will cause YHWH's wish to be fulfilled. The political fortunes of both Ishbaal and David seem to depend upon Abner's power, but the interrelations between this power, Ishbaal's accusation, and sexual contact with Rizpah are not specified.

If the story in 2 Samuel 3 gives no motive for the sexual contact, and no clear explanation for Ishbaal's reaction, 2 Samuel 16 is more informative. Here the throne of Israel is again in dispute, but the concubines involved are not associated with a dead king. The concubines are those of David, who is himself currently the king. David, fleeing Jerusalem, leaves ten concubines behind. When Absalom arrives in Jerusalem, Ahithophel advises him to have sexual relations with (literally "go in to") the concubines, so that "all Israel will hear that you have become odious" to David and "the hands of all who are with you will be strengthened" (16:21). A tent is placed upon the roof, and Absalom has sexual relations with the concubines in front of Israel.

On one level, this text is a fulfillment of YHWH's threat to David, in 2 Samuel 12:11, to take David's women and give them to David's neighbor, who will lie with them in front of Israel. However, a motivation for Absalom's actions is also supplied by Ahithophel. This motivation has two dimensions. First, by having sexual relations with the concubines, Absalom will make himself "odious" to David, as all Israel will hear. Second, those who support Absalom will be encouraged and strengthened in their task. The second motivation may be accomplished by the first: Absalom's supporters are heartened by the fact that Absalom has made himself "odious" to his father. But what, exactly, does this former motivation signify?

The term which is generally translated "become odious" refers literally to having a bad smell. The Niphal form which appears in this verse is primarily used figuratively, as seems to be the case here. Although this use is not particularly frequent, there is an important occurrence elsewhere in 2 Samuel where another subject becomes "odious" to David. In 2 Samuel 10:6 the Ammonites see that they have "become odious" or "been a stink" to David. What do they do to achieve this effect? The Ammonite king shaves the beards and cuts the skirts of David's emissaries. When the Ammonites see that, by these actions, they have "become a stink" to David, they proceed to make preparations for battle. Their actions lead to an intensification of conflict. For the moment, the intertextual link between the two stories can simply be noted; its significance will soon become apparent.

It is interesting to find that Ahithophel's words are seldom referred to when scholars account for the significance of Absalom's actions. Instead, the case is simply conflated with 2 Samuel 3 and I Kings 2 as justification for the reconstructed custom of harem possession. However, since 2 Samuel 16 is the only one of these texts which actually gives an account of the meanings involved, Ahithophel's words ought to play a more significant role in the interpretation of these passages. Ahithophel gives not so much as a hint that Absalom's action is, for example, "a state act equivalent to a declaration that the previous king is dead" (Hertzberg 1964:350). On the contrary, the king in question is explicitly the first intended recipient of the message which Absalom's actions will send. Absalom's first goal is to produce a negative effect, signified by the verb already discussed, on his father.

The meaning of Absalom's sexual practice is somewhat less ambiguous than that of Abner. We are at least aware that Absalom does intend to produce a negative effect upon his father and a positive effect upon his supporters. We know that Absalom's intercourse with the concubines is intended as a message to other men. Nevertheless, the full significance of the sexual actions involved remains unclear. We still need, as readers, some kind of grid of assumptions about the significance of various sexual actions. Some sort of frame will have to be produced by us as readers, if the text is to be contextualized and interpreted. The only question is whether we can construct a frame that is plausible, in terms of both the literary structure of the texts, and the information available to us about the range of meanings which human beings attribute, under various circumstances, to sexual practice.

One other aspect of these texts, shared in common, must be emphasized. Very little attention is given in the texts to the concubines. It is the male characters who are subjects of the verbs dealing with sexuality and, indeed, of all the other verbs as well. The concubines are represented as acted upon rather than acting. They are objects rather than subjects (cf. Bal 1988b; 1991). We do not gain any insight into their viewpoints or hear any of their words.

Now it is clearly not the case that concubines did not act sexually in ancient Israel, or that they had no perspective upon sexual practice, or that, given the chance, they would not have spoken about such matters. Yet these actions, these viewpoints, these words are absent from the narrative discourse. It is difficult to escape the conclusion that these particular texts originated from a source which was simply uninterested in such matters. The focus is rather upon the actions, viewpoints, and words of male characters. The text seems to inscribe male interests, presenting events from a perspective that is concerned almost exclusively with the male participants in sexual practice. Hence, it is important that one choose an approach which is able to analyze a discourse in terms of male-specific interests.

Constructing an Anthropological Frame

In the summary that follows, I will focus upon three theoretical notions which seem useful as interpretive tools for approaching the texts in question. These notions may be glossed as (1) the interrelation between sex, gender, and prestige structures; (2) the interrelation between a competitive notion of masculinity and a concern about female chastity; and (3) the role of the "traffic in women" in male relationships. These concepts, which overlap at numerous points, will be discussed in dialogue with anthropological discourse. I intend this summary to be suggestive rather than exhaustive. The dominant concern will be the reconstruction of possible cultural premises in terms of which a plausible reading can be defended.

(1) Sex, Gender, and the Structure of Prestige

The relation between sexual matters and the structure of prestige is emphasized by Sherry Ortner and Harriet Whitehead (Ortner and Whitehead 1981). They note that, while the realm of kinship and marriage has long been recognized as an important social context for the meanings attributed to gender and sex, the role of prestige structures in the production of such meanings has been given far less attention. Ortner and Whitehead suggest that the cultural notions in terms of which one's value and worth are analyzed, and the processes by which this analysis takes place and affects one's prestige, may be just as important in most cultures, and perhaps more important in some, for an interpretation of sex and gender. Their discussion focuses more upon gender than upon sexual activity. But this emphasis is perhaps correct, since sexual practice seems to be related to the structure of prestige through the crucial mediation of gender performance. One's prestige depends in part upon one's ability to display culturally recognized gender characteristics, including those which concern sexual activity.

Of course, gender is itself a prestige structure to the extent that prestige is allotted differently to men and women by virtue of their gender. Moreover, men often have more access than women to the roles to which prestige generally accrues. But beyond this point, Ortner and Whitehead argue that "the concepts used to differentiate men from women in terms of social worth are often identical to the concepts used . . . to grade individuals of the same gender" (Ortner and Whitehead 1981:16-17). The values in terms of which men are accorded more prestige than women are frequently the same values in terms of which some men are accorded more prestige than others.

Every culture has particular ideas about how a man or a woman ought to act *as* a man or a woman. These ideas extend not only to the sexual division of labor, but also to such things as leisure activities, clothing, body language, and so forth. Attributes considered to be "masculine" attributes in a particular culture are often accorded a higher value than attributes considered "feminine." These attributes are then used not only to allot prestige differentially to men and women, but also to allot prestige differentially to particular men depending upon the degree of their own possession of supposedly "masculine" attributes. A good example is the "active/passive" dichotomy. In many cultures, "activity" is widely assumed to be a male trait and "passivity" a female one. But the two polar terms can also be used to distinguish between men, so that a man who seems more "passive" than "active" is in danger of losing a certain amount of social prestige (cf. Gilmore 1990).

While it is often assumed that males or females naturally act like men or women by virtue of their biological sex, it is obvious that individuals of the "same sex" are actually quite varied in terms of their demonstration of gender signals. It is this ambiguity which allows members of a culture to evaluate persons of the "same" gender in terms of their possession of cultural gender signs. As Michael Herzfeld points out, in the Greek village that he studied it was not so important to be "a good man" as it was to be "good at being a man" (Herzfeld 1985:16). One can be successful or unsuccessful at displaying publicly and in sufficient quantity the appropriate gender signals.

To fail to fulfill these cultural expectations is to leave oneself open to the charge of being an inadequate case of one's gender. For the man, this amounts to the charge of being feminine; for the woman, of being masculine. What must be grasped is the extent to which, within a culture characterized by gender differentiation, this accusation affects one's prestige. For men in particular, "masculinity" is defined over against "femininity," and prestige is granted primarily to the man who can demonstrate his possession of the former (see Gilmore 1987). The situation of women is more ambiguous, since under certain circumstances women who are perceived to "act like a man" are admired rather than criticized (Blok 1981:429; Brandes 1981:231).

Sexual activities can play a crucial role in this semiotics of gender performance. The various ideas about "how men act" and "how women act" include, while extending far beyond, sexual practices. It is assumed that there are certain ways in which the gendered subject (as well as the gendered object) of sexual activity ought to act. A failure to meet these expectations in the realm of sexual practice impacts the overall estimate of one's prestige because one's socially affirmed gender is brought into question. Among men, for example, the omission or comission of a particular sexual act can raise questions about whether one is "a real man."

An important caution needs to be stressed at this point. One should always inquire about the subject of this sort of evaluation. Even within a single culture, it may or may not be true that women and men hold the same ideas about prestige and its relation to gender and sexual practice. The criteria which women use to evaluate the social worth of men or of other women may not be identical to the criteria used by men to evaluate women or one another (see Wikan 1984; 1991). For the moment, it can be noted that a discourse which betrays evidence of being primarily a discourse between men is more likely to utilize male assumptions about gender and prestige.

What are some of the implications of this line of anthropological thought for the interpretation of ancient texts? Readers tend to evaluate the actions of literary characters in terms of cultural norms. When these characters are specified as male or female, and hence gendered, then one group of norms which will be utilized in the reading process is the set of gender norms held by the reader(s) in question. One is rightly cautious about reinscribing the gender norms of another time and place as starting points for reading. However, any attempt to understand an ancient text in terms of the conventional assumptions of its own context should make an explicit methodological space for the evaluation of characters in terms of their relation to cultural gender norms. This step requires asking about the ways in which a gendered character fulfills or fails to fulfill culture-specific expectations about gender-specific behavior.

If gender and sexual practice are related to the structure of prestige, then the question of gender performance can take its place alongside other questions which biblical scholars routinely raise when we attempt to understand how the status ascribed to a particular character affects the meaning of a text. We should not only recognize that a character does or does not meet the expectations of "Levite," "king," "prophet" and so forth. We must also ask whether the character meets the expectations of "male" and "female," and base our interpretations of the possible meanings attributed to a character's actions accordingly. If sexual practice is one area in which such gendered norms play a role, then stories in which sexual acts take place ought to be considered carefully in the light of gender-based prestige.

(2) Masculine Contest and Female Chastity

One of the particular prestige structures mentioned by Ortner and Whitehead is the ideological complex often referred to as the "honor/shame" system of values. The anthropological literature on honor and shame in the Mediterranean basin is relatively well known among biblical scholars and need not be reviewed in detail. The issues raised in these discussions have already impacted the interpretation of ancient literature, resulting in readings of classical texts (Winkler 1990), New Testament texts (Malina 1981), and the Hebrew Bible (Pitt-Rivers 1977; Bal 1988a; Matthews 1992). So far as the present paper is concerned, the specific terms "honor" and "shame" are much less important than a particular aspect of the system of values which these words are supposed to signify. That aspect is the interrelation between a competitive notion of masculine sexuality and an emphasis upon female chastity.

Sex and gender have long played a key role in debates about the "honor/shame" ideological complex. David Gilmore has noted that the sexual element which recurs in the anthropological literature is actually one of the few characteristics of "Mediterranean culture" sufficiently widespread to justify treating the Mediterranean basin as a sort of unit (Gilmore 1987; see also Delaney 1987). In many ethnographic accounts of the Mediterranean and the Middle East, one finds that women's sexuality is treated by men as a sort of resource which, like other limited resources, can become the object of conflict between men (see Schneider 1971; Blok 1981). The point around which this conflict seems to coalesce is the chastity of women (Giovannini 1987), which male kinsmen are compelled to guard with vigilance. The success with which a woman's sexual purity is maintained influences the social reputation of her male kinsmen.

The required vigilance is itself justified by the belief in a competitive, predatory notion of masculine sexuality (Gilmore 1987; 1990). One of the ways in which men demonstrate their masculinity, at least in theory, is through sexual conquest. Sexual access to women, guarded ferociously by male kinsmen as a good which affects their own prestige, is desired by other men as a means with which to increase their prestige in turn. Since the honor of a woman's kinsmen is thought to depend in part upon the manner in which they control access to her sexuality, sexual relations with the woman are a potential means of attack for any man who wishes to cast doubt upon that honor. By acquiring sexual access to the woman *in spite of* the wishes of her kinsmen, a man attacks these kinsmen by showing them incapable of the vigilance required toward the sexuality of their kinswomen. The man's sexual act not only takes away from the honor of the woman's kinsmen, but it increases his own honor in turn.

The virginity of sisters and daughters is frequently at stake in this sort of sexual contest (see Schneider 1971; Giovannini 1987), but the chastity of other women may be involved as well. For example, an unfaithful wife is particularly dreaded by men (Brandes 1981) since her unfaithfulness has allowed another man to cast shame on her husband. However, the implications which seem to concern the men in this framework are those which impact themselves and other men. Aspersion on a woman's honor is not important because her prestige is considered, in and of itself, important, but rather because of the ways in which her sexual purity is tied to the honor of her husband.

Gilmore notes that this structure triangulates the social relations involved. Sexual practice is not simply a matter of a single heterosexual couple. Rather,

... the masculine experience of sexuality becomes broadened conceptually to encompass a triad involving two men—or groups of men—and a woman, who is reduced to an intermediating object. Sexual relations are experienced as a measure of comparative virtue, judged as "performance" among men. Necessarily, female sexuality becomes objectified, becoming not only a libidinal goal in itself, but a contentious and arbitrating social index for masculine reputation. (Gilmore 1987:4-5)

Two points emerge from this quote. First, the emphasis upon "masculine reputation" indicates that the reputation in question is that of the man *as a man* (see further, Gilmore 1990:30-55). In other words, it is masculinity itself, within a certain economy of gender, that is at stake. Both the kinsman and the potential sexual partner can demonstrate their ability to embody a particular sort of manhood by their actions in preventing or accomplishing sexual contact with the woman. Public awareness of a sexual act can affect the prestige of both men in this way.

Second, it is uncertain whether the more ideologically charged relation here is actually that between the man and the woman, or rather that between the men. To be sure, the woman and her sexuality are a crucial part of the picture. But it is doubtful that the importance accorded to her sexuality by the men can be registered apart from a consideration of its possible impact upon male-male relations. From the perspective of the men who share this set of assumptions, the relations between men are at least as important for the meanings attached to heterosexual contact as that between the men and the woman. It is this triangular relation which raises the notion of the "traffic in women."

(3) The "Traffic in Women" and Male Social Relations

The term "traffic in women" is taken from an important essay by Gayle Rubin (Rubin 1975) which attempts to analyze some of the structural underpinnings of the dominance of men over women. In the course of a wide-ranging discussion, Rubin produces an insightful reading of, among others, Lévi-Strauss and his theories of kinship. Lévi-Strauss had argued (Lévi-Strauss 1969) that the real function of incest taboos can be found in the imperative for men to marry women who are members of another kinship group. This imperative enforces the exchange of women between groups of men. The result of this exchange is a network of social alliances which hold kinship societies together. Lévi-Strauss even suggested that the incest taboo, and the exchange of women which it enforces, constitute the origin and foundation of culture, bringing into existence the alliances upon which society depends.

Rubin is critical of this last notion since it entails the implicit corollary that culture cannot exist without the subordination of women. Nevertheless, she insists that Lévi-Strauss' analysis is useful as a tool for understanding the symbolic logic of societies in which women are subordinate to men. One of the presupppositions of this logic is that men have the right to be agents of exchange, while women are usually reduced to the status of objects of exchange. Men establish and negotiate their relations with one another through their relations with women. Women, though vitally important to the process, serve as "a conduit of a relationship" between men (Rubin 1975:174). Rubin's analysis focuses upon marriage and kinship as the most significant points in the exchange system. However, she suggests that not only relations of alliance but also relations of conflict might be expressed through the traffic in women. Moreover, she does not limit the significance of the concept to the sorts of societies which Lévi-Strauss analyzed, but suggests instead that the same general principle appears in many different societies, including modern industrial ones.

Understood broadly, Rubin's notion of a "traffic in women" coheres well with other elements of my interpretive frame. If prestige and gender are related, then this relation has effects both upon men's relations with other men and also upon men's relations with women. A man's relations with women can be seen from the perspective of the male actor in terms of their possible impact upon male prestige (Ortner and Whitehead 1981:19-20). The range of possible relations is quite broad, as a brief summary of possibilities given by Ortner and Whitehead (1981:21) indicates:

> . . . [M]ale prestige is deeply involved in cross-sex relations. Women may be cast as the prize for male prowess or success; having a wife may be the prerequisite to full adult male status; good or bad liaisons with women may raise or lower one's status; the status of one's mother may systematically affect one's status at birth; the sexual comportment of one's sisters and daughters may polish or dull one's honor; and so forth.

If these and other relations with women can affect male prestige relative to other men, then it should not be surprising that men often manipulate their male-female relations to achieve particular goals in the realm of their male-male relations. Indeed, the notion of a "traffic in women" may extend far beyond the relatively clear example of marriage alliances. All sorts of male-female relations can be interrogated for what they tell us about all sorts of male-male relations. Sexual relations are potentially one case of a much larger set. In regard to any particular heterosexual contact, we can ask not only whether it violates or adheres to dominant ethical norms about sexual activity. We must at least raise the question whether the act reveals anything about a male-male relation; whether, that is to say, the woman involved in the sexual contact is serving as the "conduit of a relationship," in Rubin's words. If there is evidence that such is the case, then the exact nature of the relationship ought to be analyzed.

An Anthropological Reading

Anthropological discourse is based, at least in theory, upon the actions and words of real people. There are thus problems involved in "applying" such evidence to literary texts. I do not intend to claim that ancient Israelites must have always acted like the figures of ethnographic literature. Nor do I believe that literary characters always embody the conventions of the culture in which they emerge. Indeed, the effect of literature is often achieved by a transgression of cultural conventions. Yet it is literally impossible for communication to take place without some idea of the implicit meanings which circulate in a culture. The actions of literary characters are always interpreted against a background of cultural premises to which they respond in various ways. The question that remains is whether the cultural premises which I have outlined seem to cohere with the elements that appear in the text, while also being useful as tools for explaining the implicit assumptions that may underly the text.

Utilizing these concepts as an interpretive frame, we can return to the case of the disputed concubines. Right away the significance of the sexual activity appears in a different light, particularly in 2 Samuel 16. Absalom's sexual activity can be read as an attempt to attack David's prestige. By having sexual relations with the ten concubines of David, Absalom has demonstrated David's inability to fulfill a crucial part of a culturally inscribed view of manhood. As all Israel can see, David has been unable to maintain control over sexual access to the women of his house.

This demonstration has intended consequences for both Absalom and David. Absalom has attempted to increase his own prestige by showing his ability to take what David ought to be, but is not, able to control. It is not simply David's power as control that has been placed in question. Rather, it is David's social masculinity. The effects upon David's reputation can be read in terms of Gilmore's suggestion that the man who becomes a victim, through the women associated with him, of another man's sexual assertiveness has become symbolically feminized (Gilmore 1987:11). Lacking a crucial element of a cultural definition of masculinity, he falls perilously close to femininity. He is symbolically emasculated.

Here the linguistic intertextual link with 2 Samuel 10 is significant. Both the Ammonites and Absalom become a stench to David. In both instances, this is achieved in part by attacking the symbolic masculinity, and by extension the prestige, of the king. The Ammonites cut the skirts and beards of David's messengers. It may be unclear to modern Anglo-American readers that facial hair, and indeed body hair in general, is often a potent gender signifier. In other ancient Mediterranean texts, the production of body hair and the production of semen seem to have been considered the results of similar physiological processes. A profusion of body hair was a sign of virility, and a lack of body hair was a sign of effeminacy (Gleason 1990:399-402). Similar connotations occur in ethnographic accounts of Mediterranean face-to-face societies. Bourdieu can quote his informants as saying, "I've got a moustache too," when they want to assert the equivalence of their honor with that of other men. Bourdieu explains that facial hair is considered "a symbol of virility," and that the removal of the beard by another man stands metaphorically for social humiliation (Bourdieu 1979:100; cf. Campbell 1964:280).

Among Hebrew Bible scholars, McCarter has already suggested that the beard's removal "symbolically deprives a man of his masculinity." Hence, David's messengers are subjected to "symbolic castration" (McCarter 1984:270). The Ammonites deprive David's emissaries of one of the signals by which one's manhood is publicly affirmed. The treatment of the messengers seems to be an insult as well to the one from whom the messengers came. What kind of king, a Mediterranean audience might well ask, allows his subjects to be treated in such a manner? The act is a sort of challenge, for which David's own masculine honor requires a response.

If the actions of the Ammonites constitute a symbolic emasculation, such may also be the case with the actions of Absalom. Both the Ammonites and, according to Ahithophel, Absalom can produce the same effect: make themselves a stench to David. To restate this effect in anthropological terms, we might say that the Ammonites and Absalom both attempt to shame David. But if the Ammonites attack David's prestige by attacking his representatives, Absalom attacks David's prestige by attacking his women. The specific connotations are not identical, but the effect (signified by the use of the same verb) and the process ("symbolic castration") of the two cases overlap significantly.

While the Ammonites focus upon the gender connotations of body hair, Absalom focuses upon the gender connotations of the attitude taken toward the sexuality of the women of one's household. The concubines become a means with which Absalom can attack David's masculinity. If David were "good at being a man," the Mediterranean audience might assume, he would not have left himself open to this sort of attack. A properly vigilant attitude on his part would have prevented such an event from taking place. There are, as Ahithophel implies, two effects to be achieved here: David has been shamed in his own eyes, but his prestige in the eyes of other men has also been diminished, even as Absalom's has increased. The concubines themselves thus become, in Rubin's turn of phrase, the "conduit of a relationship": a relation on the one hand between David and Absalom, and a relation on the other hand between Absalom and the men who support him, who will, it is hoped, be sufficiently impressed with Absalom's manhood to fight even harder for his cause.

The demonstration of Absalom's own masculinity in terms of cultural signifiers of manhood clearly seems to be an issue in the texts. Absalom has already responded to the rape of his sister by killing the rapist. It is Absalom's vengeance, rather than David's inaction, that is most consistent with Mediterranean norms. Moreover, the notation of Absalom's own profusion of hair (2 Sam 14:26) may be more than simply a statement of his good looks. It may also hint at his virility. The narrator is careful to tell us that Absalom had to cut his hair each year because it grew so thickly and became heavy. The explanation is quickly followed by an account of the birth of Absalom's children. The signification of Absalom's potency becomes complete, as the ability to sire children is one of the most important Mediterranean signifiers of a successful manhood (Gilmore 1990:41-42).

The situation in 2 Samuel 3 is more ambiguous. We do not know that Abner intended anything by his actions with Rizpah. But the crucial points for the reading of this text are, first, that Ishbaal interprets Abner's actions suspiciously and, second, that Abner responds to Ishbaal's question with an assertion of his own power. So far as Ishbaal's suspicions are concerned, his attitude coheres well with the attitudes outlined by the Mediterranean anthropologists. Ishbaal's question is an expression of the required vigilance toward the sexuality of the women of one's household. Ishbaal assumes that sexual access to Rizpah, his father's concubine, is a matter over which he ought to exercise control. Hence, sexual actions taken toward Rizpah without Ishbaal's permission are a denial of this power, and an affront to Ishbaal's prestige. By confronting Abner, Ishbaal need not be interpreted as implying that Abner is plotting for the throne. The confrontation would instead be an entirely appropriate response from a man who, within a certain cluster of assumptions about gender, prestige, and sexual practice, wishes to assert that he is "good at being a man."

Thus, Abner's refusal to recognize Ishbaal's rights in this matter is itself a sort of attack on Ishbaal's masculine honor. Abner points out that Ishbaal is dependent for his power upon Abner and is by no means the independent, assertive subject whose role he attempts to fill. Dependence upon the power and goodwill of another man is itself often a negative signifier of manhood (cf. Gilmore 1990:49-50). The balance of power between Abner and Ishbaal is thus crucial here. By claiming the right to arbitrate in the matter of Rizpah's sexuality, Ishbaal assumes one sort of power relation. Abner's angry reply assumes another. Both men assume that the matter of sexual contact with Rizpah is a locus for such a dispute to be decided. The ideology underlying such an assumption is not, in my opinion, a "custom" about monarchical legitimacy. It is rather a complex bundle of premises about masculinity, sexual practice, and prestige which the anthropological literature helps to clarify.

The dispute here is one which Abner wins. Ishbaal, the narrator tells us, is afraid to pursue the matter further. This attitude is precisely the opposite of that competitive and assertive display which the discussions of Mediterranean notions of manhood underscore. Thus, it seems likely that Ishbaal's inability to maintain the discussion might have been interpreted as an indication of his inability to embody the "cultural poetics of manhood" (Herzfeld 1985). Ishbaal's timidity is contrasted with Abner's competence in the games of gender performance. This competence, embodied elsewhere by his military prowess but here by his interventions with a woman of Ishbaal's household, cannot but increase his prestige in the eyes of a particular audience. David himself probably embodies the views of a Mediterranean male audience when, hearing of Abner's death, he bewails the fact that a prince and a great man has fallen in Israel (2 Sam 3:38).

I wish to emphasize that this reading is not entirely at odds with a reading which links the wives and concubines of a previous king to monarchical succession and legitimacy. Rather, we now see why sexual practice could be considered relevant for male power struggles, of which the struggle for the throne is but one possible example. The books of 2 Samuel assume at numerous points that an appropriate king is not simply one whose father was king, but rather one who can embody attributes considered positive. Military skill, good looks, the ability to broker alliances (including marriage alliances) which work to one's advantage, the participation in ecstatic religious practices: all of these qualities seem to be cultural signifiers of a certain sort of man. In choosing a king who embodies such qualities, YHWH as a narrative character is simply following the implicit dictates of a culture which projected its own beliefs about "being good at being a man" onto him. A particular relation to sexual practice is simply one example of a complex of features by which such characterizations were accomplished.

Sexual activity is utilized in these stories primarily on the basis of its ability to signify in terms of prestige and gender. The connotations of sexuality which are taken up by the biblical narrator are those which impact the struggles between men for power and honor. There is little or no interest in the actual male-female relations which constitute the weapons in this struggle. On the contrary, heterosexuality turns out to be of interest for the narrator almost entirely because of its impact upon homosocial relations.

Implications: Beyond the Case of the Disputed Concubines

There is no reason to assume that biblical attitudes toward sexual practice are uniform. The sort of anthropological reading which I have attempted here would not produce even results if applied throughout the Hebrew Bible. Nevertheless, the issues highlighted shed light on a number of other stories in which sexual matters play a role.

Julian Pitt-Rivers argued years ago for the relevance of the anthropology of honor and shame to the story of Dinah, Shechem, and Jacob's sons in Genesis (Pitt-Rivers 1977:126-171). Whatever one thinks of his particular hypotheses, the story does seem to bear some relation to the ideology of sex, gender, and prestige which I have outlined. Dinah serves as the "conduit of a relationship" between groups of men who are concerned about their honor. Elsewhere, the use of homosexual rape as a signifier of radical inhospitality in Genesis and Judges can easily be read in terms of sexual practice, gender, and prestige. A man who is raped by other men is symbolically emasculated in a sense far more radical than the removal of a beard can signify (cf. Brandes 1981:232-34). Such an account helps to explain why, from the perspective adopted by the text, the rape of women was considered less offensive, even to the fathers of the women in question.

Elsewhere in 2 Samuel, the account of the rape of Tamar, while granting Tamar a narrative presence beyond most of the women in these stories, nevertheless is concerned primarily with the impact of this rape upon the relations between three men: Amnon, Absalom, and David. Even the story of David and Bathsheba appears in a different light when placed within an anthropological frame. The focus of that story is the relation between David and Uriah. David gets into trouble not because he is involved in the traffic in women, but rather because of his dishonorable actions toward a man who, due to the unequal distribution of power between king and soldier, is unable to protest. The social differential between David and Uriah is thematized in Nathan's parable. David, by attacking a man who cannot be considered his social equal, has transgressed a premise about honorable masculine behavior (cf. Bourdieu 1979:101). That the use of women in male power struggles is itself not questioned is apparent in YHWH's rebuke, where YHWH states that he is the force behind David's traffic in women (2 Sam 12:8; cf. further Schwartz 1992:47; Linafelt 1992:105).

Adonijah's request for Abishag in 2 Kings 2 is usually explained together with my two cases as an instance of the same set of ideas. Clearly, there are similarities between the stories, and the anthropological literature to which I have appealed would help to produce a compelling interpretation of 2 Kings 2. However, there is a crucial difference between the stories. This difference is the role which Bathsheba plays. Both as the Queen Mother in particular and as a mother in general, Bathsheba has an altogether different position within the narrative of 2 Kings 2 from the concubines in my texts or, indeed, from Abishag in 2 Kings. The difference in the positions of the female characters results in altogether different narrative dynamics.

Bathsheba as well as Abishag becomes the "conduit of a relationship" in 2 Kings. However, the male-female relation between Solomon and Bathsheba is not that of a man and a concubine, but rather that between a man and his mother. Hence, the male-male relation in question, that between Solomon and Adonijah, is played out in a different manner. Solomon's angry response may have less to do with the specific request for Abishag, and more to do with the route by which Adonijah attempts to achieve his goal: the manipulation of the king's own mother. The mother-son relation is an enormously complex symbol, which would require more elucidation than is possible here (cf. Gilmore 1987:14-15; Campbell 1964:168). The point is that when the "traffic in women" is recognized as an interpretive tool, the particular form which it takes must be integrated into the interpretation.

Of course, the notion that a "traffic in women" might serve as a reading hypothesis is surely a controversial one. I argue for its legitimacy here on the basis that the texts being interpreted are written from a point of view which assumes male interests and priorities. Israelite women might not have shared the attitudes toward sexual practice, gender, and prestige which underlie these texts. As I have already noted, women sometimes hold different opinions about sex and prestige than men, even within the same traditional culture (cf. Wikan 1984; 1991). The problem for the biblical interpreter is that we have little evidence upon which to decide the question. Even when one acknowledges the importance of framing by the reader, some questions can be put to the text more easily than others. Where the question of women and sexual matters are concerned, the tales of the disputed concubines give us little textual data with which to work in interpreting the impact of sexual practice upon the women involved.

A recognition of this fact is necessary for understanding the relations between power, discourse, and the biblical text. In these texts, sexual elements are able to signify because of their possible impact upon male struggles for prestige and power. However, the text does not simply represent relations of power. It is itself a discourse of power by virtue of the fact that it includes some perspectives and issues while excluding others. Narrating the power politics of male Israelite characters, it practices a power politics of its own. Questions about female prestige, sexual practice, and gender performance have been rendered almost invisible.

This fact is by no means a neutral reflection of Israelite social reality, but is rather the result of a speech act with particular effects of power. After all, the sexual relation with the concubines of David might be considered a rape. There is absolutely no reason to consider that women in such a situation would have been willing participants. Yet the violence done to the women in the text and, indeed, by the text risks being perpetuated by the analyst if one does not call attention to what Mieke Bal (1988b; 1991) might consider the subject of focalization. The perspective which shapes the narrative, by choosing particular elements for inclusion as relevant and excluding others, has helped to inscribe the dominance of male interests in symbolic reality, if not in actual socio-historical reality.

The notions about masculinity which these texts presuppose are unstable notions. Gilmore has pointed out that the definitions of masculinity which one finds in the Mediterranean area are founded upon a radical separation of "masculine" from all that is considered "feminine." This ideology of masculinity contains a paradoxical element. Its self-image requires a denial of the "feminine" within. Yet the ability to attack the prestige of another man by calling his manhood into question rests upon an implicit premise that those expelled elements can and do appear as characteristics of male human beings. These texts thus presuppose a structure of prestige that ultimately undermines the ideology of gender dualism which it inscribes.

The significance of sexual practice in these texts has very little to do with ethics as traditionally conceived. Modern ideologies of sexual behavior which claim to find their foundation in the biblical texts seldom highlight the issues which seem to be at stake in these narratives. Indeed, the homosocial aspect of heterosexuality which one finds here is generally repressed by readers of the biblical literature, scholarly and non-scholarly alike. As our understanding of the biblical assumptions about sexual practice grows, other aspects of its meaning are likely to emerge. Such an understanding can only be the result of a reading practice which refuses to deny the cultural differences between our world and that which produced the biblical texts. In the struggle to develop such a practice, anthropology will surely continue to play an important role.

References

Bal, Mieke. 1988a. *Murder and Difference: Gender, Genre, and Scholarship on Sisera's Death*. Bloomington: Indiana University Press.

_____ 1988b. *Death and Dissymmetry: The Politics of Coherence in the Book of Judges*. Chicago: University of Chicago Press.

_____ 1991. *On Storytelling: Essays in Narratology*. Sonoma: Polebridge.

Blok, Anton. 1981. "Rams and Billy-Goats: A Key to the Mediterranean Code of Honour." *Man* 16:427-40.

Bourdieu, Pierre. 1979. *Algeria 1960*. Cambridge: Cambridge University Press.

Brandes, Stanley. 1981. "Like Wounded Stags: Male Sexual Ideology in an Andalusian Town." In *Sexual Meanings: The Cultural Construction of Gender and Sexuality*. Ed. S. Ortner and H. Whitehead. Cambridge: Cambridge University Press.

Campbell, J. K. 1964. *Honour, Family and Patronage*. Oxford: Clarendon.

Culler, Jonathan. 1988. *Framing the Sign: Criticism and Its Institutions*. Norman: University of Oklahoma Press.

Delaney, Carol. 1987. "Seeds of Honor, Fields of Shame." In *Honor and Shame and the Unity of the Mediterranean*. Ed. D. Gilmore. American Anthropological Association.

Dover, Kenneth. 1978. *Greek Homosexuality*. Cambridge: Harvard University Press.

Eilberg-Schwartz, Howard. 1990. *The Savage in Judaism: An Anthropology of Israelite Religion and Ancient Judaism.* Bloomington: Indiana University Press.

Foucault, Michel. 1978. *The History of Sexuality.* New York: Random House.

———— 1985. *The Use of Pleasure.* New York: Random House.

———— 1986. *The Care of the Self.* New York: Random House.

Frymer-Kensky, Tikva. 1989. "Law and Philosophy: The Case of Sex in the Bible." *Semeia* 44:89-102.

———— 1992. *In the Wake of the Goddesses.* New York: Free Press.

Gilmore, David. 1987. "Introduction: The Shame of Dishonor." In *Honor and Shame and the Unity of the Mediterranean.* Ed. D. Gilmore. American Anthropological Association.

———— 1990. *Manhood in the Making: Cultural Concepts of Masculinity.* New Haven: Yale University Press.

Giovannini, Maureen. 1987. "Female Chastity Codes in the Circum-Mediterranean: Comparative Perspectives." In *Honor and Shame and the Unity of the Mediterranean.* Ed. D. Gilmore. American Anthropological Association.

Gleason, Maud. 1990. "The Semiotics of Gender: Physiognomy and Self-Fashioning in the Second Century C.E." In *Before Sexuality: The Construction of Erotic Experience in the Ancient Greek World.* Ed. D. Halperin et al. Princeton: Princeton University Press.

Gottwald, Norman. 1985. *The Hebrew Bible: A Socio-Literary Introduction.* Philadelphia: Fortress.

Halperin, David, John Winkler, and Froma Zeitlin, eds. 1990. *Before Sexuality: The Construction of Erotic Experience in the Ancient World.* Princeton: Princeton University Press.

Halperin, David. 1990. *One Hundred Years of Homosexuality and Other Essays on Greek Love.* New York: Routledge.

Hertzberg, Hans. 1964. *I & II Samuel.* Philadelphia: Westminster.

Herzfeld, Michael. 1985. *The Poetics of Manhood.* Princeton: Princeton University Press.

Hillers, Delbert. 1985. "Analyzing the Abominable: Our Understanding of Canaanite Religion." *Jewish Quarterly Review* 75/3:253-69.

Ishida, Tomoo. 1977. *The Royal Dynasties in Ancient Israel.* Berlin: Walter de Gruyter.

Jobling, David. 1991. "Feminism and Mode of Production in Ancient Israel: Search for a Method." In *The Bible and the Politics of Exegesis.* Ed. D. Jobling et al. Cleveland: Pilgrim.

Keuls, Eva. 1985. *The Reign of the Phallus: Sexual Politics in Ancient Athens*. Berkeley: University of California Press.

Lemche, Niels Peter. 1991. *The Canaanites and Their Land*. Sheffield: JSOT Press.

Levenson, Jon. 1978. "I Samuel 25 as Literature and History." *Catholic Biblical Quarterly* 40:11-28.

Levenson, Jon, and Baruch Halpern. 1980. "The Political Import of David's Marriages." *Journal of Biblical Literature* 99:507-18.

Lévi-Strauss, Claude. 1969. *The Elementary Structures of Kinship*. Boston: Beacon.

Linafelt, Tod. 1992. "Taking Women in Samuel: Readers/Responses/ Responsibility." In *Reading Between Texts: Intertextuality and the Hebrew Bible*. Ed. D. Fewell. Philadelphia: Westminster.

Malina, Bruce. 1981. *The New Testament: Insights from Cultural Anthropology*. Louisville: John Knox.

Matthews, Victor. 1992. "Hospitality and Hostility in Genesis 19 and Judges 19." *Biblical Theology Bulletin* 22/1:3-11.

McCarter, P. Kyle. 1984. *II Samuel*. Garden City: Doubleday.

Oden, Robert. 1987. *The Bible Without Theology*. San Francisco: Harper & Row.

Ortner, Sherry B., and Harriet Whitehead. 1981. "Introduction: Accounting for Sexual Meanings." In *Sexual Meanings: The Cultural Construction of Gender and Sexuality*. Ed. S. Ortner and H. Whitehead. Cambridge: Cambridge University Press.

Pitt-Rivers, Julian. 1977. *The Fate of Shechem or the Politics of Sex*. Cambridge: Cambridge University Press.

Rubin, Gayle. 1975. "The Traffic in Women: Notes on the Political Economy of Sex." In *Toward an Anthropology of Women*. Ed. R. Reiter. New York: Monthly Review.

Schneider, Jane. 1971. "Of Vigilance and Virgins: Honor, Shame and Access to Resources in Mediterranean Societies." *Ethnology* 10/1:1-24.

Schwartz, Regina. 1992. "Adultery in the House of David: The Metanarrative of Biblical Scholarship and the Narratives of the Bible." *Semeia* 54:35-55.

Tsevat, M. 1958. "Marriage and Monarchical Legitimacy in Ugarit and Israel." *Journal of Semitic Studies* 3:237-43.

Wikan, Unni. 1984. "Shame and Honour: A Contestable Pair." *Man* 19:635-52.

———— 1991 [1982]. *Behind the Veil in Arabia*. Chicago: University of Chicago Press.

Wilson, Robert. 1984. *Sociological Approaches to the Old Testament*. Philadelphia: Fortress.

Winkler, John J. 1990. *The Constraints of Desire: The Anthropology of Sex and Gender in Ancient Greece*. New York: Routledge.

Matthew 28:16-20, Resurrection, Ecclesiology and Mission

Pheme Perkins
Boston College

As scholars have turned their attention to literary analyses of the gospels, Matt. 28:16-20 has received new prominence as the culmination of Jesus' ministry. This pericope resolves the tension over whether or not Jesus' disciples will or can fulfil the mission entrusted to them when they were called to be "fishers of human beings" (Matt. 4:19). Obedience to the will of the Father characterizes both the disciples whom Jesus called as brothers and sisters during his earthly ministry (12:49-50) and the new disciples to be called by the eleven, referred to as "my brothers" in the summons issued through the women (28:10).[1] Jesus' command to "go and make disciples of all the nations" (v. 19a) becomes the central concern of the scene. The christological implications of the announcement that Jesus now has all ἐξουσία in heaven and on earth provides the foundation for the universal spread of his teaching. Similarly, the mission to "all nations" requires a new communal self-definition. Jesus continues to be with the disciples to the end of the age (Matt. 28:20) when disciples are gathered as a church (Matt. 18:20).

The Problem of Genre

Attempts to delineate a form-critical category to describe the genre of Matt 28:16-20 often oscillated between an enthronment model, which was heavily dependent upon echoes of Dan 7:13-14, and a commissioning model, which focused on the command to the disciples.[2] The former highlighted christological claims in the passage by comparing the implied exaltation of Jesus with the christological hymns in the New Testament. However, though Jesus could not possess "all power in heaven and on earth" without being exalted to the right hand of God, Matt. 28:16-20 lacks the terminology of exaltation. Christological hymns focus their affirmation on titles such as Lord or Son of God. The latter emerges indirectly in the baptismal formula but is

---

[1] See Michael J. Wilkins, "Named and Unnamed Disciples in Matthew: A Literary-Theological Study," *Society of Biblical Literature 1991 Seminar Papers* (Ed. Eugene H. Lovering, Jr.; Atlanta: Scholars Press, 1991) 424.

[2] See the extensive discussion of these attempts by Gerhard Friedrich, "Die formale Struktur von Mt 28,18-20," *ZThK* 80 (1983).

not the center of the passage.[3] The commissioning model turned attention to the mission given the disciples. However, the sayings which make up the commissioning are more closely related to the narrative which precedes this passage than to any of the Old Testament scenes taken to be models for this passage. Literary critics have also reminded scholars that a reader's cumulative perceptions of the characters and relationships involved, not on isolated treatments of individual sections of the gospels. Dorothy Weaver's treatment of the missionary discourse in Matthew 10 has pointed out that the disciples were already commissioned for a task that they did not perform during the earthly ministry of Jesus.[4] Therefore, the commissioning scene resolves issues that are raised by the narrative, itself.

Form-critical investigations have left many commentators with the conclusion that the pericope is *sui generis*.[5] The quest for pre-Matthean traditions behind either the scene as a whole or individual sayings from which it has been composed continues to be debated. Hans-Theo Wrege argues that most of Matt. 28:16-20 is derived from Matthew's *Sondergut*.[6] For some attempts to reconstruct the social history of Matthew's community, the implications of Matt. 28:19a are critical. Can one detect an earlier missionary effort to Israel behind the restrictions of Matt. 10:5b-6 that must be abandoned in view of growing hostility?[7] Does the mission envisaged exclude further missionary efforts among Jews or are they presumed to be among the nations evangelized?[8] Is Matthew reaffirming what is established practice in his church or arguing for an innovation that is threatened by the prestige of Pharisaic interpreters of the Law?

For some exegetes the question of how Matthew and the church for which he writes understood the relationship between Christianity and Judaism can be illuminated by appealing to christological developments that are associated with each layer of tradition in this pericope. Davies and Allison isolate three

---

3 Jack Dean Kingsbury ("The Composition and Christology of Matt 28:16-20," *JBL* 93 [1974] 573-84) uses this reference to argue that "Son of God," not "Son of Man," is the christological title implied in this passage.

4 Matthew omits the references in Mark (Mark 6:13, 30) to the disciples' mission activity. Dorothy Jean Weaver, *Matthew's Missionary Discourse. A Literary Critical Analysis* JSNTSup 38 (Sheffield: JSOT, 1990)

5 Cf. Eduard Schweizer, *Das Evangelium nach Matthäus*, NTD 2 (Göttingen: Vandenhoeck & Ruprecht, 1981); Joachim Gnilka, *Das Matthäusevangelium. II. Teil Kommentar zu Kap. 14,1-28,20 und Einleitungsfragen*, HTKNT I/2 (Freiburg: Herder, 1988).

6 Hans-Theo Wrege, *Das Sondergut des Matthäusevangeliums* (Zürich: Theologisher Verlag, 1991).

7 Terence L. Donaldson [*Jesus on the Mountain. A Study in Matthean Theology*, JSNTSup 8 (Sheffield: JSOT Press, 1985)] argues that the shift resulted from tensions engendered by the Jewish War and the Pharisaic consolidation which followed.

8 Matthew sometimes uses ἔθνη to refer to Gentiles in opposition to Jews (e.g. 10:5, 18; 20:19, 25; 21:43), though it may also be generic (e.g. 24:7, 9; 25:32). The claim that the phrase refers to Gentiles, not Jews has been defended by Douglas Hare and Daniel Harrington ("'Make Disciples of All the Gentiles' (Mt 28:19)," *CBQ* 37 [1975] 359-69). Most scholars accept the view that Matthew acknowledges a growing Gentile mission but does not intend to exclude Jews from evangelization. For a defense of the inclusive reading of "nations" see John P. Meier, "Nations or Gentiles in Matthew 28:19?" *CBQ* 39 [1977] 94-102).

stages in the tradition history of this passage: (a) a primitive appearance story; (b) its combination with Son of Man traditions based on Dan 7:13-14; and (c) reformulation to depict the new Moses commissioning his successors.[9] The primitive resurrection commissioning narrative cannot be definitively recovered. It was combined with Dan 7:13-14 to provide the emphasis on Jesus' cosmic authority as Son of Man as well as the triadic baptismal formula. Matt identifies Jesus with the Danielic Son of Man explicitly in 24:30 and 26:64. Early Christian tradition understood resurrection as exaltation to the divine throne. Dan 7:13-14 provides the necessary clue to the significance of Jesus' exaltation for the nations, the authority of the Son now extends beyond the geographical and temporal limits of his earthly ministry. Though many scholars would agree that some echoes of Dan 7:13-14 are present in this passage, the assertion that the mountain setting and emphasis on keeping Jesus' teaching demonstrates that Matthew advocated a Mosaic christology is less persuasive.

Davies and Allison treat the final episode as a deliberate echo of the commissioning of Joshua, not merely a generalized version of OT examples.[10] This parallel depends upon their argument that Matt is dominated by a Moses typology from the birth narratives through Jesus' teaching and transfiguration on mountains. The mountain in Matt 28:16 reflects the mountain on which Moses ended his life in Deut 34.[11] However, Matt does not refer to Jesus' departure from life, quite the opposite. The elements in Matt 28:16-20 that are said to depend upon Joshua traditions involve general features of the commissioning story: orders to go, commands to keep Mosaic teaching and the promise of divine presence. Davies and Allison find a stronger verbal echo if one compares Matt to the conflation of Deut 31:14-15 and Josh 1:7 in *The Testament of Moses* I 6-18. While selection of individual phrases gives the appearance of parallels to Matt 28:16-20, the sustained concern with God as creator, revelation of the written Law to make God's purposes known among the nations, depositing the Torah in the place God has chosen for worship from all eternity and the personal integrity of Joshua strike a very different tone. The reference to the day of reckoning is correlated with the creation as evidence for the eternity of the divine sanctuary and the permanence of God's will in the Torah. Thus, it does not form the striking parallel to the "end of the age" in Matt 28:20 dectected by Davies and Allison.[12]

The emphasis on going to *all nations* does not appear in the reconstruction of the pre-Matthean, Son of Man tradition that Davies and Allison present.

---

9 W. D. Davies and Dale C. Allison, "Matt. 28:16-20: Texts Behind the Text," *RHPR* 72 (1992) 89-98.

10 Davies and Allison, "Matt. 28:16-20," 90-93.

11 Davies and Allison, "Matt. 28:16-20," 91.

12 Davies and Allison, "Matt. 28:16-20," 93-94. The authors are unclear about the relationship between Matt. and *Test. Moses*. Although it is alleged to provide a model for the allusion to Joshua's commissioning in Matt., they also imply that *Test. Moses* could have been echoing Matt, "where Jesus' followers are commissioned to go forth and teach the observance of all the commandments, can cite precedent: the author of *The Testament of Moses*, when working with Deuteronomy 31 and Joshua 1, constructed a commissioning narrative in many ways reminiscent of Matt. 28:16-20" (p. 94).

They claim that Matthew has reworked a tradition which already included the following:

> Jesus appeared to the eleven. When they saw him they were glad, although some disbelieved. Then he said: "All authority in heaven and on earth has been given to me. Preach the gospel. Baptize in the name of the Father, the Son and the Holy Spirit. (And behold), I will send the Holy Spirit to you.[13]

Nor does it appear in the list of Matthean redactional additions that have been made on the basis of Joshua material: moutain setting, command to make disciples, command to keep Jesus' teaching, and assurance of eternal presence. The proposed pre-Matthean tradition contains additions that appear to be assimilations to other narratives. The command "preach the gospel" echoes the opening of Jesus' ministry (Matt 4:23; also 9:35) and the reference to the future mission of disciples (Matt 24:14). The latter contains elements in common with Matt 28:16-20: the preaching is testimony to *all the nations*; at its completion, the *end will come*. Both of these elements must be attributed to Matthew's redaction in the proposed scheme. The promised sending of the Holy Spirit must be imported through an alleged parallel between this tradition and Acts 1:6-12.[14]

Prior decisions about distinctively Matthean christology inform this construction of the tradition-history behind Matt. 28:16-20. The emphasis on christology brings back the division between exaltation/enthronement and commissioning scenes as the likely background to this passage. Jewish traditions which link Moses with Elijah and Enoch as individuals who were translated into heaven without dying provide a link between the hypothesis of a Moses typology and the resurrection context of the passage.[15] But, unlike Acts, Matt. does not depict the departure of Jesus. Instead, Jesus remains present to the disciples until the end of the age.

Other scholars have noted the eschatological tension between this promise of Jesus' presence and the apocalyptic sayings about the coming of the Son of Man in judgment (e.g., Matt. 24:7; 25:31-32).[16] The gospel which has been preached to *all the nations* (24:14) forms the basis on which they are judged

---

13 Davies and Allison, "Matt. 28:16-20," 95.

14 The case for a common tradition behind Acts 1:6-20 and Matt 28:16-20 has been argued by John P. Meier, "Two Disputed Questions in Matt. 28:16-20," *JBL* 96 (1977) 410-12. Though their reconstruction appears to depend upon that claim, Davies and Allison insist that Luke and Matt are independent ("Matt. 28:16-20," 94 n. 28).

15 Davies and Allison, "Matt. 28:16-20," 97 n. 35; see James D. Tabor, "Returning to Divinity:" Josephus's Portrayal of the Disappearances of Enoch, Elijah and Moses," *JBL* 108 (1989) 225-38. Josephus affirms that Moses' account of his death was intended to curtail rumors that he had been exalted to divinity (p. 227; *Ant.* iii 5, 7 sec. 96; viii 48 sec. 326). Philo describes Moses as one who is disengaged from the earthly elements so that his soul can return to the divine (p. 236; *De virt.* 76).

16 Terence Donaldson argues that the more realized eschatology in Matt. 28:20 corrects the apocalyptic tradition (*Jesus on the Mountain. A Study in Matthean Theology*, JSNTSup 8 [Sheffield: JSOT Press, 1985] 190).

(25:31-46).[17] While Matthew certainly reminds readers that the Church is also subject to judgment (Matt. 7:15-23; 13:40-43; 22:11-14), the abiding presence of Christ with the community implies that outsiders are condemned or rewarded on the basis of how they have treated the "little ones," the persecuted witnesses to the gospel (10:40-42). The assurance of Jesus' presence is not simply equivalent to the sayings about the Spirit's assistance (Matt. 10:20). Rather, it is an ecclesiological assertion which establishes the place of the community's mission in salvation history.[18] The lack of explicit christological titles in this pericope suggests that the evangelist has already established the authority of Jesus as Son of God and Son of Man. Scholars are certainly right to discern echoes of those passages in the gospel's conclusion. But the real concern of this concluding section does not lie in demonstrating Jesus' authority. It lies in sayings which ground the church's existence and mission in the authority of the risen Lord and in fidelity to the teaching of the earthly Jesus.[19]

This dual emphasis gives Matt. 28:16-20 the *sui generis* form which does not fit the models that have been proposed.[20] Although scholars typically speak of this passage as a resurrection appearance story, it has a number of anomalies when compared with other examples of the genre. Like the other such stories, the appearance tradition is independent of both the kerygmatic formulae and the empty tomb traditions.[21] Unlike the other examples, Matt. 28:16-20 does not elaborate on the appearance of Jesus. Only the reactions of worship and uncertainty suggest the mysterious presence typical of the genre. As a story, the episode lacks both direct participation by the disciples and a conclusion. The readers must supply their own account of Jesus' departure and the disciples' response to Jesus' words.[22]

---

17 See the discussion of the parable by John R. Donahue, "The 'Parable' of the Sheep and the Goats: A Challenge to Christian Ethics," *Theological Studies* 47 (1986) 3-31.

18 Other scholars have been more impressed with the substitution of Jesus' presence for the old sacred space of the Jerusalem temple (so Amy-Jill Levine, *The Social and Ethnic Dimensions of Matthean Salvation History*. "God nowhere among the Gentiles. . ." (Matt. 10:5b) Studies in the Bible and Early Christianity 14 [Lewiston: Edwin Mellen, 1988] 100). This concern assimilates modern anthropological studies of religion with elements of the Johannine tradition (e.g. John 2:13-22; 4:20-21). Matthew's references to "their synagogues" suggest a Jewish community which has an established tradition of holiness that is already independent of the sacred space associated with the Temple. Similarly, Donaldson's attempt to read Matthew in terms of a new Zion ideology (*Jesus on the Mountain*) is unpersuasive.

19 Rudolf Pesch ("'Wo zwei oder drei versammelt sind auf meinen Namen hin. . .' (Mt 18,20)" *Studien zum Matthäusevangelium*. Festschrift für Wihelm Pesch [Ed. Ludger Schenke; Stuttgart: Katholisches Bibelwerk, 1988] 242-43) argues that Matthew's ecclesiology centers on the conviction that the gathered community is the place where God's will is done on earth. It owes its existence to the on-going presence of the one who called it into being.

20 E.g., Donaldson, *Jesus on the Mountain*, 176. The proposal that Matthew has a commissioning scene in mind comes closest to capturing the genre of the passage.

21 John E. Alsup, *The Post-Resurrection Appearance Stories of the Gospel-Tradition*, Calwer Theologische Monographien 5 (London: S.P.C.K., 1975) 147.

22 Both the shorter and longer endings that were added to Mark's gospel provide the elements of a narrative conclusion. The disciples set about the task of preaching the gospel.

Matthean Composition in Matt. 28:16-20

Has Matthew combined diverse sayings with an introductory reference to a resurrection appearance? The disjunction between verses 16-17 and 18-20 makes a two-part structure evident. Quite unlike the earlier notice of Jesus' appearance to the women outside the tomb (Matt. 28:9-10), Jesus' words make no reference to the worship and doubt of the disciples. Worship and a word of reassurance are standard elements in an epiphany of Jesus. The reader has already encountered them in the Walking on Water (Matt. 14:25-32). In that episode, Jesus chides Peter for doubting, having little faith (v. 31).[23] All of the terminology in Matt. 28:17 appears in Matthew's version of the Walking on Water episode. Further, the verb προσκυνεῖν only designates worship/homage in response to a manifestation of Jesus when used of the Magi (2:2, 8, 11), the disciples in the boat (14:33), the women outside the tomb (28:9) and in our passage (28:17).[24] Otherwise, the verb designates the gesture of a suppliant seeking healing (8:2; 9:18; 15:25) or a favor (18:26; 20:20). Just as the Walking on Water episode attributes worship to the whole group and doubt to an individual, who nevertheless represents the possibilities for all disciples, so worship and doubt are awkwardly divided in this passage. The awkward οἱ δέ, without its matching οἱ μέν, suggests that some of the Eleven doubted.[25] Since all of the language can be found in the earlier story, the awkwardness of the expression about doubt does not provide a basis for distinguishing that clause as Matt.'s redactional addition to traditional material.[26]

Some interpreters see the distinction between the command to tell "my brothers" in Matt. 28:10 and the reference to "eleven disciples" in 28:16 as evidence that verses 16 and 17 belong to a resurrection appearance that was independent of the tomb stories.[27] Donaldson finds all earlier references to mountains to be dependent upon earlier tradition. Therefore, the mountain in verse 16 as well as the unusual expression οὗ ἐτάξατο αὐτοῖς ὁ Ἰησοῦς are derived from pre-Matthean tradition.[28] The instructions conveyed to the disciples by the women contain no reference to a mountain at all. Nor does the earlier prediction in Matt. 26:32. Matt. 28:16 refers to *the* mountain as though a specific location had been named. However, the only mountain

---

23 David B. Howell, *Matthew's Inclusive Story: A Study in the Narrative Rhetoric of the First Gospel*, JSNTSup 42 (Sheffield: JSOT Press, 1990) 256 n. 1.

24 Joachim Gnilka, *Das Matthäusevangelium. II. Teil Kommentar zu Kap. 14,1-28,10 und Einleitungsfragen*, HTKNT I/2 (Freiburg: Herder, 1988) 506.

25 Rather than another group of followers other than the Eleven. Matt. may intend to divide the Eleven into worshipers and doubters. However, the earlier example suggests that those who doubted also belong to the group which worshiped (cf. Gnilka, *Matthäusevangelium*, 506); Howell (*Matthew's Inclusive Story*, 256 n. 1) suggests that Matthew refers to the whole group of disciples, even though the expression is grammatically difficult.

26 Contrary to Hans-Theo Wrege, *Das Sondergut des Matthäusevangeliums* (Zürich: Theologischer Verlag, 1991) 129.

27 Alsup, *Post-Resurrection Appearance Stories*, 153.

28 Donaldson, *Jesus on the Mountain*, 172-73.

referred to by name in Matthew is the Mount of Olives.[29] Matthew has located healings and the feeding of the four thousand on a mountain that is alleged to be near the Sea of Galilee.[30] Therefore, though I am not persuaded by their emphasis on mountains as a sign of Moses christology, Davies and Allison rightly see the mountain in Matt. 15:29 as Matthean redaction.[31]

Since neither healing nor feeding play a distinctive role in this pericope,[32] it seems unlikely that Matthew is directing the reader toward that episode. Some interpreters assume that Mattew set the encounter on a mountain simply because mountains are associated with revelation. Donaldson points out that such general claims do not explain the use of mountains in Matthew's narrative. The mountains play distinctive roles within the passages where they are found.[33] Matthew may assume that the reader will supply one of the other mountains in Galilee as the referent, the mountain of the Sermon on the Mount (Matt. 5:1) or that of Transfiguration (17:1). Matt. 5:1 appears to have taken the reference to a mountain from the designation of the Twelve disciples in Mark 3:13.[34] The rest of the Markan scene appears in Matthew as the introduction to the missionary discourse (Matt. 10:1-4). That pericope provides the reader with the names of the Twelve. Matthew is the only evangelist who uses the designation "twelve disciples."[35] Since Jesus' teaching is to be the content of the mission to the nations, the mountain of Matt. 5:1 would appear to be the most likely referent.

The list of the Twelve disciples which Matthew has taken from Mark 3:13-16 to open the missionary discourse, provides another clue that our passage has been composed by the evangelist. Matt. 28:16 introduces an unusual numerical precision about the group which encounters the Lord. They are explicitly identified as "the eleven disciples." Despite the betrayal of Judas (26:20), the rest of the group has remained intact.[36] They can now take up the mission for which they had been called. The expression οὗ ἐτάξατο αὐτοῖς ὁ Ἰησοῦς contains a verb which only appears elsewhere in some manuscripts at Matt. 8:9. The parallel in Luke 7:8 attaches the participle τασσόμενος to the Centurion's description of himself as a "man under authority," a reading

---

[29] Gnilka, *Matthäusevangelium*, 506. Gnilka rightly rejects any attempt to associate the mountain setting with Mosaic traditions. Davies and Allison detect a Sinai association with the mount of Transfiguration because it is designated "high" as Sinai is in first century Jewish authors (Josephus, *Antiquities* iii sec. 76; Philo, *Vit. Mos.* ii sec. 70). The mountain of the feeding in Matt. 15:29 is associated with Moses through the reference to Exodus in John 6 ("Matt. 28:16-20, 91).

[30] In order to derive the mountain setting from tradition, one must argue that Matthew's tradition was not simply taken from Mark but included elements also found in John 6:3.

[31] W. D. Davies and Dale C. Allison, *The Gospel According to Matthew*. Volume II. Commentary on Matthew VIII-XVIII. ICC (Edingburgh: T. & T. Clark, 1991) 565-66.

[32] Unlike the missionary instructions in Matt. 10:1 where healing is a primary feature of the mission, neither healing nor exorcism belong to the concluding commission.

[33] Donaldson, *Jesus on the Mountain*, 175.

[34] Davies and Allison, *The Gospel According to Saint Matthew* Volume I. Introduction and Commentary on Matthew I to VII (Edinburgh: T. & T. Clark, 1988), 421.

[35] Davies and Allison, *Matthew* II, 150-52.

[36] Gnilka, *Matthäusevangelium* II, 506.

which also appears in some manuscripts of Matt. 8:9. Though scholars commonly attribute the participle to Lukan redaction,[37] the combination of the verb with a statment about authority might represent a common expression. If so, Matthew's image of Jesus as the one who has been given "all authority" (v. 18) could have brought the verb to mind in formulating an introduction for the sayings which follow.

Matthew reformulates the story of the women at the tomb, which he found in Mark. Both the women and then the disciples demonstrate more loyalty to Jesus than one finds in Mark. The women no longer flee in silence, but depart in joy to carry out the command received from the angel. The variant of the angel's words used when the risen Jesus meets the women outside the tomb highlights a similar point about the disciples. They have not left Jerusalem. Rather, Jesus must command them to return to Galilee in order to see him there (v. 10). Reference to the Eleven as obedient to orders (v. 17) ameliorates the impression of wholesale desertion and cowardice given by the Markan narrative. The credal formula in 1 Cor 15:3-5 does not provide any geographical location for appearances of the risen Lord. The extended appearance narratives in John and Luke indicate that such stories might be set in either location. Matthew's concise accounts of both the appearance to the women at the tomb and that to the disciples show no clear evidence of influence from such extended narratives. Matthew's tendency to abbreviate longer Markan narratives is not at work here. Both episodes may contain no more recoverable pre-Matthean tradition than the simple fact that Jesus was said to have appeared to women in the vicinity of the tomb and to the disciples in Galilee. The rest is Matthean composition.

Analysis of the sayings in verses 18-20 is more complex. They are the focus of the pericope as it stands. The relationship of Daniel to the authority saying and the baptismal formula remains unclear. The command to go to the nations links this passage to Matt. 10:5b-42, as we have seen. However, it also generates extensive debate about the meaning of that command. As we have also seen, the final affirmation of Jesus' abiding presence seems to be in tension with the apocalyptic vision of the Son of Man in the earlier chapters. Evaluation of these relationships cannot be separated from hypotheses concerning tradition and redaction in the sayings. We have already seen that Davies and Allison proposed a christological tradition-history for Matt. 28:16-20 that grounds the shift from echoes of the Daniel Son of Man figure to eternal presence in the hypothesis that Jesus as new Moses forms the basis of Matthew's own christology. Identification of the risen Jesus as Son of Man vindicates Jesus' assertion that all nations will see the Son of Man coming with power and glory (24:30; 26:62).[38]

Eduard Schweizer insists that the Matthean elements in verses 18-20 make it impossible to separate tradition from redaction in those cases as well.[39] This observation does not preclude the possibility that Matthew has reworked traditional material. The triadic baptismal formula which departs from the

---

[37] Davies and Allison, *Matthew* II, 23 n. 61.

[38] Davies and Allison, "Matt. 28:16-20," 97.

[39] Eduard Schweizer, *Das Evangelium nach Matthäus*, NTD 2 (Göttingen: Vandenhoeck & Ruprecht, 1981) 171.

more usual NT references of baptism in the name of Jesus and which is a cultic directive for how persons are admitted to the community can hardly be Matthean invention. A similar tripartite formula appears in *Did.* 7 and in Justin Martyr (*1 Apol.* 61). Since *Did.* 9.5 speaks of admitting to the Eucharist those who had been baptized "in the name of Jesus," both usages existed in the same community. Schaberg may be right in arguing that Matt. 28:19b need not represent the exact words pronounced over the baptized in Matthew's church.[40] She argues for allusions to Dan 7:13-14 that encompass both the bestowal of cosmic authority in verse 18 and the triadic elements in the baptismal formula of verse 19b. The reworking of Daniel behind the triadic formula would have consisted of the Ancient of Days, the angels and the Son of Man figure.[41] She suggests that it originated among hellenistic Jewish Christians to vindicate the mission to the Gentiles.[42] Thus, in contrast to Schweizer, most of the sayings represent pre-Matthean tradition.

Derivation of the baptismal formula from an alleged midrash on Dan is not overly compelling. Many scholars have also challenged the assumption that Matt. 28:18 refers to the Son of Man figure in Dan 7:13-14. David Bauer makes the most extensive case against the assumption that Matthew has simply taken over the language of Daniel.[43] In Dan 7:13-14 the ascent of the Son of Man refers to vindication and political triumph over enemies, "the nations," who will be destroyed. In that context, $\tau\grave{\alpha}\ \xi\theta\nu\eta$ clearly excludes Jews. Matthew, by contrast, assumes that they are included among those evangelized. Unlike Dan 7:13-14, Matt. 28:16-20 contains no description of the Son of Man's appearance. The evangelist is only interested in the authoritative word which Jesus speaks. Further, the use of the expression "Son" in the baptismal formula does not refer to the Son of Man but to Matthew's claim that Jesus is Son of God.[44] Therefore, this passage is better understood as Matthew's composition.

Shifting verb tenses distinguish the three sayings in verses 18b-20. The declaration that all authority has been given Jesus (v. 18b) is in the aorist. The commission opens with a participle and follows the imperative "make disciples" with two more participles specifiying what constitutes making some one a disciple (vv. 19-20a). The assurance of Jesus' presence with the disciples is introduced with $\kappa\alpha\grave{\iota}\ \iota\delta o\acute{\upsilon}$ and then follows with a verb in the present tense (v. 20b). The opening participle in the commissioning saying picks up the verb $\pi o\rho\epsilon\acute{\upsilon}\epsilon\sigma\theta\alpha\iota$ from verse 16. Matthew used the verb from the angel's command to the women (Matt. 28:7)[45] to refer to the movement of Jesus' followers in response to his command throughout the chapter (vv. 11, 16, 19). The phrase $\kappa\alpha\grave{\iota}\ \iota\delta o\acute{\upsilon}$ also appears in the angel's words. There it marks off the authoritative word of Jesus that he would go before the disciples to Galilee

---

40 Jane Schaberg, *The Father, the Son and the Holy Spirit. The Triadic Phrase in Matthew 18:19b.* SBLDS 61 (Chico: Scholars, 1982) 21.

41 Schaberg, *Father, Son and Holy Spirit*, 189-238.

42 Schaberg, *Father, Son and Holy Spirit*, 326-30.

43 David R. Bauer, *The Structure of Matthew's Gospel. A Study in Literary Design.* Bible and Literature 15 (Sheffield: Almond Press, 1988) 111-12.

44 Bauer, *Structure of Matthew's Gospel*, 112.

45 Matthew has substituted $\tau\alpha\chi\grave{\upsilon}\ \pi o\rho\epsilon\upsilon\theta\epsilon\hat{\iota}\sigma\alpha\iota$ for $\dot{\upsilon}\pi\acute{\alpha}\gamma\epsilon\tau\epsilon$ in Mark 16:7.

where they would see him (v. 7). Matthew then uses the phrase to introduce Jesus' appearance to the women (v. 9) and attaches πάσας τὰς ἡμέρας to the participle to indicate the women's compliance (v. 11) in order to introduce the pericope about Jewish rumors. Matthew binds the group of sayings together by repeated uses of πᾶς: πᾶσα ἐξουσία (v. 18); πάντα τὰ ἔθνη (v. 19); πάντα ὅσα ἐντειλάμην (v. 20a), and πάσας τὰς ἡμέρας (v. 20b).[46]

Commissioning Sayings and the Gospel Narrative

Further elements of Matthean composition and links to the earlier sections of the narrative are evident in the individual sayings. We have already seen that there is considerable disagreement over the relationship between verse 18b and Dan 7:13-14.[47] For some interpreters, absence of the title "son of Man" and of any of the imagery associated with that figure's ascent to the divine throne makes the claim that the reader is intended to supply such information unlikely.[48] The designation "son" in the baptismal formula refers the reader to Jesus as Son of God, a relationship established in the baptismal scene (Matt. 3:17).[49] Matthew's reader knows that Jesus possesses ἐξουσία on earth (e.g. 7:29; 9:6, 8; 21:23, 24, 27). Such ἐξουσία can only be conferred by God (9:8; 21:23-27). Yet, Jesus is able to grant it to the disciples, when he sends them to heal and preach the gospel (10:1). Both the sending of the Twelve (10:1) and the dispute over the source of Jesus' ἐξουσία (21:23-27) have ties to the conclusion of the gospel. Jesus responded to the question about the source of his authority with a question about the baptism of John: τὸ βάπτισμα τὸ Ἰωάννου πόθεν ἦν; ἐξ οὐρανοῦ ἢ ἐξ ἀνθρώπου; (21:25a/Mark 11:30). Heavenly authority has been contrasted with that conferred by humans. Matt. 28:18 affirms what the reader already knows about Jesus' authority, its origins are divine, not human.

The expression ἐν οὐρανῷ καὶ ἐπὶ [τῆς] γῆς recalls other examples of the expression in the gospel. The Father is Lord of heaven and earth (Matt. 11:25; 5:34-35). Discipleship implies doing God's will on earth as in heaven (6:10). The divine origin of the community's power to bind or loose on earth means that such actions will be confirmed in heaven (16:19; 18:8). Those who confess or deny Jesus on earth will find that he does likewise for them before his Father in heaven (10:32-33). By inserting the episode in which the chief priests bribe the soldiers to spread the rumor that Jesus' disciples stole the body and promise to keep them out of trouble with the governor (Matt. 28:11-15), Matthew reminds his readers of the human authorities who remain hostile to the gospel message.[50] Other examples refer to heaven and earth passing away (5:18; 24:35). The first affirms the validity of the Law; the second, that of Jesus'

---

46 Gnilka, *Matthäusevangelium* II, 502.

47 Schaberg (*Father, Son and Holy Spirit*, 111-41) provides an extensive survey of the earlier arguments over the background to this passage. She argues that the Danielic allusions are well-established by the apocalyptic Son of Man sayings earlier in the gospel.

48 E.g. Donaldson, *Jesus on the Mountain*, 176-77.

49 Bauer, *Structure of Matthew's Gospel*, 112-13.

50 God's ability to defeat such authorities is displayed when the angel's appearance strikes the guards numb (Matt. 28:4; J. P. Heil, *The Death and Resurrection of Jesus. A Narrative-Critical Reading of Matthew 26-28* [Minneapolis: Fortress, 1991] 99-104).

words. Jesus words are to endure even beyond the end of heaven and earth. The temporal reference will be picked up by the promise of Jesus' presence until the "end of the age" (28:20).

Matt. 10:1 provides a key to the link between the saying about Jesus' authority and the commissioning. The sending of the disciples follows as a consequence of the authority which Jesus now possesses.[51] Matthean language figures prominently in the commissioning saying as well.[52] With the exception of Acts 14:21, the term μαθητεύειν only appears in two other places in Matthew (Matt. 13:52; 27:57).[53] The inclusiveness of the mission to "all nations" has led some interpreters to treat the commissioning as though it revoked the limits set in Matt. 10:5b-6. As we have seen, others point to the fact that the previous mission is never described as having been completed. Just as Jesus' authority when displayed during his earthly life is not qualitatively different from the authority he now possesses, so the mission of the earlier period is not opposed to the commission which the disciples receive in verse 19. However, the content of the latter shifts away from the gospel's focus on healing and preaching the Kingdom to activities which mark the community of Jesus' followers as a group separate from others. Thus, use of the word ἔθνος may refer primarily to those who are the object of Christian witness, whether they are Jews or Gentiles. Such an understanding fits the descriptions of the community's mission in the apocalyptic discourse (Matt. 24:9, 14) and the judgment scene attached to the parable of the Sheep and the Goats (25:32).[54]

Matt. 21:25 associates the authority behind Jesus' ministry with that exhibited by Jesus in his ministry. Matthew's readers know that Jesus is to bring a baptism in "fire and the Spirit" (3:11). Jesus' own baptism provided the occasion for a heavenly confirmation of the special relationship between Jesus and the Father (3:16-17). Though that scene contains Father, Son and Spirit, it does not appear to be the model for Christian baptism.[55] Matthew's readers can be presumed to recognize their own experience in the triadic formula attached to the command to baptize. In addition, the reader knows that disciples exercise the authority to heal, exorcise and prophecy in Jesus' name. However, some persons invoke Jesus' name who will finally be rejected because they do not follow Jesus' teaching (Matt. 7:13-28; 24:5). The missionary discourse refers to both hostility and hospitality received by disciples because they bear Jesus' name (10:22, 41-42; also 18:5). The community gathers in Jesus' name (18:20). Therefore, baptism in the name of Father, Son and Holy Spirit anticipates a spectrum of other activities which take place "in the name" of Jesus.

Matthew's challenge to those in the community who invoke Jesus' name without keeping his teaching (Matt. 7:15, 22) anticipates the combination of baptism and teaching in this passage. Readers have been warned that one must "do the will of the Father who is in heaven" (7:21) in order to enter the

---

51 The οὖν in verse 19 makes this relationship clear (Alsup, *Post-Resurrection Appearance Stories*, 177-79).

52 Gerhard Friedrich, "Die Formale Struktur von Mt 28,18-20," *ZThK* 80 (1983) 174.

53 Alsup, *Post-Resurrection Appearance Stories*, 180 n. 525.

54 Gnilka, *Matthäusevangelium* II, 508-509.

55 Gnilka, *Matthäusevangelium* II, 509.

Kingdom. The final element in the commissioning charge focuses on keeping all things that Jesus taught. The gospel uses διδάσκειν with Jesus as subject at the beginning and end of the Sermon on the Mount (5:2; 7:29) and in the conclusion of the missionary discourse (11:1). Two instances of the verb are taken from Mark (Matt. 13:54/Mark 6:2; Matt. 26:55/Mark 14:49). Matthew has replaced Mark's κηρύσσων (Mark 1:39) with διδάσκων in Matt. 4:23. In doing so he creates an additional reference to Jesus teaching in the synagogue. Matthew also has the authorities interrupt Jesus to pose the question about his authority while he is teaching in the temple (Matt. 21:23). Mark had Jesus walking in the area when he was accosted. That shift links the issue of Jesus' authority with the teaching which Jesus gives.

Readers should associate Jesus' teaching with the commands of the Law. The saying about the yoke implies that Jesus has provided its true interpretation (Matt. 11:28-30).[56] Jesus tells the rich young man to keep the commandments if he wishes to enter life (19:17). Even the teaching of the scribes and Pharisees can be "kept" so long as one does not follow their practices or the heavy burdens which their teaching places on others (23:3-4). The universal authority of Jesus' teaching has already been established in the gospel, itself. The conclusion to the Sermon on the Mount has already cautioned readers that disobedient followers will be condemned regardless of any claims they make to Jesus' name.[57] The condemnation which Matthew attaches to the parable of the Wicked Vineyard Workers contains a similar warning (Matt. 21:43). The Kingdom of God will be given to a nation (ἔθνος) that will produce the fruits of it. The Jewish leaders and those who follow their teaching constitute an ἔθνος that can be contrasted with the people who will be entrusted with the vineyard. However, Matthew's readers should recognize that the warning applies to them as well. The mission entrusted to the disciples establishes the new tenants in God's vineyard.

Though individual disciples might find themselves excluded from the Kingdom when Jesus returns in judgment, the new people of God cannot fail. Jesus remains present with his followers until the end of the age. As we have seen, Jesus' identification with the persecuted preachers of the gospel means that others are judged according to their treatment of these disciples (Matt. 10:41-42; 25:40, 45).[58] Matthew's readers may also have thought that Jesus' eternal presence with the community reflected the Old Testament references to God's presence with the people (Gen 26:25; Exod 3:12; Deut 20:1, 4; 31:6; Josh 1:9; Isa 41:10; 43:5).[59] The promise of Jesus' continuing presence returns to a theme invoked when the infant Jesus was named "Emmanuel, God with us" (Matt. 1:23).[60] Throughout the concluding section of the gospel, Matthew points the readers backwards toward the preaching and ministry of Jesus of

---

[56] Graham N. Stanton, *A Gospel for a New People. Studies in Matthew* (Edinburgh: T. & T. Clark, 1992) 341; Wrege, *Sondergut*, 131.

[57] Matthew refers to conduct of life, not merely knowledge of Jesus' teaching in verse 20a (so Gnilka, *Matthäusevangelium* II, 510).

[58] Wrege (*Sondergut*, 131) suggests that Jesus' presence with the community grounds the exhortation to community leaders not to lay claim to offices and titles (Matt. 23:8-12).

[59] Gnilka, *Matthäusevangelium* II, 510.

[60] Stanton, *Gospel for a New People*, 217, 330.

Nazareth. The one who remains present to the community is that Jesus, not an unknown, transcendent being.[61]

Matt. 28:16-20 is tied to the rest of the gospel so closely, that it cannot be said to display layers of tradition-history. However, the passage does bring the narrative from the past of Jesus of Nazareth into the present of the readers. They know that their faith was derived from the mission established by the authority of the exalted Jesus. The contrast between the resurrection scenes in which Jesus encounters his followers and the manipulation of affairs by Jewish religious authorities reminds the readers that they may have to choose sides.[62] The false story set in motion by the authorities continues to be told among the Jews "to this day," (28:15). The precautions which the authorities take to insure a guard for the tomb depends upon their knowledge of Jesus' own prediction (27:63). They also show that the fraud with which Jesus' disciples are charged was not true (27:64; 28:13). Therefore, readers should follow the words of Jesus, not those of his opponents. The earlier references to missionary efforts of Jesus' followers remind the readers that like Jesus' presence, their testimony before the nations will also continue to the end (10:22b). Even the witness to Israel will remain incomplete when Jesus returns as Son of Man (10:23b).[63]

As we have seen, the emphases in Matt. 28:16-20 highlight Matthew's earlier treatments of community and mission. The narrative alienation between the followers of Jesus and the Jewish leaders makes this emphasis critical. A new people of God has to be established through the post-resurrection activity of the disciples.[64] This new gathering has been anticipated but not realized in the narrative. Scholars often treat the narrative development from the mission to Israel to the command to teach the nations as evidence for the social development of the Matthean community. However, literary analyses have pointed out the methodological weakness in attempts to turn narrative details into social history. Narratives project an image of the implied author and readers which may differ considerably from actual persons. Neither implied nor actual readers can be directly identified with a group in the narrative.[65] Michael Wilkins has shown that Matthew makes use of unnamed disciples, not part of the Twelve to expand the circle of those who are followers of Jesus.[66] These characters determine the implied reader's understanding of discipleship by requiring evaluative judgments even on the depiction of the Twelve. The tension between particularity and universality is consistently played out in favor of universality.[67]

---

[61] Bauer, *Structure of Matthew's Gospel*, 114.

[62] Heil, *Death and Resurrection*, 107.

[63] Cf. Weaver, *Matthew's Missionary Discourse*, 15.

[64] Donaldson, *Jesus on the Mountain*, 189.

[65] Wilkins, "Named and Unnamed Disciples," 424-32.

[66] Wilkins over-emphasizes the role of such disciples in the resurrection account when he asserts that those to whom the women are sent constitute a nameless group ("Named and Unnamed Disciples," 437 n. 97). The numerical designation the Eleven is sufficient to function as a proper name, since it directs the reader back to the list of names prior to the missionary discourse.

[67] Wilkins, "Named and Unnamed Disciples," 438-39.

Conclusion

Matt. 28:16-20 has been created by the evangelist in order to ground the present experience of the readers in the story of Jesus of Nazareth. All of the individual elements in the pericope refer back to the earlier narrative. Even the command to "make disciples of all the nations" summarizes a point of view that has been established earlier in the gospel. One should not speak of Matt. 28:16-20 as though it were in conflict with the earlier mission to Israel. Not only is the latter presumed to continue, it is clearly the condition for the global mission of testimony to the gospel.[68] Matthew's characterization of the Jewish leaders creates a tension in the mission to Israel because blindness and deceit make it possible for them to claim the authority to lay on others the "heavy yoke" constructed of merely human precepts.

However certain the identification of Matthew's readers with the risen Jesus, they have been warned against similar behavior. The strong affirmation of Jesus' presence which concludes Matthew's gospel should not be read as a revision of the earlier judgment sayings associated with Jesus' return as Son of Man.[69] Nor should the exaltation of Jesus as the coming Son of Man be read into Matt. 28:18b. The narrative focuses on Jesus' presence as "God with us" in its final depiction of the ideal reader as the true disciple. By adding the brief notice of doubt to the encounter between the risen Jesus and the Eleven, the evangelist creates distance between the reader and the disciples. Readers are reminded of the complex evaluative judgments which they have already made about Jesus' followers.[70] The reader has seen an encounter between the women and Jesus which did not attach the notice about doubt to the gesture of worship (28:9).

Another narrative clue that the construction of discipleship required of the reader does not exclude the mission to Israel lies in the distinctive expression $\mu\alpha\theta\eta\tau\epsilon\acute{u}\epsilon\iota\nu$ (v. 19a). The two prior instances in the gospel refer to persons outside the circle of the Twelve who belong to the religious (Matt. 13:52) and social leadership of Israel (Matt. 27:57). Matthew presents Joseph as a wealthy person from outside Jerusalem and rejects the tradition that he was a member of the Council (Mark 15:43a). Joseph is separated completely from the group responsible for Jesus' death and the misinformation about his resurrection. Just as readers were instructed to distinguish between the teaching and practice of the Pharisees (Matt. 23:3-5) so they can also distinguish between Jewish scribes and leaders who are disciples of the Kingdom and those who are its enemies. The $\xi\theta\nu o\varsigma$ to which God has now entrusted the vineyard will certainly include the former.

---

68 Ernest Best ("The Revelation to Evangelize the Gentiles," *JTS* n.s. 35 [1984] 28-29) argues that the tradition of a command to evangelize the nations given to the Twelve as a group can only have emerged after the evangelization of the Gentiles was established practice.

69 Contrary to Donaldson's assertion that the apocalyptic judgment of Matt. 24 and 25 is being countered by a more realized eschatology (*Jesus on the Mountain*, 190).

70 The instances in which Matthew creates distance between the ideal reader and the disciples suggest that the latter might be treated as narratees rather than as ciphers for the ideal reader.

Finally, if Matt. 28:16-20 encapsulates the picture of Jesus' authoritative word, the new community and its mission found in the narrative, we should be cautious about over-interpreting the resurrection/exaltation as the beginning of a new stage in Matthean salvation history. The two christological affirmations which are most easily seen in Matt. 28:16-20, Son of God and Emmanuel, belong to Jesus from his conception. Matthew's depiction of encounters with the risen Jesus lack all the elements of epiphany characteristic of the resurrection appearance narratives elsewhere. As we have seen, the saying about Jesus' authority generalizes an authority which Jesus already exercises during his ministry. Matthew's narrative provides readers with the final examples of fulfiled prophecy. Jesus has been raised and appeared to his disciples in Galilee as predicted. Even the hostile Jewish leaders are forced to acknowledge the truth of Jesus' own words by inventing an elaborate cover-up of facts that were witnessed not only by believers but by the soldiers as well.

The fact of Jesus' resurrection and exaltation is a necessary condition for both his continued presence to the community and his later return in judgment. However, it is not a sufficient condition for the existence of the church or its mission. Unlike the Fourth Gospel in which no true understanding of Jesus is possible until after the resurrection (e.g., John 2:22; 14:25-28), Matthew's narrative grounds the entire life of the community in the life and teaching of Jesus of Nazareth. Matthew has set the conditions of its mission in the missionary discourse and other instructions given by Jesus. The coming of the Magi does not function simply as a proleptic anticipation of a future Gentile mission. Rather, it signals the reader that the new age of salvation began with the birth of Jesus of Nazareth.

Matthew 28:16-20, Anticlimax or Key to the Gospel?

Robert Harry Smith
Pacific Lutheran Theological Seminary

The question driving this brief essay on the resurrection in Matthew is not that of historicity ("Did he or didn't he?"), or of tradition ("What did Matthew inherit?"), or of form ("Enthronement or Cult Legend?"). It is rather the question, "What work does Matthew assign to the resurrected Jesus at the end of the Gospel in the Great Commission (GC), and how is that work connected to everything which goes before?"

Without denying the importance of other questions or methods, I want to signal at the very start that I will focus on the text in its finished form. Furthermore, I will enter into dialogue especially with colleagues who share a commitment to working primarily in a redaction or narrative critical mode, trying to discover why their answers often differ from my own.

I. Three Readings of the Great Commission (GC)

No consensus exists concerning the precise form of 28:16-20, but almost everyone agrees that the heart of the GC is the mandate: "Make disciples."[1] Commentators fall roughly into one of three camps (let's call them "christological," "ecclesiological" and "ethical") as they interpret that imperative. The following initial paraphrase, while it is admittedly a caricature, may nevertheless provide a useful framework for discussion.

---

[1] The notion that GC is an enthronement ritual enjoyed a brief vogue but is now widely regarded as mistaken. Gerhard Friedrich, "Die formale Struktur von Mt 28,16-20," *ZTK* 80 (1983) 137-183, critically reviews the history of efforts to define the form of the GC. He himself sees close parallels to the "I-Sayings" of the Fourth Gospel, speaks of the GC as a *Christusrede*, but prefers to deal with the three statements of the GC one at a time: *Selbstproklamation, Aussendungsrede*, and *Zusage*. D. Hill, "The Conclusion of Matthew's Gospel," *IBS* 8 (1986) 54-63, swims against the stream by calling baptism the center of the GC and asserting that indicatives and not imperatives are at the heart of the GC and of Matthew's theology. Bruce Malina and Jerome Neyrey, *Calling Jesus Names* (Sonoma: Polebridge, 1988) interpret the entire Gospel of Matthew as a status elevation ritual. In the GC they see Jesus "rewarded by his Father with maximum prominence, a) being raised from the dead, b) endowed with all power, c) being made the Messiah-to-come, d) becoming the faction founder and patron, who wishes to have disciples and clients in the here and now" (98). Further on Malina's views in section I.B, "Ethical Readings" (below).

The Great Commission Paraphrased

"The resurrected Jesus, who has been exalted to incomparably high status (a widely shared presuppostion in early Christianity), expressed his will to the eleven in a post-Easter speech to them (also broadly attested), declaring that they should:

> a) 'make disciples' = preach the good news that Jesus is Son of God, so that all people may believe and be saved;
> b) 'make disciples' = preach the good news to all peoples, especially the nations, so that they may know God's new openness to them and become God's people;
> c) 'make disciples' = turn all converts and confessors from among the peoples of the world into a community of disciples obedient to Jesus' commands."

Thus, in answer to the question, "What work does the Easter Jesus perform in Matthew's Gospel," scholars tend to respond by saying either that Jesus points (a) to himself and his new status, (b) to his new universal community, or (c) to his old teachings. Each of these readings of the GC reflects a reading of the Gospel as a whole as a document whose primary aim is christological, ecclesiological, or ethical.

Certainly interpreters are not so myopic as to insist that only one or these three elements (christology, ecclesiology, ethics) has some role in the GC, but they do tend to be determined, even fiercely so, in emphasizing one as shining so brilliantly as to be the sun around which the others orbit like minor moons.

I will attempt to articulate and defend a reading of the GC and of Matthew which in shorthand fashion may be called "ethical," while I try to carry on a fair fight with colleagues whose readings are primarily christological or ecclesiological.

All three sets of actual readers do their best to read in accord with Matthew's instructions and believe that they have successfully assumed the role assigned to the implied reader.

A. *Christological Readings*

In the christological interpretation the GC is read as a command to proclaim Jesus as God's Son to people everywhere, calling them to repent, believe and be saved. For a long time the popular religious mind has seen the launchings of untold thousands of foreign mission ventures as the obedient and logical yield of the GC. Many scholars find reasons to support that cherished tenet of popular piety.

For example, David Bauer interprets the imperative, "Make disciples," to mean, "Announce publicly the messiahship of Jesus."[2] That understanding accords fully with his conviction that "christology is the central concern of Matthew's Gospel."[3]

Bauer hangs that christological conviction on his observation that the Gospel is "the story of Jesus." However, Matthew's decision to author a "story

---

2 *The Structure of Matthew's Gospel* (Sheffield: Almond Press, 1988) 128, cf. 115.

3 Bauer, 145.

of Jesus" does not necessarily indicate that settling christological debates or celebrating Jesus' high status was his uppermost concern. It is both easy and legitimate to imagine that Matthew published his version of the story of Jesus for other purposes.

John Paul Heil represents a view similar to Bauer's. For him the imperative, "Make disciples," means to call people "to authentic faith in the absolute authority of the risen Jesus" and so "make true believers of all peoples."[4] His christological interpretation of the GC is consistent with the very pronounced attention he pays to the titles of Jesus in his introductory chapter, "The Previous Narrative Prepares for Matthew 26-28." For Heil and Bauer the GC is a command to promote a certain kind of christology.

Obviously christology is not the only thing these interpreters see in the GC. Their christology has transformative consequences and is ethical in a broad sense. They combine a Son of God christology with an evangelical soteriology: trusting the good news about the resurrected Jesus as God's Son has saving effects.

This understanding of the GC reflects a particular way of reading Matthew's plot, clearly articulated in recent work by Mark Allan Powell and Jack Dean Kingsbury.

These latter point to two series of Matthean passages as key. One set (4:17 and 16:21) divides the story of Jesus into three periods (preparation, proclamation, passion). The second set articulates the intention of the Jesus who lived that tripartite life. Chief among them is the angelic word of 1:21, "He will save his people from their sins." Three other passages, uttered by Jesus (another "reliable voice"), are summoned to serve alongside 1:21 as prime witnesses to the intentions of the Matthean Jesus: 9:13; 20:28; 26:28.[5]

Working with these passages, Powell concludes that "the main plot" of Matthew can be entitled "God's plan and Satan's challenge" and may be summarized (almost entirely in his own words) as follows: God intends to save people from their sin through his Son Jesus (1:21), who (1) proclaims the nearness of the rule of heaven and declares that he has come to call sinners (9:13), and who then (2) predicts his passion and declares that he has come to give his life as a ransom (20:28; 26:28). The divine plan of salvation meets satanic resistance: religious leaders hinder the first part of the divine plan but then ironically assist in the second; the disciples assist in the first part but resist the second. The saving activity of God overcomes Satan's challenge as Jesus dies on the cross, fulfilling God's plan to save people from sin.

Powell and Kingsbury insist that it is at the cross, not at the resurrection, that Matthew's story of Jesus reaches its culmination, for "the cross is the place where God in Jesus accomplishes universal salvation."[6]

Powell therefore speaks of the final paragraph of Matthew's Gospel as "the great commission epilogue." Its purpose is merely "to inform us that these resolutions [calling sinners and giving his life as a ransom] have set in

---

4 *The Death and Resurrection of Jesus* (Minneapolis: Fortress, 1991) 107, 111.

5 Powell, "The Plot and Subplots of Matthew's Gospel," *NTS* 38 (1992) 195, 199-200; Kingsbury, "The Plot of Matthew's Story," *Int* 46 (1992) 355, cf. *Jesus Christ in Matthew, Mark, and Luke* (Philadelphia: Fortress, 1981) 63-64.

6 Kingsbury, "Plot," 355.

motion new developments that will be resolved in a story yet to be told."[7] The resurrected Jesus is thus a decidedly minor character in Matthew's plot but will have some unspecified larger role in a new story beyond the confines of Matthew's narrative.

For Kingsbury the resurrection functions within the plot as "vindication" and "exaltation." As vindication it is God's demonstration "that Jesus' death is in line with (God's) saving purposes." As exaltation, the resurrection bestows universal authority on this Jesus through whom God "will renew his covenant and proffer all humans everywhere the forgiveness of sins and salvation."[8]

However, if Matthew wanted to portray the resurrected Jesus as sponsoring a mission of spreading the good news that he is truly Son of God and that believing this gospel issues in forgiveness of sins, then he has done a poor job of choosing his words.

In fact, if Benjamin Hubbard is anywhere near correct, then Matthew has deliberately altered an appropriate formulation in order to produce the present inappropriate wording of the GC.

Hubbard believes that two earlier commissionings underlie the GC. At first "one of the eleven disciples narrated Jesus' appearance to them and subsequent commissioning so as to authenticate his right to preach the gospel of Jesus Christ." Then within 15 years "a Gentile missionary, at least one step removed from the disciple, heard the account of Jesus' appearance and commissioning and added the universalistic emphasis."[9]

The resultant "proto-commissioning" had the following wording:

> Jesus appeared to the eleven. When they saw him they were glad, though some disbelieved. Then he said: preach (the gospel) to all nations. (Baptize) in my name for the forgiveness of sins. (And behold,) I will send the Holy Spirit upon you.[10]

Hubbard thinks that Matthew then altered these words to produce the GC as a third edition of the commissioning.

Hubbard's analysis is useful in highlighting the Matthean character of the language of the GC. However, Hubbard takes all three editions, in spite of all the differences among them, to mean that the eleven are to "spread the gospel" and make converts. Like Bauer and Heil, he thinks that the GC's imperative, "Make disciples," means to "make new disciples" by undertaking a "universal mission.[11]

But why use new language ("disciple all nations!") if the GC has the same point as its predecessors? Hubbard appears satisfied to say, "It's language Matthew learned under the influence of Hebrew bible commissionings." Others appear to say that discipling is simply Matthew's word for converting people from unfaith to faith in the saving gospel.

---

7 Powell, 196.

8 "Plot," 355; cf. *Jesus Christ*, 85.

9 *The Matthean Redaction of a Primitive Apostolic Commissioning* (SBL: Scholars Press, 1974) 128.

10 Hubbard, 122f.

11 Hubbard, 127, 89.

However, the images and language of the GC do not depict the resurrected Jesus as urging reluctant disciples to venture forth on a kerygmatic mission of testimony bearing the offer of forgiveness to potential converts. That is the sort of thing with which other Gospels conclude (Luke 24:44-49; cf. Acts 1:6-8; John 20:19-23; Mark 16:9-20).

The GC lacks all the usual early Christian words associated with evangelism. Nothing is said of "sending, apostleship, or mission." Nothing about "the word" or "the gospel," nothing about "preaching" or "proclaiming." Nothing of "repenting, believing, and confessing," or of receivig the divine benefactions of "forgiveness and peace with God." As the story closes, Jesus is speaking on a mountain, not directing a fishing expedition at the lakeside. The GC is not about missionaries venturing forth with a message of grace in quest of converts.[12]

B. Ecclesiological Readings

In the ecclesiological interpretation the crucifixion and resurrection of Jesus (sometimes one of them alone, often together) constitute the turning point in God's plan of salvation, marking the moment when old arrangements crumble and God in the Son creates a fresh opening to the Gentiles.

In his investigation of Matthew's plot, Frank Matera writes that Matthew at first glance seems simply to tell the story of Jesus' life from birth till death and resurrection. However, he notes that Matthew has set the life of Jesus into a wider context stretching from Abraham to the parousia.[13]

So while Bauer says that Matthew's story is "about Jesus" and therefore about christology, Matera says that it "has something to do with salvation history."[14]

Matera sums up his study with the statement that "Matthew's Gospel can be read as a story whose plot concerns Israel's rejection of the Messiah and the consequent movement (elsewhere he says "transfer") of the gospel to the Gentiles.[15]

---

[12] See Guenther Baumbach, "Die Mission im Matthaeus-Evangelium," *TLZ* 92 (1967) 889-93, and Friedrich, 180-181.

[13] Matera, "The Plot of Matthew's Gospel," *CBQ* 49 (1987) 233-253; so also Kingsbury, *Jesus Christ*, 63.

[14] Matera, 241.

[15] Matera, 252f. Matera begins by identifying six "kernels" (Seymour Chatman's term) in Matthew's narrative: 1) The Birth of Jesus (2:1a); 2) The Beginning of Jesus' Ministry (4:12-17); 3) John the Baptist's Question (11:2-6); 4) Jesus' Conversation at Caesarea Philippi (16:1328); 5) The Cleansing of the Temple (21:1-17); and 6) The Great Commission (28:16-20). Working with the six kernels and the context of salvation history, Matera offers this plot summary (245-6): Jesus is born as the Davidic Messiah. After the imprisonment of John the Baptist, he initiates a mission of preaching, teaching, and healing exclusively to Israel. At a crucial moment in his ministry (signaled by the question of John), representatives from all segments of Israel reject him. Jesus' disciples, however, recognize him as the Messiah, and he confides to them his destiny of suffering, death, and resurrection. When Jesus arrives at Jerusalem, his action of cleansing the temple becomes the immediate occasion for his death. Jesus' passion is Israel's definitive rejection of the Messiah, and it results in the transfer of the gospel to the Gentiles.

Pheme Perkins takes the imperative, "Make disciples," in a similar way. It means to "move beyond the confines of Judaism" and "evangelize" the Gentiles, "preaching" in a missionary effort aimed at converting them.[16]

In discussing the GC, Perkins declares her agreement with Schuyler Brown that the Gospel of Matthew "has been composed to defend the mission to the Gentiles" at a time when "the mission to convert Israel" was failing.[17]

Matera, in carrying out his literary critical analysis of Matthew's plot, does not discuss the external circumstances of the composition of the Gospel, but it is easy to suspect that an extra-narrative picture of early Christian history, similar to Brown's, is intruding on his thinking.

In this interpretation the death and resurrection of Jesus, conceived as a single eschatological event, signify God's sweeping away of the old dispensation and the establishing of something new. The GC is the resurrected Jesus' own triumphant declaration of his startling Sonship and universal Lordship, articulated in a call to embrace peoples of the world formerly excluded from God's favor, including them by means of a baptismal rite which replaces circumcision, and binding them to his own words in place of the Torah.[18]

In his work on Matthew's plot, Matera never once cites the passages of prime importance to Powell and Kingsbury (1:21; 9:13; 20:28). If there is a single passage informing (or haunting) the ecclesiological interpretation of the Gospel, it is 21:43. Graham Stanton writes that "Matt 21:43 with its double emphasis on God's rejection of Israel and his acceptance of Gentiles as part of his people is one of the most important verses in the whole gospel."[19] When Israel or the religious leaders and their allies refused to bear fruit, the kingdom was taken from them and given to the Gentiles.[20]

If Matthew had intended to put the resurrected Jesus to work destroying the barrier between Jew and Gentile, eliminating circumcision and canceling purity regulations, with a view to creating one new inclusive community, better language than that of the GC was available.

Jesus might have announced that there is "no longer Jew or Greek, slave or free, male and female" (Gal. 3:28), or used the language of "peace" (Eph. 2:14-15) or "reconciliation" (Col. 1:20) or "oneness" ("one new humanity" marked by "one Lord, one faith, one baptism, one God and Father of all" (Eph. 4:5). But Matthew does not deal in such language, nor does he picture

---

16 *Resurrection* (Garden City: Doubleday, 1984) 87, 134.

17 Perkins, 134, 203-4; see S. Brown, "The Matthean Community and the Gentile Mission," *NovT* 22 (1980) 193-221.

18 See, for example, John P. Meier, *Law and History in Matthew's Gospel* (Rome: Biblical Institute Press, 1976), and Daniel Harrington, *The Gospel of Matthew* (Collegeville: Liturgical Press, 1991).

19 *The Gospels and Jesus* (Oxford University Press, 1989) 67.

20 Also of great significance for the ecclesiological understanding of the Gospel are passages which feature Jesus' bitter words about the scribes and Pharisees (e.g., ch. 23) and those passages which highlight the tension between old and new views of the Law (5:17-20 and 28:20a) and between old restriction of the mission to Israel and the new openness to the nations (10:5; 15:24 and 28:19). See Stanton, "The Communities of Matthew," *Int* 46 (1992), especially 383-85 for these and other passages.

anything like a sheet descending from heaven with all manner of creatures now declared to be clean (Acts 10:11-15).

C. Ethical Readings

Central to the GC and to the Gospel as a whole is the proclamation of an ethic or, better, a discipleship marked by a higher righteousness that does the will of God as Jesus has articulated it in his ministry of teaching, healing and suffering.

In this interpretation the verb "to disciple" does not mean "to induce people to ascribe the proper status to Jesus and confess him with the proper titles" or "to proclaim Jesus as the fulfiller of God's plan of salvation so all may know him as the ground of their new status as people of God." "To disciple" means "to turn converts and confessors of Jesus from among Jews and Gentiles into disciples, people walking the way of righteousness, trees bearing good fruit, guests wearing a wedding garment.

While christological and ecclesiological interpretations of the GC seem almost to be taken for granted, supporters of the ethical interpretation are harder to find, but their number may be increasing.[21]

In an article principally devoted to the form and structure of the GC, Malina takes seriously the word "therefore" (*oun*) and the phrase "and remember" (*kai idou*), and argues that the three main clauses of the GC (18, 19-20a, 20b) together form "a single coherent statement of Jesus." His conclusion (with which I heartily agree) may be paraphrased as follows. The GC means that (1) the authority of Jesus (2) wells up into a command which is (3) supported by a promise. The heart of the GC is the command, and the command says to "form disciples."[22]

In articulating his understanding of this command, Malina explicitly rejects the notion that the GC is "apostolic." "No one," he writes, "is sent." Therefore, to call the GC a *Missionsauftrag* as Trilling does, or a *Sendungsbefehl* as Bornkamm does is to apply a misnomer.[23]

Malina insists that the participle (*poreuthentes*) preceding the imperative (*mathēteusate*) "is essentially an auxiliary, with no force of its own at all."[24]

Malina's view needs one small modification. While the participle does not indicate a separate action from the imperative, it adds urgency to the imperative, and thus the phrase may be rendered: "Throw yourselves into forming disciples."

---

21 See especially Bruce Malina, "The Literary Structure and Form of Matt 28:16-20" *NTS* 17 (1971) 87-103; Robert H. Smith, *Easter Gospels: The Resurrection of Jesus according to the Four Evangelists* (Minneapolis: Augsburg, 1983), and also "Matthew's Message for Insiders," *Int* 46 (1992) 229-239; and Douglas R. A. Hare, *Matthew* (Louisville: John Knox, 1993).

22 "Literary Structure," 88, 96.

23 Unfortunately, by the time Malina reaches the end of his essay he is backsliding from his rejection of labels such as *Missionsauftrag*. In his conclusion he writes that the GC "presents Jesus' commission to expand and open the circle of true disciples so as to include people of all nations," that is, to "make more disciples" (102). And his study of deviance and prominence labelling (see note 1) leads him to stress the christological rather than the ethical character of the GC.

24 "Literary Structure," 90. Hubbard, 83, and others disagree and see visions of a "very extensive mission" dancing in Matthew's head.

The imperative ("form disciples") is the main verb, and the two following participles articulate the means by which the formation of disciples is to be carried out.

"Baptizing": For Matthew baptism is not the occasion for the influx of divine energy issuing in tongues-speaking, exorcisms and miracles (see Matt. 7:21-23 and contrast Acts 2:4; 10:46; 19:6; 1 Cor 12:8-10). Jesus' own baptism in Matthew's Gospel at the hands of John was the moment when Jesus stepped up onto the way of righteousness (3:15; 21:32) and of obedient sonship. Jesus, conceived by the Spirit (1:18,20) and endowed with the Spirit at baptism (3:16), focused all his charismatic energy on executing God's will and opposing demonic forces (4:1-11; 12:28; cf. 6:33).

The triadic baptismal formula, whatever its origin or precise manner of use in the community, binds the Spirit one more time to the Father (3:16; 10:20) and to the Son (12:18, 28), effectively denying to the Spirit any novel or independent mission in the days after Jesus' crucifixion and resurrection. Baptism sets a person onto the path of righteousness under the single sponsorship of Father-Son-Holy Spirit.

"Teaching": How often it is said that here in the GC the disciples receive a kind of ordination at the hands of Jesus so that they become authoritative teachers in the new community.

But in the GC Jesus does not rescind his former emphatic undermining of the whole dreary business of seeking privileged positions (20:20-28) or titles (23:7-12) in the community, nor does he repent of the warnings he earlier issued concerning spiritually powerful teachers or prophets who will arise from within the new community to lead people astray (7:15-20, 21-23; 24:11, 24).

Whatever arrangements concerning offices or leadership may have prevailed in his community, Matthew in the GC emphasizes the authority of the resurrected Jesus, not the authorizing of the eleven. Jesus alone is to be called "Teacher" and "Master" in the community (23:8, 10). He assigns neither status nor titles when he defines the function of the eleven: teaching all that Jesus has commanded.[25]

II. The GC and the Plot of Matthew's Gospel

When the resurrected Jesus in the GC calls attention to all that he has previously "commanded," he himself thereby lifts to prominence actions ignored or downgraded in the christological and ecclesiological interpretations and suggests a different reading of the Gospel as whole.

The resurrected Jesus does not call to mind his old deeds of power (healings, exorcisms or other miracles), nor does he mention the provocative way he ignored old taboos, nor does he breathe a single syllable concerning his passion. He calls attention to his authority, which embraces all places in heaven and on earth, and his presence, which encompasses all time to the close of the age, only to throw the full weight of his exalted status behind a program of disciple-making. Matthew uses the resurrected Jesus to validate

---

[25] See Edgar Krentz, "Community and Character: Matthew's Vision of the Church," *Society of Biblical Literature Seminar Papers* (Scholars Press, 1987) 565-573.

and promote a program of "teaching them to observe all that I have commanded."

Many have commented on the chiastic structure of the Gospel and the way the GC recapitulates themes trumpeted in early chapters.[26] By setting the GC on "the mountain" in the presence of "disciples" and by lacing Jesus' speech with talk of "making disciples" and "baptism" and "teaching commands," Matthew conjures up memories of the beginning of the Gospel, especially Jesus' first words and the first great action of his ministry.

A. First Impressions

First words and first acts have peculiar power in shaping the perceptions of readers, and each of our canonical evangelists has lighted upon a different utterance and a different deed in recording Jesus' first words and first great public action. These "firsts" have a programmatic quality as they inaugurate and define Jesus' ministry.[27]

Matthew's unique choice of first utterance and initial public activity of Jesus disposes readers to think that the work of Jesus has little to do with christology or ecclesiology and has everything to do with "righteousness."

First Words: The first words out of the mouth of Jesus in Matthew's Gospel appear in the exchange with John the Baptist: "It is proper for us to fulfill all righteousness" (3:15). The impression that Jesus is vitally concerned about "righteousness" is reinforced by a whole series of sayings in which Jesus speaks explicitly of his intentions for himself and God's people: "live by every word from God's mouth" (4:4), "not abolish but fulfill the law and the prophets in an exceeding righteousness" (5:17-20), "be perfect" (5:48), "do the will of God on earth" (6:10), "seek first God's kingdom and righteousness" (6:33), "do his words" (7:24-27), "desire mercy" (9:13a), "take his yoke" (11:29), "do God's will and become Jesus' family" (12:50), "grow like good seed" (13:36-43), "forgive as forgiven" (18:23-35), "yield fruits" (21:43), "put on a wedding garment" (22:11-14), "love God above all and the neighbor as oneself" (22:34-40), "feed the hungry" (25:31-46), "do God's will" (26:39, 41).

All these are sayings in the mouth of Jesus and therefore come to the reader cloaked in the mantle of reliability. Some are "I-sayings," some are quotations of scripture, and most are uniquely Matthean. In all of these sayings (and in many others in the Gospel) the impression of Jesus' first words (3:15) is restated, paraphrased and deepened but never disconfirmed.

Jesus' First Public Act: The public phase of Jesus' life in Matthew's Gospel opens not with an exorcism (as in Mark 1:21-28), not with a synagogue

---

26 Bauer offers a full discussion in his chapter on the GC, "The Structure of Matthew: Climax with Inclusio," 109-128.

27 The fact that teachers and writers have so much fun, even mounting contests year by year, with Bulwer-Lytton's line, "It was a dark and stormy night," is evidence of the conviction that openings are singularly important. Shlomith Rimmon-Kenan, *Narrative Fiction* (London: Methuen, 1983) 119-122, summarizes the researches of Menakhem Perry on "the primacy effect," the tendency of what comes first to control a reader's understanding of what comes later. For further reflections on "the doctrine of first impressions" see Mikeal C. Parsons, "Reading a Beginning/Beginning a Reading: Tracing Literary Theory on Narrative Openings," in *How Gospels Begin*, ed. Dennis Smith, *Semeia* 52 (1990) 18-21.

sermon at Nazareth (as in Luke 4:16-30), nor with a miracle at a wedding in Cana (as in John 2:1-11). In the other Gospels these are the public acts which follow immediately upon Jesus' preparation for ministry (baptism, temptation and call of first disciples). Instead of "telling," each evangelist has done a masterful job of "showing" what Jesus' program was all about.

Unlike the other evangelists, Matthew features the Sermon on the Mount as Jesus' first great public act. Fresh from his baptism at the Jordan and testing in the wilderness, Jesus summons a handful of disciples (4:18-22) and attracts a vast international crowd (4:23-25). Talk of "disciples" (5:1) and of that great throng from across many borders sets Matthew's preparatory account apart and alerts readers to central Matthean concerns.

Seeing disciples and that throng, Jesus immediately ascends the mountain and faces them. At that moment the chief actors in Matthew's drama are on the stage: Jesus and a multitude of people consisting of disciples and potential disciples. At that moment the action in Matthew's plot begins in earnest.[28]

The Matthean Jesus, seated on the mountain, face to face with that multitude, has many options: exorcise a demon, cleanse a leper, open blind eyes, feed the throng, or speak to them. And if he chooses speech, what words should fill his inaugural address? It is of utmost significance for our understanding of Matthew's plot that Jesus begins his public activity by speaking the Sermon on the Mount, with its vision of a people living lives of a higher righteousness.

B. Plot and Conflict

The suspense in the plot of the Gospel derives from that moment on the mountain. Will Jesus in his life's work live up to the promise of his name? Will he be able to rescue people so that their lives are defined not by sins but by deeds of righteousnesss? (1:21; 3:15; 21:28-32). In a plot so conceived, the discourses will play a major role and not be ignored or subordinated to other concerns as so often happens.[29]

The conflict marking Matthew's story of Jesus is regularly described, both by christological and ecclesiological readers, as mortal combat between Jesus and the religious authorities. These readers focus either on the authorities' denial of Jesus' christological claims, or on the way the authorities bring ruin on Israel by their sullen opposition.

However, the authorities are only one of the groups with whom Jesus struggles, and they do not even seriously confront Jesus until chapter 9. Futhermore, it should be obvious that it is the speaker of the Sermon on the

---

[28] Robert Funk writes that the action of a narrative begins when two characters, moving toward one another on a collision course, first meet (*The Poetics of Biblical Narrative* [Sonoma: Polebridge Press, 1988] 215).

[29] I regard the act of delivering the Sermon on the Mount as a "kernel" in Matthew's plot. Seymour Chatman defines kernels as critical moments in a plot which "cannot be deleted without destroying the narrative logic" (Chatman, *Story and Discourse* [Ithaca: Cornell University Press, 1978] 53). Powell, on the other hand, defending his christological-soteriological view of Matthew's plot, has said that "Jesus has not come to give speeches but to give his life" (*What is Narrative Criticism?* [Minneapolis: Fortress, 1990] 46. Bauer, 134, seems to agree with Powell when he says that the discourses "play a primarily formal role in the climactic development toward 28:16-20."

Mount who is rejected. As he moves from the mountain, he encounters many kinds of people and provokes many different responses, rousing scattered admiration but also deadly opposition, issuing finally in his crucifixion. Instead of a universal upsurge of repentance and renewal in righteousness, the outcome of the ministry which began on the mountain was the tragedy of crucifixion.

The final paragraph of the final discourse (25:31-46) is artfully connected to the passion narrative. The formula concluding the discourse in this instance introduces Jesus' prediction of his imminent passion (26:1-2). Here are both terrible irony and awful choice: The Judge over all humanity (25:31-46) predicts that he will be handed over to the judgment of human courts (chs. 26-27). Two judgments: his and theirs. The Judge will be judged, and how will readers judge? Will they live by his values (25:31-46) or by the values of Caiaphas and Pilate and all their accomplices? The same kind of choice confronts readers in the final two paragraphs of the Gospel: 28:11-15 embodies one set of values and 28:16-20 those of the speaker of the Sermon on the Mount who is the world's final Judge.

The end which Jesus predicted for himself was not in vain. All the way to the end Jesus models discipleship, and some few within the narrative confessed their allegiance to Jesus and his program. And far from being forever destroyed by human intransigence, Jesus was raised from the dead.

By raising Jesus from the dead, God passed judgment on Jesus' opponents, declaring them to be absolutely wrong, and wrote "God pleasing" (cf. 3:17) over Jesus' entire way (words and deeds and not his suffering alone). And God bestowed on Jesus universal authority, not that he might begin a new career but so that he might resume his old ministry of discipling but no longer under the old restrictions. Matthew portrays the resurrected Jesus as working in all times and all places with all people to fashion converts into disciples.[30]

C. Last Impressions

Final scenes are as important as first scenes in assessing an author's values and meaning.[31] The GC (the final scene of the whole Gospel) closely

---

[30] Oscar Brooks, "Matt 28:16-20 and the Design of the First Gospel," *JSNT* 10 (1981) 2-18, argues that the GC "has controlled the entire design of the Gospel of Matthew," and that the Gospel was written "to support the conclusion that Jesus is endowed with authority and that his teachings are worthy to be transmitted by the disciples."

[31] David Ball, *Backwards and Forwards: A Technical Manual for Reading Plays* (Carbondale: Southern Illinois University, 1983), with *Hamlet* as example, demonstrates the usefulness of reading backwards from the final scene in order to comprehend how all elements in a plot hang together. M. Perry (see S. Rimmon-Kenan, note 27 above) describes the "recency effect," the tendency of readers to assimilate all previous information to what they have read last of all and to modify hypotheses established on the basis of items appearing first. Matthew offers material enriching but never contradicting his first impressions. John Gardner claims that "the writer works out plot in one of three ways: by borrowing some traditional plot or an action from real life [as Matthew borrowed Mark and retells the story of Jesus?] . . .; by working his way back from his story's climax; or by groping his way forward from an initial situation. Since usually one does not work out plot all at once, but broods over it, mentally trying alternatives . . . one may in practice work both

resembles the final scenes in each of the five discourses, and all these last scenes together confirm what is here being called an ethical reading of the Gospel.

The GC and the concluding passages in the discourses do not teach a high christology but presuppose one. In these final scenes Jesus is portrayed as the great and exalted Judge of humanity and as using the language "Son of Man" (13:41; 25:31) or "Lord" (7:21-22; 25:44) or "Son" (28:19) in speaking of himself.

While the CG and the judgment scenes in the discourses make use of a high christology, christology is never the criterion of judgment. Not once does the Judge raise the question of his identity (his proper titles, for example). In fact a correct title (*kyrios*) is on the lips of the condemned in 7:21-22 and in 25:44. In spite of their correct christology the Judge disowns them (7:23; 25:41). What counts is not knowledge or language but performance (7:24-27; 25:42-43).

Community or church (16:18; 18:17) is likewise important to Matthew, but never once does judgment depend on one's corporate identity. No judgment scene even hints that membership in "the church" rather than in "their synagogues" might be a thing of value. Nothing is said of any advantage accruing to people by virtue of their being Jew or Gentile or because of their belonging to any particular social or economic class. Nor does male have any advantage over female. The GC and the discourses speak in universal terms: "everyone who" (7:24,26; 10:32), "whoever" (10:37-42), "every one of you" (18:35), "all the nations" (25:31; 28:19). Again each is judged on the basis of performance.[32]

From first (first words and first great action) to last (final scenes in the discourses and the GC at the end), Matthew's Gospel declares that the ministry of Jesus is a struggle to win for God a people liberated from sins and yielding the fruits of righteousness.[33]

The resurrected Jesus in the GC looks both backwards and forwards: back over the narrative and ahead to the world beyond the borders of the narrative. As he does so, he articulates a single overriding concern: not that the nations get their christology right, not that Gentile outsiders should become aware of their new insider status, but only that all peoples everywhere attend to his words and so begin to enact the will of God and live the life of discipleship.[34]

---

backward and forward or even in all three of the possible ways simultaneously." (*The Art of Fiction* [New York: Random House, 1983] 56-57).

[32] Amy-Jill Levine, *The Social and Ethnic Dimensions of Matthean Social History* (Lewiston: Edwin Mellen Press, 1988), 273, writes that "neither ethnic origin [the focus of ecclesiological readings] nor confessional affiliation [the focus of christological readings] will influence the final judgment." All (Jew and Gentile alike) will be "judged according to the same criterion of faith in God demonstrated in action." She seems to use the phrase "faith-in-God-demonstrated-in-action" as a single word to describe the characteristic mark of disciples in Matthew's Gospel.

[33] Powell's christological-soteriological interpretation of the GC and of the Gospel as a whole may be due in part to his reading of 1:21. 8 of 12 times, when quoting or paraphrasing 1:21, including the first time he cites the passage, he uses the singular: "He will save his people from their *sin*." He and others apparently read a Pauline interpretation into the word and take sin to be a great and singular power gripping humankind, whose grasp is broken only by the death of God's messiah.

[34] John Gardner, 192, defines a "resonant close" as "the novel's chief glory." What he says is perfectly relevant to the GC: "What moves us is not just that characters, images, and

With the GC, Matthew teaches readers to look back over the story and conclude that the ministry of Jesus reaches its goal not with Jesus' death on the cross but only when characters in the narrative step up onto the way of righteousness and discipleship.

D. Readers at the Great Commission

The GC is both conclusion and new beginning. It concludes the narrative and assists readers in exiting the story and returning to the real world.

Both Matera and Heil focus briefly on the response Matthew seeks to provoke in readers of the Gospel as they come to the GC and the end of the reading process.

Matera pursues a suggestion of Kieran Egan that the sequence of events in a plot will stimulate a sequence of emotions in the reader. On the basis of the GC, Matera concludes that Matthew's Gospel achieves its affective goal as readers worship Jesus as risen Lord (28:17) and have confidence in his authority and presence (28:20). He finds support for this conclusion in two passages at the beginning of the story: the angel's assurance to Joseph that Jesus is Emmanuel (1:23) and the Magi's act of worship at Bethlehem (2:11).

Heil, comparing 28:11-15 with 28:16-20, writes that readers are called to faith in the risen Jesus and through that faith are empowered to prevail over fraudulent authority. By Jesus' promise they are equipped to predominate over persistent unbelief, and they are invited to embark on a mission of sharing faith in the resurrected Jesus.

Matera and Heil raise important questions: What response is generated by the GC, and how does the GC achieve that response? Matera points to words describing the responses of characters in the narrative, while Heil tracks the way Matthew, by means of his sequences of interlocking scenes, takes readers "through a progressive interchange of sharply opposing themes."

At one point Heil describes readers as "identifying with the disciples" during the reading process, and in his summary of Matthew 26 he writes of the empowering benefit of "our identification with Jesus."[35]

Heil's focus on "identification" is provocative. In whose shoes do we as readers stand? Do we identify with Jesus? with the Twelve? Do we enter the narrative and try to find a character with whom we feel some measure of sympathy and then identify with that character? In the course of reading do we try out several identifications?

Or do we enter the narrative in a different way? Don't we step into the narrative and live temporarily in it, experiencing its dynamics, submitting to its values, not identifying with any particular character but always moving freely through the varied scenes as silent and invisible presences, better informed than any characters in the story, sometimes criticizing their responses and sometimes applauding? As the text moves readers to criticize or

---

events get some form of recapitulation or recall: We are moved by the increasing connectedness of things, ultimately a connectedness of values."

[35] Heil describes his work, *The Death and Resurrection of Jesus*, as narrative critical study with "a special emphasis on the responses of the implied reader" (1). The quotations cited in the text are on pages 107 and 111 of the same work.

to applaud in accord with the highest values of the narrative world, the text achieves its goal with the readers.[36]

The GC is direct discourse, and direct discourse in a narrative has peculiar power to make readers feel addressed personally. That fact together with the tendency of some readers to identify with characters in the narrative has led to one traditional way of reading the GC. Many actual readers have imagined that Jesus is speaking directly to them when he says, "Make disciples." Such readers should take more seriously the fact that Jesus speaks the GC to the eleven and not to readers. Readers are present on the mountain in the same way they are present everywhere else in the story, seeing all deeds and hearing all words.

The appropriate response to the GC does not seem to be, "Jesus is telling me to make disciples," but rather, "Jesus in his final words assigns ultimate value to discipleship." The reader is not left with the question, "Will the gospel be preached to the nations?" or "Shall I become a maker of disciples?" The crucial question raised by the GC is rather this: "Will I, the reader, perform better than the characters in the narrative and become an obedient disciple of the resurrected Jesus?"

III. Beyond the Ending

Different readers, moving through Matthew's text to the end, have reached conflicting notions of the overall meaning which makes sense of the text as a whole. Christological, ecclesiological and ethical interpreters are not seeing ghosts. They report on realities in the text but differ in their convictions about how these richly narrated realities are related to one another.

Matthew puts the resurrected Jesus to a certain kind of work in the narrative world (not easy to agree on) because he has his heart set on his narrated Jesus doing a certain kind of work in the real world (even harder to agree on). Kingsbury may be correct in saying that we should try to get the narrative world straight before we take up questions of real world. Nevertheless, I have a hunch that each reading of the Gospel reflects an interpreter's sense of what Benjamin Bacon (who had never heard of implied author or implied reader) called "Matthew's implied environment." Even in these days of literary and narrative criticism it is hard to suspend such interests.

I confess that I continue to see the environment as one in which Matthew uses the resurrected Jesus to combat not synagogue leaders but other Christian teachers who were promoting themselves and their authority in the community on the basis of their spiritual endowments (7:21-23; 23:8-12; 24:10-12). Matthew counters with a fresh use of the tradition of the resurrection

---

[36] Robert Tannehill, "The Disciples in Mark: The Function of a Narrative Role," *JR* 57 (1977) 395, describes Mark's strategy of first encouraging readers' tendency to "associate" or "identify" with the disciples and of then countering that tendency by offering negative portraits, thereby plunging readers into "a search for a new self who can follow Jesus faithfully." Janice Capel Anderson, "Matthew: Gender and Reading," *Semeia* 28 (1983) 24, distances herself from "any interpretation which insists certain readers must identify with certain character groups." She defines discipleship in terms of "the norms and values the implied author wishes the implied reader to adopt."

of Jesus, portraying Jesus as the exalted Teacher of the Sermon on the Mount who still lives in the midst of the community with all his prior words (and of course marked by all his prior action and passion).

The Great Commission was designed in large measure, I think, to demote the most powerful leaders in Matthew's community, to elevate Jesus' teaching, and to shift the energies of the community from charismatic display to deeds of righteousness, even from precision of Christological confession to the quality of community life. But "Matthew's implied environment" is a topic for another time and place.[37]

---

[37] Kingsbury, "Reflections on the 'Reader' of Matthew's Story," *NTS* 34 (1988) 442-60; B. W. Bacon, *Studies in Matthew* (New York: Henry Holt, 1930), 75. Robert H. Smith, *Easter Gospels*, 55-91; *Matthew* (Minneapolis: Augsburg, 1989; and especially "Matthew's Message for Insiders," *Int* 46 (1992) 229-239.

The Silence of the Messiah: The Function of "Messianic Secret" Motifs across the Synoptics

Neil Elliott
College of St. Catherine

Rationale

Since William Wrede's groundbreaking work on "the Messianic Secret in the Gospels,"[1] considerable attention has been devoted to the contours and purpose of that motif—or as more recent studies suggest, that complex of motifs—in Mk's Gospel.[2] Much less attention has been given to parallel materials in the other synoptic Gospels.[3] This paper explores the particular configuration of some "secret" motifs in the narratives of Mt and Lk, then compares the results with the role of "secret" motifs in Mk's narrative.

Although most of the passages that Wrede saw as components of the Markan messianic secret had parallels in Mt or Lk, Wrede gave these parallels less attention in his treatment, for several reasons. First: Wrede was convinced that Mk, as the first of the synoptic Evangelists, had created the messianic secret motif as a compositional schema within which fundamentally unmessianic traditions about the earthly Jesus could be integrated with the early Christian *kerygma* of Jesus as the exalted Lord. As creator of the motif, Mk was obviously to be made the primary focus for the study of the motif. Second: Wrede was equally convinced that Mt and Lk had used Mk in composing their Gospels (the "Two-Source Hypothesis"); consequently he declared that parallels to elements of Mk's secrecy theme that appeared in Mt or Lk "are not simply to be thought of as the expression of their own views, for the very good reason that for the most part they merely

---

[1] William Wrede, *Das Messiasgeheimnis in den Evangelien* (Göttingen: Vandenhoeck & Ruprecht, 1901); ET *The Messianic Secret*, trans. J. C. G. Greig (Cambridge and London: James Clarke and Co., 1971).

[2] For a selective treatment of research through 1976, see James L. Blevins, *The Messianic Secret in Markan Research, 1901-1976* (Washington, DC: University Press of America, 1981); more recently, Heikki Räisänen, *The Messianic Secret in Mark's Gospel*, trans. Christopher Tuckett (London: T. & T. Clark, 1986); Christopher Tuckett, ed., *The Messianic Secret*, Issues in Religion and Theology 1 (Philadelphia: Fortress, 1983).

[3] Jack Dean Kingsbury writes, for example, that "it has been customary in Mattthean studies to accept as axiomatic the view that the truth of Jesus' divine sonship is devoid of any aura of secrecy" ("The Parable of the Wicked Husbandmen and the Secret of Jesus' Divine Sonship in Matthew: Some Literary-Critical Observations," *JBL* 105:4 (1986) 643.

reproduce and rearrange material they have taken over [from Mark]."[4] His brief treatment of parallel pericopes aimed to show that neither Mt nor Lk had understood Mk's theological conception of the messianic secret, and that as a consequence, in the process of using Markan pericopes, both had reproduced parts of the messianic secret rather incidentally. And finally: Wrede's interest in turning to the other synoptics was less to explore their own appropriations of elements of the secret motif than to determine briefly that neither Mt nor Lk had been concerned to *correct* Mk's imposition of the motif on the "raw material" of the Jesus tradition. That is, Wrede sought to show that Mk's messianic secret was a theologically motivated literary innovation; his concern with the other synoptic Gospels was to show that neither of them presented a historical challenge to that argument.

Two developments since Wrede have raised the prospect of studying the "secrecy" elements in Mt and Lk with renewed interest. In the first place, although the Two-Source Hypothesis continues to dominate synoptic studies, it also continues to be challenged, particularly in recent years by proponents of the "*Two-Gospel*," or "revised Griesbach" hypothesis. This hypothesis reverses the direction of the argument from common order in the Two-Source Hypothesis, and argues instead that Mk, on either account the "middle term" in the synoptic relationship, in fact used both Mt and Lk in composing his Gospel.[5] One result of the ongoing debate has been that a number of scholars have pursued the *Two-Gospel* hypothesis with vigor; another, that some other scholars, still convinced by the *Two-Source* hypothesis, are nevertheless more cautious in presuming it.[6]

The implications of the Two-Gospel hypothesis for the study of the "messianic secret" are obvious. If Mk used Mt and Lk to compose his Gospel, then the "messianic secret" in Mk, however it is to be interpreted, is not Mk's literary innovation alone, but the result, at least in part, of his dependence on Mt and Lk and of his modifications of motifs he found there. On this theory, we might well look to Mt or Lk for clues to the origin of various secrecy motifs.

---

4 Wrede, *Messianic Secret*, 152.

5 The centrality of this argument from order is widely recognized among proponents of the Two-Gospel Hypothesis: see (in addition to references in the next note) David Dungan's article on the "Two-Gospel Hypothesis" in the *Anchor Bible Dictionary*. I consider the argument from order as a literary phenomenon far more important for deciding the question of synoptic relationships than the "external evidence" of patristic tradition; the sort of "imaginative reconstruction" offered by Bernard Orchard in which Papias' testimony to the composition of Mark is expanded to include Mark simultaneously unrolling scrolls of Matthew and Luke at best corroborates the notion that both arguments are compatible; it has no independent evidentiary value. See "How the Synoptic Gospels Came into Existence," in Bernard Orchard and Harold Riley, *The Order of the Synoptics: Why Three Synoptic Gospels?* (Macon: Mercer University Press, 1987) 263-274.

6 The programmatic statement for the Two-Gospel Hypothesis is William R. Farmer, *The Synoptic Problem* (New York: Macmillan, 1964); see further *Synoptic Studies: The Ampleforth Conferences of 1982 and 1983*, ed. Christopher M. Tuckett; JSNTS 7 (Sheffield: JSOT Press, 1984); *New Synoptic Studies*, ed. William R. Farmer (Macon: Mercer University Press, 1983).

There is another reason to look again at the presence and role of secret motifs in Mt and Lk. Whether or not the Two-Gospel hypothesis is entertained as a reasonable explanation of synoptic relationships, more recent students of the Gospels are far more disposed than the early redaction critics to a "holistic" reading of narratives as networks of interrelated meanings.[7] The newer literary-critical perspective would not allow us, for example, simply to tag elements of a "secrecy" motif in Mt or Lk as incidental byproducts of synoptic borrowing, but would require us to discern what distinctive roles these elements come to play within the narrative of Mt or Lk. Thus arises the possibility of discovering the theological significance—or at least compositional significance—for elements of possible secrecy motifs in Mt and Lk.

Distinguishing "Secrecy" Motifs

Under the term "messianic secret" Wrede sought to understand a number of phenomena in Mk. These phenomena include Jesus' commands to demons and to human beings being healed to "be silent"; his commands to his disciples to "tell no one" about his identity as the Christ or about the Transfiguration vision until after the resurrection; miracles Jesus performed "privately" or secretly; the chronic failure of Jesus' disciples to understand his identity or destiny; and the purpose the Markan Jesus attributes to his parables of *concealing* the "secret of the kingdom" (Mk 4:11-12). Wrede admitted that these features were not carried through in Mk in a consistent way so as to keep Jesus' identity secret. The fact that Jesus' efforts to remain secret were thwarted within the narrative by his ever-increasing reputation with "the crowd" (ὁ ὄχλος) was evidence, in Wrede's view, that we are dealing with Mk's (incomplete) imposition upon his source materials of a fundamentally theological conception.

After Wrede, interpreters have doubted whether all of the components that Wrede linked together in fact belong to a single theological conception of messianic secrecy, and have called attention to the equally prevalent theme of the manifestation of Jesus' authority and power in Mk. Martin Dibelius focused on Jesus' commands to silence after miracles, interpreting the "Secret" as a means for explaining why Jesus had been rejected and crucified; the manifestations of his power were "secret epiphanies."[8] H. J. Ebeling proposed that Jesus' attempts to remain secret served as a literary foil for a more fundamental theme in the Gospel, that of the revelation or manifestation

---

7 One signal of this tendency is student-level introductions to the New Testament. Luke Timothy Johnson, for example, writes that "I consider the hypothesis of Markan priority to be correct and assume it in this book. But my reading of each Gospel *does not depend* on the correctness of that hypothesis. My approach is closer to that of literary criticism. My concern above all is with the final form of the text" (*The Writings of the New Testament: An Interpretation* [Philadelphia: Fortress, 1986] 145).

8 Martin Dibelius, *From Tradition to Gospel* (New York: Charles Scribner's Sons, 1934) 230. German original, 1919.

of Jesus as the Son of God.[9] Ulrich Luz sought to separate the motif of healings performed in secret, which he took as literary devices heightening the revelatory character of these healings, from Jesus' commands to demons and his disciples not to reveal his identity as Son of God.[10] Most recently, Heikki Räisänen has argued that "only the commands to silence addressed to the demons and those addressed to the disciples" concern the secrecy of Jesus' identity as Son of God, and thus only they belong to a "messianic secret" properly so called. From those motifs we must distinguish the motif of secret healings, which emphasize "that Jesus' miraculous deeds cannot remain hidden"; the "parable theory" of 4:11-12; and the motif of the disciples' lack of understanding.[11]

In the light of these proposals, it seems prudent to distinguish and track separately the various motifs associated with Wrede's "messianic secret" theory. In what follows I distinguish among [A] Jesus' command silencing demons concerning his identity as Son of God; [B] Jesus' efforts to heal privately, or to keep healings secret, and the ironically related increase in popular interest in Jesus; [C] the "parable theory" expressed in Mk 4:11-12; and [D] Jesus' commands *to the disciples* not to make his identity known; and [E] the theme of the disciples' lack of understanding.

Aligning Secrecy Motifs

Although I have assumed that *some* literary dependence best explains the synoptic relationships, I do not presume that such literary dependence must have run the course indicated by the Two-Source hypothesis. The following table of alignments is arranged according to Markan order. Arrows indicate passages in Mk that more closely parallel one Gospel than the other, in order of pericopes and/or in content within pericopes. On the Two-Source hypothesis, these arrows would indicate places where either Mt or Lk was following Mk's order and/or wording more closely; on the Two-Gospel hypothesis, places where Mk was following the order and/or wording of either Mt or Lk more closely.[12]

Alignment of Secrecy Motifs

Key to Secrecy Motifs:

[A] Jesus' commands silencing demons concerning his identity as Son of God;

---

9 H. J. Ebeling, *Das Evangelium nach Markus* (Göttingen: Vandenhoeck & Ruprecht, 1949).

10 Ulrich Luz, "The Secrecy Motif and the Marcan Christology," in Tuckett, ed., *Messianic Secret*, 75-96; translated from *ZNW* 56 (1965) 9-30.

11 Räisänen, *Messianic Secret*, 159.

12 This format is adapted from the "Narrative Outline of the Markan Composition according to the Two Gospel Hypothesis" prepared by W. R. Farmer, D. L. Dungan, A. J. McNicol, D. B. Peabody, and P. L. Shuler, distributed to the Two-Gospel Hypothesis working group at the 1990 SBL Annual Meeting.

[B]   Jesus' efforts to heal privately or to keep healings secret (related with Jesus' increasing publicity);
[C]   the "parable theory" expressed in Mk 4:11-12;
[D]   Jesus' commands to the disciples not to make him known; and
[E]   the theme of the disciples' lack of understanding.

Matthew	Mark	Luke
	1:21-28 [A] ======>	4:31-37 [A]

(Exorcism in the Capernaum synagogue. In both Mk and Lk, Jesus commands the demon to silence [A]; nevertheless his fame spreads.)

Matthew	Mark	Luke
8:16-17 (18 [B?])	1:32-34 [A] ======>	4:40-41 [A]

(Summary statement concerning "sick healed at evening." In Mk and Lk demons are silenced "because they knew him" [A]; Mt reports neither the demons' knowledge nor Jesus' rebuke, but does indicate [Mt 8:18] that Jesus leaves when "great crowds" gather.)

Matthew	Mark	Luke
8:1-4 [B]	1:40-45 [B] ======>	5:12-16 [B]

(Cleansing of the leper. In all three Gospels Jesus tells the leper to say nothing to anyone [B], but to show himself to the priest. In Mk and Lk, but not Mt, the news spreads nevertheless, attracting crowds; in Mk, but not Lk, because the man has disobeyed Jesus. In Mk, the resulting crowd prevents Jesus from openly entering any town; in Lk, Jesus withdraws to pray.)

Matthew	Mark	Luke
(4:24-25)		
12:15-20 [B] <======	3:7-12 [A]	6:17-19

(Another summary of healings. Mk is parallel to Mt 4:24-25 and to Lk in identifying where the crowd comes from. But in Mt 4:24-25 the scene is being set for the Sermon on the Mount; Lk will first narrate the call of the disciples, and then begin the Sermon on the Plain. On the Two-Source Hypothesis, both Mt and Lk have (independently) selected this point in Mk's narrative to insert sermon material for the first time; on the Two-Gospel Hypothesis, on the other hand, Mk has turned away from Lk [to avoid the Sermon?] in order to follow Mt. The more significant parallel for secrecy material in Mk is with Mt 12:15-20, for there (not in Lk) secrecy is enjoined on those healed [B]; Mt goes on to provide a Scripture proof from Isaiah 42:1-4. Mk alone has Jesus command demons to silence because they recognize him [A]; this has been simultaneously dropped from Mt and Lk [on the Two-Source Hypothesis] or added by Mk [on the Two-Gospel Hypothesis].)

Matthew	Mark	Luke
13:10-17 [C]	4:10-12 [C] ======>	8:9-10 [C]

(The reason for speaking in parables [C]. Although Mk is closer to Mt in that both include a "parable chapter" at this point (Mk 4, Mt 13), in wording Mk is actually closer to Lk here, particularly in the phrasing of the quotation from Isaiah 6:9. Mt gives an explanation: "I speak in parables *because* 'seeing they do not see and hearing they do not hear nor understand.'" Mk and Lk state an intention: *"in order that* [ἵνα] seeing they may not see,'" etc. The parables that follow in Mt speak of an eventual divine discrimination between what (or who) is now "mixed," and it is clear that the disciples understand [13:51-52] the wisdom Jesus speaks [13:35]. In Mk 4, the disciples pointedly fail to understand [4:13].)[13]

Matthew	Mark	Luke
(8:28-34)	5:1-20 [B?!] ======>	8:26-39 [B?!]

(The Gerasene demoniac, an anomaly for the "secret" theory because in both Mk and Lk Jesus fails to silence the demons who have identified him, and commands the delivered man *to tell* what has happened to him [Mk 5:19, Lk 8:39].)

Matthew	Mark	Luke
(9:18-26)	5:21-43 [B] ======>	8:40-56 [B]

(The raising of Jairus' daughter. Mt has Jesus put the crowd outside [9:23-24], but this is because of their "tumult" [9:23]; in Mk, it follows the crowd's laughing at Jesus [5:40]. Mk reports that Jesus allowed only Peter, James, and John to enter the house with him; Lk also admits the girl's parents; and both have Jesus charge them to tell no one about the healing. Mk includes the Aramaic incantation "Talitha cumi" [5:41].)

Matthew	Mark	Luke
15:21-28 <======	7:24-30 [B]	

(Healing of the Syrophoenician/Canaanite woman's daughter; absent from Lk. Only Mk's version involves a "secret" motif in that Jesus sought to remain hidden [7:24].)

Matthew	Mark	Luke
15:29-31 <======	7:31-37 [B]	

(A deaf mute [Mk] and "many others" [Mt] healed. Again, Mk has introduced the secrecy motif, having Jesus heal the deaf mute "aside from the multitude, privately," and charge "them" to tell no one. Mk uses an Aramaic incantation, "Ephphatha" [7:34].)

Matthew	Mark	Luke
9:27-31 [B]	8:22-26 [B]	
(20:29-34)	(10:46-52) ======>	(18:35-43)

(These five pericopes report Jesus' healing of blind men. Mt and Mk each have two accounts of blind men healed, the second account in each sharing details with Lk 18. Our interest is with the first account in Mt and in Mk, for these pericopes [*not* the parallels in Mt 20/Mk 10/Lk 18] involve secrecy. In Mt 9 the blind man approaches Jesus in private [εἰς τὴν οἰκίαν, 9:28], is commanded to tell no one about the healing [9:30] yet proclaims it "throughout the land" nevertheless—the only occurrence of such

---

13 Farmer et al. align Mark 4:1-9 more closely with Mt 13:1-9 ("Narrative Outline"); but see John Bernard Orchard, *A Synopsis of the Four Gospels in Greek, Arranged according to the Two-Gospel Hypothesis* (Macon: Mercer University Press, 1983) 84-85.

disobedience in Mt: the similar story in Mt 20 has neither command to silence nor proclamation, but only the report that the men now followed Jesus. Mk 8 gives a story with some broad parallels to Mt 9: the blind man comes to Jesus [he is not sitting, as in Mt 20/Mk 10/Lk 18], is healed in secret [Jesus leads him by hand out of the village] and commanded to silence ["do not even enter the village"], yet in contrast to Mt 9 we are not told that he disobeys. That the man's sight is only partially restored at first [8:24] has led interpreters to read this story metaphorically, followed as it is by Peter's imperfect realization of Jesus' identity [Mk 8:27-30]; Mk has thus created a compositional "bracket" [with 10:46-52] for the passion predictions in Mk 8:31-33, 9:30-32, and 10:32-34.)

Matthew	Mark	Luke
16:5-12 [E]	<====== 8:14-21 [E]	

(The disciples fail to understand Jesus' saying about the "leaven of the Pharisees." This is temporary in Mt—at last they *do* understand [16:12]—not so in Mk.)

Matthew	Mark	Luke
16:13—17:13 [D, E]	<===== 8:27—9:13 [D, E]	9:18-36 [D]

(A complex including Peter's confession at Caesarea Philippi, Jesus' prediction of the passion, the Transfiguration; and, in Mt and Mk, Jesus' words on "the coming of Elijah." In Mt and Mk, not in Lk, Peter protests Jesus' prediction of his death; in both Jesus censures Peter, although in Mt this is mitigated by the divine authorization of Peter in 16:17-19. In all three Gospels Jesus then charges the disciples not to reveal his identity. Following the Transfiguration [where Mt alone does not criticize Peter], the disciples are charged not to reveal what they have seen; in Lk they comply; in Mk, they keep quiet because they do not understand "what the rising from the dead meant." In Mt, the disciples *do* understand Jesus' saying concerning Elijah.)

Matthew	Mark	Luke
17:22-23	9:30-32 [D, E] ======>	9:43b-45 [E]

(Jesus predicts his passion again; Mk and Lk report that the disciples fail to understand the saying, Lk specifying that it was "concealed from them that they should not perceive it." Mk indicates Jesus sought not to be recognized while he taught this truth to his disciples.)

We turn next to more detailed explorations of the configuration of "secrecy" motifs in each of the Gospels.

The Silence of the Messiah in Matthew

We may observe first that Mt tells no story in which a demon recognizes Jesus and is silenced. This element of Wrede's "messianic secret" (motif [A]) is absent from Mt. Jesus does command his disciples to silence about his identity as Christ after Peter's confession at Caesarea Philippi (16:20), and about the Transfiguration (17:9) (motif [D]). In these scenes the disciples are the recipients of divine revelation: "flesh and blood has not revealed this to you," Jesus tells Peter, "but my Father who is in heaven" (16:19). Similarly Jesus thanks God (11:25-26) for "hiding these things," apparently meaning his identity, "from the wise and understanding, and revealing them to babes, for thus was your gracious will."

How do the commands to silence and the theme of revelation or manifestation function within Mt's narrative?

In a number of articles and books Jack Dean Kingsbury has argued that the form and message of Mt cohere in *christology*. Discerning major turning points in the transitions at 4:17 ("From that time Jesus began to preach," i.e., the nearness of the reign of God) and 16:21 ("From that time Jesus began to show his disciples" the necessity of his passion), Kingsbury divides the Gospel into three broad segments: (I) the Person of Jesus Messiah (1:1-4:16), (II) the Proclamation of Jesus Messiah (4:17–16:20), and (III) the Passion, Death, and Resurrection of Jesus Messiah.[14]

Within this broad outline we may observe a dynamic of surprising or paradoxical manifestation of the messiah. In presenting the messiah's "credentials" (1:1-4:16), Mt manages to show, first, that Jesus is of Davidic descent, but his genealogy *from Abraham* accentuates a rhythm between the glorious reign of David and the disaster of the Babylonian exile (1:17). Isaiah's prophecy of Emmanuel (Is 7:14) is fulfilled in a virgin's extramarital conception (Mt 1:18-25). Diverse prophecies (so Mt takes them) that the messiah would appear in Bethlehem (Mic 5:2), from Egypt (Hos 11:1), and as a Nazarene (Is 11:1?),[15] are all fulfilled in Jesus by reason of his family's flight from a king's hostility. At Jesus' baptism a voice from heaven declares him to be God's Son (3:17); but the temptations visited upon him afterward show that the way of this messiah will not be the way of seeking worldly dominion nor of miraculous display (4:1-11).[16] Rather this messiah responds to conflict— specifically the arrest of John the Baptist—with what we might call "strategic withdrawal" (4:12); and thus is fulfilled the Scripture that the messiah will be manifest in Galilee (Is 9:1-2).

In Kingsbury's second major division of Mt (4:17-16:20), the messiah's manifestation in word and deed continues to be paradoxical, and brings mixed results. He invites his hearers to enter the reign of God by a way opposite to power and force: spiritual poverty, mercy, hunger for justice, peacemaking, reconciliation, nonretaliation, all constitute "entering by the narrow gate" (7:13-14), and this is contrasted with the way of "false prophets" and wonder workers (7:15-23); "the crowds" also contrast it with the teaching of the scribes (7:28-29). To be sure, Jesus also performs miracles and heals many, and commands his disciples to do the same (10:1). Yet these miracles are not unambiguous signs of the messiah in Mt. They sometimes provoke

---

14 Jack Dean Kingsbury, "Form and Message of Matthew," *Interpretation* 29 (1975) 18.

15 The problem here is that there is no scripture referring to the Messiah as a "Nazarene." On efforts to find the background to Mt 2:23 either in the Nazirite of Judges 13:5 or in the "root" (נצר) of Jesse in Isaiah 11:1, see H. H. Schaeder, "*Nazarenos, Nazoraios,*" *TDNT* 4:878.

16 John Howard Yoder declares, "all the options laid before Jesus by the tempter are ways of being king" (*The Politics of Jesus* [Grand Rapids: Eerdmans, 1972] 30).

faith (8:8-10, 27; 9:8, 28-29, 32; 12:23) and fulfill Scripture concerning the Servant of God (Mt 8:17 = Is 53:4). But they also provoke hostility toward Jesus from the Pharisees, who accuse him of exercising the power of the prince of demons (9:34, 12:24-32) and seek to destroy him (12:14); and they will provoke rejection and hostility toward the disciples as well, as they enter synagogues as sheep among wolves (10:16-18). Precisely because miracles are not foolproof signs of the messiah, Jesus must warn his disciples that they will face antagonism (10:19-42); and he pronounces a blessing on those who can witness his miracles without being scandalized (11:2-6), and woes on cities that have failed to respond to miracles (11:20-24). It is "an evil and adulterous generation" that seeks to authenticate the messiah through signs (12:38-45; 16:1-4). Jesus' refusal to authenticate himself through signs, and his warnings about the "leaven of the Pharisees and Sadducees" (16:11-12), are necessary since, as Jesus tells his disciples later, in the last days "false messiahs and false prophets will appear and produce great signs and omens to lead astray, if possible, the elect" (24:24).

Amid questions and speculations about his identity from his own disciples ("what sort of man is this?" 8:27), from John the Baptist ("Are you the one who is to come?" 11:3), from the crowds ("Can this be the Son of David?" 12:23), from his townsfolk ("Isn't this the carpenter's son?" 13:54-56), from Herod ("This is John the Baptist, raised from the dead," 14:2), and from "people" in general ("Some say John the Baptist, others Elijah, and others Jeremiah or one of the prophets," 16:14), the messiah also wins sporadic recognition: demons hail him as Son of God (8:29), as do his disciples after he comes to them walking on the sea (14:33); two blind men call upon him as Son of David (9:27), as does a "Canaanite woman" (15:22); finally Peter acclaims him "the Christ, the Son of the living God" (16:16).

Kingsbury argues that the "secrecy motif" in Mt consists in the fact that "although Mt as narrator, the implied reader, and transcendent beings such as God . . . Satan . . . and demons . . . know that Jesus is the Son of God, human characters in Mt's story do not."[17] This is slightly inaccurate: against Kingsbury's statement that Jesus is the only human to hear the divine voice at his baptism (3:16-17), the text is not so restrictive (Mt reads "this is my beloved Son," not "you are" as in Mk and Lk). Further, we have seen that other human beings acclaim Jesus as "Son of David"; and Mt gives us no reason to consider "Son of David" an *inadequate* expression of Jesus' identity.[18] Rather, I take the pattern of reactions to Jesus to indicate that in isolated instances individuals can recognize Jesus as messiah, but that these identifications remain indecisive for the story. Human beings may have insight through divine revelation into Jesus' messianic identity (11:25-26; 16:17), but the question cannot *decisively* be resolved apart from Jesus' going the way of the cross (16:21).

---

17 Kingsbury, "Parable of the Wicked Husbandmen," 643.

18 David Hill criticizes Kingsbury's tendency to exalt *one* christological title, "Son of God," as preeminent in Matthew, at the cost of other important titles: "Son and Servant: An Essay on Matthean Christology," *JSNT* 6 (1980) 2-16.

These stories—clearly a doublet (more clearly than Mk 8:22-26 and 10:46-52!)—serve a christological theme in Mt, and on the Two-Gospel Hypothesis, this theme is Mt's invention.

It is within this scheme, I suggest, that Jesus' command to silence in 9:27-31 makes sense. Two blind men follow Jesus into a house, and "their eyes were opened"; they realize that the one they have hailed as Son of David can indeed give sight to the blind. Jesus tells them not to tell anyone: the truth about the messiah cannot yet fully be told; yet they immediately "spread his fame through all that district." In so doing, however, they only add their view to an array of opinions about Jesus' identity. At this point in the story, the truth is mixed in with false opinions, and who can sort it out?

Later—*after* the messiah has spoken plainly about the way he must take to the cross, and the way those who follow him must share, and *just before* he sets his foot finally on that path—two other blind men hail him as Son of David and ask to have their eyes opened. At this point (20:29-34) there is no need for secrecy; the way of the messiah has been revealed, and the messiah will now run his course for all who can discern it. While the first two blind men went away to contribute to the discussion of who Jesus might be, these two blind men receive their sight and "follow Jesus" as he goes to the cross.

The secrecy motif in Mt 12:15-21 plays a different role. Here Jesus orders people he has just healed "not to make him manifest" (μὴ φανερὸν αὐτὸν ποιήσωσιν, 12:16). Mt gives this event an explicit theological significance: what Jesus does here fulfills Isaiah's prophecy concerning the "servant of God" (Is. 42:1-4). In light of Mt's characteristic concern with the fulfillment of Scripture, we should doubt that this is merely a "trace" of the messianic secret, a "half-unconscious inheritance from Mk."[19] It is probably the predominance of similar commands in Mk's Gospel, and their significance for Wrede's theory, that draws attention first to the command to silence in Mt 12:16. In fact, however, within Mt's narrative the emphasis lies not on the command to silence itself but on Jesus' withdrawal in response to the hostility of Pharisaic opponents (12:14).

Deirdre Good has shown that "withdrawal" in response to hostility and in fulfillment of prophecy is a prominent theme at several places in Mt:[20]

(a) In Mt 2:12-15, first the magi and then Joseph and his family "withdraw" to elude Herod. In 2:22-23, Joseph again "withdraws" to Nazareth to elude Archelaus. Mt asserts that two different messianic prophecies are thus fulfilled in the itinerary of these holy refugees.

(b) In 4:12-18 Jesus "withdraws" to Galilee after John's arrest, thus fulfilling another messianic prophecy.

(c) In 12:15-21, the opposition of Pharisees causes Jesus to "withdraw." Good points out that what is new in *this* withdrawal is that Jesus is not alone. In the intervening chapters, 5-11, Jesus has delivered "the first major proclamation of his message," and has warned his followers about

---

19 F. W. Beare, *The Gospel according to Matthew* (New York: Harper & Row, 1981) 274.

20 Deirdre Good, "The Verb *anachoreo* in Matthew's Gospel," *Novum Testamentum* 32:1 (1990) 1-12.

persecution (ch. 10); "in chapter eleven the question about his identity is specifically raised and the answer given in vv. 16-19. . . . The chapter concludes with the invitation of Jesus as Wisdom to rest (11:28-30)."[21]

(d) In 14:12-14 Jesus' disciples report to Jesus that John has been executed; he responds by withdrawing. Good suggests that the element of prophecy fulfilled is implicit in the feeding miracle that follows.

(e) In 15:21-28 Jesus withdraws from the opposition of Pharisees and scribes "to the district of Tyre and Sidon." As in the previous instance, no fulfillment of Scripture is explicit; but Good suggests that the healing of the Canaanite woman's child may fulfill the Scriptures cited in Mt 12:18 and 12:21. One might also note that another feeding miracle follows in 15:32-39.

Since explicit Scripture citations are missing in the last two instances, we might modify Good's scheme to include the elements opposition, withdrawal, and (not fulfillment of prophecy but) manifestation of Jesus as messiah *in the narrative*. Our point is that the withdrawal motif plays an important role in Mt's christological narrative, showing how the messiah fulfills Isaiah's prophecy by withdrawing again and again from conflict.

Good shows that this theme might have important resonances for an audience familiar with the Septuagint, perhaps calling to mind Moses' "withdrawal" from Pharaoh (ἀνεχώρησεν, Ex. 2:15) or Judas Maccabeus' withdrawal before a decisive victory over Greek armies (2 Macc 5:27); or again, what is more likely in Good's view, the "withdrawal" of divine Wisdom in apocalyptic passages like 1 Enoch 42, 4 Ezra 5:9, and 2 Baruch 48:36.[22] The allusions to Wisdom allow Good to suggest that in Mt "Jesus' withdrawal can be seen as both real and metaphorical" in so far as Mt "asserts the overriding providence of God in the face of what appears to be retreat."[23] Throughout the Gospel, the messiah is "aware of alternatives." It is *Matthew's* Jesus who renounces both the use of the sword (26:52) and his own recourse to angelic armies (26:53-54). Clearly the way of the cross is "an alternative to meeting hostility with opposition in order that the scripture might be fulfilled." It is "not *retreat from* hostility but rather *withdrawal for* the fulfillment of prophecy that demonstrates Mt's intention in his creation of this pattern."[24]

Our discussion of secrecy motifs in Mt have shown that for Mt the relevant question is how the messiah is to be recognized. His answer is that by God's gracious will (11:25-26) eyes will be opened (20:29-34) to recognize that the way Jesus took, a way of "withdrawal for the fulfillment of prophecy," has always been Scripture's testimony to the messiah. This message would have particular relevance within the historical context to which Mt's composition is often assigned in modern scholarship. After the Jewish War, both the ἐκκλησία of Matthew (in Antioch?) and the descendants of the Pharisees appealed to the hearts and minds of Palestinian Jews in their efforts to restore the people of

---

21 *Ibid.*, 3-4.

22 Good, "The Verb *anachoreo*," 8-10.

23 *Ibid.*, 11.

24 *Ibid.*, 12.

God. In that context, Mt seeks to identify the way of the cross as the way of the messiah, and to distance Jesus the messiah from the violence of the Jewish rebels. Perhaps because the contrast of Jesus' way and the way of the Zealots seems to him anachronistic, perhaps because he wants to disaffect his readers from the Pharisaic cause, he also shifts responsibility for the disaster onto the shoulders of (those whom he makes into) Jesus' enemies, the Pharisees (Mt 23).[25]

The Servant Empowered by God in Luke

The table of alignments offered above shows that Mk and Lk share both the motif of Jesus' commanding demons to silence (motif [A]) and a greater investment in silencing after healing (motif [B]) than Mt. Depending on the theory of synoptic relationships one accepts, this correspondence would indicate either Lk's adoption of a Markan secrecy motif or Mk's dependence on Lk for the same motif. We turn next to Lk to see how secrecy motifs function within the narrative of Luke-Acts.

The temptation scene (3:4-13) shows Jesus withstanding Satan; he will continue to exercise authority over Satan and the demonic realm until the hour of his betrayal.[26] The inaugural sermon in Nazareth (Lk 4:16-30) is programmatic for Lk's presentation of Jesus and his miracles.[27] Jesus is the Servant empowered by God's Spirit (Lk 4:18 = Is 61:1; cf. Lk 4:1, 14), and so Lk takes care to tell the reader that it is by God's Spirit or God's power that Jesus heals (4:36, 5:17, 6:19, 8:46, 11:20), that Jesus again and again retreats into prayer to God (5:16; 6:12; 9:18, 28; 11:1), and that the proper response to his healings is praise or thanksgiving directed to God (5:25, 26; 7:16; 8:39; 9:43; 13:13; 17:16, 18; 18:43).

Lk is similarly concerned in the book of Acts to emphasize that it is by the power of God, now at work through the name of Jesus, that Christians heal and cast out demons (3:12-13; 4:10; cf. 4:30; 9:34-35, 40-42). This power does not

---

25 See the discussion of Matthew in Norman Perrin and Dennis Duling, *The New Testament: An Introduction*, rev. ed. (New York: Harcourt Brace Johanovich, 1983) 263-273.

26 In what follows I depend on Susan Garrett, *The Demise of the Devil: Magic and the Demonic in Luke's Writings* (Minneapolis: Fortress, 1989). Garrett shows that "magical" and "miraculous" elements in Luke-Acts are controlled by the theme of Jesus' dominion over demonic powers.

27 In particular, the Isaiah quotation shapes Luke's description of Jesus' miracles. Exorcisms are depicted as "release to the captives" (αἰχμαλώτοις ἄφεσιν, 4:18), or even more precisely as "sending away free those who have been oppressed" (ἀποστεῖλαι τεθραυσμένους ἐν ἀφέσει). The imagery of bondage is explicit in Luke's account of the Gerasene demoniac, who was "kept under guard, and bound with chains and fetters, but [repeatedly] broke the bonds and was driven by the demon into the desert" (8:29), and in the story of the woman "bent over" by a "spirit of infirmity" (13:11), "bound by Satan," whom Jesus "looses from her bonds" (13:16). Both individuals are "sent away" released (ἀπέλυσεν, 8:38; ἀπολῦσαι, 13:12), as is the man with dropsy (ἀπέλυσεν, 14:4) and the grateful leper (ἀναστὰς πορεύου, 17:19). In addition to exorcisms, the evangelization of the poor and recovery of sight to the blind prophesied by Isaiah (Lk 4:18) are explicitly performed as well as declared when John sends to ask whether Jesus is the one awaited (7:21-22).

come from the apostles themselves (3:12-13, 14:11-18), nor is it like magical powers, behind which stands Satan (8:9-24, Simon; 9:4-12, Elymas; 16:16-18, the Philippian demoniac; 19:11-19, the sons of Sceva).

The "secrecy" motifs in Lk can be seen, then, to cluster around two interests.

(a) Lk wants to show that Jesus has authority over demons, and so relates stories in which demons acknowledge Jesus' power as Son of God and are then "rebuked and silenced" (4:35-37, 41-42), or simply rebuked (8:29). In the instances of such a command, Jesus' fame nevertheless spreads immediately; secrecy does not seem to be the point of the narrative. The instructive analog is the demoniac in Philippi, who follows Paul's entourage crying, "Here are the servants of the most high God!" (Acts 16:17), until Paul at last casts the spirit out "in Jesus' name." It is *the power of Jesus* that is thus expressed both by the demon's speech, and by the demon's silence.

(b) Jesus twice commands silence after a healing (a leper, 5:14; Jairus' daughter, 8:56); the first scene is followed by a notice that Jesus "withdrew to pray" (5:14-16). Since these commands are not given routinely, there is no reason to speak of an effort on Jesus' part to remain secret; rather Lk apparently chooses this device to show that Jesus does not act on his own, but depends on God's power.[28] Again, Acts provides the instructive parallels as the apostles point away from themselves toward the power of God or the power of Jesus' name.

Susan Garrett has discussed both Lk's concern to show Jesus' power in wresting creation away from Satan *and* Lk's concern to distinguish that power from the power at work in magic, which Lk attributes to Satan. In contrast to the self-exaltation of Satan and those who share in his power, Jesus does not seek his own glory. The commands to silence may be seen to serve what Garrett calls Lk's "insistence that it is ultimately God who is active in all Jesus' and the Christians' signs and wonders"; and Garrett declares this insistence part of "Luke's anti-magic apology."[29]

We have not yet discussed the motif of the disciples' silence regarding Jesus' identity in Lk 9. Jesus commands his disciples to tell no one that he is the Christ just before his first prediction of the Passion (9:21-22). After the Transfiguration, Lk simply reports that the disciples remain silent (Lk 9:36). After the second prediction of the Passion we are told that the disciples "did not understand" Jesus; "it was hidden from them so that they should not see the meaning of it, and they were afraid to ask him what this meant" (9:45). This failure to understand is, of course, temporary in Luke-Acts; it is remedied by Jesus himself "explaining all the passages of Scripture relating to himself" after his resurrection (Lk 24:25-27; 44-48). At this point they are commissioned as his witnesses (24:48), a commission to be fulfilled in the book of Acts.

---

28 "Luke's care in specifying God as the actor behind Jesus' and the Christians' power is prompted by an awareness that there are other such actors at work in the world . . . and Luke wants to preclude the suspicion that this 'alternative agent' had anything to do with the miracles of Jesus and the Christians" (Garrett, *Demise of the Devil*, 66).

29 *Ibid.*, 103.

Christ Revealed and Concealed in Mark

There are reasons to dispute the phrase "messianic secret" in relation to Mk's Gospel. On one hand, as Sherman E. Johnson points out, "one of the most curious features of Mk's Christological language is that he is so reserved in his use of the word χριστός." Further, if, in Mk, "Jesus is at all descended from David, he is much more; and it is possible that Mk rejects the formula 'Messiah son of David' completely." Johnson concludes that "the mystery in Mk is not so much a 'messianic secret' as a Christological one."[30] On the other hand, there is a sense in which there is no christological secret in Mk's Gospel—for the reader: the very first words make it crystal clear that what follows will be "the Gospel of Jesus Christ the Son of God."

I submit that the more relevant question to ask of Mk's narrative is not "who is Jesus" but "who are they who know who Jesus is?"

They are, first of all, superhuman beings. At his baptism Jesus is assured by God that he is God's "beloved Son," with whom God is well pleased (1:11); a few verses later, a demon recognizes Jesus as "the Holy One of God" (1:24). Here and elsewhere in Mk (1:34, 3:7-12, 5:7), the demons act in Mk as a dramatic chorus, ensuring that the reader understands the significance of developments in the story. Lk also uses the motif of demons silenced, as we have seen; but Mk uses the motif more often. At Mk 3:7-12 and parallels, for example, depending on one's theory of synoptic relationships one would conclude either that Mt and Lk have simultaneously (yet independently) declined to include the silencing (Mt 4:24-25, 12:15-16; Lk 6:17-19), or else that Mk has added the motif to stories he found in Mt and Lk.

Combined with the motifs or private healings and silence commanded after healings (motif [B]), the demons' recognition of Jesus contributes to a paradoxical dynamic of *revelation and concealment* in Mk's narrative. In a number of pericopes Mk goes beyond parallels in Mt or Lk to emphasize Jesus' rapidly increasing popularity.[31] *At the same time* Mk is more interested than Mt or Lk in Jesus *wanting* to remain hidden: commands to silence in Mk 3:7-12, 7:24-30, 7:31-37 are not paralleled in Mt or Lk; commands to silence at Mk 1:45 and 7:36 are deliberately disobeyed.

With his words as well, the Markan Jesus both reveals and conceals, speaking to "those outside" in parables, "*so that* they may indeed see but not perceive . . ." (4:11-12), but entrusting "the secret of the kingdom" to his disciples (4:11) and "privately explaining everything" to them (4:34).

---

30 Sherman E. Johnson, *The Griesbach Hypothesis and Redaction Criticism*, SBLMS 41 (Atlanta: Scholars Press, 1991) 103.

31 After an exorcism in the Capernaum synagogue, "*immediately* his fame spread, *everywhere*, throughout *all* the surrounding region." That evening, "*the whole city* gathered about the door" (1:33). The next morning, "*everyone*" is searching for Jesus (1:37). A leper, cleansed, directly disobeys a command to silence (1:45, cf. 7:36), with the Markan result that "*Jesus could no longer openly enter a town*, but was out in the country, and people came to him from every quarter." Days later, people crowd Jesus' house *so that no one can get through the door* (2:2); Jesus and disciples cross the Sea "*lest the crowds crush him*" (3:9); returning, they so crowded "*they cannot even eat*" (3:19b; again, 6:31); the crowd again impels him into a boat (4:1, 35). Even escaping to the region of Tyre and Sidon Jesus "*could not be hid*" (7:24).

A second answer to "who are they who know who Jesus is" in Mk, then, is: *those "inside."* More is at work in Jesus' commands to silence than a literary device heightening the dramatic effect of his manifestation. Jesus also *intends* to be concealed, *from some people.* Mk *is* a Gospel of "secret epiphanies" (Dibelius); but secrecy and epiphany, concealment and manifestation, are simultaneous events. It is this phenomenon that awaits explanation.

I suggest that the contours of secrecy in Mk are related to Mk's antagonism toward Judaism. Others have observed that Mk is singularly distant from Judaism, not only taking it upon himself to explain aspects of Judaism for his reader[32] but doing so fairly unsympathetically. Nor is this antagonism toward Judaism incidental in Mk's narrative; rather, as Burton Mack writes, "Mark's story is about a conflict that God and his Son Jesus had with Judaism, a conflict of apocalyptic proportions."[33] (Just this distance, or even antagonism toward Judaism, has been taken by some proponents of the Two-Gospel hypothesis to indicate that Mk represents a later stage of Christianity than that represented by Mt or Lk.)[34]

In the controversy with Pharisees in Mk 7, Jesus characterizes "the Jews" by the scrupulous washing of hands and "many other traditions, the washing of cups and pots and vessels of bronze" (7:3-4). He then speaks against them in the words of Isaiah's prophecy—immediately, that is, against the Pharisees, but by implication, against *Jews as such*: "This people honors me with their lips, but their heart is far from me, teaching as doctrines human precepts. You leave the commandment of God and hold fast human tradition." The practice of *korban* is a sufficient example to show the hypocrisy of Jewish practice: "and many such things you do" (7:13). All this Jesus says publicly. But he takes his disciples inside the house to reveal *to them* that the laws of *kashrut* are canceled ("thus he declared all foods clean," 7:19). This is the same intentional concealment, maintaining a barrier between insiders and outsiders, that characterized Jesus' teaching in parables (4:11-12). But it is also now a barrier between insiders and *Jews*, "us" and "them."[35] What the insiders now know is that the dietary regulations of Torah have been canceled by a word from Jesus.

In other ways Mk makes it clear that the Christ is concealed from the Jews (among whom we must apparently include the members of Jesus' own family, who are scandalized by him [3:21] and whom Jesus renounces [3:31-35]). In the Capernaum synagogue, *Mark alone* relates that Jesus "looked around at them [i.e., the Jews] with anger, grieved at their hardness of heart"

---

32 Aramaic is translated (ταλιθα κουμ [5:41], κορβᾶν [7:11], εφφαθα [7:34], the cry of dereliction [15:34]), yet not consistently (αββα ὁ πατήρ, 14:36; "Bartimaeus, son of Timaeus," 10:46).

33 Burton Mack, *A Myth of Innocence: Mark and Christian Origins* (Minneapolis: Fortress, 1988) 9.

34 Pierson Parker, "The Posteriority of Mark," in *New Synoptic Studies*, 67ff.

35 In her article "The Jewish Leaders in the Gospel of Mark: A Literary Study of Marcan Characterization" (*JBL* 108:2 [1989] 259-281), Elisabeth Struthers Malbon makes this point with regard to the narrator's intrusions at 7:3-4, 11, and 19: "The Pharisees—and 'all the Jews' (7:3)—are 'them'; the narrator and the hearers/readers are 'us'" (272).

(3:5). *Mark alone* specifies that the "sin against the Holy Spirit," the sin that cannot be forgiven but is "an eternal sin," is what the "scribes from Jerusalem" have just committed in accusing Jesus of having an unclean spirit (3:30; and note that Jesus' reason for concealing his meaning in parables is so that "those outside" *"should not be forgiven"* [4:12]). When asked by the Pharisees for a sign, the *Markan* Jesus "sighs deeply in his spirit" and declares that "no sign shall be given to this generation" (8:12). The other synoptics continue, "except the sign of Jonah" (Mt 16:4, 12:39, Lk 11:29); but *in Mark*, not even that enigmatic sign is offered: "this generation" is permanently in the dark.

Rejected in Nazareth, Jesus declares that a prophet is without honor "in his own country"; *in Mark* Jesus adds, "and among his own people [ἐν τοῖς συγγενεῦσιν αὐτοῦ, 6:4], and in his own house; and he marveled because of their unbelief."

It may be significant that the one occasion in Mk when Jesus does not command silence but in fact commands the healed person to "go and announce to your own house and your own people [πρὸς τοὺς σούς] how much the Lord has done for you," he is in Gentile territory, the "country of the Gerasenes" (5:1-20). When in Jewish territory, by contrast, the Markan Jesus routinely heals privately, or "in a lonely place" (the feeding miracles, 6:30, 8:4), or in the presence of his disciples alone; and he often commands silence.

That no hope is held out for Judaism is made clear in the Passion story. The cursing of the fig tree (11:12-14, 20-21) frames Jesus' "assault" on the Temple; the parable of the vineyard (12:1-12) is told "against them," i.e., "the chief priests and scribes and elders." At one place the manifestation of the Son of God and the concealment of truth from "the Jews" coincide: the high priest asks Jesus point blank, "Are you the Christ, the Son of the Blessed?", and Jesus responds with an unequivocal "Yes." Here, at the very instant the veil of secrecy is lifted and the Son of God is revealed, the high priest condemns Jesus for blasphemy. In this way Isaiah's words are fulfilled: "seeing they will not perceive, hearing they will not understand, lest they turn again and be forgiven." At the moment of Jesus' death, the Temple curtain is torn in two, presaging the Temple's destruction (15:38); a Roman soldier simultaneously recognizes the epiphany of the Son of God (15:39).

I suggest, on the basis of the observations in the preceding paragraphs, that what appear in Mk as competing motifs—secrecy and deliberate concealment on one hand, revelation and manifestation on the other—appear *simultaneously* because it is important for Mk that the appearance of Jesus have a *dual effect*. The implied reader knows, as do the demons, what "those outside," the "scribes and Pharisees," "the Jews" cannot know because it is hidden from them. This suggestion arises, in part, out of the difficulty of resolving the tension between competing motifs, i.e., concealment vs. revelation, either by incorporating secrecy as a literary device highlighting manifestation, or by emphasizing secrecy as an element in an "apologetic" theme. *Both* concealment and revelation take place *simultaneously* in Mk, and neither is subordinated to the other.

I note at this point that within this scheme, the disciples play an ambiguous role. They are "those inside," to whom "everything" is explained; they are thus comparable with the implied reader of the Gospel. On the other hand, they repeatedly show a lack of faith (4:40) and of understanding (4:13; 7:18; 8:17, 21), and are even "hard of heart" (6:52; 8:17). Predicting his passion to his disciples, he "speaks plainly" (8:32); yet Peter fails to understand (8:32-33), as do the others (9:32), and they will eventually forsake him. Mk ends (at 16:8) without narrating their rehabilitation. They thus demonstrate a level of faith less adequate than that Mk expects from his readers.

I am not convinced that the "negative" picture of the disciples functions chiefly as a narrative instrument of Markan polemic,[36] or of Markan pastoral concern.[37] In 7:18, the disciples' lack of understanding can only be overcome by Jesus privately revealing to them the abolition of *kashrut*. Jesus' warning in 8:15 to avoid "the leaven of the Pharisees and of Herod" is a warning against the blindness of "this generation," in which the Jewish leaders walk (8:18, cf. 4:12). In Mk, alone, Jesus' apocalyptic speech is provoked by his disciples' enthusiasm over the Temple's splendor ("Look, teacher, what wonderful stones and what wonderful buildings!" 13:1). I conclude that at least one function of the disciples in Mk is to distance the Christian reader from sympathy with the (now vanquished) Jewish establishment in Jerusalem. The disciples can play this role because they are *both* disciples (and so can attract the reader's initial identification) *and* are Palestinian Jews (and so can serve increasingly to distance the reader from the lost Judean cause).

This thesis about the "dual effect" of Mk's secrecy motifs might gain some indirect corroboration if we could identify a social setting in which this dual effect would have ideological cogency. I suggest that such a setting lies behind the distinctive "teaching" represented in the Letter of Barnabas (dated to the early second century) which attributes to the revelation in Christ a dual intentionality. First Barnabas establishes that Scripture as such has two components, a component directed "*to them*," that is to Israel (the Jews), in which God repudiates the error of Jewish observances (especially sacrifices and fasting) and thus brings Israel to "shipwreck"; and another component directed "*to us*," that is, to Gentile Christians as the true people of God, assuring them of salvation.[38] Scripture serves "to make all things plain to us

---

[36] So the disciples are sometimes taken to represent a *theios aner* christology (Theodore J. Weeden, *Mark: Traditions in Conflict* [Philadelphia: Fortress, 1971]) or Jewish Christianity (in Jerusalem) (Joseph Tyson, "The Blindness of the disciples in Mark," *JBL* 80 [1961] 261-268).

[37] The "pastoral" interpretation relies on increasing tension created between an initial identification with the disciples and the final distance the reader feels from them (Robert C. Tannehill, "The Disciples in Mark: The Function of a Narrative Role," *JR* 46 [1977] 392-394). The intent of this dynamic, according to Tannehill, is to move the reader toward accepting the "way of the cross" as the way of discipleship; according to Elisabeth Struthers Malbon, to display "the lively struggle between faith and doubt, trust and fear, obedience and denial" ("The Jewish Leaders in the Gospel of Mark: A Literary Study of Marcan Characterization," *JBL* 108:2 [1989] 279; earlier, "Fallible Followers: Women and Men in the Gospel of Mark," *Semeia* 28 [1983] 29-48).

[38] Note the scheme "to us" and "to them" in 2:4, 2:7; 2:10; 3:1; 3:3.

beforehand that we should not be shipwrecked by conversion to their [i.e., the Jewish] law" (3:6) and to refute the belief that "the covenant is both theirs and ours," that is, belonging to Jews and Gentile Christians alike (4:6, 13:1).

This dual intentionality is discerned more specifically in "what is written concerning [Jesus]" and the events of his life: it "relates partly to Israel, partly to us" (5:2). Jesus "endured so as to deliver up his flesh unto corruption" *both* so that Israel might be "abandoned" (4:14) *and* so that [εἰς τοῦτο] "we should be sanctified" (5:1). Jesus' teaching and miracles share in this double effect. It was necessary, Barnabas writes, for the Lord to be manifested in flesh so that human beings beholding him might be saved (5:10), *and* so that "he might complete the total of the sins of those who persecuted his prophets to death" (5:11), that is, by drawing to himself the hostility of the Jews. Barnabas explicitly lays the responsibility for Jesus' trial and death upon the Jews: it is "the synagogue of the sinners" of Psalm 22:18 that puts Jesus to death, even being assimilated to the Roman soldiers who gambled for Jesus' clothing (Barnabas 6:6). The death thus secures doom for the Jews (6:7) and blessing for (Gentile) Christians (6:8).

This dual effect is the subject of Barnabas' "teaching," and as such can even be summed up as "what is necessary for salvation" (17:1). It is a comprehensive theological concept that allows Gentile Christianity to appropriate everything written in Israel's Scripture about the covenantal promises at the same time that Judaism is *disinherited*; and this "knowledge" (γνῶσις) is routinely described in the language of "manifestation." "It was made manifest [ἐφανερώθη] both that the tale of their sins should be completed in their sins, and that we through Jesus the Lord who inherits the covenant should receive it" (14:5). This knowledge is *hidden*, however, *from the Jews*, who persist in claiming the covenant for themselves: "the things which were thus done are plain to us [ἡμῖν μέν ἐστιν φανερά], but obscure to them [ἐκείνοις δὲ σκοτεινά], because they did not hear the Lord's voice" (8:7).

I also note that for Barnabas, as for Mk, the fact that Jesus' first disciples were Jews makes them objects of some ambivalence: Barnabas declares, for example, that Jesus came to fulfill prophecies made with regard to Israel, and that "while teaching Israel and doing great signs and wonders he preached to them and loved them greatly" (6:7-8); but Israel's covenant is "fulfilled" only through the creation of "the new people" (6:7). The Jewishness of the first disciples, then, is something of a theological liability which Barnabas turns into theological virtue: "when Jesus chose out his own apostles who were to preach his Gospel, he chose those who were iniquitous above all sin to show that 'he came not to call the righteous but sinners'" (6:9). We have seen a comparable ambivalence toward the disciples in Mk: as "insiders" they receive the secret of the kingdom of God, yet (as Jews?) they remain uncomprehending.

I see in Barnabas, then, an analog for the "dual effect" that I have described in Mk's use of secrecy motifs. The analog suggests that it is plausible, within the history of early Gentile Christianity, and particularly the emergence of the theology of Gentile-Christian supersession (the "replacement theory"), for Mk's juxtaposition of concealment and manifestation to cohere with the antagonism he expresses toward Judaism.

We have seen how the distribution and arrangement of different "secrecy" motifs in Mt, Lk, and Mk contribute to distinctive perspectives on Jesus' identity. In Mt, Jesus' commands to silence and his withdrawals are parts of an alternative vision of messiahship that Mt takes pains to argue fulfills Scripture. In Lk-Acts, Jesus, and his disciples after him, engage Satan in a contest of miracles. Lk uses the motif of the silencing of demons (by Jesus *and* by Paul) to show both that Jesus has authority over Satan and his demons and that Jesus performs miracles so as to exalt God, not himself. In Mk, finally, we argued that divine concealment and public manifestation are deliberately juxtaposed insofar as the Christ is hidden from the Jews, but revealed to those who will follow him as disciples, going with him the way of the cross.

The Acts of Peter and The Acts of John: Which Came First?

Dennis R. MacDonald
Iliff School of Theology

This paper continues the discussion of the literary interconnections among the Acts, canonical and apocryphal, for the SBL Seminar on Intertextuality in Christian Apocrypha. The working criteria for mapping these interconnections appear in the paper that appears earlier in this volume entitled "*The Acts of Paul* and *The Acts of John*: Which Came First?" For the Seminar last year I proposed the priority of *The Acts of Paul* to *The Acts of Peter*, and in the paper published ealier in this volume I again supported the priority of Paul's Acts to John's. I now turn the the question of literary connections between *The Acts of Peter* and *The Acts of John*.

At a few points these Acts contain similarities with each other that cannot have derived from a common dependence on *The Acts of Paul*, at least not on *The Acts of Paul* that now survives. *Acts of Peter* 20 and *Acts of John* 98 each contain speeches regarding Jesus' polymorphism. Both speeches refer to the transfiguration story, but their distinctive wording demonstrates that they did not derive independently from the gospels; they are literarily related to each other. Both speeches mention Jesus' ability to appear to people as enormous or small or old or embodied or disembodied. Both also discuss the paradox of a divine sufferer. Notice also the similarities between these two lists of predicates.

Acts of Peter 20	*Acts of John* 98
as the <u>door</u>, light, <u>way</u>, <u>bread</u>, water, <u>life</u>, <u>resurrection</u>, refreshment, pearl, treasure, <u>seed</u>, abundance, mustard seed, vine, plough, <u>grace</u>, <u>faith</u>, <u>word</u>.[1]	as <u>word</u> or mind or Christ or <u>door</u> or <u>way</u> or <u>bread</u> or <u>seed</u> or <u>resurrection</u> or son or father or spirit or <u>life</u> or truth or <u>faith</u> or <u>grace</u>.

Of the fifteen predicates in *The Acts of John* nine appear also among the eighteen in *The Acts of Peter*, occasionally even in the same order.

The speech in *The Acts of John* is much longer, expresses a more thoroughly philosophical docetism, and gives the impression of an expansion of the speech in *The Acts of Peter*. Furthermore, the transfiguration tradition is more indigenous to the Petrine tradition than the Johannine. The canonical Gospels stress the role of Peter and 2 Peter appeals to the transfiguration in order to validate the truth of Peter's preaching. From the parallels that follow, it would appear that

---

[1] The translations of *The Acts of Peter* usually are those of Rob Stoops, created for Polebridge collection.

The Acts of Peter was not inspired by *The Acts of John* but by Matt 17:1-9 and 2 Peter 1:16-18.

Matthew 17:1-9	2 Peter 1:16-18	*Acts of Peter* 20
Six days later, <u>Jesus</u> took with him (παραλαμβάνει) Peter and James and his brother John, and led them up a high <u>mountain</u>, by themselves. And he was transfigured before them, and his face <u>shone like the sun</u>....	...but we had been <u>eyewitnesses of his majesty</u> (μεγαλειότητος)....	When our Lord <u>Jesus</u> Christ wished us <u>to</u> <u>see his majesty</u> (*maiestatem*) on the holy <u>mountain</u>, and I and the sons of Zebedee saw the splendor of his <u>light</u>.
When the disciples <u>heard this</u>, they fell to the ground and were <u>overcome by fear</u>.	I fell <u>as</u> <u>though dead</u>. We ourselves <u>heard this voice</u> come from heaven, while we were with him on the holy <u>mountain</u>.	I closed my eyes, and I <u>heard this voice</u> such as I cannot describe....
But Jesus came and touched them saying, "<u>Get up</u> and do not be afraid" And <u>when they looked up</u>, <u>they saw</u> no one except Jesus himself alone.		and <u>lifted me up</u>. When I stood, <u>I saw him</u> again in a way that I was able to comprehend.

The Acts of Peter here repeatedly displays parallels with Matthew and 2 Peter, both of which already had emphasized Peter's role in the story. In only one instance (the use of the verb παραλαμβάνει, "he took with him") does *The Acts of John* agree with the biblical texts without a parallel in *The Acts of Peter*.

Acts of Peter 20	*Acts of John* 90
When our Lord Jesus Christ	On another occasion he had James, Peter, and me
wished us to see his majesty on <u>the</u> holy <u>mountain</u>, and I and the sons of Zebedee saw the splendor of his <u>light</u>. I closed my eyes, and I heard this voice such as I <u>cannot describe</u> ...	accompanying him (παραλαμβάνει, cf. Matt 17:1) to <u>the mountain</u> on which he was wont to pray. we saw upon him a kind of <u>light</u> which a mortal of perishable speech <u>could not</u> possibly <u>describe</u>.

It therefore would appear that *The Acts of Peter* better satisfies the criterion of generative traditions.

Furthermore, the author of *The Acts of John* obviously took exception to the Petrine character of the transfiguration tradition and attempted to replace Peter with John as the recipient of special revelation. The passage that follows in John's Acts is a second transfiguration account in which Jesus speaks only to John.

"Peter and James were vexed that I [John] was speaking with the Lord and gestured that I should leave the Lord by himself and come to them" (91). Here we find a conscious polemic against Peter's primacy in the transfiguration traditions such as one finds in *The Acts of Peter*.

Unfortunately, a significant problem internal to *The Acts of John* puts this hypothesis in jeopardy. Many scholars suggest that *Acts of John* 94-102 and 109 were added to the Acts after its original composition. If this be the case, the parallels presented above would demonstrate only that *The Acts of Peter* influenced a later redaction of the Acts, not necessarily *The Acts of John* at its more generative stage. Therefore, if one were to assess the intertextual connections between the Acts about Peter and John, one should look for parallels in undisputedly early sections of *The Acts of John*.

There are indeed a few tantalizing points of overlap that meet these requirements, but once again the interpreter confronts the problem of derivative and incomplete texts. *Acts of Peter* 21-26 narrates the healing of a group of blind, elderly women and Peter's performing several other miracles in a theatre; the text survives in a single Latin manuscript. *The Acts of John* too once narrated the healing of many elderly women in a theater, but the surviving text breaks off in the middle of a speech just prior to the actual healing. Even so, it is possible to determine a likely direction of dependence.[2]

Acts of Peter 22-23	*Acts of John* 31
	"All who wish to view the power of God,
...he got up <u>to go to the forum</u>	<u>assemble in the theater</u>
(*veniret ad forum*).	(γίνεσθε ἐν τῷ θεάτρῳ) tomorrow.
<u>The brothers and sisters together with all who were</u> in	By dawn <u>the crowd</u>
Rome assembled (*convenerunt*),	had already formed (συνῆλθον).
each paying a single gold piece to	
take a seat. <u>Senators, prefects, and officials flocked in</u>	When <u>the Roman governor</u> learned what was happening, <u>he, too,</u>
(*concurrunt*) as well.	<u>hastened</u> (σπεῦσαι) to take his place among the multitude.
	Now <u>a certain chief magistrate and leading Ephesian citizen</u> . . . .

Both Acts then express the desire of the crowd for miraculous evidence of divine power. In the case of *The Acts of Peter*, the apostle must demonstrate that his powers exceed those of Simon Magus, "the magician." In *The Acts of John* the apostle must live up to the statement of Andronicus that John had promised "impossible and incredible things." In both Acts the spectators show concern that

---

2 *The Acts of Paul* also contained an episode in a theater, at Sidon, but the text is too fragmentary to permit an assessment of its relationship to these scenes in *The Acts of Peter* and *The Acts of John*. There also exist parallels between the scenes of apostolic departures in *Acts of Peter* 2-4 and *Acts of John* 58-59, but it is possible that each could have derived independently from Acts 20:17-38 (Paul's departure from Miletus/Ephesus) or more likely from *Acts of Paul* 9-10 (*Pap. Hamburg* 6-7).

the ensuing deeds are not mere magic but true miracles. Both apostles also use the opportunity to preach.

Acts of Peter 23 and 25	*Acts of John* 32-33
After a long silence	When it was very silent
(*post multum silentium*)	(σιγῆς πολλῆς γενομένης),
	John opened his mouth and
Peter said: "People of Rome	began to speak: "People of Ephesus
(*Viri Romani*), you be (*estote*)	(ἄνδρες Ἐφέσιος), you first
our true judges! . . . so that	should know (γνῶτε) . . . .
when they see they will	By his power (δυνάμει)
be able to believe that he	I shall reprove unbelief,
	even that of the chief magistrate,
is raised by the power (*virtute*)	by raising up these women."
of God."	

Peter raised the boy; John healed the women, and both crowds believed in God.

Even though these parallels are not as extensive as those treated above, they suggest that the two stories somehow are related. In favor of the priority of *The Acts of Peter* is the motif of magic which appears in both but is more native to Peter's Acts which gives center stage to the magical competition between Peter and Simon Magus. Both men perform miracles in order to produce belief, but in the end it is Peter's miracles that prove the more spectacular. The contest in the forum is the anticipated shootout, the demonstration of their powers before *senatus populusque Romanus*. The parallel episode in *The Acts of John*, on the other hand, serves primarily to set up the conversion of Drusiana and the hostility of Andronicus. Little would be lost from John's Acts if this scene disappeared (much of it has!), whereas Peter's Acts would be hollow without this contest between Peter and Simon. It therefore would seem reasonable to conclude that of the two magical contests in these two Acts, that in *The Acts of Peter* better meets our criteris of external generative traditions and internal consistency.

On the basis of the parallels discussed last year and this, I propose the following intertextual map for the relationships among the apocryphal Acts devoted to Peter, Paul, and John.

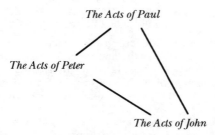

Next year we will analyze the relationship of each of these Acts to the canonical Acts of Apostles.

The *Acts of Peter* as Intertext:
Response to Dennis MacDonald

Judith B. Perkins
Saint Joseph College, West Hartford, CT

Intertextuality—referring not simply to influence, but to the way a text acquires meaning or significance by being read in the context of another text or texts—is a fruitful notion for considering the relationship between the *Acts of John* (AJ) and the *Acts of Peter* (APt).[1] These texts are obviously related—sharing so many themes and motifs that a common authorship for them has found proponents since antiquity. But in a context of circulating oral and written stories sharing the same themes, imagery, even vocabulary, the difficulty is in defining the precise terms of their relationship. In such a milieu and given the present state of evidence, certainty as to which text provides the intertext for another may be impossible, but Dennis MacDonald shows how instructive the effort to establish intertextuality can prove.

MacDonald's suggestion that the APt provides the intertext for the AJ seems correct to me. At several points the AJ seems to be contesting or offering a variant to the APt in terms that recall the APt. An extensive portion of the APt survives in an apparently faithful Latin translation—the *Actus Vercellenses*. This Latin text shows that the APt was a unified, cohesive narrative postulating three major themes: the superior power of the Christian God, his benevolent and inexhaustible mercy, and an egalitarian Christian community where Christ through his church usurps the place of the contemporary power structures as exemplified in the patronage system.[2] Treatment of one and usually several of these themes underlies nearly every episode of the APt. In this tightly focused work, if there were outside influences, one would expect the extrinsic themes to stand out. But such themes are not apparent; rather as MacDonald shows, at several points, the AJ takes up themes more germane to the APt.

MacDonald, for instance, demonstrates that the AJ's representation of John receiving special knowledge on the mountain assumes a familiarity with the

---

[1] Michael Riffaterre, "Textuality: W. H. Auden's Musée des Beaux," in *Textual Analysis*, ed. Mary Ann Caws (New York: MLA, 1986) 1-13. Riffaterre provides a useful definition: "Intertexuality is that form of reference experienced when the reader finds that a text presupposes another and that the latter provides the former with the means of interpreting it and justifying its formal and semantic peculiarities . . . This intertext represents a model on which the text builds its own variations."

[2] Robert Stoops, Jr., "Christ as Patron in the *Acts of Peter*," *Semeia* 56 (1992) 143-157 and his "Patronage in the *Acts of Peter*," *Semeia* 38 (1986) 91-100.

Petrine tradition and functions to displace Peter's primacy in the transfiguration tradition. This example clearly denotes intertextuality. If the reader is familiar with the alternative version, the text of the AJ takes on added significance and its double consideration of the transfiguration is explained. I would extend MacDonald's point here and suggest that many of the details of the AJ's transfiguration scene and its discussion of Christ's polymorphism work to challenge analogous scenes in the APt.[3]

Both the Acts introduce episodes of their apostle preaching on the transfiguration. In the APt, Peter enters Marcellus's house to find the gospel being read (vidi evangelium legi, 20); he rolls up the text and announces to the believers that they all should know how the gospels ought to be proclaimed (scitote, qualiter debeat sancta scriptura . . . pronuntiari, 20). He explains that Jesus took human form (effigie hominis) out of pity for human weakness (misericordiam suam). Peter describes the result of the incarnation in words that John picks up and echoes in the introduction to his discourse on the transfiguration. But as one would expect in an intertextual relationship, John uses these echoes not simply to recall but also to modify Peter's message.

Peter 20	*John* 88
For each of us (unus quisque nostrum) saw as he was able (capiebat videre), as he had power to see (poterat videre).	I cannot speak or write to you these things which I have seen and heard. Yet now I must adapt myself to your hearing and according to each man's (ἔκαστος ἐκείνων) capacity (χωρεί) I will impart those things of which you can be (δύνασθε γενέσθαι) hearers.

Both texts emphasize capacity, whether to see or hear. In the AJ, it is John who must adapt to his listeners' limited capacity. The text stresses that his knowledge is greater than theirs. John is unable to tell his audience what he knows, just as later in the transfiguration scene he will not tell James and Peter what he has heard. The narrative continues to underline John's superior status. When he and his brother, James, see Jesus from the boat, James sees a boy (παιδίον) while Peter sees a handsome man (ἄνδρα); as Schneider has pointed out, this difference in perception symbolizes John's more mature conception of the Lord.[4] In John's description of Jesus' other polymorphic appearances to him, he emphasizes the Lord's different sizes, ages, materiality and his difference from the human condition—his eyes never close, he leaves no footprints, and he levitates.[5]

In the APt, as Peter explains in his preaching, it is Christ who adapts himself to humankind so all can experience him as they are able. As Cartlidge points out, polymorphism in the APt fosters inclusiveness. Peter does not, as John did, withhold his knowledge; he explains what he knows (vobis exponam, 20). In fact, the narrative is framed to emphasize that Peter is as dependent on the Lord's

---

3 David R. Cartlidge, "Transfigurations of Metamorphosis Traditions in the Acts of John, Thomas and Peter," *Semeia* 38 (1986) 19-36 for a valuable comparison.

4 Paul G. Schneider, "Perfect Fit: the Major Interpolation in the Acts of John," *Society of Biblical Literature 1991 Seminar Papers* (Atlanta, GA: Scholars Press, 1991) 523-524.

5 Eric Junod and Jean-Daniel Kaestli, *Acta Iohannis* (Brehols: Turnhout, 1983) 2.466-493.

support as any other Christian. Immediately before the transfiguration account, Peter had entered Marcellus's house and encountered a blind widow supported by her daughter (*filiam eius manum ei dantem*, 20). He called out to her to rely on Jesus' support ("his right hand," dextram). When the brilliant light knocks Peter to the ground at the transfiguration, he believes himself to be blinded, but the Lord gives him his hand and picks him up (dans mihi manum elevavit me, 20). This narrative structure displays Peter as no more able than the widow to stand alone, no more able to take in God's splendor.

The APt's descriptions of Christ's human forms reinforce this egalitarian ethos. Christ is described as great and small; beautiful, but poor and ugly (magnum et minimum, formosum et foedum . . . speciosum sed inter nos humilem, 20). These terms, used to denote his earthly manifestations, belong to the social vocabulary of the time—the text verbally situates the Lord among those considered by society humble. The scene continues to reinforce this theme of all Christians' equality. Christ's brilliant light flashes into Marcellus's house; too bright, it blinds Peter and his companions, but enters the eyes of the blind widows and cures them. It is significant that it is the widows and not the apostle who have visions of the polyform Lord within this light. Peter's elated deduction after the widows relate what they have seen—"God is greater than our thoughts" (maior constans deus cogitationibus, 21)—insists on the equality of *all* Christians before the greatness of God.

The AJ reflects a different conception of the apostle's power and the Christian community; it understands a community where some have deeper levels of knowledge than others. Here again the APt appears to be the primary text; the interest in power relations is woven all through it. At a later point in the APt, for example, the imagery of the transfiguration scene occurs again. Peter, in the midst of raising two dead men, a favorite of Caesar's and a senator, is interrupted by a widow who begs him to raise her dead son, her only support. With her son gone, she asks Peter, "who will give me a hand (qui mihi manum porriget, 25)?" Peter raises the boy and tells him, not the senator, that he will be a deacon and bishop (diaconi ac episcopi, 27).[6]

As MacDonald also shows, sections of the AJ more secure than AJ 87-102 reveal signs of having been written in reaction to the APt. The AJ's use of the APt as a model, for example, can help explain the doubled resurrection of sinners in Drusiana's tomb. If an intertextual relation is recognized, this doubling can be interpreted to comment on the APt's attitude toward repentance. The constancy of divine mercy and forgiveness sustains the plot of the APt. After Paul departs from Rome, the Christian community seduced by Simon falls away, until Peter is sent to win them back. Peter does not chastise the Romans for their failure of faith, rather he identifies with them: "I denied our Lord Jesus Christ, and not once only but, three times. . . . But the Lord did not lay it to my charge; he turned to me and had compassion on the weakness of my flesh" (fui abnegans eum dominum nostrum Iesum Christum, et non tantam semel, sed et ter . . . et non mihi imputavit dominus; et conversus ad me et misertus est infirmitatem carnis meae, 7.3–5). Peter's failure in faith is a feature of the Petrine tradition, and in the APt the thrice denying Peter stands as an emblem for the Lord's repeated forgiveness. At times Peter almost appears to link the condition of

---

6 Cf. APt 28 for concern for slaves.

being human with sin: et ego ex vobis cum sum unus, carnem portans humanam sed peccator . . . (28.29-30).

The APt introduces another example of a repetitive sinner with Marcellus.[7] After Simon's arrival, Marcellus apostatizes and even persecutes the brethren. Forgiven by Peter, he immediately fails in faith again, despairing over the emperor's broken statue. Although Peter rebukes him for his lack of faith, Marcellus is immediately given another chance (11). In the APt, not even Simon who has bedeviled Peter so often is shut off from mercy. When the crowd threatens to burn him, Peter reproves them in conventional language: "we have not learnt to repay evil with evil, we have learnt to love our enemies and pray for our persecutors . . . for God will not remember evil" (deus enim non memorabitur mala, 28). Indeed, Peter treats Simon with relative gentleness. Even when he fears that Simon's flying will win him converts, he carefully stipulates in his prayer that Simon should "be crippled but not die but break his leg in three places"—Simon dies, rather, because he trusted a doctor of the same sort as he was (32).

The AP's attitude toward forgiveness helps us interpret some aspects of the AJ's tombscene. When John and Andronicus enter Drusiana's tomb they find two dead bodies. John raises Callimachus in order to discover what has taken place. He learns that a snake has saved Drusiana from necrophilic assault by killing her would-be attacker Callimachus and Fortunatus his accomplice. The revived Callimachus repents of his actions and begs to join the community.[8] Gerald Poupon has pointed out how similarly in the Acts the two sinners, Marcellus and Callimachus, are represented. Both are highborn, both are guilty of wrong doing, both are won over by marvels, both throw themselves at the feet of the apostle, both are forgiven and embraced, and both give the apostle an occasion for preaching. Nearly analogous terms describe their remorse and forgiveness.[9]

Acts of John 76-78	*Acts of Peter* 10-11
I need your help and so I <u>grasp your feet</u> (ἅπτομαί σου τῶν ποδῶν). And John seized with great gladness . . . said, . . . what unthinkable <u>glory</u> (δόξα) is ours . . . <u>So saying John took Callimachus and kissed him</u>(καὶ εἰπὼν ταῦτα . . . τὸν Καλλίμαχον ἠσπάζετο).	when Marcellus saw it he went to the door and <u>threw himself down at Peter's feet and said "I embrace your feet</u> (proiciens se ad pedes Petri et dixit: Petre, amplector tuos pedes) . . . and Peter said . . ." To thee O Lord, be <u>glory</u> (gloria) and splendor . . . <u>So saying Peter embraced Marcellus</u> (Haec dicente Petro et amplectentem Marcellum).

This similar representation of Callimachus and Marcellus—especially the linguistic echoes—suggests intertexuality. But even more indicative is the introduction of a second sinner to contrast with Callimachus (and Marcellus), a sinner who rejects repentance; and the text's response to him. Callimachus sins, is brought back to life, and repents. The addition of a second example in the AJ,

---

7 Gerald Poupon, "Les 'Actes de Pierre' et leur remaniement," *ANRW* 25.6 (1988) 4363-4383 has not persuaded me that the emphasis on second repentance is the work of a redactor.

8 Schneider, 520.

9 Poupon, 4376.

an unrepentant sinner, Fortunatus, and the description of his fate can be interpreted, I suggest, as a challenge to the repeated opportunities for mercy represented in the APt. After John has raised Drusiana, she begs that Fortunatus also be raised; Callimachus demurs, but John reminds him: "we have not learned to return evil for evil . . . and though we persecuted his brethren, [God] made no (such) return" (οὐκ ἐμάθομεν, τέκνον, κακὸν ἀντὶ κακοῦ ἀποδοῦναι . . . 81.9-10). This saying is suggestive here, especially as NT sayings are used so sparingly in the AJ. Its use, echoing the APt, in a scene where Callimachus's description recalls that of Marcellus, supports our reading that the AJ introduces the example of Fortunatus to contest the AP's attitude towards forgiveness. Unlike Callimachus who repents, when Fortunatus is resurrected and sees the faithful standing around, he wishes he were still dead and runs away. John denounces him for this, and, linking Fortunatus to Satan, curses all Satan's creatures, banning them from the Christian community: "from their practice, from their counsel, from their resurrection to God, etc." (84). Fortunatus, unlike Peter and Marcellus, is given only one chance. Retribution is swift; Fortunatus dies a second time from the bite of the divine agent, the snake.

The AJ appears to reflect those who set a limit on the availability of mercy. John explicitly preaches this later in the text: "if when you have known him and found mercy with him you resort again to such deeds, then both your former sins will be laid to your charge, and you shall have no part nor mercy in his presence" (107). Again an intertextual relation, once recognized, clarifies meaning. The peculiar introduction of an unrepentant resurrected sinner, in contrast to another who repents, gains significance if one senses as the reason for it an implicit polemic against a model-text that endorsed repeated forgiveness.

One final example of intertextuality. Junod and Kaestli note that on several occasions the AJ portrays John as physically transferring his miraculous powers.[10] The text marks John taking the hand of the person to whom he is delegating his power. Laying on of hands is a traditional method of bestowing power, but again, I suggest, the verbal stress on hands in these episodes of the AJ recall the APt as intertext. The first example occurs when Cleopatra is delegated to raise her husband, Lycomedes. The text depicts John touching and instructing her: "Then the Apostle went up to the couch on which Lycomedes lay, and taking Cleopatra's hand he said, . . . 'speak with a loud voice to your husband and say, "Rise up and glorify the name of God" . . .' and she went near and spoke to her husband as she was instructed and immediately raised him up" (24).

This physical transfer of power is underlined more emphatically in a second scene of resurrection when John empowers a man to raise his kinsman, the dead priest of Artemis. The man's hands are referred to three times. This emphasis recalls the many scenes in the APt where hands are featured; for example, Marcellus's miraculous reformation of the emperor's broken statue.

---

10 Junod and Kaestli, 509.

Peter 11	*John* 46-47
But if you are truly repentant and believe in Christ . . . take running water into your hands (manibus tuis)" . . . taking the water in his hands (manibus suis). . . . "I take water in my hands (in manibus meis)" . . . and Marcellus was uplifted in spirit, because the first miracle was done at his hands (signum primum inter manus eius factum fuisset).	John . . . took him by the hand (τῆς χειρός). . . and took his hand (τῆς χειρός). . . .and still holding the young man by the hand (τῆς χειρός) he said, "I tell you, my son, go and raise up the dead man yourself, saying nothing, but only this: John, the servant of God, says to you, Arise!'"

These two scenes use linguistic similarity to make very different points. In the AJ the repetition of χειρός marks John's physical transfer of his power. John attributes his power to the Lord (47.12), but the text explicitly represents the apostle as the mediator of Christ's power. Certain other Christians share this power. Drusiana raises Fortunatus with her own healing touch without any help from John. Junod and Kaestli explain Drusiana's ability as a result of her explicitly attested, long-term piety (θεοσέβεια, 63.5-6).[11] The AJ constructs a hierarchy of miraculous power-wielding, a hierarchy notably missing from the APt. Peter assures Marcellus, for example, that, if he believes in his heart, his hands will perform a miracle. Marcellus a recent persecutor of Christians is empowered simply by his belief; Peter does not transfer power to him. In fact, in the APt, almost anyone can effect a miracle, even Agrippa, the Roman prefect and future persecutor. Backed by Christ's power and Peter's voice, Agrippa is allowed to resurrect his servant: "And Peter said to the boy's master, 'Come, take his right hand, and you shall have him alive.' . . . And Agrippa the prefect ran and came to the boy and taking his hand restored him to life" (26). The APt seems actually to de-emphasize the apostle's power. Peter appears as simply a stand-in for the Lord.[12] When Peter tells the blind widow that Jesus's hand (dextram) will support her, she is cured and opens her eyes to see Peter's hand (manum 20).

The AJ's representation of the apostle's laying on of hands before allowing a surrogate to perform a miracle gains significance if a reader knows a text where such a transfer of power is not delineated. But other Christian texts also do not insist on the physical transfer of miracle working powers. More significant to my mind as an indicator of the intertextuality between the APt and the AJ is the four-fold repetition of χαιρός in a few lines of AJ 46-47. In the AJ repeated reference to hands is unexpected, an anomaly. Whereas the APt displays what seems to be almost an excessive attention to hands. The entire text is focused, often verbally, on Christ and his community's helping hands. The triple repetition in AJ 46-47 suggests to me the verbal influence of the APt.

---

11 Junod and Kaestli, 509, n.1.

12 Junod and Kaestli define John as a mediator, but in the APt Peter often seems simply a "front." See, for example, Marcellus's dream (22) where Peter calls for Christ and then Marcellus sees someone similar to Peter come and kill the Ethiopian but, at the same time, sees Peter looking on.

MacDonald has made a case for the APt as the intertext of the AJ, a case with which I agree. I sense, however, with a change of lens, that the AJ might well appear to be the intertext of the APt. In conclusion I suggest that, given the present state of the evidence, the nature of the Apocryphal Acts, and the culture of their creation, with respect to the priority among the early Acts, we must be satisfied by reasoned conjectures rather than firm conclusions.

Apostolic Apocrypha: Where Do We Stand with Schneemelcher's Fifth Edition?

Robert F. Stoops, Jr.
Western Washington University

The fifth edition of *Neutestamentliche Apokryphe II*, offers an overview of the state of research on apocryphal texts dealing with the careers and teachings of the apostles.[1] This new edition, edited again by Wilhelm Schneemelcher, clearly reflects the major changes in the questions which define the field. It also shows how little has been settled at this point in the discussion. The recent English translation makes Schneemelcher's work accessible to a wider range of students, if only because its cost is less than half that of the German edition.[2]

Introductory Matter

The previous German edition, which was the basis for the first English translation, appeared more than a quarter century ago. At that time, the controlling question remained the search for authentic traditions concerning the lives of the apostles in apocryphal texts. In the new edition, the apocryphal texts have come into their own as the subject of study. They are no longer seen as attempts to supplant the canonical texts. Their diversity in terms of genre and function is fully recognized. Text-critical questions are given new prominence. Schneemelcher can still speak of the importance of recognizing traditions behind the present texts, but now the influence of these texts on later

[1] Wilhelm Schneemelcher, ed., *Neutestamentliche Apokryphen in deutscher Übersetzung. 5. Auflage der von Edgar Hennecke begründeten Sammlung. II. Band. Apostolisches Apokalypsen und Verwandtes* (Tübingen: J. C. B Mohr [Paul Siebeck], 1989).

[2] *New Testament Apocrypha: Revised Edition of the Collection Initiated by Edgar Hennecke* (Trans. R. McL. Wilson; Louisville: Westminster/John Knox, 1992). The English edition is, like the German, set in a very readable type and has fewer typographical errors than the German. In general, material that is unchanged in the fifth German edition has not been modified in the new English edition. The rather stilted "thee's and thou's" have been retained in the translations of the texts. The translations of the introductory essays remain somewhat stiff, and some of the new material gives the impression of having been translated by computer. Unfortunately, the English publishers have chosen to place endnotes after each section. Endnotes are particularly cumbersome in this work because it is impossible to know whether one is being directed to an important variant reading, a vague NT parallel, or, less frequently, a discussion of a problem of interpretation. The footnotes of the German edition (and the previous English edition) are much to be preferred. Page references are to the English edition unless otherwise noted.

literature receives equal or greater attention. Schneemelcher notes that the apocryphal texts should be studied for the light they can cast on the development of popular (3–4) or even marginal (85) forms of Christianity. However, the question of how to accomplish this goal is far from settled.

In the previous edition, a significant portion of the introductory matter was given over to Walter Bauer's survey of apostolic traditions in Christian literature of all types. Organized by apostle, Bauer's essay assembled fragments of tradition with characteristic thoroughness.[3] The early apocryphal Acts were also approached as potential sources for authentic tradition. Their historical value was impugned, and their distance from the NT was emphasized with a somewhat dismissive air. The literary descendants of the early Acts were merely noted as curiosities which might, on occasion, contribute something for the reconstruction of the earlier documents. Bauer's survey of apostolic trivia has nearly disappeared from Bienert's reworking of the introductory essays. The direction of current research is demonstrated by the comparable expansion of Santos Otero's survey of later apostolic Acts (426–482).

Apostolic Pseudepigrapha

The section of the book dedicated to "Apostolic Pseudepigrapha" (28–74) has not changed much. These texts have not seen as much activity as the apocryphal Acts. The introductory essay is largely unchanged, although some bibliography has been added. The treatment of the *Kerygma Petri* is the same, but the discussion of *Kerygmata Petrou* is appropriately removed from this section to be joined with the other material from the Pseudo-Clementine romances. The section on *The Epistle to the Laodiceans* has hardly been touched. Quispel's 1950 article is still presented as a recent development (44). The treatment of the Pseudo-Titus *Epistle on Virginity* is presented as a revision, but the changes are largely limited to the addition of more recent bibliographic references in the notes and a few minor changes in the text.[4] Only the *Correspondence between Seneca and Paul* has truly been reworked. The new introduction by Cornelia Römer is accompanied by a much more readable translation.

Second and Third Century Acts of Apostles

Schneemelcher's introduction to the second and third century Acts has been revised to take account of the newer work on the apocryphal Acts (75–86). These texts are no longer assessed in terms of their differences from the canonical book of Acts, and the lengthy discussion of Dibelius's views on Acts has mercifully disappeared. Rather, their influence on later hagiographic literature is emphasized. The old uneasiness about statements covering all five texts has grown into an insistence on the distinctiveness of each text (76). Since each text is now to be treated as an independent object of study, the question of transmission has taken on a new importance.

---

[3]Bauer's essay is reason enough to retain the old volume in one's library.

[4]E.g., "eternal bridegroom" has been changed to "bridegroom forever."

Schneemelcher's discussion of genre or *Gattung* in fact covers a variety of topics (78–83). Schneemelcher stays rather close to Rosa Söder's old position and cites Vielhauer in support. The apocryphal Acts are to be understood as a type of Christian literature which is influenced by the ancient novel but not identical to it. He criticizes members of the Association for their imprecision on the question of genre, especially in light of their frequent insistence on the literary character of these texts. This observation brings him to a critique of the principles of dating put forward by Junod and Kaestli, who take the absence of biblical and ecclesiastical traditions as evidence that texts like *The Acts of John* were composed near the middle of the second century. Presumably, a crucial element is the degree to which these texts employ traditions. However, it is unwise to assume a straightline development that is uniform in all places and all communities. Other grounds for dating must be found.

Even more curiously, Schneemelcher chooses to discuss the work of a number of American scholars in this section on genre. He does so in spite of the acknowledged fact that these works are not primarily concerned with questions of genre. Schneemelcher finds the social and folklore analyses of Davies, MacDonald, and Burrus too ideological in content (81–82). Moreover, these studies leave the apostolic protagonists in the shadows, and in his mind the apostles are the figures who give these texts their distinctively Christian character. The characterization of these efforts as "ahistorical travesties" (81) may involve an over-translation of *Verzeichnungen* (perhaps Professor Wilson is registering his opinion with his choice of terms), but Schneemelcher does finds these efforts at social history misguided or "scarcely useful" (83) at best.

Schneemelcher's final section deals with the role of the apocryphal Acts in theology and Church history (83–85). This would seem to be the appropriate place to discuss the investigations into social history which American scholars have undertaken. The old issue of the gnostic or catholic character of the Acts is addressed instead. The now obvious conclusion is reached: sweeping judgments cannot be made. These Acts must be seen as a counterbalance to the interests of the theologians. They represent the interests of common people or marginal groups (85). Why women and their potential concerns should not be counted among the audience is not explained.

Schäferdiek's contribution on the question of a Manichean collection has been expanded and given separate status. He responds to the challenges of Nagel and Kaestli,[5] but still asserts that an early collection existed. In any case he distinguishes this claim from the issue of canonical status. The evidence he offers for a formal collection might equally argue against it. Most of the witnesses he cites mention only a subset of the collection.

Only two new texts has been added to the collection of early apostolic Acts: an Irish apocryphon in the John tradition, and *The Acts of Peter and the Twelve Apostles* from the Nag Hammadi library. The new arrangement of the five early Acts in alphabetical rather than in (approximate) chronological order may reflect the editor's lack of certainty concerning relative dating and the direction of possible influences. The text-critical work of members of the Association pour l'étude de la littérature apocryphe chrétienne is noted, though not always accepted in the individual introductions. Unfortunately the

---

[5]I happen to agree with Schneemelcher's caution in this case.

progress made on text-critical research is not reflected in most of the apostolic apocrypha published in the new edition. In some cases, the editor is not convinced by the suggestions (e.g., *Acts of Peter*).[6] Even where the editor has changed his assessment of an issue (e.g., the relationship of *3 Corinthians* to *The Acts of Paul*), these changes are not reflected in the texts offered. In most cases, only minor modifications have been made to the texts as printed in the previous edition. Many of these modifications are bibliographic additions to the notes.

Acts of Andrew

Prieur has provided a new introduction to *The Acts of Andrew*. It is a useful summary of contribution to Series apocryphorum. Because it is organized along similar lines, the reader can easily pursue the fuller discussion. Prieur is not convinced by MacDonald's early work that *Andrew and Matthias among the Cannibals* belongs to the original *Acts of Andrew*.[7] The discussion of *Andrew and Matthias among the Cannibals* in Santos Otero's review of later Acts should be consulted on this question as well.

Prieur interprets *The Acts of Andrew* as an individual's free composition based on philosophy rather than church tradition. The human condition is characterized by ignorance. The revealer figure functions as a redeemed redeemer. Asceticism is the natural expression of a mature spiritual understanding. Prieur offers Socrates as a point of comparison. Both Socrates (Prieur) and Homer (MacDonald) are commonplaces for later Greek literature. It is probably wise not to rest a large interpretation on a few parallels. Prieur argues for early date, along lines used by Junod and Kaestli for *Acts of John*.

In spite of the new introduction, the text Schneemelcher prints for the *The Acts of Andrew* is a disappointment. We are still offered only a summary of Gregory's epitome. The translation of the Utrecht papyrus is inferior to MacDonald's.[8] A translation of Detorakis's edition of the martyrdom has replaced the extracts presented in the earlier edition of Hennecke-Schneemelcher. This is an improvement, but the Armenian is not considered, and one is left to construct his or her own synopsis of the material in both Vaticanus 808 and the JS version.

Acts of John

Schäferdiek's introduction to *The Acts of John* is only slightly revised. He employs the seemingly standard move among the Germans of arguing that the differences between *The Acts of John* and other early Acts are too great to demonstrate literary dependence in either direction. He rejects Junod and

---

[6]See his note 15 on page 96.

[7]Dennis R. MacDonald, "*The Acts of Andrew and Matthias* and *The Acts of Andrew*" *Semeia* 38 (1986) 9-26, 35-39. MacDonald's reconstruction of the Acts of Andrew in his *The Acts of Andrew and The Acts of Andrew in the City of the Cannibals* (SBLTT, Christian Apocrypha 1; Atlanta: Scholars Press, 1990) was not available to Prieur at the time of publication.

[8]Dennis R. MacDonald, *The Acts of Andrew*.

Kaestli's theory of origin and still argues for composition in the east in the first part of the third century.

Minor improvements have been made in the translation. Junod and Kaestli's edition has allowed him to remove a number of asterisks, so that the page presents fewer distractions. An Irish apocryphon is added. It is an interesting text but rather distant from the original *Acts of John*. It remains unclear why this particular text was chosen for inclusion when other late apocrypha are not given similar treatment.

Acts of Paul

Schneemelcher's introduction to *The Acts of Paul* (213–238) adds a (negative) response to Davies's suggestions in his *Semeia* contribution. Schneemelcher is somewhat less confident of the possibility of reconstructing the contents of *The Acts of Paul*, but he continues to assume a single journey as his working model. Schneemelcher gives extensive treatment of Rordorf, but his suggestions are largely resisted. Only his contention that *3 Corinthians* arose independently of *The Acts of Paul* is accepted. The printed text is not changed to reflect this new view. Rordorf's suggestions that *The Acts of Paul* could be related to traditions in the Pastoral Epistles and to the climate of Montanism are both rejected. The fact that MacDonald had made similar proposals in his *Legend and the Apostle* is overlooked. Schneemelcher again dismisses the application of methods drawn from folklore and interests in reconstructing women's experience as "*Phantasiegebilde.*" He is not convinced by Drijvers's argument for a thoroughly symbolic interpretation either. The author is supposed to have known the canonical Acts, but the use of common traditions is said to have played a more important role. Schneemelcher in the end argues that *The Acts of Paul* constitute a collection of edifying materials assembled in Asia Minor in the last decades of the second century. For all the options surveyed, he has changed his mind only on the question of *3 Corinthians*. The accompanying text has not been significantly changed.

The Acts of Peter

Here too Schneemelcher's introduction has been revised to take note of new issues but makes no fundamental changes in his conclusions. Schneemelcher has condensed his discussion of the relationship between *The Acts of Peter* and the Pseudo-Clementine literature. His conclusion is the same, they make use of common traditions. He is also less confident than Junod and Kaestli in assessing the possible relationship between *The Acts of Peter* and *The Acts of John*, but he still follows Schmidt in arguing that *The Acts of Paul* are dependent on those of Peter.

Poupon's analysis of the composition history is discussed but not accepted (281). Schneemelcher still sees *The Acts of Peter* as a supplement to the canonical Acts based on a variety of traditions. It would be a mistake to look for theological consistency here. Only minor corrections in the translation of the text have been necessary, pending Poupon's new edition.

Acts of Thomas

The Acts of Thomas, like *The Acts of Andrew,* have received a wholly new introduction, this one from the hand of Hans J. W. Drijvers. Drijvers' introduction is one of the most valuable features of the new edition insofar as it presents a clear, alternative reading of *The Acts of Thomas.* Bornkamm's introduction was firmly placed in the *Religionsgeschichtliche Schule* of its time and found the redeemed redeemer everywhere. Drijvers' offers a different interpretive context. Tatian and Bardaisan, who witness a Syrian soteriology related to issues of freedom and gnosis, replace the Mandeans, Manicheans and even Marcosians of Bornkamm's picture. Drijvers' interpretation requires a strong reading of symbolism throughout. He seems to suspect that a parable lurks behind almost every element of any given story. The notes calling attention to Biblical parallels are far more numerous than in the previous edition.

Drijvers' completely rejects the redeemed redeemer myth as background. Bornkamm may have gone too far with the myth, but Drijvers is in danger of falling off the other end of the log. His reading of the Hymn of the Pearl, for instance, seems forced. If the pearl stands for the power of the serpent, why is it said to belong to the prince, why is he sent for it, and why does he carry it into the presence of the king? The pearl would seem to stand for something valuable. Retrieving the pearl effects a change in the prince's identity. This is very close to what is usually meant by a redeemed redeemer; in fact, it is the model case.

Drijvers does note possible influence of *The Acts of Thomas* on interpretation of Mani. Santos Otero contributes important comments on both the influence of these Acts on later texts and on the development of the textual tradition itself.

Acts of Peter and the Twelve Apostles

The Acts of Peter and the Twelve Apostles is the only text from Nag Hammadi included in the collection of early Acts. Schenke suggests a second century dating because the text contains no direct quotations from the New Testament. This argument seems to me to beg the question of genre and intended function. He rightly rejects Krause's attempt to identify this text as a missing portion of the *Acts of Peter.*

The Pseudo-Clementines

One of the more egregious faults of the earlier volume has been partially alleviated by bringing the Pseudo-Clementine material together in one place. The two introductions have been modified slightly to remove the more obvious disagreements. The separate existence of *The Kerygmata Petrou* needs a stouter defense in light of the objections raised since the introduction was written. The fact of these objections is noted, but they are left unanswered (p. 489). The selections from the texts remain the same. Beyond the updated bibliography, this section offers no new insight on this complex body of materials. Perhaps that explains why it is hidden behind Santos Otero's chapter on later Acts, even the dating argued for in the introduction would seem to justify inclusion among the second and third century Acts or at least the position it held previously, ahead of the later Acts.

Later Acts of Apostles

The shift in scholarly interest can be measured most clearly in Santos Otero's reworking of the chapter on "Later Acts of Apostles." The number of texts and text complexes discussed has doubled, but the more detailed discussions of content and especially the cataloguing of much richer manuscript resources and published editions result in an essay that is eight to ten times longer. The material is still introduced for its value in reconstructing, and as evidence for the continued influence of the early Acts. There is less stress on differences from NT and the canonical Acts in particular. The boundary between NT apocrypha and hagiography disappears in favor of "textological symbiosis," the belief that early and late productions must be studied together in order fully to understand either. Certain general tendencies, such as the association of several apostles within one story and the broad influence of *The Acts of Thomas* on later apocrypha are noted.

The Andrew apocrypha are treated at some length. *The Acts of Andrew and Matthias among the Cannibals* receives extensive discussion. Santos Otero does not fully agree with Prieur's assessment of this text and should be consulted along with Prieur's introduction. Similarly, Santos Otero's discussion of the later text development of *The Acts of Thomas* and its influence on other apocryphal traditions is an important complement to Drijvers' introduction. *The Acts of Philip* receive an extensive discussion which is independent of Bovon's study in *ANRW* II.25.6. The question must be asked whether a translation of this text should be included in future editions. Santos Otero fills out the apostolic roster with reviews of the content and manuscript sources for several dozen later texts which were not dealt with at all in previous editions. His survey provides a foundation for a significant broadening of the field of study.

Where then do we stand?

Schneemelcher's fifth edition of Hennecke is a necessary revision of a standard reference tool, but it is far from the last word on the subject of apostolic apocrypha. The editor, himself, remains unconvinced by much of the new research. Schneemelcher is to be credited for the care with which he sets out the available options on debated questions. The extreme caution with which he reserves final judgment can be frustrating, but this caution is a useful indicator of the need to strengthen the arguments put forward. On questions of the transmission history of apocryphal texts, Schneemelcher does not accept the approach of Junod and Kaestli, which suggests that heterodox ideas and a paucity of NT parallels indicate composition in the early part of the second century. Similarly, he has not been convinced by Poupon's reconstruction of the compositional history of *The Acts of Peter*.[9] In general, Schneemelcher still refuses to acknowledge literary dependence unless he finds elements that are both closely parallel and used for similar purposes. He

---

[9] I agree with Schneemelcher's reserve in these two areas.

prefers instead to speak of common traditions behind the texts. In the new edition, Schneemelcher is even more cautious than before about suggesting the nature of those traditions. Consequently, he has moved away from his earlier call for form-critical studies (80-81). On the other hand, he has not accepted the view often expressed by members of the Association that these texts should be understood and analyzed as relatively free literary creations.

The relationship between text and oral tradition in the apocryphal Acts needs continued investigation. This need, coupled with the complexity of developing textual traditions noted in Santos Otero's survey, indicates that the questions of intertextuality addressed by the SBL seminar are important for the wider field at the moment. Because traditions probably developed in many different ways, we should be looking for patterns of relationship that can help us develop a range of models for the transmission of traditions. Different sets of criteria may be necessary for discerning different kinds of relationships among texts.

While textual history may be an end in itself, it is also a necessary foundation for further investigation of the texts as sources for the history of Christianity in the times and places of their composition. It is of course not necessary to wait for the text-critical eschaton before proceeding in a provisional way. In fact, questions concerning the textual basis are only a minor element in what may be characterized as European skepticism toward the social-history approach taken by many members of the SBL seminar. For the most part, the studies criticized by Schneemelcher—and by Bovon and Junod—have been explicit about their methodology. The questions have concerned the appropriateness of these methods to the analysis of texts from late antiquity. Most of what has been offered in this area have been new interpretations of the texts or hypotheses as to their social location. The persuasiveness of such studies depends on their ability to make sense of large texts or complexes of tradition. They often result in substitute readings rather than extensions of existing scholarship. It is not surprising that they have failed to convince in many cases. We might do ourselves and our colleagues a favor if we focused our social and historical interests more narrowly on the problem of the developing text traditions. Our common interest in questions of intertextual relationships should provide opportunities for further demonstrations of the appropriateness of these methods. Reconstructions which help to explain the transformation of a specific tradition from one text to another in terms of social function are likely to be taken seriously. By the fruits of our collective labors we shall be known. For that reason, it is important to bring the social-historical perspective to bear on questions of intertextual relationships even more explicitly than we have done in the past.

Matthew and Marginality

Dennis C. Duling
Canisius College

Introduction

There is an increasing tendency in New Testament study to refer to Jesus, Jesus movements, gospel characters, and other Christian persons and groups as "marginal."[1] This tendency has also found its way into study of the Gospel of Matthew. Janice Capel Anderson has forcefully argued that the woman with the hemorrhage (Matt 9:20-22) and the Canaanite woman (Matt 15:21-28) are not only marginal because they come from marginal groups, the ritually unclean and Gentiles, but also because they are women: they are "doubly marginal."[2] From the perspective of redaction criticism, John R. Donahue contends that the "parable" of the Sheep and the Goats in Matthew 25 is the hermeneutical key to the gospel. To be sure, says Donahue, acts of mercy toward the "least of my brothers and sisters" in this parable refer to acts toward the Matthean apostles/missionaries; nonetheless, "the criterion of judgment will be works of charity and mercy shown toward the marginal, the poor and the suffering of the world."[3] Several recent social historians have viewed the Matthean community as sectarian,[4] and if one were to argue that "sects" are marginal groups, the conclusion would be that the community as a whole is marginal. Finally, from the perspective of deviance and labeling theory in the social sciences, Bruce Malina's and Jerome Neyrey's work might be seen as a contribution to analysis of Matthew from the perspective of marginality.[5]

---

[1] E. Schüssler Fiorenza, *In Memory of Her. A Feminist Theological Reconstruction of Christian Origins* (New York: Crossroad, 1983) 141; John P. Meier, *A Marginal Jew. Rethinking the Historical Jesus* (2 vols.; New York: Doubleday, 1991-); John S. Kloppenborg, "Blessing and Marginality. The 'Persecution Beatitude' in Q [6:22ab, 23ab], Thomas, and Early Christianity," *Forum* 2/3 (1986) 36-56; Robert J. Karris, *Jesus and the Marginalized in John's Gospel* (Collegeville, MN: Liturgical Press, 1990);

[2] Janice Capel Anderson, "Matthew: Gender and Reading," in Mary Ann Tolbert, ed., *The Bible and Feminist Hermeneutics*, Semeia 28 (1983) 10-17. While marginal, they are examples of faith and initiative.

[3] John R. Donahue, "The Parable of the Sheep and the Goats: A Challenge to Christian Ethics," *TS* 47 (1986) 3; see *The Gospel in Parable* (Philadelphia: Fortress Press, 1988) 125.

[4] J. Andrew Overman, *Matthew's Gospel and Formative Judaism. The Social World of the Matthean Community* (Minneapolis: Fortress, 1990); David L. Balch, ed., *Social History of the Matthean Community. Cross-Disciplinary Approaches* (Minneapolis: Fortress Press, 1991).

[5] Bruce J. Malina and Jerome H. Neyrey, *Calling Jesus Names. The Social Value of Labels in Matthew* (Sonoma, CA: Polebridge Press, 1988).

In this paper, I have two aims. First, I explore the conceptuality of marginality as it has emerged among certain social scientists. Second, I try to show from this perspective in what sense the author of Matthew is concerned about marginal people and in what sense he might be considered a marginal figure himself. First, then, some social scientific discussion about marginality.

Marginality Theory

1. "Marginal Man"

In 1928 Robert E. Park, leader of the Park School of sociology of the University of Chicago, first used marginality as a distinct theoretical concept to describe ethnic immigrants to the United States in relation to the dominant Anglo-Saxon majority.[6] Park referred to "Marginal Man," that is, a person who is condemned to live in two different, antagonistic cultural worlds, but does not fully belong to either. Such persons are not fully acculturated. The "marginal man" or "marginal woman" can also be the child of marriages from two different cultural representatives.

In 1937 E. V. Stonequist elaborated Park's insight in a fascinating and influential social psychological work titled *The Marginal Man*.[7] For Stonequist, "[T]he marginal personality is most clearly portrayed in those individuals who are unwittingly initiated into two or more historic traditions, languages, political loyalties, moral codes, or religions."[8] Stonequist organized his study around two types of marginals: racial mixtures (e.g., Eurasians of India; Cape Colored of South Africa; Mulattoes of the United States) and cultural mixtures, which were further subdivided into migrant foreigners (Europeanized Africans; Westernized Orientals), second generation American immigrants, American Negroes, and Jews emancipated from the ghetto. Stonequist also mentioned the *parvenu*, the upwardly mobile marginal, often satirized (e.g., the ancient Trimalchio) or praised (e.g., the modern Horatio Alger), and the opposite, the *déclassé*, or downwardly mobile marginal. Noted as well were the migrant from the farm to the city and women who find themselves in a new social role previously occupied only by men.[9]

In subsequent studies American sociologists discussed marginality in connection with high crime rate, family dysfunction, and emotional distress among immigrants. They eventually turned to other types of social contact, mostly subcultures within a larger culture. There was continued study of movements up and down various levels of the social ladder, ethnic subcultures

6 Robert E. Park, "Human Migration and the Marginal Man," *American Journal of Sociology* 33 (1928) 881-93; "Personality and Cultural Conflict," *Publication of the American Sociological Society* 25 (1931) 95-110; cf. R. A. Schermerhorn, "Marginal Man," in Julius Gould and William L. Kolb, eds., *Dictionary of the Social Sciences* (New York: The Free Press, 1964) 406-407.

7 E. V. Stonequist, *The Marginal Man* (New York: Charles Scribner's Sons, 1937).

8 Stonequist, *The Marginal Man*, 3.

9 Stonequist, *The Marginal Man*, 5-6.

in relation to the dominant culture, and urbanization and detribalization in Africa—in short, anything that produces "status incongruence."[10]

In line with such developments, a computer search of the word "marginality" today will turn up hundreds of titles that range from studies of the poor, particularly in Latin America, to migrant workers in Germany, French avant-garde literary figures, the handicapped, and women in higher education. For my purposes, it will be important to explore two more theoretical areas, or what I shall call involuntary marginality and voluntary marginality.

2. *Involuntary Marginality*

Gino Germani has written a useful work on theoretical sociology titled simply *Marginality* (1980).[11] He states that at the descriptive level, one can observe certain phenomena typical of urban ecological environments: segregated shantytowns, squatter settlements, poor working conditions, low standard of living, and the exclusion of such groups from the decision making process that affects their lives. Germani thinks that similar phenomena can exist in rural areas. These phenomena represent subcultures, sometimes ethnic populations, with differing norms, values, and attitudes from those held by the majority culture; such persons are dominated by economic, political, and cultural elites. They are not in "the center" (usually modern and developed), but are on "the periphery" (usually underdeveloped and archaic). When they exist side by side in a single political entity, such as a national state, these phenomena point to a kind of internal colonialism, a society within a society. Germani argues that such groups and persons are roughly equivalent to those who live in poverty and that they have some level, however minimal, of social participation; therefore, they do not represent a totally separate class unrelated to the rest of the social structure, as some analysts have affirmed.

At the explanatory level, Germani offers five basic, interrelated causal factors for these phenomena: economic and social (especially unemployment); political (limitation of participation on the basis of class, race, sex, ethnicity); demographic (overpopulation); cultural (domination of one cultural group by another; [neo]colonialism; rural-urban contrasts); and psychosocial (powerlessness; helplessness; status inferiority; inadequate early socialization). After considering the origins of the concept of marginality, and arguing for some similarity between developed and developing countries (despite the ubiquity of the phenomenon in developing countries), Germani observes certain correlations with social stratification. While there is some validity in correlating marginals with the bottom of the social hierarchy, it is also possible to think of marginals at each level of the social hierarchy in terms of a participant/nonparticipant continuum. On this basis, Germani arrives at a generalized definition of marginality:

---

10 Schermerhorn, "Marginal Man," 407.

11 Gino Germani, *Marginality* (New Brunswick, NJ: Transaction Books, 1980).

. . . we may define marginality as the lack of participation [exercise of roles] of individuals and groups in those spheres in which, according to determined criteria, they might be expected to participate.[12]

The "lack of participation" in this definition means the inability of persons to conform to expected social roles with respect to sex, age, civil life, occupation, and social life in relation to levels of status in the social system. These statuses are based on social norms, values, and expectations rooted in law and legitimated by custom. In other words, the marginal person no longer participates in what Germani calls "the normative scheme," that is:

the set of values and norms which define the categories (status), the legitimate, expected, or tolerated areas of participation and the assignment mechanisms of individuals to each category.[13]

Lack of participation often occurs because of a new and competing "normative scheme."[14] For marginal persons there are two related elements. First, the usual "objective resources," both material and nonmaterial—education, jobs, purchasing power, housing—are not unavailable. Second, the "personal conditions" needed to exercise their social roles are not present.

We refer here to psychological features on the emotional, volitive and intellectual level as well as the cognitive patrimony: attitudes, propensities, motivations, behavior patterns or more generally type of personality, intellectual capacity and general and technical knowledge.[15]

I refer to this type of marginality with the shorthand expression "involuntary marginality."

The above analysis leads Germani to a methodological approach for studying marginality:

. . . in whatever analysis, the interpretation of the data and situations, the empirical research and the diagnosis of marginality must be made explicit with regards to the normative scheme, and marginality criteria and the explanatory system utilized.[16]

Much of Germani's analysis focuses on "modernization" in relation to the Third World, that is, Enlightenment conceptions of political freedom, economic development, secure employment, and industrialization. This orientation is too Western and modern for direct application to Greco-Roman antiquity. Yet, Germani's general analysis is abstract enough to engage almost any social system. Thus, in analyzing Matthew and marginality one ought to develop the "normative scheme" in the social context of the Gospel of

---

12 Germani, *Marginality*, 49.

13 Germani, *Marginality*, 50.

14 Competing "normative schemes" sounds like competing "plausibility structures" from the perspective of sociology of knowledge; see Peter L. Berger and Thomas Luckman, *The Social Construction of Reality. A Treatise in the Sociology of Knowledge* (Garden City, New York: Doubleday & Company, 1966) 154-63.

15 Germani, *Marginality*, 51.

16 Germani, *Marginality*, 54.

Matthew, and to indicate, if possible, how and to what extent the author of Matthew and/or his group are marginal with respect to marginality criteria.

3. Voluntary Marginality

The anthropologist Victor Turner takes quite a different approach to marginality.[17] It is part of the analysis of ritual. Building on van Gennep's classic analysis of rites of passage,[18] Turner sees a common pattern in ritual:[19]

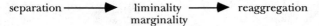

separation ⟶ liminality ⟶ reaggregation
marginality

"Separation" removes individuals or groups, usually secluded physically, from their accepted statuses or roles in a social system marked by law, custom, convention, and ceremonial—the center—to the margin. In this transitional, "liminal" phase (Latin *limen*: "threshold") individuals or groups are in limbo. They are "neither here nor there"; they are "betwixt and between."[20] In the third phase, the initiate reenters the social system as a neophyte, often with higher status. Turner characterizes the second, or marginal, liminal phase by *communitas*, a status-less, role-less phase marked by spontaneity, concreteness, intense comradeship, and egalitarianism. Those in this phase are often considered sexless and anonymous, sometimes symboled by nakedness.

Turner also views this model in terms of structure/anti-structure. "For me, communitas emerges where social structure is not."[21] Structure refers to ". . . differentiated, and often hierarchical systems of politico-legal-economic positions with many types of evaluation, separating men in terms of 'more' or 'less.' "[22] In structure, there are fixed "relationships between statuses, roles, and offices."[23] Contrariwise, anti-structure is "spontaneous, immediate, concrete"; "individuals are not segmentalized into roles and statuses but [existentially] confront one another. . ."[24]

The specifics of Germani's analysis are too modern for Greco-Roman society. Likewise, the specifics of Turner's analysis are drawn too much from small tribal societies, notably the Ndembu. Yet, as Germani generalizes, so does Turner:

> The time has now come to make a careful review of a hypothesis that seeks to account for the attributes of such seemingly diverse phenomena as neophytes in the liminal phase of ritual, subjugated autochthonous, small nations, court jesters, holy mendicants, good

---

17 Victor Turner, *The Ritual Process. Structure and Anti-Structure* (Chicago: Aldine Publishing Co., 1969); *Dramas, Fields, and Metaphors. Symbolic Action in Human Society* (Ithaca: Cornell University Press, 1974).

18 Arnold Van Gennep, *Rites of Passage* (Chicago: University of Chicago Press, 1960).

19 Turner, *The Ritual Process*, 94-95.

20 Turner, *The Ritual Process*, 95.

21 Turner, *The Ritual Process*, 126.

22 Turner, *The Ritual Process*, 96.

23 Turner, *The Ritual Process*, 131.

24 Turner, *The Ritual Process*, 127, 132.

Samaritans, millenarian movements, "dharma bums," matrilineal systems and monastic orders. Surely an ill-assorted bunch of social phenomena! Yet all have this common characteristic: they are persons or principles that (1) fall in the interstices of social structure, (2) are on its margins, or (3) occupy its lowest rungs.[25]

Turner goes further and develops another general principle: "the spontaneity and immediacy of communitas . . . can seldom be maintained for very long. Communitas itself soon develops a structure . . . ."[26] From this insight Turner distinguishes three kinds of communitas:

> (1) *existential* or *spontaneous* communitas—approximately what the hippies today [sic!] would call "a happening," and William Blake might have called "the winged moment as it flies," or, later, "mutual forgiveness of each vice"; (2) *normative* communitas, where, under the influence of time, the need to mobilize and organize resources, and the necessity for social control among the members of the group in pursuance of these goals, the existential communitas is organized into a perduring social system; and (3) *ideological* communitas, which is a label one can apply to a variety of utopian models of societies based on existential communitas.[27]

Whereas spontaneous communitas stands apart from social structures, normative communitas represents an emergent microsocial group *within* a macrosocial system.[28] Finally, ideological communitas presents communitas as *desired* vision, or what is known in Christian history as the *ecclesiola in ecclesia*. As examples, Turner analyzes the early Franciscans of medieval Europe and the Sahajīyās of fifteenth- and sixteenth-century India.

For Turner normative communitas is on the way to structure, and ideological communitas is voluntary "outsiderhood."[29] It is not *socially* imposed marginality, but *voluntarily chosen* marginality.[30] That he is not developing the concept of involuntary marginality is clear from his statement about poverty:

> Liminal poverty must not be confused with real poverty, although the liminally poor may become actually poor. But liminal poverty, whether it is a process or a state, is both an expression and instrumentality of communitas. Communitas is what people really seek by voluntary poverty . . . . The principle is simple: cease to have

25 Turner, *The Ritual Process*, 125.

26 Turner, *The Ritual Process*, 132.

27 Turner, *The Ritual Process*, 132.

28 One hears the echo of Max Weber's "charisma" and "routinization" here; indeed, Turner mentions Weber in this context. See Turner, *The Ritual Process*, 133; Max Weber, *Economy and Society. An Outline of Interpretive Sociology* (Ed. Günther Roth and Claus Wittich; New York: Bedminister Press, 1968).

29 Turner, *Dramas, Fields, and Metaphors*, 133.

30 Turner, *Dramas, Fields, and Metaphors*, 133, admits that he is not thinking of Park's and Stonequist's "Marginal Man."

and you are; if you "are" in the relationship of communitas to others who "are," then you love one another.[31]

4. Marginality Summary

The concept "marginality" in the social science literature examined above has three dimensions:

a) *the "Marginal Man"*: individuals and groups who, because of birth, migration, conquest, and the like are "doomed" to live in two different, antagonistic cultures without fully belonging to either (Park; Stonequist); this social-psychological type is closely related to

b) *involuntary marginality*: individuals and groups who for reasons of race, ethnicity, sex, "underdevelopment," and the like are not able to participate in normative social statuses, roles, and offices and their obligations and duties. They fail to share in both material and nonmaterial resources available to other members at the center of society, and thus who experience themselves as personally alienated (Germani).

c) *voluntary marginality*: individuals and groups who consciously and by choice live outside the normative statuses, roles, and offices of society because they reject hierarchical social structures, though there will be attempts to perpetuate this spontaneity by social control or in conventicles within the normative social system. Though freely chosen, they will eventually share in some of the same conditions as involuntary marginals (Turner).

The two terms I have chosen, "involuntary" and "voluntary," need to be used with caution. It is important not to transfer the modern, enlightened democratic ideology of "voluntary associations" and "freedom of assembly" to Greco-Roman antiquity and thus Christianity. Yet, within certain social restrictions Greco-Roman society had its own sort of voluntary associations: *collegia*, clubs, trade guilds, burial societies, as well as schools and mystery cults.[32] Moreover, within Judaism there existed a variety of religious sects and parties. Thus, after a further comment about method, I shall also attempt to indicate how one might approach the Gospel of Matthew through these three types of marginality.

Texts and Contexts

How is the book of Matthew related to social realities? How does one move from text to social context? This paper is not the place to develop either a social-historical or social-scientific hermeneutic.[33] Yet, I would say that there is a dialectical relationship between text and social context: economically/socially/politically located ideology generates literature; but

---

31 Turner, *Dramas, Fields, and Metaphors*, 266.

32 Frederick Danker, "Associations, Clubs, Thiasoi," *ABD* (New York: Doubleday, 1992) 1.501-503.

33 See, e.g., Piet van Staden, *Compassion–The Essence of Life. A Social-Scientific Study of the Religious Symbolic Universe Reflected in the Ideology/Theology of Luke* (HTS 4; Pretoria: University of Pretoria, 1991).

literature also challenges economically/socially/politically located ideology.[34]

I still try to discover how the narrative world is related to authorial intention and how text is related to social historical context. One possible metaphor is that Matthew's narrative is not a steamy bathroom mirror that, when wiped with a towel, allows you to see yourself better; rather, it is a foggy window that *can* be a mirror, but is nonetheless a *window*. By wiping away the fog at the appropriate places, one can see through the text to the author's social-historical context. The keys are the appropriate models and the "the appropriate places."

Matthew and Marginality

1. Normative Scheme A: A Macrosocial Model

As noted above, according to Germani the first task is to define "the normative scheme," that is, the values and norms that define status; the legitimate, expected, or tolerated areas of participation; and the assignment mechanisms of individuals to each category.[35] What is the center from which various persons and groups can be seen to be marginal? What are the missing objective and personal dimensions? This determination is not a simple task because there are competing "normative schemes" and correspondingly different marginalities in Greco-Roman and Jewish antiquity and the New Testament. As a point of departure for gaining access to one part of the normative scheme, I note first George Ritzer's macroscopic-microscopic continuum of social levels.[36]

---

34 From the perspective of Marxist literary criticism, literature as art is part of an ideological consciousness related to a superstructure that is determined by the economic base or infrastructure. Yet, literature is not the mere passive, unconscious reflection of economics. Schematically, the relation is not simply productive forces → social relations → ideology → text. This would be so-called "vulgar Marxism." Thus, art can also challenge the ideology of which it is a part, and thus the social, political, and economic order that undergirds it. Art is an expression of ideology, but it also distances itself from ideology. See Terry Eagleton, *Marxism and Literary Criticism* (Berkeley and Los Angeles: University of California Press, 1976). On ideology, see David McLellan, *Ideology* (Milton Keynes: Open University Press, 1986); Jorge A. Larrain, *The Concept of Ideology* (Brookfield, VT: Gregg Revivals, 1992 [1979]).

35 Germani, *Marginality*, 50.

36 George Ritzer, *Contemporary Sociological Theory* (New York: Alfred A. Knopf, 1983) 309.

A Simplified Macroscopic-Microscopic Continuum

Macroscopic

    1. World systems

    2. Societies

    3. Organizations

    4. Groups

    5. Interaction

    6. Individual thought and action

Microscopic

One of the highest macrosocial levels ("societies") for the writings of the New Testament period can be understood through the model of an advanced agrarian society. Several New Testament scholars have employed the model developed by Gerhard and Jean Lenski to clarify social stratification in the Roman Empire.[37] I have also used it.[38] Its main features correspond to what Ramsay MacMullen has called "verticality" in Roman society.[39] Drawing on G. Alföldy's work and using data from Josephus, archaeology, and the rabbis, David Fiensy has adjusted this same model down a level for Palestine.[40] I

---

[37] Gerhard and Jean Lenski, *Human Societies. An Introduction to Macrosociology* (5th ed.; New York: McGraw-Hill, 1993) 164-208; see also Gerhard Lenski, *Power and Privilege. A Theory of Social Stratification* (New York: McGraw-Hill, 1966). Some scholars who have used the Lenski model are John H. Elliott, "Social-Scientific Criticism of the New Testament and its Social World: More on Method and Models," in John H. Elliott, ed., *Semeia 35. Social-Scientific Criticism of the New Testament and Its Social World* (Decatur, GA: Scholars Press, 1986) 13-14; Herman C. Waetjen, *A Reordering of Power. A Socio-Political Reading of Mark's Gospel* (Minneapolis: Fortress Press, 1989) 6; David A. Fiensy, *The Social History of Palestine in the Herodian Period. The Land Is Mine* (SBEC 20; Lewiston, NY: The Edwin Mellen Press, 1990) 155-76; Anthony J. Saldarini, *Pharisees, Scribes, and Sadducees in Palestinian Society. A Sociological Approach* (Wilmington, DE: Michael Glazier, 1988) 20-27; Richard Rohrbaugh, "Social Location of the Markan Audience" (forthcoming in *Interpretation* and *BTB*).

[38] Dennis C. Duling, "Matthew's Plurisignificant 'Son of David' in Social Science Perspective: Kinship, Kingship, Magic, and Miracle," *BTB* 22/3 (1992) 99-116; "Matthew's Infancy in Social Science Perspective," Context Group, Portland, March, 1991; "Egalitarian Ideology, Leadership, and Factional Conflict in the Matthean Gospel," Synoptic Gospels Section, Society of Biblical Literature, San Francisco, November, 1992; "Matthew and Marginality," preliminary version, Eastern Great Lakes Biblical Society (regional SBL, CBA, ASOR), Pittsburgh, PA, April, 1993. See also the new edition of Dennis C. Duling and Norman Perrin *The New Testament: An Introduction* (Fort Worth, TX: Harcourt Brace and Company, 1993) Ch. 2.

[39] Ramsay MacMullen, *Roman Social Relations. 50 B.C. to A.D. 284* (New Haven: Yale University Press, 1974); cf. Wayne A. Meeks, *The First Urban Christians. The Social World of the Apostle Paul* (New Haven: Yale University Press, 1983) 51-73.

[40] Fiensy, *Social History of Palestine*, 158.

have added a few speculative percentages from various authors. It looks like Model A.[41]

Model A Social Stratification in the Herodian Period

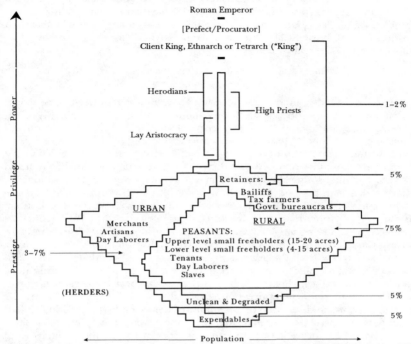

(modified slightly from D. Fiensy, *The Social History of Palestine in the Herodian Period*, p. 158, based on G. and J. Lenski, *Human Societies*, p. 203, influenced by G. Alföldy, *Die römische Gesellschaft*).

In this model the primary bases of social stratification—power, privilege, and prestige—are primarily economic and political; kinship and religion are implied—for example, succession among the ruling groups and religious support of the "state"—but they are less conspicuous. There are a very few at the top of the vertical social structure; though this is not indicated, they are urban. The vast majority are at the bottom. There is no real "middle class." Indeed, one should think of a status hierarchy rather than "social classes" based on economics.[42] The lower part of the model is divided into urban and rural sections, with rural peasants dominating. The upper strata are virtually

---

41 Lenski, *Power and Privilege*, 243-48; Saldarini, *Pharisees, Scribes, and Sadducees*, 40-45; Fiensy, *Social History of Palestine*, 155-70 *passim*; Duling and Perrin, *New Testament Introduction* (3rd ed.), chapter 2.

42 Explicit descriptions of class are rare and limited to Rome; see Meeks, *The First Urban Christians*, 53-55; Richard Rohrbaugh, "'Social Location of Thought' as a Heuristic Construction in New Testament Study," *JSNT* 30 (1987) 103-119.

all urban.[43] Retainers (mainly bureaucrats), merchants, artisans, fishermen, day laborers, and many expendables belong in or near the towns and cities, while the upper level small freeholders (15-50 acres), lower level small freeholders (4-15 acres), tenant farmers, some day laborers, and most slaves belong in the rural districts. The expendables have now been subdivided into "unclean and degraded" and "expendables." The model implies accepted institutional authority. Clearly it is, in Victor Turner's terms, a "structure," in this case a hierarchical structure.[44]

2. Matthew and Marginality from the Macrosocial Perspective: Involuntary Marginality

There are further modifications of the above model that need to be made, all of which have to do with decisions about Matthew and marginality. First, this reconstructed model roughly corresponds to certain dimensions of Palestine at the time of Jesus. It does not correspond quite as well to the usual time for the composition of the *Gospel of Matthew* itself, ca. 80-90 C.E. Thus, the Herodians should be removed and the priests have much declined in political power. Second, some client rulers may have experienced "psychological" marginality simply because they were Roman colonials ("relative deprivation");[45] nonetheless, in what follows I shall exclude the upper strata, including Idumeans and Jews (Caesar; rulers of the Gentiles; prefects/procurators; ancestral native kings; Herodian client kings; the High Priest Caiaphas; chief priests; elders). Third, for the same reasons, it is probably also best from the perspective of *this* model to exclude the retainers of the upper strata (toll collectors; Roman centurions; High Priest's guards; most priests; most scribes). Fourth, this model operates best for certain forms of economic and political oppression, especially the colonial context of the Eastern Empire, and for rural-urban contrasts, demography (population shifts), and perhaps psychosocial marginality (powerlessness; helplessness; status inferiority). Fifth, other important status criteria (based on other models) need to be considered, especially in relation to Palestinian Judaism, for example, units further down Ritzer's continuum, notably kin groups, regional and ethnic groups (Idumeans; Samaritans; Gentiles in general), religious parties (Essenes), and gender within patriarchal contexts. As an example, toll collectors and scribes would not be considered marginal from the perspective of the above macrosocial model because they were retainers of the ruling classes; yet, toll collectors, while economically and somewhat politically

---

[43] Rohrbaugh, "'Social Location of Thought,'" 103-119; see Douglas E. Oakman, *Jesus and the Economic Questions of His Day* (SBEC 8; Lewiston, NY: The Edwin Mellen Press, 1986).

[44] I have also added to the model what the Lenskis call a "specialized society" still present in Palestine, namely, the semi-nomadic herders. They represent a different, parallel social system altogether.

[45] One need only recall that Eleazar, son of Ananias the High Priest and governor of the Temple, was instrumental in the revolt against Rome (Josephus, *Wars* 2.17.2 §409). See David Aberle, "A Note on Relative Deprivation Theory As Applied to Millenarian and Other Cult Movements," in Sylvia Thrupp, ed., *Millennial Dreams in Action. Studies in Revolutionary Religious Movements* (New York: Schocken Books, 1970) 209-14; John Gager, *Kingdom and Community. The Social World of Early Christianity* (Englewood Cliffs, NJ: Prentice-Hall, 1975) 27-28.

advantaged, were universally despised by *native* peoples in the Roman Empire[46] and scribes were sometimes considered marginal if they belonged to a marginal group, e.g., Essenes. Sixth, it is not always easy to distinguish between "unclean and degraded" and "expendable" in the Jewish context. Prostitutes, those with skin diseases, and demoniacs, for example, might fall into both categories. Finally, one might make a case that in a limited good society, especially in the colonial context like Palestine, all peasants—about three-quarters of the population—were marginal. Given that this is a peasant society, I have elected to omit upper level peasants.

With these qualifications, I suggest that from the above macrosocial perspective the lower social strata would have been seen as "involuntary marginals." Here is a sample inventory implied in Matthew's gospel:[47]

1. Forced laborers (implied): 5:37.
2. Day laborers (*ergatēs*): 20:1, 2, 8; perhaps 9:37, 38; 10:10.
3. Some slaves:
   a. "Slave/servant" (*doulos*): 8:9; 10:24, 25; 13:27, 28; 18:23, 26, 27, 28, 32; 20:27; 21:34, 35, 36; 22:3, 4, 6, 8, 10; 24:45, 46, 48, 50 ; 25:14, 19, 21, 23 [twice], 30; 26:51.
   b. "Slave/son" (*pais*): 8:6, 8, 13; 12:18 [Isa 42:1]; 14:2; 17:18; 21:15?
3. Some peasants, urban poor, and destitute:
   a. "Crowd(s)" (*ochlos*): 50 references!
   b. "Tenant farmers" (*geōrgos*): 21:33.
   c. "Poor" (*ptōchos*): 5:3; 11:5; 19:21; 26:9, 11.
   d. Receivers of alms (implied by *eleēmosunē*, "alms" in 6:1-6; 19:21).
4. Unclean and degraded (dishonored):
   a. Eunuchs (*eunouchos*): 19:12 (three times).
   b. Ritually unclean: ([Jesus and] certain disciples): 15:2.
   c. Lepers (*lepros*): 8:2; 10:8; 11:5; 26:6.
   d. Women believed to be dishonored (*porneia*): 5:32; 15:19; 19:9; cf. 1:19).
   e. Woman with hemorrhage: 9:20-22.
   f. Women outside their usual home "space" (who follow Jesus).
   g. Those with "every disease and every infirmity": 4:23 and 9:35; with "various diseases and pains": 4:24; "all who were sick": 8:16; "their sick": 14:14; "sick: 14:35.
      1. Blind (*typhlos*): 9:27, 28 (two blind men); 11:5; 12:22 (and dumb); 15:14 (four times); 15:30; 15:31; 20:30 (two blind men); 21:14.
      2. Lame (*chōlos*): 11:5; 15:30-31; 18:8; 21:14.
      3. Deaf (*kōphos*): 11:5.
      4. Dumb (*kōphos*): 9:32, 33; 12:22 [twice]; 15:30, 31.
      5. Deformed (*kyllos*): 15:30, 31.
      6. Paralytics (*paralytikos*): 4:24; 8:6; 9:2 [twice], 6.
      7. Demoniacs (*daimonizomenos*): 4:24; 8:16; 8:28-34; 15:21-28.

---

[46] John R. Donahue, "Tax Collector," *ABD* (New York: Doubleday, 1992) 6.337-38; Naphtali Lewis, *Life in Egypt Under Roman Rule* (Oxford: Clarendon Press, 1983) 156-84.

[47] For a fuller, but slightly different arrangement, see Duling, "Matthew's Plurisignificant 'Son of David' in Social Science Perspective: Kinship, Kingship, Magic, and Miracle," *BTB* 22/3 (1992) 102-103.

      8. Epileptics (*selēniazomenos*): 4:24.
5. Expendables:
    a. Bandits (*lēstēs*): 21:13 [Jer 7:11]; 26:55 (contrasted w. Jesus); 27:38, 36 (mock Jesus on cross).
    b. Prostitutes (*pornē*): 21:31, 32.

A few further remarks are in order. Matthew's "crowds" are undifferentiated. Nonetheless, the writer implies that they contained women and those with all manner of debilitating disease and sickness.[48] Perhaps they also contained bandits, eunuchs, slaves, tenant farmers, and other artisans and fishermen. Matthew writes that Jesus had compassion on "the crowds" who are "like sheep without a shepherd" (9:36),[49] and the above strata represent the "lost sheep of the house of Israel" to whom Jesus and the disciples direct their activities (Matt 10:6; 15:24). They do not participate in normative social statuses, roles, and offices, and they fail to share in both material and nonmaterial resources. It could be argued that peasants and village artisans who have lost their ancestral lands,[50] and fishermen whose activities were heavily taxed,[51] should be included. Jesus and some of his disciples are from this group. Herders (*poimēnēs*) fall within another structure, but they would be marginal, though the term "shepherds" is used positively as metaphor (9:36; 25:32 [sheep/goats]; 26:31, "strike the shepherd" [Zech 13:7]). In this context, I would exclude these groups.[52] In any case, whatever decisions are made about center and margin, it is clear that the percentage of involuntary marginals would have been quite high, even omitting some peasants.

It is impossible to discuss all the remaining groups and persons in the First Gospel here. Let us take a representative example, "the poor." The plural *ptōchoi*, which in the synoptics in general refers to the destitute,[53] is used clearly as an actual social condition in four verses: 11:5; 19:21; 26:9, 11, to which one must compare "poor in spirit" (*hoi ptōchoi tō pneumati*) in 5:3. In

---

[48] Dennis C. Duling, "The Therapeutic Son of David in Matthew's Gospel," *NTS* 24 (1978) 392-410.

[49] Dennis C. Duling, "Matthew's Plurisignificant 'Son of David'," 112-13.

[50] For this reason, some analysts suggest that village artisans, despite some economic success, are below the peasants.

[51] K. C. Hanson, "Fishing," Unpublished paper of the Context Group, 1991.

[52] In this model peasants represent the majority; for the debate about whether one can speak of marginality in traditionally structured societies where those of lower social status see themselves as elites as them, for example, in caste systems, see Germani, *Marginality*, 52: "In such a society the very concept of marginality does not emerge as a social perception scheme."

[53] Luise Schottroff and Wolfgang Stegemann, *Jesus and the Hope of the Poor* (Trans. Matthew J. O'Connell; Maryknoll, NY: Orbis Books, 1986) 16. In general, see Jon Sobrino, *The True Church and the Poor* (Maryknoll, NY: Orbis, 1984); Wolfgang Stegemann, *The Gospel and the Poor* (Trans. Dietlinde Elliott; Philadelphia: Fortress Press, 1984); Wolfgang Stegemann and Luise Schottroff, eds., *God of the Lowly: Socio-Historical Interpretations of the Bible* (Maryknoll, NY: Orbis, 1984); Bruce J. Malina, "Interpreting the Bible with Anthropology: The Case of the Poor and the Rich," *Listening. Journal of Religion and Culture* 21 (1986) 148-59; Thomas D. Hanks, "Poor, Poverty (New Testament)," *ABD* (New York: Doubleday, 1992) 5.414-24.

Matthew 26:9, which simplifies Mark 14:5, the disciples are angered at the woman's "waste" of an alabaster flask of "very expensive perfume" (v. 7): "For this perfume might have been sold for much [money] (*pollou*) and given to the poor (*ptōchois*)" (v. 9). Jesus defends the woman's "good work" (v. 10: *ergon . . . kalon*) to him: "The poor (*tous ptōchous*) you always have with you, but me you do not always have" (26:11). In this passage, the perpetual presence (and pervasiveness) of the poor is assumed (*pantote*). Yet, the act of one marginal—probably a "promiscuous" woman who encounters (sits with?) Jesus at table[54]—appears to override social concern for other marginals, the poor.

One might conclude from these comments that the "preferential option for the poor" in Matthew is qualified by the woman's symbolic act of preparing Jesus for burial (Matt 26:12-13). There is probably some validity to this conclusion: for Matthew ideology—Christology and eschatology—is paramount. Furthermore, the impression is related to Matthew's apparent tendency to think in terms of the city and wealth, and to his addition of "in spirit" to "the poor" in 5:3.[55] One can conclude that the portrayal of the disciples' irritation is understandable in the light of what has gone before with regard to the young man (Matt 19:16-22; see Mark 10:17-22; Luke 18:18-23). Jesus has told him, "If you want to be perfect (*teleios*), go, sell your possessions (*ta hyparchonta*) and give to the poor (*ptōchois*), and you will have treasure (*thēsauron*) in heaven, and come follow me" (19:21). Apparently "the poor" would have had much to gain for the young man has "many possessions" (v. 22: *ktēmata polla*).[56] Here, of course, are Matthew's familiar discipleship/following terms, and with them the question of *voluntary* poverty is articulated: The true disciple is *commanded* not to store up treasures on earth, but in heaven (6:19-21).

The third passage is John's question to Jesus and Jesus' answer, reworked from Q (Q 7:18-23; Matt 11:2-5).[57] Jesus' miracle working in Matthew 11:5 is

---

54 Kathleen E. Corley, *A Place at the Table: Jesus, Women, and Meals in the Synoptic Gospels*, Ph.D. Diss., Claremont Graduate School (1992), p. 208, concludes, "Matthew, the gospel considered the most androcentric of all the Synoptics, is the only gospel which portrays women reclining with men for meals. Only in Matthew are women allowed an equal place at the table . . . Furthermore, Matthew allows for the presence of women identified as 'courtesans' among the followers of Jesus [Matt 21:31-32]. 'Sinners,' a group which in Matthew includes women, join Jesus and his disciples for meals [9:9-13] . . . In spite of the larger controversy over the 'public' behavior of Greco-Roman women [that is, in some circles, they reclined at table with men, while others continued to think of such practices as dishonorable], Matthew boldly affirms the presence of women accused of promiscuity among the followers of Jesus." See further, Anderson, "Matthew: Gender and Reading," 3-27.

55 Jack Dean Kingsbury, "The Verb *Akolouthein* ('to follow') as an Index of Matthew's View of His Community," *JBL* 97 (1978) 56-73; Michael H. Crosby, *House of Disciples. Church, Economics, and Justice in Matthew* (Maryknoll, NY: Orbis, 1988) 39-43. Crosby, pp. 154-55 argues that Matthew does not "canonize" poverty, but neither does he "spiritualize" it.

56 For the view that what is implied is the redistribution of wealth in a limited good society, see Bruce J. Malina, "Interpreting the Bible with Anthropology," 155-56.

57 It is generally accepted that *ta erga tou Christou* in Matt 11:2 refers back to Jesus' miracles in Matt 8-9; cf. the evidence cited in Duling, "The Therapeutic Son of David in Matthew's Gospel," 392-410. W. D. Davies and Dale C. Allison, *A Critical and Exegetical Commentary on the Gospel According to Matthew* (Edinburgh: T&T Clark: 1991) 2.240 argue that it also refers to Matthew 5-7 because of 11:5f., "the poor have good news preached to them"

full of allusions to Isaiah,[58] and "the poor have good news preached to them" alludes to the famous Jubilee passage in Isaiah 61:1 (1QH 18:14; Luke 4:18). That Isaiah is Matthew's favorite scriptural text suggests that he is quite aware of these scriptural allusions. While the verb *euangelizomai* is a Matthean *hapax legomenon*, its cognate *euangelion* calls forth the key Matthean summaries (4:23; 9:35) and, indeed, the central proclamation of the kingdom of Heaven.[59] There is no theme more central than this theme in the gospel. Thus, the Matthean author stresses that the poor hear the good news, but his view on *actual* poverty is somewhat mixed. It will have to be compared to his ideal of voluntary marginality.

3. Normative Schemes B, C, D: Microsocial Models

Another way to understand marginality, that is, the way that values and norms define status in relation to participation, as well as the assignment mechanisms of individuals to each category, is to move further down Ritzer's Macroscopic/Microscopic continuum to groups (No. 4). Groups are also important for involuntary marginality, but they are especially significant for voluntary marginality. In Turner's terms voluntary individuals and groups are those who spontaneously but consciously choose to live outside the normative statuses, roles, and offices of society because they reject hierarchical social structures ("spontaneous communitas"). Nonetheless, says Turner, there will be gradual attempts to perpetuate this spontaneity by social control within the group ("normative communitas") or in conventicles within the normative social system ("ideological communitas").

Ever since Weber's contrast between charisma and routinization, social theorists have persistently contrasted structured institutions with non-structured groups. Victor Turner's contrast between structure and anti-structure and his view that anti-structure tends toward structure is only one example. Bruce Malina, building on the work of the Mediterranean network anthropologist Jeremy Boissevain, contrasts "corporations" as hierarchical structures with "coalitions" as non-hierarchical structures.[60] Drawing further on the work of Ph. G. Herbst, Malina has also attempted to contrast hierarchical organizations with non-hierarchical groups on the basis of task allocation.[61]

Non-hierarchical groups are best seen with respect to their opposite, hierarchical organization, of which the macrostructure above is but one type.

---

in relation to 4:23-26. In the light of 5:16 ("*see* your *kala erga*") and 11:20 (*hai pleistai dynameis*), this conclusion seems to stretch the meaning of *ta erga* in Matthew 11:5.

[58] Isaiah 26:19; 29:18; 35:5-6; 42:7, 18; 61:1. Matthew adds "lepers," apparently in accord with Matthew 8:1-4.

[59] Dennis C. Duling, "Kingdom of God, Kingdom of Heaven (New Testament and Early Christian Literature)," *ABD* (New York: Doubleday, 1992) 4.57-58.

[60] Jeremy Boissevain, *Friends of Friends: Networks, Manipulators, and Coalitions* (New York: St. Martin's Press, 1974) 170-205; Bruce Malina, *Christian Origins and Cultural Anthropology. Practical Models for Biblical Interpretation* (Atlanta: John Knox 1986) 13-67; "Patron and Client. The Analogy Behind Synoptic Theology," *Forum* 4/1 (1988) 19-31; "A Conflict Approach to Mark 7," *Forum* 4/3 (1988) 14.

[61] Malina, *Christian Origins and Cultural Anthropology*, 66-67; Ph. G. Herbst, *Alternatives to Hierarchies* (Leiden: Martinus Nijhoff Social Sciences Division, 1976) 18-19, 29-40.

Hierarchical Organization
One Person—One Task

Assumptions
1. Organization by decomposing into smaller and smaller units.
2. Each unit or person allocated a single task.

Consequences
1. A single structure of relationships between units.
2. Uniform type of relationship: units and persons linked by superior-subordinate relationship.
3. Every unit and person has one, clearly demarcated, set of functions with sharp boundaries between units and persons.
4. Decisions are made for subordinates by superiors.
5. Principle: decision making is separated from task performance.

Hierarchical Model

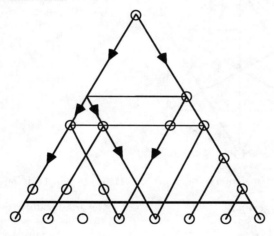

Non-Hierarchical Groups

Characteristics
1. The capacity for multi-structured functioning.
2. The capacity for achieving and maintaining "directive correlation" of ongoing activities, that is, the work of each supports and facilitates the work of others in the direction of the achievements of a joint aim.

Models B, C, D: Non-Hierarchical Groups

GROUP	TASK
1. Matrix group	Each person has a specialized function, but overlapping competence (two to four tasks each) (members work together; no necessary limit to size)

Model B

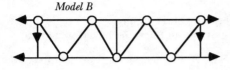

2. Composite autonomous group

Each person can carry out all tasks (members work together; each person equipotential; no specialized leadership function; no specific, ongoing structure; size relatively small).

Model C

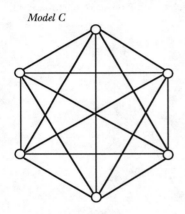

To Herbst's two non-hierarchical groups, Malina, again building Boissevain, adds a third:[62]

3. Network group

Geographically dispersed individuals or subsets (no direct control)

Model D

Patron

Broker

EGO

household
village   vicinity   outside

---

[62] Malina, *Christian Origins and Cultural Anthropology*, 67.

Except for the last, these interesting models are drawn from modern industrial relations. Yet, again, there is a kind of rough correspondence between Groups 1, 2, and 3, in reverse order and Turner's three types of non-hierarchical groups:

Turner	Herbst
ideological communitas normative communitas	
	matrix group
spontaneous communitas	composite autonomous group network group

These non-hierarchical groups can be viewed as illustrations of "voluntary marginality," though in the case of Herbst's composite autonomous and matrix groups there is some "industrial engineering." As the vertical arrow indicates, there is at the group level a gradual tendency toward hierarchy, as Turner realized. Time, size, the need for social control, and increasing division of labor (task allocation) lead toward normative communitas and eventually hierarchy.

4. Matthew and Marginality from Microsocial Perspectives: Voluntary Marginality

Where does the Gospel of Matthew belong with respect to voluntary marginality? At the microsocial level, the first gospel reveals several types of groups. There are clear indications of spontaneous sub-groups of the network type from the days of the historical Jesus. The best example is the mission charge in Matthew 10, especially 10:9-15. This text segment, which has echoes in *Didachē* 11, 12, and 16:3, represents an ideology similar to, though not exactly like, that of the itinerant Cynic philosophers.[63] The command to take "no gold" and "no bag" for food (cf. 1 Cor 9:4, 14, 17-18; *Didachē* 11.6), no change of tunic, and no sandals (a sign of wealth) are indications of *voluntary* poverty. If the "no bag" is a contrast to itinerant Cynic preachers who carried a bag that symbolized their self-sufficiency, the stress may be less on actual begging than on eating common meals with others.[64] In this regard, the

---

63 F. Gerald Downing, *Christ and the Cynics: Jesus and Other Radical Preachers in First-Century Judaism* (JSOT Manuals 4; Sheffield: JSOT Press, 1988) 47-48; see the discussions in Willy Schottroff and Wolfgang Stegemann, *God of the Lowly*, 160-67; Richard A. Horsley, *Sociology of the Jesus Movement* (New York: Crossroad, 1989) 46-47.

64 John Dominic Crossan has called this phenomenon "unbrokered egalitarian commensality." Drawing on James Scott, he states:

. . . peasant culture and religion is actually an anticulture, qualifying alike both the religious and political elites that oppress it. It is, in fact, a reflexive and reactive inversion of the pattern of exploitation common to the peasantry *as such.* "The radical vision to which I refer," he [Scott] continues, "is strikingly uniform despite the enormous variations in peasant cultures and the differing great traditions of which they partake . . . At the risk of overgeneralizing, it is possible to describe some common features of the reflexive symbolism. It nearly always implies a society of brotherhood in which there will be no rich and poor, in which no distinctions of

itinerant apostles, wise men, prophets, and scribes of Matthew's Gospel are commanded to carry on the Jesus tradition of a non-hierarchical faction. "Therefore I send you prophets *and wise men and scribes*, some of whom you will kill *and crucify, and some you will scourge in your synagogues* and persecute *from town to town. . . .*" (Matt 23:34; italics = Matthean additions). The danger, as in the *Didachē*, is false prophets (*Didachē* 11; Matt 7:15-23). Yet, one would have to modify the network model slightly since the itinerants themselves clearly have some status and authority.[65]

This is not the only non-hierarchical group in the Gospel of Matthew. I turn now to an "appropriate passage" that points to a slightly different group, one that may suggest a more settled community.

[The Pharisees love...] to be called Rabbi by the people.	8) But (as for) you (pl.),
do not be called Rabbi,	
for one is your teacher,	but (pl.) you are all brothers
9) And father do not call yourselves (pl.)	on earth,
for one is your (pl.) father,	the heavenly.
10) Neither be called (pl.) tutors,	
for your (pl.) tutor is one,	the Christ.

Benedict Viviano represents most current opinion when he says that this passage contains "a critique of synagogue offices and titles that are merging in and around the rabbinic academy of Jamnia/Yavneh at this time . . ."[66] The rejected titles of honor are "Rabbi," known from Rabbinic references to teachers prior to 135 C.E.[67] and from inscriptions[68] but are used elsewhere in Matthew only by the traitor Judas (Matt 26:25, 49); "father," also known from Rabbinic and inscriptional references;[69] and *kathēgētēs*, which Bruce Winter has shown to mean "private tutor" in Greek,[70] though it might represent the Hebrew *mōreh*, as in *mōreh hazzedek*, the "Teacher of Righteousness" (4QpPs[a]37

---

rank and status (save those between believers and non-believers) will exist. Where religious institutions are experience as justifying inequalities, the abolition of rank and status may well include the elimination of religious hierarchy in favor of communities of equal believers. Property is typically, though not always, to be held in common and shared. All unjust claims to taxes, rents, and tribute are to be nullified. The envisioned utopia may also include a self-yielding and abundant nature as well as a radically transformed human nature in which greed, envy, and hatred will disappear. While the earthly utopia is thus an anticipation of the future, it often harks back to a mythic Eden from which mankind has fallen away."

[65] See further, Gerd Theissen, *Sociology of Early Palestinian Christianity* (Trans. J. Bowden; Philadelphia: Fortress, 1977).

[66] Benedict Viviano, "Social World and Community Leadership: The Case of Matthew 23:1-12, 34," *JSNT* 39 (1990) 10.

[67] H. Lapin, "Rabbi," *ABD* (New York: Doubleday, 1992) 5.600-601.

[68] Shaye J. D. Cohen, "Epigraphical Rabbis," *JQR* 72 (1981) 1-17.

[69] Viviano, "Social World and Community Leadership," 20; Martin Hengel, "Die Synagogeninschrift von Stobi" *ZNW* 57 (1966) 145-83; Rachael Hachlili, "Synagogue (Diaspora Synagogues)," *ABD* (New York: Doubleday, 1992) 6.260.

[70] Bruce Winter, "The Messiah as the Tutor: The Meaning of *kathēgētēs* in Matthew 23:10," *Tyndale Bulletin* 42/1 (1991) 152-57.

[= 4Q171] 3:15-16; 1QpHab 2:8; CD 1:9-11).[71] Viviano notes four "run-ons" placed at the right on the above chart. I would add that since the heavenly/earthly contrast and the Christ are Matthean redactional emphases, so probably is the designation for members of Matthew's group, "brothers." This is the language of "fictive-" or "pseudo-kinship."[72] Though "crowds" are mentioned (23:1), clearly the intended recipients are "disciples"—in other words, the Matthean brotherhood—and this points to the recipients of the gospel as a "brotherhood" (cf. also 5:21-26; 7:1-15; 12:46-50; 18:15-22). This "brotherhood" has an "egalitarian" ideology. Pharisaic titles of status in relation to the central activity of teachers and those taught are rejected by the author of Matthew for the "brotherhood."

The ideology of this passage represents a version of Turner's non-hierarchical group, an ideological communitas. It also represents Boissevain's and Malina's "faction" and Herbst's "composite autonomous group." Each person can carry out all tasks; each person is equipotential; members work together; there is no specialized leadership function, and no specific, ongoing structure. One could develop this contrast of structure and antistructure much further.

It should be emphasized again that Matthew's "network" and "composite autonomous" orientations represent an *ideological* communitas. However, as Turner was aware, there are pressures toward hierarchy. Thus, despite this Matthean ideology, there appear to be in the Matthew group those who are more equal than others.[73] In the first place, there are undefined central persons with scribe-related labels and functions:

1. "Apostles" (10:2).
2. "Prophets" (5:10-12; 11:9; 10:40-42; 13:57; 21:11, 23-27; 23:29-36; all of the formula quotations, including Psalm 78:2 and 110:1, are from "prophets").
3. "Teachers" (5:19; 28:20).
4. "Scribes" (13:52; 23:34).
5. "Righteous men" (10:41-42).
6. "Wise men" (23:34).

Moreover, the ascription of honor to Peter (lower status) by Jesus (higher status) implies a transfer of authority (16:17-19).[74] Thus, like its rivals, the Pharisees, the Matthew group is not simply a non-hierarchical communitas, but is on its way toward a hierarchical structure (normative communitas). I have elsewhere attempted to represent this movement as a so-called "leaderless group."[75]

[71] Viviano, "Social World and Community Leadership," 11.

[72] Julian Pitt-Rivers, "Pseudo-Kinship," in D. L. Sills, ed., *International Encyclopedia of the Social Sciences* (New York: Macmillan, 1968) 8.408-13.

[73] Dennis C. Duling, "Egalitarian Ideology, Leadership, and Factional Conflict." Paper delivered in the Synoptic Gospels Section, Society of Biblical Literature, San Francisco, November, 1992.

[74] Dennis C. Duling, "Binding and Loosing (Matthew 16:19; Matthew 18:18; John 20:23)," *Forum* 3/4 (1987) 21.

[75] Dennis C. Duling, "Response to E. Krentz, 'Community and Character. Matthew's Vision of the Church'," unpublished paper at the SBL Matthew Section, Boston, 1987;

In short, the above models illuminate several types of groups related to marginality in the Matthean gospel. One example of what Turner calls spontaneous marginality would be the ideology of a group of the network type from the days of the historical Jesus (e.g., 10:5-15, 40-42; 23:34). Another would be the ideology of "leaderless group," or "faction" (Boissevain; Malina), or at least the group without titles of honor (23:8-10). This would be Boissevain's and Malina's "faction" and Herbst's "composite autonomous group." Nonetheless, in my view there is also a clear tendency toward structure, or what Turner calls normative marginality.

From this perspective, I return to the example of "the poor." The macrosocial model of an agrarian society offers a lens through which to view statements about those who are involuntarily marginally poor in the First Gospel. Microsocial groups offer a lens through which to see the ideal of voluntary poverty. The mission statements that fit the network model are commands to perpetuate the ideal of voluntary poverty (e.g., 10:5-15, 40-42; 23:34). A similar ideology occurs in the story of the young man: he cannot "follow" because he cannot give up his "many possessions." Many other examples could be cited, not least of which is the passage that Donahue claims is the hermeneutical key to the gospel, the "parable" of the Sheep and the Goats in Matthew 25:31-46. On the one hand, the language reflects the ideal of voluntary poverty; on the other, the ideal reflects actual poverty: "Truly I say to you, as you did it to one of the least of these my brothers (and sisters), you did it to me" (25:40, 45). At the same time, those critics who sense a step back from the ideal perceive the move toward "normative marginality": "For the poor you always have with you, but me you do not always have." Indeed, perhaps here we have the clue to Matthew's "Blessed are the poor *in spirit*, for theirs is the kingdom of heaven" (Matt 5:3).

The Author of Matthew as "Marginal Man"

If we once again define a "Marginal Man" as an individual who, because of birth, migration, conquest, and the like is "doomed" to live in two different, antagonistic cultures without fully belonging to either, how does Matthew look? Here I shall only outline a proposal.

1. The author of the gospel is a scribe (13:52). There are a several current studies on writing and writers in antiquity[76] and some of them have to do with the Gospel of Matthew.[77] Current estimates of those who could write in antiquity are quite low. From the perspective of macrosocial

---

"Egalitarian Ideology." See B. Aubrey Fisher and Donald G. Ellis, *Small Group Decision Making. Communication and the Group Process* (3rd ed. New York: McGraw-Hill, 1990).

[76] E.g., André Lemaire, "Writing and Writing Materials," *ABD* (New York: Doubleday, 1992) 6.999-1008.

[77] E.g., Saldarini, *Pharisees, Scribes, and Sadducees*; David E. Orton, *The Understanding Scribe. Matthew and the Apocalyptic Ideal* (JSNT Suppl. 25; Sheffield: JSOT Press, 1989); Antoinette Wire, "Gender Roles in a Scribal Community," in David L. Balch, ed., *Social History of the Matthean Community* (Minneapolis: Fortress Press, 1991) 87-121; Lucretia B. Yaghjian, "Was Matthew's Scribe a Social Science Critic? From Parables to Protocols of Reading and Writing Culture in Matthew 13," Society of Biblical Literature Annual Meeting, San Francisco, November, 1992.

stratification, the author of Matthew ranks at least as a retainer of the elite strata. Moreover, he has much honor from the perspective of scribalism in traditional Judaism. Yet, he is concerned about those from the lower strata and represents a tradition infused with involuntary marginality, and so stands between two cultures.

2. The scribe's opponents are Pharisees, a rival faction within Judaism. Yet, for the gospel writer, Pharisaism is becoming "normative," that is, the center; again, he is between two cultures.

3. The Matthean author "brings out of his treasure what is new and what is old" (13:52), a dominant theme in the gospel concerned especially with the Torah and its interpretation (e.g., 5:17-48). He stands between the old and the new.

4. The first two chapters suggest that Matthew knew conventional forms of the encomium of the progymnasmata,[78] as the modified *bios* form suggests. Yet, his use of the formula quotations and his stress on interpreting and making a hedge around the Torah (5:17-6:48) point to the Pharisaic scribalism. His "synagogue Greek" is derived in part from the Septuagint; yet, he uses Christian sources: Mark and Q. He improves Markan syntax, yet his language is semitizing.[79] Matthew seems to stand on the boundary of Greek and Jewish education.

5. Matthew's has concern for the "lost sheep of the house of Israel" (10:6; 15: 24), but ultimately the mission is to the Gentiles (28:16-20). Presumably his concerns are divided.

6. Is the author of Matthew a Jewish Christian or a Christian Jew?[80] Would he have understood this question? If he did, he realized he stood between two cultures.

Conclusion

In this paper, I have attempted to clarify several dimensions of the concept "marginality." I have also attempted to relate the Gospel of Matthew to these various dimensions of the term. The author of the Gospel of Matthew has an ideology of "voluntary marginality," but his gospel includes some hope for "involuntary marginals" in the real world, though it is tempered. On the basis of several multiple criteria he might be called a "Marginal Man." That will be a subject for further investigation.

---

[78] Jerome H. Neyrey, "Encomium, Progymnasmata and Description of First Century Persons: Josephus's *Vita* as a Test Case," Society of Biblical Literature Annual Meeting, New Orleans, LA, 1990.

[79] Ulrich Luz, *Matthew 1-7. A Commentary* (Trans. Wilhelm C. Linss; Minneapolis: Augsburg, 1990) 49-76.

[80] Overman, *Matthew's Gospel and Formative Judaism*; David L. Balch, ed., *Social History of the Matthean Community*.

Works Consulted

Aberle, David.
 1962   "A Note on Relative Deprivation Theory As Applied to
         Millenarian and Other Cult Movements." Pp. 209-14 in Sylvia
         Thrupp, ed., *Millennial Dreams in Action. Studies in Revolutionary
         Religious Movements.* New York: Schocken Books.

Alföldy, G.
 1986   *Die römische Gesellschaft.* Wiesbaden: Steiner.

Anderson, Janice Capel.
 1983   "Matthew: Gender and Reading." Mary Ann Tolbert, ed. *The
         Bible and Feminist Hermeneutics. Semeia* 28: 3-27.

Balch, David L., ed.
 1991   *Social History of the Matthean Community. Cross-Disciplinary
         Approaches.* Minneapolis: Fortress Press.

Bauer, David R.
 1988   *The Structure of Matthew's Gospel: A Study in Literary Design.* JSNT
         Suppl. 31. Bible and Literature Series 15. Sheffield: Almond.

Boissevain, Jeremy.
 1974   *Friends of Friends: Networks, Manipulators, and Coalitions.* New
         York: St. Martin's Press.

Cohen, Shaye J. D.
 1981   "Epigraphical Rabbis." *JQR* 72: 1-17.

Cooper, John M.
 1941   *Temporal Sequence and the Marginal Cultures.* Washington, D.C.:
         The Catholic University of America.

Cope, O. Lamar.
 1976   *Matthew. A Scribe Trained for the Kingdom of Heaven.*
         Washington, D.C.: The Catholic Biblical Association of
         America.

Court, J. M.
 1985   "Right and Left: the Implications for Matthew 25:31-46." *New
         Testament Studies* 31: 223-33.

Crosby, Michael H.
 1988   *House of Disciples. Church, Economics, and Justice in Matthew.*
         Maryknoll, NY: Orbis Books.

Crossan, John Dominic.
 1991a   "Open Healing and Open Eating. Jesus as a Jewish Cynic?"
         Biblical Research 36: 6-18.
 1991b   *The Historical Jesus. The Life of a Mediterranean Jewish Peasant.*
         San Francisco: HarperCollins.

Dahrendorf, Ralf.

    1959   *Class and Class Conflict in Industrial Society.* Stanford: Stanford University Press.

Danker, Frederick.

    1992   "Associations, Clubs, Thiasoi." *ABD.* New York: Doubleday, 1992. 1.501-503.

Derrett, J. Duncan M.

    1981   "Mt 23,8-10 a Midrash on Is 54,13 and Jer 31,33-34." *Biblica* 62: 372-86.

Donahue, John R.

    1986   "The Parable of the Sheep and the Goats: A Challenge to Christian Ethics." *Theological Studies* 47: 3-31.

    1988   *The Gospel in Parable.* Philadelphia: Fortress Press.

Donaldson, James.

    1973   "The Title Rabbi in the Gospels—Some Reflections on the Evidence of the Gospels." *JQR* 63: 287-91.

Duling, Dennis C.

    1978   "The Therapeutic Son of David in Matthew's Gospel." *NTS* 24: 392-410.

    1983   "Matthew and the Problem of Authority: Some Preliminary Observations," *Proceedings 3. Eastern Great Lakes Biblical Society* 3: 59-68; reprinted in *Explorations. Journal for Adventurous Thought* 3 (1984) 15-24; and pp. 33-42 in William P. Frost, ed., *New Testament Perspectives.* Dayton, Ohio: College Press, 1984.

    1985   "Insights from Sociology for New Testament Christology: A Test Case." Pp. 351-68 in Kent Harold Richards, ed., *SBL Seminar Papers.* Atlanta: Scholars Press.

    1987a   "Binding and Loosing (Matthew 16:19; Matthew 18:18; John 20:23)." *Forum* 3/4: 3-31.

    1987b   "Response to E. Krentz, "Community and Character. Matthew's Vision of the Church." Unpublished paper circulated at the SBL Matthew Section.

    1991a   "Review of Richard A. Horsley, *Sociology and the Jesus Movement.*" *BTB* 21: 123-24.

    1991b   "Matthew's Infancy in Social Science Perspective." Paper discussed at the Context Group in March.

    1992a   "Matthew's Plurisignificant 'Son of David' in Social Science Perspective: Kinship, Kingship, Magic, and Miracle." *BTB* 22/3: 99-116.

    1992b   "Egalitarian Ideology, Leadership, and Factional Conflict in the Matthean Gospel." Paper delivered in the Gospels Section, Society of Biblical Literature, San Francisco, November.

1992c   "Kingdom of God, Kingdom of Heaven (New Testament and Early Christian Literature)." *ABD*. New York: Doubleday, 1992. 4.56-69.

1992d   "Matthew (Disciple)." *ABD*. New York: Doubleday. 4.618-22.

1993   "Introduction and Annotations" on the Gospel According to Matthew in the HarperCollins Study Edition of the New Revised Standard Version. Ed. Wayne A. Meeks.

Duling, Dennis C., and Norman Perrin.

1993   *The New Testament. An Introduction.* New York: Harcourt Brace and Company.

Eagleton, Terry.

1976   *Marxism and Literary Criticism.* Berkeley and Los Angeles: University of California Press.

Elliott, John H.

1986   "Social-Scientific Criticism of the New Testament: More on Methods and Models." Pp. 1-33 in John H. Elliott, ed., *Social-Scientific Criticism of the New Testament and Its Social World.* *Semeia* 35. Decatur, GA: Scholars Press.

1990   *A Home for the Homeless. A Social-Scientific Criticism of 1 Peter, Its Situation and Strategy.* 2nd ed. Minneapolis: Augsburg-Fortress.

Fiensy, David.

1990   *The Land is Mine: The Social History of Palestine in the Herodian Period.* New York: The Edwin Mellen Press.

Filson, Floyd V.

1956   "Broken Patterns in the Gospel of Matthew." *JBL* 75: 227-31.

Fisher, B. Aubrey, and Donald G. Ellis.

1990   *Small Group Decision Making. Communication and the Group Process.* 3rd ed. New York: McGraw-Hill.

Gager, John.

1975   *Kingdom and Community. The Social World of Early Christianity.* Englewood Cliffs, NJ: Prentice-Hall.

Garland, David E.

1979   *The Intention of Matthew 23.* Leiden: E. J. Brill.

Germani, Gino.

1980   *Marginality.* New Brunswick, NJ: Transaction Books.

Green, H. B.

1968   "The Structure of St. Matthew's Gospel." Pp. 47-59 in *Studia Evangelica* 4. Ed. F. L. Cross. TU 102. Berlin: Akademie Verlag.

Hachlili, Rachael.
    1992   "Synagogue (Diaspora Synagogues)." *ABD* New York:
            Doubleday. 6.260-63.

Haenchen, Ernst.
    1951   "Matthäus 23." *ZTK* 48: 38-63.

Hanks, Thomas D.
    1992   "Poor, Poverty (New Testament)." *ABD*. New York:
            Doubleday. 5.414-24.

Hanson, K. C.
    1991   "Fishing." Unpublished paper of the Context Group.

Hengel, Martin.
    1966   "Die Synagogeninschrift von Stobi." *ZNW* 57: 145-83.

Herbst, Ph. G.
    1976   *Alternatives to Hierarchies.* Leiden: Martinus Nijhoff Social
            Sciences Division, 1976.

Hill, David.
    1965   "DIKAIOI as a Quasi-Technical Term." *NTS* 11: 296-302.

Horsley, Richard A.
    1989   *Sociology of the Jesus Movement.* New York: Crossroad.

Karris, Robert J.
    1990   *Jesus and the Marginalized in John's Gospel.* Collegeville, MN:
            Liturgical Press.

Kingsbury, Jack Dean
    1988   *Matthew. Structure, Christology, Kingdom.* Minneapolis: (1975)
            Fortress Press.
    1978   "The Verb *Akolouthein* ('to follow') as an Index of Matthew's
            View of His Community." *JBL* 97: 56-73.

Kloppenborg, John S.
    1986   "Blessing and Marginality. The `Persecution Beatitude' in Q,
            Thomas, and Early Christianity." *Forum* 2/3: 36-56.

Lapin H.
    1992   "Rabbi." *ABD*. New York: Doubleday. 5.600-601.

Larrain, Jorge A.
    1992   *The Concept of Ideology.* Brookfield, VT: Gregg Revivals (1979).

Lemaire, André.
    1992   "Writing and Writing Materials." *ABD*. New York:
            Doubleday. 6.999-1008.

Lenski, Gerhard and Jean.
    1987   *Human Societies. An Introduction to Macrosociology.* 5th ed. New York: McGraw-Hill.

Lewis, Naphtali.
    1983   *Life in Egypt Under Roman Rule.* Oxford: Clarendon Press.

Luz, Ulrich.
    1989   *Matthew 1-7. A Commentary.* Trans. Wilhelm C. Linss. Minneapolis: Augsburg.

MacMullen, Ramsay.
    1974   *Roman Social Relations. 50 B.C. to A.D. 284.* New Haven: Yale University Press.

Malina, Bruce J.
    1981   *The New Testament World. Insights from Cultural Anthropology.* Atlanta: John Knox.
    1986a   *Christian Origins and Cultural Anthropology. Practical Models for Biblical Interpretation.* Atlanta: John Knox.
    1986b   "Normative Dissonance and Christian Origins." In John H. Elliott, ed. *Social-Scientific Criticism of the New Testament and Its Social World. Semeia* 35: 35-59.
    1986c   "Interpreting the Bible with Anthropology: The Case of the Poor and the Rich." *Listening. Journal of Religion and Culture* 21: 148-59.
    1988a   "Patron and Client. The Analogy Behind Synoptic Theology." *Forum* 4/1: 2-32.
    1988b   "A Conflict Approach to Mark 7." *Forum* 4/3: 3-30.

Malina, Bruce J., and Jerome H. Neyrey.
    1988   *Calling Jesus Names. The Social Value of Labels in Matthew.* Sonoma, CA: Polebridge Press.

McLellan, David.
    1986   *Ideology.* Milton Keynes: Open University Press.

McNutt, Paula.
    1993   "The Kenites, the Midianites, and the Rechabites as Marginal Mediators in Ancient Israelite Tradition." Paper discussed at the Eastern Great Lakes Biblical Society, April.

Meeks, Wayne A.
    1983   *The First Urban Christians. The Social World of the Apostle Paul.* New Haven: Yale University Press.

Meier, John P.
    1991-   *A Marginal Jew. Rethinking the Historical Jesus.* 2 vols. New York: Doubleday.

Neyrey, Jerome H.

1990   "Encomium, Progymnasmata and Description of First Century Persons: Josephus's *Vita* as a Test Case." Paper given at the Social Science and New Testament Interpretation Section, Society of Biblical Literature, New Orleans, LA, 1990.

Oakman, Douglas E.

1986   *Jesus and the Economic Questions of His Day.* SBEC 8. Lewiston, NY: The Edwin Mellen Press.

Orton, David E.

1989   *The Understanding Scribe. Matthew and the Apocalyptic Ideal.* JSNT Suppl. 25. Sheffield: JSOT Press.

Overman, J. Andrew.

1990   *Matthew's Gospel and Formative Judaism. The Social World of the Matthean Community.* Minneapolis: Fortress.

Park, Robert E.

1928   "Human Migration and the Marginal Man." *American Journal of Sociology* 33: 881-93.

1931   "Personality and Cultural Conflict." *Publication of the American Sociological Society* 25: 95-110.

Pitt-Rivers, Julian.

1968   "Pseudo-Kinship." D. L. Sills, ed., *International Encyclopedia of the Social Sciences.* New York: Macmillan. 8: 408-13.

Ringe, Sharon H.

1985   "A Gentile Woman's Story." Pp. 65-72 in Letty M. Russell, ed., *Feminist Interpretation of the Bible.* Philadelphia: Fortress Press.

Ritzer, George.

1983   *Contemporary Sociological Theory.* New York: Alfred A. Knopf.

Rohrbaugh, Richard.

1987   "'Social Location of Thought' as a Heuristic Construction in New Testament Study." *JSNT* 30: 103-119.

(1993) "Social Location of the Markan Audience" (forthcoming in *Interpretation* and *BTB*.

Saldarini, Anthony J.

1988   *Pharisees, Scribes, and Sadducees in Palestinian Society. A Sociological Approach.* Wilmington, DE: Michael Glazier.

Schermerhorn, R. A.

1964   "Marginal Man." Pp. 406-407 in Julius Gould and William L. Kolb, eds. *Dictionary of the Social Sciences.* New York: The Free Press.

Schottroff, Luise, and Wolfgang Stegemann.
  1986   *Jesus and the Hope of the Poor.* Trans. Matthew J. O'Connell.
           Maryknoll, NY: Orbis Books.

Schüssler Fiorenza, Elisabeth.
  1983   *In Memory of Her. A Feminist Theological Reconstruction of
           Christian Origins.* New York: Crossroad.

Scott, James C.
  1977   "Protest and Profanation: Agrarian Revolt and the Little
           Tradition." *Theory and Society* 4: 1-38 and 211-246.

Stegemann, Wolfgang.
  1984a   *The Gospel and the Poor.* Trans. Dietlinde Elliott. Philadelphia:
           Fortress Press.
  1986   See Schottroff, Luise.

Stegemann, Wolfgang, and Willy Schottroff, eds.
  1984   *God of the Lowly: Socio-Historical Interpretations of the Bible.*
           Maryknoll, NY: Orbis.

Stonequist, E. V.
  1937   *The Marginal Man.* New York: Charles Scribner's Sons.

Theissen, Gerd.
  1977   *Sociology of Early Palestinian Christianity.* Trans. J. Bowden.
           Philadelphia: Fortress.

Thiemann, Ronald F.
  1987   "The Unnamed Woman at Bethany." *Theology Today* 44: 179-
           88.

Turner, Victor.
  1969   *The Ritual Process. Structure and Anti-Structure.* Chicago: Aldine
           Publishing Co.
  1974   *Dramas, Fields, and Metaphors. Symbolic Action in Human Society.*
           Ithaca: Cornell University Press.

Via, Dan O.
  1987   "Ethical Responsibility and Human Wholeness in Matthew
           25:31-46." *HTR* 89: 79-100.

Viviano, Benedict V.
  1990   "Social World and Community Leadership: The Case of
           Matthew 23:1-12, 34." *JSNT* 39: 3-21.

Waetjen, Herman C.
  1989   *A Reordering of Power. A Socio-Political Reading of Mark's Gospel.*
           Minneapolis: Fortress Press.

Weber, Max.
   1968   *Economy and Society. An Outline of Interpretive Sociology.* Ed.
               Günther Roth and Claus Wittich. New York: Bedminister
               Press.

White, Leland J.
   1986   "Grid and Group in Matthew's Community: The
               Righteousness/Honor Code in the Sermon." In John H.
               Elliott, ed. *Social-Scientific Criticism of the New Testament and Its
               Social World. Semeia* 35: 61-88.

Wilson, Bryan.
   1973   *Magic and the Millennium.* London: Heinemann.

Winter, Bruce.
   1991   "The Messiah as the Tutor: The Meaning of *kathēgētēs* in
               Matthew 23:10." *Tyndale Bulletin* 42/1: 152-57.

Wire, Antoinette.
   1991   "Gender Roles in a Scribal Community." Pp. 87-121 in David
               L. Balch, ed., *Social History of the Matthean Community.*
               Minneapolis: Fortress Press.

Wolf, E.
   1966   *Peasants.* Englewood Cliffs, NJ: Prentice-Hall.

A Sound Map of the Sermon on the Mount

Bernard Brandon Scott
Phillips Graduate Seminary, Tulsa, OK

Margaret E. Dean
Phillips Graduate Seminary, Tulsa, OK

This paper is an experiment in understanding the construction of the Sermon on the Mount from the standpoint of hearing. As such its first concern is the text as signifer, the sign's physical aspect. Semantics operates at the level of the sign, the unity of signifier and signified. Yet most often biblical studies neglect the signifier. Because this paper is an experiment, not all the rules are well known or known in advance, but must be discovered by trial and error. Likewise, the payoff (meaning) may turn out to be different from that in which traditional scholarship has invested.

I. Reading is *Recitatio*

The Sermon on the Mount is contextualized in the Gospel of Matthew as a speech, a common sense observation. Yet its implications are important. As George Kennedy remarks, "It was the intent of the evanglists to present speeches, and early Christian audiences listening to the Gospels read, heard these chapters as speeches."[1] Two aspects of Kennedy's quote need attention. First the Sermon the Mount is a speech and secondly the gospels were read aloud, meant to be heard. Both demand that we pay attention to the sound of the text and the implications of that sound.

Reading creates its own characteristic social,[2] conceptual space for its reception.[3] After the invention of the printing press, that space has become increasingly interior and reading a silent process. Discourse was replaced by

[1] George A. Kennedy, *New Testament Interpretation through Rhetorical Criticism, Studies in Religion* (Chapel Hill, NC: The University of North Carolina Press, 1984) 39.

[2] M. A. K. Halladay, *Language as Social Semiotic: The Social Interpretation of Language and Meaning* (Baltimore: University Park Press, 1978).

[3] "Every written text occupies physical space and at the same time generates a conceptual space in the minds of writers and readers. The organization of writing, the style of writing, the expectations of the reader—all these are affected by the physical space the text occupies. Jay David Bolter, *Writing Space. The Computer, Hypertext, and the History of Writing* (Hillsdale, NJ: Lawrence Erlbaum Associates, 1991) 85.

silent scanning.[4] This points to an essential difference between modern and ancient story-telling. Modern fiction explores a character's interior life and psychological development, while ancient fiction holds up the character as exemplar. The model is dyadic,[5] exterior, and character remains fixed.[6]

Historical criticism builds on the historical difference between the Hellenistic world and our own and increasingly social science theory is drawing even stronger differences. Literary criticism, on the other hand, has tended to miminize the difference, almost seeing the techniques of narrativity as universals.[7] This assumption needs challenging. Already rhetorical criticism is challenging it by positing and analyzing a specifically Hellenistic rhetoric.

Since ancient texts were meant to be read aloud,[8] they must employ sound to create public space. Furthermore since sound is the first encounter point for audience and text, we would expect sound to have a strongly conventional aspect. Modern readers (i.e., printing press readers) press towards the meaning, the semantics, of a text. As Eisentein notes, they read to learn.[9] The ancients recited to learn. Reading was a public, out loud activity. As Harris says about book publication at Rome, "it is assumed to be the *recitatio*, not the book, which will make a man celebrated."[10] This has important implications

---

4 Elizabeth L. Eisenstein (*The Printing Press as an Agent of Change: Communications and Cultural Transformations in Early Modern Europe* [2 vols. New York: Cambridge University Press, 1979] 1.129-136) deals with some specific outcomes of this shift "from a hearing public to a reading public."

5 Bruce J. Malina, *The New Testament World, Insights from Cultural Anthropology* (Atlanta: John Knox, 1981) 53-60.

6 Robert Scholes and Robert Kellogg, *The Nature of Narrative* (New York: Oxford University Press, 1966) 164-7. Theodore J. Weeden (*Mark, Traditions in Conflict*, [Philadelphia: Fortress Press, 1971]) was among the first to draw out the implications of this understanding of character for a study of the gospels.

7 R. Alan Culpepper, *Anatomy of the Fourth Gospel, A Study in Literary Design, Foundations and Facets* (Philadelphia: Fortress Press, 1983) is a good example. His title plays on the title of Northope Fyre's famous book, *The Anatomy of Criticism*. Robert W. Funk, *The Poetics of Biblical Narrative, Foundations and Facets* (Sonoma, CA: Polebridge Press, 1988) attempts to develop a literary criticism based on the texts themselves.

8 William V. Harris, *Ancient Literacy* (Cambridge: Harvard University Press, 1989), 36. Lentz, in dealing with poetry and drama maintains, "the Greeks continue, by ancient tradition and contemporary [i.e., Hellenistic] choice, to think of literature as an oral form" (Tony Lentz, *Orality and Literacy in Hellenic Greece*, [Carbondale, IL: Southern Illinois University Press, 1989] 147), and in regard to philosophical writings, "Reading aloud is therefore more widespread than silent reading of philosophical discourse. ... The simplest practical explanation for this absence [of silent reading] is the high cost of papyrus and the expense of having copies written upon it. Making multiple copies of discourses—for each member of a group, for example—would be prohibitively expensive" (102). Acts 7:30 and Augustine, *Confessions*, iv. 96, are both examples of private reading out loud. I am not contesting that private reading could be silent, but reading was normally out loud in the ancient world. Str-B 2:687 quotes a number of later references forbidding reading Torah silently. This indicates that the earlier tradition was reading aloud, not silently.

9 Eisenstein, *The Printing Press as an Agent of Change*, 1.65.

10 Harris, *Ancient Literacy*, 226.

for our project. A written text was written to be spoken aloud (*recitatio*), not read silently, pointing out the primary importance of sound. Modern silent readers depend on typographic conventions to guide and organize the printed word for semantic digestion.[11] An ancient reader had few such clues beyond the alphabet itself. Ancient manuscripts have few conventions and need preparation to be read.[12] Ancient reciters and audiences must first concern themselves with a text's sound because it provided their initial and primary clues as to its organization and meaning. As Michael Stubbs has pointed out, "listeners have to understand in real time."[13] They do have the luxury of re-reading.

This issue of silent reading and sound is frequently dealt with under the categories of oral culture, scribal culture, and print culture. Werner Kelber pioneered this distinction in New Testament studies drawing upon the work of Ong, Havelock, and Eisenstein.[14] In Kelber's categories, the Hellenistic Mediterranean world is a scribal culture. But this term is problematic in two ways. First, it sets up a contrast, almost contradiction, between oral culture and scribal culture. As Vernon Robbins has trenchantly shown, this was not the situation in the Hellenistic period. That situation was characterized by an interaction between oral and scribal environments. Robbins terms this a rhetorical culture, one that "is aware of written documents, uses written and oral language interactively, and composes both orally and scribally in a rhetorical manner."[15] By "rhetorical manner" Robbins means "writing traditional materials clearly and persuasively" and for recitation.[16] For

---

11 Eisenstein, *The Printing Press as an Agent of Change* 1.52: "The highly competitive commercial character of the new mode of book production encouraged the relatively rapid adoption of any innovation that commended a given edition to purchasers." She gives an extensive list with references to the typographical conventions early printers developed.

12 Henri I. Marrou, *A History of Education in Antiquity*, Wisconsin Studies in Classics. (Madison, WI: University of Wisconsin Press, [1982], 1956) 150-57, provides a detailed analysis of the teaching of reading and writing, indicating that it was not pupil friendly. "Expressive Reading" was not taught until secondary school because of the difficulty in reading a text presented by *scriptio continua* (165-66). Stanely F. Bonner in *Education in Ancient Rome: From the Elder Cato to the Younger Pliny* ([Berkeley and Los Angeles: University of California Press, 1977] 220-22) shows how the lack of punctuation created real problems in reading. On the other hand, Bruce M. Metzger, *The Text of the New Testament* (3rd ed. [Oxford: Oxford University Press, 1991] 13) seems to think this presents no real difficulty, even though he quotes no evidence to this point.

13 "[B]ut readers can refer backward and forwards in the text." *Language and Literacy: The Sociolinguistics of Reading and Writing*, Routledge Education Books (London: Routledge & Kegan Paul, 1980) 13.

14 Werner H. Kelber, *The Oral and the Written Gospel, The Hemeneutics of Speaking and Writing in the Synoptic Tradition, Mark, Paul and Q* (Philadelphia: Fortress Press, 1983).

15 Vernon K. Robbins, "Progymnastic Rhetorical Composition and Pre-Gospel Traditions: A New Approach," ed. Camille Focant. (BETL; Leuven: Leuven University Press, 1993) forthcoming.

16 Vernon K. Robbins, "Writing as a Rhetorical Act in Plutarch and the Gospels," *Persuasive Artistry: Studies in New Testament Rhetoric in Honor of George A. Kennedy*, ed. Duane F. Watson. Journal of the Study of the New Testament Supplement Series 50, (Sheffield: JSOT Press, 1991) 145-6.

Robbins scribal culture is concerned with copying and is part of the elementary writing processes in the Hellenistic world. In a rhetorical culture, one wrote in order to persuade others by reciting; in a scribal culture one copies in order to preserve. As Robbins summarizes in a forthcoming article:

> Performing oral and scribal activity in this way creates a rhetorical culture—one in which speech is influenced by writing and writing is influenced by speaking. Recitation, then, is the base of a rhetorical culture. People know that certain traditions exist in writing. They also know that all traditions, whether oral or written, need to be composed anew to meet the needs of the day. Each day as they spoke, they were interacting with written traditions: whenever they wrote, they were interacting with oral traditions. This interaction characterized their thinking, their speaking, and their writing."[17]

Again we are thrown back on the primacy of sound as the access to a composition (text).

A second problem in the term scribal concerns the effects of the technology of writing on composition. The space of a scroll is less bounded than that of a codex, it more closely mimics the indeterminancy of oral space. The codex marks a decisive break in this regard with the conventions of orality.[18] Unlike the oral saga, the scroll has a strong beginning, but shares with the oral song a tendency towards a weak ending.[19] The codex has both a strong beginning and end. It imposes a more self-contained structure. Mark seems to exhibit more of the characteristics of scroll space, while Matthew and Luke cohere more with the Codex space. The clear segmentations of Matthew cohere with the shaping of space into codex pages.[20]

In a rhetorical culture, the Sermon on the Mount would be heard as a speech. The author, then, faces a problem of verisimilitude. How is the Sermon to be cast and what should it sound like? A Jesus speaking like a Pericles in Galilee would be unbelieveable.[21] Matthew provides a number of clues as to the genre of the Sermon. Since genre is part of the conventions of language, genre would indicate to the audience how the Sermon was to be heard. The Sermon on the Mount is οἱ λόγοι τῆς διδαχῆς as the close parallelism between the Sermon's introduction (5:1-2) and it conclusion (7:28-29) attests. Both speak of words and teaching: ἀνοίξας τὸ στόμα, λέγων; ἐδίδασκεν (5:2); τοὺς λόγους and ἐπι τῇ διδαχῇ (7:28), διδάσκων (7:29). Likewise the Sermon's final parable begins each example with a reference to

---

17 Robbins, "Progymnastic Rhetorical Composition," forthcoming.

18 Bolter, *Writing Space*, 85-86.

19 Even the book divisions in Homer seem to be dictated by later copyists conforming the poem to the length of a scoll (G. S. Kirk, *The Iliad: A Commentary* [5 vols.; Cambridge: Cambridge University Press, 1985] 1. 45).

20 If in composing 5 sermons Matthew is thinking of the Pentateuch, then he probably is thinking of five books, not scrolls, regardless of their physical characteristics.

21 These matters are probably determined by context as the speeches in Acts would indicate. Paul's tone shifts to fit the context. This would cohere with the dyadic understanding of personality.

μου τοὺς λόγους (7:24, 26). Both λόγοι and διδαχή are important. Διδαχή refers to "one of the most prominent functions of Jesus"[22] and is strongly emphasized in the triad of teaching, preaching and healing in 4:23, the summary statement that precedes the Sermon. οἱ λόγοι indicates that he is imitating what he takes to be the sayings of Jesus.[23] Thus generically the Sermon is teaching (διδαχή) in the form of sayings (λόγοι).[24]

Even though the Sermon is intended to be οἱ λόγοι (oral tradition), it is not a transcription of oral tradition but an imitation by a literate scribe (Matt 13:52) of oral tradition. The quest for verisimilitude leads the rhetorical composer to imitate the teaching of a specific oral tradition, the Jesus tradition. Even though this tradition was in Greek from a very early period, it was not organized along Greek lines. Christian oral singers did not employ versification with the resultant use of formulae to sing their tales. Rather, the explicit use of Greek literary forms to preserve or develop the oral tradition occurs when the oral tradition interacts with and becomes absorbed into the rhetorical culture with the use of the chreia to frame sayings. This introduction appears to be typical of the rehearsal of the tradition in writing.[25] Yet the earliest forms of the oral tradition appear to have developed along what we may designate as Hebrew lines. This does not designate the language in which the oral tradition originated or developed, but the cultural constraint on its development. This can be observed in two ways. 1) The forms that typify the oral tradition as it appears in Q–the synoptic Sayings source, the Gospel of Thomas, as well as Mark, are forms primarily associated with Hebrew popular wisdom, parables, aphorisms, etc.[26] 2) Instead of versification,[27] parallelism and chiasm are the more prominent mnemonic devices.[28]

---

22 Karl Heinrich Rengstorf, "διδάσκω," *TDNT* 2:139.

23 Helmut Koester (*Ancient Christian Gospels* [Philadelphia: Trinity Press International, 1990] 31-33) shows the primacy of this term as a reference to the oral tradition prior to Marcion.

24 Hans Dieter Betz (*Essays on the Sermon on the Mount* [Philadelphia: Fortress Press, 1985] 1-16) describes the Sermon as an epitome which coheres with this argument, while his argument about its pre-Matthean character does not.

25 Burton L. Mack, and Vernon K. Robbins, *Patterns of Persuasion in the Gospels*, Foundations and Facets (Sonoma, CA: Polebridge Press, 1989).

26 Rudolf Bultmann (*The History of the Synoptic Tradition* [New York: Harper & Row, 1963] 106) appears to be correct in his argument that the providence of the Synoptic logia and proverbs is Jewish wisdom.

27 C. F. D. Moule, *An Idiom-Book of New Testament Greek* (Cambridge: Cambridge University Press, 1963) 199, notes the infrequency and apparently accidental nature of Greek poetic meters in the New Testament.

28 While there are some similarities between the distinctive parallelism of Hebrew poetry and parallelism in the New Testament, the basic organizational pattern is different. R. C. Tannehill, (*The Sword of His Mouth* [Philadelphia, Missoula: Fortress Press, Scholars Press, 1975] 41-42) describes some of these differences, including "parallelism of more complex structures" (e.g., Matt 6:2-6, 16-18) ... [and] ... less use of traditional word pairs. . . ." For detailed treatments of parallelism in Hebrew poetry, see J. L. Kugel, *The Idea of Biblical Poetry, Parallelism and its History* (New Haven: Yale University Press, 1981) 1-58, and L. A. Schökel, *A Manual of Hebrew Poetics* (Rome: Pontifical Biblical Institute, 1988) 48-63.

If the problem of verisimilitude is solved by imitating οἱ λόγοι, as Matthew constructed Jesus' Sermon he faced a number of problems resulting from its aural character, from the fact that the text in which the speech is embedded must be recited (*recitatio*).

1) The initial organization of the Sermon cannot be abstract (literate) but aural. Even if the author had in mind an abstract model on which to build the Sermon, à la Bornkam's elaborate chiasm,[29] such an abstract model must be implemented by means of an aural organization, and thus can be tested by whether it corresponds to an aural organization. In order to understand it, the audience will first have to hear it.[30] To recall the remark of Stubbs, listeners, unlike readers, "have to understand in real time."[31] We have already seen the careful repetition of phrases between the introduction and conclusion providing the hearer with multiple clues as to beginning and ending but also genre.

Within the Sermon itself aural clues employing repeatable phonetic/syntactial markers help the hearer group οἱ λόγοι. The Macro Outline (Appendix 1) indicates the initial aural formulae that allow the construction of a visual-graphic outline of an aural performance. The repetition of μακάριοι as the initial phrase clearly sets up the first group. As the Sermon develops, these initial formulae become more complex. The ἠκούσατε section 4 shows considerable variation in the basic initial aural formula, but the pattern of the whole is clearly implied. Section 6 is by far the most complex in its arrangment and yet a series of patterns recurs to help the hearer sort out its arrangment.

2) Since the author is not an oral singer, but a literate rhetorian, he must imitate οἱ λόγοι. He probably exaggerates the characteristics of that orality. As an example of this exaggeration a comparison with the Q parallels will show that Matthew normally increases the exactness of the parallelism in positive/negative contrasts. The final parable of Builders (Q 6:47-9) clearly indicates this tendency.[32]

There are other examples of what might be judged imitations of orality. The paratactic structure of the sentences in individual units with little subordination or the infrequent use of participles would indicate oral tradition

---

29 Günther Bornkamm, "Der Aufbau der Bergpredigt," *NTS* 24 (1978): 419-432.

30 This is true of the entire gospel narrative. The author must structure the narrative in such a way that a hearer can hear the divisions, units, and motion in a text. The so-called threefold formula in Matthew or the formula endings of the five sermons are such aural markers. They bear a striking similarity to the formulaic markers of oral versification but in fact are somewhat different. The function of the formulae in oral versification enable the singer to rapidly and automatically complete the metric cycle (Albert B. Lord, *The Singer of Tales, Harvard Studies in Comparative Literature, 24* [Cambridge: Harvard University Press, 1960] 54. See the careful analysis of John Miles Foley, *The Theory of Oral Composition, History and Methodology, Folkloristics* [Bloomington: Indiana University Press, 1988] 41-44).

31 This observation alone is enought to call into question the highly abstract pattern of Bornkamm.

32 John S. Kloppenborg (*The Formation of Q, Trajectories in Ancient Wisdom Collections, Studies in Antiquity and Christianity* [Philadelphia: Fortress Press, 1987] 172) argues that "there is little in [Q/Luke] 6:20b-49 which does not appear to be a Q text."

or more likely oral imitiation. At other times, in comparison with Q, the Sermon on the Mount appears more concrete. In 4.4 the Sermon reads "right cheek" and the Lucan parallel has the more general "on the cheek" (Luke 6:29).[33] In the Lord's prayer the Sermon has σήμερον while Luke has τὸ καθ ' ἡμέραν. In the same prayer, the better parallel structure in the Sermon may well be an imitation of orality.

3) Because the Sermon is an imitation of οἱ λόγοι and since the controlling mindset is literate, even if rhetorical, there are many examples of literacy intruding on the imitiation. As an example, one could point to the peculiar lack of paratactic connectives between sections and units.[34] The paratactic connectives *within* units is very strong. This makes the units themselves stand out. The block of material in 6:25-34 has a strong construction based on aural patterns, but it is subordinated both logically and by means of shift in markers (διὰ τοῦτο) to the heading in 6:19. It appears to have a paratactic structure (a sequential order) yet it is clearly subordinated.

Other examples abound. In the μακάριοι section, the beatitude for those who hunger and thirst (Matt 5:6) breaks the beatitude's simple pattern with a double participle and the specification τὴν δικαιοσύνην. While parallel to τῷ πνεύματι(1.1) and τῇ καρδία (1.6), τὴν δικαιοσύνην is an abstract term while the other two are concrete.[35]

We have tried to indicate why the primary organizing character of the Sermon must be aural. Now we turn to an analysis of the Sermon itself to show in detail how that organization operates.

II. Hearing is Sound

The Micro Analysis that follows exhibits in diagram the phonetic and/or syntactical features of the Sermon on the Mount that provide the hearer/reader with the aural clues for its organization. We are aware of the contradiction of exhibiting, i.e., showing, what is meant to be heard.[36] But in a printing press culture that is rapidly becoming graphically orientated, convention will not allow otherwise. The following definitions of terms are employed in the Micro Diagram.

Sections are designated by an *initial aural organizing formula* and usually have a series of *units* that share both an initial formula and a *common organizational*

---

33 In "Jesus as Sage: An Innovating Voice in Common Wisdom," (*The Sage in Israel and the Ancient Near East*, ed. John G. Gammie, and Leo Perdue. [Winona Lake, IN: Eisenbrauns, 1990] 404) I argued that such specificity in the Matthean text pointed to oral tradition and to Jesus. In light of the above arguments, I now have to change my mind.

34 By way of comparison, in the birth narrative the separate units are paratactically connected; e.g., 1:18 or 2:1 or even 3:1.

35 Leander E. Keck, "The Poor Among the Saints in the New Testament," *ZNW* 56 (1965) 100-37 argues that τῷ πνεύματι is not an abstract term, but conjures up a concrete reality.

36 Even the repertoire of words available to explain our observations tilts in the direction of graphic, visual metaphors for analysis.

pattern. There is a total of eight sections in the Sermon. The first cardinal number is always the Section Number.

A *unit's* beginning is denoted by an initial aural formula. A unit is a single iteration of the initial formula and organizing pattern. It has a completeness not only formally but thematically as well. The second cardinal number is always the Unit Number.

A *line* is the smallest element in a unit that exhibits a function or formula. It is recognizable on the basis of its phonetic/syntactial function. In some sections the function or formula of a line are standardized and recurring. The definition of a line is loosely based on the analogy of the line in Greek hexameter.

Lexie is a single printed row of exhibited text. The status of the line and lexie is derived from their usefulness for analysis. A line, defined by its function or the use of a formula, may consist of more than one lexie. For example in 4.2.3 the line is recognized by the formula ἐγὼ δὲ λέγω ὑμῖν ὅτι πᾶς ὁ + participle. In section 4, this line has a recurring formula and plays a recurring function in each unit. We have divided the line into three lexies (rows of print) for analysis. A lexie is not denoted by a cardinal number but their number can always calculated from the first lexie in a line.

The initial aural formula is a recurring phrase that denotes the beginning of a unit and its recurrence denotes a section. For example, section 4 employs the phrase ἠκούσατε ὅτι ἐρρέθη τοῖς ἀρχαίοις to introduce each unit. This initial aural formula need not be repeated verbatim at the beginning of each unit, but performancial variations are normal, typical of the compositional technique of rhetorical culture.[37] The full initial formula occurs in 4.1 but is abbreviated in a variety of ways in the other units of section 4.

Each section has a common *organizing pattern* that gives shape to the section's units. The initial aural formula is the first element in the organizing pattern. This pattern is discussed at the beginning of our analysis for each section.

The beatitudes of section 1 provide a ready example. The section is denoted by its common initial aural formula, μακάριοι οἱ. As a result there are nine units in this first section. The common organizing pattern consists of the initial aural formula + plural nominal and ὅτι αὐτοί. Because of the pithiness of the μακάριοι formula we have not divided the units into lines although technically according to our definitions each unit consists of two lines and each line has one lexie (except unit 1.9).

Epithets are fixed phrases. We have borrowed this term from Homeric studies and the correpondence is not exact since metrical needs are prominent in the classic definition of epithet and that factor is irrelevant here.[38] It is a

---

37 See John Dominic Crossan, *In Fragments: The Aphorisms of Jesus* (San Francisco: Harper & Row, 1983) 40-1 who also distinguishes between performancial and hermeneutical variations. Hermeneutical variations involve a reinterpretation.

38 Milman Perry defined the epithet formula as "a group of words which is regularly employed under the same metrical conditions to express a given essential idea." quoted in Albert B. Lord, *The Singer of Tales, Harvard Studies in Comparative Literature, 24* (Cambridge: Harvard University Press, 1960) 30.

stock pharse which allows variation to fit context and, as Foley has recently emphaized of the Homeric epithet, evokes a whole reference of meaning connected with the stock phrase.[39]

We used the Nestle Aland[26] text but have paid attention to significant textual variations in the footnotes because often our observations bring important evidence to bear on scribal changes. These at times confirm our observations about sound.

We have not employed the standard versification and chapter numbers because these frequently are misleading. They lead to a fragmentation of the text and do not represent a scientific analysis, but a convenience dictated by the printing press, even though they allow easy reference. We have employed a hierachical numbering system to indicate how each unit fits into the Sermon's overall design. In our diagram we have striven to follow a consistent set of graphic conventions to indicate relations. This has proved difficult at times, since we would have liked to illustrate more relationships than available graphic clues allow. Deviations from our own conventions are obvious or we have noted them

bold	→	initial aural formula
single underline	→	organzing pattern markers
double underline	→	same sound or word.
dotted underline	→	same sound or word.
capital letters	→	epithets

1.0-1.8. Μακάριοι(*5:3-10*)

1.1 **Μακάριοι** οἱ πτωχοὶ τῷ πνεύματι,
  ὅτι αὐτῶν ἐστιν Η ΒΑΣΙΛΕΙΑ ΤΩΝ ΟΥΡΑΝΩΝ.

1.2 **μακάριοι** οἱ πενθοῦντες,
  ὅτι αὐτοὶ   παρακληθήσονται.

1.3 **μακάριοι** οἱ πραεῖς,
  ὅτι αὐτοὶ κληρονομήσουσιν   τὴν   γῆν.[40]

1.4 **μακάριοι** οἱ πεινῶντες καὶ διψῶντες τὴν δικαιοσύνην,
  ὅτι αὐτοὶ   χορτασθήσονται.

1.5 **μακάριοι** οἱ   ἐλεήμονες,
  ὅτι αὐτοὶ   ἐλεηθήσονται.

1.6 **μακάριοι** οἱ καθαροὶ τῇ καρδίᾳ,
  ὅτι αὐτοὶ τὸν θεὸν   ὄψονται.

1.7 **μακάριοι** οἱ εἰρηνοποιοί,
  ὅτι αὐτοὶ υἱοὶ θεοῦ   κληθήσονται.

1.8 **μακάριοι** οἱ δεδιωγμένοι ἕνεκεν   δικαιοσύνης,

---

[39] John Miles Foley, *Immanent Art: From Structure to Meaning in Traditional Oral Epic.* Bloomington: Indiana University Press. See footnote 15.

[40] Some manuscripts reverse 1.2 and 1.3. Although the textual evidence is very weak, the rhetorical effect is strong. πραεῖς and πτωχοί are nicely balanced and Matthew frequently employs the contrast between οὐρανός and γῆ.

ὅτι αὐτῶν ἐστιν Η ΒΑΣΙΛΕΙΑ ΤΩΝ ΟΥΡΑΝΩΝ.

While proposals for structuring the beatitudes have proliferated, two approaches predominate. One divides eight beatitudes into two groups of four (1.1-1.4 and 1.5-1.8), contending that the initial π sound and the common passive condition of the blessed unify the first four, while the active ethical condition of the blessed unifies the second group.[41] The other posits a chiastic arrangement between the two groups of beatitudes on the basis of the inclusio established by the epithet in 1.1 and 1.8 and the use of the "divine passive" in 1.2, 1.4, 1.5, and 1.7.[42]

Both proposals ignore several important clues to the section's organization. The first does not explain why the initial π sound was abandoned with the doubling of the verb in the fourth beatitude, nor does it indicate why no distinctive sound occurs in the last four beatitudes. The second proposal fails to explain the occurrence of τὴν δικαιοσύνην at the end of the fourth and eighth beatitudes.[43] The repetition of δικαιοσύνην at the end of each group of four beatitudes suggests parallel arrangement, not a chiasm as these theorists propose.

Since our analysis focuses primarily on the Sermon's sound, its aural quality, phonetic clues govern the following outline. The eightfold repetition of μακάριοι οἱ gives the section its distinctive initial sound and each iteration of the full formula consists of μακάριοι and a nominative phrase with the subsequent ὅτι plus the third person pronoun. This pattern typifies the beatitude form.[44] Three interlocking inclusios unite 1.1 and 1.8. The first overarches 1.1 to 1.8 with the repetition of ὅτι αὐτῶν ἐστιν ἡ βασιλεία τῶν οὐρανῶν. A second inclusio of τῶν οὐρανῶν and τὴν γῆν unites 1.1-1.3. This apparent contrast is a frequent one employed by Matthew in the Sermon (see below, 5.3.7).

A third inclusio unites 1.4-1.8 with the repetition of τὴν δικαιοσύνην at the beginning and the end. Unit 1.4 claims special prominence. It initiates the longer of the two subsidiary inclusios and both the abstract character of the noun δικαιοσύνη and the doubling of the nominative element in the main clause of 1.4 signal a departure from the aural unity of the previous material.

Several phonetic features connect the two groups of units, 1.1-1.3 and 1.4-1.8. The alliterative π crosses over from the first group to the second with its occurrence in the first nominative participle 1.4, while providing a simple phonetic unity to the first four beatitudes. The -ονται ending of the future

---

41 See, for example, Eduard Schweizer, *The Good News According to Matthew* (Atlanta: John Knox Press, 1975) 82; Robert H. Gundry, *Matthew, A Commentary on His Literary and Theological Art*, (Grand Rapids: Eerdmans, 1982) 73; R. Guelich, "The Matthean Beatitudes: 'Entrance Requirements' or Eschatological Blessings?," *JBL* 95 (1976): 431-2; John P. Meier, *Matthew, New Testament Message 3*, ed. Wilfrid Harrington and Donald Senior (Wilmington, DE: Michael Glazier, Inc., 1980) 39.

42 N. J. McEleney, "The Beatitudes of the Sermon on the Mount/Plain," *CBQ* 43 (1981) 10-13.

43 W.D. Davies, and D.C. Allison, *A Critical and Exegetical Commentary on the Gospel According to Matthew*, ICC (Edinburgh: T & T Clark, 1988) 1:429-30.

44 Jacques Dupont, *Les Beatitudes* (Louvain: E. Nauwelaerts, 1958) 1:279.

passive verb in 1.2 anticipates this repeated feature in the second group. Within the second group the distinctive -ονται ending of the future and future passive verbs remains consistent in each ὅτι clause. This group also exhibits three doublets: the repeated ἐλεη- sound in 1.5, the repeated initial κα- in the main clause of 1.6, and the occurrence of θεός in the ὅτι clauses of both 1.6 and 1.7.[45] The beatitudes in this second group stand out as more abstract and less concrete than those in the first group.

1.9. μακάριοί ἐστε (5:11-12)
1.9.1 1   **μακάριοί ἐστε**[46]
    2   ὅταν   ὀνειδίσωσιν...   ὑμᾶς
    3   καὶ   διώξωσιν
    4   καὶ   εἴπωσιν
            πᾶν πονηρὸν καθ'   ὑμῶν[47] ἕνεκεν ἐμοῦ.
1.9.2 1   χαίρετε καὶ ἀγαλλιᾶσθε,
    2   ὅτι ὁ μισθὸς   ὑμῶν πολὺς ΕΝ ΤΟΙΣ ΟΥΡΑΝΟΙΣ·
    3   οὕτως γὰρ ἐδίωξαν
    4   τοὺς προφήτας τοὺς πρὸ   ὑμῶν.

A performancial variation shifts the initial aural formula in 1.9 and an expressed verb (implied in 1.1-1.8) signals a change in person. Likewise the organizing pattern shifts with a temporal clause and a pair of imperatives followed by a ὅτι clause. Its initial μακάριοι and the recurrence of οὐρανοῖς invokes the epithet ἡ βασιλεία τῶν οὐρανῶν in the inclusio of 1.1 and 1.8 and also connects 1.9 with the preceding eight beatitudes. Yet the altered form of the ninth beatitude effects a transition to section 2 and highlights important structural features. First, ἐστέ refocuses the initial structuring formula to the dominant addressee in the Sermon. In Greek oratory apostophe, the shift from a nominal addressee to the real addressee, is very common.[48] The section unfolds two sets of four lexies. The first set (1.9.1) begins with μακάριοί ἐστε and the second (1.9.2) with the doubled imperative, χαίρετε καὶ ἀγαλλιᾶσθε. The second person pronoun occurs in the second and fourth lexie of each set, employing first ὑμᾶς and then a threefold repetition of ὑμῶν. The first and fourth occurrences of the pronoun appear at the end of the phrase and the middle two occurrences appear in the middle of the phrase. The balanced repetition of the second person pronoun accents the shift to the second person after the μακάριοι in 1.9 and establishes a link to the initial aural formula of section 2, ὑμεῖς ἐστε.

The first set (1.9.1) is erected on a triplet of verbs paratactically arranged, ending in -ωσιν. The center verb of this triplet, διώκω, receives emphasis because it repeats the verb of the initial clause in the preceding eighth

---

45 Betz, *Essays on the Sermon on the Mount*, 4-5, draws attention to the importance of "seeing" in 1.7 and especially Matt 6:22-23 (Chapter 5).

46 ἐστέ is bolded to show that it anticipates the initial marker of section 2

47 Not only does ψευδόμενοι have a weak attestation (D and a few others), but it can be set aside on stylistic grounds because it breaks up the paratactic organization of the first set. The subordinating use of the participle is infrequent in the Sermon.

48 Kennedy, *New Testament Interpretation through Rhetorical Criticism,*, 41.

beatitude (1.8) and anticipates the verb in the center of 1.9.2. This second set also introduces the words μισθός and προφήτης which will become prominent in subsequent sections.

2. ‘Υμεῖς ἐστε (5:13-16)

2.1 ‘Υμεῖς ἐστε τὸ <u>ἅλας τῆς γῆς·</u>
    ἐὰν δὲ τὸ   <u>ἅλας</u> μωρανθῇ,
    ἐν τίνι   <u>ἁλισθήσεται;</u>
    εἰς οὐδὲν ἰσχύει ἔτι
    εἰ μὴ βληθὲν[49] ἔξω
    <u>καταπατεῖσθαι</u> <u>ὑπὸ τῶν ἀνθρώπων.</u>

2.2 ‘Υμεῖς ἐστε <u>τὸ φῶς τοῦ</u>   κόσμου.

     οὐ δύναται πόλις   κρυβῆναι
    ἐπάνω ὄρους   κειμένη·
    οὐδὲ   καίουσιν   <u>λύχνον</u>
    καὶ τιθέασιν   αὐτὸν
                  ὑπὸ τὸν μόδιον
                  ἀλλ’ ἐπὶ τὴν <u>λυχνίαν,</u>
    καὶ <u>λάμπει</u> πᾶσιν τοῖς ἐν τῇ οἰκίᾳ.
    <u>οὕτως λαμψάτω τὸ φῶς</u> ὑμῶν
    <u>ἔμπροσθεν τῶν ἀνθρώπων,</u>
    <u>ὅπως</u>   ἴδωσιν ὑμῶν τὰ καλὰ ἔργα
    καὶ   δοξάσωσιν ΤΩΝ ΠΑΤΕΡΑ ΥΜΩΝ ΤΩ ΕΝ ΤΟΙΣ ΟΥΡΑΝΟΙΣ.

The initial aural formula changes to ὑμεῖς ἐστε, echoing the ἐστέ of the initial formula in section 1.9.1. The new formula occurs twice, creating two units. Each unit repeats the key vowel sound of its title and ends with a variation of the same recurring formula, ὑπὸ τῶν ἀνθρώπων and ἔμπροσθεν τῶν ἀνθρώπων. Further, each unit contains internal organizing features based on aural clues.

2.1 employs a triple repetition of ἅλας. 2.2, like 1.1-1.4, uses alliteration based on κ from the title word κόσμου in the initial formula. Λύχνον and λυχνίαν form an inclusio that groups a series of four phrases ending with an -ον or -αν sound. A doubling of λάμπω follows the inclusio. Unit 2 ends with the epithet τὸν πατέρα ὑμῶν τὸν ἐν τοῖς οὐρανοῖς. This is the first occurrence of the epithet in the gospel of Matthew. In this transitional section of the Sermon, the epithet serves as a bridge by echoing[50] the three previous formulaic references to ὁ οὐρανός in section 1 and anticipating subsequent occurrences of the epithet ὁ πατήρ ὑμῶν in each successive section of the Sermon.[51] As in section 1, the last unit evidences greater elaboration of the structural pattern.

---

49 Other manuscripts read βλήθηναι ἔξω καί (see Nestle-Aland[26]). While the paratactic infinitives are attractive in a Sermon imitating oral style, Matthew does not favor paratactic infinitives, but main verbs as in 1.9.1.

50 Foley has referred to the use of such stereotypical epithets in oral compositions as "value added meaning," or "immanent art" in which the phrase stands for a much larger signified, a part for the whole which is conjured up by the phrase. Foley, *Immanent Art*, chapters 3-5.

51 The epithet occurs in units 4.5.3 and 4.5.5, 5.0, 5.2, 5.3, 5.4, 6.1.4.1, 6.1.4.4, 7.1, and 8.1.

3. Μὴ νομίσητε (5:17-20)

3.0.1 <u>μὴ **νομίσητε**</u> ὅτι <u>ἦλθον καταλῦσαι</u> ΤΟΝ ΝΟΜΟΝ Η ΤΟΥΣ ΠΡΟΦΗΤΑΣ·
οὐκ <u>ἦλθον καταλῦσαι</u> ἀλλὰ πληρῶσαι.

3.0.2 <u>ἀμὴν γὰρ λέγω ὑμῖν·</u>
<u>ἕως ἂν</u> <u>παρέλθη</u> ὁ οὐρανὸς καὶ ἡ γῆ,
ἰῶτα ἓν ἢ <u>μία</u> κεραία οὐ μὴ <u>παρέλθη</u> ἀπὸ ΤΟΥ ΝΟΜΟΥ,
<u>ἕως ἂν</u> πάντα γένηται.

<u>ὃς ἐὰν</u> <u>οὖν</u> <u>λύση</u> <u>μίαν</u>	<u>ὃς</u> δ' <u>ἂν</u> <u>ποιήση</u>
τῶν ἐντολῶν τούτων τῶν <u>ἐλαχίστων</u>	
<u>καὶ</u> <u>διδάξη</u>	<u>καὶ</u> <u>διδάξη</u>,
<u>οὕτως</u> τοὺς ἀνθρώπους,	
<u>ἐλάχιστος</u> <u>κληθήσεται</u>	<u>οὗτος</u> μέγας <u>κληθήσεται</u>
ΕΝ ΤΗ ΒΑΣΙΛΕΙΑ ΤΩΝ ΟΥΡΑΝΩΝ·]	ΕΝ ΤΗ ΒΑΣΙΛΕΙΑ ΤΩΝ ΟΥΡΑΝΩΝ.]

3.0.3 <u>λέγω γὰρ ὑμῖν</u> ὅτι
ἐὰν μὴ περισσεύση ὑμῶν ἡ δικαιοσύνη πλεῖον τῶν γραμματέων
καὶ Φαρισαίων,
οὐ μὴ εἰσέλθητε   ΕΙΣ ΤΗΝ ΒΑΣΙΛΕΙΑ ΤΩΝ ΟΥΡΑΝΩΝ.

Significant phonemes from section 2, ὑμεῖς, and οὐ/ἀλλά, form an aural
bridge to section 3. The leading phoneme of 3.0.1, μή, echoes ὑμεῖς, while the
paired negative and adversive connector, οὐ/ἀλλά, set up in section 2 the
antithetical relation that is repeated and elaborated in section 3. The initial
phrase is not repeated but the internal repetition of the ἀμὴν λέγω γὰρ ὑμῖν
formula delineates two lines, both of which are punctuated by the concluding
epithet ἐν (εἰς τὴν βασιλείαν) τῇ βασιλείᾳ τῶν οὐρανῶν. A morpheme of
ἔρχομαι figures prominently in each line of section 3: ἦλθον is doubled in the
introduction, παρέλθη is doubled in the next line (3.0.2), and εἰσέλθητε
expresses the goal in the closing statement. The introductory sentence begins
with a negative imperative and contains a doublet with the repetition of ἦλθον
καταλῦσαι. The phrase τὸν νόμον ἢ τοὺς προφήτας functions as an epithet.

Line 3.0.2 replicates the pattern. The formula ἀμὴν γὰρ λέγω ὑμῖν
introduces the line which itself subdivides into two parallel parts. The
introduction, like the initial formula, contains a doublet with the repeated
verb, παρέλθη. τοῦ νόμου abbreviates the epithet in 3.0.1.[52] The ἕως ἂν phrase
is followed by the same phoneme πα-, and the double negative οὐ μή before
the second παρέλθη nicely balances the phrase.

The two sublines within 3.0.2 exhibit parallel organizational patterns,
although the second one abbreviates by means of elipsis. This pattern
anticipates the constructions in the ἠκούσατε section wherein the specific case
law examples come in parallel units (4.1.4, 4.2.4, 4.3.4, 4.4.4, and 4.5.4.). Both
3.0.2a and b begin with a conditional clause and doubled verb, with διδάσκω
as second verb and κληθήσεται in both apodoses. The sublines set up a contrast,
foreshadowing the elaboration of contrasts in section 4. Both end with the
epithet ἐν τῇ βασιλείᾳ τῶν οὐρανῶν. The concluding double negative echoes
the initial μή. The οὕτως/οὗτος phonetic connection links the two sublines

---

52 Some scribes even spelled out the epithet; cf., Nestle-Aland[26].

and marks the elipsis. A reference to the number one in 3.0.2a establishes a connection to 3.0.1 which mentions one iota and one serif. 3.0.3 likewise begins with λέγω γὰρ ὑμῖν and ends with the epithet εἰς τὴν βασιλείαν τῶν οὐρανῶν. The unit's unpatterned phraseology uses terms important and typical of Matthew, δικαιοσύνη and τῶν γραμματέων καὶ Φαρισαίων.[53] The lack of patterning and the abstract character breaks the passage's rhythm, emphasizing the phrase's semantic value.

4. Ἠκούσατε *(5:21-48)*
The organizing pattern in section 4 consists of five lines.
1. Introductory formula:
    ἠκούσατε ὅτι ἐρρεθη [τοῖς ἀρχαίοις]
2. Statement of Torah:
    (prohibition in 4.1.2, 4.2.2, 4.3.2, implied negative in 4.4.2; positive in 4.5.2.)
3. Counter-statement (negative in 4.4.2; positive in 4.5.2):
    ἐγὼ δὲ λέγω ὑμῖν plus:
    a.) ὅτι πᾶς ὁ (participle),
    b.) μή with the aorist infinitive, or
    c.) present imperative
4. Specific examples from case law, set in parallel
    usually includes a conditional or relative clause and an imperative verb or series
    of verbs.
5. Conclusion
    In each unit but 4.4. the conclusion employs rhetorical devices for emphasis. 4.1.5
    uses an ἀμήν phrase and double negative. 4.2.5 substitutes an abbreviated form of
    the ἠκούσατε pattern. 4.3.5 and 4.5.5 use the verb εἰμί as a bracket with a
    phonetic emphasis in the center, ναὶ ναί and οὐ οὐ in 4.3.5 and chiasm plus
    epithet in 4.5.5. While 4.4 has no conclusion proper, the last line breaks rhythm
    (see below at 4.4).

4.1 *(5:21-26)*
    4.1.1 Introduction
    Ἠκούσατε ὅτι ἐρρέθη τοῖς ἀρχαίοις,
    4.1.2 Law
      οὐ φονεύσεις·
      ὃς δ' ἂν φονεύσῃ,   ἔνοχος ἔσται τῇ κρίσει,
    4.1.3 Counter-Statement
    4.1.3a ἐγὼ δὲ λέγω ὑμῖν ὅτι πᾶς ὁ ὀργιζόμενος τῷ ἀδελφῷ αὐτοῦ
      ἔνοχος ἔσται τῇ κρίσει·
    4.1.3b ὃς δ' ἂν εἴπῃ   τῷ ἀδελφῷ αὐτοῦ,
      ῥακά,   ἔνοχος ἔσται τῷ συνεδρίῳ·
    4.1.3c ὃς δ' ἂν εἴπῃ,
      μωρέ,   ἔνοχος ἔσται ΕΙΣ ΤΗΝ ΓΕΕΝΝΑΝ ΤΟΥ
                                  ΠΥΡΟΣ.
    Case Law
    4.1.4a ἐὰν οὖν προσφέρῃς   τὸ δῶρόν σου ἐπὶ τὸ θυσιαστήριον

---

53 See Gundry, *Matthew*, 81-82 and Ulrich Luz, *Matthew 1-7: A Commentary, Evangelisch-Katholischer Kommentar zum Neuen Testament* (Minneapolis: Augsburg, 1989) 56-57.

κἀκεῖ μνησθῆς ὅτι   ὁ ἀδελφός σου ἔχει τι κατὰ σοῦ,
ἄφες ἐκεῖ   τὸ δῶρόν σου ἔμπροσθεν τοῦ
                      θυσιαστηρίου
καὶ ὕπαγε πρῶτον διαλλάγηθι τῷ ἀδελφῷ σου,
καὶ τότε ἐλθὼν πρόσφερε   τὸ δῶρόν σου.
4.1.4b ἴσθι εὐνοῶν   τῷ ἀντιδίκῳ σου ταχὺ,
    ἕως ὅτου εἶ μετ' αὐτοῦ ἐν τῇ ὁδῷ,
    μήποτέ σε παραδῷ   ὁ ἀντίδικος τῷ κριτῇ
    καὶ ὁ κριτῆς[54] τῷ ὑπηρέτῃ
    καὶ εἰς φυλακὴν βληθήσῃ·
4.1.5 Conclusion
    ἀμὴν λέγω σοι,
    οὐ μὴ ἐξέλθῃς ἐκεῖθεν,
    ἕως ἂν ἀποδῷς τὸν ἔσχατον κοδράντην.

The Sermon's fourth section establishes an elaborate system of parallels labelled with the initial structuring formula Ἠκούσατε ὅτι ἐρρέθη τοῖς ἀρχαίοις. The first unit exhibits the full pattern. In 4.1.1 the introductory aural formula occurs in its complete form. In 4.1.2 the verb φονεύω is doubled[55] and the marker for a relative clause, ὃς δ' ἄν, and the phrase ἔνοχος ἔσται establish a link with the counter statement. The counter-statement section labelled by the formula ἐγὼ δὲ λέγω ὑμῖν ὅτι πᾶς ὁ and introduces the phrase τῷ ἀδελφῷ αὐτου which helps unify this unit.

Lines b and c follow a formulaic pattern: the phrase ὃς δ' ἂν εἴπῃ + τῷ ἀδελφῷ αὐτου as an indirect object (implied in the third elaboration) + a pejorative label in the vocative case + ἔνοχος ἔσται + an indirect object or prepositional phrase. 4.1.3.c ends with an epithet, εἰς τὴν γέενναν τοῦ πυρός, in a construction similar to that of the internal parallel in 3.1.1. Like the insults, the three dative phrases are set in escalating order, building on the ἔνοχος ἔσται τῇ κρίσει which concludes 4.1.2 and is repeated in 4.1.3.a. Furthermore, συνεδρίῳ and γέενναν τοῦ πυρός form a correlative binary in reverse order with the epithet ὁ οὐρανὸς καί ἡ γῆ (3.0.2).

The case law example (4.1.4.a) begins with a third class condition marked by ἐὰν οὖν. The example exhibits a series of imperatives, with three imperative verbs in the apodosis (ἄφες, ὕπαγε, πρόσφερε). A threefold repetition of τὸ δῶρόν σου (A) is interspersed with a triple reference to τὸ θυσιαστήριον (B) and ὁ ἀδελφός σου/τῷ ἀδελφῷ σου (C). This sets up the parallel pattern ABC/ABC/A, creating the expectation that B and C will follow. B (τὸ θυσιαστήριον) does follow in elipsis and ἀντιδίκος, the antithesis of ἀδελφός, begins the next subline 4.1.4.b. The verb ἔχει phonetically

---

[54] A number of texts fill in the elipsis with σε παραδῷ. Not only do the earliest witnesses not support this (Nestle-Aland[26]), but we have seen that Matthew frequently employs elipsis.

[55] Lexie 2 in 4.1.2 is unattested in the Hebrew Bible or Jewish literature. Thus it was deliberately doubled probably for phonetic reasons. Repetition allows a hearer to pick up on the theme.

reinforces the repetition of κἀκεῖ/ἐκεῖ. Πρῶτον occurs with the imperative here, the first of three such uses of πρῶτον in the Sermon.[56] The second subline (4.1.4b) begins with the imperative ἴσθι and the double reference to the accuser (τῷ ἀντιδίκῳ σοῦ, ὁ ἀντίδικος). In 4.1.4.a the protasis was elaborated into two lines before the first imperative. In 4.1.4.b the imperative comes first and the action (apodosis) is elaborated. Furthermore, the threefold motion from judge to prison parallels the threefold motion of 4.1.3, the counter-statement.

κριτής	κρίσει
ὑπηρέτης	συνεδρίος
φυλακής	γέενναν τοῦ πυρός

This last parallel evokes the Matthean epithet about being cast into outer darkness where there will be weeping and gnashing of teeth.[57] A terminal -η sound unifies the last series of phrases.

The unit's conclusion begins with the formula ἀμὴν λέγω σοι and employs the definitive form of negation οὐ μή for the future.[58] While on the surface 4.1.5 concludes the subunit 4.1.4.b, the double negative and ἔσχατον confirm the parallel of the series κριτής to φυλακής with κρίσει to γέενναν. Thus there is a semantic shift from prison to Gehenna. The concluding section employs ἐκεῖθεν, echoing the repetition of ἐκει earlier in the example.

4.2 (5:27-32)

4.2.1 **Ἠκούσατε ὅτι ἐρρέθη,**

4.2.2 οὐ <u>μοιχεύσεις</u>.

4.2.3 <u>ἐγὼ δὲ λέγω ὑμῖν</u> ὅτι πᾶς ὁ βλέπων γυναῖκα
πρὸς τὸ ἐπιθυμῆσαι <u>αὐτὴν</u>
ἤδη <u>ἐμοίχευσεν</u>   <u>αὐτὴν</u> ἐν τῇ καρδίᾳ αὐτοῦ.

4.2.4[59]

εἰ δὲ <u>ὁ ὀφθαλμός</u> σου ὁ δεξιὸς	καὶ εἰ ἡ δεξιά σου <u>χεὶρ</u>
σκανδαλίζει σε,	σκανδαλίζει σε,
<u>ἔξελε αὐτὸν</u>	<u>ἔκκοψον αὐτὴν</u>
καὶ βάλε ἀπὸ σοῦ·	καὶ βάλε ἀπὸ σοῦ·
συμφέρει γάρ σοι ἵνα ἀπόληται ἓν	συμφέρει γάρ σοι ἵνα ἀπόληται ἓν
τῶν μελῶν σου	τῶν μελῶν σου
καὶ μὴ ὅλον τὸ σῶμά σου	καὶ μὴ ὅλον τὸ σῶμά σου
<u>βληθῇ</u> ΕΙΣ ΓΕΕΝΝΑΝ.	ΕΙΣ ΓΕΕΝΝΑΝ <u>ἀπέλθη</u>.

4.2.5.1 **Ἐρρέθη** δέ,

4.2.5.2 Ὃς ἂν   <u>ἀπολύσῃ τὴν γυναῖκα αὐτοῦ,</u>
δότω αὐτῇ ἀποστάσιον.

---

56 5:24. The others are 6:33 and 7:5.

57 Matt 8:12; 22:13; 25:30. See also the last lexie in 4.2.4 conjures up the whole phrase exactly as Foley describes the functioning of an epithet.

58 F. Blass, A. Debrunner, and Robert Funk, *A Greek Grammar of the New Testament and Other Early Christian Literature*, (Chicago: University of Chicago Press, 1961) 365. This form of negation is emphatic and "virtually limited to quotations from the LXX and sayings of Jesus" in the New Testament.

59 In this parallel arrangement words that are *not* paralleled are underlined.

4.2.5.3 ἐγὼ δὲ λέγω ὑμῖν ὅτι πᾶς ὁ <u>ἀπολύων τὴν γυναῖκα αὐτοῦ</u>
παρεκτὸς λόγου πορνείας
ποιεῖ αὐτὴν μοιχευθῆναι,

4.2.5.4 καὶ ὃς ἐὰν <u>ἀπολελυμένην γαμήσῃ</u>[60]
μοιχᾶται.

The introduction to unit 4.2 abbreviates the initial formula, eliminating the indirect object. The statement of the law is similarly brief, quoting the LXX with no elaboration. The third line, the counter-statement, repeats the formula of 4.1, ἐγὼ δὲ λέγω ὑμῖν ὅτι πᾶς ὁ, and the verb μοιχεύω introduced in the legal prohibition. According to the established pattern, the elaboration of case law (4.2.4) presents two parallel examples, the first dealing with the right eye and the second with the right hand. The parallel is nearly perfect with few variations. The two examples use different verbs in the apodosis and the first and last lexies of the two examples show chiastic arrangements. In the first lexie of each example, the noun and adjective δεχιός are reversed, while in the last lines the same is true of the verb and the prepositional phrase εἰς γέενναν. The chiastic arrangement provides closure for the complex parallels of the case law line.

In place of a conclusion, this unit uses a block of material that duplicates in abbreviated form elements 1-4 of the ἠκούσατε section's organizational pattern. The introductory aural formula is reduced to ἐρρέθη δέ. A conditional statement introduces the verb ἀπολύω and delivers the statement of law in the apodosis. The formula for the counter-statement remains intact and repeats both the phrase ἀπολύων τὴν γυναῖκα αὐτου from the statement of law and the verb μοιχεύω from the law and counter-statement of 4.2.2 and 4.2.3. This verb as well as ἀπολύω are repeated in the case law example which is reduced to a relative clause joined to the previous main clause by the connective καί.

Several structural features argue for the subordination of 4.2.5 to the main unit 4.2: (1) The transitional character of the connective particle δέ;[61] (2) the abbreviation of the form of the initial aural formula and other lines; (3) the doubled verb μοιχεύω which, when matched with its twofold repetition at the beginning of 4.2.1.2 and .3, forms an inclusio that delineates the beginning and end of the unit; and (4) the lack of a conclusion for 4.2.[62]

4.3 (5:33-37)

4.3.1 Πάλιν ἠκούσατε ὅτι ἐρρέθη τοῖς ἀρχαίοις,
4.3.2 οὐκ ἐπιορκήσεις, ἀποδώσεις δὲ τῷ κυρίῳ τοὺς ὅρκους σου.

---

[60] B reads καὶ ὁ ἀπολελυμένην γαμήσας thus making the phrase parallel to the preceeding ὁ ἀπολύων. But the majority reading fits the pattern of the case law example which begins a new line and does not conclude the counter-statement.

[61] Until unit 5.1, no unit begins with a connective. See below for 5.1.

[62] Gundry, *Matthew*, 89, agrees this material is subordinate to 5:27-30, serving as an "appendix." On the other hand, Davies, *Matthew*, 504, views it as an independent unit, supplying the third element in a triad with the previous ἠκούσατε units and followed by another triad (4.3, 4.4, and 4.5). See the footnote on πάλιν in 4.3, below. Lacking criteria for the delineation of units, many consider ἐρρέθη δέ as a separate antithesis while stressing its supplementary, subordinate character. So Francis W. Beare, *The Gospel According to Matthew* (San Francisco: Harper & Row, 1981) 153; and Luz, *Matthew 1-7*, 299.

4.3.3   ἐγὼ δὲ λέγω ὑμῖν μὴ ὀμόσαι ὅλως·

4.3.4   μήτε ἐν τῷ οὐρανῷ,   ὅτι θρόνος   ἐστὶν τοῦ θεοῦ,
         μήτε ἐν τῇ γῇ,   ὅτι ὑποπόδιόν   ἐστιν τῶν ποδῶν
                                                     αὐτοῦ,
         μήτε εἰς Ἱεροσόλυμα,   ὅτι πόλις   ἐστὶν τοῦ μεγάλου
                                                     βασιλέως,
         μήτε ἐν τῇ κεφαλῇ σου ὀμόσῃς, ὅτι οὐ δύνασαι μίαν τρίχα
                                        λευκὴν ποιῆσαι ἢ μέλαιναν.

4.3.5   ἔστω⁶³ δὲ ὁ λόγος ὑμῶν   ναὶ ναί,

                                   οὖ οὔ·
         τὸ δὲ περισσὸν τούτων ἐκ τοῦ πονηροῦ ἐστιν.

The third unit repeats the initial aural formula's full form, introduced by πάλιν.⁶⁴ The statement of the law includes two verbs in the future, consistent with the expected pattern. The lack of attestation for the quote reinforces its composition to fit the form. The formulaic introduction to the counter-statement omits ὅτι πᾶς and the participle, which does not occur again in section 4. Ὅλως replaces πᾶς. Both this counter-statement and the next employ μή and the infinitive. Four case law examples follow in parallel, organized by the repetition of μήτε ἐν ... ὅτι, and, in all but the the last example, ἐστίν. Forms of the verb εἰμί bracket the subunit's conclusion (4.3.5), with the double ναί/οὖ in the center. In the first three case law examples the verbs in the claim clauses are implied, while expressed (ὀμόσῃς) in the final example. This leads to a shift from impersonal (ὅτι + noun + ἐστίν + genitive) to implied personal. The final ὅτι clause is nicely balanced with the final infinitive ποιῆσαι bracketed by λευκήν and ἢ μέλαιναν, forming a chiasm in the final two lexies of the line. The reference to white and black is part of the Sermon's concreteness, like δεξιός, ἀδελφός, and ἀντίδικος in the previous case law examples.

4.4 (5:38-42)

4.4.1   Ἠκούσατε ὅτι ἐρρέθη,

4.4.2   ὀφθαλμὸν   ἀντὶ ὀφθαλμοῦ
         καὶ ὀδόντα   ἀντὶ ὀδόντος.

4.4.3   ἐγὼ δὲ λέγω ὑμῖν μὴ ἀντιστῆναι τῷ πονηρῷ·

4.4.4 a ἀλλ᾽ ὅστις σε ῥαπίζει εἰς τὴν δεξιὰν σιαγόνα [σου],
         στρέψον αὐτῷ καὶ τὴν ἄλλην·

      b καὶ τῷ θέλοντί σοι κριθῆναι καὶ τὸν χιτῶνά σου λαβεῖν,
         ἄφες αὐτῷ καὶ τὸ ἱμάτιον·

      a καὶ ὅστις σε ἀγγαρεύσει μίλιον ἕν,
         ὕπαγε μετ᾽ αὐτοῦ δύο.

---

⁶³ B has ἔσται, an interesting reading which more closely parallels the final ἐστίν and parallels 4.5.5.

⁶⁴ Davies, *Matthew*, 504 interprets the πάλιν variation as signal of the beginning of a second set of triads in the ἠκούσατε section (triad 1, 5:21-32; triad 2, 5:33-48). Counting the ἐρρέθη δέ section (4.2.5.1) as an independent unit, he observes that the first triad of each set begins with the full form of the initial formula and the first triad uses ὅτι in each instance of the counter-statement.

c τῷ αἰτοῦντί σε
    δός,
b <u>καὶ τὸν θέλοντα ἀπὸ σοῦ</u> δανίσασθαι
    μὴ ἀπο<u>στραφῇς</u>

The fourth unit follows the established pattern except that it contains no element five, conclusion. The initial aural formula occurs in abbreviated form. The second line, the law, is set off in parallel phrases around the preposition ἀντί. Unlike other statements of law there is no verb or negative, although the ἀντί implies a negative.

The counterstatement (4.4.3), repeats the same variation of the formula as in 4.3.3, ἐγὼ δὲ λέγω ὑμῖν plus a negative and aorist infinitive. The verbal prefix ἀντι- picks up on its doubled use in 4.4.2, playing on a semantic shift in the preposition's meaning. The substantive adjective πονηρός echoes the previous unit's conclusion (4.3.5), creating an ambiguous referent.[65]

The case law portion of the fourth unit follows the expected parallel pattern. The adversative conjunction ἀλλά introduces the line, indicating a contrast with the law. The organizing pattern is: conjunction + ὅστις σε + specific action + imperative. In the second, fourth, and fifth examples a participle phrase substitutes for ὅστις, with 2 and 5 based on verbs of wishing and 2 and 4 on dative participles. This creates a strong interlocking patern, ABACB. Καί provides a regular rhythmic pattern. The series of clauses show an expansion and then a contraction: the first clause establishes the pattern, the second expands it with a double infinitive bracketing the noun, and the fourth contracts to the essential elements of the pattern, the participle and imperative without modifiers. Since this is the C element in the pattern, it is appropriate that it is the shortest thus drawing attention to itself. The simple, emphatic δός stands out as the positive of μὴ ἀντιστῆναι. The final subjunctive, the only negative, echoes μὴ ἀντιστῆναι in the counter-statement (4.4.3). While not in the form of a conclusion, the break in pattern, the subjunctive of prohibition instead of an imperative verb, and the double reference to the counter-statement, may indicate that these last two lexies function as a conclusion.

4.5 (5:43-48)
4.5.1 Ἠκούσατε ὅτι ἐρρέθη,
4.5.2   <u>ἀγαπήσεις</u> τὸν πλησίον σου
    καὶ <u>μισήσεις</u> τὸν <u>ἐχθρόν</u> σου.
4.5.3   <u>ἐγὼ δὲ λέγω ὑμῖν,</u>
    <u>ἀγαπᾶτε</u> τοὺς <u>ἐχθροὺς</u> ὑμῶν
    καὶ προσεύχεσθε ὑπὲρ τῶν διωκόντων ὑμᾶς,
    ὅπως γένησθε υἱοὶ ΤΟΥ ΠΑΤΡΟΣ ΥΜΩΝ ΤΟΥ ΕΝ ΟΥΡΑΝΟΙΣ,
      ὅτι τὸν ἥλιον αὐτοῦ ἀνατέλλει ἐπὶ πονηροὺς καὶ ἀγαθοὺς
      καὶ   βρέχει   ἐπὶ δικαίους καὶ ἀδίκους.
4.5.4

---

[65] The exact signified is difficult to specify: the evil one? the evil person? the evil? The case law examples would suggest "evil person," while the conclusion of the previous unit suggest "the evil one."

ἐὰν γὰρ ἀγαπήσητε   καὶ ἐὰν ἀσπάσησθε
 τοὺς ἀγαπῶντας ὑμᾶς,   τοὺς ἀδελφοὺς ὑμῶν μόνον,
τίνα μισθὸν ἔχετε;   τί περισσὸν ποιεῖτε;
οὐχὶ καὶ οἱ τελῶναι   οὐχὶ καὶ οἱ ἐθνικοὶ[66]
τὸ αὐτὸ ποιοῦσιν;   τὸ αὐτὸ ποιοῦσιν;
4.5.5 Ἔσεσθε οὖν ὑμεῖς   τέλειοι
  ὡς Ο ΠΑΤΗΡ ΥΜΩΝ Ο ΟΥΡΑΝΙΟΣ τέλειός ἐστιν.

The fifth unit again follows the formal pattern. It employs an abbreviated form of the initial aural formula, ἠκούσατε ὅτι ἐρρέθη. Only here is the statement of the law expressed in a positive. The law is again expressed in a doublet and the second element is unattested.[67]

The counter-statement occurs in expanded form. The epithet τοῦ πατρὸς ὑμῶν τοῦ ἐν οὐρανοῖς is elaborated into a ὅτι compound clause which includes a chiasm of opposing terms, πονηρούς/ἀγαθούς and δικαίους/ἀδίκους. The case law line again sets specific examples in parallel, first οἱ τελῶναι and then οἱ ἐθνικοί as negative examples. The first example emphasizes the verb ἀγαπάω by doubling the sound, expressing it first as an aorist imperative and then an aorist participle as direct object. The direct object of the second example (τοὺς ἀδελφούς) echoes back to the first unit of this section where ἀδελφός was a prominent organizing sound. There ἀντίδικος opposed it, here οἱ ἐχθροί. The parallel pattern of the two examples is obvious: ἐάν + connective + aorist subjunctive + direct object + interrogative phrase + negative intensive + noun + τὸ αὐτὸ ποιοῦσιν.

The conclusion (4.5.5) forms a chiasm which, like 4.3.5, is bracketed by morphemes of εἰμί. It repeats the adjective τέλειος, and places the epithet ὁ πατὴρ ὑμῶν ὁ οὐράνιος in the prominent center position. The epithet forms an inclusio with its previous occurrence in the expanded counter-statement 4.5.3. The inclusio and chaism emphasize the limit (τέλειος) to which the father and ὑμεῖς should go.[68]

5. Ὅταν ... μή (6:1-18)
5.0 (6:1)
5.0 Προσέχετε[69] τὴν δικαιοσύνην ὑμῶν
  μὴ ποιεῖν   ἔμπροσθεν τῶν ἀνθρώπων

---

[66] Later manuscripts read τελῶναι thus increasing the parallel. Parallels are not expected to be perfect and the difference points to the semantic or ideological level.

[67] Given the strong doublet form of the law statement, it seems likely that the second member is the creation of the author on the basis of the Q text. The search for an extra gospel parallel is in vain.

[68] Margaret E. Dean, "Reading Matthew's Treasure Map: Territoriality in Matthew's Five Sermons" (M.Div. thesis, Phillips Graduate Seminary, 1993), 54-56, proposes the translation of 5:48, "You must be one [who goes to] the limit, as your heavenly father is [one who goes to] the limit," arguing that τέλειος typically denotes the attainment of an end or a termination. In the Sermon it refers to the law's extension to cover a broader category of circumstance.

[69] The textual evidence for δέ probably leans towards excluding it (cf., Nestle-Aland[26]). Supporting this exclusion is that the beginnings of units do not normally employ connectives in the Sermon.

πρὸς τὸ θεαθῆναι αὐτοῖς·
εἰ δὲ μή γε, μισθὸν οὐκ ἔχετε
παρὰ ΤΩ ΠΑΤΡΙ ΥΜΩΝ ΤΩ ΕΝ ΤΟΙΣ ΟΥΡΑΝΟΙΣ.

Like the previous section, the fifth section of the Sermon organizes a large body of material with a repeating phonetic/syntactical pattern. (See Appendix 2 for a schematic display of parallel organization in section 5.) Unlike the ἠκούσατε section, however, the fifth section opens with an introductory statement which stands alone as a thematic reprise.[70] It begins with προσέχετε τὴν δικαιοσύνην ὑμῶν and employs several of the Sermon's primary words and themes: δικαικοσύνη, μισθός, being seen, acting in public, and Matthew's full epithet for God, πάτερ ἡμῶν ὁ ἐν τοῖς οὐρανοῖς. The introductory section also establishes several organizing elements that recur in the subsequent subsections: a prohibitive statement, a result clause pertaining to public behavior, and ὁ μισθός. 5.0 has few internal phonetic markers and a high concentration of abstract terms. As such it stands out and would break a reciter's and hearer's rhythm, calling attention to itself.

Four units with an initial aural formula begin with ὅταν. Tannehill observes this "repetitive pattern [which] can release words from their literal limits" and amplify their meaning.[71] It also makes it possible to hear. One of these units, the unit containing the πάτερ ἡμῶν ὁ ἐν τοῖς οὐρανοῖς, abbreviates, elaborates, and deviates from the organizing pattern while retaining several of the repetitive formal features. The phonetic/syntactical pattern includes the following elements.

1. A temporal clause, usually with ὅταν but once with a participle (5.3.1), which states the unit's topic phonetically (almsgiving 5.1, prayer 5.2, fasting 5.3).
2. A negative imperative clause or a subjunctive of prohibition.
3. A negative comparison with οἱ ὑποκριταί.
4. A causal clause with with a doublet, frequently introduced by ὅτι or γάρ.
5. A purpose clause introduced by ὅπως which refers to public activity.
6. A pronouncement introduced by the formula ἀμὴν λέγω ὑμῖν which refers to ὁ μισθός.
7. A temporal clause with συ, the connective δέ, and a present participle or a subjunctive verb (as in 5.2). The clause contains a doublet and reiterates the unit's topic.
8. A purpose clause [ὅπως] making reference usually to the father ἐν τῷ κρυπτῷ (κρυφαίῳ).
9. A formulaic ending that functions as a refrain, connected to the preceding material with καί and concluding ὁ πατήρ σου ὁ βλέπων ἐν τῷ κρυπτῷ [κρυφαίῳ] ἀποδώσει σοι.[72]

5.1 (6:2-4)

---

[70] Kennedy, *New Testament Interpretation Through Rhetorical Criticism*, 57, shows this unit functions rhetorically as a retatement of the theme, our section 3.

[71] Tannehill, *The Sword of His Mouth*, 79-85.

[72] Later manuscripts including textus receptus show at the end of this phrase in all three of its occurences ἐν τῷ φανερῷ to balance ἐν τῷ κρυπτῷ.

5.1.1 Ὅταν οὖν ποιῇς ἐλεημοσύνην,
5.1.2 μὴ σαλπίσῃς ἔμπροσθέν σου,
5.1.3 ὥσπερ οἱ ὑποκριταὶ ποιοῦσιν
ἐν ταῖς συναγωγαῖς
καὶ ἐν ταῖς ῥύμαις,
5.1.5 ὅπως δοξασθῶσιν ὑπὸ τῶν ἀνθρώπων·
5.1.6 ἀμὴν λέγω ὑμῖν, ἀπέχουσιν τὸν μισθὸν αὐτῶν.
5.1.7 σοῦ δὲ ποιοῦντος ἐλεημοσύνην μὴ γνώτω ἡ ἀριστερά σου
τί ποιεῖ ἡ δεξιά σου,
5.1.8. ὅπως ᾖ σου ἡ ἐλεημοσύνη ἐν τῷ κρυπτῷ·
5.1.9 καὶ ὁ πατήρ σου ὁ βλέπων ἐν τῷ κρυπτῷ ἀποδώσει σοι.

There is some doubt whether 5.1-5.4 are four units or should be seen as four sections of the single unit 5.0. The opening temporal clause is not as strong an initial aural formula as in other units (although it occurs in every unit) and these are the only units in which a connective occurs in the first lexie. On the basis of our evidence a case could be made for four sequential units or 4 subordinate units. To the ear the difference is not critical and this may well represent a case of the Sermon's mixed nature. These are meant to sound like paratactic units in sequence but semantically they are subordinated to the introduction 5.0.

The first unit (5.1) follows the pattern closely. Its introductory temporal clause states its topic, almsgiving, which is repeated in the second temporal clause (5.1.7) following the ἀμήν formula (5.1.6). The unit lacks the causal clause (5.1.4) following the negative imperative but the comparative clause (5.1.3) contains a doublet referring to two locations, συναγωγαῖς and ῥύμαις. The second temporal clause (5.1.7) following the ἀμήν formula employs a second doublet based on the left and right hands. The purpose clause (5.1.8) and conclusion (5.1.9) conform to the formal pattern. The constantly repeated phrases so characteristic of section 5 (see Appendix 2) and the two doublets give this unit a strong rhythmic pattern.

5.2 (6:5-6)
5.2.1 Καὶ ὅταν προσεύχησθε,
5.2.2 οὐκ ἔσεσθε
5.2.3 ὡς οἱ ὑποκριταί,
5.2.4 ὅτι φιλοῦσιν ἐν ταῖς συναγωγαῖς
καὶ ἐν ταῖς γωνίαις τῶν πλατειῶν
ἑστῶτες προσεύχεσθαι,
5.2.5 ὅπως φανῶσιν τοῖς ἀνθρώποις·
5.2.6 ἀμὴν λέγω ὑμῖν, ἀπέχουσιν τὸν μισθὸν αὐτῶν.
5.2.7 σὺ δὲ ὅταν προσεύχῃ
εἴσελθε εἰς τὸ ταμεῖόν σου
καὶ κλείσας τὴν θύραν σου
5.2.8 πρόσευξαι τῷ πατρί σου τῷ ἐν τῷ κρυπτῷ·
5.2.9 καὶ ὁ πατήρ σου ὁ βλέπων ἐν τῷ κρυπτῷ ἀποδώσει σοι.

The second unit concerning prayer follows the formal pattern exactly, except that the second purpose clause (5.2.8) preceding the formulaic ending (5.2.9) employs the aorist infinitive πρόσευξαι, a performancial variation of ὅπως. Its doublets refer to contrasting locations. The first, συναγωγαῖς and γωνίαις τῶν πλατειῶν, echoes the first doublet in 5.1.3. The second refers to the contrasting location, εἰς τὸ ταμεῖόν σου καὶ κλείσας τὴν θύραν σου, establishing a strong private vs. public contrast with the first doublet. The reference to praying occurs four times, versus three for fasting, foreshadowing the subject's elaboration in the next unit.

5.3 *(6:7-15)*
5.3.1   **Προσευχόμενοι** δὲ
5.3.2.1   μὴ βατταλογήσητε
5.3.3.1   ὥσπερ οἱ ἐθνικοί,
5.3.4.1   δοκοῦσιν <u>γὰρ</u> ὅτι ἐν τῇ πολυλογίᾳ αὐτῶν εἰσακουσθήσονται.
5.3.2.2   μὴ <u>οὖν</u>
5.3.3.2   <u>ὁμοιωθῆτε</u> αὐτοῖς·
5.3.4.2   οἶδεν <u>γὰρ</u>   Ὁ <u>ΠΑΤΗΡ...ΥΜΩΝ</u> ὧν χρείαν ἔχετε πρὸ τοῦ ὑμᾶς
                                                                αἰτῆσαι αὐτόν.

5.3.7   <u>Οὕτως</u> οὖν <u>προσεύχεσθε</u> ὑμεῖς·
   a   <u>ΠΑΤΕΡ..ΗΜΩΝ</u> Ο ΕΝ ΤΟΙΣ ΟΥΡΑΝΟΙΣ,
   ἁγιασθήτω   τὸ ὄνομά <u>σου·</u>
   ἐλθέτω   ἡ βασιλεία <u>σου·</u>
   γενηθήτω   τὸ θέλημά <u>σου,</u>
   ὡς ἐν οὐρανῷ καὶ ἐπὶ γῆς·
   b   τὸν ἄρτον   <u>ἡμῶν</u>   τὸν ἐπιούσιον δὸς <u>ἡμῖν</u> σήμερον·
   καὶ **ἄφες**   <u>ἡμῖν</u>   τὰ ὀφειλήματα <u>ἡμῶν,</u>
   ὡς καὶ   <u>ἡμεῖς</u> **ἀφήκαμεν** τοῖς ὀφειλέταις <u>ἡμῶν·</u>
   καὶ μὴ εἰσενέγκῃς <u>ἡμᾶς</u> εἰς πειρασμόν,
   ἀλλὰ   ῥῦσαι <u>ἡμᾶς</u> ἀπὸ τοῦ πονηροῦ.
5.3.8.1   Ἐὰν γὰρ **ἀφῆτε** <u>τοῖς ἀνθρώποις</u> <u>τὰ παραπτώματα αὐτῶν,</u>
5.3.9.1   **ἀφήσει** καὶ ὑμῖν
         Ο ΠΑΤΗΡ ΥΜΩΝ Ο ΟΥΡΑΝΙΟΣ]·
5.3.8.2   <u>ἐὰν</u> δὲ μὴ **ἀφῆτε** <u>τοῖς ἀνθρώποις,</u>
5.3.9.2   οὐδὲ   Ο ΠΑΤΗΡ ΥΜΩΝ   **ἀφήσει**
                                        <u>τὰ παραπτώματα ὑμῶν.</u>]

Two units on prayer (5.2, 5.3), the length and variation of the second unit, and its central placement in this section indicate its importance. Unit 5.3 presents an elaborate performancial variation of the organizing pattern.[73]

The unit opens with a present participle, a performancial variation of the regular initial aural marker for section 5, ὅταν. The participle expresses the unit's topic, prayer, and the morpheme is repeated after οὕτως οὖν in 5.3.7 where the organization of the unit shifts for the prayer πάτερ ὑμων. The repetition of the προσευχ- morpheme echoes its fourfold repetition in the

---

[73] Others have noticed the parallel pattern of 5.1, 5.2, and 5.4 and have observed many of its organizing elements in 5.3 but analyses of the pattern typically rest primarily on conceptual, thematic grounds. See, for example, Davies, *Matthew*, 572-73, 592-3, and Betz, *Essays on the Sermon on the Mount*, 56-64. Luz, *Matthew 1-7*, 369, observes some phonetic/syntactical differences between the "you" and "we" petitions but does not indicate the effect or importance of these features.

previous unit. The negative imperative (5.3.2.1 and .2), the comparative clause (5.3.3.1 and .2), and the causal clause (5.3.4.1 and .2) are doubled in this unit and οἱ ἐθνικοί rather than οἱ ὑποκριταί appears as the negative nominal in the comparative clauses (5.3.3.1 and .2). This substitution echoes the parallel in 4.5.4 of οἱ τελῶναι / οἱ ἐθνικοί and contributes to the gospel's narrative objective by building up a system of synonyms for οἱ ἐθνικοί.[74]

The doubling of the negative comparison and its accompanying elements is characteristic of the performancial variation in the first part of this unit. The second μή and comparison lines abbreviate and combine the formula into a verb of comparison (ὁμοιωθῆτε) and pronoun (αὐτοῖς). Instead of the normal doublet in the causal clause (line 4, cf. 5.2.4) there are two lines in two complete doublets of lines 5.3.2.1., .3.1, and .4.1 and 5.3.2.2, .3.2, and .4.2. The doubling signals an upcoming shift which begins with the abbreviated epithet ὁ πατήρ ὑμῶν. This abbreviated epithet is repeated in the unit's last line (5.3.9.2), forming an inclusio. Both the full epithet, πάτερ ἡμῶν ὁ ἐν τοῖς οὐρανοῖς, and a slightly abbreviated version, occur twice inside the inclusio and reinforce it. The two interior epithets are chiastically arranged and bracket the Lord's prayer.

The prayer (5.3.7) functions as a temporal clause (line 7) in the organizing pattern of this unit with οὖν and the present tense providing the temporal sense. The prayer itself reiterates the unit's theme and is also divided into two parts, thus fulfilling all the conditions of line 7. The two parts (α and β) of the Lord's prayer are organized by triplets. The repetition of the morpheme οὐραν- in the first and last lexies of the α part encloses a triplet of imperative verbs + direct object + σου. The β group triplet consists of three clauses joined by καί. The first person plural pronoun punctuates and unifies the prayer's second triplet, creating a distinct difference in voice and person between the two parts. Likewise the first triad is short and staccato in sound; the second longer and more fluid.

As we have arranged it, the second triplet (group β) consists of five lexies. The first lexie stands alone and the remaining four lexies are arranged in two doublets. In the first three lexies a form of ἡμεῖς punctuates the middle and end of each lexie. The first lexie forms a chaism with the second: direct object + ἡμῶν + imperative + ἡμῖν // imperative + ἡμῖν + direct object + ἡμῶν. The second lexie introduces the verb ἀφίημι which repeats in the third lexie in a prominent central position. In lexies 4 and 5, the first person plural pronoun serves as the direct object and precedes a prepositional phrase that completes the parallel between the two lexies. This careful organization by sound and rhythm of the prayer's two parts give each part a distinctive sound and explains it mnemonic ease.[75]

---

[74] By identifying οἱ ὑποκριταί and οἱ ἐθνκικοί the author is preparing for the bridge that leads to the command to preach the gospel to τὰ ἔθνη.

[75] Outlines of 6:7-15 offered by Davies, *Matthew*, 592, and Betz, *Essays on the Sermon on the Mount*, 56-64 do not account for the significance they ascribe to the Lord's prayer. Gundry, *Matthew*, 104, remarks on the prayer's "liturgical style" but does not furnish a basis for so classifying the prayer. Our analysis analyzes empirically the prayer's distinctive sound and advances phonetic/syntactical evidence for its semantic importance.

The unit ends with a pair of third class conditions in which ἀφίημι serves as the only verb. The protasis of both conditions (5.3.8.1 and .2) employs an expected element of line 5, the reference to ἄνθρωποι, while the apodosis implies the μισθός (here forgiveness) of line 6. A specific line 5 is missing in this unit. The doubling of the final lines serves to round out the organization of the unit and the doublet patterning also returns to the organizing pattern of the unit's beginning (5.3.2.1-.4.2). The conditions function as purpose clauses (line 8)[76] and the apodoses as conclusions (line 9). The doublet combines parallelism, chiasm, and inclusio. The protasis in both conditions includes ἐάν + a postpositive particle + ἀφῆτε τοῖς ἀνθρώποις, while the apodosis includes a reference to ὁ πατὴρ ὑμῶν (A) and the verb ἀφήσει (B). The word order of the two apodoses forms a chiasm: BA/AB. The phrase τὰ παραπτώματα αὐτῶν at the end of the protasis of the first condition and at the end of the apodosis of the second condition marks an inclusio that delineates the lines 5.3.8.1-5.3.9.2.[77]

5.4 (6:16-18)
5.4.1   Ὅταν δὲ νηστεύητε,
5.4.2   μὴ γίνεσθε
5.4.3   ὡς οἱ ὑποκριταὶ σκυθρωποί,
5.4.4   ἀφανίζουσιν γὰρ τὰ πρόσωπα αὐτῶν
5.4.5   ὅπως φανῶσιν τοῖς ἀνθρώποις νηστεύοντες·
5.4.6   ἀμὴν λέγω ὑμῖν, ἀπέχουσιν τὸν μισθὸν αὐτῶν.
5.4.7   σὺ δὲ νηστεύων ἄλειψαί σου τὴν κεφαλὴν
             καὶ τὸ πρόσωπόν σου νίψαι,
5.4.8   ὅπως μὴ φανῇς τοῖς ἀνθρώποις νηστεύων
             ἀλλὰ τῷ πατρί σου   τῷ ἐν τῷ κρυφαίῳ·
5.4.9   καὶ ὁ πατήρ σου ὁ βλέπων ἐν τῷ κρυφαίῳ ἀποδώσει σοι.

Unit 5.4 presents in skeletal form the previously established phonetic/syntactical pattern for section 5. There is no doublet in 5.4.4 but 5.4.8 is doubled. The doublet referring to the father's seeing in secret employs κρυφαίῳ rather than ἐν τῷ κρυπτῷ as elsewhere.

6. Μὴ θησαυρίζετε (6:19-7:6)
The units of section 6 employ an initial aural formula denoted by three prohibitions, μὴ θησαυρίζετε, μὴ κρίνετε, and μὴ δῶτε. The units are of unequal length. The first, under the heading μὴ θησαυρίζετε, consists of four subunits, each of which contains internal parallelism and a concluding proverb. The first three subunits show stronger organizational similarities to each other than does the fourth subunit. Subunits 6.1.1, 6.1.2, and 6.1.3 resemble each other in their use of summary statements at the beginning and the end of the subunit and antithetical parallels which illustrate these

---

76 Paraphrased: the purpose of forgiving is that God will forgive.

77 Following τοῖς ἀνθρώποις of 5.3.8.2 many excellent manuscripts (see Nestle-Aland[26]) fill in the elipsis with τὰ παραπτώματα ὑμῶν. This breaks up the chaism between the lines (so also Bruce M. Metzger, *A Textual Commentary on the Greek New Testament*, [New York: United Bible Societies, 1971] 17) and the inclusio. Furthermore, throughout the Sermon, Matthew has frequently employed elipsis.

proverbs, as in the μὴ νομίσητε section (3) and ἠκούσατε section (4). Section 6.1.4 subordinates a fivefold prohibition against anxiety to the major prohibition of 6.1, μὴ θησαυρίζετε.

6.1 (6:19-34)

1-**Μὴ θησαυρίζετε** ὑμῖν θησαυροὺς
ἐπὶ τῆς γῆς,

1-θησαυρίζετε δὲ ὑμῖν θησαυροὺς
ἐν οὐρανῷ,

2-ὅπου σὴς καὶ βρῶσις
ἀφανίζει

2-ὅπου οὔτε σὴς οὔτε βρῶσις
ἀφανίζει

3-καὶ ὅπου κλέπται διορύσσουσιν
καὶ κλέπτουσιν·

3-καὶ ὅπου κλέπται οὐ διορύσσουσιν
οὐδὲ κλέπτουσιν·

ὅπου γάρ ἐστιν ὁ θησαυρός σου,
ἐκεῖ ἔσται καὶ ἡ καρδία σου.

6.1.1. (6:19-21)
μὴ θησαυρίζετε, a new initial aural marker, signals a new section. It begins with a set of antithetical parallels contrasting treasure on earth and in heaven. The parallel phrases use identical words and syntax except in the negation. The first parallel lexies combine references to γῆ and οὐρανός, a frequent binary in the Sermon. The second and third sets of lines differ only in the addition of negatives: οὔτε/οὔτε in the second line and οὐ/οὐδέ in the third. The concluding proverb also appears in parallel rather than chiasm. It pairs the treasure with the heart and repeats both the second person singular pronoun and the verb εἰμί, which also appeared in doubled form in the concluding proverbs of units 4.3 and 4.5. It also repeats the adverb ὅπου from lines 2 and 3. The strong rhythmic repetition of the morpheme θησαυρ- signals it out as the subunit's primary theme.

6.1.2. (6:22)
6.1.2.1 Ὁ λύχνος τοῦ σώματός ἐστιν ὁ ὀφθαλμός.

2 ἐὰν οὖν ᾖ ὁ ὀφθαλμός σου ἁπλοῦς,

3   ὅλον τὸ σῶμά σου φωτεινὸν ἔσται·

4 ἐὰν δὲ ὁ ὀφθαλμός σου πονηρὸς ᾖ,

5   ὅλον τὸ σῶμά σου σκοτεινὸν ἔσται.

6 εἰ οὖν τὸ φῶς τὸ ἐν σοὶ σκότος ἐστίν,

7   τὸ σκότος πόσον.

Subunit 6.1.2 contains both an introductory proverb and a concluding one, indicating its subordinate character. The pattern of this subunit is very similar to that of the case law line in section 4 (ἠκούσατε). The opening statement introduces the subunit's key words: σῶμα and ὀφθαλμός. Two parallel third class conditions follow which contrast the sound and evil eye. The verb occurs at the beginning of the protasis of the first conditional statement (lexie 2) and at the end of the protasis in the second (lexie 4). As in the previous subunit, vocabulary and syntax are identical except where the contrast is established: the second phrase substitutes πονηρός for ἁπλοῦς and σκοτεινόν for φωτεινόν. In the protasis of the second condition, the verb occurs at the end of the lexie (4), creating a phonetic rhythm, πονηρὸς ᾖ. The concluding statement employs a first class condition and both doubles σκότος and contrasts φῶς and σκότος. Furthermore it contains monosyllabic words until the quick repetition of σκότος at the end creates a strong paratactic ending.

6.1.3 *(6:24)*

6.1.3. Οὐδεὶς δύναται δυσὶ κυρίοις δουλεύειν·

    ἢ γὰρ τὸν ἕνα μισήσει   καὶ τὸν ἕτερον ἀγαπήσει,

    ἢ   ἑνὸς ἀνθέξεται   καὶ τοῦ ἑτέρου καταφρονήσει.

      οὐ δύνασθε   θεῷ δουλεύειν καὶ μαμωνᾷ.

Subunit 6.1.3 exhibits an even tighter parallelism with short phrases. Its opening and concluding proverbs are synonymous but unfold an interesting substitution and elaboration. They parallel each other and employ a wordplay with κύριος and θεός. The proverbs differ only in that the opening statement places δυσὶ κυρίοις before the infinitive δουλεύειν whereas the closing proverb brackets the infinitive with the names of the two lords, θεῷ and μαμωνᾷ. Their recurring verbs have the same initial sound, δυ-/δου- which also occurs in the word δυσί in the opening proverb. The intervening parallel statements that apply the opening and closing proverbs contrast "the one" and "the other" lord, repeating the number one which first occurs in the opening proverb in οὐδείς. Within the parallel pattern the terms for hate/love and devoted/despise are chiastically arranged.

6.1.4 *(6:25-34)*

Section 6.1.4 contains five subparts[78] with the prohibition μὴ μεριμνᾶτε as the initial aural marker. It concludes, as do the previous three subunits, with a summarizing proverb. The μὴ μεριμνᾶτε subpart begins with διὰ τοῦτο, which clearly indicates its subordinate character with respect to the larger μὴ θησαυρίζετε unit.[79] This is an example of the Sermon's mixed character. The subpart has many of the characteristics of a section, but the variation and subordinating phrases clearly indicate that both phonetically and semantically it is to be subordinated. Matthew appears to be trying to achieve a logical subordination by a sequential arrangement.

Although the subparts do not exhibit the parallelism that is evident in 6.1.1, 6.1.2, and 6.1.3 or in the major sections 4 and 5, it does have a strong organizational pattern. At or near the beginning of each subpart is a

---

[78] Technically they are sub-sub-units, but we will refer to them as subparts to avoid confusion and give them a distinctive marker.

[79] Even though this subunit is quite long, it is not a separate unit or section. This is indicated by the placement of the initial aural marker in second position and the subordinating character of the phrase διὰ τοῦτο in Matthew (see also 12:31 and 21:43 for other occurrences of διὰ τοῦτο with λέγω ὑμῖν; διὰ τοῦτο also occurs in 12:27, 13:13, 13:52, 14:2, 18:23, 23:34, and 24:44). If the intial aural marker occurred in primary position or without the διὰ τοῦτο phrase, this subunit would be classified as a separate section. This decision is based upon the observation of Matthew's style in this Sermon, not on the need to produce a semantics and thus demonstrates the superiority of our method of *listening* to the text before *interpreting* it.

morpheme of μεριμνάω. 6.1.4.4-.5[80] exhibit identical phonetic/syntactical markers, μὴ οὖν μεριμνήσατε. Subpart 2 begins with a question, while subparts 1, 3 and 4 have questions beginning in the second lexie. Subpart 1 ends with the question, οὐχ ὑμεῖς μᾶλλον διαφέρετε αὐτῶν (1.6), and the third ends similarly to the first, with the question οὐ πολλῷ μᾶλλον ὑμᾶς, ὀλιγόπιστοι (3.5). Subpart 1 contains two initial questions τὶ φάγητε, τὶ ἐνδύσησθε, while the fourth subpart balances it with 3, adding ἢ τὶ πίωμεν. Subparts 4 and 5 both conclude with a proverb.

Although the subparts do not closely parallel each other, their phonetic/syntactical organizational features lend a formal unity to the topically unified μὴ μεριμνᾶτε subunit. The first three all open with interrogative clauses marked by the interrogative pronoun and end with a favorable comparison between the hearers and the subpart's example as grounds for the Father's care. In addition, the first subpart contains a λέγω formula, the formula μὴ μεριμνᾶτε, a negative question, and an imperative, some of which are repeated in the second subpart and the remaining ones are repeated in the third.

6.1.4.1 (6:25-26)
6.1.4.1.1b   Διὰ τοῦτο λέγω ὑμῖν,
6.1.4.1.1a   **μὴ μεριμνᾶτε** τῇ ψυχῇ ὑμῶν
6.1.4.1.2   τί φάγητε
            μηδὲ   τῷ σώματι ὑμῶν
            τί ἐνδύσησθε.

6.1.4.1.3   οὐχὶ   ἡ ψυχὴ πλεῖόν ἐστιν τῆς **τροφῆς**
            καὶ τὸ σῶμα   τοῦ ἐνδύματος;
6.1.4.1.4a   ἐμβλέψατε εἰς τὰ πετεινὰ τοῦ οὐρανοῦ
6.1.4.1.4b   ὅτι οὐ σπείρουσιν
             οὐδὲ θερίζουσιν
             οὐδὲ συνάγουσιν εἰς ἀποθήκας,
6.1.4.1.5   καὶ Ο ΠΑΤΗΡ ΥΜΩΝ   Ο ΟΥΡΑΝΙΟΣ τρέφει αὐτά·
6.1.6.1.6   οὐχ ὑμεῖς μᾶλλον διαφέρετε αὐτῶν;

Subpart 6.1.4.1 introduces a full complement of features much like the initial unit of a section (i.e., sections 1.1; 4.1; 5.1). λέγω ὑμῖν from the first lexie is repeated in 4.3.1b. The prohibition μὴ μεριμνᾶτε (1.1a) reappears in subparts 4.4.1a and .5. All but the last subpart employ the interrogative pronoun τίς, usually in series. Then the sequence repeats. After the interrogative τίς comes a negative question, here introduced by οὐχὶ (1.3), a feature repeated in 3.3; then an imperative (1.4a), an element that recurs in 4.4a; and finally the favorable comparison (1.6) with the hearer, marked by μᾶλλον.

Within this first subpart several aural features stand out. Following the διὰ τοῦτο introductory phrase, the next six lexies are interlocked by alternating and repeating morphemes and elipses. The prohibition in lexie 2 parallels

---

[80] In order to avoid number fatigue, since all the μεριμνᾶτε subparts will begin with the prefix number 6.1.4, that number will be left out in the commentary, except where it might result in confusion. That is, the first number will indicate which of the four subparts is referenced and the second number which line of the subpart.

lexie 4 which is introduced with μηδέ and the prohibition is supplied by elipsis. The final phrases of these two lexies are set in parallel, τῇ ψυχῇ and τῷ σώματι. This binary organizes the entire μὴ μεριμνᾶτε subunit. Both lexies end with ὑμῶν and are interlaced with parallel interrogatives in lexies 3 and 5 which pick up on their respective prohibitions. ψυχή asks about eating (what goes in) and σῶμα about clothing (what is on the outside). The prohibitions and questions are tied together in 1.3 where the negative question repeats the contrasting pair in the same order, introducting another parallel, τροφή and ἔνδυμα. Thus the parallel equivalences are set up:[81]

ψυχή	φάγητε	τροφή
σῶμα	ἐνδύσησθε	ἔνδυμα

The forms of the first parallel are feminine and the second are neuter, producing similar sounds[82] at the beginning and end of the lexies. The total effect is a strong phonetic, syntactical, and semantic rhythm for these six lexies.

The imperative clause of line 4 contains a triplet, οὐ σπείρουσιν, οὐδὲ θερίζουσιν, οὐδὲ συνάγουσιν (4b). The negative question and the ὅτι clause of the imperative statement set concrete examples in parallel in a style consistent with sections 4 and 5. 1.5 introduces τρέφει, parallel to τρόφη, creating the expectation that the next lexie will play on ἐνδύμα, which it does not. Unfulfilled expectation is part of the normal elaboration of parallelism.[83] Both phonetically and semantically it plays on the οὐχὶ ἡ ψυχή lexie. The epithet ὁ πατὴρ ὑμῶν ὁ οὐράνιος draws the subpart to a close.

6.1.4.2 (6:27)

6.1.4.2 τίς δὲ ἐξ ὑμῶν **μεριμνῶν**
    δύναται προσθεῖναι
        ἐπὶ τὴν ἡλικίαν αὐτοῦ
           πῆχυν ἕνα;

Subpart 2 radically abbreviates the elements set up in subpart 1 to a question and the initial aural morpheme μεριμνάω. More importantly it picks up semantically on the expected but missing final parallel of σῶμα /ἔνδυμα. ἡ ἡλικία is a measurement of σῶμα. Thus subpart 2 finishes out the parallel.

6.1.4.3 (6:28-30)

6.1.4.3   καὶ περὶ ἐνδύματος
6.1.4.3.1a/2 τί   **μεριμνᾶτε**;
6.1.4.3.4a   καταμάθετε τὰ κρίνα τοῦ ἀγροῦ

---

81 Following τί φάγητε many manuscripts insert ἢ (καὶ) τί πίητε. Besides the textual evidence problems with such an insertion, the careful structuring of lexies 2-7 speak against it. It was most likely picked up from 4.2 below.

82 The phonic similarity that results from morphemes of conjugation, person, or number in "the logical articulation of the language" is sometimes referred to as poor rhyme. See Schökel, *Manual of Hebrew Poetics*, 21.

83 Kugel, *Idea of Biblical Poetry*, 7.

6.1.4.3.4b πῶς αὐξάνουσιν·[84]
 οὐ κοπιῶσιν
 οὐδὲ νήθουσιν·
6.1.4.3.1b λέγω δὲ ὑμῖν ὅτι
6.1.4.3.3 οὐδὲ Σολομὼν
 ἐν πάσῃ τῇ δόξῃ αὐτοῦ
 περιεβάλετο ὡς ἕν τούτων.
 εἰ δὲ τὸν χόρτον τοῦ ἀγροῦ
 σήμερον ὄντα
 καὶ αὔριον εἰς κλίβανον βαλλόμενον
6.1.4.3.5 Ο ΘΕΟΣ οὕτως ἀμφιέννυσιν,
 οὐ πολλῷ μᾶλλον ὑμᾶς, ὀλιγόπιστοι;

The initial lexie of subpart 3 picks up ἔνδυμα explicitly, thus tying 2 and 3 closely together, completing the parallelism initiated by subpart 1. The first two lexies of this subpart form a phonetic chiasm with subpart 2 in which the order of the interrogative and the paralleled element are reversed, tying the two subparts even more closely together. The second lexie of subpart 1 and the first lexie of subpart 2 share a large number of sounds.

 δύναται προσθεῖναι

 καὶ περὶ ἐνδύματος

If subpart 2 abbreviates the pattern, subpart 3 repeats it fulsomely. The μὴ μεριμνᾶτε becomes a question as in 2, combining in this subpart the functions of lines 1a and 2. The imperative with three paratactic verbs (3.4b) comes forward to set up the elongated negative comparison (3.3). In subpart 1 the ψυχή/σῶμα comparison had consisted of two lexies. While it still has two parts here, they are elaborated. A new signifier (περιβάλλω in place of ἐνδύομαι) is introduced for the signified, "to clothe" in order to make a word play on βαλλόμενον at the comparison's end. It forms an inclusio for the example of the grass. The epithet (3.5) is abbreviated to the simple ὁ θεός and sets up a contrast between Solomon and God. Solomon is clothed in all his glory and ironically compared to grass. God who clothes the more beautiful grass is clothed in his reduced epithet. Σολομών and θεός form another inclusio for the example (3.3). Δόξης, here ironically ascribed to Solomon, is properly ascribed to ὁ θεός. A third signifier, ἀμφιέννυσιν, associated with God, draws an even stronger contrast with Solomon. This sets off the implicit comparison if grass, clothed by God, has greater glory than Solomon, how much more you ὀλιγόπιστοι, who are cared for by God. This accounts for the rearrangement and the placement of the subpart in the center. It likewise explains the reduction of the epithet to ὁ θεός, creating an ironic contrast between God and Solomon and his glory.

6.1.4.4 (6:31-33)
6.1.4.4.1a μὴ οὖν μεριμνήσητε λέγοντες
6.1.4.4.2 τί φάγωμεν;

---

84 The unique reading of codex Sinaiticus, οὐ ξένουσιν οὐδὲ νήθουσιν οὐδὲ κοπιῶσιν (they do not card neither do they spin nor toil) is very attractive. See Metzger, *A Textual Commentary*, 18.

ἤ, τί πίωμεν;
ἤ, τί περιβαλώμεθα;
6.1.4.4.3   πάντα γὰρ ταῦτα τὰ ἔθνη ἐπιζητοῦσιν·
6.1.4.4.5   οἶδεν γὰρ Ο ΠΑΤΗΡ ΥΜΩΝ Ο ΟΥΡΑΝΙΟΣ
             ὅτι χρῄζετε τούτων ἁπάντων.
6.1.4.4.4a   ζητεῖτε δὲ πρῶτον
6.1.4.4.4b   ΤΗΝ ΒΑΣΙΛΕΙΑΝ ΤΟΥ ΘΕΟΥ[85]
             καὶ   τὴν δικαιοσύνην αὐτοῦ,
             καὶ ταῦτα πάντα προστεθήσεται ὑμῖν.

Subpart 4. turns the interrogative clause (4.2) into a triplet by setting up the doublet φάγωμεν/πίωμεν. The subpart opens with the prohibition μὴ οὖν μεριμνᾶτε and ends with an imperative. In the comparison (4.3) the negative is not expressed but implied in that the activity of τὰ ἔθνη is to be avoided. The repetition of a πάντα ταῦτα-like phrase at the beginning of the line both in 4.3 and the final lexie in 4.4b, and at the end of the final lexie in 4.5 creates a threefold pattern to match the three interrogatives. The middle phrase is surounded on either side by an epithet, ὁ πατήρ and ἡ βασιλεία. The epithet in 4.5 again emphasizes the activity of God (knows what you need). The imperative clause introduces the triplet βασιλεία, δικαιοσύνη, and ταῦτα πάντα, matching the other triplets in subparts 1 and 3. Line 4a presents the second occurrence in the Sermon of πρῶτον with an imperative verb. A chiastic pattern draws the subpart to a close. After the interrogatives, πάντα occurs before ταῦτα, followed by a form of the verb ζητέω. The verb then recurs in imperative form, with ταῦτα πάντα in reversed order. Just as two different signifiers were employed to distinguish Solomon and God, so a compound form of ζητέω distinguishes τὰ ἔθνη from a simple form for ὑμεῖς. Within this chiastic arrangement also occur two epithets, ὁ πατὴρ ὑμῶν ὁ οὐράνιος and τὴν βασιλείαν, and a key word for Matthew, τὴν δικαιοσύνην. The chiastic form, the epithets, and the repetition of key words signal the semantic significance of the unit.

6.1.4.5 (*6:34*)
6.1.4.5.   μὴ οὖν   μεριμνήσητε εἰς τὴν αὔριον,
             ἡ γὰρ αὔριον μεριμνήσει ἑαυτῆς:
             ἀρκετὸν τῇ ἡμέρᾳ ἡ κακία   αὐτῆς,

The abbreviation of the pattern, repetition of morpheme μεριμνάω, the noun ἡ αὔριον in a chiasm, and the end rhyme tightly links the three lexies. The middle lexie participates in both the chiasm and the rhyme, interlocking the two features and phonetically unifying the concluding subpart drawing the whole subpart to a conclusion.

6.2 (*7:1-5*)
6.2 Μὴ κρίνετε, ἵνα μὴ κριθῆτε·

---

[85] The textual confusion in first two lexie of this line is considerable. Both Vaticanus and Sinaticus omit τοῦ θεοῦ, which is very strong evidence. Vaticanus likewise reverses δικαιοσύνην and βασιλείαν. Although Matthew seldom uses βασιλεία without modifier (normally the modifier is τῶν βασιλείων) and more importantly the simple θεοῦ picks up on the reduced epithet in the previous subpart.

ἐν ᾧ γὰρ	κρίματι	κρίνετε	κριθήσεσθε,
καὶ ἐν ᾧ	μέτρῳ	μετρεῖτε	μετρηθήσεται ὑμῖν.
τί δὲ βλέπεις	τὸ κάρφος	τὸ ἐν τῷ ὀφθαλμῷ	τοῦ ἀδελφοῦ σου,
	τὴν δὲ	ἐν τῷ σῷ ὀφθαλμῷ	δοκὸν οὐ κατανοεῖς;
ἢ πῶς ἐρεῖς			τῷ ἀδελφῷ σου·
ἄφες ἐκβάλω	τὸ κάρφος	ἐκ τοῦ ὀφθαλμοῦ σου,	
καὶ ἰδοὺ ἡ	δοκὸς	ἐν τῷ ὀφθαλμῷ σου;	
ὑποκριτά, ἔκβαλε πρῶτον		ἐκ τοῦ ὀφθαλμοῦ σου τὴν δοκόν	
καὶ τότε διαβλέψεις			
ἐκβαλεῖν	τὸ κάρφος	ἐκ τοῦ ὀφθαλμοῦ	τοῦ ἀδελφοῦ σου.]

Unit 6.2 opens with μὴ κρίνετε, a performancial variation on the initial aural formula for section 6 which phonetically indicates the unit's theme. Its organization evokes the formal parallelism of 6.1.1 and .2. Following the initial aural formula, the unit opens with a proverb, followed by a double question and then an imperative introducing the final two sets of doublets. In the ninth lexie πρῶτον with an imperative verb occurs for the third time.

The initial aural formula employs the repeated phoneme κρι-. The double proverbs introduced by ἐν ᾧ build the phoneme into a triple repetition and then do the same thing with the phoneme μετρ-. These two proverbs are set in parallel. Following the proverb, repeated words reverberate throughout the subunit. The phoneme βλεπ- occurs at the beginning in the first τί lexie and at the beginning of the concluding lexie (διαβλέψεις). The verb ἐκβάλλω occurs three times, once in the ἄφες lexie and twice in the ὑποκριταί lexie. The contrasting terms ὁ κάρφος and ἡ δοκός recur in three pairs of lexies. Their order is reversed in the final pair. Three references to ὁ ἀδελφός σου occur, as well as six references to ὁ ὀφθαλμός, two in each sentence. The τί sentence is arranged chiastically: verb, object, modifier//modifer, eye, object verb. After the complicated patterns and rhythms of μὴ μεριμνᾶτε subparts the relative simplicity and repetition of this unit allows the listener to relax and directs attention to the previous subparts.

6.3 (7:6)
6.3 **Μὴ δῶτε** τὸ ἅγιον τοῖς κυσίν
μηδὲ βάλητε
τοὺς μαργαρίτας ὑμῶν
ἔμπροσθεν τῶν χοίρων,
μήποτε καταπατήσουσιν
αὐτοὺς ἐν τοῖς ποσὶν αὐτῶν
καὶ στραφέντες ῥήξωσιν ὑμᾶς.

An extended proverb with two parallel parts concludes section 6. The first part begins with a third performancial variation on the initial aural formula for section 6, μὴ δῶτε, and initiates a strong pattern of internal rhyming as did the previous unit. Μὴ δῶτε rhymes with μηδὲ βάλητε. The sentence ends with ἔμπροσθεν τῶν χοίρων which rhymes with ὑμῶν at the end of the previous lexie. The opening lexie of the second parallel part begins with μήποτε which repeats the phonemes of the initial aural formula and then picks up for an internal rhyme the terminal phoneme of the proverb's first line, -υσιν/-ουσιν, which repeats the phonemes with ποσίν and ῥήξωσιν. At the end of the middle lexie of the second parallel part, αὐτῶν echoes the end rhyme ὑμῶν and χοίρων in the first part. Ποσίν and ῥήξωσιν in the last two lexies of the unit repeat the ending sounds of the first and fifth lexies.

7. Αἰτεῖτε *(7:7-20)*

Section 7 has three units denoted by the occurrence of three imperative verbs: αἰτεῖτε, εἰσέλθατε, and προσέχετε. These serve as the initial aural markers and in 7.1 the pattern is announced by three consecutive imperatives. Thus each unit will be marked by an initial imperative. But the three imperatives of 7.1 also announce the organizing pattern of this section because each imperative is balanced by a verb in the future tense. Each unit carefully balances a series of binaries and this balancing of binaries announces the organizing pattern.

7.1 *(7:1-12)*

7.1.1α   **Αἰτεῖτε** καὶ   δοθήσεται ὑμῖν,

β   **ζητεῖτε** καὶ   <u>εὑρήσετε</u>,

γ   **κρούετε** καὶ   <u>ἀνοιγήσεται</u> ὑμῖν·

α   πᾶς γὰρ   ὁ <u>αἰτῶν</u>   λαμβάνει

β   καὶ   ὁ <u>ζητῶν</u>   <u>εὑρίσκει</u>

γ   καὶ   τῷ <u>κρούοντι</u>   <u>ἀνοιγήσεται</u>.

7.1.2   ἢ τίς ἐστιν ἐξ ὑμῶν ἄνθρωπος,

ὃν <u>αἰτήσει</u> ὁ υἱὸς αὐτοῦ   ἄρτον,

μὴ λίθον <u>ἐπιδώσει αὐτῷ</u>;

ἢ καὶ ἰχθὺν   <u>αἰτήσει</u>,

μὴ ὄφιν <u>ἐπιδώσει αὐτῷ</u>;

7.1.3   <u>εἰ οὖν</u> ὑμεῖς πονηροὶ ὄντες

οἴδατε δόματα   <u>ἀγαθὰ</u> διδόναι

τοῖς τέκνοις ὑμῶν,]

πόσῳ μᾶλλον Ο ΠΑΤΗΡ ΥΜΩΝ Ο ΕΝ ΤΟΙΣ ΟΥΡΑΝΟΙΣ

<u>δώσει</u> <u>ἀγαθὰ</u>

τοῖς <u>αἰτοῦσιν</u> αὐτόν.]

7.1.4   <u>Πάντα</u> <u>οὖν</u> <u>ὅσα</u> <u>ἐὰν</u> θέλητε

ἵνα <u>ποιῶσιν</u>   <u>ὑμῖν</u>   οἱ ἄνθρωποι,

οὕτως καὶ <u>ὑμεῖς</u>   <u>ποιεῖτε</u>   <u>αὐτοῖς</u>·

οὗτος γάρ ἐστιν Ο ΝΟΜΟΣ ΚΑΙ ΟΙ ΠΡΟΦΗΤΑΙ.

The first unit (7.1) opens with a triplet of imperative verbs joined by καί to complementary verbs in the future (passive) tense, laid out in three parallel clauses. This triplet is repeated in the following πᾶς γὰρ clause where the imperative verbs become participial nouns as subjects of their corresponding verbs in the future tense. The corresponding verb for αἰτέω changes in its parallel clause, from δοθήσεται in the first occurrence to λαμβάνει in the second, differentiating between the giver and the receiver. Ζητέω in the second lexie echoes its previous highlighted occurrence in 6.1.4.4. In the first triplet ὑμῖν occurs at the end of the first and third lexies, bracketing the group.

The remainder of the unit exhibits patterned elements similar to those in the μὴ μεριμνᾶτε subpart while maintaining the doublet organization. 7.1.2

picks up phonetically and thematically on the first imperative αἰτεῖτε. A double question (7.1.2) employing only one interrogative pronoun sets two specific illustrations in parallel. A first class condition (7.1.3) follows, establishing a comparison using μᾶλλον, and finally a conclusion (7.1.4) is drawn. Each of these lines is organized in a doublet, either by way of negative or positive comparison, with a proverb as the unit's conclusion. In the two parallel examples (7.1.2) the relative clauses are chiastically arranged, reversing the order in the second one of the verb αἰτέω and the object of one's asking (fish). The main clause is identical except for the object.

The conditional statement (7.1.3) opens by addressing ὑμεῖς as πονηροί, which continues the negative name calling of the addressee that has been a feature of this part of the Sermon (cf. ὀλιγόπιστοι [6.1.4.3], ὑποκριταί [6.2]). The apodosis repeats the thematic morpheme αἰτέω and includes the epithet that opens the Lord's prayer. The verb δίδωμι and the substantive adjective ἀγαθά occur in both the protasis and the apodosis (lexies 2 and 4) and are set in chiasm with concluding dative phrases set in parallel. τοῖς τέκνοις ὑμῶν parallels τοῖς αἰτοῦσιν αὐτόν. These bracket the epithet ὁ πατήρ, creating a nice semantic bridge effect: children/Father/requesters.

This density of phonetic/syntactical, rhetorical and semantic clues signals the upcoming conclusion, the proverb beginning πάντα οὖν. As in the μὴ μεριμνᾶτε subunit (subpart 4), the οὖν signals both the conclusion and its connection with what goes before. This line, too, contains a chiasm with the repetition and reversed order of the second person pronoun and the verb ποιέω with subject and indirect object at the ends of their repective lexies. Their endings (οι/οις) create a weak rhyme. The proverb ends with another epithet, ὁ νόμος καὶ οἱ προφῆται. The epithet harkens back to its usage in section 3 and it also parallels the ὁ πατήρ epithet used in the prayer in 5.3. Thus 7.1.3 and .4 implement the common division and correlation in Matthew of ἐν τοῖς οὐρανοῖς and ἐπὶ τῆς γῆς and demonstrate the correspondence between the two.

7.2 (7:13-14)
7.2 **Εἰσέλθατε** διὰ τῆς <u>στενῆς</u> <u>πύλης·</u>

α ὅτι πλατεῖα ἡ <u>πύλη</u>[86]
β <u>καὶ</u> <u>εὐρύχωρος</u> <u>ἡ</u> <u>ὁδὸς</u> <u>ἡ</u> <u>ἀπάγουσα</u> <u>εἰς</u> <u>τὴν</u> <u>ἀπώλειαν</u>
γ <u>καὶ</u> πολλοί <u>εἰσιν</u> <u>οἱ</u> εἰσερχόμενοι δι' <u>αὐτῆς·</u>
α τί[87] <u>στενὴ</u> ἡ <u>πύλη</u>
β <u>καὶ</u> <u>τεθλιμμένη</u> <u>ἡ</u> <u>ὁδὸς</u> <u>ἡ</u> <u>ἀπάγουσα</u> <u>εἰς</u> <u>τὴν</u> <u>ζωήν</u>
γ <u>καὶ</u> ὀλίγοι <u>εἰσὶν</u> <u>οἱ</u> εὑρίσκοντες <u>αὐτήν.</u>

The imperative aural marker εἰσέλθατε begins unit 7.2 which consists of a another proverb arranged in a parallel doublet. After the initial aural formula, the saying contains two sets of nearly identical lines which highlight the

---

86 Sinaticus and many patristic quotations omit this noun and its article. But the highly repetitive way this unit is constructed indicates that it belongs.

87 Many manuscripts (including the first hand in Vaticanus and Sinaticus) read ὅτι, but τί has been widely used in the Sermon for just such an organizational marker. The correcting hand of Vaticanus and Sinaticus would seem to be right.

distinctive elements. The parallel pattern draws attention to the contrast between στενῆς and πλατεῖα, εὐρύχωρος and τεθλιμμένη, ἀπώλειαν and ζωήν, and between πολλοί and ὀλίγοι. In the case of the participles οἱ εἰσερχόμενοι (lexie 4) and οἱ εὑρίσκοντες (lexie 7), the first repeats the imperative initial aural marker noting the unit's theme, while the second refers back to the second in the series of triple imperatives that began the section: ζητεῖτε καὶ εὑρήσετε. The contrast between narrow and wide set off in a triple pattern likewise echoes the initial doublets arranged in a triple pattern in 7.1.1.

7.3 (7:15-20)

7.3 **Προσέχετε** ἀπὸ τῶν ψευδοπροφητῶν,
οἵτινες ἔρχονται πρὸς ὑμᾶς ἐν ἐνδύμασιν προβάτων,
ἔσωθεν δέ εἰσιν λύκοι ἅρπαγες.
<u>ἀπὸ τῶν καρπῶν αὐτῶν ἐπιγνώσεσθε αὐτούς.</u>

μήτι συλλέγουσιν ἀπὸ ἀκανθῶν σταφυλὰς
ἢ ἀπὸ τριβόλων σῦκα;

οὕτως πᾶν <u>δένδρον ἀγαθὸν</u>	<u>καρποὺς καλοὺς</u>	<u>ποιεῖ,</u>
τὸ δὲ <u>σαπρὸν δένδρον</u>	<u>καρποὺς πονηροὺς</u>	<u>ποιεῖ.</u>
οὐ δύναται <u>δένδρον ἀγαθὸν</u>	<u>καρποὺς πονηροὺς</u>	<u>ποιεῖν</u>[88]
οὐδὲ <u>δένδρον σαπρὸν</u>	<u>καρποὺς καλοὺς</u>	<u>ποιεῖν.</u>
πᾶν <u>δένδρον</u> μὴ <u>ποιοῦν</u>	<u>καρπὸν καλὸν</u>	

ἐκκόπτεται καὶ εἰς πῦρ βάλλεται.
<u>ἄρα γε ἀπὸ τῶν καρπῶν αὐτῶν ἐπιγνώσεσθε αὐτούς.</u>

The third unit opens with the imperative προσέχετε and contrasts the outward clothing with the inward nature of οἱ ψευδοπροφήται. The opening statement echoes the clothing theme from the μὴ μεριμνᾶτε subpart and its subsequent pattern is similar to the μὴ κρίνετε unit with its multiple repetition of a series of words. The repeated proverb ἀπὸ τῶν καρπῶν αὐτῶν ἐπιγνώσεσθε αὐτούς forms an inclusio that encloses five parallel independent clauses. Inside the inclusio on either side of the five parallel cases is a phrase of gathering (συλλέγουσιν) and casting out (εἰς . . . βάλλεται), emphasizing the strong contrast the parallels establish. The words δένδρον, καρπούς/καρπόν, and a form of ποιέω are each repeated five times, once in each clause. Of these, only καρπούς always occurs in the same position; in the second clause δένδρον and its adjective change position and in the fifth clause the participle ποιοῦν precedes καρπόν. Ἀγαθόν and σαπρόν alternate as modifiers of δένδρον, coupled with καλούς and πονηρούς as modifiers of καρπούς. This parallel arrangement emphasizes the verb ποιέω at the end of each lexie and the contrast between ἀγαθὸν/καλοὺς and σαπρὸν/πονηρου;". This unit likewise ties back to the three imperatives that initiated the section. Those who come are those who knock and one must recognize their fruit before one opens the door.

8. Οὐ πᾶς ὁ (7:21-27)
8.1 (7:21-23)

---

88 Vaticanus subsitutes ἐνεγκεῖν for ποιεῖν in an effort to improve the style by relieving the boredom of repeating the same morpheme (so Metzger, *A Textual Commentary*, 20). The very style of this section with its strong repetition of phrases would support the majority reading.

8.1 Οὐ **πᾶς** ὁ λέγων μοι,   <u>κύριε κύριε</u>,
         εἰσελεύσεται εἰς ΤΗΝ ΒΑΣΙΛΕΙΑΝ ΤΩΝ ΟΥΡΑΝΩΝ,
ἀλλ᾽   ὁ ποιῶν τὸ θέλημα
         ΤΟΥ ΠΑΤΡΟΣ ΜΟΥ ΤΟΥ ΕΝ ΤΟΙΣ ΟΥΡΑΝΟΙΣ,
      πολλοὶ ἐροῦσίν μοι ἐν ἐκείνῃ τῇ ἡμέρᾳ, Κύριε κύριε,
οὐ   <u>τῷ σῷ ὀνόματι</u>   ἐπροφητεύσα<u>μεν</u>
καὶ   <u>τῷ σῷ ὀνόματι</u>   δαιμόνια ἐξεβάλο<u>μεν</u>,
καὶ   <u>τῷ σῷ ὀνόματι</u>   δυνάμεις πολλὰς ἐποιήσα<u>μεν</u>;
καὶ τότε ὁμολογήσω αὐτοῖς ὅτι
                                       οὐδέποτε ἔγνων ὑμᾶς·
      ἀποχωρεῖτε ἀπ᾽ ἐμοῦ οἱ ἐργαζόμενοι τὴν ἀνομίαν.

A different initial aural formula, Οὐ πᾶς ὁ, indicates a new section.[89] Its
first unit consists of a set of parallel statements that draw a contrast between
confession and action, followed by three paratactic questions that repeat the
phrase τῷ σῷ ὀνόματι and end with an ‑αμεν/‑ομεν rhyme. The unit ends
with a concluding statement that negatively reprises the unit's opening. In the
initial set of parallels each statement ends with an epithet, first τὴν βασιλείαν
τῶν οὐρανῶν and then τοῦ πατρός μου ἐν τοῖς οὐρανοῖς. This latter phrase
and epithet recall the third petition of the Lord's prayer. The following line
introducing the triplet repeats κύριε, κύριε from the unit's opening lexie,
forming an inclusio that brackets the pair of epithets and linking the parallel
arrangement to the subsequent triplet. The three lexies of the conclusion
reprise in opposition to the opening. Ὁμολογήσω parallels λέγων, confirming the
contrast between confession and action. The second lexie's harsh never
knowing both echoes the ἐπιγνώσεσθε of the last unit of the previous section
and serves as the opposite of κύριε. Ἀποχωρεῖτε opposes εἰσελεύσεται. Because
the concluding statement lacks phonetic elements characteristic of the
previous repetitive patterns, its harsh condemnation receives additional
emphasis.

8.2 (7:24-27)

8.2.1 **Πᾶς** <u>οὖν</u> <u>ὅστις</u> <u>ἀκούει</u> μου	8.2.2 <u>καὶ</u> **πᾶς** ὁ <u>ἀκούων</u> μου
τοὺς λόγους τούτους καὶ <u>ποιεῖ</u>	τοὺς λόγους τούτους καὶ μὴ <u>ποιῶν</u>
αὐτούς,	αὐτοὺς
ὁμοιωθήσεται ἀνδρὶ <u>φρονίμῳ</u>,	ὁμοιωθήσεται ἀνδρὶ <u>μωρῷ</u>,
ὅστις ᾠκοδόμησεν αὐτοῦ τὴν οἰκίαν	ὅστις ᾠκοδόμησεν αὐτοῦ τὴν οἰκίαν
ἐπὶ τὴν <u>πέτραν</u>·	ἐπὶ τὴν <u>ἄμμον</u>·
καὶ κατέβη ἡ βροχὴ	καὶ κατέβη ἡ βροχὴ
καὶ ἦλθον οἱ ποταμοὶ	καὶ ἦλθον οἱ ποταμοὶ
καὶ ἔπνευσαν οἱ ἄνεμοι	καὶ ἔπνευσαν οἱ ἄνεμοι
καὶ προσέ<u>πεσαν</u> τῇ οἰκίᾳ ἐκείνῃ,	καὶ προσέ<u>κοψαν</u> τῇ οἰκίᾳ ἐκείνῃ,

---

89 Davies, *Matthew*, 693, debates whether to recognize a unit division after 7:20 but
dismisses this possibility because he judges that 7:15-23 deals with a single subject, false
prophets. His criteria for the delineation of units include thematic coherence and
conformitiy with a triadic pattern. He ignores the aural clues of the initial aural formula
which holds in 7:7, 7:13, 7:15 and changes for the units beginning 7:21 and 7:24.

καὶ <u>οὐκ</u> ἔπεσεν, καὶ ἔπεσεν

<u>τεθεμελίωτο</u> γὰρ ἐπὶ τὴν πέτραν. <u>καὶ ἦν ἡ πτῶσις αὐτῆς μεγάλη.</u>

The initial aural formula reflects the performancial variation πᾶς οὖν ὅστις/πᾶς ὁ. The section presents a parable consisting of two extended parallels in a style similar to the extended parallel examples of the ἠκούσατε section (4) and section 7. The two parts are nearly identical, drawing attention to its contrasting elements: φρονίμῳ/μωρῷ, πέτραν/ἄμμον, οὐκ ἔπεσεν/ἔπεσεν and ἐπὶ τὴν πέτραν/ἦν ἡ πτῶσις αὐτῆς μεγάλη. The double introduction sets up as correlative hearing and doing, in contrast to confessing and not doing of the previous unit. Μου τοὺς λόγους is a reference to the Sermon which establishes the will of God. The narrator's formulaic ending of the sermon will pick up on this description of the sermon: ἐτέλεσεν ὁ Ἰησοῦς τοὺς λόγους. The conclusion of the two parallels contrasts building on rock and not as expected building on sand, but "great was the fall," a type of warning about final destruction that has concluded many units.

III. Composing in Sound

Our study of the Sermon on the Mount attends to its aural quality, its *recitatio,* and the deliberate imitation of orality implicit in Matthew's construction of Jesus' speech as οἱ λόγοι. As a rhetorical composition the Sermon sustains an aural rhythm achieved through the combination of phonetic, syntactical, and semantic devices. The most basic of these is the repetition of sound and reiteration of organizing patterns.[90] Our analysis has placed strong emphasis on the initial aural formula that begins a section and repeats throughout to segment it. The sermon opens with such a formula, μακάριοι, which gives the sermon's first section its distinctive sound. The initial aural formula was Matthew's primary means of delineating units. We have therefore derived our Macro Outline (Appendix 1) from the initial aural formulae and have used them to label the sermon's sections and units.

Variations in the initial aural formula can be substantial. In section 8, for example, only a single syllable repeats, πᾶς, accompanied by various o sounds (ὁ, οὖν, οὐ, ὅστις). The formula for section 7 contains no phonetic repetition at all. Instead, a grammatical form, an imperative verb, occurs at the beginning of each unit in a predictable syntactical arrangement. The initial aural formula sometimes varies by abbreviation and elaboration. In section 4 multiple versions of the initial formula occur: a full form, ἠκούσατε ὅτι ἐρρέθη τοῖς ἀρχαίοις (4.1), a full form with a connecting adverb, πάλιν (4.3), a short form, ἠκούσατε ὅτι ἐρρέθη (4.2 and 4.4), and even ἐρρέθη δέ (4.2).

Organizing patterns can also vary by abbreviation and elaboration. Typically, the pattern appears first in full form, expands through elaboration, then abbreviates. Sections 4 and 5 exemplify this arrangement, with the full statement of an organizational pattern in 4.1 and 5.1, elaborations in 4.2

---

90 Tannehill, *Sword of His Mouth,* 41-43, argues that repeated sound creates the patterns that organize a text. "Repetition emphasizes, thus allowing a text to disclose its own points of emphasis and so providing a key to the proper interpetation of a text." This coheres with hearing because one hears in real time.

(modified conclusion) and 5.3 (rearrangement of elements and substantial expansion of one element), and abbreviations in 4.4 and 5.4. An indication of the sermon's high rhetorical character is its preference for unbalance. Its eight sections, although clearly marked with initial aural formulae, extend for quite different durations. The subordinate μὴ μεριμνᾶτε subpart unbalances the otherwise evenly balanced section 6. Section 3 is a unit that stands as its own section, and 5.0 falls outside the established structure of its section. The vocabulary of these latter two units also shifts to include abstract terms such as δικαιοσύνη. The lack of aural patterning in the conclusion of 8.1 achieves intensity by avoiding phonetic and syntactical repetition. These unbalances call attention to the units that alter organizational patterns.

Our evidence indicates distinctive stylistic features at the micro level of subunit, line, and lexie. Frequent parallels occur, such as that between salt and light (section 2), divine and human forgiveness (5.3.6.1-.7.2), the treasure and the heart (6.1.1), the one and the other (6.1.3), and the houses built on rock and sand (8.2). Parallels can admit of variation. For example, the verb placement changes from the beginning of the lexie to the end in the protases of the parallel conditions of 6.1.2. Similarly, in the triplet which introduces the verb ἀφίημι in the Lord's prayer (5.3.5), the verb occurs in a different place in each of three lexies. These variations break the monotony of exact reduplication of parallels.

Throughout the sermon, doublets, triplets, and combinations of doublets and triplets organize the material within a unit. Doublings can establish contrast, such as heaven and earth (6.1.1), the narrow and wide way (7.2), or houses built on rock and sand (8.2.1), or they can be synthetic, such as loving and greeting another (4.5.4) or treasure and heart (6.1). A triple imperative begins unit 7.1. Three interrogatives characterize what should not produce anxiety: eating, drinking, and clothing (6.1.4.4).

Doublets and triplets often interlock. In section 2, three phonetically similar lexies occur in each of two units. Each of the two units in section 2 include the triple occurrence of a dominant sound. In 6.1.4.1 the paired terms ψυχή and σῶμα give rise to the triple example of the birds who neither sow, reap, nor gather. Triplets figure prominently in 5.3.5, the Lord's prayer, which concludes with a double condition.

Inclusios, another stylistic feature, often bracket a unit or subunit, as does ὅτι αὐτῶν ἐστιν ἡ βασιλεία τῶν οὐρανῶν in μακάριοι (section 1) and ἀπὸ τῶν καρπῶν αὐτῶν ἐπιγνώσεσθε αὐτούς (section 7). Inclusios can bracket a set of lines for emphasis, as does τὴν δικαιοσύνην in the μακάριοι section and the repeated Father epithet (5.3.5).

Chiasmus occurs in the Sermon neither as prominently as inclusio nor as frequently as the interlocking doublet and triplet. Typically, chiasm combines with other stylistic features and often in conjunction with an epithet or with the rehearsal of a primary theme. The chiasm formed by πάντα ταῦτα/ταῦτα πάντα in 6.1.4.3, for example, encloses the epithet ὁ πατὴρ ὑμῶν ὁ οὐράνιος, the command ζητεῖτε δὲ πρῶτον τὴν βασιλείαν, and the distinctively Matthean τὴν δικαιοσύνην. Similarly, chiasm in 4.5.3 modifies the Father epithet and, in the same unit, the chiastic conclusion places it in the prominent central position. Chiasm combines with parallels to conclude a subunit in 6.1.3 (the love/hate terms are chiastic, δύναμαι and δουλεύω are parallel) and 6.1.4.5 (μεριμνάω and αὔριον are chiastic, ἑαυτῆς and αὐτῆς are parallel).

Various stylistic features combine to produce organizational patterns, connect material, and create closure. Repetition is the primary means of introducing an organizing pattern. Μακάριοι οἱ repeats eight times, for example, before the initial aural formula changes. Repetition with variation (sections 4 and 5) and repetitive forecasting (section 7) can also establish organizational patterns. Units and sections also often begin or end with proverbs, such as in 6.1, 6.2, and 6.3 and section 7.

Repeated key words or organizing elements forge links between sections, units, or shorter blocks of material. For example, the threefold repetition of διώκω in 1.8-1.9 and the occurrence of ἐν τοῖς οὐρανοῖς in 1.9 connect the μακάριοί ἐστε unit with the beatitudes. The repetition in 5.0 of μισθόν, which functioned as a component of an internal organizing formula in section 4, connects section 5 with the ἠκούσατε section. The specific examples set in parallel 3.1.1 and the λέγω ὑμῖν formula repeated in 3.1. and 3.2 anticipate key organizing elements of the following section.

The sermon establishes closure through a variety of means. Section 5's units conclude with a repeated refrain. Some units end with a proverb (6.1.1-.3, 4.5, and 7.3). In 6.1.4.4 and 7.1 the appearance of οὖν in the ultimate and penultimate lines highlights the upcoming conclusion. Closure appears to be a primary function of the epithet in the sermon. Epithets can signal the end of a unit or section, as in sections 2 and 3 and subpart 6.1.4.1. Epithets conclude parallel specific examples in 3.1.1 and 4.2.1. Parallel lines in 8.1 conclude with two different epithets. Epithets frequently occur within an inclusio (1.8), a chiasm (6.1.4.4 and 4.5, concluding both a unit and a section), or other stylistic feature. The closing of the Lord's prayer in 5.3 combines epithet, inclusio, chiasm, and parallelism. Unit 7.1 provides a particularly interesting example because of its double set of clues for closure. An epithet, a chiasm, a proverb, and the closing signal οὖν occur in each of its final two lines. This doubled ending balances the unit's triple beginning. Often a density of aural devices signals the end of a unit or section, with or without an epithet.

We have seen that detailed observations at the micro level of the phonetic/syntactical features of the text can begin to suggest a description of Matthew's distinctive style. The text's aural features also indicate the Sermon's overall design. (See Appendix 1). We now turn to a discussion of the Sermon's arrangement at the macro level, comparing our analysis of its organization with other outlines of the Sermon.

IV. From Sound to Outline

Our outline of the Sermon derives from the level of the signifier. As such we hope it has an empirical basis. The Sermon's sound signals the demarcation of units. Because attention to sound highlights aspects of the sermon that are difficult to see through other methods, our outline differs in significant ways from others. We have chosen for comparison four recent detailed proposals for structuring the Sermon on the Mount. We examine

Georg Strecker's scheme[91] because it represents a major monograph. We include the outlines of W. D. Davies-Dale C. Allison[92] and Ulrich Luz[93] because they represent major commentaries from English-American and German scholarship.[94] We give only brief notice to Günther Bornkamm's classic outline because of its similarity to Luz's scheme.[95]

Strecker's outline agrees with ours in most of its major divisions, except for his sectional division at 7:12 instead of 7:20. He recognizes as our outline does the sequential character of the sermon's units. He claims the sermon is thematically organized by "the conceptual structure of [Matthew's] theology" and that this structure is "expressed in the organization of the speech,"[96] but actually his outline conforms to his descriptive observations without imposing a fully developed thematic schema. Strecker contends that the demand for greater righteousness in 5:20, the demand for perfection in 5:48 and the golden rule in 7:12 represent the major dividing lines of Matthew's theological system, but his outline does not consistently reflect this scheme. Verse 5:20 comes at the end of the section he designates as the first major section, but 5:48 falls at the end of the section Strecker designates as the first subdivision of section 2, and 7:12 marks the conclusion of the same major section.

Strecker aligns 5:21-48 (the antitheses, our section 4), 6:1-18 (section 5 in our outline), and 6:19-7:12 as the three major sections of the main body of the Sermon, whereas our analysis finds no evidence at the level of the signifier to support the ascription of equivalent importance to these sections. Neither does our outline indicate a sectional break at 7:12.[97] Rather, we recognize 7:21-27 as a section unified by phonetic/syntactical qualities.

The organizational scheme first proposed by Allison and followed by Davies and Allison posits an elaborate thematic arrangement centered around the same three sections Strecker identifies as the sermon's core.[98] Allison's observation of triads in the Sermon and throughout Matthew's gospel leads him to argue for this threefold emphasis. Allison correlates this with Simeon the Just's three pillars of the Law: Torah, temple service, and deeds of loving-kindness. Allison argues that, just as many rabbis revised the three pillars

---

91 Georg Strecker, *The Sermon on the Mount. An Exegetical Commentary*, (Nashville: Abingdon, 1988) 14-15.

92 D. C. Allison, "The Structure of the Sermon on the Mount," *JBL* 106 (1987) 437-38. Davies, *Matthew* 58-65, adopts Allison's outline.

93 Luz, *Matthew 1-7*, 211-13. The outline follows that of Kürzinger and R. Riesner, "Der Aufbau der Redem im Matthäus-Evangelium," *Theologische Beitrage* 9 (1978) 173-76.

94 See Appendix 3, Comparative Outline, for a schematic display of all five outlines.

95 Bornkamm, "Der Aufbau Der Bergpredigt," 419-32.

96 Strecker, *The Sermon on the Mount*, 14-15.

97 On this point our outline differs from most analyses of the Sermon.

98 Davies, *Matthew*, 61-62, admits that "Matthew's architectonic grandeur does not appear to derive from a clear blueprint," but he does find convincing Allison's observation of a tripartite structure and he accepts Allison's outline.

after the destruction of the Jerusalem temple in 70 C.E., the Sermon represents Matthew's revision.[99]

According to Allison, Matthew's three pillars are Jesus and the Torah (5:17-48), the Christian cult (6:1-18), and social issues (6:19-7:12). The first pillar contains and introductory statement (5:17-20; our section 3) and two triads of instruction, the six antitheses (4 in our outline).[100] The second pillar contains one triad of instruction on almsgiving, prayer, and fasting (our section 5), and the third pillar contains two triads of instruction, a triad on the true treasure (6:19-24) and a triad on one's attitude toward others (7:1-6), as well as two units of encouragement, "do not worry" (6:25-34) and "ask" (7:7-11). According to Allisons's analysis, these three pillars are bracketed by an introduction (4:23-5:12) and statement of the task of God's people (5:13-16) and a concluding statement (7:12), eschatological warning (7:13-27), and conclusion (7:28-8:1).

The Davies-Allison three pillars model fits three of the occurrences of an important key word, δικαιοσύνη, which occurs in 5:20 at the introduction to the first pillar, in 6:1 at the introduction of the second, and at 6:33 in the conclusion to the third. But they ignore several crucial observations at the level of the signifier. For example, Allison argues for the formal unity of 6:19-7:12.[101] On semantic grounds, he aligns 7:1-12 with 6:19-34 as its "structural twin."[102] Further, he contends that the section ends at 7:12 because its reference to the law and the prophets forms an inclusio with a similar reference in 5:17. He contends these verses bracket the main body of the sermon, the exposition of the three pillars.

Allison's analysis of the triadic arrangement of 6:19-7:12 remains unconvincing. His proposal for the unity of 6:19-7:12 ignores the significance of the changed initial aural formula in 7:7 and 7:21. Although 7:1 and 7:6 articulate prohibitions as in 6:69-34, the imperatives change to positive form in 7:7. Nor do these two units share significant phonetic/syntactical qualities. Moreover, whereas our evidence emphasizes the density of the Sermon's aural clues to delineate a unit or section, Allison's outline assigns to a single inclusio the

---

[99] Allison, "Structure of the Sermon on the Mount," 443.

[100] This argument assumes a unit division at 5:31 beginning with ἐρρέθη δέ which our outline finds subordinate to the unit beginning 5:27.

[101] Ibid., 434. Allison claims the formal unity of 6:19-7:12 "has seemed evident to most" and is "no less obvious than that of 5:17-48 or 6:1-18." But the the Sermon's organization must be heard, not "evident," "obvious," or seen. The Sermon's aural clues indicate the sectional unity of 6:19-7:6 (section 6), 7:7-20 (section 7), and 7:21-27 (section 8), not 6:19-7:12.

[102] Ibid., 435-37, 440; Davies, *Matthew*, 64. Davies admits that the "encouragement" sections of the Sermon are the only two places where Matthew breaks his triadic pattern (625-7). Davies and Allison find the key to the structure of 6:19-34 (μὴ θησαυρίζετε, unit 6.1 in our outline) in what they take to be parallels with chapter 7:

Introduction:

exhortation	6:19-21	7:1-2
parable on the eye	6:22-23	7:3-5
second parable	6:24	7:6
Encouragement:		
the Father's care	6:25-34	7:7-11
The golden rule	7:12	

improbable burden of bracketing an extraordinarily long block of material (5:17-7:12), the main body of the sermon. He must append an auxillary category, "encouragement," to his triadic organization to acccount for all material in the third pillar section. In fact, our outline with its section 6 division at 7:6 follows a clearer triadic scheme than Allison's in that it presents first a triple prohibition (μὴ θησαυρίζετε 6:19, μὴ κρίνετε 7:1, and μὴ δῶτε 7:6) and then a triple positive command in section 7 (αἰτεῖτε 7:7, εἰσέλθατε 7:13, and προσέχετε 7:15) with a triple introduction at the beginning of section 7, αἰτεῖτε, ζητεῖτε, and κρούετε. Allison even recognizes the sound repetition in the material designated sections 6 and 7 in our outline and recognizes their theological importance as units, but does not allow these observations to influence his delineation of the sermon's sections.

Moreover, Allison's scheme does not take adequate account of the material that lies outside the three pillars inclusio. Allison's outline does not explain why the Sermon's conclusion (7:13-8:1) should be so elaborated, nor how 7:12 functions at the level of the signifier as a conclusion.

Neither does Allison's outline adequately account for the importance of the sermon's opening material His scheme draws attention to 5:13-16 as a prelude to the three pillars and relegates the beatitudes to the function of introduction, along with the framing material in 4:23-5:2. According to this arrangement, the beatitudes all but disappear. The strong aural pattern of the beatitudes and their thematic importance argues strongly against this result.

Bornkamm's outline of the sermon posits a thematic progression from the introduction to the law (5:15-20), antitheses (5:21-48), the practice of piety (6:1-18), new instruction on prayer (6:19-7:6), and the conclusion (7:7-12). Luz's outline uses the same sectional divisions and, like Bornkamm, finds a concentric ring arrangement with the Lord's prayer in the center. His scheme recognizes sound repetitions as structural clues at the beginning and end of the sermon. Luz notices the repetition in 7:28-8:1a of ὄχλοι, διδάσκω, and ἀνα(κατα)βαίνω . . . ὄρος from 5:1-2, the recurrence of the phrase βασιλεία τῶν οὐρανῶν in the beatitudes as an inclusio and in 7:21, and the inclusio with νόμος καὶ προφῆται which, for Allison, marks off the three pillars of the law (5:17-7:12). He also observes the patterned use of the second and third grammatical person in 5:13-16 and 7:13-27. For his organization of the main body of the sermon, however, Luz changes his theoretical base and relies on conceptual abstractions and observations of comparative length.

The main difficulties of Luz's and Bornkamm's schemes are their chiastic arrangement, the ascription of central status to the Lord's prayer and their designation of 7:12 as the end of the Sermon's main body. Our outline challenges the centrality for the whole Sermon of the Lord's prayer.[103] We find no evidence at the level of the signifier that the prayer organizes the surrounding material.[104] Far more significant for the sermon's organization

---

103 See the discussion of 5.3 in the Micro Analysis.

104 Luz, *Matthew 1-7*, admits that "the architectonic symmetry" which he discerns in the Sermon around the Lord's prayer is "apparent only when the Sermon on the Mount is read in context, and even then it does not reveal itself in the first reading but only to repeated perusal and, in a manner of speaking, in an 'optical' view." Luz concludes that

is the reprise, unit 5.0, that organizes by momentarily suspending the sermon's repetitive patterns.[105] Finally, Luz's outline like the other three used for comparison here offer no convincing reason to place a sectional break at 7:12.[106] The verse is subsumed in 7.1. where it functions as a proverbial conclusion to the unit. Although a unit break occurs after 7:12 the subsequent rehearsal (7:13) of section 7's initial aural formula indicates the sectional unity of 7:7-20. The new initial aural formula introduced in 7:21 and repeated in 7:24 clearly indicates a sectional break, although the unity of this section is seldom recognized.[107]

Our outline follows the Sermon's initial aural formulae which signal its basic organizational patterns. The sermon is sequentially organized, with no overarching organizing principle at the level of the signifier. This is due to the the sermon's paratactic quality that imitates οἱ λόγοι, even though Matthew avoids the common paratactic device of connectives (καί, δέ) at the beginnning of units and sections. Nevertheless, other devices link the sermon's sections and indicate its unity.

The sermon's first section, μακάριοι, exhibits strong aural clues to its unity: short, highly formulaic units and three interlocking inclusios which establish closure for units 1.1-1.8. Unit 1.9 effects the transition to section 2 with the apostrophe, a shift in grammatical person, and its repetition of διώκω and ἐν τοῖς οὐρανοῖς. Having established strong organizational patterns in its first two units, section 3 fails to repeat an initial aural formula, μὴ νομίσητε. Since the hearer has been led to expect repeated, initial aural formulae, this significant structural deviation signals the thematic importance of section 3 and indicates its organizational function. Likewise, the threefold repetition in the section of the epithet βασιλεία τῶν οὐρανῶν evokes the inclusio in section 1 that brackets beatitudes 1.4-1.8. This link as well as the section's concluding emphasis on ἡ δικαιοσύνη, indicates its importance.

"the Gospel of Matthew was intended in the first place for reading and not for hearing." We disagree and contend that Luz's symmetrical scheme is difficult to see because it does not exist at the level of the signifier and would not have been evident to an ancient auditor of the text, nor would the text have been known except by hearing. If the Gospel of Matthew was intended for silent rereading, it was the only such text in the ancient world.

105 Daniel Patte, *The Gospel According to Matthew, A Structural Commentary on Matthew's Faith,* (Philadelphia: Fortress Press, 1987) 65, acknowledges the organizational function of this unit. He labels it "framing material" and places the unit at the center of his chiastic outline of the Sermon. While we do not endorse his chiastic scheme, Patte's analysis indicates the importance of 5.0.

106 Kennedy, *New Testament Interpretation through Rhetorical Criticism,* 59-62, supports our alternative proposal. On the basis of his rhetorical analysis of the Sermon on the Mount, he finds the sectional break after 7:20 as in our outline and not after 7:12. Kennedy argues 7:12 is embedded in a third group of rhetorical headings in the sermon (6:19-7:20, our sections 6 and 7).

107 Daniel Patte, *The Gospel According to Matthew, A Structural Commentary on Matthew's Faith,* (Philadelphia: Fortress Press, 1987) 65, recognizes as we do the sectional break at 7:21, although he also designates 7:12 as the end of a section. None of the outlines selected for comparison acknowledge the unity of section 8, despite its clear phonetic/syntactical clues.

The beatitudes (1.4-1.8), identified for emphasis in section 1 and differentiated from units 1.1-1.3 by a separate inclusio and other features,[108] organize the material in sections 3 and 4. In section 3 those who hunger and thirst for righteousness (1.4) are those who fulfill the law. The merciful (1.5) are those who extend the prohibition against killing to outlaw anger (4.1). The clean of heart (1.6) are those who avoid adultery in the heart (4.2). The peacemakers called sons of God (1.7) are those who do not come ἐκ τοῦ πονηροῦ (4.3). Those persecuted for righteousness (1.8) are those slapped in the face and pressed into service (4.4). Those told to rejoice in their persecution (1.9) are told to pray for their persecutors (4.5). Thus the last five beatitudes thematically link the units in the first half of the sermon.[109]

While the initial aural formula does not repeat in section 3, yet the section's well integrated arrangement clearly defines it as a unit and reinforces the links that unify sections 1-4. The triple reference to the heavenly kingdom in section 3, its reference to heaven and earth after the λέγω formula, and its concluding reference to righteousness evoke the three inclusios that unite the beatitudes, (1.4-1.8). Two of its organizational features anticipate those elaborated in section 4, the recurring λέγω formula and the parallel case law example. Its opening doublet, frequent epithets, abstract terms, and repeated λέγω formula signal its semantic importance. Thus the hearer's attention is drawn to material that deviates from an expected pattern.

The first unit that falls outside the beatitudes' organizational scheme is the unusually unpatterned reprise, 5.0. While introducing a new organizational pattern for the rest of the section,[110] it exhibits strong aural ties with preceding and subsequent units. The reference to τοῖς οὐρανοῖς recalls the inclusio ἡ βασιλεία τῶν οὐρανῶν that brackets the first eight units of the μακάριοι section. The phrase ἔμπροσθεν τῶν ἀνθρώπων echoes its previous occurrence in ὑμεῖς ἐστε (section 2), the prohibition μὴ ποιεῖν recalls the prohibition of section 3, and μισθόν anticipates the λέγω formula in section 5 which echoes section 4's λέγω formula. The closing epithet, τῷ πατρὶ ὑμῶν τῷ ἐν τοῖς οὐρανοῖς, sets the theme for section 5 where references to the Father close each unit and 5.3 elaborates the prayer that begins with the same epithet. Thus the reprise encapsulates the foregoing material while establishing a new organizational pattern for section 5.

The sermon's remaining sections present more complex organizational patterns with subtler aural clues. Krister Stendahl speaks for many when he claims "VI.19–VII.29 offers material which has been brought into the Sermon on the Mount by Matthew in such a manner that we find no clue as to his

---

108 See the discussion of these units in the Micro Analysis for evidence.

109 One could argue that the beatitudes organize the Sermon's entire first half. Unit 1.1 labels and represents 1.1-1.9 which introduces the Sermon's initial aural formula and articulates the epithet inclusio. The mourners of 1.2 are those trodden on in public in 2.2. Those promised to inherit the earth in 1.3 are declared the light of the world in 2.2 and charged with the task of causing others to give glory to the Father in heaven, suggesting a correspondence between heaven and earth which recurs in the Sermon and is petitioned in the Lord's prayer (5.3.5).

110 Section 5 might properly be considered a single unit. See the discussion of 5.0 in the Micro Analysis.

arrangement."[111] This is to be expected in a text written to be heard because by the midpoint of a speech the speaker and hearer have rehearsed familiar conventions and have come to terms. Nevertheless, the signifier continues to instruct the hearer with phonetic/syntactical devices that disclose each section's limits and internal organization. The reprise at 5.0 signals an upcoming shift in organization and links the Sermon's two halves. After the extensive elaboration of the πάτερ epithet and theme in section 5, sections 6-8 suggest a dialectical movement: section 6 presents three prohibitions, section 7 three positive commands, and section 8 a synthesis encompassing "all."

The initial formulae of sections 6 and 7 correlate: each of the three units in section 6 opens with a negative imperative, while the three units of section 7 begin with a positive command. In the first unit of section 6, the first three subunits rehearse a similar parallel pattern, while the fourth (6.1.4) exhibits its own organizational pattern: it repeats its initial aural formula five times, thus creating five subunits of unequal duration and twice placing the initial aural formulae in the second position.

Section 7 exemplifies the technique of initial reinforcement, with three imperatives at the beginning of its first unit which signal the formulaic character of the section's subsequent imperatives and forecasts the threefold division of the section into units. Section 8 connects with section 7 through its emphasis on saying "Lord, Lord," (8.1) which evokes the knocking at the door in 7.1. The condemnation in 8.1, "I never knew you," recalls the theme of knowing false prophets by their fruits in 7.3. The Sermon's concluding unit (8.2) refers to and enforces the entire sermon with its repetition of τοὺς λόγους τούτους.

V. If It Ain't Got That Swing

To conclude this paper is nearly impossible, because it represents a first step. Since in a rhetorical world, reading is *recitatio* and writing is for the purpose of *recitatio*, then sound is the first clue in a text's reception and organization. This paper represents an experiment in the effort to understand sound as the primary receptive clue. As we become more familiar with the problems of sound, much more can be done, including the importance of prose rhythm, an issue we almost totally avoided. Two areas need to be pursued, the theoretics of sound reception, and the hellenistic rhetoricians' exposition of sound, about which there is some evidence.

The contributions of this paper are twofold. First it offers a close analysis of the Greek text as signifier. Whatever the paper's merit, that much has been acheived. Second, we have shown the possibility of a more empirical approach to issues of textual organization and division. We have begun to discover those phonographical clues that parallel modern typographical clues. Our analysis, based on the level of signifier, without any investment in the Sermon's semantics or a theological ideology, has significantly undercut the most significant recent proposals for the sermon's outline by disproving

---

111 "Matthew," in *Peake's Commentary on the Bible* (ed. M. Black and H. H. Rowley; Middlesex: Nelson, 1962) 779.

signficant linchpins in their construction. We need only point to those dependent on a chiastic structure, like Bornkamm's or Luz's built on the Lord's prayer, or those that make a major section break at 7:12.

If the analysis of sound is the first step, what should be the second? We would suggest that a comprehensive methodology would involve theoretically four steps: sound analysis, rhetorical analysis, literary analysis, and ideological analysis. Very briefly, we would like to indicate how our analysis supports these others.

The only sustained rhetorical analysis of the Sermon is George Kennedy's.[112] His outline, based solely on rhetorical figures and not sound, corresponds very closely to ours.

Proem	5:3-16	Sections 1-2
Thesis	5:17-20	Section 3
Kephalaia	5:21-7:20	Sections 4-7
Principle of the Law	5:21-48	Section 4
Restatement of Thesis	6:1	Section 5.1
dikaiosyne	6:2-6:18	Section 5.2-7
Epilogue	7:21-27	Section 8
Recapitulation	7:21-23	Section 8:1
Stir the audience	24-27	Section 8:2

These two analyses confirm each other and could enrich the observations of each. Our analysis had shown how 5:17-20 and 6:1 are both eccentric and related, a result Kennedy's analysis confirms. These units stand out because they are the thesis of a literate argument. Both our analyses deny a major section break at 7:12 as is traditional (almost universal). We both see the conclusion as beginning at 7:21. We both see 6:25-34 as a subunit of 6:19 and our two analyses intertwine in their explanations. The close fit of our analysis with Kennedy's confirms that the next step is a rhetorical analysis.

The third step would be a literary analysis, the consideration of the text as art. If one concludes with a rhetorical analysis, much of a text's power is lost. Both the sound and rhetorical analyses have a strong social referent, while a literary method is more concerned with the creative possiblity of the text itself. The various studies of the Sermon's sections as "focal instance" in Robert Tannehill's *The Sword in his Mouth* illustrate a literary method. He builds at times on observations about the text's sound qualities. Repetition "can release words from their literal limits."[113] The extremeness of the commands in section 4 breaks the literal limits. "The tension which is an essential part of metaphor gives the metaphor its power to point beyond the literal sense of words. In a similar way, the tension which is part of these commands points the hearer beyond the literal sense to the many situations in which" we encounter other people.[114] Such an analysis moves beyond the rhetorical argument about the purpose of the text as persuasive to demonstrate how it creates new meaning.

---

112 *New Testament Interpretation through Rhetorical Criticism*, 37-63.

113 *Semeia Supplements* (Philadelphia, Missoula: Fortress Press, Scholars Press, 1975) 81.

114 Ibid., 72.

A final step would involve an ideological (or mythological) analysis of the text. Our analysis surfaced a number of binaries that need investigation. A primary one is Father/Evil One. One might even conclude from our analysis that the epithet Heavenly Father is the Sermon's presiding metaphor. A second binary is Law/Kingdom. These two binaries correspond to Kennedy's argument that the *Kephalaia* deals with two topics, first the Law and then *dikaiosyne*. Law and Kingdom are binaries in Matthew and it sets up the interesting possibility that *dikaiosyne* and Father are binaries. Other binaries that receive prominence at the sound level are treasure/heart, heaven/earth, ψύχη/body. These binaries present interesting possibilites in ambiguity to develop a rich understanding of the Sermon and then its place in the gospel of Matthew.

For too long New Testament studies have ignored the most basic level of textual reception, the sound of language. It is time we began to pay it serious attention. As the old jazz song says, "it don't mean a thing, if it ain't got that swing."[115]

Appendix 1
Sermon on the Mount Macro Outline

Introduction
Ἰδὼν δὲ τοὺς ὄχλους
1. Μακάριοι
1.1-.8 Μακάριοι οἱ...
1.9 μακάριοί ἐστε
2. Ὑμεῖς ἐστε
2.1 ' Ὑμεῖς ἐστε τὸ ἅλας τῆς γῆς·
2.2 ' Ὑμεῖς ἐστε τὸ φῶς τοῦ κόσμου.
3. Μὴ νομίσητε
3.0.1 Μὴ νομίσητε ὅτι ἦλθον καταλῦσαι
3.0.2 ἀμὴν γὰρ λέγω ὑμῖν· ἕως ἂν παρέλθῃ ὁ οὐρανὸς καὶ ἡ γῆ,
3.0.3 λέγω γὰρ ὑμῖν ὅτι ἐὰν μὴ περισσεύσῃ ὑμῶν ἡ δικαιοσύνη πλεῖον
4. Ἠκούσατε
4.1 Ἠκούσατε ὅτι ἐρρέθη τοῖς ἀρχαίοις, οὐ φονεύσεις·
4.2.1 Ἠκούσατε ὅτι ἐρρέθη, οὐ μοιχεύσεις.
    4.2.2 Ἐρρέθη δέ, ὃς ἂν ἀπολύσῃ τὴν γυναῖκα αὐτοῦ,
4.3 Πάλιν ἠκούσατε ὅτι ἐρρέθη τοῖς ἀρχαίοις, οὐκ ἐπιορκήσεις,
4.4 Ἠκούσατε ὅτι ἐρρέθη, ὀφθαλμὸν ἀντὶ ὀφθαλμοῦ
4.5 Ἠκούσατε ὅτι ἐρρέθη, ἀγαπήσεις τὸν πλησίον σου
5. Προσέχετε τὴν δικαιοσύνην ὑμῶν
5.1 Ὅταν οὖν ποιῇς ἐλεημοσύνην,
5.2 Καὶ ὅταν προσεύχησθε,
5.3 Προσευχόμενοι δὲ μὴ βατταλογήσητε ὥσπερ οἱ ἐθνικοί,
5.4 Ὅταν δὲ νηστεύητε,

---

115 Duke Ellington (1929).

6.1.1 Μὴ θησαυρίζετε
  6.1.2 Ὁ λύχνος τοῦ σώματος
  6.1.3 Οὐδεὶς δύναται δυσὶ κυρίοις δουλεύειν·
  6.1.4 μὴ μεριμνᾶτε
    6.1.4.1 Διὰ τοῦτο λέγω ὑμῖν,
    6.1.4.2 τίς δὲ ἐξ ὑμῶν μεριμνῶν
    6.1.4.3 καὶ περὶ ἐνδύματος
    6.1.4.4 μὴ οὖν μεριμνήσητε λέγοντες
    6.1.4.5 μὴ οὖν μεριμνήσητε εἰς τὴν αὔριον,
6.2 Μὴ κρίνετε, ἵνα μὴ κριθῆτε·
6.3 Μὴ δῶτε τὸ ἅγιον τοῖς κυσίν
7. Αἰτεῖτε
7.1 Αἰτεῖτε καὶ δοθήσεται ὑμῖν,
7.2 Εἰσέλθατε διὰ τῆς στενῆς πύλης·
7.3 Προσέχετε ἀπὸ τῶν ψευδοπροφητῶν,
8. πᾶς ὁ
8.1 Οὐ πᾶς ὁ λέγων μοι, Κύριε κύριε,
8.2 Πᾶς οὖν ὅστις ἀκούει μου τοὺς λόγους τούτους
Conclusion
Καὶ ἐγένετο ὅτε ἐτέλεσεν ὁ Ἰησοῦς τοὺς λόγους τούτους

Appendix 2
Units 5.1, 5.2, 5.4

1 Ὅταν οὖν ποιῇς ἐλεημοσύνην,	Καὶ ὅταν προσεύχησθε,	Ὅταν δὲ νηστεύητε,
2 μὴ σαλπίσῃς ἔμπροσθέν σου,	οὐκ ἔσεσθε	μὴ γίνεσθε
3 ὥσπερ οἱ ὑποκριταὶ	ὡς οἱ ὑποκριταί·	ὡς οἱ ὑποκριταὶ σκυθρωποί,
ποιοῦσιν ἐν ταῖς συναγωγαῖς	ὅτι φιλοῦσιν ἐν ταῖς συναγωγαῖς	ἀφανίζουσιν γὰρ τὰ πρόσωπα αὐτῶν
καὶ ἐν ταῖς ῥύμαις,	καὶ ἐν ταῖς γωνίαις τῶν	
	πλατειῶν	
	ἑστῶτες προσεύχεσθαι,	
4 ὅπως δοξασθῶσιν	ὅπως φανῶσιν	ὅπως φανῶσιν
ὑπὸ τῶν ἀνθρώπων·	τοῖς ἀνθρώποις·	τοῖς ἀνθρώποις νηστεύοντες·
5 ἀμὴν λέγω ὑμῖν, ἀπέχουσιν	ἀμὴν λέγω ὑμῖν, ἀπέχουσιν	ἀμὴν λέγω ὑμῖν, ἀπέχουσιν
τὸν μισθὸν αὐτῶν.	τὸν μισθὸν αὐτῶν.	τὸν μισθὸν αὐτῶν.
6 σοῦ δὲ ποιοῦντος ἐλεημοσύνην	σὺ δὲ ὅταν προσεύχῃ	σὺ δὲ νηστεύων
μὴ γνώτω ἡ ἀριστερά σου,	εἴσελθε εἰς τὸ ταμεῖόν σου	ἄλειψαί σου τὴν κεφαλὴν
τί ποιεῖ ἡ δεξιά σου,	καὶ κλείσας τὴν θύραν σου	καὶ τὸ πρόσωπόν σου νίψαι,
		ὅπως μὴ φανῇς τοῖς ἀνθρώποις
		νηστεύων
ὅπως ᾖ σου ἡ ἐλεημοσύνη	πρόσευξαι τῷ πατρί σου τῷ	ἀλλὰ τῷ πατρί σου
ἐν τῷ κρυπτῷ·	ἐν τῷ κρυπτῷ·	τῷ ἐν τῷ κρυφαίῳ·
7 καὶ ὁ πατήρ σου ὁ βλέπων	καὶ ὁ πατήρ σου ὁ βλέπων	καὶ ὁ πατήρ σου ὁ βλέπων
ἐν τῷ κρυπτῷ ἀποδώσει σοι.	ἐν τῷ κρυπτῷ ἀποδώσει σοι.	ἐν τῷ κρυφαίῳ ἀποδώσει σοι.

Appendix 3

Scott/Dean	Strecker	Davies/Allison	Bornkamm	Luz
5:1 introduction	5:1 SETTING	4:23-5:2 INTRODUCTION	4:23-5:2 narrative setting	5:1 FRAMEWORK: situation
				5:3-16 INTRODUCTION: LEADING IN
1. Μακάριοι	5:3 OPENING			
5:3 Μακάριοι οἱ πτωχοί	5:3 beatitudes	5:3-12 beatitudes	5:3 introduction: beatitudes	5:3 beatitudes
5:11 μακάριοί ἐστε				
2. Ὑμεῖς ἐστε		5:13-7:12 TASK OF GOD'S PEOPLE IN THE WORLD		
5:13 Ὑμεῖς ἐστε τὸ ἅλας τῆς γῆς	5:13 the nature of discipleship	5:13-16 summary, salt and light	5:13 mission (relational)	5:13 "You are the salt of the earth"
5:14 Ὑμεῖς ἐστε τὸ φῶς τοῦ κόσμου.				
3. Μὴ νομίσητε		5:17-7:12 THE THREE PILLARS	INTRODUCTION	5:17-7:12 THE MAIN PART
		5:17-48 FIRST PILLAR: JESUS AND THE TORAH		5:17-20 INTROIT OF THE MAIN SECTION
5:17 Μὴ νομίσητε ὅτι ἦλθον καταλῦσαι	5:17 the new righteousness	5:17 introductory statement	5:17 the Law	
		5:17-20 general principles		
5:18 ἀμὴν γὰρ λέγω ὑμῖν				
5:20 λέγω γὰρ ὑμῖν ὅτι				

Scott/Dean	Strecker	Davies/Allison	Bornkamm	Luz
4. Ἠκούσατε	5:21 THE ANTITHESES	5:21-48 TWO TRIADS OF SPECIFIC INSTRUCTION	PIETY IN THE KINGDOM: ANTITHESES	5:21-48 MAIN SECTION: antitheses
5:21 Ἠκούσατε ὅτι ἐρρέθη τοῖς ἀρχαίοις, οὐ φονεύσεις	5:21 the first antithesis: on killing	5:21-32 FIRST TRIAD of instruction 5:21 murder	5:21 anger	5:21: higher righteousness 1; the antitheses 5:21 on killing
5:27 Ἠκούσατε ὅτι ἐρρέθη, οὐ μοιχεύσεις	5:27 the second antithesis: on adultery	5:27 adultery	5:27 adultery	5:27: on adultery
5:31 Ἐρρέθη δέ, ὃς ἂν ἀπολύσῃ τὴν γυναῖκα αὐτοῦ,	5:31 the third antithesis: on divorce	5:31 divorce	5:31 divorce	5:31 on divorce
5:33 Πάλιν ἠκούσατε ὅτι ἐρρέθη τοῖς ἀρχαίοις, οὐκ ἐπιορκήσεις	5:33 the fourth antithesis: on oaths	5:33-48 SECOND TRIAD of instruction 5:33 do not swear	5:33 oaths	5:33: on swearing
5:38 Ἠκούσατε ὅτι ἐρρέθη, ὀφθαλμὸν ἀντὶ ὀφθαλμοῦ	5:38 the fifth antithesis: on retaliation	5:38 turn the other cheek	5:38 retaliation	5:38 on nonviolence
5:43 Ἠκούσατε ὅτι ἐρρέθη, ἀγαπήσεις τὸν πλησίον σου	5:43 the sixth antithesis: on love of enemy	5:43 love your enemy	5:43 love for enemies	5:43: on the love of enemies
5 Ὅταν . . . μή				
6:1 (Interlude) Προσέχετε τὴν δικαιοσύνην ὑμῶν	6:1 ON ALMSGIVING, PRAYER, FASTING	6:1-18 THE SECOND PILLAR: THE CHRISTIAN CULT	PRACTICE YOUR PIETY	6:1 HIGHER RIGHTEOUSNESS 2: THE ATTITUDE TOWARD GOD
	6:1 on almsgiving	6:1 general principle	6:1 practice your piety	6:1-6 RIGHTEOUSNESS BEFORE GOD

Scott/Dean	Strecker	Davies/Allison	Bornkamm	Luz
6:2 Ὅταν οὖν ποιῇς ἐλεημοσύνην		6:2 A TRIAD OF SPECIFIC INSTRUCTION		
		6:2 Almsgiving	6:2 almsgiving	
6:5 Καὶ ὅταν προσεύχησθε	6:5 on praying	6:5 Prayer	6:5 praying	
6:7 Προσευχόμενοι δὲ μὴ βατταλογήσητε ὥσπερ οἱ ἐθνικοί	6:9 the Lord's prayer			6:7-15 THE LORD'S PRAYER WITH FRAME
6:16 Ὅταν δὲ νηστεύητε	6:16 on fasting	6:16 Fasting	6:16 fasting	6:16-18 RIGHTEOUSNESS BEFORE GOD
6 Μὴ θησαυρίζετε	6:19 INDIVIDUAL DIRECTIVES	6:19-7:12 THE THIRD PILLAR: SOCIAL ISSUES	6:19 PIETY IN THE KINGDOM: PRAYING	6:19-7:11 MAIN SECTION: possessions, judging, and prayer
		6:19 GOD AND MAMMON		
6:19 Μὴ θησαυρίζετε ὑμῖν θησαυροὺς	6:19 on wealth	6:19 triad on true treasure	6:19 treasure in heaven	6:19 do not collect earthly treasures
6:22 Ὁ λύχνος τοῦ σώματος			6:22 light of the body	
6:24 Οὐδεὶς δύναται δυσὶ κυρίοις δουλεύειν			6:24 God and mammon	
6:25 Διὰ τοῦτο λέγω ὑμῖν	6:25 on anxiety	6:25 encouragement: "do not worry"	6:25 anxiety	6:25 seek the kingdom of God
6:27 τίς δὲ ἐξ ὑμῶν μεριμνῶν δύναται				
6:28 καὶ περὶ ἐνδύματος τί μεριμνᾶτε;				

Scott/Dean	Strecker	Davies/Allison	Bornkamm	Luz
6:31 μὴ οὖν μεριμνήσητε λέγοντες· τί φάγωμεν; 6:34 μὴ οὖν μεριμνήσητε εἰς τὴν αὔριον				
7:1 Μὴ κρίνετε, ἵνα μὴ κριθῆτε	7:1 on judging	7:1 ON ONE'S NEIGHBOR 7:1 a triad on attitude towards others	7:1 judging	7:1 do not judge
7:6 Μὴ δῶτε τὸ ἅγιον τοῖς κυσίν 7. Αἰτεῖτε			7:6 pearls	7:6 do not give what is holy to the dogs
7:7 Αἰτεῖτε καὶ δοθήσεται ὑμῖν	7:7 on the answering of prayer 7:12 the golden rule	7:7 encouragement: "ask" 7:12 CONCLUDING STATEMENT: the golden rule	7:7 conclusion: pray 7:12 golden rule (relational)	7:7 courage to pray 7:12 CONCLUSION OF THE MAIN SECTION the golden rule
7:13 Εἰσέλθατε διὰ τῆς στενῆς πύλης	7:13 CLOSING ADMONITIONS AND PARABLES 7:13 the gate and the way	7:13-27 THREE WARNINGS, THE PROSPECT OF ESCHATOLOGICAL JUDGMENT 7:13 the two ways	7:13 sermon conclusion	7:13-27 CONCLUSION: LEADING OUT 7:13 the narrow and the wide door
7:15 Προσέχετε ἀπὸ τῶν ψευδοπροφητῶν	7:15 the false prophets	7:15 beware of false prophets		7:15 warning against false prophets

Scott/Dean	Strecker	Davies/Allison	Bornkamm	Luz
8: Οὐ πᾶς ὁ				
7:21 Οὐ πᾶς ὁ λέγων μοι, κύριε κύριε	7:21 the necessity of deeds			
7:24 Πᾶς οὖν ὅστις ἀκούει μου τοὺς λόγους τούτους	7:24 the closing parables: on the wise and foolish builders	7:24 the two builders		7:24: conclusion: the two housebuilders
Conclusion	EPILOGUE	CONCLUSION		FRAMEWORK
7:28-29 Καὶ ἐγένετο ὅτε ἐτέλεσεν ὁ Ἰησοῦς τοὺς λόγους τούτους	7:28-29 epilogue	7:28-8:1 conclusion	7:28-29 narrative climax	7:28-8:1a framework: reaction of the hearers

The Death of Christ as Divine Patronage in Romans 5:1-11

Raymond W. Pickett
Manhattan, Kansas

Method: The Convergence of Narrative and Social Worlds

The theme of Paul's letter to the Romans is succinctly stated in 1:16-17 where the gospel is defined in terms of the "δικαιοσύνη θεοῦ . . . ἀποκαλύπτεται ἐκ πίστεως εἰς πίστιν." The apocalypse of God's righteousness in the death and resurrection of Jesus Christ is the subject of the first eight chapters of the letter. Together these chapters comprise a portion of the letter which has a certain thematic coherence. Paul's point of departure in 1:18ff. is the creation of the world (v. 20), and his argument builds to a climax in 8:18ff. with a meditation on the hope which the children of God have in Christ for the redemption of the whole creation (vv. 21-25). In Rom. 8:20 he notes that "the creation was subjected to futility," but in Rom. 1:21 it is human beings who are characterized as "futile in their own thinking."[1] This "futility" of human thinking is symptomatic of all the ἀσέβειαν καὶ ἀδικίαν ἀνθρώπων which sets the stage for Paul's explication of the righteousness of God demonstrated primarily through the death of Christ.[2]

In this section of the letter Paul mounts a sustained argument which incorporates diatribe, midrash, and rhetorical conventions. Yet when viewed as whole these chapters have a certain narrative quality. Paul relates a story that is cosmic in scope, but has anthropology as its focus.[3] Through it he attempts to make sense of the human condition. An in depth analysis of human actions is set within an apocalyptic framework which posits a mutual dependence between human history and the history of God.[4] Although Romans is a letter and not a narrative per se, it nevertheless has a narrative

---

[1] In 1:21 Paul uses the verb ματαιόω, and in 8:20 he uses the noun ματαιότη."

[2] Although Paul's gospel includes the death and resurrection of Christ, it is evident from 3:21-26 and 5:1-12 that in this context the death is isolated as the locus of this revelation.

[3] Käsemann remarks that "the tension between cosmology and anthropology characterizes the whole of Paul's theology." Ernst Käsemann, *Commentary on Romans* (Grand Rapids: Eerdmans, 1980), p. 33.

[4] On the relationship between history and story see Norman Petersen, *Rediscovering Paul; Philemon and the Sociology of Paul's Narrative World* (Philadelphia: Fortress, 1985), p. 10.

world.[5] The story has actors both human and divine, a plot, and Paul tells it from a certain point of view. The narrative world, then, is "that reality which the narrator bestows upon his actors and upon their actions, a reality into which he authoritatively invites his audience."[6]

For the purposes of the reading of Rom. 5:1-11 being proposed in this paper, there is an advantage to conceiving of the context, or frame of reference of this text as a narrative world. While it is generally agreed that Paul's statements and exhortations are always spoken as a "word on target" for a particular situation,[7] there is diversity of opinion concerning the reasons Paul wrote to the Christians in Rome. In view of the lack of consensus about the specific situation(s) in the church in Rome which occasioned the letter, the narrative world of the letter provides another way of construing context. Even if we cannot be certain of the details of the historical context, it can be assumed that the language of the text references a world external to the text. The narrative world of the text, although a literary construction, can serve as a window on this outer world because narrative worlds have both literary and cultural dimensions.[8]

The values and conventions of a particular culture order narrative worlds in the same way that they govern life in the social worlds in which the literature is produced. A literary text has at least two fields of reference, an internal one and an external one.[9] The internal field of reference is another way of referring to the narrative world itself. The narrative world is virtually a self-contained world of plot and characterization which is usually intelligible without appeal to anything outside the text. The external field of reference, on the other hand, denotes a social world that exists apart from the text. Normally it is presupposed rather than explicitly stated, and therefore must be inferred from the text. Although this external field of reference encompasses what is typically identified as the historical context of Paul's letters, it also includes the cultural values and conventions which guide the actions and structure the convictions of actors in both narrative and social worlds.

This reading of Rom. 5:1-11 is more concerned with the relationship between the narrative world of the letter and the structural level of its external field of reference. It will be a contextual reading, but instead of using the text as a mirror which reflects the more immediate circumstances to which Paul was responding, the method employed here could be likened to an archaeological dig. The text will be excavated with a view to ascertaining its cultural landscape. The fundamental premise upon which the argument of this paper is constructed is that the narrative world of the letter is firmly embedded in the social world of the Roman empire. More specifically, Paul's interpretation of the death of Christ in Rom. 5:1-11 is seen to be predicated on the social institution of patronage, which was focused on the pivotal cultural value of

---

5 Norman Petersen provides a helpful description of the narrative world of letters, and I am dependent here on his work. *Rediscovering Paul*, pp. 7-17.

6 *Ibid.*, p. 7.

7 J. Christiaan Beker, "The Faithfulness of God and the Priority of Israel in Paul's Letter to the Romans," *HTR* 79 (1986), p. 10.

8 See Petersen, *Rediscovering Paul*, p. 9.

9 Robert Funk, *The Poetics of Biblical Narrative* (Sonoma: Poleridge Press, 1988), p. 288.

honor and the model in terms of which all relationships in the Greco-Roman world were structured.

This relationship between the narrative world of Romans and the Greco-Roman social world in which it is embedded can be further clarified by the semiotic method of analysis developed by Hendrikus Boers.[10] He differentiates between two types of structures in a grammar of discourse, semio-narrative and discursive. The semio-narrative structure, which pertains to the narrative world of Paul's letters, has a surface level and a deeper level. According to Boers, at the surface of a text are the figures which give expression to themes; the themes, being more general, lie at a deeper level. Together these constitute the discursive structure. At the deeper level of narrative semantics are the values to which the themes and figures give expression. At the deepest level is the micro-universe on which the text is based.

This reading of Rom. 5:1-11 aims to penetrate to the structural level of values in order to discern how Paul's interpretation of Christ's death in this passage is generated out of the values and social arrangements typical of Greco-Roman culture. The meaning Paul ascribes to this core theological symbol is not thereby reduced to a mere reflex of cultural values and conventions. Rather it is at the structural level that the interplay between this theological symbol and the cultural symbols which help to define its significance can be discerned. At this most fundamental level the narrative world tends to reflect the values of the social world. Only at the surface level where these structural values find expression in the themes and figures of the concrete text can the distinctiveness of Paul's explication of the death of Christ be seen.[11] Once it is apparent how the narrative world of Romans is embedded in the social world of the Roman Empire, it will be possible to discern how and to what extent Paul's interpretation of this symbol is at variance with prominent ideas, values and conventions in the culture. This can be done by following the trajectory from the surface level of the narrative world to the deeper structural level of values in order to delineate the cultural field of reference, and then follow the trajectory back to the surface to see how Paul departs from it.

The Narrative World of Romans

The narrative world of Paul's letter to the Romans operates on at least two levels. There is the narrative structure, or pattern, which includes plot, characterization, point of view, and the "mythic structure." The mythic structure is a deep structure of fundamental binary oppositions which are held to underlie and generate narrative texts.[12] While it is valid to discuss the narrative structure independently from the mythic structure, a working

---

[10] Hendrikus Boers, "The Meaning of Christ in Paul's Writings: A Structuralist-Semiotic Study," *BTB* 14 (Oct., 1984, no. 4) 131-143.

[11] Boers, "The Meaning of Christ in Paul's Writings," p. 133.

[12] Richard Hays compares the narrative structure, or pattern, to Aristotle's conception of the *mythos* of a drama, but distinguishes it from the structuralist conception of myth (*The Faith of Jesus Christ* [Chico: Scholars Press, 1983], p. 17).

premise of this paper is that the narrative structure is predicated on a mythic structure which attempts to reconcile the oppositions.[13] These oppositions are the key to ascertaining the narrative structure, and by the same token are an important link between the narrative world of the text and social world in which it is embedded.

Although the structure of Paul's argument in Romans 1-5 is in some instances convoluted, the basic plot of his gospel story in those chapters is relatively straightforward. In Rom. 1:16-18 Paul makes three thematic statements which disclose something of the moving plot line of the narrative world in this context: 1. The gospel is God's power for salvation, for Greeks as well as Jews. 2. In the gospel the righteousness of God is revealed, "from faith to faith." 3. The wrath of God is revealed against all ungodliness and wickedness of humankind.[14] The last two of these thematic statements are articulated in antithetical parallelism and spelled out in reverse order.[15] First Paul deals with the revelation of the wrath of God, and then with the revelation of righteousness. The antithesis between the righteousness of God and the ungodliness and wickedness of humankind expresses the fundamental opposition of the narrative structure. The gospel is "the power of God for salvation" inasmuch as it is able to resolve this opposition between the righteousness of God and the sinfulness of humanity.

The divine action through which the reconciliation between God and humanity occurs constitutes the plot of the narrative structure. Paul begins in 1:18-32 with an indictment of the Gentiles "who by their wickedness suppress the truth" (v. 18), and then in 2:1ff. addresses Jews who, despite their privileged status as God's people, are no better off than the Gentiles, for "both Jews and Greeks are under the power of sin" (3:9). The failure of Jew and Gentile alike to honor God sets the stage for a new manifestation of God's righteousness in 3:21ff. God's response to human beings, all of whom "have sinned and fall short of the glory of God" (3:23), was to redeem them through Jesus Christ, "whom God put forward as an expiation by his blood, to be received by faith" (3:25). Rom. 4 is a midrash on Gen. 15:6 dealing with the example of Abraham's faith, which serves as a paradigm of faith for the believer. In 4:25 Paul picks up where he left off in 3:25 with the death of Christ. In 5:1-11 he further elaborates on how through Jesus Christ believers "are saved by him from the wrath of God" (5:9), and "reconciled to God by the death of God's son" (5:10).

If a plot can be defined as "a set of events linked by temporal succession and causality,"[16] then the plot of the narrative structure of these first five chapters of Romans could be summarized in this way: all human beings have alienated themselves from God, but God has taken the initiative to provide the basis for a new relationship through the death of Christ. Paul says essentially

---

13 On mythic structure see Lévi-Strauss, "The Structural Study of Myth," in *Structural Anthropology* (New York: Basic Books, 1963), pp. 206-31.

14 The thematic statements are identified by Nils Dahl, "Missionary Theology in Romans," in *Studies in Paul* (Minneapolis: Augsburg, 1977), p. 78.

15 *Ibid.*, p. 79.

16 Stephen Moore, *Literary Criticism and the Gospels* (New Haven: Yale University Press, 1989), p. 14.

the same thing in 5:10: "while we were enemies we were reconciled to God by the death of God's Son." He makes it clear in 1:16 that the sequence of events is important: "to the Jew first and also to the Greek," but in his analysis of the human predicament he reverses the order in which he deals with Jews and Greeks. Attention to temporal succession is also reflected in the way that Paul's interpretation of the problem precedes his explanation of God's resolution. Nonetheless, it is not just how the events are linked temporally, but also the way they are linked causally, that constitutes the plot.[17]

In Rom. 1:20-26 Paul explains the cause of the human debasement he describes so vividly in that chapter in terms of humanity's unwillingness to "honor" (δοξάζω) God (v. 21).[18] He avers that "because they exchanged the truth about God for a lie and worshipped and served the creature rather than the creator," God "gave them up . . . to the dishonoring (ἀτιμάζω) of their own bodies." Dishonor, then, is both the reason humanity is at enmity with God, and the cause of the moral depravity which is deserving of God's wrath. The causal connection between these ideas occurs again in 2:5-7 where Paul contrasts those who are "storing up wrath for yourselves on the day of wrath" (v. 5) with those who "by patience in well-doing seek for glory and honor and immortality" (v. 7). He makes it clear in 2:10 that "glory and honor" are not only to be ascribed to God, but are also ascribed by God to "everyone who does good." In 2:23 it becomes apparent that Jews are likewise under the power of sin because they, too, "dishonor (ἀτιμάζω) God by breaking the law." Even in the midrash of Rom. 4, Abraham's faith is seen to be exemplary primarily because "he gave glory to God" (4:20).

The fundamental cause of the degenerate human condition to which Paul's gospel is a response is failure to honor God properly. The effect is that the distinction between God and humanity, creature and Creator (1:25), has been collapsed, and hence the wrath of God has been incurred. Paul has skillfully painted such a bleak picture of the impudence and impotence of humankind that he leaves no doubt in the reader's mind that only God is capable of restoring the human condition. The action which God takes to redeem sinful human beings comprises the second major movement of the plot in these chapters. The means through which God provides human beings with a new status before God, i.e. justification, is the death of Christ. The transitional verses are 3:23-25 where Paul concludes that while "all have sinned and fall short of the glory of God" (v. 23), God reestablishes a relationship characterized by honor/glory through a "gift" (v. 24). That gift is none other than God putting forward God's own Son, Jesus Christ, as an expiation through his death (v. 25).

The pieces of the plot converge in Rom. 5:1-11 where human beings who are characterized as "weak," "ungodly," "sinners," and "enemies" of God deserving of "wrath" are given a new status before God which is denoted by the terms "justified," "peace," "access to this grace," recipients of "God's love," and "reconciliation." This is accomplished through the death of Christ,

---

17 *Ibid.*, p. 14-15.

18 The RSV appropriately translates δοξάζω as "honor" because it belongs to the same semantic domain, as is evidenced by how they are virtually interchangeable in Rom. 2:7, 10.

which is mentioned no less than four times in 5:6-10. In order to perceive the line of reasoning by which this occurs in the narrative it will be necessary to see how the narrative functions at the structural level, but prior to making that move it will be helpful to look at yet one more aspect of plot.

Stephen Moore notes that plot and character are inseparably bound up in the reading experience. "Characters are defined in and through the plot, by what they do and by what they say."[19] What is surprising about Rom. 1-5 is not that God is the main character, but that even the death of Christ is in every instance conceived of as God's action. In 3:25 God put him forward (προέθετο) "as an expiation by his blood." Although it is not certain whether God is intended as the subject in 4:25, it is clear that Jesus is the object of the aorist passive verb παρεδόθη. In Rom. 5:6 Paul does say that "Christ died for the ungodly," but in v. 8 this is seen to be a demonstration of God's love. His point of view is different here than in 2 Cor. 5:14 where the death of Christ is interpreted as a demonstration of the "love of Christ," or in Gal. 2:20 where it is Christ who in and through death "loved me and gave himself for me." God is undoubtedly the protagonist in this drama, which is universal in its scope, and Paul's point of view is unquestionably theocentric, as opposed to the christocentric perspective typical of some of his other letters. These are significant aspects of the narrative world of this letter.

From Narrative Structure to Mythic Structure

The narrative world of Romans is characterized by several antitheses or oppositions which lend themselves to structural analysis. Lévi-Strauss has described the logical processes which are at the root of mythical thought as a progression from the awareness of oppositions toward their resolution.[20] This reconciliation of opposites usually occurs through a mediator. The gospel story which Paul relates in Rom. 1-5 seems to fit this pattern, and therefore it seems appropriate to interpret it in the light of the basic logic of myth.[21] The fundamental opposition which is the focus of the story is introduced in the thematic statements of 1:16-18 where the "righteousness of God" is contrasted with the "ungodliness and unrighteousness of men." Humanity dishonored God and so God "gave them up" (παρέδωκεν) to their own "dishonorable passions" (1:21-26). This relational opposition between God and humanity is what needs to be reconciled.

The other antitheses which come into view as the argument unfolds correspond to, or are variations of this root antithesis. There are some other fundamental antitheses such as death/life, slavery/freedom, and law/grace, but in one way or another they all describe the quality or means of a person's relationship to God. For example, in Rom. 6 death is a consequence of sin (vv. 16, 23), and the believer is freed from slavery to sin (vv. 20-22). Believers die to

---

19 Moore, *Literary Criticism and the Gospels*, p. 15.

20 Lévi-Strauss, "The Structural Study of Myth," p. 224.

21 Lévi-Strauss distinguishes the logic of myth from philosophical logic, but notes that it is just as rigorous ("The Structural Study of Myth," p. 230). For the suitability of myth as a category of intepretation for Paul's letters see Hendrickus Boers, "Interpreting Paul: Demythologizing in Reverse," pp. 153-172.

sin, or are freed from sin, in order that they might "live to God" (6:10, 22), which is the desired end of the righteousness manifested through the death of Christ. The polarity between sin and righteousness denotes, then, the fundamental opposition between humanity and God, which is the primary focus of Paul's argument. Although sin has a variety of nuances in this context, it is evident from the categorical indictment of humanity in 3:23 that sin here, as in 1:20-26, is associated with a "lack of honor for God" (ὑστεροῦνται τῆς δόξης τοῦ θεοῦ).

If we use Greimas' schema for classifying the elements of narrative, the structure of Paul's gospel story looks like this:

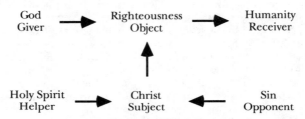

This diagram of the narrative substructure of Romans is derived from the first three chapters which culminate in 3:21-26 where Paul compresses the entire drama into a succinct theological synopsis of the plot. God (Giver) revealed God's righteousness (Object) through the death of Christ (Subject), thereby conferring on humanity (Receiver) a status in relation to God which had been precluded by sin (Opponent).

In Rom. 5:1-11 this same narrative substructure is reiterated in somewhat different language, and in a manner which recalls the analysis of the human predicament in Rom. 1:18ff. Here the new standing with God (δικαιωθέντες) mediated through Christ and obtained through faith is described in terms of "peace with God" (5:1). This verse alludes to Rom. 1:18 where Paul announces that "the wrath of God is revealed from heaven against all ungodliness and unrighteousness." The connection is made explicit in v. 9 which indicates that the net result of having been justified through the death of Christ (ἐν τῷ αἵματι αὐτοῦ) is that "we will be saved through him from the wrath of God." In v. 10 believers are characterized as "enemies" of God prior to being "reconciled to God by the death of his Son." Now through Christ they are able to approach God (προσαγωγή), and share in the "hope of the glory of God" (5:2). Christ's role as the mediator of the righteousness of God which makes this new status possible is designated principally by the preposition διά. This preposition is used seven times in vv. 1-11. Although it refers expressly to the death of Christ only twice, Paul also uses ὑπέρ (5: 6,7,8) and ἐν (5: 9,10) to emphasize that Christ's death is the focal point of the mediation.

A plausible external frame of reference for this aspect of the narrative structure of Rom. 5:1-11 are attitudes towards the gods typical of pagans in the Greco-Roman world. Robin Lane Fox argues that despite many variations in local practice, there was a common core in pagan piety. What these pagan cults shared was a fundamental aim to honor the gods in order to avert the misfortunes which might result from the gods' own anger at their neglect.

Hence the notion of divine wrath was central to pagan mythology. In Fox's view, "any account of pagan worship which minimizes the gods' uncertain anger and mortals' fear of it is an empty account."[22] The few references to the fear of God in Romans betrays similar convictions. The citation from Ps. 35:2 (LXX) in Rom. 3:18 indicates that Paul thinks there is a connection between the lack of righteousness which is characteristic of humanity (3:9-10), and the absence of a fear of God. Moreover, Rom. 8:15 suggests that previously the believer's relationship to God was characterized by fear. The advice Paul gives in Rom. 13:3-4 regarding governing authorities also reflects the view that fear is an appropriate disposition toward those civil servants who are the instruments of God's wrath.

Roman religious beliefs and rituals were important inasmuch as the Romans presumed that the safety and prosperity of their communities depended upon the gods, whose favor was won and held by the correct performance of the full range of cult practices.[23] The phrase πᾶσαν ἀσέβειαν καὶ ἀδικίαν ἀνθρώπων, which in Rom. 1:18 describes the reason for the manifestation of God's wrath, would also typify pagan ideas about the causal relation between human impiety and divine wrath. As Dunn points out, it is an all-embracing phrase which in Greek thought would include hostility to or disregard for what was generally accepted to be good religious practice, in particular failure to observe the state cultus.[24] The divine wrath which was the consequence of not honoring the gods through the appropriate religious practices was customarily abated by means of expiatory rituals.[25] That this same basic structural pattern underlies the narrative world of Rom. 1-5 is implied not only by the causal connection between wrath and impiety (ἀσέβεια), but also by the way in which Paul conceives of the death of Christ as a means of expiation (ἱλαστήριον). This idea is stated explicitly in 3:25, and also conveyed by the cultic language ἐν τῷ αἵματι αὐτοῦ in 5:9 which emphasizes the sacrificial significance of Christ's death.

If Paul's version of the gospel story in Rom. 1-5 is in some sense predicated on, or at least consonant with this pandemic mythic structure, it also departs from it at a critical point. In pagan cults the gods were propitiated by those who offered gifts to avert their anger or gain their favor, but in Rom. 3:25 it is God who presents Christ in death as a means of expiation. In contrast to the pattern typical of pagan cults, believers are saved from God's wrath and reconciled to God not by their own efforts, but by means of God's own action in and through the death of Christ. Instead of the believer offering gifts to divert God's wrath, it is God who provides the gift which allows God's "enemies" to have "peace with God." In going a step further and construing the death of Christ

---

22 Robin Lane Fox, *Pagans and Christians* (New York: Alfred A. Knopf, 1986), p. 38.

23 P. Garnsey and R. Saller, *The Roman Empire; Economy, Society and Culture* (Berkley and Los Angeles: University of California Press, 1987), p. 163.

24 James D. G. Dunn, *Word Biblical Commentary: Romans 1-8* (Dallas: Word Books, Publisher, 1988), p. 55. Although Dunn notes that Paul hardly uses ἀσέβεια and that ἀδικία is the more dominant concept, he offers no explanation of why Paul uses it here. The fact that he uses this term along with the more familiar ἀδικία is probably significant, and may indeed be an intentional reference to Greco-Roman beliefs about the connection between impiety and wrath.

25 See Garnsey and Saller, *The Roman Empire*, p. 163.

not only as a means of reconciliation but also as a demonstration of God's love (5:8), Paul is in effect revising a traditional conception of God.[26] In fact, this seems to be the primary aim of his explication of the death of Christ in Rom. 5:1-11. As a demonstration of God's righteousness, the death of Christ provides a new perspective on who God is in relation to humanity.

What is interesting about the narrative structure of Rom. 1-5 is that while it incorporates this common mythic pattern of averting divine wrath through an expiatory offering, that pattern does not explain the process by which believers are reconciled to God through the death of Christ. Since Paul conceives of the death of Christ as a gift of God, it does not follow that God is placating God's own wrath. Rather the death of Christ is interpreted in this context as a defining moment or symbol of God's character. Paul's concern about the development of the believer's character in 5:3-5 corresponds to his interest in transforming their perception of God's character. The death of Christ in these chapters is construed as a manifestation of God's righteousness (1:17; 3:21-26) and God's love (5:8), and so in order to understand Paul's rhetoric of reconciliation in Rom. 5 it is necessary to ascertain the basis of this theological claim. If the mythic pattern of propitiating divine wrath cannot account for Paul's interpretation of the death of Christ here, then the logic by which believers are reconciled to God must be informed by some other model.

From Narrative World to Social World

In his discussion of the relationship between the narrative world of Paul's letters and their social world, Petersen notes that while God and Christ are actors in the narrative world, they are absent from the social world. They are present only as objects of knowledge. He goes on to point out, however, that "because God and Christ are known in terms of role names derived from the earthly social universe, their symbolic universe is also conceived of by believers in social terms, however metaphorical they may be."[27] In other words, even though God and Christ are actors only in the narrative world, their actions and relations are nonetheless structured by and understood in terms of the values and social conventions of Greco-Roman society. The primary focus of Rom. 1-5 is the new standing, or means of relating to God established by the death of Christ, and hence the social values and conventions which shape human interaction also form the basis for the relationship between God and humanity. Since these social values and conventions provide the rationale for human behavior and intercourse, they also help to explain how human beings conceive of their relationship to God.

---

[26] Leander Keck has argued that vv. 6-7 interupt the flow of thought in the paragraph and turn it into a moralizing reflection on Christ's death. This, along with the confused manuscript tradition, leads him to the conclusion that these verses are a post-pauline interpolation. If Keck is right, and these verses are eliminated, this puts even more emphasis on the death of Christ as something which pertains more to God. See Leander Keck, "The Post-Pauline Interpretation of Jesus' Death in Rom 5,6-7" in *Theologia Crucis – Signum Crucis*, eds. C. Anderson and G. Klein (Tübingen: J. C. B. Mohr, 1979), pp. 237-248.

[27] Petersen, *Rediscovering Paul*, p. 28.

In the previous section I suggested that the mythic pattern typical of pagan piety provides a frame of reference for comprehending some of the pivotal ideas of the narrative structure of Rom. 1-5, e.g., wrath, fear, and expiation, but that it does not really explain Paul's conception of how believers are reconciled to God through the death of Christ. However, that mythic pattern does pivot upon an important social value which is also central to the narrative world of Rom. 1-5, namely honor. The chief concern of the gods of pagan cults was honor and the due offering of gifts. They were honored for their power and their capacity for benefaction.[28] In Rom. 1:20-26 it is precisely the failure to honor God which is the source of the sin that has resulted in humanity's estrangement from God. Honor, as it pertains to God, is the social value upon which the narrative world and social world of Rom. 1-5 converge.

In Greco-Roman society honor and its counterpart, shame, were associated with social status. A person's rank and status determined their place in the social hierarchy, and relationships within this framework were based on the reciprocal exchange of favors and services. Benefaction and requital were matters of honor, and the dynamics of the exchange partially determined the social status of those involved. The proper conduct of a recipient was to acknowledge and advertise the benefactor's generosity and power.[29] The predominant model for this ethic of reciprocity was that of patron-client. Patron-client relations were based on a strong element of inequality and difference in power. A patron had social, economic, and political resources that were needed by a client. In return, a client could give expressions of loyalty and honor that were useful for the patron.[30]

Paul's characterization of God and the relationship between God and humanity seem to bear the influence of the patron-client model of social relations. It will be recalled from our examination of Rom. 1:18ff. that humanity has incurred the wrath of God because of its failure to honor God. Paul virtually equates sin with dishonoring God (cf. 2:23; 3:23). Honor in this context is not a civic virtue but is exclusively reserved for God; it is God's glory (δόξα, 1:21, 23) and God's power (1:20). Nevertheless, in an honor society the term cannot be disassociated from its social connotations. As a theological value it has the same force and function that it does as a social value. As with any patron, it is humanity's due to render the honor which is due to God (1:21).[31]

In the narrative world of these first five chapters of Romans God assumes the role of divine patron. An important motive for patronage in Greco-Roman society was a desire for repute (δόξα) and honor (τιμή). This is the desire Paul imputes to God in Rom. 1:18-27 where failure to comply has resulted in a manifestation of the wrath of God (1:18). In this respect Paul's characterization of God here is no different from pagan mythology in which the gods are honored in the hope of divine help and protection, and in order to avert their anger. For Paul God is the ultimate patron who as creator expects exclusive

---

28 Robin Lane Fox, *Pagans and Christians*, pp. 39-40.

29 Garnsey and Saller, *The Roman Empire*, p. 148.

30 Halvor Moxnes, "Patron-Client Relations and the New Community in Luke-Acts," in *The Social World of Luke-Acts*, ed. Jerome Neyrey (Peabody, Mass.: Hendrickson, 1991), p242.

31 See Halvor Moxnes, "Honour and Righteousness in Romans," *JSNT* 32 (1988), p. 66.

loyalty (πίστις) from humanity. Since Paul's analysis of the human predicament in Rom. 1:18ff. is focused on images of honor, the patron-client model helps to elucidate mutual expectations in the relationship between God and humanity.

God acts as divine patron to reconcile humanity through the death of Christ. Paul's comprehensive indictment of all Gentiles and Jews as having sinned and fallen short of the glory of God (3:23) leaves them in a helpless state unable to do anything on their own to improve their standing with God. Rhetorically, it is apparent that he intends to invoke this sense of impotence in the reader/hearer in order to increase appreciation of what God has done on their behalf. This is evident, for example, in his use of the phrase ὄντων ἡμῶν ἀσθενῶν in 5:6, which is followed by the claim that Christ ὑπὲρ ἀσεβῶν ἀπέθανεν. It has already been observed, however, that throughout Paul conceives of the death of Christ as something which God does (3:25; 8:3) and which reveals who God is (3:21; 5:8). As divine patron, God provides the believer with a new status (δικαιόω) and unprecedented access (προσαγωγή) through the death of Christ.

In the light of the patron-client model, the death of Christ would be perceived as divine benefaction, but it is not clear yet just how this particular act of benefaction resolves the opposition between God and humanity. Acts of benefaction tended to reinforce the difference in status between patron and client, and so as a frame of reference for understanding Christ's death it would underscore the indebtedness of those who enjoyed its benefits. Given his remarks in 1:23, 25 about how human minds have been darkened because "they exchanged the truth about God for a lie and worshipped and served the creature rather than the Creator," Paul may well have intended his depiction of God as patron to reinforce the distinction between Creator and creature. The fact that these respective roles have been blurred is, in his estimation, a fundamental cause of the sin which has alienated humanity from God. The paradox of Paul's position in Rom. 1-8, though, is that his emphasis on honoring God as divine patron, i.e., acknowledging the sovereignty of God, is combined with an even more important emphasis on the new familial relationship with God established through the death of Christ which is characterized by love and solidarity (5:8; cf. 8:14ff.).

The inequality and asymmetry in power and status which typified patron-client relationships was often combined with expressions of mutual solidarity.[32] Presenting the death of Christ as an act of divine patronage allows Paul to emphasize God's unique status as sovereign of the world, while at the same time expressing God's solidarity with humanity. As divine patron who gives Christ over to death, συνίστησιν δὲ τὴν ἑαυτοῦ ἀγάπην εἰς ἡμᾶς ὁ θεός, that is to say, the death of Christ is a demonstration of God's solidarity with "ungodly" (ἀσεβῶν) human beings. The same idea is conveyed by defining the righteousness of God in terms of the death of Jesus (3:21-25). The term δικαιοσύνη has its origins in the Hebrew Bible, and is essentially a

---

32 S. N. Eisenstadt and L. Roniger, *Patrons, Clients and Friends: Interpersonal Relations and the Structure* (Cambridge: Cambridge University Press, 1984), pp. 48-49. According to Eisenstadt and Roniger, this is one of the paradoxical contradictions which constitute one of the major features of the patron-client nexus.

concept of relation signifying trustworthiness or loyalty in regard to the community.[33] The "righteousness of God," as Käsemann has shown, has the character of gift and power, both of which are integral to notions of patronage.[34] This new manifestation of God's righteousness is gift and power inasmuch as God, as divine patron, does for human beings what they could not do for themselves, namely restore their relationship to God.

Paul's use of the word ἐχθρός in 5:10 denotes the severity of human rebellion and implies the magnitude of the loyalty, or solidarity which God demonstrates through the death of Christ.[35] However, Paul may also have chosen this term because it signifies something about the nature of the new status obtained through Christ's death. The converse of enmity, or being an "enemy," was friendship, one of the more important types of patron-client relationships in the Greco-Roman world. The ideal of friendship was also predicated on the ethic of reciprocity, and was usually sought by equals, people of the same status, though friendship between non-equals was possible.[36] Giving between friends was done with an eye to receiving, whether it be for material gain or honor. It is conceivable that friendship is the model of patron-client relations which serves a frame of reference for Rom. 5. Since this material is preceded by the midrash on Abraham in Rom. 4, an inter-textual echo of the reference to Abraham as a friend God is possible (cf. 2 Chron. 20:7; Isa. 41:8).[37] God's solidarity with humanity through the death of Christ transforms enemies of God into friends of God. The righteousness of God, manifested in the death of Christ, is the divine patron's loyalty and faithfulness to sinful humanity. It is the gift of solidarity through which God reconciles those creatures who willfully ignored and dishonored the Creator (cf. 1:219-23). This gift, like all acts of patronage, carries with it an obligation.[38] The obligation is honor, but Paul defines the honor which God desires in terms of "the obedience of faith" (1:5; cf. 5:19).

From Social World to Historical Context

The values of honor and shame and the patron-client model of relations were central to the daily lives of everyone in the Greco-Roman world. Within the framework of the social hierarchy people of every rank and status were motivated by the desire for honor. They were guided in their interpersonal

---

33 Ernst Käsemann, "'The Righteousness of God' in Paul," in *New Testament Questions of Today* (Philadelphia: Fortress, 1969), p. 172.

34 Ibid., p. 170.

35 Dieter Georgi remarks that "Romans 5:6-8 turns martyrdom into a death that establishes solidarity with the rebel and the enemy. This view of martyrdom protests the one-sided understanding of loyalty which prevailed in contemporary social and political life." Dieter Georgi, *Theocracy in Paul's Praxis and Theology* (Minneapolis: Fortress, 1991), 97.

36 See Alan Mitchell, "The Social Function of Friendship in Acts 2:44-47 and 4:32-37," *JBL* 11/2 (1992), p. 264.

37 James 2:23 refers to Abraham as "the friend of God," and 4:4 reverses the ideas in a way reminiscent of Romans: "friendship with the world is enmity with God."

38 Käsemann's description of the divine righteousness unwittingly reflects the dynamics of patronage: "Paul knows no gift of God which does not convey both the obligation and capacity to serve" ("'The Righteousness of God' in Paul," p. 170).

relations by the ethic of reciprocity. In exchange for favors and services, the recipient honored the benefactor for his generosity and power. The same social values and conventions obtained in the context of religious worship. Pagan deities were honored for their help and protection, and in order to avert their wrath. As Garnsey and Saller assert, "in Rome, as in other societies, religious institutions and practices reflected the power relations within the community and provided the justification for the existing order."[39] It would be difficult to overestimate the extent to which these values and conventions influenced every aspect of social, religious, and political life in the Roman Empire.

Honor and the system of patronage were so much a part of the fabric of society that the Christians in Rome would undoubtedly have understood Paul's gospel story in terms of this cultural paradigm. In other words, from a reader-response perspective, this cultural paradigm would have served as the reader/hearer's frame of reference for interpreting Paul's explication of the manifestation of God's righteousness in the death of Christ. So even if these values and conventions are not always explicit in the rhetoric of argumentation in Romans, they at least comprise the sub-text upon which the letter was constructed and in the light of which it was interpreted. There is some indication though, that they may serve as more than a tacit frame of reference for interpreting the letter.

The rhetoric of honor and wrath, righteousness and power, patronage and beneficence not only denotes pivotal social values and conventions, it was also the power language of the imperial ruling elite.[40] In a recent study, Dieter Georgi has suggested that by using such loaded terms as εὐαγγέλιον, πίστις, δικαιοσύνη, and εἰρήνη as central concepts in Romans, Paul intentionally evoked their associations to Roman political theology.[41] By depicting God as divine patron in Rom. 1-5, especially in demonstrating righteousness and love through the death of Christ, Paul may indeed have been challenging the emperor's role as great patron of all.[42] Garnsey and Saller point out that "Augustus sought to establish his legitimacy not only by restoring the social order, but also by demonstrating his own supremacy in it through the traditional modes of patronage and beneficence.[43] The theocentric point of view, the emphasis on God's sovereignty, the rhetoric of peace and loyalty (πίστις), and the focus on God's beneficence (χάρις) are all features of Romans which suggest that Paul intends to engage the imperial ideology.

The phrase ἐν ὁμοιώματι εἰκόνος φθαρτοῦ ἀνθρώπου in Rom. 1:23 may be more than a general reference to idolatry, as most commentators think. Even though the argument draws on standard Jewish polemic against idolatry,[44] the singular ἀνθρώπου may allude to the cult of the Emperor. Like gods, the Emperors were agents of unpredictable powers and benefaction, and hence

---

39 Garnsey and Saller, *The Roman Empire*, p. 163.

40 See Orlando Patterson, *Freedom in the Making of Western Culture* (New York: Basic Books, 1991), p. 341.

41 Georgi, *Theocracy in Paul's Praxis and Theology*, p. 83.

42 Seneca's description of the emperor in *de Clem.* 1.13.5.

43 Garnsey and Saller, *The Roman Empire*, p. 149.

44 Dunn, *Romans 1-8*, p. 61.

they received divine honors from their subject communities.[45] According to Pliny, the good Emperor was more of a paternal protector and benefactor than an efficient administrator.[46] As Garnsey and Saller observe, "since subjects could not repay imperial benefaction in kind, the reciprocity ethic dictated that they make a return in the form of deference, respect and loyalty."[47] The sovereignal freedom of the semidivine Emperor was the basis of the personal freedom of the freedman proletariat and middle classes. Patterson maintains that "the masses promoted his divine *dignitas* and celebrated his glory not only because it guaranteed their own personal freedom, but because the greater the honor and glory of their emperor, the greater the collective honor and glory of all Roman citizens."[48] Dio Chrysostom even depicts the Emperor as a patron who acted on the basis of friendship.[49]

Together these facets of the imperial ideology form part of a larger narrative about the Emperor which would have been a requisite frame of reference for anyone in the Roman Empire, but especially a resident of Rome. They also bear a striking resemblance to the themes, plot, and characterization of the narrative world of Rom. 1-5. Paul depicts God as sovereign of the world who deserves the honor and loyalty of humanity. God acts as divine patron by demonstrating God's righteousness and love in and through the death of Christ, which is conceived as an act of beneficence (χάρις) and loyalty (πίστις). The ethic of reciprocity is also operative in this narrative. However, the honor which God desires is not the homage paid to a pagan deity or divine Emperor. It is an honor which finds expression through the "obedience of faith." Ultimately, though, it is not just the sovereignty and divinity of the Emperor that is challenged. The very idea of patronage is thrown into question. The divine patronage enacted through the death of Christ is a demonstration of solidarity with "godless" and "unrighteous" humanity which, in the end, has no conditions or contingencies. In effect, the reciprocity ethic collapses because the gift which God gives in the death of Christ is Godself. In the end, God is a patron who doesn't act like a patron, for the distance which normally separates patron from client is bridged, God's enemies are reconciled to God through the death of Christ (5:10).

---

45 Fox, *Pagans and Christians*, p. 40.

46 *Panegyric* 2.21, cited in Garnsey and Saller, *The Roman Empire*, p. 149.

47 Garnsey and Saller, *The Roman Empire*, p. 149.

48 Patterson, *Freedom in the Making of Western Culture*, p. 337.

49 *Or.* 3:86-122, cited in Moxnes, "Patron-Client Relations and the New Community in Luke-Acts," 246.

Seized by the Cross: The Death of Jesus in Paul's Transformative Discourse

Alexandra R. Brown
Washington and Lee University

> I appeal to you, brothers and sisters, by the name of our Lord Jesus Christ, that all of you be in agreement and that there be no divisions among you, but that you be united in the same mind and the same purpose. (1 Cor 1:10, NRSV)

> For the Word of the cross is folly to those who are perishing, but to us who are being saved, it is the power of God. (1 Cor 1:18, RSV)

> 'For who has known the mind of the Lord so as to instruct him?' But we have the mind of Christ. (1 Cor 2:16, RSV)

> Saying what is can effect a set of circumstances with every bit of transformational impact that Austin first invoked to show that Words do things other than what they say.[1]

Introduction

In 1 Corinthians 1-2, Paul strikes at the heart of schism in the church. His principal weapon is the "Word of the cross" (1:18);[2] with it he breaches the barriers of ego and ideology—even Christian ideology—that divide believers at Corinth. His battleground is the realm of human perception; wielding the Word of the cross he invades the perceptual landscape of his hearers, cutting across their accustomed (and, he believes, false) ways of knowing with the sharp expression of a new reality. The effectiveness of this strike, Paul's letter suggests, rests in the power of the Word he preaches to liberate both minds and bodies from the grasp of the false world to which he elsewhere refers as "this present evil age" (Gal 1:4). Paul's discourse is aimed toward reconciling the Corinthian church, but it reaches beyond the historical contingencies of ancient Corinth, revealing the power of the cross proclamation to address and

---

[1] Sandy Petrey, *Speech Acts and Literary Theory* (London: Routledge, 1990) 27.

[2] Hereafter, I will refer to the Word of the cross without quotation marks, using Word to indicate the message communicated by Paul's *words*.

transform succeeding generations of readers/hearers. How the words of the text work to reveal the Word that transforms life is the subject of this study.

Our text reveals both that the transformation in view is a perceptual one—it concerns the way one sees the world—and that it is governed by the cross. The perceptual focus is established by Paul's opening appeal for unity of mind, the density of perceptual language (especially wisdom terminology) in the text, and by the culminating noetic claim of the argument at 2:6, "But we have the mind of Christ." As we will see, perceptual terminology is especially prevalent in the part of the discourse devoted to the cross where it is also strikingly intertwined with apocalyptic language and image. The way these themes, perception, cross and apocalypse, combine in our text leaves little doubt that Paul's aim in preaching the cross is to alter his hearers' perception *of* the world in such a way as to alter their experience *in* the world. In the preaching of the cross, something is unveiled that moves the one who perceives it from one world to another, from the divided mind to the "mind of Christ."

The clustering of wisdom and apocalyptic motifs in this discourse has prompted a number of studies in recent decades, many of them driven by history-of-religions concerns to determine the position Paul encounters and opposes in Corinth.[3] Typically in these studies, an effort is made to separate Paul's theology from that of his opponents and to show how he adopts, adapts or rejects available traditions in the service of the "core" of this thought, the "theology of the cross." While these studies have made valuable contributions to understanding the text's "background," they have tended to eclipse certain rhetorical aspects of Paul's discourse on the cross, especially the function of the cross in promoting the cognitive transformation Paul strives for in the letter.

This study depends on those "background" studies but goes beyond them to explore how Paul's preaching on the death of Jesus—his Word of the cross—works in a particular social and linguistic context toward the perceptual transformation of his hearers. My focus, then, is the *function* of Paul's Word of the cross in 1 Corinthians 1-2. Faced with disintegration in the community, Paul writes a letter that he intends to have reconciling effect. As active agent of this reconciliation, he introduces in forceful, apocalyptic language, the Word he expects to have power to reconcile its hearers. The force of the Word he brings is apparent in the internal workings of the text itself; its entry into the discourse causes a disruption of the conventions of language that both shape

---

[3] In addition to the several important studies that locate Gnosticism in our test (W. Lütgert, R. Bultmann, W. Schmithals, U. Wilckens, P. Winter) there are others that employ similar methodology (research in the history of religions) and find the text's determinative background in Jewish wisdom traditions (H. Conzelmann, J. Dupont, A. Feuillet, H. Windisch), in combinations of wisdom and apocalyptic traditions (R. Scroggs), or in certain strains of Hellenistic Jewish philosophy (R. Horsley, B. Pearson), specifically Philo. These studies have yielded tremendous insight into the complexity of the Corinthian milieu and into Paul's own theological and philosophical depth. They have *not* yielded consensus either on the precise identity of Paul's Corinthian opponents or on the operative background for Paul's own formulations in 1 Corinthians. For a selected bibliography, see my dissertation, "Paul's Apocalyptic Word of the Cross" (Ph.D. diss. Columbia University, 1990) 608, nn. 6, 7, 8, 9, 10.

and reflect the world of ordinary perception. In its capacity to disrupt perceptual structures, the Word has destructive force; but this is not its only force. The discourse ends with the announcement of a newly created perceptual organ, the "mind of Christ." True to its apocalyptic setting, the Word of the cross creates anew in the rubble of destruction.

I. Speech Act Theory and the "Total Speech Situation" in 1 Corinthians

One way to talk about the effects of Paul's Word of the cross is to use his own language, the time-honored language of apocalyptic that is sounded whenever despair of the present order meets the hope of a new beginning. In these times apocalyptic language may work not only to predict destruction but to elicit hope, to create new forms, to inspire new vision. In these times apocalyptic language not only says something but does something in the saying. It does not merely describe a state of affairs, it produces hope.

Modern philosophers and literary critics have found other ways of talking about the power of words to effect conditions. The work of analytic philosopher J. L. Austin on what he called the "performative force" of certain utterances has inspired an array of inquiries from diverse quarters into how words "work." Not least among Austin's admirers are a growing number of biblical scholars who appreciate among other things, the functional nature of his method and the freedom it offers the interpreter from both formalist and metaphysical preoccupations of other methodologies.[4]

My own efforts to evaluate the function of the Word of the cross in Paul's discourse have been further stimulated by Austin's work on performatives. Although I borrow from his work very selectively, attending primarily to his insights about the conventions of language that enable it to function, I see enough parallels between Austin's performatives and Paul's apocalyptic presentation of the cross to make a formal comparison that I hope will enhance our understanding of how Paul's Word of the cross functions in a particular social and linguistic context. Paul's proclamation of Jesus' death, I will argue, has what Austin calls "performative force" to effect in the minds of its hearers the transformation it narrates. While I claim only a modest usefulness for the application of Austin's ideas, I believe the theory does have value for enhancing our understanding of the Word of the cross as a functional, indeed transforming agent of the discourse as a whole.

---

4 Hugh C. White describes the attraction of literary critics to Austin's theory: "Literary critics have been attracted to speech act theory for two primary reasons. First the theory has opened the possibility of a functional approach to literature which is less encumbered with metaphysical presuppositions than previous theories of criticism . . . Secondly, speech act theory offers the means to orient the reader away from various formalisms which detach the text from its historical and social matrix, toward its concrete context, without engulfing it once again in the psychological, social and historical conditions of its production." Hugh C. White, "Introduction: Speech Act Theory and Literary Criticism," *Semeia* 41 (1988), 2. In my own use of the theory, I wish to deny neither metaphysical implications of the text nor the importance of the historical conditions of its production. Speech Act theory is certainly not "engulfed" by these concerns, but neither are they necessarily precluded by the methods Speech Act theory engenders. My interest in historically-informed theological hermeneutics will be evident in the paper.

In what follows, I will briefly review features of Austin's theory that are relevant to my interpretation. Then, with Austin's insights in mind (yet not intending a thorough-going application of speech act theory), I will turn to the text itself to suggest how the performance of the Word of the cross takes place.

Austin's Discovery: "The Performative Utterance"

Austin's most celebrated contribution to analytic philosophy is his division of spoken utterances into two classes that he took at first to be absolutely distinct. Constatives, he said, are utterances that state or describe something; their aim is to represent reality. "The cat is on the mat" is his best-known example of a constative. Other utterances, which he called "performatives," do more than describe reality; they aim to *do* something. Some performatives, he called "illocutionary acts." These are utterances that *do* what they *say* in the saying, such as warnings, promises, bets and the like. Others, called "perlocutionary acts," bring about an effect in the hearer *by* the saying, such as when a speaker convinces, persuades or intimidates someone. The "perlocutionary act," Austin states, "is the achieving of certain effects by saying something" while the illocutionary act "has a certain force *in* saying something."[5]

Austin thought it important to distinguish between these two kinds of performance. The difference turns on whether the utterance acts *in* the saying or acts *by* the saying. The illocutionary capacity of an utterance to act *in* the saying depends entirely on the presence of conventions recognized and accepted by both speaker and hearer. The conventions that define marriage, for example, make it possible for the words "I do" to actually accomplish the joining of two people in marriage. Perlocutions, he thought at first, were non-conventional, although he admitted a certain tentativeness about defining conventions . . . "it is difficult to say," he admitted, "where conventions begin and end."[6]

As Austin's argument progresses in *How to Do Things with Words*, the sort of hedging he does on the precise definition of conventions extends more generally to the distinction between illocution and perlocution and finally even to the distinction between constatives and performatives. In fact, as he elaborates on this principal distinction, he begins to demonstrate the difficulty of holding to it absolutely and to show that many statements that appear to be constatives actually *function* as performatives. What appears to him first as the exceptional class, performatives, finally swallows the general class, constatives. One of Austin's most appreciative critics, Sandy Petrey, has captured this development in a particularly memorable way:

> Say John has a large piece of bright green vegetable matter stuck between his front teeth, while you, John, and a group of comparative strangers whom John wants to impress are discussing the federal budget deficit. If you interrupt the discussion to announce what you see to John and the others present, you have provided a description meeting

---

5 J. L. Austin, *How to Do Things with Words* (Cambridge: Harvard University Press, 1962) 52.

6 Ibid., 118.

all possible criteria of truth and accuracy. But it would be fallacious beyond belief to pretend that providing a description was the only thing you had done. Saying what is can effect a set of circumstances with every bit of transformational impact that Austin first invoked to show that words do things other than what they say.[7]

The surprising result of Austin's labors, then, is the demonstration that *all* language is potentially performative. Even statements of *fact* turn out to be acts of informing someone of something and the stating of a fact may have any number of effects on the one who is informed. Everything depends, he says finally, on the "total speech act in the total speech situation."

In order to explain what can go wrong with statements we cannot just concentrate on the proposition involved (whatever that is) as has been done traditionally. We must consider the total situation in which the utterance is issued—the total speech-act—if we are to see the parallel between statements and performative utterances, and how each can go wrong. So the total speech act in the total situation is emerging from logic piecemeal as important in special cases: and thus we are assimilating the supposed constative utterance to the performative.[8]

Despite his discovery of the performative potential of all normal speech, Austin insisted that *literary* language is by definition devoid of real illocutionary force:

A performative utterance will, for example, be in a peculiar way hollow or void if said by an actor on the stage, or if introduced in a poem, or spoken in a soliloquy. This applies in a similar manner to any and every utterance—a sea change in special circumstances. Language in such circumstances is in special ways—intelligibly—used not seriously, but in ways parasitic upon its normal use—ways which fall under the doctrine of the etiolations of language. All this we are excluding from consideration.[9]

Literary critics naturally question this exclusion of literary language from the category of true performatives. To Austin's example that "Walt Whitman does not seriously incite the eagle of liberty to soar," for example, Sandy Petrey responds,

Even if Walt Whitman doesn't "seriously" incite the eagle of liberty to soar, the influence of Whitman's poetry in the history of American discourse on liberty is a very serious matter indeed, as is the capacity of that discourse to do things with substantive impact on the reality of American life.[10]

Biblical critics have even more reason to object to Austin's exclusion since, as sacred scripture, the Bible often operates in ways not simply mimetic or

---

7 Petrey, *Speech Acts*, 27.

8 Austin, 52.

9 Ibid., 22.

10 Ibid., 104.

"parasitic" on real speech, but as real world speech act.[11] Petrey suggests that Austin betrays his own best insights when he limits the realm of illocution to "normal" face-to-face oral speech and calls for an extension of the theory in line with Austin's own assimilation of constatives to performatives:

> While Austin never did for the literary what he did for the constative—proclaim the speech-act character of what was originally excluded from speech-act theory—those of us who have ignored his strictures about literature are respecting the spirit of his writings as we ignore the letter.[12]

It is in this spirit, and recognizing the special claim of biblical literature to function as real world speech act, that I propose parallels between Austin's speech acts and the work of Paul's epistolary utterances, especially that extended utterance in 1 Cor 1:18-2:16 whose subject is "the Word of the cross." Clearly, Paul uses the discourse on the cross to bring about effects in his hearers, the most obvious being the effect of reconciliation. Here and throughout his writings he seems to be in the shadowy area between the two kinds of saying Austin labelled "performative."

On the one hand, Paul's writing is filled with expressions that *do*, within certain conventions, carry the force of acts. "I remind you in what terms I preached to you" (1 Cor 15:1), for example, is an utterance that constitutes an act. Here Paul does more than report a fact; in saying, "I remind you," he actually does remind, provided his utterance invokes the conventions that allow the expression "I remind you" to function as reminder in a given setting. Indeed, the very process of writing may be said to have illocutionary force. It is generally recognized, for example, that 1 Thessalonians functions largely as paraenesis. Here Paul's writing *in order to instruct* itself *does* the instruction, and does so within shared conventions that define his speech act as paraenesis.

On the other hand, his letters often function as persuasive argumentation designed to "achieve certain effects by saying something," i.e., Austin's perlocutionary act.[13] When he writes, for example, to the Thessalonians, "For I was gentle as a nurse" he uses a rhetorical figure to persuade the Thessalonians of his good intentions and of their own security in his care.[14] The expression itself does not do what it says, as the expression "I comfort you" might, and yet it may have the effect (among others, depending on the circumstances and conventions of the audience) of comforting.

It is not easy, and perhaps not possible, to determine exactly what role Austin allows convention in perlocutionary acts once he begins to collapse the distinction between illocution and perlocution. Surely, the conventions that define paraenesis in 1 Thessalonians are distinct from institutional

---

11 Hence, the observation of Hugh C. White that "Speech acts such as the promise of land, or the Sinai covenant, claim to be real world speech acts, in some sense, and not parasitic." White, "Introduction: Speech Act Theory," 5.

12 Petrey, 53.

13 Austin, 121.

14 On this paraenetic element in 1 Thessalonians, see A. Malherbe "'Gentle as a Nurse': The Cynic Background to 1 Thess 2," *NovT* (1970) 203-17.

conventions that make the words "I do" work in a marriage ceremony. And yet, in both cases, the performance of the words spoken depends on rather specialized social and linguistic conventions.

When Paul writes letters that state astonishment or concern, affection or anger, he relies on conventions he shares with his audience to make his words meaningful. In a different, but no less conventional manner in 1 Corinthians, he relies on agreement about certain conventionally paired opposites—e.g., wisdom and folly—to show (and by showing, make effective) the end of the world conventionally described by those opposites.[15] As I will demonstrate in my treatment of 1 Cor 1:18, he uses convention to go *beyond* convention. Here, no less than in Austin's strictest illocution, the world after the performative utterance is not the same as it was before. By stating what the cross *is*, using conventional language unconventionally, Paul "speaks" the conditions of the new world.

My reading of 1 Corinthians 1-2 will be attentive to Paul's play on conventions of language defined more broadly than the strict institutional conventions that limit Austin's illocutionary acts. Finally, it is Austin's sensitivity to the transformative interaction of language with society, his recognition that words have power to *do* things within certain conventions, and not his minute distinctions among types of conventions that will be most useful for interpreting Paul's Word of the cross as an apocalyptic speech act.

The Situation at Corinth

Austin's attention to the "total speech situation" mirrors concerns for describing social setting and contextual meaning in biblical exegesis. Since it is my thesis that Paul's message to the Corinthians depends on the potential of the Word he preaches to bring about perceptual and behavioral transformation, it is necessary to set that Word, as nearly as possible, into the context of its original use.[16]

It is, first, my working hypothesis that chapters 1-2 function as a unit devoted to the task of perceptual shift within the larger unit, chapters 1-4.[17] This judgment is based in part on the movement of the discourse from the noetic division Paul notes in 1:10, "I appeal to you . . . be united in the same *mind (en tō autō noi)*" to its opposite, the noetic denouement in 2:16, "But we have the *mind* of Christ *(nous tou Christou)*." Between these noetic markers, I suggest, Paul provides a strategy to facilitate the shift from the alienated and divided *nous* to the unified and reconciling *nous tou Christou*. While chapters 3-4 extend the experiential implications of the noetic shift and thus function within the same realm of discourse, *the shift itself* is the focus of chapters 1-2.

---

[15] On the thought in antiquity that the structure of the cosmos lies in pairs of opposites and that Paul both presupposes and disrupts this conventional epistemology when he writes Galatians, see J. Louis Martyn, "Apocalyptic Antinomies in Paul's Letter to the Galatians," *NTS* 31 (1985) 410-424, esp. p. 414, n.12 and n.13.

[16] This is not the place to review the literature on the social-historical setting of 1 Corinthians. The brief summary offered here represents widely accepted views on the situation of the letter.

[17] The larger unit is framed by the two appeals (parakalō) in 1:10 and 4:16. It is worth noting that the discourse on the cross between 1:18 and 2:16 is marked by the use of the first person plural.

I take 1 Corinthians to be a unified composition[18] that arises apparently from a conflict between Paul and certain church members in Corinth in large part over what it means to be a *pneumatikos* or "spiritual person." In Paul's view, the Corinthians' excess of spiritual enthusiasm, grounded in a theology whose catchwords are *sophia* (wisdom), *pneuma* (spirit), and *gnōsis* (knowledge) is having serious detrimental effects on the spiritual and ethical integrity of the church. Claiming both superior knowledge (*gnōsis*) of God (8:1-2) and perfection (*teleios*) in the Spirit (2:6), they separate themselves as an intellectual and spiritual elite (8:10-13), quarrel among themselves about the sources of their spiritual powers (1:10-16), and demonstrate their freedom in the Spirit by acting immorally (5:1-5) and disregarding the weak and the poor in the community (8:10-13; 11:17-22).

There is evidence in the letter that the Corinthians appeal to certain combinations of pagan, Jewish and Christian ideas favoring spiritual over bodily realities to provide the rationale for their ideology and behavior. While the precise contours of these parallel traditions will not be my focus, I assume that Paul's argument is designed with pointed references to them that would not be missed by his hearers. Indeed, Paul punctuates his discourse with what appear to be the Corinthians' own key terms and slogans, now turned ironically toward his own rhetorical purposes, e.g., in 4:8: "Already you are filled! "Already you have become kings!," and in 8:1, "We know that 'all of us possess knowledge.'" I take these slogans to indicate (at least) a Corinthian preoccupation with (knowledge *gnōsis*) as a spiritual endowment that separates some Christians (the *teleioi*) from others.

Over against the Corinthian preoccupation with an exalted spiritual *gnōsis*, Paul demonstrates another way of knowing that takes its bearings from the cross of Christ—"For I decided to know nothing among you except Jesus Christ and him crucified" (1 Cor 2:2)—construed as an event of apocalyptic import—"For the word of the cross is folly to those who are perishing, but to us who are being saved it is the power of God" (1 Cor 1:18).

As the Corinthians' perception is articulated in wisdom terminology, so is Paul's own way of knowing shaped and expressed by the language of apocalyptic. Because I take Paul's joining of apocalyptic language with the cross to be central to the performative function of his discourse, it is important to show where and how the association is made in his letters, and to suggest exactly what sort of apocalyptic language Paul employs.[19]

---

18 For a summary of the arguments for the integrity of 1 Corinthians see Werner G. Kümmel *Introduction to the New Testament* (rev. ed., Nashville: Abingdon, 1975).

19 Long before Paul's time, the motifs of perceptual transformation and apocalyptic were joined in Jewish literature. In Jewish apocalyptic texts, the visionary's perception of what is "really real" shifts before there is any change in the actual conditions of life. Because of what has been revealed, the seer is able to see and to proclaim the coming end of present worldly conditions and to encourage hope in a new world order (the "real world") to come. The new world the visionary announces is *perceived*, even experienced before it is actual. See, for example, 4 Ezra where complaint turns to praise (4 Ezra 13:48), and 2 Baruch's perceptual shift in 83:15. Paul follows in the tradition of his apocalyptic forbears when he proclaims, on the basis of a revelatory experience, the end of one world and the advent of a new creation. But for him, it is a historical event, the cross of Jesus Christ, that reveals the separation of old from new and marks the transition from one to the other. Thus, when in Galatians Paul speaks of his own transformation, he uses explicitly

The Cross as Apocalyptic Disclosure

A critical link in my argument concerns the apocalyptic setting of Paul's discourse on the cross in 1 Corinthians 1-2. I wish to suggest that Paul's language about the cross is a specific kind of apocalyptic language. Without using the apocalypse *genre*, Paul adopts and adapts the essential theological perspective of that genre, namely, the perspective characterized by expectation of a future reign of God, confirmed by present revelatory experience.[20]

It is relatively easy to demonstrate that Paul typically articulates his understanding of the Christ event in ideas and images drawn from Jewish apocalyptic thought, shaping these ideas to conform to the new historical circumstances articulated in the kerygma. He is as apt to use apocalyptic motifs in proclaiming what has *already happened* in the Christ event as he is in speculating on future events (e.g., the return of Jesus at the Parousia; see 1 Thess 4:13-5:12). For Paul, the new creation does not simply await the Parousia but is already present in the transformed life of the believer and indeed, in a hidden way, throughout the cosmos (1 Cor 7:31; 2 Cor 5:16).

Corollative to Paul's belief that the new creation is present is his conviction that the forms of this world are passing away (1 Cor 7:31) and that the believer lives at a unique vantage point (2 Cor 5:16) from which he can see both the dissolving of the old order and the emerging new cosmos.[21] Indeed, certain of Paul's rhetorical strategies seem designed primarily to make his hearers aware of their precarious stance between the ages. Among these strategies is his juxtaposition of the "already" with the "not yet" as in 2 Cor 5:16-6:2 and especially his unconventional treatment of conventional paradigms, e.g., "in Christ there is no male or female, slave or free, Jew or Greek" (Gal. 3:28), or "let those who rejoice live as though not rejoicing. . . . for the form of this world is passing away" (1 Cor 7:29-31).

Careful observation of Paul's language about the emergence of the new creation within the structures of the old world reveals that his perceptual transformation begins with the image of the cross of Christ as the turning point between the ages.[22] Often when the cross appears in his letters, it is

---

apocalyptic images, combined with a personalized language of the cross; the result of God's "apocalypse" of Jesus Christ to Paul is Paul's own death to the world (described as crucifixion) and his entry into the "new creation" (Gal 1:16; 6:14-15). Paul's experience of the Christ event as apocalypse draws upon a Jewish apocalyptic world-view even as it extends the boundaries of the classical apocalyptic vision. What is now revealed and proclaimed is not only that the turning of the ages is at hand, but that in God's action at the cross, it has already, decisively begun.

20 That Paul expects a future end is obvious throughout his writings. Paul modifies apocalyptic themes, however, when he argues implicitly that, in the death and resurrection of Jesus, the reign of God is already breaking in to the present. See 1 Cor 4:20; 7:31; 15:20-27; 2 Cor 5:16-17; 6:2.

21 In his treatment of 2 Cor 2:14-6:10, J. Louis Martyn has argued that what Paul advocates here is a way of knowing *kata stauron* ("according to the cross") that properly characterizes "epistemology at the turn of the ages." J. Louis Martyn, "Epistemology at the Turn of the Ages," in *Christian History and Interpretation: Studies Presented to John Knox* (eds. W. R. Farmer, C. F. D. Moule and R. R. Niebuhr; Cambridge University Press, 1967) 269-87.

22 J. Louis Martyn has coined the expression "bi-focal vision" to describe Paul's perception at the turn of the ages. He writes, "If we are to converse with Paul, we are

surrounded by apocalyptic and perceptual images that call for a new orientation to the old world. From the vantage point of the cross, Paul is able to proclaim God's victory over the powers of the old world while yet living provisionally in that world. Because for Paul the cross is the pivot between the ages (2 Cor 5:17-21), however, it is apt to generate misunderstanding before it generates new insight. From the conventional perspective of the old world, it is the symbol of suffering, weakness, folly and death. But from the perspective of the new creation, it is the transforming symbol of power and life. The movement of his audience from the one perspective to the other through the re-presentation of the cross in preaching (the repetition of the *kerygma*) is Paul's persisting apocalyptic (and hence, performative) objective, not only in 1 Corinthians, but throughout his writings. It is precisely this cross-inspired movement that we seek to understand.

The Cross and Apocalyptic Motifs in 1 Corinthians 1-2

A survey of the cross (*stauros*) terminology in Paul's seven undisputed letters reveals that he often places the cross in an apocalyptic frame of reference.[23] While it is more concentrated in our letter than in others, the apocalyptic and perceptual context of *stauros* terminology in 1 Corinthians is consistent with what we find in other letters. Apocalyptic associations, for example, are most obvious (and familiar) at 1 Cor 1:18 and 2:8. In the first instance (1:18), end-time apocalyptic judgment is clearly in view as Paul shows the cross (or, more precisely the *Word* of the cross) to be the divider of humanity into two groups, the "ones being saved" and "the ones perishing." In the second instance (2:8), apocalyptic significance attaches in a more obvious way to the term "rulers of this age." A third apocalyptic motif in 2:8 is the reference to the *present* age (*aiōnos toutou*) which implies *another* age (opposite the ruler's age), and thus the two-age schema typical of apocalyptic thought (cf. Gal 1:4; 1 Cor 1:12; 2:6; 3:18 and 2 Cor 4:4).

The remaining references to the cross or crucifixion in 1 Corinthians have implied apocalyptic significance in that they concern the true or false perception that arises from the cross as revelatory event. At 1:13, Paul protests the schismatic and misdirected allegiance of some he had baptized with the disclaimer, "Was Paul crucified for you?," thereby placing the cross of Jesus against all other systems of allegiance. Again, at 1:17, he places the cross at the center of his preaching in claiming that it is *solely* the cross of Christ and not baptism by any apostle (or baptism at all) that is the operative "power" in the experience of salvation. In 1:23 we find an echo of the cross as apocalyptic divider seen earlier at 1:18, "But we preach Christ crucified, a stumbling block

---

required to speak of bi-focal vision, an expression not found, of course, in Paul's letters, but one which may help us to understand his letters. The dictionary defines "bi-focal," as regards eyeglasses, as a lens having two portions, one for near vision, one for far vision. In order to find a metaphor helpful to our interpretation of Paul, we will have to imagine looking simultaneously through both of these lenses. Looking in that manner would cause you to see everything in another perspective." See "From Paul to Flannery O'Connor with the Power of Grace," *Katallagete* 6 (1981) 12.

23 I have provided a more complete survey of the use of *stauros* in the Pauline corpus in my dissertation, "Paul's Apocalyptic Word of the Cross: Perception and Transformation in 1 Corinthians 1-2," (Ph.D. dissertation, Columbia University, 1990) 44-62.

to Jews and folly to Gentiles." Here, the ones separated by their misunderstanding are the Jews and the Greeks (i.e., the whole world) whenever what they seek (signs or wisdom) is not satisfied by the preaching of the cross. Finally, at 2:2, Paul makes a pointed autobiographical statement about the connection of the cross to *knowledge*: "I decided not to know anything among you except Jesus Christ and him crucified (*estaurōmenon*)."

The emphasis Paul places on the perceptual or epistemological effects of the cross in 1 Corinthians reflects not only the apocalyptic character of his own vision, but also the special vulnerability of the gospel in the Corinthian context to perceptual error. Indeed, Paul seems to locate the Corinthian error in an insufficient comprehension and experience of the cross. Thus he adamantly emphasizes his role to "preach the gospel lest the cross be emptied" (1:17) and, over against their *gnōsis*, decides to "know *nothing* among [them] except Jesus Christ and him crucified" (2:2). As we focus now more closely on 1 Corinthians 1-2 we will observe a rhetorical strategy custom-fitted to the vulnerabilities of this particular community and yet, by virtue of its enduring linguistic patterns, able to facilitate the apocalyptic performance of the Word even beyond this first-century context.

II. Wisdom versus Apocalyptic:
The Performative Strategy of Oddly Paired Opposites

In the first seventeen verses of chapter one, Paul introduces nearly every major theme of the letter,[24] including the themes of perception (1:5,10), apocalypse (1:7), the cross (1:13) and spiritual gifts (1:7). Already in these verses, he begins the play of opposites and ironies that dominates the discourse. Then, in verse 17, he states the central polemic:

> For Christ did not send me to *baptize* but to *preach*, and not with *eloquent wisdom* lest the cross of Christ be *emptied*.

In his arrangement of the two pairs of terms, on the one hand, "baptize/preach" and on the other, "wisdom/emptiness," Paul anticipates both the strategy and the content of his message. In each paired opposite he sets something exalted by the Corinthians against something not exalted by them. Thus *baptism* and *wisdom*, both elevated by the Corinthians, are opposed to *kerygma* and *cross emptiness*. Simultaneously, we find a subtle and subversive *equation* of "wise words" (*sophia logoi*), (again something exalted in the Corinthians' world) with emptiness (*kenos*). Paul's performative strategy is anticipated in his play on conventional opposites and especially his subversion of the catch words "baptism" and "wisdom." The world in which these terms play second to the cross is a world dramatically reorganized. While the exact *content* of his "preaching" is left unstated, its subject is clear - he is sent to preach "lest the cross of Christ be emptied."

The strange pair of opposites introduced in 1:17, empty "wise words" (*sophia logoi*) versus the "not emptied cross" (*hina mē kenōthē ho stauros*) becomes the governing motif of the discourse that runs from 1:18-2:16. I am in

---

24 Notably absent in the thanksgiving section (vv. 4-9) is reference to *sophia*, one of the gifts evidently being claimed by the Corinthians.

agreement with the now widely held opinion, that Paul's use of the terms *sophia, logos*, and *gnōsis* in the text reflects his polemic against a type of wisdom theology that was influential in Corinth.[25] I am further inclined to agree with those who describe the Corinthian wisdom theology as "proto-gnostic" that is, not yet reflecting a fully developed gnosticism, but already emphasizing the soteriological powers of *gnōsis*. This would explain the urgency of Paul's appeals to perception; he opposes a tradition that not only prides itself on having already attained the perfect *gnōsis* of God and hence having already realized the resurrection in the present, but one that is gaining considerable territory in the Christian mission.

Whatever the exact contours of the Corinthian wisdom, my focus here is on how Paul addresses the ideology he encounters at Corinth. In what I take to be a deliberate rhetorical strategy, he allows the Word he preaches to make its first inroads into the consciousness of his hearers by disrupting standard expectations about the structure of language and hence, the world. Then, in a related but different strategy, most evident in 2:6-16, having once disrupted the received linguistic paradigm, he goes on to subvert particular terms within the old paradigm toward the service of a new perceptual model. Using conventions to go beyond conventions, he prepares his hearers for transformation.

The Word's Performance: A Drama in Two Acts

What makes Paul's Word of the cross an event that accomplishes "salvation" or "destruction" is not merely the shared knowledge of speaker and hearer about how the language works (its conventions), nor merely the necessary agreement about how the utterance is to be understood, but what the Word actually *says*. The Word of the cross, like Austin's performatives, is effective in more than the pragmatic sense of activating the conventions shared by speaker and hearer; it does something more to the perception of the hearer. It points the hearer toward another reality, governed by a new image of who God is, namely, the One who is present in the cross event.[26]

The two functions of Paul's message, the destructive function, accomplished through his unconventional use of standard conventions and

---

25 Numerous studies have attempted to describe this wisdom theology. There is general consensus that it was "pre" or "proto-gnostic."

26 In recent essays on the theology of 1 Corinthians, both Gordon Fee and Victor Paul Furnish have emphasized the element of divine self-disclosure in the cross. Fee writes, "Thus in his crucifixion Christ not only effected salvation for the called, but ultimately revealed the essential character of God, which is revealed further in the servant character by Paul's apostleship (3:5; 4:1-2, 9-13)." Gordon Fee, "Toward a Theology of 1 Corinthians" (Revised version of paper delivered at the One Hundred Twenty Seventh Annual Meeting of the Society of Biblical Literature, 1991) 5. See the similar emphasis in Furnish, ". . . Paul is not interpreting Jesus' death on the cross as an act of atonement for sins, even though such an idea surfaces elsewhere in the letter (15:3; cf. 8:11; 11;24). Rather, his point is that specifically the crucified Christ discloses the nature of God's power and wisdom. The cross is thus definitive for a properly Christian understanding of God." V. P. Furnish (Revised version of paper delivered at the One Hundred Twenty-Seventh Annual Meeting of the Society of Biblical Literature, 1991) 11. Both essays will be included in the upcoming volume, *Pauline Theology, Volume 2: 1 and 2 Corinthians*, ed., David M. Hay (Minneapolis: Fortress).

the constructive function, the construction of the new mind, may be understood as two "acts" in the dramatic performance of the text. In Act One, the Word of the cross works to expose and "de-center" the perceptions of the reader. This de-centering is the first step in its powerful and transformative play against what Paul calls the "wisdom of the world." At the next level of the discourse, the burden of Paul's rhetoric is to clear a path through the rubble of his hearers' now deconstructed language, building a new framework for perception. Act Two of the drama brings the completion of the new structure— in our text, Paul's re-figuring of the terms wisdom and folly, power and emptiness, psyche and spirit—and invokes the power of the Spirit to bring the hearer into the transformed mind. In this Act, the one who was seized by the cross in the first Act, now grasps what seized him.[27] Now in possession of the "mind of Christ" (having what seized him in mind) this one embodies the power of the cross to work toward salvation.

Act One: The Word Meets the Conventions of Folly and Power

The first half of Paul's performative strategy is illustrated in the topic sentence of the discourse on the cross at 1:18:

> For the Word of the cross (*logos tou staurou*) is folly to those who are perishing, but to us who are being saved it is the power of God (*dynamis tou Theou*).

On the surface this is a nicely balanced sentence; it has two parallel clauses, each consisting of subject, copulative verb, indirect object and predicate nominative. The two pairs of opposites together assert something about the single subject, the Word of the cross (*ho logos tou staurou*). On closer inspection, however, the paired opposites are strangely unbalanced; by standard expectations, they represent an *aporia*. The first pair, *saved versus perishing* presents no particular perceptual problem; that is an opposite we expect. But the second, *folly versus power* presents an unexpected and destabilizing opposition. Even in the 20th century, and perhaps all the more in the philosophical and religious context of the 1st century, the expected partner to "folly" is not "power," but "wisdom."[28]

Paul's choice of opposites is startling, especially in light of his subject, the cross; it is not simply the pairing of folly with power that surprises, but the attribution of power to what is otherwise the symbol of weakness, the cross. In making the substitution "power" for "wisdom," Paul has said something new and epistemologically offensive about salvation. It is now not the wisdom of the wise that "saves," despite the high value of wisdom in the traditions of both Jews and Greeks; in fact, this wisdom is equated with "emptiness." Rather, what saves is the "power of the cross," a formulation that is nonsensical in the

---

27 This way of expressing what happens in 1 Cor 2:6-16 comes from Gerd Theissen, *Psychological Aspects of Pauline Theology*, (Philadelphia: Fortress, 1987) 352. German Original, Göttingen: Vandenboeck and Ruprecht, 1983. The expression, "they grasp what seized them," says (and does?) more in German—"Sie *begreifen,* was sie *ergriffen* hat,"— where the verb *ergreifen* connotes not only arrest, seizure, but also to be moved by feeling, altered, changed.

28 The Book of Sirach, a product of the Hellenistic period, rehearses the familiar opposition: e.g. Sir 21:16, "Like a house that has vanished, so is wisdom to a fool."

perspective of worldly wisdom. Moreover, Paul has located the power of the cross not simply in the past event itself, but in the present Word about the event that continually re-presents it to the reader. Through the *logos*, the cross continues to break powerfully into the old world's "dominant system of convictions" wherever it is proclaimed.[29]

Already in the structure of the sentence at 1:18, we begin to see how the Word works in a particular linguistic context to dislodge readers from their accustomed perceptual worlds. This is one aspect of its dynamic apocalyptic nature; by this power to dislocate, the Word begins to create the conditions under which readers may be transformed and transferred into a new world. In his transpositions of linguistic signs, and particularly signs associated with ways of knowing—i.e., *wisdom and folly*—Paul presses previously held cognitions about God, self and world to the point of collapse. This is the first step of the transformative action of the Word–Act One of the performative drama.

The strategy is brought home to the Corinthians in 1:26-29 where Paul reminds them that their election by God was an example of creation *ex nihilo*:

> For consider your call, brethren; not many of you were wise according to worldly standards, not many were powerful, not many were of noble birth; but God chose what is foolish in the world to shame the wise, God chose what is weak in the world to shame the strong, God chose what is low and despised in the world, even things that are not, to bring to nothing things that are, so that no human being might boast in the presence of God.

This real-life example calls the Corinthians to recognize their utter dependence on God's creative and redeeming power. The strategy that began in a disruption of language and ideology thus leads the perceptive reader to the knowledge of his own un-knowing, indeed his non-being (*ta mē onta*) before God. This recognition, it seems, is required for true perception of the cross and hence for reconciliation to God, self and other.

Once conventions have done what they can do by de-stabilizing the hearer, creating the cognitive dissonance that prepares for transformation, then *what* the Word says, and what it *reveals*, can have its effect. From the rubble left by the destruction of the conventional cosmos, arises a unifying image of the One who not only calls and creates *ex nihilo*, but, by a self-giving act, sanctifies and empowers "things with no being," *ta mē onta*. The image and the utterance that gives it voice together produce the cognitive shift that enables the hearer to find herself, reoriented by image when words have failed, among the ones being saved by the Word of the cross.

III. Coming to Consciousness in the Mind of Christ

It should come as no surprise that in chapter two where Paul attempts to show *what* is revealed in the crevasse the Word of the cross creates, he resorts to heightened apocalyptic, indeed, mystical imagery. For here the

---

[29] Gerd Theissen uses this phrase to describe the opposition encountered by the word of the cross within the human psyche. *Psychological Aspects* (1987) 79.

performance moves into its Second Act, beyond the conventional concerns of shared vocabulary, even beyond the image of the cross, and into the shared experience of the Spirit who transcends human cognition to communicate the depths of God. Now Paul seeks to bring the new world to consciousness by invoking the presence of its vital force, the Spirit of God, in the experience of the believer. Here, he must move to a heightened mystical discourse taking with him only those who have been prepared for this move through the course of 1:18-2:5.

Paul's use of uncharacteristic language patterns in this chapter, i.e., his linking of the vocabulary of knowledge (*gnōsis*), mystery (*mystērion*), spirit (*pneuma*), and wisdom (*sophia*), and the absence of an explicit cross motif lead many to conclude that at this point Paul abandons the cross, turning instead, perhaps in desperation against his opponents, to a gnostic-like position approximating theirs or to an esoteric teaching intended for a few advanced believers.[30]

While each of these solutions to the difficulties of 2:6-16 is compelling in its way, I wish to offer another interpretation that preserves the integrity of the cross discourse from 1:18-2:16. By attending to the apocalyptic strategies that link the two sections, we may see that both are focussed on the cross, although certainly at two different levels of discourse, as the agent of true perception. Neither section alone is sufficient to complete the shift Paul intends. Act One brings the reader into the range of transformation and sees its beginnings through the strategies of convention and image described above. Act Two allows its completion through the transcendent action of the Spirit. Here the re-figuring of language Paul begins in chapter one reaches its full effect.

Act Two: Bringing the Cross to Consciousness

In 2:1-5, apocalyptic imagery intensifies. This "bridge" between the cross discourse 1:18-31 and the next unit, 2:6-16, makes clear the connection between them. Here Paul announces his intent to proclaim God's mystery by

---

[30] It is Rudolf Bultmann's opinion, for example, that Paul becomes so enmeshed in the world-view of his audience that his theology of the cross here gives way to a theology of gnosis (Rudolf Bultmann, *Theology of the New Testament* [New York: Charles Scribners, 1951, 1955] 175, 181). Ulrich Wilckens, too, initially argued this line although he later retracted his thesis on gnosticism at Corinth (Ulrich Wilckens, *Weisheit und Torheit* [Tübingen: Mohr, 1959]). Robin Scroggs takes a different turn that acknowledges the apocalyptic cast of the section (Robin Scroggs, "Paul: Sophos und Pneumatikos," *NTS* 14 [1967] 33-35). He argues that in 2:6-16, Paul leaves the cross kerygma to engage in an esoteric discourse on apocalyptic mysteries designed for a few advanced believers, the spiritual *teleioi*. Although Scroggs avoids the dubious assignment of gnosticism to Corinth, he, like Bultmann and Wilckens, posits a sharp disjunction between the two sections of the argument. This break signals the failure of the cross proclamation to bring the Corinthians into the unity of mind toward which the whole discourse is aimed. While for Bultmann the proclamation of the cross appears to have fallen prey to the gnostics, for Scroggs, it seems merely too elementary a doctrine for the spiritually advanced believer who now turns with Paul to the esoteric, secret doctrines of spiritual "perfection." While I admit that Paul is no stranger to rhetorical failure, there is no other place known to me where his failure is attributable to confusion about which side he is on. For both Bultmann and Scroggs, the discourse that begins with a strong plea for unity of mind in Corinth ends with a gnostic-like confirmation that the transformation of Spirit offered by the gospel is, seemingly by design, more accessible to some than to others.

knowing nothing except Christ crucified.[31] This knowledge, he goes on to say, is demonstrated in his "fear and trembling," a condition typical of apocalyptic visionaries, at the revelation of God and in the outpouring of God's Spirit and power (2:4-5). The mention of Spirit is risky in this context among self-professed "spiritualists," but its introduction at just this point is strategic. At the point of the hearer's greatest uncertainty, just after 1:18-31 and the devaluing of human wisdom over against the wisdom manifested in the cross, Paul links the cross with the Spirit. Without this link, surely the Corinthian hearers would be apt to retreat to their accustomed spiritualism— without the cross.[32] But once this link is established in 2:1-5, it causes all that Paul says about the Spirit in 2:6-16 to be read in light of the cross kerygma.

The link is reiterated in the next section; in 2:6 we read the apparently contradictory statement, "Yet among the perfect we do impart wisdom". Here the "wisdom" in question is immediately qualified as the apocalyptic wisdom hidden in the cross, i.e., "the secret and hidden wisdom of God . . . which the rulers of this age did not understand, for if they had, they would not have crucified the Lord of Glory."

The second act of the Word's performance begins with the introduction of the Spirit in 2:4. Having dislodged his audience from their customary world by deconstructing time-honored paired opposites in 1:18-31, Paul now illumines the Spirit's role as guide to a newly constructed universe. Without the link between 2:6-16 and the cross kerygma, however, the "performance" of the Word would be cut short. It is the Spirit re-figured in light of the cross— for Paul, the only true Spirit—that brings the work of the Word to completion. In his study of the psychological aspects of this text, Gerd Theissen suggests that this level of the discourse moves the hearer to a "higher stage of consciousness." He remarks on the two-stage development that occurs between 1:18 and 2:16:

> In the "initial preaching" (i.e., 1:18-2:5), Christians are seized by the symbol of the cross. But it is only through the "doctrine of perfection" that they grasp what seizes them. Both the immature and the perfect are affected by the same revelation, but only the perfect penetrate what happens to them and in them. In brief, perfect wisdom consists in making conscious a previously unconscious content.[33]

What Theissen calls "higher consciousness," I see resulting from the hearer's entry into the transformed world defined by the cross. I differ with Theissen only in that I conceive a single audience for both stages of the

---

[31] The apparent identification of the kerygma as "mystery" at 2:1 is one of the most debated aspects of the text. Although there is early and strong evidence for the variant reading *martyrion* ("witness") instead of *mysterion* at 2:1, I follow the twenty-sixth edition of Aland and a number of authorities on 1 Corinthians including Bornkamm, Leitzmann, Lührmann and Lang in choosing *mysterion*.

[32] G. Fee notes what he takes to be the "especially pointed irony" of 2:6-16 that "since the Corinthians are *pneumatikoi* (Spirit people), they should have understood the cross as God's wisdom; for the Spirit alone knows the mind of God and has thus revealed what was formerly hidden." G. Fee "Toward a Theology of 1 Cor," 9.

[33] Theissen, *Psychological Aspects*, 352.

discourse and hence a continuous, progressive line of argument through the two chapters.

My argument for the two stage performance of the Word as apocalyptic drama can be concluded by turning to the culminating verse of the section, 2:16:

> For who has known the mind of the Lord so as to instruct him? But we have the mind of Christ (*nous tou Christou*).

Here Paul's argument comes full circle as his opening call for unity of mind in the community (1:10) is echoed in the appeal to a common mind, the mind of Christ. Here the central themes of the discourse converge in a single image of transformed perception; the new world revealed in the cross and communicated by the Spirit comes to consciousness. The perceptual transformation begun in the dismantling of intellectual and social structures by the rhetoric of the cross now reaches its completion in the consciously cruciform mind. Possession of this mind is what makes possible the unity Paul calls for in 1:10, the mindful servanthood outlined in 1 Corinthians 3-4, and the mindfulness of prayer and praise in 1 Cor 14:13-16. One who has this mind has transcended old perceptual structures to enter into the visionary world revealed by the cross; apocalypse is complete when the new world enters consciousness and experience. Now the believer is compelled to live "as if" the new creation had already arrived despite signs to the contrary: "Let those who deal with the world [live] as if they had no dealings with it, for the form of this world is passing away" (1 Cor 7:31).

From Consciousness to Mindful Action

Commentators have long suspected that Paul's use of the Greek word for mind, *nous*, like his use of the word for Spirit, *pneuma*, is polemically directed against another, perhaps proto-gnostic use of the term which he deems to be in error. Indeed, that it appears as the culmination of a series of rhetorical strikes against the Corinthians' favored self-designations, leads one to suspect that the term *nous tou Christou*, used only here in Paul's letters is meant to displace another notion of *nous* operative at Corinth.

A survey of other uses of *nous* in the Pauline corpus confirms that for Paul the term carries more than intellectual or even spiritual meaning. For him, noetic disposition is intimately linked to experience and especially to relationships with God and with other human beings. Thus, for Paul, the mind reflects the orientation of the whole self toward or away from God. This noetic self may be "taken captive to obey Christ" (2 Cor 10:5), it may be ruled by the flesh (Rom 8:5), it may be renewed and restored to the service of God (Rom 12:2), or it may be fallen, *adokimos* (Rom 1:28). In Philippians 2:2, Paul calls his hearers to a state of unity in the mind of the crucified Christ (although in the expression, *to auto phronēte, nous* is not used) who "emptied himself, taking the form of a servant" (2:7). As in 1 Corinthians, so too in Philippians, the set of the mind demonstrates participation in the Spirit and participation is demonstrated in active service toward the other. When this mind and this Spirit characterize community, the new world is realized, however provisionally, in new relationships formed in the image of the Crucified, free of dominating self-concern. The perceptual transformation begun in the head-on realization of crucifixion as the wisdom of God and the breakdown of the world's wisdom is completed in the lived experience of resurrection that is mediated by the Spirit. When readers or hearers of the Word reach this stage of cognition, when they "grasp what seized them" in Act One of the drama, the performative function of the Word as agent of transformation is fulfilled.

Conclusion

I have focussed on one dimension of the performance of the Word, namely, the rhetorical strategy that makes it "work". My goal has been to demonstrate that the language of the cross functions as performative agent of perceptual transformation in an apocalyptic context extending from 1:18-2:16 and to outline the principal rhetorical strategies Paul aims at the divided community. I conclude that for Paul the revelatory Word of the cross, in all its offense to the wisdom of the world, is the sole and necessary catalyst for the transformation of mind he intends. What the cross-as-offense accomplishes in the first half of the argument, i.e., the seizure of the hearer in the break-down of conventional wisdom, the Spirit brings to completion in the second half, i.e., in the consciousness through the "mind of Christ" of what seized him.

Finally, we have seen that this consciousness is not something that can, by the logic of Paul's own argument, be reserved for an elite. The perceptual shift reflected in having the "mind of Christ" is the necessary result of the performative utterance of the cross whenever it is heard. Like the transformations in Austin's performatives, but on a radically different plane, this speech act, too, is manifestly social, issuing in changed relationships to God and others that reach deep into the life of the church and the world. The resolution of the multiple problems in Corinth depends on the apocalyptic, performative force of Paul's Word of the cross to achieve perceptual transformation in and reconciliation among all its members.

Prayers from Qumran: Issues and Methods

E. Glickler Chazon
Hebrew University, Jerusalem

A Collection of Prayers and Texts of Liturgical Import from Qumran

I.   Prayer as Worship

1) Rule of the Community (1QS IX 3-5)[1]

When these become members of the Community in Israel according to all these rules, they shall establish the spirit of holiness according to everlasting truth. They shall atone for guilty rebellion and for sins of unfaithfulness that they may obtain lovingkindness for the Land without (more than) the flesh of holocausts and the fat of sacrifice. And prayer rightly offered (an offering of the lips) shall be as an acceptable fragrance of righteousness, and perfection of way as a delectable free-will offering.

2) Damascus Document (CD XI 18-21)[2]

No man shall send to the altar any burnt-offering, or cereal offering, or incense, or wood by the hand of one smitten with any uncleanliness, permitting him thus to defile the altar. For it is written, *The sacrifice of the wicked is an abomination, but the prayer of the just is as an agreeable offering* (Prov. XV,8).

3) Rule of the Community (1QS X 1-17)[3]

(I shall bless Him) at the times ordained by Him:
at the begining of the dominion of light,
(with its circuit) and at its end
when it retires to its appointed place;
at the beginning of the watches of darkness
when He unlocks their storehouse and speads them out,

---

[1] All translations of 1QS, the Damascus Document (CD), the Prayers for the Festivals (1Q34, 1Q34bis, 4Q507–509), and the Songs of the Sage (4Q510, 4Q511) cite G. Vermes, *The Dead Sea Scrolls in English* (Sheffield: JSOT, 1987). The material is reproduced here by permission of Sheffield Academic Press. I have included alternate translations and additional passages parenthetically.

[2] The translation is by Vermes, *Scrolls*, 96.

[3] For the translation see Vermes, *Scrolls*, 75-77. The alternate translations and versifications are based on J. Licht, *The Rule Scroll* (Jerusalem: Bialik, 1965).

(at its circuit) and also at its end
when they retire before the light;
when the heavenly lights shine out
from the dwelling-place of Holiness
and also when they retire to the place of Glory.

At the entry of the seasons on the days of the new moon,
(together with their circuits) and also at their end
when they succeed to one another.
Their renewal is a great day for the Holy of Holies,
and a sign for the unlocking of everlasting mercies
at the beginning of seasons in all times to come.

At the beginning of the months of the seasons
and on the holy days appointed for remembrance in their seasons
I will bless Him with the offering of the lips
according to the Precept engraved for ever:
at the beginning of the years
and at the end (duration) of their seasons
when their appointed law is fulfilled,
on the day decreed by Him
that they should pass from one to the other—
the season of early harvest to the summer time,
the season of sowing to the season of grass,
the seasons of years to their weeks (of years)—
and at the beginning of their weeks for the season of Jubilee.
All my life the engraved Precept shall be on my tongue
as the fruit of praise and the portion of my lips . . .

Before I move my hands and feet I will bless His Name.
I will praise Him before I go out or enter, or sit or rise,
and whilst I lie on the couch of my bed.
I will bless Him with the offering
of that which proceeds from my lips
from the midst of the ranks of men,
and before I lift my hands to eat
of the pleasant fruits of the earth.
I will bless Him for His exceeding wonderful deeds
at the beginning of fear and dread
and in the abode of distress and desolation.
I will meditate on His power
and will lean on his mercies all day long.
I know that judgement of all the living is in His hand,
and that all His deeds are truth.
I will praise Him when distress is unleashed
and will magnify Him also because of His salvation.

II. Liturgies for Fixed Prayer Times

1) Daily Prayers for One Month (4Q503)[4]

Regular, Weekday Prayers (Days 5-7 of the month)

4Q503 4

And when [the sun] goes forth [to illumine the earth . . .]
[they shall bless and answer and say,
Blessed be the God of Israel . . .]
who recounts/the number [. . .]
for this day [. . .]
[appointed times of glo[ry . . .]
[Peace be upon you] Israel.

And on the sixth of the mon[th in the evening]
[They shall bless and answer and say,
Blessed be the God of Israel . . .]
night which is [. . .]
we are His holy people [. . .]
five l[ots of light . . .] and [. . .

4Q503 8–9

[And when the sun goes forth to illumine the earth
They shall bless and answer and say,
Blessed be the God of Israel . . .]
. . .] light of day to make known to us [. . .
. . .] with six gates of ligh[t . . .]
. . .] sons of Your covenant, we shall praise [. . .]
with all flags of [light . . .
a]ll tongues of knowledge, bless Your name [. . .] light
Peace [be upon you Israel . . .]

On the seventh of [the month in the evening]
they [shall bless and answer and say]
Blessed be the God of Isr[ael . . .] justice [. . .
a]ll these we have known by [. . .] which [. . .]
Blessed be the God [of Israel . . .

Prayers for Sabbaths During the Month (Days 4, 11, 18, 25)

4Q503 1

And when [the sun] goes forth [to illumine the earth
they shall bless and answer and say]:
Blessed be the Go[d of Israel . . .]

---

4 I have based my versification and translation upon the Hebrew[text published by M. Baillet (*Discoveries in the Judean Desert* VII, [Oxford: Clarendon, l982] 106-119) and the reconstructions suggested by J. Baumgarten, ("4Q503 Daily Prayers and the Lunar[Calendar," *RQ* 12 [1986] 399-407) and E. Peuch ("Recensions," *RB* 95[[1988] 405-411). All material from the *DJD* volumes is reproduced here by permission of Oxford University Press.

with four [gates of light . . .]
ten fla[gs of darkness . . .]
when it passes over [. . .],
[Peace be upon you] Israel.

4Q503 24–25
[And when the sun goes forth to illumine] the earth
they shall bless [and answer and say:
Blessed be the God of Israel]
who has chosen us from among all [the] nations [. . .]
for an appointed [time] of rest and delight [. . .].
[. . . hap]py [. . . ligh]ts[. . .

4Q503 40–41
And when [the sun] goes forth [to illumine the earth]
[the third [Sabbath] of the fir[st month]
[. . .] our glory
[. . .] holy rest [. . .]
and they praise [. . .]
and praised is [your holy] name [by] all holy on[es . . .]
holy ones [. . .] glory[. . .].

4Q503 37–38
On the fifth and [twentieth day of the month in the evening
they shall bless and answer and say:
Blessed be [the Lord of all holy one[s . . .]
holy [?day] and rest for us[. . .]
from the lot of its dominion[. . .].

[And when the sun goes forth to illumine the earth
they shall bless and answer and say:
Blessed be the Lord of all ho]ly ones [. . .
five and] twenty gates [of light . . .]
praising with us [. . .] our glory,
Peace [be upon you Israel].

Prayers for Festivals During The Month (Day 15)
4Q503 2 6–11
[On the fifteenth of the month in the ev]ening
they shall bless and answer and say,
Blessed be the God [of Israel . . .]
before Him in every division of its glory
and the night [. . . for[ever], and to praise Him
our redemption in the beginn[ing . . .]
revolution(s) of vessels of light [. . .]
this day (there are) fourte[en lots of light . . .] light of day,
P[eace be upon] you Israel.

[And when the sun goes forth] to illumine the earth
they shall bless and an[swer and say,
Blessed be the God of Israel . . .]

for festivals of joy and appointed times of gl[ory . . .]
fifteen gate[s of light . . .]
with lots of night . . .

2) Prayers for the Days of the Week ("Words of the Luminaries")[5]

Prayer for Thursday (4Q504 1-2 II 7-17)

We entreat you, Lord
    act as Yourself (in accordance with Your attributes),
    as the greatness of Your power,
    as You forgave our forefathers
    when they rebelled against You . . .
Let Your anger and Your rage turn away from Your people, Israel
    for all their sins,
    and remember the wondrous deeds which You performed
    before the nations' eyes
    because Your name is called upon us.
. . . to cause us [to return/draw near]
    with all (our) heart and all (our) soul,
    and to implant Your Torah in our heart
    [so that we may not go astray] to the right or the left
    for you shall heal us from madness and blindness and
        astonishment [of heart].
[. . .] we have been sold [in] our sins
    and in our transgressions You have called us
    [. . .] and save us from sinning against You,
    [. . .] and to make us understand Your testimonies.　[

Prayer for Friday (4Q504 1-2 V 1-VII 2)

[. . . They abandoned] the source of living water,   Col. V
    and worshipped a foreign god in their land.
Their land was also laid waste for their enemies,
    because your rage and your burning anger
    were poured out in the fire of your jealousy
    to make it desolate of all who traverse it.
But in spite of all this,
    you did not despise the seed of Jacob
    and you did not abhor Israel
    so as to violate Your covenant with them,
    because you alone are the living God
    and there is none beside You.
You remembered your covenant
    in that you took us out before the nations' eyes,

---

5 For the Hebrew text and versification see E. Chazon, "A Liturgical Document from Qumran and its Implications: 'Words of the Luminaries' (4QDibHam)," (unpublished dissertation, Hebrew University: 1992 [in Hebrew]). The text was first published in full by Baillet, *DJD* VII.

and you did not abandon us among the nations.
You were gracious to your people, Israel
    in all the lands to which you banished them
    so that they bethought themselves
    to return unto you and to heed your command,
    according to all that you commanded them
    through your servant, Moses.
For you have poured your holy spirit upon us
    to bring your blessings upon us
    so that we sought you in our distress
    and whispered in the contraint of your chastisement.

And we have come into difficult straits, blows and trails
    through the rage of the oppressor
    for we too have tired God with our iniquity,
    we have caused the Rock to weary with [our] sin;
    but he did [not] weary us
    so that we would profit from walking
    in the way in which [we should walk].
But we did not obey/if we had obeyed [your commandment . . .]

[You cast away] from us all our transgressions   Col. VI
    and you purified us from our sin for your sake.
To you, God, is righteousness
    for you have done all these things.
Now, today, when our heart is humbled,
    we have expiated our iniquity
    and the iniquity of our forefathers,
    in our unfaithfulness
    and in that we walked contrarily.
We did not despise your trials
    and our soul did not abhor your blows
    so as to break your covenant
    in all the distress of our soul.
For, You who sent our enemies upon us,
    strengthened our heart
    so that we will recount your might
    to generations to come.

We entreat you, Lord,
    as you perform wonders from eternity to eternity,
    let your anger and your rage be turned back from us,
    look upon our af[fliction] and our suffering and our oppression,
    deliver your people from [all] the lands, near and far,
        to which [you have banished them],
        all those written in the book of life.
    [. . .] to serve you and to praise you [. . .]
    from all those who harass them/from all their plagues
    [. . .] who cause them to stumble/the stumbling-blocks
    [. . .]

[Blessed be the Lord]   Col VII
    who has delivered us from all distress.
    Amen, [amen].

Songs of Praise for the Sabbath Day (4Q504 1-2 VII 4ff.)

Give thanks [to the Lord forever]
[Praise] his holy name continually.
Pro[claim his praise from day to day]
In the hea[vens and on earth recount his glory]
all angels of the holy firmament,
and [all the waters above] the heavens;
the earth and all its depths,
[all fountains of the] great [deep] and Abaddon,
and the waters and all that is [in them].
[Give thanks to the Lord]
all his created ones
continually, forever and ever.

3) Sabbath Prayers for the First Quarter of the Year

Songs of the Sabbath Sacrifice [6]

Song for the Second Sabbath (4Q400 2 2-8)
They are honored among all the camps of godlike beings
and reverenced by mortal councils,
a w[onder] beyond godlike beings and mortals (alike).
And they declare His royal splendor according to their knowledge
and exalt [His glory in all] the heavens of His realm.
And in all the lofty heights
wondrous psalms according to all [their insight do they sing,
and all] the glory of the King of godlike beings do they declare
in the habitations where they have their station.
But [. . .] how shall we be considered [among] them?
And how shall our priesthood (be considered) in their habitations?
And our ho[liness–how can it compare]
with their [surpassing] holiness?
[What] is the offering of our mortal tongue
(compared) with the knowledge of the el[im? . . .] our [s]ong,
let us exalt the God of knowledge [. . .].

Song for the Seventh Sabbath (4Q403 1 i 3-44)
By the instructor. Song of the sacrifice of the seventh Sabbath
on the sixteenth of the month.

---

6 The text and translation are by C. Newsom, *Songs of the Sabbath Sacrifice: A Critical Edition* (Harvard Semitic Studies 27 [Atlanta: Scholars Press, 1985]). For the versification and interpretation of the twelfth song see Newsom, "Merkabah Exegesis in the Qumran Sabbath Shirot," *JJS* 38 (1987) 11-30. I have versified the second and seventh songs based on her critical edition.

Praise the God of the lofty heights,
O you lofty among all the elim of knowledge.

Let the holiest of the godlike ones sanctify the King of Glory
who sanctifies by holiness all His holy ones.

O you chiefs of the praises of all godlike beings,
praise the splendidly [pr]aiseworthy God.
For in the splendor of praise is the glory of His realm.
From it (comes) the praises of all the godlike ones
together with the splendor of all [His] maj[esty.

And] exalt His exaltedness to exalted heaven,
you most godlike ones of the lofty elim,
and (exalt) His glorious divinity above all the lofty heights.
For H[e is God of gods] of all the chiefs of the heights of heaven
and King of ki[ngs] of all the eternal councils . . .

Sing with joy, you who rejoice [in His knowledge
with] rejoicing among the wondrous godlike beings.
And chant His glory
with the tongue of all who chant with knowledge;
and (chant) His wonderful songs of joy
with the mouth of all who chant [of Him.
For He is] God of all who rejoice forever
and Judge in His power of all the spirits of understanding.

Ascribe majesty, all you majestic elim, to the K[in]g of majesty;
for His glory do all the elim of knowledge confess,
and all the spirits of righteousness confess His faithfulness . . .

Sing praises to the mighty God with the choicest spiritual portion
that there may be [melod]y together with divine joy,
and (let there be) a celebration with all the holy ones,
that there may be wondrous songs together with e[ternal] joy.

With these let all the f[oundations of the hol]y of holies praise,
the uplifting pillars of the supremely lofty abode,
and all the corners of its structure.

Sin[g praise] to Go[d who is Dr]eadful in power,
[all you spirits of knowledge and light]
in order to [exa]lt together the splendidly shining firmament
of [His] holy sanctuary.

[Give praise to Hi]m, O you god[like] spirits,
in order to pr[aise for ever and e]ver
the firmament of the uppermost heaven,
all [its beams] and its walls, a[l]l its [for]m,
the work of its struc[ture. . .

Song for the Twelfth Sabbath (4Q405 20 ii-21-22)
By the Instr[uctor. Song of the sacrifice of] the twelfth
[Sa]bbath [on the twenty-first of the third month.

Praise the God of . . .] wondrous [. . .] and exalt Him . . . the Glory.
In the tabernacle of the God of knowledge the cherubim fall before
Him; and they bless as they lift themselves up.
A sound of divine stillness [is heard]; and there is a tumult of
jubilation at the raising of their wings, a sound of divine [stillnes]s.
The image of the chariot throne do they bless (which is) above the
platform of the cherubim; [and the splendo]r of the luminous
platform do they sing (which is) beneath His glorious seat.
And when the ophannim move, holy angels return; they go out
between its glorious [h]ubs.
Like the appearance of fire are the most holy spirits round about, the
appearance of streams of fire like hashmal.
And there is a radiant substance with glorious colours, wondrously hued,
blended of splendor.
The spirits of the living godlike beings move continuously with the glory
of the wondrous chariot(s).
And there is a still sound of blessing in the tumult of their movement; and
they praise (His) holiness as they return on their paths.
As they rise, they rise marvelously; and when they settle, they [stand]
still; the sound of glad rejoicing falls silent. And there is a stillness of
divine blessing in all the camps of godlike beings; [and] the sound of
prais[es . . .] from between all their divisions on the[ir] si[des . . . and] all
their mustered troops rejoice, each one in [his] station.

III. Annual Festival Prayers (1Q34, 34bis; 4Q507-509)

Prayers for the New Year and the Day of Atonement

4Q509 3, 1Q34bis 2+1[7]

. . .] The appointed time of our peace[. . .]
[For Thou hast caused us to rejoice], removing our grief,
and hast assembled (will asssemble) our banished ones
for a feast of . . .
Thou shalt gather our dispersed . . . for the season of . . .
Thy [me]rcies on our congregation like rai[ndrops on the] earth
in the season [of sowing . . .] and like showers on the [gr]ass
in the season of sprouting and . . .
[We shall recount] Thy marvels from generation to generation.
Blessed be the Lord who has caused [us] to rejoice.

Prayer for the Day of Atonement. Remem[ber, O Lo]rd [. . .]

---

[7] The concluding benediction appears in both manuscripts. The translation reflects the
fuller text in 4Q509 and follows Vermes, *Scrolls*, 233. Alternate translations are included
parenthetically. I have also translated the title, which occurs only in 1Q34bis.

4Q508 2[8]

[Prayer for the Day of Atone]ment.
Remember O Lord, the feast of (Your) mercies
and the time of return . . .
Thou hast established it for us as a feast of fasting, and
everlas[ting] precept . . .
Thou knowest the hidden things and the things reveal[ed] . . .
(You have known our inclination since [. . .]
our [rising up] and our lieing down You [. . .])

1Q34bis 3 1, 4Q508 1[9]

(. . . In the lot of righteousness and for the wicked a lot [of . . .]
. . . in their bones, a reproach for all flesh.
. . . and the righteous [. . .]
abundance in the clouds of heaven and the produce of the earth
to distinguish between the righteous and the wicked.)
Thou wilt cause the wicked to be our ransom
and the unfaithful [to be our redemption.]
[Thou wilt] blot out all our oppressors
and we shall praise Thy Name for ever [and ever].
For this hast Thou created us and [to say (respond) to Thee] this:
Blessed are Thou . . .

1Q34bis 3 II, 4Q509 97–98

. . . the Great Light (of heaven) for the [day]time,
[and the Little Light (of heaven) for the night]
. . . without transgressing their laws, . . .
and their dominion is over all the world.
But the seed of man did not understand all that Thou caused them to inherit; they did not discern Thee in all Thy words and wickedly turned aside from every one. They heeded not Thy great power and therefore Thou didst reject them. For wickedness pleases Thee not, and the ungodly shall not be established before Thee.
But in the time of Thy goodwill Thou didst choose for Thyself a people. Thou didst remember Thy Covenant and [granted] that they should be set apart for Thyself from among all the peoples as a holy thing, And Thou didst renew for them Thy covenant (founded)[on a glorious vision and the words of Thy Holy [Spirit], on the works of Thy hands and the writing of Thy Right

---

8 The title has been restored from 1Q34bis 2+1 (see the previous note). The translation follows Vermes (*Scrolls*, 232) with alternate translations and additional verses given parenthetically.

9 The translation of 1Q34bis 3 I-II follows Vermes, *Scrolls*, 231. [The first lines of frg. 3 I were not translated by Vermes and I add them here parenthetically. My translation is based on both 1Q34bis 3 I (J. Barthelemy and J. Milik, *DJD* I, [Oxford: Clarendon, 1955] 153) and the overlapping text in 4Q508 1 (*DJD* VII, 177-178). 1Q34bis 3 II overlaps 4Q509 97-98 (*DJD* VII, 198-199).

Hand, that they might know the foundations of glory and the steps towards eternity . . . [Thou didst raise up] for them a faithful shepherd . . .

IV. Liturgies of Benediction and Malediction

Covenant Renewal Ceremony[10]

Rule of the Community (1QS I 19 - II 22)

On entering the Covenant, the Priests and Levites shall bless the God of salvation and all His fathfulness, and all those entering the Covenant shall say after them, 'Amen, Amen!'

Then the Priests shall recite the favours of God manifested in His mighty deeds and shall declare all His faithful grace to Israel, and the Levites shall recite the iniquites of the children of Israel, all their guilty rebellions and sins during the dominion of Satan (Belial). And after them, all those entering the Covenant shall confess and say:

'We have strayed! We have [disobeyed!] We and our fathers before us have sinned and done wickedly in walking [counter to the precepts] of truth and righteousness. [And God] (is just in that He) has judged us and our fathers also; but He has bestowed His bountiful mercy on us from everlasting to everlasting.'

And the Priests shall bless all the men of the lot of God who walk perfectly in all His ways, saying:
'May He bless you with all good and preserve you from all evil!
[May He lighten your heart with life-giving wisdom
and grant you eternal knowledge!
May He raise His merciful face towards you for everlasting bliss!'

And the Levites shall curse all the men of the lot of Satan (Belial), saying:
'Be cursed because of all your guilty wickedness!
May He deliver you up for torture at the hands of vengeful Avengers! May He visit you with destruction by the hand of all the Wreakers of Revenge!
Be cursed without mercy because of the darkness of your deeds!
Be damned in the shadowy place of everlasting fire!
My God not heed when you call on Him,
nor pardon you by blotting out your sin!
May He raise His angry face towards you for vengeance!
May there be no "Peace" for you
in the mouth of those who hold fast to the Fathers!
And after (those reciting) the blessing and the cursing, all those
entering the Covenant shall say, 'Amen, Amen!' . . .

---

10 The translation follows Vermes, *Scrolls*, 62-63. For other ceremonies of benediction and malediction see 4QBer[a-e] (J. Milik, "Milkî-ṣedeq et Milkî-rešaᶜ," *JJS* 23 [1972] 95-144; the manuscripts have been reassigned to B. Nitzan). A parallel ceremony of benediction to be held during the eschaton is recorded in an appendix to the Rule of the Congregation (1QSb). Eschatological prayers such as these (see also those in the War Scroll) have not been included in this collection of prayers, whose primary focus is the liturgy actually in use at Qumran.

Thus they shall do, year by year, for as long as the dominion of Satan (Belial) endures. The Priests shall enter first, ranked one after another according to the perfection of their spirit; then the Levites; and thirdly, all the people one after another in their Thousands, Hundreds, Fifties, and Tens, that every Israelite may know his place in the Commmunity of God according to the everlasting design.

V. Incantation Hymns

Songs of the Sage (4Q510, 4Q511)[11]

4Q510 1 1–9

Praises [. . .] Ben[edictions for the K]ing of glory.
Words of thanksgiving in psalms of . . . to the God of knowledge,
the Splendour of power, the God of gods,
Lord of all the holy (ones).
[His] domini[on] is over all the powerful mighty ones
and by the power of his might all shall be terrified and scatter and be put to
flight away by the splendour of the dwe[ling] of his kingly glory.

And I, the Master (Sage), proclaim the majesty of his beauty
to frighten and ter[rify] all the spirits of the destroying angels
and the spirits of the bastards, the demons, Lilith,
the howlers and [the yelpers] (jackals and wild cats)
(and) they who strike suddenly
to lead astray the spirit of understanding
and to appal (incriminate) their heart and their (souls)
in the age of the dominion of wickedness
and the appointed times for the humiliation (sufferings)
of the sons of ligh[t]
but not for eternal destruction
but for (an age) for humilation (sufferings) of sin.

Exalt, O just, the God of marvels
My psalms are for the upright . . .
May all whose way is perfect exalt him.

4Q511 2 I 5–10

For the Master (Sage). [First] Song.
[Praise the name] of his holiness (his holy name);
exalt him, all who know [justice] . . .
He put an end to the chief of the dominations
without [any remnant or escapees]

---

11 Baillet, *DJD* VII, 215-262. B. Nitzan, "Hymns from Qumran—4Q510-4Q511," *The Dead Sea Scrolls: Forty Years of Research* (Leiden: Brill; Jerusalem: Magnes Yad Izhak Ben Zvi, 1992) 53-63; *Tarbiz* 55 (1985) 19-46 [in Hebrew]. The English translation is based on Vermes, *Scrolls*, 244-247. I give alternate translations and additional passages parenthetically.

. . . eternal [joy] and everlasting life,
to cause light to shine . . .
his [l]ot is the best of Jacob
and the inheritance of God . . . of Israel . . .
. . . they who guard the way of God
and the pat[h] of his [hol]iness for the saints of his people.
By the discerning knowledge [of Go]d,
he placed Israel in twelve camps . . .
the lot of God with the ange[ls] of the luminaries of his glory.
In his name the praises . . .
he has established for the feast(s) of the year
and for a common government (dominion *yahad*)
that they may walk [in] the lot of [God] according to [his] glory
[and] serve him in the lot of the people of his throne.

4Q511 28–29 2–4

And I [will thank Th]ee
for, because of Thy glory, Thou has [s]et knowledge
on my foundations of dust to pr[aise Thee]
. . . of a shape [of clay] was I moulded
and from darkness was I kneeded
and iniquity is in the limbs of my flesh . . .

4Q511 30 1–3

Thou (my God) hast sealed . . . the [e]arth . . . and they are deep.
[The heavens and the heavens of the] heavens,
and the abysses and the dar[k places (depths) of the earth] . . .
Thou, O my God, hast sealed them all
and there is none to open (them).

4Q511 35 1–2

. . . and an avenging judgement to destroy wickedness
and for the raging anger of God.

4Q511 37 3–5

(their foundations [will shake] and the earth will writhe
all its depths [will] shout
and al[l . . .] will shall be terrified and scattered away . . .)

4Q511 63 III–IV

As for me, my tongue shall extol Thy righteousness,
for Thou hast released it.
Thou hast placed on my lips a found of praise and
in my heart the secret of the commencement of all human actions
and the completion of the deeds of the perfect of way,
and the judgements regarding all the service done by them,

justifying the just by Thy truth
and condemning the wicked for their guilt.
To announce peace to all men of the Covenant
and to utter a dreadfull cry of woe for all those who breach it . . .

May they bless all Thy works always
and blessed be Thy name for ever and ever. Amen, amen.

VI. Psalms, Hymns, and Literary Prayers of Liturgical Import

1) Hymn to the Creator (11QPsᵃ XXXVI 9-15)[12]

Great and holy is the Lord,
the holiest of holy ones for every generation.
Majesty precedes him,
and following him is the rush of many waters.
Grace and truth surround his presence;
truth and justice and righteousness
are the foundation of his throne.
Separating light from deep darkness,
by the knowledge of his mind he established (the) dawn.
When all his angels had witnessed (it) they sang aloud;
for he showed them what they had not known:
Crowning (the) hills with fruit,
good food for every living being.
Blessed be he who makes (the) earth by his power,
establishing (the) world in his wisdom.
In his understanding he stretched out (the) heavens.
and brought forth [wind] from his st[orehouses].
He made [lightening for the rai]n,
and caused mist[s] to rise
[from] the end of [the earth].

2) Psalm of Joseph (4Q372 1 16-32)[13]

My father and my God,
do not abandon me in the hands of the nations;
do justice for me lest the afflicted and the poor perish.
You have no need for any nation or people for any help;
[your fin]ger is greater and stronger than anything in the world.
For you select the truth,
and in your hand there is no violence.
Your mercies are abundant,
your kindnesses great for all who seek you;

---

[12] J. Sanders, *The Dead Sea Psalms Scroll* (Ithaca: Cornell, 1967) 130-131. Cf. also Sanders, *The Psalms Scroll of Qumran Cave 11* (*DJD* IV; Oxford: Clarendon, 1965) 89-91.

[13] E. Schuller, "The Psalm of 4Q372 1 Within the Context of Second Temple Prayer," *CBQ* 54 (1992) 67-79; "4Q372 1: A Text about Joseph," *RQ* 14 (1989) 349-376. "4Q372 1: A Text about Joseph," *RQ* 14 (1990) 349-376.

they are stronger than I
and all my brothers who are joined with me.
A hostile people is dwelling upon it, and . . .
and they opened their mouth
against all the sons of your friend Jacob
with vexations to . . .
the time of their destruction from the entire world,
and they will be given . . .
And I will arise to do justice and right[eousness . . .]
the will of my creator,
and to sacrifice sacrifices of [thanksgiving . . .]
my God; and I will tell [his] kindnesses . . .
I will praise you YHWH, my God, and I will bl[ess] you . . .
the former things,
and to teach sinners your laws
and all who abandon you [your] Tor[ah . . .]
and evil so that your testimonies do not reproach me,
and to tell the words of [your] righteousness . . .
For God is great, holy, mighty and majestic,
awesome and marvellous . . .
and the earth and also in the depths of the Deep;
splendor and [majesty . . .]
And [I] know and I understand and [. . .]

Prayer in the New Testament in Light of Contemporary Jewish Prayers

James H. Charlesworth
Princeton Theological Seminary

In this paper I will examine some Jewish prayers roughly contemporaneous with Jesus and the authors of the New Testament. After reviewing the characteristics of early Jewish prayers two questions will be highlighted: Did the authors of the New Testament exhort believers in Jesus to pray to him? How is early "Christian" prayer different from other prayers within Judaism?

I. NT Prayers Addressed Directly to God

Definition. In the present paper I have chosen to focus on New Testament prayers which are addressed by the author, or one who recorded them, directly to God. Prayer is thus a literary unity in which the believer is in communication with God. The vehicle is not some verbal utterance; it is language in which one heart speaks supra-orally directly to another heart (*cor ad cor loquitur*).

Examples:

Matthew 6:5-14 (cf. Luke 11:2-4)

And whenever you pray, do not be like the hypocrites; for they love to stand and pray in the synagogues and at the street corners, so that they may be seen by others. Truly I tell you, they have received their reward. But whenever you pray, go into your room and shut the door and pray to your Father who is in secret; and your Father who sees in secret will reward you.

When you are praying, do not heap up empty phrases as the Gentiles do; for they think that they will be heard because of their many words. Do not be like them, for your Father knows what you need before you ask him.

Pray then in this way:
Our Father in heaven,
　hallowed be your name.
　Your kingdom come.
　Your will be done.
　on earth as it is in heaven.
　Give us this day our daily bread.
　And forgive us our debts,
　　as we also have forgiven our debtors.

And do not bring us to the time of trial,
   but rescue us from the evil one.
For if you forgive others their trespasses, your heavenly Father will also
forgive you; but if you do not forgive others, neither will your Father
forgive your trespasses.

Mark 14:36

He said, "Abba, Father, for you all things are possible; remove this cup from
me; yet, not what I want, but what you want."

Acts 4:24-30

When they heard it, they raised their voices together to God and said,
"Sovereign Lord, who made the heaven and the earth, the sea, and everything
in them, it is you who said by the Holy Spirit through our ancestor David,
your servant:
   'Why did the Gentiles rage,
      and the peoples imagine vain things?
   The kings of the earth took their stand,
   and the rulers have gathered together
      against the Lord and against his Messiah.'
For in this city, in fact, both Herod and Pontius Pilate, with the Gentiles and
the peoples of Israel, gathered together against your holy servant Jesus, whom
you anointed, to do whatever your hand and your plan had predestined to take
place. And now, Lord, look at their threats, and grant to your servants to speak
your word with all boldness, while you stretch out your hand to heal, and
signs and wonders are performed through the name of your holy servant
Jesus."

Romans 8:15

For you did not receive a spirit of slavery to fall back into fear, but you have
received a spirit of adoption. When we cry, "Abba! Father!"

Revelation 11:17-18

We give you thanks, Lord God Almighty,
who are and who were,
for you have taken your great power
and begun to reign.
The nations raged,
but your wrath has come,
and the time for judging the dead
for rewarding your servants, the prophets
and saints and all who fear your name,
both small and great,
and for destroying those who destroy the earth.

II. Roughly Contemporaneous Prayers

1. Prayer of Manasseh

Although this prayer was once considered a Christian composition, because of the expressed need for forgiveness and the affirmation that only God can forgive, we now know, thanks to a refined perception of Jewish piety during the time of Hillel and Jesus, that it was composed by a Jew, perhaps in Greek but probably in Hebrew or Aramaic. The precise time is unknown; but it was probably written sometime between the second century B.C.E. and the first century C.E. My own dating would place the prayer during the time of Herod the Great, or sometime in the late first century B.C.E. The provenience is probably Palestine. Because the concepts in this prayer are similar to many now assuredly found in Palestine, thanks to the discovery of the scrolls in the eleven Qumran caves, it is probable that the prayer was composed in Jerusalem or its environs.[1]

The Prayer of Manasseh (1-8, 11-15; Charlesworth, OTP 2.634-35)

O Lord, God of our fathers,
    God of Abraham, Isaac, Jacob, and their righteous offspring;
He who made the heaven and the earth
    with all their beauty;
He who bound the sea
    and established it by the command of his word,
he who closed the bottomless pit
    and sealed it by his powerful and glorious name;
You (before) whom all things fear and tremble;
    (especially) before your power.
Because your awesome magnificence
    cannot be endured;
none can endure or stand before
    your anger and your fury against sinners;
But unending and immeasurable
    are your promised mercies;
Because you are the Lord,
    long-suffering, merciful, and greatly compassionate;
and you feel sorry over the evils of men.
You, O Lord, according to your gentle grace,
    promised forgiveness to those who repent of their sins,
    and in your manifold mercies
appointed repentance for sinners as the (way to) salvation.
You, therefore, O Lord, God of the righteous,
    did not appoint grace for the righteous,
    such as Abraham, Isaac, and Jacob,

---

[1] For more information, see *OTP* 2. 625-37. *OTP* = *The Old Testament Pseudepigrapha*, 2 vols., ed. J. H. Charlesworth (Garden City, New York: Doubleday, 1983, 1985). All quotations of prayers from this collection will be cited according to translator, volume, and page. I am deeply grateful to Doubleday for the permission to quote extensively from this collection.

> those who did not sin against you;
> > but you appointed grace for me, (I) who am a sinner . . .
> And now behold I am bending the knees of my heart before you;
> and I am beseeching your kindness.
> I have sinned, O Lord, I have sinned;
> and I certainly know my sins.
> I beseech you;
> > forgive me, O Lord, forgive me!
> Do not destroy me with my transgressions;
> do not be angry against me forever;
> do not remember my evils;
> and do not condemn me and banish me to the depths of the earth!
> For you are the God of those who repent.
> In me you will manifest all your grace;
> and although I am not worthy,
> > you will save me according to your manifold mercies.
> Because of this (salvation) I shall praise you continually
> > all the days of my life;
> because all the hosts of heaven praise you,
> > and sing to you forever and ever.

2. Psalms of Solomon

The Psalms of Solomon were composed by devout Jews most probably in Hebrew (less likely Greek), sometime during the middle or later part of the first century B.C.E., since the 18 psalms (or prayers) refer to the demise of the Roman general Pompey. They were probably recited by Jews living in Jerusalem. The group behind them is not to be facilely identified with the Pharisees or Essenes. The following is an excerpt from this important pre-70 Palestinian hymnbook.

Psalms of Solomon (Wright, OTP 2.651-70)

> I cried out to the Lord when I was severely troubled,
> > to God when sinners set upon (me).
> Suddenly, the clamor of war was heard before me;
> > "He will hear me, for I am full of righteousness."
> I considered in my heart that I was full of righteousness,
> > for I had prospered and had many children.
> > > (1:1-3)
> I shall prove you right, O God, in uprightness of heart;
> > for your judgments are right, O God.
> For you have rewarded the sinners according to their actions,
> > and according to their extremely wicked sins.
> You have exposed their sins, that your judgment might be evident;
> > you have obliterated their memory from the earth.
> God is a righteous judge and he will not be impressed by appearances.
> For the gentiles insulted Jerusalem, trampling (her) down;
> > he dragged her beauty down from the throne of glory.
> She put on sackcloth instead of beautiful clothes,
> > a rope around her head instead of a crown.

She took off the wreath of glory which God had put on her;
    in dishonor her beauty was thrown to the ground.
(2:15-21)

And I did not wait long until God showed me his insolence
    pierced on the mountains of Egypt,
    more despised than the smallest thing on earth and sea.
His body was carried about on the waves in much shame,
    and there was no one to bury (him), for he (God) had despised
    him with contempt,
He did not consider that he was a man,
    for the latter
    do not consider (this).
He said, "I shall be lord of land and sea";
    and he did not understand that it is God who is great,
    powerful in his great strength.
He is king over the heavens,
    judging even kings and rulers,
(2:26-30)

Praise God, you who fear the Lord with understanding,
    for the Lord's mercy is upon those who fear him with judgment.
(2:33)

For the Lord is good to those who persistently call upon him,
    to treat his devout in accordance with his mercy,
    to bring them (constantly) before him in strength.
Praised be the Lord forever before his servants.
(2:36-37)

The confidence of the righteous (comes) from God their savior;
    sin after sin does not visit the house of the righteous.
The righteous constantly searches his house,
    to remove his unintentional sins.
He atones for (sins of) ignorance by fasting and humbling his soul,
    and the Lord will cleanse every devout person and his house.
(3:6-8)

May God banish those who arrogantly commit all (kinds of) unrighteousness,
for the Lord our God is a great and powerful judge in righteousness.
Lord, let your mercy be upon all those who love you.
(4:24-25)

And you will listen. For who is good and kind but you,
    making the humble person happy by opening your hand in mercy?
(5:12)

Those who fear the Lord are happy with good things,
    In your kingdom your goodness (is) upon Israel.
May the glory of the Lord be praised, for he is our king.
(5:18-19)

He prays to the Lord for all his household,
    and the Lord has heard the prayers of all who fear God.
And the Lord fulfills every request from the soul that hopes in him;
    praised is the Lord, who shows mercy to those who truly love him.

(6:5)

Because of this God mixed them (a drink) of a wavering spirit,
  and gave them a cup of undiluted wine to make them drunk.
He brought someone from the end of the earth, one who attacks in strength;
  he declared war against Jerusalem, and her land.
The leaders of the country met him with joy. They said to him,
  "May your way be blessed. Come, enter in peace."
They graded the rough roads before his coming,
  they opened the gates to Jerusalem, they crowned her city walls.
He entered in peace as a father enters his son's house;
  he set his feet securely.
He captured the fortified towers and the wall of Jerusalem,
  for God led him in securely while they wavered.
He killed their leaders and every (man) wise in counsel,
  he poured out the blood of the inhabitants of Jerusalem
  like dirty water.
He led away their sons and daughters, those profanely spawned.

(8:14-21)

And whose sins will he forgive except those who have sinned?
  You bless the righteous, and do not accuse them for what they sinned.
And goodness is upon those that sin, when they repent.

(9:7)

The Lord is faithful to those who truly love him,
  to those who endure his discipline,
To those who live in the righteousness of his commandments,
  in the Law, which he has commanded for our life.
The Lord's devout shall live by it forever;
  the Lord's paradise, the trees of life, are his devout ones.
Their planting is firmly rooted forever;
  they shall not be uprooted as long as the heavens shall last,

(14:1-4)

When I was persecuted I called on the Lord's name;
  I expected the help of Jacob's God and I was saved.
  For you, O God, are the hope and refuge of the poor.
For who, O God, is strong except he who confesses you in truth;
  and what person is powerful except he who confesses your name?
A new psalm with song with a happy heart,
  the fruit of the lips with the tuned instrument of the tongue,
  the first fruits of the lips from a devout and righteous heart.

(15:1-3)

Lord, you chose David to be king over Israel,
  and swore to him about his descendants forever,
  that his kingdom should not fail before you.
But (because of) our sins, sinners rose up against us,
  they set upon us and drove us out.
Those to whom you did not (make the) promise,
  they took away (from us) by force;
  and they did not glorify your honorable name.

With pomp they set up a monarchy because of their arrogance;
    they despoiled the throne of David with arrogant shouting.
But you, O God, overthrew them, and uprooted their descendants from
    the earth,
for there rose up against them a man alien to our race.
You rewarded them, O God, according to their sins;
    it happened to them according to their actions.
According to their actions, God showed no mercy to them;
    he hunted down their descendants,
        and did not let even one of them go.
The Lord is faithful in all his judgments
    which he makes in the world.
The lawless one laid waste our land, so that no one inhabited it;
    they massacred young and old and children at the same time.
In his blameless wrath he expelled them to the west,
    and he did not spare even the officials of the country from ridicule.
(17:4-12)
See, Lord, and raise up for them their king,
    the son of David, to rule over your servant Israel
    in the time known to you, O God.
(17:21)
He will gather a holy people
    whom he will lead in righteousness;
and he will judge the tribes of the people
    that have been made holy by the Lord their God.
(17:26)
He will judge peoples and nations in the wisdom of his righteousness.
Pause.
And he will have gentile nations serving him under his yoke,
    and he will glorify the Lord in (a place) prominent (above)
    the whole earth.
And he will purge Jerusalem
    (and make it) holy as it was even from the beginning,
(for) nations to come from the ends of the earth to see his glory,
    to bring as gifts her children who had been driven out,
and to see the glory of the Lord
    with which God has glorified her.
And he will be a righteous king over them, taught by God.
There will be no unrighteousness among them in his days,
    for all shall be holy,
    and their king shall be the Lord Messiah.
(For) he will not rely on horse and rider and bow,
    nor will he collect gold and silver for war.
Nor will he build up hope in a multitude for a day of war.
The Lord himself is his king,
    the hope of the one who has a strong hope in God.
(17:29-34)
May God dispatch his mercy to Israel;
    may he deliver us from the pollution of profane enemies;

The Lord Himself is our king forevermore.

(17:45-46)

May God cleanse Israel for the day of mercy in blessing,
> for the appointed day when his Messiah will reign.

Blessed are those born in those days,
> to see the good things of the Lord
> which he will do for the coming generation;

(which will be) under the rod of discipline of the Lord Messiah,
> in the fear of his God,
> in wisdom of spirit,

and of righteousness and of strength,

to direct people in righteous acts, in the fear of God,
> to set them all in the fear of the Lord

A good generation (living) in the fear of God,
> in the days of mercy.

Pause. (18:5-9)

3. Selected Prayers from the Jewish Apocalypses

The Jewish apocalypses contain numerous prayers. Only two are chosen for examinations now.

The Prayer of Enoch (1Enoch 84:1-6). This prayer was composed by a Jew in a Semitic language, sometime in the early second century B.C.E. (because it belongs to the Dream Visions [83-90] which antedate 161 B.C.E. It was most likely composed in Palestine).

The Prayer of Enoch (1 Enoch 84.1-6; Isaac, OTP 1.62-63)

Then I raised up my hands in righteousness and blessed the Holy and Great One; and I spoke with the breath of my mouth and the tongue of flesh which God has made for the children of the flesh, the people, so that they should speak with it; he gave them the breath and the mouth so that they should speak with it.

Blessed are you, O Great King,

you are mighty in your greatness,

O Lord of all the creation of heaven,

King of kings and God of the whole world.

Your authority and kingdom abide forever and ever;

and your dominion throughout all the generations of generations;

all the heavens are your throne forever,

and the whole earth is your footstool forever and ever and ever.

For you have created (all),

and all things you rule;

not a single thing is hard for you—(absolutely) not a single thing or wisdom;

Your throne has not retreated from her station nor from before your presence.

Everything you know, you see, and you hear;

nothing exists that can be hidden from you, for everything you expose.

The angels of your heavens are now committing sin (upon the earth),
and your wrath shall rest upon the flesh of the people until (the arrival of)
the great day of judgment

"Now, O God, and Lord and Great King, I pray and beg so that you may sustain my prayer and save for me (a generation) that will succeed me in the earth; and do not destroy all the flesh of the people and empty the earth (so that) there shall be eternal destruction. Do now destroy, O my Lord, the flesh that has angered you from upon the earth, but sustain the flesh of righteousness and uprightness as a plant of eternal seed; and hide not your face from the prayer of your servant, O Lord."

The Lament and Prayer of Ezra (4 Ezra 8:20-36). It was composed by a Jew, most likely in Hebrew. In its present form it postdates the destruction of 70 C.E. and antedates 100 C.E. It was most likely composed near Jerusalem or its environs.

The Lament and Prayer of Ezra (4 Ezra 8.20-36; Metzger, OTP, 2.542-43)

The beginning of the work of Ezra's prayer, before he was taken up. He said, "O Lord who inhabits eternity, whose eyes are exalted and whose upper chambers are in the air, whose throne is beyond measure and whose glory is beyond comprehension, before whom the hosts of angels stand trembling and at whose command they are changed to wind and fire, whose word is sure and whose utterances are certain, whose ordinance is strong and whose command is terrible, whose look dries up the depths and whose indignation makes the mountains melt away, and whose truth is established forever— hear, O Lord, the prayer of your servant, and give ear to the petition of your creature; attend to my words. For as long as I live I will speak, and as long as I have understanding I will answer. O look not upon the sins of your people, but at those who have served you in truth. Regard not the endeavors of those who act wickedly, but the endeavors of those who have kept your covenants amid afflictions. Think not on those who have lived wickedly, in your sight; but remember those who have willingly acknowledged that you are to be feared. Let it not be your will to destroy those who have had the ways of cattle; but regard those who have gloriously taught your Law. Be not angry with those who are deemed worse than beasts; but love those who have always put their trust in your glory. For we and our fathers have passed our lives in ways that bring death, but you, because of us sinners, are called merciful. For if you have desired to have pity on us, who have no works of righteousness, then you will be called merciful. For the righteous, who have many works laid up with you, shall receive their reward in consequence of their own deeds. But what is man, that you are angry with him; or what is a mortal race, that you are so bitter against it? For in truth there is no one among those who have been born who has not acted wickedly, and among those who have existed there is no one who has not transgressed. For in this, O Lord, your righteousness and goodness will be declared, when you are merciful to those who have no store of good works."

4. Selected Prayers Found in the Qumran Caves

From Qumran caves I and IV have come copies of the hymnbook of the Qumran sect. It is the well-known Hodayot, or Thanksgiving Hymns. This work is composite, reflecting the life of the Qumran community. Some prayers or hymns were most likely composed by the founder of the sect, the Righteous Teacher, who was surely one of the leading priests in the Jerusalem cult before he led a band of priests into the wilderness. The following prayer or hymn was most likely composed by him in Hebrew sometime after 150 B.C.E. and following the settlement in the wilderness at what is now Khirbet Qumran.[2]

1QH 8.4-11

I [praise you, O Lord, because you] placed me
  as an overflowing fountain in a desert,
  and (as) a spring of water in a land of dryness,
  and (as) the irrigator of the garden.
You [have plant]ed a planting of cyprus, and elm,
  with cedar together for your glory;
  (these are) the trees of life hidden
  among all the trees of the water
  beside the mysterious water source.
And they caused to sprout the shoot [*nsr*]
  for the eternal planting.
Before they shall cause (it) to sprout they strike root,
then send forth their roots to the river [*ywbl*].
And its trunk shall be open to the living water;
and it shall become the eternal fountain.
But upon the shoot [*nsr*]
  every [beast] of the forest shall feed.
And its trunk (shall become) a place of trampling
  for all those who pass over the way [*drk*].
And its branches (shall be) for every bird.
And all the tre[es] of the water
  shall exalt themselves over it,
because they shall become magnified in their planting.
But they shall not send forth a root to the river [*ywbl*].
And he who causes to sprout the hol[y] shoot [*nsr*]
  for the planting of truth is concealed
with the result that he is not esteemed,
and the sealing of his mystery is not perceived.

This prayer or hymn was certainly used in the cultic ceremonies of the Qumran sect. This hymnbook celebrates the cosmic unity of prayer and praise, known especially from Qumran by the Angelic Liturgy. The Sons of Light are joined with the Angel of Light. The hymnbook also demonstrates how the Qumranites experienced the presence of the future day, the end of days, and eschatological salvation. They felt that angels were present in their religious services. In fact heaven and earth, the present and the future were

---

2 Translated by Charlesworth; published in *"Shaʿarei Talmon": Studies in the Bible, Qumran, and the Ancient Near East Presented to Shemaryahu Talmon*, ed. M. Fishbane and E. Tov, with W. W. Fields (Winona Lake, Indiana: Eisenbrauns, 1992), 295-307. I thank Eisenbrauns for the permission to quote from my translation.

not conceived as separate dualities; they were experienced as a synthetic whole.

5. *Prayer of Joseph*

The Prayer of Joseph was conceivably composed by a Jew. According to Nicephorus' *Stichometry* the prayer contained 1100 lines. The mere 164 words which are extant only in Greek quotations that derive directly or indirectly from Origen do not allow an answer to the question of whether the original was composed in a Semitic language or in Greek. The work clearly antedates the third century C.E.; it may have been composed in the first century C.E. The provenience may be Alexandria, but Palestine seems far more likely.

Prayer of Joseph (Frg. A, 1-9, J. Z. Smith, OTP 2.713)

I, Jacob, who is speaking to you, am also Israel, an angel of God and a ruling spirit. *Abraham* and Isaac *were created before any work.* But, I, Jacob, who men call Jacob but whose name is Israel am he who *God called Israel* which means, a man seeing God, because I am the *firstborn of every living thing to whom God* gives life.

And when I was *coming up from Syrian Mesopotamia,* Uriel, the angel of God, came forth and said that 'I [Jacob-Israel] had *descended to earth* and I had tabernacled among men and that I had been called by the name of Jacob. He envied me and *fought with me and wrestled with me* saying that his name and *the name that is before every angel* was to be above mine. I told him his name and what rank he held among the sons of God. Are you not Uriel, the eighth after me? and I, Israel, *the archangel of the power of the Lord* and the *chief captain* among the sons of God? Am I not Israel, the *first minister before the face of God?* And I called upon my God by the inextinguishable name.

Most striking among the concepts in this prayer is the disclosure that Jacob is none other than the earthly incarnation of the Angel Israel, who is a ruling spirit. Indeed, he is the chief of the angels. Jacob, Israel, is declared to be the firstborn. The archangel Uriel is revealed to be jealous and the one who wrestled with the Angel Israel, who descended to earth and "tabernacled" among humans. The Angel Israel is superior to Uriel, who is merely eighth after him. Even considering the elevation of the Angel Israel, the prayer is not addressed to anyone except God.

6. *Prayer of Jacob*

The little known Prayer of Jacob was composed by a Jew, who refers to himself as from the race of Israel. It was composed in Greek sometime before the fourth century since it is preserved only in one fourth-century C.E. papyrus (Deutsche Staatsbibliothek, Berlin). Perhaps the prayer was composed in the second or first century C.E. The provenience seems to be Egypt.

For our purposes it is important to observe that the prayer is directed to God, the Father of the Patriarchs, the Creator of all. God is declared to be "King." As did Solomon (1Kings 3), the author asks for wisdom. The author reveals his self-understanding: he prays as an angel on earth, as one who is immortal. It is imperative to note that he does not state he is an angel; he uses a simile. The Greek is ὡς. The dramatic aorists that follow seem to indicate that the author has received God's gift, has become immortal, and is really an angel on earth.

We should probably not think that the author is comparing unlike things; he is most likely portraying himself as if he were an angel.

Prayer of Jacob (1-3, 5-6, 8, 10, 17-20; Charlesworth, OTP 2.720-23)

Father of (the) Patria[rch]s,
Father of al[l] (things),
[Fathe]r of (the) powe[rs of the co]sm[os];
Cr[e]ato[r of a]l[l . . .],
Creator of the angels and archang[e]l[s],
the C[r]eator of (the) re[deeming] nam[es];
I invoke you,
O Father of powe[r]s altogether,
Father of the [wh]ole [co]s[m]os
    [and of] all creation, both the inhabited and uninhabite[d,
    to whom the] ch[erubim are sub]j[e]c[t]e[d];
He who showed favor to [Abr]aham
    by [giving the] kingd[om to him].
He[a]r me,
(You) the God o[f the p]owers,
the G[od of ang]els a[nd a]r[cha]ngels,
ki[ng . . .];
You who s[i]t upon (the) mountain of h[oly] [S]inaios; . . .
[you] who sit upon the s[e]a, . . .
you who sit [upon] the s[er]pen[t] gods,
the [God who s]i[t]s [upon the s]un, *Iao,*
you who si[t upon . . .]
you who [si]t [u]pon th[e . . .] . . .Abriel, Louel
    [. . .t]he [r]esting place of (the) che[r]u[b]i[m . . .]
    f[o]r ever and e[ve]r.
God *Abaoth, Abrathiaoth, [Sa]ba[oth, A]donai, astra* . . .
    the L[or]d of all (things).
I summon you, . . .
Fill me with wisdom,
empow[e]r me, Lord;
Fill my heart with good things, Lord;
As an ear[th]ly angel,
as [hav]ing become immortal,
as having recei[ved] the gift which (is) from [yo]u, [a]men, amen.
[S]ay [the p]r[a]y[e]r o[f] Jacob seven times to (the) Nor[th] and E[a]st.

III Problems, Definitions, Methodologies, the Canonization Processes

Numerous problems have attended the historical and critical study of Jewish prayers contemporaneous with Jesus and the authors of the books in the New Testament. None of them has been more detrimental to the perception of early Jewish piety as the presupposition that Christianity is superior to Judaism. Hence, Jesus was seen not as a devout Jew, but as one who transcended an evil people. The beauty of Jewish prayer was not perceived, and Jewish prayers like the Prayer of Manasseh were judged to be

"Christian." The theological justification was that Jews earned salvation through the observance of the Law, which was defined legalistically, and that Christians were given salvation by grace through faith in Jesus' efficacious suffering. Major truths were miscast and Judaism was placarded as degenerate. Now, we known that there is not one Jewish text from the time of Hillel, Jesus, and Paul that affirms the Law saves the Jew. In fact running through the Jewish prayers excerpted here is the dual expression of sin and the affirmation that God, and he alone, forgives the sinner.

During the first century C.E. the canonical process was continuing in Judaism. It had not begun within "Christianity," which indeed up until 70 at least was still a "sect" within Judaism; most of the books in the New Testament had not yet been composed. Hence, it is anachronistic to cavalierly refer to the prayers already mentioned as "extracanonical." That means it is unwise to categorize them as inferior to prayers in the Hebrew Bible, the Greek New Testament, or in Rabbinics. The authors who composed the prayers already mentioned most likely considered them authentic, inspired, and genuine. The communities who recited the Psalms of Solomon and the Hodayot probably phenomenologically acted out the fact that these collections were their communal hymnbook.

IV Prayer and the Believer Today

The most important insight we obtain from studying the prayers already discussed is that religious individuals are challenged to move beyond thinking about God, and beyond believing in God. They are shown how to experience God as one who hears and answers prayers. God is one who speaks to them and purifies them of their infirmities.

V Conclusion

The prayers in the New Testament studied at the outset indicate that prayer is to be directly addressed to God. According to Matthew 6:5-14 Jesus is reported to have instructed his followers to "pray to your Father" in simple, direct, and personal speech. After these words in Matthew he gives them the Lord's Prayer. According to Acts 4:24-30 Jesus' followers prayed to God with the address "Sovereign Lord." According to Paul, in Romans 8:15, the believer in Christ is to pray not to him but to God: "Abba! Father!" According to Revelation 11:17-18 prayer is to the "Lord God Almighty." These prayers carry on the Jewish tradition in which the devout is to pray to God, and to him alone.

In the New Testament there are Christological hymns in which Jesus is deified—in the words of the author of Colossians—"in him all the fullness of God was pleased to dwell" (1:19). In Philippians 2:5-11, which is in one of Paul's authentic letters, Jesus is depicted as one who is worthy to receive adulation from all. God has "bestowed on him the name which is above every name." At the name of "Jesus every knee should bow, in heaven and on earth and under the earth, and every tongue confess that Jesus Christ is Lord, to the glory of God the Father" (2:10-11).

In this christological hymn or prayer is Jesus portrayed as the one to whom the believer is to pray? In light of the insights received from studying Jewish prayers—and the lack of an explicit exhortation to pray to Jesus—I think we should not read into the hymn in Philippians 2 what later Christians would understand it to denote. It is clear that the Lamb in Revelation is worthy of all praise. He is depicted as enthroned in Revelation and in Hebrews. A study of Jewish prayers contemporaneous with Jesus and the authors of the New Testament, the presence of Jesus' own exhortation to pray to God, his habitual praying directly to God in the Synoptics and in the Gospel of John, and the lack of a clear injunction in the New Testament to pray to Jesus and not to God, it is not wise to say that early Christianity broke with Judaism by praying to Jesus and not to God.

Is that conclusion warranted? In what ways, then, did early "Christian" prayers differ from Jewish prayers? Here may well be some major questions to discuss in the seminar.

The Phenomenology of Greco-Roman Prayer

David E. Aune
Loyola University, Chicago

The following translations of Greek and Latin prayer texts are intended to accompany and illustrate my paper on the phenomenology of prayer in the Greco-Roman world. One of the major purposes of the paper is to demonstrate the fact that the traditional distinction between "religious" prayer and "magical" prayer is problematic and consists primarily in the differing social contexts in which prayer occurs.

Text 1: *Iliad* 1.35-42; translation in Richmond Lattimore, *The Iliad of Homer* (Chicago: University of Chicago, 1951) 60. The prayer exhibits a threefold structure: (1) initial listing of the god's titles and local associations, (2) special claims on his favor, (3) the request.

> Over and over the old man [Chryses] prayed as he walked in solitude
> to King Apollo, whom Leto of the lovely hair bore: "Hear me,
> lord of the silver bow who set your power about Chryse
> and Killa the sacrosanct, who are lord in strength over Tenedos,
> Smintheus, if ever it pleased your heart that I build your temple,
> if ever it pleased you that I burned all the rich thigh pieces
> of bulls, of goats, then bring to pass this wish I pray for:
> let your arrows make the Danaans pay for my tears shed.

Text 2: *Iliad* 7.179-80; translation in Lattimore, *Iliad of Homer*, 173. This prayer is extremely short and exhibits a twofold structure: (1) the god addressed is briefly named, (2) the request immediately follows expressed with an imperatival infinitive.

> Father Zeus, let Aias win the lot, or else Diomedes,
> Tydeus' son, or the king himself of golden Mykenai.

Text 3: *Iliad* 10.277-82; translation in Lattimore, *Iliad of Homer*, 225.

> And Odysseus was glad at the bird-sign, and prayed to Athene:
> "Hear me, daughter of Zeus of the aegis, you who forever
> stand beside me in all hard tasks, nor am I forgotten
> as I go my ways: now give me the best of your love, Athene,
> and grant that we come back in glory to the strong-benched vessels
> when we have done a great thing that will sadden the Trojans."

Text 4: *Iliad* 10.283-94; translation in Lattimore, *Iliad of Homer*, 226-26.

> Diomedes of the great war cry spoke in prayer after him:
> "Hear me also, Atrytone, daughter of great Zeus.
> Come with me now as you went with my father, brilliant Tydeus,
> into Thebes, when he went with a message before the Achaians,
> and left the bronze-armoured Achaians beside Asopos
> while he carried a word of friendship to the Kadmeians
> in that place; but on his way back he was minded to grim deeds
> with your aid, divine goddess, since you stood in goodwill beside him.
> So now again be willing to stand by me, and watch over me,
> and I in turn will dedicate you a heifer, broad-browed,
> one year old, unbroken, that no man ever led under
> the yoke. I will drench her horns in gold and offer her to you."

Text 5: *PGM* I.195-222; translation in H. D. Betz (ed.), *The Greek Magical Papyri in Translation including the Demotic Spells* (2nd ed.; Chicago: University of Chicago, 1992) 10.

This, then, is the prayer of deliverance for the first-begotten and first-born god:
> "I call upon you lord.
> Hear me, holy god who rest among the holy ones,
> at whose side the Glorious Ones stand continually.
> I call upon you, [fore]father,
> and I beseech you, eternal one,
> eternal ruler of the sun's rays,
> eternal ruler of the celestial orb,
> standing in the seven-part region,
> CHAO CHAO CHA OUPH CHTHETHONIMEETHECHRINIA MEROUMI
> ALDA ZAO BLATHAMMACHOTH PHRIXA EKE . . . PHYEIDRYMEO
> PHERPHRITHO IACHTHO PSYCHEO PHIRITHMEO ROSEROTH
> THAMASTRA PHATIRI TAOCH IALTHEMEACHE;
> you who hold fast to the root,
> [who] possess the powerful name which has been consecrated by all
>   angels.
> Hear me, you who have established the mighty Decans and archangels,
> and beside whom stand untold myriads of angels.
> You have been exalted to heaven,
> and the lord has borne witness to your wisdom and has praised your
>   power highly
> and has said that you have strength in the same way as he,
> as much strength as he [himself] has.
>
> I call upon you, lord of the universe, in an hour of need;
> hear me, for my soul is [distressed],
> and I am perplexed and in want of [everything.
> Wherefore, come] to me,
> you who are lord over all angels;
> shield me against all excess of magical power of aerial
> daimon [and] fate.

Aye, lord, because I call upon your secret name which
reaches from the firmament to the earth,
ATHEZOPHOIM ZADEAGEOBEPHIATHEAA AMBRAMI ABRAAM
THALCHILTHOE ELKOTHOOEE ACHTHONON SA ISAK
CHOEIOURTHASIO IOOSIA IICHEMEOOOOAOAEI,
rescue me in an hour of need."
Say this to Helios or whenever you are forced to do so.

Text 6: *PGM* I.296-327; translation in Betz, *The Greek Magical Papyri*, 11.

O lord Apollo, come with Paian.
Give answer to my questions, lord. O master
Leave Mount Parnassos and the Delphic Pytho Whene'er my priestly lips
    voice secret words,
First angel of [the god], great Zeus, IAO
And you, MICHAEL, who rule heaven's realm,
I call, and you, archangel GABRIEL.
Down from Olympos, ABRASAX, delighting
In dawns, come gracious who view sunset from
The dawn, ADONAI. Father of the world,
All nature quakes in fear of you, PAKERBETH.
I adjure God's head, which is Olympos;
I adjure God's signet, which is vision;
I adjure the right hand you held o'er the world;
I adjure God's bowl containing wealth;
I adjure eternal god, AION of all;
I adjure self-growing Nature, mighty ADONAIOS;
I adjure setting and rising ELOAIS:
I adjure these holy and divine names that
They send me the divine spirit and that it
Fulfill what I have in my heart and soul.
Hear blessed one, I call you who rule heav'n
And earth and Chaos and Hades where dwell
[Daimons of men who once gazed on the light].
Send me this daimon at my sacred chants,
Who moves by night to orders 'neath your force,
From whose own tend this comes, and let him tell me
In total truth all that my mind designs,
And send him gentle, gracious, pondering No thoughts opposed to me.
    And may you not
Be angry at my sacred chants. But guard
That my whole body come to light intact,
For you yourself arranged these things among
Mankind for them to learn. I call your name,
In number equal to the very Moirai,
ACHAIPHOTHOTHOAIEIAEIA
AIEAIEIAOTHOTHOPHIACHA.

Text 7: *Hymni Homerici* 24; LCL translation.

To Hestia
Hestia, you who tend the holy house of the lord Apollo,
  the Far-shooter at goodly Pytho,
with soft oil dripping ever from your locks,
come now into this house,
come, having one mind with Zeus the all-wise—
draw near, and withal bestow grace upon my song.

Text 8: *Hymni Orphici* 1; translation in Apostolos N. Athanasakis, *The Orphic Hymns* (SBLTT 12; Missoula: Scholars Press, 1977) 5-5-7.

To Hecate Lovely Hekate of the roads and crossroads I invoke;
in heaven, on earth, and in the sea, saffron-cloaked,
tomb spirit reveling in the souls of the dead,
daughter of Perses, haunting deserted places, delighting in deer,
nocturnal, dog-loving, monstrous queen,
  devouring wild beasts, ungirt, of repelling countenance.
You, herder of bulls, queen and mistress of the whole world,
leader, nymph, mountain-roaming nurturer of youth,
maiden, I beseech you to come to these holy rites,
ever with joyous heart and ever favoring the oxherd.

Text 9: Lead tablet inscribed in Greek. Translation in John G. Gager (ed.), *Curse Tablets and Binding Spells from the Ancient World* (New York and Oxford: Oxford University, 1992) 62-63, no. 10; first few lines only.

I invoke you, whoever you are, spirit of the dead,
IONA, the god who established earth and heaven.
I bind you by oath, NEICHAROPLEX,
the god who holds the power of the places down beneath.
I bind you by oath, . . . ,
the god . . . of spirits.
I bind you by oath, great AROUROBAARZAGRAN, the god of Necessity.
I bind you by oath, BLABLEISPHTHEIBAL, the firstborn god of Earth "on
  which to lie(?)"
I bind you, LAILAM, THE GOD OF WINDS AND SPIRITS.

Text 10: Lead tablet, 2nd cent. BCE to 2nd cent. CE (Gager, *Curse Tablets*, 167, no. 75), side B.

Lady Demeter, I appeal to you as one who has suffered wrongs.
Hear me, goddess, and render justice, so that you bring the most terrible and painful things (on) those who think such things about us and who rejoice together against us and bring suffering on me and my wife, Epiktesis, and despise us. Oh Queen, lend an ear to those of us who suffer and punish those who look happily on such as us.

Text 11: Tin tablet, 350-400 CE (Gager, *Curse Tablets*, 197, no. 99).

To the God Nodens. Silvianus has lost a ring. He has given half of it (its value) to Nodens. Among those whose name is Senicianus, do not permit health until he brings it to the temple of Nodens.

Text 12: *PGM* IV.939-55; translation in Betz, *The Greek Magical Papyri*, 56-57.

> "Hail, serpent, and stout lion, natural
> Sources of fire. And hail, clear water and
> Lofty-leafed tree, and you who gather
> Clover from golden fields of beans, and who
> Cause gentle foam to gush forth from pure mouths.
> Scarab, who drive the orb of fertile file,
> O self-engendered one, who because you are
> Two-syllabled, AE, and are the first-
> Appearing one, nod me assent, I pray,
> Because your mystic symbols I declare,
> EO AI OU AMERR OOUOTH IYIOE MARMARAUOTH LAILAM
> SOUMARTA.
> Be gracious unto me, first-father, and
> May you yourself send strength as my companion.
> Stay allied, lord, and listen to me through the charm that produces direct
> vision which I do today, and reveal to me concerning those things I ask
> you through the lamp divination for direct vision which I do today, I,
> NN, IY EYE OO AEE IAEE AIAE EAI EY EIE OOOOO EY EO IAOAI"
> (repeat).

Text 13: Catullus *Poems* 34; LCL translation.

We girls and chaste boys are lieges of Diana. Diana let us sing, chaste boys and girls. O child of Latona, great offspring of greatest Jove, whom thy mother bore by the Delian olive-tree, that thou mightest be the lady of mountains and green woods, and sequestered glens and sounding rivers; thou art called Juno Lucina by mothers in pains of travail, thou art called mighty Trivia and Moon with counterfeit light. Thou, goddess, measurest out by monthly course the circuit of the year, thou fillest full with goodly fruits the rustic home of the husbandman. Be thou hallowed by whatever name thou wilt; and as of old thou wert wont, with good help keep safe the race of Romulus.

Text 14: Livy 1.32.10; LCL translation. Declaration of war.

"Hear, Jupiter, and thou, Janus Quirinus, and hear all heavenly gods, and ye, gods of earth, and ye of the lower world; I call you to witness that this people"—naming whatever people it is—"is unjust, and does not make just reparation. But of these matters we will take counsel of the elders in our country, how we may obtain our right."

Text 15: Aristophanes *Thesmophoriazusae* 295-305; translation in Louis Bruit Zaidman and Pauline Schmitt Pantel, *Religion in the Ancient Greek City* (Cambridge: Cambridge University, 1992) 42. Parody of prayer said before silent citizens before orators addressed them from the rostrum.

Pray silence, pray silence. Pray to the two Thesmophoroi [Demeter and Persephone], to Ploutos [god of Wealth] and Kalligeneia [Demeter "bearer of fair offspring"] . . . that this Assembly and gathering of the day may have the most beautiful and beneficial outcome . . . Address your vows to heaven and pray for your own good fortune. Hail, Paian, hail! Let us rejoice and be glad!"

Text 16: Aeschylus *Seven Against Thebes* 266-79; LCL translation.

"May the gods fight on our side!"
And now first hear my vow, and then ring out the loud and solemn cry of jubilance, our Grecian wont of sacrificial shout heartening to our friends, and remove the terror of battle. And now "To the guardian gods of our country, whether they haunt the plain or keep watch over the market-place, to Dirce's springs, and to Ismenus' stream, I make my vow that, if all go well and the city with its burghers be preserved, they shall stain with blood of sheep the hearths of the gods and offer trophies, while I will bedeck their hallowed abodes with the spoil of the spear-smitten vestments of the foe."

Text 17: Aeschylus *Libation Bearers* 124-51 (LCL trans.). Prayer to a deified ancestor (Electra's murdered father Agamemnon).

Herald supreme between the world above and world below, O nether Hermes, come to my aid and summon me the spirits beneath the earth to attend my prayers, spirits that keep watch o'er my father's house, aye, and Earth herself, that bringeth all things to birth, and having nurtured them receiveth their increase in turn. And I the while, as I pour these lustral offerings to the dead, invoke my father and thus voice my prayer: "Have compassion both on me and on dear Orestes! How shall we be lords in our estate? For now we are vagrants, as it were, bartered away by her that bare us, by her who in exchange hath bought Aegisthus as her mate, even him who was her partner in thy murder. As for me, I am no better than a slave, Orestes is an outcast from his substance, while they in insolence of pride wanton bravely in the winnings of thy toil. Yet may Orestes come home—and with happy fortune! This is my prayer to thee, and do thou hearken unto me, my father. For myself, oh grant that I may prove in heart more chaste, far more, than my mother and in hand more innocent. These invocations on our behalf; but for our foes I implore that there appear one who will avenge thee, father, and that thy slayers may be slain in just retribution. ('Tis thus I interrupt my prayer for good, for them uttering this prayer for evil.) But to us be thou a bringer of blessings to the upper world by favour of the gods and Earth and Justice crowned with victory." Such are my prayers, and over them I pour out these libations. 'Tis your due service to crown them with flowers of lamentation, raising your voices in a chant for the dead.

Text 18: Vergil *Aeneid* 6.264-67 (trans. Frank O. Copley, *Vergil, The Aeneid* [2nd ed.; Indianapolis: Bobbs-Merrill, 1975]; prayer for revelation.

O gods who rule all souls! O silent shades!
Phlegethon, Chaos, regions of voiceless night!
Grant me apocalypse! Grant me right and power

to show things buried deep in earth and darkness!

Text 19: Sappho *Frag.* 1 (Dionysius of Halicarnassus *De comp. verb.* 173-79); trans. D. A. Campbell in *The Cambridge History of Classical Literature,* Vol. 1: *Greek Literature* (Cambridge: The University Press, 1985), 204.

Ornate-throned immortal Aphrodite, wile-weaving daughter of Zeus, I entreat you: do not overpower my heart, mistress, with ache and anguish, but come here, if ever in the past you heard my voice from afar and acquiesced and came, leaving your father's golden house, with chariot yoked: beautiful swift sparrows whirring fast-beating wings brought you above the dark earth down from heaven through the mid-air, and soon they arrived; and you, blessed one, with a smile on your immortal face asked what was the matter with me this time and while I was calling this time and what in my maddened heart I most wishes to happen for myself: "Whom am I to persuade this time to lead you back to her love? Who wrongs you, Sappho? If she runs away, soon she shall pursue; if she does not accept gifts, why, she shall give them instead; if she does not love, soon she shall love even against her will." Come to me now again and deliver me from oppressive anxieties; fulfil all that my heart longs to fulfil, and you yourself be my fellow-fighter.

Text 20: Menander Rhetor 1.336 (trans. D. A. Russell, *Menander Rhetor* [Oxford: Clarendon Press, 1981] 13); an *apopemptikos hymnos* is one used to dismiss a deity.

Apopemptic hymns, as the name indicates, are the converse of cletic. This is a very rare form, and in only found in the poets. Such hymns are delivered over actual or supposed departures of gods, like what are called the departures of Apollo at Delos or Miletus and of Artemis at Argos.

There are apopemptic hymns also in Bacchylides. The basic theme of such hymns is the country, cities, or nations which the god is leaving, and likewise the city or country to which he is going, together with topographical descriptions and the like. The speech should proceed with charm, since a valedictory situation demands a certain relaxation and geniality of style. It admits more extensive treatment of topics, not less, as the cletic hymn does, since in the latter we desire the god to be with us as soon as possible, whereas in the apopemptic we wish his departure to be postponed. There must also be a prayer for return and a second visit.

Text 21: Gold phylactery; trans. Roy Kotansky, "Incantations and Prayers on Inscribed Greek Amulets," in *Magika Hiera: Ancient Greek Magic & Religion,* ed. C. A. Faraone and D. Obbink (New York and Oxford: Oxford University, 1991) 118 (modified).

Lords, archangels, gods, and divine "characters," drive away all evil and all epilepsy and every headache(?) from [. . .]os, whom ore[. . .] bore . . . .

Text 22: Hymn to Zeus in Aeschylus *Agamemnon* 160-83; translated in Eduard Fraenkel, *Aeschylus, Agamemnon: Edited with a Commentary* (Oxford: Clarendon Press, 1950) 1.101.

Zeus, whoever he be—if to be called and invoked by this name is pleasing to him, even thus do I address him. I have nothing whereto to liken him, weighing all in the balance, nothing save Zeus if there is need to cast the burden of vain thought from the care-laden mind in real truth.

And he who aforetime was mighty, swelling with the boldness of a victor in every contest, shall not even be reckoned, since he is of the past; and he who afterward came into being met his thrower and is gone. But anyone who gladly shouts "Hail to Zeus the victor!" shall hit full on the target of understanding:

It is Zeus who has put men on the way to wisdom by establishing as a valid law "By suffering they shall win understanding." Instead of sleep there trickles before the heart the pain of remembrance of suffering: even to the unwilling discretion comes. There is, I think, a blessing from the gods, who, using force, sit on the dread bench of the helmsman.

Text 23: *PGM* XCII.1-16; translation in Betz, *The Greek Magical Papyri*, 303.

Your great name, for favor. "Everyone fears your great might. Grant me the good things: the strength of AKRYSKYLOS, the speech of EUONON, the eyes of Solomon, the voice of ABRASAX, the grace of ADONIOS, the god. Come to me Kypris, every day. The hidden name bestowed to you(?) [is this]: TOATHOETHATHOOYTHAETHOUSTHOAITHITHETHOINTHO; grant me victory, repute, beauty toward all men and all women.

Text 24: *PGM* LXII.24-38; translation in Betz, *The Greek Magical Papyri*, 293.

Come to me, god of the gods, the only one who appears from fire and wind, you who have truth on your head, who disperse the darkness, you the lord of the winds LOTH MOOULOTH PNOUT EI ESIOTH, hail, lord LAMPSOURE IAAO IA . . . D."

Say these things many times. If, while you are reciting, the apparition delays: "Open up, open up, Olympos; open up, Hades; open up, Abyss. Let the darkness be dispelled by command of the highest god and let the holy light come forth from the infinite into the abyss." Whenever it still delays, cry out in this way and again close the eyes of the boy: "Hail, holy light! Hail, eye of the world! Hail, brightness of the dawn of the world, ABRA A O NA BABROUTHI BIE BARACHE, god. Come in, lord, and reveal to me about the things I request of you." Then ask what you wish. . . .

Dismissal: "I give thanks to you because you came in accordance with the command of god. I request that you keep me healthy, free from terror and free from demonic attacks, ATHATHE ATHATHACHTHE ADONAI. Return to your holy places.

Text 25: Thucydides 6.32.1-2; LCL translation.

When the ships had been manned and everything had at last been put aboard which they were to take with them on the voyage, the trumpeter proclaimed silence, and they offered the prayers that were customary before putting out to sea, not ship by ship but all together, led by a herald, the mariners as well as the officers throughout the whole army making libations with golden and silver cups from the wine they had mixed. And the rest of the throng of people on the shore, both the citizens and all others present who wished the Athenians well, also joined in the prayers. And when they had sung the paean and had finished the libations, they put off, and sailing out at first in single column they then raced as far as Aegina.

Text 26: Plato *Cratylus* 400d-e; LCL translation.

By Zeus, Hermogenes, we, if we are sensible, must recognize that there is one most excellent kind, since of the gods we know nothing, neither of them nor of their names, whatever they may be, by which they call themselves, for it is clear that they use the true names. But there is a second kind of correctness, that we call them, as is customary in prayers, by whatever names and patronymics are pleasing to them since we know no other.

Text 27: *PGM* IV.1748-1812; translation in Betz, *The Greek Magical Papyri*, 70.

I call upon you, author of all creation, who spread your own wings over the whole world, you, the unapproachable and unmeasurable who breathe into every soul life-giving reasoning, who fitted all things together by your power, firstborn, founder of the universe, golden-winged, whose light is darkness, who shroud reasonable thoughts and breathe forth dark frenzy, clandestine one who secretly inhabit every soul. You engender an unseen fire as you carry off every living thing without growing weary of torturing it, rather having with pleasure delighted in pain from the time when the world came into being. You also come and bring pain, who are sometimes reasonable, sometimes irrational, because of whom men dare beyond what is fitting and take refuge in your light which is darkness. Most headstrong, lawless, implacable, inexorable, invisible, bodiless, generator of frenzy, archer, torch-carrier, master of all living sensation and of everything clandestine, dispenser of forgetfulness, creator of silence, through whom the light and to whom the light travels, infantile when you have been engendered within the heart, wisest when you have succeeded; I call upon you, unmoved by prayer, by your great name: AZARACHTHARAZA LATHA LATHAL Y Y Y LATHAI ATHALLALAPH IOIOIO AI AI AI OUERIEU OIAI LEGETA RAMAI AMA RATAGEL, first shining, night-shining, night rejoicing, night-engendering, witness, EREKISITHPHE ARARACHARARARA EPHTHISIKERE IABEZEBYTH IO, you in the depth, BERIAMBO BERIAMBEBO, you in the sea, MERMERGOU, clandestine and wisest, ACHAPA ADONAIE BASMA CHARAKO IAKOB IAO CHAROUER AROUER LAILAM SEMESILAM SOUMARTA MARBA KERBA MENABOTH EIIA. Turn the "soul" of her NN to me NN, so that she may love me, so that she may feel passion for me, so that she may give me what is in her power. Let her say to me what is in her soul because I have called upon your great name.

Prayer of Early Rabbinic Tradition: Representative Texts

Asher Finkel
Seton Hall University

I. Purview: The governing determinants for foundational consideration of liturgical study.
- A. The Literary Witness
  1. Oral Transmission: Fluency and Accuracy, Coinage and Order.
  2. Citing Prayers: Initial Words, Seals and Themes.
  3. Mnemonic Devices and Poetic Forms.
  4. Dual Recensions, Long and Short Forms.
  5. Liturgical Phraseologies in Religious Works (Mishnah and Midrash), Epistles and Homilies, Apocalypses and Mystical Writings (see also II. H).
- B. The Experiential Dimension
  1. Academic and Synagogal Settings.
  2. Collective and Private Settings.
  3. Phenomenological Aspect: Spoken Word and Ritual Act, Liminality, Attitudes and Moods, the Numinous Experience, Roles and Responses.
  4. Pedagological Aims: Worship and Study, Recitation and Interpretation.
  5. Theological and Ethical Aims: Kavannah and Ma'aseh, Names of God and Human Acts.

II. Texts
- A. Scriptural Reading and Torah Blessings
- B. Shema' Recitation and Accompanying Blessings.
- C. Tefillah (Long Prayer): the Daily 18 Benedictions and the Fast-Day's 24 Benedictions.
- D. Tefillah Qeṣarah (Short Prayer): the Abbreviated Form and the Brief Form.
- E. Numinous Prayer: the Keddushah (Trishagion) and the Kaddish.
- F. Blessings at Mealtime.
- G. Targumic Forms as Related to Prayer.
- H. Prayer Formulations of Synagogal Inscriptions.

II. The Texts in Translation

Note: M.=Mishnah; Tos.=Tosefta; TB=Talmud Bavli; TY=Talmud Yerushalmi; Sof.=Soferim; Hil.=Hilkhoth ʾEreṣ Israel (Genizah) ed. M. Marglolioth, Kook: Jerusalem, 1973; *S. S. Jew. Lit.=Contributions to the Scientific Study of Jewish Liturgy,* ed. J. Petuchowski, Ktav: New York, 1970; Ver.=Version; Mid=Midrash.

A. Blessings of Torah-Reading (Collective)

Refer to Second Temple practice of High Priest and King (M. Sotah 7); see Sof. 13, M. Berakhot 7:4 and *S. S. Jew. Lit.,* p. 403.

Introit: "Let us bless the Lord, the blessed One."

Doxological antiphon: "Blessed is the Lord, the blessed One, for all eternity."

1. Blessing before Torah-Reading: "Blessed are You, O Lord, King of the universe,"
    ver. a: " who gives Torah from heaven, eternal life from High."
    ver. b: "who chose us from all the people and gave us His Torah."
    "Blessed are You, Giver of the Torah." Response: Amen.

2. Blessing after Torah-Reading: "Blessed are You, O Lord, who gave us the Torah of truth; thereby He implanted eternal life within us. Blessed are You, O Lord, Giver of the Torah." Response: Amen.

3. Blessing before the Concluding Prophetic Reading (Hafṭara) "Blessed are You, Lord our God, King of the universe, who chose good prophets and favored their words that were spoken in truth. Blessed are You, O Lord, who chooses the Torah and Moses His servant, Israel His people and the prophets of truth and righteousness." Response: Amen.

4. Blessing after the Hafṭara: "Blessed are You, Lord our God, King of the universe, Rock of all aeons, Righteous throughout all generations, the faithful God who says and does, who speaks and fulfils, for all His words are true and righteous."
    Communal response: "You are faithful, Lord our God, and Your words are faithful. O faithful One, who lives and exists eternally, let You reign over us everlastingly."
    Blessing of Reader continues: "You are faithful, Lord our God, and Your words are faithful. Not one word of Your words in the past will be rendered unfulfilled, for You are a faithful God. Blessed are You, O Lord, the faithful God in all His words." Response: Amen.

5. Eschatological Blessing concerning Jerusalem: "Comfort/ Have mercy, Lord our God, on your city Zion for it is the abode of our life, and to the deeply humiliated bring salvation speedily in our days. Blessed are You, O Lord, Rebuilder of Jerusalem. (Ver. b. "who gladdens Zion through her children.") Response: Amen. Note: See TY Berakhot 4:5, 8c.

6. Eschatological Blessing on Messiah: "Let us rejoice, Lord our God, with Your servant, Elijah the prophet, and with the kingdom of the House/the Son of David Your servant. Let him come speedily and gladden our hearts. Upon his throne no stranger shall sit and let not others anymore inherit his glory. For You swore to him by Your holy name (Ps 132:11) that his light will never be extinguished forever.

Blessed are You, O Lord, Shield of David." Response: Amen. Note: See Mid.Psalms 18, TB Pesahim 117b.

7. "For the Torah (-Reading), for the (prayer-) service, for the prophetic (-Reading) and for the day [of rest,] (Sabbath or name of holiday), that You, Lord our God, gave us for holiness and restfulness, for glory and splendor. For all these, Lord our God, we thank You and bless You. May Your name be blessed by the mouth of all the living always forever. Blessed are You, O Lord, who sanctifies the Sabbath [on the holidays say: "who sanctifies Israel and thereby the (festival) seasons."]." Response: Amen.

B. Shemaᶜ Recitation (collective). Refer to Second Temple practice M. Tamid 5:1, see TB Berakhot 49b, Sifre Deut. 32:3, *S. S. Jew. Lit.*, p. 373f., TY Berakhot 1:7, 3c.

Introit: "Let us bless the Lord, the blessed One."

Doxological Antiphon: "Blessed is the Lord, the blessed One for all eternity."

1. Blessing before dawn: "Blessed are You, Lord our God, who formed light and created darkness, made peace and created all (Isaiah 45:7, last word, "evil" is changed to "all," signifying cosmos.) He who gives light on the earth and to the inhabitants upon her with compassion. Through His goodness He renews daily always the work of creation. As it says (Psalm 136:7) '[Give thanks] to Him who makes the great luminaries, for His kindness endures forever.' Blessed are You, the Fashioner of luminaries." Response: Amen.

2. Blessing before Shemaᶜ Recitation: "With everlasting love You loved us, Lord our God, with great compassion You have shown us. For our fathers' sake who trusted You and whom You taught the statutes of life, be gracious our Father, the merciful Father, show compassion towards us. Let us heed and do, learn and teach all the words of the Torah-Study with love. Let our eyes be enlightened by Your Torah and let our hearts cleave to worship You in truth. Let us declare Your unity with awe. Blessed are You, O Lord, who chooses His people Israel." Response: Amen.

3-4. Shemaᶜ Recitation: Begins with the act of Accepting God's Kingship (Deut. 6:4-8)* "Hear O Israel; the Lord our God, the Lord is One" (with eyes closed and covered to effect Kavannah). Doxological Response (in whisper) "Blessed be the name of the glorious kingdom for all eternity."

5-6. Continue with Deut. 11:13-22 and Num. 15:37-42.

*During Second Temple period the Decalogue was also read, Deut. 5:1-18.

7. Concluding Blessing of Confirmation, ending with a conflated Blessing of Redemption: "True and firm, established and enduring, right and faithful and good is this word (= recitation) upon us and upon our fathers and upon our children, upon our generation and all generations of Your servants, the seed of Israel. Upon the former and later (generations) forever, it is a statute not to be passed away. (It is) true that You are the Lord our God, the God of our fathers forever. You are our king, the king of our fathers. For the sake of your Name redeem us, as You redeemed our fathers. (It is) true that from everlasting is Your name, and upon us it is called in love. There is no

other God beside You." "O Powerful king, who is like You a god, who split the mighty waters. Then they all said with joy, with song and great happiness: 'Who is like You among the gods, O Lord! Who is like You, glorious in holiness, awesome in praises, doing marvels' (Exod. 15:11). Your kingship, Your sons witnessed as You split the sea before Moses. 'This is our God,' they responded saying, 'this is the Rock of our salvation.' God our king, a living and enduring king, Your name is upon us. 'God reigns, God reigned, God will reign everlasting' (Tar Exod. 15:18). God our king is our savior. He will redeem us with complete redemption. Blessed are You, O Lord, the Redeemer of Israel."

C. Long Tefillah: Daily 18 Benedictions and Fast-Day's 24 Benedictions. See M. Taᶜanith 2:2-11; Tos. Taᶜanith 1:8-14; TB Megillah 17b; TB Rosh Hashanah 32a; TY Berakhot 2;4,4d, *S.S. Jew. Lit.*, pp. 375, 378, 416. Refer to Apostolic Constitution Vol. 7, Sirach 51; 2 Macc. 1:24-29. Opening three Praise formulations:'Avoth, Gevuroth, Qeddushot.

1. "Blessed are [Bow] you, Lord our God, 'the God of our fathers, the God of Abraham the God of Isaac and the God of Jacob' (Exod. 3:15), 'the great, mighty and awesome God' (Deut. 10:13), 'Most High God, who owns heaven and earth' (Gen. 14:19). Our shield and the shield of our fathers, our refuge in every generation. Blessed are [Bow] you the Shield of Abraham." Response: Amen.

2. "You are powerful who brings low the haughty, mighty who punishes the tyrants, Life of the worlds who raises the dead, the mover of wind who brings down dew (in winter: "who brings down rain"), the sustainer of life who revives the dead, with a wink of the eye let redemption sprout for us. Blessed are You, the Reviver of the dead." Response: Amen.

3. Ver. a. "You are holy and awesome is Your name and there is no god beside You." Ver. b. "You are holy and Your name is holy ones (=angels) praise You daily, Selah."

"Blessed are You, the holy God." Response: Amen. Note: ver. b. leads to Qeddushah, see below E.

Middle Petitions (first six are existential, last six are eschatological).

4. Ver. a. "Grace us our Father with knowledge from You, understanding and insight from Your Torah."

Ver. b. "You grace the human being with knowledge and teach the person understanding. Grace us from You, knowledge, understanding and insight."

"Blessed are You, who graces us with knowledge." Response: Amen.

5. Ver. a. "Return us our Father to Your Torah, draw us near our King to Your worship and bring us in perfect repentance to Your presence."

Ver. b. "Return us O Lord unto You and we shall return; renew our days as of old (Lamentations, end)."

"Blessed are You, who favours repentance." Response: Amen.

6. Ver. a. "Forgive us our Father, for we erred against You, wipe away and remove our transgression from Your sight. For Your mercies are abundant."

Ver. b. "Forgive us our Father for we erred, pardon us our king for we transgressed. For You pardon and forgive."

"Blessed are You, the merciful One who abundantly forgives." Response: Amen.

7. "See our afflictions, address our conflict and redeem us for Your name sake. Blessed are You, the Redeemer of Israel." Response: Amen.

—See below the additional six Benedictions in time of crisis, on a Fast-Day, to be inserted here. The above Blessing of Redemption opens the series.—

8. "Heal us, Lord our God, from the pain of our hearts. Agony and anxiety, remove from us and advance a therapy for our wounds. Blessed are You, the Healer of the sick. Response: Amen.

9. "Bless the year upon us, Lord our God, for the best with all types of produce. Give us dew (in winter add: "and rain") upon the face of the land: Blessed are You, O Lord, who blesses the years." Response: Amen.

10. "Sound a large Shofar for our liberation and raise a banner for the gathering of our exiles. Blessed are You, O Lord, who gathers the dispersed of His people Israel." Response: Amen.

11. "Restore our judges as in former period and our counsellors as at the beginning. Blessed are You, O Lord, who loves justice." Response: Amen.

12. "Unto the apostates there shall be no hope and the wicked Kingdom (=Rome) will speedily be uprooted in our own days." [End of Second Century: "The Christians"] "and the Minim (=heretics) be destroyed swiftly (added in First Century.) Blessed are You, O Lord, who breaks the enemies and defeats the wicked." Response: Amen.

13. "Towards the righteous and the pious Your tender mercies will be stirred, O Lord our God. Towards the righteous proselytes, who trust in you give them good reward with us, with those who do Your will. Blessed are You, O Lord, the mainstay and refuge of the righteous. Response: Amen.

14. "Unto Jerusalem Your city return with compassion and dwell thereon, as You have spoken. Blessed are You, O Lord, God of David and the builder of Jerusalem." Response: Amen.

14b. A separate Benediction on the theme of "God of David," for Exilic Jewry: "Speedily cause the shoot of David, Your servant, to sprout and exalt his anointment through Your salvation. For unto Your salvation we hope daily, Blessed are You, who causes the horn of salvation to sprout." Response: Amen.

15. "Hear the voice of our prayer, Lord our God, and fulfill speedily our petitions. Blessed are You, O Lord, who hears our prayer." Response: Amen.

The concluding three Thanksgivings ('Avodah, Hoda'ah and Shalom.)

16. Ver. a (earlier). "Be pleased O Lord with the prayer of Your people Israel. The burnt offerings of Israel and their prayers receive favorably in love. Be pleased with the Tamid service of Israel Your people. Blessed are You, O Lord, for You alone in awe we worship." Response: Amen.

Ver. b. (later) "Be pleased, O Lord our God. Let Your Shekhinah dwell in Zion and let Your servants worship You in Jerusalem. Blessed are You who restores the Shekhinah to Zion." Response: Amen.

17. "We thank [Bow] You, O Lord our God, the God of our fathers, for all the good things since creation and for Your love and mercy since days of lod. When we say our feet have tottered, Your love O Lord, will give support. Blessed are [Bow] You, O Lord, it is good to thank You." Response: Amen.

—Blessing of the Priests: Num. 6:24-26, to be said with their hands lifted.—

18. In response the concluding Benediction. "Grant peace upon Israel Your people. Bless and keep us all as one.

For it is good in Your eyes to bless Your people Israel with peace. Blessed are You, O Lord, the Maker of Peace." Response: Amen.

C2.   The Inserted Six Benedictions on Fast Day, at Time of Famine or Crisis (Collective) follow with Benediction of Redemption (#7): "See our affliction, address our conflict and redeem us for Your name sake." [Priests blast the Shofar.] "The One who answered our father at Mount Moriah will respond to your crying voice on this day. [Teki'ah, Teru'ah, Teki'ah.] Blessed are You, O Lord,* the Redeemer of Israel." Respond: Amen.**

Add the following Benedictions:

1. Recite the Zikhronoth of New Year liturgy [or I Kings 8:35-4]. [Priests make a breaking sound of Shofar.] "The One who answered our forefathers at the Reed-Sea will respond to your crying voice on this day. [Teki'ah, Teru'ah, Teki'ah.] Blessed are You, O Lord,* the One who remembers the forgotten." Respond: Amen.**

2. Recite the Shofroth of New Year Liturgy [or Jer. 14:1-10]. [Priests blast the Shofar.] "The One who answered Joshua at Gilgal will respond to your crying voice on this day. [Teki'ah, Teru'ah, Teki'ah.] Blessed are You, O Lord,* the One who hears the breaking sound of Shofar." Respond: Amen.**

3. Recite Psalm 120, [Priests make a breaking sound of the Shofar.] "The one who answered Samuel at Miṣpah will respond to your crying voice on this day. [Teki'ah, Teru'ah, Teki'ah.] Blessed are You, O Lord,* the One who hears the crying voice." Respond: Amen.**

4. Recite Psalm 121. [Priests blast the Shofar.] "The One who answered Elijah at Mount Carmel will respond to your crying voice on this day. [Teki'ah, Teru'ah, Teki'ah.] Blessed are You, O Lord,* the One who hears prayer." Respond: Amen.**

5. Recite Psalm 130. [Priests make a breaking sound of the Shofar.] "The One who answered Jonah in the belly of the fish will respond to your crying voice on this day. [Teki'ah, Teru'ah, Teki'ah.] Blessed are You, O Lord,* who answers in time of distress." Respond: Amen.**

6. Recite Psalm 102. [Priests blast the Shofar.] "The One who answered David and Solomon his son in Jerusalem, etc. [Teki'ah, Teru'ah, Teki'ah.] Blessed are You, O Lord,* who shows compassion for the land." Respond: Amen.**

*During the Second Temple Period add: "God of Israel from (this) World to the World (to come)."

** During the Second Period say the doxology: "Blessed be the Name of
the glorious kingdom for all eternity." See M. Berakhot 9:5.

D. Tefillah Qeṣarah: Short form of prayer. See M. Berakhot 4:3,4; Tb Berakhot
29; Tos Berakhot 3:11; TY Berakhot 4d, 8a, b; Hil. pp. 144-5; *S.S. Jew. Lit.*, p.
420.

1. The Abbreviated form of Eighteen Benedictions.

"Blessed are You, Lord our God, the God of our fathers, the God of
Abraham, the God of Isaac, and the God of Jacob, the great, mighty
and awesome God, the Most-High God, who owns heaven and earth.
[1]The shield of our help, [2]the reviver of the dead, [3]who is sanctified in
righteousness, [4]grace us with knowledge, [5]accept our repentance,
[6]forgive our transgressions and [7]redeem us from the hand of 'Adinah'
('the luxuriant one,' a sobriquet for Rome.) [8]Heal us and [9]bless our
years. [10]Gather our dispersed and [11]judge us with love and mercy.
[12]Defeat our adversaries, [13]for You are the refuge of the righteous.
[14]Build Jerusalem, Your city soon and there we will worship You.
[15]There You will hear our prayer and show compassion upon us.
Restore Shekhinah to Zion speedily and the order of Your service to
Jerusalem Your city. For You have chosen us and we know that You
are good and benevolent to all. Spread upon us Your tabernacle of
peace. Blessed are You the Maker of peace."

There is also a Babylonian recension of 'Havinenu,' attributed to Mar
Samuel of 3rd Century. As there is also a Babylonian recension of the
Long Prayer of 19 Benedictions.

2. The short form of prayer, in place of danger on the road.

R. Yehoshua of 1st Century: " Save, O Lord, Your people Israel, at any
occasion of turbulance let their needs be before You. Blessed are You
who hears prayer." R. Eliezer of lst Century: "Do Your will in heaven
and give spiritual serenity to those who revere You on earth. Do what is
good in Your eyes. Blessed are You who hears prayer."

R. Meir of 2nd Century: "The needs of Your people Israel are numerous
and their forbearance is short. Let it be Your will, O Lord our God of our
fathers, that You will mete out to each creature its needs and to each
body what is necessary. Blessed are You, O Lord, who hears prayer."

R. Yose of 2nd Century: "Hear the voice of prayer of Your people Israel and
fulfill speedily their petition. Blessed are You, O Lord, who hears
prayer."

E. Numinous Prayer (Qeddushah and Qaddish)—Collective only BT
Berakhot 21b, Tos Berakhot 1:11; sof. 19; Hekhalot Rabbati 2:5; 3:1, 2, 4; 4:1;
7:2; 10:3, 5; 27:5; 31:4.

1. Qeddushah DeYeshivah (to be recited antiphonally during the first
Blessing of Dawn, before Shema' Recitation, corresponding to the time
the Heavenly Hosts offer their praise. Tar Neof and Y Gen. 32:27). "All
receive upon themselves the yoke of heavenly kingdom, one from the
other, and they give permission to one another to sanctify (in praise)
their Creator. With a pleasant spirit, with a clear speech, with a holy
chant, all in unison respond and say awesomely: 'Holy, Holy, Holy
the Lord of Hosts! The whole world is full of His glory' (Isaiah 6:3).

The Wheels and Holy Beasts with great thunder lift themselves facing the Seraphs. As they face them they praise and say: 'Blessed be the glory of God from His place' (Ezek 3:12)."

2. Qeddushah DeAmidah (to be recited antiphonally following the third Benediction of Praise during the Long Prayer of 18 Benedictions)— Collective only. Brief ver. a. "Let us sanctify Your name in the World, as they sanctify Him in high heavens. As it is written by Your Prophets (Isa. 6:3): 'One calls unto the other saying: Holy, Holy, Holy the Lord of Hosts! The whole world is full of His glory. Facing them, they say Baruch (Ezek 3:12): 'Blessed be the glory of God from His place.' In Your Hagiographa, it is written (Psalm 115:10): 'Let God reign forever, Your God in Zion from generation to generation. Praise be YH (= Halleluyah)." Elaborated ver. b. "Let us sanctify and exult You, like the melodious speech of the Holy Seraphs, who thrice repeat Qaddosh. As it is written by Your prophet (Isa. 6:3): 'Holy, Holy, Holy the Lord of Hosts! The whole world is full of this glory.' Then with a loud noise, overwhelming and strong, they produce a sound (while) lifting themselves against Seraphs, (as) they face them they say Baruch (Ezek. 3:12): 'Blessed be the glory of God from His place.

From Your place our King appear and You reign over us; for we await You. When will You reign in Zion? Soon, in our days forever You'll dwell! May You be exalted and sanctified in the midst of Jerusalem Your city, from generation to generation and for all eternities. Let our eyes witness Your kingdom, as it is expressed in the mighty songs of Your servant David, Your righteous Messiah (Psalm 146:10): 'The Lord will reign forever; Your God, O Zion, from generation to generation. Let us praise YH' (= Halleluyah)."

There is a third Babylonian version of Qeddushah DeAmidah, as well as the Exilic version of Qeddushah DeSidra (following Scriptural Reading.)

3. Kaddish (originally it followed the Scriptural Reading)—Collective only.

The full version: "Magnified and sanctified be His great Name, in the world that He will renew. He will revive the dead and bring us into everlasting life. He will rebuild the city of Jerusalem and will beautify the Temple therein. He will uproot the strange worship from the land and restore the heavenly worship to its place. Let the Holy One Blessed be He reign in His glorious kingdom, during your lifetime of the entire house of Israel, soon in a short while. And say ye: Amen."

Doxological Refrain: "Let His great Name be blessed for all eternity." Continue: "Blessed, praised, glorified, exalted, extolled, honored, magnified and lauded be the Name of the Holy Blessed be He, above all blessings, songs, praises and consolations that are said in the world. And say ye: Amen."

"Let there be abundant peace from Heaven and life, upon us and upon all Israel. And say ye: Amen." —In 2 recensions, Aramaic and Hebrew.

F. Blessings after meal. M. Berakhot 7:3, TB Berakhot 48b, *S. S. Jew. Lit.*, p. 445f. Compare Didache 9, 10.

When three or more are present begin with invitation to bless: "My masters
let us bless [the Lord]." Doxological Response: "Let the name of the Lord be
blessed for all eternity."

Continue: "With permission of my masters: Let us bless (with ten: "our God;"
with ten thousand: "Lord our God, God of Israel, the Lord of Hosts, throned
on the Cherubs) for the food we ate. Response: "Blessed be He (as above in
view of the number of participants) for the food we ate."

1. "Blessed are You, Lord our God, king of the universe, who feeds us and
not by our doing, who sustains us and not by our merits, who bestows
His great goodness upon us; as it says: 'He opens His hand and satisfies
every living thing with favor (Psalm 145:16).' Blessed are You, O Lord,
who feeds all." Amen.

2. "We give thanks unto You, Lord our God, that You gave us our fathers
inheritance, a desirable, good and ample land, as well as Torah, life
and food, and for taking us out of Egypt and delivering us from land of
bondage, and for the Torah you taught us and for the covenant You
sealed in our flesh. For all these, Lord our God, we thank You and bless
Your name. May Your name be blessed always forever; as it says: 'You
shall eat, be satiated and you shall bless the Lord Your God' (Deut.
8:10). Blessed are You, O Lord, for the land and the food." Amen.

3. "Have mercy, Lord our God, upon us, upon Israel Your people, upon
Jerusalem Your city and Zion, the dwelling of Your glory and upon
the Great House (= Temple), upon which Your name is called and
upon the kingdom of the House/son of David, Your Messiah. Speedily
You shall restore it to its place. For unto You, O Lord, our eyes yearn
and You alone will reign over us. Although we ate and drank we did
not forget the destruction of Your great and holy House (= Temple) and
may we not be forgotten ever. For it says: 'God will build Jerusalem
and the dispersed of Israel He will gather' (Psalm 147:2). Blessed are
You, O Lord, who builds Jerusalem."

Concluding response: Amen in our lifetime, Amen speedily; in our days
Zion will be built with song and the service will be restored in
Jerusalem and the palace in its place, while the Evil Rome will fall.

4. Following Hadrianic war with Bar Kochba (135 C.E.), a fourth Blessing
of Theodicy was added.

G. Targumic material (reflecting a synagogal setting of Torah-study).

1. Anamnesis Reflection of the Binding of Isaac:

Gen. 22:14 (from the Torah lection for New Year Day) "And Abraham
called the name of the place the Lord will see." Tar Neof (Tar Y and
PJ): "Abraham worshipped and prayed in the name of God's Word
and said: With a plea of mercy from You, O Lord, to whom all is
known and manifest, that I had no conflict in my heart when You first
told me to sacrifice my son Isaac and render him dust and ashes
before You. Upon dawn I rose to do Your will with joy, to fulfill Your
command. Therefore, when my son Isaac's descendants will face the
hour of tribulation, You will recall the Binding of Isaac, their patriarch.
Hear the voice of their prayers and respond to them, saving them from
tribulation." Compare the concluding prayer of Zikhronot for the New

Year: "The Binding of Isaac, You will recall mercifully today in behalf of his descendants."

2. Pedagogical Hymn on Works of Loving-Kindness (the Emulation of God's Way)

Gen. 35:9 (After the death and burial of Deborah): "God appeared again to Jacob upon his return from Padan-Aram and blesses him."

Tar Neof (Tar. Y; compare Tar PJ to Deut. 34:6, the death and burial of Moses)

"God of the universe" or "Blessed be the name of the Master of the Universe."

Doxological Response: "Let His name be blessed for all eternity."

"Your humility, honesty, righteousness and glory never cease. For You taught us to bless the groom and the bride (= the Marriage Blessing) from (the way You blessed) Adam and his mate (Gen. 1:28). Again You taught us to visit the sick from (the way You visited) our patriarch Abraham, the righteous, when You appeared to him in the field of Mamre in the heat of the day, when he was in pain from circumcision (18:1). Again You taught us to comfort the mourners from (the way You did) to Jacob, the righteous, upon the passing of Deborah, the nurse of his mother Rebecca, as he sat crying and wailing. You with compassion appeared to him and blessed him with the Mourners Blessing, and comforted him."

3. The Lesson of Shema^c Recitation with the Doxological Response on Gen. 49:1, 2.

"Jacob called his sons and said to them . . . gather together and hearken the sons of Jacob, hearken to your father Israel" (read instead: "hear: God of Israel is Your Father.")

Tar. Neof, Tar. Y. "The twelve tribes of Israel gathered as one and said: Hear our father Israel, the Lord our God, the Lord is one. Jacob replied: Blessed be the name of the glorious kingdom for all eternity (Neof)," or "let His great name be blessed for all eternity (Y)."

4. Hymn the Messiah and His Works. Gen. 49: 10, 11, 12. "A rod will not depart from Judah, nor the staff from between his feet, until he comes to Shiloh and to him shall nations be obedient. Binding his foal to the vine and his colt to the choice vine, he washes his garments in wine and his cover in the blood of grapes. His eyes shall be red with wine and his teeth white with milk."

Tar Neof (Tar. Y and PJ): "Kings will not cease from the tribe of Judah, nor scribes who teach the Torah, from his descendants. Until the King Messiah will come; for unto him is the kingdom and unto him all kingdoms will submit.

How majestic is the King Messiah, who will arise from the tribe of Judah. He girds his loins and goes out to battle his enemies, to kill their kings and tyrants. The hills will become red from the blood of casualties and their clothing will drip blood, as red juice pressed from grapes. How beautiful are the eyes of the King Messiah like clear wine; for they do not see adultery, nor bloodshedding. His teeth are white from milk, for they do not eat stolen food, nor slayed meat."

5. Song at the Sea: the Torah lection for Seventh Day of Passover. Exod. 15:1.

Tar. Neof, Tar. Y. "Then Moses and the children of Israel sang the praise of this song before God. They said: Let us give thanks and praise before God. For He is exalted above all that are exalted. He is supreme above all that are supreme. Anyone who is arrogant before Him will receive punishment from Him.

Verse 3. "The children of Israel say: the Lord is a warrior doing battle. Every generation, He makes His power known to His people Israel. Lord is His name, so is His power. Let His name be praised for all eternity."

Verse 18. "The children of Israel say: O Lord, how befitting it is for You to receive a crown of kingship. For when Your children saw the miracles at the sea and Your power on the waves, they opened their mouths, as one, and said: Unto the Lord is the kingship from the beginning of time and until time everlasting. Let His great name be blessed for all eternity."

H. Phraseologies of Synagogal Inscriptions (Compare also phrases in epistles of Bar Kochba from Murabbaat findings).
1. Theme of Shalom
   a. "Let there be peace in this place and all places and all places of Israel."
   b. "Peace upon Israel, upon us and upon our children."
   c. "Peace upon Israel" (see Murabbaat)
   d. "With abundant peace, loving kindness in peace."
2. Blessing and Curse
   a. "Bestow blessings on their work."
   b. "Let him/her /them have blessing."
   c. "Blessing from heaven."
   d. "Show wrath upon that person and his descendants."
3. Rememberance
   a. "Remember him/her/them favorably."
   b. "Remember them favorably with blessing."
4. Reward
   a. "let them be inscribed in the book of life with all the righteous."
   b. "let them have a portion with the righteous."
   c. "Let them have a portion in this holy place."
5. Amen Formulations
   a. "Amen."
   b. "Amen, Amen, Selah."
   c. "Amen, Selah, shalom."
   d. "Shalom, Amen."
   e. "All the people say Amen, Amen, Selah."
6. Names of God
   a. "Master of the Heaven."
   b. "Heaven" (Murabbaat).
   c. "King of the Universe."
   d. "The Compassionate One."
   e. "The One, whose eyes scan the world and see all the hidden."

7. Descriptions (visual depictions)
    a. Holy objects of the Inner Sanctum of the Temple.
    b. Depiction of Akedah.
    c. Depiction of calendar.
    d. List of Priestly Watches.
    e. Sabbatical laws.
    f. Warnings.

Consult J. Naveh, *On Stone and Mosaic: Aramaic and Hebrew Inscriptions from Ancient Synagogues.* Karta: Jerusalem, 1978.

The Praying Logos and the Christian at Prayer in Clement of Alexandria: Critical Issues in the Patristic Prayer Corpus

Pamela Bright
Concordia University, Montreal

From the immense corpus of prayers in early Christianity I have selected a number of writings of Clement of Alexandria as a springboard for discussing issues central to Christian prayer: prayer mediated through Christ and the New Testament injunction to pray always. Active in the latter part of the second century, Clement, a convert to Christianity, found in Alexandria a confluence of many traditions of prayer in Late Antiquity—Jewish, Gnostic, and philosophical syncretism. The texts from Clement have been chosen with an eye to the double theme to be discussed in the presentation in November— the centrality of Christ/Logos in Christian prayer and the centrality of prayer in the life of the Christian (for Clement the "true Gnostic).

As a point of comparison with the Clementine texts, I have included a number of texts from Nag Hammadi, and brief selections from monastic writers, much later than Clement, but illustrating comparative elements in monastic prayer.

In the analysis of these texts, four points will be kept in mind:
1. Prayer as a reflection of the *culture* which it presupposes. In the case of Clement of Alexandria, it is the gnostic and syncretistic culture proper to educated Alexandrians in the second and third centuries CE.
2. Prayer as a form of *spiritual authority*, based on the religious experience of the person who prays. The religious components of the experience basic for any given prayer need clarification.
3. Prayer belongs to a specific *social setting*, by its language, the needs it expresses, by the individual and community links it established with deity.
4. Prayer derives from the decisions and convictions out of which the believing person shapes his/her self-definition. A critical perception is needed of the *intellectual history* behind the praying discourse.

(A) PRAYER IN CLEMENT OF ALEXANDRIA

1. *The Song of the Word from* Exhortation to the Heathen

Behold the might of the new song! It has made men out of stones, men out of beasts. Those, moreover, that were as dead, not being partakers of the true life, have come to life again, simply by becoming listeners to this song. It also composed the universe into melodious order, and turned the discord of the elements to harmonious arrangement, so that the whole world might become harmony. It let loose the fluid ocean, and yet has prevented it from encroaching on the land. The earth, again, which had been in a state of commotion, it has established, and fixed the sea as it boundary. The violence of fire it has softened by the atmosphere, as the Dorian is blended with the Lydian strain; and the harsh cold of the air it has moderated by the embrace of fire, harmoniously arranging these the extreme tones of the universe. And this deathless strain—the support of the whole and harmony of all—reaching from the centre to the circumference, and from the extremities to the central part, has harmonized this universal frame of things, not according to the Thracian music, which is like that invented by Jubal, but according to the paternal counsel of God, which fired the zeal of David. And He who is of David, and yet before him, the Word of God, despising the lyre and harp, which are but lifeless instruments, and having tuned by the Holy Spirit the universe, and especially man—who, composed of body and soul, is a universe in miniature—makes melody to God on this instrument of many tones; and to this instrument—I mean man—he sings accordant: "For thou art my harp, and pipe, and temple"—harp for harmony—a pipe by reason of the Spirit—a temple by reason of the word; so that the first may sound, the second breathe, the third contain the Lord. And David the king, the harper whom we mentioned a little above, who exhorted to the truth and dissuaded from idols, was so far from celebrating demons in song, that in reality they were driven away by his music. Thus, when Saul was plagued with a demon, he cured him by merely playing. A beautiful breathing instrument of music the Lord made man, after His own image. And He Himself also, surely, who is the supramundane Wisdom, the celestial Word, is the all-harmonious, melodious, holy instrument of God. What, then, does this instrument—the Word of God, the Lord, the New Song—desire? To open the eyes of the blind, and unstop the ears of the deaf, and to lead the lame or the erring to righteousness, to exhibit God to the foolish, to put a stop to corruption, to conquer death, to reconcile disobedient children to their father. The instrument of God loves mankind. . . .

This is the New Song, the manifestation of the Word that was in the beginning, and before the beginning. The Saviour, who existed before, has in recent days appeared. He, who is in Him that truly is, has appeared; for the Word, who "was with God," and by whom all things were created, has appeared as our Teacher. The Word, who in the beginning bestowed on us life as Creator when He formed us, taught us to live well when He appeared as our Teacher; that as God He might afterwards conduct us to the life which never ends. He did not now for the first time pity us for our error; but He pitied us from the first, from the beginning. But now, at His appearance, lost as we already were, He accomplished our salvation. For that wicked reptile monster, by his enchantments, enslaves and plagues men even till not; inflicting, as seems to me, such barbarous vengeance on them as those who are said to bind the captives to corpses till they rot together. This wicked tyrant and serpent, accordingly, binding fast with the miserable chain of superstition whomsoever he can draw to his side from their birth, to stones, and stocks, and images, and such like idols, may with truth be said to have taken and buried living men with those dead idols, till both suffer corruption together.

Therefore (for the seducer is one and the same) he that at the beginning brought Eve down to death, now brings thither the rest of mankind. Our ally and helper, too, is one and the same—the Lord, who from the beginning gave revelations by prophecy, but now plainly calls to salvation. In obedience to the apostolic injunction, therefore, let us flee from "the prince of the power of the air, the spirit that now worketh in the children of disobedience" (Eph 2.2), and let us run to the Lord the Saviour, who now exhorts to salvation, as He has ever done, as He did by signs and wonders in Egypt and the desert, both by the bush and the cloud, which, through the favour of divine love, attended the Hebrews like a handmaid, by the fear which these inspired He addressed the hard-hearted; while by Moses, learned in all wisdom, and Isaiah, lover of truth, and the whole prophetic choir, in a way appealing more to reason, He turns to the Word those who have ears to hear. Sometimes He upbraids, and sometimes He threatens. Some men He mourns over, others He addresses with the voice of song, just as a good physician treats some of his patients with cataplasms, some with rubbing, some with fomentations; in one case cuts open with the lancet, in another cauterizes, in another amputates, in order if possible to cure the patient's diseased part or member. The Saviour has many tones of voice, and many methods for the salvation of men; by threatening He admonishes, by upbraiding He converts, by bewailing He pities, by the voice of song He cheers. He spake by the burning bush, for the men of that day needed signs and wonders.

He awed men by the fire when He made flame to burst from the pillar of cloud—a token at once of grace and fear: if you obey, there is the light; if you disobey, there is the fire; but, since humanity is nobler than the pillar or the bush, after them the prophets uttered their voice—the Lord Himself speaking in Isaiah, into our minds, and writing them on our hearts. What laws does He inscribe? "That all shall know God, from small to great;" and, "I will be merciful to them," says God, "and will not remember their sins" (Heb 8:10-12; Jer 31.33, 34). Let us receive the laws of life, let us comply with God's expostulations; let us become acquainted with Him, that He may be gracious. And though God needs nothing let us render to Him the grateful recompense of a thankful heart and of piety, as a kind of house-rent for our dwelling here below.

> "Gold for brass,
> A hundred oxen's worth for that of nine:" (Il. 6.236)

that is, for your little faith He gives you the earth of so great extent to till, water to drink and also to sail on, air to breathe, fire to do your work, a world to dwell in; and He has permitted you to conduct a colony from here to heaven: with these important works of His hand, and benefits in such numbers, He has rewarded your little faith. Then, those who have put faith in necromancers, receive from them amulets and charms, to ward off evil forsooth; and will you not allow the heavenly Word, the Saviour, to be bound on to you as an amulet, and, by trusting in God's own charm, be delivered from passions which are the diseases of the mind, and rescued from sin?—for sin is eternal death. Surely utterly dull and blind, and, like moles, doing nothing but eat, you spend your lives in darkness, surrounded with corruption. But it is truth which cries, "The light shall shine forth from the darkness." Let the light then shine in the hidden part of man, that is, the heart; and let the beams of knowledge arise to reveal and irradiate the hidden inner man, the disciple of the Light, the familiar friend and fellow-heir of Christ; especially now that we have come to know the most precious and venerable name of the good Father, who to a pious and good child given gentle counsels, and commands what is salutary for His child. He who obeys Him has the advantage in all things, follows God, obeys the Father, knows Him through wandering, loves God, loves his neighbour, fulfils the commandment, seeks the prize, claims the promise. But it has been God's fixed and constant purpose to save the flock of men: for this end the good God sent the good Shepherd. And the Word, having unfolded the truth, showed to men the height of salvation, that either repenting they might be saved, or refusing to obey, they might be judged. This is the proclamation of righteousness: to those that obey, glad tidings; to those that disobey, judgement. . . . .

12. "Hear, ye myriad tribes, rather whoever among men are endowed with reason, both barbarians and Greeks. I call on the whole race of men, whose Creator I am, by the will of the Father. Come to Me, that you may be put in your due rank under the one God and the one Word of God; and do not only have the advantage of the irrational creatures in the possession of reason; for to you of all mortals I grant the enjoyment of immortality. For I want, I want to impart to you this grace, bestowing on you the perfect boon of immortality; and I confer on you both the Word and the knowledge of God, My complete self. This am I, this God wills, this is symphony, this the harmony of the Father, this is the Son, this is Christ, this the Word of God, the arm of the Lord, the power of the universe, the will of the Father; of which things there were images of old, but not all adequate. I desire to restore you according to the original model, that ye may become also like Me. I anoint you with the unguent of faith, by which you throw off corruption, and show you the naked form of righteousness by which you ascend to God. Come to Me, all ye that labour and are heavy laden, and I will give you rest. Take My yoke upon you, and learn of Me; for I am meek and lowly in heart: and ye shall find rest to your souls. For My yoke is easy, and My burden light."

2. Hymn to the Word from The Instructor

Bridle of untamed colts, Wing of unwandering birds, sure Helm of babes, Shepherd of royal lambs, assemble Thy simple children to praise holily, to hymn guilelessly with innocent mouths, Christ the guide of children. O King of saints, all-subduing Word of the most high Father, Ruler of wisdom, Support of sorrows, that rejoicest in the ages, Jesus, Saviour of the human race, Shepherd, Husbandman, Helm, Bridle, Heavenly Wing of the all-holy flock, Fisher of men who are saved, catching the chaste fishes with sweet life from the hateful wave of a sea of vices—Guide [us], Shepherd of rational sheep; guide unharmed children, O holy King, O footsteps of Christ, O heavenly way, perennial Word, immeasurable Age, Eternal Light, Fount of mercy, performer of virtue; noble [is the] life of those hymn God, O Christ Jesus, heavenly milk of the sweet breasts of the graces of the Bride, pressed out of Thy wisdom. Babes nourished with tender mouths, filled with the dewy spirit of the rational pap, let us sing together simple praises, true hymns to Christ [our] King, holy fee for the teaching of life; let us sing in simplicity the powerful Child. O choir of peace, the Christ-begotten, O chaste people, let us sing together the God of peace.

3. The Prayer of the (true) Gnostic from The Stromata

Now we are commanded to reverence and to honour the same one, being persuaded that He is Word, Saviour, and Leader, and by Him, the Father, not on special days, as some others, but doing this continually in our whole life, and in every way. Certainly the elect race justified by the precept says, "Seven times a day have I praised Thee" (Ps 119. 164). Whence not in a specified place, or selected temple, or at certain festivals and on appointed days, but during his whole life, the Gnostic in every place, even if he be alone by himself, and wherever he has any of those who have exercised the like faith, honours God, that is, acknowledges his gratitude for the knowledge of the way to live.

And if the presence of a good man, through the respect and reverence which he inspires, always improves him with whom he associates, with much more reason does not he who always holds uninterrupted converse with God by knowledge, life, and thanksgiving, grow at every step superior to himself in all respects—in conduct, in words, in disposition? Such an one is persuaded that God is ever beside him, and does not suppose that He is confined in certain limited places; so that under the idea that at times he is without Him, he may indulge in excesses night and day.

Holding festival, then, in our whole life, persuaded that God is altogether on every side present, we cultivate our fields, praising; we sail the sea, hymning; in all the rest of our conversation we conduct ourselves according to rule. The Gnostic, then, is very closely allied to God, being at once grave and cheerful in all things—grave on account of the bent of his soul towards the Divinity, and cheerful on account of his consideration of the blessings of humanity which God hath given us.

Now the excellence of knowledge is evidently presented by the prophet when he says, "Benignity, and instruction, and knowledge teach me" (Ps 119.66), magnifying the supremacy of perfection by a climax.

He is, then, the truly kingly man; he is the sacred high priest of God. And this is even now observed among the most sagacious of the Barbarians, in advancing the sacerdotal caste to the royal power. He, therefore, never surrenders himself to the rabble that rules supreme over the theatres, and gives no admittance even in a dream to the things which are spoken, done, and seen for the sake of alluring pleasures; neither, therefore, to the pleasures of sight, nor the various pleasures which are found in other enjoyments, as costly incense and odours, which bewitch the nostrils, or preparations of meats, and indulgences in different wines, which ensnare the palate, or fragrant bouquets of many flowers, which through the senses effeminate the soul. But always tracing up to God the grave enjoyment of all things, he offers the first-fruits of food, and drink, and unguents to the Giver of all, acknowledging his thanks in the gift and in the use of them by the Word given to him. He rarely goes to convivial banquets of all and sundry, unless the announcement to him of the friendly and harmonious character of the entertainment induce him to go. For he is convinced that God knows and perceives all things—not the words only, but also the thought; since even our sense of hearing, which acts through the passages of the body, has the apprehension [belonging to it] not through corporeal power, but through a psychical perception, and the intelligence which distinguishes significant sounds. God is not, then, possessed of human form, so as to hear; nor needs He senses, as the Stoics have decided, "especially hearing and sight; for He could never otherwise apprehend." But the susceptibility of the air, and the intensely keen perception of the angels, and the power which reaches the soul's consciousness, by ineffable power and without sensible hearing, know all things at the moment of thought. And should any one say that the voice does not reach God, but is rolled downwards in the air, yet the thoughts of the saints cleave not the air only, but the whole world. And the divine power, with the speed of light, sees through the whole soul. Well! Do not also volitions speak to God, uttering their voice? And are they not conveyed by conscience? And what voice shall he wait for, who, according to His purpose, knows the elect already, even before his birth, knows what is to be as already existent? Does not the light of power shine down to the very bottom of the whole soul; "the lamp of knowledge," as the Scripture says, searching "the recesses"? God is all ear and all eye, if we may be permitted to use these expressions.

In general, then, an unworthy opinion of God preserves no piety, either in hymns, or discourses, or writings, or dogmas, but diverts to grovelling and unseemly ideas and notions. Whence the commendation of the multitude differs nothing from censure, in consequence of their ignorance of the truth. The objects, then, of desires and aspirations, and, in a word, of the mind's impulses, are the subjects of prayers. Wherefore, no man desires a draught, but to drink what is drinkable; and no man desires an inheritance, but to inherit. And in like manner no man desires knowledge, but to know; or a right government, but to take part in the government. The subjects of our prayers, then, are the subjects of our requests, and the subjects of requests are the objects of desires. Prayer, then, and desire, follow in order, with the view of possessing the blessings and advantages offered.

The Gnostic, then, who is such by possession, makes his prayer and request for the truly good things which appertain to the soul, and prays, he himself also contributing his efforts to attain to the habit of goodness, so as no longer to have the things that are good as certain lessons belonging to him, but to be good.

Wherefore also it is most incumbent on such to pray, knowing as they do the Divinity rightly, and having the moral excellence suitable to him; who know what things are really good, and what are to be asked, and when and how in each individual case. It is the extremist stupidity to ask of them who are no gods, as if they were gods; or to ask those things which are not beneficial, begging evils for themselves under the appearance of good things.

Whence, as is right, there being only one good God, that some good things be given from Him alone, and that some remain, we and the angels pray. But not similarly. For it is not the same thing to pray that the gift remain, and to endeavour to obtain it for the first time.

The averting of evils is a species of prayer; but such prayer is never to be used for the injury of men, except that the Gnostic, in devoting attention to righteousness, may make use of this petition in the case of those who are past feeling.

Prayer is, then, to speak more boldly, converse with God. Though whispering, consequently, and not opening the lips, we speak in silence, yet we cry inwardly (1 Sam 1.13). For God hears continually all the inward converse. So also we raise the head and lift the hands to heaven, and set the feet in motion at the closing utterance of the prayer, following the eagerness of the spirit directed towards the intellectual essence; for and endeavouring to abstract the body from the earth, along with the discourse, raising the soul aloft, winged with longing for better things, we compel it to advance to the region of holiness, magnanimously despising the chain of the flesh. For we know right well, that the Gnostic willingly passes over the whole world, as the Jews certainly did over Egypt, showing clearly, above all, that he will be as near as possible to God.

Now, if some assign definite hours for prayer—as, for example, the third, and sixth, and ninth—yet the Gnostic prays throughout his whole life, endeavouring by prayer to have fellowship with God. And, briefly, having reached to this, he leaves behind him all that is of no service, as having now received the perfection of the man that acts by love. But the distribution of the hours into a threefold division, honoured with as many prayers, those are acquainted with, who know the blessed triad of the holy abodes.

Having got to this point, I recollect the doctrines about there being no necessity to pray, introduced by certain of the heterodox, that is, the followers of the heresy of Prodicus. That they may not then be inflated with conceit about this godless wisdom of theirs, as if it were strange, let them learn that it was embraced before by the philosophers called Cyrenaics. Nevertheless, the unholy knowledge (gnosis) of those falsely called [Gnostics] shall meet with confutation at a fitting time; so that the assault on them, by no means brief, may not, by being introduced into the commentary, break the discourse in hand, in which we are showing that the only really holy and pious man is he who is truly a Gnostic according to the rule of the Church, to whom alone the petition made in accordance with the will of God is granted, on asking and on thinking. For as God can do all that He wishes, so the Gnostic receives all that he asks. For, universally, God knows those who are and those who are not worthy of good things; whence He gives to each what is suitable. Wherefore to those that are unworthy, though they ask often, He will not give; but He will give to those who are worthy.

Nor is petition superfluous, though good things are given without claim.

Now thanksgiving and request for the conversion of our neighbours is the function of the Gnostic; as also the Lord prayed, giving thanks for the accomplishment of His ministry, praying that as many as possible might attain to knowledge; that in the saved, by salvation, through knowledge, God might be glorified, and He who is alone good and alone Saviour might be acknowledged through the Son from age to age. But also faith, that one will receive, is a species of prayer gnostically laid up in store.

But if any occasion of converse with God becomes prayer, no opportunity of access to God ought to be omitted. Without doubt, the holiness of the Gnostic, in union with [God's] blessed Providence, exhibits in voluntary confession the perfect beneficence of God. For the holiness of the Gnostic, and the reciprocal benevolence of the friend of God, are a kind of corresponding movement of providence. For neither is God involuntarily good, as the fire is warming; but in Him the imparting of good things is voluntary, even if He receive the request previously. Nor shall he who is saved be saved against his will, for he is not inanimate; but he will above all voluntarily and of free choice speed to salvation. Wherefore also man received the commandments in order that he might be self-impelled, to whatever he wished of things to be chosen and to be avoided. Wherefore God does not do good by necessity, but from His free choice benefits those who spontaneously turn. For the Providence which extends to us from God is not ministerial, as that service which proceeds from inferiors to superiors. But in pity for our weakness, the continual dispensations of Providence work, as the care of shepherds towards the sheep, and of a king towards his subjects; we ourselves also conducting ourselves obediently towards our superiors, who take the management of us, as appointed, in accordance with the commission from God with which they are invested.

Consequently those who render the most free and kingly service, which is the result of a pious mind and of knowledge, are servants and attendants of the Divinity. Each place, then, and time, in which we entertain the idea of God, is in reality sacred.

When, then, the man who chooses what is right, and is at the same time of thankful heart, makes his request in prayer, he contributes to the obtaining of it, gladly taking hold in prayer of the thing desired. For when the Giver of good things perceives the susceptibility on our part, all good things follow at once the conception of them. Certainly in prayer the character is sifted, how it stands with respect to duty.

But if voice and expression are given us, for the sake of understanding, how can God not hear the soul itself, and the mind, since assuredly soul hears soul, and mind, mind? Whence God does not wait for loquacious tongues, as interpreters among men, but knows absolutely the thoughts of all; and what the voice intimates to us, that our thought, which even before the creation He knew would come into our mind, speaks to God. Prayer, then, may be uttered without the voice, by concentrating the whole spiritual nature within on expression by the mind, in undistracted turning towards God.

And since the dawn is an image of the day of birth, and from that point the light which has shone forth at first from the darkness increases, there has also dawned on those involved in darkness a day of the knowledge of truth. In correspondence with the manner of the sun's rising, prayers are made looking towards the sunrise in the east. Whence also the most ancient temples looked towards the west, that people might be taught to turn to the east when facing the images. "Let my prayer be directed before Thee as incense, the uplifting of my hands as the evening sacrifice" (Ps 141.2), say the Psalms.

In the case of wicked men, therefore, prayer is most injurious, not to others alone, but to themselves also. If, then, they should ask and receive what they call pieces of good fortune, these injure them after they receive them, being ignorant how to use them. For they pray to possess what they have not, and they ask things which seem, but are not, good things. But the Gnostic will ask the permanence of the things he possesses, adaptation for what is to take place, and the eternity of those things which he shall receive. And the things which are really good, the things which concern the soul, he prays that they may belong to him, and remain with him. And so he desires not anything that is absent, being content with what is present. For he is not deficient in the good things which are proper to him; being already sufficient for himself, through divine grace and knowledge. But having become sufficient in himself, he stands in no want of other things. But knowing the sovereign will, and possessing as soon as he prays, being brought into close contact with the almighty power, and earnestly desiring to be spiritual, through boundless love, he is united to the Spirit.

Thus he, being magnanimous, possessing, through knowledge, what is the most precious of all, the best of all, being quick in applying himself to contemplation, retains in his soul the permanent energy of the objects of his contemplation, that is the perspicacious keenness of knowledge. And this power he strives to his utmost to acquire, by obtaining command of all the influences which war against the mind; and by applying himself without intermission to speculation, by exercising himself in the training of abstinence from pleasures, and of right conduct in what he does; and besides, furnished with great experience both in study and in life, he has freedom of speech, not the power of a babbling tongue, and which neither for favour nor fear conceals aught of the things which may be worthily said at the fitting time, in which it is highly necessary to say them. He, then, having received the things respecting God from the mystic choir of the truth itself, employs language which urges the magnitude of virtue in accordance with its worth; and shows its results with an inspired elevation of prayer, being associated gnostically, as far as possible, with intellectual and spiritual objects.

Whence he is always mild and meek, accessible, affable, long-suffering, grateful, endued with a good conscience. Such a man is rigid, not alone so as not to be corrupted, but so as not to be tempted. For he never exposes his soul to submission, or capture at the hands of Pleasure and Pain. If the Word, who is Judge, call; he, having grown inflexible, and not indulging a whit the passions, walks unswervingly where justice advises him to go; being very well persuaded that all things are managed consummately well, and that progress to what is better goes on in the case of souls that have chosen virtue, till they come to the Good itself, to the Father's vestibule, so to speak, close to the great High Priest. Such is our Gnostic, faithful, persuaded that the affairs of the universe are managed in the best way. Particularly, he is well pleased with all that happens. In accordance with reason, then, he asks for none of those things in life required for necessary use; being persuaded that God, who knows all things, supplies the good with whatever is for their benefit, even though they do not ask.

For my view is, that as all things are supplied to the man of art according to the rules of art, and to the Gentile in a Gentile way, so also to the Gnostic all things are supplied gnostically. And the man who turns from among the Gentiles will ask for faith, while he that ascends to knowledge will ask for the perfection of love. And the Gnostic, who has reached the summit, will pray that contemplation may grow and abide, as the common man will for continual good health.

Nay, he will pray that he may never fall from virtue; giving his most strenuous co-operation in order that he may become infallible. For he knows that some of the angels, through carelessness, were hurled to the earth, not having yet quite reached that state of oneness, by extricating themselves from the propensity to that of duality.

But him, who from this has trained himself to the summit of knowledge and the elevated height of the perfect man, all things relating to time and place help on, now that he has made it his choice to live infallibly, and subjects himself to training in order to the attainment of the stability of knowledge on each side. But in the case of those in whom there is still a heavy corner, leaning downwards, even that part which has been elevated by faith is dragged down. In him, then, who by gnostic training has acquired virtue which cannot be lost, habit becomes nature. And just as weight in a stone, so the knowledge of such an one is incapable of being lost. Not without, but through the exercise of will, and by the force of reason, and knowledge, and Providence, is it brought to become incapable of being lost. Through care it becomes incapable of being lost. He will employ caution so as to avoid sinning, and consideration to prevent the loss of virtue.

Now knowledge appears to produce consideration, by teaching to perceive the things that are capable of contributing to the permanence of virtue. The highest thing is, then, the knowledge of God; wherefore also by it virtue is so preserved as to be incapable of being lost. And he who knows God is holy and pious. The Gnostic has consequently been demonstrated by us to be the only pious man.

He rejoices in good things present, and is glad on account of those promised, as if they were already present. For they do not elude his notice, as if they were still absent, because he knows by anticipation what sort they are. Being then persuaded by knowledge how each future thing shall be, he possesses it. For want and defect are measured with reference to what appertains to one. If, then, he possesses wisdom, and wisdom is a divine thing, he who partakes of what has no want will himself have no want. For the imparting of wisdom does not take place by activity and receptivity moving and stopping each other, or by aught being abstracted or becoming defective. Activity is therefore shown to be undiminished in the act of communication. So, then, our Gnostic possesses all good things, as far as possible; but not likewise in number; since otherwise he would be incapable of changing his place through the due inspired stages of advancement and acts of administration.

Him God helps, by honouring him with closer oversight. For were not all things made for the sake of good men, for their possession and advantage, or rather salvation? He will not then deprive, of the things which exist for the sake of virtue, those for whose sake they were created. For, evidently in honour of their excellent nature and their holy choice, he inspires those who have made choice of a good life with strength for the rest of their salvation; exhorting some, and helping others, who of themselves have become worthy. For all good is capable of being produced in the Gnostic; if indeed it is his aim to know and do everything intelligently. And as the physician ministers health to those who co-operate with him in order to health, so also God ministers eternal salvation to those who co-operate for the attainment of knowledge and good conduct; and since what the commandments enjoin are in our own power, along with the performance of them, the promise is accomplished.

And what follows seems to me to be excellently said by the Greeks. An athlete of no mean reputation among those of old, having for a long time subjected his body to thorough training in order to the attainment of manly strength, on going up to the Olympic games, cast his eye on the statue of the Pisaean Zeus, and said: "O Zeus, if all the requisite preparation for the contest have been made by me, come, give me the victory, as is right." For so, in the case of the Gnostic, who has unblamably and with a good conscience fulfilled all that depends on him, in the direction of learning, and training, and well-doing, and pleasing God, the whole contributes to carry salvation on to perfection. For us, then, are demanded the things which are in our own power, and of the things which pertain to us, both present and absent, the choice, and desire, and possession, and use, and permanence.

Wherefore also he who holds converse with God must have his soul immaculate and stainlessly pure, it being essential to have made himself perfectly good.

But also it becomes him to make all his prayers gently with the good. For it is a dangerous thing to take part in others' sins. Accordingly the Gnostic will pray along with those who have more recently believed, for those things in respect of which it is their duty to act together. And his whole life is a holy festival. His sacrifices are prayers, and praises, and readings in the Scriptures before meals, and psalms and hymns during meals and before bed, and prayers also again during night. By these he unites himself to the divine choir, from continual recollection, engaged in contemplation which has everlasting remembrance.

And what? Does he not also know the other kind of sacrifice, which consists in the giving both of doctrines and of money to those who need? Assuredly. But he does not use wordy prayer by his mouth; having learned to ask of the Lord what is requisite. In every place, therefore, but not ostensibly and visibly to the multitude, he will pray. But while engaged in walking, in conversation, while in silence, while engaged in reading and in works according to reason, he in every mood prays. If he but form the thought in the secret chamber of his soul, and call on the Father "with unspoken groanings" (Rom 8.26), He is near, and is at his side, while yet speaking. Inasmuch as there are but three ends of all action, he does everything for its excellence and utility; but doing aught for the sake of pleasure, he leaves to those who pursue the common life.

(B) Prayers from Nag Hammadi

1. *Prayer of the Apostle Paul*

. . . Your light, give me your mercy!
My Redeemer, redeem me, for I am yours: from you have I come forth.
You are my mind: bring me forth!
You are my treasure house: open for me!
You are my fullness: take me to you!
You are my repose: give me the perfection that cannot be grasped!

I invoke you, the One who is and preexisted, by the name which is exalted above every name, through Jesus Christ the Lord of lords, the King of the ages: give me your gifts which you do not regret through the Son of man, the Spirit, the Paraclete of truth.

Give me authority when I ask you; give healing for my body when I ask you through the Evangelist, and redeem my eternal light-soul and my spirit.

And the Firstborn of the pleroma of grace—reveal him to my mind! Grant what no angel eye has seen and no archon ear has heard and what has not entered into the human heart, which came to be angelic and came to be after the image of the psychic God when it was formed in the beginning, since I have faith and hope. And place upon me your beloved, elect, and blessed greatness, the Firstborn, the First-begotten, . . . and the wonderful mystery of your house; for yours is the power and the glory and the blessing and the greatness for ever and ever. Amen.

2. *The Three Steles of Seth*
The First Stele of Seth.

I bless thee, Father, Geradama(s), I, as thine (own) Son, Emmacha Seth, whom thou didst beget unconceived, as a blessing of our God; for I am thine (own) Son. And thou art my mind, O my Father. And I, I sowed and begot; [but] thou hast [seen] the majesties. Thou hast stood, being unceasing. I bless thee, Father. Bless me, Father. It is because of thee that I exist; it is because of God that thou dost exist. Because of thee I am with that very one. Thou art light, since thou beholdest light. Thou has revealed light. Thou art Mirotheas; thou art my Mirotheos. I bless thee as God; I bless thy divinity. Great is the good Self-begotten who stood, the God who was first to stand. Thou didst come in goodness; thou has appeared, and thou hast revealed goodness. I shall utter thy name, for thou art a first name. Thou are unconceived. Thou hast appeared in order that thou mightest reveal the eternal ones. Thou art he who is. Therefore thou hast revealed those who really are. Thou art he who is uttered by a voice, but by mind art thou glorified, thou who has dominion everywhere. Therefore [the] perceptible world too knows thee because of thee and thy seed. Thou art merciful. And thou art from another race, and its place is over another race. And now thou art from another race, and its [place is] over another race. Thou art from another race, for thou art not similar. And thou art merciful, for thou art eternal. And thy place is over a race, for thou hast caused all these to increase, though because of my seed. For it is thou who knows it, that its place is in begetting. But they are from other races, for they are not similar. But their place is over other races, for their place is in life. Thou are Mirotheos.

I bless his power which was given to me, who caused the malenesses that really are to become male three times, who was divided into the pentad, the one who was given to us in triple power, the one who was begotten unconceived, the one who came from what is select; because of what is humble, he went forth in the midst.

Thou art a Father through a Father, a word from a command. We bless thee, Thrice Male, for thou didst unite the all through them all, for thou hast empowered us. Thou hast come from one through one; thou hast moved, thou hast come to one. [Thou] hast saved, thou hast saved, thou hast saved us, O crown-bearer, crown-giver! We bless thee eternally. We bless thee, once we have been saved, as the perfect individuals, perfect on account of thee, those who [became] perfect with thee who is complete, who completes, the one perfect through all these, who is similar everywhere, Thrice Male.

Thou has stood. Thou wast first to stand. Thou wast divided everywhere. Thou didst continue being one. And those whom thou willed, thou hast saved. But thou dost will to be saved all who are worthy.

Thou art perfect! Thou art perfect! Thou art perfect!

3. *The Discourse on the Eighth and Ninth*

O my son, that I am Mind. I have seen! Language is not able to reveal this. For the entire eighth, O my son, and the souls that are in it, and the angels, sing a hymn in silence. And I, Mind, understand."

"What is the way to sing a hymn through it (the eighth)?"

"Have you become such that you cannot be spoken to?"

"I am silent, O my father. I want to sing a hymn to you while I am silent." Then sing it, for I am Mind.

I understand Mind, Hermes, who cannot be interpreted, because he keeps within himself. And I rejoice, O my father, because I see thee smiling. And the universe [rejoices]. Therefore there is no creature that will lack thy life. For thou art the lord of the citizens in every place. Thy providence protects. I call thee father, aeon of the aeons, great divine spirit. And by a spirit he gives rain upon everyone. What are you saying to me, O my father, Hermes?

Concerning these things I do not say anything, O my son. For it is right before God, that we keep silent about what is hidden.

O Trismegistus, let not my soul be deprived of the great divine vision. For everything is possible for you as master of the universe.

Return to <praising>, O my son, and sing while you are silent. Ask what you want in silence.

When he had finished praising he shouted, "Father Trismegistus! What shall I say? We have received this light. And I myself see this same vision in you. And I see the eighth and the souls that are in it and the angels singing a hymn to the ninth and its powers. And I see him who has the power of them all, creating those <that are> in the spirit."

"It is advantageous from [now on] that we keep silence in a reverent posture. Do not speak about the vision from now on. It is proper to [sing a hymn] to the father until the day to quit (the) body."

"What you sing, O my father, I too want to sing."

"I am singing a hymn within myself. While you rest yourself, be active in praise. For you have found what you seek."

"But is it proper, O my father, that I praise because I am filled in my heart?"

"What is proper is your praise that you will sing to God so that it might be written in this imperishable book."

"I will offer up the praise in my heart, as I pray to the end of the universe and the beginning of the beginning, to the object of man's quest, the immortal discovery, the begetter of light and truth, the sower of reason, the love of immortal life. No hidden word will be able to speak about thee, Lord. Therefore my mind wants to sing a hymn to you daily. I am the instrument of thy spirit. Mind is thy plectrum. And thy counsel plucks me. I see myself! I have received power from thee. For thy love has reached us."

4. The Letter of Peter to Philip

Then, when the apostles had come together and thrown themselves upon their knees, they prayed, saying, "Father, Father, Father of the Light who possesses the incorruptions, hear us just as [...] in thy holy child Jesus christ. For he became for us an illuminator in the [darkness]. Yea hear us."

And they prayed again another time, saying, "Son of Life, Son of Immortality who is in the light, Son, Christ of Immortality, our Redeemer, give us power, for they seek to kill us."

Then a great light appeared so that the mountain shone from the sight of him who had appeared. And a voice called out to them, saying, "Listen to my words that I may speak to you. Why are you asking me? I am Jesus Christ who is with you forever."

Then the apostles answered and said, "Lord, we would like to know the deficiency of the Aeons and their Pleroma." And: "How are we held in this dwelling place?" Further: "How did we come to this place?" And: "In what manner shall we depart?" Again: "How do we have the [authority] of boldness?" [And]: "Why do the powers fight with us?"

(C) Monastic Prayers

1. Prayers of John of Apamea

(1) Praised are you
O Christ our Teacher,
for you enrich
with absolutely everything those who cleave to you.
Lord, if someone gives his possessions to the state,
then he receives in return great honour;
how much more will you, Lord,
magnify and praise
that person who offers his whole self to you,
possessing nothing besides you!

Make our souls grow by your grace, Lord,
so that we may grow in you

and give praise to you, for no one can grow
except in you,
and no one can excel
except in you.

Praise to you,
without whom everything is empty;
praise to you,
for apart from the paise of you,
all praise is but idle.
Praise to you,
the One who magnifies,
but it is you who are thereby praised,
for you are the object of praise
of everything.
Praise to you,
Perfecter of everything, O Christ.
By your divine teaching you gave wisdom
to all who are instructed by you
to deprive themselves of everything
that belongs to this world
—then they shall be attached to you.
Otherwise, as they travelled after you
while still cleaving to the world,
they might be drawn back by the world into it. Praise to you who bade us
    release ourselves
and then cleave to you,
seeing that, when we are not bound up with anything,
nothing will separate us from you.

(2) Direct the course of our lives, Lord,
straight towards you,
so that in you we may reach you,
and so that in you we find you.
Make us worthy to attain to you,
in you; and let us behold nothing beside you.
Hide everything from our mind's vision
by means of the manifestation of your glorious light.
For whoever gazes upon you
does not need to look upon anything else;
but whoever does not gaze upon you
is in need of all kinds of other sources of illumination
in order to be able to see.

Praise to you,
for you are the Light,
and in you our souls have illumination.
You illumine all
with knowledge of yourself.

Draw back the veil of falsehood from our souls
so that we can see your light clearly,
for our minds are not totally dark
owing to love of you,
for whoever desires the sight of you
does not see himself alongside you,
being deprived not only of his possessions,
but also of his very limbs
as he longs to take up more
than his human nature is capable of doing.
For whoever has really loved you
yearns not only after your poverty,
but also after death for your name's sake,
so that with his death
he may lose himself in order to find you.
He loses himself
and all that belongs to the world
in order to find you who have found him.
All the time he is eager
to take up your love for him
into himself,
so that with your help
he may love you.

2. *Prayer of Isaac of Nineveh*

(1) As my soul bows to the ground
I offer to you with all my bones
and with all my heart
the worship that befits you,
O glorious God who dwells in ineffable silence.
You have built for my renewal
a tabernacle of love on earth
where it is your good pleasure to rest,
a temple made of flesh
and fashioned with the most holy sanctuary oil.
Then you filled it with your holy presence
so that worship might be fulfilled in it,
indicating the worship
of the eternal persons of your Trinity
and revealing to the worlds which you have created in
your grace
an ineffable mystery,
a power which cannot be felt or grasped
by any part of your creation that has come into being.
In wonder at it
angelic beings are submerged in silence,
awed at the cloud of this eternal mystery
and at the flood of glory
which issues from within this source of wonder,

for it receives worship
in the sphere of silence
from every intelligence that has been sanctified
and made worthy of you.

(3) I beseech You, O God,
send me help from your highest heavens
so that I may keep afar from my heart
every evil intention and every carnal wish.
Do not cast me, Lord, from your protection
lest my adversary find me
and trample upon me just as he desires,
destroying me utterly.
It is you who grants repentance and a sorrowing heart
to the sinner who repents;
in this way
you ease his heart of the weight of sin
that is laid upon it,
thanks to the comfort which comes from sorrowing
and from the gift of tears.

(5) O name of Jesus,
key to all gifts,
open up for me the great door to your treasure house
so that I may enter and praise you
with the praise that comes from the heart
in return for your mercies
which I have experienced in latter days;
for you came and renewed me
with an awareness of the New World.

(6) I give praise to your holy nature, Lord, for you have made my nature
a sanctuary for your hiddenness
and a tabernacle for your Mysteries,
a place where you can dwell,
and a holy temple for your divinity.

(7) O Mystery exalted beyond every word
and beyond silence,
who became human in order to renew us
by means of voluntary union with the flesh,
reveal to me the path
by which I may be raised up to your mysteries,
travelling alone a course
that is clear and tranquil,
free from the concerns of this world.
Gather my mind into the silence of prayer,
so that all my wandering thoughts
may be silenced within me

during that luminous converse
of supplication and mystery-filled wonder.